Contents

Illustrations

PLATES

The Diaries of
SOFIA TOLSTAYA

Edited by O. A. Golinenko, S. A. Rozanova, B. M. Shumova,
I. A. Pokrovskaya and N. I. Azarova

Translated by Cathy Porter
With an Introduction by Professor R. F. Christian

JONATHAN CAPE
THIRTY-TWO BEDFORD SQUARE LONDON

First published 1985

Jonathan Cape Ltd, 32 Bedford Square, London WC1B 3EL

British Library Cataloguing in Publication Data
Tolstaia, S.A.
The diaries of Sofia Tolstoy.
1. Tolstaia, S.A. 2. Wives – Soviet Union – Biography
3. Novelists, Russian – 19th century – Biography – Marriage
I. Title II. Golinenko, O.A.
891.73'3 PG3385.T6
ISBN 0-224-02270-9

Printed in Great Britain by
Butler & Tanner Ltd, Frome and London

Illustrations

The publishers would like to thank Tania Albertini Tolstoy for the use of all photographs herein excluding nos 3, 5, 10–12, 14, 16, 18 and 20 which appear by permission of VAAP, the Central Soviet Copyright Agency.

Introduction
by Professor R. F. Christian

S. A. Rozanova, in an excellent introduction to the Russian edition of Countess Tolstaya's diaries published in 1978, recalls the words written by her in 1913, three years after her husband's death: 'Let people be indulgent to the woman whose strength was perhaps insufficient to bear on her weak shoulders from youth onwards the burden of a high destiny, namely to be the wife of a genius and a great man.' Not everyone would agree with her that her husband was 'a great man', despite his unquestioned status as one of Russia's two greatest novelists. Rebecca West once described him as a monster who had earned the contempt of the whole world. One of his recent biographers, Edward Crankshaw, called him the greatest novelist in the world, 'a blazing genius', but at the same time a person who was very far from admirable – indeed an intolerable man. For many years biographical opinion tended to favour the husband rather than the wife when it came to apportioning the blame for their much-publicised difficulties and disagreements. More recently the balance may have swung a little in the other direction, and the appearance for the first time in English of a complete translation of the Countess' diaries together with a selection of her so-called 'daily diaries' (*yezhednevniki*) will be welcomed by many people, not only of a feminist persuasion, who feel that the time has come to re-examine the evidence from the woman's point of view.

Sofia Andreevna Tolstaya, née Behrs, was born on August 22, 1844 at her parents' estate of Pokrovskoe, near Moscow, the second of three daughters in a family of eight children. Her father was a Moscow doctor who was eventually appointed court physician with a residence in the Kremlin. Her mother's family had known the Tolstoys for many years and the young Lev Tolstoy had not only played as a boy with his future mother-in-law, but had allegedly even pushed her off a balcony in a momentary fit of jealousy! Over the years Tolstoy became something of a familiar figure in the Behrs' household while Sofia was growing up – a vivacious, intelligent and cultured young lady by all accounts. At the age of eleven she began to keep a diary. When only sixteen she wrote a story, 'Natasha', which, according to her sister, contained in embryo the characters of Countess Rostova and her daughters Vera and Natasha in *War and Peace*, and which was read with interest and approval by her future husband. Both her early diaries and her first story were burnt by her before her marriage, much to her later regret, but her account of a visit to the Troitsa monastery in present-day Zagorsk has survived and is translated in this volume. In 1861 she passed an examination at Moscow University which entitled her to give private tuition; there is no evidence, however, that she put her qualification to immediate use.

The following year she was to see much more of Tolstoy, who had by then become a frequent visitor to the Behrs' residence. It was assumed at first that he was paying court to Sofia's elder sister – or even to her mother, as Dr Behrs sometimes thought – but it was to Sofia that he eventually proposed on September 16, 1862. A week later they were married. She was eighteen; he was thirty-four. On the same day they left for Tolstoy's estate at Yasnaya Polyana, some 130 miles from Moscow, which was to be their main home for the rest of their lives.

Shortly before they were married Tolstoy gave Sofia his bachelor diaries to read. The frank record of his youthful sexual promiscuity and venereal disease shocked her profoundly, and her jealousy was further aggravated when, as a young wife, she discovered that the peasant woman with whom he had had a liaison and who had borne him a son still worked in her new home. It was an inauspicious beginning. Indeed the marriage was hardly a week old when husband and wife had their first of many quarrels, and after only ten months the distraught Sofia wrote in her diary that 'These past nine months have been practically the worst in my life'. Nevertheless, the evidence of other witnesses suggests that as a rule the storm clouds were quick to disperse, that both partners were very much in love and that they both shared a strong belief in the traditional virtues of family life which made the 1860s and early 1870s the happiest and most fruitful period of their long life together. Eight children were born in the first eleven years of their marriage and five more followed in the next fifteen. (The last survivor, Aleksandra, died in America as recently as 1980 at the age of 95.)

In the 1860s Tolstoy the novelist was at the height of his creative powers and was happy in his work. His wife idolised him as a writer and was more than willing to assist him in every possible way: by copying, re-copying and discussing what he was writing, shielding him from distractions and assuming the main burden of running a large household. It was she who looked after their rapidly growing family, saw to their education, made their clothes and supervised their meals. She made toys for them and put on puppet shows and other entertainments. She made jam, bottled fruit, kept the accounts, did embroidery and still found time to read quite widely. Her energy was prodigious, her sense of duty exceptional. It was not until the late 1870s that relations between her and her husband seriously deteriorated as he became more and more remote, neglected her and the children, and passed through a spiritual and moral crisis in the course of which he sought to devise for himself a religion based on the teachings of

Christ as he understood them, but purged of miracle, mystery and ecclesiastical authority. Sofia was upset by the increasing presence in her house of her husband's disciples, especially the more uncivilised. She resented his newly adopted vegetarianism, which meant that she had to prepare two menus, and she was quick to notice the occasions, especially in their sexual relations, when he failed to practise what he preached. When he decided to renounce his property and the copyright of all his future works, the responsibility for managing the estate and producing an income from his books published before 1881 fell very largely on her shoulders. At the same time the purchase of a town house in Moscow and the need to spend part of each year there when the children went to school added to her financial and domestic worries. Nevertheless, despite a particularly unhappy and depressing period in the middle 1880s when Tolstoy was on the point of leaving home, her loyalty to her husband never wavered and she continued to be in effect his literary agent and publisher, producing admirable editions of his earlier, copyright novels and stories, bringing out new works of his, handing over his manuscripts and letters to the Rumyantsev Library in Moscow for safekeeping, pressing for the removal of censorship restrictions on those of his writings which had been banned (she once obtained an audience of the Tsar to plead successfully for permission to publish *The Kreutzer Sonata* which she found so odious), writing to the press in his defence and regularly copying out his latest articles and stories, even those most alien to her sensibilities and beliefs. During the disastrous harvest failure of 1891–2 she gave him loyal and active support in his work on behalf of the famine victims. As she grew older she acquired new hobbies – photography and water-colour painting in particular – and devoted more time to what was perhaps her favourite recreation, playing the piano. She translated Tolstoy's *On Life* into French, and at his request made translations for him from English and German. During the 1870s and early 1880s she made a number of valuable notes about her husband's work on the unfinished historical novels *Peter I* and *The Decembrists*, on *Anna Karenina* and on the famous quarrel between Turgenev and Tolstoy. In 1895 she published a story, 'Grandmother's Treasure', in a children's journal, and in 1904 a group of nine poems in prose under the significant pseudonym, *A Tired Woman*. She also published an anthology of children's tales and wrote two other stories which were not published, one on the subject of *The Kreutzer Sonata*. Over the years 1904–16 she wrote her autobiography, *My Life*, on the basis of her diaries and letters – a partial translation by S. Koteliansky and Leonard Woolf appeared in London in 1922 – and she was also the author of the first printed biographical essay on her husband, as well as several letters to the press.

In 1895 the Tolstoys' youngest child Ivan (Vanechka), an exceptionally gifted boy from whom great things were expected, died a month before his seventh birthday. His death was probably the greatest shock which Sofia had experienced since reading her husband's bachelor diaries, and her overwhelming grief coupled with the generally unhappy atmosphere at home was the prelude to an intense but platonic infatuation with the composer and family friend Sergei Taneev, which provided the basis of her other unpublished story. His music seemed to bring out in her an almost hysterical emotional response to the loss of her son and her own need for moral support; but her innocent attachment aroused Tolstoy's bitter jealousy and further exacerbated the already strained relations between them.

Sofia's married life was lived almost entirely in Yasnaya Polyana and Moscow. She never travelled abroad and her journeys within Russia were largely confined to short visits to St Petersburg and Kiev, and a nine month stay near Yalta in 1901–2. When, in the summer of 1901, it was feared that Tolstoy's life was in serious danger, Countess Panina put her luxurious estate on the Black Sea coast at the Tolstoys' disposal, and there Sofia nursed her husband – an exceptionally demanding patient by her accounts – back to health with her customary tireless and single-minded devotion. It was in the Crimea, incidentally, that she remarked in her diary that she had been on board ship for the first time in her life!

In the late 1900s the relationship between Sofia and her husband was further complicated by the constant presence of Tolstoy's most famous, dedicated and fanatical disciple, Vladimir Chertkov, who had finally returned from exile in England in 1908 to settle near the man he worshipped. Tolstoy had first met this wealthy aristocratic Guards officer and friend of the royal family in 1883, when the latter's own life was undergoing a 'Tolstoyan' transformation, and Chertkov, profoundly influenced as he was by the older man's religious, moral and social ideas, soon became the dominant figure in his life – much to his wife's dismay. As he became more and more involved in Tolstoy's daily routine and made it his mission to collate and preserve all his papers for the benefit of posterity, he inevitably came into conflict with the Countess, especially over questions concerning Tolstoy's will (which was frequently being amended under Chertkov's influence) and the eventual disposal of his diaries and manuscripts. With Chertkov's reappearance on the scene Sofia began to show increasing signs of neurotic instability, culminating in more than one attempt at suicide, and her condition in 1909–10 required constant medical attention as the stresses and strains of her life became almost intolerable. The final blow came in October 1910 when Tostoy left home in the middle of the night, exasperated beyond all measure by his wife's alleged spying and eavesdropping; and although she was able to follow him to the railway station at Astapovo where he lay dying, she was deliberately prevented from seeing him until almost the very end.

For some weeks after Tolstoy's funeral Sofia was confined to her bed.

Physically unwell, she was also inwardly tormented by feelings of guilt and remorse, blaming herself for the tragedy of her husband's death. For the rest of her life she devoted herself almost exclusively to honouring his memory and came to sympathise more with many of his ideas – his pacifism, his attitude to the private ownership of land, even his vegetarianism, which had at one time been a source of constant friction between them. Though ageing rapidly and losing much of her phenomenal energy, she outlived Tolstoy by nine years. Despite the Bolshevik revolution and the nationalisation of land, she was allowed to continue living in the house at Yasnaya Polyana (the estate itself had already been bought by her daughter Aleksandra and given to the peasants), but her wish to be buried by her husband's side in the grounds of their home was not respected and she was interred in the village cemetery two miles away.

Such is the bare outline of Countess Tolstaya's life, which has been well documented by herself and others and about which there is little disagreement. But what sort of person was she, and what picture of her character and personality emerges from her diaries?

Before attempting to answer this question it will be necessary to say something about the diaries themselves. The first edition, in four volumes, was published in Moscow between the years 1928 and 1936. The diaries span the years 1862 to 1910, but with significant gaps. There are no entries, or virtually none, for 1868, 1880–1, 1884, 1888–9, 1893, 1896, 1898, 1905–7 or 1909. The introduction to the first volume (1860–91) by M. A. Tsyavlovskii warned readers of the need for caution in view of Sofia's morbid, suspicious and jealous disposition and referred to her impressionistic entries, temperamental outbursts and vehement language. The same author, in introducing the second volume (1891–7), spoke of the 1890s as the most painful period of her life. The story of her relations with her husband, he said, was a story of quarrels, great and small, and evidence of her nervous disorder. Sergei Tolstoy, however, who helped to edit and wrote the introductions to volumes three and four, remarked that most people had condemned his mother and that it was time for her voice to be heard. He conceded that her diaries were not always truthful and impartial and that they reflected the illness of her later years which, he believed, was not paranoia but hysteria. Nevertheless in his opinion the tragedy of 1910 was not due to his mother's illness, but to the wide gulf separating his parents and their beliefs and way of life. This first edition of Sofia's diaries was not entirely unabridged. Some passages of a particularly intimate nature were omitted, as well as entries which, although conceivably of use, as her son said, to literary historians and biographers of his father, might be tedious for the general public – entries about the weather, the family's state of health and the arrivals and departures of friends and relatives.

This first edition has long been out of print, but in 1978, in connection with the 150th anniversary of Tolstoy's birth, a new, revised two-volume edition appeared in the Soviet Union, which restored some of the cuts but also introduced new ones, which are unfortunately not indicated in the text. Unlike its predecessor, this new edition (from which the present translation is done) includes a selection of Sofia's so-called 'daily diaries' – brief entries which she made over the years 1893–1919 as a supplement to, or a substitute for, her main diary. Much of this selection appeared in print for the first time in Russian in the 1978 edition, and is now translated for the first time into English. It should be added that some of the entries in this 'daily diary' were not written on the day in question but composed later with the benefit of hindsight, especially in the year 1910.

This new English translation by Cathy Porter is more comprehensive than its predecessors, namely: *The Diary of Tolstoy's Wife, 1860–1891*, translated by A. Werth, 1928; *Countess Tolstoy's Later Diary 1891–1897*, also translated by A. Werth, 1929; and *The Final Struggle, being Countess Tolstoy's Diary for 1910*, translated with an introduction by Aylmer Maude, 1936. The diaries for the period 1898–1908 have not previously appeared in English, while the Russian text of 1910 was somewhat abridged by Maude. These earlier translations were extensively reviewed and made a great impression on both sides of the Atlantic. 'An extraordinary human document', 'a strikingly candid account of the diarist's emotional life', it was said of the first volume; and of the second – 'the most savage, shameless and shattering record of married life', 'the most moving and tragic book I have read for years'. Most reviewers, however, felt obliged to comment on their unreliability as source material for the last years of the Tolstoy marriage – a point reinforced by the editors of the new Russian edition, who preface their notes to the years 1901–10 by a warning of their subjective and partisan nature and a reminder of the need to use them with great caution.

With the course of time the mood and direction of Sofia's diaries inevitably underwent changes. At first she wrote primarily in order to express her spontaneous feelings, to talk to herself about herself and her relations with her husband, to register her momentary unhappiness at the apparent intellectual gulf between them and the fear that he might cease to love her. She frankly admitted (and her husband confirmed) that she usually resorted to her diary when quarrelsome or depressed; when things were going smoothly, as they often were, there was no need to say so. Indeed her sole entry for 1868 says: 'It makes me laugh to read my diary. What a lot of contradictions – as though I were the unhappiest of women! But who could be happier? Could any marriage be more happy and harmonious than ours? [. . .] I always write my diary when we quarrel.' By the 1870s the content of the diary becomes less brooding and introspective and more a record of daily life at Yasnaya Polyana, the humdrum details of her husband's and her children's activities, a chronicle of comings and goings, of temperatures and illnesses and the state of the weather. But as though afraid that these mundane particulars might seem to reflect unworthily on a great novelist, she also kept separate notes about his creative work, plans and ideas which have already been referred to and are translated below under the title 'Various Notes for Future Reference'. The diary entries proper for the 1880s are sparse. For the early 1890s they are much fuller, but at the same time more querulous, exaggerated and unjust than for any other period of her life except the last few months of 1910.

So much for the background to the diaries. What, then, of the woman who wrote them? Countess Tolstaya was without doubt an exceptionally practical, versatile and conscientious woman with an immense capacity for hard work. She had an intelligent and perceptive mind and a heightened literary and musical sensibility, without being herself a particularly gifted writer or performer. She was an excellent judge of her husband's work and had a keen appreciation of all that was best in nineteenth-century Russian literature. Like many women of her class she valued social refinements, good manners, *le bon ton*. She liked good clothes and the outward trappings of her class and status in society. 'When I am in Moscow I shall feel ashamed', she confessed, 'if I don't have a carriage and horses with a liveried footman in attendance, a nice dress to wear, a fine apartment to live in and all the rest of it. Lyovochka is an extraordinary man; he cares nothing for any of this.' She was strikingly attractive in her youth and middle age and enjoyed being admired. It was important to her what other people thought of her – especially people who mattered – and in this respect she was not so very different from her husband, at least until his later years. She was not too proud to use the good offices of people in high places when her children's careers or her husband's interests were concerned – she was intensely loyal to her family, and their welfare was always uppermost in her thoughts – but she never sought any favours for herself. A paragon of conventional moral virtue, she could at times be prudish and straitlaced. Pious by nature, her religious beliefs were strictly orthodox; she believed in the need to give children a religious upbringing and was offended by her husband's blasphemy and hostility towards the Orthodox Church – which did not prevent her from standing up for him when that Church excommunicated him for his heresies.

Sofia's character was not without its unattractive sides, as she was well aware. She was quick-tempered and impulsive and had a sharp tongue. Her moods changed rapidly from elation to despair, and when depressed she gave vent to her feelings impetuously and with great vehemence. She was jealous and possessive and liked to dominate. Maxim Gorky once wrote in this connection: 'I detected in her a jealous, always stubborn and, I suppose, morbidly tense desire to underline the incontestably great part she played in her husband's life. She reminded me of a man who, exhibiting an old lion at a fair booth, starts by making the audience terrified of the beast's strength, and then demonstrates that he, the tamer, is the only man on earth whom the lion obeys and loves.' She had more than a modicum of social snobbishness – 'he disgusts me with his talk of the "people"', she wrote two months after they were married – and she had little patience with the representatives of the lower classes, the 'dark ones' as she called them, who inflicted themselves in growing numbers on the Count, or the village boys and girls with whom her teenage sons, to her embarrassment and shame, liked to keep company. She failed to give credit to her husband for the genuine, deeply-felt and often laudable convictions he came to hold, and the virtually impossible task he had of trying to reconcile them with his obligations to his wife and children. Above all she was morbidly suspicious, neurotic, and on several occasions close to suicide – features of her character and illness which Tolstoy was well aware of, but towards which he was often inconsiderate. As she once said in a moment of self-pity: 'If only I were more normal.'

Those who take Sofia's side over the very Russian question 'Who was to blame?' argue justifiably that she had a great deal to endure. Sociable by nature and fond of lively company, she felt lonely and bored during her first months at Yasnaya Polyana. She wanted to be the centre of attention – she admitted to being an egoist – but instead she found that her husband was so absorbed in his work that she was left alone for hours on end. When there was nobody to talk to she took out her diary and talked to herself. Disposed when lonely towards self-analysis and confession, she often brooded over what seemed to have gone wrong with their relationship, alternately reproaching herself and her husband, masochistic and sadistic in turn. Companionship in marriage was what she longed for, and she acknowledged that the physical side of love meant far less to her than to him. Soon after their first child was born she complained that he only needed her for his own satisfaction, that she was a nurse, a piece of furniture, *a woman* – nothing more. And not only was Tolstoy sensual by her standards; he was not always particular about personal cleanliness (although it is hard to believe that she was not exaggerating when she wrote some years later that to wash was quite an event for him; or that she was surrounded in their Moscow house by dirt, boots, shoemaker's tools and chamber pots). Sofia did not find it easy at first to accustom herself to her new environment at Yasnaya Polyana, for although the grounds were delightful, the house itself left something to be desired. The furniture for the most part was primitive, there were no good pictures in the rooms and the floorboards were often bare or cheaply carpeted. What was worse, however, were the rats and mice, against which she had to wage intermittent war. If the rodents were unwelcome intruders, they could at least be exterminated. But the same was not true of the many visitors who came to call and sometimes to stay: not the cultured men and women who came to pay tribute to the famous novelist, but the 'dark ones', unkempt peasants and artisans. It was one thing to enjoy civilised company; another to have to clean up after the Tolstoyans! Finally the counsel for Sofia's defence would argue that she was right to complain that Tolstoy was hypocritical in professing love for mankind, but apparently denying it to his own wife and family, and that as far as sexual relations between them were concerned his practices did not always accord with his principles.

But what compensations did Sofia enjoy for the sorrows and disappointments so often recorded in her diaries? First, without question, the knowledge that she had married a writer who was already famous and soon to become a world celebrity. She loved to talk to him about his work and to know that he valued her judgement and woman's intuition. She was the first critic and the first reader of most of his major works. She loved to feel that she was indispensable to him, that she could serve him, look after him, be everything to him – could 'make a personal sacrifice' for him, as she put it. Indeed, she would have been happy to possess him absolutely, and only regretted that 'He can never be entirely mine as I am his'. She took great pains to defend him in public, even over causes uncongenial to her. Any little kindness he showed her, such as picking a flower, was a source of disproportionate pleasure, and she even planted the pips of two apples he once gave her, to commemorate his allegedly 'rare display of tenderness' towards her. The vicarious fame of being the wife of a celebrated novelist meant much to Sofia, and made up for many moments of bitterness and depression.

From an early age Sofia had wanted to have a big family. She was an exceptionally conscientious and loving mother ('the ideal wife', said Tolstoy, 'in a pagan sense – in the sense of loyalty, domesticity, self-denial, love of family . . . ') and her children were always near the centre of her thoughts. Of course they caused her anxiety and suffering. She quarrelled with Tolstoy over his insistence on breast-feeding and his unorthodox views on education. Five of their children died in infancy or childhood. The younger boys were lazy and undisciplined and lacked a firm paternal hand. The girls were slow to find acceptable husbands and took opposing sides in the ideological issues which divided their parents. But despite Sofia's occasional regret that her children had not turned out as she would have liked and despite her difficult relationship with her youngest daughter, Aleksandra, she was undoubtedly devoted both to the ideal and the reality of family life, imperfect as it was. Whether this was adequate compensation for her many trials and tribulations, only she herself could know.

In trying to assess the importance of Sofia's diaries, it must be said that despite their admitted exaggeration and unfairness it would be unthinkable to write a serious biography of Tolstoy without drawing on them extensively, and that nobody except his wife could have written about him with such intimate knowledge and frankness. Some readers indeed find her diaries more valuable for what they say about *him* than about her. Some argue on the strength of them that the early years of their marriage were reasonably happy ones and that it was Tolstoy's 'crisis' and the intervention of Chertkov in their lives that caused the rift so apparent in the 1880s and 1890s. Others again take the view that the marriage was an impossible one from the start, given the incompatibility of their temperaments and the ideological gulf separating them on so many fundamental issues. Tolstoy himself once said, when repeating his repudiation of the angry remarks made about her in his own diary in moments of exasperation, that 'every husband gets the wife he needs'. Certainly he *needed* Sofia, and she needed him. She might have been happier with another man. Another woman might have been happier with him. It must be doubted, though, whether another woman would have made *him* happier.

St Andrews, 1984

Translator's Introduction

Sofia Andreevna Tolstaya started keeping a diary at the age of sixteen. But it was two years later, in 1862, shortly before her marriage to the great writer, that she embarked in earnest on the diaries she would keep until just a month before her death in 1919, at the age of seventy-five. In this, their first complete English translation, she gives us a candid and detailed chronicle of the daily events of family life: conversations and card games, walks and picnics, musical evenings and readings aloud, birthdays and Christmases; the births, deaths, marriages, illnesses and love affairs of her thirteen children, her numerous grandchildren and her many relatives and friends; friendships and quarrels with some of Russia's best-known writers, musicians and politicians; and the comings and goings of the countless Tolstoyan 'disciples' who frequented the Tolstoys' homes in Yasnaya Polyana and Moscow. She records the state of the writer's stomach and the progress of his work. And she describes the fierce and painful arguments that would eventually divide the couple for ever. All this is in the foreground. In the distant and muted background are some of the most turbulent events of Russian history: the social and political upheavals that marked the transition from feudal to industrial Russia; three major international wars, three revolutions and the post-1917 Civil War.

But it is as Countess Tolstaya's own life story, the story of one woman's private experience, that these diaries are so valuable and so very moving. Half a million words long, they are her best friend, her life's work and the counterpart to her life and marriage.

Indeed throughout the Tolstoys' forty-eight-year marriage diaries were the very currency of their relationship, and both wrote them in order that the other should read them. In the early days she tried desperately to hide her troubled moods from him, recording them instead in her diary. When he expected her to merge with him and become his shadow, she stood out for her independence – in her diary. When he insisted on revealing to her all the ghosts of his past, demanding 'truth' and confessions from her at every turn, she would keep silent and record her wretchedness in her diary, and communicate it to him in this way. And as time went on, and communication between them became more difficult, it was increasingly to her diary that she confided her worst fears, her deepest anxieties and her tormented desires for revenge – in the hope that he might see it there. The happy periods – and there were many of them – were rarely recorded.

In 1847, at the age of nineteen, Count Lev Nikolaevich Tolstoy became master of the 4,000-acre estate of Yasnaya Polyana and the 330 serfs living on it. He was a restless and changeable young man. An enthusiastic maker and breaker of good resolutions, he dreamt of social equality while enjoying to the full his aristocratic privileges ('serfdom is an evil, but a very pleasant one!'). Yearning for purity yet craving fame and women, he was constantly lured from his peaceful country existence with his beloved Aunt Tatiana to the brothels and gipsy cabarets of Moscow and Tula, where he would drink, gamble and sow his wild oats.

At the age of twenty-three he decided it was time he brought some order to this aimless life, and kissing his aunt good-bye, he moved to Moscow. His purpose there, spelt out in his diary, was: 1) To gamble, 2) To find a position, and 3) To marry. The first two resolutions he pursued enthusiastically enough. As for the third, although he did for a while entertain dreams of the woman he would marry, and fell rapidly in and out of love in search of a wife, his hunger for gipsy and peasant women soon got the better of him and after a few months he gave up Moscow as a bad job and left with the army for the Caucasus.

There it was that he started to write. By the time he left to serve in the Crimean War, his *Childhood*, *Boyhood* and *Youth* had been published, and his reputation as a writer was assured. His experiences as an officer during the bloody siege of Sevastopol provided yet more inspiration, and by the time he returned to Moscow in 1856 his name as the author of the *Sevastopol Tales* had preceded him.

But now it was the simple peasant life he wanted. On his return to Yasnaya Polyana he put on a peasant shirt, let his beard grow, abandoned writing for the plough and opened a school for peasant children based on Rousseauesque principles. He also fell deeply in love with a peasant woman named Aksinya, who in the summer of 1858 gave birth to their son, Timofei. He longed increasingly now for a respectable wife to save him from sin. 'I must get married this year or never!' he wrote in his diary on New Year's Day, 1859. 'A wife! A wife at any price! A family and children!' he wrote the following year. But he was still a bachelor when, in the summer of 1862, he fled to Moscow.

By then he was thirty-four. His books had made him famous, he had travelled widely in Russia and Europe, and he was more than ready to settle down. He had no one particularly in mind, but he was determined to marry out of his own aristocratic class, and to choose a young girl. Property-owner, womaniser, hunter and gambler, he was a rake ready to be reformed.

Sofia Behrs was eighteen at the time, the daughter of his old childhood friend Lyubov Behrs, in whose crowded hospitable Kremlin flat Tolstoy was a regular visitor. Lyubov was the daughter of an illegal marriage, and though she was of an ancient aristocratic family her name had been changed at birth. At the age of sixteen she had married Andrei Evstafovich Behrs, a distinguished doctor eighteen years her senior, who was attached to the court. (Although as the grandson of a German military instructor who had settled in Russia in the eighteenth century, he was definitely not of the aristocracy, and the Russian aristocracy tended anyway to look down on the medical profession.)

Between 1843 and 1861 Lyubov Behrs bore eight children, three of them girls: Lisa, her eldest child, clever and rather distant, Sofia, a year younger, poetic and graceful, and Tanya, a lively laughing tomboy. The Behrs watched strictly over their daughters, but they had fairly progressive ideas on girls' education, and they arranged for them to take lessons in foreign languages and literature, music, painting and dancing, so that by the time she was seventeen Sofia had received her teacher's certificate. She and her sisters were also taught to keep accounts, make dresses, sew and cook, in preparation for marriage – for it was on this that all three girls' thoughts were focused. And in 1862 all three of them were of marriageable age.

Tolstoy, who had never had any proper family life of his own, was drawn again and again to the Behrs' warm and unaffected family circle, and he would later use them as his model for the Rostovs in *War and Peace*. As for the girls, he found them all enchanting. But by the time he left Moscow that summer for his estate he knew Sofia was the one he wanted. They were in many ways very similar: impetuous, changeable, wildly jealous, romantic, high-minded and passionate. And they both idealised family life. When Tolstoy met Sofia again later that summer he had become the centre of her thoughts, and – though she was barely old enough to know what she wanted – the wedding was fixed for September 23.

But not before he had insisted (with her parents' permission) on showing her his bachelor diary (and insisting that she keep one too). Sofia was a very childish 18-year-old who had led an extremely sheltered life, and what she read there shattered her. For his diaries were one long catalogue of lurid, guilt-racked confessions: of casual flirtations with society women, loveless copulations with peasants, his passionate affair with Aksinya, who now lived on his estate with their son, professions of homosexual love, disgusted diatribes against women, himself and the world in general – not to mention a desperate round of gambling sessions and drunken orgies. Sofia had dreamed of the man she would love, 'completely whole, new and *pure*'. She never forgave him for thus shattering her dreams and assaulting her innocence, and forty-seven years later she was still referring bitterly to Aksinya.

Youthful promiscuity and gambling were not in fact so uncommon amongst young Russian aristocrats, but even so Tolstoy and his family had a certain reputation for fast living. His brother Dmitrii had bought a prostitute from a brothel and died in her arms at the age of twenty-nine. His brother Sergei lived with a gipsy woman by whom he had eleven children. And his sister Maria left her despotic husband and lived in sin with a Swedish Count, by whom she had a daughter. Sofia's family did not live in this way – and Tolstoy would always apply a double standard when dealing with his wife and with the world at large (including his own family). She could never really forget his sordid, loveless past, and was deeply scarred by the episode, to which she would refer again and again in her diaries.

At their magnificent wedding in the Kremlin, Sofia could not stop weeping for the family she was leaving behind. She wept all the way to her new home. And she wept when, crushed and terrified by Tolstoy's clumsy attempts to embrace her, they finally arrived at Yasnaya Polyana, where she would spend the next fifty-seven years of her life.

Waiting for them on the steps of the large, white-painted wooden house were Tolstoy's old aunt, Tatiana Ergolskaya, holding an icon of the Holy Virgin, and his brother Sergei, bearing the traditional welcome of bread and salt. Sofia bowed to the ground, embraced her relatives and kissed the icon. (She would be guided to the end of her life by the simple rituals of the Russian Orthodox Church.) Then Aunt Tatiana handed her new mistress the keys of the house, and these she hung on her waist and carried there until the day she died.

The house, cold, spartanly furnished and infested with mice, had been Tolstoy's home all his life. There was a large farm, with cattle, sheep, pigs and bees, and until the 1880s Tolstoy took a keen interest in its management. But he was not a successful farmer. The pigs kept dying of hunger, the sheep proved unprofitable, and the cows were neglected and did not give enough milk. The only profit came from the apple orchards, but even so the estate was always running at a loss. Yasnaya Polyana's greatest asset was its forests ('my daughters' dowry', Sofia would call them), but these too were neglected. Tolstoy's other estate, in Nikolskoe, was even more dilapidated and even more forested, and in these forests, inhabited only by wolves and birds, Tolstoy loved to hunt, for until the 1880s he was a passionate sportsman.

Sofia was determined to like her new home and to be a good wife. She took over the accounts, organised the housekeeping and marshalled the small army of dependants and domestics living there who comprised her new family. There was Aunt Tatiana, with her personal maid and companion Natalya Petrovna; there was Maria Arbuzova, Tolstoy's old nanny, with her two sons, one of whom was Tolstoy's personal servant; there was Agafya Mikhailovna, who had been Tolstoy's grandmother's maid and was now the 'dog's governess'. There was Nikolai the cook, Pelageya the laundress, and many, many others who came and went, and lived either in the house or in the village of Yasnaya Polyana.

Tolstoy's young bride made a stern mistress. Tolstoy never lost his temper with the servants; she was constantly doing so, for she lacked his authority. She was also desperately worried lest he resume his old passion for teaching the peasants. She thought it improper for a count to associate so closely with the common people and feared that they might take him from her. Had his diaries not revealed to her just how ruthlessly he had exercised his power over the women on his estate?

But of course she did not talk to him of such things, and she remained for many weeks very much in awe of her new husband, always addressing him in the formal 'You'. She supervised all the domestic work. She sewed everything, including her husband's trousers and jackets. She attended to all the peasants' medical needs (for which she had quite a talent). She was supported, to be sure, by a large staff of servants, but her upbringing had taught her to be extremely self-reliant, and so she washed, boiled, gardened, pickled and sewed all day long in the eager desire to serve her husband.

The revelations in his diaries had badly shaken her sexual confidence. She yearned for tenderness and was shocked by his coarseness, hurt by his outbursts of passion, followed by coldness and withdrawal, but she submitted uncomplainingly to his fierce embraces. Since he believed that sexual intercourse should be for purely procreative purposes, they did not use any form of contraception. She became pregnant almost immediately, and her diary for this first year of marriage established the regular cycle of pregnancies and births that would fill her life. (She bore sixteen children in all, of whom thirteen lived.) Tolstoy, who held that sex during pregnancy was 'both swinish and unnatural', kept out of her way as much as possible, and Sofia grew increasingly desperate.

Her mother, uncomplainingly bearing her eight children and tending her home, had provided her with an excellent model of the selfless role women were traditionally expected to play in marriage. Orthodox religion had for centuries endowed women with this special capacity for self-sacrifice, and Sofia would throughout her life look to the Church, with its emphasis on suffering, selflessness and humility, to give dignity to her wifely role. But by the mid-1860s attitudes to women and the family were already undergoing a profound change, and Sofia too, in this first year of marriage, felt the stirrings of change within her.

Alexander II's emancipation of the serfs in 1861 had spelt the end of the old feudal Russia and the orthodox religious values underpinning it, and the start of a process that would affect every area of people's lives. Thousands of women, forced to make themselves financially independent of husbands and fathers, left their families behind for good to find work and education in the cities. Conservative men jeered at them as 'nihilists', but amongst the men of the intelligentsia there was now a new and serious commitment to treat women as equals and support their desire for education and autonomy. Debates raged about women's social role and the future of marriage and the family. More radical women would go so far as to reject love and marriage altogether, since to them marriage meant inevitably being trapped in endless domestic chores, while sexual relations, in the absence of reliable contraception, inevitably led to endless pregnancies. But even respectably married women were now claiming that husband and children were no longer enough to fill their lives, and that only through work could they find the emotional and economic independence they longed for. The 'woman question' was the burning issue of the day.

For Sofia it meant the discovery of a wholly unexpected dissatisfaction with her new life. Despite her endless labours for Tolstoy, toiling in the house and caring for him body and soul, she felt she was merely his toy. 'If I do not interest him, if he sees me as a doll, merely his *wife*, not a human being, then I will not and cannot live like that,' she writes in her diary. 'I am left alone morning, afternoon and night,' she complains later on. 'I am to gratify his pleasure and nurse his child, I am a piece of household furniture, I am a *woman*!' She longed to find her own interests outside the house and could not, and feeling increasingly inadequate, she alternately toyed with thoughts of suicide and nursed murderous feelings for Aksinya and her son. Pregnant and wretched, she was even jealous of her beloved younger sister Tanya.

But Tolstoy, for all his extraordinary sensitivity to the women in his novels, had no apparent desire to understand his wife's feelings. And for all his optimistic faith in the virtues of equality, simplicity and hard work, he would to the end of his days use his enormous moral authority in Russia to preach a particularly savage kind of New Testament asceticism, which equated sexuality with godlessness and proclaimed that women existed merely to arouse the beast in men and then frustrate it. In countless interviews, articles and plays he would make abundantly clear his view of women's weakness, their inferiority and moral subordination to men, and would indulge in countless ironic, contemptuous or frivolous comments on the 'woman question'. These anti-feminist views, many of which Sofia records in her diary, became more violently and lengthily argued as time went on, and help to explain the early tensions between the Tolstoys, which would remain so remarkably constant throughout their long life together.

On June 28, 1863, Sofia gave premature birth to their son Sergei, a sickly baby who had difficulty feeding. Her nipples grew inflamed and she longed to hire a wet-nurse. But Tolstoy, who held advanced views on the matter, would not hear of it: not to breastfeed was disgusting and unnatural, to hire a wet-nurse to do so was obscene; besides, a woman who abandoned her maternal duties so lightly would surely have no qualms about abandoning her wifely duties. Terrified of losing his love, Sofia struggled on in agony until eventually ordered by the doctor to stop, and

Fillip the coachman's wife was asked to help out. (The woman's son, Sergei's 'milk brother', was to be his lifelong friend.)

Tolstoy angrily withdrew from her and wrote a five-act comedy called *The Infected Family*, about a woman who could not breastfeed her baby because she was an 'unnatural, emancipated woman' and a 'nihilist'. (Thankfully, he could not persuade the Maly Theatre in Moscow to put it on, and soon dropped it.) He grew increasingly possessive towards Sofia, and increasingly obsessed by the ideal of marital chastity. He was terrified by the new egalitarian attitudes to women – taken by some to their logical conclusion of demanding for women an equal right to commit adultery. He thought of the great writer Herzen, whose wife had claimed her right to fall in love with a poet, and he concluded that Herzen's tragedy was that he had lightheartedly betrayed his wife with housemaids and prostitutes, and the more emancipated sexual attitudes of the 1860s had avenged him.

Tolstoy's past too was catching up with him, and he became wildly jealous. Not that he had any reason to be, of course; Sofia had dedicated her life to him, and needed him as much as he needed her to care for him and create the family he had never had. But perhaps more importantly, she represented for him a moral purity he felt he had long ago lost, or never had, and which he desperately needed for his own moral regeneration. And despite everything, relations between them began to improve. For that autumn he started writing *War and Peace*, and she was able to devote herself entirely to him.

She assumed responsibility for everything that concerned his everyday life, supervising his diet, ensuring that he was not disturbed while he sat hour after hour in his study, and gladly going without sleep or food to care for him when he was ill. She assumed all responsibility for the servants, the housekeeping and the accounts, and she arranged and catalogued the books in the large library.

These were just some of her responsibilities over the next forty-five years. But the task she cherished most throughout these years (helped later on by her daughters and Tolstoy's secretaries) was copying out his voluminous writings. Every night after the baby had been put to bed, she would sit at her desk until the small hours, copying out his day's writing in her fine hand, telepathically deciphering (sometimes with the aid of a magnifying glass) the scribble that only she could read, and straining her eyes to the point of damaging her sight. Every morning she would place the fair copy, along with fresh sheets of writing paper, on Tolstoy's desk. And back they would come to her every evening to be recopied, black with corrections, swarming with margin notes, a chaos of crossings-out, balloons and footnotes. In the six years he was writing *War and Peace* she would copy some passages over and over again. (Her son Ilya later wrote that she had copied parts of it seven times.) Yet she rarely knocked at his door to ask for help, and she never complained of fatigue.

They were happy together. The quarrels between them became less frequent, her diary entries rare. She felt she was not just his secretary but his colleague and confidante, for he always asked her advice and deeply respected her judgement. Even when he was away a couple of days he would write her daily letters, and only when he was writing did he forget her. As for her, his writing captured her childhood experiences, her own thoughts and words, and as she copied she relived her past. 'Nothing touches me so deeply as his ideas, his genius,' she wrote in her diary. And when their friend the writer Sollogub praised her as the 'nursemaid of Tolstoy's talent', she was humbly grateful for the compliment.

In the spring of 1864 she became pregnant again. She was 20 years old, strong, healthy (she thought nothing of falling out of a carriage when four months pregnant), and by all accounts extremely attractive. And when her second child Tanya was born that October she was delighted to be able to feed her herself.

Between 1864 and 1871 she gave birth to three more children: Ilya and Lyova, healthy boys, in 1866 and 1869, and a sickly girl called Maria in 1871. In those years family life was very happy. Everyone commented on what an exceptionally united couple they were. 'Sonya couldn't look for greater happiness,' wrote Tolstoy's niece Varya in her diary in 1864. 'Sonya and Lyova were an exemplary couple,' she said, 'but such couples were rare; all one ever hears about these days is husbands leaving their wives or wives divorcing their husbands.' And Sofia's brother Stepan wrote in his memoirs: 'The mutual love and understanding between them has always been my ideal and model of marital bliss.' Their relationship was charged with passion. And although his was a passion of the flesh, while hers was a passion of the spirit, and for babies, the strength of their feelings for one another remained undiminished (though often horribly distorted) throughout their marriage.

This was surely the source of her remarkable energy. She organised everything, often ignoring his instructions. Gardening, painting, bottling, upholstering, playing the piano, copying – she was always busy. Her son Sergei later recalled a certain lack of spontaneous gaiety about her: she had always found it hard to be happy, even as a young girl. 'For me "*aimer*" never meant playing with feelings,' she wrote before her marriage. 'Both then and later on it was something closer to suffering.' And shortly after her marriage she wrote: 'Love is hard – when you love it takes your breath away, you lay down your whole life and soul for it, and it's with you as long as you live.' She rarely laughed or enjoyed jokes, and as a deeply religious woman she tended to see the business of loving and caring for her husband and children as bound up with inevitable suffering, sorrow and sacrifice. Perhaps this explains why the children always addressed her in the formal 'you', even though she was always there to scold or reassure them, while their father, who was much more distant and inaccessible, was always 'thou'.

She made herself responsible for the children's education too, teaching them Russian grammar, French, history, geography, painting and music. (There was an English governess to teach them English, while their father taught them Russian literature and arithmetic.)

To escape from the demands on her she would withdraw into the 'private inner world' or her diary. And when they quarrelled, writing it would open up a 'peaceful, poetic existence, free of excitements and the material things of the so-called physical world; a life of prayer, holy thoughts, dreams of self-perfection, and a quiet love that has been trampled underfoot'.

The year 1871 was not a good one. The couple's second daughter Maria was born prematurely on February 12, and Sofia almost died of puerperal fever. (She never really felt much warmth for her daughter, and throughout Maria's life there was constant tension between her and her mother.) As Sofia, weak and thin, her head shaved, struggled back to life, Tolstoy was haunted increasingly by fears of death. Two years before he had finished *War and Peace*, and after this mighty labour he felt dazed and drained. Fearing that he might have consumption, he gave up all idea of writing, and in the summer of 1871 he set off south to Samara (now Kuybyshev) with Sofia's younger brother Stepan. There they lived a simple life on the steppes in a felt Bashkiri tent, and drank health-giving fermented mare's milk (*kumis*). Tolstoy worshipped the romantic nomadic Bashkirs, he loved the vast open steppes, and he decided on impulse to buy an estate there. In the summer of 1873 he persuaded Sofia to travel south with the children to stay in their new property. First they travelled three hundred miles to Nizhnii Novgorod (now Gorky), then another five hundred to Samara, and thence another 120 miles by carriage to their new property.

Sofia had just given birth to her fifth child, Petya, and was still feeding him. She and the younger children settled into the main house, which was more like a large peasant hut, with a leaking roof, smoking fireplace and swarming flies, while Tolstoy and Stepan camped out in the felt tent they had bought, and the boys and their tutor lived in the shed. Tolstoy loved this primitive life, and his depression melted away, but Sofia did not enjoy herself, and bitterly regretted that the estate had even been bought.

Between 1873 and 1876 the Tolstoys lost three babies. In November 1873 Petya was carried off by the croup. 'The darling, I loved him too much!' wrote Sofia, wild with grief. 'He was buried yesterday. What emptiness!' Tolstoy's grief was more restrained, and his main desire seemed to be to escape from his wife and her weeping. In April 1874, the couple's sixth baby, Nikolai, was born, but ten months later he died in agony of meningitis. In 1875 the children all fell ill with whooping cough, and Sofia, pregnant yet again, came down with peritonitis, was prescribed quinine, and gave birth prematurely in November to a baby girl called

Valya, who died immediately afterwards. Sofia's diary entries dwindle to almost nothing.

Tolstoy had just started work on a new novel, and Sofia was able to bury her grief in devotedly copying out his day's writing for him. It was in 1877, as *Anna Karenina* was nearing completion, that his depressions became even more frequent and alarming. He was prone to violent rages against Sofia and the world, pursued by fears of death and feelings of guilt, racked by a sense of his own worthlessness. Surrounded by poverty and wretchedness on all sides, he continued to be served and pampered by the peasants (and, of course, his wife). The only solution, he decided, was to find some link, through religion, to the peasants, to accept everything, rites, miracles and all, that reason repudiated, and humbly to abide by all the Church's teachings.

The consequences of Tolstoy's long and painful 'conversion' were both deeply impressive and utterly intolerable; for Sofia it was a disaster. He became increasingly doctrinaire in his religious views, railing against those who smoked, hunted and ate meat (though continuing to do so himself), and preaching the virtues of living by one's own labour (though still waited on hand and foot by his wife and servants). His philosophy was changing – and he was requiring Sofia to change too – yet his life remained very much the same, and his inability to live by his principles made him acutely depressed, while his inability to carry through these principles to his wife and children spelt tragedy to his family.

He was unable to give Sofia any advice as to how she might adapt to his change of course. And when he finally renounced property, sexuality and wordly affairs, his publishers, his children and the estate, he merely made her take responsibility for it all. She was at first genuinely puzzled by his change of heart, and demanded guidance as to how far she should simplify the housekeeping and limit expenses. What about the children's education? And the servants? And his copyright money? But he gave no clear answers, merely demanding repeatedly that she follow his example, give away his money and abandon material concerns. His disregard for her feelings threw her into despair: 'I have been discarded like a useless object, impossible, undefined sacrifices are expected of me, in my life and in my family, and I am expected to renounce everything . . . '

But perhaps the greatest blow was when he renounced the creative writing she had always so loved, and turned instead to moral tracts, pamphlets and articles attacking the hypocrisy of the Church and preaching against those who lived in luxury off the labour of the peasants. In the late 1870s, as revolutionaries urged the peasants to rise against their masters, Tolstoy was claimed as their spokesman, and several of his more outspoken works, banned by the Tsar and circulated underground, aroused enormous interest. Increasing numbers of his visitors were uncompromising opponents of the tsarist society – Yuriev, a left-wing slavophile, Fyodorov, an ascetic and mystic, Syutaev, a self-educated peasant who refused to pay his taxes, and many, many more. Bohemians, pacifists and revolutionaries, visionaries, students and eccentrics, peasants, artisans and factory-workers, the disaffected and the disinherited – they arrived in their hundreds to meet the great writer and prophet; and they stayed and stayed. Sofia hated these 'dark ones', as she called them, for they took him from her; they filled the house day and night, creating extra work and worries for her; they had to be entertained, reassured, paid or thrown out; they surrounded Tolstoy with an unpleasantly worshipful atmosphere; and they brought the whole family to the unwelcome attention of the police. Sofia was outraged, shocked to her conservative soul, and deeply frightened.

But mainly she hated what she saw as the hypocrisy of this conversion of her husband's. He now rose early, tidied his own room, pumped his own water from the well and took it home in a barrel; he chopped wood, made his own boots and worked in the fields with the peasants. But for all his proclamations of universal love and brotherhood, she had to endure his calculated slights and insults. He refused to help her with the education of their children or the management of the estate (at which she was no more successful than he, being opposed to any sort of technical innovation in farming, and unable to tell a good steward from a bad one). And when he gave up hunting, drinking and eating meat, this merely involved her in preparing two menus every day.

Her diaries are merciless; again and again she refers unforgivingly to his old diaries, accusing him of merely seeking fame and fortune under another name: 'He would like the eyes of the world to see him on the pedestal which he took such pains to erect for himself. But his diaries cast him into the filth in which he once lived, and that infuriates him.'

When terrorists assassinated Tsar Alexander II in 1881, Tolstoy wrote to his heir begging him not to hang them. Sofia was distraught, terrified that the whole family would be thrown into jail. We read her diaries now with an increasing sense that her days are numbered and the social order supporting her has not long to run. At this point she appears so tragically blind, yet so powerfully sympathetic that we long to step in, alter the course of history and save her.

In the years that followed the discord between the two became more acute. He wrote in his diaries (which of course she read) about his loneliness in his family and his domineering wife, with her sharp tongue and her hostility to his changed philosophy of life. Sofia, tired, bewildered and pregnant yet again, retorted in hers that she could no longer do both a man's *and* a woman's work. After nineteen uninterrupted years in the country she was also beginning to chafe at her solitary life, and she longed to visit Moscow, to be with Sergei during his first term at the university, and Tanya, who was about to start an art course in the capital and had to be introduced to the social life, as well as Ilya and Lyova, now aged 15 and 12, who were old enough to enrol in secondary school. But she also wanted to enjoy herself a little, meet some friends and attend some concerts. All this would cost money. And there were also three new children now to consider – Andrei (born in 1877), Mikhail (in 1879) and Aleksei (in 1881). And so in the autumn of 1881 a house was bought in Moscow, and thereafter the family spent the winters there.

But this was the source of yet more bitter arguments. There existed for Tolstoy three types of woman: 'femme du temple', 'femme du foyer' and 'femme de la rue'. His wife had moved swiftly through the first two categories, and her outrageous wordly desires had now clearly placed her in the third. The girl he had married had been an angel of modesty and obedience. Now that she was beginning to assert herself against him and claim her own needs, for privacy, music, her own friends – even her own sexual needs, for she was now apparently discovering some of the tormenting desires of the flesh – he turned her into the devil, everything he hated in himself, and withdrew from her, devoting himself more and more to the endless visitors who came to see him in Yasnaya Polyana and Moscow with all their religious, personal and political problems. It was to them that he complained of his tyrannical wife. But it was in his story *The Kreutzer Sonata* that these complaints were spelt out with their greatest cruelty and clarity, for all the world to read. Yet when the story was banned as obscene it was Sofia who went in person to the Tsar and pleaded successfully for the ban to be revoked.

When in 1884, at the age of forty, Sofia became pregnant for the fifteenth time, in spite of all Tolstoy's vows of chastity, her shame was so intense that she tried to have the baby aborted. (The abortionist refused in horror to proceed on learning who she was.) And when she finally went into labour with the unfortunate Aleksandra, Tolstoy packed his bag after a petty quarrel and announced that he was off to make a new life in America. (He returned to finish the quarrel shortly before the baby was born.)

Sofia was exhausted. Her diaries record her endless labours: managing the estate and the family's increasingly complicated financial affairs, copying all Tolstoy's voluminous writings, worrying constantly about his every little cough and always fearing the worst, tending him tirelessly through his frequent illnesses (for she never allowed anyone else to care for him when she was ill, and only when he was ill did she forget her bitterness).

Endless domestic tasks and suffocating confinement breed a boredom as vast as the steppes, a narcotic depression for which there is no cure or release but the madness which gradually and terrifyingly comes on her.

From 1891 there is more and more talk in her diaries of nervous troubles – headaches, sleeplessness, 'evil spirits'. She is a prey to physical symptoms – neuralgia, eyestrain, stomach-aches, fevers and asthma attacks. Quickened pulse-rates and heightened temperatures are obsessively recorded. And these problems are complicated by the onset of the menopause, with its hot flushes and unspecified 'gynaecological problems', for which she consults specialists. She talks frequently of suicide, and makes numerous attempts to kill herself – throwing herself in the pond, poisoning herself with opium, lying in the snow to freeze, refusing to eat.

She writes constantly in her diaries now of Tolstoy's ill-treatment of her. He writes of her too in his diaries, with some anger, but also with pity and despair, and long periods of estrangement between them alternate bewilderingly with periods of passion. Now, in her fifties, with the fear of pregnancy behind her, her physical passion awakens. Yet it is all so late, and makes her feel so sad, incomplete and unworthy. 'His passion dominates me, but my whole moral being cries out against it . . . All my life I have dreamed spiritual dreams, aspired to the perfect union, a spiritual communion, not *that*!'

There was still some tenderness and friendship left too, and during the disastrous harvest of 1891 the two worked together in the countryside on behalf of the peasant victims of the famine. Yet amid the last flickerings of their love there is always the sensation of fast approaching death. Indeed fears of illness and death are always present in an atmosphere almost completely ignorant of 'scientific' medicine. Her daughter Maria has seven babies die before birth, her beloved eldest daughter Tanya gives birth to three dead babies, and three of her own infants die before the age of seven. These children are frail, spiritual creaturs, cherished intensely and mourned inconsolably. It is when her adored youngest son Vanechka dies in 1895 at the age of seven that Sofia's spirit is finally broken, and dazed by despair she longs only to join her dead children in the other world.

Music becomes the focus of her life. It is with its help that she regains her sanity. And it is through her friendship with the composer Sergei Taneev that she finds peace of mind and the strength to survive. All her thoughts and feelings become focused on her dead son and the gentle undemanding Taneev ('the man at the centre of my disgraceful untimely madness'). Yet the relationship could never conceivably be consummated: 'How much spent passion, how many tragic feelings of love pass between decent people and are *never* expressed! And these feelings are the most important of all!' Tolstoy tries furiously and helplessly to intervene against Taneev, as do her friends and her children, but she refuses to be ruled. She visits Moscow to attend concerts and meet Taneev and his friends, she invites musicians back to the house to play, and she spends hours herself at the piano.

Away from music and Taneev, despair breaks through. Her diaries, fragmented, confused, charged with emotion, turn now into a sad catalogue of female complaints – of loneliness and powerlessness, jealousy and self-pity, love rejected and work unappreciated, fears of confinement, illness and madness. Endless outpourings of emotions, moods, descriptions and reflections are all jumbled up, the poetic and the prosaic flung recklessly together with a breathless and desperate incoherence, often without so much as an 'and' or 'but' to help us interpret them.

While Tolstoy soars above the world she remains chained to earth by all the problems he leaves there for her to deal with – and thus she comes to represent to him everything he is trying to rid himself of: 'If he is protesting against humanity as a whole, the entire existing social order, he can hardly be expected not to protest against me, a mere weak woman.'

The old Tolstoy had died in 1881, he explained, leaving his property to his wife and children, and a new Tolstoy had been born. He had hoped that his family would change with him then – that was why he stayed with them – but they had not. So all he asked now was that the copyright on all his post-1881 works be given away. Sofia refused. She had the estate to run and nine children to support, and she had no wish to line the pockets of his publishers merely for the privilege of finding work as a laundress. Yet his words always carried so much more weight than hers. ('If one were to say which of us caused the other more pain, it would be he: his weapons are so much more powerful and more authoritative.')

Her diaries melt into self-pity at every turn. Her labours for him, once performed so gladly, now turn into mere drudgery. 'Everything wears out in the end, even a mother's love.' Her endless responsibilities bring her no freedom, and the lack of it becomes increasingly oppressive to her: 'I am free to eat, sleep, be quiet and submit,' she writes in 1898, 'but I am not free to think as I please, to love whom I please, to come and go according to my own interests and intellectual pleasures, to pursue my music . . . ' Meanwhile Tolstoy is writing in his diary: 'A woman can be free only if she is a Christian. An emancipated woman who is not a Christian is a wild beast.' Again, to his son Lyova, he warns: 'A sound healthy woman is a wild beast.' And to all three of his elder sons: 'The most intelligent woman is less intelligent than the most stupid man.'

Meanwhile Sofia muses on her wasted talents: 'I was wondering why there weren't any women writers, artists or composers of genius,' she writes in the same year. 'It's because all the passions of an energetic woman are consumed by her family – love, her husband and especially her children. When she has finished bearing and educating them her artistic needs awaken, but by then it is too late, for her abilities have atrophied.' She does not mention the main obstacle to her self-fulfilment – perhaps because even at the age of fifty-six, she still admits to feeling afraid of her husband. But Tolstoy's views on women are all too painfully familiar to her – and all too typical in tsarist Russia: 'He announced that he was against women's emancipation and so-called "equal rights", and that no matter what a woman did – be it teaching, medicine or art – she had only one real purpose in life and that was sexual love. So that whatever she might strive to achieve, her strivings would merely crumble to ashes.' Women should not raise the issue of their own emancipation, he goes on, this would be unwomanly and impertinent. They should not talk of women's inequality at all, in fact, but of people's inequality in general. Sofia agrees: 'It's not freedom we women need, it's *help*, help mainly in bringing up our sons.'

Her cries for help become more frequent, but they are unheard. She is bitterly angry about Tolstoy's cynical views on women, which have made her suffer so and which she feels he has come by simply because he did not meet a decent woman until he was thirty-four and married her. And in her powerlessness she clings to Taneev.

Tolstoy's disciples all dislike her – particularly Vladimir Chertkov, the most persisent, unimaginative and dogmatic of them all. And it is while the conflict between the couple is at its most intense that Chertkov enters their lives to set them against one another in earnest. His purpose is to gain Tolstoy's confidence, his copyright and his soul.

Chertkov is utterly unscrupulous. Humourless, unimaginative and rude, pathologically attached to Tolstoy and pathologically hostile to his wife, his purpose has always been to divide them. As long ago as 1887 Sofia read a letter he wrote to Tolstoy 'describing in joyful tones his deep spiritual communion with his wife, and commiserating with L.N. for being deprived of this joy'. While Tolstoy enjoins Chertkov: 'Let everyone try not to marry, and if he be married, to live with his wife as brother and sister . . . you will object that this would mean the end of the human race? . . . What a great misfortune! The antediluvian animals are gone from the earth, human animals will disappear too . . . I have no more pity for these two-footed beasts than for the ichthyosaurus.'

Chertkov manages to wheedle out of the old man his diaries, which have until then belonged unquestioningly to Sofia. Then he prevails on Tolstoy to alter his will in his favour. From 1910 onwards her diaries are dominated by Chertkov's evil genius. (The more normal everyday events of her life for this year are reserved for her Daily Diaries.) Sofia's condition worsens with every moment. Sleepless nights are followed by days blurred by opium and anxious depression, and her obsessional prying and spying drives Tolstoy yet further from her. While he weeps and suffers and rails against her, Chertkov seizes on this discord to exacerbate it: 'The shadow of this crazy woman, mad with greed and wrath, hovers over our friendship', he writes to a friend. Lev Nikolaevich had merely proved by his fortitude that it was truly possible to carry in one's heart a truly indestructible love: he evidently needed a cruel and ruthless warder to bind him hand and foot.

Chertkov does all he can to encourage Tolstoy to leave his wife and make a new life for himself elsewhere. And in 1910, at the age of eighty-two, this is what he does, and on October 28 he leaves Yasnaya Polyana with his doctor and his youngest daughter Aleksandra, and boards a train heading south. When she finds him gone, Sofia throws herself into the pond. She is dragged out and taken to her bed, where she lies semi-delirious and refusing to eat. By the time she learns that Tolstoy is lying ill at the stationmaster's hut at the station of Astappovo, it is too late. She manages to see him only ten minutes before he dies, and there is no time for them to speak.

She lies for many months after his death in a fever, and when she resumes her Daily Diaries the entries are short and matter-of-fact. With Tolstoy's death she regains her clarity, but loses all her old wild, mad energy. She works hard to the end, copying his writings, dashing off endless articles, supervising the estate, tending and visiting the grave, entertaining the hordes of visitors who come to pay their respects to Tolstoy's widow. And to the end she resents this household drudgery, which takes her from her *real* work – of the intellect and the spirit.

In the last nine years of her life she sees the outbreak of world war, two revolutions and civil war. Yet her life and her preoccupations remain much as before. She greets the revolution of 1917 with bewilderment, but is grateful to the Bolsheviks for providing her with everything she needs and not expropriating the estate. And when Bolshevik soldiers and commissars are billeted in the village during the Civil War she finds them unexpectedly sympathetic. She remains as indomitable as ever into her seventies, making little of her own discomforts and going off to the fields to pick potatoes when the shops empty. As her strength declines her diary dwindles and she leaves us in October 1919 with the unforgettable image of civil war refugees trailing down the highway on their way from Oryol to Tula.

Sofia Tolstoy is a complex woman, a human dynamo with an iron constitution and a poetic soul. The 'dark ones' who fill her house see her as a tedious, self-centred, complaining woman, who threatens to drag her husband down with her. And this is the judgement that has been passed down to us. True, one's sympathies are often strained by her exasperating snobbishness, her anti-semitism, her sentimentality and her conservatism. But her diaries reveal her as someone of immense subtlety, intelligence, dignity and courage. She refuses to be resigned when all are against her, refuses to accept decisions taken over her head, refuses to be mocked, exploited or silenced. Her diaries are the writings of a confused psyche, battered but indomitable, clinging desperately to her self-esteem and the better things of life. She longs to improve herself (though she dreads change), and her writing is informed by her search for clarity, balance and goodness, through love, pain, and increasingly death.

Like Anna Karenina, she asserts the finer feelings in a barbaric society hostile to enlightenment. Her struggle too is against sexual hypocrisy, but it is also against herself, against her own split psyche and her unloving husband. 'If personal salvation and the spiritual *life* means *killing* one's closest friend, then Lyovochka's salvation is assured,' she writes. 'But is this not the death of us both?' Her diaries are a terrible reminder of the price of genius and the sacrifices made in its name.

The translation of these immense diaries has given me an all too uncomfortably close understanding of Sofia Tolstaya's despair. The burden has been lightened by help and encouragement from many people too numerous to mention, but I am especially grateful to Professor Reginald Christian, of St Andrews University, for his invaluable suggestions and corrections; to Della Couling, for her patient and sensitive editing; to Barbara Alpern Engel, of the University of Colorado, for her inspiring work on women in nineteenth-century Russia; to Lily Feiler, for sharing with me her enthusiasm for Sofia Tolstaya, and to Dr Faith Wigzell, of the School of Slavonic Studies, London University, for her help with the translation.

In a work of this length, problems of accuracy seem to multiply exponentially, and all such errors are my responsibility. However, because I have opted whenever possible for a literal translation, I have tried not to alter Sofia's own inconsistencies and inaccuracies, particularly when these are clarified in the notes, so that when a name, date or book title in the text does not correspond with that given in the notes, it is the note version which should be taken as correct.

A final word on transliteration and dates. There are several approved systems for transliterating Russian, but non-Russian readers tend to find the results impenetrable and unpronounceable. So my transliteration of Russian names, places and so on corresponds with that commonly used by British historians, rather than with any standard convention. (Names already familiar in an anglicised version, such as Tchaikovsky, Rachmaninov – even Sofia and Tolstoy – have been thus rendered.) Unless otherwise stated, dates given in the diaries correspond to the old (Julian) calendar, twelve days behind the western (Gregorian) calendar in the nineteenth century, and thirteen days behind in the twentieth. Russia did not adopt the Gregorian calendar until 1918, one year before Sofia Tolstaya's death.

I

DIARY 1862–1910

· 1862 ·

Tsar Alexander II's emancipation of the serfs the previous year ushers in the 'era of great reforms' – of law courts, the army and local government. Radical intellectuals call for the overhaul of every institution, and liberals urge yet more reforms. Early in 1862 a new political group emerges, Land and Liberty, whose members, populist socialists, denounce the emancipation as a fraud and dedicate themselves to peaceful propaganda in the countryside. The following decades witness increasing social tensions. Also increasing international trade, the expansion of the railway, postal and telegraph systems, and a massive increase in large industrial enterprises – which bring enormous hardship to the men and women working them. For the art, literature and journalism of the 1860s and 1870s, the trend is towards greater social realism.

On September 23, Lev Nikolaevich Tolstoy and Sofia Behrs are married in Moscow, and move immediately to Tolstoy's estate at Yasnaya Polyana, near Tula. December to February 1863, the Tolstoys visit Moscow to see The Cossacks *published.*

October 8 My diary again. It's sad to be going back to old habits I gave up since I got married. I used to write when I felt depressed – now I suppose it is for the same reason.

Relations with my husband have been so simple these past two weeks, and I felt so happy with him; he was my diary and I had nothing to hide from him.

But ever since yesterday, when he told me he didn't trust my love, I have been feeling truly terrible. I know why he does not trust my love: I don't think I shall be able to say or write what I really think. I always dreamt of the man I would love as a completely whole, new, *pure* person. In these childish dreams, which I still find hard to give up, I imagined that this man would always be with me, that I would know his slightest thought and feeling, that he would love nobody but me as long as he lived, and that he, like me and unlike others, would not have to sow his wild oats before becoming a respectable person. These dreams have always been so sweet to me. It was thanks to them that I almost fell in love with P.; for in loving my dreams I made P. a part of them.[1]

It would not have been hard to take these feelings further and be quite carried away by them – but then I have never really stopped, I've just gone ahead without thinking. Since I got married I have had to recognise how foolish these dreams were, yet I cannot renounce them. The whole of his (my husband's) past is so ghastly that I don't think I shall ever be able to accept it.[2] Unless I can discover other interests in my life, like the children I long for, since they will give me a firm future and show me what real purity is, without all the abominations of his past and everything else that now makes me so bitter towards my husband. He cannot understand that his past is like another world to me, with thousands of different feelings, good and bad, which can never belong to me, just as his youth, squandered on God knows what or whom, can never be mine either. Another thing he doesn't understand is that I am giving him everything; not one part of me has been wasted elsewhere, and only my childhood did not belong to him. And even that belonged to him. My fondest memories are of my first childish love for him, and it is not my fault if this love was destroyed, how can it be? Was it so wrong of me? He had to fritter away his life and strength, he had to experience so much evil before he could feel anything noble; now his love for me seems to him something strong and good – but only because it is such a long, long time since he lived a good life, as I do. There are bad things in my past too, but not so many as in his.

He loves to torment me and see me weep because he does not trust me. He wishes I had lived as evil a life as he, so that I might more fully appreciate goodness. It instinctively irritates him that happiness has come so easily to me, and that I accepted him without hesitation or remorse. But I have too much self-respect to cry. I don't want him to see how I suffer; let him think it's easy for me. Yesterday while Grandfather[3] was here I went downstairs especially to see him, and I was suddenly overwhelmed by an extraordinary feeling of love and strength. At that moment I loved him so much that I longed to go up to him; but then I felt that the moment I touched him I should not feel so happy – almost like a sacrilege. But I never shall or can let him know what is going on within me. I have so much foolish pride – the slightest hint that he misunderstands or mistrusts me throws me into despair. It makes me so angry. What is he doing to me? Little by little I shall withdraw completely from him and poison his life. Yet I feel so sorry for him at those times when he doesn't trust me; his eyes fill with tears and his face is so gentle and sad. I could smother him with love at those moments, and yet the thought haunts me: 'He doesn't *trust* me, he doesn't *trust* me.' Today I began to feel that we were drifting further and further apart. I am creating my own sad world for myself and he is making himself a practical life filled with distrust. And I thought how vulgar this kind of relation was. And I began to distrust his love too. When he kisses me I am always thinking, 'I am not the first woman he has loved.' It hurts me so much that my love for him – the dearest thing in the world to me because it is my first and last love – should not be enough for him. I too have loved other men, but only in my imagination – whereas he has loved and admired so many women, all so pretty and lively, all with different faces, characters and souls, just as he now loves and admires me. I know these thoughts are petty and vulgar but I can't help it, it is his past that is to blame. I can't help it, I can't forgive God for so arranging things that people must *sow their wild oats* before they can become decent people. And I can't help feeling bitterly hurt that my husband should come into this common category of person. And then, he thinks I don't love him; why would I care so much about him if I didn't love him? Why else would I try to understand his past and his present, and what may interest him in future? It's a hopeless situation – how can a wife prove her love to a husband who tells her he married her only because he *had* to, even though she never loved him? As if I had ever, for one moment, regretted my past, or could so much as dream of not loving him – it's unimaginable! Does he really enjoy seeing me cry when I realise how difficult our relations are, and how we shall gradually drift further and further apart spiritually. Toys for the cat are tears for the mouse. But this toy is fragile, and if he breaks it, it will be he who cries. I cannot bear the way he is slowly wearing me down. Yet he is a wonderful and good person. He too loathes everything evil, he cannot bear it either. I used to love everything beautiful, my soul knew the meaning of ecstasy then – now all that has died in me. No sooner am I happy than he crushes me.

October 9 Yesterday we opened our hearts and now I feel much better, even happy. We went horse-riding today, which was splendid, but I feel downcast all the same. I had such a depressing dream last night, and it is weighing on me, although I do not remember it in detail. I thought of Maman today and grew dreadfully sad, but I am happy enough on the whole. I do not regret my past. I shall always bless it, for I have known great happiness. My husband seems much calmer now and I think he trusts me again, God willing. It is true, I realise, I do not make him very happy. I seem to be asleep all the time and unable to wake up. If I did, I am sure I would be a completely different person, but I do not know how to. *Then* he would realise how much I love him, for I should be able to *tell* him of my love. I should be able to see into his soul as I used to, and know how to make him completely happy again. I must wake up at once, I must. This sleep came over me that summer when we drove from Pokrovskoe to Ivitsy. I woke up briefly, then fell asleep again when we went to Moscow, and have been unable to wake ever since. Something is weighing on me. I keep thinking that at any moment I might die. It is so strange to be thinking such things now that I have a husband. I can hear him in there sleeping. I am frightened of being on my own. He will not let me go into his room, which makes me very sad. All physical things disgust him.

October 11 I am terribly, terribly sad, and withdrawing further and further into myself. My husband is ill and out of sorts and doesn't love me. I expected this, yet I could never have imagined it would be so terrible.

Why do people always think I am so happy? What no one seems to realise is that I cannot create happiness, either for him or for myself. Before when I was feeling miserable I would ask myself, 'What is the use of living when you make others unhappy and yourself wretched?' This thought keeps recurring to me now, and I am terrified. He grows colder and colder every day, while I on the contrary love him more and more. His coldness will soon be unbearable to me. Of course, he is much too honest ever to deceive me. If he does not love me he would never pretend to do so, but when he does love me I can see it in his every movement. He upsets me all the time. When Grisha talked today of his 'papa' I felt so sorry for him – for he is not his real son – that I almost cried.[4] I keep thinking of my own family and how happy my life was with them; now, my God, it breaks my heart to think that nobody loves me, just Auntie,[5] who merely does so because she feels obliged to, and my husband, who does not love me at all. Darling mother, Tanya – what wonderful people they were, why did I ever leave them? Poor Liza, it gnaws at my conscience to think of all she has had to endure. Lyovochka is a wonderful man and I feel that absolutely everything is my fault; yet I am afraid to show him how sad I am for I know how bored men are by such foolish melancholy. I used to console myself that it would all pass and everything would soon be all right again, but now I feel that things will never get better, and will merely become a great deal worse. Papa writes to me: 'Your husband loves you passionately.'[6] It is true, he did love me *passionately*, but passion passes, and what nobody realised is that he was attracted to me without loving me. I have only just realised this myself. Why did I not see then that he would have to pay a heavy price for this attraction, for it is intolerable to have to live your whole life with a wife you do not love. Why have I ruined this dear man, whom everybody loves so much? For once, it was pure selfishness on my part that made me marry him. I look at him now and think what he used to think about me: I wish I could love her, but I no longer can.

Yes, this time has passed like a dream. 'You'll be happy, you'll see,' people used to tease me. 'Don't worry so much!' they said. Now I have lost everything I once possessed, all my energy for work, life and household tasks has been wasted. Now I want only to sit in silence all day, doing nothing but think bitter thoughts. I wanted to do some work, but could not; why should I dress up in that stupid bonnet which makes my head ache? I long to play the piano but it is so awkward in this place; upstairs you can be heard all over the house and downstairs the piano is too bad to play. He suggested today that I stay at home while he went off to Nikolskoe.[7] I should have agreed and set him free from my presence, but I simply could not. I can hear him now playing a piano duet upstairs with Olga. Poor man, he is always looking for something to divert him and take him away from me. What is the point of living?[8]

November 13 An unlucky date – this was the first thing that came into my head. But I have spoken to him, and like a true egoist, I always feel much better after I have had him into my room and set my mind at rest.

It is true, I cannot find anything to occupy me. He is fortunate because he is talented and clever. I am neither. One cannot live by love alone, but I am too stupid to do anything but sit and think about him. He has only to feel slightly under the weather, and I immediately think, 'What if he dies?' and these hideous thoughts then make me feel wretched for the next three hours. When he is cheerful, I worry only lest this mood passes, and am so happy that I can again think of nothing else. Whenever he is away or busy I again think of him constantly, listening out for him and watching the expression on his face. It is probably because I am pregnant that I am in such an abnormal state at present; it has some effect on him too, I know. It is not difficult to find work, there is plenty to do, but first you have to enjoy such petty household tasks as breeding hens, tinkling on the piano, reading a lot of fourth-rate books and precious few good ones, and pickling cucumbers. I am sure all this will come once I have forgotten my idle girlhood ways and grown used to living in the country. I don't want to fall into the common rut and be bored all the time – and I shan't. I wish my husband had a greater influence on me. It is strange that I should love him so terribly and yet feel his influence so little. I sometimes have lucid moments when I understand everything, when I see how splendid life is and how many responsibilities I have, and how pleasant this is, but these moments soon pass and I forget everything. I am waiting for that bright day when things run as smoothly as a machine and I can start to live – that is, live an active life. It is strange, I look forward to this time as I look forward to some events, like the holidays or the coming of summer. I am asleep now, since nothing brings me any excitement or joy – neither the trip to Moscow nor the thought of the baby. I wish I could take some remedy to refresh me and wake me up.

I have not prayed for a long time. Before, I used to love even the external aspects of religious ritual. When nobody was looking I would often light a wax candle before the icon, put some flowers there, lock the door, kneel on the floor and pray for one or two hours. It all seems rather silly and ridiculous now, but I love remembering it. My life is so serious now, yet my early memories are still so vivid that it is hard to part with them, even though it's impossible to return to them. Over the next few years I shall make myself a serious *female* world, and I shall love it even more than the old one because it will contain my husband and my children, whom one loves more than one's parents and brothers and sisters. But I haven't settled down yet. I still swing between my past and my future. My husband loves me too much to tell me how to live my life; besides, it is difficult, and it is something I must work out for myself. And he too feels that I have changed. With patience I shall again be as I was before, although no longer a young girl but a woman; I shall wake up then, and both of us will be happy.

I am sure that Moscow will refresh me; surrounded by my old life I shall view the present in a better light, for I am the cause of all this trouble. If only he would be patient with me during this painful time in which I have to change so much . . . I am alone now, and as I look around me I feel sad. It is terrible to be alone. I am not used to it. There was so much life and love at home, and it's so lifeless here without him. He is almost always on his own and cannot understand me. He is used to it, and finds pleasure not in the company of those close to him, as I do, but in his work. Well, I shall get used to it too. But now there is never a happy voice to he heard, as if everyone had died. And then he gets angry when I complain about being left alone. He is so unfair, but then he never had a family, so he cannot understand. I shall do all I can to please him because he is a splendid man and I am a far worse person than he, and because I love him and have nothing, nothing in the world but him. And if I am bored it is because I have few talents and no inner resources, and because I am used to a more boisterous life, while there is nothing here but deathly silence. But I shall get used to it, one can get used to anything. And in time I shall turn this into a cheerful noisy house and live for my children. I shall make a serious and purposeful life for myself and enjoy my young ones.

November 23 He disgusts me with his talk of the 'people'. I feel it is either me, representing his family, or the people, whom L. loves so passionately.[9] This is selfish. So be it. I live through him and want him to live for me, otherwise I feel cramped and suffocated in this place. Today I ran out of the house because everyone and everything disgusted me – Aunt, the students,[10] Natalya Petrovna,[11] the walls, life – so I just slipped out and ran off alone, and I wanted to laugh and shout for joy. L. no longer disgusted me, but I suddenly realised how far apart we were: his 'people' could never absorb all my attention, and I could never fully absorb his as he does mine. If I do not interest him, if he sees me as a doll, merely his *wife*, not a human being, then I will not and cannot live like that.[12] Of course I am idle at present, but I am not so by nature; I simply have not discovered anything I could do. He gets impatient and angry. Let him, I feel happy and free today because I am on my own, and although he has been very morose he has left me alone, thank God. I know he has a brilliant nature, he is poetic and intelligent, and he has many and various talents, but it makes me angry that he is preoccupied only with the gloomy side of things. Sometimes I long to break free of his rather oppressive influence and stop worrying about him, but I cannot. I find his influence oppressive because I have begun thinking his thoughts and seeing with his eyes, trying to become like him, and losing myself. And I have changed too, which makes it even harder for me. In future I shall always leave the house or go for a drive whenever I am depressed. Sometimes when I go out I suddenly feel free. At other times I cannot stop imagining him anxiously running around to look for me, and I get so worried that I go straight home. He has been so gloomy these days, I could have wept. He will not talk to me. It is terrible to live with him – he'll suddenly get carried away by his love for the common people again and I shall be done for, because he loves me merely as he used to love his school, nature, the people, maybe his writing, all of which he loved a little, one after the other, until it was time for something new. Aunt came in and asked why I had run out and where I had been, and I wanted to needle her and said I was escaping from the students, for she always defends them. But that was not true. I am not the least bit angry with the students, it is only old habit that makes me grumble and complain like this. I went out simply because I was bored with doing nothing – I am not used to staying at home all day. Here it is nothing but Aunt, Natalya Petrovna, Aunt, Natalya Petrovna, and then the students, one after the other. My husband is not mine today, he will not talk. It's as if he wasn't here. If only I could leave, go off and see how my family is and then return. I shall go and play the piano now. He is in the bath. He is a stranger to me today.

December 16 One of these days I think I shall kill myself with jealousy. 'In love as never before!' he writes. With that fat, pale peasant woman – how frightful![13] I looked at the dagger and the guns with such joy. One blow, I thought, how easy it would be – if only if it weren't for the baby. Yet to think she is there, just a few steps away. I feel demented. I shall go for a drive. I may even see her. So he really did love her! I should like to burn his diary and the whole of his past.

I have returned and am feeling much worse; my head aches, I am distraught, my heart is heavy, so heavy. I felt free outside in the open air – if only I could always think, breathe and live as freely as that. But life is so petty. Love is hard – when you love it takes your breath away, you lay down your life and soul for it, and it's with you as long as you live. It would be narrow and mean, this little world of mine, if it were not for him. Yet it is impossible for us to join together our two worlds. He is so intelligent, he has such energy, and then there is that dreadful, endless past of his. And mine is so small and insignificant. I felt terrified today by the thought of our journey to Moscow, for I shall become even more insignificant there. If I am to have a life and a world that will satisfy me I think it will be here, in Yasnaya, without visitors, with only our family and whatever I can create for myself. I have been reading the openings of some of his works, and the very mention of love or women makes me feel so disgusted and depressed that I would gladly burn everything. I want never to be reminded of his past again. I really would not care about his books, because jealousy has made me terribly selfish.

If I could kill him and create a new person exactly the same as he is now, I would do so happily.

· 1863 ·

Reforms introduced over the following decade by Alexander II's Minister of War, Milyutin. Constitutional reforms in Finland. A charter is passed barring women from the universities. Many go abroad to study.

June 23 – birth of the couple's son, Sergei. Shortly afterwards Tolstoy talks of going to war (possibly to put down the Polish uprising against Russian domination, possibly to take part in the continuing war in the Caucasus). But instead he starts on War and Peace. *Summer – Sofia's 17-year-old sister Tanya Behrs visits Yasnaya Polyana and embarks on a romance with Tolstoy's brother Sergei, twenty years her senior.*

January 9 Never in my life have I felt so wretched with remorse. Never did I imagine that I could be so much to blame. I have been choked with tears all day, I feel so depressed. I am afraid to talk to him or look at him. I love him deeply, he has never been so precious to me, and I have never felt so worthless and loathsome. Yet he is not even angry and he still loves me, and his face is so gentle and saintly. A man like this could make one die of happiness and humility. I feel very ill. Mental pain has made me physically ill. I thought I would miscarry, I was in such pain. I am demented. I have been praying all day, trying to lighten my crime and undo what I have done. I feel a little easier when he is not here, for then I can cry and love him. When he is here my conscience tortures me; it is agony to see his sweet face, which I have avoided looking at since yesterday evening and which is so precious to me. How could I have treated him so badly? I have racked my brains for some way of making amends for that stupid word[1] – or rather, not so much make amends as make myself a better person for him. I cannot love him any more than I already do, for I already love him to such excess, with all my heart and soul, that there is no other thought or desire in my mind apart from my love for him, nothing. There is absolutely no evil in him, nothing I could ever dream of reproaching him for. He still doesn't believe me, he still thinks I cannot do without constant diversions, but I need nothing but him. If only he knew how joyfully I contemplate the future, not with a lot of entertainments but with him and everything that is dear to him. I try so hard to love even the things I dislike, like Auerbach.[2] But yesterday I was being especially wilful – I surpassed even myself. Have I really such a vicious character, or is it all merely the effect of pregnancy and bad nerves? Things must get a little better now that I know I am 'guarding our happiness' – if I haven't already ruined it. It is all terrible, when things could be so happy. He is healthy now. That was my doing. Tanya,[3] Sasha,[4] and Kusminskii have arrived, and I simply cannot stop crying. I would not let them see me for anything, for they are children and have never been in love. I so long to see him. Lord, what if he loses interest in me altogether? Now absolutely everything depends on him. What a worthless person I am; how depressing this mental pettiness is. I am sure he must suddenly have realised just how vile and pathetic I am.

January 11 I am calmer now because he is being a little kinder to me. But my unhappiness is still so fresh that every little memory of it brings on a terrible physical pain in my head and body – I feel it passing through my veins and nerves.

He has said nothing and has not even referred to my diary. I don't know whether he has read it. I think my diary was vile, and I have no desire to re-read it.

I am quite alone, and afraid, which is why I wanted to write sincerely and at length, but fear has confused my thoughts. I am afraid of being frightened now that I am pregnant. My jealousy is a congenital illness, or it may be because in loving him I have nothing else to love; I have given myself so completely to him that my only happiness is with him and from him, and I am afraid of losing him, as old men fear to lose an only child on whom their whole life depends, when they know they can never have another. People always told me I was not at all egotistical, but this is really the most complete egotism. I am not generally an egotist, yet in this respect I am frightful. But I love him so much that this too will pass. Only I shall need a lot of patience and strength of will, otherwise it will be no good. There are days when I am morbidly in love with him, and this is one of those days. It is always so when I have done something wrong. It hurts me to look at him, listen to him or be with him, like a devil in the presence of a saint. When I manage to please him and make him love me as before, then our relations will be easier again. But now it is because our merits are not equal that our relations are not equal. People's merits are never equal, of course, but I do wish there were just a little less evil on my side! I used to love him boldly, and rather assertively, but now I thank God for his every kind word and caress, for every indulgence and friendly look.

This is how I live now, and I must expect nothing more and be content. I used to feel some pride that I was bearing a child and would soon bring it into the world, but this is merely my fate, a law of nature, and even that is no consolation. My husband (i.e. Lyovochka) is everything to me, he is responsible for all that is good in me, because I love him deeply and care for nothing in the world but him.

January 14 (Moscow) I am alone again, and sad again. Yet we have managed to make peace again. I do not know what has reconciled him to me – or me to him. It happened of itself. All I know is that I have my happiness back. I want to go home. I have so many plans and dreams of how I will live in Yasnaya with *him*. I feel rather sad to have broken so completely, body and soul, from the Kremlin crowd. I see terribly clearly how much my world has changed, yet I love my family more than ever, especially Maman, and it sometimes saddens me that I am no longer part of their lives. I live completely through him and for him, and it's often painful for me to realise that I am not *everything* to him and that if I were suddenly to die he would certainly be able to console himself somehow, for he has so many *ressources*,* whereas I have such a weak nature: I have given myself to one man and would never be able to find another world for myself.

Life in this hotel depresses me. I am happy only when I am sitting with my family, and with *Lyovochka*, of course.[5] I could leave for home at once I know, it is largely up to me, but I have not the heart to say goodbye to my family so soon after arriving, and I am too lazy to move. I had such a bad dream last night. Our Yasnaya peasant girls and women were visiting us in some huge garden, all dressed up as ladies, then started going off somewhere, one after the other. A. came last, wearing a black silk dress.[6] I began speaking to her and was seized with such violent rage that I picked up her child from somewhere and began tearing it to pieces. I tore off its head and its legs – I was like a madwoman. Then Lyovochka came up and I told him they would banish me to Siberia, but he picked up the legs and arms and all the other bits and told me it was only a doll. I looked down and saw that it was indeed, with just cloth and stuffing for a body. And that made me furious.

I often torture myself thinking about her, even here in Moscow. It is his *past* that torments me, not his present. He can never be entirely mine as I am his, for his past is so full, rich and varied, that even if he died this instant his life would have been a full one. The only experience he has not yet had is that of being a father. As for me, I could never have imagined that life would suddenly give me all this, and cannot believe it will last. I keep thinking it is all merely accidental and passing, for it is too good. How terribly strange that one man, on the strength of his personality alone, and regardless of any other reasons or personal qualities, could have taken me in hand and made me completely happy.

Maman was right when she said I had become sillier than ever – rather, I think, my mind is just lazier. It is an unpleasant feeling, this physical lethargy. And the physical lethargy produces mental lethargy too.

I regret my former liveliness. But I think it will return. I feel it would have as good an effect on Lyovochka as it once had on the Kremlin crowd. When I first went to Yasnaya I was my old lively self, but now I have

*French in original.

deteriorated. Lyovochka used to love me even when I behaved outrageously. He seems to be mentally asleep, although I know his soul never sleeps but is always grappling with some great work. He has become very thin and this worries me. I would give anything to creep into his soul. He is not even writing his diary, which makes me very sad.

I sometimes have a sly unconscious desire to experience my power over him and make him obey me. But whenever I do, he always manages to outwit me, and I am glad he does; and it soon passes.

January 17 I have been feeling out of sorts and angry that he should love everything and everyone, when I want him to love only me. Now that I am alone in my room I realise I was just being wilful again; it is his kindness and the wealth of his feelings that make him good. The cause of all my whims and miseries and so on is this wretched egotism of mine, which makes me want to possess his life, his thoughts, his love, everything he has. This has become a sort of rule with me. The moment I think fondly of something or someone I tell myself no, I love only Lyovochka. But I absolutely *must* learn to love something else as he loves his *work*, so that I may turn to it when he grows cold towards me. These times will become increasingly frequent; imperceptibly it has been like this all along. I see this clearly now – why should Lyovochka study all the subtleties of our relations as I do, for want of anything else to occupy me? From this I also learn how I should behave with him, and I do this not as a duty but quite involuntarily. I cannot yet put this knowledge into practice, but everything comes in time. We must get back to Yasnaya very soon; there he devotes himself more to me, for there is nobody else but Aunt and me. Our life there is terribly precious to me, and I would not exchange it for any other; I would make any sacrifice for it. I shall gradually arrange things better, and if I succeed I shall be completely happy. I know I can make the house a happier place, as long as Lyovochka does not want visitors, for I do not know where I should find the right people to ask, and besides I don't like them. But if Lyovochka wants, then I will entertain whomever he cares to invite; anything to keep him happy and not bored, for then he will love me and there is nothing else I want. It is hard to live together without quarrelling, but I must try not to all the same, for he is right, our quarrels make a *cut*.[7] My misfortune is my jealousy. He must try to spare me this, and I must control myself and spare him. I understand why he doesn't always want to take me out with him – my hat and my crinolines get in his way – but I hate being alone without him. It's terrible to cling, but it saddens me that he no longer needs to be with me when we are not apart. My need to be near him grows stronger every day.

I have waited and waited for him and have now sat down again to write. There are people who live in solitude. But it's terrible to be alone. I don't suppose we shall go to that lecture now. Perhaps I got in his way. This thought often torments me, for I am often guilty of this. I have grown so terribly fond of Maman, and it frightens me, for we can never live together now. I have begun to love Tanya rather condescendingly – what right have I to do so?

I am dreadfully sad to have to leave them. Lyovochka doesn't understand and I say nothing. I shall be glad to see Aunt. I feel very fond of her these days, for I haven't talked about her to Lyovochka. He is so changeable. I have behaved badly to her and must be nicer, if only because she once looked after Lyovochka and will look after my children too. Anyway it is always wise to try to please people, as they love you for it. My trouble is, I am always afraid of flattering and dissembling. But there can be nothing insincere in wanting to make friends with a good, kind old woman. How narrow-minded I have become. Nothing interests me outside *our* life, and all the things and people that fill it. It is almost three and he still hasn't come. Why did he promise then? Is it good to be so unpunctual? I suppose it must be, for it shows he is not petty. I hate him to be angry with me. When he badgers me and blames me for everything I want to run away, for his words can pierce my heart. But his bad moods generally pass quickly and he doesn't often grumble.

January 29 Kremlin life is oppressive; it evokes the oppressive, lazy, aimless life I led here as a girl. All my illusions about the aims and duties of marriage vanished into thin air when Lyovochka let me know that one cannot be satisfied merely with one's family, one's husband or wife, but that one needs something more, a larger cause. ('I need nothing but you. Lyovochka talks a lot of nonsense sometimes.' [L. N. Tolstoy's note])

March 3 Still the same old story – writing on my own. But I am not lonely now, I have grown used to it. And I am now happy in the knowledge that he loves me, and loves me constantly. When he gets home he comes up to me so kindly and asks me something or tells me something. My life is cheerful and easy now. I read *his* diary and it made me happy.[8] There is me and his work – nothing else matters to him. Yesterday and today he has been preoccupied. I am afraid to disturb him when he is busy writing and thinking. I am afraid he will get angry and my presence will be unbearable to him. I am glad he is writing. I wanted to go to Mass this morning, but instead I stayed at home and prayed here. Since my marriage every form of ceremony and artificiality has become even more loathsome to me. I long with all my heart to manage the household and *do* something. But I haven't yet learnt how, I don't know how to go about it. It will come in time. It would be horrible to bustle around trying to deceive myself and others that I was *busy*. Who would I deceive anyway? What would be the point? Sometimes I see quite clearly *what* I ought to do, and how to spend my time usefully, but then I forget and am distracted. How easy and simple my life has become! I feel that my life and *my duty* is here, and I want nothing more. And even if I asked myself what I wanted when I was depressed, I wouldn't know how to reply. I do not think my love for Aunt is genuine, which distresses me. She is so old, and this irritates me more than it touches me. This is bad of me, I know. Yet she is always getting angry and is often insincere. How sunny it is outside, as sunny as in my heart. I am gradually reconciling myself to everything – the students, the common people and of course Aunt, and everything else I used to abuse. The power of Lyova's influence over me is strong and I am happy.

March 26 I am unwell and apathetic. He left for Tula this morning; I feel as if I haven't seen him for a month, and haven't been happy for a long, long time either. And when I do see him, it's as though it's only his shadow, an apparition. My love for him lies deep within me, but I feel it very strongly and know it is the only thing in my life. I visited the servants' quarters and now my heart is heavy. They are sick, they are unhappy, they complain, this one is ill, that one has some grief to talk about. And there are many cunning ones too, which made me even sadder. Aunt is kind and in a calm state, but I find her very tedious – she is so old. I have been thinking a lot about my family. Their life is so full. I often feel sad not to be with them, but I never regret my past life. I am so happy now. I am often afraid to love him. It would be easy to spoil such happiness. I'm beginning to get anxious that he's not back yet. It's always the way, when I don't go out with him I always blame myself afterwards. Better he should be angry, I think, better I should get in his way than torment myself waiting for him to return. Always the same story. He must not go to Nikolskoe or I shall go out of my mind. If only people could understand how slowly time passes. Aunt just came in and kissed my hand. I wonder why? But I was deeply touched. She really is very kind, and is sorry for me here alone, and if she is out of spirits it is because she is feeling bilious. And I am young and should be more tolerant of these weaknesses, and I often feel guilty that I am impatient and irritable with her. He was annoyed yesterday and wouldn't say why. So I suppose we are not being quite open with one another either. As for me, I always want to tell him what's worrying or annoying me, and am often afraid to. I am spoilt. Lyova gives me too much happiness. I love his cheerfulness, his moroseness, his good, good face, his gentle kindness, and his vexation, for he expresses all these things so wonderfully that he *hardly* ever insults my feelings. Now I am sitting here pleasantly, almost mechanically putting pen to paper as I think about him. Images of him pass through my mind as I imagine him from every angle and all the expressions that cross his face. Writing all this down is only a pretext for absorbing myself in him and dreaming about him. I always feel sick with happiness when he returns home. However much he says he loves me it couldn't possibly be as much as I love him. I am sure he has never waited for me with such desperate impatience.

April 1 I am unwell and in low spirits. Lyova has gone off again. I have a very great misfortune: I have no inner resources to draw on. And this is indeed necessary and important in life. The weather is wonderful, it is almost summer, and my mood is like the summer – sad. It is so bleak and lonely here. Lyova has his work and the estate to think about while I have nothing . . . What am I good for? I cannot go on living like this. I would like to *do* more, something *real*. At this wonderful time of year I always used to long for things, aspire to things, dream about God knows what. But I no longer need anything, no longer have those foolish aspirations, for I know instinctively that I have all I need now and there is nothing left to strive for, even though it is a little dreary here sometimes. So much happiness and so little to do. One grows tired even of good things and needs to do something useful as a contrast. What was previously replaced by dreams and the life of the imagination must now be replaced by some sort of work and a *real* life, not the life of the imagination. Everything seems stupid now and I get irritable.

April 6 We have started attending to the estate together, Lyova and I, he taking it all very seriously, me so far pretending to. It was all very pleasant and not at all petty. It interests me greatly and sometimes gives me pleasure too. He seems subdued, preoccupied and unwell, and this makes me constantly anxious and depressed. I am afraid to let him know how much these blood rushes of his worry me. It is a terrible thought, but I can't help worrying that this life of ours and our immense happiness together is not real happiness at all but just a trick of fate, and will suddenly be snatched away. I am afraid . . . It's stupid, but I cannot write it down. I wish this fear would pass quickly, for it poisons my whole life. He has bought some bees, which pleases me very much; managing the estate is interesting, but hard work too. The Auerbachs are so dull, we don't need anyone here. She has made me feel quite depressed. Yet I am sorry for her somehow. Does she love her husband? You can never really discover a person's 'marriage secrets'. Lyova certainly has something on his mind; he is being so unstraightforward and secretive. Or is it just that he has a headache? What is the matter with him? What does he want? I would do anything he wanted if only I could. He is out now, but I fear that when he comes back he will be in a bad temper and will find something to irritate him. I love him desperately, I know it, for I feel I could endure anything for his sake if I had to.

April 10 He has gone to meet Papa in Tula and I already feel miserable. I have been re-reading his letters to V. A.[9] They seem so youthful. It was not her he loved but love itself and her family life. I recognise him well – his moral precepts, his splendid strivings for all that was noble and *good*. What a wonderful man he is! And reading through these letters I almost stopped feeling jealous, as if it were not *V*. at all but *me*, the woman he *had* to love. I put myself into their world. She was apparently rather a pretty girl, essentially empty-headed, morally good and lovable only because she was so young, while he was just as he is now, not really in love with V. so much as with his love of life and goodness. Suddenly I saw Sudakovo* clearly too, with the piano, the sonatas and a pretty little dark-haired girl, kind and trusting. Then there was her youth (but what is this? Am I already thinking of myself as old?), nature, rural solitude. Anyway, I understood everything and was not at all unhappy. Then I read his plans for their family life together. Poor man, he was still too young to realise that happiness can never be planned in advance, and you will inevitably be unhappy if you try to do so. But what noble splendid dreams these were nevertheless.

April 24 Lyova is either old or unhappy. He seems to think of nothing but money, the estate and the distillery – nothing else interests him.[10] If he is not eating, sleeping or sitting in silence he is roaming about the estate alone the whole day. And I am wretched and alone, always alone. He shows his love for me merely by kissing my hands in a mechanical fashion, and by being kind to me and not cruel.

It is beautiful weather and generally more prepossessing outside, but something is gnawing at me. In the old days Tatiana and I knew how to appreciate spring and summer; we both used to enjoy it so much, the more so as we could be together and share our thoughts, without worrying about what this factory cost, or what kind of machinery that was, for such matters are desperately dull. I shall be terribly glad when she comes. I love young people in general, and especially such a dear person as Tanya. I feel so awkward with Lyova, bashful and ashamed of myself. I do not know why, for I have nothing on my conscience and have done him no wrong. I write this now, because this is what I think, yet the thought that he might read it disturbs me. I am afraid of loving him – afraid that he will see this, I suppose: that he will see how bored I am, and that this doesn't really matter to him. If I knew what I wanted I would ask for it, but I don't know. It will happen of its own accord.

April 25 The same wretchedness all morning, the same premonition of something terrible. I still feel very shy in my relations with Lyova. I cried as if demented and afterwards could not understand why this was always happening – I knew only that I had good reason to cry, and even possibly to die, if Lyova had stopped loving me as he used to. I did not mean to write

*The estate where Valeria Arseneva lived.

today, but I am all alone downstairs and have given in to my old habit of scribbling. I have been interrupted . . .

April 29, evening I get irritable over trifles – over some parcels, for instance. I make great efforts not to be irritable, and shall soon achieve this. Towards Lyova I feel terribly affectionate and rather shy – a result of my petty moods. Towards myself I feel a disgust such as I have not felt for a very long time. I desperately want to go out and look at the bees and the apple trees and work on the estate,[11] I want to be active, but I am heavy and tired, and my present infirmity tells me to sit still and look after my stomach. It's infuriating. And it distresses me that this infirmity should make Lyova so unkind to me, as if it were my fault I am pregnant. I'm no help to him at all at present. And there is another thing which makes me disgusted with myself. (One must above all speak the truth in a diary.) It made me happy to recall the time when V. V.[12] was in love with me. I wonder if it could make me happy if someone fell in love with me now? Oh, how trivial and loathsome. I always laughed at him then and never felt anything for him but revulsion and utter contempt. Lyova ignores me more and more. The physical side of love is very important for him. This is terrible, for me it is quite the opposite. At least he is morally sound, that is the main thing.

May 8 My pregnancy is to blame for everything – I am in an unbearable state, physically and mentally. Physically I am always ill with something, mentally there is this awful emptiness and boredom, like a dreadful depression. As far as Lyova is concerned I do not exist. I feel I am hateful to him, and want only to leave him in peace and cut myself out of his life as far as possible. I can do nothing to make him happy, because I am pregnant. It's a cruel truth that a wife only discovers whether her husband really loves her or not when she is pregnant. He has gone to the beehives and I would give anything to go too but shall not, because I have been having bad palpitations and it is difficult to sit down there, and there will be a thunder-storm any moment, and my head aches and I feel bored – I feel like weeping, and I do not want him to see me in this tedious and unpleasant state, especially as he is ill too. I feel awkward with him most of the time. If he is occasionally kind to me it is more a matter of habit, and he still feels obliged to continue the old relations even though he does not love me any more. I am sure it would be terrible for him to confess that he did once love me – and not so long ago either – but that all this is over now. If only he knew how much he has changed, if only he could step into my shoes for a while, he would understand how hard life is for me. But there is no help for it. He will wake up again after the baby is born, I suppose, for this is what always happens. This is that terrible *common rut* into which everyone falls, and of which we used to be so afraid. Unfortunately, though, I still love him very much, even more so than before. Will I fall into this wretched rut too?

May 9 He promised to be here at twelve o'clock and now it is two. Has something happened? How can he take such pleasure in tormenting me so? You don't drive out a dog that licks your hand. Maman endured a rather similar fate to mine in the first year of her marriage. Only it was worse for her, for Papa was always travelling around visiting patients and playing cards, whereas Lyova merely travels and walks around the estate. But I am also lonely, also bored, also pregnant, and also ill. You learn so much more from experience than from the intellect. Youth is a misfortune, not a blessing, at least if you are married. You simply cannot be happy just sitting there sewing or playing the piano alone, completely *alone*, and gradually realising, or rather becoming convinced that even though your husband may not love you, you are stuck there for ever and there you must sit. Maman told me her life got much happier as she got older; when her youth passed her children arrived and she found something to focus her entire life on. That is how it will be with me too. I am moody and bad-tempered only because I am bored with waiting for him since twelve o'clock alone, anxious and frightened. It is wicked of him not to have pity on me, as any moderately decent person would have for another suffering fellow-creature.

May 12 I have been making a great effort not to feel sorry for myself, and although I am not very happy, I am at least calm and no longer bored.

May 22 When you walk into the study thinking of nothing, its dreary chilly atmosphere overwhelms you. But if you go in there imagining it full of life, as it used to be, then it feels quite different. Now I feel cold and dreary in here – or rather afraid. Afraid of death, afraid that our past has died. There is no life here, no love and no life. I ran into the garden yesterday and thought I might miscarry. But I have an iron constitution. There is not a drop of love in him. He is unwell at present – but he will feel terrible when he gets better too. It is always the way, the richer the imagination the poorer the life. One can *imagine* anything – thousands of different worlds – yet one has to *live* in one's own little circle. I have grown to love mine and want nothing more, but he is tired of it and again has *longings*. I felt convinced today that I needed nothing but him – yet how often did I have to convince myself it was true? Maman often used to say there was nothing worse than tying a man to your apron strings. Those were her very words, and how true they are. I should worship her – she has endured so much. Life is hard, you need to be made of steel. And you have to work out *how* to live. Before I was married I wisely reasoned with myself that it would be best not to fall in love. I knew myself so well – I knew I could never love someone just a little, and that a great love is hard. Tanya understood this perfectly; she does not find happiness easily either. She is happy at present, for she is young, and her soul is alive – and she has a great soul. Someone will crush her though. But she won't easily reconcile herself to a life which gives her too little. It is hard to curb one's spirits. But she is capable of inspiring more love than I. I merely 'cut myself'. I do not mean to, and it costs me dear. Each new cut takes a bit of my life, my strength, my youth, my energy and a great deal of my happiness, and makes me despise myself even more. These cuts can never be healed. I must guard *his* love, for there is so little of it – maybe none left at all. It's a terrible thought, and it is constantly on my mind. I have been ill since yesterday. I am afraid I may miscarry, yet I even take pleasure from the pain in my stomach. It is like when I did something naughty as a child, and Maman would always forgive me but I could never forgive myself, and would pinch and prick my hand. The pain would become unbearable but I would take intense pleasure in enduring it. It is at times like this that love is put to the test. Soon the good weather and my health will return, I shall take pride in the house and re-establish some order here, I shall enjoy my new baby and also enjoy physical pleasures again – how disgusting.

He may think his love for his wife has returned, but it will be merely a memory. And once more he'll be sick, once more he'll be harassed by his hateful wife, who has the gall to be in his sight all the time, once more he'll be wretched. This is what life has in store for him. As for me, I have no life of my own, although I used to have one, when I loved him and comforted myself with the thought that he would love me too. What a fool I was to think so – I only made myself miserable. Everything here seems so depressing. Even the clock sounds melancholy when it strikes the hour; the dog is mournful, Dushka[13] is unhappy, the old women are wretched and everything is dead. But if Lyova . . .

June 6 The young folk have arrived[14] to disturb our life and I am sorry. They don't seem very cheerful. Or maybe it's just the chilly atmosphere here. It isn't at all as I expected. They haven't cheered me up a bit, they've merely made me more anxious, and things seem even drearier now. I love Lyova intensely but it angers me that I should have put myself in a relationship in which we are not equals. I am entirely dependent on him, and God knows I treasure his love. But he either takes mine for granted or does not need it, for he seems to be alone in everything. I keep reminding myself that autumn will soon be here and all this will soon be over. I do not know what I mean by 'all this', though. And what sort of winter we shall have after the autumn – or whether there will be a winter at all – I just cannot imagine. It is terribly depressing that I should wish for nothing and nothing should make me happy, as though I were an old woman, and how unbearable it would be to be old. I did not want to go for a drive with them after he said: 'You and I are old folk, let's stay put.' And it seemed such fun to stay at home with him, just the two of us, as though I had fallen in love with him against my parents' will. Now the others have driven off, Lyova has gone out and I am alone with my melancholy thoughts. I am angry too, and am prepared to reproach him for not giving me a carriage, which means I can never go out for a drive, not thinking about me, and so on. It's much simpler for him just to leave me on the sofa with a book and not bother his head about me. If I can stop being angry for a moment, though, I realise of course that he has a mountain of work – which has nothing to do with me – and that running the estate is a gruelling labour; then there are the common people visiting him all the time and never giving him a moment's peace. That loathsome Anatolii[15] is always hanging around. And then there are those people who cheated him over the carriage, and it wasn't *his* fault – no, he is a *wonderful* man and I love him with all my heart.

June 7 I love him madly, this feeling has taken a hold over me and overwhelms me. He is on the estate all the time, but I am not moping now and I feel very happy. And he loves me, I think I can sense that. I fear this means I shall die – how sad and terrible it would be to leave him. The more I get to know him the dearer he becomes to me. I think each day that I have never loved him so much – and the next day I love him even more. Nothing exists for me but him and everything that concerns him.

June 8 Lyova is very cheerful nowadays. He was dying of solitude, and the company has cheered him up. No sir, I am stronger than you! It was only the boredom that made him ill. Tanya is not well and the two Sashas, especially mine,[16] are in extremely delicate health.

July 14 It is all over, the baby[17] has been born and my ordeal is at last at an end. I have risen from my bed and am gradually entering into life again, but with a constant feeling of fear and dread about my baby and especially my husband. Something within me seems to have collapsed, and I sense that whatever it is it will always be there to torment me; it is probably the fear of not doing my duty towards *my family*. I feel terribly timid with my husband, as though I had wronged him in some way. I feel I am a burden, a foolish person (the same old theme!), even rather vulgar. I have become insincere, for I am frightened by the womb's vulgar love for its offspring, and frightened by my somewhat unnatural love for my husband. All of this I try to hide, out of a feeling of shame I know to be stupid and false. I sometimes comfort myself with the thought that most people see this love of one's husband and children as a virtue. I shall never go any further than this, I fear, although I should like to be a bit better educated – my education was so bad – again if only for my husband's sake and that of my children. But how strong these maternal feelings are! It strikes me as quite natural and not at all strange that I am now a mother. He is Lyovochka's child, that's why I love him. Lyova's present state of mind makes me very anxious. He has such a wealth of ideas and feelings and it is all being wasted. I truly appreciate all his great qualities, and God knows I would give anything to make him happy.

July 23 I have been married for ten months and my spirits are flagging, it's terrible. I automatically seek support as my baby seeks the breast. I am in agonising pain. Lyova is murderous. He cannot run the estate – I'm not cut out for it, he says. He is restless.[18] Nothing here satisfies him; I know what he wants and cannot give it to him. Nothing is sweet to me. Like a dog, I have grown used to his caresses, but he has grown cold. I console myself that there are bound to be days like this. But they are all too frequent. *Patience.*

July 24 I went on to the balcony and was overwhelmed by an almost morbid joy. The countryside was so fine, wide and vast, and I thought of God . . . My family has gone and my mother, my best friend,[19] has left. I didn't cry much, I felt numb. My husband has cheered up, thank God. I have prayed a lot for him. He loves me, may God grant us lasting happiness. I am in even worse pain, and have withdrawn into my shell like a snail, determined to endure it to the end. I love my baby deeply; it would be a great grief that would poison my life if I had to stop breastfeeding him. I long to rest and enjoy myself in the fresh air – I feel imprisoned here. I am so impatient for my husband to return from Tula. I love him with all my heart, with a firm, deep love, and am rather in awe of him. I shall now go and sacrifice myself to my son . . .

July 31 What he says is so *banal.* I know things are terrible, but why should he be so angry? Whose fault is it? Our relations are frightful, and at such a painful time as this too. He has become so unpleasant that I try all day to avoid him. When he says, 'I'm going to bed' or 'I'm going to have a bath' I think, thank God. It breaks my heart to sit with my little son.[20] God has taken both my husband and my son from me – to think how devoutly we used to pray to Him. Now I feel everything is over. Patience! I keep telling myself. We were at least blessed with a happy past. I have loved him so much and am grateful to him for everything. I have just been reading his diary. At that wonderful poetic moment everything seemed vile to him. 'These past nine months have been practically the worst in my life,' he wrote – to say nothing of the tenth. How often he must secretly have asked himself why he ever got married. And how often he has said aloud to me, 'What has become of my old self?'[21]

August 2 It was not written for me to read. Why am I idling my life away?

You'd do well to clear out at once, Sofia Andreevna. A grief like this can wear you down. I have sternly forbidden myself ever to mention his name again. Maybe it will pass.

August 3 I spoke to him and felt a bit better, for my guess has proved correct: it is abnormal not to feed one's baby, who could deny it? But what can I do about a physical infirmity? I instinctively feel he is being unjust to me. Why does he continually torture me? I've felt so angry that today even the joy of looking after the baby has been spoilt; just as he wants to wipe me from the face of the earth because I am suffering and am not doing my duty, I want not to see him at all because he is not suffering but just goes on writing. This is yet another aspect of husbands' cruelty – it had never occurred to me before. At this moment I really think I no longer love him. How can one love an insect which never stops stinging? Well, I cannot mend matters, I shall go to my son and do all I can for him, not for Lyova's sake of course – let him suffer as much as he has made me suffer. It is a strange weakness in him that he can't be patient with me for a while, until I get better. I have to be patient, though – ten times more patient than he. I wanted to write this down because I felt so angry.

It has started raining and I am afraid he'll catch cold. I am not angry any more. I love him, God bless him.

> Sonya, forgive me, I have only just realised that I am to blame and have wronged you greatly. There are days when one seems guided not by one's will but by some irresistible external law. That was why I treated you like that then – to think I could have done such a thing. I have always recognised that I have many failings and very little generosity of spirit. And now I have acted so cruelly, so rudely, and to whom? To the person who has given me the finest happiness of my whole life and who alone loves me. I know this can never be forgotten or forgiven, Sonya, but I know you better now and realise how meanly I treat you. Sonya darling, I know I have been vile – somewhere inside me there is a fine person, but at times he seems to be asleep. Love him, Sonya, and do not reproach him too much. [L. N. Tolstoy's note]

Lyovochka wrote that, begging my forgiveness, but then he lost his temper and crossed it out. He was talking of that terrible time when I had mastitis and my breasts hurt so much I was *unable* to feed Seryozha, and this made him angry. It wasn't that I didn't *want* to – I longed to, it was what I wanted more than anything else. I deserved those few lines of tenderness and remorse from him, but in a moment of rage with me he crossed them out before I had even had a chance to read them.

August 17 I have been day-dreaming, recalling those 'mad' nights last year, and other mad nights too, when I was so utterly free and in such a splendid state of mind. If ever I have known complete happiness it was then. I loved and experienced and understood everything, my mind and my being were completely in tune, and the world seemed so fresh. And then there was the dear poetic *comte*[22] with his wonderful deep bright gaze. (That was the impression he made on me then.) It was a heavenly time. I felt pampered by the hint of his love. I certainly must have felt it, otherwise I would not have been so happy. I remember he was rude to me one evening when Popov was there and I was terribly hurt, but I pretended I didn't care and went out and sat on the porch with Popov, straining to hear what the *comte* was talking about inside, while all the time pretending to be fascinated by everything Popov was saying. I grew even fonder of the *comte* after that and made a point of never dissembling to him again. I was just thinking about all this when I suddenly realised with incredulous joy that this very same *comte* was now my husband. Lizka knew what happiness was all right, but Sonechka Behrs was never able to understand these things.[23] She does now though, with all her heart. My goodness, how silly he was to be jealous[24] – as if that could have given him any reason for jealousy! I am sorry he spent that poetic August last year alone and not with me, for it would have been even finer then. He is out now, and I always mope when he is not here. I don't know when I'll get used to it. I want to be better and to return to life, my life with Lyova – now we are always apart. When he doubts my love for him, I feel so stunned that I lose my head. How can I prove it, when I love him so *honestly*, so steadfastly?

September 10 I feel slightly nostalgic about my youth, slightly envious and very bored. Endless sufferings and ordeals, and a life confined by these four walls, while outside it's so splendid and I feel so carefree and so happy with my family life. The moon is shining again and the evenings are again warm and gentle, but these things are not for me. Natalya's[25] child is dying. What a ghastly tragedy. Why should a mother and child have to suffer so? The father is sobbing too. It breaks my heart and I have been crying. Lyova's gaze pursues me everywhere. He startled me when I was playing the piano yesterday. What *was* he thinking of then? I have never seen that look on his face before. Was he remembering something? Or was it jealousy. He loves . . .

September 22 It will be a year tomorrow. Then I had hopes of happiness, now only of unhappiness. Before I thought it was all a joke, but now I realise he means it. So he is off to war.[26] What sort of behaviour is that? Is he unbalanced? No, I think not, merely erratic. I don't know whether it is intentional, but he seems to do his utmost to arrange life in such a way as to make me thoroughly unhappy. He has put me in a position where I have to worry from one day to the next lest he go off and I find myself abandoned with my baby, and maybe more than just one. It is all a joke to them, a fleeting fancy. One day they decide to get married, enjoy it, and produce some children – next day it's time to leave it all behind and go off to war. I only hope now that my child will die, for I shall not survive without him. I have no faith in this love for the 'fatherland', this *enthousiasme* in a man of thirty-five. Aren't his children also the fatherland, aren't they also Russian? But no, he wants to abandon them so he can enjoy himself galloping about on his horse, revelling in the beauties of battle and listening to the bullets fly. His inconsistency and cowardice have made me respect him less. But his talent is almost more important to him than his family. If only he would explain to me the true motives of his desire. Why did I marry him? Valerian Petrovich[27] would have been better, as I would not have minded so much if he left me. What did he need my love for? It was just an infatuation. And I know he's blaming me, for now he is sulking. He blames me for loving him and not wanting him to die or to leave me. Let him sulk. I only wish I had been able to prepare myself for it in advance, i.e. to stop loving him, for the parting would then have been much easier. If he is going to push me aside I too shall withdraw from him. A year of happiness is enough for him and now he fancies a change. Life here bores him. Well, he will not have any more children – I shall not give him any more merely so he can abandon them. What despotism! 'This is what I want,' he says, 'don't you dare say a word!' The war has not started yet, and he is still here. So much the worse, with nothing to do but wait and worry. It will all be the same in the end anyway. And I love him, that's the worst of it, when I see him he looks so depressed, forever morosely searching his soul.

October 7 What gloom. At least my son gives me some joy. But why is the nurse always fussing over the baby's clothes and distracting me? Of course he can see how low I feel, it's no use trying to conceal it, but he'll soon find it insufferable. I want to go to the ball, but that is not the reason I feel low. I shan't go, but it irritates me that I still want to. And this irritation would have spoilt all the fun, which I doubt it would have been anyway. He keeps saying, 'I am being reborn'. What *does* he mean? He can have everything he had before we were married, if only he can be rid of his terrible anxieties and restless strivings to go hither and thither. 'Reborn'? He says I'll soon understand. But I get flustered and cannot understand a word he is talking about. He is undergoing some great change. And we are becoming more and more estranged. My illness and the baby have taken me away from him, this is why I don't understand him. What else do I need? Am I not lucky to be so close to all these inexhaustible ideas, talents, virtues and intelligence, all embodied in my husband? But it can be depressing too. It's my *youth*.[28]

October 17 I feel I don't understand him properly, that's why I am always jealously following him – his thoughts and his actions, his past and his present. I wish I could understand him fully so that he might treat me as he treats Alexandrine, but I know this is impossible so I must not be offended and must accept the fact that I am too young and silly and not poetic enough. To be like Alexandrine, quite apart from any innate gifts, one would need to be older anyway, childless, and even unmarried. I would not mind at all if they took up their old correspondence, but it would sadden me if I felt she thought Lyova's wife was fit for nothing but the nursery and humdrum superficial relationships. I know that however jealous I may be of her soul, I must not cut her out of his life, for she has played an important part in it for which I should have been useless.[29] He should not have sent her that letter. I cried because he did not tell me everything he'd written in it, and because he said, 'Something which I alone know about myself. And I'll tell you too, only my wife doesn't know anything about it . . .' I should like to know her better. Would she consider me worthy of him? She understands and appreciates him so well. I found some letters from her in the desk and they gave me a clear impression of what she was like, and of her relations with Lyova. One was particularly fine. Once or twice it has occurred to me to write to her without telling Lyova, but I can't bring myself to. She interests me greatly and I like her a lot. Ever since I read Lyova's letter to her I have been thinking about her constantly. I think I could love her.[30] I am not pregnant, judging by my state of mind, and long may this continue. I love him to distraction, and it worries me to think I shall love him even more in the future. I feel so happy, clear-headed and calm today, probably because he loves me at present. I do not believe he has deteriorated. But I am patiently waiting for his present agitation and dissatisfaction with himself to pass. I am glad that his mental state has improved, for I was afraid. This emotional strain shortens his life, which is so precious to me.

October 28 Something is wrong, I feel so depressed. It's as though our love had fled and nothing was left. He is being cold, almost calm now and deeply preoccupied, but not cheerfully so, and I feel crushed and angry. Angry with myself, with my own character and my attitude to my husband. Was this what I wanted, and promised him in my heart? Dear darling Lyovochka. All these squabbles weigh so heavily on him; was he made for *this*? But God forgive me, I am still furious. I love him terribly, I am unhappy, I don't know how to make myself happy, and I don't know how to make others happy. I loathe my own mental weakness; I hate myself. My love cannot be very strong if I am so weak. But no, I love him terribly, there can be no doubt about it. If only I could raise myself up. My husband is so good, so wonderfully good. Where is he? Probably working on *The History of 1812*. He used to tell me about his writing, but now he thinks I am not worthy of his confidence. In the past he shared all his thoughts with me, and we had such blissful, happy times together. Now they are all gone. 'We shall always be happy, Sonya,' he said. I feel so sad that he has had none of the happiness he expected and deserved.

November 13 I feel sorry for Aunt – she won't last much longer. She is always sick, her cough keeps her awake at night, her hands are thin and dry. I think about her all day. He says, let's live in Moscow for a while. Just what I expected. It makes me jealous when he finds his ideal in the first pretty woman he meets. Such love is terrible because it is blind and virtually incurable. There has never been anything of this ideal in me and there never will be. I am left alone morning, afternoon and night. I am to gratify his pleasure and nurse his child, I am a piece of household furniture, I am a *woman*. I try to suppress all human feelings. When the machine is working properly it heats the milk, knits a blanket, makes little requests and bustles about trying not to think – and life is quite tolerable. But the moment I am alone and allow myself to think, everything seems insufferable. He does not love me, I couldn't keep his love. How could I, it was fate. In a moment of grief, which I now regret, when nothing seemed to matter but the fact that I had lost his love, I thought even his writing was pointless; what did I care what Countess So-and-So said to Princess So-and-So?[31] Afterwards I despised myself. My life is so mundane, and my death. But he has such a rich internal life, talent and immortality. I have become afraid of him, and at times I even feel he is a complete stranger. It may be my fault, for my character has deteriorated – but I have felt for some time that I am no longer what I was to him and that is why he has abandoned me. I do not fret as I used to, thank God, I have learnt to be more patient. But then nothing excites me or cheers me up either. I do not know what is wrong with me. I know only that my instinct is correct.

December 19 I have lit two candles, sat down at the table and feel perfectly happy. I am a craven empty-headed person. But at present I am too lazy and happy to care. Everything seems funny and unimportant. I feel like flirting, even with someone like Alyosha Gorshkoi, or losing my temper with a chair. I played cards with Aunt for four hours, which made him furious, but I didn't care. It hurts me to think of Tanya, she is a thorn in my flesh.[32] But I have put even this thought out of my mind today, I am feeling so silly. The baby is better, maybe *that's* why I am so happy. At this moment I should love to go to a *dance* or do something amusing. I shall reproach myself later, but I cannot change the way I feel now. It infuriates me how little Lyova cares, and how unaware he is of how much I love him; I'd like to pay him back. He is old and self-absorbed, whereas I feel young and long to do something wild. I'd like to turn somersaults instead of going to bed. But with whom?

December 24 Old age hovers over me; everything here is old. I try to suppress all youthful feelings, for they would seem odd and out of place in this sombre environment. The only one who is young, or younger in spirit than the others, is Seryozha,[33] which is why I like it when he comes. I am gradually coming to the conclusion that Lyova wants only to restrain me; this is why he is so reserved, and why he constantly frustrates my spontaneous outbursts of love. Anyway, how *can* I love him in this quiet, sober, sedate atmosphere? It is so monotonous here, so lacking in love. But I won't do anything. I complain as though I were really unhappy – but then I *am* really unhappy, for he doesn't love me so much. He actually told me so, but I knew it already. As for myself I am not sure. I see so little of him and am in such awe of him that I can't be sure how much I love him. I dearly want to marry Tanya off to Seryozha, but the idea frightens me today. What about Masha?[34] All Lyova's pronouncements on the compartments of the heart are nothing but fanciful idealism – as he is – and are no comfort to me.

· 1864 ·

January 1 – local government statute creating new organ of self-government, the zemstvo, *under the control of local nobles, to levy rates, attend to roads, hospitals, education, medical care and other local needs which central government has hitherto ignored. June – five students shot in Kazan, and many more arrested, for attempting to incite a peasant uprising. November – 'statutes of the judiciary' reforming the law courts and introducing trial by jury. These judicial reforms in many places takes decades to enact, and trial by jury suffers a partial eclipse. Nevertheless the government has strengthened its hand, and organised protest wanes; intense debates within Land and Liberty on the way ahead. In London, Marx's International Workingman's Association (the First International) formed.*

October 4 – the Tolstoys' daughter, Tatiana (Tanya, Tanechka) is born. At the end of the year Tolstoy visits Moscow for an operation on his broken arm.

January 2 Tanya, Tanya, this is all I can think about. I am worn out with grieving and planning and wrestling with it all. Lyova, Aunt and I are all in God's hands. Yet I desperately, passionately, want them both to be happy. I am in a dismal mood, I know. Tula was so cheerless today, it has quite exhausted me. I wanted to buy up the whole town, how pathetic, but I soon came to my senses. Lyova is being sweet; there was an almost childlike expression on his face when he was playing the piano. I thought of Alexandrine and understood her perfectly; I realised just how much she must adore him. 'Grandmother',[1] he calls her. He annoyed me just now when he said, 'When you're cross you take to your diary.' What does he care? I am not cross at the moment. Yet the slightest sarcastic remark from him hurts and offends terribly; he should cherish my love for him more. I am afraid of being ugly, morally and physically.

March 27 My Diary is all covered in dust, it is so long since I opened it, and today I decided to creep off furtively, like a child playing hide-and-seek, and while nobody was watching, to write whatever came into my head. I want desperately to love everyone and enjoy everything, but someone only has to brush against me when I am in this state and it goes away. I feel a sudden love, trust and tenderness for my husband, perhaps because it occurred to me yesterday how easily I might lose him. Today I firmly resolved never to think of it ever again, come what may. I shall refuse to listen if anybody, even he, so much as mentions it. I love Tanya so much, why are they trying to ruin her? Although they needn't bother, for she'll never be spoilt. We'll be so happy together, I'll see to that. I can give her a lot of emotional support but can do almost nothing about the situation she is in. At any rate, I shall do my utmost to distract her. I shall have my two children, Tanya and Sergushka,[2] to look after, and it will be splendid. I think I am less selfish than I was a year ago. Then I moped around with my stomach, depressed because I couldn't have fun with the others. Now I have my own joy and am happier than anyone else.

April 22 I am all alone. All day long I have been trying hard not to brood here on my own, but now that evening has come I feel impelled to focus my thoughts, have a good cry and write everything down in my diary, although I would feel much happier if I could write this to him – if he was here and I could. There's nothing to write about; it's so bleak and empty here, there's no life in the place. I can control myself when I am looking after Seryozha, but in the evening, when he has gone to sleep, I bustle about frantically as though I had a million little tasks to do, when in fact I am simply trying to avoid thinking and worrying about things. I keep imagining he has just gone out hunting, or to look at the estate or see to the bees, and will return at any moment, for I am so used to waiting, and he always seems to return at the point when my patience is just about to give out. I am always trying to think of something unpleasant in our life together so as not to feel so sorry for him all the time, but I cannot, for the moment I think of him I realise how deeply I love him, and I want to weep. The moment I catch myself thinking I am *not* sad, it is as if I deliberately make myself so. Tonight for the first time in my life I am going to bed completely alone. They said I should put Tanya's bed in my room but I did not want to – I want no one but Lyova beside me, ever. He could die easy in his mind that I would always be faithful to him. But I have such trust in him, it almost frightens me. How ridiculous I am, sitting here and choking back the tears as though

I was ashamed of crying for my husband because I miss him. And I shall cry for the next four days too, or I'll do something silly like going to Nikolskoe. I could easily do so if I don't watch myself and my tears. My diary and writing this have upset me even more. What am I good for if I have so little strength of character and capacity for endurance? I don't want to know what he is doing. He is sure to be having a good time – I don't suppose *he* is depressed and crying. I needn't be ashamed of my feelings for I am alone, and I hardly ever write my diary these days, and he never reads it now to find out whether I have been writing and if so, what. I cannot bring myself to go to bed alone, I am so feeble. I keep thinking that Tanya will soon hear me crying from the sitting-room and I shall feel ashamed, and I have been so sensible all day.[3]

November 3 It is odd that in these happy surroundings I should be feeling so disconsolate, so filled with dread about Lyova. And these feelings grow stronger every day. Last night, and every other night too, I was stricken with such fear and grief that while I was sitting with my little girl I cried,[4] for I could picture his death so clearly. It all started on the day when he dislocated his arm[5] and I suddenly realised the possibility of losing him; and ever since then I have thought of nothing else. I almost live in the nursery now, and looking after and feeding the babies sometimes distracts me. I often think too that he must find this female world of ours insufferably boring, and that I cannot possibly make him happy, that I am a good nursemaid, but nothing more. No intelligence, education or talent, nothing. I wish something would happen soon, for I sense something is about to. Looking after the children and playing with Seryozha can be delightful, but deep in my heart I sense that my old happiness has fled for good and nothing can give me joy any more. I often have premonitions of Lyova's bad moods with me; now he secretly hates me.

· 1865 ·

April 6 – 'Provisional Rules' on the press (in force for the next forty years). Most books and journals exempt from preliminary censorship, but punitive censorship continues, under the control of the Ministry of the Interior. The excitement over the 'great reforms' is over, and is followed by intense disillusionment. Some Land and Liberty members favour violence, and form a secret society, the Organisation, bent on assassinating particularly hated officials.

June – Tanya Behrs betrothed to Sergei Tolstoy, who deserts her at the last moment for the gipsy woman with whom he has been living for many years. July –

first part of War and Peace *(called* The Year 1805*) published. November – publication of the second part.*

February 25 I am so often alone with my thoughts that the need to write my diary comes quite naturally. I sometimes feel depressed, but today it seems wonderfully pleasant to be sitting here alone with my thoughts, not having to reveal them to a soul. Yesterday Lyovochka said he felt very young and I understood exactly what he meant. Now I am well again and not pregnant – it terrifies me how often I have been in that condition. He said that for him being young meant '*I can achieve anything*'. For me it means *I want and can do anything.* But when the feeling passes, other considerations come into my mind, and reason tells me that there is nothing I either want or can do beyond nursing, eating, drinking, sleeping, and loving and caring for my husband and babies, all of which I know is happiness of a kind, but why do I feel so woeful all the time, and weep as I did yesterday? I am writing now with the pleasantly exciting sense that nobody will ever read it, so I can be quite frank with myself and not write for Lyovochka. He is away at the moment; he spends so little time with me now anyway. But when I feel *young* I prefer not to be with him, for I am afraid he will find me stupid and irritating. Dunyasha[1] says, 'The count has grown old.' Is this true? He is never cheerful now, I often annoy him, he is absorbed in his writing, but it gives him no pleasure. Can it be that he has lost all his capacity for enjoyment and fun? He talks of spending next winter in Moscow. I am sure he will be happier there, and I shall try to make the best of it. I have never admitted this, but even with Lyovochka, my own husband, I am sometimes unconsciously a bit devious in order that he won't see me in a bad light. I have never admitted to him just how vain and envious I am. When we are in Moscow I shall feel ashamed if I don't have a carriage and horses with a liveried footman in attendance, a nice dress to wear, a fine apartment to live in and all the rest of it. Lyovochka is an extraordinary man; he cares nothing for any of this. That is true wisdom and virtue.

The children are my greatest joy. When I am alone I disgust myself, but the children awaken the possibility of better feelings in me. Yesterday I prayed over Tanya, but I've now forgotten why or for what I was praying. With the children I don't feel *young*, but calm and happy.

March 6 Seryozha is ill. I am in a dream. Nothing is real. It's all an illusion. Better or worse, that's all I understand. Lyovochka is young, energetic, and independent, with the strength of mind to carry on writing. I feel he is strength and life itself, and I am a worm crawling over him and feeding off him. I am afraid of being weak. My nerves have been bad since I was sick, and I feel ashamed. That last 'cut' of Lyovochka's is still very painful. I can only wait, knowing that it was all my fault, yet it frightens me to wait, for what if his love for me never returns? I have such reverence for him, but I realise I have fallen so low as to want sometimes to pounce on his weaknesses. Everything seems so odd this evening. He has gone for a walk, I am alone and everything is silent. The children are fast asleep, the big stove is burning, upstairs it's so clean and bare that the vivid, strongly-scented orange-blossoms seem out of place here and even the sound of my own breathing and footsteps frightens me. Lyovochka came in for a moment and I felt brighter. He is like a breath of fresh air.

March 8 I am feeling much gayer. Seryozha is better and the illness has passed. Lyova too is better, and is in thoroughly good spirits, but to me he is cold and indifferent. I am afraid to say he *does not love me*. Yet the thought torments me, and that is why I feel so hesitant and bashful in my relations with him. I was in a frightful state during those sad days when Seryozha was so ill. Suffering does not subdue me, and that is bad. I was pursued by ghastly thoughts which I am frightened and ashamed to admit. As Lyovochka was treating me so coldly and was forever going out of the house, I got it into my head that he was going off to see A.[2] This thought has been tormenting me all day, but now Seryozha has managed to take my mind off it and now when I think about it I feel terribly ashamed of myself. I should know him better by now. If it were true, how could he be so calm, open and natural with me? It must be said, however, that as long as she and I live in close proximity every bad mood or cold word from Lyova will instantly reduce me to an agony of jealousy. What if he were suddenly to return and tell me . . . ? Oh, what a lot of nonsense I talk, I ought to be ashamed. I just felt obliged to confess this terrible thought which dimly but persistently hovers in my mind.

March 9 Lyovochka is as distant as ever. I have a cold, and I feel vile and wretched. I shall soon forget how to speak altogether. I sit here silently all day long, delving into my thoughts, staring out of the window, admiring and identifying with nature and looking forward to spring. The children still have coughs and colds, and Seryozha is pathetically thin. I feel such tenderness for my children that I try to restrain myself for fear of appearing vulgar. Lyovochka is killing me with his indifference, his total lack of interest in anything I do. He simply demands that *I* be interested in everything *he* does – as if it wasn't precious to me anyway. I am feeling calm and even submissive, which is rare for me. I think constantly of my family in Moscow, but Lyovochka cannot understand these feelings. I long to see them, but every time I propose a trip to Moscow he makes some objection. He thinks only of what *he* would gain by it, and no longer has the slightest desire to give *me* any pleasure. I wonder whether I am a selfish person. I don't think I am, for I would do anything in the world for Lyovochka. He says I have a weak character. Perhaps that is just as well, for I can submit to anything if need be, and ask nothing for myself. But I am making great efforts not to be so feeble. Lyovochka is off hunting, and I have been busy copying all morning. I look forward to Aunt's visit, for I am very fond of her,[3] but I am sorry it will disrupt this solitary life which I have now grown used to and now love, for I can only be completely free and honest when I am alone. I am afraid of Lyovochka. He is always commenting on my faults now, and I am beginning to think there is very little good in me.

March 10 Lyovochka has a headache; he has ridden off to Yasenki. I am not well either, and both the children have coughs and colds and look utterly pathetic. I cannot think how to make Seryozha better. He is so thin and dejected – he eats nothing and has continual diarrhoea. I have just had a letter from Aunt; she says that she was very touched by my letter,[4] and that she too has a cough and is unwell. For Mashenka I nurse a 'silent hatred', as Lyovochka puts it, although for her children I have a special and very genuine love (not, however, without a tinge of condescension).[5] Lyovochka has been much more affectionate today. He actually kissed me for the first time in days. I am doing a lot of copying and am glad to be of some use.

March 14 I have had a terrible headache for several days now; it is only in the evenings that I feel better, eager to do things and enjoy myself. Lyovochka is playing some Chopin preludes. He is in fine spirits, although with me he is distant and wary. The children absorb me completely. They both have diarrhoea; it's driving me frantic. Our friend Dyakov came, still the same irrepressible 'nightingale', as Tanya calls him. I am very fond of him, and find him sympathetic and easy to talk to. There is no sign of spring and it is still cold winter, which is seriously affecting both our emotional well being and the children's health. I long for the blessings of spring, but it is late in coming this year. Lyovochka has been feeling the urge to visit Tula, as he apparently needs to see more people. I do too, but not people in general, just Tanya, the Zefirots,[6] Mother and Father.

March 15 Lyovochka has gone off to Tula and I am glad. Seryozha's child is dying and I am feeling desperately sad. My headache is better today and I feel strong and full of energy. The children are not completely well yet but they're a bit better. The sun came out for a moment and its effect on me was like the bars of a waltz on a sixteen-year-old girl. I long for spring, for country walks, for summer. It's such ages since I heard from my family. What can my lovely poetic Tanya be doing? Lyovochka and I are happy and straightforward with one another again. He told me he had felt very dissatisfied with himself recently . . . I love him terribly, I could never become a wicked person with him. His confession, and his knowledge of himself, make me feel very humble, and force me to search out every single one of my faults.

March 16 I have a frightful headache and the children are poorly. Seryozha has been feverish, and I simply cannot understand what ails him. Lyovochka is out of the house the minute he wakes up. Where is he now? What is he doing? Yesterday I got a letter from Tanya, along with *her luggage*. I felt so happy at the thought of seeing her again, for seeing one's family is always a very special kind of joy, and when I saw her things I came across some girlish little bits and pieces of mine too. Seryozha's son has died.[7] I have been in tears all morning. I feel so terribly sorry for him. I cannot do a thing while I have this headache. It's an unbearable tic.

March 20 For the past two days I have had a fever in the morning and a frightful headache. Lyovochka makes me feel like a mangy dog. I try not to get in his way, but he pays me no attention anyway. I find this terribly painful, as far as he is concerned I might as well be dead. But I still have all the same powerful jealous feelings for him. I am spoilt. I was just reading a review of *The Cossacks*[8] and thinking about the novel, when I suddenly realised it was *I* who stood in his way, and that his youth and his love were all spent, wasted on Cossack girls and other women. My children cling terribly to me, I have given myself to them, and it is a great joy to know I am indispensable to them. When Tanya lies at my breast, or Seryozha hugs me with his little arms, then I feel no jealousy, no grief, no regrets, no desires, nothing. Now that they are both sick nothing makes me happy. The weather is wonderful, spring is here, but I am not destined to enjoy it. I admire Lyovochka, happy and strong in mind and in body. It's a terrible thing to feel so inferior. My only resources, as weapons to match his, are my children, my energy, my youth, and the fact that I am a fine healthy wife. Now I am just his mangy dog.

March 23 My fever has gone, and with it my depression. My tic still torments me, though. The children are still unwell, and Lyovochka has driven off to Tula for the doctor. We are on good terms; I feel easy and happy with him; I haven't the slightest doubt that he loves me, and I don't feel jealous. Spring is here, the weather is delightful, the streams have thawed, yet I am locked indoors. Lyovochka is very busy with the dairy-yard, and is writing his novel without much enthusiasm.[9] He is bursting with ideas, but when will he ever write them all down? He sometimes talks to me about his plans and ideas, which is always a tremendous joy. I always understand him too. But what am I talking about? I shan't put his ideas down here, anyway.

March 26 In a sudden fit of domesticity I tidied everything up – I always feel like that when I have put Seryozha and Tanya to bed. They are almost well now. I feel terrified for Tanya, I cling to her, but am haunted by fears of death, the eternal grief that haunts almost all of us. Lyovochka is in a bilious mood, and sometimes I cannot help feeling a little irritated with him. Today a terrible thought occurred to me: what would he do if, after taking my love and devotion for granted for so long and caring so little for my feelings, I were suddenly to grow cold towards him? It is not possible, of course, which is why I can speak of it so lightly, and why he will continue to disregard me. Seryozha has spent the past few days with us. He is very unhappy at present, and I am growing extremely fond of him. I feel so happy and comfortable with him. It is dull and cloudy outside, but I am in a state of childish excitement and in a 'holiday' mood. Tomorrow is Palm Saturday, a day I used to love at home. After that it will be Easter Saturday, which nowadays is just the same as any other weekday in Lent. But in the past I used to cry so much, whereas now I am much calmer. Yesterday Seryozha said: 'The only good things in life are love, music, nightingales and the moon,' and we had a long talk in which I did not feel at all shy with him; whereas when I talk to Lyovochka about such things, he always looks at me as if to say, 'What right do you have to discuss such things? You can't *feel* it.' Sometimes, it is true, one *dares* not feel these things. Lyovochka loves a solitary poetic existence, maybe because there is so much fine poetry in him and he wants to keep it all to himself. This has taught me too to cultivate my own little life of the soul. I can hear him writing now – his diary too, probably. I hardly ever read it now. As soon as you read each other's diaries you become dishonest. And I have become much more honest lately, which makes my life much happier and easier. He puts down all his latest ideas about his novel, and it's all so *clever*[10] that it makes me horribly aware of my pettiness and inferiority.

April 1 Lyovochka is in Tula and I am depressed and beset by morbid thoughts, because he keeps complaining of blood-rushes, poor digestion and buzzing ears. All this scares me dreadfully, and I am even more a prey to these fears when I am on my own like this, especially on such a lovely warm, bright spring day. The children are almost well and I have been taking them for walks, one at a time; Tanya has now seen God's world for the first time in her six-month existence. I have done nothing all day, just kept trying to escape my gloomy thoughts. He says bad health has shortened his life by a half. And his life is so very precious. I love him intensely and it annoys me that I can't do more for him to make him completely happy. I feel no bitterness towards him, just the most total and terrifying love.

May 3 It is a terrible spring, Tanya has come, and the hunting, riding and snipe shooting has all started again. Everyone had been in good health and

I had been getting on well with them all, but today everything went wrong and I quarrelled with Lyova; I am a spiteful, wilful person and must mend my ways. The children are ill. I am angry with Tanya for meddling in Lyovochka's life. They go to Nikolskoe, or go off hunting, riding or walking. I actually made a jealous scene for the first time in my life yesterday. I am now bitterly regretting it. I shall let her have my horse, which I think is very nice of me. He is much too self-indulgent, though. The two of them have gone off to the woods alone to shoot woodsnipe and I am imagining God knows what.

June 9 The day before yesterday everything was settled: Tanya and Seryozha are to be married. They are a joy to see. Her happiness gives me more pleasure than my own ever did. I have been playing chaperone as they stroll about the garden together, a role which both amuses and irritates me. Because of Tanya I now love Seryozha too – it's all quite splendid. The wedding will be in twenty days or so.[11] I wonder how things will work out. She has loved him for a long time, she is a lovely person and has such a splendid character, and I am so glad we'll be even closer friends now. It is terrible weather; Lyova and Tanya both have colds, and Seryozha has gone off to Pirogovo with Grisha and Keller.[12] It has been dreary and depressing ever since morning. But then waiting for something is always tedious. I shall be glad to see them both happily settled down together. We shall shortly be going to Nikolskoe, where the wedding will be held. I have just been reading her old diary. I was often close to tears as I read about all her past sufferings and I kept having to stop – but she thought I did not want to read on because I found them dull. Lyova is not at all cheerful at present. The children are delightful and are making good progress.

July 12 (Nikolskoe) Nothing has come of it. Seryozha has betrayed Tanya. He has behaved like a swine.[13] It has been almost a month of constant grief – it breaks one's heart to look at Tanya. To think that such a sweet, poetic, talented person should be ruined. And there are symptoms of consumption, which worry me terribly. I shall never be able to write the whole sad story in my diary. But my anger with Seryozha knows no bounds. I shall do everything in my power to have my revenge on him. Tanya has behaved extraordinarily well throughout. She loved him very much, and he deceived her into believing that he loved her too. Whereas, of course, he loved the gipsy woman more. Masha is a good woman, and I feel sorry for her and have nothing against her. But he is loathsome. Wait a bit, wait a bit, he kept saying, and all the time he was merely toying with her emotions and mocking her feelings for him. In the end she also began to feel sorry for Masha and the children, she could stand being made a fool of no longer, and above all, she loved and pitied *him* so much – and she broke it off. And that was twelve days after they had become engaged, and they had kissed, and he had promised her the usual silly things, and made all sorts of plans. What a brute. I shall tell everyone about it, including my children, in the hope that it will teach them never to behave like that.[14] My own family life is so wonderfully calm and happy. What did I do to deserve such happiness? The children have been well, as has Lyova, and he and I are on the best of terms, and outside it is gloriously warm, summer is here, and everyone and everything is perfect. If only this vile business with Seryozha had not disturbed our peaceful, honest life. We have been here in Nikolskoe ever since June 28, Seryozha's birthday. We have already had the Dyakovs here, and Mashenka and the little girls,[15] and yesterday dear Dyakov came again and managed to divert Tanya for a while. This morning a neighbour of ours called Volkov paid his first visit. He is a shy, agreeable, quiet, fair-haired, snub-nosed man. I like him well enough. Life here is merely a series of impressions – swimming, the river, the hills, the heat, contentment of soul, red berries, Tanya's grief. I am consoled by my children and my darling Lyovochka, who is in a wonderfully poetic mood. I am happy – who knows for how long?

July 16 I have quarrelled with Nurse[16] and feel desperately, unforgivably, ashamed of myself, for she is a good woman. I tried to make it up and as good as apologised to her, but one must not get too deeply involved with these people, for they would not understand. The Fets are here. They are pleasant people, although he is a little pompous; she is rather plain, but very good-natured. Poor Tanya troubles me terribly. She is still in a daze and we fear consumption. Little Tanya too has been ill, and I have been worried about her; she is better now. She is a sweet, lively baby, and her eyes and smile are adorable. Seryozha has been naughty recently, probably because he was ill; he is generally the sweetest, most good-natured child. I was terrified by the thunder-storm today. Lyova is reading the war scenes in his novel; I do not care for these parts at all.

Why ever did I quarrel with Nurse? I am just like Maman. I have recently discovered an alarming number of things about myself which are like her, and which I disliked in her. Mainly it is my habit of announcing to everyone what a good woman I am, then expecting all my faults to be forgiven. But I really *do* want to be good and to recognise my faults, and I don't want people (least of all me) to make allowances. That is my new resolution.

October 26 It is nice to be writing in my diary again – because I love my own private world so much, I suppose. Why, though, should the general rule be that a husband who was so much in love at first should grow cold with the passing years? I have just discovered that a woman only becomes a *real* woman when she has been married a few years, and that only one in a million is unchanged by marriage; if a woman can remain just as sweet and charming as she was before, then her husband, if he is a good man anyway, will be in love with her all his life. I have changed very much for the worse – did I ever pretend I hadn't? No, I have become much, much worse and Lyova's coldness no longer distresses me now, for I have well deserved it. He no longer reduces me to tears of despair as he used to, for in the old days I was a kinder, gentler more compliant person. Now for a brief account of our life here, for future reference. We have been in Yasnaya since October 12, and Tanya has been staying with the Dyakovs. She is far from well, and we must always face the dreadful possibility of losing her. I just try not to think about it. Lyova was ill but he is now better, and is writing. The children are well. I am trying to wean my little girl and it makes me feel so sorry for her, and so sad. Lyovochka has always taught me to attribute everything to physical causes, and it's very depressing, but I too now see almost everything in this way. Auntie[17] is weak and pathetic. And I am so cold to her. Haven't I an ounce of affection in me? I think I must be pregnant, and I'm not happy about it. I am frightened of everything and think badly of everyone. I long to have power over others. It is hard for me to understand, but there it is.

· 1866 ·

April 4 – a former student, Dmitrii Karakozov, makes an attempt on the Tsar's life. Hundreds of people rounded up and arrested. October 3 – Karakozov publicly hanged. The end of the 'era of reforms' and the start of a period of repression known as the 'White terror', which lasts until 1868.

May 22 – the Tolstoys' second son, Ilya (Ilyusha), is born.

March 12 We spent 6 weeks in Moscow and returned here on the 7th,[1] and in Yasnaya I immediately felt the old security, slightly melancholy, but imperturbably happy none the less. I enjoyed myself in Moscow, I loved seeing my family, and they loved seeing my children. Tanya is a clever, healthy, affectionate little girl. Seryozha is much stronger now, he is a reasonable child, less amenable than he used to be, but very sweet-natured. I am afraid I tend to over-indulge my children, but I am delighted by them. Lyova and I have been cold and awkward together ever since P. behaved so rudely in Moscow in response to my inept treatment of him. It has put a great strain on our relations.[2] I now feel horribly ashamed, but it is not as though there were the slightest blot on my conscience, now or at any moment in my marriage. Lyova has judged me too harshly. Yet even so it pleases me, for it proves that he cares for me, and in future I shall be a hundred times more careful, and shall enjoy being so. Yet it is terrible to think that this incident is yet another 'cut' in our relationship. I now feel even more contemptible, even more liable to abase myself, which means that I make even fewer claims on the happiness and self-esteem I need to survive.

We spent most of our time in Moscow in the Kremlin. In the morning the carriage would come for the children, and we would go and see my parents for the whole day. Lyova would go off to his sculpture classes and his gymnastics.[3] The friends of ours I saw most of were the Perfilevs, the Bashilovs and Princess Gorchakova; we also developed an acquaintance with Princess Obolenskaya. I went to some concerts and very much enjoyed the classical music. It was a nice life and I loved everything in Moscow, even our hotel on Dmitrovka Street, and our stuffy bed-sitting room and study, where Lyova modelled his red clay horse and where the two of us sat talking in the evenings. Petya[4] is a dear creature and I have grown to love him. I often think of them still, and it breaks my heart that I cannot see them now.

March 22 One does not seek experiences when one is young, which is why they are so precious, and so over-abundant too, but now it's different, and one is constantly thinking things over and striving for the more serious and worthy experiences of life. Which is a shame.

April 28 When a man gets married he says, I'll take such-and-such a girl, with such-and-such a personality, but what he does not realise is that this girl will change utterly, and when she does the entire mechanism breaks down. So there is no point in saying 'I am happy with her' until the old mechanism has completely broken down, and has been replaced with a new one. Moreover, a woman's character is not nearly such an important consideration as all the influences on her in the early part of her marriage. Everyone envies our happiness, and this makes me wonder what makes us happy and what that happiness really means.

June 9 On May 22 I was unexpectedly delivered of my second son, Ilya. I was expecting him in the middle of June.

June 19 We have a new bailiff here, with his wife.[5] She is an attractive young woman and a 'nihilist'. She and Lyova have endless lively discussions about literature and politics. This is quite improper in my opinion; their conversations go on far too long, and they may be flattering for her but for me they are a complete torture. He was the one who preached against admitting any outsider, especially a young and attractive person, into the *intimité* of our family circle, yet now he is the first to do so. I haven't let him know how much I hate it, of course, but I don't have a moment's peace of mind. We have been sleeping in separate rooms since Ilya's birth, which is wrong, for if we were together I would have it out with him this evening and blurt out all my simmering resentments, whereas I shan't go into his room now, and he won't come in to see me. The children are the joy of my life. Having experienced the happiness that they give me it would be a sin to ask for anything more. Loving them is such a joy. Yet it still grieves me that Lyovochka does not observe his own rules. And why was he saying only today that a man always worries lest he accuse his wife of something she did not do – as if one suffered only when one's husband actually *did* something wrong. For even the most momentary private doubts about his love for his wife can be just as disastrous. It is very wrong of Lyovochka to honour Maria Ivanovna with all these ardent speeches. It is almost one o'clock in the morning but I cannot sleep. I have a horrible premonition that this nihilist woman will be my *bête noire.*

July 22 Lyovochka invented some excuse for visiting *that* house earlier today. Maria Ivanovna told me so, and also that he had stood beneath her balcony talking to her. What reason can he have had for going over there in the rain? It is obvious: because he likes her. The very thought is driving me insane. I wish her every conceivable ill, although I am always especially nice to her for some reason. I wonder if her husband will turn out to be unfit for the job, so they will have to leave? At the moment I am wild with jealousy. He treats me with the utmost coldness. My breasts hurt, and it is agony for me to feed the baby. Today I had to call in Mavrusha to give him some extra milk so as to allow my breasts to heal. These ailments of mine always make him act so cruelly towards me. And when he is cold to me they are compounded by emotional sufferings which are far worse than any physical pain. She is in the drawing-room with the children and I have shut myself in my room. I simply cannot endure her. It enrages me to see her beauty and high spirits, especially in the company of Lyovochka.

July 24 Lyovochka visited her house again today, and came back saying how he pitied the poor woman and her dull life. Then he asked me why I hadn't invited them to dinner. If I had had my way I would never have had her in the house in the first place. Oh Lyovochka, can't you see you've been caught! My aching breasts rob me of so much time and happiness. And the worst thing is that I have completely withdrawn from Lyovochka, and he has withdrawn even further from me. It disturbs him that I have got Mavrusha to help me feed Ilyusha, and it grieves me too to see him suckling another woman's milk as well as my own. God only knows when my breasts will heal. Everything is going wrong. My heart rejoices whenever Lyova expresses his dissatisfaction with the way the farm is being run. Maybe he will dismiss the bailiff, and then I shall be rid of my tormenting jealousy for Maria Ivanovna. I would be sorry for his sake, but her I hate.

August 10 There are days when you feel so happy and light-hearted that you long to do something to astonish people and make them love you. When I hear of others' misfortunes I count myself very fortunate. Yesterday Bibikov told us the dreadful story of the regimental clerk here in Yasenki who has just been shot for hitting his company commander in the face. Lyovochka was a defence witness at the open court-martial, but of course the defence was unfortunately a mere formality.[6] I have just heard today that *Constance's* little boy had died;[7] how tragic for her.

We had a lot of visitors all on the same day: the two Princesses Gorchakova, nice Prince Lvov and that fat Sollogub with his two adolescent sons. He told me I was the perfect wife for a writer, and that a wife should always be 'the nursemaid of talent'. I appreciate that, and shall try to be an even better nursemaid of Lyovochka's talent from now on. All my jealousy of Maria Ivanovna has vanished – it was virtually groundless anyway – and our relations are much simpler and happier, if still somewhat reserved. My children are such darlings. Seryozha has begun to call me 'thou'. But I am disappointed with him for forgetting his alphabet over the summer; he knew it so well last winter.

August 27 I love my children with a passion that is often painful; every little sorrow drives me frantic, and every little smile and glance brings tears to my eyes. Ilyusha is unwell, and I am waiting for Tanya, the Dyakovs, and Mashenka and her little girls to arrive. They have moved into the new wing, where they will be staying from now on.[8] Breastfeeding the baby is a trial, and often exhausts me. It would be so much easier if I did not love the children so much.

November 12 Lyova is in Moscow and has taken Tanya with him.[9] She is very poorly and I am desperately worried about her. The more hopeless her health is, the more intensely I love her. She will probably visit Italy with the Dyakovs.[10] I am afraid I failed to realise just how ill she was this autumn. We were having such a good time here in the first three weeks of September that I instinctively repressed all sad thoughts. When I do not open my diary for a long time I always think what a pity it is I do not record the happy times. The Dyakovs were here those three weeks, as well as Mashenka and the little girls, and Tanya, and there was so much friendship between us, so much simple affection, that I am sure it is not often one enjoys such happiness with friends. I shall always remember my name-day, September 17, with special joy. To my surprise and delight, a band struck up a tune for me just as we were eating dinner,[11] and there was dearest Lyova gazing at me so tenderly. That evening we sat out on the verandah, which was lit by lanterns and candles. I shall never forget the young ladies darting about in their white muslin dresses, and good-natured little Kolokoltsev; but it is Lyovochka's sweet cheerful face I remember most clearly, as he rushed here, there and everywhere, doing everything he could to ensure that we all enjoyed ourselves. I quite surprised myself, normally so staid and serious, dancing away with such abandon. The weather was perfect and everyone had a wonderful time. Tanya stayed on with us for another month after our guests left, and only then did it become obvious how ill she was. I feel so sad for her, especially now Lyova is away, but then I am always dejected when he is not here. I do not believe any two people could be closer than we are. We are terribly fortunate, in every way – in our children, our relationship, our life. Now he is away I am living even more through my children. But they are still so small; they are asleep now, soon they will wake and eat, and this evening they will go back to sleep. Meanwhile I cherish and encourage every expression of their personalities. I now spend most of my time copying out Lyova's novel (which I am reading for the first time).[12] This gives me great pleasure. As I copy I experience a whole new world of emotions, thoughts and impressions. Nothing touches me so deeply as his ideas, his genius. This has only been so recently. Whether it is because I have changed or because this novel really is extraordinarily good, I do not know. I write very quickly, so I can follow the story and catch the mood, but slowly enough to be able to stop, reflect upon each new idea and discuss it with him later. He and I often talk about the novel together, and for some reason he listens to what I have to say (which makes me very proud) and trusts my opinions.

· 1867 ·

May – a Polish emigré, Berezowski, attempts to kill the Tsar in Paris. Summer – a small group of populists travel to the villages to teach the peasants.

July – Tanya Behrs marries Aleksandr Kuzminskii, a young magistrate. December – first three volumes of War and Peace *published.*

January 12 I am in a terrible state of agitated depression, as though something were coming to an end. There are indeed many things that must soon come to an end, and that terrifies me. The children have been continuously ill, and I still find the Englishwoman awkward and gloomy.[1] I do not warm to her. They say one becomes very anxious when one is about to die. Well, I feel extremely anxious and keep rushing about and have so much to do. Lyovochka has been writing all winter, irritable and excited, often with tears in his eyes.[2] I feel this novel of his will be superb. All the parts he has read to me have moved me almost to tears too; whether this is because, as his wife, I feel so much for him, or because it really *is* very good I cannot say for certain – although I rather think the second. His family generally gets nothing but his *fatigues de travail*; with me he is often impatient and bad-tempered, and I am beginning to feel very lonely.

March 15 At ten o'clock last night, when I was already asleep, a fire broke out in the hothouses and everything was burnt to ashes. Lyova woke me up and I stood and watched the blaze from the window. He dragged the gardener's children and their possessions from the building, while I ran to the village to fetch some peasants. But there was nothing they could do: everything was burnt, all those plants which Grandfather had so lovingly cultivated all those years ago, and which had given pleasure to three subsequent generations; the little that is left is probably frozen and charred too. I was not so upset about it last night but today I had to struggle to control my feelings, otherwise I would have been in floods of tears. What a blow. I feel desperately sorry for Lyovochka; he looks so crushed, and every little tribulation of his weighs so heavily upon me. He had lavished so much love on those plants recently, and everything he had planted was just beginning to flourish again. But nothing can bring them back now, and time alone will ease the pain.

August 29 We have quarrelled and we haven't made it up. 'It's my fault,' I said, 'if I still don't know what my husband likes and what he can tolerate.' And all the time I just wanted to end it as quickly as possible. But it got worse and worse. I kept contradicting myself, trying to get at the truth and it was agony – but I didn't have any malicious intentions. And now all that's left is jealousy, the fear that it is all over, ruined.

September 12 Yes, it *is* ruined. There's such coldness, such a glaring emptiness and a sense of loss, for the old love and openness. I feel it constantly, I am afraid of being on my own, yet I am afraid too of being with him, and I sometimes shudder when he starts talking to me, for I think he's going to tell me how much I disgust him. But he says nothing, he's not angry and he never mentions our relations. But he does not love me. I never thought it would come to this, I never thought I would suffer such agony. Sometimes, in a proud and angry mood, I tell myself it is not right that I should love him so if he is unable to love *me*, but mostly I am angry because I *do* love him so intensely, so humbly, so painfully – and all to no avail. Maman often boasts of how long Papa has loved her. But it's not that *she* did anything to inspire such devotion, it was he who had this great capacity for loving. And that is a very special capacity. How does one inspire devotion anyway? It cannot be done. It was drummed into me that I should love my husband, and that I should be a good and honourable wife and mother. All this is written in our ABCs – and what complete rubbish it is too. I know now that one should learn *not* to love, to dissemble, to be cunning and to hide one's faults (for absolutely everyone has their faults).

The main thing, though, is not to love. Why did I love him so intensely! And what can I do with this love, which has brought me nothing but suffering and humiliation? He thinks I am merely being foolish. 'You keep saying that but you never do anything,' he says. I argue back, yet I have nothing but my stupid humiliating love for him, and my bad character, which both conspire to make me unhappy, for the latter distorts the former.

September 14 Nothing has changed. I might even learn to endure it – today I actually resolved to do so. It is rather a peaceful, poetic existence, free of excitements and the material things of the so-called physical world; a life of prayer, holy thoughts, dreams of self-perfection, and a quiet love that has been trampled underfoot. Nobody, not even Lyovochka, shall enter this inner world of mine, and nobody shall love me; yet I shall love everyone else, and shall be stronger and happier than they.

September 16 All day I have been unable to stop thinking of September 17 last year.[3] God knows I don't need parties or music or dancing – all I need is for him to want me and to love giving me pleasure, as he used to; if only he knew how much I appreciated his kindness to me last year – I shall remember it as long as I live. Then I felt so sure of myself, so happy and strong and beautiful. Now I feel equally sure that I am worthless, weak and ugly.

This morning we had a friendly discussion about the estate, and we agreed about everything and were such good friends, just as though we were *one* again, yet we so seldom talk to each other about anything these days. I think of nothing but my children and my own trivial preoccupations. Seryozha came up to me just now and said, 'What's that you're writing in your little book?' And I told him he could read it when he grew up. What will he make of it? Will he think badly of me? Will the children stop loving me too? But it's because I am so demanding that I can never make people love me.

· 1868 ·

Universities of St Petersburg and Moscow in ferment. September – first issue of Bakunin's periodical, the People's Cause, *published in exile in Switzerland.*

Tolstoy immersed in the last part of War and Peace. *Sofia assumes most of the responsibility for the household and estate. Autumn – entire Tolstoy family travels to Moscow, where Sofia's father is dying.*

July 31 It makes me laugh to read my diary. What a lot of contradictions – as though I were the unhappiest of women! But who could be happier? Could any marriage be more happy and harmonious than ours? When I am alone in the room I sometimes laugh for joy and cross myself, and pray to God for many, many more years of happiness. I always write my diary when we quarrel. There are still days when we quarrel, but this is because of various subtle emotional reasons, and we wouldn't quarrel if we didn't love one another. I have been married for six years now, but I love him more and more. He often says it isn't really *love*, but that we have grown so used to one another that now we cannot be separated. But I still love him with the same passionate, poetic, fevered, jealous love, and his composure occasionally irritates me.

He has gone off hunting with Petya. It's hard for him to write in the summer. Afterwards they will go to Nikolskoe. I am unwell and have stayed indoors almost all day. The children go out for long walks and come back only to eat their meals on the verandah. Ilya is a perfect darling. Tanya is completely absorbed with Dasha and hardly comes in to say hello. Kuzminskii is neither flesh nor fowl.

(New repressive rules introduced into the universities in 1869. Student unrest intensifies. A young student, Sergei Nechaev, produces his Revolutionary Catechism, *which urges students to adopt terror tactics. Land and Liberty regroups in St Petersburg, formed of young intellectuals and students whose first priority is to carry their peaceful propaganda into the factories, schools and universities.*

May 20, 1869 – Sofia Tolstaya gives birth to her third son, Lev (Lyolya, Lyova). Tolstoy finishes War and Peace. *December 4, 1869 – the sixth and final volume published.)*

· 1870 ·

*First strikes in St Petersburg, followed by similar disturbances elsewhere. Numerous people arrested and imprisoned. June 16 – law passed whereby every town is to have a council (*Duma*) elected by local residents on the basis of their tax assessments (with the larger tax-payers' influence predominating). July – France declares war on Prussia. Russian section of the First International formed in Geneva.*

Tolstoy starts work on a novel about Peter the Great, writes a series of readers for peasants and learns Greek. Sofia writes a short story called 'Sparrows', and Russian and French grammars for her children.

June 5 I have been weaning Lyovushka for four days now.[1] I am almost sorrier with him than I was with all the others. I blessed him, and I cried and prayed for him. It is very hard, this first separation from one's baby. I think I must be pregnant again. With each new child one sacrifices a little more of one's life and accepts an even heavier burden of perennial anxieties and illnesses.

· 1871 ·

Franco-Prussian War ended in February, and the Third Empire overthrown by a revolution. May – defeat of the Paris Commune. June – new Russian education policy, with less humanities, more classics and religion.

February 12 – premature birth of the Tolstoys' second daughter, Maria (Masha). Sofia nearly dies of puerperal fever. Shortly after the birth, Tolstoy leaves for a health cure in Samara, and buys a 67,000 acre estate near Buzuluk.

August 18 I saw Tanya and her children off to the Caucasus yesterday evening. My soul is empty, sad and afraid at the prospect of living apart from my dearest friend. We have never been parted before. I feel as if part of my soul had been torn out, and nothing can comfort me. There is no one else in the whole world who could make me smile, comfort me when I am sad, and lift my spirits when I feel low. I look at nature and at my life stretching ahead of me, dismal and desolate, for everything seems dead without her. I cannot find words to express what I feel. Something has died in me. It is not a grief which one can forget through tears, and whose memory will make my heart ache for years to come.[1] I worry constantly about Lyovochka's health. For two months he has been on a *kumis** diet, which has done him no good at all;[2] he is still ill, I know – intuitively rather than intellectually – from his complete lack of interest in life ever since last winter. A shadow seems to have passed between us and separated us. I feel that if I don't force myself to be cheerful, endure Tanya's departure with fortitude, busy myself with the children, lead an active life, and refuse to pine, he will not be able to lift my spirits; for he constantly drags me down into his own hopeless melancholy. He would never admit this, but my feelings never deceive me. It is always I who suffer most from his moods, and I know I am not mistaken.

Last winter, when Lyovochka and I were both so ill, something between us was broken. I know that what was broken in me was my faith in our old life and happiness. I have lost that confidence, and now I am permanently

*Fermented mare's milk, believed to have health-giving powers.

beset by fears that something will happen. And it has indeed: Tanya has gone and Lyovochka is ill; these are the two people I love most in the world and I have lost them both, Lyovochka because he is no longer the person he was. He says it's old age, I say it's illness. But that 'something' has cut us off from one another.

· 1872 ·

June – group of Austro-Hungarian officers attend Russian army manoeuvres near St Petersburg. Gradual rapprochement *of the imperial courts of Germany, Austro-Hungary and Russia. Marx's* Capital *(first published 1867) appears in Russian, its first foreign translation.*

Tolstoy, disillusioned with fiction, opens a school for peasant children in the house, and writes his peasant ABC. *He is increasingly haunted by fears of death. Spring – he abandons his peasant school and turns to teaching his own children. June – a bull on the estate gores a herdsman to death. Later that year Tolstoy's* ABC *is published. It is not a success.*

It has been a happy winter; our souls have been in harmony again, and Lyovochka's health has not been bad.

April 1 Lyovochka returned from Moscow on March 30.[1] The children have brought yellow and purple flowers in from the garden.

I fasted, returned from Tula by train, then took the carriage. There's snow only in the gullies and it's terribly muddy, but warm and sunny. Lyovochka hunted woodsnipe this evening; he shot one and Mitrofan sent us another.[2]

April 3 Still warm. He shot two woodsnipe. We sat up until almost four a.m. getting the proofs of the *ABC* ready to send off.[3]

April 5 He shot another woodsnipe. Before dinner he took the children out to the beehives, but they couldn't cross the ford. I turned back and took Lyolya for a walk near the house. Very warm, with a warm wind.

April 6 A bright windy morning followed by thunder and a violent hail-storm. Lyovochka has had a chill for the past three nights and is still unwell.

April 8 There was a terrific thunder-storm in the night, followed by a downpour of rain. Lyovochka still has a chill in his back and feels unwell.

But he is in good spirits, and says he has enough work to last a lifetime.[4] Everything is green. The leaves are bursting out, the lungwort is in flower, and the grass is already tall.

April 9 It could be summer.

April 12 We took Ilyusha to the Zakaz clearing to watch the snipe-shooting. It was a heavenly evening, warm and clear, and we had a splendid time. A full moon appeared above the treetops.

April 16 Easter Sunday. There was rain and thunder last night, and by morning it had turned cold and dull.

April 18 L. went out with Bibikov to shoot snipe at Zaseka and got three. Still cold.

April 19 Lyovochka looked at the stars all night until dawn.

April 20 Drove out with Varya and the children to pick violets. Everything is very fresh. I feel slightly feverish. Lyovochka is well. Varya's fiancé came this evening.[5]

April 21 I drove out to pick morels with Varya, Nagornov and the children. We got a whole basketful. It is still cool. Lyovochka, Varya and her fiancé went off to shoot snipe. The sun set like a blazing ball of fire. It is a warm, still evening, 11 ° above zero. The limetree is almost in leaf and all the other trees (apart from the oak) have opened up. This morning Lyovochka brought in a huge bunch of flowers and branches he had picked from various different trees.

April 23 A cold night and a bright, fresh, still morning with a clear sky. Lyovochka said yesterday that one or two of the oaks were beginning to come into leaf, and a few of the limetrees are already quite green.

April 27–28 Lyovochka left for Moscow last night.[6] Masha is very sick.[7]

April 30 Unbearable heat, thunder-storms night and day.

May 13 Lyovochka brought in a bunch of sweet briar covered in flowers.

May 14 Lyovochka, Styopa[8] and Seryozha went to Nikolskoe.

May 15 We had a swim, made coffee, then picked mushrooms for our basket. Very hot.

May 16–17 They have returned from Nikolskoe; it's cold and overcast.

May 18 Hannah has gone to Tula to buy toys for the children. We went out to pick mushrooms, and were caught in a shower – we got chilled through. Lyovochka is very upset that they haven't yet sent the proofs, and wrote yesterday to Moscow[9] telling them to return the original, which is with Ries. Today he wrote a letter to Lieven about Sasha.[10] There are huge pods on the acacias. Dry, windy and cold.

May 20 Terrible heat. Lyovochka and Ilyusha went to Tula in the train and I took the children swimming. The sweet briar has lost its blossom. Yesterday they sold the hay from the orchard.

· 1873 ·

Summer – young Land and Liberty members flock 'to the people', travelling to the villages dressed as artisans and peasants to teach literacy classes, give medical help and spread socialist ideas. Hundreds of Land and Liberty members arrested and await trial. An imperial ukase *orders all women studying abroad to come home.*

Spring – Tolstoy gives up work on his Peter the Great novel and starts work on Anna Karenina. *Another bull on the estate gores a peasant to death. June 13 – Sofia gives birth to her fourth son, Pyotr (Petya). Shortly afterwards, the whole family travels south to Samara, to stay on their new estate. November – publication of the third edition of the* Complete Works of L. N. Tolstoy, *in eight volumes. November 9 – Petya dies of croup. Tolstoy haunted by fears of death.*

February 13 Lyovochka has gone to Moscow[1] and all day long I have been sitting alone here wretchedly staring into space, a prey to sickening anxieties which leave me no peace. I always take up my diary when I am in this sort of mental turmoil, for I can pour out all my emotions and then feel calmer. But my present mood is sinful, stupid, spiteful and insincere. Where would I be without the support of this good, honest man, whom I love with all my heart, and whose thoughts are always so fine and pure? Yet in moments of anxiety I sometimes search my heart and ask myself what I really want. And to my horror, the answer is that I want gaiety, smart clothes and chatter. I want people to admire me and say how pretty I am, and I want Lyova to see and hear them too; I long for him occasionally to emerge from his rapt inner existence which demands so much of him; I wish he could briefly lead a normal life with me, like a normal person. But then my heart cries out against the Devil's temptations of Eve, and I think even worse of myself than before. I hate people who tell me I am beautiful. I never believed them, and now it would be too late anyway – what would be the point of it? My darling little Petya[2] loves his old nanny just as much as he would love a great beauty. And Lyovochka could get used to the plainest wife, so long as she was docile and quiet, and lived the sort of life that suited him. I want to turn my character inside out and demolish everything that is mean and false in me. I am having my hair curled today, and have been happily imagining how nice it will look, even though nobody will see me and it is quite unnecessary. I adore ribbons, I would like a new leather belt – and now I have written this I feel like crying . . .

The children are waiting upstairs for their music lesson, and here I am in the study, writing all this stupid nonsense.

We went skating today. The boys kept bumping into Fyodor Fyodorovich[3] and I felt sorry for them and had trouble pacifying Fyodor Fyodorovich, while at the same trying to comfort them. I do not take to the new Englishwoman[4] who arrived here the other morning; she is too lethargic and *commune* for my liking. But it's too early to know.

April 17 It snowed all morning, 5 ° above zero, no grass, no warmth, no sun, none of the bright aching joy of spring, for which we have been waiting so long. My heart is as cold, gloomy and sad as the countryside. Lyovochka is writing his novel, which is going well.

November 11 On November 9 at nine in the morning, my little Petyushka died of a throat infection. He died peacefully, after two days' illness. He was born on June 13, 1872, and I had fed him for fourteen and a half months. What a bright, happy little boy – I loved my darling too much and now there is nothing. He was buried yesterday. I cannot reconcile the two Petyas, the living and the dead; they are both precious to me, but what does the living Petya, so bright and affectionate, have in common with the dead one, so cold and still and serious. He loved me very much – I wonder if it hurt him too to leave me?[5]

· 1874 ·

Land and Liberty members continue to go 'to the people'. By the end of the year some 800 are rounded up and arrested, and Land and Liberty is virtually wiped out. Winter – a group of women who had been studying abroad return to Moscow to form a secret revolutionary society, whose members carry their message into the factories. They too are arrested.

April 22 – Sofia gives birth to a son, Nikolai. June 20 – Tolstoy's Aunt

Tatiana dies after living for fifty years at Yasnaya Polyana. Her companion, Natalya Petrovna, becomes deranged and is moved to an old people's home. Tolstoy's Aunt Pelageya moves in. Tolstoy's spiritual crisis deepens and his religious doubts multiply.

February 17 When I think of the future I see a blank. I am haunted by the gloomy premonition that as soon as the grass grows over Petya's grave they will have to plough it up for me.

·1875·

Two large strikes in Odessa, supported by the Union of South Russian Workers, the first working-class organisation in Russia. Peasants in the Chigirin area near Kiev, dissatisfied with the land allocated to them after the emancipation, start to redistribute it amongst themselves and despatch one of their number to St Petersburg to petition the Tsar.

January – chapters 1–14 of Anna Karenina *appear in the* Russian Herald. *February 2 – ten-month-old Nikolai dies in agony of meningitis. November 1 – Sofia gives birth to a baby girl, Varvara, who dies immediately afterwards. December – Aunt Pelageya dies after a fall. Tolstoy prone to ever more severe doubts and depressions.*

October 12 This isolated country life is becoming intolerable. Dismal apathy, indifference to everything, day after day, month after month, year after year – nothing ever changes. I wake up in the morning and just lie there wondering who will get me up, who is waiting for me. The cook is bound to come in, then the nurse, complaining that the servants are grumbling about the food and there is no sugar, which means we must send for more, so then I get up, my right shoulder aching, and sit silently darning holes, and then it's time for the children's grammar and piano lessons, which I do with pleasure, although with the sad realisation that I am not doing it as well as I should. Then in the evening more darning, with Auntie[1] and Lyovochka playing endless horrible games of patience together. I get some brief pleasure from reading, but how many good books are there? On days like today I feel I am living in a dream. But no, this is life, not a dream. In dreams I go to vespers and pray as I never pray in real life, or else see the most marvellous flowers, or picture galleries, or crowds of people whom I neither hate nor avoid but love with my whole heart.

This year, God knows, I have struggled with these shameful feelings of boredom, and have tried, all on my own, to assert my better self, and to reassure myself that it is best for the children, emotionally and physically, to live in the country, and I have managed to subdue my own selfish feelings, but I then realise to my horror that this turns into a terrifying apathy and a dull animal indifference to everything, which is even harder to struggle against. Besides, I am not on my own, I am tied to Lyovochka and the bonds have grown even tighter with the passing of the years, and I feel it is mainly because of him that I am sinking into this depression. It's painful for me to see him when he is like this, despondent and dejected for days and weeks on end, neither working nor writing, without energy or joy, just as though he had become reconciled to this condition. It is a kind of emotional death, which I deplore in him. Surely it can't go on much longer.[2] It may be vulgar and wrong of me, but I feel oppressed by the terms of our life which he has laid down – by this terrible monotony and solitude which reduce us both to such apathy. Whenever I think of the future, when our children are grown up, when I think of their education and all the things they'll need in life, I realise that Lyovochka is far too apathetic and indifferent to be any help to me, for nothing touches his heart, it's always I who take all the emotional and moral responsibility for our children, and must suffer for their failures – how *can* I be expected to take sole responsibility, and how can I help them at all when Lyovochka is in such a dazed and hopeless state that I despair of rousing him? But there is no life without hope, and my hope is that God will light the spark of life in Lyovochka and he will once more be the person he used to be.

·1876·

Troops sent into Chigirin to put down the rebellious peasants, and a permanent garrison established there. Spring – demonstrations in St Petersburg to mourn the death in custody of a populist student. December – Land and Liberty organises its first demonstration, outside the cathedral of Our Lady of Kazan in St Petersburg. Revolutionaries become more militant.

Summer – Tolstoy visits Samara again to buy horses for a stud farm he plans to start. October – Sofia starts work on a biography of Tolstoy, on which she works until 1878. Tolstoy resolves his religious doubts by strict observance of the religious rituals.

September 15 We live in such isolation, and here I am again with my silent friend, my diary. I intend to write it every day without fail from now on. Lyovochka went off to Samara, and from there to Orenburg, a town he had always wanted to visit. I got a telegram from him there.[1] I miss him a lot and worry even more. I try to tell myself I am pleased he is enjoying himself, but it isn't true. I am hurt that he has torn himself away from me just when we were getting along so well and were such good friends, and has sentenced me to two sad, anxious weeks without him.

But I have decided to make the best of it, and am throwing myself into the children's lessons. But my goodness, how impatient I am! I keep losing my temper and shouting at them – just today, I became annoyed beyond endurance by Ilya's laziness and all the spelling mistakes in Seryozha's essay on the Volga and I burst into tears just as the lesson was ending. The children were dismayed, but Seryozha was sorry for me and I found that very touching; afterwards he kept following me around, and was so quiet and attentive. Tanya and I are not getting on. How sad to have this endless battle with one's children. I mean no harm, I should merely like more freedom and variety in my life. I get terribly tired, I am not well, my breathing is laboured and I have indigestion and a stomach-ache. I am suffering from the cold and feel pinched.

September 17 My name-day. One more day has passed without Lyovochka, or so much as a word from him. This morning I got up feeling lazy and unwell, plagued by minor worries. The children went off with Styopa[2] to fly the kite and ran back red-faced and excited to beg me to go and watch. But I didn't go, for I had ordered all Lyovochka's papers to be fetched out of the gun-closet and was immersed in the world of his novels and diaries. I was very excited, and experienced a wealth of impressions. But I realised I could never write that biography of him as I had intended, for I could never be impartial; I avidly search his diaries for any reference to love, and am so tormented by jealousy that I can no longer see anything clearly. I shall try to do it, though.[3] I am afraid of my resentment of Lyovochka for leaving me just when I loved him so much, but in my soul I blame him constantly for causing me so much worry and misery. It seems odd that although he is always so anxious that I should not fall ill, he should torture me by going away at a time when my health was so poor. I now cannot sleep for worrying, and eat practically nothing. I just choke back the tears, or hide away several times a day and weep with anxiety. I have a fever every day and a chill at night, and am so agitated I feel my head will burst. I have thought about so many things the past two weeks. I have been getting on better with the children. I am afraid I may often exploit their pity for me. But their concern is so delightful. Tanya is becoming quite pretty; I'm rather disturbed by her childish adoration of Ippolit Nagornov[4] the violinist. I did not give them their lessons after breakfast today; I suddenly felt drained of energy and could do nothing. God help me survive, perhaps for several more days. 'What is he punishing me for?' I keep asking myself. 'Why, for loving him so much.' And now all my happiness is in pieces, and I feel very bitter that my good humour and my spontaneous loving feelings have once again been crushed.

September 18 I had a telegram from him in Syzran today saying he will be home the day after tomorrow in the morning.[5] I suddenly felt more cheerful, and the house was all happiness and light, the children's lessons went well, and they were adorable. But I have a pain in my chest – I wonder if I'm going to be ill, it reduced me to tears today and I feared for our peaceful life together. Talking and explaining things to the children during lessons was agony. I keep catching my breath. The children were in a bad mood when they came upstairs after M. Rey's class.[6] Apparently they had misbehaved, and had all been given 'twos' for bad conduct. I told Seryozha that as he had been naughty he was not to go hunting, and that I hoped this punishment would teach him a lesson. But he just lost his temper, and shouted '*Au contraire*!' I found this very hurtful; but later, when he was saying goodnight, he asked me if I was still angry with him, and I was very pleased and forgave him. Styopa is so sweet and such a help to me with the children, making them learn and go over their lessons. My heart leaps when I think that the day after tomorrow Lyovochka will be coming back, lighting up the house.

· 1877 ·

January – trial of those arrested for demonstrating in St Petersburg. March – great public trial opens of those (mainly women) arrested for propagandising in the factories of Moscow (Trial of the 50). April – Russia declares war on Turkey. Hundreds of revolutionaries volunteer to fight with the Bulgarian partisans in the Balkans. October to January 1878 – second great public trial (Trial of the 193), of those arrested for propagandising in the villages.

Final chapters of Anna Karenina *published in the* Russian Herald, *earning Tolstoy huge royalties. July – he makes a pilgrimage on foot to the Optyna Pustyn monastery. The discord between the couple increases. Sofia assumes yet more of the burdens of running the farm and the house. December 6 – Andrei Tolstoy (Andryusha) born.*

February 27 As I was reading through some of Lyovochka's old diaries today, I realised I would never be able to write those 'Notes for a Biography', as I had intended to.[1] His inner life is so complicated and his diaries disturb me so much that I grow confused, and cannot see things clearly. Sadly, I must abandon this dream of mine. I can record our present life, though, and what he says about his intellectual activities, and I shall try not to shirk and to do it conscientiously. He has gone to Moscow to correct the proofs for the February instalment of his book,[2] and to consult Zakharin about his headaches and blood-rushes.[3]

The other day, when I asked him to tell me about something from his past, he said: 'Please don't ask about these things; it disturbs me to think of my past and I'm much too old now to relive my whole life in memories.'

· 1878 ·

January 24 – a young revolutionary called Vera Zasulich attempts to kill General Trepov, hated governor-general of St Petersburg. February–March – student demonstrations in Kiev. March 31 – Zasulich tried, acquitted and a warrant issued for her rearrest, but by then she has fled to Switzerland. The affair provides the impetus to yet more assassination attempts. August 4 – Sergei Kravchinskii kills General Mezentsev, head of St Petersburg secret police. November – student riots in St Petersburg.

April – Tolstoy visits Samara and buys more land. He starts work on a novel (never published) on the Decembrists' uprising. Sofia Tolstaya finishes her biography of him.

September 21 Nikolenka Tolstoy has been staying with us, and we have been discussing our plan to visit Moscow with him and his young wife-to-be.[1] She's a 'little star'.

September 22 Lyovochka and Ilyusha went hunting with the borzois and brought back 6 hares. Andryusha had his smallpox vaccination.

September 23 Our 16th wedding anniversary; I gave the children their German lesson, which went very well; it's a warm, bright, peaceful day. Andryusha is a joy.

September 24, Sunday I got up late. Lyovochka went to Mass[2] and the three of us, Lyovochka, his sister Mashenka and I, drank coffee together. After lunch the children walked over to Yasenki, and Mashenka drove to Tula with Seryozha's classics tutor, the high-school teacher Ulyaninskii. Lyovochka and Seryozha took their guns and the hounds and went hunting, and I stayed at home cutting out jackets for the boys. Then Mashenka, Annie[3] and I all went off in the carriage to Yasenki to look for the children. Just before I left Prince Urusov[4] appeared with his gun, and went off to look for our huntsmen. I found the children in the shop at Yasenki, having bought themselves some sweets. We all congregated for dinner, then we had a game of croquet in the twilight, with Lyovochka,

Ilyusha and I playing M. Nief, Lyolya and Urusov; they beat us. After that Lyovochka and Urusov played a game of chess, the children ate their sweets and were rather rowdy, and I read Octave Feuillet's *Journal d'une femme.*[5] It is all very fine and idealistic, although the ending is a bit forced. But the whole thing seems to be written in deliberate contrast to the excessive realism of some contemporary literature. It is midnight. Lyovochka is having some supper, and after that we shall go to bed.

September 25 I taught the children this morning, then Mashenka came to dinner bringing Anton, Rossa and Nadya Delvig with her. The children were in ecstasies. After dinner we danced a quadrille, and I partnered little Lyolya to make up a third couple. Lyovochka and Aleksandr Grigorevich played for us.[6] Then Masha and Aleksandr Grigorevich played a piano and violin duet, which was quite successful. (They did that delightful Mozart sonata, with the andante which always moves me to tears.) Then Lyovochka played some Weber sonatas. But for me Aleksandr Grigorevich's violin-playing was by then beginning to compare badly with Nagornov's. Finally they did Beethoven's *Kreutzer Sonata* – badly; now that should be truly something when played properly!

Afterwards the children and I played a hand of 'fate' with the others. Rossa is a dear, candid soul, though rather plain. They all stayed the night here.

The following day, September 26 I woke up with a headache. Lyovochka and Auntie went to Mass, while the rest of us played a jolly game of croquet. The days are fine, the trees have all turned yellow but still have their leaves on, and it's all very beautiful. The nights are moonlit and frosty. After lunch we played another game of croquet, with Rossa and me playing Anton and Seryozha. Then Lyovochka persuaded the children to walk the borzois over the fields. They each took a dog on the lead, one of the huntsmen rode along beside them, also with a dog on the lead, and Annie, Mlle Gachet and M. Nief all followed behind. It made a very pretty picture. After we had finished our game of croquet the others joined them, and I went to visit Vasilii Ivanovich.[7] I felt awkward and depressed with them this time. Seryozha looked in on his way back, and was amazed to see me there. Seryozha is very fond of Vasilii Ivanovich and always remembers to visit him, which delights me. Lyovochka went hunting and shot a grouse in the new birch plantation. The children played croquet until dinner while I watched. After dinner the Delvigs went home and the children all crowded into Lyovochka's sitting-room laughing and chattering and pushing one another. They went to bed early.

September 27 It's still clear and dry. I did a lot of cutting and sewing, gave Liza[8] a French lesson, and Masha and Tanya a German lesson. I am in an orderly, domestic mood. Andryusha had his smallpox vaccination on Friday and is sick and restless; my nipples are hurting. Lyovochka rode off beyond Zaseka with the borzois, but didn't even see anything; his work is still not progressing and he has a back-ache. Masha is irritable, shivering and out of sorts.

October 1, Sunday, Festival of the Protection of the Virgin Lyovochka went to Mass this morning, while Ulyaninskii gave Seryozha his classics lesson. I slept late, for Andryusha's vaccination has upset him and he has not been sleeping well. The children had put on their best clothes and were waiting anxiously for me to get up, for the weather was clouding over and they had planned to visit Delvig. It was fairly warm, though, so I let them go, and the four of them drove off with Mlle Gachet. Urusov came to visit, and went off with Lyovochka and M. Nief to shoot snipe. Mashenka is ill, and has been sitting downstairs treating herself with homeopathic remedies, so I have been all on my own; I trailed around the garden, the croquet lawn, and the house, then sat down with some sewing. We dined at seven, then sat talking pleasantly about serious matters while Lyovochka and Urusov played chess and I embroidered a dress for Andryusha. It was after nine when the children got back; they were in high spirits and delighted with their day, which they told us all about.

October 2 I was just giving the children their lesson when someone arrived at the house. It turned out to be Gromov and his daughter Nadya, Nikolenka's fiancée. She is a sweet girl, unaffected and very serious, and I'm sure I shall love her. They left straight after dinner. I worked all evening, and later Tanya and I took a bath together. Life here is peaceful and happy and not at all dull. The weather is still fine, and the nights are enchanting and moonlit. Andryusha is better.

October 3 I have been sitting indoors all day, despite the marvellous weather. I gave the children their lessons, and had to scold and punish Tanya for refusing to take a walk and running away from Mlle Gachet. Mashenka came and sat with me and was in a very good mood. Lyovochka went hunting and shot 5 hares. His horse fell under him, although he only hurt his arm, thank God, but it was at full gallop and he flew over its head, and the horse twisted its neck, and lay there for a long time unable to get up. Lyovochka has put a plaster on his right side – I am still rather anxious about him. Andryusha is an adorable child; he feeds himself now with his bread and milk. Nikolenka is coming tomorrow. The children played croquet after their lessons. While Lyovochka was having supper after the hunt, a letter arrived from my sister Tanya; I was so happy, and when I read it to the others, I couldn't stop smiling with delight. We all burst out laughing at the part where she sent her regards to 'our kind, gentle, devout, fair-skinned papa', which was how our little fortune-telling book *The Oracle* described him, and what we always jokingly call him when we play croquet.

October 4 Tanya's fourteenth birthday. As soon as I got up I walked to the little plantation where the children were having a picnic. M. Nief was there with his sleeves rolled up, making them *une omelette* and some hot chocolate, there were four bonfires and Seryozha was roasting *shashlyk*. We all had enormous fun and ate a lot, and we had magnificent weather. We got home and were just starting a game of croquet when what should we see but a procession of horses and donkeys filing along our 'prospect' on their way from Samara. The children were tremendously excited and immediately rushed over, leaped on to the donkeys and started riding about on them. Nikolenka came to dinner, with Baroness Delvig and Rossa, and we drank Tanya's health in champagne; she blushed but was very pleased. Later that evening Tanya and I drove our guests back to Kozlovka in the carriage, so we didn't get to bed until late. On our way home we met Lyovochka, who had come out to meet us on foot.

October 6 I am ill. I have rheumatism all over and a swollen cheek. I went downstairs this morning to see Lyovochka, busily writing at his desk. He told me this was his tenth attempt to start his new novel. It is to open with a cross-examination in a trial involving some peasants and a landlord. He got the details of the trial from the actual recorded documents, and is even leaving in the relevant dates. The trial, like a fountain, will precipitate events – for the peasants and for the landowner, in St Petersburg and in all the other places where the various characters will play their part.[9] I very much like this *entrée en matière.* The children are studying, but they are in a lazy mood and keep thinking up different games.

October 8 Yesterday was Nikolenka's wedding. As Lyovochka was best man, he set off for Tula this morning; Tanya and I left that evening and went straight to the church, where the marriage ceremony was just beginning. Tanya was most struck by the choristers' singing and the service. We left immediately after it was over. Seryozha had been hunting and caught two hares. The children rode over to Yasenki this morning on the donkeys.

October 9 Bibikov has just returned from Samara with a piece of bad news: there's practically no money from the estate again. I was terribly angry when I found out that they had rented some land and hadn't even told me about it. They bought some cattle too, and the harvest wasn't good either. I had a frightful argument with Lyovochka.[10] I think I have been very ill-used, and I still don't think I've done anything wrong, but I hate everything: myself, my life, my so-called 'happiness'. It is all dreary and disgusting.

October 11 D. A. Dyakov visited us this morning. He has been travelling around looking for an estate to buy for his daughter. Lyovochka went hunting, but didn't kill anything. Yesterday he shot two snipe and a hare, which was ripped to pieces by the hounds. We read aloud every evening, and M. Nief is at present reading us Alexandre Dumas' *The Three Musketeers*. It is highly enjoyable and the children listen fascinated, and are always impatient for the evenings to come.[11] Lyovochka is busy reading background material for his new work, but keeps complaining that his head is heavy and tired, and he still cannot write. We are good friends again,[12] and I intend to take good care of him from now on.

October 13 Lyolya, Liza and I were sitting studying, when the other children burst into the room shrieking with joy. Apparently Sergei Nikolaevich had arrived from Tula, where he had gone on business. We spent the day talking.

October 14 Mashenka left today. Sergei Nikolaevich went to Yasenki to see Khomyakov about a new bailiff, while Lyovochka went out hunting and saw six black grouse. Sergei Nikolaevich repeatedly asked after my sister Tanya and said he had not forgotten her and never would; he told me how much he had longed to speak to her that time he met her at the station. Seryozha hit Lyolya for throwing a stick at him. (Seryozha wanted the stick and was trying to grab it from Lyolya.) I got very angry and gave Seryozha a good talking-to. The hunchbacked drawing master came this afternoon and gave Tanya, Ilya and Lyolya their lesson. Tanya worked away studiously but the boys merely giggled and played around. Seryozha had his Greek and Latin lesson with Ulyaninskii and after that we read another instalment of *The Three Musketeers*, which still holds the children's interest. I am in a rather strange mood – very preoccupied with my appearance, and dreaming of a completely different sort of life. Once again I wish I were better educated, able to discuss clever ideas and read a lot of books; I also wish I were prettier, and keep thinking of clothes and other silly things. I long to go to Moscow with the children. I adore Andryusha.

October 15 When I went into the drawing-room for my morning tea, I found Lyovochka, his brother Seryozha, and the children all sitting there with the two teachers, the hunchbacked drawing master and Ulyaninskii the tutor. One feels slightly constrained by the teachers' presence. Lyovochka then drove to Mass.

Preparations started for the hunt. Seven horses were saddled up, and Lyovochka, the two Seryozhas, Ilyusha, a couple of servants and M. Nief all rode off with the hounds, while Tanya, Masha, Lyolya, Mlle Gachet and Liza rode the donkeys over to Kozlovka. I stayed behind on my own and played with Andryusha for a while, but when he fell asleep I grew restless, and ordered them to harness up the cart for me to go and meet the children. I found them at the boundary of the estate, and managed to persuade Mlle Gachet to drive home with me. There we ordered some grated horse-radish and sour milk, which we ate; we decided not to have dinner until our hunters were back. It was almost seven when they returned, looking very pleased with themselves and triumphantly bearing six hares strung up on a stick, which they gave to us. Later on we read more Dumas. Everyone was exhausted. Seryozha is most pleasant, and says such nice things to me about the children. I am going to bed.

October 16 I got up late. The children came one by one into the bedroom to see me as usual, followed by Lyovochka. Then the nurse came to take Andryusha, who had been sleeping with me since I had given him his morning feed. Then I tried on my new dress, which looked very charming, then I went downstairs to talk to my brother-in-law Seryozha, who is very depressed and low; he left for Pirogovo shortly afterwards and we saw him off. I read some German with Lyolya and Ilyusha. After dinner Lyovochka went off to a meeting of the Tula High School, of which he is a trustee. I have agreed to write a short biography of him for the new Russian Library series. It will consist mainly of various extracts from his works, chosen by Strakhov, and will be published by Stasyulevich.[13] I now realise, however, that writing a biography is by no means an easy task, and the little I have done is no good. I was hindered by the children, the noise, feeding Andryusha – and simply not knowing enough details of Lyovochka's life before I married him to write a biography. I am modelling mine on the biographies of Lermontov, Pushkin,[14] and Gogol.[15] I am transported by their works; it is a joy to immerse myself in the world of poetry, which I so love. Yet sadly, poets are human too, with all sorts of faults and blemishes, and Lermontov's biography has ruined him for me. We read some more Dumas; the children are increasingly fascinated by him. I sewed a little flannel shirt for Andryusha. At present I am reading *L'Idée de Jean Têterol* by Cherbuliez,[16] which I do not like at all. Mlle Gachet kept me company this evening, as Lyovochka is away. He did not work today, but this morning he said to me: 'It is going to be so good!'[17]

October 18 Andryusha has been ill, shivering and feverish, with an upset stomach. I got up late. The children have gone out: the boys took the dogs to the fields to catch mice, and Lyolya and the girls went out on the donkeys; Lyovochka has gone hunting with the borzois. I played croquet with Mlle Gachet and Vasilii Ivanovich – we won one game and Mlle Gachet won the other. It is beautifully mild and clear, dry and beautiful, with the wind from the south. I have resumed Lyolya's music lessons. Dinner was frightful: the pie was dry, the potato soup greasy, the *levashniki*[18] like shoe-leather, and hare I never eat. I just had a salad, and afterwards gave the cook a piece of my mind. Just then Lyovochka returned, with four hares and one fox. He is lethargic, silent and lost in thought; he does nothing but read. Today a length of Caucasian silk arrived from Tanya, and from Schuyler his translation of *The Cossacks*, which is quite good.[19] This evening we read more Dumas while I cut out and tacked a white cashmere dress I am making for Andryusha; I think I shall embroider it in red silk. Ilya and Lyolya were romping and laughing downstairs in the bath, and when I went to see them in bed they looked so happy and clean and splendid. I had gone in pretending that I wanted to examine Ilya's nightshirt, which he had said was too short. I feel mentally oppressed – I yearn for new experiences, new *émotions*.

October 21 Andryusha was very sick indeed yesterday: his little hands and feet grew cold, and he ran a high fever, he tossed and sobbed in his sleep, his lips twitched and his eyelids fluttered. This morning the fever had passed, but now he has diarrhoea, his sleep is still disturbed and I feel terribly worried. A certain Navrotskii, editor of a new journal called *Russian Speech*, came from Petersburg to visit us. He has been reading us his poems, and some extracts from his play – it wasn't too bad.[20] He also told us all the Petersburg news, which was quite interesting. The tutors came again today (Saturday). We had pancakes. I had a serious talk with Seryozha. Yesterday I had scolded him for making fun of people, and told him how much it distressed me; today I explained that I scolded my children only because I loved them and wanted them to be happy, and our happiness, I said, depended chiefly on being loved by others. I was thinking what a pity it is that tsars were embalmed. Everyone should be buried in the earth immediately after they die – 'earth unto earth'. All these embalming rituals and burial vaults are a curse. Lyovochka went out hunting and caught a hare. He did a little writing yesterday, but has not shown it to me yet. The weather has broken and it is drizzling outside. For the last three days Seryozha has had cramps again in his side.

October 22, Sunday The children went over to Yasenki today; some walked, some rode the donkeys, and Masha drove the little cart, drawn by Kolpik.[21] They bought themselves some sweets there and ate them. Annie and I stayed behind with Andryusha. He is still poorly. I cut out a pinafore for him, and moped at home all day on my own. This morning the hunchbacked drawing master told us the interesting story of how he started his career, as a draughtsman in a silk-factory. Lyovochka went to Mass, then went hunting with Seryozha. But they had no luck. Nurse is in Tula, and I have been with Andryusha since seven this morning and am exhausted. Lyovochka had intended to write several letters but was not in the right mood, so he wrote only to Turgenev and Strakhov.[22] This evening the children played hide-and-seek and various other games, while I read *L'Idée de Jean Têterol* by Cherbuliez – it is quite good. Lyovochka read, then went to bed.

October 23 After drinking his morning coffee with me, Lyovochka took the borzois off to Zaseka to hunt. I gave Masha a Russian lesson, Liza a French lesson, and Lyolya a German lesson. Lyovochka was back for dinner with three hares, and afterwards Seryozha played a Haydn sonata – quite well – with Aleksandr Grigorevich accompanying him on the violin. Then this evening Lyovochka played some sonatas, by Weber and Schubert, also with a violin accompaniment; I embroidered Andryusha's white cashmere robe in red silk, while enjoying the music. The weather is windy and unpleasant. Lyovochka was just saying that he had read his fill of historical material, and was going to start on Dickens' *Martin Chuzzlewit* for a rest.[23] I happen to know, however, that when Lyovochka turns to English novels he is about to start writing himself.

The children are well. Lyolya is making good progress with his lessons, Ilya is eagerly practising his embroidery, and Masha never stops smiling; she is a quiet, obedient child, and I find her as enigmatic as ever. Tanya is lazy and distracted; she has no vitality, but no silly moods either.[24] (A peasant has just brought in the rats and mice he had killed, for which we paid him five rubles.)

October 24 It was raining when we got up, but it cleared shortly afterwards and we went out to watch Mishka being lowered into the well on a rope to bring up the buckets and pails which had been lost down there. They managed to bring up two old ones, but couldn't find the new one. Then we went to the box-room to look over some things being stored there in suitcases for the winter. I gave the children their lessons and embroidered the baby's dress. When I was carrying him around the house today I noticed how much he loved all the pictures and portraits on the walls; he shrieked with joy at the sight of them. After dinner the children and I had a lively discussion about the play we plan to put on here over Christmas. We are still reading an abridged version of *The Three Musketeers*. Earlier today Lyovochka went to Zakaz with the hounds, but didn't catch anything. He is in a bilious and apathetic state, but he and I are getting on well. He is still unable to write. 'Sonya,' he said to me today, 'if I ever write anything again, it will have to be in such a way that the children can understand every single word of it.'

October 25 I gave Lyolya a music lesson and searched Haydn's symphonies for an easy menuetto for him to play. I read with Masha, helped Liza with her lesson, and worked on a white piqué dress for Andryusha. Lyovochka took the borzois hunting. He returned with a hare and a tiny white creature rather like a weasel. Later the two of us went over Lyovochka's entire life for his biography,[25] and I took notes while he talked. We worked cheerfully and well, and I am glad we did it. The children are studying hard. The wind is blowing and it is pouring with rain. We read some more Dumas this evening.

October 27 This morning I sent ten letters off to the post for Lyovochka, then came down to my usual, lonely morning tea. The weather was fine, and I was wretched, and choking back the tears. I drank my tea and went out for a walk. Lyovochka had left first thing to go hunting. I played with Andryusha for a while, then went out to look for the children. The 3 boys I discovered playing in the corn-stooks on the threshing floor, while M. Nief lay in the straw reading his book; I had no idea where the little girls were. The garden was heavenly. Just before dinner I discovered that Ilyusha and Lyolya had stolen some caviare, which made me very angry, and I smacked Ilya and gave them both a good talking-to. This evening the tutors, the children and I all went off in several carriages in the moonlight. It was a lovely night. Then I worked on my biographical essay. Andryusha was sick and feverish yesterday. Aleksei Alekseevich Bibikov payed us a visit. I shall have some boiled pike for my supper; after that I shall feed Andryusha and go to bed.

October 28 I drank tea alone, then Tanya came in complaining of a sore throat. I was very alarmed and told her to gargle with Bertholet salts, one teaspoonful dissolved in a glass of hot water. Aside from this, though, she seems quite well, so I don't feel so anxious now. I went to the woods to watch them making barrels. (We have agreed to make 6,000 for Gil.) We took the forest path, and it was enchanting – clear, frosty and silent. Then I went for a walk with Masha, Mlle Gachet and Annie, and the boys went back to the threshing-floor to play in the straw. The teachers again arrived while we were having dinner. Tanya did a rather good charcoal drawing of a woman's head. I sewed a christening-gown for Parasha's[26] baby boy and gave Andryusha his first bath since his vaccination. Lyovochka went out with the hounds and killed a hare.

October 29 It snowed today, then it became warm and the snow turned to mud. The children played hide-and-seek and made a great noise, but they enjoyed themselves. Everyone stayed indoors all day because of the weather. Lyovochka tried to do some work and I wrote all day and finished my biographical essay. This evening we had more reading aloud and I finished the christening-gown.

November 1 Lyovochka read me the beginning of his new book yesterday morning. It is an immense, interesting and serious undertaking. It begins with a case of some peasants and a landowner, who are in dispute over a piece of land, the arrival in Moscow of Prince Chernyshev and his family, the laying of the foundation-stone of the Cathedral of the Holy Saviour, a woman pilgrim, a peasant's wife, an old lady, etc.[27] Dyakov came for dinner. Lyovochka killed a hare, and later that evening we sat around discussing all the estates Dyakov has been looking at for his daughter Masha.[28] Seryozha and Tanya were both godparents at the christening of Parasha's son on Monday; they behaved with great dignity, but Ilyusha started giggling, and soon had Lyolya laughing too. I went to Tula this morning with Dmitrii Alekseevich, Seryozha and Tanya: it was fine and frosty. We bought some fur to make a coat for Tanya and a sheepskin jacket for Seryozha (costing 12 silver rubles); Seryozha was then measured for a winter overcoat (65 silver rubles), and we ordered some boots for Tanya, a fox jacket for me (to be made from our own furs) and various other things. Lyovochka had been working at home all day, and just as we were nearing the house he came out to meet us. It's always such a joy to return home and see his grey overcoat in the distance. Andryusha had not been at all sick or fretful. I had bought some tops for the boys (costing 10 kopecks each), a thimble for Masha, some beads, ear-rings and a brooch for the dolls, warm gloves and various other little things for the rest of them. I was terribly tired by then, for we had had nothing to eat all day but some sweet cakes and a piece of soft bread. This evening I gave Andryusha a bath; his fontanelle is very large and still has not grown over properly, which worries me. We read the final instalment of *The Three Musketeers* with great interest, after which Lyovochka sat for a long time improvising at the piano – yet another of his gifts. I got a letter from Tanya; her Miss MacCarthy has left and she wants Annie to replace her, but I cannot let her go and don't know what to do.

November 4 I didn't write my diary yesterday, I was too distracted. Lyovochka took Seryozha out hunting and the mist came down – they lost their way in the hills and did not return until 9 o'clock at night, by which time I was desperately anxious. They had missed three foxes, but brought back one hare. Today I walked out to see Lyovochka and the hounds off hunting again. The girls rode there on the donkeys. Then the teachers arrived and we read aloud from some rather dull book. Lyovochka does practically no writing and is in low spirits. I started on some flannel drawers for Tanya, and embroidered Andryusha's initials on his handkerchiefs with red silk. I gave the children their lessons and had an argument with Lyovochka about Seryozha's French, for I maintain that he should be taught literature but he does not agree. Andryusha's nurse pierced Masha's ears, so now she can wear her ear-rings.

November 5 A long, lonely, foggy Sunday! Lyovochka and Seryozha went out hunting with the hounds and Seryozha killed a hare. The other children took the donkeys and cart and went off with Mlle Gachet and M. Nief to Yasenki, where they bought themselves quantities of sweets. I worked hard and played with Andryusha; I am still worried about his large head and his large fontanelle, which hasn't yet grown over. This evening we played a Mozart trio as a piano duet. Lyovochka read while eating his evening meal – he always reads at morning coffee and supper. I had some tea and sauerkraut, then finished reading *Les deux Barbeaux* in the *Revue des Deux Mondes*,[29] which I found quite interesting. Tanya, Ilya and Lyolya had a drawing lesson with their teacher this morning, and Seryozha had a classics lesson with Ulyaninskii. Tanya is becoming quite good at shading (i.e. putting in the shadows) – I suppose I gave her a good start; this is only her fourth lesson with the teacher, but with me she had three years.

November 6 Fog, air oppressive. I read some German first with Lyolya, then this evening with Ilyusha. I gave Masha a Russian lesson, and she recited Pushkin's poem 'The snow has veiled the sky in mist . . . ' quite nicely. Her written work was atrocious, though, and I tore the page out of her exercise-book. Aleksandr Grigorevich came; he is not teaching Ilya and Lyolya a thing. Lyovochka went hunting and brought back 2 hares. He is fretful because he cannot write; this evening, while he was reading Dickens' *Dombey and Son*,[30] he suddenly announced to me: 'Aha! I've got it!' When I asked what he meant he would not tell me at first, but eventually he said: 'Well, I've been imagining this old woman – her appearance, her manner, her thoughts – but I haven't been able to find the right *feelings* to give her. And I suddenly realised: it's the constant awareness that her husband, old Gerasimovich, is languishing in prison, with his head shaven, for a crime he did not commit.' Then he sat down at the piano and started improvising. I read an article on art and artists in the *Revue des Deux Mondes*, and quilted an eiderdown for Andryusha. This evening the children had a discussion about affectation, and they all criticised Tanya for putting on airs when they were at the Delvigs'. Everyone here is well.

November 7 I cut out shirts for Lyovochka and helped Liza with her studies. There was an unpleasant incident: I thought someone had cut a piece off my length of linen, but in fact I was wrong; I measured it and it turned out to be a full *arshin*.* Lyovochka went to the bath-house with Ilyusha and Lyolya this evening; he is much more cheerful now, and clearer in his mind about his writing. I keep worrying about Andryusha's head. Tanya still has a slightly sore throat; I asked her to repeat her history lesson about Aleksandr Nevskii, and she did not do it particularly well. I

*Twenty-eight inches.

gave Lyolya a scripture lesson about Moses and the plagues of the Egyptians.

November 10 I haven't written anything because I have had a headache. Andryusha was poorly yesterday, with a cold and a dry, hoarse cough, but he is a bit better today. Lyovochka also has a bad cold and a chill and is staying indoors, which is not like him. I set Lyolya an English translation and heard him repeat his lesson on the exodus of the Jews from Egypt, after which we played the piano together; we're practising a Haydn piano minuet for four hands. Masha wrote an essay describing the class-room, read out loud, and learnt by heart the poem that goes 'On the twelfth night of Christmas the girls were telling fortunes . . . ' She had her first arithmetic lesson with her father today; it was a great struggle for her to understand the higher numbers like 20, 40, 50 and so on. We both scolded Tanya today for being so lazy. I played duets with Lyovochka this afternoon, made Masha a calico pinafore and read *Le Roman d'un peintre*,[31] which is rather dull. For supper we had salted fish (this being Friday, Lyovochka will eat no meat), and have just drunk our tea. Nurse's granddaughter Akulka has been given a place at the orphanage, thanks to me, and tomorrow Uncle Sergei[32] will take her to Tula. We are getting out our skates; the sky is grey, the clouds are racing, there is a frost and it looks like snow – if only it would! I feel like a machine. I should so like a little time to myself, but that's out of the question, impossible, I'll say no more, not another word . . .

November 11 It's a pity that I always write in my diary at the end of the day, when I am worn out. Andryusha woke up wheezing and coughing at four this morning and went on until eight. I was at my wits' end. He is slightly better now, but still has diarrhoea and a harsh rasping cough. I gave him three drops of antimony, and bandaged his neck with a piece of flannel soaked in oil, lard, soap and camphor. Today Lyovochka said that all his characters were coming to life, and he saw it all much more clearly. He is cheerful and working again, now that he *believes* in it.

The drawing-master and Ulyaninskii the high-school teacher came again today. Tanya is doing quite a good drawing of a shepherd boy's head, but Ilya and Lyolya merely play at it. I have done a lot of sewing, have finished a flannel vest for Andryusha, as well as a pillow and 2 pillow-cases for him. I had a letter from Mother.

November 14 On Sunday, the day before yesterday, Seryozha, Tanya, Ilyusha, Lyolya and I all went to Tula. It was overcast and warm, and the roads were muddy. The children had a wonderful time. We didn't reach the Delvigs' until six and were met there by Seryozha, who had set off earlier with the teachers. The children played and danced, and I enjoyed myself watching them. Earlier in the day Obolenskii had visited us; Lyovochka spent the evening at home with a headache, and later on he walked out to meet us on our return. I borrowed some of Sollogub's comic sketches from the Delvigs, so as to select a suitable one for the children's Christmas play. We read one yesterday called *The Russian Painter's Studio*, which I thought would do – although the fun is in the plans and rehearsals.[33] Yesterday evening Lyovochka and Aleksandr Grigorevich played some piano and violin duets together. This morning, after a night filled with the most frightful dreams and nightmares, I had tea with Lyovochka (a rare event nowadays) and we had a long philosophical discussion about death, religion, the meaning of life and so on. These discussions with Lyovochka have such a soothing effect on me. I interpret his wisdom on these matters in a very personal way, and can always pick out things he says which will lay my doubts to rest. I should set his ideas down on paper but I cannot, especially now, when I have a headache and am tired.

Lyovochka goes hunting every day. Yesterday the borzois hunted down 6 hares, and today he took the hounds out and shot a fox. Dmitrii Dmitrich Obolenskii paid us another visit; his affairs are going badly and he seems to pour out all his sorrows when he is with us.[34] Lyovochka is not entirely well yet and Andryusha still has diarrhoea, although he is cheerful.

November 16 Lyovochka said: 'All the characters and events and ideas are here in my head.' But he is still unwell and unable to write. He started eating Lenten fare yesterday; I strongly opposed this as I was sure it would do his health no good. Yesterday he went out with the borzois and caught 3 hares and a fox, and today he stayed at home all day. I gave Lyolya a Russian reading and parsing lesson, after which Tanya repeated very badly her Russian history lesson on Ivan III. Masha did some reading and copying. I finished stitching my rug. Seryozha and Tanya both long to have *fun*, and I'm sorry there's so little I can do about it, but I shall do my best. This evening the six children, Lyovochka and I all gathered in the balcony room and I suddenly felt how sad it was that the time would come when we would all have gone our separate ways and would look back on this moment. I had a letter today from Tanya and two letters yesterday, from Strakhov and Liza Obolenskaya. I keep begging Lyovochka to help me improve my brief biography of him, but I get no response.

November 19 Lyovochka went hunting again yesterday and caught 4 hares and a fox; today he worked all morning and went to Mass. I have managed to persuade him to abandon his Lenten diet, thank God – his stomach has been terribly upset. He read my biography of him and said it wasn't too bad, although he still hasn't corrected it. Seryozha, Ilyusha and M. Nief rode to Yasenki to watch the Tsar travel past,[35] but all they saw was the train '*et le marmiton*',* as M. Nief jokingly put it. Tanya and Lyolya rode over too, to their great delight, and Masha went by cart with Mlle Gachet. Tanya enjoyed herself today trying on the train of my black skirt, and could not take her eyes off it. We had a lot of trouble with Ilyusha on Friday. He was not doing any work, was being rude and naughty to M. Nief, and kept throwing a wet sponge at him. So his father told him he was to go without dinner. When I went down to the nursery I found him lying on his bed with his head and stomach hanging over the edge, sobbing inconsolably. I felt so sorry for him; M. Nief and I tried to comfort him and he eventually stopped crying, although he got no dinner all the same. And what an appetite the poor fellow had for his roast beef later on! This evening I played the piano while the children danced quadrilles. They did enjoy themselves, the older ones starting off, and the little ones joining in.

The autumn has brought on my usual depression. I sit here in silence, doggedly stitching my rug or reading; I feel cold, dull and indifferent to everything – and ahead lies nothing but darkness. I know this mood will pass when winter comes, but at present it is unendurable. The drawing-room window is open and outside it is still, warm and foggy.

November 21 Various troubles. Firstly Nurse is pregnant and will have to leave in two months, so I shall have to find another nurse for poor little Andryusha. Then Grigorii[36] has given his notice. Lyovochka went hunting with Ilyusha today and caught 6 hares. Seryozha has a cough and played waltzes on the piano with Tanya all day; he played Beethoven's *Sonata Fantasia* too. This evening the children danced quadrilles and various other dances. Andryusha has diarrhoea, and in one day has become frightfully weak. It is warm outside – the children have brought in some willow branches still in leaf.

November 24 For three days I have been ill with a fever, a toothache and a cough. It is still warm, with still no sign of snow. Grigorii has left. Andryusha still has diarrhoea; he is starting to crawl. I was hearing Lyolya repeat his lesson on the Jews in the wilderness this morning and he began to falter, and realising that even though the lesson had already lasted an hour, he would have to say it all over again, he started sobbing, 'I *can't* do it, I *can't*! I don't care if I do get a "one"!' I was gentle with him, though, thank God, and did not make him go on, but postponed it until the following day.

I am still sick at heart. I have been a prey to terrible jealous suspicions about Lyovochka. This is the stuff of madness, I sometimes think. 'God help me!' I whisper to myself. For I would certainly go mad if such a thing should happen.

Tonight I sat feeding Andryusha in the silence, with only the icon-lamp

*'And the kitchen-boy.'

lighting the darkness. The nurse had just gone off to hang up the swaddling clothes when I heard Annie shouting from the nursery next door: 'Serosha, dare not! Serosha!'* I was terribly alarmed, laid Andryusha in his cradle and hurried into the nursery, to find that Annie had been shouting in her sleep. I tucked up Tanya and Masha, who had kicked off the blankets in their sleep, and went to bed. I was shivering and feverish all night and did not sleep a wink. Tanya's fur coat arrived from Tula today, as well as my hat and my fox jacket. The jacket is too narrow at the back and the sleeves are too short.

Lyovochka has stayed at home the last two days; on Wednesday he had dinner with the Samarins in Tula. I finished the second version of my biographical essay today, but it's too long, so once more it won't do.[37]

· 1879 ·

February 9 – Grigorii Goldenburg's assassination of Prince Kropotkin, governor of Kharkov. March 13 – Leon Mirskii's unsuccessful attempt to kill the chief of security police, General Drenteln. April 2 – Aleksandr Solovyov fires five shots at the Tsar. Conflicts within Land and Liberty over the use of terror tactics lead to a split, the majority joining the new People's Will party, formed in October and dedicated to the assassination of Tsar Alexander II. November 18 and 19 – two more attempts to kill the Tsar.

Tolstoy abandons work on the Decembrists for a series of articles on religious faith, including 'What I Believe' and 'An Investigation of Dogmatic Theology'. Sofia Tolstaya prepares the fourth edition of Tolstoy's Complete Works. *At the end of the year her biography of him is published in the Russian Library series. December 20 – Mikhail Tolstoy (Misha) born.*

December 18 More than a year has passed. I sit waiting for my confinement, which may start at any moment and is overdue. The thought of this new baby fills me with gloom; my horizons have become so narrow, and my world is such a small and dismal place. Everyone here, including the children, is in a tense state, what with the approach of the holidays and the suspense about my confinement. It has been terribly cold, more than 20° below zero. Masha has had a sore throat and a fever for the past week. She got up today. Lyovochka has gone to Tula to authorise Bibikov to go to Moscow to deal with the new edition,[1] and he has promised to buy something for the Christmas tree. He is writing a lot about religion. Andryusha is the light of my life and an utter delight.

*English in the original.

Two days after writing this, at 6 in the morning on December 20, 1879, Misha was born.*

(January 1880 – People's Will printing press discovered. February 5 – Stepan Khalturin gains access to the Winter Palace and attempts to kill the Tsar. February 12 – decree announcing the coordination of all government activities and the establishment of a Supreme Executive Commission, headed by Count Loris Melikov, formerly governor of Kharkov and now vested with comprehensive powers. Hundreds arrested and tried. February 20 – a People's Will member makes an unsuccessful attempt to kill Loris Melikov.

Fourth edition of the Works of L. N. Tolstoy *published (in eleven volumes). Tolstoy starts work in March on 'A Collation of the Gospels'.*

March 1, 1881 – revolutionaries assassinate Tsar Alexander II. A statute is immediately issued empowering the government to declare a state of emergency, the power of military tribunals is extended, and administrative officials are granted wide powers. A huge round-up starts, and on April 5 five assassins, one of them a woman, are publicly hanged. The reign of the new Tsar, Alexander III (1881–94) sees the reassertion of absolutism, bureaucracy, orthodoxy and nationalism. Extreme reactionaries are appointed to government, on which the chief influence is Pobedonostsev, formerly the Tsar's tutor, now Procurator of the Holy Synod. Alexander presides over a population impoverished by a sick economy, crushing taxes and a vast public debt. There is a wave of pogroms.

Tolstoy writes to the new Tsar begging him not to hang the assassins. His popularity protects him from the consequences of his plain speaking, but in official circles feeling against him is growing. June 1881 – Tolstoy makes a second pilgrimage to the Optyna Pustyn monastery. He gives up hunting and smoking and criticises his family's wordly aspirations. September – the Tolstoys rent a flat in Moscow, and until 1901 they spend their winters in the city, where Sergei attends the university, Tanya attends art school, and Ilya and Lev go to secondary school. Tolstoy becomes increasingly distant from his family, and the discord between husband and wife is at its most intense when he meets Syutaev, a peasant, Christian and socialist, who has a great influence on him. October 31 – Sofia gives birth to Aleksei (Alyosha).)

·1882·

May – 'provisional rules' forbidding Jews to settle in rural districts, even within the pale. June – first Factory Act, prohibiting employment of children under

*This was added by Sofia Tolstaya later.

twelve, and setting an eight-hour day maximum for minors. Factory inspectors appointed to enforce the new rules (which remain largely ignored). August – 'provisional rules' on the press, strengthening the censors' powers. A State Peasant Bank established to help peasants buy their land.

August – Ilya Tolstoy seriously ill with typhus. Arguments between the couple intensify, and Tolstoy threatens to leave. He starts writing 'What Then Must We Do?' and continues 'What I Believe'. October – the Tolstoys buy a house in Dolgokhamovnikheskii Street in Moscow.

February 28 We have been in Moscow since September 15, 1881. We are staying in Prince Volkonskii's house on Denezhny Lane, near Prechistenka.[1] Seryozha goes to the university, and Tanya attends an art school on Myasnitskaya Street, while Ilya and Lyolya go to Polivanov's secondary school, which is virtually next door to us.[2] Our life in Moscow would be quite delightful if only it did not make Lyovochka so unhappy.[3] He is too sensitive to survive the city, and his Christian disposition cannot reconcile all this idle luxury with people's struggling lives here. He went back to Yasnaya with Ilya yesterday, to have a break and do some work.

August 26 It was 20 years ago, when I was young and happy, that I started writing the story of my love for Lyovochka in this book: there is virtually nothing *but* love in it in fact. 20 years later, here I am sitting up all night on my own, reading and mourning its loss. For the first time in my life Lyovochka has run off to sleep alone in the study. We were quarrelling about such silly things – I accused him of taking no interest in the children and not helping me look after Ilya, who is sick, or making them all jackets. But it has nothing to do with jackets, and everything to do with his growing coldness towards me and the children. Today he shouted at the top of his voice that his dearest wish was to leave his family. I shall carry the memory of that heartfelt, heartrending cry of his to my grave. I pray for death, for without his love I cannot survive; I knew this the moment his love for me died. I cannot prove to him how deeply I love him – as deeply as I loved him 20 years ago – for this love oppresses *me* and irritates *him*. He is filled with Christian notions of self-perfection, and I envy him . . . Ilyusha has typhus and is lying in the drawing-room with a fever. I have to make sure he is given his quinine at the prescribed intervals, which are very short, so I worry in case I miss a dose. I cannot sleep in the bed my husband has abandoned. Lord help me! I long to take my life, my thoughts are so confused. The clock is striking four.[4]

I have decided that if he doesn't come in to see me, it must mean he loves another woman. He has not come. I used to know what my duty was – but what now?

He did come in, but it was the next day before we made it up. We both cried, and I realised to my joy that his love for me, which I had mourned all through that terrible night, was not dead. I shall never forget the heavenly cool clear morning, the silvery dew sparkling in the grass, as I walked through the woods after a sleepless night to the bath-house. Rarely have I seen such a miracle of natural beauty. I sat for a long time in the icy water, hoping to catch a chill and die. But to no avail. I returned home to feed Alyosha, [5] who smiled with joy at seeing me.

September 10 Aunt Tanya and her family have left us for Petersburg,[6] and Lyovochka has taken Lyolya to Moscow.[7] Today was the last warm day of summer. I went for a swim.

· 1883 ·

May – law on religious dissenters, granting them a modicum of rights, but greatly increasing the powers of the Minister of the Interior to deal with them.

Summer – Alexander III's coronation in Moscow. All members of the People's Will behind bars or in exile. Plekhanov, who split from Land and Liberty when it adopted terror, founds Marxist Liberation of Labour Group in Geneva, while in Russia small groups of students and intellectuals form Marxist discussion groups in the cities.

Spring – big fire in the village of Yasnaya Polyana. May 21 – Tolstoy signs over to Sofia full power of attorney to conduct all matters concerning the property. Hordes of 'disciples' start to visit Tolstoy – including Vladimir Grigorevich Chertkov.

March 5 (Moscow) The spring sun always has a bracing effect on me. It is shining into my little study upstairs, where I sit and look back, in the calm of this first week of Lent, on the events of last winter. I went out into society a bit, enjoying both Tanya's successes and my own; I felt youthful and gay, and I enjoyed everything about this sociable life. Yet no one would believe me if I said that the moments of despair outweighed the happiness – moments when I would say to myself, 'It's not right, I shouldn't be doing this.' But I was *unable* to stop. I simply couldn't. It is clear to me that I am not free to act and live as I want, but am guided by the will of God, or fate – whatever one chooses to call the supreme will which controls even our smallest affairs.

It was three days ago, March 2, that I weaned Alyosha, and I am again suffering the pangs of separation from my previous baby. It comes on me again and again, and there is no way I can be rid of it.

Our life at home, away from the crowded city, is much easier and happier than it was last year. Lyovochka is calmer and more cheerful; he does sometimes get in a rage and blame me for everything, but it doesn't last so long now, and doesn't happen so often. He is becoming nicer every day, in fact.

Only God knows what I felt last year. All through the summer and autumn I dreaded going to Moscow, for I didn't think I would have the strength to shoulder on my own all the burdens and responsibilities of our life in the city. Besides, I would be abandoning everything I loved and knew in Yasnaya. And how precious it all was to me when we had left. Yet we could have returned home last year . . . But this second trip to Moscow was nothing to do with me, it was what the children and their father wanted. It was God's will, the family's happiness depended on it . . . I cannot imagine why. Lyovochka continues with his religious writings.[1] They are never-ending because they can never be published, but he must do it, it is God's will; and they may even serve His great purpose.

(August 1884 – law abolishing university autonomy, increasing fees, restricting entry of women and ruling that all staff be appointed directly by Ministry of Education. Many professors dismissed and education becomes more imbued with religion and nationalism.

Tolstoy starts making boots, chopping wood and drawing his own water from the well. He spends more and more time with Chertkov, and arguments with Sofia become increasingly ugly. He talks increasingly of leaving her to lead an ascetic life. Sofia, pregnant again, is beside herself with shame and misery. June 18 – Aleksandra (Sasha) born. Soon afterwards, Sofia gains Tolstoy's permission to borrow money to bring out new edition of his novels. Tolstoy finishes 'What I Believe', and all copies of the first edition seized by police at the printer's.)

· 1885 ·

May – disciplinary powers of Minister of Justice over judges strengthened. State Bank of the Nobility founded to provide favourable mortgage credit for landowners and check the liquidation of large estates. Spring – huge strikes in two textile factories near Moscow. June – law prohibiting night work in textile mills for women and young people under seventeen.

February – Sofia visits St Petersburg and unsuccessfully petitions the Empress for permission to publish Tolstoy's banned works. She converts an empty shed near the Moscow house into a warehouse and publishing office, and assumes responsibility for all the proof-reading and publishing of Tolstoy's works. Chertkov sets up his own publishing house, the Intermediary, to offset Sofia's by publishing cheap books for the masses. As Chertkov moves into the role of Tolstoy's executor, secretary and confidant, Tolstoy describes his relationship with his wife as 'a struggle to the death'. In December, he again threatens divorce after a terrible argument, then leaves with his daughter Tanya to stay with friends.

March 24 Holy Easter Sunday. Lyovochka returned yesterday from the Crimea, where he went with Urusov, who is ill.[1] The Crimea brought back many of his old memories of Sevastopol and the war, and he spent a lot of time walking in the mountains and gazing at the sea. On the road to Simeiz, he and Urusov passed the place where he had been stationed with his cannon during the war. He had fired it, just once, in that very spot. That was thirty years ago.[2] He and Urusov were travelling along, and he suddenly jumped out of the carriage and started searching for something. It turned out that he had seen a cannon-ball lying near the road. Could it really be the same one he had fired during the battle of Sevastopol? Certainly no one else, either then or later, could have fired a cannon in that very same place, and there was only one cannon at the time. Now it is evening; the elder children are visiting the Olsufievs and Lopatin is singing.

· 1886 ·

March – law forbidding peasant households to break up unless approved by a two thirds majority of the village. June 6 – law tightening up labour contracts, while stiffening up penalties for striking. June 12 – law making breach of contract by agricultural labourers a criminal offence.

January 18 – four-year-old Aleksei Tolstoy dies of quinsy. Tolstoy writing 'Walk In the Light', 'The Death of Ivan Ilich' and a very long essay called 'On Life and Death', and finishes 'What Then Must We Do?' He also dictates to Sofia his play, The Power of Darkness. *Sofia preparing eighth edition of his works (which Chertkov hopes to produce more cheaply). November – Sofia's mother dies in the Crimea. The Archbishop of Kherson and Odessa denounces Tolstoy as a heretic.*

October 25 (Yasnaya Polyana) Everybody in this house – especially Lev Nikolaevich, whom the children follow like a herd of sheep – has foisted on me the role of *scourge*. Having loaded me with all the responsibilities for the children and their education, the finances, the estate, the housekeeping, indeed the entire material side of life – from which they derive a great deal more benefit than I do – they then come up to me with a cold, calculating, hypocritical expression, masked in virtue, and beseech me in ingratiating tones to give a peasant a horse, some money, a bit of flour, and heaven knows what else. It is *not* my job to manage the farm – I have neither time nor aptitude for it – so how can I simply give the peasant a horse if I don't know if it will be needed at the farm at a particular moment? All these tedious requests, when I know so little about the state of affairs here, irritate and confuse me.

My God, how often I long to abandon it all and take my life. I am so tired of living, struggling and suffering. The egotism and unconscious malice of the people one loves most is very great indeed! Why do I carry on despite all this? I don't know; I suppose because I must. I can't do what my husband wants (so he says), without breaking all the practical and emotional chains that have bound me to my family. Day and night I think only of how to leave this house, leave this life, leave all this cruelty, all these excessive demands on me. I have grown to love the dark. The moment it is dark I feel happier, for then I can conjure up all the things I used to love, all the ghosts from my past. Last night I caught myself thinking aloud, and was terrified that I might be going mad. Surely if I crave the dark I must crave death too?

Although the last two months, when Lev Nikolaevich was ill,[1] were an agonising time for me, strangely enough they were also a very happy time for me. I nursed him day and night and what I had to do was so natural, so simple. It is really the only thing I can do well – making a *personal* sacrifice for the man I love. The harder the work, the happier I was. Now that he is on his feet again and almost well, he has given me to understand that he no longer needs me. So on the one hand I have been discarded like a useless object, and on the other, impossible, undefined sacrifices are, as always, demanded of me, in my life and in my family, and I am expected to renounce everything, all my property, all my beliefs, the education and wellbeing of my children – things which not only I, a fairly determined woman, but thousands of others who *believe* in these precepts, are incapable of doing.[2]

We have been in Yasnaya longer than usual this time. I have not the strength to organise anything. But my conscience is still alert and blames me for my lack of energy. I know one should take the path one considers to be right, but I merely carry on as before through inertia. I shall go to Moscow again, I think, to try and keep the family together, have business meetings with publishers, get some money for Lev Nikolaevich, who constantly comes up to me with that air of indifference, malevolence, and even hatred, and demands that I give him more money to give to all his minions and paupers, like Konstantin,[3] Ganya,[4] Aleksandr Petrovich,[5] and the rest, who are not really poor but have learnt that sheer brazen audacity is the best way of getting what they want. The children criticise me for opposing their father, and they too ask for as much as they can get . . . Oh, to leave it all behind – I *shall* leave, somehow or other. I have neither strength nor love for all this labour and struggle. For the time being I shall write my diary; I shall feel calmer and gentler if I can pour out my distress here.

It is a grey and miserable autumn. Andryusha and Misha have been skating on the Lower Pond. Both Tanya and Masha have toothache. Lev Nikolaevich is starting on a new play, about peasant life.[6] I pray to God that he may take up this kind of work again. He has rheumatism in his arm. Mme Seuron is a pleasant, cheerful woman, very good with the children.

The boys, Seryozha, Ilya and Lyova, live such mysterious lives in Moscow and it worries me. And they have such strange views about human passions and their own weaknesses: according to them, these things are completely natural, and if they *do* manage to resist them they consider themselves very fine fellows indeed. But why are people *bound* to have these weaknesses? Naturally one struggles to overcome one's failings, but this is something that happens once in a lifetime, not every day of one's life. And it is well worth the struggle too, even though it often destroys one's life and breaks one's heart. But it has nothing to do with nasty commonplace little passions like cards, or wine, or Strelna.

I often wonder why Lyovochka is always blaming me, when I'm not guilty of anything? I think it's because he doesn't want me to have any life of my own; he wants me to suffer and immerse myself in poverty, sickness and suffering – actually to *seek it out* if it does not occur naturally. He demands this from the children too. Is it necessary? Is it necessary for a perfectly healthy man to keep visiting hospitals to watch people writhing in agony and listen to them groan? If a sick person is actually there, then of course one does everything one can to make him better, but why seek him out?

I am reading the lives of the philosophers.[7] It is terribly interesting, but difficult to read calmly and sensibly. One always searches for the philosophical teachings that approximate to one's own convictions, and ignores anything incompatible with them. As a result it is difficult to learn anything new. But I try not to be so prejudiced.

Buturlin has just come. He is a reliable person and sees things clearly.

October 26 Lyovochka has written the first act of his play and I am going to copy it out. I wonder why I no longer blindly believe in him as a writer. He has gone for a walk with Buturlin. It is dark and damp.

I spent too long chatting with Buturlin, and forgot my rule: '*Garde le silence le plus souvent, ne dis que les choses nécéssaires et toujours en peu de mots*', in the words of Epictetus.* But this Buturlin is a clever man, and he understands a lot.

Andryusha and Misha are playing with the peasant boys Mitrosha and Ilyukha, which I dislike for some reason – I suppose because it will teach them to dominate and coerce these children, which is utterly immoral.

*'Keep silent as often as possible, say only what is necessary, and always in few words.'

I read through Urusov's letters yesterday and felt so sad he was no longer with us. I always longed to know what he thought of me when he was alive, and I have been trying to discover this.[8] I only know that for some reason I always felt happy and relaxed with him, why that was I don't know.

I think a lot about the older boys – it grieves me that they have grown so distant. Why do fathers not grieve for their children? Why is it only women whose lives are burdened in this way? Life is so confusing.

October 27 I have copied the 1st act of Lyovochka's new play. It is very good. The characters are wonderfully portrayed and the plot is full and interesting; there will be more too. This evening Lyovochka read Buturlin his *Critique of Theology*.[9] I was listening, but thinking of other things. It does not touch me – either my heart has hardened or there's some other reason. A letter came from Ilya mentioning marriage. Surely this is just an infatuation, the first awakening of physical feelings for the first woman with whom he has been in close relations? I do not know whether to welcome this marriage or not – I cannot approve of it, quite frankly, but I trust in God.[10] I gave Andryusha and Misha their lessons today without much enthusiasm or success – they are both so dear to me. I have been correcting the proofs for the cheap edition[11] and am very tired. I am afraid of leaving Yasnaya, mainly because I fear this may interfere with the work Lyovochka has just started upon. Meanwhile Masha runs about and does no lessons, the boys harass me and things are in a bad way. If Lyovochka can work in Moscow I shall be perfectly happy. I must be careful and considerate with him, and save him for his work, which is so dear to my heart.

October 30 Act 2 is now finished. I got up early to start copying it out, and recopied it this evening. It is good, but rather *flat* – it needs more theatrical effects, and I told Lyovochka so. I gave Andryusha and Misha their lessons, corrected some proofs, and the whole day was taken up by work. I read *The Source*[12] and *Echoes of the Homeland*[13] to the little ones, who loved the verses and pictures and cheered up. The two little girls sat downstairs reading and writing as usual. There were moments today of the old familiar melancholy, and I felt cramped and confined. Aniska[14] came and told me about her sick mother; I felt too lazy to visit her today, but shall do so tomorrow without fail. Just as I was sitting down to dinner the girls asked me for some money, on Lyovochka's behalf – for some old woman and for Ganya the thief. I wanted to eat my dinner and was annoyed with everyone for being late, and I had no desire to give any money to that Ganya woman. So I lied and said I didn't have any – although I did in fact have a few rubles left. But later I felt ashamed, and after I had had my soup – as I later recalled – I went and got the money. I said nothing, just sat and pondered: can one *really* find it in one's heart to love everyone and everything, as Lyovochka demands? Even that woman Ganya the thief, who has systematically robbed every single person in the village, has a hideous disease, and is a thoroughly vile person. I had a flickering of pity for her, but it soon passed. Feinerman[15] came; his presence bothers me less than it used to. We got some letters from old Gué;[16] I still distrust him: there's something stiff and affected about him.

Buturlin left and I cannot say I am sorry, although he was good company while he was here. Tanya angrily reproached me for not giving her father the money. And I suddenly thought how odd it was: I hadn't given it to *him*, yet it was he who asked me for it – although he had been far from my thoughts at that moment. But the money was not for him, and I simply could not imagine how my refusing it to Ganya could have anything to do with him. This sort of thing happens to me so often.

· 1887 ·

February – Ministry of Justice empowered to order the hearing of any case in camera to 'protect the dignity of state power'. March 5 – five students hanged for attempting to assassinate Tsar Alexander III. A quota is set for Jewish university students: 10 per cent of the student body within the pale and 5 per cent outside, except for Moscow and St Petersburg, where it is 3 per cent. The boundaries of the pale revised to exclude Rostov-on-Don and Taganrog. Schools in the Baltic provinces ordered to teach in Russian.

February – Power of Darkness *forbidden to be staged in Russia, but produced as a pamphlet. Tolstoy receiving hundreds of visitors from all over the world. Sofia takes up photography.*

March 3 We have heard some shocking news: four students in Petersburg have been discovered with some bombs, which they were intending to throw at the Tsar while he was returning from his father's funeral service.[1] It agitated me so badly that it has driven everything else from my mind. This evil will beget many others. And *any* sort of evil distresses me so much at present! Lyovochka heard the news in despondent silence. He had so often imagined it happening.

The play is a huge success, and both Lyovochka and I are quite satisfied with it.[2] I was writing my diary when he first started on it, but I soon had to do so much copying of the play that I had to break it off. On November 11 my mother died in Yalta (and was buried there).[3] On the 21st I travelled to Moscow with the family. Lyovochka has written a story about the early Christians,[4] and is now working on an article entitled 'On Life and Death'.[5] He keeps complaining of stomach pains. We had a peaceful and happy winter. The new cheap edition has come out,[6] but I have completely lost interest in it. The money brought me no joy – I never thought it would. Miss Fewson, the new English governess, has arrived. Masha is ill and I have been reading *King Lear* to her. I love Shakespeare, even though he sometimes does not know where to draw the line – witness all those brutal murders and innumerable deaths.

March 6 I have finished copying out 'On Life and Death' and have just read it through carefully. I tried hard to discover some new ideas in it, but although I found many apt expressions and beautiful similes the fundamental idea seemed to me the same unquestionable eternal truth as before: that one should forswear the material, personal life for the life of the spirit. One thing I do find intolerably unjust, however, is the idea that one should have to renounce one's personal life in the name of universal love. I believe that there are obligations which are ordained by God, that no one has the right to deny them, and that these obligations actually promote, rather than hinder, the spiritual life.

My soul is oppressed. It grieves me to think of Ilya and his nasty mysterious life, full of idleness, lies, vodka and bad company – and more importantly, the complete lack of any spiritual dimension. Seryozha has gone off to Tula again, to attend tomorrow's meeting of the peasant bank.[7] Tanya and Lyova irritate me by playing vint*. The younger children I seem to have lost all ability to *educate* – I always feel so terribly *sorry* for them, and I fear I may be spoiling them. I have an old woman's anxiety for them and an old woman's tenderness for them. Yet I still take their education very seriously. I have quite lost my bearings, yet there are some beautiful moments in my life when I contemplate death in solitude, moments when I clearly perceive the duality of the spiritual and the material consciousness, and know that both are immortal.

Lyovochka often says he is going back to the country, but always ends up staying. I never say anything, though, as I feel I have no right to impose my wishes on him. He has changed greatly: he is good-natured and calm, joins in games of vint, sits down at the piano again, and is no longer driven to despair by life in the city. We had a letter from Chertkov.[8] I do not like him – he is sly, malicious, obtuse and narrow-minded. L.N. warms to him only because he is so obsequious. As for Chertkov's work on popular reading, however, inspired by L.N., that I do respect; I must give him credit for that.[9] Feinerman is in Yasnaya again. He has left his pregnant wife and his child somewhere – and has come to us, without a penny to his name. Now I support the principle of the family, so for me he is not a person and is lower than an animal. However fanatical his beliefs may be, and however beautifully he may express them, the fact of the matter is that he has left his family to eat at others' expense, and that is grotesque.

*A card game, rather like whist.

March 9 Lyovochka is writing a new article, 'On Life and Death', which he is to read to the University Psychological Society.[10] He has been on a vegetarian diet[11] for the past week, and his present state of mind is ample evidence of this. He deliberately started talking about the evils of money and property in my presence today, hinting that I wanted to hold on to it for the children's sake. At first I kept quiet, but then I lost my temper: 'I sell 12 volumes for 8 rubles,[12] and you sell *War and Peace* alone for only 10!'[13] I shouted. This made him very angry, but he said nothing. All these so-called friends of his, these 'new Christians', are trying desperately to set him against me – and not always unsuccessfully either. I read Chertkov's letter describing in joyful tones his deep spiritual communion with his wife, and commiserating with L.N. for being deprived of this joy: what a sad thing it was, he wrote, that L.N., of all people, should be denied this sort of communion[14] – this was so obviously referring to me I felt quite ill when I read it. To think that this sly, devious, stupid man has fooled L.N. with his flattery and now wants (like a 'good Christian', I dare say) to destroy all the things that have kept us together for nearly 25 years! The two months when Lev Nikolaevich was ill were just like the old days. It was an emotional rest for him; all his old creative powers were reawakened, and it was then that he started writing his play. But then he became entangled with all those sycophantic 'new Christians' again. I could see the effect this had on his soul, as he began pining for the country and his creativity was smothered.

He must end this relationship with Chertkov, for it involves nothing but lies and rancour; we must get as far away as possible.

We had some guests today, all young. We ate dinner together, after which they played vint. What a sorry thing this passion for vint is! Cold, and up to 14 ° below zero at nights.

March 14 (Moscow) I am sitting here all on my own, the house is quiet and I am enjoying myself. The three little ones are asleep. Tanya, Masha and young Lyova are out visiting the Tatishchevs, Ilya has been confined to barracks for three days for being late for drill,[15] and Lev Nikolaevich has gone off to a meeting of the University Psychological Society with Nikolai Gué (the son), to read his new article, 'On Life and Death'. Gué and I had to copy it out in a great rush and I was busy writing all day.[16] L.N. is unwell; he has bad indigestion and stomach-aches, yet he eats such a senseless diet, first it's rich food, then vegetarian, then rum and water, and so on and so on. He is gloomy but kind. We had a visit from the gentleman sent from Petersburg to Yasnaya Polyana for the costumes for our play.[17] I had a letter yesterday from Potekhin, who said it was not yet certain whether or not they would allow the play to be performed.[18] But rehearsals have started, and they are going ahead. I can't decide whether to attend the dress rehearsal! I should love to, but am afraid to leave the house. I have not made up my mind yet – it all depends on Lyovochka's health. I took the children skating but did not skate myself. All the pleasures of youth are gradually forsaking me. Lyovochka worked very hard on that article, and I like it a lot. This is the second time he has spoken at the university, and he is now beginning to bend some of his more eccentric rules: Grigorii[19] often cleans his room for him nowadays, when he is ill he sometimes eats meat, and when we play vint he too occasionally sits down for a game. All his old rancorous obstinacy has left him, and he has become so much more cheerful and good-natured. He is no longer angry about the sale of his books either, and is pleased that the collected edition is selling for eight rubles.[20]

March 30 Lyovochka is still in bad health – for 3 months now he has had pains in the pit of his stomach. I eventually decided to write to Zakharin, asking him to call, but L.N. forestalled his visit and took himself off to see him yesterday evening. Zakharin diagnosed catarrh of the stomach and prescribed the following, which I am jotting down from memory:

1) To wear warm clothes
2) To wear a piece of unbleached flannel around the stomach
3) To avoid all butter
4) To eat little and often
5) To drink half (½) a glass of fresh Ems Kranchen or Kesselbrunn water, heated up, three or four times a day i) on an empty stomach, and ii) an hour before and a quarter-of-an-hour after lunch – and the third an hour before dinner. He should follow this regime for three consecutive weeks, then stop, and repeat again if necessary. It should be as hot as he can drink it without burning himself, hotter than fresh milk.
6) To fight his fondness for smoking.

June 18 Many people blame me for not keeping a proper diary, a record of my life with Lev Nikolaevich, since fate has ordained that I should live my life with this extraordinary person. But it is so hard to renounce my *personal* feelings about him, so hard to be impartial, and my time is so terribly occupied – and has been so all my life. I thought I would have time this summer to sort out Lev Nikolaevich's manuscripts and do some copying; but I have been here more than a month, and Lev Nikolaevich has kept me constantly busy, copying out his article 'On Life and Death', which he has laboured over so tirelessly and for so long. No sooner do I copy it out than he covers it with scribbles and it has to be done all over again. What patience and thoroughness he has. I should keep some notes about his life, if only to explain the things about it that people find so hard to understand. That letter he wrote to Engelhardt, for instance, the manuscript of which was passed on to Strakhov. Now he had never met this Engelhardt, a young man who, like many others, merely wanted to write a letter to the famous Lev Nikolaevich Tolstoy. It just so happened, though, that L.N. was in a gloomy mood at the time, and felt that he had written about ideas that he could not possibly realise in his own life. So he poured out all his loneliness and his misery in a letter to a complete stranger, just as though he were writing his diary.[21] But then he maintains equally strange relationships and correspondences with people who have the most frightful reputation, people generally regarded as downright criminals – like Ozmidov, for example.[22] The other day I saw an envelope with Ozmidov's address on it, and when I asked Lev Nikolaevich why he continued to write him friendly letters when he knew quite well what a scoundrel he was, he replied: 'Well, if he is a scoundrel, I am more use to him than I am to the others.' So that explains his friendship with all those good-for-nothings, obscurities, total strangers and 'dark ones', who gather about us in such vast numbers.[23] Yesterday we had another visit from that fourth-year medical student and revolutionary fanatic, whom Lev Nikolaevich tried to convince of the error of his ways.[24] Whether he was successful I do not know, for I was not there. Today we had a number of letters from America, along with Kennan's[25] article in *The Century* about his visit to Yasnaya Polyana and his conversations with Lev Nikolaevich, and also a review of L.N.'s translated works. All very flattering and favourable. How extraordinary and marvellous to find that people in these faraway places have such a genuine understanding and sympathy for his work.

Lyovochka walked to Yasenki with his two daughters and the two Kuzminskii girls. It started raining, so I sent the carriage and some warm clothes after them. Now that Lyovochka is no longer surrounded by Chertkov, Feinerman and all the rest of his apostles, he is just as he used to be before, a sweet, happy family man. The other evening he played the piano accompaniment to some violin sonatas by Mozart, Weber and Haydn; he played with such feeling, and clearly enjoyed himself immensely. The violinist was the young man I have hired to teach young Lyova. He is called Lyassota; he is only eighteen and is from the Moscow Conservatoire.

When we got back from Moscow on May 11 I firmly insisted that Lyovochka should drink the waters, as Zakharin had ordered him to; he consented, and I now silently hand him a glass of heated Ems, which he silently drinks. When he is out of sorts, though, he says: 'They tell you to pour this stuff down me and you believe them. I'm only doing it because I don't suppose it can do me much harm.' But he has been taking the waters for three weeks now, and has not resumed his vegetarian diet. In my view his health has improved considerably; he walks about, is much stronger, and the only problem now is that he gets a mere seven hours' sleep a night, which is not enough – I suppose this is because his work is so intellectual and sedentary.

He is delighted by his success, or rather by the favourable response to him in America – although fame and success generally have very little effect on him. He looks radiantly happy, and keeps saying: 'How good life is!'

I miss Ilyusha and am sorry not to have visited him yet.[26] But he has had so little time for his family this past year, and has been so distant from us, that it must be supposed that he has no need of us. The poor fellow is drifting and has deteriorated mentally; this is why he seems so despondent and sick at heart. I must visit him very soon.

Hordes of sick people visit me every day. I try, with the help of Florinskii's book, to treat them all[27]; but what torture it is when I cannot recognise what is wrong and don't know what to do! It happens so often that I sometimes feel like abandoning the whole business, but then I go out and the sight of their sick pleading eyes and their touching trust makes me so sorry for them that although I dread to think I may be doing the wrong thing, I hand the poor dears their medicine and then try to put them right out of my mind. The other day I did not have the medicine I needed and had to give the poor woman a note and some money to take to the chemist. She burst into tears, returned the money and said: 'I know I'm dying, so take back your money and give it to someone worse off than me. Thank you all the same, but I don't need it.'

June 21 The warm weather is here at last and I went swimming for the first time this year. Yesterday evening the actor Andreev-Burlak[28] came to make Lev Nikolaevich's acquaintance, and he told stories, rather like those of Gorbunov, about peasant life.[29] Everyone then went off to bed, leaving Lev Nikolaevich, Lyova and me downstairs, and we sat up till two in the morning. The stories were so marvellously funny – Lyovochka laughed so much that we grew quite alarmed for him. He was correcting his article 'On Life and Death' all today, and after dinner he went out to mow the hay. I read Strakhov's book attacking spiritualism; it is heavy reading and, alas, not at all convincing – either that or I have not understood it fully.[30] Before going for my swim today I sent for the young people and read them Lermontov's *A Hero of Our Time.* What remarkable, mature ideas it contains. I love Lermontov. Apparently as a person he was unpleasant and bilious, yet he was so clever, and so *very* far above the average human being. Everybody misunderstood *him*, but *he* saw through everybody.

I feel physically and emotionally debilitated, overwhelmed by a mass of memories and regrets. There is nothing worse than that.

July 2 I went to Moscow to see Ilya – I was so happy to see his friendly face, and I could see he was overjoyed to see me too. He lives in a hovel; his landlord and landlady are very fond of him, yet he leads such a disorderly life. As his mother, who can still remember feeding him at her breast, I felt very sad that he should be spending all the money I send him to repay his debts. And he never has a proper dinner, just buys snacks and sweets on credit. But it doesn't bother him. All he can think about is Sofia Filosofova, and he lives on memories, letters and hopes. He is here at the moment – he has just been hunting and has killed three snipe – but he is leaving tomorrow. This makes me very sad; I must simply accept that the fledglings have flown the nest.

Strakhov is here; what a clever, pleasant person![31] Lyovochka is busy with the mowing, and spends 3 hours a day writing his article.[32] It is almost finished now. The other evening he came into the room when Seryozha was playing a waltz on the piano, and said: 'Shall we take a turn around the floor?' And away we danced, to the delight of all the young folk. He is very lively and cheerful, although he is not so strong as he used to be and tires more quickly when mowing or walking. He has been having long conversations with Strakhov about science, art and music; today we had a discussion about photography, as I have bought a camera and intend to do landscapes and family portraits. My daughter Tanya is in Pirogovo.

July 3 Seryozha is playing Beethoven's Kreutzer Sonata, with Lyassota on the violin. What power! It expresses every conceivable human emotion. There is a bunch of roses and mignonettes on my table, we are just sitting down to a splendid dinner, the storm has passed and it is mild and calm outside, and my dear children are with me; Andryusha has been hard at work upholstering the chairs in the nursery, sweet gentle Lyovochka will soon be back – this is my life and I revel in it and thank God for it, for in it I have found true *goodness* and *happiness*. And when I copy out Lyovochka's article, 'On Life and Death', I realise that he has given me a completely different kind of happiness. I remember when I was very very young, long before I was married, I longed to live for others: I yearned with all my soul for the joys of renunciation, even asceticism. But fate granted me a family, so I lived for them – only now I am forced to admit that this *wasn't* what I had longed for, that this wasn't *life*. Shall I ever be able to see it as such?

Strakhov left yesterday, and Ilya today. Yesterday Seryozha and I made some experiments with my newly acquired camera.

July 19 The past few days have been turmoil. Seryozha was in Samara but didn't settle anything.[33] We had a visit from Pavel Dmitrievich Golokhvastov, an extreme orthodox and Slavophile; he and Lev Nikolaevich had a discussion about religion and the Church, and it was all most unpleasant. Golokhvastov described with great pathos the magnificent cathedral in New Jerusalem (Voskresensk), with its beautiful construction and up to 10,000 worshippers. After listening to him talk on and on, L.N. said: 'And they go there to mock God.' He was being ironic, not to say malicious, and I then spoke up and said it was arrogant to say that 10,000 people would go merely to mock, and to assume that he alone professed the true faith, and

1 On previous page: Sofia Tolstaya in 1863

2 Above: Sofia Behrs and her younger sister Tatiana, photographed some time in the early 1860s

3 Below: Yasnaya Polyana, the general view of the Tolstoys' estate, 1897

that he must admit that such vast numbers of people must have a more honourable reason for attending the cathedral than that. After dinner Golokhvastov started talking about the Patriarch Nikon, and his fascinating life and personality. Lev Nikolaevich read his newspaper throughout all this, then suddenly burst out, in the same tone as before: 'He was a Mordvinian peasant, and if he did once have something to say he certainly didn't say it.' At that Golokhvastov flushed crimson and said: 'Either you are laughing at me, or – since I am accustomed to respecting what other people say – I should ponder upon that remark.' All in all a very difficult evening.

We also had a visit from Butkevich, a former revolutionary who has twice been in prison, once for political activities and the second time under suspicion. This young man, the son of a Tula landowner, had written to Lev Nikolaevich telling him how after his release from jail he had passed on the street a lady of his acquaintance who had pretended not to recognise him, and this had mortified him. I did not announce him when he came before, and he had to sit downstairs, but this time I felt sorry for him and asked him in for some tea. He then stayed for the next two days, in which time I grew to dislike him intensely. He is very dark and very silent, has a squint and a fixed expression on his face and wears blue-tinted spectacles. From the few words he does utter there is no way of knowing what he believes in. And now he is a 'Tolstoyan'. What unattractive types Lev Nikolaevich's followers are! There is not one among them who is normal. And most of the women are hysterics. Like Maria Aleksandrovna Schmidt, for example, who has just left. In the old days she would have been a nun – now she is an ecstatic admirer of Lev Nikolaevich's ideas. She used to be a schoolmistress at the Nikolaevskii Institute but left because she lost her faith in the Church, and now she lives in the village, supporting herself by copying out Lev Nikolaevich's banned works, and bursting into hysterical sobs every time she greets him and says goodbye to him. Pavel Ivanovich Biryukov is also staying: he is an excellent man – serene, clever and also a proponent of 'Tolstoyism'.[34] Golokhvastov's wife was here too with their ward,[35] as well as my nephew Andryusha and his tutor.[36]

All very noisy, difficult and tedious. I long to be alone with my family, and for life to resume a more sensible, leisurely course. These guests take up all my time. Abalamek also paid us a visit, accompanied by the Helbigs, mother and daughter; she was born Princess Shakhovskaya, but married a German professor, and she and her daughter also wanted to visit Tolstoy, the famous Russian. They turned out to be very pleasant people, and good musicians too, but it is a severe trial never being able to *choose* my own friends, and having to entertain anybody and everybody. The days are hot, the nights are cool. We go swimming, there is an abundance of fruit.

August 4 Countess Aleksandra Andreevna Tolstaya left today; she has been staying with us since July 25.[37] On July 16 Lyovochka had a bad liver attack, from which he has not yet fully recovered. Yesterday afternoon Pavel Biryukov took his article 'On Life' to the printers. He had deleted '. . . and Death', since after he had finished it he decided that 'there is no death'.[38] We have had a few showers, but it has cleared up a little now.

August 19 The painter Repin visited on the 9th and left on the night of the 16th. He did two portraits of Lev Nikolaevich; the first he started painting in the study downstairs, but he was not satisfied with it and started on another in the drawing-room upstairs, against a bright background. It is extraordinarily good, and is still drying. The first he finished in a rough and ready fashion and gave to me.[39] The printers started working on the article but the type was no good, so they are having to reset it. Lyovochka's health is satisfactory at the moment, although he sometimes complains of liver pains. It's marvellous fine weather. Ilya came to visit on the 15th and 16th; he was in the best of health and very cheerful, which is good; some people manage to be ill, out of sorts and wretched the whole time. My pregnancy is a torment, physically and emotionally. Lyovochka's health is worse, our family life is so complicated, and I feel drained of emotional energy. My brother Styopa came to see us with his wife.[40] He travelled on to Petersburg yesterday to apply for a transfer to European Russia, and she stayed here. It's hard to know what to make of her, she's always so cautious and restrained. Lyovochka's dark ones are here: Butkevich, Rakhmanov and that student from Kiev. What peculiar and disagreeable people they are, and what a strain they put on our family life. And what a lot of them there are too! This is the price we must pay for Lyovochka's fame and the originality of his ideas.

Lyovochka has been reading Gogol's *Dead Souls* aloud to us in the evening.[41] I have neuralgia.

August 25 I spent the day sorting out Lyovochka's manuscripts and setting aside the ones I want to take to the Rumyantsev Museum for safekeeping.[42] I had a terrible job trying to put in order that jumble of papers, which I am *sure* will never be properly sorted out and read. I also want to take along his letters, diaries, portraits, and all the other things relating to Lev Nikolaevich. I am only being *sensible*, but for some reason it makes me feel sad. Or am I tidying up because I am about to die?

Styopa and his wife are here, as well as dear Strakhov. It is a frightfully hot day and I have a sore throat. Lyovochka has been very weak and has been taking Ems water since the 20th. Verochka Tolstaya and Masha arrived here wanting money for Lyovochka's brother Seryozha. Lyovochka sits working on his article all day, but he seems to have no energy for it.

Lev Nikolaevich started taking Ems Kesselbrunn water on June 17, 1888.

He drank these waters for four weeks starting in June 1889, and for four weeks starting on May 8, 1890, and he drank mare's milk all summer.

Lyovochka brought me this flower in October 1890, at Yasnaya Polyana.*[43]

(February 28, 1888 – Ilya Tolstoy marries Sofia Filosofova. March 31 – Sofia Tolstaya gives birth to Ivan (Vanechka), her last child, and her ninth son. Tolstoy starts writing The Kreutzer Sonata. The Power of Darkness *produced in the Théâtre Antoine in Paris.*

July 7, 1889 – various offences (murders and assassinations of officials, etc.) to be tried by juryless courts. July 12 – creation of 'land captains', hereditary nobles and local landowners appointed by the Ministry of the Interior to manage peasant institutions of self-government. Justices of the peace dismissed, except in a few large cities, and land captains now hear most criminal cases. November – admission to the bar of non-Christians (i.e. Jews) allowed only with the permission of the Ministry of Justice.

Autumn 1889 – Tolstoy finishes The Kreutzer Sonata. *November – 800 copies secretly lithographed in Intermediary offices and circulated in St Petersburg before being passed by the censor. This (and the story's contents) provokes furious arguments between the Tolstoys. Sofia's eleventh edition of Tolstoy's* Complete Works *published, Volume 12 separately, and Volume 13, containing* The Kreutzer Sonata, *still not passed by the censors.)*

· 1890 ·

April 24 – law empowering factory inspectors to lift ban on night work for women. June 12 – law bringing zemstva *under state control, by altering basis of franchise in favour of provincial governors and officials. Jews banned from* zemstva.

Sofia Tolstaya involved in litigation with priest from nearby Ovsyannikovo over some disputed land. Tolstoy working on The Kingdom of God is Within You. *November –* The Kreutzer Sonata *published. Sofia writes her story 'Who Is To Blame?', her riposte to* The Kreutzer Sonata. *Vanechka becomes the centre of her affections.*

November 20 (Yasnaya Polyana) I have been copying Lyovochka's diaries, which cover his whole life, so I decided I would start writing mine again; because I've never been more lonely within my family than I am

*The last three sentences were added later by Sofia Tolstaya, and a dried flower attached to the page.

now. My sons are all over the place: Seryozha in Nikolskoe, Ilya and his family in Grinevka, and Lyova in Moscow. Tanya too has just gone for a visit there. I stay here with the little ones and give them their lessons. Masha and I have never been close; I don't know whose fault it is,[1] my own most likely. And now Lyovochka has broken off all relations with me. Why? What can the reason be? I simply cannot understand. When he is ill he lets me nurse him, but only in the most rude and grudging manner, and only so long as he needs his poultices and so on. I have done everything in my power to achieve a slightly deeper and more spiritual intimacy with him – it's what I want more than anything else in the world. I secretly read his diaries too, in the hope of discovering how I could help him, and myself, understand how best we might be reunited. But these diaries have reduced me to even greater despair; and he must have discovered that I was reading them, for he has started hiding them away. He has not mentioned it though.

I used to copy out everything he wrote, and loved doing so. Now he carefully conceals everything from me and gives it to his daughters instead. He is systematically destroying me by driving me out of his life in this way, and it is unbearably painful. There are times in this useless life of mine when I am overwhelmed with violent despair, and long to kill myself, run away, fall in love with someone else – anything not to have to live with this man whom for some reason I have always loved, despite everything, although I now see just how I have idealised him, how long I have refused to realise that there is nothing in him but sensuality. Now my eyes have been opened, and I see that my life is destroyed. I so envy people like the Nagornovs, for they are *together*, and have things in common besides the physical bond. And plenty of other people live like them. As for us – my God, he is always so unfriendly, so querulous and so artificial when he speaks to me! How can he treat me like this when I am so open and cheerful with him, so eager for his affection!

Tomorrow I am going to Moscow on business. I generally find such expeditions hard work and nerve-racking, but this time I am pleased to be going. They ebb and flow like waves, these difficult times when I realise just how lonely I am and I want only to cry, and know that I must somehow put a stop to it, make it easier. I pray for a long time every night nowadays, and find this a good way to end the day. I gave Andryusha and Misha their music lesson today and was cross with them. Andryusha sulks whenever I am irritable, but Misha always takes pity on me. I love them both; educating them is a pleasant duty, although I obviously handle it very clumsily. Vera Kuzminskaya is staying with us; I feel very close to her, no doubt because she is so like my sister Tanya. I love the peace and leisure of the countryside and am happy to be living here – if only *someone* was slightly sympathetic to me! Days, weeks, months pass when we say not so much as a word to one another. I am so used to running up to him with whatever is on my mind – about the children, some book I am reading or some new idea. But he merely snubs me with a look of grim surprise, as if to say: 'So you still hope to come crawling up to me with your silly ideas!'

Can there be any spiritual intimacy left between us, or has it died? I think that if only I could go up to him as I used to, go through his papers, read his diaries and discuss it all with him, he would help me go on living; how splendid it would be if he would just speak plainly to me, and everything would be as it was before. But now, even though I am innocent, and have always loved him, and have never done him any harm, I am desperately afraid of him and feel like a criminal. I am afraid of his silent disapproval, sullen, severe, indifferent and unloving, which is far more painful than any words. He is incapable of loving, *he never learnt to* when he was young.

December 5 I am going on with my diary. I went to Moscow, saw a lot of people and enjoyed a lot of hospitality, for which I thank my good fortune. Tanya was there too; I am always so happy to see her, and I value her company. Lyova is still very jumpy; whenever I go near him he recoils from me, which I find very hurtful. Yet he always senses when he is doing so, which is some compensation. I am sure he will manage to put this anxious, pessimistic state behind him somehow or other. When I got back, on the morning of the 25th, Lyovochka was just leaving for Krapivna with Masha, Vera Tolstaya and Vera Kuzminskaya. It was cold outside and there was a blizzard, but I hadn't the strength to stop them. There was a trial there, and thanks to Lyovochka's influence the murderers received a very light sentence – deportation instead of penal servitude. So they all returned well pleased.[2] Misha was ill for five days with a high fever and an upset stomach. I spent all my time looking after him, which exhausted me, and I hadn't rested properly after my visit to Moscow. We have guests at the moment: Rusanov, who is sick, Boulanger, Butkevich and Petya Raevskii. They're all strangers except Petya, and I find them tedious company. Lyovochka is being less distant towards me, but then everything always depends on his mood. Today I played Beethoven's *Una Fantasia* and *Adelaide*, and sight-read some Schubert. This evening I read aloud some poems by Fet to entertain our guests. But I enjoyed the music and poems too. Tanya and Masha accompanied Vera Kuzminskaya back to Tula and returned home in time for dinner. I myself was in Tula yesterday about the sale of the timber, the division of Ovsyannikovo with the priest,[3] putting money in the bank, shopping. It always makes me irritable and depressed when I have to waste all my energy on these practical matters. There are so many better things to do with it.

December 6 Today is a holiday, Andryusha's 13th birthday. We all walked up the hill and went skating. The girls and boys all looked so smart and cheerful; they had a marvellous time. I dragged myself around on the ice, I don't enjoy it any more. Tanya went off to Tula for a name-day party given by the Zinovievs and the Davydovs. The same guests here: Rusanov, Boulanger, Butkevich and Petya Raevskii, who went off with Tanya. I feel physically destroyed: my chest hurts, my breathing is laboured, and my female condition is also painful and distressing. I was delighted to receive a letter from Sofia Alekseevna Filosofova about my eldest sons. A mother only wants her children to be *happy*, and it really does seem as though they are happy at the moment. Lyovochka is still unsociable and cold to everybody, although this affects me far more painfully then anyone else. I did almost no work, just copied out a little of Lev Nikolaevich's diary, then entertained our guests and played with the children. Vanechka takes up a lot of time.[4]

December 7 I have been writing all day, I am not well. Davydov visited with the local magistrate, on their way to Krapivna. I read a story by Leskov called 'One Godly Hour'; talented, but rather contrived.[5] I hate any form of falsehood. Lyovochka is cheerful and seems well.

December 8 I am still copying out Lyovochka's diary. Why did I never read and copy it before? It has simply been lying in my chest of drawers all this time. I don't think I ever recovered from the shock of reading Lyovochka's diaries when I was engaged to him – I can still remember the agonising pangs of jealousy, the horror of that first appalling experience of male depravity. May God save all young hearts from such wounds, for they never heal. I gave Andryusha and Misha their music lesson today. Andryusha was so spiteful and stubborn that I was on the point of losing my temper with him, but I was determined to be patient and managed not to get angry, but suddenly burst into tears instead. Then he started to cry, promising to work harder, and he turned over a new leaf then and there. I felt ashamed of myself, but maybe it was all for the best. I read a stupid story in *Revue des Deux Mondes*, and this evening, at Lyovochka's request, Tanya read us a dull story translated from Swedish. I long to read something really worthwhile, by some really great thinker, but cannot imagine what. I am in a happy, gentle mood just now, and want to see things in a pleasant light. But I have sinful dreams and little peace of mind – especially at certain times.

December 9 Once more I am ending the day with a heavy heart. Everything makes me anxious. I have been copying out Lyovochka's youthful diary.[6] Today I went for a walk and thought – it was a marvellous day, 14° below zero, frosty and clear, and every tree, bush and blade of grass was covered in thick snow. I passed the threshing-floor and took the path into the plantation. On my left the sun was already low in the sky, and on my right the moon was rising. The white treetops gleamed, the sky was blue, everything was bathed in a rosy light, and in the distant clearing the fluffy snow was dazzling white. What *purity*. And what a fine and beautiful thing this whiteness and purity is, whether in nature, in one's heart, morals and conscience, or in one's material life. I have tried so to preserve it in myself – and all for what? Wouldn't the mere memory of love – however sinful – be preferable to the emptiness of an immaculate conscience?

I played a Mozart symphony on the piano today, first with Tanya and then with Lyovochka. We didn't get it right at first, and he went for me peevishly; it was all very brief and insignificant, but I found it so hurtful that I lost all enthusiasm for playing duets and just felt sad, terribly sad. Then Biryukov came and we had to stop. The girls were highly excited, Tanya for Masha's sake and Masha for her own. Everyone became very stilted and talked a lot of affected nonsense, and it was most unpleasant. I do hope he leaves soon, and that Masha will settle down again. Now this silly business has started it won't be so easily laid to rest.[7] I read a novel in the *Revue des Deux Mondes* which describes a young girl's joy at staying in the house of the man she loves, surrounded by all *his* furniture, *his* things, *his* life. How true that is!

But what if these things are boots, boot-making tools, chamber-pots and mud, what then? No, I shall never grow used to it.[8]

December 10 I have to endure such a sad time in my old age. Lyovochka has surrounded himself with the most peculiar circle of friends, who call themselves his disciples. One of them arrived just this morning; this man, called Butkevich, has been in Siberia for his revolutionary ideas, wears dark glasses and is himself a dark and mysterious person, and has brought his Jewish mistress with him, whom he refers to as his wife merely because she lives with him. As Biryukov was here too, Masha went downstairs to prance around and make herself agreeable to this Jewess. It made my blood boil – to think that my daughter, a respectable girl, should associate with such rabble, apparently with her father's approval too. I shouted at him in a rage: 'You may be used to spending your life with any old riff-raff but I'm not, and I don't wish my daughters to associate with them either!' He sighed, of course, was furious, said nothing and walked away. Biryukov's presence is also oppressive; I cannot wait for him to leave. Masha was lingering in the drawing-room this evening after we had left, and I thought I saw him kiss her hand. When I mentioned it to her, though, she angrily denied it. I suppose she was right, but how is one to know what is right amidst all the secrecy, lies and artificiality? They have worn me down. Sometimes I feel like letting Masha go. 'Why hold on to her?' I think. 'Let her go with Biryukov, then I can take her place beside Lyovochka; I shall do his copying, put his affairs and his correspondence in order, and gradually, without him noticing, send this whole hateful crowd of "dark ones" packing.'

Lyova still hasn't come; I wonder how his health is. Andryusha, Misha and I thought that for our Christmas play we might put on a translation from a Japanese story. I knitted Misha a blanket, did some copying, gave the children two hours of religious instruction and shall now do some reading.

December 11 I have spent the whole day copying out Lyovochka's diary, which always evokes a profusion of thoughts. I thought, amongst other things, that one never loves the person who knows one the best, with all one's weaknesses, for one cannot reveal just *one* side of oneself to him. That is why couples so often grow estranged in their old age – for then it is in the interests of neither of them to have *everything* exposed and clarified. I was kind and patient with the boys when I gave them their music lesson. Biryukov is staying yet another day. Masha came to explain about yesterday, and I said I was sorry if I had offended her for no good reason. Today, amongst other things, she said with a flippant laugh: 'If you let me marry him that'll be an end to the matter. You know you really think he is a good man.' If only that were enough! I have noticed that most mothers are themselves practically besotted with their future sons-in-law, and that means that the couple is bound to remain on good terms. For Biryukov, however, I feel nothing but revulsion, and I am sure it wouldn't be long before Masha felt the same way. But she cannot see this – or she is not my daughter.

Lyova has arrived and I feel cheerful and festive, although he himself is far from cheerful – he is just like his father, preoccupied solely with himself, to the exclusion of everything else. Vanechka's delight at seeing him was so touching, and he looked at him so lovingly, yet Lyova was very gruff with him. One can see how children and adults have all the gentleness and affection crushed out of them. Long ago, when Lyova himself was young and tender, he wept at being taken away from the English governess and sent downstairs to the tutor, and said he would 'become a bad person' downstairs, and I wanted to take him back. But his father talked sternly to him and left him with his tutor – God knows what effect this had on him, whether it made him less loving, less joyful and emotionally strong. This evening we all sat together in the drawing-room. Tanya has a back-ache and is in a strange, despondent state. Now *there* is someone who needs to get married and start a new life; I pray every day for this to happen. I was just thinking what a sin it was to bemoan my fate; even if one is denied *one* happiness, there are so many others, and I can quite sincerely say 'God be thanked for everything!'

At the dinner-table Lyovochka told me that the peasants who'd been arrested for felling 30 trees in our birch wood were waiting outside to see me.[9] Whenever I am told that someone is waiting to see *me*, and that I have to take some decision, I am seized with terror, I want to cry. Being expected to manage the estate and the household '*in a Christian spirit*' is like being gripped in a vice, with no possible escape; it is a heavy cross to bear. If personal salvation and the spiritual *life* means *killing* one's closest friend, then Lyovochka's salvation is assured. But is this not the death of us both?

December 13 I did not write my diary yesterday – I was too distressed all day by thoughts of the peasants who were found guilty, although I did not know this until the evening. Biryukov left and an Englishman named Dillon arrived; he has translated *Walk in the Light*, etc. I copied Lyovochka's diaries all day yesterday, and there were moments when I felt quite sorry for him – how lonely and helpless he was! But he has always, throughout his life, followed the same path, that of the intellect. Today I learnt that the peasants had been sentenced to 6 weeks in jail and a 27-ruble fine. Once again a sob rose in my throat, and I have felt like weeping all day. I am sorry mainly for *myself*: why should people be harmed in *my* name, when I have nothing against them and would never wish anyone any harm? Even from a practical point of view, it is not my property, yet I have become a sort of scourge! I taught the children for three hours without a break and was patient with them. Lyova and I had a talk about Tanya and Masha yesterday; we both want them to get married, though not to Biryukov, of course.[10] I almost never see Lyovochka; he seems quite happy that we are estranged, but it makes me so sad that I sometimes think I can't go on living. Tanya, Masha, Lyova, Liddy, Andryusha, Misha and I all took a walk up the frozen hillside late yesterday afternoon. The children went there by carriage but I wanted to walk. It was an astonishing moonlit night, 15 ° below zero; the dazzling purity of the snow, the trees and the moonlight was so beautiful, that we stood there marvelling at it, unable to leave. 'It's enough for me just to look at this,' I said to Lyova. And he said: 'Well, it's not enough for me.'

December 14 I copied Lyovochka's diaries up to the part where he wrote: 'There is no such thing as love, *only the physical need for intercourse and the practical need for a life companion*.'[11] I only wish I had read that remark 29 years ago, then I would never have married him. I spent the day much as usual: gave Misha his lesson, played with Vanechka, chatted with Dillon; we had a visit from a student called Aleksandr Zinger. I taught Sasha[12] her 'Our Father', and I did only a little copying. I had a talk with Masha about Biryukov. She assured me that if I didn't let her marry him she would not marry anyone. Then she added: 'But there's no need to worry. Anything might happen!' And I felt she actually wanted to be released from this accidental entanglement with him. Tanya was deep in some long mysterious discussion with her today, and they seemed to be having a good time. I wrote some letters – one to my sister Tanya, and one to a French newspaper about an article of November 21, 1890 in *Le*

Figaro,[13] about the money I was supposed to be making out of the foreign editions of Lev Nikolaevich's works; I wrote also to Dunaev and Aleksandr Behrs.

December 15 An unproductive day. Our music lesson was interrupted by the arrival of the *zemstvo* chairman, a man named Sytin, whom Tanya had invited here to discuss the Yasnaya school with her. Then Bulygin arrived for dinner. I took the children out for two walks, the second with Sasha, who was crying this evening because it was all so *boring*. All of us here feel weighed down by a great melancholy.

Lyovochka is even more sullen and out of sorts now that the peasants have been sentenced to hard labour for felling the trees in the plantation. Yet the moment it happened, immediately after the village policeman called, I asked him what I should do and whether they should be charged, and he pondered a while, then said: 'They should be given a good fright and then forgiven.' It soon turned out that this was a criminal offence, and that there was no chance of a pardon – so once again it was all my fault, of course. He is furious and won't speak, and I can't imagine what he is planning to do.[14] I feel depressed, I'm sick and tired of the whole thing – I've had it up to my ears, as they say. I thought today of setting off to see Ilya and saying good-bye to everyone, then calmly lying down on the railway-line, as Agafya Mikhailovna is always threatening to do. But I am afraid to – it would be so easy.

Dillon left first thing today and Bulygin and Zinger left this evening. No more guests.

December 16 Yes, I have completely lost the power to concentrate – on my thoughts, feelings or actions. This chaos of innumerable petty worries, all jostling with one another, is driving me insane. I am losing my judgement. It's easily said, yet at every moment of the day I have to worry about my children's illnesses and studies, my husband's medical and (more importantly) his mental state, the older children's affairs, their debts, jobs and children, the sale of the Samara estate, and the plans – which I have to get hold of and copy for the buyers – the new edition and Volume 13, which contains the banned *Kreutzer Sonata*,[15] the petition for the division of the land with the Ovsyannikovo priest, the proofs for Volume 13, Misha's night-shirts and Andryusha's boots and sheets; I must make sure not to default on the household expenses, I must see to the servants' passports, make sure the jobs are done on the estate, keep the accounts, copy them out . . . and so on. And for all this I am directly, inescapably responsible. And when there is an incident like last night's, I realise I have done the wrong thing, I have lost my judgement and have quite inadvertently caused Lyovochka pain. Last night's 'incident' was the inevitable result of the peasants' six-week prison sentence. We had lodged a complaint with the chairman of the *zemstvo*, imagining that we could pardon them after the sentence. But it turned out to be a *criminal* case, which meant that the sentence couldn't be revoked, and Lyovochka was in despair at the thought of Yasnaya peasants going to prison on account of *his* property. He did not sleep all last night and kept jumping up, pacing about the drawing-room, sighing; he blamed me, of course, and in the cruellest tones too. I didn't lose my temper with him, thank God, for I realised he was ill, but what amazed me was the way he kept trying to arouse my pity for *him*, yet he had absolutely no feelings for me, no desire to understand *my* side, and to accept that the last thing I wanted was to cause him or the thieving peasants pain.[16]

This self-adoration runs through all his diaries. It is strikingly obvious that people exist for him only if they directly concern him. And as for the women! I caught myself thinking a wicked thought today. I have been copying out his diaries in a frenzy, drunk with jealousy and agitation whenever I read anything to do with women. I still haven't regained my peace of mind – I shall never be rid of those memories, never. Something else struck me in his diary today: along with all the debauchery, he actually seeks out opportunities to 'do a good deed' every day. So now, in his frequent walks along the highway, he is always giving a drunkard a horse, helping to unload a cart or harness a horse – and all because he wants to 'do his good deed for the day'.

Today is Sunday. My heart has been as heavy as lead all day after last night's reproaches. The time has dragged. There was a snowstorm and nobody left the house apart from the boys, who went for a walk. Young Lyova set off to visit Ilya, but turned back just past the village. This evening we read a French translation of *The Chinese Fairy Tales*. Very odd. I played the piano a little. Vanya and Sasha danced together this evening, and people became slightly more cheerful.

December 17 Lyovochka is beginning to worry about me copying out his diary. He would like to destroy his old diaries, as he wants to appear before his children and the public as a patriarchal figure.[17] Still the same old vanity!

Some 'dark ones' have arrived: silly Popov, some weak, lazy Oriental, and stupid fat Khokhlov, who is of merchant origin.[18] To think that these people are the great man's disciples – these wretched specimens of human society, windbags with nothing to do, wastrels with no education. Tanya and young Lyova went off to see Ilya last night. The children's lessons were interrupted by the arrival of Eduard Kern, who used to be a forester on the Zaseka estate and is now a landowner; he gave me some very useful advice on the forests and orchards.

December 19 Yesterday morning Andryusha, M. Borel and I went off to Tula. It was very cold and I kept worrying about Andryusha. We rushed about buying and ordering things, then briefly called on the Raevskys, but only the boys were at home. We got back just in time for dinner. This evening Aleksei Mitrofanovich[19] read us some very dull piece about German communities here, and then we looked through *The Review of Reviews*. I am tired, and have felt anxious; Popov and Khokhlov irritate me, they're such mute and insipid characters.

I got up late this morning for I did not sleep last night. Waiting in the drawing-room was a stiff young officer called Zhirkevich, who had come to make Lyovochka's acquaintance, and who also wrote poetry and prose. He is evidently very pleased with himself and his future prospects, but at least he is not stupid and one can understand what he says, unlike the 'dark' ones. I took Vanechka for his first walk this winter, and Sasha came too. I taught Misha his prayers and told him about the New Testament. And now I am writing my diary – even though I have only copied two pages of Lyovochka's and have not nearly fulfilled my daily quota of ten pages. I had an unpleasant scene with Andryusha: he often *deliberately* misunderstands, and simply *refuses* to make the slightest effort to think or remember. This evening I shall help to entertain our guests, then take a bath.

December 20 I could not sleep last night and got up late this morning. I am suffering from the most horrible physical agitation, and a back-ache. I took the children skating but the ice was bad and I was worried that they would fall. Some peasant girls, the gardener, my own three children and I all scattered snow on the ice and I gave Sasha her first skating lesson. After we got back I taught the children for three hours: Andryusha learnt about Holy Mass, and the two boys had a music lesson. It is Misha's 11th birthday today. Lyova came back from Ilya's and brought Sasha Filosofova along with him. Masha went to Pirogovo with Fillip the coachman.[20] Tanya, Natasha[21] and Ilya all went there too and will be returning tomorrow. Lyova has been muttering and grumbling about everything; he told us the sad story of how Seryozha and Ilya fell out – all on account of a silly horse.

This evening I copied out part of Lyovochka's article on the Church.[22]

The Church as an idea, as the true religion, which guards the gathering of the faithful, cannot be denied. But the existing Church, with all its rituals, is unacceptable. Why should one have to poke a stick in a piece of bread instead of simply reading the Bible story about the soldier who pierced the rib of Christ? There is such a profusion of these primitive rituals, and they have killed the Church. It is 10 o'clock, we shall have some tea, then read. I have not copied out Lyovochka's diaries today, and consequently feel much calmer and fresher.

December 23 A lot has happened these past few days. The day before yesterday we were woken up at 6 a.m. by two telegrams, the first saying that Sonya was ill, the second announcing that she had had a son.[23] I was excited and delighted by the news, but not for long, for I soon started thinking what an unreliable father Ilya would be, despite being so sweet and kind. I always feel a special tenderness for Sonya, mainly because unlike all of us, who are restless, nervous, hot-tempered and forever picking quarrels, she is gentle and even-tempered. Ilya, Tanya and Natasha Filosofova came back from Kursk on the train. I had the usual unpleasant discussion with Ilya about money and property, and he left this evening. I spent all yesterday in Tula, dined at the Davydov's and wearily bought some things for the Christmas tree. Christmas used to be fun, but now I am tired of it. The Filosofov girls left today and Masha Kuzminskaya arrived with Erdeli; I wasn't at all pleased that she had come with *him*, and didn't pretend to be. We made flowers for the tree, gilded nuts, and the whole day passed in a rather dreary, futile manner. I received a very flattering letter from Fet which was almost a love letter; I felt terribly pleased, although I have never loved him in the slightest – I have always found him rather unattractive, in fact.[24]

December 24 I got up late; Vanechka came into my room and I played with him for a whole hour. Then I went downstairs. Seryozha arrived and played the piano. He is being very affable and kind, like a man who has *achieved* something and can now take a rest. Masha Kuzminskaya and Erdeli are so tiresome; it's neither one thing nor the other: they can't announce their engagement, yet they behave just as though they had. My Masha is pathetically thin and wretched. Tanya, Liddy, the children and I all made the Christmas pudding. We had a cheerful dinner and afterwards Lyovochka read the Bible, much of which made us laugh. I cut out cardboard puppets for the children's play I am putting on – what foolishness. Dunaev has just come. It's late.

December 25 Christmas Day. Everyone has been in a festive mood all day, and I have been busy decorating the Christmas tree. Lyova and Lyovochka started a heated discussion over morning coffee about happiness and the meaning of life, which all began when Lyova commented on the change of mealtimes here and his general dissatisfaction with the formalities in *our* life. Lyovochka replied in a reasonable and friendly manner that it all depended on the individual, on a person's *inner* needs rather than *external* appearances. All this was very true, but when he points to his disciples as examples it makes me so angry.

We had a cheerful party around the Christmas tree, to which about eighty peasant children came; we gave them a wonderful time, and our children enjoyed themselves too. I talked to Erdeli for the first time about his relations with Masha Kuzminskaya and their future marriage.[25] They both look so wretched; they long to be married and something is always preventing it. Lyovochka is happy and well, though he occasionally complains of indigestion.

December 27 I didn't write my diary yesterday. I dislike holidays, when people do nothing but lounge about and rush around trying to have a good time. I glued and painted puppets all day in preparation for the puppet-show I am putting on for the little ones. By evening I felt depressed at having wasted the whole day in such a foolish way. I had a toothache last night and could not sleep. I picked up *Le Sens de la vie* by Rod this morning and have been unable to tear myself from it.[26] What a sensitive, intelligent, sincere view of life's problems! How honestly and simply he deals with all the complicated questions of everyday life. And his language is beautiful too. This book has reawakened my long-buried interest in questions of life and the spirit, for I suddenly sensed new hope, and the possibility of creating my own spiritual world, independent of Lyovochka's crushing sermons.

In the evening the servants all came in dressed as mummers, and danced to the harmonica and piano. It was Tanya who had arranged this, for she wanted some really *silly* fun. She and Masha dressed up too, but when Masha walked through the door Lyova and I simply gasped: she was dressed as a boy, in a pair of tight trousers which showed her behind, yet she showed not an ounce of shame. What a strange, foolish, inscrutable creature.

These rowdy parties always make me depressed. I went off to my room, opened the window, gazed out at the bright, frosty, starry sky, and suddenly remembered poor U.[27] And I felt so sad, so unbearably sad, that he had died and that I was robbed for ever of that refined, pure, discrete friendship, which was so much more than friendship, yet left nothing on my conscience, and filled so many years of my life with happiness. Who needs me now? Where will I ever find such affection and consideration? There is only Vanechka, I thank God for that joy.

December 28 Rod's book ends badly. The chapter entitled 'Religion' is obscure, and it is hard to believe that he really found the conclusion, '*le sens de la vie*', which he was looking for. None of us has found it, and *never will*. Life consists in the search. And afterwards God, the source of all life, receives us back to Himself again. Yes, life would indeed be impossible without this constant awareness of God within us. I myself have the habit of saying, before I take so much as a single step: 'God help me, forgive me and take mercy on me . . . ' Yet I know that my life is not a godly one. I keep thinking: *now* I shall start being good and loving everyone; there will be an aura of goodness around me and people will love to be near me. Yet I cannot be like that. When I look at my son Lyova I see a person of such intelligence, experience and talent, yet so little sense of self-protection: everything interests, excites, agitates and torments him. That is always the way with young people. Lyovochka is a married man and has learnt to guard his own inner life, but he never had a family and the lack of this family feeling has stayed with him for ever.

Yesterday I read through his letters to me as I had to make corrections for Al. Tolstaya.[28] There was a time when he loved me so deeply, when he was my entire world and I looked for him in every child we had. But surely on his part it was nothing but a physical attraction, which has dwindled over the years to the point where nothing remains but this emptiness between us. Yesterday in the drawing-room he was telling Lyova about the narrative form he was trying to create when he started writing *The Kreutzer Sonata.* This notion of creating a genuine *story* was inspired by that extraordinary story-teller and actor Andreev-Burlak.[29] He had told Lyovochka about a man he had once met at a station who told him all about his unfaithful wife and how unhappy she was making him, and Lyovochka had used this as the subject-matter of his own story. He is not very well today and has indigestion and stomach-ache.

I copied out Lyovochka's diaries all day, and this evening we all sat down for a good family talk together. We have been waiting for Davydov, the Lopukhins and the Pisarevs, who are due from Tula at any moment. Cold and windy, 12°.

December 29 A heavenly bright, frosty day. Blue sky, hoar-frost on the trees, utter silence. We spent almost the whole day outside. The little ones and the girls turned the benches into toboggans and Erdeli, Masha K., Lyova and I all went skating. I am a clumsy, timid skater, but I loved the heady but soothing movement. The Zinovievs came for dinner, with Mme Giuliani and her son. The Zinovievs are pleasant, straightforward people. Lyuba played the piano nicely enough, although too much like a beginner to give real pleasure. Mme Giuliani sang a duet with Nadya, then a solo. Her voice has great passion – her nature too, I expect. Lyovochka is still not very well and is silent and uncommunicative. Seryozha is going off to the Olsufievs'. Tanya is being nervously cheerful.

December 30 I played with Vanechka all day until dinner-time, as Nurse was visiting her mother. I finished reading Rod, and once again his prayer seemed perfectly honest and clear to me. After dinner Andryusha and Misha helped me get the theatre ready. My mind is asleep. We all spent the evening together and had a quiet, amicable talk about music. Lyova has gone to a party in the village.

December 31 I am so used to living for Lyovochka and the children rather than for myself that I feel empty and uneasy if a day passes when I do not do something for them. I have started copying out Lyovochka's diaries again. How I regret now that my perpetual emotional dependence on the man I love has killed all my other talents – my energy too: and I had such a lot of that once.

I have been putting the accounts in order, but still cannot balance our total income over the past 20 months with our expenditure. But it doesn't bother me, for I keep the accounts so badly. A telegram arrived from Ilya asking me to be the baby's godmother. Sofia Alekseevna[30] declined, so did Tanya, so now it's my turn, *faute de mieux*. But I don't care. It's my little grandson I care about, not the others, and I am delighted to be his godmother. I shall leave tonight, or rather at 5 a.m., which is New Year's Day. I did some copying today, and sat with the children. Everyone here is quiet and friendly. We shall see in the New Year quietly on our own.

· 1891 ·

Trans-Siberian railway line, the greatest state-built line, starts construction, opening up vastness of Siberia to colonisation and providing impetus for Russia's ambitions in the far east. June – Tariff Act, marking high point in Russian protectionism. Law forbidding Jewish artisans to trade in towns. Disastrous harvest, followed by famine in which thousands die.

February 25 – Volume 13 of the Complete Works *(published separately, containing* The Kreutzer Sonata*) seized and banned. March – Sofia goes to St Petersburg and successfully petitions the Tsar against the ban. (The volume is published in June, with many textual changes.) April – Tolstoy's property redistributed amongst his family (the process finalised only a year later). Spring – Lyova Tolstoy forced to leave the university by a nervous illness. Autumn – Tolstoy works in the countryside, setting up canteens for victims of famine. Sofia joins him. Tolstoy denounced as 'impious infidel' by Archbishop of Kharkov.*

January 2 I have just returned from seeing Ilyusha and christening the baby. The ceremony, renouncing Satan and so on, was as dull as usual. But the baby, his eyes tightly closed, had such a touchingly contented expression on his little red face, and I was so deeply moved by the mystery of his soul and his new life that I prayed for him. There were crowds of Filosofovs in Grinevka, all very large and stout, but astonishingly sweet-natured both in their manners and in the way they lived their lives. There is so much genuine, unassuming simplicity about them, and they are so completely without malice. And that is splendid. Ilya was somewhat distracted and seemed almost deliberately inattentive, rushing about on small errands. It was so sad to get home, for it was obvious nobody was interested to see me back. I often wonder why they do not love me when I love all of them so dearly. I suppose it is because of my outbursts of temper, when I get carried away and speak too sharply. Then everyone gathered round me, although they hadn't even bothered to make me anything to eat. But that didn't bother me. Only Vanechka was glad to see me again, and Sasha, he with noisy delight, she with quiet pleasure. I found Kolechka Gué and Pastukhov here. I was delighted to see the former – I love his honest face and happy soul. Misha is not well. The Davydovs came. We tried to entertain them, but I fear they found it dull. He is very likeable and I am always pleased to see him.

Masha and I have just had another angry argument this evening about Biryukov. She is doing all she can to re-establish contact with him, but I cannot alter my views on the matter: if she marries him she is lost. I was harsh and unreasonable with her, but I cannot discuss it calmly, and Masha really is the most terrible cross God has sent me to bear. She has given me nothing but pain from the moment she was born. She is a stranger to her family and to God, and her imaginary love for Biryukov is completely incomprehensible.

January 3 I worked all day on the puppet theatre. The drawing-room was packed with children but it was not a success. How disappointing that they liked Punch best when he was fighting. What horrible coarse values! I am tired and bored. We have guests – Pastukhov and young Gué. Lyovochka is cheerful; he did a lot of writing this morning on the subject of the Church. I am not very fond of these religious and philosophical articles of his – I love him best as an artist, and always shall. There is a blizzard, 7° below freezing.

January 4 Terrible snow-storm all day, 10° below freezing. The wind is howling in the stoves, outside everything is buried in snow. We had some unpleasant news this morning: Roman, the head forester, got drunk last night and rode down to the marshes, where he and his horse fell into the lake. He got soaked through, but a Yasnaya peasant called Yakov Kurnosenkov managed to drag him out. The horse was drowned, however. It's most annoying and a great pity, for it was a young horse. Roman himself ran home in a terrible state. Berger cannot be found either. I am very displeased with him indeed for he is frightfully lazy and a liar. Masha has bought a washtub and scrubs her own underwear. I angrily told her she was ruining her health and would be the death of me too, but she answered me with calm indifference. All four of the young ones have coughs and colds, but they are up and about and in good spirits. Where can Seryozha be in this blizzard? He was visiting the Olsufievs – I only hope he didn't leave. Lyovochka has been complaining that he cannot write. I have been tidying my things, clothes and papers all day, and sorting my letters, and now that everything is in order I can die in peace. I am not at all well; I have palpitations, I feel sick, keep gasping for breath, and I have a back-ache.

Lyova and the bailiff went to look for the missing horse, but they got lost and returned without finding it. Lyova is so precious to me. I only wish he were not so distressingly thin and melancholy – although at present he is looking much more contented, which is a relief.

January 5 I am feeling ill, my back aches, my nose keeps bleeding, my front tooth is aching, and I am terrified of losing it, for a false one would be horrible. I copied out Lyovochka's diary all morning, then tidied his clothes and underwear and cleaned his study until it was spotless; then I darned his socks, which he had mentioned were all in holes, and this kept me busy until dinner-time. Afterwards I played with Vanechka. Earlier today Lyovochka and Nikolai Gué (the son) visited Bulygin, and Petya and Vanya Raevskii came here. I sat and darned socks: a dull job, but necessary until I buy more. This evening I was angry with Misha for hitting Sasha. I was much too hard on him, and pushed him in the back and made him kneel in front of everyone. He cried and ran off to his room, and I felt sorry then both for him and our friendship. But we soon made it up. Masha Kuzminskaya read me a letter from Erdeli. What a lot of gossip and unpleasantness; poor young things, what unnecessary aggravation.

It is almost two in the monring but I am not sleepy. Lyovochka is being very affectionate, which makes me so happy. I notice I have been very irritable lately, and quick to lose my temper with everyone. It is because I am ill, but it is not good enough, I must be more careful.

January 6 I am still ill: my head and back ache, and I did not sleep last night. I haven't stirred all day, just sat dumbly darning Lyovochka's socks. I was sent some Spinoza but cannot read it: I shall wait for my head and the black spots in front of my eyes to clear. We had guests – Bulygin and Kolechka Gué. Seryozha returned by express train and is kind and genial. We chatted about frivolous matters, his visit to the Olsufievs, and business. He is going to Nikolskoe tonight.

Andryusha and Misha went to the village to look in on a party. They evidently didn't have a good time, for the village lads were shy and wouldn't play. I am sorry they didn't enjoy themselves. It's all very difficult with Masha. She goes out on her own with a village girl to visit typhus patients. I am worried about her and the risk of infection, and I have told her so. This desire of hers to help the sick is all very well – I do so myself frequently – but she always goes too far. But today I reasoned gently with her, and began to feel so sorry for her, so sorry too that we are now irreconcilably estranged. Lyovochka has just read his article on the Church to Gué, Lyova and Bulygin.[1] I copied out part of it, and read the rest. I am not growing any fonder of these unartistic, tendentious, religious articles. They make me angry, they undermine me, and they plunge me into a state of useless anxiety.

January 7 Masha's words to me yesterday have been in my mind all day: she is going to marry Biryukov next spring, she says. 'I shall go and grow potatoes,' were her words, by which she meant she was going to plant them. I have now adopted the habit of waiting until the following day to respond. So today I wrote Biryukov a letter, enclosing the money for a book he had sent her. I said I did not want Masha marrying him, and I asked him to stop writing her letters and coming to see her. Masha overheard me telling Lyovochka about the letter and was furious with me, saying she took back all the promises she had made me. I was upset and in tears too. Masha really is a torment, everything about her, her deviousness and now her imaginary love for B.[2]

Lyova left for Pirogovo with Mitrokha this morning.[3] Tanya went to Tula, and there she had her money stolen. And last night 2 cartloads of firewood were stolen from the shed. I copied out L.'s diaries this morning, then taught the children, darned some socks, and now I can't do another thing. What infernal drudgery! This evening I read aloud two tedious and horrible stories which that stupid and insensitive Chertkov sent. Kolechka Gué left with Bulygin yesterday and still hasn't returned. What a good, clever, bright man. What an air of happy contentment he has. He must have gone through a lot of suffering before he learnt to live as he does now, although he has never claimed that his present life is perfect, merely that it is right for him. 'There can be no going back,' he says. And how true that is. Masha Kuzminskaya has no mind of her own. Her love for Erdeli is her whole world, and now that world no longer exists for her.

Today I was thinking that nine-tenths of all that happens in this world is caused by love in all its various aspects, yet people are always anxious to conceal this fact since otherwise all their most private emotions, thoughts and passions would be revealed. At this very moment I could cite several such cases, but am afraid to: it would be like appearing naked in public. There is no mention of *love* in Lyovochka's diaries, not as I understand it anyway – he seems to have had no experience of it. I did not express very clearly what I meant about love as the motivation of human behaviour. What I meant was that when we are possessed by love we put it into everything we do, our life and work, a book, relationships with others. And we put such energy and joy into everything that not only are we motivated by it, but everyone around us too. So I cannot understand Masha Kuzminskaya's kind of love. She seems crushed by it. Maybe it has just gone on too long.

January 8 Overwhelmed with work all day. I went through the accounts for Yasnaya Polyana and the timber sales, and checked them. Then Nikolai Gué (the son) and I read the proofs for Volume 13 of the new *Collected Works*.[4] Then I gave Andryusha and Misha a music lesson which lasted two hours, and after dinner I wrote down some chords for the children. Then I worked out our expenses on butter and eggs, and wrote yet more rough drafts of my legal petition regarding the division of the estate to the Ovsyannikovo priest and the transfer of the Grinevka estate. So now I have put everything in perfect order – as if before death? I really should pay a visit to Moscow about Volume 13, but I have no desire to go. My heart is heavy, though it shouldn't be: everyone is well and happy, thank God. Sasha, Vanechka and I all said our prayers together. Tanya and Masha drove off to Kozlovka with Kolechka Gué. I have seen almost nothing of Lyovochka: he spends all his time downstairs reading and writing, and comes out only to eat and sleep. He is happy and well.

January 9 I was not so energetic today, even though I didn't get up before 10 again. I felt too lazy to do much copying, and gave Misha just one lesson. Then I taught Andryusha how to play duets, then we had dinner, then after dinner I wrote for a while, and read a story by Zasodimskii called 'Beside the Blazing Fireside', which was rather good, and written with a sincerity that moved me to tears.[5] Tanya and I played the Kreutzer Sonata as a piano duet – badly; it is a very difficult piece to play without any practice beforehand. This evening Andryusha had a toothache and I carried Vanechka about in my arms, as he had lost his voice. What a gentle, affectionate, sensitive, clever little boy he is! I love him more than anything in the world and am terrified that he will not live long. I dream constantly that I have given birth to another son. My letter to *Le Figaro* has been translated and published in the *Russian Gazette*, but it misrepresented the original, and the word 'reputation' was clumsily translated.[6] I wrote letters to my sister Tanya and Gué senior. I am going to bed now. I have got the documents, the plans and the money ready, and shall go to Tula tomorrow on business.

January 10 It was almost 10 when I got up, so I did not go to Tula; there's a terrible wind. This morning I cut out some underwear for Sasha and did some copying. I gave the children a music lesson and gave Andryusha religious instruction. I took great pains with them and it went very well. Andryusha is stubborn and absent-minded, and seems quite deliberately not to listen or understand. The more I put my heart into the lesson the more inattentive and rude he is. How he distresses me! He will have a hard life with that character, poor boy! After dinner the three girls went off to Yasenki to meet Erdeli off the express train. He is going to see his mother. He and Masha sat together all evening cooing like a couple of birds. We read Solovyov's article on Fet and on 'Lyrical Poetry'; quite clever, but insubstantial.[7] We also read a silly story. Then Lyovochka and

Nikolai Nikolaevich[8] played chess with Aleksei Mitrofanovich[9] who played without looking at the board, to our great amazement. I wrote a letter to my brother Vyacheslav. Lyovochka is well and in a cheerful, lively mood. We talked about the ways in which censorship always prevents writers from saying what is most important to them, and I argued that there *were* free works, works of pure literature which the censors were unable to silence – take *War and Peace*, for instance. Lyovochka angrily replied that he had renounced all those works.[10] It was obviously the banning of *The Kreutzer Sonata* that was making him so bitter – he had just mentioned it.

January 12 Yesterday I went to Tula, traded in the coupons, handed in my application for the transfer of the Grinevka property, settled the bills, and, mainly wore myself out discussing the division of the Ovsyannikovo estate with the priest's wife, who shares the rights to the land with us. Four times I walked from the district court to the provincial offices and back again, as each place sent me back to the other, saying that the matter was not under their jurisdiction. So I left without accomplishing a thing. It is a long time since I felt as depressed as I did yesterday, waiting in Davydov the magistrate's office for the barrister, who was late. These *business* matters are so tedious and difficult – it's much easier to say: 'I am a Christian and can do nothing, it's against my rules!' I must hire a proper businessman to see to it for I cannot be continually going to Tula. I am tired, and the wind was terrible, a real gale. I called briefly on the Davydovs and Chelokaeva was there, and was such pleasant company, so lively and clever. It was Misha's name-day party this evening – Vanechka was overjoyed to see me and they had waited for me to return before starting dinner. At 3 this morning Vanechka started coughing and running a high fever. I dragged myself out of bed, went into his room and tried to soothe him. I got up late this morning. Today is Tanya's name-day, but we both gave the children their lessons; Andryusha played the piano quite nicely, but Misha just scowled stubbornly. Lyova returned from Pirogovo with Vera Tolstaya, and Vanya and Petya Raevskii arrived while we were having dinner. It was a bit like a name-day: we played games with the children and Vanechka was in ecstasies. We looked after him all day; he still has a cough and a temperature but he does not complain. Later on we all drove back to Kozlovka with Kolechka Gué. The post brought a letter from Varya Nagornova, as well as the proofs for *The Kreutzer Sonata*. The affair has now reached some sort of dénouement – what *will* happen? Will it be banned? What should I do?

There's no time for anything – no time to read or work. Tomorrow I must do the proofs and cut out some underwear. My soul is empty and lonely.

January 13 Vanechka is ill. He did not get up at midday, and by 2 he had a temperature of 39.4 – and the same at 9 this evening. Last night he was running a fever and choking on a thick phlegmy cough. He has a bad cold, and this morning he had an ear-ache. I feel so sorry for him, and so exhausted. In my free time I managed to correct a lot of the proofs for Volume 13, which includes *The Kreutzer Sonata.* Masha Kuzminskaya helped too. Vera Tolstaya left today and the girls accompanied her home. Lyovochka and Lyova drove over to Kozlovka this evening. It is 24° below freezing. When Vanechka was choking last night I ran into Masha's room to ask her for an emetic. She was asleep but she woke at once and jumped out of bed with alacrity to get some ipecacuanha. When she turned to me her face looked so touchingly thin and sweet that I had a sudden impulsive longing to hug and kiss her. That *would* have surprised her! She has had that sweet expression on her face all today, and I love her. If only I could always feel like this towards her, how happy I would be! I must try.

January 14 Vanechka is better. His temperature rose to 38.4, but then it went down, his cough improved and he grew more cheerful. Lyova went to Moscow. Klopskii arrived. He is utterly repulsive, and a dark one.[11] I wrote back to Misha Stakhovich and Varya Nagornova, and did a little copying. I taught Andryusha the Liturgy and Misha the Holy Communion. After dinner I sat with Vanechka for a while, copied Lyovochka's diary and reached 1854, then sat downstairs with the girls. My mind is asleep. This evening we saw Mitrokha off to Moscow; Andryusha and Misha both helped him get ready and gave him an overcoat and 50 kopecks of their own money. There is a hard frost. Lyovochka is so irritable and unkind. I am terrified of his merciless sarcasm – it cuts me to the quick.

January 15 It is a hard struggle at times. This morning the children were downstairs doing their lessons and that Klopskii was there. 'Why are you doing your lessons?' he asked Andryusha. 'Do you want to destroy your soul? Surely your father wouldn't want that!' The girls then piped up and asked him if they could shake his noble hand for saying so, and the boys ran up to tell me about it. I then had earnestly to assure them that since we did no real, *peasant* labour, without intellectual labour there would be nothing for us but total idleness; that this intellectual work was the justification for the grand life we led. I told them that I had to educate them all on my own, that if they turned into bad people all the shame would be mine, and that I would be very hurt if all my labours were in vain.

January 16 I went to Tula on business again, ran all over the place frantically, saw a lot of people and did a lot of talking. My business there was to settle the dispute with the priest's wife over the Grinevka transfer and the division of the Ovsyannikovo estate, and sell the firewood. I also got Petya Vasilevich's passport.[12] I visited Raevskaya, then went on to see

Zinovieva, who was having dinner when I arrived. Little Manya[13] reminds me of Vanechka; she sat on my knee and kissed my cheek.

On my way home I thought of my enemies and prayed for them. I decided to write a friendly letter to Biryukov – and did so. I decided to come to a friendly agreement with the priest's wife – and wrote to her too. I also replied to Baroness Ikskul's letter asking for permission to publish 'Kholstomer' and a popular edition of 'Polikushka'. I refused her first request but agreed to the second.[14] I wrote to Seryozha too, enclosing the documents for the Grinevka transfer.[15] Everybody was in high spirits when I got home and nothing untoward had happened. I have decided to send Masha to help the families of those peasants who are in jail for stealing the wood.

January 17 I was feeling lazy this morning and got up late. I was worn out from my trip yesterday. I wrote a letter to Lyova and copied to the end of Lyovochka's Caucasus diaries. I gave Andryusha a lesson on the Church service, then gave them both a two-hour music lesson. We worked well and amicably together. After dinner I did more copying, then sat with Vanechka, who had an ear-ache and was crying. We then read from a rather dull French novel. Over dinner we had a frivolous discussion about what would happen if the masters and servants changed places for a week. Lyovochka scowled and went downstairs; I went and asked him what the matter was and he said: 'That was a stupid discussion about a sacred matter. It's agony for me to be surrounded by servants, and very painful that this should be turned into a joke, especially in front of the children.' I tried to pacify him. But he then started arguing irritably with Aleksei Mitrofanovich, and defending Strakhov.

January 18 I am unwell. All the muscles in my stomach ache and I have a slight temperature. I had a dreadful scene with Nurse. She has been very rude to me ever since yesterday, and has been neglecting the baby. She is driving me desperate. I was feeling ill and told her that I would not be insulted by a hussy. At that she said something so appallingly vulgar that were I not so foolishly besotted with Vanechka I would have sacked her on the spot. The poor little boy, sensing an argument, clung to her skirt and would not leave her, saying, 'Maman good, Maman good!' If only we were all like children! I gave Misha a lesson and did some copying. I did not go to bed although I was groaning with pain and could eat nothing. This part of Lyovochka's diaries, about the Crimean War and Sevastopol, is so interesting. One page, which had been torn out, struck me particularly: what coarse, cynical lechery! A woman wants *marriage* and a man wants *lechery*, and the two can never be reconciled. No *marriage* can be happy if the husband has led a debauched life. It is astonishing that ours has survived at all. It was my own childish ignorance and my capacity for self-preservation that made it possible for us to be happy. Instinctively I closed my eyes to his past, and I deliberately, in my own interests, didn't read all his diaries and asked no questions. If I had, it would have destroyed both of us. He does not know this, or that it was my purity that saved us, but I know now that it is true. Those scenes from his past, that casual debauchery, and his casual attitude to it, is poisonous, and would have a terrible effect on a woman who hadn't enough to keep her busy. After reading these diaries a woman might well feel: 'So this is what you were like! Your past has defiled me – *this* is what you get for that!'

January 19 I am still ill; I have a stomach-ache and a temperature. Almost in my sleep, I taught the children music for two hours and corrected the proofs for *The Kreutzer Sonata*. I don't know how I manage to work so hard and for so long! What a pity I have been unable to direct it towards something worthier and more elevated than this mechanical drudgery. If only I could write stories or draw pictures, how happy I would be! I had a lovely letter from Lyova, but oh Lord! what a melancholy, sensitive soul he is. He does not know how to enjoy himself and will never be in harmony with himself, either in his life or his work. How sad!

I have observed a connecting thread between Lyovochka's old diaries and his *Kreutzer Sonata*. I am a buzzing fly entangled in this web, sucked of its blood by the spider.

January 20 My health is better but I have a cold. Misha has influenza but Sasha and Vanya are much better. Erdeli came; his mother won't let him marry Masha for another 3 years. Masha is distraught, and so apparently is he. We all cried and felt very sorry for them, but could not think what to do for the best. He is such a weak, pathetic boy. After dinner the children played, the little girls did some writing and I did some too. Before dinner I was reading Spinoza. I have neither grasped him properly nor grown to like him any better, although I find his definition of God perfectly satisfactory and compatible with my own.[16] I also read a few pages of a French novel. The proofs for the final part of *The Kreutzer Sonata* have arrived; I read them through – without feeling so agitated this time, thank God – and made just one correction. Lyovochka is sleeping badly and cannot write. It was warmer this morning – only 1½° below freezing; now it is 7° again.

January 23 I haven't written my diary for three days. The day before yesterday we had guests: Raevskaya, Erdeli and Aleksandr Aleksandrovich Behrs. It was an uneventful day and I was in a foolish excitable state. Lyovochka walked to Tula yesterday morning – it was quite warm. Raevskii had walked over to our house to meet his wife, and that was what gave him the idea. He dined at the Zinovievs (Zinoviev himself was away), and spent the evening with the Raevskiis. He returned on the train with Aleksei

Mitrofanovich. Seryozha had been in Tula, and today he came here. He, Tanya and I all sat down, just the three of us, and had a good talk – about business, marriage, and the business with Masha Kuzminskaya and Erdeli. He left after dinner and I ran up some underwear on the sewing-machine. Head, eyes, everything aches in this terrible cold. We all have influenza. Being ill makes me utterly listless.

January 25 I got up early this morning, despite being unwell and having a bad cold, and drove to Tula. It was a bright, warm day. At the footbridge I met Lyovochka, bright and cheerful, already returning from his walk. I love meeting him, especially unexpectedly. I had various things to attend to in Tula. I collected the payment for the timber, came to an understanding with the Ovsyannikovo priest, acceding to all his claims and virtually agreeing to the division of the land.[17] I visited the Raevskiis, the Sverbeevs and Maria Zinovieva, at whose house I met Arsenev, the local marshal of the nobility. For two years now I have noticed people treating me like an *old woman*. It feels strange, but doesn't greatly bother me. What a powerful habit it becomes, feeling one has the power to make people treat one with a certain sympathy – if not admiration. And I need even more respect and affection from people these days.

It occurred to me this evening, as I was correcting the proofs for *The Kreutzer Sonata*,[18] that when a woman is young she loves with her whole heart, and gladly gives herself to the man she loves because she sees what pleasure it gives him. Later in her life she looks back, and suddenly she realises that this man loved her only when he needed her. And she remembers all the times his affection turned to harshness or disgust the moment he was satisfied.

And when the woman, having closed her eyes to all this, also begins to experience these needs, then the old sentimental, passionate love passes away and she becomes like him – i.e. passionate with her husband at certain times, and demanding that he satisfy her. She is to be pitied if he no longer loves her by then; and he is to be pitied if he can no longer satisfy her. This is the reason for all those family crises and separations, so unexpected and so ugly, which happen in later life. Happiness comes only when will and spirit prevail over the body and the passions. *The Kreutzer Sonata* is untrue in everything relating to a young woman's experiences. A younger woman has none of that sexual passion, especially when she is busy bearing and feeding children. Only once in every two years is she a real woman in fact! Her passion awakes only in her 30s.

I returned from Tula at about six and dined alone. Lyovochka came out to meet me but we missed one another, which was sad. He has been more affectionate lately, but I have deceived myself time and again about this, and I cannot help feeling it's for the same old reasons: his health is better and the usual old passions are aroused.

I worked hard all evening correcting the proofs for *The Kreutzer Sonata* and the Postscript, then did the accounts. I made a list of everything I had to do in Moscow: seeds, shopping, business.

January 26 I got up at 10. Vanechka came upstairs, was dressed and taken out for his walk. I checked the proofs which I'd corrected yesterday and went on to the end, then looked through the seed catalogue, noting the ones I wanted. I gave Andryusha and Misha their music lesson. Andryusha was dreadfully stubborn and unpleasant; he has now adopted a new manner which will be hard to correct. The Sverbeev children visited with their English governess, as well as the two Raevskii children and Seryozha Berger. They played games and went tobogganing on the hill. I called on Ivan Aleksandrovich, who is as wretched and helpless in his suffering as a child. I went in to see Lyovochka to read over old Gué's letters with him,[19] and I told him that of his followers I liked only Prince Khilkov and Gué's son Nikolai Nikolaevich. These people were educated at the university, I said, in the old tradition, and that was their strength and their charm. Just wait and see how *their* children develop, he answered irritably and the conversation turned unpleasant. I merely pointed this out to him quietly, but left the room feeling angry with him. If only people knew how little genuine goodness he has in his heart, how much he puts on, *not from the heart but the principle of it.*

Everyone has gone to bed, and I am going too. Save me, Lord, from the sinful dreams which woke me up this morning.

February 4 A lot has happened to me recently. On the night of the 27th I left for Moscow. My adventures there were of no great interest. On my first day I dined with the Mamonovs, and that evening I went to a concert with Tanya, Lyova and the Urusovs. *The Kreutzer Sonata* was first (Grzimali and Poznanskaya) followed by a piano recital by Poznanskaya. It was very hot and tiring and I simply could not concentrate on the music, even though I realised they were performing well. The following morning I paid 7,600 rubles into the Moscow Bank and redeemed the Grinevka estate, then delivered the mortgage papers to the Bank of the Nobility. I dined with Fet and prattled on far too long, stupidly and wickedly complaining that Lyovochka didn't love me enough. I returned home that evening to find Dunaev there, and we both settled the accounts with the secretary. Uncle Kostya once described Dunaev as 'the man who pines for you', which completely spoilt him for me, even though I know he is a good and artless person. On Tuesday morning Kuzminskii arrived with Masha; they had just come from Yasnaya and I was delighted to hear the news from home. We sat chatting cheerfully for three hours, had lunch and laughed a lot. Tanya, Lyova, Vera Petrovna and Lily Obolenskaya came too. Then Urusov came and we went off to visit the Shidlovskiis. On Wednesday I visited the Severtsevs; Uncle Kostya and the Meshcherinovs were there, and we had a discussion about love and marriage. On Thursday I visited Dyakov; Liza, Vanya and Masha Kolokoltseva were there and made me feel quite at home in that simple, friendly atmosphere. I finished my business quickly, but my main preoccupation was not business or people but Lyova, his complicated inner existence, his attempts to write, and his completely joyless attitude to life. He read me a short story he has written called 'Montecristo', which was very touching and affected me deeply – more of a children's story really. He has sent another to *The Week*, which Gaideburov has promised to publish in the March issue.[20] He has begged me not to tell anyone, though, as it is still a secret. It suddenly occurred to me what a wonderful thing it was that if I should survive Lyovochka all the things I had lived for, the artistic world that has always surrounded me, would not be lost. I shall still be involved, through my son, with all the fascinating things that have filled my life, and loving him I shall love my own life better, and his father too. But it is all God's will!

Another disturbing thing was that on my return home I found Misha Stakhovich there, and he confessed to me for the first time, much to my amazement, his longstanding love for Tanya: '*J'ai longtemps tâché de mériter Tatyana Lvovna, mais elle ne m'a jamais donné aucune espoir.*'* We had always imagined that he wanted to marry Masha, and when I told Tanya I could see she was deeply upset. I would be so happy if Tanya married him, though, as I am very fond of him. I like him more than any other young man I know in fact, and who else would I want my favourite daughter to marry but my favourite young man?

We are all very cheerful these days. Kern and his wife visited, as well as the Raevskii boys, Dunaev and Almazov. But it was Stakhovich who made us cheerful. Last Sunday and February 2 were both holidays. The children went tobogganing all over the countryside on upturned benches,[21] and I called on blind Evlania, the mother of Lyova's servant Mitrokha, and told her all about him; I was glad to be able to do her this favour.

I taught the children today: Andryusha had done no work while I was away and hadn't learnt anything. I lost my temper and sent him out of the room. Lord, how he torments me! Lyovochka is not very bright, but he rode over to Yasenki today, and after dinner he played some Chopin. Nobody else moves me so much on the piano; he always plays with such extraordinary feeling and such perfect phrasing. Lyovochka was telling Tanya that he was planning a major new work of fiction;[22] he told Stakhovich about it too. Masha suddenly made up her mind to go to Pirogovo today, but I am not letting her go because she has a sore throat and it's cold – 15° below freezing. I wonder if she was distressed to hear that Stakhovich loves Tanya best; for so long everyone led her to believe it was her he loved.

*'I have long tried to be worthy of Tatiana Lvovna, but she has never given me any hope.'

Tanya went to Tula with Miss Lydia to have another photograph taken; Stakhovich had asked for her picture and she eagerly agreed. She is certainly very excited. But once again, it is all in God's hands . . .

February 6 I got up at 10. I had been dreaming of my little son Petya, who died; Masha had brought him from somewhere, and he was all torn and mutilated. He was already as big as Misha, and bore a great resemblance to him. We were overjoyed to see one another, and all day I have been seeing him as he was when he was ill, lying in the darkness. I cut out, tried on and sewed some trousers for Andryusha and Misha; I worked all day and had finished both pairs by evening. Later on Lyovochka read us Schiller's *Don Carlos*[23] while I knitted. It is now 11 and he has ridden to Kozlovka to collect the post. The girls have gone to bed; both of them are upset and slightly unhappy about Mikhail Stakhovich's declaration of love. I am reading *La Physiologie de l'amour moderne.*[24] I haven't fully grasped what it's about yet as I have only just started it, but I don't like it.

Lyovochka adores Vanechka and plays with him. This evening he put first him, then Sasha, into an empty basket, shut the lid and carted it around the house with Andryusha and Misha. He *plays* with all the children, but he never *looks after* them.

February 7 Tanya is ill: she has a temperature of 39.2, and her legs, back and stomach are aching. I gave Andryusha and Misha a lot of lessons today. Misha always has a headache, which worries me. Still no news from Lyova, which is depressing – maybe he is ill. We had a letter from Manechka Stakhovich – I had been expecting one from Misha. These past two evenings I wanted to drive to Kozlovka with Lyovochka, but on both occasions he rode over on his horse, as if deliberately to spite me. He is being stiff, sullen, and unpleasant again. I was silently angry with him last night, for he kept me up until two in the morning. He spent such a long time washing downstairs that I thought he must be ill, for washing is quite an event for him. I try to see only his spiritual side, and I can do this when he is being good to me.

February 9 Yesterday evening my wish was finally granted and I drove to Kozlovka by sledge in the moonlight. There were just the two of us, Lyovochka and I. There weren't any letters, though, and no news from Lyova. Tanya seems a little better, although she still has a temperature of 38.6. My darling little Vanechka has been ill too with a temperature. The weather is windy, 1° below zero. I am sad and apathetic today. I made Vanya a sailor suit, gave the children a two-hour music lesson, and read Beketov's pamphlet *On Man's Present and Future Nourishment.*[25] He predicts universal vegetarianism and I think he is right. Vanechka is coughing and it distresses me to hear him.

February 10 Tanya was groaning from morning to dinner-time with a terrible headache, then her temperature went up to 38.5 again. Vanechka too had a temperature this morning, it was 39.3. What a strange mysterious sickness! I cannot say I'm *too* anxious about my patients, but I do feel sorry for them. I don't feel very well either, and couldn't sleep last night. Today I copied out Lyovochka's Sevastopol diaries,[26] which are very interesting, then took my knitting and sat with the two invalids. I examined Andryusha on this week's lesson, which he hadn't learnt. Masha has opened a school for the riff-raff in 'that house',[27] and the children have all been flocking over there for lessons. Sasha has been going there for her lessons too while Tanya is ill. Misha has a new watch and is terribly pleased, as only children know how to be. I see almost nothing of Lyovochka. He is writing about art and science again.[28] He showed me an article today in *Open Court* which accused him of living at variance with his teachings, and handing over his property to his *wife*. 'And we all know how people in general, and Russians in particular, treat their wives,' they wrote. 'A wife has no mind of her own.' Lyovochka is very upset, but it's all the same to me – I'm used to this sniping.[29]

February 11 Now Andryusha is ill. Vanechka was a lot better all today, but was feverish again this evening. Leonila Annenkova came. Tanya is much better. A short letter from Lyova. I copied out a very long and very interesting part of Lyovochka's diary, from the Sevastopol War.

I worked, and taught the children.

February 12 All the children were ill today, with various ailments: Tanya and Masha have stomach-aches, Misha has a toothache, Vanechka has a rash and Andryusha has a fever and has been vomiting. Only Sasha is happy and well. I have been copying out Lyovochka's diary. He took it away this evening and read it. He has told me several times that he did not like me copying it out, but I thought to myself, 'Well, you'll just have to put up with it then, since you've lived such a disgusting life.' Today he brought it up again, and said I didn't realise how much I was hurting him, he wanted to destroy the diaries – how would *I* like to be constantly reminded of everything that tormented me, and every bad deed? He said much more besides, to which I replied that if he found it all so painful I was not a bit sorry for him, and if he wanted to burn his diaries, let him – I put no value on my own labours; but if one were to say which of us caused the other more pain, then it was he, for he hurt me *so* deeply when he published his latest story to the entire world that it would be hard for us ever to be quits. His weapons are so much more powerful, more authoritative. He wants the world to see him on the pedestal he has so laboriously built for himself. But his diaries cast him down into the filth of his past, and that infuriates him.[30]

I do not know how or why everyone connected *The Kreutzer Sonata*[31] with our own married life, but this is what has happened, and now everyone, from the Tsar himself down to Lev Nikolaevich's brother and his best friend Dyakov, feels sorry for me. And it isn't just other people – I too know in my heart that this story is directed against me, and that it has done me a great wrong, humiliated me in the eyes of the world and destroyed the last vestiges of love between us. And all this, when not once in my whole married life have I ever wronged my husband, with so much as a gesture or glance at another man! Whether or not I ever had it in my heart to love another man – and whether or not this was a struggle for me – is a different matter, and that is *my* business. No one in the world has the right to pry into my secrets, so long as I have remained pure.

I don't know why, but today I decided at last to let Lev Nikolaevich know my feelings about *The Kreutzer Sonata*. He wrote it so long ago, but he would have had to know sooner or later what I thought about it, and it was after he had reproached me for 'causing him so much suffering' that I decided to speak up about *my* suffering.

Masha's birthday. What a dreadful day it was, and it's still just as dreadful twenty years later.[32]

February 13 Yesterday's discussion distressed me deeply. But it ended with a reconciliation, and we agreed to try to live the rest of our lives as peacefully and amicably as we could.

The children are still ill: Andryusha has had a temperature all day, Tanya and Masha are very weak and have headaches, and Misha has neuralgia. I spent the day sitting with Annenkova and the children, and did some work: I finished sewing a pillow-case, cut out a dressing-gown for Andryusha, and darned some socks. Lyovochka read to the end of Schiller's *Don Carlos* this evening and two letters arrived, one for me from Lyova and one for Lyovochka from Countess Aleksandra Andreevna Tolstaya – both splendid letters.[33] Tanya is in a strange hysterical mood. This mundane life, and all my cares about the children and their illnesses, have once again paralysed my spiritual life and my soul is asleep. It is a hateful feeling.

February 15 Lyovochka has virtually forbidden me to copy out his diaries, and I am furious, for I have already copied so much that there's almost nothing left of the book I'm working on now. I shall go on with it while he is not looking, for I *must* finish: I made up my mind long ago that it *had* to be done. The children are all well. We had a telegram from Lyova saying that he wouldn't be going to Grinevka tomorrow as he had business in Moscow. We also had a letter from Misha Stakhovich about the duel between Lomonosov and Vadbolskii, which he considers, quite rightly, as murder, just like any other.[34] He again urged me to go to St Petersburg for an audience with the Tsar, to discuss with him the censors' attitude to

Lyovochka. He puts great faith in this visit. If only I could feel easy in my mind about the house and the children, if only I liked *The Kreutzer Sonata*, if only I believed in the future of Lyovochka's *literary* work – then I would go. But now I don't know where I'll find the energy and enthusiasm I'd need to exert my influence on the Tsar and his rather inflexible view of the world. I used to have a great sense of power over others, but no longer.

We went to Kozlovka to collect the mail, Lyovochka on horseback and Tanya, Masha, Ivan Aleksandrovich and I by sledge.

A heavenly moonlit night, the gleaming snow, the smooth road, frost, silence. It was 12° below freezing – it's always colder in the open countryside. On the way home, I thought with horror of life in the city. How could I ever live without this natural beauty, and the vast space and freedom one enjoys in the country.

February 16 Stakhovich's letter must have agitated me, as I keep dreaming of the Tsar and Tsarina and think constantly about visiting St Petersburg. Vanity plays a major part in all this – I shall not give in to it and shall not go. Lyovochka was going to Pirogovo with Masha, but stayed here instead. I know why, I can sense it from the way he has been behaving to me.

I have been busy all day, cutting out underwear and sewing on my machine. I am still reading *La Physiologie de l'amour moderne*, and am interested by this analysis of sexual love. I gave the children a music lesson; we are progressing slowly but progressing none the less. Andryusha is playing a Beethoven sonata and Misha one of Haydn's. Misha is incomparably more gifted. Masha, Andryusha and Aleksei Mitrofanovich taught the peasant girls and the housemaids in the 'little house' this evening. Masha is very pale and wretchedly thin; there's something so touching about her. Tanya is distracted and on edge, and is waiting for something to happen.

February 17 We had a letter from Lyova in Moscow saying that he had been ill, apparently with the same thing the children had here in Yasnaya. It may be something entirely different, of course. In any case, I still feel very worried, even though he writes in person, in a straightforward manner, and says it's not serious. Ilya is also in Moscow, selling clover. I wrote three letters, all bad, one to Lyova, one to my sister Tanya and one to M. Stakhovich. Nikolai Nikolaevich Gué came with his wife, and brought his latest painting, of Judas Iscariot gazing at a group of people withdrawing into the distance.[35] The moonlight, the subject-matter and the ideas are all splendid, but it is poorly executed and unsatisfying, more of a canvas than a real painting. It looks better under a strong light. I spent the day with Anna Petrovna Gué, and I was bored without my usual occupations. Lyovochka rode off to Tula but returned soon afterwards as he didn't find the

Davydovs in; he left a message with their servant inviting them to come and see the painting. He is cheerful, but in an agitated state. First he goes to Pirogovo, then to Tula; one moment he refuses meat soup again, next he demands oat coffee – being healthy evidently bores him. I personally find his fussiness worrying and unpleasant. He keeps saying he cannot write. Masha gave another evening class today; she was the only teacher there, and was exhausted.

February 18 Bad news from Lyova. A telegram came saying that the doctor had called and had diagnosed the same feverish condition he had 2 years ago. Then came a letter saying he was much better, but according to Ilya, who has just come from Moscow, Lyova has the same illness as we had here in Yasnaya. I hope to God it doesn't drag on. Tanya is going to Moscow tomorrow to see him, and I am going to Tula to discuss the division of the land with the Ovsyannikovo priest. All dreadfully dull and disagreeable.

Gué, Butkevich and I read aloud a story called 'The Clock', by some little-known writer.[36] Ilya and I had some unpleasant discussions about business and property. Masha is fading away; I am very worried, and feel so sorry for her. Monotonous days, filled with anxieties. I taught the children scripture today, which went badly. I then embroidered stripes on a blanket and talked to Anna Petrovna.

There's a frightful wind making an unearthly noise.

February 19 I went to Tula and saw nothing but shops, the notary, the priest, the streets, the District Administrative Offices. The priest and I had a discussion about the division of the land, but reached no conclusion. Ivan Aleksandrovich came too. Tanya went to Moscow to look after poor Lyova. I am very pleased for his sake, but I am not so worried now as I am sure he will soon be better. I love him so much and cannot bear to think of anything bad happening to him.

I did some embroidery, ate, and chattered away foolishly. Raevskii came to inspect the painting. I saw Davydov briefly on the street, which gave me great pleasure; of all the people I am especially fond of, he is quite the nicest; he is really quite *different* from the rest.

February 20 We have just taken the old Gués to Kozlovka. I had two letters today, one from Tanya and a pencilled note from Lyova saying that he was much better – 37° in the morning, and 38.6° at night. There was a telegram too. Misha worries me; during lessons he sometimes becomes quite hysterical, laughing and crying at the same time. But it always passes quickly. Could it be that I am working them too hard? Andryusha is lethargic too. Lyovochka, Masha and I went to Kozlovka; it was a warm and windy day. This evening, Lyovochka, the two Gués and I had a painful discussion about our marriages and how much husbands suffer when their wives don't understand them. Lyovochka said: 'You conceive a new idea, give birth, with all the agony of childbirth, to an entirely new spiritual philosophy and all they do is resent your suffering and completely refuse to understand!' I then said that while they were giving birth in their imagination to all these spiritual children, we were giving birth, in real pain, to real live children who had to be fed and educated, and needed someone to protect their property and their interests; one's life was much too full and complicated to give it all up for the sake of one's husband's spiritual vagaries, which one could never keep up with anyway, and could only regret. We both said much more besides in the same reproachful vein, yet in our hearts we both wanted the same thing – at least I always do: to stop opening up old wounds and to try to live together as friends. For any person – not only one's husband, whom one loves – will be treated kindly if they are truly good, in word and deed. It may be a slow business and take some time, but it cannot be otherwise if a person really means well.

February 23 We have Gorbunov here, and Annenkova has come too. Sasha is ill with a cough and a temperature; I am very worried about her and am taking special care of her. Annenkova said she had seen Tanya and Lyova in Moscow; he was quite well, although still afraid to leave town. We received a letter from Polonskii, together with a book of poems entitled *Evening Chimes*.[37] Lyovochka was sewing boots this evening, and complaining of a chill. There is a terrible wind outside, a real gale. I spent all day looking after Sasha and playing with Vanechka. I gave Andryusha and Misha a two-hour music lesson and worked on my blanket. I am persecuted by sinful thoughts; I have the strange sensation that they have nothing to do with my life or soul – all my life I have felt as though they were something quite independent of me, without the power to touch or harm me.

I was pleased with Misha today, for he played very well. We started practising the serenade from *Don Giovanni*, arranged for four hands, and he beamed with pleasure at the melody.

He and Andryusha are always whispering *secrets* to one another, which I find dreadfully upsetting. Maybe Borel has corrupted them – goodness only knows! Purity, sublime purity, this is what I value more highly than anything else in the world.

February 25 Lyovochka, Masha, Petya Raevskii and Gorbunov all set off for Kozlovka with Annenkova. Masha greatly enjoyed herself with Petya. He is not indifferent to her, and this delights her. Their youthful flirtation is a joy to watch.

Yesterday we had a rather gloomy letter from Lyova about his illness, and a slightly more cheerful one from Tanya. They are still afraid to travel.

Vanechka woke me up at about 4 in the morning with a rasping cough. Masha and I both leapt out of bed and gave him some hot seltzer water to drink, then we boiled up some water and turpentine, poured it into a basin, covered all our heads in a sheet and made him inhale the steam. This relieved the choking, but his temperature shot up to 40° and he started coughing again. I thought it would be a long illness but it was all over in twenty-four hours, and today he was singing 'The Lyre' in the drawing-room. Sasha is much better, too, and has got up.

I gave the children a scripture lesson and spent a long time explaining the notion of God to Misha. He has heard so many ideas denied – particularly concerning the Church – that he is now thoroughly confused, but I tried my best to explain the true meaning of the Church, as I understand it: an *assembly of the faithful*, a *repository* of holiness, contemplation and faith, not a mere ritual. Lyovochka is happy, calm and well. Our relations are friendly and straightforward – superficially: it does not go very deep. But it's certainly much better than it was at the beginning of the winter. The wind is still howling. Olga Ershova's little girl has died in the village. She was her mother's favourite, seven years old and such a darling. I feel dreadfully sorry for her; Lyovochka and Annenkova went to see her but I couldn't go.

February 28 The last few days have sped past. Vanechka was poorly, I worked, taught the children, read and was also ill. I am better today; but Vanechka still has a bad cough. Last night Tanya, Lyova and Sonya Mamonova arrived. Lyova is terribly thin but doesn't look ill. He is just highly-strung and has a weak constitution. Tanya is very lively and is looking much prettier. The three Raevskii brothers came from Kozlovka, and the children all went to meet them. The road is in a terrible condition. The weather is fine with a south wind and about 2° above freezing. Lyovochka drove to Tula, took Ivan Ivanovich Gorbunov to the station, then called on the Raevskiis. He is full of exuberance, but this exuberance is a little like the spring – there is something selfish and materialistic about it. He has not looked so healthy and cheerful for a long time, though. I do not know what he is working on at present as he doesn't like to talk about it. The news from Moscow is that the whole of Volume 13 has been banned.[38] I cannot think how it will all end, and still haven't decided what to do.

This evening Lyovochka read us a story by Nefedov, called 'Daughter of Eulampius'.[39] It was dreary and badly written. I am going to bed. I feel wretched and apathetic.

March 2 Yesterday was a lazy holiday. The children and the Raevskiis went to the Rovskie barracks for tea.[40] They took their things with them and played games after dinner. Vanechka was utterly adorable and tried seriously to understand all the games and to join in the fun. The dear, pale, clever little mite is particularly touching when he is with grown-ups, especially the Raevskiis. Seryozha and Ilya arrived here today with Tsurikov, Seryozha's colleague and their neighbour. Ilya invariably asks me for money, which is most unpleasant. He has such a frivolous attitude to money and lives such an extravagant life. Lyovochka is wretched; when I asked him why, he said his writing wasn't going well. And what's he writing about? About non-resistance.[41]

So it doesn't surprise me at all! Everybody, including him, is sick of the subject – it has been examined and discussed from every conceivable viewpoint. He wants to work on some *fictional* subject but doesn't know how to go about it. That wouldn't demand a lot of *philosophising*. Once he let his true creative powers pour forth he wouldn't be able to stop the flood, and he would then find all this non-resistance most awkward – he's terrified of letting it go, yet his soul yearns for it.

Lyova took great offence when Seryozha and I told him we thought he was looking unwell. I had wanted to humour him because I felt so sorry for him, but I hurt his feelings instead.

Today I finished Bourget's *Physiologie de l'amour moderne*, in French of course. It is clever but it bored me; it all centres on one thing and a life which is alien to me.

March 3 The last day of Shrovetide. Andryusha rode over to Kozlovka. Misha and Masha went by sledge to visit the patients at the Yasenki hospital, then to Telyatinki to visit a peasant who has been in bed for several months with a terrible wound. It is good that Masha is taking an interest in him and comforting him; that is genuine charity.[42] Lyova is slightly more cheerful, but I am so worried, for he looks so ill. Sonya Mamonova sang, and then Seryozha and Ilya played the piano. A lot of chatter with Tsurikov, and as usual I am now regretting that I talked so much. I sewed all day, since it was impossible to do anything else in this hubbub. It was a joy to see all 9 children gathered around the dinner-table.

March 6 Seryozha went to Nikolskoe and Masha took a sick peasant woman to Tula, and Sashka the village girl went too, to keep her company. Life has resumed its normal course. But it was lovely to see my nine children all sit down at the table with us old folk on Saturday and Sunday. I have been sitting at home all day doing various tasks. As I wanted some exercise after dinner I joined Lyovochka, who was playing with the little ones, Sasha, Vanechka and Kuzka. Every evening after dinner he puts them, one at a time, into an empty basket, closes it and drags it about the house. Then he stops and makes the one in the basket guess which room they are in. Lyova is all skin and bones and my hearts aches for him, although he is more cheerful now; he must go on a strict *kumis* diet this summer.

The others read a Russian story called 'Sunset',[43] and I read some Spinoza on my own. His interest in the Jewish people does not particularly excite me; we shall see what happens in the part which contains his *éthique*. I love any sort of abstract or general ideas, not *analyses* of this or that area of knowledge.[44]

Over tea we had a talk about food, luxury and the vegetarian diet which Lyovochka is always preaching. He said he had seen a vegetarian diet in some German magazine which recommended a dinner of bread and almonds. I am quite sure that the man who wrote that keeps to his diet in much the same way as Lyovochka practises the chastity he preaches in *The Kreutzer Sonata*.

March 8 The March issue of *The Week* arrived, containing Lyova's story.[45] This is the first time he has ever had anything published, and it appears under the name 'L. Lvov'. I haven't yet had time to re-read it, as the magazine has only just come and I have been in Tula all day. I am very excited by Lyova's writing, especially its future development. I do not know whether this is a chance thing arising from his impressionable nature, his new experiences in life and the novelty of it all, or whether it really is the beginning of a literary career. How wonderful it would be if writing *did* become his life's work, for then he would love life itself. His health and general appearance have much improved but he is still very thin.

Yet more business in Tula: negotiating the Grinevka mortgage, collecting the timber money from the factory, depositing Nurse's money at the Bank of the Nobility, shopping, and finally visits to the Zinovievs and the Davydovs. Expeditions are always exhausting. *Social* calls ought to be brief, an hour or so, no longer; otherwise they disrupt family life, time drags and everyone senses it.

March 10 Lyovochka was having his breakfast today when the letters and papers were delivered from Kozlovka. 'Still no news about Volume 13,' I said. 'What are you fussing about?' he said. 'No doubt I shall be forced to renounce the copyright on all the works in Volume 13.' 'Just wait until it comes out,' I said. 'Yes, of course,' he said, and left the room. I was seething at the thought that he was intending to deprive me of badly-needed money for my children, and I tried to think of a spiteful reply. So just as he was going out for his walk, I said to him: 'Go ahead, publish your renunciation. But I shall publish a statement immediately below it, saying I hope the publisher is sufficiently sensitive not to exploit the copyright which belongs to your children.' He then told me that *I* was being insensitive, but he spoke gently and I made no answer. If I really loved him, he went on, I myself would publish a statement that he had surrendered the copyright on his new works. He then left the room and I felt so sorry for him: all those material considerations seem so paltry compared to the pain of our estrangement. After dinner I apologised to him for speaking so maliciously and said I would not publish anything, for the idea of distressing him was unbearable to me. We both cried, and Vanechka, who was standing there, looked frightened. 'What's the matter, what's the matter?' he kept asking. 'Maman hurt Papa,' I told him, 'and now we're making it up.' This satisfied him, and he said, 'Ah!'

A cold and windy day. The drawing-master came; he asked me to lend him some money and I refused, for he is a very bad teacher.

My back and chest ache and I feel frightfully weak. Tanya, Masha, Vanya, Sonya Mamonova and even Misha all danced to the piano and the harmonium after dinner, and Sonya dressed up as a peasant woman. Aleksei Mitrofanovich went to Tula with his four pupils.

I read an extraordinarily sensitive and intelligent article on *The Kreutzer Sonata*, by M. de Vogué.[46] He says, amongst other things, that Tolstoy had taken his analysis to extremes ('*analyse creusante*'), and that this had killed all the personal and literary life of the work. This evening Lyovochka read us Potapenko's story 'The General's Daughter'[47] – not bad. I did some knitting, and Sonya and I cut out and sewed a jacket for Agafya Mikhailovna.

Lyovochka is correcting and rewriting his piece 'On Non-resistance', and Masha is copying it out for him. It is hard for him, as an *artist*, to write these weighty articles, but he cannot do his own artistic work.

March 11 Sonya Mamonova left and Vyacheslav[48] arrived. I am so happy to see him again – he reminds me of Mother, who loved him so much. Tanya drove with Sonya to Tula, and had dinner with the governor there. Lyovochka rode to Tula also, to discuss various peasant matters with Davydov and Zinoviev. I spent the whole day with my brother. This evening we read aloud.

March 12 We had a visit from an American from New York who edits a paper called *Harold**.[49] Also a 'dark one', called Nikiforov. Nothing but talk, endless talk. I have been informed by the Moscow censors that Volume 13 has been irrevocably banned. I shall go to St Petersburg to appeal. I dread the thought of it. I am sure I shall achieve nothing, and feel as if all my faith, strength and happiness have been wasted. But maybe the good Lord will come to my rescue. Snowing, wind and frost – just the weather for a ride in the sledge.

March 13 I went to Tula, where I saw nobody but business people. More

**New York Herald.*

negotiations with the priest. This evening I had a talk with the American. He needs information about Lyovochka for his newspaper, and I was able to help him, although I have learnt my lesson, and did not tell him too much. Vyacheslav left early this morning; I am sorry he had to tear himself away. I had a letter from Countess Aleksandra Andreevna Tolstaya, who said the Tsar did not receive ladies but that I should wait a week or ten days for him to reply.[50]

I am going to Moscow. I shall bring out the 12 volumes with an announcement that Volume 13 has been delayed.[51] I wish I did not have to move, what a worry this business is! But who else can do it?

Cold, wind, some snow. We all went out in the sledge again.

March 20 I spent the 15th and 16th in Moscow with Lyova. He is overjoyed because they are publishing another story of his, called 'Montecristo', in the April number of *The Source*. I am overjoyed too. I take such a delight and interest in his literary efforts and his success with the publishers, who seem to like these first efforts of his. When I was in Moscow I heard that Volume 13 had been banned in St Petersburg. (In Moscow only *The Kreutzer Sonata* was proscribed.) I shall have to go to St Petersburg and do all I possibly can to see the Tsar and vindicate Volume 13. I saw the Olsufievs and Vsevolozhskii in Moscow, which was a great pleasure; they are splendid young people. Dunaev was ill and strange. I brought Varya Nagornova back to Yasnaya with me. She is such a sweet, sunny creature, and everyone here was overjoyed to see her. She left today, and Tanya and Masha have just driven off with her in the new carriage to Tula, where they will spend the night at the Zinovievs and see the travelling art exhibition. I am going on Sunday with the boys. But I can think of nothing while the fate of Volume 13 is in the balance. In my mind I keep composing speeches and letters to the Tsar, imagining what will happen and thinking endlessly about what I should say. I am only waiting now for Aleksandra Tolstaya's letter telling me whether or not the Tsar will agree to receive me, and if so, when. Lyovochka says his mind is asleep, and his writing is going badly. He has a stomach-ache but looks cheerful.

Windy, thawing, 5° above zero, muddy. We have taken the carriage out.

March 21 I have been reading Spinoza and was deeply impressed by two of his arguments, the first about authority and laws: people should respect authority not out of fear of punishment, but because it represents an ideal, something to aspire to and inspire virtue, not just for each individual but for society as a whole. The other argument is about miracles: the uneducated (*'le vulgaire'*) see the hand of God only in what lies *beyond* the laws of nature and probability, and simply do not see God in the whole of Nature and Creation. This is why they expect miracles – i.e. something that lies beyond nature.

The girls spent the night in Tula at the Davydovs', saw last year's art exhibition and returned home chilled to the bone. There's a terrible wind, a real blizzard, but only one degree of frost and it's thawing. I had another nasty scene with Andryusha. During his music lesson he never knows what he is meant to be *doing*, and knows everything that is going on around him; he rudely jerks his hand when I touch his arm, turns his head away, and so on and so forth. I put up with this as long as I can, then start to seethe, and end up either shouting at him or smacking his hand, and get terribly upset.

Tanya had a letter from Lyova. Lyovochka is in an extraordinarily sweet, cheerful, affectionate mood at the moment – for the usual reason, alas. If only the people who read *The Kreutzer Sonata* so reverently had an inkling of the voluptuous life he leads, and realised it was only this that made him happy and good-natured, then they would cast this deity from the pedestal where they have placed him! Yet I love him when he is kind and normal and full of human weaknesses. One should not be an animal, but nor should one preach virtues one does not have.

March 22 I was busy all day measuring and sewing new clothes for the children. Lyovochka and I played duets after dinner; later on, instead of playing patience he wound some unbleached balls of cotton for me, which he found highly entertaining. I wrote a letter to Sonya. I am ill and tired.

March 23 I felt spring in the air for the first time today. Although it was still freezing, there was a bright sunset, the birds sang and the trunks of the young birch trees at Chepyzh looked particularly beautiful and spring-like. After dinner I took Andryusha and Sasha out and we cleared the snow from the stone terrace in front of the house. Lyovochka rode off to Tula, saw nobody but Davydov and returned here at eight in the evening. He is well and happy. He was having breakfast this morning while I was working in the drawing-room. 'Listen,' he said, 'I've just had such a silly thought: "*Quand est-ce qu'on se porte bien? – Quand on a une bonne et qu'on ne lui donne pas du thé, c'est à dire qu'on a une bonne sans thé (bonne santé)*"'* He had been eating a chocolate pudding and I had told him the chocolate was harmless, *santé* not vanilla, and that was what put the pun in his mind.

I gave the children a music lesson, and played a Bach gavotte as a duet arranged for children. Petya Raevskii has come. Still no news from St Petersburg, and I am sick with uncertainty and anticipation.

March 24 I wrote 3 letters this morning, 2 in reply to Lyova and Dunaev, and one to Countess Aleksandra Tolstaya; I thought I had better make some more enquiries, as the suspense has been tormenting me. Lyova's letter

*Untranslatable French pun: 'When does one feel well?' 'When one has a nanny and does not give her tea, then one is well.'

was long and detailed. I am glad he is not breaking off relations with his family, and writes so openly about himself. After I had finished I sat down on my own and read a splendid article in the *Russian Gazette* called 'Schopenhauer's Ideas on Writing'.[52] He divides writers into 3 categories: 'those who take ideas directly from other people's books; those who decide what they are going to say only *after* they have sat down to write; and lastly those who give a great deal of thought to what they are going to write, and only do so when they have a lot of ideas. Those writers are very rare.' How wise that is.

The children all went over to the Rovskie barracks for tea. Davydov arrived here at about 3 with his daughter and little Buchman, and after dinner we went for a walk. We looked at the cows and pigs, went to the threshing-floor and clambered over the straw. When we got back I played piano duets with Davydov, then we all played games and had a very lively evening. Relations with Lyovochka are friendly and simple. He is well; he went for a walk and wrote a little of his article. If only he would finish it and get it off his hands! 2° above freezing, with a light frost towards evening. Still a lot of snow everywhere, especially in the wood.

March 27 On the 25th I went to Tula with Misha and Andryusha, and we visited the Wanderers' art exhibition. I always love looking at paintings, but there were few good ones, apart from some lovely landscapes by Volkov and Shishkin.[53] Afterwards we visited the pastry-cook's, the educational suppliers, and the Raevskiis. Ivan Ivanovich and Elena Pavlovna were going off to have dinner with Sofia Dmitrievna Sverbeeva, and I went with them. The six boys all dined alone. There was a spare concert-ticket at the Sverbeevs, so I went with one of their dear girls, Lyuba, and Raevskii collected all the boys and came along too. The concert and reading were undistinguished, as one would expect in the provinces, but I was not bored, just tired. The children loved it, though.

Afterwards I went back to stay the night with the Davydovs, and the children stayed at the Raevskiis'. Next morning they returned home, and I got up early and I went to town to attend to my business. Just as I was walking down Kievskaya Street who should I meet but Ilyusha. I was very surprised to see him, and asked if he would come with me to inspect a barouche that was for sale. It was a long, tedious business. Afterwards I visited the senior notary to collect the mortgage documents, then went home with Ilya. He had come to find out about the auction of the estate and to ask me for 35,000 rubles, which I refused him. This caused some unpleasantness, but it did not last long. I had gone into Tanya's room to sit with the children after dinner, when Ilya suddenly shouted: 'Well, I shan't give you that *kumis* mare then!' I lost my temper. 'I shan't ask you for it anyway – I'll just ask the bailiff!' I said. At that he too lost his temper. 'But I am the bailiff here!' he says. 'Well, I am the estate-manager here,' say I. I

4 Above, left to right: Sofia Tolstaya, Lev Tolstoy, Sofia's younger brother Stepan Behrs, Sofia's daughter Maria, and Maria Petrovna Behrs, Stepan's wife, 1887

5 Below: Peasant women gathering apples in the Tolstoys' orchard at Yasnaya Polyana, 1888

6 Above left: Sofia Tolstaya with her children Tatiana and Sergei, 1866

7 Above right: Ivan Tolstoy (Vanechka), the Tolstoys' youngest child, photographed in 1893 in Moscow by the firm of Scherer and Nabholz

8 Below: Sofia Tolstaya with her younger children. Left to right, Mikhail (Misha), Andrei (Andryusha), Aleksandra (Sasha), and Ivan (Vanechka).

don't know whether it was because I was tired, or whether he had driven me to exasperation with his talk of money and property, but I became absolutely furious with him. 'You've got to the point where you even grudge your father a *kumis* mare – I can't think why you came! You can go to the devil – you torment me!' And I slammed the door and went out. I felt so sick and ashamed, and so angry with my son – it was quite horrible.

Then for the first time we had a serious discussion about it all, and agreed that things couldn't go on like this, and that we would have to divide up the property between all of us. I am delighted by the idea, but agree only on condition that the children draw lots; I don't expect Ilya will accept this, as he wants to hold on to Nikolskoe and Grinevka, but I will not deprive my defenceless little ones. It is really only Ilya who is being so difficult. He is terribly selfish and very greedy, maybe because he already has a family of his own. The other children are all very sensitive, and will agree to anything. Lyovochka has always had a special fondness for Ilya and will never see his faults, and this time too he was agreeing to all his demands. I am afraid there will be no end of unpleasantness. Fortunately, though, Grinevka is in my name, and if the others won't agree to draw lots, I shall refuse to hand over Grinevka and Ovsyannikovo. I simply will not allow my little ones to be slighted. Lyovochka finds all these discussions a great trial, but they are ten times worse for me, as it is I who have to defend the younger children against the older ones. Then Tanya always takes Ilya's side, which distresses me. Tomorrow I am going to St Petersburg. I am dreading it, for I know I shall not succeed. The very thought terrifies me. It is warmer now, although windy. Today it was 7° above freezing.

April 22 I haven't written my diary for almost a month. It has been a particularly interesting and eventful month, but it's always the same: I had so little free time, my nerves were so strained and I had to write so many letters home, that I didn't manage to write my diary.

Today is the second day of Easter and the second warm summery day of the year. In just two days all the bushes and trees have changed from brown to a soft green, and for the first time this morning I heard a nightingale singing at the top of its voice. Yesterday evening he was just tuning up.

I got back from St Petersburg early on Palm Sunday. I was not well, and for the first part of Holy Week I rested in bed in the peace of our family circle, and gave the children a few lessons. Then we resumed our discussions about dividing the property, with the children, especially Ilya, all grabbing for the biggest bits. This is how we eventually decided to divide it: Ilya will have Grinevka and part of Nikolskoe, Seryozha will have another part of Nikolskoe, and either Tanya or Masha will have the third and largest part, with responsibility for paying off its debts. Lyova will have the house in Moscow and the Bobrov estate in Samara, either Tanya or Masha will have Ovsyannikovo and 40,000 rubles, and Andryusha, Misha and Sasha will each have 2,000 *desyatins* in the Samara region. Vanechka and I will have Yasnaya Polyana. At first I insisted that we draw lots for everything, but Lev Nikolaevich and the children protested so I had to agree with them. The Samara land is good for the children since it will gain in value, and besides there is nothing to steal, chop down or damage there, and it is all run by the same hands. Vanechka and I were given Yasnaya because his father must not be moved; and where I am, Lev Nikolaevich must be, and Vanechka too.[54]

Ilya was here for three days, and brought Tsurikov and Naryshkin with him. Seryozha is still here, and so is Lyova. Seryozha has grown very distant from his family, and again says that he wants to serve as a *zemstvo* official in Moscow,[55] and that he is bored with Nikolskoe, which is hardly surprising, considering he is on his own there. Lyova is leaving today, as he has to prepare for an examination in Moscow. He is still very thin, but emotionally well. He had his story 'Montecristo' published in the April issue of *The Source*, and was paid 26 rubles for it. His story 'Love' was published in the March issue of *The Week*, and they paid him 65 rubles for that. This is the first money he has earned! 'Montecristo' has been praised by everyone, including Lyovochka.

Over Holy Week I made Andryusha and Misha fast, although I could not do so myself. They were calm and natural about it, like the common people. We had a service performed here on Saturday, at the request of all the servants. Lyovochka was out. When I asked him that morning if he would find it at all unpleasant if we held a service in the drawing-room, he said, 'Not a bit'.

Yesterday, after breakfast, I ordered the new carriage to be brought round and gathered up all the children, Lydia, Nurse, Tanya, Masha and both little girls (the two Sashkas). Then we all drove off down the road to pick morels at Zaseka. I stayed with Vanechka and Sasha all the time. Although I saw almost no morels because I'm so shortsighted, I love the forest, the wild profusion of nature in spring and the silence in the depths of the trees, and I enjoyed myself enormously. Lyova and Andryusha went fishing, but they didn't get so much as a bite and Lyova broke his rod. Today and yesterday the children were playing *pas de géant* in the meadow in front of the house and romping about in front of the byre.

Yesterday evening our boys played games with the village children. It's strange the way these lads of 11 and 13 already treat the village girls as *girls*, no longer as friends. How sad and hateful that is!

Dunaev is staying here. Lyovochka is somewhat melancholy, and when I asked him why, he said, 'My writing isn't going well.'[56] But then of course there's my trip to St Petersburg, the children's fast and the service we held here – all this goes against his *faith* and makes him wretched. My attitude to it all is rather odd. I cannot help feeling enormously sympathetic to all these moral rules which Lyovochka lays down for himself and others. But I cannot possibly see how to carry them out in practice. I cannot stop half-way – it is not in my nature to do that. Yet I haven't the strength to go on to the end.

Quite apart from all this, the children are growing up without any religious training. Children need *forms*, as do the common people, to express and contain their relationship with God. This is what the Church is for. And only those with the most lofty and abstract of faiths can separate themselves from it, for without it we feel nothing but the most hopeless emptiness.

I have just seen Lyova off to Moscow. Tanya and Vanechka accompanied him as far as Yasenki.

Now I shall try to recollect and faithfully record my visit to St Petersburg in connection with the banned Volume 13 of the *Complete Collected Works*, and the audience I had with the Tsar on April 13, 1891.

My visit to St Petersburg

I left Yasnaya Polyana on the night of March 28–29, and arrived in Moscow the following morning. I sat and talked to Lyova for a while, then went off to the State Bank to convert my 5 per cent bonds to 4 per cent ones. By 4 that afternoon I was at Nikolaev Station. I found myself a very comfortable second-class compartment which I shared with one other lady, a landowner from Mogilyov whose husband was marshal of the local nobility. We had a very pleasant journey together. When I arrived at the Kuzminskiis' house they were just getting up. Sasha was away on a tour of inspection in the Baltic provinces, Tanya was getting dressed and Masha and the children were receiving the Eucharist. Tanya and I were overjoyed to see one another, and she put me in her bedroom. We sat down at once and wrote a note to Misha Stakhovich. When he arrived he told me that he had already written asking me to attend an audience with the Tsar, since Elena Grigorevna Sheremeteva (née Stroganova), the cousin of the Tsar and the daughter of Maria Nikolaevna (Lichtenburgskaya), had managed to persuade him to receive me. The reason they gave for my application to see the Tsar was that I wanted him to be personally responsible for censoring Lev Nikolaevich's works. M. Stakhovich's letter to me was either lost or he did not write it at all. He is not a very straightforward person, so I have my doubts. He showed me the letter to the Tsar which he had sketched out. I did not like it at all, but took it all the same. I should add, by way of explanation, that Sheremeteva had arranged my audience with the Tsar at the request of Zosya Stakhovich, whom she is very fond of. The morning after my arrival I called on Nikolai Nikolaevich Strakhov in his apartment, which is completely filled with the marvellous library he has collected. He was surprised and delighted to see me, and we at once sat down to discuss my letter and my forthcoming discussion with the Tsar.

He did not like Stakhovich's letter any more than I did and he drafted another version, which was sent round at 5 that evening. But I did not like this one any better, so I decided to write a third version myself, based on the other two. My brother Vyacheslav arrived and made the final corrections to my letter, and it was his version that we sent, on March 31. Here is the text of the letter:

Your Imperial Majesty,
I make so bold as to enquire very humbly about the audience Your Majesty has so graciously granted to me in order that I may bring to Your Majesty's notice my personal petition on behalf of my husband, Count L. N. Tolstoy. Your Majesty's gracious attention gives me the opportunity to specify the conditions under which my husband would be able to return to his former artistic and literary endeavours, and to point out that some of the very grave accusations made against his work have been unfounded, and have stolen the last ounce of spiritual strength from a Russian writer who is already losing his health, but who might possibly still bring some glory to his country with his writings.

Your Imperial Majesty's faithful subject.

Countess Sofia Tolstaya.

March 31, 1891

As I was not sure how to send this letter, my sister Tanya made enquiries on the telephone of a good friend of hers called Skalkovskii, who occupies a senior position in the Post Office, and the following morning Skalkovskii sent his messenger round with a note assuring me that my letter would be delivered to the Tsar that evening in Gatchina. The letter arrived there on April 1. On the same day Grand Duchess Olga Fyodorovna, who was in Kharkov on her way to the Crimea, died of pleurisy and a heart attack. Her death, together with the marriage of her son Mikhail Mikhailovich to Countess Merenberg without permission either from the Tsar or from his parents, was the talk of St Petersburg. People could think of nothing else. Tradition and etiquette demanded a complete cessation of activity at the court for nine days, and the entire royal family went into full mourning. We stood at the window of the Kuzminskiis' apartment and watched as the Grand Duchess's coffin was borne along the Nevskii Prospect on its way from the station to the Peter and Paul fortress. The Tsar and Mikhail Mikhailovich went straight to the graveside. The soldiers and priests were inseparable (there was a particularly large number of the latter). For instance, when they stopped in front of the Church of the Annunciation to read the litany and the prayer they *beat the drum* and played a strange sort of whistling music. I have never heard anything like it. It reminded me of some pagan ceremony.

As I wanted to find out how best to address the Tsar, and plead with him for Volume 13, I decided to visit Feokistov at the censorship committee, to find out why it had been suppressed. My sister Tanya accompanied me there. We went in, and when we had greeted Feokistov (whom I had first met in Moscow as a young man, just after he had deceived his mother and eloped with his beautiful wife), I asked him why the *whole* of Volume 13 had been banned. He responded in a cold mechanical fashion by opening up some book and reading from it in a monotonous voice: 'The book *On Life* is banned by the Church censors on the orders of the Holy Synod. The article "What Then Must We Do?" is banned by the Police Department. And *The Kreutzer Sonata* is banned on the orders of the Tsar.' I then pointed out indignantly that I had already had several chapters from *On Life* published in *The Week*,[57] and there had been no complaints from the censors then. And it was they themselves who had passed some chapters of 'What Then Must We Do?', which were published in Volume 12. That left only *The Kreutzer Sonata*, and I was hoping to obtain the Tsar's permission to publish that.

Feokistov was very embarrassed to discover that *On Life* and 'What Then Must We Do?' had already been published in abridged forms. He called for his secretary, ordered him to look into the matter and promised me a reply in two days' time. I then complained about the careless and contemptuous way in which a great writer like Lev Nikolaevich Tolstoy had been treated by the censors. They obviously did not even bother to read the *contents* page, and had brought both the author and me a great deal of trouble and grief. Feokistov realised he had done something stupid, and on April 3 he brought me Volume 13 in person and told me it had been passed for publication.

Meanwhile the *New Times*[58] newspaper published the repertoire of the plays being performed that season at the imperial theatres, and these included *The Fruits of Enlightenment*, by L. N. Tolstoy. Knowing that the play had been banned from the imperial theatres, I visited the Theatre Committee to find out what was happening. It turned out to be true. I asked them whether they had been in communication with the author about it or asked him what his wishes were, and they said they had not. I was furious, and told the official there that this was a tactless and discourteous way to treat an author. I also asked him, amongst other things, if he would kindly negotiate with *me* in future, not with the author. The following day I had a visit from the producer, who handed me a piece of paper listing various conditions. There were a vast amount of obligations I was to take on: for instance, I was to *guarantee* that his plays would not be performed at private theatres, *indemnify* them with a fine of 2,000 rubles if it was, and so on and so forth. I was outraged by all these conditions, and next morning I set off again to the Theatre Committee and told the official I was not prepared to accept *any* of their terms, they could stop the production – nothing would make me sign. He told me I should say that to the director, so I ordered them to announce me to the director, Vsevolozhskii. He refused to see me. 'Well, this is a peculiar state of affairs you have here – one can see the Tsar, but the director, whose *job* it is to receive people, refuses to see one.' He was very disconcerted by my high and mighty manner and went off to announce me. 'You boors,' I kept saying to myself. 'One has to shout at people like you.' Vsevolozhskii received me in a somewhat overfamiliar manner and introduced me to his assistant, a person named Pogozhev. 'So you don't want to give us your plays, eh, Countess?' he said. 'I merely do not want to take on a lot of obligations which I cannot fulfil,' I replied. 'But all that's just a formality!' he said. 'It may be a formality for someone', I said. 'But for me it is a matter of conscience and I shall sign nothing.' At that point Pogozhev intervened: 'If you don't sign those conditions you will receive only 5 per cent of the gross takings, instead of 10 per cent.' At that I turned on him in a fury: 'I do not live on Merchants' Row and am not accustomed to haggling with shopkeepers, so kindly leave aside all questions of money since they do not interest me, or, more importantly, the Count. And I shall not give you that play.' I then turned to Vsevolozhskii and said: 'What is this? How is it that a person of our circle like you does not understand that one cannot treat Lev Nikolaevich as one would treat a music-hall writer? We must all take his wishes into account, especially I, as his wife and a respectable woman, and that is why I cannot sign your conditions or undertake that his plays will *never* be performed on a private stage. It is Lev Nikolaevich's greatest joy that he hasn't made a single kopeck out of this play so far, and this undertaking here would deprive people of the right to perform it at charity benefits . . . ' I was becoming so heated that Vsevolozhskii eventually suggested deleting several of the conditions. But I would not agree to that either, so he proposed that I write an unofficial letter instead, giving the Imperial Theatre the right to perform the play against 10 per cent of the gross takings. This I did.

My son Seryozha suggested that this money be donated to the Empress Maria's Charitable Institutions. I should have been delighted to do this, but I had to think of my 9 children who need the money so badly – where else would I find it for them?

I profited from my free time in the capital to visit two art exhibitions, the Wanderers' and the Academy.[59] I don't know if I was in a bad temper or just tired, but neither of them made a great impression on me. Afterwards I went shopping with Tanya, sewed my dress and sat with my family and their guests. I saw Countess Aleksandra Andreevna Tolstaya three times, which was a great pleasure. I had long talks with her about religion, Lyovochka, the children and my position in the family, and her attitude to me was so affectionate and sympathetic. I dined once with the Stakhoviches, once with the Mengdens, once with the Trokhimovskiis, once with the

Auerbachs and once with Countess Aleksandra Andreevna. The rest of the time I stayed at home. They tried to tempt me to go to the theatre and see Duse, the celebrated Italian actress, but my nerves were shattered, and besides I could not afford it. All the time I was there I never slept more than five hours a night.

Eventually, on Friday the 12th, I could wait no longer for my audience with the Tsar. Holy Week was approaching, I was feeling homesick, and my nervous condition was growing worse: I decided to return home that Sunday. I dressed and drove over to Sheremeteva to thank her for her pains and tell her I could not wait any longer. But she had Princess Mecklenburg with her, and thinking that this Countess Sofia Tolstaya must be the younger sister of Aleksandra Andreevna, she did not receive me. I then went on to visit Zosya Stakhovich to tell her that I was leaving on Sunday and ask her to send a message to Sheremeteva so that she might inform the Tsar. From there I went on to see Aleksandra Andreevna to take my leave of her.

At eleven that evening I had just gone to bed when a note arrived from Zosya informing me that the Tsar had sent me an invitation, through Sheremeteva, to see him at 11.30 the following morning at the Anichkov Palace.

My first feeling was of enormous relief, that I could go home the next day. I then started packing, wrote various notes and sent a message to Mme Auerbach asking her to send round a carriage and servant for me. I eventually got to bed at 3 in the morning, feeling very agitated. I was quite unable to sleep and kept brooding and repeating all the things I was going to say to the Tsar.

Early that morning I checked that I had paid all my bills, asked Tanya to settle the rest for me, got dressed and sat waiting for the time when I had to leave. I had on a black mourning dress I'd made myself, a veil and a black lace hat. At a quarter to eleven I set off. My heart was pounding as we approached the Anichkov Palace. I was saluted at the gates, then at the porch, and I bowed back. I entered the ante-chamber and asked the doorkeeper whether the Tsar had instructed him to receive Countess Tolstaya. No, he said. He then asked someone else, and got the same reply. My heart sank. Then they summoned the Tsar's footman. A handsome young man appeared, wearing a bright red and gold uniform and a huge three-cornered hat. 'Do you have instructions from the Tsar to receive Countess Tolstaya?' I asked him. 'I should think so, Your Excellency!' he said. 'The Tsar has just returned from church and has been asking about you.' (The Tsar had apparently been at the christening of Grand Duchess Elizaveta Fyodorovna who has just converted to Orthodoxy.) The footman then ran up a steep stairway, covered in an ugly bright green carpet, and I followed him up. But I had not realised how fast I was running, and when he left me with a deep bow at the reception-room my heart was pounding so wildly that I thought I should die. I was in a terrible state. The first thought that came into my head was that this business was not worth dying for. I imagined the footman coming back to summon me to the Tsar and finding my lifeless body. I should be unable to say a word, at any rate; my heart was beating so violently that it was literally impossible for me to breathe, speak or cry out. I sat down and longed to ask for a glass of water, but could not. Then I remembered that the thing to do when a horse has been driven too hard is to lead it about quietly for a while until it recovers. So I got up from the sofa and took a few paces around the room. That did not make it any better though, so I discreetly loosened my stays and sat down again, massaging my chest and thinking about the children. How would they take the news of my death, I wondered. Fortunately the Tsar had not been informed of my arrival and had received someone else before me. So I had time to rest and get my breath back, and I had fully recovered by the time the footman returned, and said: 'His Majesty begs Her Excellency the Countess Tolstaya to enter.' I followed him into the Tsar's study and he bowed and left. The Tsar came to the door to meet me and shake my hand, and I curtseyed slightly.

'Do forgive me, Countess, for keeping you waiting for so long,' he said. 'It was impossible for me to receive you earlier.'

I replied: 'I am deeply grateful to Your Majesty for doing me the honour of receiving me.'

Then the Tsar began to talk about my husband (I do not remember his exact words), and asked me the precise nature of my request. I then spoke, in a quiet but firm voice:

'Your Majesty, I have recently observed that my husband seems disposed to resume his literary endeavours. Only the other day he was saying to me: "I have moved so far beyond these philosophical and religious works now that I think I might start on some literary work – I have in mind something rather similar to *War and Peace*, in form and content." Yet with every day that passes the prejudice against him grows stronger. Volume 13 was banned, for instance, although it has now been decided to pass it. His play *The Fruits of Enlightenment* was banned, then the order was given for it to be performed on the Imperial stage. *The Kreutzer Sonata* was banned . . . '

'Surely, though, you would not give a book like that to your children to read?' the Tsar said.

I said: 'This story has unfortunately taken a rather extreme form, but the fundamental idea is that the ideal is always unattainable. If the ideal is total chastity, then people can be pure only in marriage.'

I also recall that when I told the Tsar that Lev Nikolaevich seemed disposed to write *literary* works again, he said: 'Ah, how good that would be! What a very great writer he is!'

After defining what I took to be the main point of *The Kreutzer Sonata*, I went on to say: 'It would make me so happy if the ban was lifted from *The Kreutzer Sonata* in the *Complete Collected Works*. That would be clear evidence of a gracious attitude to Lev Nikolaevich. And who knows, it might even encourage his work.'

To this the Tsar replied: 'Yes I think it might very well be included in the *Complete Works*. Not everyone can afford to buy it, after all, and it will not have a very wide circulation.'

On two separate occasions in the conversation (I don't remember exactly when), the Tsar regretted that Lev Nikolaevich had left the Church. 'There are so many heresies springing up amongst the simple people, which are having a very harmful effect on them,' he said.

To this I replied: 'I can assure Your Majesty that my husband has never preached any philosophy either to the people or to anyone else. He has never mentioned his beliefs to the peasants and not only does he not distribute the texts of his manuscripts to other people, he is actually in despair when other people distribute them. For instance, there was a certain young man who stole a manuscript from my husband's file, copied various pages out of his diary and two years later had them lithographed and distributed.' (Although I did not mention him by name, I was of course referring to Novoselov and the 'Nikolai Palkin' affair.[60])

The Tsar was astounded. 'Why that's disgraceful, absolutely disgraceful! People should be able to write whatever they want in their diaries – it's a wicked thing to do, to steal someone's manuscript!'

The Tsar is rather shy and speaks in a pleasant melodious voice. His eyes are warm and kind, and he has a friendly bashful smile. He is very tall and somewhat stout, but he is sturdily built and looks strong. He is almost completely bald, and his head is very narrow at the temples, as though it had been squeezed in at the top. He reminded me a little of Vladimir Grigorevich Chertkov, especially his voice and manner of speaking.

The Tsar then asked me how the children felt about their father's teachings. I replied that they could not but feel the greatest respect for the lofty moral standards which their father preached, but that I considered it important for them to be educated in the faith of the Church. I had fasted with them over August, I said, but in Tula, not the village, as several of our priests, far from being our spiritual fathers, were in fact police spies who had been sending in false reports about us.

'Yes, I have heard about that,' the Tsar said. Then I told him that my eldest son was a leading *zemstvo* official, my second was married and had his own home, my third was a student, and the others still lived at home. Oh, and I forgot to note that when we were discussing *The Kreutzer Sonata* the Tsar said, 'Could your husband not alter it a little?'

I said: 'No, Your Majesty. He can never make any corrections to his works, and besides, he says that he has grown to hate this story and cannot bear its name to be mentioned.'

The Tsar then asked: 'And do you see much of Chertkov, the son of Grigorii Ivanovich and Elizaveta Ivanovna? It seems your husband has completely converted him.'

I was quite unprepared for this question and for a moment I was at a loss for words. But I soon regained my composure. 'We have not seen Chertkov for more than two years now,' I said. 'He has a sick wife, whom he cannot leave. His relations with my husband were not initially based on religion but on other matters. Seeing how many stupid and immoral books were being published for popular consumption, my husband gave Chertkov the idea of transforming this popular literature and giving it a moral and educational direction. My husband wrote several stories for the people which sold millions of copies, but were then suddenly found to be harmful and not sufficiently pious, and were also banned. Besides this they published a number of scientific, philosophical and historical books. It was a very successful venture and doing very well – but this too has been persecuted by the authorities.'[61]

The Tsar said nothing to this, and finally I made so bold as to add: 'Your Majesty, if my husband *should* start writing works of fiction again, and I should publish them, it would be a very great pleasure for me to know that the final verdict on his work rested with Your Majesty in person.'

To this the Tsar replied: 'I should be most happy to do so. Send his works directly to me for my perusal.'

I cannot remember now whether anything more was said. I think I have written down everything. I do remember, though, that at the end he said: 'Rest assured, everything will be for the best. I am so happy to have met you.' And he stood up and gave me his hand.

I curtseyed again, and said: 'I am so sorry that I did not ask to be presented to the Empress. I was told she was not well.'

'No, the Empress is quite well today and will receive you. I shall give orders for you to be announced,' he said.

I then turned to go. The Tsar stood in the doorway leading to the little room next to his study and took his leave of me. 'Will you be staying in St Petersburg for a while?' he asked.

'No, Your Majesty, I am leaving today.'

'So soon? Why is that?'

'One of my children is sick.'

'Really? What is the matter?'

'Chicken-pox.'

'Well, that's not dangerous, so long as he doesn't catch a chill.'

'Yes, Your Majesty, I am afraid they might let him catch a chill in this cold weather if I am not there.'

The Tsar shook my hand very warmly, then I bowed yet again and went out.

I went back to the reception-room, which was upholstered in red satin, with a statue of a woman in the middle, two statues of boys at the sides, and two pier-glasses in the arches separating this room from the main hall. Everywhere there was a profusion of plants and flowers. I shall never forget that mass of bright-red azaleas which I had looked at when I thought I was dying. Outside the window there was a desolate view of a cobbled courtyard with two waiting carriages and some soldiers on parade.

An elderly footman, who looked and spoke like a foreigner, was standing at the door of the Tsarina's reception-room. On the other side stood a Negro in national costume. There were also a number of Negroes, three I believe, standing by the door of the Tsar's study. I asked the footman to announce me to the Tsarina, telling them that the Tsar himself had authorised it. He told me that the Empress was with another lady at the moment, but that he would announce me the moment she left.

I waited for fifteen to twenty minutes. The lady came out, the footman told me that the Tsar had spoken to the Empress and told her that I wanted to be presented to her, and I went in.

The Empress, a slim woman, quick and light on her feet, came to meet me. She had a lovely complexion, and her beautiful chestnut-coloured hair was wonderfully neatly arranged, as though glued to her head. She was neither very tall nor very short, and was wearing a high-necked, narrow-waisted black woollen dress, very narrow at the arms. She gave me her hand, and like the Emperor, immediately invited me to sit down. Her voice was loud and rather guttural.

'*Je vous ai déjà vu une fois, n'est-ce pas?*' she said.

'*J'ai eu le bonheur d'être présentée à votre majesté il y a quelques années à l'Institut St Nicolas, chez Mme Shostag,*' I replied.

'*Ah, certainement, et votre fille aussi. Dites-moi, est-ce vrai qu'on vole les manuscrits du comte, qu'on les imprime sans lui demander la permission? Mais c'est une horreur, c'est très mal, c'est impossible.*'

'*C'est vrai, votre majesté, et c'est bien triste. Mais que faire?*'*

Then the Empress asked me how many children I had and what they all did. I said I was happy to hear that her son, Georgii Aleksandrovich, was better, and told her that I had suffered for her, knowing how hard it must have been for her to be separated from her two sons when she knew one of them was so ill. She said that he was fully recovered now; he had had pneumonia, the illness had been neglected, he had not looked after himself properly, and she had been extremely worried. I expressed my regret that I

*'I have already met you once before, I believe?'

'I had the pleasure of being presented to Your Majesty several years ago at the Institute of St Nicholas, in Mme Shostag's house.'

'Ah yes, of course, and your daughter too. Now do tell me, is it really true that people have stolen manuscripts from the Count and published them without his permission? But that is horrifying – what a frightful thing to do!'

'It is indeed true, Your Majesty, and it is very sad. But what can one do?'

had never met any of her children, and the Empress replied that they were all in Gatchina at present.

'*Ils sont tous si heureux, si bien portants*,' she said. '*Je tiens qui'ils aient des souvenirs heureux de leur enfance*.'

I said: '*Dans une famille comme celle de sa majesté, tout le monde doit se sentir heureux*.'

The Empress went on: '*Ce petit Michel aux joues roses, il joue une grande fille à 16 ans*.'*

Then the Empress stood up, gave me her hand and warmly took her leave of me. '*Je suis très contente de vous avoir revue encore une fois*,' she said.†

I bowed and went out.

The Auerbachs' carriage was waiting to take me back to the Kuzminskiis'. I got back and raced up four flights of stairs, my feet scarcely touching the ground.

My sister Tanya greeted me, then Zosya, Manya and Misha Stakhovich, Erdeli, Aleksandr Mikhailovich and all the Kuzminskii children, and made me tell them everything. They were delighted for me and I was congratulated on all sides. I then sent two telegrams, one to Lyova in Moscow and one to the family at home, had lunch, then set off to catch the 3 o'clock train. They all took me to the station. When I saw Tanya's careworn face and realised all the trouble I'd caused her and all the sympathy she'd given me, I felt dreadfully sorry to be leaving her.

There was one thing I forgot to mention in my discussion with the Tsar. In connection with his question about Lev Nikolaevich's influence on the common people, he enquired about his young converts. I told him that practically all these young people had been on a false and sinful political path, and that it was thanks to Lev Nikolaevich that they had abandoned this and turned to non-resistance, universal love and the cultivation of the earth. So that even if they were still misguided, they were now at least on the side of order.

The train arrived at the Kursk Station in Moscow on Sunday, April 14, and I was met there by Lyova, Dmitrii Alekseevich Dyakov and Dunaev. We had lunch, and I again recounted my adventures to them. Lyova and Dmitrii Alekseevich listened with great interest. On the platform, just as the train was leaving, I met Nadya Zinovieva, who was getting into the same carriage. She invited us into her family compartment and Lyova, Nadya and I had a cheerful journey home with two ladies, mother and daughter, landowners from Kharkov. The daughter was in tears at first, as she had just parted from her fiancé.

*'They are all so happy and healthy – I think they will have happy memories of their childhood.'
'Anyone would consider themselves happy in a family like Your Majesty's.'
'My little rosy-cheeked Michel now behaves like a big girl of sixteen.'

†'I am very happy to have met you once again.'

Tanya and the younger children welcomed us home. Lyovochka had gone to Chepyzh and then gone out to the park to wait for me. I got back before him, though, and it was a long time before he returned. Masha was in her room. I was delighted to be home again, but Lyovochka was displeased about my adventure and my meeting with the Tsar. He said we had now taken on all sorts of responsibilities which we couldn't possibly fulfil. He and the Tsar had managed to ignore each other up to now, he said; all this could do us a lot of damage, and might well have some disagreeable consequences.[62]

April 23 Early this morning I went out to the park to plant the fir saplings dug up yesterday from the Chepyzh plantation, and the acorns which Vanechka and Nurse had collected for me. Vanechka and Lydia accompanied me, and Dunaev helped too. We planted them beside the lower pond. It makes me so sad to see the old trees going to ruin; I hope new ones soon grow up to replace them. I have an odd aversion to Dunaev, although he is a good person.

The Zinovievs all came to dinner today. We went for a walk and talked, and after dinner the two Zinoviev girls sang and played for us. Seryozha played a Chopin ballade, very beautifully.

I was thinking about Urusov this evening (I always think of him when summer is approaching), and was filled with unbearable sadness at the thought that he was gone and would never return. He had such a capacity for filling others' lives with joy; he quite spoilt me with his constant sympathy, his conviction that I was worthy of the best, that I was capable of doing anything I wanted, that everything I did was excellent. Yet my own family treated me with such contempt, such coldness, such selfishness and jealousy. Why is one's *own* family always so much more severe on one than others? How sad that is, how sad that they should spoil one's life and relationships like this. It is a cold fine day. Tanya has just gone past my door and told me that Lyovochka asked her to tell me that he had lain down and put out the candle.

April 24 I accompanied Seryozha and the Zinoviev girls to Yasenki today; they were all on their way to Tula, and our girls, Tanya and Masha, have gone on from there to Pirogovo. I took Sasha and Vanechka with me to Yasenki. It started to rain, a north wind sprang up and I was terrified that the children would catch cold. After we got back I wrote letters to Lyova, Zosya Stakhovich, Fet and Gaideburov (in response to his enquiry about the new edition).[63] We had a quiet dinner, Lyovochka, Dunaev, Lydia, the 4 boys and I. Afterwards Lyovochka suddenly decided to walk to Tula with Dunaev. The north wind was so strong by then that I begged him not to go. But he insisted – never in my life has he done anything *I* have asked him to, especially where *his* health is concerned. So off he went with Dunaev, wearing nothing but a light coat. I went out for a little walk in the garden with the children, and there, just by the lower pond, on the very spot where yesterday I'd planted all the oaks and firs, I saw a whole herd of village cows. Some village woman and girls were calmly tending them, until I let out a loud scream. I was furious about my little trees and my wasted labours. I then went to Vasilii and told him to drive away any cows that got into the estate. The village people are very hard to deal with, for they have been spoilt by Lyovochka. When we got home I ran a bath for Vanechka, bathed him myself and put him to bed. Then I copied out Lyovochka's diaries. It is now 11 o'clock. The wind is howling outside and I am afraid for those who are out in it. I sent the carriage to Kozlovka to fetch Lyovochka, but he will barely make it to Tula and catch the train. Lyovochka and Dunaev did catch the train and are now back. It was so cold that Lyovochka was glad of his fur jacket.

April 29 I haven't written my diary for several days. The evening before last I had another asthma attack. I felt as though something were blocking my chest, and had dreadful palpitations and giddiness. I threw myself at Nurse and said: 'I am dying!' Then I kissed Vanechka and ran downstairs to Lyovochka to take leave of him before I died. Physically I was terrified, but not mentally. Lyovochka was not there, so I crossed myself and waited, unable to breathe, for death to come. Then I went back to my room. On the way I managed to ask for some mustard for my chest and a pulveriser, and when I lay down and inhaled the steam I began to feel much better. But even now my chest feels heavy and I do not think I have long to live. I have overstrained myself and broken something; I've used up my allotted share of energy – at my age it is all too much for me.

The day before yesterday the old Gués were here on their way back from St Petersburg. I wrote a letter to the Minister of Internal Affairs, asking him to remind the Tsar that he had given me his personal permission to publish *The Kreutzer Sonata* in the *Complete Collected Works*.[64] We had a wretched letter from Lyova, saying he did not wish to take his exam and was leaving the university.[65] Both Lyovochka and I wrote advising him not to abandon his university studies until he had clearly decided what he wanted to do when he left. I don't expect he will take any notice though. Let him do what he thinks is best, the main thing is for us to support him. Tanya is going to Moscow the day after tomorrow. We are all well and cheerful here, and the children started lessons again today. It was cold and wet all day. I have been sitting at home ill for the past three days, but outside it is already quite green, the grass and leaves are coming out and the nightingales are singing.

April 30 The Gués have left and the family is alone again, which is very pleasant. The nights are cold and frosty. I sit at home all day, mostly on my own. It's a long time since I felt so free and unconfined as I do today. My mind is unfettered, my spirits are free and I understand everything – my thoughts soar up over the boundless expanse. There are some days when it's just the opposite: when you feel cramped, stifled and imprisoned. I was reading *La Vie éternelle*, a marvellous book, not new. Lyovochka rode over to Yasenki and collected it in the post. Nikiforov sent it to him.[66]

It is very bad that I lived such an isolated life when I was young. I remember how every little trifle, like the food being under- or over-cooked, used to take on enormous significance; how every grief was exaggerated, while every joy, lacking anything to compare it with, passed unnoticed; every guest was extraordinarily interesting, and one monotonous day followed another, like a dream, without rousing one's energy or interest in anything that was happening. No, I was not made for solitude, and it has crushed all my spiritual strength.

May 1 Tanya left for Moscow this morning. Ilya arrived and went off to Tula to see about the division of the property. Davydov came for dinner with his daughter and Prince Lvov. I find them both very pleasant, and the day would have passed most enjoyably had I not been unwell. I have catarrh in my respiratory passages, am feverish at night and feel very sluggish.

I copied Lyovochka's diary and continued reading *La Vie éternelle.* It is very good and very interesting. After dinner we all went for a walk, and afterwards I played Mendelssohn's *Lieder ohne Worte* and a Beethoven sonata for about two hours. It always annoys me that I play so badly, and I sometimes wish I could take lessons and learn properly. Lyovochka went off to meet Davydov. He spends all his time going for walks and writing his article.[67] Over tea we had a discussion about education. I don't want to send my children to the gymnasium, yet I see no alternative. I don't know what to do for the best. I cannot educate them on my own, and Lyovochka is always very good at *talking* about such things, but when it comes to *acting* on it he never does a thing. A gentleman came with a letter from Orlov,[68] and is just about to leave. It has become warmer, and everyone keeps bringing bright fresh violets into the house. We have been eating morels, the nightingale is singing and everything is slowly coming into leaf. It is rather a dismal spring, slow, sluggish and cold. Davydov is such a sensitive, sympathetic person.

May 15 Again, I haven't written my diary for a long time, and again a lot has happened. On May 2 or 3, we had a visit from Urusova (née Maltseva) with her two elder daughters, Mary and Ira. Their presence reminded me so painfully of the late Prince Urusov himself that I simply could not get him out of my mind. When we were having dinner I kept seeing him sitting opposite me, next to Lyovochka, or sitting beside me while we waited for his family to arrive: 'You will love them Countess, won't you? You will love my *poor* wife?' he said, pronouncing the word 'poor' with a foreign accent. I do indeed love his poor wife and her children, especially Mary, who is strikingly like him, and who played a Beethoven sonata so well as to leave us in no doubt about her exceptionally fine musical ability. And how naive they both are, and how very civilised too! The princess has changed very much for the better, is more resigned, and full of remorse. I don't know why she is always telling me of the exceptional love her husband felt for me. This time she told me in especially grave and earnest tones, that he had loved me even more than he loved Lyovochka, and that it was I who had given him all the things that she, his wife, should have given him – true family happiness, sympathy, friendship, affection and concern. I told her she was quite wrong to imagine that her husband had loved me, he had never told me so, and we had never been anything more than very good friends. She replied: '*Jamais il n'aurait osé vous avouer son amour, et il aimait trop le comte pour s'avouer à soi-même.*'*

We spent three happy days together and parted on friendly terms.

They left for the Crimea, and I then got a letter from Tanya summoning me to Moscow to make arrangements for Andryusha and Misha to take their examinations. On the 6th the boys, Aleksei Mitrofanovich and I set off for Moscow by express train. It was very hot, and I sat knitting while the children went into the other compartments making friends with the passengers, who gave them things to eat. We arrived at Khamovniki Street that evening, and I went off immediately to see Polivanov and make enquiries about the examination. Andryusha was so nervous he could not sleep, but Misha, unperturbed, went to sleep at once. The first exam, on religious knowledge, went well – at any rate they became less nervous. We stayed five days in the apartment, and spent every moment of our free time in our wonderful garden. The children did badly in their exams. I am not sure of the reason for this – whether it's bad teachers or their own poor abilities. Andryusha was accepted into the 3rd form and Misha into the 2nd. But I still cannot decide whether to send them to the gymnasium. I feel so sorry for them, and so afraid of what will happen to them there – yet I am afraid not to. I am just leaving it for fate to decide. How different the two boys are! Andryusha is nervous, shy and cautious. Misha is excitable, talkative and loves the good things of life.

We went to a French exhibition, but it was not quite ready when we went and apart from a dazzling fountain the only things we saw were some bronzes and porcelain.

Driving past the Kremlin, I saw an enormous number of carriages at the Small Palace. Grand Duke Sergei Aleksandrovich has just been appointed Governor General of Moscow, and has been receiving the whole city.

The censors are still refusing to release Volume 13 and are cavilling at

*'He would never have dared to confess his love to you, and he loved the Count too much to confess it even to himself.'

three passages, which go approximately: 'From the Eiffel Tower to universal conscription . . . ' 'When all the European nations were busy teaching their young people how to murder . . . ', and lastly, 'Everything is managed and controlled by people who are half drunk.' But these phrases had already appeared in the same article, which was published in the form of a prologue to Alekseev's book *On Drunkenness*.[69] I wrote to the Moscow censor informing him of this fact, and also to Feokistov in St Petersburg. A letter arrived for me in Yasnaya from the Minister[70] while I was away, announcing that he had given permission for *The Kreutzer Sonata* and the 'Epilogue' to be published in the *Complete Works*. In Moscow I learnt of this at the press where it was printed. I cannot help secretly exulting in my success in overcoming all the obstacles, that I managed to obtain an interview with the Tsar, and that I, a woman, have achieved something that nobody else could have done! It was undoubtedly my own personal influence that played a major part in this business. As I was telling people before, I needed just one moment of inspiration to sway the Tsar's judgement as a human being and capture his sympathy, and the inspiration came, and I did influence his will – although he is a kind man anyway, and obviously quite capable of yielding to the correct influence. Anybody who read this and thought I was boasting would be quite wrong and unjust.

Volume 13 will come out any day now, and I should dearly love to send the Tsar a copy, enclosing a group photograph of my family, in whom he showed so much interest. Both he and the Tsarina asked in great detail after all my children.

Spring fills the air. The apple trees are covered in flowers – there is something mad and magical about these blossoms. I've never seen anything like it. Every time one looks out of the window one sees an amazing airy cloud of white, pink-fringed flowers, set against a bright green background.

The weather is hot and dry. Bunches of lilies-of-the-valley fill the room with their intoxicating scent.

Poor Lyovochka has inflamed eyelids, and has been sitting alone in a darkened room for the past two days. He was a bit better today. Yesterday I sent for Doctor Rudnyov and he prescribed bathing the eyes in Goulard water, which he sent us. Yesterday Lyovochka dictated to Masha a letter on religious matters for Alekhin (a dark one), and I was amazed by how good it was and how totally it corresponded to my own feelings.[71] It dealt with questions of immortality and the after-life: we shouldn't worry about such things, he said, once we had placed ourselves in God's hands and said 'Thy Will be Done!' We can never answer these questions anyway, however much we may worry about them.

The Kuzminskiis are coming tomorrow. The children were very annoyed when they heard about this at dinner today, and they don't want these outsiders – even if they are family – coming into our house and disrupting our quiet, happy family life. But I love my sister so much that I can never consider anyone in her family as a burden, and am always terribly pleased to see her. Seryozha was here, and has just left for Tula. He, Tanya and Lyova stayed up until almost two a.m. last night, and they all seemed to be having a good time together.

Lyovochka yesterday dictated to Tanya a romantic opening to something or other, she wouldn't tell me what, and I wouldn't want to make her or Lyovochka tell me about something that is scarcely born; that's always irritating.[72]

May 22 Another busy week has passed. The Kuzminskiis came, and so did Masha's fiancé, Erdeli. The usual summer activities – swimming, lounging in the heat, admiring the beauty of the countryside, crowds of noisy, jostling children with nothing to do. Fet was here with his wife and read us some of his poems – nothing but love, love, love; he was in raptures over everything here at Yasnaya Polyana, and seemed well pleased with his visit and with Lyovochka and me.[73] He is 70 years old, but his lyrics are eternal, lively and melodious, and they always arouse in me the most suspiciously youthful and poetic feelings. Yet they are so good and innocent and always remain in the realms of abstraction – what if these feelings *are* inappropriate?

Masha went off with the Filosofov girls to stay with them at Paniki. Let her enjoy herself, poor girl, she's only 20 but so serious and old for her age. We went out for a walk, but it started to rain and one by one we all made our way back to the house. Instead of reading, we spent a most interesting evening talking about novels, love, art and painting. Lyovochka said there was nothing more horrible than those paintings which depicted lust in everyday situations, like the one of the monk looking at the woman, or the Tartar and the lady riding off on horseback together to the Crimea, or the father-in-law casting lascivious glances at the young bride; all this is bad enough in real life, he said, but in a painting you have to look at this filth *all the time.* I completely agree with him. I only like paintings which depict beauty, nature and lofty ideals.

Today is Ilya's birthday. The poor fellow lives in such a muddled and senseless fashion, preoccupied with his household, his family and his doubts, and permanently dissatisfied with his fate. It is so sad that these disagreements over the property have put such a strain on our relations, but I hope they will pass in time. There's a vagueness about him which conceals much; if one were to clarify a few things, one might be forced to describe them as downright dishonest, and both he and I are afraid of doing this.

May 27 Annenkova is staying with us. She has brought a young girl with her, whom she has recommended as a replacement for Nurse and a governess for Sasha and Vanechka. But I don't like her and find her sickly and artificial. Ilyusha arrived in a much happier and gentler mood, to collect the plans for Nikolskoe; he took Lyova off with him. Lyova asked me yesterday if I could remember when we had had those marvellous winter days when the sun and moon met in the sky and gave off such a beautiful light. I copied out a page of my diary, dated December 9, 1890, and gave it to him, for I had described just such a day there. I expect he needed it for something he is writing. We took a walk to Kozlovka yesterday, with Annenkova, Lyovochka and the young lady, and there we met Zinoviev and his two daughters, who were just driving Tanya and the two Kuzminskii girls back to our house. The Zinoviev girls sang and we had a very enjoyable evening. My sister Tanya sang too; her voice has a timbre unlike anyone else's . . .

The Raevskiis, father and son, walked here from Tula today and stayed for dinner. We walked back with them after we had eaten, and on the highway we met the editor of the *Kursk Leaflet*,[74] who came up to Lev Nikolaevich wheeling a bicycle. He had long dreamt of making his acquaintance, he said, and asked whether he might visit us. As we approached the house we met Mikhail the coachman, who was taking the chambermaids out for a gallop in the cart, which he had harnessed to the children's horse. I was furious that they had got up to this while I was out, and I sent them home. It transpired that it was Tanya who had organised it, and I gave her a good scolding. I spent the rest of the evening correcting the proofs for *The Kreutzer Sonata*; I don't like the work, I never have been fond of it.

Very cold and cloudy. There has been such a strong north wind over the past three days that we have all stayed indoors. Vasya Kuzminskii fired at Sasha's eye with his toy pistol, and left a red bruise. Vanechka had a stomach-ache last night, and didn't sleep. I got up at 3 a.m. to be with him, and didn't get back to sleep myself until 5. The lilacs and lilies-of-the-valley are over now. Vanechka and Nurse brought some night violets into the house, and the white mushrooms are out. It is very dry and the grass is withering. Raevskii was saying there was a drought in the Epifania district. We had a letter from Masha. She is evidently enjoying herself at the Filosofovs, which I am very pleased about.

June 1 Endless guests. First Annenkova's husband,[75] a landowner, much preoccupied with legal affairs, and an odd, vulgar sort of man, although said to be infinitely kind and sensitive. He brought with him a man called Nelyubov, a thin dark idealist full of ecstasy and gloom, and the magistrate of Lgov, their county capital. Then Suvorin, editor of *New Times*, came for the evening. He struck me as a shy man, interested in everything. He asked whether he might bring with him or send along a Jewish sculptor from Paris, to do a full-length sculpture of Lev Nikolaevich. I begged him to send him here, although Lyovochka said nothing as usual. I am sure he would like it.[76] Yesterday P.F. Samarin was here, as well as Davydov and General Bestuzhev. Lyovochka walked over to Tula to inspect the abattoir, but they weren't slaughtering anything so he just looked round the building. Davydov brought him back in a cab. This evening we went for a walk. Relations with Davydov are increasingly friendly and open, he is such a nice man. I had to tell Samarin and Davydov about my visit to the Tsar, and about our discussion. Everybody is so terribly interested to hear about it! Yet nobody knows my real motive for visiting St Petersburg. It was *The Kreutzer Sonata* that was at the bottom of it all. That story cast a shadow over my life. Some people suspected that it was based on our life, others felt sorry for me. Even the Tsar said: 'I feel sorry for his poor wife.' Uncle Kostya told me when I was in Moscow that I had become '*une victime*', and that everyone pitied me. So I wanted to show that I wasn't a victim at all; I wanted people to say that my visit to St Petersburg was something I had done instinctively. I knew in advance that I would be successful and that I'd be able to prevail upon the Emperor, for I have not yet lost my powers of winning people's sympathy; and I certainly made an impression on him, with my words and my demeanour. But it was also for the sake of the public that I had to vindicate the story. Everyone now knows that I *pleaded with the Tsar* for it. If that story had been written about me and my relations with Lyovochka, then I would hardly have begged him to let it be published. Everyone will see this now. I have had various reports of the Tsar's flattering comments about me. He told Sheremeteva that he was sorry he'd had urgent work to attend to that day and had been unable to spend longer with me, as he found our discussion so interesting and enjoyable. Countess Aleksandra Andreevna Tolstaya wrote to tell me that I had made an *excellent* impression. And Princess Urusova said that Zhukovskii had told her that the Tsar found me sincere, simple and sympathetic, and that he had not realised I was still so young and pretty. All this flatters my female vanity, and avenges me for all the years in which my husband not only failed to promote me in society but actually did his utmost to drag me down. I can never understand why. It has been raining all day, and it is cold and windy. I am about to give the children their first music lesson of the summer. Lyova and Masha have not yet returned. But everything is going well here; relations with Lyovochka are simple and friendly and the children are being quiet and good. About three days ago we had a visit from a mother and her two sons who were selling *kumis*. They weren't the same people who came last year – they were quiet and looked very poor. Lyovochka keeps insisting that he doesn't want *kumis* and refuses to drink it, but he has had a bad stomach upset these past few days.

June 3 A German from Berlin came and spent the whole of yesterday with us.[77] He had come to 'take a look at Tolstoy', and ask Lev Nikolaevich for an article which he could take back and translate for his German Jews –

Loewenfeld and the others. He himself is a merchant and travels around Russia buying wool. He was a most unpleasant, ingratiating fellow, and ruined the whole day. That evening Lyovochka, my sister Tanya and I had a discussion about abstract matters. Lyovochka maintained that there were certain actions which were simply *impossible*, and this was why some Christians were martyred; they were *unable* to worship sacrificial idols, the peasant was *unable* to spit out the communion wafer, and so on. I said that of course one couldn't do such things, but that for some cause, or to help or save a person close to one, anything was possible. 'Like killing a child, you mean?' he said. 'No, not that,' I said, 'because *that* is the worst crime one could possibly imagine, and there couldn't be any possible justification for it.' He did not like this at all, and contradicted me in a terrible, angry voice. Then he began shouting hoarsely: 'Ah, ah, ah!' he went, and I grew so exasperated by this that I said a lot of unpleasant things to him. I told him one could never hold a conversation with him – his friends had realised that long ago – for he always *preached* at people, I couldn't talk to him when he shouted and made all those horrible noises, I said, any more than I could talk to a barking dog . . . I was far too hard on him, but I was feeling very angry.

I went to Tula today, where I had a long discussion with the notary about this loathsome division of the property. I looked in on the Raevskiis and dined with the Davydovs. Zinoviev (the Governor) arrived this evening with his brother, the engineer.

Lyovochka has only two 'extreme' topics of conversation now: against heredity and in favour of vegetarianism. There is a third subject which he never mentions, but which I think he is writing about, and that is his ever more bitter denunciation of the Church.

My children are out walking and riding all day and I see almost nothing of them, which is a pity. Vanechka, Sasha, Tanya and the two Kuzminskii girls came out to meet me and my sister Tanya. Young Zinger is visiting us. It is still cold, and not at all like summer.

June 5 A warm fine day and a moonlit night. My soul is uneasy, I am dissatisfied with my life, and nothing I do seems right. I need to do something else, but don't know what or how. This morning Tanya and I read aloud Potapenko's story 'The General's Daughter', which Lyovochka is so fond of. After lunch, Lyova and Tanya started dicussing with Masha and Vera (Kuzminskaya) the idea of a journey across Russia. They were very enthusiastic about it and I fully sympathised with them, for I have seen so little myself. But my sister Tanya said angrily that it was only because they had been 'living off the fat of the land for too long' and had been 'thoroughly pampered and spoilt'. The young folk then went off to see the Zinovievs, while Lyovochka and I went to the village to look in at the bootmaker's and visit poor sick Timofei Fokanov. I sometimes long to be close to Lyovochka and talk to him, but he makes this quite impossible at the moment. He has always been severe, but now one is always touching on old wounds – as happened last night. We started talking about the children's journey, and he declared that such ideas sprang from over-indulgence and bad upbringing. Soon an altercation had started as to whose responsibility that was. I said it was his – the whole way he himself had been brought up, and the way this affected the course of our family life. He said that twelve years ago he had undergone a great change, and that I too should have changed with him, and brought up the children in accordance with his new beliefs. I replied that I could never have done so on my own – I simply wouldn't have *known how to* anyway – and that he had always *talked* a lot, and over the years he had *written* a lot, but in fact he'd not only not brought up the children himself, he'd actually quite often forgotten about them altogether.

It ended quite amicably, however, and we parted as friends. Lyova and Andryusha rode over to Pirogovo today. I have just finished yet another page of proofs for *The Kreutzer Sonata*. It is now 2 in the morning.

June 6 I went to Tula today with Sasha, Vanya, Misha, Nurse and Liddy. Liddy needed a passport, I had the younger children's photograph taken, and I had to discuss the division of the property. What a laborious, tiresome, complicated business this is, both in principle and in practice. I was mortified to discover that two thousand-ruble bonds had been drawn two years ago and hadn't collected any interest.

I went swimming this evening for the first time this summer, with Tanya, Masha and Masha Kuzminskaya. Lyova and Andryusha returned from Pirogovo at 11 last night. A hot day and a cool night. I thought a lot about death, and imagined it quite clearly. Petya Raevskii is staying with us. He finished at the gymnasium today, and is feeling very happy. Aleksandr Vasilevich Zinger is also here.

June 7 Misha Kuzminskii is ill, and it looks very much like diphtheria. My heart is like lead. I am terrified both for him and for all the other children. My sister Tanya simply shrugs off any idea of danger, but I cannot do that. When grief does come, she is totally unprepared for it and succumbs to the most utter despair. We have sent for Doctor Rudnyov.

Lyovochka went to Tula at the request of one of the 'dark ones', some follower of his whom I don't know by the name of Dudchenko, to visit this gentleman's mistress who is being transported from Tula, where she has been in exile, to Tver. They told her she could make the journey there on her own if she wanted, at her own expense; but she refused, so now she will travel with the other prisoners. Why is he going? So he can brag and boast about his 'principles', or from a sense of conviction? I won't decide which before seeing for myself. It turned out that the girl wasn't in Tula anyway, and Lyovochka was evidently pleased to have done his *duty* without actually having had to see her. He went to the slaughter-house again,[78] and told us in great agitation what a frightful spectacle it was, how terrified the bulls were when they were led out, and how the skin was ripped off their heads while their legs were still twitching and they were still alive. It is indeed terrible – but then all deaths are terrible! Lyovochka's sister, Maria Nikolaevna, came. She talks only of monasteries, Father Ambrosius, priests and nuns, John of Kronstadt and the holy powers of this or that icon, but she herself likes to eat well and frequently loses her temper, and seems to have no love for anyone. We went swimming this evening. It was terribly hot all day. I was cutting Vanechka's hair and accidentally nicked his head with the scissors. The blood spurted out and he cried and cried. 'Forgive Maman, careless Maman,' I said, but he went on crying. Then I stretched out my hand to him and said: 'There, hit it!' But he seized it and kissed it fervently, still sobbing. What a dear little boy he is. I fear he will not live long.

June 9 Whit Sunday. A heavenly summer day, bright, hot and beautiful, and an equally lovely, warm, moonlit evening. To think of all the Whitsuns I have lived through! The children went off to church this morning in the carriage, looking very solemn in their best clothes, and carrying flowers. Sister Maria Nikolaevna, the tutor and the governess went with them. When they came back both families drank coffee on the croquet lawn, and then a long discussion started up, with my Tanya talking heatedly and irritably about how married people ought to behave. Then everyone dispersed, some to write and some to swim; Masha Kuzminskaya went off with her fiancé Erdeli, who had just arrived. He is a fine boy, kind and good-natured – but he's just a boy! That is why everyone is so worried – he's only 20. After I had had a rest and a read, I took Vanechka and Mitechka into my room and told them fairy-stories in bed. One must develop their minds. Then suddenly we heard the strains of peasant women singing as they approached the house, and we went out and followed this bright, smartly-dressed crowd to Chepyzh, where they wove crowns. There is something sad but very moving about this endlessly repeated spectacle. Every summer, for almost thirty years, ever since I have been at Yasnaya, they have woven crowns and thrown them into the water. Almost three generations have grown up here before my very eyes, and this is the one time in the year I see them all together. Today I felt such tenderness for these people with whom I have lived for so long and for whom I have done so little.

We had a cheerful dinner, and we were all happy to be together. It was especially pleasant to have with us Masha and Lenochka, from the Tolstoy side of the family, and I am always glad to have Seryozha here. Ilya came yesterday and in the evening we had yet another discussion about the division of the property. We still cannot decide how best to divide things up. First it's one thing which someone finds unsatisfactory or worrying, then it's another. I find it all terribly upsetting, but Lyovochka takes a most casual and unwilling part in it all. He really is extraordinarily indifferent to the whole business. Yesterday and today he was stitching himself some boots; in the mornings he writes his article.[79] He is eating very badly and won't touch eggs, milk or *kumis*, just stuffs his stomach instead with bread, mushroom soup and chicory or rye coffee. He has made himself a spade and says he is going to dig the wheatfield instead of ploughing it. Yet another mad scheme of his – wearing himself to death digging up the dry earth, which is hard as a stone. Seryozha is playing the piano and Sister Maria is listening and encouraging him; it's a joy to hear him play. We drove to the river for a swim, while Lyovochka went off somewhere on his own. I was thinking about him today: I should be so happy to see him healthy again – instead of ruining his stomach (in the doctor's words) with all this harmful food. I should be so happy to see him an artist again – instead of writing sermons which masquerade as articles. I should be so happy to see him affectionate, attentive and kind again – instead of this crude sensuality, followed by indifference. And now this new fantasy of digging the earth – why, it will be the death of him! And in this heat! He is a continual torment to me with his restless heart and his perpetual daydreams.

June 12 I have not written for three days. On Whit Monday there was an unpleasant episode here. Erdeli was leaving in the morning and Masha was going as far as Yasenki with him. I had to collect some documents from the priest – I needed the children's birth certificates in connection with the division of the property. Then someone told me that Masha was going to Tula with her fiancé. 'Oh that's not possible,' I said, but I asked Masha anyway, so that if she was going there I could tell the coachman to call in on the priest. (I wouldn't bother her if she was returning, since she would be feeling too sad after saying goodbye to her fiancé.) 'Are you going to Tula?' I asked her when she came in. 'No I'm not,' she said. So I decided to go. When the carriage had been harnessed I asked Berger if anyone was going past Kozlovka, as I had to send a telegram. Fillip replied that Maria Aleksandrovna had told him to meet them off the suburban train. I was furious, both because she hadn't told me the truth about what she was doing, and because she had given the coachman orders. It turned out, however, that she had done no such thing, but merely asked if her own horse could be sent. She had forgotten what she had said to me – what with saying goodbye to her fiancé she'd had quite enough on her mind. I love her very much, and took it all terribly to heart. And as if this weren't enough, Sanya and Vasya made me and Mashenka wait in the carriage, and when my sister Tanya finally appeared I started complaining bitterly to her about her children. She asked me what the matter was, and I said I simply couldn't understand why Masha had lied to me. Tanya then grabbed Mitya, jumped out of the carriage and ran off. I felt even more wretched, the tears came to my eyes, and I picked up Vanya and was about to get out. But then I felt sorry for him and decided to go on. Lyova got in, and Mashenka got in, and then there was a huge *row*. What set it all off was Lyova's remark that I was in a bad mood today. I was very hurt, especially as I'd been working so hard on the proofs and the housework all morning that I'd given myself a headache and a nose-bleed. Anyway, we eventually made it up, but it still rankled. Later on M.I. Zinovieva came with her daughters, they all sang, and we had a very enjoyable evening.

Yesterday we had a visit from two 'dark ones' (disciples of Lyovochka's), called Khokhlov and Alekhin. Alekhin used to be a learned chemist and university teacher, but he now wears a peasant shirt and wanders around the country with his comrades in the faith. The same old Russian pilgrims served with another sauce – this wandering life is in the Russian blood. But it seems sad that he spent ten years working at the university and is now going to waste. Khokhlov is a technician, young and somewhat unformed. They are a silent, gloomy pair, like all the disciples; they won't eat meat, and wear rough peasant clothes. I cannot understand that scientist. He must realise that this is no way to live, wandering about and living off others. Lyovochka keeps telling me that they *do* work, but I have yet to see any serious evidence of this: as far as I can see they do nothing but sit around in silence with downcast heads.

I went to Tula yesterday. I took sister Mashenka back, got some money, deposited it in the bank, paid a visit to the other notary – the one at the district court – did some shopping and was absolutely exhausted. I had dinner on my own, then went for a walk and a swim. Being alone helped me to clear my thoughts about my life and affairs.

This evening we all sat together and read aloud a silly Russian story in the *Northern Herald*.[80]

Everyone is asleep now. Andryusha, Misha and M. Borel are leaving first thing tomorrow to visit Ilya.

June 13 I got up at four this morning to see the children off to Ilya's. It was a bright and cold day. Then I went back to bed but couldn't get to sleep for a long time. This morning Lyovochka announced that he and his 'dark ones' were setting off on foot to see Butkevich, some 40 *versts** away. I am afraid it will exhaust him and I'm unhappy about the friendship, but I realise that he's in a restless mood, and if it's not this it will only be something else – some wild venture he'll think up just for a change, I suppose. So they slung their rucksacks over their shoulders and all three

*One *verst* = 3,500 feet.

set off in the blazing heat. The nights are very cold, but the days are hot and dry. It is dreadful to hear people complaining on all sides about the drought and the probability of famine. I cannot imagine how most Russians are going to get through this year. In places there has been an almost complete crop failure, and they have had to plough the land all over again. The situation at Yasnaya Polyana is still tolerable, but there are parts of the country where people have no crops for themselves or their cattle.

After dinner I gave the whole house a thorough clean and swept the rubbish out of all the corners with the help of Fomich and Nikita; I then fetched Ivan Alexandrovich and one gardener, and the three of us went out to the orchard to count the fruit on the apple trees and make a rough calculation of the year's yield. This took us until evening. I shall do the same thing tomorrow.

We all gathered on the verandah this evening to drink tea shivering in the cold while Masha told us in horrified tones about the debauchery that goes on amongst the servants. I was appalled that Masha and the little girls should know about such things but it could hardly be avoided, I suppose, considering the sort of life she has led. She spends all her time with the common people, and they talk of little else.

Then Lyova arrived, and Ivan Aleksandrovich and Misha Kuzminskii returned from the Lodyzhenskiis', and we changed the subject. Everyone is asleep now, and I am going to read. I miss Andryusha and Misha, and am worried about them and Lyovochka.

June 14 I had a pleasant, busy day, although I didn't sleep at all last night. This morning I read some Russian stories in a journal, then tidied up the house until it was all neat and clean. I don't know why, but whenever Lyovochka is away I am always filled with energy. Then we all went for a swim. Before dinner I read the German proofs of a biography of Lyovochka which Loewenfeld had sent us.[81] After dinner I gathered up Sasha, Vanya, Mitya Kuzminskii, Vera and the nurses, and we all walked across the rye-field, picking cornflowers as we went, to the Cherta forest. There we gathered bunches of night-violets, then sat down to marvel at the evening. How extraordinarily lovely, peaceful, clear and fresh it was! Then I took another turn around the park and examined the oaks and firs I'd planted. I went into the house, read through the Russian proofs of the *Second Reader*,[82] wrote some letters and drank tea alone with Tanya. The young folk went off to Kozlovka, and Fillip went to Krapivna for me to see the Board of Trustees and to get the documents authorising me as the guardian of the four minors, in the division of the property. Three *versts* from Krapivna, at five in the evening, he had seen Lyovochka walking down the road. He was quite safe, thank God. He brought news of the children too. It's 2 in the morning and I am going to bed. The nights are very cold.

June 15 I went to Tula with my daughter Masha, to attend to the division of the property, and to apprentice the boy Filka to a bootmaker – which she did. My affairs there were to do with the fact that Masha has refused to accept her share of the property. I realise that the poor girl simply doesn't know what she is doing, and cannot imagine what it will be like to be left without a kopeck after the life she's been used to. But she is acting under hypnotism, not conviction. She is waiting for her father to return so she can ask his advice, since she has at least to sign some papers and to accept my guardianship.

This evening we discussed death and dying, premonitions, dreams, and all the things that affect our imaginations. We were interrupted by a visit from a lady from the Caucasus, the wife of Doctor Kudryavtsov. She had come to see Lyovochka, and she missed him. Then Misha Kuzminskii arrived and told us some fascinating stories about a madwoman here. What happened was that various things of Tanya's had disappeared from the pavilion,[83] and there was clear evidence that it was the mad sister of Mitya's wet-nurse who had made off with them. So Misha went off with the wet-nurse to see the woman, and tactfully questioned her as to what she'd done with the things. It was a highly peculiar business. Gradually she showed him where everything was: she'd buried the little work-box with its keys in the cemetery near the church, and covered it with stones; she'd hidden two towels and a shirt under the bridge; she'd trampled her own peasant dress and a pair of her husband's trousers into a muddy ditch; and she'd hung an antique silver ink-pot, on its chain, from a tree in the orchard at Telyatinki. She remembered exactly where everything was, and slowly went round collecting it, all except for the ink-pot, which they could not find in the dark. It rained this evening, and got a bit warmer. But it didn't rain enough – God grant us more.

June 16 It rained all day, and there was a thunder-storm; the countryside and people are all looking more cheerful now. Lyovochka has returned from the Butkeviches in a sombre and silent mood. My daughter Masha is learning the most frightful things from the workers and peasant girls in the village. All this moral corruption grieves and shocks her dreadfully, and she insists on bringing this degenerate filth home with her and telling us all about it. It is quite horrifying! When I told Lyovochka, he said we must not turn away from such things, we must help them to forsake their vile ignorance. Help them – yes indeed, he and I might possibly try to help them, but not she, an innocent girl of 20! It is he who has pushed her into this disgusting world, and he will have to answer to God and his conscience for her. I am temperamentally incapable of meddling in their lives – I should suffocate and die in that environment, and I can see how she is being affected by things which any other girl would recoil from in horror, and avoid for ever more.

I spent the whole day upholstering the screens and furniture in Sasha's and Liddy's room – there are times when I feel the need for hard physical labour. That will keep me happy for some time now.

June 18 Sasha's seventh birthday. I gave her some presents this morning, then drove with her, Vanechka and Vasya Kuzminskii to Yasenki, where we met Andryusha, Misha and M. Borel, who were on their way back from Ilyusha's. We had a cheerful drive home with the children, who told us what a lovely time they'd had with Ilya and how nice it had been to see him. When we got back I started on the translation of the preface to an English book on vegetarianism.[84] I laboured away, and made some progress. Masha returned from Tula in time for dinner, and brought me various papers from the notary which I sat over for more than an hour after dinner.

This evening we packed up some plates and crockery, the samovar, some berries, and various other nice things to eat, and all went off to Chepyzh, where we made a bonfire and had a 'picnic', as the children say. The little girls played rather half-heartedly, but we had great fun. Then, just as it was growing dark, two women came rushing out of the Kuzminskiis' house and told us that the bull had escaped and was charging towards Chepyzh. We gathered up our things in a flash and raced home. It turned out that the bull had indeed escaped and had gone for the cowherd, who was very nearly gored to death. I was just worried about Lyovochka, who was out swimming. But he soon came back, put on his dressing-gown and announced that he had a stomach-ache and a chill and wasn't feeling well. It is hardly surprising, considering his abominable diet recently – almost nothing but bread, stuffing his stomach with it despite the doctor's warning that it won't do him any good. He's completely given up eggs, drinks enormous amounts of rye coffee – and on top of that he insists on walking to Butkevich's, about a hundred versts there and back, carrying a heavy rucksack that bends his back and strains his stomach. I've never met anyone more stubborn once he gets some outrageous idea into his head. For instance, he wants to thwart me so he refuses to drink *kumis*, but he won't tell me the reason. It is infuriating to have to look on while a person destroys himself like this. This morning my daughter Tanya said some very angry and unpleasant things to me about the way I had brought up the children, and this evening she was angrily attacking everyone for the way the horses are mistreated. I said nothing on either occasion, though, thank God.

Yesterday evening everyone went off to visit the Zinovievs, with Lyovochka on foot, and I sat on my own all evening reading *La Vie éternelle*, which I had not looked at for some time. I don't like his definition of *God*, there's something materialistic about it: '*Dieu est dans la vie éternelle et universelle, dans l'infini du temps et dans l'infini de l'espace; dans tous les siècles,* *comme dans chaque instant; dans tous les mondes, comme dans chaque atome.'** This is God as an existing entity – but where is the God of love, the God of spirit and goodness to whom I pray?

Lyova is writing something and Masha Kuzminskaya is copying it out for him. I should dearly love to know what it is and how it is going, but I am afraid I might disturb the progress of his work if I ask to read it or say anything about it.

June 29 Everything has been going smoothly and happily without guests, excitements, joys or griefs; although the younger children were ill from the heat for a day. Repin and Kuzminskii arrived today. I took Sasha and Vanya for a walk after lunch. Nurse went to see her mother in Sudakovo, but Lydia was too tired to leave the house. Repin came with us, and when we sat down to rest in the plantation he did a pencil drawing of us in his album. It wasn't very lifelike, but rather picturesque.[85] It was a magnificent sunny day and there were flowers everywhere. The children picked more berries and we had interesting discussions; Repin is obviously jaded by life.

Tanya left with Lyovochka to visit Seryozha for his birthday, and will probably be back tomorrow.

Repin is going to do some sketches, and wants to draw Lyovochka writing in his study.

We are expecting Aleksandra Andreevna on Tuesday.

July 16 Aleksandra Andreevna came, but left in a hurry for Tsarskoe Selo when she learnt that her blind sister, Sofia, was ill there.

She was her usual cheerful self, affectionate and interested in everything. But she is a lady of the court to her fingertips. She loves the court, the Tsar and all the Tsar's family, firstly because she is inclined to love *everyone*, and secondly because they are our rulers and she believes in the Orthodox Church and in those whom the Lord has anointed.

The day after she left I went to Moscow to order 20,000 copies of Volume 13;[86] they had printed only 3,000, and these had sold out almost immediately. I exhausted myself getting the paper and finding a printer prepared to do it in 2 weeks. I also ordered some silver for Masha Kuzminskaya's dowry. Vera Kuzminskaya came with me, and we stayed with Dyakov, who is living in our house. Vera and I went to the French exhibition.[87] I wanted to see the paintings but it was closing for the evening when we got there, so we hardly saw anything. I was terribly tired, and decided not to go up in a balloon as I didn't want to waste my 5 rubles.

Lyovochka wrote to me in Moscow saying he wanted to make Volumes 12 and 13 public property,[88] so that anyone could print them. On the one hand I don't see why my family should lose the money, and on the

*'God is in life eternal and universal, in the infinity of time and the infinity of space, in every century and in every moment; in all worlds and in each atom.'

other, since the censored articles in these volumes have been allowed to appear only in the *Complete Collected Works*, I think it would be wicked to release these to the public, and would involve them in all sorts of expense and confusion. But it grieves me more than anything else to annoy Lyovochka, so yesterday I told him he could do what he liked, print what he wanted, I wouldn't stop him. He hasn't mentioned it again, and hasn't yet done anything about it.

We have had crowds of visitors here. Repin left today; he has finished a small head and shoulders of Lyovochka writing in his study, and has started a larger full-length painting of him standing barefoot in the forest with his hands in his belt.[89] He is going to finish this one at home.

Ginzburg is sculpting a large bust of him, which is most unsuccessful, but he has also done a smaller figure, writing at his desk, which is not so bad.[90] Varya Nagornova visited us, as well as Vera and Varya Tolstaya, the Zinovievs, and now the Helbigs are here, brother and sister. Young Helbig and I took photographs of Repin's painting today, and of Mitya and Vanya, but they did not come out very well.

We had two rather dreary letters from Lyova, who is on his way to Samara. Seryozha has gone to Samara too, to do some business for me. Belobrodov the notary arrived with some papers the day before yesterday, and the division of the property is going ahead. Figner was here on Sunday night and sang for us, not very well.

Lyovochka is out of sorts. Today I was told that he had said he wasn't going to Moscow. I simply don't know what to do or how to sort things out. My heart is torn with anxiety, uncertainty, and the terrible responsibility of making up my mind one way or another. How I am supposed to bring up the boys here in the country I cannot imagine – it cannot be done. And what about Lyova when he leaves the university, what if he is on his own again? Then there's Tanya – she stands a far better chance of getting married in Moscow. And then there's Lyovochka, who finds it so hard to live in the city. I simply wait for God to push me this way or that, to force me to do one thing or another.

It's hot and terribly dry, the nights are cool, and people talk of nothing but this dreadful, terrible famine, it preys on my mind every moment of the day. The situation seems to me to be utterly *hopeless*.

Lyovochka is in poor health. He ate such quantities of green peas and water-melon yesterday that I was quite alarmed. He paid for it in the night with an upset stomach. He still refuses to drink *kumis*.

I took Vanya and Sasha for a walk yesterday evening and today; yesterday I went to the ravine at Zakaz, today I walked to the well by the felled plantation. Vanya loves to exercise his imagination – he was pretending to be terrified that there were wolves in the forest, and that the water in the well was 'special'.

Ginzburg is doing a very bad bust of Lyovochka.

July 21 I must write down the whole foolish, improbable, sad story of what happened today. I don't know whether it is I who am foolish, or the life I am forced to live, but I now feel utterly crushed, exhausted in body and soul.

Just before dinner today Lyovochka told me he was sending a letter to various newspapers to renounce the copyright on his latest works.[91] The last time he mentioned doing this I decided to endure it meekly, and that is what I would have done this time too. But when he did mention it again, just a few days later, I was simply not prepared, and my immediate feeling was of outrage; I felt how terribly unfair he was being to his family, and I realised too for the first time that this protest of his was merely another way of publicising his dissatisfaction with his wife and family. It was this more than anything else that upset me. We said a great many unpleasant things to one another. I accused him of being vain and greedy for fame; he shouted at me, saying I only wanted the money, and that he'd never met such a stupid, greedy woman. I told him he had humiliated me all my life, for he had never learnt how to behave towards a decent woman; he told me I would only spoil the children with the money. It ended with him shouting 'Get out! Get out!' So I went out and wandered about the garden not knowing what to do. The nightwatchman saw me crying, and I was so ashamed. Then I went into the apple orchard, sat down in the ditch, and signed his statements with a pencil I had in my pocket. Then I wrote in my notebook that I was going to Kozlovka to kill myself; I was exhausted by these endless quarrels with Lev Nikolaevich and no longer had the strength to settle all our family business on my own, so I was going to put an end to my life.

When I was younger, I remember, I always felt like killing myself after an argument, but I never thought I could. Today though I would have done it – if circumstances had not saved me. I ran to Kozlovka completely deranged. For some reason I kept thinking about Lyova. If I were to receive a letter or a telegram now, I thought, telling me that for some reason or another Lyova was no more, that would quicken my resolve. When I had almost reached the footbridge across the great ravine, I lay down to get my breath back. It was beginning to get dark but I was not at all afraid. It was strange, but my main feeling now was that I would be *ashamed* to go home without carrying out my plan. So I got up and walked on, in a calm, dispirited way and with the most frightful headache, as though my head were in a vice. Then I suddenly caught sight of a figure in a peasant shirt, walking towards me from Kozlovka. I was overjoyed, thinking that this was Lyovochka and we would be reconciled. But it turned out to be Aleksandr Mikhailovich Kuzminskii. I was furious that my plan had been thwarted, and felt sure he would not let me go on alone. He was greatly surprised to meet me on my own, and saw from my face that I was upset. I certainly hadn't expected to see him, and tried to persuade him to go home and leave me, assuring him that I would soon be back myself. But he wouldn't go, and urged me to walk with him, pointing to a crowd of people in the distance and saying they might frighten me, for God knows who was wandering about these parts.

Then he told me that he had intended to take the roundabout route back, through Voronka and Gorelaya Polyana, but that he had been attacked by a swarm of flying ants, and had had to run for cover into a thicket and take off his clothes. After waiting there for a while he'd decided to set back along the same road. Realising that God did not want me to commit this sin, I had no choice but to meekly follow Kuzminskii. But I didn't want to go home and decided to walk alone through Zaseka and go for a swim. There is another way out, I thought, I can drown myself; for I was still pursued by the dull despairing desire to leave this life with all its impossible problems. But then it was quite dark in the forest. Then all of a sudden, just as I was approaching the ravine, a wild beast leaped at me, intending to cross the path. I could not see what it was, a dog, a fox or a wolf – I am so short-sighted I can see nothing from a distance – but I screamed at the top of my voice. At that the animal jumped away and darted off with a great rustling of leaves. At that point all my courage deserted me and I set off home. I got back and went straight in to Vanechka, who was already in bed. He kissed me and said, 'My Maman! My Maman!' over and over again. In the past, when I used to go to my children after these episodes, they seemed to give meaning to my life. Today I realised to my horror that on the contrary, my despair merely grew deeper, and the children made me even more sad and hopeless.

I lay down in my bed; then I was seized with anxiety about Lyovochka, who had gone out, and I went into the garden to lie in the hammock and listen for his returning footsteps. One by one all the others came out onto the verandah, and eventually Lyovochka returned. Everyone was chattering, shouting and laughing, and Lyovochka was as merry as if nothing had happened; for him these are *rational* issues, in the name of some idea, which have no effect whatsoever on his heart. As for the pain he caused me – he has already hurt me so often in the past. As for the fact that I was close to killing myself – he will never know about that, and if he did he wouldn't believe it anyway.

Exhausted by the emotional and physical torment I had endured, I dozed off in the hammock. Masha then came looking for something with a candle and woke me up, so I went in for tea. We all gathered together and read Lermontov's play *A Strange Man*.[92] Later on, when Ginzburg and the rest of them had all gone off, Lyovochka came up to me, kissed me and tried to make the peace. I begged him to print his statement and say no more about it. He said he would print it only when I *understood* why it had to be. I said I had never lied and never would, and that I would never 'understand'. Days like these are hastening my death. Something inside me has broken, and has left me feeling sad, hard and old. 'Let them strike but let them finish me off quickly!' I thought.

I am haunted again and again by thoughts of *The Kreutzer Sonata*. Today I again told him I could no longer live with him as his wife. He assured me this was exactly what he wanted too, but I did not believe him.

He is asleep now and I cannot go in to him. Tomorrow is Masha Kuzminskaya's name-day and I have got the children to rehearse a game of charades. I hope to God that nothing goes wrong and no one quarrels.

July 23 This latest quarrel has broken something in me that will never mend. I went in twice to ask him publicly to renounce the copyright on his recent works. Let him tell the world about our family arguments! I am not afraid of anyone, my conscience is clear. I spend all the money from his books on *his* children; I merely regulate the amount *I* give them, since if they had it all at once they might spend it unwisely. Now I have but one desire: to clear myself of this charge, this crime I am accused of. I have too much on my shoulders already: the division of the property, foisted on me against my will, the education of the boys, for whose sake I should go to Moscow, all the business with the publishers and the estate, and the entire emotional responsibility for my whole family. These past two days I have felt crushed by the weight of my life; were it not for the flying ants which attacked Kuzminskii and forced him to return along that path, I might not be alive on this earth today. I was never so calmly determined about it as I was then.

Yet despite this stone on my heart, I organised the children's charades yesterday. We did 'horse-pond'. Masha, Sanya, Vasya Kuzminskii, Boris Nagornov, Andryusha and Misha all joined in. Sasha appeared briefly as an angel, and also made a *tableau vivant*.

They all played nicely together; these games are essential for the boys, I think, for they develop their imaginations and occupy their minds. There can be nothing wrong in them enjoying themselves. Besides the family and Erdeli watching, there were the young Zinoviev girls, the Bashkirs, the coachmen and all the servants. It was a huge success and everyone was delighted. When it was all over I was staggering with exhaustion, yet the stone still lay heavy on my heart, and there it has stayed.

Yesterday it was decided that Masha Kuzminskaya's wedding should take place at Yasnaya Polyana on August 25. I am so glad; this will make the whole thing much simpler and cheaper for me. Now we won't have to go to St Petersburg, and everyone will have a merry time here instead.

Still very dry and windy outside, although the nights are cool. Everything is parched and shrivelled – the orchards, the gardens, the meadows, the leaves on the trees. Lyova writes from Samara to say it is the same there too.

Ginzburg has finished his bust – dreadfully bad. But then Ginzburg himself is a vulgar plebeian; I am glad he has gone.

I have completely changed my mind about Ginzburg. He is a good and honest man.

S.T.*

July 26 A young peasant woman died in the village – the wife of Pyotr, Fillip the coachman's son. Masha, who was looking after her, had mentioned that she had a bad sore throat, and eventually told us she thought it was diphtheria. I told her she wasn't to go there again. But if she has been infected, it will be too late anyway. I was so sorry for that dear little peasant woman, but also very angry with Masha for exposing two families and several small children to the risk of infection. Judging from her reports, it certainly seems like diphtheria, but she was keeping it to herself in her usual sly way. Now she is distraught, complains of a sore throat, and is obviously terrified. This daughter of mine brings nothing but grief, anxiety, irritation and pity; she was sent to me as the cross I must bear.

I spent all day working on the proofs for the *ABC*.[93] The Academic Committee has not approved it in view of various words, like 'lice', 'fleas', 'bedbugs' and 'devil', and also because of a number of mistakes. They have suggested that we delete the stories about the fox and the fleas, the stupid peasant, and one or two others, but Lyovochka won't hear of it.

Vanya, Mitya, Vasya and Lyovochka all have colds. It poured with rain and there was a thunder-storm, but now it is fresh and cool. Lyovochka rode to Tula yesterday to fetch some doctor known for his charitable works, but the man turned out to be in Moscow, and the peasant woman on whose behalf he went died in the meantime. Tanya and Masha Kuzminskaya left on the 24th for St Petersburg, where they will visit the dressmaker's and order clothes for the wedding.

July 27 Horribly dissatisfied with myself. Lyovochka woke me this morning with passionate kisses . . . Afterwards I picked up a French novel, Bourget's *Un Coeur de femme*, and read in bed till 11.30, something I normally never do. I have succumbed to the most unforgivable debauchery – and at my age too! I am so sad and ashamed of myself! I feel sinful and wretched, and can do nothing about it although I do try. Because of all this, I did not get up early, see off the Bashkirs and make sure they didn't miss their train, write to the notary and send for the papers, and visit the children to see what they were doing. Sasha and Vanya romped about with me for a long time on the bed, laughing and playing. Then I told Vanya the story about Lipunyushka,[94] which he loved. He has a cold and Sasha has

*The last sentence was added later.

an upset stomach. Afterwards I gave Misha a music lesson, which went quietly and well. Andryusha is doing an English translation and has given up music for good. Sonya Mamonova and Khokhlov are here. The weather is fine and cool.

Ah, what a strange man my husband is! The morning after we had had that terrible *scene*, he told me he loved me passionately. He was completely in my power, he said; he had never imagined such feelings were possible. But it is all *physical* – that was the secret cause of our quarrel. His passion dominates me too but I do not *want* it, my whole moral being cried out against it, I never wished for *that*. All my life I have dreamed sentimental dreams, aspired to a perfect union, a *spiritual* communion, not *that*. And now my life is over and most of the good in me is dead, at any rate my ideals are dead.

Bourget's novel fascinated me because I read in it my thoughts and feelings. A woman of the world loves two men at the same time: her former lover (virtually her husband, though not officially so), noble, affectionate and handsome; and her new lover, who is also handsome and also loves her. I know how possible it is to love two men, and it is described here very truthfully. Why must one love always exclude another? And why can one not love and remain honest at the same time?

July 29 Strakhov is here, wonderfully pleasant and clever as always. Basilevich came too, as well as some woman student from Kazan, who asked Lyovochka all sorts of questions about life and morality.[95]

Lyovochka has a stomach upset and was feverish in the night. Tanya is in Pirogovo. It is a dull rainy day. I am worried about Lyova and Seryozha. I wrote letters to Tanya, Ginzburg and the Samara steward.

August 12 Lyovochka rode to Pirogovo today. There is an oppressive atmosphere in this house; the strain of settling our affairs is telling on everyone. Lyovochka told Masha that he would stay here all winter and would not go to Moscow. He then tried to persuade her not to apply for the nursing course for which she wanted to enrol. This seems to have had a depressing effect on Tanya, as it has on me, but she says nothing.

My soul is in torment! What am I to do?

All my energy is exhausted by the struggle to educate the children at home. I can do no more – I cannot go on! I don't know where I am to find teachers and whether Andryusha will ever do any work – he has been asleep all winter. I don't know what will become of Lyova. How can I abandon him again? How can I live without Lyovochka and the girls? And how will they live without us if I go to Moscow with the boys? Lord, tell me what to do! On the other hand, if Lyovochka is moved to Moscow he will only be angry and fretful. Well, so be it, we shall have to separate; I'll live with the children, and he'll live with his ideas and his egotism. What is destroyed can never be mended.

My trust is in God; He will guide me when the time comes to decide.

I try to keep busy, but suicidal urges keep returning, and I long to end this double life with all its responsibilities and decisions. Yet today I ran out to the garden to pick mushrooms with little Sasha, and the other day I went to a concert at the Figners with Vera Kuzminskaya, Andryusha and Misha. I met a lot of friends, everyone sang well, and I felt cheerful.

We had a letter from Lyova in Astrakhan. He is going to sail across the Caspian Sea, but won't be visiting Pyatigorsk in the Caucasus as he had intended, as there has been a landslide on the Georgian Military Road, and it won't be passable until September 10. I miss him constantly and worry about him.

There is an enormous crop of apples, and a colossal number of mushrooms – edible *Boletus*, browncaps and *Boletus aurantiacus*. We picked some honey agarics today.

August 14 I went to Tula; Andryusha and Misha were measured for their new suits at the tailor's, I drew out some money to pay off the Nikolskoe debts (2,000 rubles), and Masha Kuzminskaya met her fiancé and brought him back here. My Masha is in bed with a fever and looks pale and wretched. I had a telegram from Lyova asking when Masha's wedding was. I wrote several business letters and one to Countess Aleksandra Andreevna. Then I ran out to the garden with Sasha and Vanechka for half an hour to pick saffron milk-caps. It was still very wet from the recent rain. I sat with Masha this evening, then we all had a discussion about love, marriage and women.

My sister Tanya says: 'You must definitely go to Moscow and stay there. Believe me, your husband and the girls will grow bored and join you soon enough.'

August 15 Marvellous weather. The children lured me outside to pick mushrooms and I was out for 4 hours. How beautiful it was! The earth smelt heavenly and the mushrooms were so lovely: shaggy-caps, sturdy browncaps and wet milk-caps glistening in the moss. The soothing forest silence, the fresh dewy grass, the bright clear sky, the children running about with happy faces and baskets full of mushrooms – this is true happiness! I had a letter from Lyova in Vladikavkaz today and a telegram from him in Kislovodsk. Thank God he is alive and well. Masha is better.

I spent the evening with the Kuzminskiis – Tanya, Masha and Vanya Erdeli. We were having a discussion about marriage, and as I was telling them the story of my own marriage I felt as though I were re-living the whole of my dismal past. And never has my life been so wretched as it is now. If two people are in love when they are young, they should live as friends when they grow older. With us, though, outbursts of passion are followed by periods of prolonged coldness, passion again, then coldness. There are times when one needs something quiet and tender, a mutual friendship and affection, and I keep thinking how good this would be, and that it's never too late to to try, but when I do try to get close to him so that we might be more simple and sincere with one another, and share our interests, I get nothing, nothing in return but a look of cold, severe astonishment, withering contempt and terrible icy coldness. And his explanation for our sudden estrangement is always the same: 'I live a Christian life, and you cannot accept this. You are ruining the children . . . ' and so on.

What sort of *Christian* life is this, I should like to know? He hasn't a drop of love for his children, for me, or for anyone but himself. I may be a heathen, but I love the children and I unfortunately still love him too, cold Christian that he is, and now my heart is torn in two with doubts: should I go to Moscow or not? How can I possibly please everyone? Because as God is my witness, *I* am happy only when I am making others happy.

August 20 Two Frenchmen have arrived here: Richet, a learned psychologist, and a relative of his.[96] They were brought here by Professor Grot. Masha went to collect Lyovochka from Pirogovo yesterday, but took to her bed again today with a temperature of 39.6 °. Yesterday morning we went for a picnic in the forest with our neighbours; there were several showers, which spoilt the children's games, and we packed up early. Lyovochka is being quiet and friendly at the moment – and extremely *amorous*. I was very interested to listen to his discussion with Richet and Grot. This evening I mentioned the idea of sending the boys to the gymnasium and moving to Moscow, and Lyovochka said: 'Well if the matter has already been decided, what more is there to say?' But nothing has been decided – the same tormenting questions are still unanswered . . .

September 19 It always happens that when life is most eventful I have no time to write my diary, yet this is just when it would be most interesting. So I shall now record everything that has happened.

Before August 25 we were all cheerfully preparing for Masha Kuzminskaya's wedding. We went shopping, and made lanterns, decorations for the horses, flags, and so on. On the morning of the 25th, my brother Sasha and I blessed Vanechka Erdeli, and I then drove with him in the carriage to the church. We were both very moved. I felt so sorry for this gentle boy, so pure, so young to be taking on all these responsibilities and so alone in the world. I was not there to see Masha being blessed but they told me she cried a lot, and so did her father. Then there was the ceremony. I kept swallowing the tears; I was thinking of my own past, her future, and the possibility of parting with Tanya – and even my own poor Masha, who I feel so sorry for, and so guilty that I cannot love her more.

Then we had dinner on the croquet lawn. It was a heavenly day, fine and warm, and everyone – family, neighbours and relatives – was in high spirits. We spent the evening playing games, dancing and singing, and Figner sang particularly well that evening. All day I kept looking at Tanya and her former suitors – all the men who have proposed to her, I mean – and at Stakhovich. I would be so happy to see her married to him. I am sure he would love and cherish her. The party went on very late, and I sat up until dawn with the guests, who were afraid to go home in the dark. My daughter-in-law Sonya stayed up too, as well as Tanya and Stakhovich, who had some harsh things to say to Sonya about young children and all the trouble they caused. Lyovochka was ill two days before the wedding, but quite well on the day. I was overjoyed to have all my children together again, and determined to put aside all my anxieties for the time being. The two young people spent that night in their old rooms: Masha with her sister and Vanechka Erdeli with Lyova. The following morning everything was just as usual, and it wasn't until six that evening that we took the young people to Yasenki, where everyone cried a lot. It was cold and windy, my spirits are overcast, and life has resumed its old course, with even more things now to worry about. It wasn't until the 29th that I once again raised the question of the move to Moscow. It was already getting late, and there was now no time to lose, so on the evening of the 29th I asked Lyovochka if we could have a talk, and asked him to give me his decision about the move to Moscow, and whether we should send the boys to the gymnasium. I told him I realised how hard it was for him, and that I just wanted to know how much of his life he was prepared to sacrifice for me by living in Moscow with me. 'I am definitely not going to Moscow,' he said.

'Splendid,' I said. 'The question is decided. I won't go either in that case, and won't take the boys, but will look for tutors instead.'

'But I don't want that!' he said. 'You *must* go to Moscow, and send the boys to school, for that's what you think is right.'

'Yes, but that means a separation – you wouldn't see me or your 5 children all winter.'

'I see little enough of the children as it is, and you can always come and visit me here.'

'Me? Not for anything!'

At that moment I felt overwhelmed with regrets: all my life I had loved nobody but him, belonged to him alone, and even now, when I was being thrown out like a threadbare garment, I was still in love with him and couldn't leave him.

My tears embarrassed him. If he had had one iota of the psychological understanding which fills his books, he would have understood the pain and despair I was going through.

'I feel sorry for you,' he said. 'I see you suffering but don't know how to help you.'

'Well, I know!' I said. 'I consider it immoral to tear your family in two, there's no reason for it. I shall sacrifice my children, Lyova and Andryusha, their education and their fate, and stay with you and our daughters here in the country.'

'You keep talking about *sacrificing* the children – then you blame me for it.'

'Well, what should I do then? Tell me what I should do!'

He was silent for a moment, then said: 'I cannot tell you now. Let me think it over until tomorrow.'

We parted on the Grumond field, and he went off to visit a sick man in Grumond while I walked home. The heartless, cynical way he had thrown me out of his life hurt me deeply. Yet another funeral of my happiness. I walked home sobbing. It was growing dark. Some peasant men and women drove past, looking at me in amazement. I walked through the forest, terrified, and eventually reached the house. There the lights were on and everyone was drinking tea. The children ran up to meet me.

The following day Lyovochka calmly said: 'You go to Moscow and take the children. I shall naturally do whatever you want.' Whatever I *want*? Why, the word was ridiculous. When did I last *want* something for myself, rather than thinking only of *their* health and happiness?

That evening I packed my things and the children's and collected my papers, and on the evening of Sunday September 1, the boys and I travelled to Moscow. I am still beset with doubts and fears as to whether I have done the right thing. But I really had no choice. Just before we set off, Lyova told me the most terrible story about Misha Kuzminskii, who has sinned with Mitechka's wet-nurse – and my boys apparently know all the details. One blow after another. My heart was filled with disgust, grief for my sister, and anxiety for my innocent boys. This pain went with me when I left, and was with me throughout my stay in Moscow. But material worries and the need to help the boys in their new life had a somewhat soothing effect on me. Then Lyova arrived and told me that my sister had taken the news very hard and was in despair. By then I had lived with this bitterness for so long that I was becoming inured to it; and Tanya was hurt because she felt my response was cool and insufficiently sympathetic. But this was unfair. Calm compassion can be just as genuine as passionate sympathy, which is all very well at the time, but may last no longer than a couple of weeks.

Lyova was in Moscow too, to take his postponed second-year examination. He is really too good for words: delicate, pure, clever, and so sweet with the children. He immediately involved himself in their classes and their new life, helped Andryusha with his lessons, explained the moral issues of the Misha Kuzminskii episode, and reassured them about it.

I stayed with them in Moscow for two weeks, had the house papered and painted, the furniture re-upholstered and the rooms re-arranged, made sure the children had settled in, and then left. My three sons are still there, along with M. Borel, Aleksei Mitrofanovich and now Fomich.

I arrived home on the morning of the 15th, and that very morning Lyovochka accused me of leaving the children 'in a cesspool'. Another argument flared up, but it soon calmed down for this was no time for quarrels. I told Tanya how disgusted I was with Misha, and mentioned the possibility of us living apart until the following summer – Lyova had assured me that this would be best for the children's sake, but I found the idea terribly painful, and I knew Tanya would too. She flushed and said: 'Don't, Sonya! You've made me suffer quite enough as it is.' So we have decided to leave it until next spring, and see how Misha behaves in the meantime. Then Lyovochka and I discussed the letter he had written to the newspaper on the 16th, renouncing the copyright on the articles published in Volumes 12 and 13. The source of all he does is vanity, the greed for fame and the desire for people to talk about him all the time. Nobody will persuade me otherwise.

The letter was sent. Then that evening a letter arrived from Leskov with a cutting from *New Times*, headed 'L. N. Tolstoy and the Famine'.[97] Leskov had taken extracts referring to the famine from a letter that Lyovochka had written to him, and allowed them to be published. Lyovochka's letter was extremely clumsy in parts, and quite unsuitable for publication. He was terribly upset that they had printed it and didn't sleep that night. The following morning he said he was tormented by thoughts of the famine; we should organise canteens where the hungry could be fed, he said, but above all people should take some personal initiatives. He hoped I would donate money (when he'd just posted his letter renouncing the copyright on Volumes 12 and 13, which meant there wouldn't be any! What is one to make of him!) and said he was going immediately to Pirogovo to organise and publicise the campaign. Since he couldn't write about something of which he had no first-hand experience, he would start by setting up two or three canteens, with the help of his brother and some local landlords, and then publicise them.

Before going off he said to me: 'Please don't imagine that I'm only doing this to be talked about. It's just that one cannot stand aside and do nothing.'

Yes indeed, if he were doing it because his heart bled for the suffering of the starving, I would throw myself on my knees before him and give him everything I had. But I don't feel, and never have, that he was speaking from the heart. Well at least he can move people's hearts with his pen and his brain!

My sister Tanya and I are living quietly here with Masha, Vera, Vasya, Vanya, Sasha and Mitya. The weather is wonderful, bright and calm. We have had nice letters from the boys. I am happy to be resting on my own; I am concentrating on my inner life, reading, thinking, writing and praying. Yesterday my husband again aroused violent passions in me; today everything is bright, holy, quiet and good. Purity and clarity – these are my ideals.

September 21 I had letters from Lyova and Misha. Yesterday and today I went for long walks, yesterday with Sasha, today with her, Vera and Liddy. These past few days have been extraordinarily beautiful. It's so warm that we are too hot even in our summer clothes. I picked bunches of flowers, wrote letters to the children in Moscow, and am happy to be living in this refreshing silence and resting my body and soul. I don't want to do a thing. I read the whole of Rod's book *Les Trois Coeurs* in one sitting.[98] It is depressing and not very good, although absorbing. I can't read anything serious, I have been feeling too morally and physically shattered. Yesterday I wrote a long outline for a story I should very much like to write, although I doubt if I shall be able to.[99] I have heard nothing from Lyovochka or Tanya and miss them both, especially Tanya. It's strange, when Lyovochka first refused to go to Moscow and persuaded me to go without him, he killed my feelings for him so thoroughly that I do not find this present separation nearly so painful as I imagined it would be. I'll just have to get used to it. When his *amorous* life with me is over, he will quite cynically and pitilessly throw me out of his life. And this will happen very soon. I must guard my heart against this blow by learning to love others, in other words my children, more than my husband. Thank God there are so many of them, and so many of them are good too.

I am feeling very bad about my poor sons in Moscow while I am here enjoying the weather and the peace of the countryside. But then we were brought up in the city, and it's now our turn to rest.

October 8 I couldn't wait, and went to Moscow to collect the boys. It happened like this: Tanya and I had a falling out over the Misha Kuzminskii business. She thought I didn't show her enough sympathy or concern, and I was very hard on Misha, for I was furious with him for corrupting my boys with his stories. So I decided to accompany Tanya as far as Moscow. Everyone was well at home, and Liza Obolenskaya and her daughter Masha were staying there. So on September 26 we set off. Our own separate carriage was attached to the train at Tula, the Tsar's suite was made available to us at the station, and Zinoviev saw us off. In Moscow I went with Vasya to visit Aunt Vera Aleksandrovna, where my three boys soon returned from an exhibition in a lively, cheerful mood. They had been expecting Tanya, and Misha didn't recognise me at first. He peered at me for a long time, then cried, 'Maman!' We all had a very merry evening together. I spent the next day with them too, and on Saturday the 28th I took the children back to Yasnaya with me. Liza and Misha Olsufiev came with us. I was terribly upset about Tanya, and so were all the children, especially the girls. Lyova did not come with us, as he was immersed in his lectures and his music, and didn't want to be disturbed. The following day (Sunday), we had more guests: Zinoviev, Davydov with his two daughters, and Misha Stakhovich. The two Mikhails were there, both of whom I think Tanya had at one time seriously considered marrying. But however closely I observed them, I couldn't see either of them paying her any special attention; between the two men, however, there was an unspoken hostility, like a silent duel. On Monday everyone left. Then Andryusha ran a fever. On Wednesday I accompanied him and Misha from Yasenki to Tula, where Zinoviev took charge of them and travelled back to Moscow with them. On the way back from Tula to Yasenki, Masha, Seryozha and I discussed the question of Tanya's marriage.

I felt utterly wretched again when the children had gone. For three nights they had slept near my bedroom, I'd been able to hear them and hadn't worried about them. Now they'd left I felt so dejected. There's never a kind word from Lyovochka, he never says a kind word to me, and never shows the slightest sympathy or concern. The nerves of my heart are so exhausted that I have had an asthma attack and neuralgia in my temple. I cannot sleep, speak, enjoy myself, do my work – nothing. I go off and weep for hours on end, weeping for everything that has happened to me, weeping for this period of my life which is over. And if I was asked what was at the heart of my grief, I would say it was Lyovochka's complete lack of affection: it isn't only *now* that he ignores and torments me, he has *never* loved me. One can see it in everything: his indifference to his family, his children, their life and education, our interests. We were just talking about various letters we had written and he started by reading his – to some dark ones.[100] I asked him where Popov was, and Zolotaryov, and Khokhlov. The former is a retired officer of Oriental appearance, and the other two are young men from the merchant class. All of them call themselves disciples of Lev Nikolaevich. 'Well, Popov is with his mother,' he replied, 'because that was what she wanted. Khokhlov is at the technological institute, because that was what his father wanted. And Zolotaryov is stuck in some small town in the south with his father, who is an Old Believer, and is having a very hard time of it!'

So they are all having a 'hard time', living with their parents because that is what their parents want. 'Where *wouldn't* they have a hard time?' I asked. Now I know that this Popov, whose mother is an extremely coarse woman, found it hard to live with his good and beautiful wife, so he left her. He then went to live with Chertkov for a while, but Chertkov could not abide him and he found it hard there too. He now lives with his mother, where he is also having a 'hard time'. I know for a fact that Lyovochka has a 'hard time' living with me – his peculiar principles make it hard for him wherever he is and whomever he's with. There have been a number of those Tolstoy communities, but they all collapsed because people had such a 'hard time' living there. It was on this unpleasant note that our discussion ended. Lyovochka went off to Kozlovka. My chest was heaving and I was choking back the tears; but I quickly managed to calm myself, for I was determined not to fall sick or lose heart. I have *so* much to do and *so* many responsibilities! I must either work hard and live for my family, or if I cannot endure it, I must simply put an end to it.

I was just looking at an earlier passage in my diary, where I wrote about Lyovochka and Tanya's visit to the famine-stricken areas around Pirogovo.[101] Lyovochka's brother Seryozha greeted them very coldly in Pirogovo and said they'd come to lecture him: you're much richer than I am, you can afford to help, he said, I am just a pauper, and so on and so on. Lyovochka and Tanya then travelled on to the Bibikovs', where they wrote down the names of all the starving people. Tanya stayed with the Bibikovs while Lyovochka went on to visit Svechin and a certain woman landowner.[102] This woman and Bibikov both responded very coolly to the idea of canteens for the starving. They are all preoccupied with their own affairs and say they have no money to spare, although the Svechins were more sympathetic than the others.

Lyovochka and Tanya returned home after five days, and on the 23rd (our 29th wedding anniversary), Lyovochka set off again by train, this time with Masha, to the Epifania district. They stayed with Rafael Alekseevich Pisaryov, and went on from there to inspect the starving villages. Raevskii met them there, and they discussed how best to go about setting up canteens. There and then Lyovochka decided what to do so he and his two daughters would have to move to the Raevskiis' for the winter. He gave them the hundred rubles I had given him, to buy potatoes and beetroot.

When they came back and announced that they wouldn't be going to Moscow but would be spending the winter on the steppes, I was appalled. This meant us being separated all winter, them living 30 *versts* from the nearest station – with his indigestion and bad intestines too – the little girls alone in the middle of nowhere, and me endlessly worrying about them. I felt particularly crushed by the news since, with a great deal of pain and effort, we had just settled one question, and I had agreed, so as to make it easier for Lyovochka to live in Moscow, that he should print his announcement about Volumes 12 and 13. And now there was a new question, a new decision to be made. It made me quite ill. And on top of this, Lyova, not knowing about this decision to stay with the Raevskiis, wrote urging us all to remain in Yasnaya, saying that my presence in Moscow would disturb the three boys in their studies, and that I wasn't needed there. This was yet another grief. For 29 years I have lived *only* for my family, denying myself all the joys and pleasures of youth, and now *nobody* needs me. I have cried so much recently! I suppose I must be very bad, yet I have loved so much, and love is said to be a noble feeling . . .

This evening I read with Sasha and played with her and Vanechka. Then we looked at the picture-book and I told them about history. Today they planted 2,000 fir trees at Chepyzh, and tomorrow they'll plant 4,000 birches. I took Nikita and Mitya into the garden and planted a few things – pines, firs, larches, alders and birches. I shall put in some more tomorrow. I am planning to go to Moscow on the 20th. I do wish I didn't have to go! I have no idea what Lyovochka and the girls intend to do. Personally I have doubts about these canteens. It is the free, strong, healthy people who will go there for food, while the children and the old people, the pregnant women and those with babies won't go, and it's they who need it most.

Before Lyovochka published his statement about the copyright on the Works in Volumes 12 and 13, I had intended to give 2,000 rubles to the starving; I wanted to choose one district and give every starving family there so many *poods** of flour, bread or potatoes per month. Now I simply don't know what to do. I cannot act on someone else's initiative with this spoke in the wheels (his statement). If I do donate money it will be for Seryozha to dispose of, for he is secretary of our local Red Cross. He has a clear duty to do famine relief work; he is free, young and honest, and is here on the spot.

October 16 I went to Tula to finalise the partition of the estate with Sokolova, the priest's wife – although I do not know whether the senior notary will ratify it. I also discussed with Belobrodov, the other notary, the division of our family property. It is an extremely tedious, difficult business. It was snowing all day. I drove to Tula in the large sledge, harnessed to a pair of horses, and when I came back it was 8 ° below freezing. Some gipsies had put up their tents and were camping just outside our estate, with children, hens, pigs, about 40 horses and a large crowd of people. The girls went to see them and brought them back to the side kitchen. Last night Lyovochka sent off his article 'On the Famine' to Grot's journal *Questions of Philosophy and Psychology*.[103] Sasha and Vanya have just drawn lots: Sasha drew her own, and got the left half of Bistrom. Vanechka drew for Misha and Andryusha; Misha has got the land at Tuchkov and Andryusha the right half of Bistrom and . . .

On the 13th I went to visit Seryozha and Ilya. I spent the whole of the first day with Sonya, and Ilya came back that evening. They made a sad impression: they have so little love for one another, their interests are so worthless, and they manage their estate so badly. Ilya looks harassed and unhappy, and I feel very sorry for him. God knows which of them is to blame, but there is clearly very little happiness there. But worst of all is the effect it is having on poor little Nikolai. He has been starved and neglected by his mother; it is all too plain that she is a bad mother and does not love

*One *pood* = About 36 lb.

him. Annochka is a lovely child. But little Nikolai might die or grow up a cripple, and it's a heavy weight on my heart.

Seryozha is cheerful, calm and good in every respect. I kept looking round his house to see if there was something I might give him, for I would so like to make his life even better. He is very preoccupied with his job as a *zemstvo* official and with his new responsibilities as secretary of the Red Cross. His place is cosy and clean, and he lives a decent honest life, although it's rather sparse and impoverished. May God give him the strength to continue living a good life. Lyova was suddenly seized with the desire to go off and do famine relief work in Samara. I am disturbed by this excitability of his: rushing about, throwing up the university, dashing off empty-handed into the unknown, just for something to do.

The directors of the St Petersburg theatres have refused to hand over the royalties for *The Fruits of Enlightenment*, and I was furious both with them and with Lev Nikolaevich for depriving me of the pleasure of giving this money to the starving. Yesterday I wrote to the Minister of the Court, Vorontsov, requesting that this money be paid to me, but I don't know what will come of it.[104] We are packing our things and preparing for the journey to Moscow. I feel apathetic and unwell. Wherever I look – in our family, all over the place – I see nothing but arguments and strife. Everything and everyone is oppressed by this famine.

October 19 Complete apathy. I haven't packed, I'm not going, spent the day drawing in Vanechka's picture-book.

Petya Raevskii is here, as well as Popov (the dark one) and some other itinerant intellectual, sent here by Syutaev. A glum, dissatisfied, disillusioned, sickly fellow.[105] Lyovochka is strangely, selfishly cheerful – physically cheerful, but not emotionally.

November 12 I have been in Moscow since October 22, with Andryusha, Misha, Sasha and Vanya. On the 26th my husband Lyovochka left with his daughters for the Dankovskii district to visit I.I. Raevskii at his estate in Begichevka, and on the 25th my son Lyova left for the village of Patrovka, in the province of Samara. We all had but one thing on our mind: to help the starving people. For a long time I didn't want them to go, and hated the idea of parting with them, but I knew in my heart that this had to be and at last I agreed. I even sent them 500 rubles when they had gone, on top of the 250 I had already given them. Lyova took just 300 and I sent another 100 to the Red Cross.[106] But how little all this is, compared to what is needed! I felt terribly homesick when I arrived in Moscow, and was in the most frightful emotional state. Words cannot describe how bad I felt. My health was shattered, and I was close to suicide. And then Dmitrii Dyakov died. And in him we lost Lev Nikolaevich's oldest and closest friend; I saw him virtually in his death agony, and went to the funeral. Then I had all four children in bed with influenza. One night I was lying in bed unable to sleep, and I suddenly decided to issue a public appeal for charity. The next morning I jumped out of bed, wrote a letter to the editors of the *Russian Gazette*, and set off at once to deliver it.[107] On the following day, Sunday, it was published. Suddenly I began to feel well and cheerful again. Donations poured in from all sides. I was so moved by people's compassionate response; some were crying when they brought the money in. Between the 3rd and the 12th I received no less then 9,000 rubles, of which I sent 1,273 off to Lyovochka, and 3,000 yesterday to Pisaryov to buy rye and maize. I am now waiting to hear from Seryozha and Lyova, who will tell me what to do with the rest of the money. All morning I receive donations, record it in the books and talk to people, and it is all very absorbing. But there are times when I suddenly lose heart and long to see Lyovochka and Tanya, even Masha, although I know she is always much happier when she is away from home. It's strange, when Lyovochka and I are together he is so cold, so totally uninterested in his family, that I feel as though I had had cold water poured all over me. 'Well what did I want?' I ask myself. 'And why is he here?' Yet when we are apart I can think of nothing but him. This is because the things I have loved about him are far greater than anything he could possibly give me.

I couldn't sleep again last night because of some articles in the *Moscow Gazette*. They have made their own interpretation of Lyovochka's article 'A Terrible Problem', which appeared the other day in the *Russian Gazette*. They discuss it in terms of the 'birth of a new political party with liberal tendencies', and all but accuse him of revolutionary intentions. For the *Moscow Gazette*, this hint of the mere possibility of some other movement, apart from this move to help the people, is a revolutionary activity in itself.[108]

Then they refer to those idiotic revolutionaries who, they claim, *might* imagine that Tolstoy and Solovyov were in solidarity with them. In my view this is merely the spark that circle needs to incite them to rebel.

What a vile, appalling paper! Anyone with a drop of intelligence regards it with contempt. I thought of writing a letter to the Minister, and the Tsar too, to complain about the harm they were doing, and I thought of going to the editorial office and threatening to sue them. But since I had nobody to consult I did nothing about it.

Andryusha and Misha are studying at the Polivanov gymnasium; Misha is doing poorly, Andryusha is average. I always feel sorry for them; I want to cheer them up and entertain them, and in general am prone to spoil them, which is no good. I was sitting down to dinner with the children today when I thought how selfish, fat and sleepy our bourgeois city existence was, without any contact with the people, never doing anything for others! I couldn't eat. I felt so wretched thinking of all those at that moment dying of hunger, while the children and I were mentally dying in this atmosphere, without any useful work to do. But what can we do?

I received a reply from the Minister of the Court. In view of the fact that I want the money for charity, he has promised to give me the royalties on *The Fruits of Enlightenment*, and I have already written to Vsevolozhskii the director about this.

· 1892 ·

Government forced to allow zemstva *to participate in famine relief work, thus encouraging popular initiative and opposition. Famine also encourages formation of populist groups, who join liberals in calling for some form of representative government. June – Municipal Government Act, restricting the franchise with more stringent property qualifications. Jews banned from local government.*

December to January – Sofia Tolstaya again joins Tolstoy in setting up canteens in famine-stricken areas. Government campaign against Tolstoy intensifies, with local priests exhorting peasants to refuse his bread.

February 16 Another three months have passed remarkably quickly and I am alone in Moscow with Andryusha, Misha, Sasha and Vanechka. Lyovochka, Tanya and Masha visited us twice: the first time from November 30 to December 9, the second from December 30 to January 28. We also had a lot of guests. We were all happy to be together, though that only made it harder to part afterwards. Then I decided to visit Begichevka myself with Lyovochka and Masha, leaving Tanya in Moscow to look after the children. The day we left someone brought us an article in issue 22 of the *Moscow Gazette*. They had paraphrased Lyovochka's article 'On the Famine' (written for *Questions of Philosophy and Psychology*), treated it as a proclamation, and declared Lev Nikolaevich to be a revolutionary. Lyovochka and I sat down and wrote a denial,[1] which he made me sign, then we set off.

When we arrived in Tula we found Elena Pavlovna Raevskaya with whom we were staying, ill in bed with a high fever and a frightful pain in her leg. She never recovered from the death of her husband, poor woman. Ivan Ivanovich died of influenza on November 26 at his estate in Begichevka while our folk were staying there.[2]

On the 24th we caught the train from Tula to Kletkotka, travelling on the desolate Syzran–Vyazma line. On the train I had asthma and a nervous attack. Lyovochka was restless, and taciturn, and kept going into the corridor. The weather was ghastly; it was raining and thawing, a heavy grey sky bore down on us and a fierce wind howled. We finished the journey in two sledges: Masha, Maria Kirillovna and Fedot the Raevskiis' cook in one, and Lyovochka and I in the other, which was smaller. It was dark and eerie, and very cramped. Masha was sick the entire journey and I was worried that Lyovochka would catch cold in the wind.

It was night-time before we got there. We were met at the Begichevka house by Ilya, Gastev, Persidskaya, Natasha Filosofova and Velichkina.[3] Ilya was in a strange, jumpy mood, terrified of seeing the ghost of Raevskii. He left the following morning, and we stayed on with our two women volunteers.

Lyovochka and I lived in one room. I took on all the book-keeping and tried to put it in some order, then went to inspect the canteens. I went into one hut; there were about ten people there, but there were soon about 48. They were all in rags, wretched and thin-faced. They came in, crossed themselves and sat down quietly. Two tables had been moved together, with long benches to sit on. There was a basket filled with slices of rye bread. This was taken round by the serving woman, and everyone took one slice. Then she put a big dish of cabbage broth on the table. There was no meat in it, just a bit of hemp oil. The young boys all sat together on one side of the table, laughing and enjoying their meal. Afterwards they get potato stew or peas, wheat gruel, oat porridge or beetroot. They generally have two dishes for lunch and two for supper. We drove out to inspect various canteens. At first I wasn't sure what people really thought of them. In the second canteen I visited I met a pale wan peasant girl who looked at me with such sadness that I almost burst into tears. It cannot be easy for her, or the old man with her, or any of them, to accept this charity. 'Lord, let us give and not take' – how true the old popular saying is. Then I began to feel easier in my mind about the canteens, without which things would have been so much worse.

The hardest thing for us is having to decide which people are the neediest, who should go to the canteens, who should get the firewood and clothes that have been donated, and so on. When I made my list a few days ago there were 86 canteens. Now as many as a *hundred* have been opened. The other day Lyovochka and I drove out to the neighbouring hamlets; it was perfect weather, bright and clear. First we visited the mill and enquired about the grinding; then we called in on another foodstore where we told them to release the millet (from Orlovka) and made general enquiries about distribution; and finally we opened a canteen in Kulikovka, where there had been a fire. We visited the village elder, asked him which families were the poorest, and told him to call the other elders and peasants to a council meeting. They came in and sat down on benches, and we began by asking them which families were worst off, then decided how many people per family were to be fed at the canteen. While I was taking down their names, Lyovochka told them to come on Tuesday to fetch their provisions, and suggested to the elder's wife that she set up a canteen in her own house for the victims of the fire.

We got back at dusk. On one side the red sun was setting, and on the other the moon was rising. We drove along the steppes, following the course of the Don. It is a flat, bleak place, but there are several old and new estates picturesquely scattered along the banks of the river.

In the mornings I helped the tailor make coats for the men from material people had donated. I managed to do 23. The boys were delighted with their new coats and fur jackets. They were *warm and new* – some of them have never in their whole lives had such a thing.

I stayed in Begichevka for 10 days. We had some snow-storms; once our women volunteers went off and didn't come back at night, and we were very worried. They were good young ladies, both of them. Persidskaya, a Cossack, red-cheeked and full of energy, gave the people medical treatment and they all called her 'Princess'. The other, a priest's daughter, a sickly, pale little thing, was rather squeamish and sentimental, but also a hard worker. They were sent all over the place visiting or opening canteens, distributing clothes and taking down the names of those who needed firewood, food or clothing.

When I got back to Moscow I heard more and more reports about Lyovochka's letters to England about the famine. Apparently this had incensed them, and I even had letters from St Petersburg saying they had threatened to send us into exile, and urging me to go there immediately and do something about it. I delayed doing anything for a long time as I was having to visit the dentist almost the whole of that week. But eventually I grew uneasy. I wrote to Durnovo, Minister of Internal Affairs, and Plehve, his deputy, as well as to Sheremeteva, Kuzminskii, and Aleksandra Andreevna. In all these letters I explained the true facts, and refuted the lie put about by the *Moscow Gazette*. They refused to publish my denials in the newspapers, even though I had written to the *Government Herald*.[4] So I made an appointment to see Grand Duke Sergei Aleksandrovich, and asked him to order them to publish my denials. He said that this was not in his power, and that Lev Nikolaevich should himself write to the *Government Herald*: this would 'soothe excited minds and satisfy the Emperor', he said. So I wrote to Lyovochka begging him to do so. I have just received his letter today,[5] and have sent it off to the *Government Herald*; I am now waiting impatiently to hear whether or not it will be published.

Lyovochka, Tanya, Masha and Vera Kuzminskaya have all gone back to Begichevka. Lyova has returned from Samara and I am expecting him here at any moment. I have no idea what he is intending to do now. I have grown quite used to my position here, living only for my four children, having no interests but theirs. I have started writing a story,[6] I collect donations, I have a vast correspondence, I draw money from the bank to buy grain, and I conduct various financial transactions, as well as all my own affairs. At times I feel depressed, but there are happy moments too.

Tomorrow is the first day of Lent, and I shall fast.

· 1893 ·

June – law restricting activities of village communes. Formation of the Siberian Rail Company encourages migration to Siberia. Several large new Orthodox churches built in non-Orthodox areas. Jews forbidden to use Christian given names. State monopoly of spirits introduced into some provinces (extended by the end of the century to the entire empire, and bringing in a vast revenue). December – law forbidding sale of land owned by village communes without the consent of administrative officials.

The Kingdom of God is Within You *finished in April; banned by the censors, it circulates unofficially none the less.*

August 2 I have just learned from Chertkov that most of Lev Nikolaevich's manuscripts are either with him or in St Petersburg – with General *Trepov* of all people. Our children must be told about this at once.

Chertkov subsquently removed all of Lev Nikolaevich's manuscripts and took them with him to Christchurch, in England.[1] [This last paragraph was added later.]

November 5 (Moscow) I believe in good and evil spirits. The man I love has been taken over by evil spirits, but he does not know it. His influence is pernicious: his son is being destroyed, his daughters are being destroyed, and so is everyone he comes into contact with. I pray day and night for my children and it is a hard spiritual struggle, and I am growing thin and am physically exhausted, but my spirit will be saved, because my communion with God can never be destroyed, so long as I do not fall under the evil influence of people who are blind and cold, too proud and presumptuous to acknowledge their God-given responsibilities. I do not have to pray for the younger ones, for they are not yet old enough to be ruined. Lyova is more cheerful and healthy here in Moscow. He is untouched by any influence save my prayers. God sent us a good man when he sent us Lyova. Just so long as I can sustain the power of my prayers – otherwise all is lost. Forgive us Lord, and save us from all influences but Thine.[2]

· 1894 ·

Passport law denying peasants the right to passports (necessary to move outside one's place of birth) without the consent of the household elder or land captain. Vigorous government action against members of such increasingly popular religious sects as the Stundists (much like the Baptists) and the Dukhobors (whose primitive communal brand of Christianity, denouncing hierarchies, sacraments and violence, is considered especially subversive). Hundreds of them harassed and imprisoned, yet this does little to check the huge and growing population of religious dissidents. November – Tsar Alexander III dies of nephritis. His 26-year-old son Nicholas becomes Tsar.

Sofia Tolstaya brings out ninth edition of Tolstoy's Complete Works.

March 2 Tanya has left for Paris to stay with Lyova. His health is worse. I am haunted by the appalling thought that he is not long for this world. He is too exceptional, too good and too unbalanced. I live from day to day – but it is no life. Worries about Lyova – and now about Tanya too – have driven away all other interests in life. My health is now shattered. Today I coughed up blood – a lot too. Feverish nights, painful chest, sweat. Lev Nikolaevich is depressed too. But at least his life goes on as usual: he gets up early, cleans his room, eats a bowl of oatmeal cooked in water, then goes off to work. Today I found him playing patience. He ate a hearty lunch, while Dunaev told stories at the top of his voice, oblivious to the fact that nobody was at all interested. Then Lev Nikolaevich went off and had a sleep. He woke up in an extraordinarily cheerful mood. Looking out at the bright sun and picking a handful of dates from the windowsill, he set off with Dunaev for the mushroom market to take a '*coup d'oeil*' at the people selling honey, mushrooms and cranberries.[1] Masha is tense, thin and depressed. Seryozha is very affable, and I am sorry he has to leave so soon for Nikolskoe.

August 4 Zakharin has found that Lyova is very ill. I always knew it in my heart. How am I to survive the loss of my son, so young, so good and so dearly loved? My heart is breaking with the strain; I live from one day to the next, and feel as though my strength were about to fail me at any moment. But I must live – for little Vanechka, for Misha, for Sasha, even for Andryusha, who still has a glimmering of love and tenderness for me even though so much in him has been destroyed. But it is all so hard. My husband has worn me down over the years with his coldness, and has loaded absolutely everything on to my shoulders, absolutely everything: the children, the estate, the house, his books, business affairs, dealing with the people, his books, and then, with selfish, critical indifference, he despises me for doing all this. And what about *his* life? He walks and rides, writes a little, does whatever he pleases, never lifts a finger for his family, and exploits everything to his own advantage: the services of his daughters, the comforts of life, the flattery of others, my submissiveness, my labours. And fame, his insatiable greed for fame, continually drives him on. You have to be heartless to live such a life. My poor Lyova, how deeply he has suffered from his father's unkindness. The sight of his sick son spoilt his easy sybaritic life – and that annoyed him. It's painful for me to recall Lyova's dark suffering eyes, the sad reproachful look he gave his father when he blamed him for being ill, and would not believe he was really suffering. He has never experienced such pain himself, and when he is ill he is always impatient and demanding.

Tanya is also in Moscow with Lyova, and I miss her and feel wretched without her here, for I haven't a single *friend* in the house – although Lev Nikolaevich and his disciples have put a heavy burden on her happy, healthy, lively nature too, and have tried to turn her against me. Strakhov left today. The house is hot, I went swimming with Sasha, attended a peasants' meeting, and raced across the unharvested fields in the heat till I was gasping for breath. A heavenly moonlit night, warm and painfully beautiful. Lev Nikolaevich went off to Potyomkino to find out about the fire and donate some money to them. Andryusha has gone to Ovsyannikovo to visit Maria Aleksandrovna Schmidt, Misha is keeping me company, Masha and Maria Kirillovna have gone to Kozlovka.

November 23 The whole family is staying in Moscow. Poor sick Lyova is the centre of my life and concerns. I shall never get used to this grief. I think constantly of his sad sick state, and I suffer painfully for him. I see almost nobody and almost never leave the house. We have a new English girl, a Miss Spiers. Lyovochka, Tanya and Misha have gone over to the Pasternaks to hear some music. His wife is to play with Grzimali and Brandukov. Andryusha has given me a lot of trouble recently, but has at last settled down. His health is not good: he has had 14 boils and keeps having stomach upsets. Misha is bright and happy, but does no work.

It hasn't snowed yet and we haven't taken out the sledges. 2° below freezing, and windy. I am preparing Volume 13 for publication,[2] and reading *Marcella*.[3] Lyovochka and I have been on friendly terms for some time, although there has been some unpleasantness recently. I was angry that he was so indifferent to Andryusha's activities and never gave me any help with him. But it's my own fault if after 32 years I still hope that Lyovochka will do something for me and the family. I should be pleased and grateful for all the good qualities he *does* have.

· 1895 ·

Nicholas II, a militant conservative, dismisses as 'senseless dreams' rumours of increased participation of zemstvo *representatives in national affairs. Liberal oppositionists to the autocracy gather around the* zemstva, *and in the cities the factory workers become increasingly militant. Revolutionaries form clandestine*

Marxist discussion groups, dedicated to taking their propaganda into the factories. Autumn – Marxists in the capital unite into the Union of Struggle for the Emancipation of the Working Class, led by Lenin. November – privately supported Literacy Committees taken over by the government. The entire Moscow student council arrested. Students in Moscow, St Petersburg and Kiev refuse to take the oath of allegiance to the new Tsar. Lenin and other revolutionaries arrested, imprisoned and exiled. The Dukhobors in the Caucasus refuse to bear arms and continue to be arrested and persecuted.

January – Tolstoy protests against the Tsar's 'senseless dreams' speech, and attends a meeting organised by liberal zemstvo *landowners. February – Lyova Tolstoy has electrical treatment for his nervous illness. February 23 – Vanechka dies. March – Tolstoy makes his first will, leaving his unpublished papers to his wife and Chertkov. He resumes work on* Resurrection. *Summer – Anton Chekhov visits Yasnaya Polyana; the composer Sergei Taneev spends the summer there; Chertkov moves to a nearby estate. July – Sergei Tolstoy marries Maria Rachinskaya. September – Nicholas II authorises production of* The Power of Darkness, *at St Petersburg's Aleksandra Theatre (opening shortly afterwards in Moscow's Skomorokh People's Theatre).*

January 1 and 2 I must write in my diary – what a pity I have written so little during my life.

Yesterday Lyovochka left with Tanya for Nikolskoe to visit the Olsufievs. Whenever I am on my own without my husband I feel suddenly free in spirit, alone before God. I find it so much easier to understand myself and sort out all the chaos and confusion in my life when I am alone. News: Lyova has started having electrical treatment and is now much calmer. He has gone off to the Shidlovskiis.

Masha is in bed, Sasha and Vanya have influenza; they are very bored and are running around with little Verka and Kolya (the labourer's children). Andryusha is staying with Ilya in the country, and Misha has gone off to visit the Martynovs with his violin. There was a snow-storm, it's 7 ° below freezing.

I was woken at 4 this morning by a ring at the door. I waited, terrified, and then there was another ring. The servant went to open the door, and who should it be but Khokhlov, one of Lyovochka's followers, who has gone out of his mind and keeps pursuing Tanya and proposing marriage to her! Poor Tanya cannot go out on to the street now, for this *dark one*, dressed in rags and covered in lice, follows her around everywhere. These are the people Lev Nikolaevich has brought into our intimate family circle – and it's I who have to send them packing.

How strange that it should be these weak, foolish people, who for whatever morbid reason have strayed from the path of normal life, that throw themselves into Lev Nikolaevich's teachings, and then follow the road to certain ruin.

I am afraid that I cannot resist complaining about Lev Nikolaevich whenever I write my diary. But I must complain, for all the things that he preaches for the happiness of humanity only complicate life to the point where it becomes harder and harder for me to live.

His vegetarian diet means the complication of preparing two dinners, which means twice the expense and twice the work. His sermons on love and goodness have made him indifferent to his family, and mean the intrusion of all kinds of riff-raff into our family life. And his (purely verbal) renunciation of wordly goods has made him endlessly critical and disapproving of others.

When it all gets too difficult I fly into a rage and say harsh things which I then regret; but by then it is too late, and that makes me even more miserable.

Elena Pavlovna Raevskaya was here recently; she spent the evening with me, and asked if she could see my story. I looked it over and realised then how much I loved it. I know this is bad of me, but it's nice all the same!

I have very tender feelings for Masha. She is a sweet, gentle good creature, and I should so love to help her with Petya Raevskii! I do not love Tanya quite so much as I used to, as I feel she has been contaminated by the love of the 'dark ones', Popov and Khokhlov. I pity her, she has grown old and withered. I am sorry that her youth is behind her – so full of beauty, happiness and promise. I am sorry she never married. How little my lovely big family has given me. I mean, how little happiness they have had. That is the most painful thing for a mother.

I wrote three letters today, a business letter to Prague and replies to Baroness Mengden and Sofia Filosofova. It is 3 a.m. and I am going to bed. This morning I read Jules Verne's *20,000 Leagues Under the Sea* to Sasha and Vanya.[1] 'It's difficult, you won't understand it,' I said to them. But Vanya said, 'It doesn't matter, Maman. Read it, and you just see how clever we get after that and *The Children of Captain Grant*.'

Lyova returned from the Shidlovskiis looking depressed and complaining about his health.

January 3 I got up late. I went in to see Masha and Lyova, scolded Misha for not practising his violin and not getting up until midday. Then Lyova went off to the clinic for his electrical treatment, and from there to visit the Kolokoltsevs. I was very vexed with him because he did not send the horse back for a very long time. I then called on Martynova, Sukhotina, Zaikovskaya and Yunge.

The Zaikovskiis brought back memories of my youth. But it made a hideous, sad impression, this spinsterish life of theirs. Will my daughters really never marry? This evening the children came in to play, and I read Lyova Fonvizin's story 'Gossip'.[2] But it wasn't much good – crude and insensitive. I sent Raevskaya my story to read. I should like to write more but I never have any peace, my nerves are strained, and besides, I don't want to deprive the children of my time when they do so love being with me. The streets, the courtyards, the garden and the balcony are all covered in snow; 4° below freezing.

January 5 I didn't write yesterday as I was reading Fonvizin's story to Lyova. We found it interesting but rather coarse.

Then I did the accounts till 3 in the morning and got in a great muddle. I can't get it right. I spent a lot of the day sitting with Vanya and reading to him, then we went for a walk to the Tolstoys together.[3] He has been ill all day today. Everything terrifies me nowadays, but especially Vanechka's fragile health. My life is inextricably bound up with his – there is almost something wrong, dangerous about it. But he is such a weak, delicate little boy – and so good! Yesterday I went to see Varya Nagornova and Masha Kolokoltseva. I am wretched wherever I am. It's my nature to need either activity or new impressions, otherwise I start to languish. Now I spend all my time looking after my sick children, and there is nothing worse than that. I am not pining for Lyovochka or Tanya at present. Ilya and Andryusha have just arrived. Rain, 1 ° above zero. Sasha went skating none the less with Misha and Miss Spiers.

January 8 Vanechka has been ill for three days with a fever and a bad stomach. It breaks my heart to see him suddenly grown so thin and pale. Andryusha, Misha and Sasha went to a children's party at the Glebovs' yesterday, while Vanechka sat on my knee all evening weak and feverish. I hated to make him miss the party. Before this he was ill in bed with influenza, and it's three weeks now since he had any fresh air. I have given up trying to teach the older boys a sense of their responsibilities; the struggle to do so has quite set my heart against them. Oh how painful it is, how painful to see Ilya ruining himself in this stupid vulgar way, and Seryozha with his immoral life, and Lyova ill, and my daughters unmarried, and poor darling little Vanechka with hardly a flicker of life in him.

Busy all day; I paid the laundresses and the others; gave the labourers in the workshop their orders; the servants asked for leave to attend a wedding; some documents arrived from the police station about the theft at Yasnaya Polyana;[4] then wages, overdue passports, and so on and so on. Then Lyova, Vanechka and I sat together and looked at the pictures in the history books; I told him everything I could remember about the Egyptians, then read him some Grimms' fairy-stories.[5]

Veselitskaya [6] came, and sat with Lyova. I took Vanya's temperature – it was 37.8.

Ilya, Veselitskaya and the Nagornovs all stayed to dinner. Afterwards Manya Rachinskaya arrived, such a nice, clever little thing. I gave Ilya 500 rubles. It won't do him any good; my children are utterly lacking in moderation, they're unbalanced, and have no sense of duty. They take after their father there – but at least he has struggled against it all his life, whereas the children have always simply done as they pleased – like all young people nowadays.

I spent two hours this evening correcting a very poor précis Misha has done of *The Captain's Daughter*. I have just seen to my horror that he hasn't copied out half of it, and hasn't even got to the end. One more bad mark; that means he'll have to do half the year's work all over again.

Later Storozhenko's children came, with Storozhenko himself. Then Mitya Olsufiev arrived. I had a long talk with him and he understood exactly what I was talking about, but I always feel guilty about chattering away so freely.

The episode with the photograph still hasn't died down. Posha came and blamed me, and I blamed all the others. They had persuaded Lev Nikolaevich, on the sly, without telling us, to have his photograph taken with a group of 'dark ones'. The girls were highly indignant, all his friends were horrified, Lyova was grieved, and I was furious. Group photographs are taken of schools, picnics, institutions, etc., so I suppose that means that the Tolstoyans are an 'institution'! The public would seize on it, and they'd all want to buy pictures of 'Tolstoy with his pupils' – that would make them laugh! But I was not going to let them drag Lev Nikolaevich from his pedestal into the mud. So the following morning I went to the photographer and got all the negatives from him before a single print had been made. The photographer, an intelligent sensitive German called Mey, was very sympathetic, and gladly handed over the negatives.

I have no idea what Lev Nikolaevich thought of all this.[7] He has been very affectionate to me, but he'll blame me 'on principle' in his diary, where he never has a sincere or kind word to say nowadays.

Masha was not so nice today as she has been recently. She is always unpleasant when she has to act a 'part' for other people. When she was with Veselitskaya today she had to act according to the opinion the others had of her.

The Englishwoman, Spiers, is not nice. She is dry, unfriendly, keeps her distance from the children and is concerned only with learning Russian and having a good time. I am reading a bad English novel, which I won't finish. I want to read history, so I can explain the pictures to the children. It's late, I am going to bed.

January 9 Misha Olsufiev brought a letter from Lev Nikolaevich.[8] He reproaches me for being unhappy – when it's he who has spoiled and complicated our life! But it is a kind letter and I loved reading it, although I love him much less than I used to! Not only am I not bored when he is away, I actually feel more comfortable. How often I used to pine and fret when he was not here, begging him to stay with me and wait either for my health to improve or for something else. And how often he cruelly threw my love back in my face. If I am not happy now it is because I have grown tired of loving, tired of always making the peace, of having to please others and suffer for them. Now only two things touch me and they are both painful – Lyova's condition and little Vanechka. I feel his little hands and feet which have grown so thin, and kiss his pale sick cheeks, and suffer and grieve for him. He eats almost no dinner, and I cannot eat either. I am worn out with worry and anguish.

Ilya has left. Veselitskaya and I had a nice, quiet, intelligent talk, and she told me the whole story about her divorce. I am angry that Mitya Olsufiev is not to marry Tanya, although it would grieve me to have to part with her.

Dunaev came, Masha Zubova was here this morning, Manya Rachinskaya has left. I had a lazy day talking to the guests. I am tired, nervous and debilitated. The weather is fine, 3 ° below freezing.

January 10 If asked what I felt, I would say I had stopped living. Nothing brings me pleasure; everything brings me endless sorrow.

The day dragged past: I sat with Lydia Ivanovna (who has now left), read Vanya some Grimms' fairy-stories, and went to the chemist's and to the market to buy soft caviare for Vanya and Lyova. Andryusha and Misha are being very good. Sasha played a waltz on her mouth-organ and Misha accompanied her on the violin. He has an impressive musical ear and style. Lyova went to see the Shidlovskiis. He is calmer now, but as thin and poorly as before. While Vanechka was listening to the music he said: 'I would so like to do something *very, very* well! Will you teach me music, Maman, please?'

This evening I went to the bath-house and took a bath. Then Masha and I drank tea together and talked about the Olsufievs and Tanya. It is pouring with rain, 3 ° above freezing, and very muddy.

This evening I smashed the negatives of the photographs of the dark ones. I had tried to scratch Lev Nikolaevich's face out of it with my diamond ear-ring, but couldn't. I went to bed at 3 a.m.

January 11 Vanya has a rasping cough. I have been sitting with him and reading him Grimms' fairy-stories. I then tried to draw our garden, but was out of practice. I went out and swept the snow from the skating-rink, mainly for the exercise. Through the window I could see that Vanya had jumped out of bed and was running about without any clothes on. I went in and shouted at the nurse, she screamed back at me, and Vanya started crying. We all dined at home. It is Misha's name-day; I gave him 10 rubles. This evening they took Ilya's peasant coachman, Abramka, to the circus, and were enchanted by his naive enjoyment of it. (Ilya had sent the boy to collect the horse he'd just bought.) This evening I sat with Lyova and inadvertently mentioned that Doctor Belogolovy had told me that his was just a bad case of nerves. At that, Lyova jumped up cursing and swearing at me – stupid, wicked, old liar, and I don't know what else. How can one endure such things! I feel less and less sorry for him, he has become so spiteful and cruel – although it's only because he is ill, and I still feel sorry about that.

To make up for it, Andryusha came in after the circus and told me that no one appreciated me, that I was a wonderful person, and he loved me more than anyone in the world.

I sorted through Lev Nikolaevich's letters to my sister Tanya, and my own to her, until 3 in the morning. I then read through his letters to Valeria Arseneva, whom he was going to marry at one time. They are splendid letters but he never loved her.[9]

5° below freezing, bright and beautiful.

January 12 I got up early and gave Vanya some apomorphine for his cough, which is worse. I opened the ventilation pane in the window – it was 10 ° below freezing – and had a wash in cold water, but did not feel any livelier. I was in very low spirits. I sat with Vanya and read to him, then received guests. Chicherin came, and Lopatin, with whom I had an interesting talk about death. He said, among other things, that life would not be so interesting if we were not faced with the eternal mystery of death at the end of it. Then Petrovskaya and Tsurikova came. Tsurikova dined and spent the night here. She is one of those aristocratic, old-fashioned unmarried ladies who tells fortunes with cards, has a huge circle of acquaintances and falls in love at the age of 40.

This evening Vanechka again had a temperature of 38.3, and I was dreadfully worried. Something has broken in me – I ache inside and cannot control myself. I took myself in hand, however, and attended Lopukhina's funeral service, went on to collect Misha from the Glebovs', then paid a brief visit to the Tolstoys. I walked home in an anxious mood. Lyova is more docile, Masha is very sweet and keeps offering to help, and the boys are very kind. Chicherin was talking about Lyovochka today; there are two men in him, he said, a writer of genius and a mediocre philosopher who impresses people by talking in paradoxes and contradictions. He cited several instances of this. Chicherin loves Lev Nikolaevich, but that is because he has known him for so long. He sees in him the Lev Nikolaevich he knew as a young man, who wrote him a vast number of letters which he treasures.[10]

January 13 I sorted through all the letters I received from people who sent money during the famine. I tore up those referring only to money or making sententious remarks, and put aside those which expressed genuine thoughts or feelings. Vanya helped me very sweetly. Poor little mite, he has a temperature every day and he has grown even paler and thinner.

January 14 I sat with Vanya and read to him. Bugaeva, Zaikovskaya and Litvinova were here this evening. A lot of stupid chatter. Vanya was 37.8 this morning, 38.5 this evening. Cough less harsh, cold worse. My life has stopped – my body and soul have come to a halt. I am waiting to be awakened.

January 15 I have still not awakened, I am sinking deeper and deeper into depression; it is probably because I am exhausted after days spent looking after Vanechka and Lyova, and this is affecting my nerves and my mood. I spent the whole day frantically trying to entertain Vanechka. Doctor Filatov came this afternoon and didn't find any complications in either his lungs or his throat, and said his spleen was not enlarged. It's influenza, nothing more. I drove to the Glebovs' to collect Sasha, who had just had her 1st dancing lesson there. My brother came this evening with his sad, thin wife.[11] Afterwards I told Masha's fortune with cards. I told Misha Olsufiev's too, and it showed death. I was very upset, and afraid for Tanya and Lev Nikolaevich. If only they would come back soon. How I would love Lev Nikolaevich if only he were a little kinder to me and more attentive to the boys.

Lyova is rather jumpy, but today he seemed brighter than he has been for a long time. Masha is pathetic and touchingly eager to help.

January 16 and 17 Vanya is just the same. He becomes feverish at noon and this lasts until night. His cough is better, but his cold is the same. Sasha also has a cold now. Misha Stakhovich was here yesterday and today, but he didn't cheer me up. Masha Kolokoltseva also came yesterday evening, and her genuine warmth and affection were a great comfort. This evening Dunaev and Elena Pavlovna Raevskaya came. I am exhausted by Vanechka's illness and my own situation. I feel weak, and breathless from the slightest exertion. Andryusha has been complaining of pains in his stomach. Misha is sleeping in Lyova's room. Masha is being gentle, sweet and helpful.

There is a snow-storm, the wind is howling, it's 6 ° below freezing. Lev Nikolaevich and Tanya promised to return from the Olsufievs' tomorrow. I am reading *Les Rois*;[12] so far quite interesting. I sewed, and spent the whole day sitting with Vanya. My life is empty and cheerless.

January 18 I always remember that today is the anniversary of my little Alyosha's death. He died nine years ago.

I got up at 6 a.m., gave Vanya 4 g. of quinine, then went back to bed. I got up again at 8.30, and took his temperature – which was 36.7. Then I lay down again and dozed off. I got up late, and my temple was aching. I went out shopping and bought cloth, stockings, bobbins and various other essentials. I also bought the children some more pieces for the ariston.[13] After dinner I accompanied Misha, who played first a Mozart violin sonata, then one by Schubert. It was a pity I sight-read so badly. He was enjoying it enormously and I was sorry to have to tear him away and make him revise his lessons with his tutor. Andryusha has a stomach-ache, but his illness makes him lazy and disagreeable.

Lev Nikolaevich and Tanya have returned from the Olsufievs'.[14] It wasn't a very joyful reunion, after 18 days apart – not as it was in the old days. Tanya has a sharp, censorious manner, and Lyovochka is indifferent to everything. They had a very merry time, didn't worry about a thing, paid a lot of visits, and Lev Nikolaevich even played vint and duets. He could live more simply there, free of the critical gaze of his followers, and he enjoyed having a rest from all the posing and insincerity he has created for himself in the company of his dark ones. I had a talk with Miss Spiers this morning about her general inadequacy. She is very disagreeable and doesn't like children. I shall have to part with her. There are no good governesses to be had these days. It's all very depressing.

January 19 I got up early and sat with Vanya. He did a still life drawing of some baskets, without any help, and I tried my hand at a water-colour sketch of our garden – with disastrous results. I have never learned to do anything properly! How sad. I read more of *Les Rois* – it's no good. We all had dinner together, which was very pleasant. I cannot live alone, I have got used to living with Lyovochka and my family, and I soon grow bored on my own with the little ones.

After dinner I tackled the Samara documents and accounts. Goltsev is with Lyovochka, reading him the Tver address and the petition presented to the new Tsar.[15] Dunaev is also here. Vanya is still ill. His temperature shoots up at 3.30 every afternoon. It's fine, 6 ° below freezing, a moonlit night. So beautiful! But I am still depressed, and my soul is asleep.

January 20 Vanya is very ill, with a high temperature. I went to see Doctor Filatov this evening, and he prescribed large doses of quinine. Lyovochka is annoyed that I consulted him, although he evidently has no idea either what to do. He is healthy, draws his own water from the well and writes; this afternoon he read, and has just gone off to see Sergei Nikolaevich. 17 ° below freezing, with a mist and hoar-frost; a fine day and a bright night. My heart is so heavy, it's quite unbearable!

January 26 Vanechka has had a high temperature for the past week. It tortures me, body and soul, to look at him. He is a little better today, but we have been giving him 4 g. of quinine twice a day. I left the house for the first time in many days, and bought some sheet music, toys, cheese, fresh eggs and so on. I sat with Vanya for a little while, played duets with Lev Nikolaevich after dinner and chose a piece for Sasha and Nadya Martynova to play at the forthcoming children's musical evening. Then everyone left but Lyova, who told me about the house he wants to build in the courtyard, and curtly asked me for the money to do so. When I refused, he soon changed his tune and became more friendly. Then Masha and I corrected and transcribed the proofs for Lyovochka's story 'Master and Man'. I am angry that he gave it to the *Northern Herald* to publish. What is one to make of him? If he'd published it for *nothing* in the *Intermediary* I would have understood, for then anyone could have bought it and read a story by Tolstoy for just 20 kopecks. But now the public is going to have to pay 13 rubles to read it. This is why I cannot share my husband's 'ideas' – because he is dishonest and insincere. His whole philosophy is so strained, artificial and unnatural, based as it is on vanity, the insatiable thirst for fame, and the compulsive desire for ever more popularity. No one ever believes me when I say this, and it's painful for me to recognise it too – especially when others don't see it. But then what does it matter to them!

It's now 2 in the morning. Lyovochka has gone off to some meeting – I don't know what about – called by Prince Dmitrii Shakhovskoi.[16] The lamps are still burning, the servant is waiting up, I have boiled his porridge and pasted up the proofs. Meanwhile they just sit there *talking*. Tomorrow I shall get up at 8, take Vanechka's temperature and give him his quinine, while he sleeps on. Then he'll go and draw his water from the well, without even asking whether his child is any better or whether his wife is exhausted. Ah, how little kindness he shows his family! With us he is never anything but severe and indifferent. His biographers will tell how he helped the porter by drawing his own water, but no one will know that he never once thought to give his wife a moment's rest, or his sick child a drink of water; how in 32 years he never once sat for five minutes by his sick child's bedside to let me have a rest, or a good night's sleep, or go for a walk, or simply sit down for a while and recover from my labours.

11 ° below freezing, hoar-frost, silence, moonlight.

February 1 Vanya hasn't had a temperature for 3 days, and for 4 days I have been giving him 5 or 6 drops of arsenic twice a day after dinner. I feel much happier about him now. I am still concerned about Lyova. Relations with Lyovochka are good.

I measured him the other day, by the way. He is 2 *arshins* 7¼ *vershoks* tall.*

It's warm. It was 25° below zero recently, but yesterday it was 5° below and today it was just 1½ ° below. I am in poor health, constantly bothered

*About 6 feet 3 inches.

by asthma and palpitations. If I walk fast my pulse shoots up in five minutes from 64 to 120.

I read Chicherin's article 'On Space and Time'.[17] It is dull and unintelligent. I went to the gymnasium to see Polivanov, who had complained to me about Misha playing about and misbehaving during lessons. I wrote a letter to Kandidov,[18] and to the bailiff.

February 5 Either I have a bad character or I am being perfectly reasonable. Lev Nikolaevich wrote a marvellous story called 'Master and Man'. Now that scheming half-Jewish Gurevich woman is always buttering him up and trying to inveigle him into sending her things for her magazine. Since he now refuses to accept money for his writing, he might as well have had it published in a cheap little Intermediary edition: that way *everyone* would have got a chance to read it, and I would have understood and sympathised. He wouldn't give it to me for Volume 13, so that I wouldn't get any money for it; but why then did he give it to Gurevich? It has made me furious, and I am now trying to find a way to make amends to the public, not to benefit Gurevich but to spite her. And I *shall* find a way too.

Once on my name-day Lev Nikolaevich brought me a file containing 'The Death of Ivan Ilich', for the new edition.[19] Then he took it away again, and published an announcement saying he was making it public property. That made me so angry, and I wept bitterly. Why does he give so little thought to *my* feelings? How sad it all is! Yesterday Masha visited Professor Kozhevnikov, who was not at all reassuring about Lyova's health. This morning I told Andryusha off for deceiving his father and me the other day and going off with Kleinmickel and Severtsev to see the gipsies, rather than coming straight home as he had promised. Andryusha flared up and said the reason he'd deceived his father was that for the past year the only two words he'd heard from him were 'Come home!' His father never took any interest in them, he said, and never had anything to do with them or gave them any help. It made me sad to hear this – but there's much truth in it.

Mamonov was here, and dear Countess Kapnist, so thin and distressed by the upheavals at the university. Lyovochka has a bad cough and has been correcting the proofs for 'Master and Man'. We had Misha's friends here yesterday evening, and Sofia Martynova read Turgenev's *Faust* to us.

I started thinking about Turgenev, and remembered that spring when he stayed with us in Yasnaya Polyana and we went out shooting snipe.[20] Lyovochka was standing behind one tree and he and I were behind another, and I asked him why he didn't write any more. And he stooped down, looked around in a rather comical way and said, 'Nobody can hear us but the trees I think, my dear.' (He called everyone 'my dear' as he got older.) 'So I shall tell you. You see, before I write something new I need to be inflamed by love – and that is all over now!'

'What a shame!' I said, adding as a joke: 'You can fall in love with me if you like, then you could write something!'

'No, it's too late!' he said.

He was such good company. That evening he danced a sort of Paris can-can with my daughters and the Kuzminskii girls, and argued good-naturedly with Lev Nikolaevich and the late Prince Leopold Urusov. I remember he asked me if we could have chicken soup with semolina, and beef and onion pie, saying that was something only Russian chefs knew how to make. He was gentle and affectionate with everyone and to Lev Nikolaevich he said: 'What a good thing you did when you married your wife.' He was always urging Lev Nikolaevich to write more fiction, and spoke passionately about his supreme talent as a writer. It's painful to recall all this now, and I regret that I have written so little in my life; no one ever suggested to me that it might be important, and I have lived in childish ignorance for so long.

Today's edition of *New Times* carried the shocking news of Mary Urusova's death. She was only 25. There was something exceptional about her – artistic, musical and gentle. Now her soul is with her father. Poor little girl, she could never accept her mother's vulgarity!

February 21 I am passing through yet another painful period. I don't even want to write about it, it is so terrible, so difficult and so clear to me now that my life is going into a decline. I have no desire to live and thoughts of suicide pursue me ever more relentlessly. Save me Lord from such a sin! Today I again tried to leave home; I think I must be ill, I cannot control myself. All my sufferings are as nothing compared to the one great grief in my soul – Lyovochka's indifference to me and the children. Surely there are some happy old couples, who have loved each other as passionately as we have for the past 33 years, and have now developed a relationship based on friendship and affection? As for us – I keep having stupid outbursts of sentimental passion for him. When I was ill he brought me 2 wonderful apples, and I planted the pips in memory of this rare display of tenderness towards me. Will I ever see those pips grow into trees, I wonder?

Yes, I was going to relate the whole dreadful *episode* between us. It is all my fault, of course, yet how did I get dragged into it in the first place? Just so long as the children don't blame me, for no one will ever be able to understand our marital relations. If, in spite of my apparent happiness, I want to end my life, and have attempted so many times to do so, surely there must be some reason for it? If only people knew how painful it is – these endless outbursts, these attempts at love, which is painfully wearing out, for it never receives anything but physical gratification; and even more painful is the realisation in the *last* days of our life together, that there are no mutual feelings between us, that for the whole of my life I have singlemindedly and unwaveringly loved a man who was utterly selfish and returned all my feelings with a withering and pitiless scorn.

Anyway, this is the 'episode' I spoke of. As I said earlier, I was upset about his story 'Master and Man'. But I tried to keep this to myself, and worked hard on the proofs with Lyovochka. Then just as they were about to be sent off I asked him if I could take a copy for myself, so I could publish them in Volume 13 of the *Complete Collected Works.*

Since I didn't want to delay them being sent off to St Petersburg, I said I would do this copying at night. For some reason, however, Lyovochka was incensed at the idea, insisting that they would be sending copies anyway, and angrily protesting against my copying it out, saying only that it was insane. I couldn't bear the idea of the *Northern Herald* having the sole rights; I recalled the words of Storozhenko, who said that Gurevich (the editor) must have bewitched the count, since she'd got two articles out of him in one year,[21] and was quite determined that come what may I would see that my own edition and the Intermediary's were published simultaneously. We were both furious and upset. Lyovochka got so angry that he rushed upstairs, put on his clothes and said he was leaving home for ever and wouldn't be returning.

Since I felt that my only crime was wanting to copy it out, it suddenly flashed across my mind that there must be some far more serious reason why he should want to leave me, and that this was just an excuse. I immediately thought of that woman and lost all my self-control, and so as he should not be the one to leave me, I ran out of the house and tore off down the road. He came chasing after me, I in my dressing-gown, he in his pants and waistcoat, without a shirt. He pleaded with me to go back, but at that point I had only one wish and that was to die, never mind how. I remember I was sobbing and shouting: 'I don't care, let them take me away and put me in prison or the mental hospital!' Lyovochka dragged me back to the house, I kept falling in the snow and got soaked to the skin. I had only a night-dress on under my dressing-gown, and had nothing on my feet but a pair of slippers, and I am now ill, demented and choked, and cannot think at all clearly.

Somehow or other we smoothed things over. The next morning I again helped him to correct the proofs for the *Northern Herald*. He finished them after lunch and was about to take a nap. 'Well I'll take a copy now if I may,' I said. He was lying on the sofa, but when I said that, he leapt up, glared at me and again refused to let me do it, without giving any reason. (I still don't know what it might be.) But I didn't lose my temper, and merely begged him to let me copy it out; I had tears in my eyes, and could hardly speak. I promised I wouldn't release the book without his permission; I was only asking him to let me copy it out. He didn't refuse in so many words, but his anger stunned me. I couldn't understand anything. Why were Gurevich and her journal so precious to him that he wouldn't let his story be published simultaneously in Volume 13 and by the Intermediary?

Feelings of jealousy and rage, the mortifying thought that he *never did anything for me*, the old grief of having loved him so much when he had never loved me – all this reduced me to a state of utter despair. I flung the proofs on the table, threw on a light overcoat, put on my galoshes and hat, and slipped out of the house. Unfortunately – or perhaps fortunately – Masha had noticed my distraught face and followed me, although I didn't realise this at the time. I stumbled towards the Convent of the Virgin, intending to freeze to death in a wood on the Sparrow Hills. I remember I had liked the idea that Vasilii Andreich had frozen to death in the story, and that I too would meet the same end. I didn't regret what I was doing. I had staked almost my whole life on one card – my love for my husband – and now the game was lost and I had nothing to live for. I wasn't sorry about the children either. I always feel that however much *we* may love them, *they* never love *us*, and I was sure they would survive quite well without me. Masha, as it turned out, had not let me out of her sight, and she eventually managed to take me home. But my despair did not subside, and for two days I kept trying to leave. The following day I just hailed a cab in the street and set off for the Kursk station. How my children guessed that I had gone there I shall never know. But Seryozha and Masha caught up with me and once again took me home. Each time I got back I felt so foolish and ashamed of myself. That night (February 7) I was very ill. All the painful feelings inside me intensified to a point of unbearable anguish. I vaguely recall thinking that anybody Lyovochka touched was doomed to perish. I became morbidly sorry for poor Khokhlov, who had gone out of his mind, and wanted to pray for them all to be released from Lyovochka's influence. I still feel that my love for him will be the end of me, and will destroy my soul. If I do manage to release myself from it – from loving him I mean – I shall be saved. If not, one way or another, I am done for. He has killed my very soul – I am already dead!

After I'd been sobbing for a long time he came in, kneeled before me on the floor and begged me to forgive him. If he could keep just a fragment of that compassion for me alive, then I might still be happy with him.

Having tortured my soul, he then called in the doctors to examine me. It was comical the way each one prescribed medicine according to his own speciality. So the neurologist prescribed bromide and the specialist in internal diseases prescribed Vichy water and drops. Then the gynaecologist Snegirev was called in, referred cynically to my 'critical time of life' and prescribed *his* particular medicine. I haven't taken any of it. I don't feel any better either. I've been running around the streets for three days and nights with barely a stitch on, in 16° of frost, frozen to the marrow and at my wits' end – naturally I'm ill. The girls were timid with me, Misha sobbed and

Andryusha went off to share his grief with Ilya. Sasha and Vanya were childishly puzzled, Lyovochka was alarmed. The nicest of all was Seryozha – gentle, affectionate and completely uncensorious. Lyovochka, Christian that you are, I saw in you more judgement than love or compassion. This whole *episode* was due only to my limitless love for him. He is always seeking *evil* in me; if only he would realise that this isn't one of my vices, although there are plenty of others to be sure. Is it my fault that God has given me such a restless, passionate temperament?[22]

Sister Maria Nikolaevna was also very sweet and kind, and said that what I'd said in my frenzy was all quite true, but that I'd gone too far. Yes, but this frenzy is an unforgivable, incorrigible vice![23]

We have made the peace again. Lyova has left for Ogranovich's sanatorium[24] and hasn't written so much as a word. He is morbidly resentful of his family and doesn't want anything to do with us, which may be for the best while he is in this nervous condition. A doctor arrived from there yesterday, and spoke reassuringly about him. God grant that I don't live to see any of my children die, and that I may be the first to join Him in the place where all is love, joy and an end to suffering.

The story has been given to both me and the Intermediary.[25] But at what a price!

I am correcting the proofs. I feel very humble and happy to be involved in this great work, which often brings tears of joy to my eyes.

February 22, morning Vanya has been ill ever since yesterday evening. He has now developed scarlet fever, a sore throat and diarrhoea. Filatov came and diagnosed it.

February 23 My darling little Vanechka died this evening at 11 o'clock. My God, and I am still alive![26]

(May 18, 1896 – Tsar Nicholas II marks his coronation with the distribution of presents to his subjects on the Khodynka Field, near Moscow. 1,300 people crushed to death in what becomes known as the 'Khodynka catastrophe'. The 1890s see an unprecedented rapid growth (supported by foreign capital) of mining, metallurgical and manufacturing industries, railways and oilfields with a corresponding growth in the working class. May to June – a huge wave of textile workers' strikes in St Petersburg (spreading to other places in Russia) against the 15-hour working day. Some two hundred and sixty factories hit; hundreds of strikers and revolutionaries arrested. November – large demonstration to mourn the Khodynka victims, in which over seven hundred people arrested. Pobedonostsev, reactionary Procurator of the Holy Synod and the Tsar's chief adviser, exhorts Nicholas II to imprison Tolstoy.

Tolstoy working on Hadji Murat. *May 15, 1896 – Lyova Tolstoy marries*

Dora Westerlund in Sweden. Taneev again spends the summer at Yasnaya; his friendship with Sofia provokes Tolstoy's jealous rage.)

· 1897 ·

First comprehensive census in Russia. June – law (resulting from the strikes) enforcing 11½-hour day in the factories and the restriction of overtime. Another disastrous harvest, followed by famine.

January – Tolstoy starts work on What is Art? *(also referred to in the text as* On Art*). February – Tolstoy's disciples Biryukov and Chertkov arrested and sent into exile. Summer – Tolstoy proposed as candidate for Nobel Peace Prize. June 2 – Maria Tolstaya marries Nikolai Obolenskii (Kolya). Tolstoy refuses to allow Taneev to spend the summer at Yasnaya, and threatens to leave. Sofia working on fourteenth edition of Tolstoy's* Complete Works. *November – first part of* What is Art? *published, to storms of protest.*

June 1 It was two years ago, on February 23, that my little Vanechka died. Since that time I closed the last page of my diary as I closed my life, my heart, my feelings, my joy. And I haven't yet recovered, but this utter spiritual solitude has made me want to write my diary again. Let my words give a picture of this last period of my life – particularly my *married* life. I shall keep strictly to the facts, and later on, when I am able to, I shall describe those two years of my life, so rich in emotion and significance.

Today is Whit Sunday, bright and lovely. This morning I saw Tanya and Seryozha off to Moscow for Masha's wedding, which is tomorrow.[1] Then I read the proofs for Volume XII of the new edition I am bringing out.[2] Lev Nikolaevich is writing an article about art,[3] and I see nothing of him from breakfast to dinner-time. We ate at 2. At 3 Lev Nikolaevich asked me to go out for a ride with him. I said no, but then I became terribly keen to go, mainly because I hate being left alone. So the three of us set off (the third being Dunaev), and rode through some lovely parts of Zaseka. We visited the mines, where a Belgian company is digging for ore, and the abandoned 'Kingdom of the Dead', then rode down the ravine, and up again. Lev Nikolaevich was extraordinarily kind and attentive to me, and I was so grateful to him, although in the past his kindness would have filled me with joy, whereas now that I've learnt from his diaries what his true attitude to me is, I am merely touched by this kindness in his old age – for I'll never again abandon myself to those paroxysms of love, those outbursts of happiness and despair, as I did before reading his diaries. One day I must tell the story of those diaries, which have completely transformed my emotional life.[4]

Our ride lasted about three and a half hours, and was very lovely. When we got back we found A.A. Zinoviev waiting for us. Lev Nikolaevich and his guests then read some German letter together,[5] while I corrected more proofs. Andryusha arrived, and alas he and Misha went off to the village dance. Sasha has Sonya Kolokoltseva staying with her, and they both went for a walk with Mlle Aubert.

June 2 Same as yesterday: proofs all day, a walk this evening with Lev Nikolaevich, Dunaev and Maklakov. Dunaev kept talking (very loudly) about the import and export of goods from abroad. A beautiful sunset: a fiery ball and one black cloud against the clear sky. Happy thoughts and pleasant memories. But our present life is unhealthy – literally too: Lev Nikolaevich terrifies me at times, he is so thin, so prone to headaches, and now this morbid jealousy . . . I don't know if I am guilty. When I first grew close to Taneev I thought how nice it would be to have such a friend in my old age: calm, kind and clever. I liked his relationship with the Maslovs, and I wanted the same . . . Now look what has happened!

Zinoviev was here this evening, as well as Feret and his wife. Sasha and I drove over to Kozlovka, where we met Miss Welsh. The moon is out, it's damp and cold . . . and oh so melancholy!

June 3 Masha and Kolya have arrived, as husband and wife. Taneev came, and Turkin, to teach Misha. All other feelings are overshadowed by the dread of scenes over Sergei Ivanovich's visit. I feel sorry for Masha, and this makes me terribly fond of her, and of course I shall love her and do everything I possibly can for her. Kolya makes the same impression as before – a nice young man, but the thought of him as my daughter's husband immediately excludes any good feelings I might have for him. He couldn't possibly be the mainstay of her life. Well, we shall see. My husband's *strength* has been the death of me, and has broken both my spirit and my personality – and it's not as though *I* lacked strength or energy! My heart is happy and at peace at present. But it was deeply painful to see the horror on Lev Nikolaevich's face when he heard of Taneev's arrival. He is morbidly jealous, and his suffering is unbearable to me too.[6] And as for my own . . .

June 4 A distressing conversation this morning with Lyovochka about S.I. Taneev. The same unbearable jealousy. I choked back the tears, bitterly reproached my suffering husband and ached with regret for the rest of the day. I read the proofs for 'The Power of Darkness';[7] what a pure, whole, truthful work of art. Then I went for a swim and met Taneev, which sadly reminded me of our daily meetings last year. After dinner he played Tanya some of his songs. I love his music and I love his character, calm, noble and good. Then I copied out Lev Nikolaevich's article on art for him.

Later he came in and invited me so nicely to take a walk with him, and we had a delightful stroll together. Then an unpleasant scene with Andryusha over money. He cried and I felt sorry for him, although I find this weakness of his distasteful – it's so unmanly.

Taneev played two of Mendelssohn's 'Songs Without Words', and transported my soul. I copied out some more of Lev Nikolaevich's article before bed-time.

Masha and Kolya have been staying here, both so sad, thin and weak . . . Tanya is very dear to me – but what has happened to all her strength and energy? I seem to have such endless supplies of it!

June 5 Sergei Ivanovich left today, and Lev Nikolaevich immediately became calm and cheerful again, and I am calm too, for I have seen him. It is only because Lev Nikolaevich is suffering that he makes these jealous demands that I have nothing more to do with Sergei Ivanovich. But to break off relations with him would make me suffer too. I feel so little guilt and so much calm joy in my pure peaceful friendship with this man, that I could no more tear him out of my heart than I could stop seeing, breathing or thinking. I read proofs this morning, then waited on the balcony for Sergei Ivanovich to have coffee with me. He came just when I'd gone out to the garden to talk to Vanechka in the watch-tower. I asked him whether there was anything wicked in my feelings for Sergei Ivanovich, and today I sensed that he wanted to draw me away from him, probably out of compassion for his father; but I know he doesn't judge me and wouldn't want to take Sergei Ivanovich from me, for it was he who sent him to me in the first place.

Later on Maria Vasilevna and I went for a swim. I am horrified by my strength and my capacity for exercise! After dinner, Lev Nikolaevich, Sergei Ivanovich, Turkin and I all went for a walk. I picked a wonderful bunch of flowers, and I was amazed to hear Lev Nikolaevich expound his views on art to Sergei Ivanovich with such lively enthusiasm after all those jealous scenes. I feel bad that I haven't yet corrected the translation I set Sasha for her homework. Vera and Masha Tolstaya came. I worked all evening: first reading proofs with Maria Vasilevna, then after supper copying out Lev Nikolaevich's article on art for three hours without a break.

There is very little life in the house at present; there are not many of us here, and I miss Sergei Ivanovich more than anything.

June 6 I couldn't sleep last night; my head and back ached, and I felt unbearably depressed. I suppose this painful physical condition is due to my critical female time of life. I went swimming with Tanya, Vera and Masha Tolstaya. There are no proofs to correct at present, so I spent the whole day today busily copying for Lev Nikolaevich. It's a fascinating article, and has given me all sorts of new ideas.

The others drove out to Ovsyannikovo, while Lev Nikolaevich and I stayed at home. I was just going upstairs to write and he was going to his study, when we stopped to have a talk about Masha, who has apparently given up her religious views, which once had such an influence on her life. Lev Nikolaevich commented that *his* life had been utterly transformed by religion. I said, his *inner* life maybe; externally it hadn't changed a bit. That made him furious, and he shouted that in the past he used to hunt, farm, teach and accumulate money, whereas now he didn't do any of those things. And a great pity too, I said. It had been much better for his family in the past; it had been a great deal better for the district when he farmed the estate, for he had planted trees and improved the land; and it had been a great help to me when he had made money and taught the children; now, although he lives the same life – i.e. the same rooms, food and furniture – he bowls about on his bicycle after work (as he has done for the past few days), goes out on whichever of his horses he feels like riding, eats the large meals that are cooked for him, and not only refuses to bother himself with his children, but frequently forgets about their existence altogether. At this he exploded with rage. I know I shouldn't have reminded him of these cruel truths; he should be allowed to relax in his old age. But I couldn't help myself after all those bitter recriminations he had flung at me – saying that I had ruined his life, when I have lived only for him and the children.

I haven't experienced such spiritual anguish for a long time. I ran out of the house intending to kill myself, go away, die, anything not to have to suffer like that again. What joy it would be to live out the rest of one's days amicably with a good quiet man, not to be tormented by any more insane jealous scenes, like the day before yesterday, any more cruel mutual recriminations, like today. Yet the sky is so clear, the weather is radiantly beautiful and peaceful, and nature, so rich, bright and abundant, it seems to have reached the very pinnacle of perfection, as though to show man how insubstantial are his endless passions and griefs beside her splendour.

This evening we made it up without explanations. Towards dusk I went for a swim in the Voronka. Lev Nikolaevich collected me in the little cart and spoke to me so kindly, and said it was time for us to stop loving and quarrelling so passionately. I had never expected such an offer of tender spiritual friendship from him. Later that evening I walked alone through the forest, weeping and praying for Vanechka, for the love we had had for each other, the one truly great and sacred love of my life. I shall never again know such love – now it's merely this insane jealous physical passion, which drives all other attachments out of my heart.

June 7 My feelings for the beauty of nature today reawoke for the first time. These feelings of mine are utterly *chaste* – without memories, without regrets for people with whom I have loved this beautiful Yasnaya countryside in the past. Recently I devised a complete theory for myself concerning this *chaste* attitude to *religion, art* and *nature.*

Religion is chaste and pure when it isn't linked with all those Father Johns, Father Ambroses, and a lot of Catholic priests and confessors, but is focused within one's own soul, alone before God. Only then does religion help us.

Art is chaste and pure when one loves it for its own sake, regardless of the personality of the artist (like Hoffmann, Taneev and Gué, for whom Lev Nikolaevich has such a high regard, or my own feelings for L.N., for that matter). Only then can art be a truly pure and lofty joy.

The same with *nature.* If all the oak trees, flowers and beautiful places are linked with memories of people one has loved and lived with and are no more, then we cannot see nature as she truly is, but will merely identify her with whatever mood we happen to be in at the time. We should love nature as God's supreme gift – the gift of beauty. Only then will she give us that pure joy.

I worked hard copying for Lev Nikolaevich all morning. Then I gave Sasha her lesson. I enjoy working with her – but oh what an insufferable temper she has – with everyone but me: with me she is always good. She hits her governess, the little girl, Maria Vasilevna – anyone who happens to cross her.

This morning I went swimming with the others, did more copying, went swimming again this afternoon, clipped the hedge along the avenue, tied back the roses and the limes and spent the rest of the day peacefully on my own.

Lev Nikolaevich is also calm: he wrote, went for a bicycle ride, then rode off on horseback to Ovsyannikovo, although he didn't reach there, for he met Masha and Kolya at Kozlovka. This evening he enjoyed himself looking at the pictures in a magazine of Tanya's called *Salon.* Tanya walked to Kozlovka with Maria Vasilevna, and Misha rode over to Goryachkino to see a friend of his called Kulishov.

It has been dry, hot and thundery; it rained a little this evening.

I long desperately for music; I'd like to play myself, but I never have the time. I did play two of Mendelssohn's 'Songs Without Words' today, however. Oh, those songs! One of them in particular moves me to my very soul.

June 8 I must make a great effort to regain my energy, not for the sake of being happy but simply because of all the work I have to do. Proofs all morning, then a walk to the Voronka for a swim. I put on a white dress for dinner. (Why? For whose benefit? Well, one mustn't let oneself go!) And after dinner I walked to the tennis court to watch Tanya, Masha, Misha, Kolya, Sasha and Lev Nikolaevich playing a game. The place is so empty without Taneev or Chertkov! I went to the rose-beds, tied back the bushes and cut off the dead heads, did some pruning and picked a great bunch for Lev Nikolaevich. Then more proofs. Later on we drove to the river in the trap, and had a swim. Then I sorted out the accounts, checked the table of contents for the new edition, and did more proofs. It is now 2 in the morning. The weather is splendid: warm. bright, hot and beautiful. Tanya is also trying to keep her spirits up. Poor thing, she is *entitled* to want love, the love of a husband and friend, the love of children. The latter are certainly a great and pure joy; the former, however, is nothing but impure pleasures, deceptions and . . .

I was going to bed last night feeling calm and happy, and I began talking to Lev Nikolaevich in a low, gentle voice. He responded affectionately: 'How sweet and feminine your voice is tonight,' he said. 'How I hate it when you shout.'

I was proof-reading *The Kreutzer Sonata* today, and again it made me so sad. How cynical it is, how blatantly it exposes the evil side of human nature. Pozdnyshev is always saying it's *we* who indulge our swinish passions, it's *we* who feel sated – *we* do this, *we* do that, it's always *our* fault. But a woman's emotions are quite different from a man's, and besides, one should never generalise about feelings, even sexual ones: there is far too much difference between a man's experiences and those of a pure woman.

It's growing light, I don't feel sleepy, it's striking two, the moon is shining into the room. It's so bright today, so high in the sky, so stately, as it vies with the early June dawn.

June 10 I did not write yesterday; one day follows another so monotonously. Maria Aleksandrovna Schmidt was here yesterday. She simply lives for L., whom she worships fanatically. She used to be an extreme adherent of the Orthodox faith, but then she read all Lev Nikolaevich's articles, took down her lamps and icons, and hung up portraits of Lev Nikolaevich in their place. Now she possesses a complete collection of his banned works, and earns her living by copying them out and selling them. She is incredibly thin, works herself practically to death, does everything for herself and delights in her kitchen-garden, her cow Manechka, her calf, and all of God's creatures. We women cannot live without our idols, and hers is Lev Nikolaevich. Mine used to be Vanechka, but now . . . my life is empty. I no longer *idolise* Lev Nikolaevich. I am still deeply fond of him, and it would hurt me terribly to lose his constant love for me. Wherever he is, whatever he is doing, he is always running to look for me, and it's always a joy to see him. But *happiness*, true happiness, is something he can no longer give me.

The same as yesterday: proof-reading and swimming morning, noon and night, nothing new. Before dinner I cut out and made up a linen peasant shirt for Lev Nikolaevich. This evening I checked and completed the table of contents for the last volumes. After dinner I invited Lev Nikolaevich,

Turkin and a young artist who is staying with us to come out for a walk and enjoy the beauties of nature, and it was lovely. Seryozha cycled here from Nikolskoe, and Semyon Ivanovich came over in the cart to collect Masha. It is marvellous weather: stormy, warm, bright and showery, lush, fresh and green.

I feel crushed, and am making great efforts to stifle all sorts of memories. Today I was looking at a portrait of Vanechka and burst into tears. No consolation, nothing, nothing. A telegram from Lyova: he is worried about his family. Does he love us, I wonder? How can he, when he torments us so? What pain he has brought me in this short time! Tanya is in better spirits too. Help her, Lord, I love her, feel for her and long to help her, but it's not in my power.

June 11 Everyone is cheerful and well. I got up late after a sleepless night, and went swimming with Sasha and Miss Welsh. I did some proofs with Maria Vasilevna, inspected the apple orchards and flower-beds with the gardener, did some pruning and grafting, and planted a few fir trees. I told Dunyasha off for wasting the bran flour I had brought specially from Moscow for Lev Nikolaevich. Tanya and I went for a swim this evening, and we had a talk about sexual love. She seems troubled about it, and I am dreadfully afraid for her. She has such a virginal, innocent nature; God save her from marrying some man who does not love her, or that peevish Sukhotin. As we were walking along the avenue in the park this evening, we met Seryozha and old Semyon Ivanovich. We've all been enjoying ourselves singing, dancing and playing games. As I was going into the house today, Seryozha started playing the piano, and I suddenly longed painfully for that music which put me in such a wonderful mood before, and gave me such pleasure. More proofs this evening, then some photography, letters and preparations for the trip to Tula. It is 2 in the morning.

June 12 I went to Tula with Seryozha and Nurse. I went with Nurse to the savings bank to collect her interest, settled Masha's financial affairs[8] with Seryozha and got the application forms for Misha to appoint me as his guardian. Then I did the family shopping. Heat, dust and frightful depression! I kept thinking of last year's trip to Tula with Tanya, Sasha and Sergei Ivanovich – the boat ride, dinner at the station, the journey back that night on the train, Andryusha's unexpected appearance in Tula, and everyone in such a happy carefree mood. I found them all in high spirits when I got back this evening, and sat down to some proofs. Then I went for a swim on my own. I came out of Zakaz to the most extraordinary sunset. Pure, bright, silent, the dark woods stark against the brilliant sun. Sublime! I swam sadly in the milky mist. Then I walked home, and although it was quite dark I didn't feel at all frightened on my own. I stopped for a moment as I always do at Vanechka's mound, where we used to rest and he used to find white mushrooms, and there I recited the Lord's Prayer. I no longer feel lonely when I walk alone, for my soul is with those I loved when they were alive. This is something no one can take from me, whatever happens, however harshly they may treat me.

Olga Friederichs came this evening and she and Seryozha shared sentimental memories of the past – oh, how unhappy they both are! It may be that Tanya has chosen a kinder fate.

Turkin and I looked at old photographs, and my heart ached once more with regret for the past.

Lev Nikolaevich is cheerful and happy. Lord help me guard his peace of mind, and let me not burden my conscience with anything for which I might blame myself. I have written to Lyova. There are several bad mistakes in the table of contents for the new edition.

June 13 I slept badly, got up late and ran straight out for a swim. On the way to the river I came across some peasant children taking lunch to the haymakers. They were such adorable little creatures, with those gentle, serious, inquisitive eyes, that they reminded me of Vanechka and I walked on with my heart full of tears. When I got to the bathing-hut Tanya said to me:

'Fancy that, I was just thinking of you.'

'Yes? What were you thinking?' I said.

'Oh, about Vanechka,' she said. 'I was remembering the way he puckered his little lips when he cried – the way he never cried from anger or naughtiness but always because he was unhappy – and I was thinking, if *I* have painful memories of him, how much more painful it must be for *you*.'

And I said: 'Was it those peasant children who put you in mind of him?'

'Yes,' she said. And at that we both burst into tears. It often happens that I hear echoes of my own soul in Tanya's words. We hadn't spoken to one another, yet we both experienced the same feeling at the same moment, prompted by the same thing.

Meanwhile Sasha was spluttering in the river by the bathing-hut, and Tanya only just managed to get to her and drag her out. When I got home I went straight in to Lev Nikolaevich. He is cheerful and full of energy today, for his work is going well. I then sat down and copied out his article on art for about four hours without a break.

This afternoon we all went for another swim, and Maklakov arrived. After dinner we piled into the trap and drove over to the Belgian iron foundry near Sudakovo. We watched the machines and saw the molten cast-iron being poured out, and it was all highly interesting – although depressing too, to see people being roasted day and night in this inferno. The place was crowded with people, including a high-spirited Frenchwoman, the heat was intense, and the ground beneath our feet was littered with iron and rocks. Some horses broke away, but were caught. Lev Nikolaevich is tender and attentive to me, and that is my greatest joy. How long will it last? It is a fresh, peaceful night, the glow of evening will soon be followed by the glow of dawn, and my head is filled with memories of the drives we took in the carriage last year.

Something very irritating happened: the sheet music arrived from Moscow extremely badly bound, and what is worse, they had torn the cover off Sergei Ivanovich's quartet on which he had inscribed his name. I all but wept.

It displeased Lev Nikolaevich to see me so upset and I tried not to let it show, but I have such a hot, ungovernable temper and have never learnt to control my feelings. I wrote an angry letter to the binders, and don't regret a word of it.

June 14 I worked hard with Sasha all morning. I corrected her English translation and her essay, entitled 'Domestic Animals', then I asked her to repeat her geography lesson, on China. She is a quick, attentive student, and never gives me any trouble. I love teaching, and am so used to doing it now. Tanya, Sasha, Maria Vasilevna and I went for a swim. Then dinner, proof-reading and more proof-reading until bed-time. This afternoon Sasha, Miss Welsh, Mlle Aubert, Maria Vasilevna and I ran down to the river for another swim, while Tanya, Kolya, Masha and Misha all went over to Pirogovo, some of them on horseback and the others in the cabriolet. Maklakov and Turkin left for Moscow. Lev Nikolaevich, Seryozha and I drank tea together this evening. I feel lonely all the time. I see almost nothing of Lev Nikolaevich. He sits writing in his study all morning until dinner time, which is at 2. After dinner he goes out on his bicycle or on horseback, then comes back for a nap. Today he walked over to Kozlovka to see off some young man from Kiev[9] who had evidently been hoping to stay with us, until Lev Nikolaevich firmly gave him to understand that this would not be possible. He came back after we had had our supper, so he had his alone, then went to bed early, and I am sitting up late.

I live for the beauty of nature, and for hard work. But for this, life would be dull and lonely indeed; but I do try to be cheerful in company, and I feel guilty when I think how much kinder fate has been to me than to many others.

June 15 I didn't sleep a wink all night. Towards morning I dozed off, but was shaken awake by my own sobbing. I was dreaming of Vanechka; Nurse and I were going through all his toys, and I was weeping. Intense grief, like intense love, is something you can never suppress, however hard you try. There are days when I feel as though I cannot make my life stretch far enough. Life is like a piece of cloth which has to be stretched over something. Sometimes it's too big, and there's a surplus; sometimes, there's exactly the right amount you need to be happy, and sometimes, there just isn't enough, and when you stretch it, it tears.

I went in to see Lev Nikolaevich the moment I got up. He was playing patience, and said his work was going splendidly. Then he looked at me with a smile, and said, 'You know you were telling me how bent I was? Well from now on I'm going to stand up straight!' And so saying, he stretched his back and sat bolt upright.

It rained during the night, but it has now cleared up and there is a cool breeze. After coffee I did more proofs – soon I'll have finished them. Pavel Aleksandrovich Boulanger came, and my sister Liza with her daughter. I was delighted to see them. We went swimming twice, despite the cold north wind. This evening Boulanger was talking about Lev Nikolaevich, whom he described as a great reformer. Neither my sister Liza nor I agree in the least with his denial of the Church, or with this latest article of his on art, in which he says that a work of art's significance lies merely in its 'infectious' powers. One has only to ask *who* is supposed to be 'infected' for his entire argument to be destroyed. A peasant is affected by a song on the accordion, for example, while I am affected by Beethoven or Mendelssohn's 'Songs Without Words', Strakhov is affected by *Ruslan and Ludmila*, Mme Helbig by Wagner, and the Bashkiri shepherd by his reed pipe.

Cool, windy and cloudy.

June 16 I got up late and didn't see Lev Nikolaevich until dinner. I worked hard on the proofs. The others returned exhausted from Pirogovo in time for dinner. My sister Liza came back with them, and we had a talk about religion. I wish I hadn't spoken my mind so openly. We should jealously guard our private and exclusive relationship with God; we should take from the Church what the holy fathers and God Himself have put there; above all we don't need a lot of forms or moral laws – for they are of little importance – but what is important is that we *strictly develop the inner feelings which guide our actions*, that we see the truth clearly and honestly, and that we recognise for *certain* and without compromise what is right and what is wrong. I ran to the Voronka for a swim with Maria Vasilevna, my one and only companion all summer. It's little better than being on my own, for she is a loud, vulgar woman, and would be quite insufferable if she had not such a good heart. More proofs this evening – and now the day is over.

Cool, overcast and windy.

June 17 I dreamt last night that I was lying in a strange bed in a strange room. Sergei Ivanovich comes in, and goes straight to the table without seeing me; on the table there is a bundle of torn-up scraps of paper – notes or bills – and he puts on his glasses and hurriedly starts writing on them. I lie there quite still, terrified that he will see me. Then, having covered all the bits of paper with his writing, he bundles them up again, takes off his glasses and leaves the room. I jump out of bed, run to the table, pick up the pieces of paper and read. On them is a detailed description of the state of his soul, his struggles and his desires. I am hurriedly reading them when there is a loud knock at the door and I wake up. I hadn't managed to read to the end, and I was annoyed at being woken up, for I had wanted to sleep on and continue reading – but of course I couldn't.

More proofs, then a swim in the cold river and a solitary walk home in the cold along that path which has witnessed so much during the 35 years of my marriage. After tea Tanya, Sasha, Vetochka, Aleksandr Aleksandrovich Behrs, Turkin, Miss Welsh, Mlle Aubert and I all walked to Kozlovka. I enjoyed our walk; Turkin and I talked about philosophy all the way, and he told me about the latest tendencies in English philosophy. I thought of our walks to Kozlovka last year. What a difference! How cheerful, happy and energetic I was then!

The other difference is that at this very moment, instead of the sweet elegant music Sergei Ivanovich played for us last year, Lev Nikolaevich is banging away on the piano in a highly unnatural manner, trying to pick out some chords to accompany Misha on the balalaika – which he plays quite nicely, although I am not particularly fond of these Russian folk-songs. I could not help making the comparison – and it could hardly be to the advantage of the latter! One thing I am glad about, however, is that Misha is at home – although he sees little enough of his father even then. I shall correct more proofs now, and that will be another day gone.

Relations with Sasha are no better. She is rude, wild and wilful, and she has worn me down by mocking me and insulting my finer feelings. Lev Nikolaevich went to visit a dying peasant called Konstantin twice today. When we went out for a walk he kept scribbling notes, then he went for a bicycle ride. He is cheerful and well.

June 18 Today is Sasha's 13th birthday. What dreadful memories I have of her birth! I remember we were sitting that evening having our tea – the Kuzminskiis were still staying with us, and Mme Seuron the governess was there with her son Alcide (the poor boy later died of cholera) – and we were talking about horses. I said to Lev Nikolaevich that he was always losing money: he bought the most marvellous stud horses from Samara, then bred them to death – no pedigree, no money, nothing, and it cost him thousands. It was true, of course, but that wasn't the point. He was always finding fault with me when I was pregnant. Because he didn't like the look of me I suppose, and he had been especially irritable with me in the last months. This time, however, he completely lost his temper with me and said a number of truly terrible things, and putting some things into a linen bag, he said he was leaving for good, possibly for America – and despite my pleading, he left.

At that point my labour pains started. I was in agony – for he wasn't there. I went into the garden and sat down alone on a bench. The contractions came stronger and stronger – and still he didn't come. My son Lyova came to me, and Alcide, and they both pleaded with me to go in and lie down. But I felt paralysed by grief. Then the midwife came out with my sister and the little girls, who were in tears, and they took my arm, led me upstairs and put me to bed. By that time the contractions were coming stronger and more frequently. At last, at 5 in the morning, he returned.

I went downstairs to him, and he glared sullenly at me. 'Lyovochka,' I said, 'the contractions are very strong – I'm about to give birth. Why are you so angry? If I'm to blame, forgive me, for I may not survive this labour . . . ' Still he didn't speak. Suddenly it flashed across my mind that he might be jealous again, or suspicious of something I'd done. So I said to him: 'It doesn't matter if I live or die, but if I do, I shall die pure in body and spirit; I have never betrayed you, never loved anyone but you . . . '

He jerked his head round and stared at me, but not one kind word did he say to me. I went out of the room, and within an hour Sasha was born.

I gave her straight to the wet-nurse. How could I breastfeed my baby when Lev Nikolaevich had handed all the work over to me, and I was having to labour both as a woman and as a man?

What an agonising time that was! It was then that he was undergoing his conversion – to *Christianity*! For this Christianity the *martyrdom* was mine, of course, not his.

I got up late this morning, and went swimming with Tanya and Maria Vasilevna. It's dreadfully cold, only 5 °. I spent a lazy day, just did a few proofs, then thought about a story and made a few notes for it. Later on we drove to Ovsyannikovo in the carriage to see Masha, and spent an enjoyable evening there. At Kozlovka the peasants were dragging a wagon across the railway line to make a temporary home, singing as they worked. The Behrs, father and daughter, went with us, as well as Turkin, Sasha, the two governesses and Maria Vasilevna; Tanya and Misha followed on horseback. Later on I developed the photographs I took today of Sasha and Vetochka.

Lev Nikolaevich went for a swim this morning in the middle pond, then went indoors to write. After dinner he played a game of tennis with Misha and the little girls, then went off on his own for a bicycle ride. Then he got on his horse and came out to meet us. While I was developing my photographs he was having a discussion with Behrs and Turkin about art. He is deeply preoccupied with it at the moment; I completely disagree with many of his views on the subject.

Behrs also accompanied Tanya on the mandolin, then played some dance music while Misha and the three little girls danced, and I danced a waltz with Misha and was astonished by my own agility. It has just struck one.

June 19 The moment I got up this morning, even before dressing, I made prints of my photographs of Sasha and Vetochka. I saw Vetochka and her father off, then sat down to some proofs. Maria Vasilevna and I went for a swim. The water was icy – it was only 5 ° at 9 last night. More proofs after dinner, then we went to Kozlovka to collect the mail. I talked all the way there with Misha's tutor, Turkin, about education, and about various human types and personalities. On the way back we met Lev Nikolaevich, walking with some man who had been imprisoned for writing a poem about the Khodynka catastrophe.[10] Lev Nikolaevich took his leave of the man and walked home with us, which made me very happy. I am not well. My temperature keeps shooting up, my legs ache – the general opinion is that it is all due to my critical period. The most terrible thing is this depression which often makes me feel so helpless. Yet again something in me has broken.

I dealt today with the unpleasant business of the felled trees, with the poor Grumond peasant coming in dressed in rags, throwing himself to the ground and begging my forgiveness. I could have wept, but I felt furious too (I don't know with whom) to have been forced into this position of having to run the estate, which means I have to guard the woods – which means I am now responsible for punishing these wretched peasants. I never liked running the estate, I never wanted to, I never knew how to. All I know is that estate management means defending private property against the people, and that is something I am simply not capable of.

It was decided that the matter would not be reported to the village policeman, that they would keep the trees, which they had already used for building, and would repay us with labour.

Another unpleasantness was a letter we had from Kholevinskaya, the woman who was exiled to Astrakhan for giving some banned books to a clerk in Tula, after Tanya had sent her a note asking her to do so. Kholevinskaya is worn out and very bitter, and has begged me to help her.[11] I cannot think what more I can do, but I should dearly like to get her released.

Lev Nikolaevich is feverishly writing *On Art*. He is already close to finishing it, and can think of nothing else. This evening he read us a French comedy from *La Revue Blanche*.[12]

June 20 Proofs all morning, worked hard on them all day, and now, joy of joys, I have finished! I have been working on them for six months, and today they're done. I just hope they're all right. I went for a swim with Tanya and Maria Vasilevna – the water is 12 ° and the nights are cold. Lev Nikolaevich went to Tula this evening to send a telegram to Chertkov in England.[13] Apparently Chertkov has been worrying about Lev Nikolaevich's *feelings* for him. But Lev Nikolaevich simply *loves* him! This evening I played some of Mendelssohn's 'Songs Without Words', and as I listened to them I remembered how Sergei Ivanovich had played them.

Later I read my letters from Lyova in Switzerland, and from Stasov.[14] Then I pasted in some photographs and wrote a letter to Lyova.

I enjoyed living completely alone with Lev Nikolaevich, for it reminded me of my youth, and that pure spiritual peace; maybe it was apathy, but it was without sin, emotions or passions.

Now I struggle constantly to stifle all this and stem the volcano of my ungovernable nature.

Tanya did some copying, played the guitar, and then the mandolin. Sasha tidied up her room, made jam and arranged flowers. Misha has taken 22 rubles and gone off somewhere. He has been singing at the top of his voice, banging out chords on the piano, walking around in Sasha's dress, and doing almost no work.

June 21 I didn't sleep, got up late, and sat down at once to work with Sasha. But I saw she was looking very pale and she said she felt sick and had a headache. So that was unfortunately the end of the lesson. Then she vomited and had to lie down. She often gets migraines, like her father. I called Tanya and Maria Vasilevna, and the three of us went for a swim in the Voronka. I cut out a dress, then we had dinner. The Obolenskiis came and they all played lawn tennis, while I wandered off on my own to sit in the watch tower. I sat there for a while talking to Vanechka, then picked a bunch of flowers for his portrait – I started back and saw them all coming in my direction, but I went home alone, sat down at the piano, stretched my fingers and was just about to start playing when Ilyusha arrived; I feel very sorry for him, I know his affairs are going badly, but I really cannot blindly hand money over to the children without having any control over their affairs. I never know what they want it for, or where I should draw the line. I have tried not to refuse – but then I realise there is no limit to their demands. I need what money I have now to live on and to pay for the new edition – and I don't have enough even for that. Financial matters are the bane of one's life.

Later on we took a walk to Grumond; it was a lovely evening and my soul was at peace.

Maybe life isn't always full of mad joy, maybe it isn't always a *holiday*, but peace of mind is also precious, and for this we should thank God.

I am not well: when I arrived here I felt that something in me had broken, and I still feel this. The strangest sensations are lurking inside me – as though I were just waiting for a pretext to take my life. It has been ripening within me for some time now, and I fear it as I fear madness. Yet I love it too, even though superstition and simple religion cry out against it. I know it's a sin, and I am afraid of killing myself, for then I would deprive myself of communion with God, and thus with the angels' souls, and thus with Vanechka. So as I was walking along today, I fell to thinking how I would write hundreds of letters, which I would send out to everyone I could think of, including the most unlikely people, and in these letters I would explain why I had killed myself. When I actually began to think what I would say in this confession of mine, I found it so touching that I all but wept for myself . . . I am now terrified of going mad. Now, after every grief, or reproach, or unpleasantness, I joyfully think to myself: you can do as you please – I'm off to Kozlovka to kill myself, I don't want to suffer any more, I cannot, I cannot, I cannot, I cannot, I cannot. Either a life without suffering, or death – and death is by far the nobler course. Forgive me, Lord!

And now I have to write out the menu for dinner: *soupe printanière* – oh, how I've grown to loathe *soupe printanière*! For 35 years, day in day out, it's been *soupe printanière* . . . I don't want to have to write *soupe printanière* ever again, I want to listen to the most difficult fugue or symphony, I want every day to listen to the most complicated musical harmonies and to strive with all my soul to understand the composer's own private, complicated musical language, and what he experienced in the depths of his being when he was composing these works.

Misha and Ilya have been banging out chords on the guitar and the piano, and bawling Russian folk-songs at the top of their voices . . . Music, like speech, can express everything, from the simplest needs – I want to eat, dance or kiss – to the most complicated philosophical questions – what is my relation to eternity? Is there a connection between my soul and God the life eternal? What is my relation to Him? A simple melody or song is like simple words, understandable to Misha, Ilya, a peasant or a child. A complicated melody – a symphony or a sonata – is like a philosophical speech, accessible only to a cultured person. I would dearly love not to have to listen to this ugly banging, and to hear once again those elegant sounds which brought me back to life last summer. Yes, that was a true holiday. I thank my good fortune merely for the memories.

June 22 A lovely bright summer day. This morning I played scales, studies and exercises on the piano. Then we went swimming. Ilya and Kolya Lopukhin stayed for dinner, and afterwards I played the piano again for an hour. After tea all of us women went for a walk. Sasha grumbled at me for calling her away from the tennis court, even though she was only watching.

Tanya ran to catch us up, and I was so pleased to see her. 'You know, mother,' she said, 'I'm growing closer and closer to you all the time – why, I shall soon become an infant again and start sucking at your breast!' Yes, I am growing more and more attached to her too. I didn't give Ilya the money. He said a great many cruel things to me: it made no difference that Lev Nikolaevich had made over the property to me by deed of purchase rather than for life, he said, I would start hoarding money in my old age . . . and much more besides. My God! Is there nothing more to my relations with my elder sons than money, money, money? And Andryusha is exactly the same – it's nothing but give me money, give me money! It's frightful!

I wrote 6 letters this evening: to Stasov, Kholevinskaya, Andryusha, Kushneryov the printer, Raevskaya, and the shops.

June 23 The beauty of nature has stirred my soul, driven out the pain that was lodged there and filled it with light. I had been peering into my heart for so long that I had grown blind and indifferent to the spring. But no more, and how good it is! Mown grass everywhere, the scent of hay, bright days, a clear, fine sickle moon (reflected today in the Voronka), the brightly dressed haymakers, their tents in the fields and their cauldrons slung over camp fires, the sleek cattle, and the dark, rich, ripe leaves on the trees this year.

I played exercises on the piano for an hour this morning, then we went swimming. After dinner I copied out Lev Nikolaevich's article 'On Art' for him from 3 to 7, and managed to get a lot done. After tea we all walked to Gorelaya Polyana, where we crossed the bridge to the main road. Under the bridge there is a new bathing-hut beside the river, and Sasha and I went for a swim there. It was cold but pleasant. We drove home in the carriage. Lev Nikolaevich came out to meet us on his bicycle, then complained of feeling tired. Misha was rude to the servant at dinner; his father rebuked him, he continued talking to him in the same tone, and Lev Nikolaevich eventually lost his temper, picked up his plate and went off to his own room. It was most unpleasant. I received a letter from Andryusha with yet more demands for money. It's the only thing I ever hear from him! Lord, what pain my children cause me! Tanya is the only one of them who doesn't bring me grief; she is my greatest joy – at present, anyway.

When we got home we found Maria Aleksandrovna waiting for us. She worships Lev Nikolaevich fanatically and lives only for him. It is this worship of him that gives her the strength to live, work and endure her life. How else could that sick, wasted, emaciated body of hers derive such strength? The power of love is an extraordinary thing! It is the mainspring of all life.

This evening after supper Lev Nikolaevich read aloud to us about the last days of Herzen,[15] and I finished copying out his chapter for him. We then shared our memories of Nikolai Gué, and argued about his *Crucifixion*.[16] I loathe this painting of his, but Lev Nikolaevich and Maria Aleksandrovna both think it is marvellous. We all took up extreme positions, so the conversation ended quickly I received a letter from Lyova in Sweden.

June 24 It rained all day. My right arm was aching in the night and I got up late. I taught Sasha very well today, and she attended well. What she needs is not knowledge so much as moral training, which I am doing my best to provide. We studied for two hours. Then I sat with Maria Aleksandrovna and altered the sleeve on my dress; we talked about our family affairs, and she was so kind and understanding. Then Sasha, Maria Vasilevna, Miss Welsh, Mlle Aubert and I drove out for a swim. The horses kept stumbling and it was quite unbearable. The water was cold, clear and swollen by the rain. Lev Nikolaevich is terribly absorbed in his work, and the world doesn't exist for him. But then all my life I have always felt alone when I was with him. He needs me at night, but not during the day, and it's so sad, and I cannot help pining for my dear friend and confidant of last year. Lev Nikolaevich rode off on his own to Ovsyannikovo, then sat downstairs all evening. I went in to see him and he was laying out a game of patience. I played two Beethoven sonatas while no one was in, and one of Mendelssohn's 'Songs Without Words'; I love it so much, I always finish with it, like a prayer. I have been copying for Lev Nikolaevich since supper, and have done a lot. It's now 2 in the morning, and I am going to bed.

A letter from Sukhotin – his wife has died. Both Lev Nikolaevich and I are extremely distressed by Tanya's relations with Sukhotin and their correspondence.

June 25 I didn't sleep a wink last night; I was so feverish I felt as though I was in a hot steam bath. This is a very difficult time for me physically. I sat at the piano for more than two hours today and played some Mozart sonatas and some exercises. I did a lot of copying for Lev Nikolaevich. I do not like his article at all, I am sorry to say. There is an unpleasant, irascible tone to all these articles of his, as though he were attacking some imaginary enemy (it might almost be Sergei Ivanovich, since he is so jealous of him), whom he was out to destroy. I walked to the Voronka for a swim, quietly enjoyed the beauties of nature, and didn't speak a word to Maria Vasilevna all day. Today was like every other day this summer, dull and uneventful. Masha and Kolya drove over, Nadya Ivanova came, and everything and everyone is dull and boring . . . I am reading a disgusting French book which I found lying around. I picked it up and was absolutely horrified by its lewd contents. The title was bad enough – *Aphrodite.*[17] What debauched people the French are! And yet reading this book does give one a true assessment of a woman's physical beauty – and of my own too.

The greatest happiness a beautiful woman can hope for, however, is to live her whole life, until she is old, in complete ignorance of her beauty and her body, for then she will remain morally pure and fresh. Books like this would be her ruin.

June 26 Heat, haymaking, I have a bad headache. I went for a swim with Nadya Ivanova this morning, and was telling her I thought each person had some vital driving force in the depths of his soul. For men it's a love of fame and gain, and for a few exceptional men it's a love of art and science for their own sake; for women it's love, often to the point of fanaticism. There was a nun at Shamordino convent, for instance, who grew two trees from the two apricot stones which Father Ambrose had spat out. She now worships those trees and lives for them. Then there's that young aristocratic girl student, and there's Maria Aleksandrovna, who worships Lev Nikolaevich. Lev Nikolaevich loves fame more than anything else, and so on.

After dinner I played the piano with Miss Welsh; I'm going to learn Beethoven's E flat Major Sonata. It's a pleasure to work with her. Tanya and Sasha have gone to Tula. Seryozha has arrived, and tomorrow Sasha and I will visit him and Ilya. I spent the whole evening copying for Lev Nikolaevich. I've seen almost nothing of him, as usual. He rode his bicycle to Tula to be mended, walked back part of the way and was taken the rest of the way back in some carts that were going in his direction. My health is getting steadily worse.

June 30 Sasha and I returned yesterday evening from visiting Seryozha and Ilya. It was Seryozha's birthday on the 28th, and I wanted to spend it with him and make at least that day a little less lonely for him. I find him very pathetic and touching in his grief, for it seems to have made him gentler; he is meek, quiet and melancholy, kinder and more deferential than he used to be. His confused runaway wife, who is now expecting his child, hasn't an ounce of pity in her icy heart for her poor husband who never did her any harm. Ilya and his way of life I found utterly depressing: four lovely children (Misha especially), and what ideas does he put into their heads, apart from horses, dogs, whether or not the hounds were in good voice, and whether or not they hunted down old Velvet? Then he goes off drinking at every opportunity with the most unspeakable characters – and that's all he ever does! If he doesn't change, his children will turn out very badly indeed. Sonya his wife vaguely senses this, and I feel very sorry for her. She does all she can to make things better, and works hard at it too – but he is no help to her, and she is simply not up to managing the house and the children's education all on her own.

At Nikolskoe with Seryozha we went for a lovely walk through some picturesque places, guests came, Seryozha and I had a discussion about musical theory; he told me something of what he knew on the subject, and gave me a number of musical pamphlets and textbooks to read. I spent the rest of the day happily with Varya Nagornova. On the train back I read a frightful book by Prévost, called *Les Demi-vierges*;[18] I felt ashamed and almost physically disgusted, as I always do when I read a dirty book. Love without purity is a terrible thing, yet even the noblest love is inevitably reduced to this same desire for possession and intimacy. But what is so disgusting in this French book is not the woman's fall, it's her life of semi-debauchery: she doesn't actually take the final step, but she does everything but, and that's the worst thing of all.

When I got back to Kozlovka I met Tanya, who was going to visit the Olsufievs. I am glad she managed briefly to escape this dismal existence which Sukhotin has forced her into; let her have a good time and see some decent people.

At home I found that Misha had a bad attack of dysentery, and there was nobody here to look after him, since Masha was busy with her young husband and Tanya had gone off. And as for his father, well, my children haven't had a father for a long time.

Lev Nikolaevich himself was rude and unwelcoming when I got back, and I was mortified to realise yet again how utterly uninterested he is in me and my life when I am simply sitting at home with the family and seeing no one; for him to pay me any attention and value me he has to feel he is in danger of losing my love, or sharing it, even in the most chaste and innocent way, with another man. As if my not seeing other people could destroy the love I have for them in my heart, or strengthen my affection for him!

The one pleasant thing today was a talk I had with Turkin. We discussed education, the character of children and Rousseau's *Émile*.[19] Then he told me about his travels, and about the Crimea. A pointless day; I did a lot of sewing. It has poured with rain all day, and still hasn't cleared.

July 2 I didn't write yesterday, Lev Nikolaevich had a bad stomach and liver. I was sitting in my room copying his article when Misha rushed in terrified, and said: 'Papa is screaming and groaning with pain!' I ran downstairs. He was sitting in his chair, bent double and groaning, and the sweat was simply pouring off him. So I at once got him into a clean shirt, then Masha, Misha and I got busy with linseed poultices, soda-water and rhubarb. But it didn't do him any good; the medicines we gave him made him vomit, and the vomiting induced excruciating pains. He didn't sleep all night, the pain got no better, and that night I feared for his life. And I thought how dreadfully lonely I would be without him. For although I suffer because his love for me is only physical, not emotional, he is none the less a part of my life and I couldn't live without him. He stroked my hair when I was changing his poultice today, and when I'd finished he kissed my hands, then followed me round the room with his eyes while I tidied up for him.

Doctor Rudnyov came today and said that Lev Nikolaevich had an excellent constitution. He had a severe catarrh of the stomach and liver, he said, but was in no danger. It will be hard to keep him on a sensible diet. It was eating all those radishes and cucumbers that made him so ill in the first place, although I had begged him not to while there was an epidemic going around and he had a stomach-ache. Misha is ill too – his dysentery still hasn't cleared up. His illness makes him so sweet, childish and quiet. I went swimming, it's warm and damp, and there's a wonderful moon – but fate has ordained that instead of walks, the wonders of nature, music, and everything else that makes life beautiful, I must fuss around with compresses, struggle against sleep and try to conquer my longing for happiness and beauty. I read Lev Nikolaevich a stupid story from the *New Times*,[20] and finished *Les Demi-vierges* on my own.

July 3 Lev Nikolaevich is better today, he has moved his bowels and is no longer in pain, and my soul is relieved of a terrible anxiety. But he stayed in bed all day. A young man came to visit him, a sectarian, and stayed talking to him for a long time.[21] He was extremely dogmatic and narrow-minded, like all sectarians, but he has read a lot and is fascinated by abstract questions and the wisdom of the ages. He has read Epictetus, Plato, Marcus Aurelius and others, all in the Intermediary edition.

Today I left the room in which I have slept for almost 35 years and moved into Masha's old room. I have started to want more privacy, besides it was stiflingly hot in the bedroom, and I am drenched in sweat all day as it is. This evening I walked to the Voronka on my own for a swim, and Turkin met me on my way back, thinking I might be afraid to walk home alone. We all sat outside on the balcony; it was so warm, and the moon was extraordinarily lovely. Masha and Kolya have left for Ovsyannikovo.

I coached Sasha for a while this morning; she has been much better ever since I threatened to send her to the institute. Misha is studying hard and is very affable, although I am sometimes alarmed by his wild behaviour – putting out candles with his gun, making strong liqueurs, thumping out chords on the piano and yelling folk-songs in a stupid, ugly voice. But he is still young, and he may well become more sensitive as his soul matures. I had a cool little note from Sergei Ivanovich to say he would be coming this Sunday. I haven't yet told Lev Nikolaevich, for I fear the news will distress him. I just hope he won't be jealous again – what a dreadful thought! But the main thing is that he is ill, and I am terrified of making him worse. If only Sergei Ivanovich knew, how shocked he would be! As for me, I cannot hide my joy at the thought of having music in the house again, and my dear, cheerful, honest friend here to talk to. He has written some songs for Tanya, and is obviously very fond of her.

July 4 Everyone has been a lot better, but there have been more unpleasant scenes. At dinner today Misha happened to mentioned Sergei Ivanovich's visit, and at that Lev Nikolaevich flushed crimson and said: 'Well that's the first I've heard of it!' After dinner there were yet more painful discussions, accusations of lying and demands that I either extinguish my special feelings for Sergei Ivanovich or break off all relations with him. Both suggestions are utterly preposterous. One cannot simply *extinguish* the feelings one has for a person. As for *actions*, which *are* under one's control, I have done nothing I could be reproached with, however furiously they might search for something to cavil at. To demand that I break off relations with this kind, honest, sensitive man would be needlessly to insult him and needlessly to compromise his own wife – to say nothing of whether she has done anything *wrong*.

I played Mozart for about four hours today and greatly enjoyed it. It was late by the time I went swimming with Miss Welsh. Pomerantsev came, and was roundly cursed; he is a pupil of Sergei Ivanovich's.

There was a thunder-storm and rain.

July 5 Neither my tender caresses, nor my loving care, nor my patience in the face of Lev Nikolaevich's rude and unjustified accusations, can soften his rage over Sergei Ivanovich's visit. So now I have decided to keep quiet. It is my own business after all, and concerns no one but God and my own conscience. Pomerantsev came, and Muromtseva. A desultory day, with a lot of talk. Muromtseva is a talented creature and understands a lot, if not intellectually then intuitively.

Lev Nikolaevich started talking about art while Pomerantsev, Muromtseva and Misha were in the room, and began attacking Wagner, modern music and the later works of Beethoven. When he launches into these denunciations he always becomes so irritable that I cannot bear to listen and have to leave the room.

July 6 Talked with Muromtseva this morning, then we drove out for a swim. I've never known it so hot, and I love it. On our way back, we met Sergei Ivanovich and Yusha walking through the woods to the swimming pool, as they did last summer. I went in to see Lev Nikolaevich the moment we got home. He was angry, sullen and jealous, and no amount of gentle reassurance on my part could soften his heart.

Muromtseva has just left. She was cuddling up to Sergei Ivanovich in the carriage in the most repulsive fashion: I have now seen a new and unpleasant side to her nature.

Mitya Dyakov came, and the boys all went off the the village dance. Tanya returned, sweet and pleasant. Sergei Ivanovich ate nothing for supper, saying he had a headache. Oh Lord, I hope he hasn't noticed anything!

July 10 I have had some very, very painful experiences. My worst fears about Tanya have come true: she is in love with Sukhotin and they have discussed marriage. She and I came to the subject in the most natural fashion, quite by chance. She evidently felt a great need to talk about it, for she is on the road to ruin and is desperately seeking salvation. She has also talked to Lev Nikolaevich about it. When I first told him he was stunned, and he suddenly looked quite wizened with grief – only it wasn't grief, it was despair. Tanya has been weeping a lot, but she does seem to realise now that this marriage would bring her nothing but grief, and she has written to refuse him.

My relations with Lev Nikolaevich have improved again.

July 13 Sergei Ivanovich left today. The past few days have been so peaceful and happy. Sergei Ivanovich played several times. The first time, on the evening of the 10th, Lev Nikolaevich had gone in to Tanya to talk about Sukhotin, and I begged Sergei Ivanovich to play a Mozart sonata for me. We were alone in the drawing-room, and it was wonderfully peaceful. He played two sonatas – what joy! Then he played the lovely andante from his own symphony, which I heard in Moscow and love so much.

Later that evening, when everyone had gathered for tea, he played again, this time a Chopin sonata. Nobody in the world plays like he does. What nobility, what integrity, what a sense of timing. Sometimes it's as though he forgets himself, abandons himself, reaches out for something beyond himself, and then he captivates his audience. The next morning, the 11th, he played again – a Beethoven rondo, Mozart's variations on the theme of '*Ah! vous dirai-je maman*', some Schubert, Marguerite's song from *Faust*, and a polonaise and ballade by Chopin.

He was obviously trying to choose pieces that would appeal to Lev Nikolaevich. His playing tore me apart; when he had finished the polonaise I could no longer hold back the tears, I was so inwardly shaken by sobs. Yesterday, at 12, he again played the Chopin sonata.

Today the weather broke. I have spent such a happy week with Sergei Ivanovich. We took two walks to the Belgian foundry, and one to Gorelaya Polyana by the roundabout route, and went swimming under the bridge by the main road. We strolled over to the mines, and through the lovely Zaseka woods, and yesterday we walked through Lemon Groves to Kochak and back again. Every day we made up a party to go swimming. Turkin and I took photographs of everyone yesterday and today, and most of mine came out very well indeed. I took a lot of Sergei Ivanovich, and Lev Nikolaevich didn't mind so much this time. In fact he has suddenly grown calm and kind. Yesterday he went for a spin on his bicycle and for a ride, and he didn't once lose his temper with me. But why should he? What possible harm can there be in my friendship with this pure, kind, talented man? How sad it is that our relations have been ruined by Lev Nikolaevich's jealousy!

Tanya has had a reply from Sukhotin – he has doubtless written her all those sentimental banalities with which he has already seduced many another woman! Masha and I wept today for this mad, blind love of Tanya's.

Andryusha visited us on his way from Moscow. He stayed only an hour but it's always the same thing with him – give me money, give me money! He was looking weak, delicate and pathetic. We went for a swim this evening. My heart aches for our walks, the music, and the soothing presence of that dear man – I cannot believe they will *never* return. It is as God wills. I believe in His will – His *good* will.

I did a little copying for Lev Nikolaevich, developed some photographic plates, and saw Maria Aleksandrovna very briefly, which I regret. It is two in the morning and I can hardly see out of my right eye. I am terrified not by the thought of death – for I welcome that – but of a helpless old age!

Pomerantsev has dedicated some songs to me, and Taneev brought me some of his duets. I shall start practising again.

The weather is changeable; this week it was terribly hot, but today it was warm, although with a slight drizzle and a north wind.

What a warm, bright, happy week it has been – apart from Tanya's grief.

July 14 I have been developing photographs all day, and making prints of the ones people have asked for. Here is a picture of me, cut out of an unsuccessful group with Tanya.* People say I actually look much younger, probably because I have a high colour. We walked to the river for a swim. There was a north wind and the sky was clear. I was exhausted all evening. Lev Nikolaevich invited me out for a walk, and I was delighted to accept. Misha started talking to me today with unwonted frankness and passion about his tormenting sexual urges, which are making him feel quite ill; he longed to remain pure, he said, but feared that he would succumb. My poor boys! They have no father, and what advice can I possibly give them in these matters? I know nothing of this side of a man's life. Tanya went to Tula today. Lev Nikolaevich is in high spirits; he was telling me all about his cycle ride to Tula to attend a meeting of the cycle club, where they discussed races and various other bicycle matters. Yet another interest of his! I feel so apathetic. I wrote to Lyova, replied to various business letters, paid the wages, did the accounts and copied out more of Lev Nikolaevich's article *On Life* for him. I try to be cheerful and keep feverishly busy. I was copying for Lev Nikolaevich until 3 in the morning.

July 15 I got up late, developed some prints, then went swimming with Sasha and the governesses. Afterwards I did some more developing and gave Sasha her lesson, which went very well today; I set her an essay to write on 'The forest', and we read various extracts from Turgenev and others who have described the forest. I pointed out to her that the beauty of these

*A photograph of Sofia and Tanya Tolstaya is glued to the diary here, with a note underneath, in Sofia Tolstaya's hand: 'I am 53.'

writers' descriptions lay in the detail, in *personal impressions* rather than *artistic imagination*. She appeared to understand perfectly. I then corrected her English translation – a story about the ancient philosophers – and asked her questions on the geography of America.

After tea we all walked over to Ovsyannikovo. We have a Swedish student staying with us, a good fellow.[22] On the way Nikolai Vasilevich Turkin took various photographs – of some sheep, the railway station and the carriage and horses. I hope they come out. We sat talking to Masha for a while, then came home in the carriage. It was a fresh and lovely evening, with the sun setting like a fiery ball against the pure bright-blue sky. Lev Nikolaevich and the Swede came back on horseback. He ate an amazing amount today: a whole saucepan-full of porridge, a large plate of salad and some fruit salad, followed by 8 cups of tea!

It is now 2 in the morning and I am still copying. It's dreadfully dull, laborious work, and everything I copy out today is bound to be crossed out and re-written by Lev Nikolaevich tomorrow. What astounding patience and industry he has!

I thought a lot about Sergei Ivanovich today; I was talking about him with Nikolai Vasilevich, and the Swedish student, who had known S.I. in Moscow, was ecstatically singing his praises. There is something about him that everyone loves. I can think calmly of him now; it's always the way after I've seen him. But my life feels constantly empty without him, especially in the summer.

I long passionately for music, and to play myself. But there's never any time, and besides Lev Nikolaevich is always working or sleeping, and every sound disturbs him. I try to convince myself that true happiness comes from fulfilling one's *duty*, and I force myself to copy out all his writings and do all my other duties, but sometimes I weaken, and yearn for some *personal* happiness, a private life and work of my own, rather than constantly toiling away for others as I have done for the whole of my life... And then the feeling goes and I feel wretched.

July 16 I got up late today as I had stayed up copying until 3 a.m. I went on with it all morning until dinner-time. I then went out to the apple orchard to watch the gardener grafting the trees, and walked through the plantation with him giving him various essential instructions. I picked some russula mushrooms on my way back, and came across the man who has rented the orchard from us. I shouted at him disgracefully for failing to prop up the trees, which means that many of them have now collapsed. I'd intended to lodge an official complaint with the president of the *zemstvo*, but hadn't done so. Later on we all went for a swim. I kept active and cheerful all day, but was suddenly overwhelmed by a wave of painful, horrifying despair. One should live an active life – forwards, ever forwards, no looking back, no regrets, and trust always in God, who always knows best. I walked home through the wood praying passionately, abandoning myself heart and soul to God's will and infinite goodness.

I spent the evening pasting photographs into the album. I shall give them all away tomorrow, and shan't waste any more of my time on my photography. I did about 80.

Turkin, Misha's tutor, has left today, and I am very sorry, for he is a splendid man and teacher. What a heavenly, warm, bright summer! Lev Nikolaevich sits in his study all day working on his article, writing letters and reading, then cycles off to the river for a swim. He takes no interest in anything or anyone.

July 17 I did more copying and developed more photographs. I gave them all away today, and shall soon give up this hobby. We went for a swim; later on we had a visit from the Shenshins, our neighbours from Sudakovo, and went for a walk with them around the plantation and to the bathing-hut. It was a marvellous evening, the deep pink sun setting against the pure bright sky, Tanya was sad, Lyovochka somewhat distant – and I was sad at heart. Misha went off to bless Ivan the servant's baby daughter. Sasha is making jam for Masha and has written her composition. She giggles all day, she's fat, red and rude to everyone. Masha and Kolya were here and played tennis.

My granddaughter Annochka arrived with her Russian governess, Sonya is arriving tomorrow with the 3 boys, and Ilya will be here on Saturday. They all leave Ilya's estate now whenever the neighbours come round for a drinking bout. I love and admire Sonya for trying to remove Ilya and her family from this hideous immorality. I am glad for the sake of my grandsons, especially Misha. I had dreamt of spending the whole of today alone, writing, playing the piano, reading – then guests arrived, and now Ilyusha's family is here, and I have to give up everything to be with my little grandchildren. I have just finished copying out a long chapter of more than 50 pages. It's dull, painstaking work. But never mind! I shall do my *duty* to the end. My life has never been happy – least of all now.

July 18 The 18th already! I don't know if I want the time to pass quickly or stand still – I don't really want anything! Tanya was sitting on a chair in the drawing-room today weeping bitterly. Maria Aleksandrovna and I came in and started crying too. Poor thing! She doesn't love him boldly, joyfully, as young people love when they have faith in the future and the feeling that everything is possible, everything is happy and the world is theirs. She is almost 33 and is morbidly in love with an old, weak-willed man of 48! I know those *morbid* feelings, when love doesn't light up God's world but darkens it – when it is *wrong* and even *evil*, but one just hasn't the strength to change things. God help us!

Sonya my daughter-in-law has arrived with all my grandchildren. I am delighted to see them, but alas they cannot fill my life. All my love for my own children has run dry and I can no longer live only for them. The three little boys went to bed, the others all drove off to Ovsyannikovo and I went to practise the piano. But then Obolenskii arrived with young Count Sheremetev and interrupted me. I am always being disturbed, and this is very painful and annoying.

Both Lev Nikolaevich and I have stomach-aches today and feel physically under the weather. I attended to a lot of business – wrote to the Samara steward, wrote to the newspaper announcing the imminent appearance of the new edition, drafted a petition to the president of the local *zemstvo* about the dilapidation of the apple trees, sent some books off to Lyova, sorted out various business papers and passports and sent them to Moscow, wrote back to Loewenfeld in Berlin, made a list of the things I had to do in Tula tomorrow, and so on and so on. All these things have to be done, but oh how tedious, how tedious it all is! Lev Nikolaevich wrote this morning, then lay reading on the sofa in his study. Neither his grandchildren nor his children give him any pleasure. He needs nothing and no one. Meanwhile everyone around him is busily defending their interests, their right to life and excitement . . .

July 20 I did no writing yesterday, for first I played with my grandchildren, then I stayed up late working on some photographs which had come out unsuccessfully. I slept badly and woke early. Today was a day of disasters. Sasha pinched Annochka and Tanya lost her temper with her. Sasha then burst into tears and wouldn't come down for dinner. I was angry with her for spoiling Ilyusha's name-day dinner and shouted at her to come down, threatening to punish her if she didn't. She came eventually, but cried all through dinner and wouldn't eat a thing. I remembered how darling little Vanechka used to suffer so when Sasha was unhappy, he couldn't bear to see another person suffer – and then I too felt so sad, so sad. I wasn't particularly sorry for Sasha, though, for I had heard her tormenting Nurse from three rooms away while she was dressing for dinner.

The same as usual: we went swimming, and I did a lot of copying. I feel a calm tenderness for Lev Nikolaevich. I still seek comfort and support from him and cling to him in moments of grief and distress – although I know how rarely he responds, and even more rarely tries to help. My God, to think of all the emotional and family problems I have had to solve all on my own!

Just today, for instance, I had a telegram from Andryusha saying, 'For God's sake send me 300 rubles.' What should I do? We all discussed it together and finally decided we shouldn't send it. Ilyusha volunteered to go to Moscow tomorrow to see Andryusha in the barracks, and I am very grateful to him.

Then yet another misfortune: Misha's tutor, N.V. Turkin, whom we all like so much, simply cannot continue his lessons with Misha. The Sabaneevs are both ill, and he is the only person capable of looking after the family and the journal, *Nature and Hunting.* What bad luck for Misha! This may adversely affect his examinations for the 7th class. He won't do any work on his own, and we'll never find another teacher for him!

We tried out some songs and duets of Taneev's this evening, but could make nothing of them. They are complicated and difficult, and will have to be learnt right from the beginning.

Terrible heat, 43° in the sun, 30° in the shade. I love having Ilyusha's family here, and am so grateful to darling Sonya for bringing them. What a dear she is, a *real* woman, wife and mother; and what a sweet nature she has.

Tanya has been weeping for the past two days, but seems a little calmer now.

I played the piano for an hour both yesterday and today, but it's not enough! I get no better at it, but it's good for my nerves and as a pastime.

July 21 I dreamed of Vanechka yesterday, lying in bed looking so thin, and stretching out his pale little hand to me. Today I dreamed of Sergei Ivanovich. He was lying in bed too, smiling and stretching out his arms to me.

Masha told me that Ilya was mortified to discover that my intimacy with S.I. was the talk of Kiev – he said they were all talking about it at my sister Tanya's and at the Filosofovs'. Public opinion is so odd! Why should it be wrong to *love* someone? But I'm not at all troubled by this gossip. I am happy and proud to have my name associated with such a fine, moral, kind, gifted man. My conscience is clear before God, my husband and my children; I am as pure in soul, body and thought as a new-born child. I know that I have never loved anyone as purely, deeply and intensely as I love Lev Nikolaevich, and I never shall. Whenever I suddenly see him somewhere unexpectedly I always feel so happy – I love his personality, his eyes, his smile, the way he talks, which is never the slightest bit vulgar (except when he is angry, of course, but I won't mention that), and his perpetual desire for perfection.

Misha and Mitya Dyakov have gone to Poltava to see the Danilevskiis. Ilya has left for Moscow to see Andryusha, and Masha and Kolya Obolenskii have gone off to visit his family.

We went swimming, and I took more group photographs in the carriage and in the water. I made prints of the ones I took yesterday, then copied for about 3 hours without a break for Lev Nikolaevich. Howling gale, columns of dust, distant peals of thunder and the sound of a fire alarm not far off. The heat was exhausting – 28 degrees in the shade, 43 in the sun and 20½ in the house.

Tanya is pale and unwell. My God, how I pity her and love her! I long to hug her and seize her in my arms and take her far away from here. Ah, how much love and care we have lavished on you, Tanya and Seryozha, my oldest and dearest children, what dreams we had for you – yet God has not looked kindly on you! They weren't destined to be happy.

July 22 Lev Nikolaevich was ill again last night. He had a violent gastric upset in the middle of the night and was vomiting continuously for four hours. He wasn't in great pain, however, and towards morning it stopped. He ate an unbelievable quantity of baked potatoes yesterday, and drank *kvass** even though he had a stomach-ache, and the day before yesterday he'd eaten nothing but Ems water and a peach. His lack of self-control and ignorance of hygienic matters is remarkable in one so clever.

Seryozha came and played the piano charmingly. I live like an automaton. I eat, walk, swim, copy, and have absolutely no life of my own, no time just to rest, play or think. It's always been like this, all my life. But what sort of life is it? '*Hélas, la plus grande partie de notre vie n'est pas vie, mais durée.*'† It's true, I am not living, *je dure.*‡

Today Seryozha said: 'Maman is in her second childhood. I shall give her a doll and maybe a china tea set too.' That may sound very funny, but in fact it's anything but funny, it's tragic. I never had time to do anything of my own, I never had time to do anything for *myself.* I've always had to subordinate my energy and time to the demands of my husband and children at any given moment. And now old age has crept up on me and I have used up all my mental and physical strength on my family, and have remained a child as Seryozha says. I have laboured away all my life for my family, bemoaning the fact that I wasn't better educated, that I never produced one work of art, that I've known so few people and have learned so little from them. But now it's all too late.

The weather has changed: it's windy, and the sky is grey. I wrote to Turkin, copied out a whole chapter of *On Art* for Lev Nikolaevich. One more day out of my life. Lev Nikolaevich was better this afternoon, and he is now sitting in the drawing-room playing chess with his son Seryozha.

July 23 Ilya and Andryusha arrived this morning with Misha's new tutor, Sobolev, who has come to replace Turkin. How I miss Turkin! This man is an enthusiastic chemist, a lively free-and-easy man, who had a long discussion with Seryozha about chemistry and the university. Andryusha has squandered all his money on the gipsies again, and has borrowed 300 rubles. I am depressed and disgusted by his appalling life. What will become of him? He has already gone to the bad, and the worst of it all is that he has taken to drink, and he's a complete dare-devil when he is

*A popular Russian soft drink made of fermented bread.

†'Alas, the greater part of our life is not lived but endured.' ‡I endure.

drunk. Ilyusha came into my room today and accused me of having changed, of no longer loving the children, and of having shut myself off from them. I denied this and reminded them (Tanya, Sonya and Andryusha were there too) that I had spent my entire life labouring away for the children, copying for their father and being constantly at his beck and call; I reminded them of that dreadful time just after Vanechka was born: Lyova was taking his final examinations, the boys had no governess, and I was having to feed my poor sick baby with aching breasts, see to the spring cleaning, look for tutors, do the packing – when I was still weak from the birth, and Lev Nikolaevich had set off on foot for Yasnaya and abandoned me, ignoring my tears and pleas for help, and I reminded them of all the difficulties, sleepless nights, tears and doubts I had endured, all the years I had moved to the city in the spring so as not to abandon my boys while they were taking their examinations – and now all I got was reproaches and criticisms. I had listened long enough, I wasn't going to justify myself any longer, I couldn't endure any more – and I burst into tears.

However much my children may criticise me, I can never again be as I was. I am worn out, my passionate maternal feelings are exhausted, I don't want to suffer any more for their weaknesses, their inadequacies, their unsuccessful lives. I feel happier with outsiders, I need new, more peaceful and straightforward relationships with people now: family relationships have made me so *ill*!

They were attacking me over Sergei Ivanovich too. Well, let them! This man has brought such richness and joy to my life; he has opened the door to the world of music, and it was only through hearing him play that I found happiness and consolation. His music brought me back to life after Vanechka's death, when life had deserted me. His gentle and happy presence has soothed my soul, and even now I feel so peaceful, so comfortable, after I have seen him. And they all think I am in love with him! How quick they are to cheapen one's feelings. Why, I'm far too old – it would be quite inappropriate.

After tea I went for a walk with Lev Nikolaevich, Seryozha, Tanya, Sasha and the governesses. Lev Nikolaevich was talking to Seryozha about the meaning of science in an unpleasant querulous voice, and I kept my distance from him, for I cannot bear that voice, which threatens at any moment to start an argument, and even a quarrel. But Seryozha was very restrained and it passed. It was dark when we got back. The men played chess and I read a little, for I had been copying all day.

It turned quite cold and dry, with a north wind, becoming clearer towards evening. We went swimming all the same. It's impossible to play the piano, and life is very tedious. I shaved my grandsons' heads and played with them all afternoon. They're very sweet but I am not consumed with *grandmotherly* feelings for them. One has to be near the earth and learn to love earthly things when one is with children, but I've left all that behind now, and childhood no longer fascinates me as it used to. I've had enough of it!

July 24 I taught Sasha this morning and corrected her composition on 'The Forest'. Then we went swimming. After dinner I did some copying for Lev Nikolaevich. This evening Ilya, Andryusha, Lev Nikolaevich and Vaka Filosofov all played tennis, my grandsons ran about brandishing whips, and Tanya, Sonya and I kept an eye on them and followed the game. But I don't like sitting still for long, so I got a saw and some scissors and cut off all the dry and dead branches on the avenue. The rain soon drove us all indoors. Before that I went to inspect the mess our wretched gardener has made of things. When I got back I had a serious talk with Ilya, Andryusha and Vaka, warning them all of the evils of alcohol and strongly urging them not to touch it. All my sons' failings and mistakes have been due to the excesses of wine. Tanya went to Tula and came back in fairly lively spirits; but I find this forced cheerfulness very sad. Our darling Tanya has left us, abandoned her old happy, peaceful life, and is walking towards her ruin. Will she get there? Or will she turn back in time? Oh how sad it is, how sad!

I am now going to read A. Rubinstein's *Letters on Music.*[23] Lev Nikolaevich has a dark one with him called Yartsev. He seems to find him insufferably tedious. He is also ill, and still has a stomach-ache and feels weak. He just lies downstairs reading and is morose and sombre. He is very distressed about Tanya.

July 25 Lev Nikolaevich still has a stomach-ache, and is depressed, unable to work and out of sorts – he even asked me to forgive him for losing his temper. I spent the day rather idly. I copied out a song which Sergei Ivanovich had written at Tanya's request to that poem of Fet's which goes: 'What joy to be alone at night with you.' I read Rubinstein's *Letters on Music* and longed to play, but didn't have time. After tea this evening I badly wanted to go for a long walk. Tanya and Seryozha had gone out in the boat, Sasha and her governesses had driven to Kozlovka and Lev Nikolaevich had a visitor, some student from the Ecclesiastical Academy, sent here by Annenkova.[24] I invited Lev Nikolaevich out, but the magnificent sunset was over by then, and it had grown cold. He went as far as the village, then felt chilled and turned back on his own, and Sonya and I walked on. It wasn't a proper walk – much too short. But I was grateful to dear Sonya, who only came out for my sake – and I always enjoy her company. Tanya and I bought some Russian lace from an old woman in the village. After supper Lev Nikolaevich read us a rather foolish play from *La Revue blanche.*[25] Sonya and the children are leaving tomorrow morning and I am very sorry. They didn't disturb me a bit, they brought me great joy.

I was sitting alone on the balcony today, thinking how fortunate I was: Yasnaya Polyana is so beautiful, my life is so peaceful, my husband is so devoted to me, I am financially independent – why am I not completely happy? Is it my fault? I know all the reasons for my spiritual suffering: firstly it grieves me that my children are not as happy as I would wish. And then I am actually very lonely. My husband is not my friend; he has been my passionate lover at times, and especially as he grows older, but all my life I have felt lonely with him. He does not go for walks with me, for he prefers to ponder in solitude over his writing. He has never taken any interest in my children, for he finds this difficult and dull. He has never travelled anywhere with me, or shared any experiences with me, for he has already experienced everything and been everywhere. And I have obediently lived my whole life with him – a smooth, empty, featureless life. And now I often long painfully for new landscapes, new information and knowledge, intellectual development, art, contact with people – and yet again I must suppress these longings and uncomplainingly live out the rest of my life without any sense of purpose or any interests of my own. To each his fate. Mine was to be the auxiliary element to my husband. And that is good; at least I have served a great writer who is worthy of the sacrifice.

I went to visit a sick boy in the village. I put a compress on his stomach and gave him his medicine, and he was so grateful to me for everything.

July 26 I copied out music all morning, then went for a swim. Very cold and windy. Boulanger, Zinoviev, Nadya Feret and the Englishman Maude came. Maude is a dull, ponderous man; Zinoviev is lively and intelligent, but not particularly likeable; Boulanger is clever and kind and absolutely devoted to Lev Nikolaevich and our family. He is currently involved with various Intermediary publications.

We were talking about death and people's different attitudes to it. My own personal feelings about it are as follows: for a long time I have felt that my soul existed outside my body, and had renounced all earthly interests. This has given my *spiritual* 'I' a boundless freedom – in other words infinity and eternity. Moreover, my connection with the Divine Source is so firm and so unwavering, that I feel I know the path on which I shall return to that place whence I came. And I sometimes experience moments of great joy, when I imagine that mysterious journey to the place where there will surely be an end to all the sufferings which torment me *here*. I cannot express this very well, but I feel as though when I die I shall *shake off* all superfluous worries, all my burden of cares, and fly off, free and light.

I played a lot this evening – I re-read various passages from Beethoven's sonatas with great interest and curiosity, and worked on a Bach invention. I have almost finished Rubinstein's *Letters on Music*. Lev Nikolaevich is still not well. His vegetarian diet does not give him nearly enough nourishment. He rode over to Kozlovka and had a long talk with our guests.

Sonya and the children left early this morning, and Andryusha drove over to see Bibikov. He keeps promising not to drink, yet he cannot go two days without seeking out the company of drunken dissolutes like the Bibikovs. Tanya seems a bit calmer, but how thin she is! Sasha went to pick nuts with her governesses. It is colder. There's a huge number of apples and they look lovely; they're being picked today.

July 27 We went for a swim this morning. It was very cold: 14 degrees in the water and 11 outside. Lev Nikolaevich is still under the weather, but managed to ride over to Yasenki. Tanya and I also went for a ride, to Ovsyannikovo. A pure clear sunset, a bright moon – towards evening the wind died down, and it was very lovely. If all is well at any given moment, I thank God for it – this is the way I live at present. I found Maria Aleksandrovna in a weary, oppressed state – she works too hard. Zinoviev, Maude and Boulanger were here again. Boulanger told me at great length that if I had given away all our property and gone out to work in accordance with Lev Nikolaevich's theories, people would not have let us starve or work; money would have poured in from all sides, as well as love and help.

What naivety! Here we are, living, writing, working, and nobody, apart from me and my daughters, has ever done any copying for us, or looked after the sick, or given us any help whatsoever.

I played the piano for a while; I practised Bach's 'Invention', sight-read the *Oberon* Overture and played my favourite pieces: Rubinstein's 'Melody', Mendelssohn's 'Songs Without Words' and Davydov's 'Romance'.

July 28 I lead a lazy, indolent life, although superficially my life is busy. I went for a swim; Ginzburg and Raevskii visited, and this evening Aleksandr Vasilevich Zinger came. Ginzburg wants to sculpt a little full-length statue of me.[26] He praised my build and my figure, and said I hadn't changed at all in 6 years. I can't think why he says such things, but this flattery pleases my vanity – if it is flattery. Everyone, including Lev Nikolaevich, played lawn tennis; I played the piano for two hours, and unburdened my soul. After the tennis we walked to Gorelaya Polyana; we crossed the stream by the little footbridge, and walked through Zaseka to the main road. We sat down for a while in the Crown plantation and returned home. A splendid moon had risen, bright and almost full, while in the west the clear evening sky was flooded with a heavenly, gentle pink light, so that my eyes kept darting from the moon to the sky, they were both so lovely. The Englishman Maude evidently felt obliged to walk with me and make conversation, when I longed to walk alone in silence and think my own thoughts . . .

I played duets this evening with Misha's tutor Sobolev. We did a four-handed arrangement of Mozart's 8th Symphony, and made a start on a Beethoven septet which we did not finish.

I got a letter from Sergei Ivanovich. I had been expecting to hear from him; I had sent him some photographs and I knew he would write to thank me, for he is such a courteous man.

Tanya and I had another talk about Sukhotin, and I was very distressed to discover how far she has already gone with him. Lev Nikolaevich is well, but not cheerful. He played tennis earlier on, and is now playing chess with Maude.

I am annoyed that Misha has not come home. Andryusha is leaving tonight, as he has to get back to his regiment.

An affectionate letter from Lyova: he misses Russia, and worries that his wife may miss her parents. You never get everything you want in life!

July 29 Another tedious day! What have I done? This morning I taught Sasha unenthusiastically, then went swimming. This takes a lot of time, but keeps one fit and is very agreeable. After dinner I wrote letters to Lyova and Sergei Ivanovich. I had to write my letter to him twice, and both versions were clumsy. Tanya was angry with me today for writing to Lyova about her and Sukhotin. I was so upset about it at the time that I simply had to tell my son. Besides, she had told Nurse and all the governesses. I worked on a black tricot hat I am making for Lev Nikolaevich, and we walked over to Kozlovka where I posted my letters and sent Misha a telegram telling him to come home. Later this evening I did some copying for Lev Nikolaevich. I didn't play the piano today, which is why I feel so melancholy.

Maude the Englishman was here all day and we had a visit from Fletcher,[27] the editor of the *Northern Herald*. (They both require Lev Nikolaevich's collaboration, which I find offensive.) We went for a walk, but Lev Nikolaevich went on ahead with them and left us women behind, so I didn't hear what they were saying. Not that they said anything new or interesting. I am so tired of all this intellectualising – attacking this and denying that, and searching not for truth, for that would be good, but for anything startling, shocking or original, anything that hasn't been said before – and it is so tedious. When people endure heart-ache and suffering in their search for truth, that is fine and honourable, but it's wrong merely to try and shock others. Each person should seek the truth for himself.

Fine days again, terribly dry, wonderful moonlit nights. If only all this natural beauty could be put to some *use*! As it is the days pass in such a mundane fashion . . .

July 30 The moon is so lovely, shining through my window! How I used to love looking at the moon when I was young, speaking in my heart to the man I loved who was far away, and knowing that he was gazing at the same moon and that his eyes too were bewitched by her beauty, so that through her we seemed to be secretly speaking to one another.

I played the piano for four hours today; music lifts me off the ground and makes all my worries and difficulties easier to bear. Today, however, there were two worries: a telegram from Danilevskaya saying that Misha was well and happy and would not be back before Saturday. This tactless, dishonest, self-indulgence of Misha's drove me to despair. His teacher is here. I managed to persuade the director of the lycée to let him take his exams in the autumn, so while Misha enjoys himself strolling around Poltava, it's I who have to endure my son's disgrace, first with his teacher, then with the director. No, I can no longer bear the burden of bringing up my weak, wretched sons! They torment me! I wept when I received that telegram today. Even Lev Nikolaevich, generally so indifferent to everything concerning the children, was indignant. I sent a third telegram to Misha, but almost two weeks have been wasted already!

The other worry is Sasha. Her work with me has been going very badly, and I made her repeat her lesson, and again she failed to learn it, so I did not let her go out riding with Tanya. I don't like punishing the children, but all the governesses have given up with Sasha.

Today passed much as usual: I swam, copied and played the piano. Lev Nikolaevich rode over to Myasoedov to enquire about the people burned out in the fire. Ginzburg the sculptor came. A terribly dry day, African heat. An owl is hooting – an evil, piercing sound. But what a marvellous night, and how still it is!

July 31 The same as usual: I did a lot of copying for Lev Nikolaevich. Some parts are fascinating, but some parts I don't agree with at all and they make me powerlessly angry, as I cannot bear to discuss it with Lev Nikolaevich. He always gets so angry when one disagrees with him that every conversation has to be brought to a speedy end. I agree with the argument in *On Art* that art used to serve religion and the Church because it was sincere, and that when that faith was lost art went astray.[28]

But there is nothing new in this, it seems to me. I remember that even I, when I was being shown around the Church of the Saviour, said I didn't like it, because the whole building – including the precious icons and paintings – had evidently been constructed without religious feeling, so it was nothing but a pagan temple; whereas the Cathedral of the Assumption is permeated with the old faith, naive but genuine, which is why it is so much better – and a true temple of God.

We went swimming and I practised the piano for an hour. This afternoon Lev Nikolaevich rode over to Tula for the post and Tanya rode to Yasenki. Goldenweiser came and played me the songs, preludes and other pieces of Taneev's which I had transcribed. He interprets them beautifully. Ginzburg was working on his statuette of me today. It's ugly, tasteless and so far not at all lifelike. I don't know how it will turn out. Misha hasn't returned, to my great annoyance. This evening I made myself a night-shirt and altered Lev Nikolaevich's cap. Then I did yet more copying. It's so dull, and I feel so unwell! Lev Nikolaevich played chess with Goldenweiser this evening. He is well and happy, thank God! A letter from Lyova, who is returning on the 12th.

August 1 Today I was copying out Lev Nikolaevich's *On Art*, in which he keeps referring to the excessive importance of love (the erotic mania) in all works of art. Yet only this morning Sasha said to me, 'How cheerful Papa is today – when he's happy everyone else is too!' If only she knew that her 'papa' was always cheerful after enjoying the love he denies.

The days are still fine and very dry. Dust and poverty everywhere. We went swimming, I posed standing up for Ginzburg. We went for a walk in the moonlight. Goldenweiser played the Chopin 'Sonata and Funeral March' beautifully. What a marvellous, heart-felt musical epic! It tells the whole story of death – the monotonous funeral knell, the wild notes of agony, the tender poetic memories of the dead one, the wild cries of despair – you follow the whole story. I should hope even Lev Nikolaevich would recognise *this* as a true work of art. Goldenweiser went on to play some Chopin preludes, Beethoven's Sonata Opus 90 and some Tchaikovsky variations. What a delight!

The Obolenskiis came. Tanya has already started making up to the new tutor, so powerfully accustomed is she to flirting. Lev Nikolaevich played lawn tennis energetically for about three hours, then rode to Kozlovka; he had wanted to go on his bicycle, but it is broken. He also did a lot of writing today, and in general he's so young, cheerful and active. What vitality he has! Yesterday he told me sadly that I had aged recently. I don't expect I shall outlive him, despite our sixteen-year age difference and my healthy, youthful appearance (as everyone tells me). I haven't played the piano, I haven't read, I have no time for anything, with this enormous amount of copying I have to do. I was overcome with melancholy again this evening, and escaped the house to go for a walk. One is so powerless at times against the passion of one's desires, so agonisingly powerless! This is how it must feel to be locked up, immured, unable to escape. This is how I felt after Vanechka's death, and at times I feel like this even now. How painful these times are, and how I long then for death!

August 2 Misha returned from the Danilevskiis in Little Russia this morning. I had meant to scold him for delaying, but I didn't have the heart: he came back so cheerful, so full of his experiences of the journey. How lovely it is to be young; one's impressions of nature and people – especially nature – are such a *novelty*. And he needed a break in his life, for he has been painfully worried by sexual temptations recently.

I went swimming with Nadya Ivanova today and swam a long way. Then I came back and copied for several hours and managed to get a lot done. 'How well you copy for me and tidy up my papers,' Lev Nikolaevich said to me today. Thank you for those few words; one never expects gratitude from him, however hard one works. I posed again for Ginzburg's statuette; it's tasteless, quite hideous and not at all like me, and I am sorry to have wasted my time. The statuette of Lev Nikolaevich[29] is also hideous and unlike him. This Ginzburg is a most untalented sculptor. This evening Sasha and I walked over to Kozlovka to meet Masha and Kolya in the carriage. Poor, poor Masha, married to that long-eared lazy-bones! She is such a sad, thin, sickly little thing – and she has all the responsibilities, while he just strolls around playing and eating at others' expense without a care in his head.

Lev Nikolaevich has some factory-worker visiting him,[30] and although he keeps saying what an intelligent man he is, he seems to find him very boring and evidently has no idea what to do with him or how to get rid of him. I finished A. Rubinstein's book on music and told Sasha about it on our walk.

This evening Misha's tutor Sobolev told us some fascinating things about the gold and platinum mines in the Urals. It is warm and still and there is a moon, although the sky is rather overcast. Lev Nikolaevich was very annoyed today because his bicycle was broken, so he couldn't ride it to the bathing-hut and had to go on horseback instead. He astonished me too by playing lawn tennis all morning. He, who so treasures his mornings, is so carried away by this game that he went out to play the moment he got up. There's still so much of the young man in him! The only things that absorb me now are music and working in the garden, sawing, planting, pruning – nothing else.

August 3 This morning I sorted out my letters to Lev Nikolaevich and his to me. I must now copy them out and hand them over to the Rumyantsev Museum in Moscow. Some I have already given them.[31] I went swimming on my own, then posed again, and after dinner I played the piano; I just sight-read a few pieces: Schumann, Beethoven and Tchaikovsky. I am alone downstairs, and it's quiet and peaceful. This evening I sorted and copied Lev Nikolaevich's manuscript *On Art*. I am completely at his service at present, and he is calm and happy. Once again he consumes my whole life. Does this make me happy? Alas, no. I do my duty towards him, there's some happiness in that, but at times I yearn for something different and have other desires.

August 4 Crowds of people all day. The moment I got up Lev Nikolaevich had a visit from a Frenchman who had been travelling around Europe doing geological research;[32] he is a cultured but uneducated man, a landowner, who lives on an estate in the Pyrenees. Then Kasatkin the artist arrived and showed us his huge collection of photographs, paintings and drawings he has brought back from abroad. This was a great aesthetic pleasure for me. I swam on my own again, and again posed for a while. Lev Nikolaevich also posed a while, standing up, for his statuette. This evening we went for a walk; it was dry and quiet, the sun was setting in a rosy sky, and now the moon is up. Two more guests came for half an hour, doctors from Odessa on their way to a medical conference in Moscow. One was called Schmidt, the other was an army doctor called Lyubomudrov. They were both very unpleasant. Goldenweiser played us a Beethoven sonata and Schumann's 'Carnaval' before retiring. Lev Nikolaevich complains of feeling weak and chilled. He went swimming and drank a lot of tea; he really shouldn't swim.

August 5 The days fly past, one after another. I went for a swim this morning, taking Sasha and Verochka in the trap with me. We took photographs of a herd of horses, and of the two little girls in the pony trap. This took a lot of time. I posed for two hours after dinner for Ginzburg, who works enthusiastically although it still bears absolutely no resemblance to me. After dinner Kasatkin, Sobolev and I took photographs of Lev Nikolaevich on horseback. But none of them came out: in mine the horse moved and it was underexposed. This evening we all went for a walk, and Lev Nikolaevich rode to Myasoedov to give money to victims of the fire there. We walked round the village and visited a number of peasant huts. Tanya was particularly anxious to call on Pyotr Osipov, the son of Lev Nikolaevich's wet-nurse, a peasant who reads books and newspapers, despises the gentry and the intellectuals, and considers himself their intellectual superior. An odious man. We walked back in the dark, developed some photographs and had supper. I had a letter from Andryusha today, and one from Gurevich,[33] asking me to send her Lev Nikolaevich's article for her journal. Why ask me? He has always gone his own way – and most of the time he deliberately does the opposite of what I want. Anyway I don't like that Gurevich, and shall certainly not do anything for her. At the moment he is reading this article to Kasatkin, Ginzburg, Sobolev and Goldenweiser. His language sounds very turgid when it's read aloud. A dry, warm, sunny day. Masha is ill. Tanya still cherishes hopeless dreams of devoting her life to Sukhotin and his family, although she is calmer now, thank God, and more cheerful.

Sasha's lesson went very well today. I corrected her essay 'A Description of Our Garden', made her repeat her geography lesson and explained to her at length the various forms of government.

August 6 I am exhausted, having just copied out a long chapter of *On Art* for Lev Nikolaevich. Then Ginzburg worked on his sculpture of me for a long time, which was also tiring. All these things dull the spirit; all my weariness and my labours are for *others* – however interesting it may be.

How much easier and more enjoyable it is to do something of one's *own*. I drove out for a swim with the children – Sasha, Lenka and Mashka. For children everything in the world is so unquestionably important, happy and fair. Ginzburg did some comic impersonations this evening: of a tailor, an Englishman speaking and a German reading. Everyone laughed – some even pretended to be doubled up with laughter – but I can never laugh and always miss the joke. This is a great failing, I know. Goldenweiser played the Grieg Piano Concerto beautifully; it is a powerful, original work, and I enjoyed it immensely. Then he played two Chopin nocturnes, something of Schubert's and a waltz by Rubinstein. Kasatkin is doing a small portrait of Tanya.[34] Sobolev took our photographs again today, and I made several prints from his best negatives. I too wanted to take photographs today, but had absolutely no time after all the copying and posing.

Masha and Kolya are here. Masha is wretched, pale and thin, and I would love to be able to help her, poor thing. About Tanya I prefer to say nothing. I am still terrified for her. Misha is very upset by all the gossip at Yasnaya, with everyone hounding everyone else to death and out for what they can get. It distresses him terribly – but it's always like this! It's better not to think about it.

Lev Nikolaevich rode to Yasenki with Kolya. He is being sculpted too, but it's nothing like him. This evening he read his guests the first three chapters of *On Art*, then played chess with Goldenweiser and his son Seryozha. He is well and cheerful.

August 8 Masha has fallen ill, Doctor Rudnyov has diagnosed typhus. This news has filled my heart with such grief; I am choking back the tears, terrible familiar tears of fear and alarm, constantly ready to flow. She had been dreaming of Vanechka – maybe he will call her to him and release her from her wretched difficult life, married to that lump of a husband. She lived a good, useful, self-sacrificing life before she married Kolya – God knows what lies in store for her now. But I feel so sorry for her personally, she has been so pitiful ever since she left home. I couldn't help recalling Sasha Filosofova's death, also from typhus, and that made me even more terrified.

The house is seething with guests. Masha and Nikolai Maklakov have come, the two Stakhovich sisters, and the two Natashas, Obolenskaya and Kolokoltseva, as well as Ginzburg, Goldenweiser and Kasatkin. There were 20 people at the table today. Individually they're all very nice, it's just a pity there are so many of them all at once. No walks, no time to oneself, no work, no copying – just this dense crush of people. I posed again, developed photographs and went for a swim, but I am not doing any real *work*; something has disappeared irrevocably, something has taken the wrong turning, something has gone wrong.

Yesterday I accidentally left my diary on the table. Lev Nikolaevich had another read of it and was annoyed by something in it. Why should *he* be annoyed? I never loved anybody in the whole world as I love him – and for such a long time too!

There was a telegram from Lombroso the learned anthropologist,[35] who has arrived in Moscow for the medical conference and wants to pay Lev Nikolaevich a visit.

Ginzburg is also sculpting Lev Nikolaevich and they read *On Art* together during sittings. It's a good thing that Lev Nikolaevich attacks the modern decadent movement in his article.[36] This vile senseless tendency must be put a stop to, and who better to do it than he.

August 11 I haven't written anything for three days. They brought poor Masha here from Ovsyannikovo the morning before yesterday. She has typhus, and for several days now she has had a fever of around 40 °. At first we were all very frightened, but we have now got used to the idea of her being ill. Doctor Rudnyov came and said it was a mild case, but I feel so sorry for her, tossing and turning and unable to sleep at night. Yesterday I sat with her till 3 in the morning copying out Lev Nikolaevich's article. I had already done a lot when Masha suddenly had violent stomach pains. Lev Nikolaevich got up and said he would put on the samovar to make poultices, but he found the oven hot enough to warm up some napkins instead. It always makes me laugh when he embarks on some practical task, for he is always so clumsy and crude about it. Yesterday he got soot all over the napkins, singed his beard with a candle and was furious with me for trying to put it out with my hands.

At 3 in the morning Tanya took my place by Masha's bed. Lombroso arrived this morning, a little old man with weak legs, who looks very decrepit for one of 62. He speaks bad French, with a lot of mistakes and an appalling accent, and even worse German. He is Italian and very learned; as an anthropologist he has done a lot of work on human criminality. I tried to draw him into a discussion, but he had little of interest to say to me. He said that crime was on the increase everywhere except in England, and that he didn't trust statistical information about Russia as we didn't have a free press. He also said that he had studied women all his life and still could not understand them. French and Italian women – '*la femme latine*', as he put it – are incapable of working, their sole interests in life are clothes and the desire to please, he said. '*La femme slave*', however, which includes Russian women, is capable of doing any kind of work and is far more moral. He then spoke about education; he feels it has almost no influence on innate qualities, and I quite agree.

Ginzburg left today. He has finished his statuettes of me and Lev Nikolaevich. He was working on the one of Lev Nikolaevich yesterday when three young ladies arrived and begged Vasya Maklakov to let them have a look at Tolstoy. They were taken into his study and he enquired whether they had any questions to ask him, they said no, they just wanted to see him. So they looked at him and left. A little later some young man arrived with the same thing in mind, but was told that Lev Nikolaevich was out. Then just as we were having our tea a man, wheeling a bicycle and covered in blood, arrived at the house asking for Lev Nikolaevich. He turned out to be a teacher from the Tula gymnasium who had fallen off his bicycle and hurt himself. He was taken into the pavilion, where his wounds were washed and bandaged, and he then stayed for supper.

The two Natashas left yesterday – by tomorrow there'll be almost no one here. I long to be alone. Yesterday Misha went to Moscow for his teacher, who has to be a juror for some court case. It has been hot, dry and dreadfully dusty. I am not well; I have rheumatism all over my body and pains in my liver and kidneys. Lev Nikolaevich is well, and played lawn tennis for a long time today. Will I ever be happy or cheerful again? My life is one endless misfortune. Yet I need so little to be happy: a couple of hours to play the piano, and 5 days to go to Kiev and see my sister Tanya, nothing more. Masha's illness has made all this impossible. It's perfectly natural for her to be staying here in her parents' house, it was I who said she should be brought here when she first fell ill. But it infuriates me that Kolya has settled in here too, and I always want to brush him aside like a pestering fly. I don't like these phlegmatic, parasitical types, who aren't even ashamed of their laziness.

August 13 Masha still has a high fever – over 40° all day. Poor girl, I feel so sorry for her, and so powerless against the implacable course of this terrible illness. I have never before seen such a bad case of typhus. The doctor called again – Lev Nikolaevich rode over to fetch him yesterday; he said she was in no danger, but I have a great weight on my heart none the less.

I have copied out a great deal of Lev Nikolaevich's manuscript *On Art* recently. I spoke to him about it yesterday, and asked him how he expected art to exist without all the specialist 'schools' he attacks. But one can never have a *discussion* with him; he always gets dreadfully irritable and shouts, and it all becomes so unpleasant that one loses sight of the subject under discussion, and merely wants him to stop talking as soon as possible. And that's what happened yesterday.

When our guests were here he read them this article and no one said a word. They were right to let him think they agreed with it all. And it does contain some admirable ideas, such as that art should inspire, not merely entertain; this is unquestionably true. And that drawing, music and all the arts should be taught in the schools, so that every individual with talent may discover his own path; another splendid idea.

Terrible heat and drought. They sowed the rye in dust, and the grass and the leaves are all withered. We go swimming, which is some relief. No news yet from Misha in Moscow.

August 14 Lyova and Dora have arrived from Sweden looking cheerful and well. Thank God – they'll cheer us up too. The doctor came and said Masha was in no danger, which reassured us. I also consulted him about my own health; he said my nervous system was in a bad state, but there was nothing organically wrong with me, and he prescribed bromide.

Lev Nikolaevich rode to Baburino at the invitation of some schoolmistress from St Petersburg. I spent a lazy day, for I had an exhausting night sitting up until 4.30 a.m. with Masha, who was very restless and had a fever of 40.7. I went for a swim, pasted up some photographs, read a little of Taine's *Philosophie de l'art*,[37] and sat with Masha. Still this terrible drought continues.

August 16 Life is getting harder and harder. Masha is still very ill. I felt quite dazed when I got up today. I had watched over her all night in a state of terror until 5 a.m. She was terribly delirious, and has been so all this morning. At 5 a.m. I went to my room, but couldn't sleep. Nothing but trouble on all sides. Tanya had a meeting with Sukhotin in Tula and sat with him in his hotel, then travelled back with him on the train. As far as I can see, she has never for one moment given up the idea of marrying him. Misha didn't go to Moscow, where his teacher is waiting for him – he's doing absolutely no work and is bound to fail his exams. He just loafs around the village playing his harmonium until 2 in the morning with the peasant lads and that silent, stupid Mitya Dyakov. Andryusha arrived this morning, and will stay for a month and a half. He said he wanted to go to Samara and to visit Ilya, which is good. But the hardest thing is my relationship with Lev Nikolaevich. There's no pleasing him, one can say nothing to him. Boulanger was here yesterday; we talked to him and agreed it would be a good idea to go through Lev Nikolaevich's article *On Art* with the censors in mind, discard a few passages to which they might object, then publish it simultaneously in the Intermediary and in Volume 15 of the *Complete Collected Works*. I did not want to be the first to suggest this, as I am terrified of the angry way he almost always speaks to me – and to almost everyone else who dares to contradict him.

Boulanger talked it over with him and told me that Lev Nikolaevich had agreed. But Lev Nikolaevich was furious when I mentioned it to him, and said that Chertkov had expressly asked that none of his works should be published here before they had appeared in English.[38] That Chertkov has Lev Nikolaevich completely in his power again, even from England!

Today we had a talk about Tanya. Lev Nikolaevich said we should keep our thoughts to ourselves – we might want the wrong thing for her or give her the wrong advice. But I said we shouldn't lie, and should tell her what we thought, even if we were wrong, and shouldn't be dishonest merely for fear of being mistaken. I don't know which of us is right – maybe he is, but it's not a question of being right, it's a question of being able to say what one thinks without losing one's temper.

Just today, as he was coming out of his study, he simply went for Misha and said some terribly – though deservedly – harsh words to him and Mitya Dyakov. But what did he achieve by it? How much better it would have been if he'd had a quiet talk with Misha this morning, and firmly told him to go to Moscow, stop shirking and work for his exams. As it was, this rebuke only made his sons angry; they were saying that their father never gave them any sympathy or advice, and did nothing but scold them and shout at them. Only their mother had the right to scold them, they said, for she was the only one who cared for them. I have indeed cared for them – but what good has that done, what have I achieved? Absolutely nothing! Andryusha has failed to do anything so far, and I cannot think what will become of Misha – he has absolutely no strength of character . . . Oh, how sad it all is, how terribly sad . . .

Lyova and Dora are settling in here and unpacking their things. Dora must find it very hard, poor dear, living in a foreign country in this dismal family of ours. I often long to run away, I am so exhausted by this life! Yet I suppose I must bear the burden of my labours, my eternal *labours*, to the end. I ought to do some more copying for Lev Nikolaevich, but I can do no more, so resentful am I of the way that he has enslaved me for life, has never shown the slightest concern for me or the children, and continually drives me like a slave even though I no longer have the strength to work for him all the time and be constantly at his beck and call.

I sat with Masha tonight, but managed nevertheless to copy out the whole of Chapter 5. I always do the work of two.

It rained a little today, but it's still oppressively hot. I read a little Taine. I had been reading it before, but Lev Nikolaevich needed those books and hid them away. I have just found them and shall now finish them. His definition of art is very good: '*L'art a pour but de manifester le caractère capital, quelque qualité saillante et notable, un point de vue important, une manière d'être principale de l'objet.*'*

Lev Nikolaevich does not have a high opinion of Taine.[39] It was Sergei Ivanovich who recommended him to me.

August 17 Lev Nikolaevich and I are on good terms again (we hadn't actually quarrelled. I just felt mortified by his attitude to me). A nurse has arrived to look after Masha; she is a little better today, and her temperature is down to 38.6 °. Lyova and Dora are both rather lethargic and under the weather. Poor Dora, I feel so sorry for her. It's very hard for her in Russia,

*'The purpose of art is to reveal the fundamental character, some striking or remarkable quality, an important point of view, the chief characteristic of the object.'

so far from her family. Another dry, windy day, but much cooler since morning. I walked back from the bathing-hut with Tanya, and we had a talk about Sukhotin. She says she hasn't yet come to any definite decision. Misha left for Moscow yesterday evening, and Andryusha has gone off to some mysterious destination. I have been copying again for Lev Nikolaevich, and sitting with Masha, but there's no satisfaction in merely fulfilling my duties, and I feel melancholy. Then there was distressing news of another fire on Ilya's estate; the whole of this year's harvest was burnt, as well as the barn, the farm implements and various other things. Oh, how cruel life is! Dunaev and Mitya Dyakov are here. I asked myself today why I found it so irksome to copy out Lev Nikolaevich's article, when it is obviously *necessary*. And I came to the conclusion that any kind of work one does requires one to take an interest in whether or not it is well done, and what the end result will be. When I sew something, I can see the result and am interested in the process of the work, whether it goes quickly or slowly, whether I do it well or badly. It's the same when I teach the children – I see the results when they make progress; or when I play the piano – I always feel I am learning something, discovering something new, revealing something beautiful. I am not talking here of creating an original work – like a painting, even the most primitive – merely of the work one does in one's everyday life. But when one copies out the same article ten times, there is nothing – no sense of accomplishment, never any end in sight, just the same thing over and over again, endlessly altered and shuffled around. And there's no interest to carry one along, as there used to be in his *literary* works. I remember how I used to wait for my pages of *War and Peace* to copy after Lev Nikolaevich had finished his day's work on it. I used to write on and on in a state of feverish excitement, discovering new beauty in it as I went on. But now I am bored. I must work on something of my own, or else my soul will wither.

August 18 Yesterday afternoon Lev Nikolaevich, Dunaev and I took a lovely walk through Zaseka, then along the railway tracks to Kozlovka. In the forest I was in a state of poetic peace such as I have not felt for a long time. But then I overtired myself; we covered about 12 *versts* and it became dull and hard going.

Masha is much better. Maria Aleksandrovna Schmidt came. There was a shower. We went swimming. The nurse arrived in the evening yesterday (or rather the day before yesterday), to take Masha's pulse and to keep an eye on her, and Doctor Rudnyov came. I visited Lyova in 'that' house, saw to various tedious domestic matters – mattresses, lamps and jam-making – and put the house in order. I then did some copying for Lev Nikolaevich and managed to do a great deal. My lower tooth is loose, which has put me in a bad mood. Oh, how I dread growing old – but I must get used to the idea. I did nothing all day. I shall read some Taine now.

August 21 I have been terrified for Masha these past three days. First she had a temperature of over 40°, then this morning it suddenly dropped to 35.6°. We got her to take some wine and champagne, but today she couldn't drink a thing, and everything made her vomit. She started shivering and we sent for the doctor, then her temperature shot up to 40° again. It's frightful! Poor thing, I feel so sorry for her, she's utterly worn out. Liza Obolenskaya has come to help look after her, and we have hired a nurse to keep an eye on her general condition and help out at night. We had a visit from that dull Prince Nakashidze from the Caucasus, the brother of Princess Nakashidze, who gave money to the Dukhobors in Tiflis and then went to visit the Chertkovs in England. Mitya Olsufiev is coming today.

I took photographs all yesterday and today – flowers, the apple harvest, the apple trees, a hut and so on. I took a walk with Rudnyov; a pure, beautiful sunset, rosy little clouds edged with fire drifting across a clear sky – and the most horrifying drought! Lev Nikolaevich went for a ride through some beautiful parts of Zaseka. He is revising his article on art from the very beginning. He is being gentle and attentive to me, but I am completely cold and cannot feel a thing; anxieties about Masha and nights without sleep have shattered my nerves.

I taught Sasha this morning, although not enough. She is embroidering a table-napkin which she is giving me for my birthday tomorrow, August 22. I shall be 53.

August 23 Masha is better now, and everyone is more cheerful. But I have another weight on my heart: Sukhotin is coming tomorrow and Tanya is very excited. Lyova, Dora, Kolya and Andryusha went to Tula to visit the handicrafts exhibition. Yesterday we took a long walk to the landslide at Zaseka, and came home in the trap. Lev Nikolaevich had gone out on horseback looking for the loveliest places, and took me out to show them to me, determined that I should enjoy myself on my birthday. We certainly saw some delightful places, but unfortunately I was absolutely exhausted yesterday, and couldn't conceal the fact. This hurt Lev Nikolaevich's feelings, which I deeply regret. But we took a long rest in the hut of some peasants who were working in the forest; they had a bonfire blazing, and those dark, ancient, majestic oaks soon made me forget my tiredness and I went home feeling happy and energetic. I waste my time on unsuccessful photographs and do no copying, which makes me feel very guilty. Boulanger came; Liza Obolenskaya is leaving.

Tomorrow I am going to Moscow, where I have a mass of things to attend to, as well as staying with Misha for the two days he sits for his exams. I have absolutely no desire to go, it's a great nuisance, but I feel I must.

August 26 This is my second day in Moscow. I went to the banks yesterday, withdrew the interest and paid in 1,300 rubles for the mortgage on Ilya's property. I shall soon have to pay the same again, and then he had a fire, and he lost a further 2 thousand rubles on the deposit on an estate he and Seryozha rashly decided to buy in the province of Volhynia. How depressing and annoying it all is. Ilya is incapable of doing *anything* – studying, managing his affairs or conducting any sort of *business*.

Seryozha's wife, Manya, gave birth to a son on the 23rd. Poor Seryozha, and that poor little boy with a mother like her!

Moscow is quiet and dull with everyone away. Dear N.V. Turkin came and he and I had such an enjoyable talk about children's education. Sergei Ivanovich isn't in Moscow yet, and I am very sad that I won't be seeing him.

I sat on the sofa all day going over the accounts with the accountant. Figures, endless figures – it's a frightful strain making sure one doesn't make any mistakes or forget anything.

It rained, and now it's cold and overcast. Tomorrow Misha will sit for his exams; I have an appointment with the board of censors, then with the accountant at home.

August 28 Today is Lev Nikolaevich's 69th birthday. This must be the first time in the whole of my marriage that I haven't spent it with him. How sad. I wonder what sort of state he is in today? Yesterday I kept thinking about his article *On Art*; it torments me, for it could be so good, but so much of it is unjustified, paradoxical and provocative.

Misha took his last exams today, and I am anxiously waiting for him to return. Will he go up to the 7th form?

For the whole of the past two days I have been busy with the accounts, adding up endless rows of figures with the accountant. Yesterday I took the Intermediary edition of Spire's book to the censors[40] and did some shopping, but I did nothing in the house and it's very dirty.

I am living a calm and healthy life on my own, and shall return here on September 10. It has become cold – or rather cool – and cloudy. I went to the bath-house today.

August 31 It's all so sad, everything has gone wrong. Misha failed, and will now have to stay down in the 6th form. Andryusha made another painful scene in Moscow and the poor boy went off in tears with Misha to visit the Gruzinskiis. I thought he might have been slightly drunk, for he was veering most oddly between extremes of violence and tenderness. Misha's attitude to his failure also saddened me: he was completely unperturbed, and went straight out to the garden with Andryusha, Mitya Dyakov and Boris Nagornov, where they started yelling folk-songs in coarse, tuneless voices. My children haven't turned out at all as we would have liked: I hoped that they would be cultured with refined aesthetic tastes and a sense of duty. Lev Nikolaevich wanted them to lead simple lives of hard work. And we both wanted them to have high moral standards. But alas this has not happened! I set off for Yasnaya Polyana the morning before yesterday feeling exhausted, worn out and depressed. Lev Nikolaevich met me not far from the house, got into the carriage beside me, and did not ask once about the children. How painful that always is! The house was packed with guests: Dunaev, Dubenskii and his wife (Tsurikova), Rostovtsev and Sergeenko. The rooms were full of bustle and chatter, and it was all extremely tiresome. These gentlemen come here expecting to get something out of Lev Nikolaevich, and now he has decided to write an open letter to be published abroad.[41] It so happens that a Swedish kerosene merchant named Nobel has left a will bequeathing all his millions to the person who makes the greatest contribution to peace (*la paix*), and against war. They held a meeting in Sweden to discuss it, and decided that Vereshchagin had made a powerful protest against war with his paintings. But further investigation revealed that he hadn't really been protesting on principle, this was merely fortuitous. So they then said that the inheritance should go to Lev Nikolaevich. He would never accept the money, of course, but he did write them a letter, saying that it was the Dukhobors who had done most for the cause of peace, by refusing military service and suffering cruelly for doing so.

Now I would have had nothing against that, but in this letter Lev Nikolaevich went on to abuse the Russian government in the most crude and provocative terms imaginable – quite inappropriately too, merely for the love of being outrageous. I was terribly distressed by this letter, my nerves were overwrought, and I became quite desperate, sobbing and blaming Lev Nikolaevich for risking his life by needlessly provoking the government. I actually wanted to leave; I cannot live this nerve-wracking life any longer, under the constant threat that Lev Nikolaevich will write something truly desperate and evil against the government, and get us all deported.

He was touched by my despair and promised not to send the letter. Today, however, he decided that he would, although a modified version of it. But all of a sudden I no longer cared – simply from a sense of self-preservation. One cannot endure endless sleepless nights such as I endured yesterday, one cannot endlessly weep and torture oneself. Grief on every side. Ilyusha was here. He had a fire and is evidently expecting me to help him out. But I am overwhelmed with bills at present, and have only just paid 1,300 rubles into the bank for him; I shall have to pay the same again this winter, too. He didn't actually ask me for the money, merely hinted at how badly off he was. Eventually he said to Lyova: 'I asked Mother for 1,000 this spring' (I had already given him 2,500 for the winter) 'but she wouldn't give it to me, which meant that I didn't insure the property, and now everything has gone up in smoke and I shan't get a thing for it.'

'So Mother's to blame again for your property burning down, is she? That's not fair,' said Lyova, and left the room. I then reminded Ilyusha that he and Seryozha had decided that in order to avoid the unpleasant business of constantly asking their mother for money, I should undertake to pay 2,000 rubles a year for the mortgage, without another word said, and that he had been quite satisfied by this at the time.

But now he was berating me for not handing the money over to him, saying it would be better if I didn't pay it into the bank but gave it straight to him instead. At that, I regret to say, I completely lost my temper with him; it was despicable of him, I said, first to ask me to pay money into the bank, then to blame me for doing so. I now feel so ashamed and sad that we quarrelled over money. It's not as though I mind giving it to him, just that I don't have any at the moment.

September 1 All the guests have left and we are on our own again, I'm glad to say. I had a short but unpleasant conversation with Lev Nikolaevich yesterday evening. I had been feeling unwell, he kept finding fault with me and we brought up the subject of our diaries. (I keep meaning to tell that old story.)

But we are friends again today; I copied out two chapters for him, tidied his room and put a lovely bunch of flowers there. I went swimming with Sasha. The water is 11 °, the nights are cold and bright, with little clouds passing across the moon; the days are beautiful, dry and sunny. Tanya went to Tula to visit an exhibition. Masha is better. Sasha is upset about the disappearance of her pet hare, who was living in the barn. Lev Nikolaevich went for a ride and received a visit from a Catholic canon who has come here to make a study of Russian monasteries.[42]

I have been yearning for music all day – I *dream* of it. I shall soon be going to Moscow, where I shall hire a piano and play; and I hope that Sergei Ivanovich will come and play to me. How good that will be, the very thought of it revives my spirits.

Today I was thinking about the sort of places we love best, and I thought it was probably those which have been untouched by human hands, like rocks, hills, the sea, mighty rivers, great forests and ravines. We love *dreams*, even in nature. We do not love huge fields, gardens and meadows which have been cultivated by the hand of man, we love untouched, mysterious places – dreams, even in nature.

September 2 I sorted and arranged the books in the library, had a swim – the water was 11 ° – went for a walk with Verochka, took a photograph of the apple trees covered in apples, and copied out a rewritten and modified version of Lev Nikolaevich's letter in which he says that the Nobel inheritance should go to the Dukhobors. I haven't finished it yet, but the first part is quite moderate. My two loose teeth have put me in a bad mood, and I cannot bear the prospect of false ones. But what can one do? One must get used to growing old.

I am going to bed now, and shall read some of Spire's philosophical book. There was a shower but it's not cold yet.

September 4 I try and try, but I just cannot stretch life far enough. Every single member of our family feels isolated, however friendly we may appear to be. Even Lev Nikolaevich complains of loneliness, of feeling 'abandoned'. Tanya is in love with Sukhotin, Masha has got married, and I haven't felt close to any of them for a long time. And we're all tired of devoting our whole lives to the service of Lev Nikolaevich. He considered himself fortunate to have enslaved the lives of three women, his two daughters and me. We wrote for him, looked after him, diligently supervised his elaborate vegetarian diet (which can be extremely inconvenient when he is ill), and never left him alone. And now we have all suddenly announced that we have a right to some life of our own, his friends have been deported,[43] there are no new followers – and he is wretched.

I strain every last drop of my energy to help him: I copy out his article; yesterday I copied a long 15-page letter calling for the Nobel Prize to be awarded to the Dukhobors;[44] I look after him. But at times I find it quite intolerable to have no work, no friends or interests of my own, no free time, no music, and I lose hope and lapse into depression.

Lev Nikolaevich is forever writing and preaching about universal love, and about serving God and the people, but it always puzzles me to hear him say these things. He lives his entire life, from morning to night, without any sort of contact or involvement with others. He gets up in the morning, drinks coffee, goes for a walk or a swim without seeing anyone, then sits down to write; later he goes for a bicycle ride or another swim, eats dinner, plays a game of lawn tennis, goes downstairs to read, and spends the whole of the afternoon in his study; it's only after supper that he comes and sits with us for a while, reading newspapers or looking through the illustrated magazines. And so this ordered selfish life goes on, day after day, without love, without any interest in his family or in any of the joys and griefs of those closest to him. His coldness is a torture to me, and I have started to seek other things to fill my inner life, and have learnt to love music, to read into it and discern the complicated human emotions contained in it; but not only is music disapproved of in this house, I am bitterly criticised for it, so once again I feel that my life has no purpose, and bowing my back I copy out some boring article on art for the tenth time, trying to find some consolation in doing my *duty*, but my lively nature resents it and I long for a life of my own, and when there's an icy wind blowing I rush out of the house, run through the forest to the Voronka and throw myself into the freezing water, and there's some pleasure in the physical emotion.

Lev Nikolaevich rode over to visit Bulygin in Khotunka, 16 *versts* away, without saying a word to me about it. Some American professor has come, but I haven't seen him yet. I looked through Lev Nikolaevich's manuscript with horror and started copying again. What a lot of work still to be done!

I taught Sasha for an hour and a half this morning and corrected her essay 'A Visit to the Troitsa-Sergievskaya Monastery'. I initialled Misha's handkerchiefs, read, cut out clothes and was busy all day long, but I feel as though I haven't accomplished a thing. That's what comes of not having one's heart in one's work.

As I was walking back from the bathing-hut today I again fell to thinking about how man lives on dreams alone. If a cabdriver, who spends years of his life driving around in an unfriendly town, didn't have his head filled with dreams of the country – of his family and his village, of how the harvest was going, how many stooks of rye they'd gathered, whether they'd bought a horse or a cow – his life would be insufferable. As it is he endures it for years on end.

It's the same with everything in this life, and the sweetest dream of all is of the heavenly kingdom awaiting us after we die, the dream of being united with God and reunited with our loved ones.

Ah Vanechka! Today I came across a scrap of cloth from his blue sailor jacket, and I wept bitterly. Why did he leave me alone on earth without love? I cannot live without him – I often feel as though he'd taken my soul with him, and my sinful body was merely dragging out its life here on earth.

September 8 A lot of commotion and a new crowd of guests: Dunaev, Boulanger and an Englishman named St John, evidently sent here by Chertkov.[45] Boulanger is being deported; he has been charged with dangerous activities – propagating Lev Nikolaevich's ideas and writing and publishing a letter in the *Stock Exchange Gazette* about the wretched condition of the Dukhobors.[46] He was summoned to St Petersburg, to the 3rd Department (in other words the police), which is responsible for administrative order (in other words administrative tyranny), and they reprimanded him.

Now Boulanger is a very clever man, lively and full of energy, and they were quite daunted by him. But heavens, what a despotic government we have! It's as though we had no Tsar at all, just a lot of ignorant blackguards like Pobedonostsev and Goremykin (Minister of Home Affairs), who behave in such a way as to bring down people's wrath on the head of the young Tsar, which is a great pity. Lev Nikolaevich is plagued by a pimple on his cheek and keeps talking about death. I feel quite alarmed, he has such a terror of dying. He is coming to the end of his article *On Art*, and we have a young lady staying here who is copying it out on the Remington; they want to send an English translation of it to Chertkov in England so he can publish it there.

Tanya has left for Moscow; she felt like the journey, and she also wanted to publish some pictures, which must appear before Boulanger's departure – i.e. before October 1. My tooth has fallen out – I suppose I shall have to go to Moscow to have a new one put in, but I don't want to move, I don't want to go to the dentist and have to bother with my teeth.

I have been busy taking photographs for Boulanger and sister Tanya. Today I photographed the apple orchard and the peasant women at work there. I went for a swim and didn't find it at all cold.

I am so bored with all these material cares, seeing that our guests have beds and food and so on. I played the piano for two hours yesterday: I forced myself to find the time.

Andryusha and Misha have gone to the village where Sashka Arbuzova is receiving her 'education'; Misha didn't go to the lycée, and I am terribly annoyed with him.

September 9 I was longing to play the piano, read, take a walk, even drink some tea. But instead I copied out Lev Nikolaevich's article *On Art* for hours on end, while he rode off to see the Züssermans, and when he got back he didn't so much as thank me, and went off in a bad temper when I asked him to explain a passage where I couldn't read his handwriting.

It infuriates me to have to sacrifice everything for him, and this resentment devalues my work. I didn't give it to him, I just let him take it himself. As Seneca says: '*Qu'il s'est laissé prendre ce qu'il n'a pas su retenir.*'*

It was warm and bright today, with spiders' webs waving and glistening in the air. I went swimming and Lev Nikolaevich went for a bicycle ride.

What a strange story this Züsserman business is. He was a retired general, 70 years old, who had fought in the wars – and a tree they were felling in his garden hit him on the head and killed him outright. He left a widow and several sons and daughters. How sad they must be feeling!

I feel badly that I didn't do any work with Sasha today; I had so many domestic tasks to attend to.

September 12 I've been in Moscow for 2 days, completely alone with Nurse, and am thoroughly enjoying myself. Misha goes to the lycée and comes home only for dinner, Tanya is staying with the Wulfs and I see hardly anything of her. I spend the mornings at the dentist, who measures my mouth and tortures me with a hot red mastic and various other nasty things. The painful moment has come when I need false teeth – another one in the front has fallen out now and the ugliness and inconvenience is quite unbearable. I am going to find my false teeth a real trial, I can see that. The main reason I like it so much here is that there are none of those tiresome guests and strangers who are constantly coming to visit Lev Nikolaevich in Yasnaya, none of those complicated family and conjugal

*'He lets them take from him only what he could not keep.'

relations, no conversations about the Dukhobors and the government, about sending articles and letters abroad to expose the activities of the government, no reproaches and criticism against me . . . How tired I am of it all, and how badly I need a rest! I played the piano this afternoon, and scribbled down some notes for a story I want very much to write.[47] I've had no news from home yet. I still haven't seen anyone here, but I very much want to see Sergei Ivanovich and hear him play. I hope he'll come on my name-day and play for me.

September 14 I went to the dentist again yesterday, and spent the rest of the day reading and sewing at home. I played the piano this afternoon; I am learning two pieces, a Bach two-part invention and a Beethoven sonata. I play badly and must practise a lot. I had arranged to meet Tanya at the Kolokoltsevs this evening to see Varya Nagornova, but she hasn't arrived from the country yet, so we spent the evening talking and dancing with the children and young folk. I danced a waltz with Sasha Behrs, and was foolishly delighted when they told me how gracefully I moved.

Today was a very busy day. I hurried out first thing this morning with my basket and took a tram to the Smolensk market to buy mushrooms. There was an enormous quantity of them. I bought some to give Tanya to take back to Yasnaya Polyana, where these white mushrooms are not to be found. I also bought some grapes. I took everything round to the Wulfs, where Tanya has been staying, then I summoned a cab and went with Nurse to visit the graves of Vanechka and Alyosha. Their little graves always fill me with sweet, tormenting memories and a grief that will never heal.

I longed desperately to die, to be borne off into the unknown where my little boys had gone. Nurse sobbed and sighed, while I recited the Lord's Prayer, striving to unite my soul with my infants and asking them to pray for us wretched sinners, then fled from my grief.

Wanting to please Nurse, I took her and the village girls to look for mushrooms in the woods. But we didn't find any. I arrived home for dinner to find a crowd of boys who had come to see Misha: Mitya Dyakov, Sasha Behrs, and the Danilevskiis. After dinner Nurse and I made jam and boiled and pickled mushrooms. We finished late, and I spent the rest of the evening playing the piano; I sight-read some songs by Taneev, Pomerantsev and Goldenweiser that they'd given me. Taneev called here today, by the way, but I was out. I was so excited when I heard that he had called; I long to see him, but I just don't see how it's to be done. God will help me; maybe I won't see him – whatever is best.

I have heard nothing from home; Lev Nikolaevich hasn't written and Lyova doesn't mention him in his letter, just asks me to do some things for him.

September 15 I got up late and scurried around the house all day. The double windows had to be put in, the floors and doors washed, the mattresses and upholstery beaten, the mushrooms and grapes pickled, etc., etc. It was impossible to do anything with all the commotion, and all the hired workers, painters and floor-polishers here, and Anna Stepanovna in charge. Then I went to the dentist; he fitted my false teeth, which look perfectly satisfactory, but I bruised my lip so painfully that I shall have to make yet another visit. How tedious it all is! When I got home I discovered that Sergei Ivanovich had again called while I was out, and I was so excited again – I longed to see him. I went to visit Prince Urusov at Princes' Court but unfortunately he had already left for the country; I also called at Konyushki to see whether Varenka or Masha Kolokoltseva had arrived, but there was no one there. I just wanted to see some friendly person. At about 8 in the evening Sergei Ivanovich arrived. Misha had had his dinner with me and had gone off with Dyakov for the evening, so the two of us spent the evening alone together. It is very sad that Lev Nikolaevich should persecute me for knowing Sergei Ivanovich, for we have such a good, calm, profound friendship. We talked all evening about art, music, Lev Nikolaevich's writing – Taneev is so fond of him – of how we'd spent the summer, of how complicated life was, but how it gets narrower as one gets older, and all the boundless hopes of one's youth – those boundless aspirations, that determination, that faith in education and in one's own physical and mental strength – all that disappears and in its place appears a wall, the boundary of life and strength.

It is then that we have to transfer this sense of boundlessness from the realm of *this* life into the realm of the life *to come*. I have already done this, to a very limited extent. May God help me to develop my aspirations for that spiritual, religious infinity ('*l'infini*') which lies beyond the grave. Sergei Ivanovich played me his beautiful symphony, which affected me deeply. It is a marvellous work, such lofty, noble music.

September 17 My name-day, I've been foolishly busy with it all day. I rearranged the furniture, bought some inexpensive flowers, and tidied and decorated the house just like a child getting ready for a holiday. My darling Vanechka did so love to 'celebrate', as he used to say in imitation of his Nurse – his own name-day and others' too. I received a letter from Sasha, which delighted me. Lyovochka still hasn't written, as though he were deliberately ignoring me, and that hurts me. Today the house is in a real 'name-day mood'; I cooked a meal for the servants too, which they appreciated, with pie, goose, tea and biscuits. Uncle Kostya, Aleksei Maklakov, S.I. Taneev, Pomerantsev and Kursinskii came this evening, followed by various friends of Misha's – Golitsyn, Butyonev, Dyakov, the Danilevskiis, Lopukhin – who all sang in chorus, jumped around, fought, ate and drank. Uncle Kostya begged Sergei Ivanovich to play (I couldn't bring myself to), and he played his symphony again. Sergei Ivanovich's music has a quality that one finds in certain people: the better you know it the more you love it. I have listened to this work three times now, and I discover new beauty in it every time, which is a very interesting thing.

I paid a visit to Aunt Vera Aleksandrovna. It was her name-day, and she was ill in bed with influenza, completely alone. Her granddaughter, Vera Severtseva, is staying with her at present, but will soon be leaving. It is most instructive to see a woman who has borne eleven children left completely on her own in the world like this. One must be prepared for this and not grumble.

I read a little today, played the piano a little, went to the market to buy mushrooms; all in all a useless, empty day.

September 18 I got up late, sat down to play the piano, and diligently practised the Bach two-part invention. When the rain stopped I left the house to visit the dentist and the Gubner factory for some fustian. But totally unexpectedly I met Sergei Ivanovich! I didn't recognise him at first, then I was amazed. Fate is always playing these tricks on me! He was on his way to the Monastery of the Virgin; we got into conversation and I accompanied him to the tram stop. I didn't get to the factory, but I arrived in good time at the dentist's, who seems to have done a splendid job on my teeth. I should not have told Sergei Ivanovich about the time I tried to kill myself by freezing to death on the Sparrow Hills. (Although I spared him all the causes and details of course.) It's just that those agonising memories evoked the need to talk about them.

A new statue of Pirogov has gone up outside the clinic[48] – the most hideous work! It's ugly from whichever direction one looks at it, and has no artistic merit at all.

I got home, had dinner with Misha, then practised for four hours, by which time I was exhausted. Misha came into the room with Butyonev and settled down to his lessons, while I embroidered some initials and Butyonev read me some French *Maximes et Pensées* in a stammering voice. I received a belated greetings telegram from my family. At times I long to be in Yasnaya, but the moment I think of all the problems and complications in our family I am glad I am not there, and would rather just sit here quietly on my own, as I am now. Those peculiar visitors are enough to turn one completely off the idea of living there.

September 19 A talented man puts all his understanding, all the sensitivity of his soul, into his work, while his attitude to real life is obtuse and indifferent. I immersed myself yesterday in Sergei Ivanovich's songs, trying to understand them more deeply. (I now have so many of them.) The music corresponds not only to the mood of the poem but to almost every word too (so powerful in places), yet Sergei Ivanovich's own personal style and character are never lost; I'd recognise his music anywhere now. But in real life he is so calm and reserved, never expressing his feelings, seldom speaking his thoughts, and always appearing so indifferent to everyone and everything.

And as for my incomparably more gifted husband! What extraordinary understanding of people's psychology in his writings, and what incomprehension and indifference to the lives of those closest to him! Me, the children, the servants, his friends – he doesn't know or understand them.

It is windy, overcast and cheerless. I long for music and more music, I feel ill and lonely and want love and company – but where is it to be found? Everyone wants love, but there are so few who can give it. Or else you offer it passionately, selflessly, and it's rejected, your love is not wanted, it's a burden. Usually it's like this ══════ , the lines of love are parallel and never meet, and it's almost never like this —————— —————— . And it's always the case that one person *loves*, while the other merely *lets* himself be loved.

September 22 I am back at Yasnaya Polyana, and have left Misha in Moscow with Nurse and Ivan the drunkard. I am sorry to have ended my solitary life, where I could play the piano, and to have returned to the hectic existence Lev Nikolaevich has organised for me here. We had a visit from some Molokans whose children were taken away from them because of their sectarian beliefs. Lev Nikolaevich has already written to the young Tsar about it, but there has been no response. He has just written again, but fortunately the Tsar is abroad and the letter will probably not reach him.[49] I would do anything in the world to console the mothers and soothe their children, but what is the point of risking one's life when it's *impossible* to do *anything*. Then there was that letter of his to the newspapers appealing for aid to the Dukhobors.[50] He is always seeking noise, publicity, risk. I simply do not believe in his goodness and his love of humanity, for I know what is at the bottom of it all – fame, the insatiable, boundless, frantic desire for yet more fame. How can one believe in his love, when he doesn't love his own children, his grandchildren, his *family*, but has suddenly developed this great love for the Molokans' children? He has a boil on his cheek and his face is tied up in a handkerchief. He looks wretched, and is terribly worried about it.

He paid two visits to the doctor while I was away, and the third time he asked him to call. He kept insisting that he had cancer and would soon die, and he was very depressed and couldn't sleep. He is better now. Poor man, how he hates suffering, and how hard it will be for him to leave this life. God help him! I hope I am not there to see his death or to survive it.

Tanya is leaving for Yalta; her nerves are still weak. Masha is very weak, emotionally and physically. Lyova is happy with his Dora. Kolya Obolenskii has left for Moscow on business.

I have just done a little copying for Lev Nikolaevich. I developed some prints for Misha, and cut out a dress for little Vera, Ilya the footman's daughter. I long desperately for music, but the moment I mentioned that I might go and play, my two daughters attacked me furiously.

September 26 The days rush past. The 23rd was our wedding anniversary and we spent it very pleasantly, although we didn't arrange any special celebration. We have been married 35 years, and however hard my life has been at times, I thank God that we have remained faithful to one another, and now live peacefully, even affectionately, together. My two eldest sons came and all the family was together except Misha, who has now arrived, I am pleased to say. Our guests included Sergeenko and Boulanger, with his 9-year-old son. Boulanger is leaving for England on the 28th; he is being deported for spreading the ideas of Tolstoy.

Lev Nikolaevich has already written the conclusion to his article on art, and has made yet more changes to it, so I shall copy it again. Apart from that, I have just finished copying his letter to the *Russian Gazette*.[51] Various papers have published articles saying it is unthinkable that the missionaries' conference in Kazan should have proposed that the sectarians' children should be taken away from them. But since this did in fact happen, and since the parents who have lost their children have been visiting Lev Nikolaevich to ask him to take up their cause, he has decided to publicise the whole story in the *Russian Gazette*. Whether they will publish it or not is another matter.

We have had two quiet days with just the family here. Today we had more visitors, an officer named Prince Cherkasskii and a schoolteacher called Tomashevich. Liza Obolenskaya arrived last night and today we went for a walk with her. How beautiful it was! We walked through the fir plantation to the river, came out at the bathing-hut, walked through the great fir trees, returning home by a circular route along the forest path. The bright yellow tints, shading into green, red, dark brown and all the colours of the autumn foliage, were extraordinarily lovely. A few young birch trees have grown up here and there amongst the tall dark firs, and their brilliant leaves are etched against the black background like transparent lace. Liza and I kept stopping to exclaim in wonder at the beauty. The sunset was wonderful, bright and clear, and we could see as far as Grumond.

On the way home I told Liza, at her request, about my friendship with Sergei Ivanovich, about Lev Nikolaevich's jealousy and my feelings for him now. It upset me to talk about it, and there were yet more trying discussions at home with Masha about her future, and the fact that they are planning to live with his mother in Pokrovskoe, and I told her I didn't approve, and said he, that is, Kolya, should go out and earn his own living or enter government service, rather than living first off her mother, then off his own. Tanya, Kolya and Masha are all packing to go to the Crimea.

September 29 Masha and Kolya Obolenskii left for the Crimea yesterday. I was not too sorry to see them go, although I am fonder of them now than when they were first married. My fears for Masha's life when she was so ill have brought me closer to her. And Kolya's a good, kind boy, just terribly lazy and phlegmatic. He cannot and will not work, and that is not a pleasant sight.

Vera and Masha Tolstaya were here, and a prison priest who came from Tula to visit Lev Nikolaevich, a gentle, sickly, naive man. He said he had much in common with Lev Nikolaevich's views and wanted to talk to him. I was astonished to learn that he had had to ask the bishop for permission to come here. Is Lev Nikolaevich really considered such a heretic? Some more Molokans came. They have been in St Petersburg, where they took Lev Nikolaevich's letters to Koni, as well as to various other people who were out of town. The case of the Molokans' children is to be taken up in the Senate, and Koni is hopeful that it will be decided to return the children to their parents; but their case may be passed on to the State Council, which means it would drag on for a couple of years.[52] The Molokans were telling us that one little girl of two was being cared for by a nun who loved her very much and was incensed that she had been taken away from her parents, but was looking after her very well. This little girl had said to her father: 'Quick, let's take a cab and get away!' The boys have also been sent to a monastery but are being badly cared for; their clothes are filthy and they're covered in lice. They asked the monks to let them go outside the gates to watch for their parents' horses, but the monks had told the Molokans that they would only be allowed to see their children in church, so they were taken there. When they got to the church their children were not there, just some other Molokans who were being converted to Orthodoxy as an example to them. The Father Superior embraced them when they came in, kissed them and said: 'Just as you grieve for your children who have left you, so Mother Church grieves for you who have left her.' But the Molokans stood their ground.

Today everyone has left: Andryusha, Liza Obolenskaya, the Tolstoys, the Molokans and that young Popov, who has been staying with Chertkov in England. It's raining. Peace, quiet and solitude.

The only worry now is the boil on Lev Nikolaevich's face, a great red, bloody, pussy lump which still hasn't closed. It has been hurting him for three weeks now and shows no sign of improvement.

The rain has kept us all indoors, which is good for work. I have to check the final chapters of *On Art*, and then send them off to be translated.

The day before yesterday I went to Tula and made arrangements, as Andryusha's and Misha's guardian, for Yasnaya Polyana to be transferred to my sons' names after Vanechka's death. I had a number of other matters to attend to there too.

Yesterday we took a marvellous walk through Zaseka to Gorelaya Polyana, and back home through the Crown nurseries. There was a magnificent sunset. The highway was packed with noisy peasants driving their empty clattering carts back from the Tula bazaar, and with day-labourers walking home from the Crown plantation where they had been planting saplings. We walked back with this noisy, festive crowd, with the triumphant glow of the setting sun in our faces.

This evening we drank tea with Lyova in the side-wing. We went out onto the balcony – it was a heavenly moonlit night, warm, with a south wind and small transparent clouds racing across the moon, now veiling, now revealing it. Tanya, Liza Obolenskaya, Vera and I sat up late sewing, foolishly telling each others' fortunes with cards and chatting about intimate matters. Women can be open with one another about *everything* – one can only be weak and unguarded with people one has loved since childhood, when one knows every detail of their character, every event of their life. I am closer to my sister Tanya than to anyone else.

September 30 Tanya has left for the Crimea, and taken Ilya's son Andryusha with her. The house is empty with only Sasha here, and Lyova and Dora in their wing. I feel dreadfully sorry for poor Lev Nikolaevich. For years he spent the quiet months of autumn with his daughters: they served him, wrote for him, became vegetarians for him, and sat through the long, dull autumn evenings with him. I always used to spend the autumn in Moscow, to be with my sons while they were at school, and I used to miss my husband and daughters terribly and was with them in spirit, since Lyovochka and my daughter Tanya were always my favourites. But now all that has changed: Masha has married and poor Tanya has fallen in love, and this disastrous love for a man who is unworthy of her has exhausted both her and us. She is going to the Crimea to think things over. God help her! And in 6 days I am leaving for Moscow with Sasha. I have put it off as long as possible, but it's high time she went to school; she is 14 now, and is doing next to no work. I am concerned about Misha too; I fear he is being morally corrupted, and I feel that family life is really the best thing for the boy. Lev Nikolaevich will be staying here with Lyova, but it is plain that neither of them is overjoyed at the prospect. I shall take Sasha to Moscow, settle her in there, then come straight back to be with Lev Nikolaevich. Oh how trying and complicated it all is! God give me strength not to neglect my duties, to understand what these are, and to extricate myself with the same energy from the innumerable difficulties of my increasingly difficult life.

Warm, slight rain; a few leaves are completely yellow now, although the oak and the lilac are still covered in lush green leaves. I tidied the house, did the housekeeping, checked the accounts and printed my photographs of Masha and Kolya setting off. They're all asking me for copies now, so I have to make prints for everyone. I did a little work with Sasha, who wrote a very bad essay. This evening I shall copy the conclusion to the article *On Art* for the fifth time, then I shall mend my petticoat; the lace is worn out, and I also want to make some little tucks and lace inserts. I curse myself for my fondness for pretty and elegant things!

I try not to think of Tanya but I cannot help missing her dreadfully. She has been my friend for 33 years; the whole of my marriage and all my past happiness is connected to her, she has shared all my griefs and all my joys, she has experienced everything with me. There is no one in the world I am closer to.

October 2 The peace of autumn, with the yellow leaves turning to gold in the sunlight. I had a good day today; this morning I read Seneca's *Consolation à Marcia* and *Consolation à Helvini*, then I tidied up the books in the library. After dinner we walked to Kozlovka and back; the road looked so sad and deserted – what memories that road evokes! Oh, I don't need memories, or regrets . . . ! Why am I so constituted that every experience leaves such a deep impression on my heart? When I got home I heard that Lyova had gone off to Krapivna leaving Dora on her own, so I ran in to keep her company. Then Lyovochka gave me Chapter 10 of his article on art, and using that as a model I was able to revise the other chapters. It's hard work, laborious, exacting and mechanical, and I was at it for three hours. I am so glad he has attacked the decadents and exposed their tricks. He cites some utterly meaningless poems by Mallarmé, Griffin, Verhaeren and Moréas among others, by way of example. Lyovochka invited me out for a game of shuttlecock this evening for some exercise, but I asked him to play a duet with me instead. We played a Beethoven septet quite nicely, and I was in such high spirits afterwards! We went to bed late and I read Menshikov's article 'On Sexual Love' in *The Week*.[53] This matter will never be settled, however much they may talk about it.

The best, the most painful and the most powerful thing in the world is love, and love alone; it guides and determines everything else. Love gives life to the artist, the scientist, the philosopher, the woman, even the child; love lifts up the soul, gives us all strength and the energy for work, inspiration and joy. And I don't mean just *sexual* love, but any kind of love. In my case the best, most powerful, most unselfish love of my whole life was for my little Vanechka. And my affection for my husband and for other people too has always sprung from the spiritual, intellectual, artistic realm rather than from physical attraction. With my husband, however much he repelled me with his slovenly habits and his immoderate physical inclinations, it was his rich inner existence that made me love him all my life; and I closed my eyes to the rest. I loved U . . . [54] for introducing me to the world of philosophy, and for reading to me the works of Marcus

Aurelius, Epictetus, Seneca and others. It was he who showed me and shared with me a whole new world of lofty human thoughts, which have been such a consolation to me throughout my life. My attachment to Sergei Ivanovich too was based not on his physical appearance but on his extraordinary musical talent; the nobility, purity and seriousness of his music flows from his soul.

It was for this reason that of all my children I loved Vanechka the best: he was all soul, such a tiny, disembodied child, so sensitive, tender and loving – he was made of the very finest spiritual material, and was not made for this world.

May God help me too to leave behind this physical life, to cleanse my soul, and with a purified heart to pass over into that world where my Vanechka is now.

October 6 I have come to Moscow with Sasha and Mlle Aubert. I left Lyovochka yesterday with a heavy heart; I have rarely felt so sorry for him as I did then. He is so old, lonely and bent. (He stoops more and more these days, probably because of the sedentary life he leads, writing hunched over his desk, sometimes for days on end.)

I tidied up his study, sorted out his things and his linen, and made sure he had all his small household needs: porridge oats, coffee, saucepans and dishes, honey, apples, grapes, Albert rusks and all the things he likes. He said goodbye to me affectionately, almost shyly, and didn't want me to go; so I shall be back in 6 days, and then we shall both go over to Pirogovo to visit his brother Sergei Nikolaevich. I am relying on young Lyova and Dora to look after him. His boil is better, but now his nose is hurting, and he is terribly shaken. I hope it's nothing serious.

I went to the dentist today, then to the Kolokoltsevs, then to the bank to see Dunaev on Lev Nikolaevich's behalf. I asked him to see that Lev Nikolaevich's letter about the Molokans' children was published, to get it back from the *Russian Gazette*, which had refused to print it, and send it to Prince Ukhtomskii at the *St Petersburg Gazette*.[55]

I am tired, I am writing badly . . .

October 10 I haven't written for four days, days filled with hectic activity and a mass of things to attend to. No music, no reading, no happiness, nothing. How I hate this life! A lot of my time has been taken up with Lev Nikolaevich's article. I transferred corrections from one text to the other, then copied out the entire 'Conclusion'. Then I started looking for suitable Russian governesses for Sasha; today I decided to hire Sofia Nikolaevna Kashkina, the daughter of Seryozha's former music teacher, Nikolai Dmitrievich Kashkin. Misha has fallen and hurt his leg; he has been off school for three days, and has been lying in bed doing absolutely nothing. These drunken footmen are quite insufferable. First one drinks himself into a stupor and has to leave, then another is blind drunk for three days on end. I've never known anything like it, it's infuriating and so tedious.

Sergei Ivanovich spent this evening with me, and there was something unsatisfactory about our relations, even a certain coldness. I didn't feel happy with him, in fact I felt awkward and even uncomfortable at times. Perhaps it's because of the kind letter I received from Lev Nikolaevich today, which transported my soul back to him in Yasnaya, or perhaps it's because it torments me that Sergei Ivanovich's intrusion into my life should have brought Lev Nikolaevich so much grief – and may be distressing him even now, but whatever the reason, something has changed in my feelings for Sergei Ivanovich, even though I always defied Lev Nikolaevich's displeasure and refused to give up my freedom to feel and behave as I liked, seeing there was never anything wrong in it.

My teeth have been badly set and they'll have to be done again, which means that I spent an entire week at the dentist's for nothing. What a tedious and exasperating business!

Tomorrow is the Czech concert. They're playing quartets by Beethoven, Haydn and Taneev. That will be nice!

October 11 I received letters today from Lev Nikolaevich, Lyova and Dora, all saying that Lev Nikolaevich was not at all well, so I made up my mind to leave for Yasnaya Polyana this evening. The concert was marvellous. They did a wonderful performance of the Beethoven quartet, and Taneev's quartet was a real musical triumph. What a delightful piece! It's absolutely the last word in modern music, but so profound and so intricate too, with such unexpected harmonic shifts and such a wealth of ideas and skill. A truly sublime musical experience. The audience called for Sergei Ivanovich twice, and they warmly applauded the Czechs too, who played the work so impeccably. After this wonderful musical experience I went home, packed my bags, and within a quarter of an hour I was at the railway station. The music put me in a happy mood which remained with me on the train, on the road to Kozlovka the following morning, and for the whole of that day at Yasnaya. (Written after the 11th.)

October 20 I stayed with Lev Nikolaevich at Yasnaya from the 12th to the 18th, during which time his health improved greatly. By the 17th he was riding over to Yasenki and had stopped drinking Ems water. I lived with him in two rooms on the ground floor, going up to my cold bedroom only to dress and undress, and I caught a bad cold and was quite ill, first with neuralgia in my head, then with frightful pains in my arm and shoulder, and finally with influenza. That week in Yasnaya was so grey and dreary. Outside, it was damp, dark and overcast; inside, the house was forlorn, cold and dirty. I wrote for days on end without drawing breath, despite being ill, and there were moments when I felt like laughing, screaming or crying from exhaustion. First I transferred the corrections from the ten revised chapters on to the fair copy. Then I did an unbelievable amount of fresh copying. Then Lev Nikolaevich scribbled yet more corrections on my copy, so I had to make all these changes in the fair copy. He has such tiny, untidy, illegible handwriting, he never completes his sentences or puts in any punctuation . . . What a strain it is trying to decipher this muddle and make sense of all his footnotes, signs and numbers!

It was dreadfully tiring, especially with neuralgia and a cold. The last two days Maria Aleksandrovna Schmidt came and helped me a bit, so we *almost* finished all the copying and correcting.

There were no servants, apart from a little peasant, virtually an imbecile, who was the coachman's assistant and came in to heat up the stove and put on the samovar. I sometimes put on the samovar myself, but I did it clumsily and it irritated me that Lev Nikolaevich's rules about doing everything for oneself should leave me with less time to help him and copy for him. I swept and dusted the rooms too, and forced myself to clean two rooms which had been left to get into an utterly filthy state in my absence.

We took dinner and supper with Dora and Lyova in their bright, clean wing. At first we felt strange and awkward there, but we soon felt quite at home.

My husband Lyovochka was so kind to me; he sweetly put compresses on my aching arm and shoulder, thanked me for copying his article, and when I was leaving he kissed my hand, something he hasn't done for a long time.

There was yet another unpleasant scene at Yasnaya Polyana while I was there. Our neighbour Bibikov, that stupid, immoral, drunken young scoundrel, appropriated some land we bought 33 years ago from his father, on which there is a plantation of 30-year-old trees. He called the district surveyor, dug a ditch marking the new boundaries and put up posts with an official seal on them. As well as this he took our brushwood and chopped down two birch trees, swearing that the land was never sold to us in the first place and had been his all along. There were visits from the village policeman and the marshal of the *zemstvo*, endless discussions and petitions and a great deal of unpleasantness. Poor Lyova and Lev Nikolaevich were terribly upset, which made it all the harder for me too.

The affair has been settled for the time being, although we still don't know how it will end. Our courts are so bad.

I returned to Moscow on the 18th. I rushed around all that morning attending to all my affairs and was fitted for my new dress. That evening I went to the First Symphony Concert. It was an all-Mendelssohn programme: his 4th Symphony, *A Midsummer Night's Dream*, with a choir, and his Violin Concerto. But I thought Safonov conducted very poorly.

The 19th was Vanya Raevskii's wedding. A sad and solemn occasion, but the mother and son were a touching sight. They are both deeply affected by the marriage, and this first separation; now she will have to share her son's love with his young wife. I can't make her out at all – a thin, sickly girl with a shy smile. It was rather a tedious affair, but my heart went out to Elena Pavlovna. She could not help recalling her late husband on this momentous day, and we talked about him and even wept a little. It was a long time since I had dressed up, and for a moment a little of my old vanity returned again, but only for a moment.

Sergei Ivanovich has fallen and hurt his leg, and will be in bed for several days. I couldn't resist going over to pay him a visit, as I felt quite concerned about him. Anna Ivanovna Maslova said to me at the concert: 'You must call on him, he'll be delighted to see you.' But I don't know if he really was pleased to see me, it may have been quite the reverse. A.A. Maklakov was there and they were playing chess together. Sergei Ivanovich himself was looking pale and wretched, like a punished child, and complaining that lack of exercise and fresh air was making it impossible for him even to work.

I had letters from Tanya and Masha. Still the same sorry news from my daughters, Masha with that lazy foolish boy-husband of hers, and Tanya with her morbid infatuation for Sukhotin. I feel as though I have lost both daughters at once.

Sasha is working hard and doing very well with her new teacher.

I rushed around today doing Dora's errands and the Bibikov business with the notary. Dora is pregnant. She is so gentle, attentive and affectionate with Lev Nikolaevich and me, and she is especially sweet and touching with her pregnancy and her sickness.

I spent this evening with Uncle Kostya and Maklakov. A pointless, useless evening, even though they're better than most.

October 21 I called on Sergei Ivanovich. He has fallen over and his leg is quite swollen, so he has to stay in bed for a few days, and I couldn't but go and see him. We talked together in our usual serious, simple, quiet fashion. He told me about a sect called the Self-Burners and I told him about the decadent poems from which I had been copying out quotations for Lev Nikolaevich in Yasnaya. Then we talked about music, and about Beethoven, and he told me various things about his life and gave me a two-volume biography to read.[56] As always I left him with a feeling of peace and contentment. He begged me to call again, but I don't know whether I can bring myself to. I went on to visit Natasha Dehn but didn't find her in, although I did see the wretched hole she lives in. All these daughters of ours go off and lead impoverished lives to be with the man they love, yet they are used to grand houses, numerous servants and good food . . . Well, there's obviously nothing more precious than love. I called on Elena

Pavlovna Raevskaya. She has clearly taken her son's marriage very hard, but she is a little more cheerful now. I spent the evening with my brother Sasha and my sister Liza. I was horrified by my sister's talk of property and profits, her extreme materialism, and her complete lack of intellectual or artistic interests. Despite the guests, the fruit, and biscuits, the carefully prepared tea, Anechka's hospitality, the dear young girls and the Kolokoltsev couple, at the end of it all the whole day was wasted, squandered, frittered away.

I received a cold and haughty letter from Lev Nikolaevich – he was trying to be friendly but didn't succeed. I expect he's angry with me for living here in Moscow rather than with him in Yasnaya, where I would be copying for him from morning to night. But I cannot do it any more, I simply cannot! I am tired and old, my spirit is crushed, and maybe I'm spoilt. I remember that week I spent there: the filthy yard, the two filthy rooms where I lived with Lev Nikolaevich, the four mouse-traps which never stopped snapping, and mice, mice, endless mice . . . the cold bleak house, the grey sky, the drizzle, the darkness; traipsing through the mud with a lantern from one house to another to eat dinner and supper with Lyova; writing, writing, morning, noon and night; smoking samovars, no servants, deathly silence . . . What a dreadful, depressing, difficult week it was. I prefer it here; I must simply live a fuller, more *useful* life.

October 23 I spent the morning at the dentist's – everything will have to be done all over again. Then I called on Aunt Vera Aleksandrovna Shidlovskaya, and chattered away about nothing with Masha Sverbeeva. Uncle Kostya came to dinner, and afterwards he and I went off to see Sergei Ivanovich. I felt bored and guilty – this *must* be the last time. We didn't spend long there, however, for Anna Ivanovna Maslova arrived, outspoken and facetious as ever, and I felt even more bored and guilty. I left to go to a concert of chamber-music. They played two Brahms quintets, so drearily that I actually dozed off.

I have been very upset by this news of Andryusha's illness, which is apparently quite serious; it's a great weight on my heart. I have also been thinking a lot about Tanya, especially today – I am quite sure that something special has happened to her today. I had a letter from M.A. Schmidt, saying that Lev Nikolaevich was well and cheerful, that he had had some peasants to tea, and so on and so forth. It suits us perfectly well to live apart, although this never used to be the case. But it's not easy for me to be without a friend, someone to take an interest in what I do, share his soul with me. Lev Nikolaevich has shared only his *body* with me, and his love for me has been merely physical. And now this side of our marriage has started to ebb, and with it our desire to live together inseparably.

I have just read a biography of Mendelssohn,[57] and have started on the two-volume biography of Beethoven. But what of biographies! What can they tell us about a man's soul? It is his soul which creates the work of art. Art draws life from its creator's spiritual life – his material life is often immoral or merely insignificant.

What is so interesting about Lev Nikolaevich's life? Or Sergei Ivanovich's? We love them not for their lives, or how they appear to us, but for that *dream*, deep and endless, from which their art flows; it is this we love to sense and idealise in them.

I feel unbalanced, unhinged. Today I felt so melancholy I could have killed myself or done something truly absurd and desperate . . .

October 24 Yet another visit to the dentist. I got up late, and am in my usual melancholy autumn mood. It is as if the threads connecting me to the world have snapped, leaving me alone, directionless, unoccupied, tied to nothing, needed by no one . . . Maklakov came to visit this evening and brought Plevako, the well-known barrister. All outstanding people are interesting, and he is no exception. He is sensitive, serious, and immediately understands what one is talking about; he is clearly someone to whom one doesn't have to *explain* things. He has a broad head, and a prominent, bumpy forehead; he is a large, ugly man, but seems pleasant, despite the bad things they say about him.

This evening I started on the first chapter of my story. I think it will be good. But who can I ask for an opinion on it? I would like to write and publish it without telling a soul.

My eye is aching – I never go to bed before three in the morning. I have heard nothing from home, but I wrote to them all yesterday and sent money. I try not to worry, for I could exhaust my nervous energy if I worried about them all. Yet I don't feel happy about any of them, and I can't help feeling uneasy . . .

October 25 I long to see Lev Nikolaevich, I have missed him all day. I played the piano for about four hours to distract myself. I spent a long time being tortured by the dentist, but my false teeth still hurt. So here I am, reduced to the misery of wearing false teeth – how I have always dreaded this . . .

I called on Masha Kolokoltseva and we had a talk about my daughters which cast another shadow on my heart. Pomerantsev and Igumnov came this evening. Igumnov played for us – his own overture, some Scriabin pieces, a Bach fugue (for the organ) and something or other by Pabst. He also played us some songs by Sergei Ivanovich Taneev and Yusha Pomerantsev. But I am deaf to music today, and half-asleep. On Monday I want to go back to Lev Nikolaevich, and visit Pirogovo with him.

October 26 I took Sasha and Sonya Kolokoltseva to a public concert held in memory of Tchaikovsky, and from there to an exhibition of Russian paintings at the Historical Museum. There was nothing outstanding. I was struck by the enormous number of autumn landscapes. Autumn was indeed very lovely this year; the leaves were on the trees for a long time, the days were long and sunny – a truly golden autumn. Seryozha came to visit. My love and tenderness for him is always checked by a certain embarrassment. I long to kiss him, tell him how much I love him and how I suffer for him. This evening Goldenweiser came, with Natasha Dehn and her husband. Goldenweiser played marvellously – a Chopin nocturne, various short pieces by Rachmaninov, some Schubert impromptus, and several other things. He has such taste, such a lovely delicate touch. It was a truly great pleasure – I have had a lot of *art* today, and am happy.

October 27 It has snowed and the garden is dazzling white in the sunshine. But I no longer feel that leap of energy, that simple uncomplicated joy I used to experience at the sight of the 'first snow'.

Went to town on business; played the piano a little; leaving now for Yasnaya Polyana.

November 2 I have been in Yasnaya Polyana with Lev Nikolaevich. As I rode there from Kozlovka by sleigh on the morning of the 28th, I was so full of energy and love, so looking forward to working and helping Lev Nikolaevich. It was a bright, sunny day, the snow was dazzling, a huge moon was setting and a brilliant sun was rising – a beautiful, magical morning!

But the moment I arrived at Yasnaya everything went wrong and my wings were clipped. Lev Nikolaevich was surly and hostile to me. Then something very unpleasant happened. While I was cleaning out the room I re-set one of the innumerable mouse-traps, which snapped shut and struck me in the eye so that I fell to the ground and thought I had been blinded.

So instead of copying for Lev Nikolaevich I had to lie down with a compress on my eye for a day and a half. The next day Lev Nikolaevich rode over to Tula; it was 15 degrees below freezing, and I felt very anxious, but I had to lie there all on my own in that great stone house, with my eyes closed, pursued by gloomy thoughts about my children and my relationship with them and with Lev Nikolaevich.

I got up several times to write, using only one eye, and I managed despite this slowly to copy out the whole of Chapter 12 of *On Art*. I had dinner and supper with Dora and Lyova in their wing, which made me feel a bit more cheerful.

The next day Lev Nikolaevich and I went to Pirogovo to visit his brother, Sergei Nikolaevich. But the evening before our departure we had a dreadful row which made one of those *cuts* which always leave such a deep scar and manage to drive two people who love one another still further apart. What was it all about? Impossible to say. Nothing at all really, yet the result was that I shuddered, as so often before, to realise what an icy heart he has, and how utterly indifferent he was to me, the children and our life. When I asked him whether he would be coming to Moscow or not, and if so when, he replied vaguely and evasively; when I said I wanted to be closer to him, to help him with his work, copy for him, cook him healthy vegetarian food and generally look after him, he peevishly told me that he needed nothing and asked for nothing, that he enjoyed being alone and didn't need any copying done either – he wanted, in other words, to deprive me in every possible way of the pleasure of thinking I could be of any use, let alone pleasure, to him. But it is the most precious thing in the world for us women to know that we can help and please our loved ones.

At first I cried, then I became hysterical, overwhelmed with a despair so extreme that I wanted only to die.

But the worst thing is that Lev Nikolaevich's iciness makes me yearn to attach myself to someone else, someone to fill the void in my heart left by this man, my lawful husband, who has spurned and rejected my love. This is a great tragedy which men will neither acknowledge nor understand.

After I had almost gone mad with tears and grief, we managed somehow or other to patch it up, and by the time we got to Pirogovo the next day I was already copying for Lev Nikolaevich again. Then he needed his warm cap which I'd thought to bring for him, as well as fruit, dates, my body, my labours and all the copying he wanted me to do for him. It was all suddenly indispensable to him! Help me, oh Lord, to do my *duty* towards my husband to the end of his life, in other words to serve him patiently and humbly. But I cannot stifle my need for the sort of quiet, friendly, considerate relations which should exist between two people who are close to one another.

And despite the pain Lev Nikolaevich caused me, I still went through agony when he rode the 35 *versts* to Pirogovo on horseback, and worried that he'd get tired and cold! He stayed on in Pirogovo with his brother, while I left yesterday and went to a delightful symphony concert: Tchaikovsky's C Major String Serenade and the Schumann Concerto. I met a number of people but not Sergei Ivanovich, who still has a bad leg.

Sasha is doing well, although she doesn't get on with Mlle Aubert. Misha told me that he got nothing but twos for his unseen translations, and I lost my temper with him, or rather I flared up and scolded him, at which he raised his voice and was rude.

I was very disturbed yesterday to learn that Seryozha had gone, at his wife's request, to visit her and his little son. When I asked him what exactly was happening between him and his wife, he said: 'A little bit of everything,' and declined to go into details of their meeting. But he does seem calmer now.

Tanya has a cough and is leaving for Cannes.

I feel much calmer and happier here in Moscow, but today I have to leave for Pirogovo. The day after tomorrow we'll return to Yasnaya, where I shall spend just one day, Dora's birthday, and then, at 6 in the morning on Thursday, I shall return to Moscow and here I shall stay. If Lev Nikolaevich wants to live apart from me, that's his business. I have Sasha's education to see to and Misha to keep an eye on – I cannot go on living at Yasnaya anyway. My old life there with the children was a full and satisfying one; but to be Lev Nikolaevich's *slave*, and an unloved slave at that (for he loves no one), with no work of my own, no life or interests of my own – no, it's not to be borne. I'm so tired of life!

November 7 My plans fell through. I returned to Pirogovo on Monday morning, and we didn't leave until yesterday, Thursday. Staying with Lev Nikolaevich's brother was a great strain. He is 71 years old, mentally alert, but the most dreadful despot with his family and a terrible misanthropist; he is widely read and takes an interest in everything, but he curses the whole world – apart from the gentry, that is. He never stops railing against the professors ('sons of b...s', 'scoundrels'), and merchants ('thieves and swindlers') – and as for the common people, they come in for every foul word he can think of. The musical world too is nothing but fools and villains . . . It was dreadfully difficult with him. They live like paupers, and the food is terrible; his poor daughters never say a word in front of their despotic father, but they long in that backwood of theirs for some human contact with living souls. So Vera organises magic lantern shows for the village children and gives a peasant boy English lessons, and they talk about philosophy and religion with the peasants, the saddlers and the carpenters. This used to enrage their father, and now their mother (the gipsy) gets very upset about it. Besides this the three girls have a horse and two cows which they feed and milk themselves, and they drink the milk too, since they are vegetarians.

Lev Nikolaevich continued with his writing there, and I copied for him all day long. One evening I played their out-of-tune piano and everyone was in ecstasies, so long was it since they had heard any music.

We had intended to leave on Tuesday, but it rained and the roads were covered in ice, so we stayed. The next day there was a frightful wind and I was afraid Lev Nikolaevich would catch cold, so we again decided to stay. By yesterday, however, my depression was so extreme that we decided to leave for Yasnaya. There was still a strong wind, but Lev Nikolaevich cheerfully rode the 35 *versts* home on horseback, while I sat in the sleigh and worried about him – more than I've worried for a long time. How insignificant all my other interests, fantasies and friendships seemed beside the fear that my husband might catch a cold, fall ill or die!

The journey back took three hours and we did not catch a cold, thank God. Lyova and Dora were waiting for us and warmly welcomed us home, and Yasnaya seemed such heaven to me after Pirogovo! We had dinner with them, and that evening we lit the stove in our part of the house. Lyovochka made some more corrections to Chapters 12 and 13 and told me to enter these into the other copy.

We sat cheerfully together and drank tea. This morning soft feathery flakes of snow were falling; there was no wind, just a light frost in the clear air. We drank coffee together, tidied our rooms, received letters from almost all the children, which delighted us, and looked through the newspapers. Then I got into the sleigh, drove off to Yasenki station, and left for Moscow. Lyovochka and I parted on very friendly terms, and he even thanked me for all my help, and for copying out his article *On Art*. Today we sent off Chapters 12 and 13 to England for Maude to translate. Lev Nikolaevich will have Dora and Lyova there with him, as well as his old copyist Aleksandr Petrovich Ivanov, a retired lieutenant who turned up 19 years ago begging for alms, and stayed on after Lev Nikolaevich's spiritual conversion to copy his articles for him.

On the train to Moscow I read the Beethoven biography, which I found extraordinarily interesting. He is one of those geniuses whose own creativity is the centre of his world – all the rest is merely the setting, the accessory ('*l'accessoire*') to his genius. Beethoven gave me a much clearer insight into Lev Nikolaevich's egotism, his utter indifference to the world. For him too it is merely the background to his own genius, he too takes from it only what will serve as an auxiliary to his talent, his work. Everything else he discards. From me, for instance, he takes my labour, my copying for him, my concern for his physical wellbeing, my body . . . As for my spiritual life, it is of no interest or use to him, so he has never bothered to investigate it. His daughters too served him, and so long as they did so he took an interest in them, but his sons are complete strangers to him. All this is very painful for us – yet the world bows before such men . . .

A lot to do in Moscow with publishers and banks – all very tedious. Sasha and Misha were delighted to see me, but they're not doing well; they do no work, and Sasha is persistently rude to her governesses.

This evening I managed again to play a little . . .

November 10 I returned today from Tver, where I had been to visit Andryusha. I left yesterday morning. He met me at the gates; he had been waiting for me all morning, he said, and fondly told me over and over again how pleased he was to see me. He had burned himself with carbolic acid and was in bed for three weeks, but the burns are all healed now. We spent a very pleasant day together; he sat with me while I worked, and then we had a talk about intimate matters and his personal life. He has matured a lot – life seems to have had a sobering effect on him. He is alert, does not drink or lead a disorderly life, and is very good company and full of energy. I am going to apply, at his insistence, for him to be transferred to Moscow, to the Sumskii regiment.

The journey back would have been dreadfully trying were it not for the Beethoven biography, which I am reading with growing fascination. The life of every man is interesting; how much more so that of a genius!

I received a telegram and a letter from Tanya, who has been held up in Yalta where Andryusha (my grandson) has fallen ill. I am expecting a visit from Vera Kuzminskaya; I shall be delighted to see her again.

I had a letter from Lev Nikolaevich. He says he has completely finished *On Art* now, and wants to start on something new. He also writes: 'I have been thinking about you and I *understand* you (?) and feel so *sorry* for you.'[58] Firstly, I wonder in what sense he 'understands' me: he has never taken the trouble to understand me and he simply doesn't know me. Whenever I used to ask him to tell me what to read, he always gave me books that interested *him*, never considered what might be useful or interesting to *me*. On the question of books the late Prince L. Urusov was always a great help to me, and now Sergei Ivanovich helps me. Whenever I was aggrieved with him, he always said it must be because I had an upset stomach (mine is always perfectly well); and whenever I wanted something he either paid no attention or said I was just moody or out of sorts. And now he says he 'understands' and 'feels sorry' for me. Well, his pity is insulting and I don't want it. If he has no pure, genuine, tender love for me, then I don't need anything from him. I am quite strong enough now to find my own purpose and pleasure in life.

November 11 I visited the lycée to discuss Misha, and was deeply distressed by their complaints of his laziness and bad behaviour. What a great misfortune it is that all my life I have had to listen, suffering and blushing with shame, to all these directors and schoolteachers criticising and belittling my sons.

Yet there are some fortunate mothers who hear very different things about their sons! At home I had yet another painful discussion with Misha and decided to do all I could to get him taken in as a boarder. He doesn't like the idea at all, but I shall stand my ground.

I went out to do some errands; it was sleeting and windy. This evening I sight-read some Beethoven sonatas – without much success but with much interest. I am still totally absorbed in the biography of Beethoven – that consummate musical genius. Vera Kuzminskaya came and I don't feel so lonely now. Anyway, I am not lonely. I have a whole new world within me, a whole new life, in which I no longer need anything or anyone to *entertain* me. I enjoy seeing my family, I look forward to seeing Tanya and Lev Nikolaevich, but they contribute very little to my inner happiness. Quite the opposite, alas . . .

November 12 I went to a musical evening at the Conservatoire with Sasha. It was delightful and not at all dull. There are some excellent women pianists being trained there. The director, Safonov, was very affable, and in the interval he took my arm and invited me into his office, where he introduced me to a foregin music professor called Ritter to whom I had to speak in German. Mme Dehn came to see me, otherwise I have seen almost no one. This morning I went to the bath-house. I don't want to see anyone either.

November 13 Went shopping for Dora and wrote her a letter, then had my 1st music lesson with Miss Welsh. I am feeling depressed today, and long for the friendly company of someone I love.

Vera Tolstaya has come. Vera Kuzminskaya is wretched because of this breach with her father. Misha has gone to the theatre, and Sasha is doing her lessons. I am going upstairs to play the piano. Maybe that will lift my dismal spirits.

I played the piano all evening, although without much success. What endless pleasure there is in the music of Beethoven!

November 14 Spent the whole day from morning to night doing dull accounts with the accountant. Maklakov came this evening and we did some duets, but he's quite hopeless. We attempted a Mendelssohn symphony, some Schubert (his lovely Tragic Symphony) and some Mendelssohn overtures, but we made a terrible job of it. I could have wept – I am incapable of playing anything properly.

Andryusha has come for a couple of days. He was so bored and lonely in Tver after I'd left that he applied to his squadron commander for leave. An affectionate letter from Lev Nikolaevich.[59]

Vera Kuzminskaya had a letter from her mother telling her that M., whom she is in love with, was about to be married. She has been weeping bitterly and is utterly pathetic. She and her father have fallen out, and yesterday she was crying over a letter he wrote her.

10 ° below freezing, rising to 7½ °, and windy. I did not go out today. Tomorrow there's a symphony concert . . .

November 15 Music all day, but little pleasure. This morning I took Vera and Sasha to the rehearsal. I didn't want to get up and go out, but did so for their sakes. Then I did some piano exercises. Misha Olsufiev came, and asked me about Tanya and Sukhotin. I told him she had refused him, and gradually, through various indirect references, we started talking about her. He became very agitated. Did he ever intend to marry her, I wonder? He probably considered it, but could never make up his mind. 'Your daughters are passionate, clever and interesting,' he said, 'but one would be afraid to marry them.' I too felt terribly agitated.

Boratynskaya and Uncle Kostya came to dinner. This evening Misha had some friends here and I went to the symphony concert: Glazunov's

Carnaval, Berlioz' *Childe Harold*, Rubinstein's 'Andante' and an excellent singer who sang some Grieg songs and something by Handel. But it was generally rather a dull concert. More unpleasantness with Misha over his lack of will-power. But this morning he was sincerely penitent, and that touched me. What will become of him? Oh, how hard it all is!

I feel sad and angry that Lyovochka isn't coming. I have seen nothing of S.I. Taneev; his leg is still bad, but I shall not visit him as I don't want to hurt Lyovochka, although it often irritates me that he still manages to circumscribe my activities and friendships, even though he isn't living with me and is enjoying his solitary life without me. Why should he care what I do when he isn't living with me?

November 16 Music again all day. I was busy all morning with the ledgers and accounts, then played the piano for about two and a half hours, and still didn't master that 8th Invention by Bach. After dinner I sight-read a Schubert symphony and played a Beethoven sonata. Then Goldenweiser, Dunaev and Varya Nagornova came. Dunaev read us a Chekhov story,[60] and Goldenweiser played a Beethoven sonata (the 'Appassionata') and some Chopin preludes and nocturnes, and he played beautifully; I love his elegant, intelligent style – although when I remember Taneev's interpretation of that sonata, the difference between them is as between earth and heaven. Ah, I have such a desperate, helpless desire to hear that man play again – will it *never* again be granted me? When Goldenweiser had left, Varya and I tried out Schubert's Tragic Symphony, and once we started there was no stopping us. We played with more inspiration than skill – I can't think how we did it. We were both in ecstasies. What a sweet, sensitive, clever girl Varechka is!

Andryusha has just left; I always feel so sorry for him. Misha has gone to a gipsy concert. Sasha has been romping around with Sonya Kolokoltseva. No news from anyone today. I didn't leave the house all day. Snow, 1 ° of frost.

November 19 I had my 2nd music lesson with Miss Welsh, and afterwards I couldn't tear myself away from the piano, and played for another 4 hours. I had a great urge to play Schubert's last, unfinished symphony as a duet, but there was no one to play with. Vera Kuzminskaya is in a hysterical state and has been utterly wretched. Seryozha has a cough and he and Styopa are busy negotiating the purchase of some estate or other – I am strongly against it. I had a letter from Lev Nikolaevich; he says that although he is missing me, he needs to be alone to write now that he is getting old and hasn't much longer to live and work.[61] These arguments may ring true for humanity at large, but it would take a lot to persuade me personally that writing articles is more important than my life, my love and my desire to live with my husband and find happiness with him, rather than seeking it *elsewhere*.

I visited Aunt Shidlovskaya this evening. She is over 72 years old and extremely dull; but I often imagine myself alone at that age, and it horrifies me.

The roads are icy – the slippery city streets are treacherous for carriages; yesterday it rained and today it was all frozen, dazzling in the sun by day and glittering in the moonlight at night.

I was just telling my fortune with the cards, and twice I drew 'death'. And suddenly I felt so terrified of dying; yet only recently I was longing for it! Well it is all in God's hands! It hardly matters whether it comes sooner or later.

November 23 (Moscow, Khamovniki Street) I am starting a new notebook on a terrible day. It is certainly true that there is a great deal more grief than joy in this world. Yesterday evening Andryusha and Misha invited a large crowd of boys here, and they all set off together to Khilkova's house on the Arbat to lie in wait for a ghost. That, at any rate, was the reason they gave for disappearing all night long and not returning until 9 this morning. I waited up all night for them, until 8 a.m., simply choking with exasperation. Then I wept, raged and prayed . . . When they finally woke up (at one o'clock), I went in to them and gave them a severe talking-to, then burst into tears, which brought on an asthma attack and palpitations in the heart and throat, which meant I had to take to my bed all day, and I now feel destroyed.

The boys were very subdued, especially Misha, whose conscience is younger and purer. There was a letter from Lyova; he is distressed by his father, who keeps arguing, shouting and losing his temper.

A telegram yesterday from Tanya in Sevastopol saying she was coming home. I wonder what she will do? Poor Masha is no better, and is still very poorly. I had a letter from her. Seryozha is so quiet and congenial – intelligent, musical and sensitive.

Frost and snow. I am reading part 3 of the Beethoven biography, and am delighted by it. I had another music lesson, my 3rd, then practised from 11 to 1 o'clock.

November 24 This morning I went to the lycée to talk to the director about Misha. He again urged that he attend as a boarder; more attempts to persuade Misha, his objections – I feel utterly defeated.

Then I posted off his application to the Duma to enrol as a volunteer.[62] Then I took Lyova's article – a translation from the Swedish – to the *Russian Gazette*.[63]

I got home, changed, then went off to a name-day celebration for Dunaev, Davydov and Ermolov. I love this worldly brilliance, lovely clothes, masses of flowers, refined company, cultured conversation and good manners. As always, as at every age in my life, there was general astonishment at my unusually youthful appearance. Istomin was particularly agreeable. I got back and played the piano for about an hour and a half. This evening Raevskii came with my brother Petya and his daughter. Tonight I played the piano again, from midnight until 2 a.m. I do so want to make progress, but I can never find the time. Seryozha played very nicely. 10° of frost, there's a moon.

Sergei Ivanovich hasn't once come to see me. He must have heard reports about L.N.'s jealousy, and his cordiality towards me has changed to extreme coldness. How sad, and how sorry I am! There is no other possible explanation for his aloofness – why else would he not come to visit? Could L.N. have written to him?

November 25 Tanya has returned from Yalta in a much better state, both emotionally and physically. Ilyusha came – wanting money as usual. This evening Sergeenko and the Dehns were here – a lot of noise and discussion, and I was very tired. A wasted day – no piano, no work, no reading, nothing. I ran out for some shopping, sent Andryusha a clock for his name-day and my grandsons some sweets, then collected some concert tickets.

Tanya tells me that L.N. has described life in Moscow as 'suicide'. So if he comes to Moscow for my sake, *I* shall be killing him. But that's frightful! I wrote to tell him so and begged him not to come.[64] I want to live with him because I love him, but according to the way he sees it, I am 'killing' him. I *have* to live here, for the children's education, yet he always reproaches me for this! Oh, I am so tired of life!

November 26 I spent all day in theatres. This morning I took Sasha, Vera Kuzminskaya and Zhenya Behrs to the Korsh theatre to see Griboedov's *Woe from Wit*. It was a poor production and I was terribly bored. Then this evening Tanya persuaded me to accompany her to see the Italian actress Tina di Lorenzo. She is a beautiful woman, with an Italian temperament, but since I did not know the language or the play (*Adrienne Lecouvreur*), I did not find it very interesting. I was exhausted today and hardly played at all; all I want now is to sit at home.

My brother Petya was here with his daughter, as well as Dunaev and Sulerzhitskii . . . Very windy and cold; Misha's throat is inflamed.

November 27 I had a good day. This morning I took the tram to Yakimanka and had my 4th music lesson with Miss Welsh; I had called on the Rusanovs, but hadn't found her in. When I got home I read, or rather re-read Parts 1 and 2 of the Beethoven biography, then worked on my story, which I am very dissatisfied with,[65] and read Seneca's 'Consolation à

Marcia'. I love this letter, it comforts me so.[66] After dinner I was going to play a Mozart violin sonata with Misha, but Seryozha arrived, so I sat him down at the piano instead. I am so pleased that Misha is taking up the violin again – it was a joy to see the two brothers practising my favourite art. Misha's playing has deteriorated, but not completely. If only he would take up his music again. He'd find it such a joy and consolation!

No news from Lev Nikolaevich. My heart is heavy with a dull apprehension and anxiety about him – but also resentment, that he has voluntarily chosen to live apart from his family, and openly abandoned all interest in us. I shall not write to him any more. I cannot live apart from him like this, corresponding only through letters. I miss Sergei Ivanovich dreadfully. I've heard nothing from him; I don't know if he is well, or whether L.N. has written to him. He must have done, otherwise I cannot imagine why he hasn't come to see me. I played the piano for a long time today – about four hours altogether – which was very soothing. I live for Beethoven at present, his thoughts, his soul, his music; I love and admire him more and more, with a new and deeper understanding.

November 29 I received a long, kind, reasonable letter from my husband yesterday.[67] I tried very hard to absorb what he was saying, but there was such an old man's coldness about it that it made me wretched. I often forget that he will soon be 70 – I forget this discrepancy in our ages and the degree of tranquillity we have attained; and this fault of mine isn't mitigated by my youthful appearance and emotions. *Tranquillity* is more important than anything to L.N. now; but I still want him to long impetuously to see me, and to live with me again. I have been pining for him these past two days – but I have got over it: something in my heart has snapped shut . . .

I had a whole day of music. This morning I went with Sasha to the symphony rehearsal, and this evening I went to the concert. They did Beethoven's 9th, which I enjoyed enormously, and Weber's *Oberon* overture also gave me great pleasure. This morning, to my great joy and surprise, I met S.I. at the door. He is coming to lunch tomorrow. He suggested it himself and I cannot say I am pleased, for it will be for such a short time; I always wish we could spend a long time together at some point – as we did over the past two summers – and most of all I want to hear him play! Aleksei Stakhovich came for dinner. I am worried about Tanya again: they seemed somewhat awkward with one another, and he is so handsome, and he sang Don Giovanni's serenade with such passion.

I am re-reading Seneca, and continuing with the Beethoven biography. It's so long, and there's so little time.

November 30 S.I. came for lunch, and was his usual delightful self, calm, gay and kind. I was observing him with Tanya, but detected nothing.

Safonova also came with her two little girls to visit Sasha, and Sonya Kolokoltseva came too, and all the girls cheerfully went skating in the garden. Then Makovitsky[68] arrived from Yasnaya and told me in his broken Russian that L.N. was well and working hard, and was sending a long, long article to the *Northern Herald*. I could hardly believe my ears, and asked him to repeat what he'd said – which he did with the greatest pleasure.

Almost three years ago, two weeks before Vanechka's death, L.N. and I had the most terrible, shameful quarrel over that wonderful story of his, 'Master and Man', which he gave not to me (as I had asked him to), or to Storozhenko (as *he* had asked him to), but to Gurevich, to publish in her journal. Although at the time I defended both my right to publish it in Volume 14 and their right to publish it in the Intermediary edition, and although we did manage to publish it simultaneously with Gurevich – which absolutely enraged her – that episode all but cost me my life and my reason.[69] And it was then that he swore solemnly to me that he would never hurt me again with a repetition of this dreadful incident, and *he would never again publish anything in the* Northern Herald. So what is his word of honour worth if his promise so clearly means nothing to him? I wanted to write to him immediately and remind him of his promise, but then I had second thoughts. But today I again re-lived the whole thing – all the pain, all the suffering.

At first I thought I would kill myself, then I thought I would go somewhere far away, then I played the piano for five hours and fell asleep exhausted in the drawing-room – having eaten nothing all day – and slept like a stone, as one does when deeply unhappy or worried.

It is quite impossible for me, particularly at present, to write about the tragedy of my life, the affairs of my heart and my love for L.N.

December 10 I haven't written my diary for ten days. What has happened? It is hard to assemble all the events on paper, especially since it has all been so painful – and now yet more painful facts have come to light. But I shall try to recall everything.

On December 2, I went to a Beethoven evening. Auer and d'Albert played four of his violin sonatas. It was an utter joy, and balm to my soul. But the following day I saw in the papers an advertisement for L.N.'s article in the *Northern Herald*. Then on top of this Tanya picked an argument with me, reproaching me for my supposed relations with S.I. – when I haven't seen him for a whole month. I felt dreadfully hurt; my family is always so quick to accuse me of crimes I haven't committed the moment I stop serving them like a slave and submitting to their demands, as I have done all my life, and instead pursue some interest of my own, like my present interest in music. And that is a crime!

The next day there was a telegram from Dora and Lyova to say they were arriving – but nothing from L.N. He did not come, he told me afterwards, because of his jealousy for Sergei Ivanovich. (But what sort of 'jealousy' is this, at our age? It's more like *envy* – that I've learned to love another art apart from literature, and through another person, not him.)

I was waiting so eagerly for L.N. to come, I so longed to write to him, to help him in every way, to love him, not to cause him any more unhappiness, and to see no more of S.I. if it was really so painful for him, that the news that he wasn't coming to see me after a whole month's separation – and that he was publishing his article in the *N.H.* – reduced me to the very depths of despair. I packed my things and decided to go off somewhere. I got into a cab, not knowing where I was going. First of all I went to the Petersburg station, intending to go to St Petersburg and take the article from Gurevich, but then I thought better of it and set off for Troitsa. That evening, alone in a dirty hotel room lit by just one candle, I sat alone as if turned to stone, overwhelmed by feelings of grief and resentment for my husband, and his utter indifference to me and my love for him. I tried to console myself with the thought that one's feelings are less passionate when one is almost 70 – but why the deception, why all these secret negotiations behind my back with the *N.H.* over his article. I thought I would go mad.

I went to bed and had just fallen asleep when I was woken by Nurse and Tanya knocking at the door. Somehow Tanya had guessed that I had gone to Troitsa, and had grown worried and decided to come and fetch me. I was very touched, but it did nothing to dispel my despair. Tanya told me that Lyova and Dora had arrived, and that L.N. was coming the next day. But the news left me completely unmoved. I had waited for him too eagerly and for too long, and now something inside me had snapped, and I felt morbidly indifferent to everything.

Tanya left and I went to Mass. I spent the whole of that day – nine hours – in church. I prayed fervently to be delivered from the sin of killing myself or avenging myself for all the pain my husband had caused me; I prayed for a reconciliation, for a miracle to unite us in love, trust and friendship; I prayed for my sick soul to be healed.

My confession was before God, since Father Fyodor, the Church elder, was so decrepit that he couldn't hear a word I was saying, and just let out a short sob of nervous exhaustion. There was something so mysterious and poetic about this monastic existence: the stone corridors and cells, the monks wandering about, the simple folk – prayers, long services and complete solitude amidst a crowd of supplicants who did not know me. I went back and spent the evening poring over the precepts and prayers in a book I found at the hotel. The next morning I received the Eucharist at the Trapeznaya Church. It was a royal day (December 6), and a magnificent dinner was being prepared for the monastery – four fish dishes, honey and beer. The tables were covered in tablecloths, the plates, dishes and mugs were all of pewter, and the meal was served by novices dressed in white aprons.

Having stood through the service, I went off to wander around the monastery buildings. A gipsy woman pursued me as I was walking across the square: 'A fair-haired man is in love with you, but dares not tell you. You are a noble, distinguished lady, refined and educated, and he is not of your class . . . Give me 1 ruble and 6 10-kopeck pieces and I'll give you a charm! Come to my house, everyone knows Maria Ivanovna, everyone knows where I live; come to my house and I'll give you a charm to make him fall in love with you like your husband . . . '

I was quite unnerved and wanted to take her charm. But when I got back to my room I crossed myself and realised this would be very foolish and wicked of me.

I felt very depressed – there was still no telegram from Tanya to inform me of L.N.'s arrival. After I had had something to eat I drove to the telegraph office, and there were two undelivered telegrams waiting for me: one from Tanya, and the other a long touching one from L.N. asking me to return home.[70]

I went straight to the station.

At home Lev Nikolaevich was waiting for me in the hall with tears in his eyes, and we fell into each other's arms. He agreed not to publish his article in the *Northern Herald* (he had already said this in the telegram to me which Tanya had sent); I promised faithfully not to see S.I. again, and to serve and care for him and do all I possibly could to make him happy.

We had such a pleasant talk, it was such a joy for me to promise him this, I loved him so very deeply and was so eager to love him . . .

Yet today in his diary he writes that I had 'acknowledged my crime' for the first time, which had brought him much joy![71] God help me to endure this! Once more he has to present himself to future generations as a *martyr*, and me as a *criminal*. But what is my *crime*? L.N. was angry with me for visiting S.I. with Uncle Kostya a month ago when he was in bed with a bad leg. It was because he was so furious about this, apparently, that he did not come to Moscow; this, according to him, was my 'crime'.

Yet when I told him that considering my pure and blameless life with him he could surely forgive me paying a visit to a sick friend – and with my old uncle too – the tears came to his eyes and he said: 'Of course that is true, your life has indeed been a pure and blameless one.' No one saw his tears of contrition, no one knows about our life together, and in his diaries he writes only of my 'crimes'! God forgive him for his cruelty and injustice to me.

We have guests every day, a lot of tedious coming and going. Lyova is out of sorts here in Moscow. Yesterday we went to the Maly Theatre to please him and Dora, and saw a performance of *The Gentleman* by Prince Sumbatov.[72] Beaunier (a correspondent for the French papers *Le Temps* and *Les Débats*) is dining here today.[73] I haven't had a chance to play the piano; I am hard at work correcting proofs, copying for L.N. and doing as much as I possibly can for him.

Terrible neuralgia last night . . .

December 11 Gurevich came, weeping and telling Tanya how wretched she was. L.N. didn't go out to see her. He has now asked her for his article back. What will happen now! I no longer have any faith in L.N.'s honesty after that deceitful business of sending his article to the *Northern Herald*.

If I wasn't living under this domestic despotism I would go to St Petersburg for the Nikish concert. As it is, I've had to abandon my music again. Dora and Lyova left for Yasnaya today. He was very irritable in Moscow.

Yesterday evening L.N. had a visit from a German actor called Levinskii; Goldenweiser came and played us Beethoven's 'Appassionata', and I remembered again how incomparably better Sergei Ivanovich played it. I saw him at the Igumnov concert, where by some trick of fate we turned out to be sitting next to one another. I had bought my ticket two weeks before, and his was a complimentary ticket which Igumnov had given him on the day of the concert. These coincidences do happen. I didn't tell. L.N., for fear of distressing him. As for me, I really couldn't care less!

December 14 L.N. has indigestion and a bad liver. I myself have just had a bad liver and stomach upset and I am afraid he may be falling ill with the same thing. There was a terrible snow-storm today; maybe L.N.'s illness is caused by the weather.

He bought himself some skates, and yesterday and the day before he went off skating. He was delighted to find that it didn't completely exhaust him; he really is full of energy, although he has been plunged in gloom since yesterday, I don't know why. A letter came from Gurevich, in despair because L.N. has taken back his article,[74] and L.N. is probably angry with me about this. So because I don't want to incur his blame I keep begging him to do what he wants, promising not to interfere or criticise. But he just frowns stubbornly and says nothing.

Today I took Vera Kuzminskaya and my Sasha to Gluck's *Orpheus*. It is a marvellous opera, graceful and melodious, and the choruses, the dances and the sets are all so airy and decorous. Yesterday I went to a symphony concert – Beethoven's lovely 'Pastoral', Tchaikovsky's 1st Symphony, and some other works of no interest.

The fact is that although I put a brave face on it I feel a deep grief in my heart that L.N. and I are not on better, friendlier terms, and a lot of anxiety about his health too. I have done my best – I did truly want us to be friends. But oh how difficult it all is! As I was leaving for the theatre today I was waylaid by some woman – the wife of a chemist – sobbing and imploring me to give her 600 rubles, then 400 rubles, to settle her debts. It's even harder for her. But we are all tempting the Lord . . .

December 16 I had a frightful headache this afternoon. The two Maslova girls, Anna and Sofia Ivanovna, came, so sympathetic, lively and kind. Then Stakhovich and Gorbunov. Liza Olsufieva came to dinner today and Fyodor Ivanovich Maslov was here with some views of the Caucasus which he brought L.N. for his story.[75] Then Natasha Dehn. I went out to do some business and shopping. L.N. has influenza and is in low spirits. I played a little – that marvellous rondo from the Beethoven sonata.

Yesterday I paid social calls. Everywhere I go it's the same question: 'What is the Count writing at present?', '*Qu'est-ce que vous faites pour rester toujours jeune?*'* and so on. My youthful appearance has become an almost invariable subject of conversation in society. But what is it to me when my soul is sad? And Lev Nikolaevich is so unfriendly – worse than that, there's definitely something he is keeping to himself and concealing from me. I would do anything in the world for him if only he *asked* me kindly. But his sullen silent defiance merely evokes the same defiance in me, and the desire to protect myself and create my own inner world, my own pursuits and friendships. I see nothing of S.I. and try not to think about him.

L.N. has a cough and is hoarse.

December 17 This morning I had a piano lesson with Miss Welsh. Then a call from Annenkova and a visit to the bath-house. Lev Nikolaevich has influenza and cannot write; he is taciturn, sullen and disagreeable; today he spoke of leaving to see Masha. This feverish life is so hard; if he comes to Moscow he only gets angry, and spends all his time here pining to be somewhere else. There is none of that friendly, peaceful family life I so long for – nothing is certain . . .

An astonishing incident at the bath-house today: there has been a lot of talk in Moscow recently of a certain family, the Solovyovs, whose three children all died of scarlet fever in one week. Well, I just happened to be sitting in the same compartment as the mother of these children. We got into conversation and I shared with her my painful memories of Vanechka's death; I told her of my grief, and of the (religious) solution which I had sought and partly found, and this consoled her a little. The she asked me who I was, and when I told her she burst into tears and threw her arms around me, kissing me and begging me to stay with her a little longer. What a dear, lovely, pitiful woman.

This evening there were guests: Chicherin, Masha Zubova, Annenkova,

*'How do you manage to stay so young?'

Rusanova and S.I. Taneev. His appearance alarmed me for Lev Nikolaevich's sake, and at first I felt very awkward and anxious. Then I had to preside at the tea-table. I was happy to see him of course, and would have been even happier to hear him play. But he didn't.

I had a dream last night; there was a long narrow hall, and at the end of it was a piano, on which S.I. was playing one of his own compositions. I observed him more closely and saw that Vanechka was sitting on his knee; I could only see him from the back, his golden curly hair and his white shirt, and he was leaning his head against S.I.'s right shoulder. And I felt so peaceful and happy listening to the music and seeing Vanechka and S.I. together. Then someone banged the shutters and I woke up. The tune he was playing stayed clearly in my mind even after I had woken up, but I didn't manage to retain it for long.

And I was overwhelmed with sadness that Vanechka was gone, that there would be no more of that music which soothes my soul, that Lev Nikolaevich would never be cured of his tormenting jealousy, and that my relations with him, and my simple, friendly relations with S.I., were ruined, through no fault of mine, just because of his jealousy. How hard life is! What a trial!

Lev Nikolaevich was telling us today about a woman who was giving birth in the Kremlin. It was a difficult birth and she was thought to be dying, so they sent to the monastery for a priest. A monk came with the sacraments, and it turned out that this monk had once been a doctor. He saw that he could save the mother and baby with the usual forceps procedure. It was the middle of the night; he went back to his cell, fetched his surgical instruments, the operation was performed and both mother and baby were saved. It is said that when this news reached the ears of the metropolitan he was going to defrock this monk, but in the end he was merely transferred to another monastery in another town.[76]

Sonya Mamonova showed me a photograph of Manya and Seryozha's two-year-old son today. Both L.N. and I were very upset. That poor little boy, and his poor father.

December 18 I got up late and walked to the bank to attend to the children's financial affairs. I feel ill and weak, both mentally and physically. After dinner I played a little, then read aloud a pamphlet called *Life*.[77] Then Lev Nikolaevich read to me and Sonya Mamonova from a new collection of French plays, as well as the contents page.[78] They're all trying to write something startling and original, with a lot of dramatic effects, but there's little real *content* in them.

Tanya visited the Golitsyns, painted and played her mandolin; Misha is here. He has such a weak character – he just sits there vacantly playing patience or thumping out some wretched Russian folk-song on the piano, over and over again. So depressing! An unpleasant scene with Sasha over her rudeness to her French governess and her poor French *extrait*. Seryozha Danilevskii and the Dehns came to dinner, and Dunaev came this evening.

December 20 Both yesterday and today I did the shopping for the Christmas holiday. My children and grandchildren, my daughters-in-law, the governess – they all have to have something, and I find it so difficult and tedious to do it all myself. I woke up sobbing yesterday. I was dreaming that Vanechka had come back and was happily playing with Sasha. I was overjoyed and ran up to him. Then he lay down and I bent over and kissed him, and he gave me a kiss, as he always used to, and I said to him: 'How long you've been away, and how good that you're back.'

And it was all so real, so lifelike, that I woke up sobbing, and couldn't stop crying for a long time afterwards. L.N. was astonished, but I just cried and cried and couldn't stop. This grief is so painful! They say it is a sin to weep for an infant; that may well be so!

Lev Nikolaevich rode off yesterday to the printing-house which is printing his article *On Art*, for the *Journal of Philosophy and Psychology*. He then went skating and in the afternoon we walked to the telegraph office together to send a wire to his translator in England.[79]

He is full of energy. I brought his saddle horse round for him, as he had begged me to.

December 21 Where is it, human happiness?

Today was yet another painful, dreadful day. Tanya had a letter today from Gurevich, insisting that L.N. should give her the article.[80] Both Tanya and Seryozha, who came today, berated me for my unwillingness to do so (I find these dealings with the *Northern Herald* so disagreeable), and they sent me to L.N. to beg him to let her have his 'Preface' to the translated Carpenter article. So I went in to him and asked him to give it her, since he and his family wanted this so much. I almost got him to agree. But of course with L.N. this is always the best way of achieving the opposite result, for he will invariably do the contrary just to be difficult.

But when I foolishly said something to the effect that I found his relations with Gurevich as unpleasant as he found mine with Taneev, I looked at him and was terrified. He face has changed so much recently: his thick, bushy eyebrows beetle over his angry eyes, and his expression is wild, ugly and full of suffering; his face is pleasant only when it has an expression of kindly sympathy or passionate affection. I often wonder what he would do to himself or me if I really did do something wrong! I thank God for sparing me from sin and temptation. I don't have a high opinion of myself; it was God who saved me.

Today I went out and returned some calls; this evening I saw Misha off to the country, Vera Kuzminskaya to Kiev, and Sonya Mamonova to her home in the Kaluga province; Tanya went to a society concert and I took Sasha to her dancing class at the Butyonevs. All very humdrum and tedious. When I got home I found Chicherin with Lev Nikolaevich. I played for an hour or so today.

This morning L.N. swept the skating rink in the garden and went skating; then he rode over to the Sparrow Hills. He is doing no work at present.

December 25 Have I really not written my diary for four days? So much has happened in this time. The day before yesterday Lev Nikolaevich went off to the Nikolaev station as he wanted to catch Sulerzhitskii and the Englishman St John to give them some money for the Dukhobors, whom they were going to visit. But he didn't find them. He walked home, chilled and exhausted, and went straight to bed, and when I got back he was already quite ill, with a temperature of 38.5. It went up in an hour to 39.4, then 40.2. The day before he had been to the bath-house, and all this activity had made him ill. I went myself for the doctor, young Usov, and L.N. willingly submitted to being examined, having his lungs listened to, and so on. The doctor prescribed Ems water as usual, and said he should have a warm massage and keep his stomach warm. It has all gone to his liver, stomach and intestines, and he has a bad chill, a result of excessive perspiration caused by overwork. I did all I could, and yesterday he was a little better and his temperature went down to 38.6; today it is 37.5. He is still very weak but no longer ill, and today he had something to eat. At 3 o'clock I gave him his Ems water and at 3.30 I brought him some puréed oatmeal soup. 'How clever of you to think of bringing me soup,' he said. 'I was beginning to feel a little weak.' Then he ate dinner with the rest of us; there weren't many of us – just us two old folk, Seryozha, Tanya and Masha – and Sasha Behrs and Mlle Aubert too. But we had a nice, quiet, friendly meal together. Seryozha is so wretched at present, poor thing! Before dinner the children went skating and visited the zoo, while L.N. slept and I diligently practised the piano.

We received an anonymous letter. This is what it said:

> Dear Count Lev Nikolaevich,
> There can be no doubt that your sect is growing and is putting down deep roots. However misbegotten it may be, you have nevertheless succeeded, with the aid of the devil and the stupidity of the people, in insulting our Lord Jesus Christ, whom we must now avenge. In order to do underground battle with your underground sect, therefore, we have formed a secret society, the Second Crusaders, whose aim is to kill you and all your disciples, the leaders of your sect. We fully recognise that this is not a Christian act – may the Lord forgive us and pass judgement on us in the next world! But once our hand is infected with gangrene it

must be sacrificed, however much it grieves us. I grieve for you too, as a brother in Christ, but you must be annihilated if we are to weaken the forces of evil! It has fallen to me, unworthy as I am, to kill you! The day I have appointed for your death is April 3 of the coming year, 1898. In doing this I am fulfilling my great and sacred mission, and enabling you to prepare for your journey to the other world.

You may well ask me, quite logically, why we attack your sect alone. It is true that all sects are an 'abomination before God'! But their instigators are numbskulls, and are no match, Count, for you. And secondly, you are the enemy of our Tsar and country! So until April 3.

The Second Crusader who drew the First Lot, December 1897, Bold Village.

It was sealed in wax with the initials E.S. and a royal crown. The postmark was Pavlograd, December 20.

I am so worried about this letter that I can think of nothing else. I thought of informing the governor of Ekaterinoslav province and the local police chief, Trepov, so that they could take appropriate measures against these dangerous people and order a police search if they wanted to.

But Lev Nikolaevich is totally unperturbed, and says we mustn't notify anyone and that it is all in God's hands.[81]

The Kolokoltsevs, Butyonev and Vera Severtseva came this evening. Lev Nikolaevich has a temperature of 38.5 and is still very weak.

December 26 I saw Tanya and Sasha off to Grinevka and Nikolskoe this morning, and Seryozha left yesterday evening. We rushed about packing boxes: I filled one with Christmas presents for my grandchildren, one with gifts and fruit for Dora, and one with some silver and a fur coat for Masha. All these will travel with Tanya; I also packed a basket with food and fruit for them to eat on the journey. Lev Nikolaevich and I are all on our own now; there's nothing to do, and it's nice and quiet. He is much better; he had a temperature of 36.9 this morning, and this afternoon it went up to 37.5. This evening he asked for some soup and a baked apple and was in much better spirits. I am haunted by that letter.

I spent the whole day playing the piano. This wordless musical conversation with Beethoven, Mendelssohn, Rubinstein and so on gives me enormous pleasure, even though I play so poorly. I was interrupted by a visit from Mitya Olsufiev, and we had a frank, friendly talk together. Then my cold, beautiful, sensible cousin, Olga Severtseva, came, accompanied by clever Maria Nikolaevna Muromtseva, who is so gifted and lively (and temperamental too). She has a lot of faults, but I always find her such fun. I had four invitations for me and the children: one from the Trepovs, one from the Glebovs, one from my brother Sasha, and one from Muromtseva,

Koni and a group of musicians. She said she had invited S.I. too. But I know that he has gone off to a monastery to work.[82]

Anna Levitskaya came this afternoon; then I developed and ruined a print of the group photograph I took in our garden yesterday. Tomorrow is the symphony concert, which I am looking forward to.

December 27 I went to the concert. The pieces were all quite new to me: a symphony by Franck, *Le Roi s'amuse* by Delibes, the first performance of Glazunov's *Stenka Razin*, a symphonic poem, and so on. New music interests me but doesn't give me pleasure. Lev Nikolaevich is better. He went into the garden today and ate well. It's hard to feed him properly on his vegetarian diet when he is ill. One has to devise ways of fortifying his food. Yesterday, for instance, I gave him some mushroom bouillon with rice soup, artichokes and asparagus in it, almond milk with semolina and chopped nuts, and stewed pears.

Nikolai Vasilevich Davydov came to see us; I told him about the anonymous letter, and he is the only person who has taken it at all seriously. I received various social calls – from Golitsyn, Samarin, the Khovrins, etc. – and this evening I had a pleasant talk with young Sofia Nikolaevna Kashkina. Annenkova, Dunaev, Zinger and Popov came, and they kept L.N. company while I went to the concert.

L.N. told me today that on the day he fell ill he was walking along Prechistenka when a grey kitten suddenly jumped out at him, ran up his coat and settled on his shoulder. L.N. evidently sees this as a bad omen.

A telegram from Masha thanking me for the coat and the silver. It is warm, 2 °, and sleeting.

December 29 I was busy all morning developing photographs, then I practised the piano a little. After dinner I played a duet arrangement of Schubert's Tragic Symphony with Lev Nikolaevich. He started by saying that it was all a lot of nonsense and music was dead, but was soon playing with great abandon. He soon grew tired, however. He is still weak after his illness; he has a stomach-ache and is so thin that it hurts me at present to look at him. I went out for a couple of hours this evening to a piano recital given by Gabrilovich. He played well, of course – his *piano* is quite extraordinary – but I was constantly aware of all the effort and calculation behind it, and so I wasn't moved. No one is as good as Hoffmann or Taneev.

How I yearn to hear him play again – maybe I never shall! Andryusha and Misha have returned from the country. Andryusha has a cough, which worries me.

Yesterday L.N. and I went to visit my brother Sasha: L.N. played vint while a young woman pianist played for me. She did that Chopin polonaise which S.I. played for us last summer, and I was transported by memories of his wonderful playing and delightful company. And now it's all over – for good!

Yesterday I went to visit old Stolypin. He had a group of young people there singing *Norma*. What a lively old man – to think he's 76!

I was thinking about L.N., who finds so much in the Church that is superfluous, superstitious and even downright harmful, and ends up by renouncing *all* it stands for. And it's the same with music: he listens to all the rubbish currently being offered us by our modern composers, and then renounces *all* music. This is a great mistake.

For decades people have rejected everything superfluous, all the musical dross, and the real talents have always survived. It's the same with modern music: once one has thrown out all the second-rate material a few things will still remain. And these will undoubtedly include the works of Taneev.

· 1898 ·

March 1–3 – founding in Minsk of Marxist Social Democratic Labour Party. Founding of the Second Socialist International.

Tolstoy finishes What is Art? *The complete work appears, mutilated by the censor, in the fourteenth edition of his works (and also in an Intermediary edition). Sofia writes a romantic short story, 'Song Without Words'. Tolstoy works in the villages to alleviate the famine, and appeals for funds. He also helps the Dukhobors raise money to emigrate, and supports the Molokans (another persecuted religious sect). December – Sergei Tolstoy accompanies a shipload of two thousand Dukhobors to Canada.*

January 1 Lev Nikolaevich, Andryusha, Misha, Mitya Dyakov, the Danilevskii boys and I all saw the New Year in together. Danilevskaya happened to be ill yesterday, so instead of seeing in the New Year at their house the two boys came here. We had a nice, quiet, friendly time. We drank Don champagne, and Lev Nikolaevich drank tea with almond milk.

This morning I played the piano and kept an eye on Misha to make sure he studied. Then I went to visit my old aunt Vera Aleksandrovna Shidlovskaya, and chatted for a while with her and my cousins; I also called on the Istomins. Lev Nikolaevich and I had dinner on our own. He is not yet fully recovered and hardly ate a thing, just a bowl of mushroom soup with rice, some semolina with almond milk, and coffee. He is lethargic and bored, for he is not used to being ill and debilitated. How hard it will be for him when he finally loses his strength and grows even weaker! He has such an appetite for life! Yet he'll soon be 70 – in August of this year, in fact, i.e. in 6 months. He has been reading alone in his study upstairs and writing a few letters; today he walked over to visit Rusanov, who is ill – and simply worships him. Lying on the sofa in his study is Tanya's black poodle, a gift from Countess Zubova. He took it out for a walk today.

Our Masha is arriving tomorrow for a consultation with the doctor. Tanya and Sasha are still in the country; they'll probably go to Yasnaya Polyana tomorrow to visit Lyova and Dora. I should like to go to Yasnaya too. How I love it, and what a lot of good experiences I have had there!

January 3 Stasov, Ginzburg the sculptor, a young painter and Vereshchagin (a bad writer) were here yesterday morning. Stasov took advantage of his 74 years to fling his arms round me and kiss me, repeating 'Oh, how pink and how slender you are!' I was so embarrassed – I just couldn't get away from him. We then went upstairs to the drawing-room and discussed Lev Nikolaevich's article *On Art*. Stasov said he thought L.N. had got it all back to front.[1] He didn't have to tell me that, he certainly hit the nail on the head!

L.N. and I had a nasty argument because I was deploring the fact that the public should have to take out a two-year subscription to the *Journal of Philosophy and Psychology* in order to read his article, which is contained in the November–December and February–March issues, when if I had brought it out in the *Complete Collected Works* I would have sold it for 50 kopecks and everyone would have been able to read it. L.N. then started shouting in front of everyone: 'I shan't give it to you! I'm giving it to everyone! Everyone has criticised me ever since I started giving my things away for nothing!'

But he never gives me anything. He sent 'Master and Man' to the *Northern Herald* behind my back;[2] he also returned the Preface[3] on the sly, and he has been at pains not to let me have his article on art either. God be with him! He's quite right, they're *his* works, *his* inalienable property – but he oughtn't to shout at me like that.

Masha arrived yesterday with Kolya. She is completely taken up with her husband, we hardly exist as far as she's concerned – and she means very little to us too. I was pleased to see her; I am sorry she is so thin, but I'm happy that she is living for love, for that is a great joy! For a long time I too lived for this simple love, without judging or criticising. I regret that I am now more experienced, have lost so many illusions. I would have preferred to remain blind and besotted to the end of my days. What I tried to accept as love from my husband was nothing but sensuality, now degenerating into sullen severity, now flaring up into jealousy, demands – and occasionally tenderness. What I would like now is to travel through life with a quiet, kind friend. I long for affection, friendship, tranquillity, sympathy . . .

This evening I went to a performance of *Sadko*.[4] A beautiful, entertaining opera, the music is marvellous in places and very clever; the composer was wildly applauded and there were numerous ovations. I enjoyed the whole thing enormously – yet how much more I would have enjoyed it if, like so many others there, I'd had a dear quiet friend – my husband – sitting beside me.

I receive and make endless calls, and find it a great strain . . .

Evening. Stasov, Kasatkin, Ginzburg (the sculptor) and Mathieu (the engraver) came to dinner.[5] Muromtseva arrived after dinner in a yellow dress and decked out in flowers, but she didn't appear to be sober – it always shocks me to see people in this condition. Later on Rimsky-Korsakov came with his wife,[6] and Muromtseva left.

There were noisy, heated discussions about art. Stasov said nothing, L.N. shouted, and Rimsky-Korsakov launched into a passionate defence of *beauty* in art, saying that people must be educated to appreciate it. All this is discussed in his article.[7] None of us agreed with L.N.'s denial of beauty, and the level of development required to understand art. The Korsakovs mentioned Sergei Ivanovich several times, and obviously have a great affection and respect for him, like everyone else – apart from my fierce husband of course. How he shouted in the discussion today! I am always afraid he'll offend someone with his sharp tongue.

I am exhausted – I spent the whole day with company . . . The boys are at the Luginins' dance.

January 5 Yesterday I went to a morning dance at the Shcherbatovs', where all Moscow's so-called 'society' had gathered. I wanted to take Sasha – she and Tanya returned this morning from seeing their brothers in the country – and I wanted to see my sons dancing. It was a very good-natured morning, and so stylish too – not at all offensive.

I went to Muromtseva's party late this evening, as I didn't want to offend her, and was received very civilly there; there was singing, music and it was all very pleasant. But this chaotic social life is making me stupid. And quite apart from that, my three daughters are ill: Masha with terrible headaches and hysterical attacks, Sasha with a painful abscess in her ear which has just burst, and Tanya with a toothache, a fever and worries about Sukhotin, who is coming tomorrow.

Lev Nikolaevich is well again and is up and about; with me he is being affectionate. Today I walked to the students' art show; it's dreadfully bad, only a few landscapes are passable and convey something of the summer, the forest, and the water. Repin dined here today and spent the rest of the day with us.

January 6 I drove to Patriarch Ponds today and went skating for a long time with the Maklakovs and Natasha Kolokoltseva. Then it started to rain and thaw. Skating is such a bracing, healthy activity. This evening I did some reading, sat with Sasha, then listened to an unknown young man named Pol, from Kiev, playing us some of his works – very well too.[8] L.N.

is gloomy because he is still unable to work. He went skating too – at some institution for young waifs and strays. This isn't the first time he has been there. I was crying this morning, remembering Vanechka when he was alive, and this evening I was again in the throes of despair, thinking of all the things I had wanted out of life, everything which never was and never will be . . .

L.N. is reading all he can find about the Caucasus at present – Caucasian life, Caucasian scenery, everything.[9]

January 8 Repin dined with us yesterday and kept asking Lev Nikolaevich to suggest a theme for a painting. He said he wanted to devote his last efforts in life to a good work of art, something really worth working on. Lev Nikolaevich hasn't suggested anything to him yet, but is thinking about it.[10] He himself can do no work. The weather is frightful: there's a terrible wind, and water everywhere – even more than during a Moscow spring; it's 3 ° and dark.

Yesterday I read Kashkin's glowing review of *Sadko*.[11] I did so love it and I longed to see it again. L.N. urged me to do so and was so sweet about it that I felt even more guilty about being so frivolous. In fact I would have been quite happy if I hadn't managed to get a ticket, but it would so happen that mine was the *last* one left at the box-office. It was for the 3rd row of the stalls, and I wanted a balcony seat as it's so noisy downstairs and I had an ear-ache, so I went upstairs to find someone to change seats with me. Someone called out my name, and who should it be but Sasha's teacher Kashkina, a sweet girl. She sent her brother downstairs and sat me between her and her mother. In the interval Anna Ivanovna Maslova also called out to me. She was there in the dress-circle too, but further forward than me, and she was with her cousin and Sergei Ivanovich. I almost fainted when I remembered the kind way L.N. had urged me to go. Fate is always playing these tricks on me. There were 3,000 people in the theatre; I am terribly short-sighted and can see no one more than two steps away; from the stalls it's impossible to see people sitting in the second row of the balcony – yet I found myself in a seat where I could see Sergei Ivanovich. When we were collecting our coats he exchanged a couple of words with me, saying that he had finished his orchestral symphony, and that he would pay a visit one of these days.

When I got home I wanted to tell L.N. that I had seen Sergei Ivanovich, but I simply couldn't. When I went in to see him his face seemed so thin and sad that I longed to throw myself into his arms and tell him I could never love anyone as I loved him, that I'd do anything in the world to make him calm and happy; but that would have been folly – there's no knowing what he would have thought; maybe he'd think, like Masha, that I'd done something wrong, that I was plotting and planning and making assignations . . .

Sasha is ill; she has an abscess in her ear and I am very sorry for the little companion of my present life. I love Tanya as passionately as before; I am deeply sorry for her, and watch her emotional struggles with great sadness. Andryusha has left for Tver, Misha has gone to the lycée. L.N. wanted to go for a ride, but his horse was lame so he went for a walk instead.

January 10 I went with Marusya Maklakova to the annual exhibition of paintings,[12] and although few of them were any good I do so love art. And on the subject of art, A. Stakhovich, an adjutant to Gr. Duke Sergei Aleksandrovich, was saying yesterday that the Grand Duke and company were reading Lev Nikolaevich's article *On Art* and were saying that it was 'deeply regrettable that this should have been produced by the brilliant pen of Lev Tolstoy'. They mentioned our family too, and the Grand Duke, after meeting me on Wednesday at Glebova's, told Stakhovich that he had been struck by my extraordinarily youthful appearance. I am so used to hearing this, however, and it's such a cheap compliment, that I no longer attach any value to it. If only I were *something* more than merely 'Tolstoy's youthful wife', how happy I should be! I am referring to spiritual qualities.

L.N. is calm and healthy, but still cannot work. We are getting on well, and it's a long time since relations have been so straightforward. I am so happy! But will it last?

January 13 Yesterday was Tanya's name-day, and we bustled around all morning organising a *party*. First Tanya invited some guests, then I invited some. One has a *duty* to one's society friends. I was sorting through some cardboard this morning, with my hair all awry and my morning cap on, when Sergei Ivanovich and Yusha Pomerantsev suddenly came into the room. I hadn't heard a thing, and I was so agitated I blushed crimson and couldn't say a word. I had given express orders that no one should be admitted, but for some reason they had been let in. They sat there for almost an hour, talking about *Sadko* and Rimsky-Korsakov, amongst other things. When Sergei Ivanovich left I felt deeply depressed – to pacify L.N. I should hate this man, or at least treat him as a stranger. But that is impossible.

At the party Stakhovich and Muromtseva-Klimentova sang, Igumnova and Goldenweiser played, there were bright lights, refreshments, supper, some princesses, a general and some young ladies – and it wasn't very gay and it wasn't too dull, but it was a lot of hard work. L.N. played vint with Stolypin, my brother Sasha and the others.

Masha and Kolya left today.

January 14 Lev Nikolaevich has been more cheerful these past two days.

Sasha has recovered, thank God, and has started lessons again. Misha also did some work today, and went to the Maly Theatre for a performance of M. Tchaikovsky's *Fighters*.

I live conscientiously, but often with a sense of deep despair in my heart . . . Help me, Lord!

January 16 Tanya is leaving for St Petersburg. I mentioned that I should like to attend some of Wagner's operas there, but this provoked from Lev Nikolaevich such an angry flood of criticisms and biting references to my insane love of music, my stupidity, my ineptitude, etc., etc., that he has completely killed my desire to do anything.

I spent the whole day checking the accounts with the accountant, and diligently set all my publishing, family and household affairs in order, but I am now exhausted, and my head is aching. Late this evening Lev Nikolaevich and I walked Marusya Maklakova home and Dunaev and my brother Styopa came too.

Seryozha and Ilyusha arrived. A painful discussion with Lev Nikolaevich this evening. He is becoming more and more difficult, suspicious, jealous and despotic. He resents every independent move I make, every innocent pleasure, every hour spent at the piano.

Marusya Maklakova and our Tanya were looking through photographs of various men today and discussing which of them they would marry. When they came to Lev Nikolaevich's portrait they both cried, 'No, no! Not for anything!' Yes, it is difficult to live under any sort of despotism, but jealous despotism is frightful!

January 17 L.N. has been nagging me all day, begging to be 'released' to go back to the country; he wasn't necessary to me here, he said, life in Moscow was sheer murder for him – on and on in the same vein.[13] The word 'released' is absolutely meaningless – as though I could 'hold' him here! I wanted him to come to Moscow because it is quite natural for me to want to live with my husband, and it's a pleasure too, for I am used to loving and caring for him. I have done all I could to spare him from his tormenting jealousy, but I still haven't earned his trust. If he went to the country he would torment himself even more; if we all went, what would happen to Misha and Sasha? What about their studies? I have been racking my brains . . . But Lev Nikolaevich's apathy and indifference to his children's education is always so painful to me, and I blame him bitterly for it. How many fathers not only educate their own children, but also support them with their own labour, as my father did? But L.N. considers that even for him to *live* with his family would be murder.

I walked to the bank on business this morning, and then to the shops. There's a terrible wind, 6 ° below freezing. Ilyusha has come for the dog-show, and for some money; Seryozha is here. My brother Styopa has left; Sonya Mamonova has come.

I was reading the newspaper while waiting in the bank this morning, and was moved to tears by a story about some workers killed in a gas explosion at the Makeevka Mines, in Kharkov province. They described the funeral, the relatives' grief, the dead horses, the crippled workers – it was terrible! Those dead victims, what a hard life they endured, endlessly toiling away underground, without light, without happiness! And now they are dead. And then they wail about the Dreyfus affair in Paris.[14] How unimportant that seems beside this Russian catastrophe.

January 18 Lev Nikolaevich swept the snow off the skating-rink in the garden and flooded it, then wrote a lot of letters. He is very taciturn and unsociable, and now that he has insulted me I expect he is complaining about me in letters to his friends.

January 20 Yesterday morning Sasha was collecting money for the young son of our footman Ivan, who has just left. This little boy, Lyonya, was badly burnt by some scalding water from the samovar, and is now in hospital.

An extraordinary thing happened the day before yesterday. My sons had gone to the theatre – Seryozha to see *Sadko* at the Solodovnikov. I had a sudden overwhelming fear that this theatre would burn down, and told Lev Nikolaevich of my premonition of a fire, and sure enough, that night after the audience had left, the theatre burnt down and the roof collapsed.

Today I took Sasha to buy her some shoes and a corset. Then I swept the snow off the skating-rink in the garden; Lev Nikolaevich joined me and we both swept together, then he took a turn on his skates while I went indoors and practised the piano for an hour and a half.

This evening we had a great treat. Maria Nikolaevna Muromtseva brought the young pianist Gabrilovich to the house and he played beautifully for us all evening: he did a ballade and a nocturne by Chopin, a Schubert impromptu and a rondo by Beethoven. Misha Olsufiev came too, and Marusya Maklakova. Lev Nikolaevich enjoyed the music enormously and thanked this clever, cheerful young twenty-year-old for playing to us.

Sonya Mamonova is staying, and she and I read a review of L.N.'s article *On Art* together. The critics have all been quite guarded about it.[15]

January 21 I was going to read the proofs for the new edition of *Childhood* and *Boyhood* today, but I realised when I looked at it that it hadn't been set with the right type, so I had to send it back to the printers to be reprinted.[16]

This evening I worked hard on my Beethoven sonata. Then I grew too tired to go on and went upstairs to see Lev Nikolaevich, who had some factory-worker with him, as well as a soldier and some other dark one. I am SO BORED with this endless wall of guests (especially ones like these) perpetually standing between me and my husband.

Sonya Mamonova and Lev Nikolaevich have spent the whole day

discussing the idea of a village newspaper for the people. Its purpose would be to provide them with something *interesting* to read.[17] News like train crashes, steamer accidents, mine disasters, the arrival of overseas visitors from China, Abyssinia and so on, then meteorological, agronomical and historical articles; then news of our Tsar and the royal family, a short list of holidays, and a feuilleton for light reading. Lev Nikolaevich is so enthusiastic about the idea that he has written to Sytin (a publisher of popular books and pictures) inviting him to come and discuss the financial side with him. But the main thing is that he wants to involve *me* in the paper. Now I have every sympathy with the idea, but I could never embark on something like this with *him* – our views are too different, and L.N. would ruin the whole thing for me by being so impractical. I would only take Lev Nikolaevich on as a fiction writer, not as an editor.

I am tired and depressed, I shall go to bed to live in my imagination the life I do not live in reality. I don't sleep much, but I think a lot and remember – and I still contemplate the future too, what lies in store for me.

Today Misha passed his half-yearly Greek exam.

January 22 I played the piano all morning. I feel intensely anxious. I didn't sleep all last night, just lay there in the dark trying not to disturb my husband. When I sat down at the piano today I suddenly thought that L.N. might die, for they have threatened to kill him, and I burst into tears . . .[18] Yet however severe he is with me, I still have so much love in my heart for him.

This evening I went to a concert – four professors from the Vienna Conservatoire who have formed a quartet.

L.N. took Tanya's black poodle for a walk round the garden; his skating-rink has thawed. Then he received a letter from a woman in Voronezh province telling him that there was a famine there and asking him for help and advice. He wrote a letter to the *Russian Gazette* about it, but it's unlikely that they'll publish it.[19] This evening he visited Rusanov, who is sick. Popov has come; he is on his way to visit Biryukov and is taking something from L.N. to give him. Biryukov is leaving Bauska for England.[20] Wiener, Prince Khilkov's former mistress, also left for England yesterday, and he too has been deported.

January 26 I have been ill these past few days. It started as terrible neuralgia on the right side of my head, and was followed by a high fever and a sore throat. Young Doctor Usov came; he feared at first that it might be diphtheria, but when he had examined me it proved not to be. These young doctors are quite extraordinary. Malyutin refused to take any money for treating Sasha, and now Usov too refuses to be paid. I have sent him a signed copy of L.N.'s works instead. As Tanya is still in St Petersburg, L.N. sweetly offered to paint my throat, which he did very cautiously and clumsily. My illness has frightened him, and he has suddenly started to look older and sadder. How strangely we love one another! He is happy when I sit quietly at home, bored and inert, copying or reading. And the moment I become more lively, tackle something new or make new friends, he becomes anxious, and then angry, and starts treating me harshly. Yet it is sometimes very hard for me to stifle my natural spontaneity!

I was lying in bed yesterday when three more Molokans from Samara came to see L.N. again, begging for letters of introduction to take to St Petersburg. They are going there to plead once more for their children, who were taken away from them by the government and sent to monasteries.[21] Those poor children, and their poor mothers! What a barbaric way to convert people to Orthodoxy! It won't convert them at all, quite the opposite.

My sister arrived from St Petersburg today, bringing her articles on tariff, finances and the peasant community, which she read to us. I can't imagine why a woman should concern herself with such matters! But she is utterly engrossed in Russia's financial affairs and is in constant touch with Witte, Minister of Finances. L.N. and Dunaev consider much of it very clever, especially her articles on the tariff which was recently introduced into Russia and has already proved such a complete disaster.[22]

I was invited to a musical evening at Muromtseva's today, but couldn't go. I shall miss the symphony concert on Saturday too; I was sorry to miss Beethoven's *Egmont*, but I gave my ticket to Seryozha, and am glad he was able to enjoy it.

Yesterday and today I was lying in bed reading the proofs of *Childhood*, which always touches me so deeply. My back aches, I feel weak and am afflicted by constant gnawing depression.

L.N. just came in and said: 'I've come to keep you company for a bit.' Then he showed me the two seven-pound weights he bought today for his gymnastic exercises. He is very lethargic at present and keeps saying: 'I feel as though I were 70.' But in 6 months, that is in August, he *will* be 70. He went skating today and swept the snow. But he cannot do any mental work, and that mortifies him beyond words.

January 27 I read proofs during the day, and this evening we had guests – Tsurikov, old Boborykin, the former governor of Oryol province, Professor Grot, Sulerzhitskii, Gorbunov and various others. I am still ill and was absolutely exhausted; I couldn't do a thing or join in any of the discussions. L.N. went skating briefly, and corrected the proofs of *Art*.[23]

January 28 I got up with great difficulty, still feeling very ill. My body aches, I feel sick and I have a headache. But I managed despite this to do a lot of work on the proofs and on the children's affairs; yesterday and today I have been copying accounts from the general housekeeping book into three separate ledgers – for Andryusha, Misha and Lyova. Dear M.E. Leonteva came to see me and we had a frank and intimate discussion about the serious matters of life.

Sergei Ivanovich sent his dear old nurse, Pelageya Vasilevna, to ask after my health.

L.N. has over-exerted himself again. First he swept the snow off the skating-rink, then he went skating. He also started on his weight-lifting. As a result of all this his liver began to trouble him again, and he also ate an enormous quantity of lentils and porridge at the wrong time of day, and ate nothing for dinner. I have just sent for some Ems water and given him some, which he drank gladly. He is now reading in his study. I am reading *Désastre* by Paul Margueritte and his brother, which appears to be set during the Franco-Prussian War.[24]

Lev Nikolaevich had a visit from a lady named Kogan, and they discussed lofty matters concerning human purpose and happiness, and the paths to its attainment.

All the copying and correcting work (negligible at present) is being done by Sulerzhitskii, an extremely able, intelligent, independent young man who used to study art with Tanya at the Myasnitskaya school. L.N. is very pleased with his work.

January 29 Tanya has returned from St Petersburg. She went in order to get her paintings published,[25] and she had a very pleasant time there. She visited Pobedonostsev to discuss the case of the Samara Molokans who were robbed of their children. He told her that the local bishop had exceeded his authority, adding that he would write to the governor of Samara about it, and that he 'hoped the whole matter would soon be settled'. What cunning! He pretended not to know that Tanya was Lev Nikolaevich's daughter, and when she was already on her way downstairs, he asked her, 'Are you the daughter of Lev Nikolaevich?' And when she said 'Yes,' he said: 'Ah, so you are the renowned Tatiana Lvovna!' To which Tanya replied: 'Well, I certainly didn't know I was renowned!'[26]

My brother Styopa has come again with his sick, deaf, sad wife. He and Seryozha have concluded their negotiations over the property they are buying in the Minsk province. The question is, is it worth it? M. Stakhovich had dinner with us. Lev Nikolaevich corrected the proofs of *What is Art?* all day. It is now evening; he has taken the black poodle for a walk and is now eating porridge and drinking tea.

A blizzard all day, between three and five degrees of frost. I am still unwell and have a back-ache. I played the piano for a couple of hours, just sight-reading, and managed to pick out a number of Chopin waltzes, nocturnes and preludes. But oh so badly! How much hard work it takes to play even reasonably well, and I play so badly and progress so slowly.

9 Lev Tolstoy and Sofia Tolstaya at Yasnaya Polyana, with eight of their children, 1887. (Sofia's photograph)

10 Above: Lev Tolstoy and Sofia in his study

11 Below: Sofia Tolstaya copying a portrait by Repin, 1904

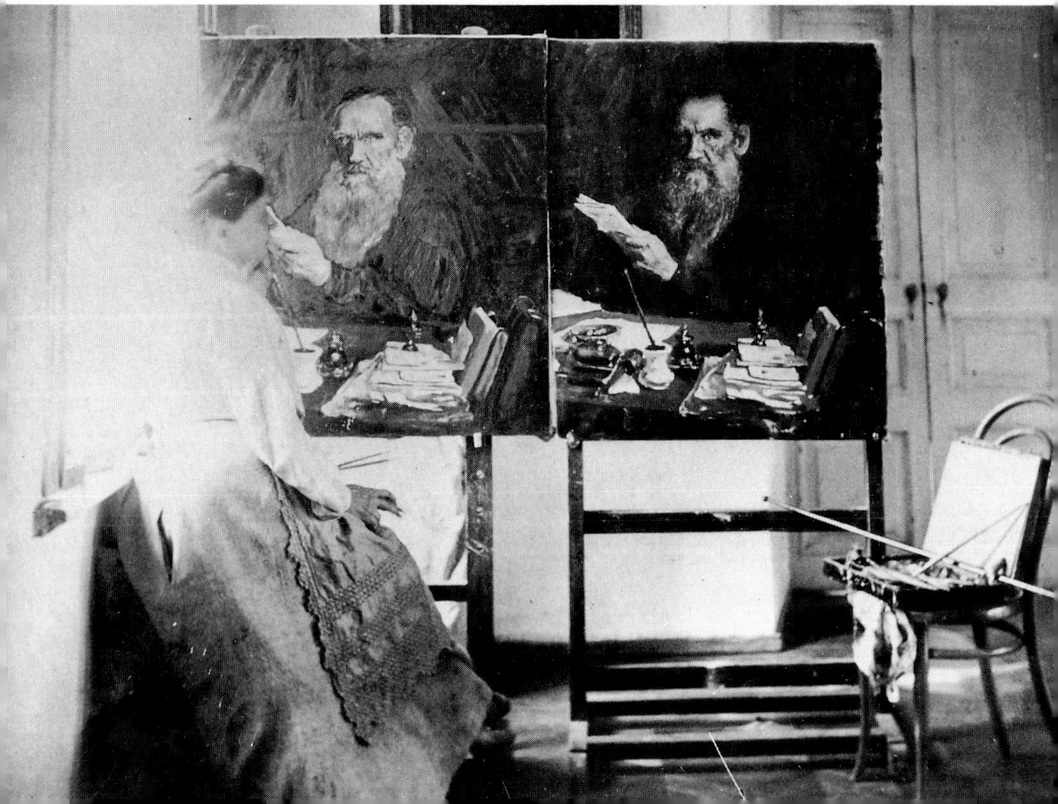

January 30 Today Sergei Ivanovich came to see me – he has an undoubted power and influence over me, I must confess. We were alone together for only a short while as my brother Styopa and my son Seryozha came in; but when he left my nerves felt so soothed, and I felt a calm joy such as I haven't experienced for a long time. Was this wrong of me? We talked only of music, of his compositions and of the musical range of the alto, soprano and tenor voices. He explained to Seryozha and me the difference between the voices. Then we spoke of the way one assuages one's conscience by dealing severely with one's own actions; and how terribly hard it is when someone close to us dies to accept the wrongs we did him. He enquired with such sympathy and affection about my recent illness, my children, and what I had been doing recently – and there was so much simple, calm kindness in it that it made me extraordinarily happy. What a pity it is that Lev Nikolaevich is too jealous to tolerate our friendship, or to allow himself and our family to be friends with this marvellous idealistic man. Seryozha was so sweet with him, very friendly and straightforward. He speaks very warmly of him, and would love him if it weren't for his father. As for himself, he told me that he was revising his opera and composing a new quartet,[27] and had sent his symphony to St Petersburg, where it will be performed from March 18 to 20. I would so love to go!

Styopa's wife has been here; her deafness is very trying. I copied out for Lev Nikolaevich the new corrections he has made to *On Art*, which took me about three hours. Then Marusya Maklakova came to dinner and read me the proofs of *Childhood*. We have received a copy of *The Source* containing Lyova's article 'Yasha Polyanov' ('Memories of Childhood').[28] It was very moving for me to read these memoirs through my children's eyes: so much of it reminded me of the pious hard-working life I lived when I was younger, caring for my children, devoted to my husband. But I wouldn't want my youth back. There was so much *grief*, so much *tragedy* in that selfless life of endless sacrifice, effort, struggle and love, such a complete lack of interest in *my* personal life, my youthful pleasures, even my need for an occasional *rest* . . . Not to mention my spiritual development or aesthetic pleasures . . .

January 31 I have been out for the first time since my illness. I paid 1,000 rubles into Ilyusha's account at the Bank of the Nobility, withdrew the interest and made various other payments. *Business* – all very dull but necessary. Andryusha came, more discussions about money and why he perpetually needs so much of it. Will the happy moment ever come when I am free of these financial ordeals with my children? I thought I would be spared all this when the property was divided up, but in fact this division has been the ruin of my children.[29]

L.N. finished correcting the proofs of *On Art*, then he energetically swept the snow-drifts off the skating-rink, put on his skates and took a turn. He now sits quite happily with our guests in the evenings, occasionally going off to his study to read and rest.

February 1 I slept badly, got up late, corrected proofs and entered yesterday's transactions into the account-books. I then overcame my laziness and drove to the skating-rink at Patriarch Ponds, where my Sasha, Andryusha and Misha had gone skating. They were all there, as well as several other acquaintances; soon my older children, Tanya and Seryozha, arrived too, and we all had a marvellous time on the ice. I enjoyed skating with Yusha Pomerantsev best of all. What a fine, open, clever, cheerful fellow this Yusha Pomerantsev is. I love him dearly, and see many good qualities in him which promise well for his future.

My children, especially the boys, were embarrassed at first to see me skating, but when they saw that I didn't draw attention to myself they relaxed, and Andryusha even took a turn with me.

But I was exhausted by the exercise and fell asleep after dinner, which I normally never do. I woke up to find that we had guests – Butyonev, Maslov, Baratynskaya and the artist Kasatkin. We had an excellent discussion about art, Slavophiles, sectarians, and Tanya's visit to St Petersburg. Lev Nikolaevich again has an upset stomach and a bad liver; he thinks it's those apples he ate – I am convinced it's because he over-exerted himself yesterday clearing the snow. He didn't even eat any dinner. I cannot bear to see him so thin; when he is asleep in bed he looks so small, with all the bones sticking out of his back and shoulders. His face looks much fresher these days, and he is very fit and active, but he is so thin. I try to give him extra nourishing food, but it's difficult; yesterday, for instance, I ordered some asparagus and a light puréed soup for him, but he is still ill today. I try very hard not to upset him; I don't contradict him, and I don't go out.

Speaking of art, L.N. was today mentioning various things which he considers to be true works of art: Shevchenko's *The Hireling*, for example, the novels of Victor Hugo, that painting by Kramskoi of a regiment marching past, with a young woman, a baby and a wet-nurse looking at them through a window;[30] then that painting by Surikov of some Siberian convicts sleeping, and an old man sitting beside them – an illustration to L.N.'s story 'God Sees the Truth'. He also mentioned a short story by Hugo (I don't remember its name) about a fisherman's wife who dies after giving birth to twins, and another fisherman's wife, who has five children of her own, takes the babies in. And when her husband comes home she shyly tells him about the death of the mother and the birth of the twins, and he says: 'Well, we must take them in then.' And the wife then draws back the curtain and shows him the babies she has already taken.[31] And many more works besides were mentioned and discussed.

Despite his ill health, L.N. went skating in the garden and took a short walk with Dunaev.

I am depressed without music, but what's to be done!

February 2 We went to bed late yesterday, and I hardly slept at all. It's a long time since I've been in such an exalted, religious mood. All those feelings I experienced after Vanechka's death reawakened in me and swept through my soul. It was as though I had raised a curtain and looked at the light – at that pure, disembodied, spiritual state besides which all earthly concerns are as nothing. And this mood inspired me to pray, and prayer brought consolation.

This morning I did some proof-reading, then went to visit Ofrosimova (Stolypina), and learnt that on January 31 she had been successfully delivered of a son. Then I called on my old aunt Shidlovskaya and sat with her for a while. The young Maklakovs came to dinner, and this evening Tanya, Sasha and Marusya all went off to see *Sadko*. I was just sitting down to play the piano when Andryusha came in, and I felt so sorry for him that I sat down with him and we had a good talk together. Later, when the poor boy had left to return to his regiment in Tver, I managed to play for about an hour and a half. L.N. was busy all day; this evening he was reading the Dukhobors' letters and a book about Mary Urusova written by her mother.[32] Then he wrote some letters, and was delighted to be on his own.

I had a letter from Masha and Lyova.[33] Cold and windy, 12 ° of frost.

February 3 Today is Nurse's name-day. She and I have been avoiding each other all day for fear of both bursting into tears, as we did last year and the year before, and stirring up memories of Vanechka, who was always so eager to 'celebrate' Nurse's name-day, as he called it, and would always ask me to buy a cup, some handkerchiefs or some sweets for her. All day I restrained my grief and spoke to no one of it, though it was choking me, and it was only in the evening that I sat down to pour out my feelings into those pieces of music which soothed my grief before, when that man made himself so dear to me by playing them for me.

The whole crowd came to see Lev Nikolaevich this evening – Gorbunov, Popov, Menshikov from St Petersburg and two new ones: one was a friend of Boulanger's, I don't know who the other one was.[34] These people never speak! There were no interesting discussions; they talked about art, and merely enumerated various important paintings. L.N. has a cold. This morning he suddenly remembered something they had omitted from the proofs of *What is Art?* He went first to Grot, then to the editorial board of the *Journal of Philosophy and Psychology*, where he replaced the omitted passage.

February 4 I had a piano lesson from Miss Welsh and played a lot.

Menshikov came this evening. I fell asleep in the drawing-room, then went off to bed.

February 5 I went to a concert given by the conservatoire students. I arrived late unfortunately, as I hadn't realised it was meant to start at 8. I sat beside Sergei Ivanovich throughout – I love his explanations and interpretations of almost every piece of music. I gave him a lift and he was naively delighted by the horses' brisk trotting.

When I got home I suddenly felt afraid, as though I were concealing some shameful secret. But I felt so sorry for Sergei Ivanovich wearing that thin coat in the wind and cold, and it seemed only natural to give him a lift. Besides, he still has a bad leg and is hobbling about with a stick.

Tomorrow he and Goldenweiser are coming to play us his symphony and the *Oresteia* overture, arranged for four hands.

February 6 A rather tense and difficult evening. Sergei Ivanovich and Goldenweiser played Taneev's symphonic overture *Oresteia* as a duet. The whole family listened with patronising indifference and no one praised it. It was all terribly awkward. Thankfully Lev Nikolaevich, with his customary good breeding, did go up to them afterwards to tell them how much he had liked the *theme*. The only ones who liked it and were excited by it were Anna Ivanovna Maslova and myself. We had heard the *Oresteia* before, and had heard the overture performed by an orchestra, so for us the piano version was only an echo of the original.

I have seen almost nothing of L.N. today. He read, visited Grot, delivered the proofs of *What is Art?*, wrote a lot of letters, and spent the evening with us. He is well again, but there is something reserved and withdrawn about his behaviour at present. I don't know where he put that notebook containing his last diary – I am afraid he may have sent it off to Chertkov.[35] I am afraid even to ask him. My God, my God! We have lived together all our lives, I have given him all my love and all my youth, and the result of our life together is that I am *afraid* of him! I am afraid – without having done anything wrong! I try to analyse this *fear*, but I soon stop analysing, for there are some things I am beginning to understand all too well as time passes and I grow older.

I know for instance that he has thoroughly slandered me in his diaries, cleverly delineating all my weaknesses with short, malicious strokes; how *cleverly* he gives himself the martyr's crown, and turns me into the scourge of Xantippe.

You alone can judge us, Lord!

February 7 Marusya Maklakova and I spent almost the whole day reading the proofs of *Boyhood* and *What is Art?* Lev Nikolaevich is completely immersed in the proofs of *What is Art?* Seryozha played the piano all evening, occasionally very well. A fierce blizzard all day.

February 8 L.N. again complains of feeling ill. His back aches from the neck down and he has felt sick all day. It must be his diet – it's terrible! Today he ate pickled mushrooms, marinated mushrooms and stewed dried fruit – all of which produces a lot of fermentation in the stomach, and there's no nourishment in it so he loses weight. This evening he asked for a mint infusion and drank a little. He is in low spirits too. Today he was saying that his life was coming to an end, the machine had broken down, it was all over; but I can also see he has a very hostile attitude to death; today he reminded me a little of his aunt Pelageya Ilinichna Yushkova, who died in our house. She also dreaded death and was violently angry when she realised it had come. L.N. has not actually said as much, but surely his depression and his indifference to everything and everyone mean that the thought of death is terrible to him. He didn't go out all day, just slept in his study, corrected proofs and read. Now it is evening. Professor Grot brought him the proofs of *What is Art?* and is now talking to him in his study. L.N. has been longing for a game of vint, but has been feeling too sick to play.

When I looked in on him this evening, there were some complete strangers sitting there – a factory-worker, some peasants and another 'dark one'. This is the wall that has stood between me and my husband over recent years. I overheard their conversation: the factory-worker was naïvely asking, 'And what are your views, L.N., on the second coming of our Lord Jesus Christ?'

My Misha has vanished for the whole day and I am very displeased about these disappearances from the house. But an eighteen-year-old boy finds it dull to be with factory-workers and old men, and he misses the company of young people. Fat, sulky Sasha is too young for him and doesn't interest him as a companion. What a difference between her and our lively, sensitive, clever little Tanya at her age!

February 9 My brother Styopa was talking to Lev Nikolaevich and Seryozha today, and when I went in they fell silent. I asked them what they had been talking about and they just mumbled something . . .

Poor, poor me! What has always bothered him about me is my love of elegance, my love of *purity* in everything – both internal and external. But he doesn't need that. What he needs is a passive, healthy, dumb woman with no will of her own. And now my music torments him, he condemns me for putting flowers in the room and for loving art, he ridicules me for reading the Beethoven biography[36] and the philosophy of Seneca . . . Well, I have lived my life, there is no point in raking up old griefs now.

February 12 For two days I haven't written. For two days I have been toiling over the proofs of *What is Art*? I have inserted all the new translations and corrections, and have now completely finished the proofs for *Childhood* and *Boyhood*. Two evenings ago L.N. walked over to see Rusanov and I had a visit from his nieces, Liza Obolenskaya and Varya Nagornova, and the artist Kasatkin, who brought some magnificent paintings, illustrations to the Gospels by the French painter Tissot. Tanya and the rest of us examined these fascinating, original paintings, which were so ethnographically remarkable and so full of imagination.[37]

I walked over to the Kuznetskii Most yesterday, and returned to find L.N. skating in the garden. I quickly put on my skates too and joined him. But after Patriarch Ponds I found our garden cramped and dreary. L.N. skates very confidently and well; he has been much healthier and happier these past three days. I was on my way to a concert yesterday when I suddenly had a vivid picture of the peasant poverty which will follow the bad harvest and crop failure that is on everyone's lips at present. I saw it as clearly as though it were before my very eyes – children begging for food when there is no food, mothers suffering to see their children starve, when they themselves are starving – and I was consumed with horror and the most helpless despair . . . Nothing grieves me more than the thought of starving children. Probably because when I was breastfeeding my own children my heart would bleed for any child who was hungry, and ever since then I have felt sorry not only for my own children but for all children on earth.

This morning there was a very unpleasant scene with Misha. He had stayed out all night, I scolded him, he answered back, I lost my temper and he went off whistling. I then burst into tears, completely beside myself, and said: 'Your mother cries and you whistle. Have you no heart?' He felt ashamed then, and apologised. To soothe my nerves and my heart I went to the piano and played Beethoven's 'Pathétique' Sonata. I played for an hour and a half and practised another sonata too. Then L.N. came in and I started telling him about Misha, but he wasn't interested in this for he had come in to give me some work – copying corrections from one copy of *What is Art?* on to another.

This took about two hours. He then went off to take these pages to the printer's, while Verochka and I tidied up Lyova's and Dora's room.

After dinner I played the piano for a while, then Lyova and Dora arrived. We all sat and talked, and later on Grot came and we discussed the article. No one likes it. I felt quite outraged today when I read his condemnation of Beethoven. Not long ago I read Beethoven's biography and learnt to love and appreciate this genius more than ever before. But my love is always quick to arouse Lev Nikolaevich's loathing, even for the dead. I remember when I read Seneca and was so enchanted by him, and he promptly told me that Seneca was nothing but a pompous Roman fool with a fondness for fine phrases.[38] One must conceal all one's feelings.

Poor Tanya is rather melancholy; she went out skating with Sasha but it didn't cheer her up. Seryozha has gone to see the Olsufievs, and I miss him; I am so fond of him.

I had an affectionate letter from Andryusha. I wrote to Masha yesterday. It's her 27th birthday today. And to think she's my *fifth*! I can never feel old – I am still young in every respect: in my eagerness for work, my impressionability, my capacity for love and grief, my passion for music, my delight in skating and parties. My step is light, my body is fit – only my face has aged . . .

February 13 I worked on the proofs all evening, transferring corrections and translations from one copy of *What is Art?* to another. Yesterday I agreed that L.N. should let Gurevich publish in the *Northern Herald* his preface to Seryozha's translation of Carpenter's article on the meaning of science. I have done so because I want to publish his views on science after *What is Art?* in Volume 15, as this will continue the sense of the article perfectly.[39] L.N. was delighted by my suggestion.

He wrote a great many letters this evening. Today and yesterday he had nothing but dry *blinis* and soda-water for dinner. Poor man! His principles won't allow him to eat butter or caviare. This restraint of his is all very fine, but it's much worse if the temptation is there.

February 14 Hectic preparations for Shrovetide. I went to buy some things for this evening, then went skating with Tanya, Sasha, Lyova and Dora, who just stood and watched, as she is pregnant. We had a family dinner, and everyone was in a very good mood, which was pleasant. L.N. is still working on the proofs of *What is Art?* This evening he visited an old merchant of seventy-two, a follower of his, who has cancer of the liver.[40] He complained to L.N. how bored he was living with his family, and told him that his wife and son both prayed to the 'boards' (i.e. the icons).

A large crowd of boys and children came round this evening. At first they were rather listless, but then they played games, organised charades, sang together and did gymnastic tricks, while some of the boys sat down to a hand of vint. In the middle of the party some complete strangers arrived in masks and domino costumes who we later learnt were the Ustinovs and the Kalachevs, whom we don't know. The evening was a disappointment, as usual. I was sorry not to be able to give Dora and Lyova a little pleasure.

My mood and my *emotional* life are the same – the same overwhelming sadness for Vanechka. I was driving down Novinskii Boulevard yesterday when I was suddenly reminded of that frightful day when L.N. and I drove down that road with Vanya's little coffin . . . That memory always makes me pray that God may help me to purify and lift up my soul in readiness for death, so that I may be reunited with my dead infants in Him . . .

And I still have my love of music, which alone sustains my spiritual equilibrium and helps me to live. And my deep fondness for certain people who have sustained my faith in human goodness, and in their capacity to help one with their lofty spiritual qualities.

The evening ended with Goldenweiser playing a nocturne and a scherzo by Chopin, followed by a Liszt étude.

February 15 Heavy snow all day, overcast; the house is silent; Andryusha was telling me the most frightful tales of debauchery and fallen women; how sad that such things should interest him. L.N. again sat at his proofs. Tanya is sad, Sasha is unwell. I sat here all day immersed in household business, and ordered seeds, which always demands a lot of thought. I didn't go out. I wanted to play the piano but kept being interrupted. Glebova came with Pavel Stakhovich. I don't judge anyone, and simply say: 'God grant me to see *my own* sins and not condemn my brother.' Vera Sollogub and Lyova Sukhotin dined here, and Andryusha and Misha were home, so we had a friendly family dinner. This evening I did some writing, then the Belskii girls came, and the Butyonevs, father and daughter. L.N. played shuttlecock with Butyonev and the girls; he is well and cheerful. We discussed *The Decembrists*; L.N. read a great deal about them that time when he was going to write something about them, and he told us everything he could remember.[41]

Seryozha has returned from the Olsufievs and poor Andryusha has left for Tver – how he dreaded going! While they were playing shuttlecock I was overcome yet again by sad memories of Vanechka. It's so strange, the less music there is the more I grieve for Vanechka, and the more there is the less I grieve for him. Sergei Ivanovich's music completely extinguishes the grief. It's like dumbbells: they pull you to them wherever you put them.

February 16 It is Monday in the first week of Lent. I love this time; I love the quiet orderly atmosphere and the religious calm. I used to love it because spring was near – but I have lost that feeling now. What's spring to me! It doesn't add anything to my happiness, it lessens it with its compelling pressure to search for a happiness that doesn't exist and never will.

I spent the morning altering a dress of Sasha's, then played the piano for two and a half hours. I called on Sofia Filosofova before dinner, and we chatted about our children and grandchildren, our trials and tribulations, and various family matters. When I left her I longed for some fresh air, exercise, solitude and freedom, so I set off for a walk. I was late for dinner; when I got back the others were all sitting round the table and scolded me good-naturedly while I ate my Lenten soup. I shall fast all through Lent,

God willing. After dinner we all looked at some pictures in a journal which L.N. received from Philadelphia, and talked about the buying of property. Then I went off for a couple of hours and finished copying L.N.'s article on art, which is being sent to England.[42]

L.N. was reading Schiller's *The Robbers* this evening, and loved it.[43] Today I saw his black oilcloth notebook lying on the table in his study, which I know contains the openings of some short stories.[44]

February 17 This morning I again managed to play the piano for over two hours. Afterwards I bought a saddle to give Lyova tomorrow for his name-day, and for Lev Nikolaevich I shall buy some honey, dates, special prunes, pears and pickled mushrooms. He loves to keep a supply of these things on his windowsill so he can eat fruit or dates with bread when he is hungry. He wrote a lot today, I don't know what, for he won't say.[45] Then he went skating with his son Lyova. We had a cheerful dinner together. Dunaev sat here this evening while I did my embroidery – I can't bear to do nothing, no matter who our guests are. And I have certainly had a lot of them foisted on me today. There was a certain Aristov who arrived to see L.N. But Lev Nikolaevich had disappeared off to the bath-house with Sergeenko and didn't return for two hours, so I had to listen to this Mr Aristov's endless tales about irrigation, fish-breeding and his family affairs, and advise him as to whether or not he should let his twenty-two-year-old daughter marry a rich old man of fifty. What a very strange question to ask a woman he has never met before! Then Sergeenko told me about his plan to publish a book about Lev Nikolaevich with a lot of reproductions and portraits of him, his family, his life, etc.[46] This would be most unpleasant in the present circumstances.

February 18 It is Lyova's and Lev Nikolaevich's name-day, although L.N. never recognises any special days, particularly name-days. I gave Lyova a very fine English saddle from Zimmerman's, and spent the whole day working; I altered and mended Lev Nikolaevich's grey flannel shirt, then sewed a band of embroidery on to some white linen – my old, beautiful, stupid work. It's best to have some sewing to do when all these guests are here, otherwise it can be very dreary.

We had a family dinner, with Uncle Kostya Islavin and Lev Nikolaevich's nieces, Liza Obolenskaya and Varya Nagornova. A lot of the children were here too – Seryozha, Tanya, Lyova, Dora, Misha and Sasha. I love celebrating these family occasions.

We drank their health in Don champagne. But there was a certain emptiness about the day.

L.N. delivered the proofs of *What is Art?* to the printers, then revised his preface to Carpenter for the *Northern Herald*.[47]

I was astonished by what L.N. said yesterday evening about the woman question. He announced, as usual, that he was against women's emancipation and so-called 'equal rights', and went on to say that no matter what work a woman did – teaching, medicine, art – she had only one real purpose in life, and that was sexual love. So that whatever she might strive to achieve, all her strivings would merely crumble to ashes.

This made me terribly indignant, and I admonished him for his perpetually cynical attitude to women, which had made me suffer so. I told him that the reason he regarded women like this was that he hadn't known a single decent woman before he was 34. It's precisely this lack of friendship and spiritual affinity (rather than physical intimacy), this indifference to my spiritual and emotional life, which torments me to this day. All this has become blatantly obvious to me over the years – it has spoilt my life, disillusioned me, and has now made me love my husband less.

February 19 Sergeenko spent the day with us. He is writing a play with Tanya,[48] but his main business here is to compile a biographical anthology about Lev Nikolaevich, and he keeps asking questions. Today L.N. drew him a plan of the original house at Yasnaya Polyana in which he was born and grew up, and which he sold to pay off a gambling debt to a landowner named Gorokhov, in the village of Dolg.* The house still stands there, half ruined, and Sergeenko is going there to photograph it for his anthology.[49]

L.N. had such a sweet, tender expression on his face when he was drawing this plan of the house, remembering where Praskovya Savishna lived, where the nursery was, and the great drawing-room, his father's huge study, the 'bachelors' room', the servants' hall, the boudoir, and so on. It was a large house. Sergeenko asked me what Lev Nikolaevich would like for his 70th birthday, on August 28th this year. He considered buying him the house, bringing it back to Yasnaya and rebuilding it on the same spot. Or building an asylum for infants whose mothers went out to work . . . We didn't manage to think of anything, but there is evidently some money tucked away.

L.N. is carefully hiding his diary somewhere. I always used to be able to guess where it was, or search it out. But now I am at a complete loss to know where he has put it.

February 20 For three days this blizzard has cast a depression. We are all doing the same things: Lev Nikolaevich is hard at work revising Chapter 20 of *What is Art?* and I am still playing the piano.

Misha is fasting at the lycée. I haven't been to church once this week, and am not happy about this.

L.N. had two visitors today, both peasants – what can he find to say to them! It's now midnight; he wanted to take the proofs to Grot at Novinskii Boulevard, and we had a hard job persuading him not to.

*Literally 'debt'.

February 21 I had a music lesson with Miss Welsh this morning, then went on playing. The blizzard continues. I went out for a walk for an hour and a half. L.N. is still doing the proofs of Chapter 20. He took his granddaughter Annochka to the Rumyantsev Museum today and showed her the paintings and the ethnographical department, with its wax dolls dressed in Russian regional costumes. Crowds of people here this evening – some boys to see Misha and some children to see Sasha and Annochka. Sulerzhitskii sang, a conservatoire student called Szaz played the cello, and Nagornov played the piano. There were some moments of musical pleasure, but I was very tired.

February 22 I visited Rusanov, who is sick, and we talked about L.N., vegetarianism and Chertkov, whom the Rusanovs strongly disapprove of; they said that he was an abnormal person, prone to attacks of insanity, manifested by his extreme suspiciousness, garrulousness, fussiness and despotism. There's really very little good in him. I then visited Filosofova. We had a lot of people to dinner, and there were *blinis*; I arrived home half an hour before dinner and was told that Count Olsufiev and Sergei Ivanovich Taneev were there. I was delighted, ran straight upstairs and found them both sitting with Tanya, who was lying on the couch. Sergei Ivanovich had brought me *The Sunrise*, his work for four voices, set to words by Tyutchev,[50] and he played it to me. It is beautifully written and is divided into two moods: waiting for the sun, and its final triumphant appearance.

We saw little of each other, and spoke little. We shall have more conversations together later, during those long evenings when I am here on my own with Misha and maybe Sasha, but without Lev Nikolaevich or Tanya. Tanya said a great many spiteful things to me yesterday about Sergei Ivanovich's visit. That's the way to stop a good sympathetic friendship between two people!

February 23 The anniversary of Vanechka's death – three years have passed since he died. The moment I got up I went to church, and prayed and thought about my dead infants, parents and friends. I had a requiem service performed for me. Then we went to the maternity home to visit the cook's wife, Masha, who earlier today had given birth to a baby boy. From there I called on Zhilyaeva, the wife of a poor landowner from Kursk, to find out how she was getting on; but she wasn't in. She has an extraordinarily musical son, a pupil of Sergei Ivanovich's. I bought some flowers to put round Vanechka's portrait, and some rolls and honey for Nurse. When I got home L.N. was clearing the snow off the skating-rink in the garden. Then he went skating, and was so worn out afterwards that he slept all through dinner and dined later on his own. He has finished the proofs and is not going to do any more work on *What is Art?* He wants to make a start on something new. But he has started so many things – if only he would finish off some of the things he has begun!

L.N. played vint with Count Olsufiev, Sofia Filosofova and my brother Sasha this evening. I saw Sonya and Annochka off home today. Seryozha came from Tula for the day.

All day I have been overwhelmed with sadness. When I was walking up to the church this morning, the birds, all huddling together in the sunshine under the eaves and doors, suddenly burst into song. The sun was as bright and cheerful as spring, despite the frost. And at that moment I was reminded of Lermontov's words: 'Indifferent nature gleaming with eternal beauty!'[51] She is indeed indifferent – indifferent to human emotions, indifferent to our tortured and turbulent, but never indifferent hearts.

February 24 Lev Nikolaevich is complaining of a bad stomach again: he has heartburn, a headache and no energy. I was horrified when I saw what he ate for dinner today: to start with he had some pickled milk-agarics, all glued together from being frozen, then four slices of buckwheat toast, some soup and some black bread, all in enormous quantities, and all washed down with fermented *kvass*.

I eat only one meal with him at present, as I am fasting for Lent, and I have constant indigestion, although I eat only half as much as he. An old man of sixty-nine really shouldn't eat this sort of food, which just blows him up and doesn't give him any nourishment at all!

Both Lev Nikolaevich and I were deeply upset by a letter we received from Sergei Nikolaevich. It appears that his daughter Vera has consumption.[52] One more sacrifice to L.N.'s principles! She didn't eat enough, she grew weak, she worked beyond her strength teaching the peasant boys at the school, she shouted herself hoarse telling the children stories for her magic-lantern shows. And now both she and Masha are collapsing from illness and exhaustion, from vegetarianism and over-work. I always warned them, especially Masha, that they wouldn't be strong enough to survive, should they fall ill. And now that is what has happened.

L.N. has been reading about the Caucasus and wants to write a Caucasian story, but he doesn't have the energy.[53] Is his soul happy? All one hears of his followers is that this one has been deported, this one is ill, this one has collapsed. Today we heard that St John had been ordered to leave Tbilisi, and had been deported back to his own country. He too is a follower, an Englishman, who took the Dukhobors some money and preached L.N.'s principles.[54]

Today I managed to sight-read *The Sunrise*. It is written for a choir, with words by Tyutchev and music by Taneev. It is a fine, solemn piece, and wonderfully conveys the two separate moments of two different emotions.

February 25 L.N. went skating and wrote a great many letters – to

Biryukov, his brother, a peasant, and so on.[55] This morning I had a long music lesson with Miss Welsh (my second). I spent the whole of this evening correcting Volume 15 of my edition of *What is Art?* Will the censors let me publish it? I read 6 printed pages and felt exhausted. Sulerzhitskii talked most interestingly about his world tour. We had tea quietly together, just the family – L.N., Misha, Sasha, Tanya and I, and Sulerzhitskii too.

February 26 This morning I received a copy of *Russian Leaflet* with an article by some correspondent who somehow managed to slip in to see Lev Nikolaevich the other day, then described the conversation he had with him. In this article he writes that Pobedonostsev had agreed to Tanya's request to settle the business with the Molokans. This made a very disagreeable impression on me, as he simply doesn't mention what the affair is about. He also reports L.N.'s views on Zola, Dreyfus, and that whole affair.[56]

I started to tell L.N. about the concert but he interrupted me in the most unpleasant manner and said it was all rubbish – or words to that effect. I said nothing. Then he told me that Grot had come to see him, and they had spent a very pleasant evening together.

February 27 My arm hurts terribly and the sinew has swollen up like a pine-cone, but I was brave and didn't even cry.

This evening Igumnov played us a Chopin barcarolle and fantasia, a polonaise by Liszt and some variations on a theme by Schubert. He is beginning to play beautifully, and has grown wiser too – what a fine young fellow he is. I did a lot of shopping and business: I ordered some boxes to be sent to the Rumyantsev Museum with yet more of Lev Nikolaevich's diaries, manuscripts and letters.

I saw little of Lev Nikolaevich today. This evening he had guests – Gorbunov, Doctor Butkevich, and some other man who has had a few dealings with the Intermediary.

March 1 Two nights ago, Tanya and I had just undressed for the night and the servants were all asleep, when suddenly there was a long, ominous ring of the electric bell. Tanya went to the front door and unlocked it – then there was a long silence. I called out to her and she quietly came into my room and handed me a telegram.

'Our Liza is dead. Olsufievs.'

I shall never forget the impression this news made on me. A painful sadness for this bright, sweet creature, this dear friend of our whole family whom I should never see again, sorrow for her suffering family, and sheer horror as to why this dear girl, so universally loved and so helpful to everyone, should have been taken from us – all these feelings will return again and again to my memory and reverberate there throughout the years.

Tanya and Seryozha went there yesterday. We still don't know the details, only that Liza Olsufieva died of scarlet fever, just like my Vanechka.

I have been weeping bitterly, and my eyes and throat are filled with tears. Tanya was as if turned to stone and did not cry at all, and Seryozha grew very quiet, and sat for an hour at the piano yesterday, running his fingers over the keys, and his face was so sad, so very sad . . .

What is death? We go off somewhere and fuse with eternity, guided by the same Will which guides us here on earth.

Lev Nikolaevich is also suffering.[57] It is strange that our life flows on as before, through sheer inertia.

This evening I went to a lecture given by Professor Dokuchaev, from St Petersburg, on various complicated questions including the simplicity of the earth's construction, the laws of gravity and repulsion, and the laws of struggle, love and so on which ensue from these. When I got home I found the entire Butyonev family there, as well as Pisaryov and his wife, Sofia Filosofova, Kasatkin and Prince Nakashidze (who was deported from the Caucasus for communicating with the Dukhobors). They chattered away all night – but they are all extremely respectable people and I was glad to see them.

L.N. cleared the skating-rink in the garden with Ivan, then went skating, and before dinner he went for a ride. He took a nap this evening, then came and sat quite cheerfully with our guests. He wrote some letters and made more revisions and additions to my edition of *What is Art?*[58]

March 4 I have been grieving and weeping for Liza. I went to the clinic, where Professor Levshin and his assistants examined my arm with X-rays to find out whether I might have a needle in it, for it is terribly painful. They didn't find anything there, but they discovered that I had an aneurism of the artery, and they bandaged it up and wanted to cut it. Professor Dokuchaev travelled back with me and spent the evening with us. He is a most abnormal man, mentally sick; he came to look at my photographs today and begged me to give them to him. I went to a funeral service for Liza in the church, where all her Moscow friends and relatives had gathered.

Yesterday evening my nerves were so fraught that I could sit at home no longer, and I went out to see the two dear old Maslova ladies. I saw Sergei Ivanovich there, but only briefly. He was eating some sausage in a most unattractive manner, it was quite impossible to talk to him and he soon left. There's no doubt that he is avoiding me, I am sure of it. But why? At the Verdi Requiem concert his ticket was for the stalls, but he went up to the gallery . . . Maybe because all the 'high life'* was there, and he always tries to avoid it.

*In English in the original.

This evening I developed a photograph of Lev Nikolaevich skating. It didn't come out well.

Bad news about *What is Art?* The secular censors passed it, but there was a telegram from St Petersburg saying that it must now be presented to the church censors.[59] Which means that this article, the second part of it anyway, is sunk for good. It's exasperating! So now I've printed and corrected it all for nothing. It will just have to be published abroad.

March 7 L.N. is listless and fractious. He cannot work, he is exhausted by all his visitors, who are often most unwelcome, and despite my pleading with him to send them away and enjoy his leisure hours, he stubbornly refuses to do so. He has a boundless *curiosity*, which makes him receive absolutely everyone who comes to see him, as well as that eternal stubbornness, and the desire to contradict and defy me all the time.

I realised today that all L.N.'s works of the last few years have been nothing but *defiance* and *protest*, pure and simple. If he is protesting against humanity as a whole, the *entire* existing order, he can hardly be expected not to protest against me, a mere weak woman.

I saw Sergei Ivanovich at Goldenweiser's concert, and had a note from him today, asking me to leave the second part of L.N.'s article with Modest Tchaikovsky, whom he is going to visit in Klin over the next day or so.[60]

I had a very unpleasant conversation with L.N. this morning. He wants to make a lot of additions to his article, but I am afraid the censors will seize on these additions and stop the book again, and I want to print 30,000 copies. One word led to another and soon we were shouting at one another; I blamed him for depriving me of my freedom and not letting me go to St Petersburg; he blamed me for selling his books; I replied that it wasn't me who took that money, most of it went to his children whom he had abandoned, and had neither educated nor trained to work. I also said that it was with this money that I paid for his saddle-horse, his asparagus, his fruit, his charity work, his bicycles and so forth, and that I spent less on myself than on anyone else . . . But I wouldn't have said all this if he hadn't shouted at me that I had forgotten myself, that he could *forbid* me to sell his books. Very well, I said, forbid me, I shall be delighted to support myself by going out to work as a schoolteacher or a proof-reader, or some such thing. I love work, and I do *not* love this life, which doesn't suit me at all and has been organised, through sheer inertia, to suit my family – my husband and children.

I photographed L.N. on his horse, then worked on my other photographs. I cut out and tacked a dress for Sasha, and visited old Uncle Kostya with Sofia Filosofova.

L.N.'s article *What is Art?* has apparently returned from the church censors. They have underlined one or two things, but have passed it. L.N.

and I didn't argue after that – in fact we were both thoroughly ashamed and made it up.

March 8 L.N., Seryozha, Styopa and I talked over tea today about the fear of death, partly in connection with an article by Tokarskii called 'The Fear of Death', and partly in connection with Liza Olsufieva's death. L.N. said there were four kinds of fear: fear of suffering, fear of the torments of hell, fear of losing the joy of life and fear of extinction. I have few of these fears: I fear suffering a little, but what terrifies me is the thought of 'the pit', the lid of the coffin, 'the darkness' . . . I love light, purity, beauty. The grave is all darkness, earth, dirt and the ugliness of the corpse.

L.N. rode over to Grot's, then to see us at Patriarch Ponds. He is reading about the Caucasus, but I don't know whether he is writing and am afraid to ask.

They have passed the article, just deleted a couple of pages.[61] Sergei Trubetskoi has made a complaint about this and is highly indignant about the base veniality and cunning of these church censors, who are virtually priests.

It was thawing today, the thermometer is at freezing-point.

I am battling with myself, my soul is torn between the passionate desire to go to St Petersburg for the Wagner and various other concerts, and the fear of distressing Lev Nikolaevich and having this on my conscience. I cried last night for this painful *lack of freedom*, which is becoming more and more oppressive. Materially, of course, I am free: I have money, horses, dresses – everything. I go to bed, sit down, drive around. I am free to read proofs, buy apples for L.N., make Sasha's dresses and my husband's shirts, take his photograph from every conceivable angle, order dinner, manage the family affairs – I am free to eat, sleep, be quiet and submit. But I am not free to *think* as I please, to *love* whom I choose, to come and go according to my own interests and intellectual pleasures; I am not free to pursue my music, I am not free to drive away all these unnumerable, unwanted, boring and often extremely evil people, and instead receive people who are good, clever, gifted and interesting. We have no need of such people in our house – for one would have to take them seriously and treat them as equals, whereas he likes to enslave people and preach at them . . .

And I'm not happy, and my life is hard . . . No, that wasn't the right word: I don't need *happiness*, what I need is a life that is *full* and *peaceful*, not this difficult, anxious, pointless existence.

March 9 The Day of the Forty Martyrs. On the morning of this day when I was a child, and when my children were young, Trifonovna, our old cook in my father's house, and Nikolai, the cook at Yasnaya Polyana, would bake delicious rich lark-cakes, with black-currants for eyes and crisp beaks. There was something so poetic about them. And then the live larks would fly up and settle on the thawed patches of brown earth poking through the snow, before soaring into the sky again with their sweet silvery song. I used to love springtime in the country. But in those days spring always brought all those happy, impractical hopes for the future . . . Now it brings nothing but sad memories and helpless, impossible longings . . . Ah, old age is no joy!

This evening, to my great delight, L.N. gave me *Hadji Murat*, his story about the Caucasus, to copy. I copied with great enthusiasm, despite the pain in my right arm, until Sergeenko came in and interrupted me. Then Dunaev and Uncle Kostya came, and my brother Sasha, and Seryozha. We had a long talk about government affairs, and about this new fleet of ships it has bought for 90 million rubles. Sergeenko told us that the Japanese had ordered these ships from the English for 130 million, but the Japanese could not pay on time as the money was held by the Chinese-Russian Bank, which delayed in handing it over. So the contract lapsed, and the Russian government then offered 90 million, and with that they bought an entire fleet from the English.

L.N. rode over to ask Miss Shanks to translate into English a letter he wants to send to someone in America.[62] He has been writing a lot of letters and is very burdened by them.*

March 10 I didn't sleep all night. At two in the morning I managed to drop off, and got up late. Oh these nights! They reveal my true spiritual state with such terrifying clarity! I am utterly exhausted. By day one is caught up in life's whirlpool, and it's impossible to come to one's senses. Then it's yet another night without sleep, with yet more thoughts and worries . . .

I loved copying out L.N.'s Caucasian story *Hadji Murat*. I think it will be very good: it's an epic work, without being *provocative*, I hope, or slyly *polemical*.

My painful right arm was very tired, so I decided to go to a chamber-music concert this evening. They played three Beethoven trios and his C-major violin sonata, and it was very enjoyable and not at all tiring. Marusya Maklakova went with me. When I got home I found Sergeenko, Professor Preobrazhenskii, Sulerzhitskii and Nakashidze there, and Lev Nikolaevich was looking very tired. He wrote more letters today, and looked through the proofs for my edition of *What is Art?* He is calm and well.

March 14 I can't remember a thing. All I can remember is more long sleepless nights. One night I sat up happily copying out *Hadji Murat* for L.N. until 4.30 in the morning. The past few days I have either stayed at

*Below is affixed a photograph of Lev Tolstoy on his horse in the courtyard of the Khamovniki house, with an inscription in Sofia Tolstaya's hand: 'Taken by me on March 6, 1898, Moscow, Khamovniki Street No 21.

home, working and proof-reading, or gone out shopping for summer clothes. L.N. writes endless letters, which he finds a great strain, and reads a lot, especially the Caucasian anthologies F.I. Maslov got for him.[63] I have spent the last three evenings so differently that one can only wonder at the contrast between my apparently equable family life and our truly momentous emotional life. L.N. hadn't been so gentle and affectionate to me for a long time, then the other day his voice suddenly changed. I was terribly busy with the proofs for Volume 15, I had been working all day, and had not been attentive to his mood. I went on working that evening, with short rests (I had 12 printed pages to read), and as I knew that my insomnia wouldn't let me sleep anyway, I asked my husband to go to bed without me, then got undressed, put on my dressing-gown and slippers and promised to come in quietly just as soon as I had finished the proofs. L.N. threw a tantrum: go to bed, he said, and let that be the end of it. Well, my work had to be done urgently – it had to be sent to the printers that morning – so I didn't pay him any attention and went on working. He then jumped out of bed, put on his dressing-gown and went up to his study. I continued reading, not realising that he had gone upstairs. An hour and a half later he came in and started shouting at me: I was torturing him, he said, he wanted to sleep and I wasn't letting him, and he had a headache. I just sat there and patiently heard him out, then went into the bedroom (I had been sitting in the dining-room, which is adjacent to it), and went to bed, without finishing the last page. But there my nerves snapped. All that hard work, that unpleasant scene, and most of all my husband's unfairness to me, produced such feelings of despair in my already suffering soul that I suddenly felt a terrible spasm in my heart and chest, and barely managed to say 'I am dying' into the darkness, before I started to choke; my heart was pounding, I had spasms in my chest and a feeling of utter horror, as though my life had stopped – it was terrifying. I have never before had such an attack. I splashed cold water on my heart and made enormous efforts to control myself, which helped me eventually to stop the attack. Lev Nikolaevich was beside himself, and began to shudder and sob . . . We slept badly, for we were both exhausted . . . But why, oh why should these things happen! Lord help me care for my husband and be patient to the end . . . The following morning I went to him and said I was sorry about what had happened. He seemed to apologise, and the peace was restored. But will it last?

Yesterday S.I. Taneev came, and his presence had an immediately soothing effect on me. He is such a calm, kind, even-tempered, gifted man. He played us his lovely symphony and asked Lev Nikolaevich for his opinion of it. L.N. considered the question with great seriousness and respect, then expounded his views: namely, that this symphony, as all modern music, was completely lacking in consistency, in either the melody, rhythm or harmony. The moment you began to follow the melody, it stopped short, the moment you mastered one rhythm, it jumped over into another, so that you felt constantly dissatisfied. Whereas in a genuine work of art you feel it could not be *otherwise*; one thing flows from another, and you think to yourself: 'Why, I would have done it just like that.' Sergei Ivanovich listened attentively and respectfully to what he had to say, but was obviously mortified that L.N. hadn't liked it. Today he is going to St Petersburg, where his symphony will be performed by an orchestra.[64]

Yesterday morning I got up feeling exhausted after our argument the night before. Then L.N. brought my grandson Misha in to me, and I was so pleased to see this pure, fresh element, this sweet, healthy, clever child. I spent the whole day with him; I took him to the Zoological Gardens, the toy shops, the cake-shop and the Kremlin, and he was delighted by everything but surprised by nothing. So yesterday was God's reward for last night's unpleasant scene with my husband.

March 17 Yesterday I copied out Lev Nikolaevich's letter 'Aid to the Dukhobors'. (They are now hoping to emigrate.) L.N. thinks the *St Petersburg Gazette* will publish it, but I am sure they won't. He appeals for two kinds of aid: finding them a place to emigrate to, and collecting the money for this.[65] There are 10,000 of them – how much money will they need?

The famous sculptor Antokolskii was here this evening, and we had a discussion about art. L.N. quoted from his article, and Antokolskii said that Art's greatest task was to portray the human *soul*.[66] I am reading all the proofs for Volume 15; they still haven't delivered any today; I shall soon be finished. I copied out L.N.'s letter again, as he had scribbled all over it, and am now going out on business and to buy summer dresses. Relations with L.N. are friendly and pleasant. But will it last? I am going to St Petersburg for several days to hear some Wagner, and also Sergei Ivanovich Taneev's symphony. This is his first symphony, and its first performance will be on the 21st.

Andryusha has come. Ilya and my little grandson Misha left two evenings ago, and I was very sorry to part with Misha, although I know I shouldn't grow attached to children now, for it's so painful to lose them if they die.

L.N. said today: 'I feel 32 years old, I slept excellently and my head is clear.'

It is a great pity he is wasting all his spiritual energy on these letters.

There isn't a trace of literary inspiration there! I suppose his age is telling on him.

Still the same harsh winter weather. It was 10 degrees below freezing today, and very windy and cold, despite the sun.

March 18 Things were going so well and we were on such good terms. But today I was reading the proofs of Lev Nikolaevich's 'Preface' to

Carpenter's article 'Contemporary Science', when I suddenly realised that it was all different, everything had been changed. I was astonished and hurt. When the *Northern Herald* took this article I begged L.N. to give me the *final* proofs, so that I could send the *final* version off to be printed in Volume 15. I went to him and reproached him, quite mildly, for deceiving me, and he grew terribly angry. These arguments open up old wounds and it was utterly unbearable. He had concealed these final proofs from me merely out of consideration for the *Northern Herald*'s profits, because he didn't want to delay its publication. It would have taken him just one day to make those corrections in my edition.

Many, many guests this evening – Belskaya and her daughter, Toliverova and her daughter, Maklakov and his sister, Varya Nagornova and Gorbunov. Toliverova, the editor of *Playthings*, wants to publish a journal called the *Woman's Cause*, and the woman question was discussed. L.N. said that before one spoke about women's inequality and oppression one should first talk about *people's* inequality in general. And he said that if a woman raises this question herself, there is something immodest, unwomanly and impertinent about it. I think he is right. It's not freedom we women need, but *help*. Help mainly in educating our sons, setting them on the right road of life, influencing them to be brave, independent, hard-working and honest. A mother cannot educate her sons all on her own, and the reason why the younger generation is no good is because their fathers are no good. They are too lazy to educate their own sons, and would gladly throw themselves into anything which would enable them to evade their most important duty – educating the future generation, which must go forward and continue humanity's work.

April 2 Two weeks have passed since I last wrote my diary! Why does life pass so quickly at present – almost unconsciously, like a dream? If only I were more normal, I would live more *consciously*, more purposefully. As it is, in years to come I shall look back on the past and, as always, I shall understand it, value it and also (for this always happens too), I shall *regret* both my past and my *inability* to profit from it. My entire life, with rare exceptions, has passed in desires and regrets.

Tomorrow is the day appointed by that anonymous letter for Lev Nikolaevich's murder. I am worried, of course, but I don't really believe it can happen. Two Dukhobors came to see L.N., strapping peasants, strong in body and soul. We told them to go and see Suvorin and Prince Ukhtomskii in St Petersburg, so that these two influential newspaper editors can give them advice and help. They have promised to do so, but it's unlikely that they will.[67]

L.N. is writing a petition for them addressed to the Tsar, to allow all the Dukhobors to settle abroad – those that were exiled, those that were recruited into the army, and those that were imprisoned.[68] It terrifies me –

it's as if we were being exiled too! These Dukhobors are now sitting with L.N., along with a young factory-worker called Bulakhov who is being sent with the petition and 300 rubles to Verigin, their exiled leader.

I spent four days in St Petersburg. Ever since autumn I had had the fixed idea of going there to hear Taneev's symphony – which he played several times for me on the piano – performed by an orchestra. I thought it would be magnificent. I had also long dreamed of hearing some Wagner, and there was a visiting German opera company performing him in St Petersburg at the time. At first L.N. refused to let me go, which resulted in depression, sleepless nights and apathy. Then he agreed to release me, but the trip was no pleasure. It rained incessantly; Taneev's symphony was atrociously performed and conducted by Glazunov; I didn't hear any Wagner; my health was destroyed; and life with my sister Behrs, who is on bad terms with her husband and servants, and is interested only in the management of Russia's financial affairs (a strange interest indeed for a woman), was so depressing, and the whole trip was so unsuccessful that I was delighted to get back to L.N. and my own life in this house, which is at least free in spirit, and I shan't be in a hurry to leave again.

Someone has come to visit every evening: first professor Storozhenko, who told us a lot about foreign literature and all the latest news in this department; then young Zinger, so lively and clever. Then Grot came for the evening, and Sergeenko (whom I don't trust for some reason), and Ekaterina Fyodorovna Yunge (of whom L.N. says, in the words of Anatole France: '*une laideur terrible et grande*'*). But she's a clever, gifted, lively woman. Young Prince Seryozha Urusov was here too, the son of Prince Urusov who died, and whom I loved so much. And Goldenweiser, who played that marvellous Chopin sonata with the 'Marche Funèbre', as well as some preludes and nocturnes.

The floor-polishers were here all day, and the locks were cleaned: noise, visitors, Dukhobors. Sulerzhitskii is here; the children are outside in the sunny garden playing muskets; Sasha is singing with the Friedman children and thumping out dance tunes on the piano; L.N. is chatting with the Dukhobors, and composing a long petition to the Tsar which I have been copying out. These past few days I have been making clothes for L.N. I embroidered his handkerchiefs in satin stitch, made him a new shirt and am about to make him some trousers. When my friends ask me why I have 'collapsed' and become so silent and sad, I reply: 'Look at my husband, that is the reason he is so cheerful and energetic.'

And no one realises that when I am *alive*, absorbed or transported by music, art, books or people, my husband becomes unhappy, anxious and angry. And when I make him shirts, as I am now, or copy, and quietly fade away, he is happy, even cheerful. That's what breaks my heart! I have to

*'A great and terrible ugliness.'

smother everything that's alive in me in the name of my husband's happiness, to suppress my natural passionate temperament and go to sleep – I don't live, '*je dure*',* as Seneca described this empty life. Part 15 of *On Art* returned from the censors today, and I have written some notices for the newspapers.[69]

April 3 Well, the day is almost over, it's gone ten and there have been no attempts on L.N.'s life. This morning I cut out some trousers for him and stitched them on the machine. He then decided to go for a walk, and I went with him so as not to stay at home worrying. First we called on old General Boborykin, who walked on with us, and I was exhausted by his slow pace, and by having to talk to him against the rumble of the cabs. Then on to the editorial office of the *Russian Gazette*,[70] then we bought some galoshes, then we went on to see the Rusanovs at Ostozhenko. I was so worn out I had to take a cab home. Throughout my life, summer and winter, it has always exhausted me to walk anywhere with L.N. He never pays the slightest attention to the person he is with: if you linger for a moment he just races ahead without slowing down, so you have to hurry to catch him up and you lose your breath, but he never waits – what an ordeal! Sergeenko and Sulerzhitskii also stood guard over him today, and Menshikov, who arrived this evening from St Petersburg. The Gorbunov brothers came too, as well as Nakashidze, and Dunaev. This never-ending stream of people is dreadfully trying. The whole day passed in discussions with them all. Oh, my poor nerves! First it was the Dukhobors, who left yesterday, now it's these fears for Lev Nikolaevich's life; then there are the young people shouting all evening over their games of vint. My whole life passes in a way that's not to my liking. L.N.'s life and interests are so particular, so personal, that they just don't concern his children; they can't interest themselves in the sectarians and the Dukhobors, or the renunciation of art, or ideas about non-resistance. They need their own personal life, which they can initiate. And since they have no leader in their father, no ideals within their grasp, they create their own undisciplined life, with card games, idleness and entertainments, rather than any serious work or art. I have neither the strength nor the skill to make a better life for them – and I doubt it would be possible anyway, with a father who renounces *everything*!

April 5 Easter Sunday. It used to be such an important, joyful day. This year I felt nothing special about it at all. Yesterday evening I sat silently sewing; Sasha had gone to matins at the orphanage with Marusya Maklakova, Tanya was also working at home, and I fell to thinking how before, when I was young, life had been divided into various periods by

*'I endure.'

various important, or apparently important, events: the holidays, the move to Yasnaya, more significantly the birth of a child, and so on. Now everything has converged in one elusive, quickly passing span of time – and nothing is important, nothing really matters so long as there isn't any trouble or unhappiness. The last three years since the death of my angel, my darling Vanechka, have been so difficult and nerve-racking for me.

This morning I had a nasty scene with Andryusha and Misha. They demanded some money, *after* I had just given them both 15 rubles. I was furious and cried, and Misha was sorry, but Andryusha, looking utterly ridiculous in a new frock coat, went off to pay some calls as though nothing had happened. That night they both went off to Red Square with a crowd of friends to listen to the bells pealing and watch the procession winding around the cathedrals. They are recklessly burning out their lives, without pausing to think or ask themselves any serious moral questions.

Feeling very distressed I went in despair to see L.N., told him with tears in my eyes about my sons, who demand money from me and then insult me, and begged him for some advice. But as usual, this man who preaches his truths to the whole world didn't have one word to say to his family, or any advice to give to his wife.

I called on the Kolokoltsevs, then spent the whole evening copying out Lev Nikolaevich's story *Hadji Murat*. I have written 20 pages now, perhaps more. L.N. is chilled and complains of feeling poorly, although he took a spin on Misha's bicycle today when everyone was out.

April 6 I devoted the whole day to the children. I went to the fair with Sasha, Verochka (the maid) and the Litvinov and Kolokoltsev children, and we watched the marionettes and the theatre, and went on the toboggans and the merry-go-rounds. After dinner we rolled eggs. The children had a lovely day. Tanya is ill, with a fever and a swollen cheek. There was a letter from Masha. The boys paid some calls. After dinner Varya Nagornova and I played Taneev's quartet as a duet; the more one studies his music the more one loves it – and him, for his profound and noble soul.

L.N. went for a bicycle ride before dinner; this morning he was writing about war;[71] this afternoon he rode over to see Brashnin, the merchant who is dying. He is *curious* to watch people dying, for his own death is not so far off, and he also likes giving comfort and sympathy to a dying man.

April 7 Koni came, and will dine with us tomorrow. It is drizzling, and it's warmer. An interesting letter from Menshikov. He says the government is concerned about the Dukhobors, but that connecting Lev Nikolaevich's name with them is putting everyone in an extremely bad temper.[72] The police have served notice on the *Russian Gazette* that they are not to accept any money for the Dukhobors in the name of Lev Nikolaevich.[73] But despite this we had 300 rubles from them today. L.N. is very good-humoured at present, but my heart is uneasy and fearful.

April 9 Yesterday was a bright and happy day. I got up and took Sasha to a rehearsal of Nikish's concert, at which the *Freischütz* overture was performed so exquisitely that I simply wept with emotion.

Sergei Ivanovich, Goldenweiser, Koni, Igumnov, Sasha, Professor Preobrazhenskii and I all walked home from the rehearsal together. We chattered away happily, the sun peeped out, and it was so good being amongst these happy people, with the spring weather and the music still ringing in my head! Anatolii Fyodorovich Koni had dinner with us this evening as well as Professor Grot, my brother Sasha, Dehn and his wife, and Miss Welsh. Koni talked splendidly, first about the late F.I. Gorbunov, the famous story-teller, and repeated some of his comic stories, then he told us some interesting cases from his legal work. He told us the suicide statistics, and said most of them were widows and widowers, living in the north, and most took place in the spring . . .

In the evening Sasha, Marusya Maklakova and I went again to Nikish's concert, which gave me enormous pleasure. L.N. spent the day with his guests: he couldn't work this morning but he wrote some letters and went out on his bicycle and his horse. Brashnin, the old merchant he has been going to visit, has died, and Lev Nikolaevich was telling me today that he was *curious* to find out all about his final hours. All along he was merely *curious* to see this old man die.

L.N. told me today that Doctor Rakhmanov was very interested in his story (*Resurrection*), and had had a long talk about it with him and given it to him to read, then re-read it himself and realised that if it were published everywhere it would be possible to raise 100,000 rubles for the Dukhobors' emigration fund. But he said this had only been an idea of his, it wouldn't actually work in practice. I said nothing. It's his *right* to do so of course, not mine, although it's a strange thing for a family to be discussing *rights*, after living together for 36 years. His children will live in poverty, for he hasn't trained them to work, but I shall not perish. And what is more, I don't need money. It's not money that makes me happy nowadays, it's certainly not money!

April 10 I should go mad if I had to live like Lev Nikolaevich. He writes all morning and wears himself out mentally, and all evening he talks non-stop, or rather preaches, as his listeners generally come to him for advice or instruction.

There were thirteen people here after dinner today – two factory-workers, three young schoolteachers, a lady studying the market for Russian handicrafts in England, a doctor, a correspondent for the *Messenger*, Sergeenko, Dunaev and various others.

Seryozha came today and sat down at the piano to compose a piece of music. Tanya is not well: her cheek is still swollen and she has a stomach-ache. Andryusha left yesterday. It rained all day. I visited the sales again and bought some furnishing material. At home I attended to *business* – accounts, banking matters, all the book-keeping for my trusteeship of the children, letter-writing, etc. I didn't touch music or my story all day.[74]

There were moments today when the old familiar grief welled up in my soul – it is still with me, after all these years I have still not really recovered from it. Varechka was here.

April 15 The past few days have been filled with activities outside the house. On the 11th A.F. Koni gave an excellent lecture on Odoevskii,[75] at which he discussed various related topics so subtly, in such an apt and truthful way.

We had guests this evening, including Professor Preobrazhenskii, who took our photographs with magnesium plate and read us a long lecture on illusions of light and colour. I was worn out and grew sleepy, something that rarely happens to me. Earlier on I had taken Sasha to the travelling art show: there was nothing outstanding, apart from some good late landscapes by Shishkin,[76] and the general poverty of subject-matter and content was appalling. Yesterday I spent two and a half hours at an exhibition of St Petersburg painters, with an enormous painting by Semidarskii of a woman martyr tied to a bull in a circus, with Nero, etc.[77]

I was fascinated by this exhibition. There was a great variety of landscapes, taking me first to Italy, then to the Crimea, then to the River Dnieper, then to the island of Capri – to wild Oriental countries, or the Russian or Little Russian countryside, or the Caucasus. It was extremely interesting, especially for me who have never travelled anywhere. Almost all the paintings were well and carefully executed – though not all of them showed evidence of talent. *Circe the Christian in Nero's Circus* was a huge painting occupying one large wall. People have expressed various guarded opinions about it, but I personally thought it very beautiful and vivid, and the characters, colours and proportions very harmonious and intelligent. But it's cold; one doesn't pity the martyr being torn to pieces, one doesn't pity the bull with the beautiful head, one doesn't feel angry with Nero – one doesn't feel the public is affected by it. But the exhibition in general gave me immense pleasure.

I did various jobs in town today – took some things to be mended and altered, left some books to be bound, etc. This evening we had a visit from young Prince Trubetskoi, a sculptor born and educated in Italy. An extraordinary man, exceptionally talented, but utterly primitive. He hasn't read a thing, doesn't even know *War and Peace*, hasn't studied anywhere – he is naïve, rough and totally engrossed in his art. He is coming here tomorrow to start on a sculpture of Lev Nikolaevich, and he will dine with us.

Sergei Ivanovich came, and it was all wonderfully calm, straightforward and ordinary. He talked in my room with Seryozha about some musical translation about which Seryozha was asking him various questions.[78]

L.N. announced today that he was leaving for the country to see Ilyusha the day after tomorrow, that it was a great strain for him to live in town, and that he had 1,400 rubles which he wanted to give to the needy. It was all perfectly reasonable of him, but I felt so wretched at the thought of living here on my own with horrid Sasha, and Misha, who is never here, that I simply burst into tears and pleaded with him not to leave me yet and to stay with me just one more week. If only he knew how fragile my soul is, how terrified I am of myself; I am terrified of suicide, despair, my desire to be entertained . . . everything *terrifies* me, and mainly I terrify myself . . . I don't know whether he'll listen to my entreaties. Even when I am with him I am often sunk in gloom. It's difficult to live in the light, there are so many of us in the family, my relations with L.N. bring me such *pain*. I am *tired* of this never-ending battle, and all the hours of hard work I devote to the house, the children's education, business affairs, publishing, managing the children's estates, looking after my husband, keeping the family peace . . . None of this would be evident to an outsider, but it's all *too* evident to my exhausted heart! It really is such a difficult situation: L.N. is always insisting that he only lives in Moscow *for my sake*, and that it's sheer torture for him! Which is to say that I torture him. Yet he is far gloomier in Yasnaya Polyana, and I know that despite what he says he actually finds city life very interesting and entertaining, and it only occasionally tires him.

April 16 Lev Nikolaevich was sculpted today by Prince Trubetskoi, who has come from Italy and is in fact an Italian citizen. He is apparently considered a very good sculptor. Nothing visible so far. He has made a start on a huge bust. L.N. is being kind to me again, and we are on good terms. Yesterday evening my nerves were in a terrible state – almost abnormal.

April 18 Lyova has come. He has suddenly decided to sell the house through some broker, without consulting me in advance. Any sort of trouble or change terrifies me at present. And I am very sorry about this house, as I had reserved it for myself,[79] and shall now be left almost penniless, with money owing on the new edition. It would cost me a great deal to buy this house too – almost 58,000 rubles. Trubetskoi has done more work on his sculpture of Lev Nikolaevich, and I can now see how exceptionally talented he is.

April 19 Tanya had an extremely painful operation on her nose. They pulled out a tooth and got through the opening to her nose to let out the pus. She is now very ill, weak and pale. I feel so sorry for her and long to stroke her, comfort her and kiss her, but one never does, and just feels wretched instead. I dismissed Mlle Aubert today and hired a new governess for Sasha, who is much quieter already. Trubetskoi is still working on his bust of Lev Nikolaevich, and it's extremely good – majestic, distinctive and very lifelike. This Trubetskoi is a naïve fellow, completely absorbed in his art; he has read nothing and is interested in nothing but sculpture.

We had a visit from S.T. Morozov, an ailing merchant, who has just finished a course at the university and wants to lead a better life. He gave Lev Nikolaevich 1,000 rubles for the starving peasants. On Wednesday I am going with L.N. to visit Ilya at Grinevka, where L.N. will stay and help the poverty-stricken peasants in the surrounding countryside.

April 20 Life's forced bustle continues. I am being virtually compelled to buy this house. I saw how sorry Lev Nikolaevich and the children were about it, and L.N., who almost never states his opinions, actually advised me straight out to buy it – 'It's a shame to sell it,' he said. But as far as I'm concerned, it's both expensive and unprofitable. I have lost two of my children here, and the last two years of my life, which I have spent here, have not been especially happy ones; my happiest times were at Yasnaya, during the early years of my marriage.

I spent the whole day at various banks, selling securities and transferring my money to Lyova's account. I had to be very careful not to sell the securities too cheaply, so as not to lose money on the deal. At home another mass of people had come for dinner – Preobrazhenskii, Trubetskoi, Butyonev, Sonya Mamonova, Misha Kuzminskii; later on the Princesses Trubetskaya, the Kolokoltsevs and Sukhotin!

L.N. has written a letter about war – in reply to some Italian.[80] He is not busy with any literary work, and this is very hard for him; but he is so used to *preaching* by now that he cannot live without it. After dinner he goes and poses for Trubetskoi. The bust is artistically conceived and excellently executed, but unfortunately L.N. is in a hurry to leave, and it is still unfinished. We are leaving the day after tomorrow; I shall come back to Moscow but L.N. will go on to Yasnaya. It is still cold.

April 21 L.N. and I were going to leave for Nikolskoe and Grinevka yesterday to see our sons, and I was so excited by it all – the trip, the spring and our grandchildren. But we decided to postpone it again until tomorrow evening, as Trubetskoi hadn't finished his bust and it was so good it seemed a pity not to let him do so. He has caught perfectly the tilt of the head, the expression of the eyes and body – it is beautifully and expressively conceived, although I am disturbed by that unfinished quality which the sculptor is so pleased about. Lev Nikolaevich is in a great hurry to leave, as he has 2,000 rubles in charitable donations, which he wants to give to peasants in the most poverty-stricken areas.

I visited the notary and the bank this morning, and when I got back I packed my things and my husband's. (I had laid in a good stock of vegetarian supplies, bread and so on.) Sergei Ivanovich called this evening, and L.N. and he had a fascinating and very lively conversation in which Trubetskoi also took part. They talked about art and the conservatoire, about how short life is and how best to make use of one's time so as to spend each moment profitably – for work, service, people (I put that in myself), and happiness.

I was delighted to see that L.N. no longer treated this marvellous man as an enemy. At the moment he is busy publishing various things in connection with his beloved conservatoire; he criticises its director, Safonov, for incorrectly handling its affairs, but he does not fear or quarrel with anyone for he has such an extraordinarily honourable and fair way of seeing things, and wants only to serve the cause.

Then V. Maklakov came, and we philosophised about happiness. We came to the same conclusion today with him as we did yesterday with Sonya Mamonova: happiness is rare and fortuitous, seize it when it is there, thank fate for small moments of joy, don't seek to recover it, don't mourn it, but go on and live your life. And even in this humdrum life, so full of adversities, it is possible to find happiness if your conscience is clear, if you live for others and for work, and if you don't do anything shameful or immoral, or anything you would later be forced to regret.

There is another kind of happiness too: the striving for self-perfection, for some moral and religious ideal. But I don't like scrutinising myself; I love others, not myself, so I find it very difficult.

Pyotr Ivanovich Bartyonev came and brought me a book containing the letters of my great-grandfather, Count Zavadovskii,[81] whom he praised very warmly to me. He is so interesting. He is an absolute walking archive and knows simply everyone, all the genealogies, all the court intrigues of all the Russian reigns, all the armorial bearings, all the estates, family connections, and so on.

April 29 Trubetskoi finished his bust of Lev Nikolaevich on the 23rd,[82] and it is excellent. That evening L.N. and I left for Grinevka, seen off by Dunaev, Maslov, my Sasha and Sonya Kolokoltseva. We travelled 1st class; it was very crowded everywhere. That evening on the train I heated up some porridge for L.N. which I had brought ready-cooked. First he said he would do it himself and grabbed the hot saucepan lid, burning three of his fingers. I offered to get him some water to ease the pain, and he stubbornly refused. But without saying anything I just brought him a mug of water anyway, and the moment he dipped in his fingers he felt better. But it meant that he slept badly that night.

In Grinkevka we were met by our sons Ilya and Andryusha, who were on horseback, and by our grandchildren Annochka and Misha, who were on foot. It was delightful to see them again and arrive in their village. L.N. set to work at once. He travelled round the villages making enquiries about the famine. It is worst of all in Nikolskoe and the Mtsensk district. There they eat bread once a day, and that's not enough, and the cattle have either been sold or eaten, or are frightfully thin. There is no disease. L.N. is organising canteens.[83] We sent Andryusha off to Oryol to discover the price of bread. We walked around Grinevka a lot; I read some French with Annochka, sewed for the boys, looked after all four children and did some painting and drawing with them; I also had to keep an eye on their atrocious cook to make sure he didn't prepare anything too horrible for Lev Nikolaevich. But Ilya and Sonya's housekeeping is so wretchedly meagre and inadequate; *I* don't mind, but I am afraid Lev Nikolaevich's stomach won't tolerate the bad food and he'll fall ill.

I didn't at all like Ilya's behaviour at home. He takes absolutely no interest in the children, he is rude to the peasants, he has no serious interests and cares for nothing but horses. Sonya, on the other hand, is kind to the peasants, gives them medical treatment, takes the trouble to see they are properly fed, and distributes flour and buckwheat to the women and children.

We also visited our son Seryozha in Nikolskoe. He is still wretchedly miserable. He keeps busy with his music and has written a lovely song, which Sonya sang very sweetly for us with her attractive young voice.

L.N. wasn't in a happy state. There was something dispirited, despondent and reserved about our relations, which saddened me very much.[84] And I couldn't have been gentler or more attentive with him all that time.

I was so sorry to have to leave him in Grinevka. But then perhaps it's better for us to part for a while!

On my way back I stopped briefly at Yasnaya Polyana, and after Grinevka I was in ecstasies over the beauty of the Yasnaya countryside. I dashed about the garden and woods, picking lungwort at Chepyzh, planting saplings in the park and flowers in the flower-beds; then I tidied the house and prepared a room for Lev Nikolaevich

On the 28th, yesterday, there was the first thunder-storm and the first cuckoo. The trees were just turning green, and there was cheerful hard work going on on all sides, planting out the kitchen garden, digging round the apple trees and clearing the orchards. Dora and Lyova were so friendly and cheerful. She is a lovely woman, cultured and even-tempered. They too are digging their newly laid-out little garden and decorating the house, in readiness for her confinement and the arrival of her parents.

I returned to Moscow this morning . . . and am wretched here. Sergei

Nikolaevich came with his daughter Masha. Lyovochka will be so sorry to have missed his brother.

May 1 I didn't write yesterday, my life is empty. This morning a pupil from the 1st Gymnasium called Veselkin brought round 18 rubles and 50 kopecks, which his comrades had collected to give to the starving. These contributions from young souls and poor people move one to tears. Then Brashnin's widow brought 203 rubles, and a woman called Kopteva from Zurich sent me another 200. I am sending it all on to Lev Nikolaevich.

I had a letter today from Sonya saying that L.N. was fit and well and was continuing to travel around visiting the needy;[85] but I still haven't had a word from him. My warm feelings for him are again beginning to cool; I have written him two letters, filled with sincere love and expressing my desire for spiritual closeness. And he hasn't written me so much as a word!

There were a lot of guests here today – the Kolokoltsevs, the Maklakovs, Aristov, Dunaev, our Obolenskiis and Tolstoys, the Gorbunovs, Butyonev, Sasha Behrs, Maria Aleks. Schmidt and S.I. Taneev. We all drank tea in the garden; the young people raced about, shrieking when they found some rotten luminous wood; there was a discussion about love, in which Marusya and Sergei Ivanovich burst out laughing. It was all very tiresome, noisy and pointless, and I couldn't help thinking of my serious life in Grinevka, teaching the children, helping the starving, planting the garden, looking after the house, and so on. And then in Yasnaya, with the spring work, the splendid, peaceful spring countryside and the interest in the new baby Dora is about to have.

Mlle Aubert left today; I am sorry to lose her, but not very sorry – what a pathetic, empty creature!

May 3 I went to Petrovsko-Razumovskii yesterday, and I saw Manya and Seryozha's little son. I was terribly upset. That little boy had such a sweet expression in his eyes. I also met various social acquaintances who were having a picnic there, and Sasha was upset that they hadn't invited her. We walked around the park and wood, then dined with my old aunt Shidlovskii, who is 77 and still very agile. We spent the evening with the Kolokoltsevs. What a tragedy motherhood is! First all the tender love one lavishes on one's young (such as I saw yesterday in Manya for her son), then the intense care one takes to bring up healthy children, then the effort to educate them, then the grief and anxiety when they grow lazy and one foresees their empty, idle future, then the estrangement, the reproaches, the rudeness from one's children – and a feeling of despair that all one's life, youth and labours have been for nothing.

I receive letters regularly now from L.N. At least he's now feeding several hundred hungry peasants.[86] But he has abandoned his own children, and that is an unforgivable crime.

May 5 I had two letters from L.N. today. He is cheerful and well, thank God. He says he has opened eight canteens and has no more money.[87] It always seemed to me that it was enough to feed one or two people – not several hundred. But today nine canteens suddenly seemed so paltry beside all the millions of poor people. We haven't appealed for money, as L.N. isn't strong enough now to do all the work; but if we did, people would certainly send us a lot.

May 9 Today Sonya Mamonova asked me if I would write to Sergei Ivanovich and invite him here this evening to meet her. And he came, and at last I was granted the joy I had been waiting for, and he played – a Beethoven sonata ('Quasi una Fantasia') and a Chopin nocturne. What a delight it was, and *how* he played! He was in a particularly tender mood, and there was something so profound, so telling about his performance . . . I knew he was playing for me, and I was so grateful to him! But why stir up these terrible feelings which have been lying asleep in my heart? It's too painful . . .

I wrote to Lev Nikolaevich,[88] and it hurt me to think about him. The pleasure I get from Sergei Ivanovich's playing makes my husband suffer, and that's an appalling thought. Why can't one reconcile things, be happy and loving to everyone, take from everyone as much happiness as he can give?

Seryozha came; he played his song to Sergei Ivanovich, then played chess with him.

May 10 This morning I read proofs, then went to collect theatre tickets, then on to the Dunaevs' to try and find an assistant for Lev Nikolaevich in his famine relief work.[89] They suggested Strakhov, who would be excellent. Today I read Chertkov's letter to L.N. as I wanted to find out about Shkarvan, who is dying.[90] The whole letter is unnatural – all the same old arguments about the struggle with the flesh, money and the sin of possessing it, but the fact is that he is in debt all over the place, and is asking Tanya for a loan of 10,000 rubles.[91]

It's such utter *hypocrisy*, *that's* what I can't endure. Which of us does *not* struggle with our passions? And what a struggle it is too! Sometimes you feel as if it is draining you of all your strength, and you have none left. What sort of passions do they have anyway? They're all so dull and austere . . . Besides, if you have passions you should keep quiet about them, not perpetually shout about them.

This evening I went to the theatre with Seryozha, Andryusha and Sasha, to see a benefit performance of *Der Freischütz*, which the conservatoire students had put on to raise money for the starving.[92] I was sitting in the second row of the stalls, the same row as Sergei Ivanovich.

May 19 (Yasnaya Polyana) A lot of coming and going these last few days. I packed up and moved the whole house, Sasha, and her new Swiss governess, Mlle Kothing, to Yasnaya. The servants all left Moscow on May 15, and Sasha and I arrived at the empty Yasnaya house on the morning of the 16th. This is the second year I have come here like this! The horses, the cow, the grand piano and the boxes arrived later the same day and we all threw ourselves into the unpacking and tidying up; we had dinner and supper with Lyova and Dora, who made us very welcome. I was off again to Grinevka to see Lev Nikolaevich on the morning of the 17th, and was delighted to see him and my children and grandchildren. But my warm feelings are always drowned in cold water. When I arrived, Lev Nikolaevich had some sectarian sitting with him to whom he was reading his article. My arrival interrupted him, and he was slightly cross about this, although he tried hard not to show it. I went out for a long walk in the garden with my darling little grandsons Misha and Andryusha, and we wandered all over the place while I told them nature stories about the flowers, the apple trees and the insects. I enjoyed myself with them for about three hours, and after dinner I again went in to see Lev Nikolaevich; that sectarian was with him again, this time reciting some long verses of a spiritual nature which had been composed for sectarians to sing; and once again L.N. irritably sent me packing. I left the room and burst into tears; we hadn't seen one another for nearly three weeks; our life in Moscow, our children, Misha's exams, Tanya – none of it means a thing to him. When he realised that I was upset he came looking for me and excused himself with some embarrassment.

Life at Grinevka was exciting, and I wish I could have taken some part in it. Twenty canteens have been opened, and flour is being distributed to the peasants; they arrive at the house all day, their carts piled with sacks, some bringing things they have bought, like flour, potatoes or millet, some receiving their weekly supplies, which they then go and distribute amongst the canteens. While I was there a load of potatoes was bought, and piled up for the canteens. Ilya's wife Sonya works with great enthusiasm, although L.N. sometimes scolds her for being muddle-headed. He took another hundred rubles of mine; that is the fourth already – I simply cannot give him any more of my own money. These hundred rubles were given to Seryozha for famine relief work in Nikolskoe. There was a stupid mix-up with the local authorities: Trubnikov, the governor of Oryol province, delivered an official document to Ilya granting them permission to open *canteens*, and actually expressed his gratitude to them for doing so. But the captain of the *zemstvo* then came along and forbade them to do so, saying he had confidential instructions not to allow any such thing and to arrest and deport all who took it into their heads to live amongst the people and help them.[93] What sort of government is this! Who is deceiving whom?

I returned to Yasnaya today, having spent about four hours in Tula seeing to various business matters: suing Bibikov over the right to the land,[94] complaining about the bridge and the embankment on the Chern highway which were washed away in the floods, investigating the subcontract and the survey, and so forth. All terribly tedious and trying! Sasha was on her own with her governess all day, and I was feeling sorry for her.

We all had tea on the terrace together this evening, then set off to meet Dora's parents, who didn't arrive till late at night.

L.N. was not entirely fit at Grinevka, and had a high back-ache and heartburn. He was better today, though. He is working hard to develop his muscles, doing gymnastics with his dumbbells, swimming in the pond and washing on the bank. He eats so poorly and so little – then grumbles and panics and groans, wraps himself up in his quilted dressing-gown and talks about death, which terrifies him.

It is fine and cool, especially at night. A bright moon in a clear sky, dry and dusty again – we'll have another bad harvest!

A telegram from Tanya to say she is arriving tomorrow. Misha continues to pass his exams, thank God! I shall go to see him the day after tomorrow.

May 20 (Yasnaya Polyana) What a dazzling, beautiful spring! Fine sunny days, bright moonlit nights, lilac blossoms, extraordinarily thick and white this year, drifting apple blossom, nightingales . . . It enchants and intoxicates us, we try to grasp these fleeting impressions of the beauty of spring, and regret them eternally.

Dora's dear kind parents, the Westerlunds, arrived yesterday. How pleased she was to see them, that dear little girl with her big stomach, her domestic worries and her concern for their comfort.

My Tanya came this morning looking pale and listless, and talking of nothing but love, her desire to have children and the difficulties of being unmarried. She heard a great deal about these particular difficulties from Vera Tolstaya, who is by now so desperate for love, and especially for children, that she is prepared to love anyone. Poor girls, little did they know when they were young what awaited them.

Today is Lyova's 29th birthday. We had dinner with him and drank champagne, and Dora happily decorated the whole house with flowers.

I am going to Tula tomorrow to see to this business with the odious Bibikov, who is plotting to cut us out of our land; in the evening I shall travel on to Moscow. Today I sent the cook off to Lev Nikolaevich with some provisions, and wrote him a long letter.[95] Tomorrow I am sending Sasha and her governess off to stay with my sister Liza, otherwise she won't have anyone to stay with, for Tanya is leaving for Grinevka on the 22nd to see her father.

I feel comfortable and happy with Tanya. We know one another through and through, and we love and understand one another.

I have before me a portrait of Lev Nikolaevich with such an expressive look on his face that it always draws me to him. Yet as I go on looking at it all I remember are his reproaches and his kisses, never his tender words, or the friendship and trust between us . . .

Did they ever exist . . . ? He has been my passionate lover at times, or my stern husband and judge, but never my friend – and I don't have one now, less then ever before.

Ah, the nightingales are singing!

Sasha and I took a walk through the woods today; we picked a few mushrooms in the plantation and in Chepyzh the beautiful lilies-of-the-valley were still in flower. I love lilies-of-the-valley, they're such noble little flowers.

What a still moonlit night! The days are hot again, and the nights warm. I re-read the life and teachings of Socrates,[96] with new understanding. All great people are alike: their genius is a deformity, an infirmity, because it is exceptional. There is no harmony in people of genius, and their unbalanced characters are a torment to others.

May 22 I arrived in Moscow this morning.

May 25 Whit Sunday. Misha has gone to the Martynovs. He has passed his exams – just. I went with Nurse to Nikolskoe to visit the graves of Alyosha and Vanechka. We planted some flowers there and edged them with turf. I then said the Lord's Prayer, and silently begged my infants to pray to God to forgive my sick and sinful soul.

It was a bright and cheerful day and the peasants were in a festive mood. A little girl took me to a nearby convent, where I chatted with the nuns. One of them said that she had been 'in love with Christ' from an early age, and was possessed by the notion that she should remain in every way the 'bride of Christ' and of no one else.

There was absolutely no 'atmosphere' about this place, with its neatly laid out little garden, the peasants, and the countryside and dachas so near by. We returned to Moscow late that evening.

May 26, 27, 28, 29 (Moscow) Proofs, solitude, sadness. I was playing the piano in the corner room one evening, longing to see Sergei Ivanovich again and hear him play, when through the window I saw three figures approaching; I didn't recognise them at first, then saw to my amazement that it was Maslov, Pomerantsev and Taneev. Maslov left first, and Pomerantsev played to me. Then Sergei Ivanovich played his songs, and he and Yusha played his quartet as a piano duet.

He came to see me again on the evening of the 29th, with Goldenweiser, but he only stayed a short time and left hurriedly, looking rather flustered.

May 30 Speech-day at the conservatoire. A hot, sunny day. A Schumann sonata, the Saint-Saëns concerto and various minor pieces were beautifully performed by the women students Friedman, Bessy and young Gediker, and gave me enormous pleasure. There wasn't a single person who didn't come up to me afterwards and say: 'How young you look today!' or 'Oh, you look so fresh!' or 'It makes one cheerful just to look at you . . . ' This was all largely thanks to my new, light, pale lilac muslin dress. But I always find it very pleasant, I am ashamed to say, when the public comment on my youthful appearance and say friendly things to me.

Safonov forced me to attend some committee meeting or other – he begged me to go, as he didn't have enough musical people attending. I simply couldn't make any sense of his accounts, but I signed something all the same, then felt thoroughly guilty.

I arrived home, went out on to the balcony, and whom should I see but Sergei Ivanovich sitting on a bench in the garden reading a newspaper. I was terribly pleased. Dinner had been laid in the garden for Misha and me, and they laid a third place for him. And what a nice cheerful dinner we had. We were all so hungry, and it was so delightfully cosy and fresh outside! After dinner the three of us strolled around the garden together. Sergei Ivanovich told us stories about the Caucasus, and Misha, who was leaving the next day, was fascinated. Then Misha went off and left the two of us together. We drank tea, and Sergei Ivanovich played me some variations composed by Kolya Zhilyaev, a pupil of his. Then we sat and talked, as people talk when they trust one another completely – frankly, seriously, without shyness or stupid jokes. We talked only of things that genuinely interested us both, and there wasn't a dull or awkward moment.

What an evening it was! It was my last in Moscow – and perhaps the last such evening in my life.

At nine o'clock he stood up to go and I didn't hold him back. He took his leave, merely saying wistfully: 'One has to go some time.' I didn't reply – I wanted to cry. I saw him to the door, then went out to the garden. Then I packed, tidied and locked up, and at midnight we set off for Yasnaya.

May 31 A dismal reception at Yasnaya this morning. No Tanya, no Lev Nikolaevich, just three telegrams announcing that he was ill and was staying with the Levitskiis! He had promised not to go off anywhere and to come and meet me at Yasnaya, and instead he sets off in the barouche with Sonya his daughter-in-law to gallivant around visiting neighbours and finding out about the famine and the approaching harvest in the region. They visited the Tsurikovs, the Afremovs and the Levitskiis, where L.N. eventually came down with dysentery and a high fever.[97]

June 1 Lev Nikolaevich didn't return. I wept all day, then feeling quite ill I set off with Maria Aleksandrovna Schmidt first for Tula, via Kozlovka, then took the Syzran-Vyazma line train to Karasei, where I arrived early this morning, hired a coach and went straight to the Levitskiis. Lev Nikolaevich was very ill and weak, and it was unthinkable that he should go home.

June 2, 3, 4, 5 (at the Levitskiis) A wonderful family, busy, liberal in a good sense, him especially – a clever, strong-minded man.

It's so hard nursing and caring for L.N., and cooking his complicated vegetarian diet, in a strange house. I sent for the doctor, and we gave him bismuth with opium and applied compresses. It was dull, dreary, cold and exasperating. Lev Nikolaevich was already ill when he left. What sort of folly is this? He should be ashamed of making a nuisance of himself in another person's house, and making a lot of complicated and outlandish demands for things like almond milk, rusks, porridge oats, special bread, and so on.

June 6 When we returned to Yasnaya I had a bad cough and felt weak, worn out and exhausted from looking after Lev Nikolaevich.

We spent the night at the house of the Ershovs, who were not at home. A dreadful thing had happened! A young woman called Tulubyova (born Ershova), threw herself into the river there in a fit of depression and drowned herself. I envied her courage. Life is very, very hard.

June 8 At 12.45 today Dora gave birth to a son. How she suffered, poor girl, how she pleaded with her father, in her guttural young voice, to give her something, noisily gabbling away in Swedish. Lyova was very gentle with her and reassured her, and she was so sweet and loving with him, pressing herself close to him as if begging him to share her suffering. And he did, and so little Lev was born, a normal and successful birth.

June 11 I have had the grand piano moved into Tanya's studio. I played there for three hours today and wept bitterly, overcome with a sudden helpless desire to hear Sergei Ivanovich's music just once more. How happy those two summers were[98] after the death of Vanechka! And to think that after such a frightful tragedy I should have been sent such a consolation! I thank thee, Lord, for that joy.

Masha and Kolya have arrived, and Ilya is here with my grandson Misha. He and I walked over to Cherta and picked night violets; we talked about his parting with his Nurse and about the little nest we had kept guard over with Vanechka – at first with eggs in it, then baby birds. It was so quiet, such balm to my soul after all the tears and despair.

Westerlund and Lyova had supper with us and we had a full table, which I love because I am so used to it. I dream of paying my sister Tanya a visit, and calling on the Maslovs on the way. Shall I manage to go? When Maslov was saying goodbye to me in Moscow, he invited me most warmly to visit them, and thanked me profusely for something or other. I am so fond of this kind, strong-minded, comforting family. They are all unmarried, but I am sure that beneath the quiet exterior their lives are not without emotional turmoil and anxiety. How I should love to stay in that quiet haven, where Sergei Ivanovich would come and play for me and I could have more serious talks with him about important matters of life and death.

L.N. has still not recovered from his illness. He is listless, sleepy and very quiet, displaying neither joy, grief, anger nor love. This last illness seems to have frightened him thoroughly, for he seems to have glimpsed the possibility of dying, and that terrifies him.

The famine and all the business with the canteens and donations suddenly seem no longer to interest him.[99] Westerlund has diagnosed an enlarged liver and has ordered him to drink very hot Vichy water every morning.

June 12 I got up late, practised my exercises assiduously and realised how badly I had fallen behind. I walked over to the fir saplings at Chepyzh with my grandson Misha, and we picked some little brown mushrooms and saffron milk-caps. The silent forest, the flowers, the bright sun, the clear sky – it was utterly glorious! Then I played the piano again, and after dinner I sat with Misha in the tower. I then went off in the cabriolet with Sasha to visit the joiner and the graves of my infants and L.N.'s aunt and parents; we picked cornflowers in the rye as we walked back, laughing, chattering and joking with the children. L.N. sat on the balcony this evening setting us problems, and remembered his favourite one about the haymakers. It goes like this.

There are two meadows, a large and a small one. The haymakers come to the larger one and mow all the forenoon. In the afternoon half the haymakers are sent to the smaller meadow. At the end of the day the larger meadow is completely mown and in the small one there's still another day's work left for one man. How many haymakers are there? Answer 8. $\frac{3}{4}$ of them mowed the large field, $\frac{3}{8}$ did the small field, that is $\frac{2}{8}$ and $\frac{1}{8}$ – which is one man. So if one man is $\frac{1}{8}$, then there must have been eight in all. This is one of Lev Nikolaevich's favourite problems and he asks everyone he knows to solve it.

I was wondering today why there were no women writers, artists or composers of genius. It's because all the passion and all the abilities of an energetic woman are consumed by her family, love, her husband – and especially her children. Her other abilities are not developed, they remain embryonic and they atrophy. When she has finished bearing and educating her children, her artistic needs awaken, but by then it's too late, for by then it's impossible to develop anything.

Young girls often develop spiritual and artistic powers, but these powers remain isolated and cannot be carried on by subsequent generations, since girls do not create posterity. Geniuses often have older mothers, who developed their talents early in life, and Lev Nikolaevich is one of these. His mother was no longer young when she married and had him.

June 13 It seems that fate has again granted that L.N. should live and we should rejoice – if only my poor heart were still capable of rejoicing. But thank God we are all in good health and on good terms. Lev Nikolaevich rode to Yasenki today; he is glad to be better, and that God has allowed him to live a little longer, and even live quite energetically. I am just beginning to settle in here, tidy the house, arrange the furniture and go for walks. Today I walked to the plantation with my grandson Misha; we picked flowers, mushrooms and berries, and I had a long talk with him about Vanechka and wept as I told him about his life.

Then I went for another walk with Lyova, Ilyusha and the Westerlunds. I had a nice quiet talk with Ilyusha about his arrangements and his plan to spend the winter with his mother-in-law. The poor fellow has got in a dreadful muddle over his financial and household affairs.

It was a magnificent clear evening – there are masses of flowers everywhere, and we picked bunches of them for tomorrow.

Tomorrow my little grandson Lev is being christened.

June 14 I spent the day with my children. Lev was christened at 1 o'clock. Dora was very agitated and the Swedish grandparents were horrified by our primitive Russian christening ceremony.

We all dined very grandly in the garden, with fruit, bunches of flowers and champagne on the table, and the weather was lovely and sunny. Then everyone played tennis, including L.N.; he is not flagging, and his health is completely restored, thank God. Masha and Kolya left this evening, and Ilya left with Misha, whom I was terribly sorry to part with. Yet the feeling that *he isn't mine*, that loving him will bring nothing but sorrow, and that I won't be the one to bring him up, makes me afraid to love him, and I deliberately withdraw from him.

I played the piano for three hours non-stop today, and I tried to learn Chopin's A Major Polonaise; it is hard, but oh, what a magnificent piece it is! Later Nadya Feret arrived and sang very pleasantly for us. I read my son Lyova's short story 'Chopin Prelude' in the *New Times*.[100] He has no special ability – it's a small talent, sincere and naïve. I finished the day with L.N. and we behaved like children.

June 17 It's all so difficult and depressing again! I can't help remembering a remark the French philosopher Charles Richet once made to me: '*Je vous plains, madame, vous n'avez pas même le temps d'être heureuse.*'*[101]

*'I pity you, madame, you have no time even to be happy.'

I have spent all yesterday and today with poultices and compresses looking after Lev Nikolaevich who is sick . . . He didn't restrain himself after his dysentery and ate much too much and much too greedily; he went bicycling, despite the doctors' orders not to, and swimming, and exhausted himself riding, and yesterday he had excruciating stomach pains and persistent and painful vomiting, and this evening he had a temperature of 38.2 and has eaten nothing all day, just groans continuously and is very impatient.

He is shortening his life with this obstinacy and immoderation, and undermining mine too. This time I feel angry; I nursed him through one dysentery attack with a great deal of care and patience, and now he is ill all over again. I am not well either – I am depressed and worn out, I have a pain in the pit of my stomach and a bad cough.

L.N. received from his bed some married couple from Voronezh, who had come to him as a spiritual doctor, asking him for advice. This has worn him out.

Yesterday, before Lev Nikolaevich fell ill, I went swimming with Sasha for the first time this year, and we were regretting that so few people make use of our lovely swimming pool and our comfortable summer life in Yasnaya. We discussed this and decided laughing that when we live as we want, we shall have many, many people of all kinds to stay here who will enjoy living with us, and we shall be delighted to have them.

June 18 Sasha's 14th birthday. An unbearably hot day – 40 degrees in the sun at 2 this afternoon. L.N. is still ill, with bad heartburn all day and a temperature of 38.3. This evening he improved a little and his temperature dropped to 37.5; he ate two plates of porridge and drank some coffee.

I raced down to the Voronka with Sasha for a swim. It was a wonderful evening, and I couldn't stop gazing at the glorious countryside, the sky and the moon.

When I got home I found L.N. dictating a newspaper article to Tanya, which they subsequently decided not to send.

It concerned 6 girls and boys, gymnasium pupils, who arrived at Yasnaya with 100 rubles which they wanted to give to the needy peasants. L.N. sent them to a priest, who is the guardian of this area, and this man told them which peasants were the poorest. The girls and boys then went to Yasenki and bought some flour, which was to be given to the poor peasants. But then the sergeant and the district police-officer appeared and strictly forbade the Yasenki merchant to give any flour to the peasants in exchange for the credit-notes which we and the children had given them.[102] It's completely outrageous! Don't anyone in Russia dare give alms to the poor – the district police-officer won't allow it! Tanya and I were deeply distressed, and would both willingly have gone straight to the Tsar or his mother and warned them against the anger which may arise amongst people exasperated by such measures.

The Tolstoy girls came, and M.A. Schmidt.

June 20 Lev Nikolaevich is still ill. He has only a slight fever, 37.8, but he is burning hot and still very thin and weak. His stomach aches only when he moves or puts pressure on it. Last night I massaged it for a long time with camphor oil, then we applied spirit of camphor compresses and I gave him some bismuth with soda and morphine. He ate a plate of porridge today, some rice gruel made with half almond milk and half ordinary milk (without telling him), and an egg, which Doctor Westerlund finally, after three days, managed to persuade him to eat.

The district police-officer was here enquiring about the Kharkov school-girls and boys who came here wanting to help the peasants in some way and work with them. They have all disappeared without trace, but two more little girls, one of whom was only 13 years old, arrived here today with the same purpose. They have all been banished from the district, and I gave the police-officer a piece of my mind for forbidding the merchant at Kolpny to supply the peasants with flour in exchange for credit notes. The priest had ordered that these notes should be given to the poorest inhabitants of our area, and the flour is paid for.

K.A. Abrikosov, from England, also came and told us quite a lot of new and interesting things about Chertkov and the other Russians living there.

I went swimming with Tanya and Sasha. Frightful heat, dry thunderstorm, black clouds, lightning, no rain, terrible drought. These past few days I have been playing a little, in fits and starts, in the studio above the servants' room.

I felt very despondent about Lev Nikolaevich today. I was thinking that if he recovered from *this* illness he would soon be 70 years old; he cannot live for much longer after that – and then I shall be left on my own in the world without him. This suddenly conjured up a vision of such terrifying solitude and helplessness that I all but burst into tears. However hard I sometimes find it living with L.N., he has never loved anyone but me, he has supported and defended me, even against the children at times. It will be dreadfully hard for me when he goes. I pray that he will live a little longer, and that I shall either not survive him at all or for as short a time as possible.

I read four pages of proofs; my eyes are getting weaker.

June 21 What with all these illnesses and anxieties I have made a terrible mess of Volume 15 of the 9th expensive edition, and I am very worried about it; I cannot think how to extricate myself from it. I forgot that what stands as the *appendix* to Volume 13 was not included in the expensive edition, and I went straight into Volume 14 without including it. Now I

12 On previous page: Maria Tolstaya (Masha) haymaking at Yasnaya Polyana, 1895. Photograph by P. I. Biryukov

13 Above: Yasnaya Polyana, 1896. Sofia Tolstaya's photograph

14 Below: The house in Dolgokhamovnicheskii Lane, Moscow

shall have to add it at the end, regardless of any system or chronological sequence.[103] I have too much to hold in my head. It's all right so long as everything else is going successfully. But 'even the old woman has a blunder up her sleeve', as the saying goes, and I really have blundered this time. And it's all because of Lev Nikolaevich being ill, and having to travel all over the place to nurse him.

I sent for Nadya Ivanovna and did some proof-reading with her, then played the piano for about three hours. Lev Nikolaevich is much better now; his temperature is decreasing every day, and today it was only 37.3; but he still complains of feeling very weak, and today he was irritable and out of sorts all day. On Westerlund's advice he now eats an egg a day for medicinal purposes, which he dislikes, but he also dislikes his weak and debilitated state.[104]

This evening we all went for a swim. I walked back through the forest alone as dusk was falling, and was suddenly overwhelmed with yearning for Vanechka, for my sister Tanya, for everything I had lost in my life, for all those spoilt and wasted emotions, for my daughter Tanya, yet another friend who is leaving me and breaking that powerful thirty-four-year-old bond of love uniting us.

Sobs rose in my chest and throat and I burst out sobbing all on my own in the middle of the forest. I think even the birds were frightened by my howls and groans. The most painful tears are those shed alone, which nobody ever knows about. Then I grew afraid. I kept hearing someone else howling in the forest – my own sobs echoed by absent friends or departed souls.

Dunaev arrived, accompanied by Dieterichs, Galya Chertkova's brother, who has just left military service in accordance with his principles.

There's an eclipse of the moon, which I can see through the window . . . It is already moving away . . .

June 22 Peasant women have been begging at the porch all day for flour, money, a bit of bread to eat, a little tea, medicine, and so on. I try patiently to give them what they want, but am exhausted. It's impossible to help them. I spent the whole day running up and down the stairs, looking after Lev Nikolaevich and attending to business, and by this evening I was half dead. As I massaged L.N.'s stomach I was dreaming of the sea and the rocks and hills of Norway, where we have been invited to stay with the Westerlunds, who are leaving tomorrow.

June 26 I spent an extremely difficult afternoon yesterday. Our young neighbour Bibikov has appropriated the land we bought from his father, and we now have to defend ourselves, and the court case has started. Yesterday they had to collect all the local witnesses, but the only witnesses called were from the village of Telyatinki, which belongs to Bibikov, and he is supposed to be our enemy. It was quite obvious that the witnesses, the judge and the land-surveyor had all been bribed and feasted by Bibikov yesterday, and the whole trial was conducted in the most corrupt fashion. At first I was distressed, then I was utterly bewildered: the judge, the questioning, the oath – it was all chicanery, from beginning to end.

I stayed out of curiosity, though, sitting until late that night in the village elder's cottage. Everyone, judge and peasants, seemed to grow rather confused and subdued towards the end of the twelve peasants' interrogation: we were all too obviously in the right.[105]

Afterwards I wrote a petition to the Tula drawing-office asking them to set boundaries to the estate, otherwise the peasants will simply appropriate more and more of our land every year.

I am still not happy about L.N.'s health. Today he had another stomach upset, and this evening he had a bad chill. And he is dreadfully weak too.

My son Lyova is also irritable and anxious – and his writing is anxious too. I do wish he enjoyed life more and had more peace of mind, less arrogance and inner turmoil.

Dora and little Lev are very sweet and touching together.

I was so pleased yesterday because a strong wind and a terrible thunder-storm sprang up while I was out, and L.N. was very worried about me, wouldn't eat supper and asked them to send the carriage and some warm clothes for me. After he is gone there will be no one to worry about me, and that is a painful thought.

And what a storm it was! Lightning flashed on all sides, the wind forced the carriage back after we had left Telyatinki for home, and there was the ominous glow of a fire in the distance.

There have been many fires, and many victims who have come to us for help.

Now the night is so still, and the moon is shining through the open window. I love being alone at night with my thoughts, in spiritual communion with my loved ones who are absent or dead.

June 27 This thundery atmosphere is insufferable; we are quite debilitated by the heat and the electricity in the air. L.N. has a stomach-ache again. My God! Help me not to grumble, and to bear my responsibilities to the end with patience and dignity.

I gave him a bath today, ran it myself, and tested the water with the thermometer. I then laid tea in the drawing-room and he brightened up considerably. I very much wanted to go and visit Seryozha tomorrow just for the day, for his birthday, but I couldn't bring myself to leave my husband. I tried to take my grandson's photograph, but failed to do so, for he fell asleep, and then the thunder-storm made it impossible. I practised my Bach Inventions, but only managed to play for an hour. The sick peasant women, work and business; I wrote a letter to some peasant at L.N.'s request.[106]

Marusya Maklakova left with Ilyusha; she, Sasha and I all went swimming in a thick white fog this afternoon.

Westerlund said I spoilt my husband terribly. I was astounded today by something L.N. wrote in his notebook concerning women: 'If a woman is not a Christian she is a wild animal.'[107]

That means that throughout my life I have sacrificed all my personal life to him and suppressed all my own desires – even a visit to my son, like today – and all my husband can see is animal behaviour.

The real animals are those men who through their own egotism completely consume the lives of their wives, children, friends – everyone who crosses their path.

June 28 Misha has just returned from the Caucasus in ecstasy over his trip, the magnificent scenery, the friendliness of the people and all the parties they organised for Andryusha and him. He arrived with Sasha Behrs, looking manlier and uglier than before. Misha and Lyova left to visit Seryozha for his birthday.

My life pursues the same excruciatingly dull course. I see hardly anything of Lev Nikolaevich, for he is always alone in his study writing letters to all and sundry, tirelessly weaving the web of his future glory, since these letters will make mighty volumes. I read a letter he wrote to a sectarian the other day and was horrified by its *hypocritical* tone. He is not so keen to write his diary now as he knows I may read it, but his letters fly all over the world and are copied at home by his daughters.

He is looking very pinched, thin and subdued.

He regarded Doctor Westerlund as a bourgeois, dull-witted German peasant, whose medical thinking was 30 years behind the times; he didn't see the doctor's goodness, his self-sacrificing life in the service of humanity, his eagerness to help every peasant woman and anyone he met, his concern for his wife and daughter, his unselfishness . . .

June 29 Lev Nikolaevich has been getting slowly and steadily better. Today he went for a walk and brought back a bunch of cornflowers. He does nothing but write letters all day.

July 1 Annenkova came today and we went over to Ovsyannikovo. We called first on Maria Aleksandrovna Schmidt, then the Gorbunovs. Maria Aleksandrovna has a large portrait of Lev Nikolaevich over her bed. She has a fanatical faith in his ideas and is in love with him as only a woman can be, and this gives her the strength to endure her austere and hard-working life. Without that she would have died long ago, so weak is her organism and so thin is she. I love her ardent nature; Annenkova is calm and kind by nature.

I didn't go swimming today. I played for half an hour and wrote 6 letters, including one to Sergei Ivanovich asking where I should send the English translation of L.N.'s *What is Art?* which he had asked me for.[108]

This was the first day Lev Nikolaevich felt completely well; he had a good sleep last night and has been writing something enthusiastically all day.

I am very dissatisfied with my life: the days pass in idle gossip (which I find truly boring) and petty affairs – distributing medicine and money, worrying about meals, housekeeping, the estate, publishing business. No ideas, no books, no art, no real work which might have some useful results . . .

Butyonev and Lev Bobrinskii came to see Misha in a barouche and a troika. One seemed to have drunk a great deal and the other smoked fat cigars, which Lev Nikolaevich found both ridiculous and pathetic.

That unsympathetic Jew Loewenfeld has arrived; he has written a biography of Lev Nikolaevich and is now writing the second part.[109]

I did so want to see my son Seryozha; Tanya has turned away from us for a while, but she will come back. My two elder children are my favourites. They have been my friends for almost the whole of my married life and youth.

July 2 I read Tanya's play; it is very *clever* but lifeless – you don't love or believe in any of the characters.[110]

Talked to Loewenfeld this evening. He was telling me about the Ethical Society in Berlin. Total atheism and a concern for people's material well-being. This concern would be a fine thing if it was practised on a wide, universal scale, but why should faith in God stand in the way of that? Without the idea of God I should lose all ability to love or understand anything. These ideas of God and eternity are utterly necessary to me.

July 4 The day before yesterday I sat up until three in the morning happily writing my story 'Song Without Words'. I played the piano for about three hours both yesterday and today. I was thinking about Taneev's songs today, for Sasha was humming them on the way to the swimming pool, and I then began to sight-read them.

Lev Nikolaevich walked to the factory with Dunaev – over 6 *versts* both ways. He has certainly got back his health and strength now, thank God

I am unforgivably depressed, and I seem to smell corpses everywhere, and it's sheer torture. Only music can save me from melancholy and from this terrible stench.

July 5 A lovely walk with L.N., Dunaev, Annenkova and three young ladies whom I didn't know, around Gorelaya Polyana to Zaseka, under the bridge to the highway, back through Zaseka to Kozlovka and home again.

A clear and beautiful evening. Tanya is still ill, and her heart is still aching. I go in and sit with her and think: 'Are we really about to part for good?'

July 6 Rain, cold; Tanya is still in bed with a stomach-ache. I strolled around the garden and picked a lovely bunch of flowers for her. I played the piano for about two and a half hours, but badly. I corrected proofs all day. I have a lot of running about to do, and a mass of petty boring matters: sending documents to the council, paying the servants' wages, buying mushrooms and raspberries, tending the sick, giving food to the beggars, ordering dinner and supper, keeping Dora and my grandson company, giving the servant girls their work for the day. I should do some copying for Lev Nikolaevich, but there's a pile of proofs to do first. And I have to look after Tanya, who stubbornly refuses to take any medicine.

July 12 I left the house to make some visits, and called first on my daughter Masha. It pierced my heart to see her, so bent, weak and nervous, tearful and as thin as a skeleton. It is such an impoverished life, and the food there is disgusting.

July 13 Early this morning I left for Selishche to see the Maslovs. Fyodor Ivanovich met me at the station, and all his family were up to welcome me – Sergei Ivanovich too. It's the most delightful place, near the Bryansk forest, the river Navlya and numerous fresh springs. It's all so vast and beautiful, especially the pine and oak forests. I took a long walk with Anna Ivanovna, and that afternoon we all read Lev Nikolaevich's wonderful article 'On the Famine',[111] which everyone liked very much. Later Sergei Ivanovich answered my prayer and played Chopin's A Major Polonaise for me – and then twice more. He also played Schubert's 'Morgenständchen' twice, as well as something by Handel. And what a joy it was! Personally, however, I did not like him at all at the Maslovs; there is a certain lack of restraint and moderation about people who have grown old living exactly the same lives as when they were children, people for whom looking at nature has merely become a habit. The following day, the 14th, we all drove to the forest, and I had my photograph taken beside an ancient hollowed-out lime tree. In the afternoon Anna Ivanovna and I worked on our photography, and we all went to bed early.

July 15 We got up early. Anna Ivanovna took me in the carriage to Navlya station, and late that evening I was met in Kiev by my sister Tanya. I spent the night with her in town, and the following morning we took a cab to Kitaev.

July 16 A warm welcome from the Kuzminskiis. They have a pretty, well-appointed little dacha, her sweet boys were there, and Sasha the cordial host, and my beloved, my dear, sweet beloved sister Tanya. The sight of little Mitechka tore at my heart: he was the same age as Vanechka, his first friend, his first childhood comrade. And Mitya is already a big boy of ten – and Vanechka is gone!

I went for a walk through the Kitaev forest, through ancient pines and old oaks, past hills and monasteries . . . Sasha, Vera, Mitya and little Volodka came too. We went swimming in the pool of a monastery, drank tea and rambled in the hills. It is so pleasant being a guest. Everything is new, there is nothing to worry about.

July 17, 18, 19, 20 I have spent the past four days with the Kuzminskiis. We had a picnic with some other dacha folk on an island in the river Dnieper, went to the peasant theatre in Kitaev, and went swimming in the Dnieper. On the 20th I went into Kiev with my sister Tanya and we visited the Vladimirst Cathedral. The best painting there was *The Raising of Lazarus*, by Svedomskii. Vasnetsov's paintings – especially the *Baptism of Vladimir and the People* – were beneath criticism: one was amazed by the complete lack of formal elegance. Eve's legs, for instance, when she is being tempted by the serpent in Paradise, are utterly frightful.

The monument to Vladimir stands in a charming place, with a lovely view on to the Dnieper below. Ancient monuments, like the one to Bogdan Khmelnitskii in Kiev, are generally so much better than the modern ones, like that hideous statue of Pirogov in Deviche Pole in Moscow.

I also visited the caves in Kiev. I forced myself to go this time, but I felt so nervous as soon as we had walked a little way down that dark, airless underground passage, illuminated only by the candles we held in our hands. It was impossible to turn back, and it suddenly came into my head that the devil was obstructing my path, and just then the monk who was leading us said to me: 'No need to be afraid, Mother! Why, people used to live here, and you're afraid just to walk through. Look, this is a church, so pray!' So I mechanically crossed myself and repeated the words of some prayer, and my fear actually vanished and I walked on fascinated. It was extraordinary to see those little round windows into the walled up cave rooms where holy people used voluntarily to immure themselves. People would hand them food through the windows once a day, and there they would die, in these cells, these living coffins.

My sister's family made such a good impression on me; I particularly envied the fact that the father was so concerned about his sons, and was such good friends with them too. That is the true meaning of the saying 'duty's duty, but friendship's friendship'. Tanya and her husband's concern for each other was also very touching.

I persuaded Tanya to accompany me back to Yasnaya, to my great joy.

July 22, 23, 24, 25 Early in the morning of the 22nd my sister Tanya and I arrived in Tula; it was cold and wet and they hadn't sent any horses for us, so we hired a cab and drove back. Then the trouble started – a whole series of unpleasant remarks from L.N. about my visit to the Maslovs and my meeting with Sergei Ivanovich.[112] Yet I had actually asked him before I left whether he would mind, and said I wouldn't go if he did. I had leant over him to say goodbye, kissed him while he was still half-asleep, and put it to him quite candidly. And he snapped back ironically: 'Why should I mind? By all means go,' adding: 'It's your business anyway.'

There is a huge wall painting at the threshold to the cave in Kiev, which depicted the forty ordeals to which the soul of Saint Theodora is subjected. The pictures alternate: two angels with the soul of Theodora as a young girl dressed in a white robe, followed by a group of devils in inconceivably hideous poses. And these devils, forty groups of them, portray the forty sins, which are inscribed in Slavonic beneath.

So I suppose L.N. is cursing me for committing all the forty sins in those three or four days.

Above this painting is one of another soul, that of a young girl in a white robe prostrating herself on the steps of a dais, on which Christ is sitting with his apostles. Further off are the gates of Paradise – then the Garden of Eden itself. It's an entire poem, and it's extremely interesting – especially for the common people, I imagine.

Eventually we calmed down, and I tried hard not to poison my sister's stay in Yasnaya. We had many talks together, and she criticised me for my attachment to Sergei Ivanovich, my love of music and all the distress I had caused my husband.

It's hard for me to subordinate my emotions to my husband's demands, but I must try.

July 28 I took my sister Tanya to Yasenki and she left for Kiev, apparently quite happy with her stay in Yasnaya. We have grown even closer, if that is possible. I feel bereft – I have no one to cling to now.

I walked through the forest alone, swam and wept. Late that night we resumed our discussion about jealousy, with yet more shouting, cursing and recriminations. Suddenly my nerves snapped. Some valve maintaining the equilibrium in my brain flew open. I lost all self-control and had the most terrible nervous attack. I was terrified, shaking, sobbing and raving. I don't remember what happened to me, only that I ended up stiff with cold.

July 29, 30 I have been lying in bed in a darkened room for the past day and a half, without food or light, without love, hate or emotions, just the deathly gloom of the grave. They all came in to see me but I didn't love or care about any of them, I just wanted to die.

I pushed the table a moment ago and Lev Nikolaevich's portrait fell on the floor, just as this diary of mine has pushed him off the pedestal he has spent his entire life erecting for himself.

July 31 Lev Nikolaevich rode 35 *versts* to Pirogovo to visit his brother Sergei Nikolaevich.

August 1, 2 I am delighting in my solitude and in life's comforts – a quite unprecedented experience for me.

August 3 I spent yesterday and the day before industriously copying out L.N.'s story *Father Sergei*, an artistic work written in a lofty style, excellently conceived although still unfinished. It takes from the *Lives of the Saints* the story of the saint who sought God and found Him in the most ordinary, lowly woman, who sacrificed herself entirely to work and toil. In this story Father Sergei, a proud monk who has experienced all life's vicissitudes, finds God in Pashenka, a woman no longer young, whom he has known since childhood, who leads an industrious life in her old age and lives for her family.

There is some hypocrisy in the story though – the ending in Siberia. I hope it won't be left like that, for it really is very well devised and constructed.

I spent the whole of last night, from 1.30 to 5 a.m., copying it out, by which time it was growing light and my head was spinning, but I finished the whole thing, so L.N. can start working on it the moment he gets back.[113]

He wants to finish *Hadji Murat, Resurrection* and *Father Sergei* together, publish the 3 stories simultaneously and sell them for as much as possible in Russia and abroad, so he can use the profits to finance the Dukhobors' emigration scheme.[114]

This is an insult to us, his family: he would do better to help Ilyusha and Masha, who are both extremely poor. And two Dukhobors came here whom I had to hide in the pavilion, which was most unpleasant.[115]

Windy, dry, fine and beautiful.

I have been keeping Dora company and getting to know my little grandson Lev. I have lost that direct, almost animal passion for small children, and in my grandchildren I love only my *dreams* for the future and for the continuation of our life.

August 5 I copied L.N.'s article all yesterday: the same rejection of absolutely everything, and all under the pretext of Christianity too – it's pure socialism.[116]

This morning I went to Tula, where I had a lot of business to attend to – at the drawing-office, the bank and the council, visiting the notary, looking for a teacher for Misha and going to the shops. I was so exhausted that my legs were shaking. I was longing for a rest when I got home, but a huge crowd of guests unexpectedly arrived – Sergeenko, the two Dieterichs girls, my sister Liza with her daughter and governess, Zvegintseva with her daughter, Volkhonskii, Prince Cherkasskii and the boys – and they all stayed to supper. My heart sank. Goldenweiser came for the evening too and played some Chopin. The music awakened that wonderful mood of elation which I have lived for these past two years.

A lot of noise and shouting and mindless youthful merriment. I am very tired. L.N. on the other hand is extremely cheerful and excited; he enjoys guests and Misha Kuzminskii's balalaika, and Princess Volkhonskii's chatter, and everything that makes for entertainment and diversion.

August 11 I have been ill for three days: all my limbs hurt, I have a headache and a stomach-ache, my chest is stuffed up, I cannot sleep, and I cannot eat.

Yesterday I felt guilty about lounging around ill in bed and not doing anything, so at mid-day I got up and forced myself to copy out almost the whole of Lev Nikolaevich's article. He is working on his hateful *Resurrection* at present; maybe he will revise it.

Gorbunov and Goldenweiser are here, and Orlov-Davydov, whom L.N. was expecting. I went out to sit on the balcony for a breath of fresh air, but felt terribly weak; then L.N. suddenly decided to go off for a nap and left his guest with me for an hour and a half.

I said that I was going back to bed, and that he could take the Count in to sit with the young folk. I really haven't the strength to make conversation with guests I have never met before, who haven't come to see me but the writer Lev Tolstoy.

Bad news from the censors, who've seized the last volume of the expensive edition which I have just had printed. It won't be passed unless I make a fuss. I have written to Solovyov, the chief censor, in St Petersburg.[117]

August 19 I have been ill with a high fever and stomach pains. I stayed in bed until yesterday, and barely managed to get up even then. The time flashed past so quickly – I have only a dim memory of it. Everyone was very kind to me, looked after me, stayed with me constantly, anticipated all my needs and comforted me. There was one day when I thought I was dying but was quite happy about it. Now I am up again, back in life's whirlpool, with all its demands, griefs, worries and unresolvable questions which need to be resolved.

I am reading an interesting book called *Le Réveil de l'âme*. I also read Anatole France's *La Bûche* and *La Fille de Clémentine*. Being ill didn't bore me at all; I enjoyed the solitude, being able to concentrate on my thoughts, and the absence of material anxieties.

Wonderful fine weather, moonlit nights, masses of flowers: all would be well if it weren't for people, with all their spite, vices, temptations, jealousy, idleness, etc.

I was moved to tears today by the beauty of summer, and felt sad that I was still too weak to walk, swim and enjoy myself actively. Mikhail Osipovich Menshikov came. Misha has developed a passion for photography, which pleases me. Andryusha has written to this Caucasian bride he has dreamed up, declining to marry her, and he is now very worried about it.[118] Tanya is in Moscow staying with the Olsufievs. L.N. rode over to Zaseka for news about the Myasoedovo peasants burnt out in the fire, but he wasn't allowed to cross that stretch of the railway-line as the Tsar was passing through on his way back from Moscow, where he had been unveiling a monument to Alexander II.

I played a Haydn symphony as a duet with Sasha, who is an extremely poor sight-reader. I made some corrections to Loewenfeld's German article about his second visit to Yasnaya Polyana,[119] and made prints of Misha's photographs. I have a stomach-ache.

August 21 I am trying to resume my old life after being ill, but nothing interests me. We are getting ready for the 28th; the worst of it is not knowing how many guests there'll be. I played the piano a little today, and was vividly reminded of what a wonderful, familiar, soothing effect it always has on my nerves and heart, and reminded too of everything music has given me over the years. The beauties of summer, moonlit nights and flowers have a melancholy effect on me, for the days rush past at such a pace, advancing inexorably towards autumn, cold weather and winter. I am not yet strong enough to go for walks, and cannot swim. Lev Nikolaevich rode all the way to Myasoedovo; but they wouldn't let him across the railway-line yesterday as they were waiting for the Tsar to pass.

My little grandson Lev has the mumps, and Rudnyov came. Andryusha has influenza, Misha is very excited about his photography.

Menshikov spent several days here, but we didn't have many interesting conversations with him this time. Today he told Masha that he disapproved of L.N. begging money from wealthy people in aid of the Dukhobors.[120] What I could never understand is how one could continue to live, speak and write so completely inconsistently as L.N.

The day before yesterday his horse trod on his foot. And that evening how terrified he was of the pain, how he groaned, and rubbed himself, and couldn't sleep, and applied compresses, and took his temperature – he was plainly very afraid, but absolutely nothing happened, and today he was dashing about again and going riding.

August 22 My 54th birthday. Tanya, Masha and Sasha all gave me presents; Tanya and Sasha gave things they had made themselves, which was nice, but Masha bought me a little table, which I didn't like, for I know she has no money, and it's a pity to waste it on things I don't need. But I suppose it was a kind thought. She is always ill, first her head aches, then her stomach, then something else . . . She thinks too much about her health – it's simply *neurasthenia*.

Zosya and Manya Stakhovich are here, such charming lively girls. Vera Kuzminskaya came this morning, and later this evening my sister-in-law Maria Nikolaevna arrived. Dora and Lyova had dinner with us, and we celebrated my birthday rather grandly. The others then walked over to Sudakovo to see Feret, while I went to the orchard to prune the young fruit trees. Then I went inside and played the piano for two hours alone in the studio. L.N. was such lively scintillating company all evening, telling everyone stories as though he were giving each of us the subject for a tale – the mother, the coupon, Kuzmich, Alexander I and so on.[121]

It is fine and warm. Misha took photographs of us all, and one of me holding a large bunch of flowers.

August 24 Windy, raining and cold, we all stayed indoors talking. Everyone is very interested in this latest statement from the Tsar in favour of universal peace and disarmament. L.N. actually had a letter from *The World* in America, asking his opinion of it. So far it was only *words*, he said; first of all one had to abolish taxes, military service, and much more besides.[122] I think that many generations will need to be educated to hate war if it is to be eradicated.

Some Munich professor came to visit, a stocky red-faced German.[123] Sulerzhitskii came here after seeing the Dukhobors, and is going on to England for more information. Meanwhile the Dukhobors, all 7,000 of them, are living by the sea shore in Batumi, waiting for a decision as to where they should go. And from whom? Why, from Chertkov of course.[124] It's an appalling, disgraceful situation – it's all so frivolous.

L.N. had a long talk with the German. He is still working on *Resurrection*, and Aleksandr Petrovich has appeared just in time to copy it for him.

I feel very apprehensive about Lev Nikolaevich's birthday, which is fast approaching. I am afraid there will be a great mob of people and a great deal of inconvenience. I am also rather anxious about my forthcoming visit to Moscow: I don't want to disrupt my peaceful life here in Yasnaya, and I am worried about the Taneev situation.

August 26, 27 I spent the whole day shopping in Tula with my sister-in-law Maria Nikolaevna, buying provisions, straw mattresses, crockery and so on for our guests.

Some more Dukhobors came; they are still waiting for something to happen, and hope for both a favourable response to their petition from the

Tsar, *and* help from Lev Nikolaevich.[125] This is quite ridiculous, since help from one necessarily excludes help and sympathy from the other.

How the day of August 28, 1898 was spent Today Lev Nikolaevich is 70 years old. I went in to greet him this morning while he was still in bed, and he looked so pleased, as though this was his own special day. All the family was here, with their wives and children – except Seryozha's wife Manya and her son, and Ilya's youngest boys Andryusha and Ilyusha. We had guests too – Potapenko, Sergeenko, Prince Volkhonskii, Mikhail Stakhovich, Mitasha Obolenskii, Prince Ukhtomskii, Muromtseva, Goldenweiser, etc., etc. Altogether we had about forty people here for dinner. P.V. Preobrazhenskii started to drink Lev Nikolaevich's health in white wine, then made a clumsy speech which everyone deliberately ignored. One can hardly *drink* L.N.'s health, since he preaches total abstinence. Then someone proposed a toast to me, and in a sudden, unanimous, noisy show of affection they all raised their glasses to me, which agitated me so much that my heart started to pound. It was a very cheerful dinner, and remained a completely *family* affair, which was just what we had all wanted. L.N. was writing *Resurrection* all morning, and was very pleased with his day's work. 'You know,' he said when I went in to see him, 'he doesn't marry her after all. I finished it today, or rather I decided that, and I know it's right!' And I said: 'But of course he doesn't marry her! I always told you that if he did it would just be *hypocrisy*.'[126]

We received about a hundred telegrams from an enormous variety of people. This afternoon the sun came out and we took all the children, grandchildren and guests out for a walk. Then Muromtseva sang at length, but was unpleasantly over-excited. And then Goldenweiser played, very badly. More guests arrived for supper, but it remained just a simple, good-natured family party.

Prince Ukhtomskii was particularly affable, intelligent and unaffected. He said the young Tsar had greatly liked Lev Nikolaevich's article 'On the Famine', but that when Ukhtomskii asked whether it could be published in the *St Petersburg Gazette*, the Tsar had said: 'No, better not publish it or we'll both get into trouble.'[127]

It is odd that the Tsar's peace proposal should be linked in so many foreigners' minds with the name of Lev Nikolaevich, and that they should attribute it to the influence of his ideas on the Tsar.[128] This simply isn't true. Apart from anything else, it is highly unlikely that the Tsar has ever read or considered any of L.N.'s ideas about war: it is a mere coincidence.

The day finished with singing – chorus and solo songs. We were all very tired, and the food and sleeping arrangements required a great deal of work . . .

August 29 The servants have all been drinking and quarrelling. It is raining. My sons, my grandchildren, Ukhtomskii and a few others are still here. Misha left for Moscow to re-sit an examination.

August 30 I received such a clever charming letter from Sergei Ivanovich this morning, and I showed it to Lev Nikolaevich, who thought the same. He writes that one doesn't have to be a follower of L.N. to be stirred by his works, for his ideas imperceptibly enter one's mind and remain there.[129] Then just an hour after I got his letter Sergei Ivanovich himself arrived. (Almost all the guests had left the day before, along with Sonya and my sons.) This evening, after he had taken a short nap, Sergei Ivanovich played a game of chess with Lev Nikolaevich, then sat down at the piano. And oh, how marvellously he played! Such depth, such intelligence, such seriousness, such experience – it would be impossible to play better. Both L.N. and Mashenka were in ecstasies – and so of course was I. He played Schumann's *Davidsbündlertänze* (I think), Beethoven's Sonata Op. 30, a Chopin mazurka and barcarolle, Rubinstein's '*Près d'un Ruisseau*' and an aria by Arenskii. Lev Nikolaevich said that his performance was superb, quite the last word in music – no one else could possibly match Sergei Ivanovich's playing, he said. The following morning, the 31st, I fell ill with a fever. I looked at the thermometer, and saw that I had a temperature of 38.4. Sergei Ivanovich left that morning, and I took to my bed. Lev Nikolaevich was so touchingly anxious about me. My dear, sweet old man! Who else could ever love me or need me as much as he does? I was moved to tears as I thought of him, and I lay in bed praying that God would prolong his precious life.

I was ill all day, so I couldn't go to Moscow as I had intended, to visit Misha and do my business.

September 1 I am better. It's a lovely warm day and there are masses of bright fragrant flowers in the garden . . . I am full of the joys of life again, and I love people and nature and the sun. I was deeply touched by the love everyone lavished on me, and rejoice in my recovery.

I went out with my camera, and dashed about taking photographs of the park, my grandchildren, L.N. and his sister, the forest, the path to the swimming pool and the charming Yasnaya countryside . . .

This evening I quickly packed my things, made a note of all the errands I had to do and left for Moscow, carrying the bunches of flowers Sasha had given me. L.N. and Sasha took me to Kozlovka in the carriage. I was tired, tearful and overwrought; I bade Lyovochka a tender farewell, then Nurse and I got into the train. That night who should come into our compartment but Seryozha; he had gone back to Yasnaya to talk to his father, and he is now leaving for England to discuss the Dukhobors' emigration scheme, for it seems from our correspondence that their plans are no further advanced, and we don't know how seriously and efficiently Chertkov is dealing with the matter; and there's so little money besides.[130] On the subject of money, Lyovochka discussed his story behind my back with Marx, the editor of *Cornfield*. Marx proposed a legal contract whereby he would have *exclusive* rights to the story, at 1,600 rubles a page. When I heard this I said he should do no such thing, since he had publicly renounced all the rights.[131] L.N. thought that since he was selling it in aid of the Dukhobors it was all right, but I said it was all wrong. So on the very day I was leaving L.N. suddenly changed his mind. Marx has now offered him 500 rubles per page, *without* insisting on exclusive rights, and L.N. appears to have accepted.[132]

September 2 I arrived in Moscow this morning with Nurse. It was raining, the house was dark and gloomy and my soul was oppressed . . . I unpacked, hired a cab and went out shopping, and oh dear, I was so jolted and shaken!

But this afternoon the lights were on, the house was filled with flowers, I had cleaned and tidied everything, and hired a piano. Misha came; he has passed the examination he was re-sitting, and is now going up to the 7th class, but I am sure he is keeping something from me. Things became more lively later on. Sasha Behrs, Danilevskii, Uncle Kostya, Yusha Pomerantsev and Sergei Ivanovich came, and we had a merry evening.

Sergei Ivanovich astonished me by something he said. He told me that when I was at the Maslovs' this summer I had deeply offended him by laughing at his ugly white cycling socks, and saying they made him look like a clown.

September 3 More shopping and business . . . Seryozha was here and has now left for England . . . It keeps on raining. No guests. Misha and I both went to the bath-house.

September 4 I spent the whole day in my dressing-gown going over the bills with the accountant, checking the sales of books and entering figures into ledgers; I didn't even take a walk. But Uncle Kostya came to dinner and prevented me from finishing, which was a nuisance, as it means I probably won't be able to leave for Yasnaya tomorrow, and shall have to pay more calls instead.

This evening the tedious, alien Nakashidze couple came to visit, and it was most annoying for Sergei Ivanovich was here, and thanks to those tedious foreigners and loud-mouthed Dunaev he and I had no chance to talk; we simply exchanged a few words intelligible only to us, and he explained various passages in a Bach aria which had been giving me some trouble. L.N. loves this aria of Bach's and I wanted to learn to play it properly for him. I read my future in the cards today, and drew death on the King of Clubs. I was terrified. I longed suddenly to be with Lyovochka again, to make him happy, not to waste one moment of my life away from him – yet when Sergei Ivanovich left, the thought that I wouldn't be seeing him again for some time made me quite wretched. And torn between these two conflicting emotions, I longed to run off somewhere and take my life. I stood alone in my room in a state of torment . . . Oh, if only one could see into a person's soul at such moments and *understand* what takes place there . . . But gradually suffering passed into prayer, I prayed long and earnestly, summoning up all my best thoughts, and I began to feel better. No letters from home, which makes me sad.

September 5 I went to visit my aunt: Vera Meshcherinova's five-year-old child is dying of dysentery. Vera Severtseva is making her trousseau for her marriage to Istomin (a Molchalin type*). More business and shopping today. Misha visited the Gruzinskiis. Clever, lively Marusya Maklakova came over this afternoon and we both cheerfully jotted down the latest book sales together, finished in a mad rush, and I went off to catch my train – and missed it. I returned home. It was a cold and windy night, and I had great difficulty getting them to open the door. I went straight to bed.

September 6 This morning I corrected one or two mistakes made yesterday in my calculations with the accountant, and left by the fast train. Home was friendly, peaceful and familiar, and I was glad to be back. I force myself to pray constantly, and I rely on God to help me in my weakness.

A lot of Obolenskiis are here – Liza and her three children.

September 7 Lev Nikolaevich is healthy, energetic and apparently calm. I love him very much, I enjoy being with him and would gladly never go to Moscow again. It always excites me, and I am not strong enough for this kind of excitement.

September 11 So many days have passed, and it has all gone splendidly; we've been so cosy and cheerful, although completely idle. Stakhovich always livens us up; all the little girls are ecstatic about him.

Sister Maria Nikolaevna is such friendly, cheerful, sympathetic company – I am so fond of her. The day before yesterday she and L.N. sat together all evening reminiscing about their childhood and it was such fun. Mashenka told us about the trip they had all made to Pirogovo when Lyovochka, then a boy of about 15, decided to run behind the carriage for five *versts* to *impress* everyone; the horses were trotting along but Lyovochka didn't fall behind, and when they stopped the carriage he was gasping so heavily that Mashenka burst into tears.

Another time he wanted to *impress* some young ladies (they were staying

*Molchalin was the hypocritical, obsequious character in Griboedov's play *Woe from Wit*.

in Kazan at the time, in the village of Panovo, their uncle Yushkov's estate), and he threw himself fully clothed into the pond. But he couldn't swim back to the bank, so he tried to touch the bottom, found he was out of his depth, and would have drowned had it not been for some peasant women haymaking in the fields nearby, who saved him with their rakes.

Then there was the time he was locked up as a punishment in the Shcherbatovs' house in Plyushchika Street, and jumped out of a second-floor window. He was twelve years old at the time. A servant standing below saw him, picked him up and put him to bed, where he slept for twenty-four hours.

Yes, he always wants to *impress* and *impress* – he has been like that all his life. Well, he certainly has *impressed* the world, as no one else!

The Obolenskiis have left. L.N. has a touch of influenza, and is feverish at night. Maria Aleksandrovna Schmidt came, and the Tula prison priest.[133] It is damp and windy. Stakhovich keeps bringing us sweets, pears, plums and peaches. I wish he wouldn't, but the young folk love them. I have been working away at my photography – too singlemindedly. I live for my family, but something has been gnawing at my heart – feelings of regret and a wild, painful longing for music.

September 12 Complete chaos at home. The footman has fallen in love with Sasha the dressmaker and is going to marry her; Verochka, a mere baby of eighteen, is going to marry the bailiff on the 18th; the chef is leaving and the cook has been taken off to hospital; Ilya and Nurse are in Moscow. There has never been anything like it. Meanwhile a never-ending stream of guests keep arriving and staying. Today Maslov and Dunaev came too.

This morning L.N. read us *Resurrection*, the story he is currently working on. I had heard it before – he said he had reworked it, but it's still exactly the same. He read it to us three years ago, the summer after Vanechka's death. And then as now I was struck by the beauty of the incidental details and episodes, and the hypocrisy of the novel itself – Nekhlyudov's relationship with the prostitute in jail and the author's own attitude to her. It's just sentimentality, toying with strained, unnatural feelings which don't really exist.[134]

September 13 Rain all day and guests – an Englishman, a Mr Right, I believe, and a stupid old maid called Ivanova who believes in spiritualism. These guests are a terrible burden imposed on our family, and especially on me. Only one thing interests me about them, the fact that they have been staying in England with Chertkov and the rest of the exiled Russian community. They found them in a terribly bad way, and told us they couldn't possibly stay there much longer, such are the emotional tensions between them and the general hardships of their life. L.N. has been at pains to keep this from me, but I always sensed it . . .

Maslov has left; we went for a walk in the rain, which pours dismally without ceasing. I was just about to play the piano, when I was startled by a frightful noise at the window; it was Lev Nikolaevich, summoning me to come and hear him read the end of his story. I was sorry to have to abandon the piano and the beautiful Bach aria I have been studying and learning to appreciate, but I went all the same.

Music has such a strange effect on me; even when I play myself it suddenly makes everything clear, fills me with peaceful joy, and enables me to see all life's worries in a new light, calmly and lucidly.

Not at all the effect L.N.'s story has on me. Everything in it is disturbing and worrying, everything induces discord . . . And it torments me that L.N., an old man of seventy, should describe with such extraordinary gusto, like a gastronome relishing some particularly delicious piece of food, the scenes of adultery between the chambermaid and the officer. I know he is describing here his own liaison with his sister's chambermaid in Pirogovo, for he told me about it himself in great detail. I have since seen that Gasha, now an old woman of almost seventy, for he has pointed her out to me, to my deep despair and disgust. It torments me too that Nekhlyudov the hero should be described in terms of his transformation from a state of degradation to a state of grace, for I see Lev Nikolaevich himself in this, and this is the way he sees himself too – when in fact he describes all these moral transformations very well in books, but never actually achieves them in his life. While he was telling everyone about these beautiful feelings of his, he was moved to tears by his own words, yet he went on as he always had, with his fondness for sweet food, his bicycle, horse-riding and physical love . . .

All in all, as I thought the first time, this story contains some brilliant descriptions and details, and a deeply, bitterly hypocritical state of affairs between hero and heroine.

The story put me in such a distressed frame of mind that I suddenly decided that I would leave for Moscow, that I couldn't possibly *love* this work of my husband's, that we had less and less in common . . . He noticed my mood, and accused me of never liking the things he liked and was working on. I replied that I loved his artistic work, that I had been in ecstasies over *Father Sergei*, was fascinated by *Hadji Murat*, highly valued *Master and Man*, and cried every time I read *Childhood* – but was repelled by *Resurrection*.

'Yes but you don't like me working with the Dukhobors either,' he said reproachfully.

'I simply can find no pity in my heart for people who refuse military service, force the poorest peasants to enter the army in their place, and then demand millions of rubles to enable them to leave Russia,' I replied.

I helped the *starving* in 1891, 1892 and this year too – I felt for them, worked for them and gave them money. No, if one is going to help give money to anyone it should be to our own humble peasants who are dying of hunger, not to those arrogant revolutionary Dukhobors.

'It makes me very sad that we don't agree on everything,' said L.N.

Me too! I have worried myself sick about this breach between us. But Lev Nikolaevich has dedicated his *entire* life to people and causes that are alien to me, whereas I have given my *entire* life to my family. And I cannot accept, in either my heart or my head, that after renouncing all authorial rights and publishing this in the newspaper, it should now be necessary for some reason to sell this story for a huge sum of money to Marx's *Cornfield*, and to give this money not to his grandsons, who don't even get any white bread to eat, nor to his impoverished children, but to the Dukhobors, complete strangers, whom I simply cannot imagine loving more than my own children. But this means of course that the whole world will now know about Tolstoy's part in helping the Dukhobors, and it will be in all the newspapers and history-books. Meanwhile his children and grandchildren have to eat black bread!

September 15 Yesterday I felt so sad that L.N. and I had been on such bad terms the day before, and he listened so meekly to my criticisms of his story and the way it was being sold, that a sudden compassionate impulse made me go down to him in his study and tell him how sorry I was for all the sharp things I'd said, and how much I longed for us to be reunited as *friends*. We both wept, and both felt that despite all the things that separated us *externally*, we had none the less been bound together these past thirty-six years by *love*, and that was more precious than anything.

Today I packed my bags and tomorrow I shall leave for Moscow, for I am very concerned about Misha. I walked through the forest for three hours, found some little saffron milk-caps in the fir plantation, picked flowers and was enchanted by the beauties of nature, the sun and the sky. The weather has brightened up.

September 17 (Moscow) I arrived in Moscow yesterday evening.

I went out first thing to buy provisions, then paid some calls, and this evening some young lads came round to see Misha, while I entertained Natasha Dehn, Miss Welsh, Goldenweiser, Dunaev and his wife, the Maklakovs, Uncle Kostya and Sergei Ivanovich. According to Yusha Pomerantsev, he had practised for three hours earlier today in order to play for me this evening. Marusya begged him to, and at first he refused, then he played Schumann's *Davidsbündlertänze*. But the boys were sitting beside him playing cards, their shouting irritated him and he made this quite plain. 'I'll come and play for you alone some time,' he said to me. 'That will be much more pleasant.'

I thanked him, and am now looking forward to this pleasure.

September 18 Shopping and errands all day. Elena Pavlovna Raevskaya came this evening.

September 19 I went to three banks today, paid in Ilya's money and closed the account I had opened three years ago in Vanechka's name. The little darling won't need money or worldly goods now! Oh, when shall I too pass over into that blessed state!

A letter from Mashenka, who says that Lyovochka was sad on my name-day.[135] This was because he knew Sergei Ivanovich would be playing for me, and was jealous again. But what could be more pure and innocent than the aesthetic pleasure of listening to marvellous music?

I myself played until 3 a.m. today. Misha has left for Yasnaya Polyana. I talked with Sergeenko for three hours nonstop, and now regret wasting my breath.

September 20 This morning I went to Petrovsko-Razumovskii to see Manya, and was enchanted by Seryozha's son – also called Seryozha. What an adorable little boy, so sensitive, clever and cheerful. I am a stranger to him, yet he took to me as if he had known and loved me all his life – and he is only a year old! When he hugged his mother he straightaway put his little arms round my neck too, so as not to offend me. When he gave his nurse a bite of apple, he immediately pushed it at me too for a bite. He was just like Vanechka, who never forgot the servants or footmen when he was offering his sweets around, and was always so generous to others. He loved and hugged everyone equally too.

When I got home I learnt that Sergei Ivanovich had called, and I was sorry I had missed him. Goldenweiser came this evening and played for three hours.

September 22 Ilya and Andryusha arrived to prepare me to receive Olga Dieterichs, to whom Andryusha has just proposed.[136]

I hired a new governess for Sasha today, an elderly lady, the mother of three daughters. I have been busy with practical matters. I played the piano for about three hours.

I made a grave mistake and I personally delivered some books to Sergei Ivanovich. I very much regret this now, but I have been quite beside myself recently, lying awake until four in the morning, haunted by the stench of corpses, the misery of loneliness and the vanity of life, and desperately searching for something to grasp hold of, something to save me from this depression. I wrote a letter to Tanya – and wept. I talked to Andryusha – and wept. I talked to Misha about his low spirits and tried to cheer him up – and again I felt so depressed. I longed for some sympathy, some advice, a friendly word, so I put the books into Sergei Ivanovich's hands and told him all about Andryusha's marriage. And he discussed the subject with so much calm wisdom that I immediately felt calmer.

Andryusha and I stayed up talking until gone two in the morning.

September 23 My wedding anniversary. Today I have been married to Lev Nikolaevich for thirty-six years – and we are apart.

It saddens me that we are not closer. I have made so many attempts to achieve some spiritual intimacy with him! There is a strong bond between us – I only wish it was based on something more congenial. But I am not complaining; it is good that he's so concerned about me, guards me so jealously and is so afraid of losing me. With no cause. Whomever else I might love, there is no one in the whole world I could *compare* with my husband. Throughout my life he has occupied far too great a place in my heart.

September 27 I am staying in Moscow. Uncle Kostya came as well as Marusya, Dyakov, Meshcherskii – and Sergei Ivanovich. He and I strolled about the garden together, and I asked his advice about various matters. What a dear friend he is! He responded so seriously and thoughtfully to all my doubts and questions, gave me his advice and comforted me. After lunch he played a Beethoven sonata and the andante from a Tchaikovsky concerto. He played formidably well, especially the last work. His visit, his advice, his sympathy and his music gave me strength to live, gave courage to my spirit and peace to my soul.

This afternoon I attended Vera Severtseva's wedding and experienced the sin of vanity. They all put me in the best place and sat me at the head of the table, and everyone praised my outfit and my youthful appearance. Vera was married in the church in the governor's residence, and both Grand Duke Sergei and Grand Duchess Elizaveta Fyodorovna were there. Vera was unaffected, serious and touching. She wants to reassure everyone that she will be happy with Istomin.

September 28 (Yasnaya Polyana) I have come home. I turned off the highway at Yasenki and drove towards the church. It was such a dismal journey in the dark through the melting snow, along the bad road, and I was weighed down with worries about Misha, whom I had left in such a despondent state. But then it was a treat to get back to the brightly lit house at Yasnaya, filled with my dear ones who love me. I went straight in to Lyovochka's study, and we fell into each other's arms as we used to when we were young, and kissed one another over and over again. And L.N.'s eyes shone with joy and love – it's a long time since I have seen him so happy. Varya Nagornova was there to my great delight, and Mashenka still hadn't returned to her convent, and Misha Stakhovich was visiting again.

He had brought Lev Nikolaevich back from Oryol, where he had gone to inspect the prison for his story.[137] We had such a friendly, cheerful family evening together, working, reading and chatting.

October 3 Yesterday evening I played symphonies by Beethoven and Schubert with the two Levs, father and son. I took a photograph of my little grandson Lev. There was a letter from Misha. He has been carousing and is in the doldrums, and now wants to come to Yasnaya to collect his wits. I have said he can, but will it help?

Tanya has left for Moscow with Vera Kuzminskaya to give Sukhotin her reply. I think of her constantly, suffer for her and fear for her. I wonder what this reply says. L.N. is buried in his work; he keeps putting more finishing touches to *Resurrection*, and has sent several chapters abroad to be translated. Today he was talking to a wandering man who was thrown into jail for four months after a strike, and was then deported. L.N. was mesmerised by his stories.

October 5 We have had news of Tanya. She has apparently refused Sukhotin, but they were both crying; Nurse writes that Misha told her she was pining and weeping.

Misha has arrived very depressed; he has been carousing in Moscow, and has returned to his family in the country to come to his senses. We had an interesting French couple here called M. and Mme de Gercy. They are extreme socialists and atheists, and have instigated several strikes in Paris. They are both passionate people, very fond of one another and very French, with their lively, temperamental natures, their capacity to live entirely for some cause, something beyond themselves.[138]

We also had a visit from one of the *Cornfield* editors, who wanted to negotiate a contract for L.N.'s *Resurrection*. L.N. is asking for 1,000 rubles per quire, without the editor having exclusive rights, but they haven't agreed to this so far. I find all these negotiations over his works so abhorrent – *especially* after he published his renunciation of the rights in all the newspapers – that I can barely restrain my indignation or remain on good terms with him. He is back to his old ways – writing fiction and wanting a lot of money for it. Only previously this money would have been given quite lawfully to his family, whereas now some fellow-thinkers called Dukhobors are dreamed up and all the money goes to them and all the newspapers write about it. It would be a great deal more natural to take pity on the Vlas in one's own village, whose cow and children are dying of hunger. Today even our French guests shed a tear over them and gave them a ruble.

October 6 This morning I had a talk with Misha about his recent disorderly life, and he said how remorseful he felt and how much he longed to do better and lead a more disciplined life. What I found so touching was that he had come to be with his family in the country, and sought salvation in nature – and he seems to have found it too.

Pasternak the artist came; L.N. invited him here as he wants him to do some illustrations for *Resurrection* for a French journal – called *Illustration*, I believe. What a lively, clever, educated man this Pasternak is.[139]

L.N. had yet another visit from the publisher of the *Cornfield*, and was trying to negotiate the sale of *Resurrection* with him. They discussed terms, wrote and re-wrote the contract, but still came to no conclusion. Lev Nikolaevich has asked for 20,000 rubles for the story, but it won't amount to as much as twenty quires and he hasn't got anything else ready yet, so they have delayed writing the conditions for another week.[140]

While all these transactions were going on downstairs I was sitting upstairs copying out this same *Resurrection* as I wanted to help Masha out with some of the copying – L.N. always gives her far too much. L.N. came upstairs several times to tell me how the discussion was going, but I said nothing. In the end, however, I spoke my mind.

When I was just a little girl, I remember L.N. coming to tell us that he had lost 1,000 rubles at Chinese billiards, adding that he had sold *The Cossacks* in advance to Katkov and had already been paid for it. And I wept bitterly.

It has been the same throughout my marriage whenever they have started negotiating over L.N.'s works; it hurts me so much that they should bargain for a human soul which is so close to me, and put a value in rubles and kopecks on all those brilliant works he has created. I feel exactly the same now.

Selling his *books* is not so hard. There is a large public there after all, who gladly buy their favourite author – or don't buy him. But in the case of journals, the editor is interested only in acquiring as much money as he possibly can by exploiting a well-loved author.

A raging blizzard all day, and a heavy fall of snow. This afternoon L.N. read us a short story by Anton Chekhov called 'Love', the most wonderfully subtle description of the most commonplace love affair between a man and a young married woman. He becomes a friend of the family – husband, children, servants. Meanwhile the love between them grows, without words, without a liaison, and is expressed only at the moment when they leave one another for good, when they fall into each others' arms sobbing and kissing – and part.[141]

How much silent passion, how many tragic tortured feelings of love pass between decent people and are *never* expressed. And these emotions are the most powerful of all!

October 17 Sasha and I have been in Moscow since Sunday evening, the 11th. She is studying hard and behaving well at present. Long may this continue. It's very hard having to keep an eye on Misha all the time, and it's a constant strain and worry lest he does something wrong, yet I feel he relies on me to worry about him. I feel both responsible and inadequate, and my soul is weary of it. My life is constantly busy: first selling the oats according to the plan, then tidying the house, then publishing business, and work: I am also copying Lev Nikolaevich's diaries, which is one more torment for my soul.

For the past two days I have lived for music, once again possessed, intoxicated and enchanted by it.

Yesterday morning was the rehearsal and that evening Uncle Kostya and the Maklakovs lured me out to a delightful concert of sacred music set to the prayer 'I believe in one God'.

This morning I went to another rehearsal with Uncle Kostya. The Interlude to Taneev's new opera *Oresteia* is really quite extraordinarily fine.

The news from home is superficially good; what interests and concerns me is Tanya's and Lyovochka's inner lives. My husband keeps his distance from me because he has sold *Resurrection* to the *Cornfield* for 12,000 in aid of the Dukhobors. I disapprove of this transaction and he knows it, just as he disapproves of my music. How sad that we have grown so apart! Which of us is to blame?

October 20 My son Seryozha has come, he wants to buy an estate. I'm so happy for him, and so fond of him. He played some Grieg delightfully. I had a nice letter from L.N.[142] and was going to write back, but I had a headache and was shivering with nervous tension. Misha is better now; he and I had a talk about inner conflicts and the struggle for self-perfection, and I reproached him for not aspiring to this. 'How do you know?' he said, and there were tears in his voice. He is not lost yet.

Sergeenko came yesterday, and again today with his little girl. He invited me out for a walk, he invited me to the theatre . . . As though I'd go with *him*! Such a dull, unsympathetic character.

I am in the throes of a real autumn depression. I am struggling to get the better of it, but feel I am about to perish one way or another. The anguish in my heart has reached a critical point . . .

I had a visit the other day from Princess Tserteleva the singer, born Lavrovskaya. She has just lost her only son at the age of 22, and we had a long talk about her inconsolable grief. How much grief there is in the world! I did my best to comfort her, but the doors in my own heart are closed too, and when I beat against the walls I only hurt myself.

A warm, grey, damp, cloudy day.

October 22 Something ripens, then falls. My depression came to a head – and yesterday it fell away. I wrote Lev Nikolaevich a bad letter,[143] and today I had one from Lyova, who writes that his papa has a headache and is exhausted by all this business with the Dukhobors and his work on *Resurrection*.[144] Oh, why did he involve himself with these Dukhobors! It's so unnatural. We have quite enough to worry about within our own family; our children need a father who takes an interest in them, instead of searching the world for sectarians. How true that Russian saying is: 'Mother Sokhya pines for the world, while at home they sit and starve.'* And L.N. doesn't even 'pine' either.

Today I was examining a photograph of him, looking at his thin old arms which I have kissed so often and which have caressed me so many times, and I felt so sad – it's an *old man's* caresses I long for now, not a lover's.

Uncle Kostya, Marusya and Sergei Ivanovich visited yesterday evening and we had a splendid time. We read some poems of Tyutchev's and Sergei Ivanovich was in ecstasies over them. He was in such a tender mood – he seemed quite inspired, and he had the idea of setting the words of one of these poems to music. We all made various unsuccessful suggestions, then Marusya opened up the book at random, at the verse: 'Do not trouble me with your just reproaches' and Sergei Ivanovich immediately started composing, wrote a song to these words and played it to us. Such a clever man.

Pomerantsev was telling us about a soldier on the Arbat square who did not salute his drunken officer, and this officer slashed him to death with his sabre. What hideous brutality!

October 23 I played the piano for three hours this afternoon and copied out Lev Nikolaevich's diary for 4 hours. The copy is for Yasnaya, and the original is for the Rumyantsev Museum. Discussions about L.N. Seryozha says: 'Give Papa the copyright.' I say: 'Why should I? To line the pockets of wealthy publishers? It's downright dishonest.[145]

October 26 I travelled to Yasnaya this morning via Kozlovka. Rain and slush, everything grey, I was chilled and soaked. At home everyone was asleep. I went straight in to see L.N. The room was dark and he jumped out of bed and kissed me.

In the mornings (L.N.) was working hard on his *Resurrection*; he says that for the past few days he couldn't work for thinking of me, and that on the morning of my arrival he dreamt about me. Every so often he comes in to see me, smiles and kisses me. Tanya and Vera are both very sweet and cheerful. Tanya is her old lively, playful, laughing self, so lovable and cheerful. To tease Dunechka they took everything out of the larder and hid it in the cupboard, so that when she got back from Tula she was convinced that everything had been stolen and was just about to go to the fortune-teller. Having made her thoroughly worried, they then opened the

*An untranslatable pun on 'Sokhya' and 'sokhne' – 'pine'.

cupboard, roaring with laughter, and showed her all the bread and jam and other things inside. Then they brought a herring from Lyova's wing, and roaring with laughter again, began to eat it. The general atmosphere at Yasnaya is good, and I have felt healthy, happy and carefree.

October 27 L.N. went to Ovsyannikovo to see M.A. Schmidt, and I walked along the path to the swimming pool with Dora, then strolled around the park on my own. Then I issued various instructions. Frosty and windy, cheerless blustery weather. We dined with Lyova. This evening we read an extremely vulgar story by Sergeenko called 'Daisy', and after being thoroughly shocked by various unbelievably tasteless passages, we had a good laugh.[146] L.N., who was playing chess with Lyova, was also laughing. We slept badly last night, as it was so cold. L.N. has a chill. We are being friendly and straightforward with one another. I have asked him a lot of questions about *Resurrection* and have approved of the ending and a number of other things. It's much less *hypocritical* now.

I am copying out L.N.'s diaries, and don't like him as he was then. Unashamed debauchery; a hatred of people; vanity.

October 28 I bade a tender farewell this morning to L.N., Tanya, Vera and Lyova. It was frosty and windy, and Adrian the coachman regaled me all the way to Yasenki with a hideous story about the murder of four people at Kosaya (Rudakova) Hill. Our neighbourhood has been ruined by that Belgian factory. It was a tedious journey; I read Maksimov's book on hard-labour convicts, all about their lives, the convict trains and so on.[147] A depressing picture!

October 30 (Moscow) Turmoil: Seryozha has arrived with Tsurikov; Sulerzhitskii has arrived from the Caucasus, where he saw the Dukhobors, and has been talking most interestingly about them; Andryusha has left for St Petersburg. Misha is frightfully lazy and apathetic and evidently has no desire to work. Seryozha had a good fatherly talk with him today and urged him to pull himself together and get down to some work. Marusya Maklakova came this afternoon. I feel my life is empty – all my days are taken up with pressing business. I read *The Influence of Music on Man and Animals*.

October 31 This morning I played the piano a little, then took a drive, and this evening Sasha and I went to a chamber music recital at which they did the Tchaikovsky trio. Delightful, but that fellow Kvast played badly.

I received affectionate letters from Masha and Lev Nikolaevich.[148] I had an interesting discussion with Tsurikov about married couples whose beliefs are not in every way identical, and we came to the conclusion that it was quite possible for them to live happily together even so.

Seryozha and Tsurikov have left. Seryozha is planning to visit the Caucasus with Sulerzhitskii to help the Dukhobors to leave Russia for Canada.

I had a brief and unexpected meeting with Sergei Ivanovich at the concert. We barely greeted one another, and he rather discourteously went on talking to some old man he was with.

November 6 I have only two interests now: my morbid anxiety about Misha, and making the arrangements for an evening in honour of *Tolstoy*. L.N. has sent me an excerpt from a beautifully conceived short story called 'History of a Mother'. This tells of a mother of eight children, a beautiful, tender, considerate woman, who at the end of her life is all on her own and goes to live near a convent, with the bitter, dramatic, unacknowledged awareness that her entire life has been wasted on her children, and that not only do they give her no happiness, but they too are unhappy.

The evening is being organised by the Society for Popular Entertainment, under the presidency of Kirpichnikov, whose assistant Pogozheva came to see me yesterday. Tomorrow I am taking this excerpt to the censors;[149] Sergei Ivanovich has been asked to play, and he will be asked again. He said to me: 'I would gladly spend the time and effort if it would give Lev Nikolaevich pleasure. But *who* will I be playing for, and what can one play apart from the Kreutzer Sonata?' He and Lavrovskaya are coming on Sunday evening to console me with music, and I am terribly happy.

I am sewing, cutting out clothes and mending underwear; I made myself a black silk skirt and altered something of Sasha's, then played the piano for a long time – but I hadn't touched it for two days. Today I received the children's money and payed the dentist for Andryusha's treatment, bought a cloak for Sasha, bought some new plants and repotted my old ones. Safonova visited, and Sulerzhitskii, who has left for Yasnaya, and Aleksei Mitrofanovich, and Pogozheva, and clever M.A. Sabashnikova, whose company I enjoyed best of all.

My health is better and my soul is calmer.

November 8 I am starting on another book of diaries, the fifth. I wonder if I'll live to finish the whole of this thick book? Is it possible under these circumstances that I will? I did no writing yesterday. I went to rather a dull symphony concert, and Marusya, Sergei Ivanovich and I walked home together under the starry sky. Now is the time of year when falling stars simply pour out of the sky. Marusya and I both wanted to look at them through binoculars; then Sergei Ivanovich happened to join us. But the stars were glimmering motionlessly in the sky, and only the firmament seemed to be swaying. When I got home I stood in the garden and gazed at the sky through binoculars for the first time in my life, amazed by the extraordinary spectacle of the innumerable stars.

This morning I drove off to visit my brother and collect some theatre tickets. Then I started making preparations for the evening. Sergei Ivanovich came, and Lavrovskaya, and my brother and his wife, and various other people, and I had a whole delightful evening of music. Lavrovskaya sang songs by Sergei Ivanovich, some of which were charming, especially 'My restless heart is beating . . . '[150] So much passion and power, such richness of content. Then Sergei Ivanovich played a Beethoven sonata.

The finale was performed so exquisitely, so originally, that it was quite unsurpassable. Yes, someone with this sort of musical gift has enormous power!

At the beginning of our gathering I read them all the excerpt Lev Nikolaevich had sent me for his evening. It's a lovely artistic piece of writing, and it gave everyone great pleasure. They all said how well I read it too, which pleased me.

What a lovely warm morning it was! As I drove down the boulevards the sun was so bright, the grass so green, the sky so blue. A complete illusion of spring! But only an illusion; in a day or so nature will be dead, and everything will be covered in snow, like that poem 'Last Love', which Tyutchev wrote in his old age. This last love blazes up like a bright sun, with all the vigour of youth, and *must* die with the snows of grey hair, toothlessness, wrinkles, impotence and so on. No, I don't welcome you, old age!

It was extremely unpleasant at the symphony concert yesterday: I asked Safonov to release Grzimali (the first violin) so he could play the Kreutzer Sonata at our Tolstoy evening, and he seized both my hands and pressed them to his breast, saying: 'For you I would do anything in the world,' but then that Grzimali could be released only from his lessons, at which I indignantly withdrew my hands, realising only too well that Safonov simply wanted to display to all those present his (completely non-existent) intimacy with 'Countess Tolstaya', wife of the famous author.

From now on I shall avoid him at all costs. I visited Pogozheva; she organises popular schools, entertainments for the people, literacy classes, tea-rooms and so on. A good and useful woman.

November 9 I remember I once used to say that when a person reached a certain age he stood between two roads and had to decide whether to reach upwards, towards moral perfection, or to sink into weakness and moral deterioration. And I feel that I am now taking this last path, and it frightens and saddens me. I want to be entertained, I want to dress up, yet there's no satisfaction in that, my soul is not happy and I yearn constantly for happiness and fulfilment.

I received a letter from my husband, a dear, kind letter,[151] and I felt so guilty for some reason – although I have nothing to feel guilty about, thank God, but my frivolity.

November 10 Misha was very cross and rude at dinner today, and grumbled that there was no fresh bread. This afternoon I went to the theatre with him for a production of A.K. Tolstoy's *Tsar Fyodor Ioannovich.*[152] It was well acted, although caricatured, and they overdid the desire for realism with a lot of shouting and bustling about on stage. Sergei Ivanovich was there. I was able to have a long talk with him this evening, and this time I felt more convinced than ever of how completely lifeless, inflexible and passionless he was. This is not to vilify him, merely to state that he really could with some reason be called 'just a fat musician' – as L.N. has frequently called him in a jealous rage. His superficial kindness conceals a total indifference to the world, and to everything but sounds and music, composing and listening to it.

November 11 Misha came home late today. I was sitting up sewing, waiting for him. He was so touching and seemed so genuinely contrite, kissing me and begging me not to cry (for I could not restrain my pent-up tears by then) that for the time being I felt consoled.

But I myself am bad too. I fear my mania for spending money, I fear my foolish love of dressing up – those are *my* sins, which I cannot control.

November 13 I had S.A. Filosofova, E.P. Raevskaya, Uncle Kostya and Goldenweiser to dinner yesterday. We read Khomyakov's article about L.N.'s preface to the works of Maupassant, and there was a reference there to his article *On Art.*[153] Khomyakov was evidently disconcerted by the word 'Catholicism', which replaced 'the Church' in order to satisfy the censors, and this prevented him from following the general sense of Lev Nikolaevich's article.

I am writing this later: Marusya, Sasha, Misha and I left on the 13th for Yasnaya Polyana. We enjoyed the journey and laughed all the way. We arrived at Kozlovka Zaseka on the mail train at 11 at night, and drove in the moonlight to Yasnaya through drizzle, white fog and frightful slush. But it was nice in the country and even nicer to be at Yasnaya. We found them all well and friendly. Masha appears to be all right. The doctors say the baby couldn't possibly have moved yet, but that it will soon; so either she *imagined* the movement or simply lied to herself and us. She is very cheerful and full of energy, and so pale, delicate and pretty.

L.N. was very tender and passionate with me but I could not respond.

November 14 I had a long talk with my husband Lyovochka about Misha, about me and about L.N.'s work. He says he hasn't been in such a creative mood since writing *War and Peace*, and is very pleased with his work on *Resurrection*. He rode over to Yasenki and is full of energy; his body is fit and his spirits are high, and all because he is doing the sort of *artistic* work to which he is temperamentally suited.

November 15 I spent the whole day outside. The rain has eased, and it's terribly muddy, but quiet and warm, and I strolled to the fir plantation with Vera Kuzminskaya; it was enchantingly lovely among the fresh green saplings. Then this evening, i.e. after dinner, we all took a long walk through the forest; we came out at Chepyzh, then back into the firs, around the plantation and home by the swimming pool path. It was dark when we got back, and we had tea with Lyova and admired our grandson, a delightful little boy. Later on we read Chekhov's 'Sakhalin';[154] What ghastly descriptions of physical punishment! Masha burst into tears, and I felt as though my heart were breaking. Once again we all ended the day on friendly, affectionate terms.

November 16 I woke up this morning in tears. I dreaded returning to Moscow and having to leave L.N. We were deeply, genuinely touched to see one another this time, and these past few days we were such good friends and in such harmony with one another – even loving.

I was sorry too to leave Tanya, whom I love so much, and I was sorry to leave calm, beautiful, familiar Yasnaya Polyana. L.N. was astonished to see me crying, caressed me and shed some tears too, promising to join me here in Moscow on December 1. I would dearly love this, but it would be wicked to make him come here, to tear him away from his urgent work, from his daughters who are such a help to him, and from Aleksandr Petrovich, who does so much copying for him. I shall try not to be selfish and shall let L.N. stay in Yasnaya. But I think he too wants to come here – he probably needs to be in the city to collect material for his story.

Sasha, Marusya and I left by the fast train; at first we were rather despondent, but then we cheered up.

Misha was there to meet us in Moscow, but he immediately got ready to go out somewhere. I was very distressed. And I was even more distressed when he came home at three in the morning and I was again obliged to give him a scolding, and was made to feel that it had all been for nothing, that all my sacrifices – living in Moscow, admonishing him, begging him to work, exhorting him to lead a more moral life – had been in vain, and that he was simply *refusing* to pay any attention.

So the moment I arrived I was waiting up for him, darning linen and grieving.

November 17 This morning Marusya, Ivan and I planted some little birches and limes which we had brought from Yasnaya, some seventy trees in all. Then we pruned the acacias, cut off all the dead wood, swept the paths and cleared a place for a skating-rink. It is warm and still, and it isn't raining; the sun peered out for a moment today and the birds are twittering. It's lovely in the garden, better than if it didn't exist.

November 18 Misha didn't return until three a.m. again; I waited up listening for him, then couldn't sleep all night for worrying about him. This morning I went to see the director of the lycée,[155] and asked him to take him on as a full boarder. '*Nous jouons gros jeu*,'* he replied, meaning that Misha might well go off for good. He looked very crestfallen when he eventually returned, said I was right about everything, but that he simply forgets all about my anxiety when he is sitting up all night with his comrades. This evening he suddenly presented me with three pears.

Unpleasant problems with the copied excerpt.[156]

Sergeenko is doing his utmost to get it out of me for his biography of L.N.,[157] but I am saying nothing.

The news of the day is that I had a letter from Lev Nikolaevich[158] – Vera Tolstaya brought it. A tender letter, full of love. But all my *tenderness* was gone – it's too painful to sustain. Just go forward, and reach the end as quickly as possible. Life has *nothing* more to offer. Falling leaves, old age – it's better to end it all.

November 19 Pasternak brought good news from Yasnaya this morning and a kind letter from L.N.[159] But he cannot write and is lethargic. I wonder if my visit was bad for him? I stayed at home all day. I played the piano for about three hours, then wrote three letters – to Lev Nikolaevich,[160] my brother Styopa and Andryusha. I did a lot of sewing and altered the sleeves on Sasha's fur jacket. Misha is in a good mood – he got another 5 for Greek, and 5 for religious studies. He visited the Baranovs. Sasha is also very sweet. I have set my children on the right path for a little while, and I feel easier in my mind, as though I had accomplished some task. I copied a little of L.N.'s diaries. I am in a calm, everyday state of mind.

November 22 If my diary could express the groans in my soul, I would just groan and groan. Misha is ruined. His moments of remorse are short-lived. The day before yesterday he again disappeared all night with the gipsies and didn't return until seven in the morning; yesterday he stayed at home, and today he went off again, and where he is or who he is with, I have no way of finding out. He has a new set of companions every day, wild, rough strangers.

I paid some dull essential visits, played and wrote. Marusya and Sasha went to the Maslovs'; I didn't go although I knew Sergei Ivanovich was there. I told them to drive and not walk, but they walked back and brought

*'We are taking a big risk.'

Sergei Ivanovich with them. I was furious with Marusya. Then Sergei Ivanovich played us his quartet and a Chopin nocturne. He quelled my rage, he was so affectionate to everyone, so cheerful and good-natured. But even he couldn't quell my anxieties about Misha. I had good reason to cry when I left Yasnaya Polyana. How I dreaded leaving L.N., how badly I needed him to help me, to defend me against life and against myself . . . In the eyes of the world he can do no wrong for he is a *great writer*, but that doesn't make it any easier for me: he is no husband to me, for he doesn't help me, and more important, he is no father to his growing children, and that is a terrible misfortune for their mother.

November 24 I went to greet Ermolova, the Davydovs and Dunaeva on their name-day, then visited Natasha Dehn who has just borne a son and has been ill since the birth. At Ermolova's my vanity was flattered both by the warm welcome they all gave me, by the beauty of the flowers and the dresses, and by the elegant manners of the worldly life and society. I had a talk with Grand Duchess Elizaveta Fyodorovna, a lovely, sweet-tempered, affable woman.

November 25 I dragged myself round Moscow all day in the rain. Such depression, wandering senselessly, nervously, aimlessly through the mud – oh the depression is insufferable! This afternoon I lay down for a sleep. I got up, Sasha came in. 'Are you ill, Maman?' I said no. She threw herself into my arms and kissed me. 'Oh, if only you knew how pink and pretty you are when you've been asleep.' Am I really *pretty*? Or is it her love that sees beauty in her darling Maman? This evening we went to the theatre to see *Mozart and Salieri*, and *Orpheus*.[161] Sergei Ivanovich was with us, as well as Marusya, Sasha, Goldenweiser, and Butyonev. Various other acquaintances were in the boxes. It started off cheerfully and interestingly enough, but I was soon bored again by the atrocious singing in *Orpheus*, and barely managed to sit through it.

November 27 Letters from home, from Lev Nikolaevich (who still plans to come to Moscow on December 1),[162] and from Tanya. Mine to her was lost – what a nuisance! I had written to urge L.N. not to come to Moscow.[163] I can't bear to think of him suffering in the city: he cannot endure the visitors, the noise, the crowded streets, the lack of leisure, being away from the country and his daughters, who have been such a help to him. Besides, it would be hard for me to curtail *my* interests – the children's education, my music, my friends, my visits, rare as they are, to concerts and theatres – and that will annoy him. And then my failing eyesight and frequent bloodrushes now make it quite impossible for me to go on copying his endlessly revised writings as I used to, and he will be angry and sad about this too, but then in Yasnaya he has his daughter, Aleksandr

Petrovich and Kolya Obolenskii to write for him. I shall go there to dissuade him from coming, and shall bring him here myself if he still insists.

Pogozheva came this morning and told me they have been given permission to hold the Tolstoy evening, but they are not to announce that it is being held in *honour* of Tolstoy, there is to be no reading of material about him, they are to read only from his own writings, and various other gross and stupid stipulations.

S.I. Taneev arrived this afternoon while Masha, Misha and I were having tea together.

How pleased I was to see him! I love him best when he comes like this, just to see me. He had composed the most beautiful impressive work today for two choirs, set to words by Tyutchev, and had come to play and sing it through for me.[164] Then he played the andante from his own symphony. We sat chatting quietly, and read an article of music criticism. One always has such a peaceful, sincere, interesting time with him. We get on so well – it is a great shame that L.N.'s jealousy weighs so heavily on this pure, simple friendship with Sergei Ivanovich.

November 28 At a symphony concert today I learnt of the death of the Safonovs' eldest daughter Nastya, at the age of seventeen, and was horrified by the news.

Goldenweiser was playing Rachmaninov's 'Trio' and the marvellous Mozart clarinet quintet. I saw many friends, including Sergei Ivanovich.

An open letter from Lev Nikolaevich announcing his arrival on the 1st.[165] Sasha and I were wildly happy, and danced around the room.

November 29 Visited the Safonovs this morning. One daughter of theirs lies dead, and another, Sasha, is dangerously ill. The four doctors there have no idea what it is. It seems something like peritonitis. I took Doctor Flerov with me. The father has just returned from St Petersburg, the mother is in a state of dull, dry-eyed despair. A terrible picture! Sasha and Marusya went to an exhibition. I played for a long time this evening, while the two girls, especially Marusya, capered about in the drawing-room in wildly boisterous spirits. At one a.m. I left for Yasnaya.

November 30 (Yasnaya Polyana) Tanya has lost her voice and has a slight fever. Still nothing definite about Masha, but she seems calm and well. L.N. rode to Pirogovo (35 *versts*) the day before yesterday, and rode back the following day, which is why he's worn out and lethargic now. Having promised to come to Moscow on December 1, he now seems to be trying to wriggle out of it. And I was so counting on the pleasure of taking him back to Moscow and living with him there. I had brought some dates, spirits and bran bread with me for the journey, I had told them to prepare a room for him in Moscow, and had ordered the dinner and the fruit, and I was going to pack his things myself and organise his journey to Moscow as inconspicuously as possible. By evening it was decided that he wasn't going; I cried, my head was aching and I took to my bed. I wasn't upset by his not wanting to come to Moscow – that I quite understood; in fact it was I who suggested that he shouldn't come before Christmas – what hurt me was that first he writes: 'We have just received your letter to Tanya' (in which I had suggested that he shouldn't come). 'I am definitely coming on the 1st by express train, and am looking forward to being with you once more.' And after this letter, which aroused all my suppressed feelings of joy and excitement at the prospect of seeing him and being with him again, he now suddenly says he isn't coming after all.

December 1 I am in Moscow again. I didn't sleep all night because of the uncertainty. 'I'm coming to Moscow on the first,' L.N. wrote to me. Today is the 1st and I prepare to catch the fast train to Moscow, thinking to myself: he can't not be packing and coming with me. My heart was pounding and I was in a fever, and this morning he got up and went downstairs without saying a word to me. I got up at about 10 to discover that L.N. wasn't packing and wasn't leaving. Choking back the tears, I get dressed and order the carriage to be harnessed – he doesn't say a word. Then Maria Aleksandrovna Schmidt, Tanya and L.N. all start clamouring – why am I leaving? What do they mean – why? I had already arranged to go, the horses have been sent, and the children and grandchildren are expecting me in Moscow. I am suffocated by uncontrollable sobs. I pick up my bags, order the carriage to catch up with me and start walking, for I don't want to upset them by letting them see me in this state, and I don't want to give Lev Nikolaevich the pleasure of achieving his goal year after year and seeing me so unhappy when he refuses to live with me in Moscow. But this is impossible, for it's his cruelty that is driving me to despair. Then I see him in his sheepskin coat driving towards me in the carriage: 'Wait! Don't go!' he shouts. We return home. He reads me a lecture in a hateful tone of voice. I am choking back the sobs. We sat together for half an hour, while I suffered the most unspeakable pain and struggled with my despair. Tanya came in and said: 'I understand how difficult it is for you.' Eventually I said goodbye to them all, asked them to forgive me and left. I shall never forget that journey to Yasenki as long as I live. What a terrible wind there was! I was doubled up all the way, sobbing so hard that I thought my head would split open. How could they let me go like this! Only one thing prevented me from lying down under the train, the thought that then I wouldn't be buried next to Vanechka, and that is my *idée fixe*. In the train the other passengers all stared at me weeping – then I dozed off. Not a bite of food had passed my lips all day. I arrived home to a cheerless welcome from my children and grandchildren, and wept again. I had a telegram from L.N.: 'I'll come the day after Sonya arrives.'[166]

December 2 I had a letter from Lev Nikolaevich this afternoon;[167] he asks me to forgive his apparently unintentional cruelty to me, the misunderstandings, his tiredness and the various other reasons why he couldn't come and why he tormented me so. Then he himself arrived . . . I have neuralgia in my right temple, all my insides are aching, I didn't sleep all night, and I am completely cold and numb, I don't feel a thing, no joy, no anger, no love, no energy for life, nothing. I just want to cry and cry – for my lost health and freedom, for my friends, since if I do manage to see them now it's simply not the same as if I were alone and they belonged entirely to me. One day of suffering has utterly destroyed me!

I shall try to do *my duty*. I shall look after L.N., copy for him, satisfy his physical love – for I don't believe in any other sort now – and there's an end to it! And what then?!!! Patience, faith and kind friends.

December 4 I was ill in bed all yesterday. My organism could not endure the unpleasantness, and all my internal organs collapsed: my liver was enlarged, my stomach was upset, I felt sick and my temple ached with neuralgia. So that's one day out of my life.

This morning I went to the funeral of Sasha Safonova. That poor little fifteen-year-old girl, so talented and passionate, died in the most terrible agony within three days of her sister, who was only seventeen. Their mother was a tragic sight. She has six other children, but these two were her eldest.

The house is cheerless and depressing; L.N. is ill-tempered, I no longer have any life of my own, with the children, or with *my* friends, interests and music; and as for my life with L.N., so far it's nothing but dull copying and a grim atmosphere that weighs upon everyone in the house.

December 5 Still the same depression, which even the grandchildren are unable to lift. Misha has fallen ill with influenza, although everything terrifies me after the Safonova girls, and I no longer trust the doctors for there were so many of them there. A Dukhobor has come from Seryozha to ask L.N. to advise them whether they should go to Kansas instead of Canada, as a man has just been sent from there to invite them over. L.N. urged them not to change their plans but to go to Canada as arranged.[168]

There was a most unpleasant discussion; Sonya (my daughter-in-law) wanted to hear some good music. So I suggested inviting Lavrovskaya, Goldenweiser and Taneev to play for us and organising a musical evening at home. Sonya and I then shyly told L.N. that we wanted some music. He looked furious. 'Well in that case I'm going out of the house,' he says. 'God forbid that you should be driven out of the house,' I say. 'We'd better not have any music in that case.' 'No, that's even worse – that would be as though I was stopping you.' Well, it soon led to an argument, and a very nasty one, after which, of course, there was no point in thinking about music.

December 6 Sonya, Sasha, my grandchildren and I all went to the theatre to see Rimsky-Korsakov's *May Night*. The music lacks any consistency of character – first it's lyricism, then it's recitatives, then it's a Russian – or rather Little-Russian – *trepak*; nothing connects to anything else, and there are very few nice melodies. There is none of the interest of modern music – the sort of complex harmonies one finds in Taneev for example – and there is none of the sheer *delight* of a wealth of melodies. So all in all I found it dull. But my head is empty anyway – my nerves still haven't recovered from the emotional shock.

December 10 Relations with L.N. have improved, but I don't believe they are either pure or lasting. I am copying the latest chapters of *Resurrection*. My eyes ache, I have no free time, yet still copy.

I went to the bank with Andryusha and handed him all his money and documents. I also gave him a fur coat and 2,000 rubles, and ordered a dozen pieces of silver for his bride. And after everything I'd done for him and all my presents he not only didn't say thank you, he actually looked disgruntled.

December 12 Copied all day. Went to a concert of chamber music this evening. The Schumann quartet was charming. Blindness – how frightful.

December 13 I invited Lavrovskaya to sing, Taneev to play and some close friends to listen. Raevskaya, the Kolokoltsevs, Uncle Kostya, my brother and his wife, the Maslovs and various others came. Sergei Ivanovich played delightfully, and also accompanied. Lavrovskaya sang a lot, and beautifully too. It would have all been so pleasant and cheerful if one didn't always feel that Lev Nikolaevich was angrily condemning every entertainment I organised.

December 14 I copied for Lev Nikolaevich for 7 hours without stirring from my chair; then I answered his letters. My head was spinning. Nikolai Gué came. Lev Nikolaevich is gloomy and sullen. He has been complaining of an ache in the small of his back. Misha is a trial: he disappears off every evening to dances, stays out all night, sleeps till three in the afternoon and hasn't been to school.

December 15 Spent all day with the accountant going over bills and checking book sales. At five I went with Sasha to the christening of the

Dehn boy, who already has a thick shock of hair. Then visitors, and I went to the bath-house. This evening L.N. read us a translation of Jerome K. Jerome – no good. It's thawing heavily.

December 16 Spent the day going over the bills with the accountant again. I have put all my practical affairs in excellent order, answered all my letters and brought the account books up to date. Varya Nargornova came and I was delighted to see her. Nikolai Gué is here too. What a good, intelligent fellow he is – and how wretchedly unlucky. L.N. read us some more of the Jerome K. Jerome – I haven't seen him roar with laughter like that for a long time.

December 19 We have just returned from an evening at the Korsh Theatre which was supposedly in honour of the seventy-year-old Tolstoy. And what a wretchedly unsuccessful evening it was! Bad singing, bad reading, bad music and some appalling tableaux vivants utterly lacking in truth, beauty, artistry or anything else. Mikhailovskii received shattering ovations for some reason, then they began shouting for Tolstoy and sent him a telegram . . . It was all so vulgar, so trite – one had no sense of this as a genuine cry from the people's heart. L.N. himself had earlier today set off alone for Yasnaya Polyana on the mail train. He worked all morning, ate some porridge and drank some coffee at one, then left, asking that no one but Gué should accompany him. He called in on the way at the Myasnitskaya art school, at Trubetskoi's request, so that the master bronze-worker there from Italy could make some alterations to his bust from the life.[169]

I went to a symphony concert rehearsal this morning, and this evening I listened again to the whole concert, apart from the Borodin symphony. I saw Sergei Ivanovich; there is so much simple trust and friendship between us – the very best sort of relations between people.

Ilyusha and Andryusha have arrived. Andryusha is terribly anxious: this summer in the Caucasus he frivolously proposed to a certain Princess Gureli, then wrote her a letter of rejection. The princess shot herself, the parents sprang to her defence and Andryusha now lives in fear of being murdered or having to fight a duel. It's been nothing but sorrow for them! Misha left for Oryol, and from there will visit Ilyusha, then Yasnaya.

The princess has since died.*[170]

December 20 I discovered that those taking part in yesterday's so-called Tolstoy evening, Ilya included, all went off to the Hermitage to dine, i.e. get drunk – and this *in honour of Tolstoy*! It's absolutely disgraceful!

I went to the conservatoire with Sasha today for a concert in memory of

*This sentence was added later.

Rubinstein; they didn't play many good pieces, although the aria from Gluck's *Iphigenia* is good and dramatic. Sasha, A.I., Sergei Ivanovich and I all walked home together; we had a marvellous time chatting and laughing away. A light wet snow was falling, everything was white, the moon peered through the clouds . . . how good it was! I fell, but it didn't hurt . . .

Numerous distressing discussions at home about this Princess Gureli who has shot herself; Andryusha proposed to her when he was in the Caucasus, then refused her, and now fears the Caucasian parents' revenge.

December 23 I left for Yasnaya Polyana with Sasha and Sonechka, and Ilya came too. We were very cramped in the train, and Ilya kept playing the fool, telling jokes and making everyone laugh. Tanya and Lyova met us at Yasenki. General irritation over our luggage, which was left on the train; Lyova has a difficult character, both for himself and for those around him, and he doesn't realise this. We drove through water; it was thawing and there was almost no snow.

Masha was at home, looking thin, weak and heartbreakingly sad. Kolya looks sad too when he is with her. Tanya is trying to keep her spirits up, but she still has not forgotten her own unhappy love affair and she too is unhappy.

L.N. is also miserable because he is unwell. He has a pain in the pit of his stomach and a slight fever. I arrived full of energy and joy at the prospect of living quietly with my family in Yasnaya, free of emotional turmoil and the distractions of music, and no longer on my own, and I was delighted at the prospect of being with Lev Nikolaevich again – but everyone was so dejected that I soon felt utterly wretched myself.

December 24 (Yasnaya Polyana) I got up early, massaged L.N.'s back and stomach again and gave him his Ems water; again my closeness disturbed him. Terrible weather – damp and windy, even though there are 3 degrees of frost. L.N. is more cheerful and was able to do some work again today, but he hasn't written anything recently and has grown terribly weak and lethargic. Whenever I am away he is unable to write, is prone to illnesses, sleeps badly and deteriorates.

Today he is like another person, and when I said this to him he smiled and agreed. I am happy to be here, but not all my family are in good spirits, and I fear that *my* energy alone isn't enough to go round and to compensate for the generally sour mood here. I went to 'the other house' to see Lyova and Dora and my darling adorable six-month-old grandson Levushka. I took a walk round the garden in a prayerful mood, filled with all my old sentimental feelings about Yasnaya and memories of my youth and recent past.

I have been in weak spirits lately, unable to feel either joy or grief. My soul has grown sensitive, filled with compassion for everything and everyone, feelings of guilt, and an incapacity for protest, patience, calmness, or, more importantly, any religious feelings. My soul is too burdened with other things.

Tanya, Lyova, Sasha and Sonya Kolokoltseva went skating today. The whole pond has frozen over, although it hasn't snowed, and I'm sorry I didn't bring my skates with me from Moscow.

December 25, Christmas (Yasnaya Polyana) Everyone has been in a holiday mood today: we made presents and unpacked all the good things we had brought from Moscow. The moment I enjoyed best was my walk through the woods. It was especially lovely in the young fir plantation – three degrees of frost, silence, and brief moments when the sun peered out after disappearing all autumn. Everything was covered with fresh pure snow that had fallen during the night, the young green fir saplings were also lightly covered in snow, across the horizon stretched the broad black band of the old Zaseka forest, frozen for the winter, and everything was quiet, still and severe. It was deeply enjoyable; nature and art are the best things in life. How well Sergei Ivanovich understands this. With one's family and in the company of others there is so much unnecessary aggravation, so much pain and spite . . .

We had a nice, cheerful family dinner. M.A. Schmidt came. At five o'clock Dora and Lyova entertained us around the Christmas tree with tea and refreshments. Poor Dora was so tired, but she loved the whole thing – she is only nineteen, virtually a little girl still, and she *needs* this holiday. My little grandson Levushka was startled and amazed. A splendid, adorable little baby.

But by eight o'clock everyone was in low spirits again, for L.N. had a temperature of 38 °; he has been running a temperature for the past few evenings, and earlier too, but it was only 37.7 before, whereas this evening it was much higher. So everyone felt depressed.

December 26 L.N. was feverish all night. He was shrieking, groaning and tossing around and I didn't get a wink of sleep. Dunyashka says: 'The others are all so sweet, not a bit like you.' It would indeed be hard to find a more impatient, selfish invalid. And the worst of it is that he is so stubborn. He wouldn't take his rhubarb yesterday but took it at 11 today. This means he cannot take his quinine for the fever now, on a full stomach, but must wait another twenty-four hours – all because of his stubbornness and his unwillingness to listen to me and take his laxative at the proper time. Oh, how bored and weary I am of putting all my energy into *persuading, convincing* and getting angry with him, with the sole purpose of saving and helping a cross, grumbling, stubborn man for whom I have sacrificed my entire life and killed every personal desire, even the simple need for peace, leisure, reading and music – not to mention the fact that I have never travelled anywhere, neither abroad nor within Russia.

Some Tula working man came here with an extraordinary picture by a peasant icon-painter. It is a pencil drawing, an *arshin* and a half wide.* Lev Nikolaevich is sitting in the middle, to his left is a school and some children, beyond them is an angel, above them is Christ in the clouds and angels, then further off are various wise men – Socrates, Confucius, Buddha and so on. On the right is a church with a gallows and some hanged men in front of it. In the foreground are some bishops, priests and gentlemen-in-waiting, and beyond them in the background are some soldiers on foot and on horseback. Then there are various national types reading books, and in the foreground for some reason there is a Turk in a turban reading a huge book. L.N. is not strictly true to life but his general appearance is. He is sitting cross-legged.

Appalling stories about the Yasnaya peasants: one brother has stolen from another, a widow has killed her illegitimate child, a father pushed his little son through a narrow crack into a store-room and told him to steal things and hand them out to him, the windows in our library have been smashed and some children have made off with our books. It is both sad and infuriating. Oh, the power of darkness!

There is a light frost. It is quiet and calm – if only it weren't for people and their sins . . . How I have grown to love quietness, quiet people, and quiet friendships with them!

I am reading a wonderful book about Buddhism entitled *The Soul of a People.*†[171] What beautiful truths there are in Buddhism. It is as though one knew them already, but to see them written down and the laconic way they are expressed is a delight to the soul.

I just wrote that I loved *quietness*, then remembered the following words underlined in this book:' . . . the greatest good for your heart is to learn that beyond all this turmoil and fret is the great peace.'†

A letter from Seryozha with a wonderful description of the Dukhobors' departure from Batumi with Sulerzhitskii. 2,000 people left and Seryozha too has now left for Canada; he sent us a telegram with the 2,000 Dukhobors.[172] I worry about him, but his is a good cause, noble, interesting and just. This government is utterly senseless – fancy deporting these marvellous folk from the outlands of Russia! They are beautiful people with a highly developed moral sense, who neither swear nor sin. According to Seryozha, there was something truly terrible and triumphant about their departure. They sang hymns, the steamer cast off – and who knows what awaits this population of seven thousand, setting off on a twenty-five day journey for places unknown, without knowing the language and without money . . . What astonishing fortitude. Is it all a question of faith? I mean religious faith?

*Forty-two inches. †In English in the original.

I went for a long, long walk; the whole of nature was utterly silent and still. There was a light frost and very little snow, so it was possible to walk all through the woods, not just in the fields. So beautiful!

We had guests here this evening – Zosya and Pavlik Stakhovich and S.N. Glebov. Lev Nikolaevich is better and everyone is more cheerful now.

December 27 I took a walk this morning, then sat with my grandson Levushka and copied a little of L.N.'s diaries. Tanya, Sasha, Sonya Kolokoltseva and I left at five for Grinevka to visit Ilya. Misha was there looking thin and somewhat restless and confused. It's nice and friendly with Sonya and Ilya. The children were all asleep, apart from Annochka.

December 28 This morning we all decorated the Christmas tree and gave one another presents. My three grandchildren are such healthy, fair-haired youngsters – they're a joy to behold. But one's grandchildren are not the same as one's children. Their lives are just repetitions of the children's, without the simple love, worries and *dreams*, and the search for resemblances to oneself and one's beloved husband. One doesn't dream about one's children's future – it's enough that they exist.

We went for a long walk; the fresh snow which had fallen that night on the boundless fields gleamed in the bright sun, and it was all so silent, pure and beautiful. I walked off a long way on my own, thinking of the people and things I love. My soul too is pure, peaceful and happy.

This evening there were guests, a magnificent Christmas tree (I had brought everything from Moscow), neighbours, servants and peasants, singing, dancing, and mummers, with a rough and ready performance of *Tsar Maximilian and his Unruly Son Adolf*. Sasha and Annochka dressed up and danced around in masks. Sasha is so fat and clumsy, she's a sorry sight. What is nice at Ilya's is that they keep open house for *everyone* to come and enjoy themselves. They had laid in quantities of food, so the guests could eat and drink all day long, and had covered the floor of the office with straw and fur jackets, so people could just lie down and sleep. It was all very hospitable, friendly and chaotic, and they live in grand style, but I couldn't live like that.

December 29 A heavenly day; the trees and fields were all covered in a thick hoar-frost, everything was white, and sky and earth were fused into one vast kingdom of whiteness. I took a long walk on my own, and the children went tobogganing on the hill. The only genuine, serious interest in Ilya's life is horses and dogs, and that is very sad. We left at six o'clock, taking my granddaughter Annochka with us. It was a fearsome journey from Yasenki to Yasnaya; I was not used to this country road in winter; we got lost on the way from Grinevka to the station too, and ended up at the house again. All is well at Yasnaya. L.N. is healthy and passionate.

December 30 A blizzard all day. Poor little Masha is so pale, thin and quiet; she looks so fragile that my heart went out to her and I was filled with tenderness for her.

Bulygin was bawling to Kolechka Gué that they ought to send their children to Switzerland to be educated; they have both fathered illegitimate children whom they have not baptised, and they are both forty now, and don't know what to do with them.

December 31 The last day of the year. What will the New Year bring! Masha collapsed this morning. We are waiting in anguish for her either to miscarry or to deliver a dead baby. It is now gone nine p.m.; the midwife is here and we are waiting for Doctor Rudnyov. The house is silent, and everyone is in a state of agonising suspense.

At five minutes to midnight Masha was prematurely delivered of a four-month son.

Then everyone cheered up and the whole family calmly gathered together to welcome in the new year. Goodbye old year, which brought me so much grief – although a few joys too. And thanks to those that caused them.

· 1899 ·

February – University of St Petersburg convulsed by student riots and demonstrations, which spread to Latvia and Poland. All universities in Russia closed. Students expelled and drafted into army. Law Society taken over by government (a blow to liberals). Finnish constitution abrogated.

January 8 – Andrei Tolstoy marries Olga Dieterichs (the sister of Chertkov's wife.) March 13 – first part of Resurrection *published in* The Cornfield, *and the money sent to the Dukhobors. November 14 – Tanya Tolstaya marries Mikhail Sukhotin. End of the year – Tolstoy finishes* Resurrection.

January 1 A disappointing start to the new year. We got up late, and I drove Sasha, Sonya Kolokoltseva and my grandchildren Misha and Annochka to the woods in the big sledge with my camera. It was lovely in the woods, and the children were such fun. We laughed and photographed; the shaft of the sledge broke, but strong Sasha repaired it. We got back for dinner. This afternoon I had tea with Dora and Lyova and lit up the Christmas tree again. Back in our house the children and both sets of servants dressed up and danced, first to dance tunes on the piano, then to two concertinas. I went off to sit with Masha, developed photographs and made a peasant shirt for Lev Nikolaevich.

We had assembled for supper. Afterwards we all played *rublik*, and everyone joined in, even Lev Nikolaevich. This was all very jolly, but my soul longs passionately for something else, something *different* – and it's a sad, painful feeling.

Thawing again – two degrees above freezing and windy, with water and puddles everywhere.

We had a visit from Volkhonskii (who is married to Zvegintseva); Masha is recovering, thank God. Lev Nikolaevich's work is going badly. He always ascribes every emotional state – his own, mine and everyone else's – to physical causes.

January 4 More guests this evening – the three Cherkasskiis, the two Volkhonskiis and the Boldyryovs – Mary is utterly delightful. Accordions, dancing, some unsuccessful choral singing . . . Dreadful! For someone of my age and with my emotional needs it's a real ordeal. One yearns for serious relationships, serious music – anything but this dreadful accordion music which I have always loathed. The appalling Princess Cherkasskaya is an ageing sinner who doesn't want to grow old. She and I woke up Masha, who then had a hysterical attack. It was extremely regrettable and annoying, and it was partly my fault for making such a lot of noise with that old harridan.

Lev Nikolaevich has again been in a good mood for work.

January 5 During the day I worked on my photography and wrote a long letter to Seryozha,[1] whom I miss. He must be sailing the Atlantic Ocean by now.

January 6 I left with Sonya Kolokoltseva for Moscow. The house is nice and quiet. I have dear Nurse and my familiar solitude, with my own beloved inner world, and memories of quiet friendly talks in the evenings.

January 7 I did shopping and business in Moscow all day, and left tonight for Tula. This evening I read *The Origins of Life* by Menshikov, on the meaning of children's lives.[2]

January 8 I spent the morning in Tula alone in my room in the Petersburg Hotel. It was so cheerless, and I felt so depressed and upset about Andryusha's wedding.[3] I read a French pamphlet about Auguste Comte, which was sent to Lev Nikolaevich and written as a letter to Emile Zola. It preached peace, brotherhood and sociology.

Then my sons arrived – poor thin Lyova, plump jolly Ilya, anxious Andryusha and wild Misha, incoherent, noisy and selfish, who hadn't received his uniform and was searching for a tail-coat to wear.

Ilya and I blessed Andryusha there in the hotel room. He was as if in a dream, deeply affected, yet bewildered as to why he was getting married or what would happen. I still can't make Olga out. A wedding is always a frightening, mysterious, moving occasion. I kept wanting to cry.

We dined at the Kuhns', got a little drunk, then took them to the station; Lev Nikolaevich rode there wearing his fur jacket. The public surrounded us: Tolstoy and a wedding; they were all fascinated. We accompanied the couple as far as Yasenki, then Tanya and I travelled on by cab. There was a slight blizzard, a little snow, and a moon. The house was gloomy and Masha had a headache. But dear Dora, darling skinny Lyova, lethargic Kolya, bold Marusya and Kolechka Gué were well. The Dieterichs' parents came back with us to Yasnaya. Lev Nikolaevich has grown to love his fame. He loved the sight of those people at the station, I could see he did. He is well, but is being rather cold.

January 9 (Yasnaya Polyana) Spent the whole day packing and tidying up at Yasnaya Polyana. I sat with Levushka in the wing – I love the little mite dearly. It's warm, raining and thawing. The snow has almost gone. Lev Nikolaevich's stomach aches and I massaged it vigorously this evening. Work on *Resurrection* is progressing. Masha is better and tried to get up.

January 10 We arrived in Moscow on the fast train today. We had a very cramped journey, Lev Nikolaevich, Sasha, Tanya, Marusya Maklakova and I. Dear Mary Boldyryova (née Cherkasskaya) also sat in our compartment. Relations with Lev Nikolaevich are very friendly and straightforward – how I love it when there are no anxieties on my side and no ulterior motives and fault-finding on his. If only it were always like this! He seemed willing, even happy, to go to Moscow.

I read Sudermann's comedy *A Quiet Corner*[4] on the train. I haven't been feeling well. I am worn out by all the packing, unpacking, travelling, tidying the house and worrying about everything – indeed life has really been very hectic and tiring recently.

January 11 I am quite poorly. I have influenza, my chest is burning and my head is aching. Lev Nikolaevich still has a stomach-ache. We are still just as friendly and comfortable together.

January 12 Tanya's name-day. A lot of tedious guests arrived at midday with a great deal of chocolate and chatter, and an endless number of boys – schoolfriends of Misha's, etc. I feel even worse. I was expecting Sergei Ivanovich all day, but he didn't come; I have been told he is in Klin working on a production of Tchaikovksy's ballet *The Sleeping Beauty* with the composer's brother. This afternoon Masha Kolokoltseva, Liza Obolenskaya and the pianist Igumnov came, just back from Tiflis. He played us a Chopin tarantella and nocturne, Rubinstein's 'Ballade', the andante from a

Schubert sonata and something by Mendelssohn – but I wouldn't have recognised his playing, it was so lifeless. Either that or I was so ill that I couldn't listen properly.

I have seen almost nothing of Lev Nikolaevich all day. He wrote a lot of letters and was busy with his own writing.[5] He still complains of a stomach-ache and I gave him another massage.

January 13 Misha arrived; he was telling me that a crowd of drunken students, magistrates, old men and all sorts of other people had gathered yesterday at the Hermitage and Yar's night clubs to celebrate St Tatiana's Day (the university holiday), and 200 people had danced the *trepak* together. They ought to be ashamed of themselves! I spent half the day in bed.

January 14 Lev Nikolaevich is well; he writes all morning, drinks tea and is quite calm. Aleksandr Petrovich has appeared and is copying for him again. I am delighted, for it would have been too much for me at present.

We had a splendid evening: Lev Nikolaevich read us two Chekhov stories, 'Darling' and one whose name I have forgotten, about a suicide, more of a sketch really.[6] Igumnov (the pianist) came and played more Chopin – a barcarolle, a ballade, a nocturne and a mazurka. He played superbly, and he did that lovely barcarolle best of all.

January 15 M.I. Tchaikovsky, two Englishwomen,[7] Nakashidze, Goldenweiser, Pomerantsev and Taneev came this evening. Taneev and Lev Nikolaevich had a long talk together, I don't know what about.[8] Then Lev Nikolaevich read Chekhov's 'Darling' again: he read it beautifully and made us all laugh. I didn't manage to talk to Sergei Ivanovich, I never do when there are a lot of people here. Lev Nikolaevich was polite to him, thank God.

January 16 A telegram from Sulerzhitskii saying that he has arrived safely in Canada with the Dukhobors, and that they like the country and have been very well received there. Our Seryozha ought to be there in six days' time. I am waiting impatiently for his telegram, I think constantly about him and even tell his fortune.

I went with Modest Tchaikovsky to a rehearsal of Tchaikovsky's ballet *The Sleeping Beauty*. Lovely music, but I am too old for ballet now, and I soon grew bored and left.

January 17 Lev Nikolaevich had a visit from Myasoedov[9] and the inspector of the Butyrki prison fortress, who gave him a lot of technical information about prison affairs, the prisoners' lives and so on for *Resurrection*.[10]

January 18 Yesterday I just wrote down the date – and there's nothing to write about today either. This evening we had guests – the Boldyryovs, Goldenweiser, Nakashidze and an interesting man called B.N. Chicherin. He read us his article about two old men from his district of the Khlyst sect* who had been wrongfully arrested, and at whose trial he alone of all the witnesses was disqualified, although this was quite unlawful, as one of the old men had worked as a forester on his estate. The masseur came at 8 this evening to see Lev Nikolaevich, who seemed rather embarrassed.

The prison inspector called again to give him more information about jails, deportations and so on.

January 19 Business all morning: deposited some money into Ilya's account and paid some bills. Lev Nikolaevich is in good spirits and is talking to the prison inspector. My head aches.

January 20 I didn't sleep all night. We had some wonderful news this morning – a telegram from Seryozha in Canada saying he has arrived safely with the Dukhobors; three died on board, one was born, and there was an outbreak of smallpox, which means they are all in quarantine.

I went to the annual art exhibition:[11] Trubetskoi's sculptures were very fine, I was outraged by all the prizes awarded to decadent paintings. Some of the landscapes are lovely, and two portraits of women – Morozova and Muromtseva – are good. There are some delightful wild flower studies too.

Lev Nikolaevich has been entertaining some dark ones – Nikiforov, Kuteleva, a midwife who did famine relief work, a certain Zonov, Ushakov . . .

January 21 I went to the Belgian art show.[12] It seemed cold, nothing captured the imagination, there was a lack of feeling, colour and passion. I have grown to love landscapes. And I love foreign exhibitions because you feel you enter into the country of the paintings and see their clothes, homes, customs, work, games – not to mention the scenery. Today I was struck by a painting of *Walzen Castle* standing on a cliff.

Taneev came this evening and played. This is now my greatest joy. He played marvellously – a Bach fugue, a Chopin polonaise, then a Beethoven rondo, two Chopin waltzes and an impromptu.

Lev Nikolaevich went out for a long ride before dinner today, and I grew anxious for he was so late back. The masseur came for the third time this evening and is massaging the small of his back.

January 22 I paid seven calls today, and this evening endless guests arrived. I am utterly exhausted. I called on Sergei Ivanovich to thank him

*A sect practising self-flagellation.

for giving us such pleasure yesterday and to enquire about his fingers, which he hurt badly when he was playing for us yesterday.

The Annenkovs, taciturn Rostovtsev, dear Davydov, pathetic Boratynskaya, Sukhotin the student and Butyonev-*père*, but my temple aches insufferably, which makes me depressed and listless, and my soul is melancholy.

A kind letter from Andryusha, to which Olga added a few lines.[13] At the moment they are quietly happy. Who knows what the future holds!

I have no contact with Lev Nikolaevich all day. He writes all morning, then takes a walk, this afternoon he went off to see Misha at the lycée, then there is this great wall of guests permanently separating us, which is very depressing. Misha is bored, he cannot sleep at the lycée and I fear he will not last long there.

January 23 I spent a quiet day on my own. And I found time for everything – read a little of *The Greek Conception of Death and Immortality*, did some work, played the piano for about four hours, sat with Lev Nikolaevich, even did a little copying from the revised proofs for him. Not a soul here all evening – heavenly! Tanya took Sasha to a dancing party and Misha went too – Misha Mamonov that is, such a nice intelligent boy; I love children, I never really grew up and joined the adults, and children are so grateful, so forgiving, they observe God's world with such eager, inquisitive eyes. Sonya Mamonova is staying with us; her fine upbringing and lovely character make her very pleasant company.

January 24 10 degrees of frost, fine. This morning, I paid some unsuccessful calls, and this evening a crowd of guests came – the Naryshkins, Princess Golitsyna, Count Sollogub, Stakhovich, Olsufiev, Ermolova, the boys, and so on – 30 people in all. I was in bed with neuralgia when Tanya got me up and called me to our guests. It seemed quite fortuitous, but in fact she and Sonya Mamonova had apparently arranged this party between them. Lev Nikolaevich was there throughout, reading Chekhov's 'Darling' to the ladies, and chatting animatedly to everyone. Then Goldenweiser played a Mozart sonata and some things by Chopin. We went to bed late, then Misha called me out to tell me he didn't know how much longer he could go on living at the school boarding-house. I'm sure he'll leave.

January 25 I stayed in all day. But I couldn't do a thing because of all the visitors. The Olsufiev brothers came, read *Resurrection* and drank tea. Then Stakhovich came to dinner. He seems rather gloomy. Tanya went to see Chekhov's *The Seagull* with Trepova.[14]

I chatted to the Tolstoy girls, and played the piano, during the day on my own, and this afternoon first with Sasha then with Tanya on the harmonium. Chicherin and Strakhov were here. Lev Nikolaevich had another massage and Doctor Usov called in to see him. His back is better, but L.N. is now very anxious to add some passages from the Gospels as epigraphs to his *Resurrection*, and he asked me to write to Marx, editor of the *Cornfield*, about it.[15]

Wind, frost, fires on the street. Sitting at the dinner table today I scolded myself for being unable to be completely happy. There was a heated discussion. Lev Nikolaevich said it was important to have principles and to strive for spiritual perfection, but that one's actions might nevertheless be inadequate, the result of human passions. I said that if despite all these principles it was still possible to sin and succumb morally, then what could I stake my faith on in future? It was better to have no principles at all, I said, just an inner sense which would lead one along the right path. Lev Nikolaevich said that the desire for spiritual perfection automatically led one along the right path. And I said that while he was perfecting himself a man could sin twenty times or more. No, I said, better to *know* what is right and what is wrong, and not to sin, rather than to expect some sort of perfection. Only the very wicked need this long path, for someone who isn't especially wicked it's much easier simply not to sin in the first place.

It is almost two a.m. Lev Nikolaevich has just sent for Maklakov for some reason,[16] and has ordered some food to be heated up for him. What a lot of trouble he makes for others, without even realising it.

January 26 I was copying the revised proofs of *Resurrection* for Lev Nikolaevich, and was repelled by the calculated cynicism of his description of the Orthodox service. For instance: 'The priest extended to the people the gilt image of the cross on which Jesus Christ was executed – *instead of the gallows*.' The sacrament he calls '*kvass* soup in a cup'. It's scurrilous and cynical, a crude insult to those who believe in it, and I hate it. I read a little today, and copied out a little of his diaries. There were no guests – what a blessing!

January 29 I don't remember the past two days: I paid visits with Tanya, played a little, pined and fretted for my absent children. I cut out and sewed today and am very tired. I thought about my son Seryozha and remembered him composing and playing for me his song which begins: 'We met once again after a long parting . . . ', and ends: ' . . . we pressed each other's cold hands, and we wept and wept . . . '[17] I know he was expressing his own fears, his own emotional state at the time. He is *awkward* but so profound in his feelings, and in all his other faculties too. He just hasn't been able to *make the best* of his good qualities. We women – and especially his wife – love to act like characters out of a *novel*, even at times with our husbands; we love sentimental strolls, we love to walk off somewhere far away, we love simply to be emotionally cherished. But one doesn't expect this from the Tolstoys. So often one feels a sudden outburst of tenderness for one's husband – but if, God forbid, it is expressed he recoils with such disgust that one feels mortified and ashamed of one's feelings. And he only cherishes one when his passions are aroused – which, alas, is not the same!

This morning I went to a rehearsal and found happiness in Lavrovskaya's singing of Bach. She sings so beautifully, and I was in just the right mood for her serious, slightly sombre voice in that empty hall, with nothing and no one to break my silent solitude.

This evening Lev Nikolaevich went to the bath-house with the Dunaevs, and I called on the Maslovs and sat for a while with Varvara Ivanovna and Yulia Afanasievna. These two are my favourites in the family, compassionate, kind and intelligent.

January 30 I sewed all morning, first a sash for the coachman, then a silk skirt for myself on the machine. Lev Nikolaevich had a visit from old Soldatenkov, who brought him 5,000 silver rubles for the Dukhobors.[18] I greatly dislike this business of asking rich people for money – considering that L.N. actually wrote an article denouncing the *evils* of *money* and refusing to have anything to do with it.[19] It doesn't bother him that while he now curses music, just to be contrary, Modest Tchaikovsky told me that he once wrote a letter to Pyotr Ilich Tchaikovsky saying that he considered music the supreme art, and that he gave it *first* place in the world of art.[20]

I often think to myself: Lev Nikolaevich should be *ashamed* of living a life of such contradictions. Everything with him is *ideological*, everything is for a purpose – the main purpose being to *describe* everything, as he did in that wonderful article of his last summer about the famine.[21] And maybe he's right: to each his own path and his own cause.

I visited the lycée the other day and talked with the director. This splendid man, Georgievskii, treats Misha better than his own father does. Misha is in good spirits; he has left the boarding-house again to be a day-boy, but has started to work. 12 degrees of frost, bright and sunny; the trees in the garden are covered in hoar-frost.

This evening I dropped Misha Mamonov off at the lycée, and rather reluctantly went on to a symphony concert, but I enjoyed the experience far more than I had anticipated. This was the five hundredth symphony concert, and they played the same programme as at the inaugural concert, when the conductor was N. Rubinstein.[22] I was in raptures over Beethoven's Fourth Symphony and the Bach cantata. And I realised with joy that beyond all earthly considerations and relations there is music, so virginal and pure, and the spiritual pleasure that it gives me.

January 31 Guests all morning. Savva Morozov came here with his wife;

Lev Nikolaevich, much to my disapproval, continues to ask rich merchants for money for the Dukhobors.[23]

February 1 Lev Nikolaevich complains of pains in the small of his back – he rode over to see Rusanov again, against the doctor's orders, and hurt his already painful organ. Yunge came to dinner, and Uncle Kostya. Dunaev, Almazov and the student Strumenskii came this evening and there were discussions again: about disarmament and whether the Tsar was sincere in his talk of peace, about Marxism, about music, and I wasn't bored, for they talked very interestingly and without acrimony. E.F. Yunge is a clever, talented woman, interested in everything.

February 2 I went skating during the day with Sasha, Marusya and some friends. I felt so happy and agile on my skates! We dined without Lev Nikolaevich – he is always late these days, and usually eats alone. Afterwards I sat down to some sewing and asked him if he would like to keep me company, but he said he was going off to his room to read. This made me terribly sad for some reason, and I burst into tears. No one is as lonely as I am: I'm alone in the morning, alone for dinner, alone in the evening. So I drag myself out to a concert, just to meet people who will talk to me seriously and sympathetically.

I don't know if L.N. was aware of my hurt feelings, but he soon came in to see me, by which time Annenkova was sitting with me.

A magnificent recital by the Czechs. I am organising a trio here on Sunday and have just invited the musicians.[24]

February 3 I was pacing about aimlessly, with an anxious heart. Then at dinner what joy, a letter from Seryozha in Canada. There was an outbreak of smallpox on the boat, and Seryozha and the Dukhobors were put down on a small island and quarantined for nineteen days. About himself he writes almost nothing, but he is evidently exhausted by his role as interpreter, and worn out by sea-sickness, anxiety and so on.

There was a special symphony concert this evening in honour of Paderewski, the famous and utterly loathsome pianist. Sergei Ivanovich was there.

At home Lev Nikolaevich was entertaining young Rusanov, who gave him a massage, and later on Butyonev and a stranger called Matveev came. I read *My Meeting with a Celebrity*, memoirs of Dostoevsky by Mikulich (Veselitskaya), which was excellent.[25]

February 4 A hectic day: first dear Manya Stakhovich called, then A.I. Maslova came with her camera to photograph some excellent biblical paintings which Butyonev had brought us – illustrations to the Gospels by a certain Prince Gagarin.[26] Then I attended to my damaged camera and took a photograph of Anna Ivanovna. It was a warm day (the water was 4 °), and we took photographs outside in the garden.

Marusya came and copied for Lev Nikolaevich. Misha didn't go to school today; he said he felt sick and stayed at home all day. Annenkova and Sergeenko came to dinner. I went this evening to hear the Czechs again. They played beautifully but the only good thing on the programme was the Beethoven quartet. I met Sergei Ivanovich when we were taking off our coats and we had a most unpleasant exchange: he said he had walked there yesterday and had driven back with M.N. Muromtseva, and he told me all this with such a foolish laugh. I was seething with rage – what business was it of mine? I was very haughty and disapproving with him and he understood, looked embarrassed and went off. But my heart missed a beat and I was infuriated, mainly with myself.

When I got home I found Lev Nikolaevich standing at the long table in the drawing-room, which had been laid for tea, and around it was a group of Molokans who had just arrived from Samara. Dunaev, Annenkova, Gorbunov, Nakashidze and some peasant or other were all there drinking tea, Lev Nikolaevich was explaining something about the St John's Gospel to them, and I overheard a discussion about religion going on.

I don't understand religious discussions: they destroy my own lofty relations with God, which cannot be put into words. There is no precise definition of eternity, infinity and the after-life – there are no words for these things, just as there are no words to express my attitude and feelings about the abstract, indefinable, infinite deity and my eternal life in God.

But I have no objection to the Church, with its ceremonies and its icons; I have lived amongst these things since I was a child, when my soul was first drawn to God, and I love attending mass and fasting, and I love the little icon of the Iversk mother of God hanging over my bed, with which Aunt Tatiana Aleksandrovna blessed Lev Nikolaevich when he went to war.

The Molokans are staying the night here, and I dislike this.

February 5 A most tedious Paderewski concert, paid calls this morning, took photographs of Anna Ivanovna Maslova. An interesting conversation with Maslov and Scriabin about music. Terrible depression all day: I cannot bear to think I have brought about a break with Sergei Ivanovich. I didn't sleep all night.

February 7–27 I haven't written my diary for twenty days, and as always there has been so much happening, so many experiences and important moments. On the morning of Sunday the 7th I received a telegram from Vera Kuzminskaya in Kiev: 'Pneumonia. Maman very ill,' it said. I left for Kiev on Monday morning.[27] On Sunday evening, however, Goldenweiser, Almazov and Szaz came and played Beethoven's third trio and a Grieg sonata, young Vera Almazova sang, and L.I. Veselitskaya and Annenkova came with various other guests, and it was all extremely difficult.[28] In Kiev I found my sister Tanya with spreading pneumonia of both lungs; she was very weak, her face was inflamed and she was in great pain, but she was delighted to see me. I shall not describe her illness here, or the effect my presence had on her, the terror I felt at the prospect of losing my best friend and the sudden *insight* I had into the question '*what is death*?' One's feelings can only be truly described directly, and this I have done in my letters.

I returned to Moscow on the 19th. I visited Yasnaya Polyana on the way just to see Lyova's little nest which I love so much, with Dora and Levushka, and to look in on Yasnaya, which has always been so dear to me.

In Moscow I found everyone well. But no sooner had I arrived than Lev Nikolaevich reduced me to tears by saying: 'Well, I'm glad you're back, now I can go off to the Olsufievs'.' I was worn out by the journey from Kiev, and this was more than I could endure. 'But I was so looking forward to living quietly with you again!' I sobbed. He was alarmed by my tears and said of course he was pleased to be with me too, and that he wouldn't go, so he won't leave for a while. I am painfully sorry for my daughter Tanya. She has to keep syringing out her nose through the hole left by the teeth she had taken out, and it has broken her spirits; she still pines terribly for Sukhotin, too, and simply cannot forget him. Her life is poisoned by a series of minor misfortunes. An interesting letter from Seryozha about his life in quarantine with the Dukhobors. They still haven't been cleared to enter Canada.[29]

We have an artist staying here, a useless, contemptible little Frenchman called Sinet, whom they invited while I was away.[30]

I happened to see Sergei Ivanovich at the Maslovs', and we are friends once more.

March 10 And again I haven't written for a long time. On February 28 I fell ill with influenza, took to my bed and stayed there for eight days. Then complications set in and I developed pneumonia of the left lung.

Nothing of interest happened, it seems. At three in the morning Lyovochka himself ran out for Doctor P.S. Usov. I was running a very high fever and was choking. I was delighted that Lyovochka was worried about me and was taking care of me. Sasha too was clumsily attentive and gentle, and Marusya Maklakova nursed me skilfully and selflessly and sat up for two nights with me.

Lev Nikolaevich goes to the Myasnitskaya art school every day to visit Trubetskoi in his studio, who is doing two sculptures of him simultaneously, one a small statuette and the other of him sitting astride an unfamiliar horse.[31] This is very tiring for him and I am amazed that he agreed to pose. He works away every morning on *Resurrection* and is well and cheerful; he still stubbornly and silently eats his breakfast on his own, at two in the afternoon, and dines, also on his own, at about 6.30, sometimes as late as 7. We simply never see him; the cook just has to seize an opportune moment to give 'the count' his food, and the servants never get a moment's peace or free time.

Today three young ladies came wanting to do something to help the starving peasants in the Samara region; Lev Nikolaevich gave them a letter for Prugavin.[32] There was a telegram from Seryozha in Winnipeg asking for money for the Dukhobors in Canada. But Lev Nikolaevich has already sent the donations to Chertkov to help the Cyprus Dukhobors, who are also planning to emigrate to Canada.[33] My sympathies are with the starving Russians and those wretched Kazan Tartars, who are dying of scurvy and swollen with hunger; they need help far more urgently than the Dukhobors, whose hard lives have been of their *own* making.

March 11–June 21 I fainted at a symphony concert on March 11. I was confined to my bed until April 8. I stayed in bed and was very weak for a long time afterwards. I haven't really been well ever since my return from Kiev. On February 27 I collapsed with influenza, forced myself to get up, then took to my bed again.

June 21 I haven't written my diary for almost three months, and for these three months I have been more dead than alive, sick in mind and body. The doctors talked about a 'weakening of the heart'; at times my pulse-rate was just 48, I was fading away, and was filled with a quiet joy at this gradual departure from this life. I had a lot of love and sympathy from my family, friends and acquaintances during my illness. But I did not die; God ordained instead that I should live. For what . . . ? We shall see.

Can I remember anything of significance in these three months? No, not really. Seryozha has returned safely from Canada, which was a relief.[34] Then there were three magnificent concerts given by the Berlin Philharmonic and conducted by Nikish, which were a great pleasure.

On May 14 Lev Nikolaevich went off to the country, travelling with Tanya; first to Pirogovo, then on the 19th to Yasnaya. Sasha and I left for Yasnaya on the 18th. On May 20 poor Tanya left with Marusya for Vienna; Hajek operated on her; she suffered greatly, and I suffered doubly for her.

On May 30 Lyova, Dora and Levushka left for Sweden. We are in Yasnaya with Andryusha, his wife Olga, Sasha, Miss Welsh, Nikolai Gué (who copies *Resurrection* uninterruptedly for Lev Nikolaevich), Misha and his teacher, a young student called Arkhangelskii.

Sergei Ivanovich and Lavrovskaya visited us on the way from Moscow. He played my favourite Beethoven sonata in D Major, the Chopin nocturne with six sharps – he picked out all my favourite pieces – and something else; next day he played his new quartet and interpreted it so interestingly for my son Seryozha. It was an absolute joy.

Then Lev Nikolaevich fell ill with a stomach-ache and was in great pain during the whole of June 14, and he still hasn't recovered from it.

A cold, rainy summer.

Lev Nikolaevich leads such a monotonous life at present, working every morning on his *Resurrection*, sending the finished chapters to Marx at the *Cornfield*, correcting now the proofs, now his manuscript. He is drinking Ems, and he is thin, quiet and has aged much this past year.

Relations between us are good – peaceful and considerate, without reproaches or fault-finding. If only it could always be like this! Although I am occasionally saddened by a certain coldness and indifference on his part.

I had a depressing experience yesterday: Lev Nikolaevich had given some self-educated peasant a number of books to bind, and in one of these he had accidentally left a letter, which I saw. Something was written in L.N.'s hand on a blue envelope, which was sealed. I was utterly horrified when I saw what it said: he wrote to me on the envelope that he had decided to take his life as he could see that I didn't love him but loved another, and he couldn't endure it . . . I wanted to open the letter and read it, but he snatched it out of my hands and tore it into little pieces.

It transpired that he had been so jealous of my relationship with T . . . that he wanted to kill himself. Poor darling! As if I could ever love anyone as I love him![35] But how I have suffered from this mad jealousy of his throughout my life! And how much I have had to give up on account of it – friendships with good people, travelling, improving myself and generally everything interesting, valuable and important.

I fainted again the day before yesterday. I welcome you, death, and am ready for you – I do not feel that this is the end. For me it is the replacement of one moment of eternity (our earthly life) by another; and this other is *interesting*, as my friend said to me.

26 My soul is torn and tormented. I have accumulated so much depression and remorse, such powerful longings for love and a different life, that I don't think I can bear this strain for much longer.

'Grant me the spirit of wisdom, humility, patience and love.'

Very hot, I swam today for the first time.

June 26 Yet another warning. Yesterday I choked several times, and that evening and night I had such a bad asthma attack, that it was almost more than I could endure. I had a terrifying and uncontrollably violent burst of hiccoughs and yawning – I was suffocating, gasping for air and simply couldn't breathe. Then it passed. There were plenty of reasons for it: Lev Nikolaevich's suicide letter, and Misha letting loose a flood of reproaches two evenings ago about the fact that no one *understood* or *sympathised* with him.

I have exercised all my maternal devotion, my energy and skill, and I have achieved nothing. It wasn't as though I didn't *want* to – I have evidently been *unable* to do so.

I haven't been able to educate my children (having married as a young girl, and spent 18 years shut up in the country), and this often torments me.

While I was playing the Beethoven 'Variations' yesterday I remembered Andryusha saying half-joking the other day: 'Do give me a music lesson, Maman, then you can slap me again . . . ' It made me unbearably sad to remember this. If I had children now I would be far too tender-hearted to lift a finger to them, but when I was young I had *goals* to achieve, the children were stubborn and lazy, it was hard to teach them, I wanted them to know everything and more, I had such a lot to do, such a lot of time was wasted and I would get upset and lose my temper and slap them – lightly of course, for a mother would never hurt her children badly. Yet they still remember it, and I longed to say: 'Forgive me, children, I am so sorry I hit your soft little heads. I wouldn't do it now – but now it's too late!'

I am leaving today to see my eldest sons and my grandchildren. If I die on the way, I greet you, death, I am ready for it. Yet something is choking me, I cannot breathe and I feel *physically* strange.

Lev Nikolaevich is stuck at the Senate trial in his *Resurrection*: he badly needs to ask someone about the sessions of the Senate, and jokingly says to us: 'Quick, find me a senator!' He might as well not exist: he lives completely alone, immersed in his work. He walks alone, sits alone, emerges half-way through dinner or supper merely to eat, then disappears again. His mind is obviously working all the time, and it has exhausted him – he is working too hard and I have advised him to take a break. Although his stomach is better, this illness has aged and weakened him and made him terribly thin. He swam yesterday for the first time.

October 4 Tanya's birthday. She went yesterday to Moscow where Sukhotin too is staying, and now feels she must decide once and for all whether or not she will marry him. My poor Tanya! 35 years old today, brilliant, clever, talented, happy and loved by all – and she hasn't found happiness. She is utterly miserable – thin, pale, nervous. Her treatment in Vienna did no good at all in my view. She still has to keep rinsing out her nose through the cavity in her mouth and forehead, and her general health is wretched.

The Ilich grandchildren have been staying with us for over two weeks, and we are thrilled and delighted to have them. Yes, my grandchildren are darlings, but they aren't *mine*! My heart is no longer swelled by that *morbid* maternal love, just as the apple tree does not blossom twice in one summer.

I went to Moscow twice. The first time Nikolai Gué and I worked out that the accountant had robbed us of 6,000 rubles. The second time I arranged for Misha to be enrolled in the Sumskii regiment. I visited Grand Duke Sergei Aleksandrovich and asked him to accept Misha despite the lack of vacancies. He was exceedingly courteous and affable and despite the irregularity of the enrolment, Misha was accepted into the Sumskii regiment.

Settling up with the accountant was very emotionally trying. I had to be both Christian and just, and not destroy our good and efficient business relations. But God came to my aid.

I saw much of Sergei Ivanovich. Our relations of trust and friendship seem firmly established now. Lev Nikolaevich is no longer jealous. Romances at our age? It's absurd!

I had thought of spending the winter at Yasnaya, if Misha hadn't been accepted in a regiment stationed in Moscow, but I can't bring myself to leave him now and shall again spend the winter in Moscow. Lev Nikolaevich says he doesn't mind where he lives. I hope he means it.

His life is as monotonous as ever: he writes all morning, dines at two, sleeps, goes for a walk or a ride, reads all evening.

His health is better.

October 11 Yet more busy monotonous days have passed at Yasnaya. We had one letter from Tanya, saying she is calm and happy in the knowledge that she is in good hands. This means she has decided to marry Sukhotin.[36]

Two days ago Lev Nikolaevich went out for a walk in the afternoon without telling me where he was going. I thought he had gone for a ride – when he'd just had such a bad cough and cold. Then a storm blew up, it rained and snowed, roofs and trees were smashed, the window-frames rattled, it grew dark – there was no moon yet – and still he didn't appear. I went out to the porch and stood on the terrace, waiting for him with a spasm in my throat and a sinking heart, as I used to when I was young and he went out hunting and I would wait hour after hour in an agony of suspense. Eventually he returned, tired and sweating after his long walk. It had been hard going through the mud and he was worn out, but in good spirits. I burst into tears, reproaching him for not looking after himself and for not telling me he was going out and where he was going. And to all my passionate and loving words his ironic reply was: 'So what if I went out? I'm not a little boy, I don't have to tell you.' Yes, but you're ill,' I said. 'Well, I always feel better for a bit of fresh air,' he said. 'But there's a storm, it's raining and snowing . . . ' 'But it's always raining and windy . . . '

I felt hurt and angry with him. I devote so much love and care to him, and his heart is so icy.

My life goes like this: work and letters all morning. Then from 12 to 2 I pose for a very crude, bad portrait which Igumnov is doing of me. After lunch I take a walk or print photographs; and every other day I teach Sasha German. Then I play the piano, and Olga and I spend the evening copying *Resurrection* for Lev Nikolaevich. Yesterday Olga and I played Beethoven's

5th and 8th symphonies arranged for four hands. What beauty, what a wealth of sounds! I felt completely calm and happy after the music.

A muddy, cold autumn. I am leaving for Moscow.

December 31 The last day of a sad year! What will the new one bring?

On November 14 our Tanya got married to Mikhail Sergeevich Sukhotin. We should have expected this. One had the feeling that she had simply come to the *end* of her unmarried life.

For us her parents, this marriage was a tragic blow such as we hadn't experienced since Vanechka's death. Lev Nikolaevich lost all his outward calm; when Tanya, tormented and grieving herself, went upstairs in her simple little grey dress and hat to say goodbye to him before leaving for the church, he sobbed as though he were taking leave of the most precious thing in his life.

Neither he nor I went to the church, but we could not be together either. Having seen Tanya off I went into her empty room and sobbed, feeling more hopeless than I felt since Vanechka died.

There were almost no guests, just our children – minus Lyova and Misha – and his children – two sons and one or two others.

As they were unable to get a sleeping compartment on the train, Tanya and Sukhotin couldn't leave for the continent that day and Tanya spent another night in her parents' house, while Sukhotin went off to stay with his sister.

The following day we saw them off for Vienna, which they have now left for Rome. Is she happy I wonder? I cannot tell from her letters, which are very long, but more descriptive than personal.

Lev Nikolaevich grieved and wept terribly for Tanya, and on November 21 he eventually fell ill with bad stomach and liver pains; his pulse was very weak for two days and his temperature was 35.5. We gave him stimulants – wine, coffee, Hoffman drops, caffeine – which we sprinkled into his coffee without telling him. He was treated by dear kind Pavel Sergeich Usov, who treated me too last spring. I shall not describe how we looked after him, and the emotional and physical effort this cost me. It was morally very hard. Spoilt by the flattery and admiration of the whole world, he accepted my backbreaking labours on his behalf merely as his due . . . But it's not *fame* we women want from our husbands, it's love and affection.

Almost six weeks have passed now, and Lev Nikolaevich is better, but he's not fully recovered yet. He still has weak intestines, a sick liver and bad catarrh of the stomach.

We gave him Ems water, Ceria powder, sparkling Botkin powder, caffeine and wine. Then some Kissingen Rakoczi. Oh, yes, and I forgot – for the first three days he drank Karlsbad water, and once, with great difficulty, (after I had wept and pleaded with him) we managed to get him to drink some bitter Franz-Josef water.

Throughout Lev Nikolaevich's illness I found distraction from my grief in painting. I had never painted in water-colours before, and had never had any lessons, but at my son Ilya's request I copied Sverchkov's two paintings of horses – young Kholstomer, and Kholstomer as an old horse.[37] They came out so successfully that everyone praised them excessively and I was delighted.

I suffered a great deal emotionally. For the first time in my life I clearly realised that I might well lose my husband and be left alone in the world. And that was an agonising realisation. If I thought about it too much I might well fall ill myself again.

Masha and Kolya are staying, as well as Andryusha and Olga, who is five months pregnant and has just buried her father.

And here too there is nothing but suffering: Andryusha is so rough, despotic and critical with dear, clever, compliant Olga. I cannot bear to see her sad and suffering; I am forever shouting at him and scolding him, but he is more like a madman than a normal person at present, for he has a bad liver. The poor girl will have to suffer a lot more from that wretched inherited complaint; Lev Nikolaevich also suffered a lot from his liver, and I suffered too because of it.

Life is so hard! Where is happiness? Or peace of mind? Or joy? In the world of children, which I have just glimpsed in a visit to my grandchildren in Grinevka, where I organised a Christmas party and immersed myself in this dear, serious childhood world, which compels one, despite oneself, to believe in the importance of life. Then there is pure, peaceful nature, with which I have again been living these past three days, marvelling in the boundless white fields and the hoar-frost which gleams in the sun and covers all the woods and the park.

I live from day to day, without any goal or serious purpose in life, and I find this terribly exhausting. I am writing a long novel, which interests me.[38] If I cannot please those around me, I try not to poison their lives, and to bring peace and love to my family and friends.

My eyes ache, I am losing my sight. But in this, as in everything else: '*Thy* Will be Done!' The end of 1899.

· 1900 ·

Russian language made compulsory in Finnish senate. Russian police set up labour organisations to combat workers' militancy. Kiev University paralysed by student riots. Summer – Socialist Revolutionary Party, heir to the People's Will, established in Kharkov. December – Marxist RSDLP brings out its first paper, Spark, *in Stuttgart.*

Discussions within the government about Tolstoy's excommunication. Sofia becomes trustee at a Moscow orphanage.

November 5 I haven't written my diary for almost a year. I shall not go over all the events of the year. The hardest thing has been my failing sight. There is a broken vein in my left eye and, according to the eye specialist, an almost microscopic internal haemorrhage. I now have a permanent black circle in front of my left eye, a rheumatic pain and blurred sight. This happened on May 27, so all reading, writing, working and any sort of strain was forbidden. A difficult six months of inactivity and ineffective treatment, with no swimming, no light and no intellectual life at all.

I have hardly played the piano, but have done a lot of exhausting work on the estate. I planted a number of trees, including some apple trees, and painfully observed our endless struggle for existence with the peasants: their thieving and debauchery and the injustice of our rich lives, making them work for us in the rain, cold and mud, and not only adults but children too, for 15, sometimes 10 kopecks a day.

On October 20 I left with Sasha for Moscow in high spirits, looking forward to enjoying myself, meeting people, and the pleasure of seeing my beloved friends. But now I have lost heart again.

Lev Nikolaevich left Yasnaya Polyana to see his daughter Tanya in Kochety on October 18, and returned to Moscow on November 3 – ill, of course. The roads were icy after a month of rain and mud, and it would have been an impossibly bumpy journey. So he set out for the station on foot, but he didn't know the way, and for four hours he wandered along, completely lost and covered in sweat, eventually getting a ride in a jolting cart which took him to the station. Now there are yet more stomach-aches, vigorous massages and the rest of it.

It was pure joy when he arrived. He had been gloomy, anxious and unable to work ever since we parted. Yet before this he had been so cheerful and full of energy, happily writing his play *The Corpse*[1] and generally working hard.

When I met him at the station he gazed at me and said, 'How lovely you are! I had forgotten you were so lovely!'

All yesterday and today he was putting his books and papers in order. Then *his* friends came – Gorbunov, Nakashidze, Boulanger, Dunaev and the rest of them. They are thinking of starting a journal with contributions from talentless scribblers like Chertkov and Biryukov, and they want Lev Nikolaevich to give his spiritual support to the scheme.[2]

I went to see Misha at his new property and felt very sorry for him – he is so childish and shy, and has made such a clumsy start in life. I spent the summer with Tanya and the autumn with Andryusha. They're all *starting* new lives. Today I took Sasha and Misha Sukhotin to a rehearsal of Koreshchenko's *The Ice-House.*[3] V.I. Maslova was there, as well as the

Maklakovs, Sergei Ivanovich and various other friends. Things have changed somewhat with Sergei Ivanovich. We seldom see one another, but when we do it's as though we'd never parted.

My heart has been heavy all autumn – no snow, no sun, no joy, as though I were sound asleep. Shall I wake up to new joys, or to death, or will some great grief arouse my joyless soul? We shall see . . .

This evening I prepared an enema for Lev Nikolaevich with castor oil and egg-yolk, while he lectured the obsequiously attentive Goldenweiser about the European governments, which he said were becoming increasingly shameless and provocative in their statements and actions.[4]

November 6 I got up early and visited the Krutitskie barracks on behalf of a woman who had begged me with tears in her eyes to intercede for her son, a soldier named Kamolov, who wanted to stay in Moscow. I arrived at a huge building, whose courtyard was milling with young recruits, their wives and mothers, a huge crowd of people. I asked a soldier where the military commander was. 'There he is!' the soldier said, and pointed. And sure enough, two men were approaching. If I'd come two minutes later I couldn't have done anything, but now I was able to plead my case, which was heard very courteously, and then I went on to demand the royalties due to the author of the *Fruits of Enlightenment*. This money has always gone either to the starving or to peasant victims of fires. It is now going to the latter. I received 1,040 rubles, covering several years.[5]

I got home exhausted and sat down to check the accounts on the book sales. I was interrupted first by E. P. Raevskaya, then a schoolboy called Okulov, asking me to buy tickets for a show, then my nephew, officer Behrs, and finally Varya Nagornova, whom I was delighted to see. So I had to abandon my work. Dunaev visited this evening and Lev Nikolaevich came down and sat chatting with us. Varya and I played the larghetto from Beethoven's Second Symphony – delightful! When I went out into the dining-room I found Lev Nikolaevich's copier Aleksandr Petrovich, standing by the door drunk and cursing. I quietly urged him to go to bed, but he cursed even louder, so I had to restrain him even more energetically. What an emotional ordeal this is for me! Ever since I was a child I have always been terrified by the sight of drunken people, and to this day the sight of them makes me want to cry. Lev Nikolaevich tolerates them quite easily and when he was young, I remember, he used to laugh at old Voeikov the landlord monk when he had had too much to drink, and would make him jump around, talk nonsense and do all sorts of tricks to make him laugh.

So the experience of the Beethoven symphony was obliterated by that of drunken Aleksandr Petrovich.

November 12 This morning I visited the orphanage where I am a guardian,[6] and took a specially good look at these children picked off the streets and from the drinking houses, children carelessly born to fallen girls or drunken women, children who are congenital idiots, children born with fits and defects, hysterical children, abnormal children . . . And it occurred to me that this work I was involved in wasn't really such a splendid thing after all. Is it necessary to save lives which offer absolutely no hope for the future? And according to the rules of the home, we only have to keep them till they are twelve.

I returned home tormented by neuralgia, in one place after another. I sat down to practise Beethoven's Fifth Sonata, but was interrupted by the arrival of Glebov, whose daughter is to marry Misha. Then Lavrovskaya came. People always say how stupid she is, but I think there's a lot of good in her and I find her creative and sincere.

Seryozha has come; he sits absorbed in chess problems for days on end. Most odd! This evening I went to the Maly Theatre with Sasha to see *The Fruits of Enlightenment*. I don't like comedies, I can never laugh – it's my great failing. We returned to find Igumnov there, who had played – while I was out, unfortunately – and dear Doctor Usov, who had had a game of chess with Lev Nikolaevich.

A heavy, wet snow is falling. At last!

The day before yesterday, the 10th, Sergei Ivanovich came and played his symphony, arranged as a duet, with Goldenweiser.[7]

On the 9th I took Sasha, Varya Nagornova and Misha Sukhotin to a recital by Tonio and Auer.

Lev Nikolaevich told me today that when he had left Tanya's in Kochety the roads were so bad that he had decided to walk to the station, but he didn't know the way and got lost. He saw some peasants and asked them to walk with him, but they were frightened of wolves and didn't want to, although one finally agreed to walk with him to the main road, where Sukhotin and the Sverbeevs overtook him on their way to the station. But by then he had been wandering around for about four hours and by the time he got back to Moscow he was ill and exhausted.

Then on the way he pinched his finger in the train, the nail came off and he has been going to the clinic ever since he got back to have it dressed; so he has been unable to write now for three weeks.

November 13 Tanya came with her husband and visited Snegiryov, who diagnosed a completely normal pregnancy. Lev Nikolaevich was so overjoyed to see Tanya that he could hardly believe his eyes, and kept repeating: 'So she's back, she's back! How astonishing!'

Lev Nikolaevich, Mikhail Sergeevich, Misha and Seryozha went off to the bath-house this afternoon and later we all sat with Tanya; she has become a stranger to us now, and is totally absorbed in material worries about the Sukhotin family. As she herself was saying only today, 'I've become a perfect Martha.'[8]

The young Maklakovs, Masha and Nikolai, were here too. Lev Nikolaevich played chess this evening with Mikhail Sergeevich. But Seryozha is in a sorry state: he sits with a long face in front of the chess-board all day, sometimes till late at night, working out chess problems.

My soul is weary and my body aches with neuralgia. It's a hard life, very hard; the inner fire which should warm my life devours it instead, for one has to smother it as soon as it bursts through.

Lev Nikolaevich was writing again today, the first day he has been able to write.[9] Now that he's living with me and I'm taking good care of him, he has got better and his mind is flourishing.

November 15 I am ill, with a cold, nausea and headache, I have stayed at home for three days. Today I played the piano for about three hours – Mendelssohn's studies, *Auf Flügeln des Gesanges* and a Beethoven sonata. We have had guests all day – the Pisaryovs, Raevskii and Zinger, the Naryshkins, brother and sister, Butyonev with his daughter, Marusya, the Petrovskiis, Boulanger, Strakhov, Gorbunov . . . Much too much commotion for my poor head; worries about food, a lot of talk.

I see almost nothing of Tanya, who is completely absorbed in her husband. Lev Nikolaevich feels slightly unwell; he has a stomach-ache and has had no dinner. Both he and I are in low spirits. It makes him angry and anxious whenever I see Sergei Ivanovich but I miss both him and his music – I don't want to hurt Lev Nikolaevich, but I can't help missing him dreadfully. It's all very sad and irreparable.

November 20 Our guests yesterday were a man from the island of Java who spoke French, and another from the Cape of Good Hope who spoke English. The first talked interestingly about Java, and told us that in the capital there were electric trams, an opera house and higher educational institutions, while in the provinces there were cannibals and real heathens. This Malayan had read all of Lev Nikolaevich's philosophical works and had come here *especially* to talk to him.[10]

The house is quite full: my daughter-in-law Sonya has come with her two sons Andryusha and Misha, Tanya is here with her husband and stepson, and Yulia Ivanovna Igumnova, Seryozha and Misha are here too. Yesterday there were two romances: Misha and Lina, who spent the whole day in our house for the first time yesterday, such a sweet, serious girl; and Sasha, who has fallen in love with Yusha Naryshkin. Who knows what *that* will lead to?

I love it when there is a lot of passion and excitement going on around me, but I can no longer join in as I used to. My own intense, impetuous, varied life, and my relations with my family and with outsiders, have burnt out my heart, and it is exhausted.

Yesterday I visited Marusya, who is sick, then sat around at home. I listened to Goldenweiser playing (Beethoven's 'Appassionata', some Chopin and so on), which was a great pleasure, but I went to bed with an empty soul, and I still feel ill. Lev Nikolaevich also has a cough and a cold: he amuses himself in the evenings by playing chess for hours at a time, first with Mikhail Sergeevich, then with Seryozha, then with Goldenweiser, and so on.

November 21 Another frantically busy morning, I visited the Glebovs; Lina is a splendid, charming girl.

This evening Sonya took my grandchildren to see *Ruslan and Ludmila*, while I practised Chopin's E Major Etude and Mendelssohn's *Auf Flügeln des Gesanges*. Then Martynova visited, and Goldenweiser and Taneev arrived.

They played a Mozart symphony as a duet. I am sorry Sergei Ivanovich didn't play on his own. Lev Nikolaevich was very talkative and affable with Sergei Ivanovich, and I was delighted. I love them both.

November 22 I printed photographs, tried on dresses and walked at length around the town. I called on Sergei Ivanovich to examine his gymnastic equipment, and he played me two choral works he has just completed. As usual I didn't understand them straightaway; one was set to words by Tyutchev, the other to the words of Khomyakov's 'The Stars'.[11]

As usual, his '*intérieure*' made a very good impression. His student Zhilyaev was sitting there busily immersed in some musical proofs, his old Nurse was asleep in her semi-darkened room, and Sergei Ivanovich came out to greet me, calm, serious and affectionate. We had a quiet talk together, and he took such an affectionate, unaffected interest in everything: Tanya, Lev Nikolaevich, whom he had found sad and thin, and our hectic life together, which has such an upsetting effect on my nerves.

This evening Suvorin came with Obolenskii and Doctor Rakhmanov, whom the Sukhotins are taking off to their house in the country. Suvorin was telling Lev Nikolaevich what a huge increase there had been in the reading public, and what a great demand there was for his books.

Sonya came back late; I stayed up chatting with her, Tanya and *Julie* (Igumnova), and we all went to bed at around two in the morning.

November 23 Tanya and her husband returned to their house in the country today, intending to return to Moscow for the birth. We won't be seeing her again until the end of January at any rate, and if it weren't for my apathy this parting would again have been quite unbearable. Seryozha and Misha are leaving too, and Sonya will leave tomorrow with the grandchildren. But again my apathy is such that I don't care about any of them, and I'm not particularly keen to see any of them – there's just this nagging sense of something irretrievably lost, a helpless tearful sense of the emptiness and pointlessness of existence, the absence of a close friend, the absence of love and concern.

I struggle to elicit from my husband or to guess just *what* he lives for. He never tells me what he is writing or thinking, and he takes less and less interest in my life.

November 24 More coming and going this morning: Sonya and the grandchildren left; my noisy brother Styopa came; Seryozha reproached me for not going to the notary at that precise moment. Then Lev Nikolaevich came down to breakfast exhausted, rowdy Sulerzhitskii also walked in, Buryonin arrived, and they all started talking about the theatre and modern literature: I wanted to listen, but the din of their voices made it impossible.

Then I found to my annoyance that I had sewn my dress wrong; then visits to various Ekaterinas on their name-day. Ekat. Mikh. Davydova is ill, Ekat. Fyod. Yunge is in tears because her son has been taken into the army for three years, Ekat. Adolf. Dunaeva is in deep mourning for her beloved brother-in-law. More cheerful at Ekat. Petr. Ermolova's, with a lot of flowers, fine gowns and social brilliance. The dear Sverbeevs and their friends were good-natured but dull.

This evening I visited sick Marusya, and Lev Nikolaevich went out to a musical evening at the lunatic asylum.[12] I often feel so sorry for him: he apparently sometimes wants music and entertainment, but his principles and his peasant shirt prevent him from going to concerts or the theatre or anywhere else.

Later this evening Lev Nikolaevich, my two brothers, Seryozha and I sat at home and drank tea. We discussed the benefit concert for the orphanage;[13] I would like to read from some unpublished works of Lev Nikolaevich, but my family is against it.

November 27 Ill again: stayed in bed all of the 25th, stayed in bed yesterday till three in the afternoon and could barely get up, barely walk, no thoughts, no desires, depression . . . This evening Prince Shirinskii-Shikhmatov, Dunaev, Sneserev, secretary of the *New Times*, and someone else. We talked about Eskimo dogs and the fire at Muir and Merrilees – so dull! Lev Nikolaevich today visited Chicherin, who still hasn't recovered from the fire which has devastated the house at his estate in Karaul. Seryozha has left.

Today I am a little better. I spent the day going over bills with the accountant, checked the book sales, got receipts for everything. He tried to cheat me out of 1,000 rubles, but I spotted it just in time. Maria Vasilevna and *Julie* helped me. Lev Nikolaevich just sits reading his books which people send him from all over the world; he writes nothing himself, he complains he hasn't the energy.

This evening he rode his horse to the bath-house with Dunaev; he came back and ate a hearty supper, on his own as usual; he is cheerful and in high spirits, partly because I am so quiet and lifeless. He hates me to be lively – it frightens him.

I was lying in bed this morning listening to the wind howling, and all at once a cock crowed. And I had a sudden vivid memory of Easter Sunday at Yasnaya Polyana; I looked out of the window and saw a red cockerel standing on a heap of straw and crowing. I opened the ventilation window and heard the distant bells ringing for Mass, and thought: in the old days no one in our home cursed the Church, no one condemned the Orthodox faith as Lev Nikolaevich did yesterday with Shirinskii-Shikhmatov. The Church is the idea which preserves the deity and unites all who believe in God. The Church has created its fathers and its worshippers, those who fast and appeal to God with purified souls and with prayers such as: 'Our Father, Lord of Life, grant me not the spirit of idleness, sorrow, self-love and empty talk, grant me instead the spirit of wisdom, humility, patience and love . . . '

November 30 This morning I went to buy shoes and jerseys for my grandchildren, wool for blankets, dresses for Dora and Varenka and plates and dishes in the sale. For two days I have been cutting out underwear and making a layette for Tanya's baby, but I don't enjoy it, I hate it, I've had enough of working.

The secretary of the orphanage was here: things aren't going well there. Some little boys were brought in yesterday and turned away because they were too young.

Today I went to a recital of Beethoven quartets. Lev Nikolaevich had guests. He played chess with Prince Tsertelev, and later he had all his friends here – Dunaev, Boulanger, Gorbunov, the student Rusanov, the artist Mikhailov; he read them an article by the peasant Novikov.[14] He is somewhat poorly, and says: 'I've had enough of my *body* – it's time to be rid of it.' Belka, our lost dog, has been found, to everyone's joy.

December 3 Nothing of special interest. On Friday the 1st I went to a rehearsal of a concert with Ziloti (conducting), Chaliapin and Rachmaninov; I saw Sergei Ivanovich, who was in a strange, sardonic, unfriendly mood. Yesterday was the concert itself, which had a most interesting programme – Tchaikovsky's *Elegy*, the overture to his *Romeo and Juliet*, the new Rachmaninov piano concerto, performed by the composer himself, Arenskii's *Dream on the Volga*, and Chaliapin's magnificent voice – although the choice of songs was unfortunate.

It was hot and stuffy in the balcony.

Lev Nikolaevich has been a little more cheerful these past two days. He played chess with Goldenweiser, who then played some Chopin. It was good but lifeless.

Ziloti came and didn't play, but had an interesting talk with us about conducting, music in general, and in particular the music of Rachmaninov and Taneev, whom he, like me, esteems highly both as a composer and a (musical) scholar.

I have been busy with the orphanage, but without success. I went there today, and for the first time since I was made a guardian I felt so sorry for these children. I want to organise a concert to raise money for it, but it will be hard, I'm too late, and it's such an unusual scheme. I went to see Strekalova, and questioned Princess Lieven closely about the concert she organised yesterday. I then visited poor E.P. Raevskaya, who is fading away from this earthly life, the Maslovs and Lavrovskaya. I have hardly played, haven't worked and haven't read.

I am worried about Seryozha; he has been elected town councillor[15] and was supposed to be here on the 1st, but he still hasn't come. Misha was here, and has left to go elk-hunting with Ilya.

December 4 Lev Nikolaevich said today that he was much better and felt motivated to work again. He said, joking, that he had been drained of all his talent by *Puzin*, and that Puzin would now be all the wiser for it. This Puzin, a nobleman and horse-dealer, is a young ignoramus who lives with the Sukhotins. Lev Nikolaevich stayed in his room and slept in his bed when he visited the Sukhotins, and afterwards said that he must have been invaded by Puzin's soul, for he couldn't work and had grown as stupid as Puzin. But today this passed. Lev Nikolaevich resumed his old life, now that I am looking after him, and is physically amd mentally fit again.

I went to greet the Varvaras on their name-day: I spent a long time at the Maslovs; all very good-natured, friendly, simple and interesting, with refreshments, chocolate and a lot of guests. Sergei Ivanovich came and immediately livened things up.

Then we went on to see Safonova – merchants' wives, finery, a priest, a lot of artificiality and affectation. She herself is unaffected and sympathetic, though. Then we went to see my dear Varechka Nagornova, shining like a diamond in that vile company – hot, noisy and crowded, with their son's wife's parents laboriously making conversation.

This evening I practised the Chopin study and did some exercises. Lina Glebova came with her mother, the Malay came with the Englishman,[16] and Shakhovskoi came and talked about the woman question. I am very preoccupied with the concert for the orphans' home.

December 5 and 6 Lev Nikolaevich is writing a letter to the Tsar appealing to him to allow the Dukhobors' wives who emigrated to Canada along with the others to be reunited in Yakutsk with their husbands, who were exiled there for refusing to do military service.[17] He is in low spirits again. He is so thin – he now weighs only 4 *poods* 13 pounds,* and to think what a powerful man he used to be!

I returned some essential calls, then sent invitations to a meeting at my orphanage and asked members to pay their dues. If only I was in more cheerful spirits I would devote more energy to this concert. As it is I feel defeated.

On the 6th a group of young folk came to see Sasha, and I read them an excerpt from the story which Lev Nikolaevich gave me for the orphanage benefit concert. It is a great pleasure to read, and wonderfully imaginative, although the themes are repeated rather often.[18] I chattered away far too long with young P. Volkhonskii, and now regret it.

December 7 Lev Nikolaevich was invited to the Glebovs for a concert of 23 balalaikas conducted by Andreev. The orchestra also includes *zhaleiki*,† psalteries and bagpipes.

It was splendid, especially the Russian folk-songs; then a waltz, Schumann's 'Warum?' This was played for Lev Nikolaevich's benefit, as he had expressed a desire to hear it. The dear Trubetskoi children were there. V.I. Maslova, Dunaev and Usov came this evening.

There was a slight unpleasantness with Lev Nikolaevich. We had planned to spend the holidays with Ilyusha, near Moscow, but Lev Nikolaevich now says he wants to go to Pirogovo to see Masha and his brother. Ilya's estate is so close to Moscow, I could have looked after him there. But Pirogovo is such a god-forsaken hole and Sergei Nikolaevich, that proud and despotic man, is in terrible pain. Lev Nikolaevich is so sorry for him and will suffer so to see him; then there's the exhausting journey and the bad food, and he'll be living away from me so I won't be able to look after him. I felt very hurt and I told him so: he would ruin the holidays for me if he went, I said, I couldn't and simply wouldn't go to Pirogovo, which I hate, I wanted to visit Ilya, Andryusha and Lyova and to see my grandchildren.

Lev Nikolaevich kept a cold and stubborn silence throughout – a murderous new habit of his. But I was sobbing all night until 4 in the morning, trying not to wake him.

December 8 I went to town to do some errands for my children, and to the bath-house. The driver turned the horse too abruptly on the Kuznetskii

*157 lb.

†Russian folk wind instrument rather like a fife, made from a young branch of willow, or a reed or cane, with a mouthpiece of cow-horn or birch-bark.

Most and tipped over the sledge, tumbling off the coach-box and throwing me on to the ground. It was a very busy street, with trams jingling and carriages dashing past, and a large crowd soon gathered around me. I hurt my elbow, leg and back, but it doesn't seem too serious. Lev Nikolaevich was very upset, though, which pleased me. I sewed a kidskin finger-guard for his sore finger and carried it upstairs to give to him; he took it and drew me towards him, kissing me and smiling. How seldom he shows me any affection these days! But thanks for this kindness, anyway.

This evening's guests were Gagarina, Gayarinova, Martynov, Gorbunov and a peasant writer called Semyonov. Lev Nikolaevich started a discussion with Sofia Mikhailovna about children. She loves and idealises them but he says that both woman and children are egotists and that it is only men who are capable of self-sacrifice. We said it was only women who were capable of self-sacrifice, and there was a nasty argument.

December 10 A meeting at the orphanage. Very flattering for me, because the other members told me I was the life and soul of their society, it was a joy to work with me, and I inspired them all with my passionate devotion to our cause.

But what made me happiest was that when they showed the children to Tsvetkova, the wife of our *benefactor*, the little ones all jumped into my arms, and hugged me and kissed me. That means the children *like* me, and that's the most precious thing for me.

This evening there was a concert. They played the interlude to Taneev's *Oresteia*, a marvellous work, but badly performed by Litvinov's orchestra. Then Sobinov sang a song which Pomerantsev had dedicated to me.

Throughout the concert I was making enquiries about the meeting-hall, finding out the conditions, when it was free, how much it cost, and so on. I was in a businesslike frame of mind; I want to organise this benefit concert for our orphanage, but I don't know whether it will be possible. I went home with Sergei Ivanovich, again quite by chance – we happened to meet on the stairs. I begged him to play at my concert, but he refused, logical, self-centred and perfectly correct, as usual, as to his reasons for not doing so:

'I am composing at present and cannot play,' he said. 'In order to play one needs to practise a piece for two months; I feel absolutely no pity for your orphans, and in order to play for just a quarter of an hour I would have to waste two months of my time practising.' He is quite right of course, but I am so sorry that no one will agree to play or sing.

At home I found Glebova there with her daughter, as well as Lazurskii and Goldenweiser. Good-natured Ilya arrived today with his endless jokes, childish Misha has brought his gramophone, which amused everyone greatly with its horrible tinny repetition of sounds. And Seryozha has come too; he played a piece by Grieg beautifully and is such affable company.

Lev Nikolaevich, to my horror, is visibly ageing and weakening; he is again complaining of stomach-aches, he grows tired after his walks and is simply at a low ebb physically.

A mass of errands for Tanya, my own business, and all the usual frantic bustle. Tomorrow I have to go to Yasnaya, although I don't want to and it's going to be difficult; I also ache all over – my arm, leg and back.

December 17 I returned yesterday evening from Yasnaya, worn out mentally and physically. When I got there I found my grandson Levushka in a fever, and Dora was anxious and also ill. Lyova left for St Petersburg to buy a house while I was there, and it was pitiful to see the worried mother with her baby, crying and groaning day and night.

I spent two days paying out money for some casual labour we had had done, entering it all into the book and checking the accounts. Then I walked around the estate. It's a never-ending struggle with the peasants; all this thieving is so justified from the poor peasants' point of view, but so unpleasant. What was particularly annoying was that the Grumond peasants had chopped down the birch trees on the bank of the pond where we so often used to have picnics, drink tea and fish. I wanted to pardon the peasant who pulled up some apple trees at the threshing barn, as he had asked permission to do so, but the case had already been referred to the village policeman while I was away.

I spent almost four days with Dora and helped her with the children, but it's hard for me to re-live old experiences with my grandchildren. From Yasnaya I drove to Ovsyannikovo to see Maria Aleks. Schmidt, and from there to Taptykovo, 20 *versts* by coach, to see Olga. It was a frosty evening, with a beautiful sunset, hoar-frost, the sharp outline of the half-moon, boundless expanses of snow, and everything so silent, stern and cold. Towards evening there was a fierce frost of 24 degrees. I was absolutely frozen and my soul was lonely and despondent. Maria Aleksandrovna seemed weighed down by her earthly life after her illness. Young Abrikosov is also there, living an ascetic life, although I cannot think what reason he had to settle there, in an alien village, with no purpose in life and no work, simply making some sort of chest for a local peasant for money, when his father owns a sweet factory and a wealthy estate in the Crimea, and lives in luxury.

I found Olga alone in Taptykovo, as Andryusha was out on a wolf-hunt. She just sits there alone with her little daughter all day, like a bird in a cage. I feel so sorry for her. I spent the night there and left the following day; still 24 degrees of frost. The train was cold and I lay down and thought – but still felt wretched.

At home in Khamovniki Street I found Lev Nikolaevich playing chess with Sukhotin and looking so thin and ill that I grew even more melancholy, and felt so sorry for him. Sukhotin left today to go abroad with his doctor and his son, leaving Tanya in the country with his children.

December 23 Yet more tense and terrible days. It turns out that Levushka has tuberculosis of the brain and is dying. One more sweet creature to whom my soul had grown attached is leaving this life. *This* child, with his delicate moral constitution, wasn't made for this world either, just like my Vanechka.

Lev Nikolaevich is constantly besieged by people. Yesterday seventeen Americans, fifteen women and two men, came to look at the famous Tolstoy. I didn't see them, I had no wish to.

Some Molokan sectarians came too; they wanted to follow the example of the Dukhobors and emigrate to Canada, and have asked Lev Nikolaevich to advise them. These crowds of people tire him out. He is so pleased to see people of his *own* circle, like Butyonev, or to have a game of chess with someone, as he did today with Vas. Maklakov and his son Ilya.

Ilya has brought his young son Misha with him, which was very pleasant for me. Anna Ivanovna was here and told me that Sergei Ivanovich had intended to visit me on Tuesday after her lesson, but that he spent such a long time looking for some book that in the end he left it too late. How like him!

S.A. Filosofova is also dying, and Sonya has gone to be with her. How terrible and frightening everything is! Death, grief and suffering on all sides!

· 1901 ·

Socialist Revolutionary Party forms Fighting Organisation. February – a Socialist Revolutionary shoots dead Minister of Education. Students demonstrate to applaud the deed. More students drafted into the army. Tolstoy writes open protest letter to the Tsar. March – S. R. Lagovskii shoots at Pobedonostsev, but misses. June – Finnish army disbanded. Government reduces taxes payable to zemstva *(a severe blow to liberals and radicals). Formation of extreme right-wing nationalist organisation, the Russian Assembly.*

February 22 – Tolstoy excommunicated, excommunication order appearing on all church doors in Russia. Sofia Tolstaya writes to Pobedonostsev and the Metropolitans to protest. Tolstoy is revered and reviled. He works on 'Notes for Soldiers' (published the following year in England). Sofia starts work on her autobiography, My Life. *June – Tolstoy seriously ill with malaria. September – Tolstoy family goes to Crimea for him to convalesce. He is mobbed along the way.*

January 6 The old year ended and the new year started with a great tragedy. On December 25, Christmas Day, I heard of Levushka's death. He passed away the previous day, at nine in the evening.[1] Despite being ill I packed immediately and set off for Yasnaya, accompanied by Ilya. I arrived that evening and Dora threw herself into my arms, sobbing hysterically, while Lyova stood there looking thin and distraught, blaming himself, his wife and everyone else for his son's death. He blamed them for letting him catch cold, for letting him go out in a thin coat, for neglecting his poor health and delicate constitution; and these accusations were harder to bear than anything else. But their grief was unspeakable! All the emotional agony I had endured with Vanechka's death surfaced from the depths of my soul, and I was suffering both for myself and for my children, the young parents. I was unable to help them; Westerlund, Dora's father, arrived and managed to relieve Lyova's conscience a little. Dear Maria Aleksandrovna Schmidt was with them all the time, and Andryusha arrived for the funeral. And then once again it was the open pit, the little waxen face surrounded by hyacinths and lilies, the harshness of death and the frantic grief of the mourners.

Then news came that Tanya had given birth to a dead baby girl.[2] I was simply stunned. No sooner had I attended Levushka's funeral than I had to set off again, that very evening, to see Tanya; Andryusha came with me. It tore my heart to see her so ill and grief-stricken, her husband away and her hopes of being a mother cruelly dashed. She bore it so bravely too, playing with the children, reading, knitting and chatting as though nothing had happened. But I could see the grief and despair in her eyes, for now she has neither husband nor a child. Her stepchildren, especially Natasha, are very sweet to her, but she said to me: 'Looking at my dead baby gave me a mere hint of the maternal instinct, and I was horrified by its power.'

I returned to Moscow on January 3. Sasha, L.N. and the servants gave me a very warm welcome, and I felt calm and happy to be at home. We have announced Misha's wedding to Lina Glebova. She is madly in love with him. I went to the Glebovs' today for the blessing, which moved me to tears. Lina is radiantly happy.

We have had Stasov staying here for the past few days – he's an interesting old man, but tiring in large doses. Yesterday evening Goldenweiser played for us, and as always the music had a wonderfully soothing effect on me.

Lev Nikolaevich is suffering from a rumbling stomach and a pain in his liver. He eats very little and always at the wrong time; he stays in bed a lot and feels sleepy and lethargic, but he is incapable of looking after himself. He ate some red cabbage today and felt even worse. He is writing letters to various people and doing no work at all.

I sent Sasha and Marusya Maklakova off for the day to visit Dora and Lyova in Yasnaya, then on to see Olga in Taptykovo.

Ilya came this evening, and I drank tea and chatted with my three sons Ilya, Seryozha and Andryusha. Ilya misses his wife, who is away in Yalta looking after her sick mother. First he reproached me angrily, then started singing my praises. Seryozha was as restrained and correct as ever. Ilya always goes to extremes, Andryusha is gentle and sentimental. He wrote to his wife saying how sorry he was not to be with her on the 8th, their wedding anniversary.

Dunaeva was here today, and Wipper the nun, and Chernogubov, who came to see us about his biography of Fet.[3]

January 8 I spent the whole day doing essential tasks. I went to the bank and deposited the money received from M.M. Stasyulevich. The poor old man is having to investigate his own affairs now that Sliozberg has robbed him and muddled up all the accounts in his warehouse. I ordered an enlarged portrait of Levushka. Sasha and Marusya have returned from seeing Lyova, Dora and Olga, who were delighted to have them. I went to the bath-house, did some shopping and took my dress to the cleaners ready for Misha's wedding. This evening I sorted through L.N.'s letters to me and gave them to Maria Vasilevna Syaskova to copy, under my supervision. I replied in person to Stasov[4] and Stasyulevich, and wrote letters to the bailiff and to Sonya Mamonova. Then I developed the photographs that Sasha and I took this morning. Mikhailov and Dunaev were here. L.N. is ill – first it was a chill, now it's a stomach-ache. He is feeling terribly wretched. He doesn't want to die – the idea clearly terrifies and depresses him.

January 10 Life is dreary and depressing. L.N. has a bad liver and his spirit is oppressed. He is looking old and sick, and I feel so sorry for him.

I went to the Rumyantsev Museum and took out an unpublished comedy called *The Nihilist, or The Infected Family*, which I think I shall read at my charity concert. I looked through a few things with An. Al. Goryainova this evening and there really doesn't seem to be anything interesting to read all the way through. We decided on Friday that we would all read something aloud.[5]

Misha's fiancée, Lina Glebova, dined with us, and this evening we had all Lev Nikolaevich's intimates here – Boulanger, Gorbunov, Dunaev, Mikhailov. Kolechka Gué came too, looking old and terribly thin – he is worn down to a shadow.

I read a humorous article by Doroshevich in the eighth issue of *Russia*. The characters in it were Expense, Cash, Revenue, Road to Siberia, and the Chinaman, and he described the relationship between them all.[6] L.N. is trying hard to find something jolly and entertaining for us to read. Today we were talking about a play called *The Straw Hat*, which makes everyone laugh and which he wanted to take a look at.[7]

My sight is failing. It is a sad life without any reading or intellectual work.

I played the piano for a long time yesterday, but that too is a strain on my eyes.

January 14 L.N. is visibly thinner and weaker this year, and this grieves me terribly; he wants to do nothing, he needs nothing, nothing matters to him. My life has been so bound up with worrying about him that I wouldn't be alive if it wasn't. And now that my eyesight is failing I shall soon be unable to sort out his papers.

We had a meeting at the orphanage today. Pisaryov spoke at great length – and so loudly and confidently too! We shall see what he actually does about it. The main thing is that there is almost no money, nothing to feed the children with, yet they all keep talking about *educating* the children of the street.

This warm wet winter has a bad effect on people's health: everyone is listless and depressed. Andryusha has come for the dog-show and Misha has arrived from Yasnaya, where he will be returning after the wedding.

January 19 Very worried these days about Lev Nikolaevich's health. He has been taking quinine for three days and seems to be feeling better, but his legs ache in the evening. His mind has simply dried up, and this depresses him. All these family griefs have taken their toll. Then all the arrangements for Misha's wedding – little bags to be sewn, invitations to be printed, endless worries about humdrum matters and young folk. Lina and Misha spend the whole time swooning over each other most unpleasantly.

The whole of yesterday was filled with *art*. In the morning I went to a rather bad exhibition of Russian artists at the Historical Museum[8] – although there was a lovely panorama of Golgotha in the twilight by Styka. What impressed me about it was that the artist hadn't overlooked one figure, one detail. Everything had been thought of, '*tout est soigné*'.[9]

This evening there was a chamber music recital. They did an Arenskii quintet, a cheerful, tuneful work, and a Mozart Divertimento, which was excellent. I did not like the Schumann quartet so much. I have now definitely decided to go ahead with this charity concert for the orphanage. I have hired the hall for March 17, and yesterday in the trustee's office I was personally granted permission to read the opening of Lev Nikolaevich's story 'Who is Right?'[10] I worry that the evening won't be a success. I am busy sorting out and copying all the letters I have written to L.N. that I have been able to find. What a sad tale these letters tell of my love for Lyovochka and my life as a mother! One is an extraordinarily characteristic lament for my lost mental and spiritual life, which I am afraid to wake up to in case I overlook my duties as a wife, housewife and mother. The letter was written under the influence of the sunset, reflections about religion and some Schubert melodies which Mashenka, L.N.'s sister, was playing at the time.[11]

January 21 My life is a whirlwind of activities. I work and take notes all day, pay visits, and today I received guests.

I have written a great many letters – to Stasov,[12] Rutzen, my brother Styopa and various other people.

Lev Nikolaevich is a little better; Doctor Usov called and found him in good shape. There has been a thaw and it's muddy and slushy outside, which is a great nuisance. We had guests this evening – Timiryazev, the Annenkovs, Maklakov and Goldenweiser. I have no energy, and keep waiting for something to happen.

January 28 A whole week spent on preparations for Misha's wedding, paying visits, going shopping, making clothes, sewing little bags for sweets and so on.

Today we heard from poor Masha; her baby has just died inside her, and she is in bed in a state of collapse, grieving inconsolably, like Tanya, for her lost hopes.[13] I just want to cry all the time. I feel so terribly, terribly sad for my two little girls, starved by their father's vegetarian principles. He couldn't have known, of course, that they would be too undernourished to feed the children in their wombs. But he has always gone against *my* wishes and my maternal instinct, which is never mistaken if a mother loves her children.

L.N. himself has been more cheerful recently and is feeling better. Yesterday evening he went to a dance at the Martynovs'; our Sasha danced too. I did not go; nothing gives me pleasure these days, there's nothing I want to do with so much grief on all sides.

January 31 Misha and Lina Glebova were married today. It was a splendid society wedding. Grand Duke Sergei Aleksandrovich came specially from St Petersburg for the day, the Chudovskii choristers sang, there was a mass of flowers and fine clothes, some beautiful prayers for the newly-weds and a lot of vanity and glitter. What an unemotional way to introduce these two young creatures, so in love with one another, to their new life together.

Nothing *amuses* me any more. I am only too aware of all life's difficulties by now, and feel sorry for my darling young Misha embarking so *irrevocably* on this new life. Still, he has a wife who is worthy of him, thank God, and who loves him too.

We left the church for the Glebovs', where the Grand Duke was particularly affable to me, and I am ashamed to admit that this flattered my vanity, as did people's comments as we were leaving the church: 'That's the mother of the bridegroom, she's still a very beautiful woman, isn't she,' and so on.

Misha was very happy, and Lina too. We went to see them off at the station with the best men and all the young people who had loved Misha. There were quantities of flowers and sweets, and they all drank champagne and shouted 'Hurrah!'. I am so glad that the young people went to Yasnaya, where Dunyasha will have everything ready for them, and Lyova and Dora will make them welcome.

The weather is good too. It has been 10 ° below freezing and the days are clear at last. I missed my daughters today. The only person there from our side of the family was Misha Kuzminskii, who came specially from Kiev.

L.N. stayed at home during the wedding, but came out at four to say goodbye to Misha and Lina. This evening he entertained some sectarians from Dubovka and various 'dark ones', and they read aloud that article by Novikov the peasant about the suffering people.[14]

February 12 Yet another series of events: bad news today from my daughter Masha Obolenskaya, who has given birth to her dead baby boy. Poor, suffering creature! She is in a satisfactory condition.

Tanya and I visited Yasnaya together. My darling, kind Tanya was determined to visit Lyova and Dora after their grief. They are a little more cheerful now, especially she, and they love and care for one another. Maria Aleksandrovna Schmidt was also in Yasnaya, and Olga, who is feeling very lonely at present. Aren't we all!

I have been feeling acutely so today. The children are always so eager to judge me – Tanya was criticising me for all the untidiness at home, Misha berated me when he and Lina were leaving for foreign parts for worrying about them on their travels. And they simply don't see anything! How can one keep things tidy when there are people constantly coming to visit and stay, and dragging yet more guests after them. At present we have Misha Sukhotin here, and Kolechka Gué, and Yulia Ivanovna Igumnova, and Tanya herself – crowds of people milling around from morning to night.

And I do all the work for everyone on my own. I take care of all the business on my own, without any help from my husband or sons. I do a man's work: I run the estate, supervise the children's education and deal with them and the servants – all on my own. My eyesight is failing, my soul is weary, yet there are all these endless, endless demands on me . . .

I am organising a concert in aid of the orphanage. There have been a lot of setbacks. L.N. gave Mikhail Aleksandrovich Stakhovich a quite unsuitable excerpt to read aloud. But both he, Mikhail Sergeevich Sukhotin, Tanya and I all considered it quite wrong – at least for reading aloud to a large audience in the great Assembly Hall. I begged L.N. to give us something else, perhaps from *Hadji Murat* or *Father Sergei*. At first he was angry and refused, then he relented and promised to find something.[15]

His spirits are gloomy these days, because he is in poor health and is terrified of death. He asked Yanzhul the other day whether he was afraid of dying.[16] Lev Nikolaevich really doesn't want to leave this life.

We had a musical evening here on the 9th. Sergei Ivanovich played his *Oresteia*, Muromtseva sang Clytemnestra's aria with a choir of her pupils, and Melgunova and Khrennikova sang too. Everyone enjoyed the evening immensely. But L.N. tried hard to cast it in a negative and ridiculous light, and as usual my children were infected by his hostility to me and my guests.

Long after all the respectable people had left and L.N. had put on his dressing-gown and gone to bed, some students, one or two young ladies and Klimentova-Muromtseva stayed on in the drawing-room. They had all had a great deal to drink at supper, and they now broke into rowdy Russian folk-songs, gipsy songs and factory ballads, whooping, dancing and generally going wild . . . I went downstairs and who should I see there but L.N. sitting in the corner and urging them on. He sat up with them for a long time too.

February 15 I have just seen Tanya off to Rome with her family. It's a long time since I've cried when parting with my children, for I seem to be forever meeting them or seeing them off somewhere. But today with the bright sunset lighting up our garden and Lev Nikolaevich's sad, grey, balding head as he sat by the window seeing Tanya off with such mournful eyes that she came back twice to kiss him and say goodbye – it broke my heart, and I am weeping even now as I write. We evidently need suffering to make us better people. Even the small grief of today's parting had the effect of ridding my heart of spite and anger, especially with my family, and I wished them all well and just wanted them all to be good and happy. I feel terribly sorry for L.N. at present. Something is tormenting him, I don't know if it's the fear of death or if he's unwell, or some secret worry. But I don't remember ever seeing him like this, constantly dissatisfied and depressed by something.

February 16 Sasha has a sore throat. Doctor Ilin called and said she had a fever and swollen tonsils, but nothing serious. I went with Sem. Nik. the cook to the mushroom market and got mushrooms for myself, Tanya and the Stakhoviches, then bought myself some Russian furniture. Crowds of people, folk handicrafts, and a lot of peasant atmosphere. They were ringing the bell for vespers when I drove home. Then I changed my dress and went out again on foot with L.N.; he went to buy 500 grams of quinine for the Dukhobors, and I went to church. I listened to the prayers and prayed fervently to myself; I love being alone in a crowd of strangers and leaving behind all cares and earthly concerns. From the church I went on to the orphanage, where the children all surrounded me, welcoming and kissing me. I stayed there a long time finding out how they were doing and what they needed. I feel lonely at home, but relations with L.N. are friendly and straightforward. After dinner Mlle Lambert read me Ohnet's *La Ténébreuse.*[17] Then Almazova, Dunaev and Usov arrived to see Lev Nikolaevich. He has an enlarged liver and his legs and arms ache.

Usov gave him powders and Karlsbad water for the pains.

It was almost 2 a.m. and we had just gone to bed, when there was a sudden desperate ringing at the doorbell. Some woman, a widow called Berg, who had been in a lunatic asylum for 13 years, wanted to see Lev Nikolaevich. I did not let her, but she talked to me for a whole hour, in a terribly agitated state, recalling amongst other things, how my Vanechka had picked some little blue flowers in the garden of the lunatic asylum seven years ago, and asked her if he could keep them. A pathetic, neurotic Polish woman. We got to bed very late, but on calm, friendly terms. At 6 in the morning I painted Sasha's throat.

February 17 I got up late. The doctor came to see Sasha again and painted her throat; her tonsils are still swollen but her fever has gone down. A lovely fine day, which brings back happy memories of spring and the joys of life. I went to the market again with Marusya and bought masses of cheap wooden and porcelain toys for the children in the orphanage. Then I took them over there. They were overjoyed. I put away the baby clothes I had made for Tanya and Masha – to think that both babies were born dead! How unspeakably cruel! Children bring so many worries and so few joys!

February 18 I went to bed late yesterday, burdened by oppressive memories of a discussion between Lev Nikolaevich and Bulygin about religion. They were saying that a priest in a brocade cassock gives you bad red wine to drink, and people call this 'religion'. Lev Nikolaevich was jeering and raging against the Church in the coarsest possible tones, and Bulygin said he thought the Church was the devil's work on a massive scale.

These remarks made me both angry and sad, and I loudly protested that *true* religion saw neither the priest's brocade cassock, nor Lev Nikolaevich's flannel shirt, nor the monk's habit. Such things simply do not matter.

February 20 Seryozha has got back safely, thank God. He is attending the Duma again, and sits here working out chess problems. Sasha has recovered, but L.N. is still suffering from liver pains and is losing weight; he fills me with melancholy.

He was having dinner on his own today, and I went to him and kissed his head, and he gave me such a blank look that my heart sank. There is a sense of hopelessness in my soul. It is wonderful weather, with fine days and moonlit nights. It is wildly beautiful. There's something so stirring and exciting about this weather, already so spring-like. The orphanage was photographed this morning, with me and the directress, for a poster advertising my concert. I came back and played the piano for a long time, and this afternoon I went for a walk . . .

March 6 We have lived through a number of important public, rather than domestic, events. On February 24 it was announced in all the newspapers that Lev Nikolaevich had been excommunicated. I am attaching the announcement here, on the preceding page, as it is of historic significance.[18] This document incensed public opinion and bewildered and dismayed the common people. For three days Lev Nikolaevich was given ovations, brought baskets of fresh flowers and sent telegrams, letters and salutations, and these expressions of sympathy with him and indignation with the Synod and the Metropolitans are still pouring in. That same day I myself wrote and circulated a letter to Pobedonostsev and the Metropolitans. I am attaching it here.[19]

This stupid excommunication on the 24th coincided with the upheavals in the university. For the past three days the students and population of Moscow had been in turmoil. The Moscow students had risen up because students in Kiev had been sent into the army for rioting. But what was unprecedented about these disorders was that whereas people had previously all been against the students, now everyone's sympathies are with them, and the cabdrivers, shopkeepers and above all the workers are saying that the students are on the side of truth and the poor.[20]

That same Sunday, February 24, L.N. was walking to Lubyanka Square with Dunaev, and there they met a crowd of several thousand people. One of them saw L.N. and said: 'Look, there he is, the devil in human form!' At this a lot of people turned round, recognised L.N. and began shouting, 'Hurrah L.N.! Greetings L.N.! Hail to the great man! Hurrah!'

The crowd grew bigger, the shouts grew louder, the cabdrivers fled . . .

At last some technical student managed to find a cab and put Dunaev and Lev Nikolaevich inside, and a mounted gendarme, seeing people grabbing the horse's reins and holding its bridle, stepped in and dispersed the crowd.

For several days now there has been quite a festive spirit in our house, with an endless stream of visitors from morning to night . . .

March 26 It's a great pity that I have not kept an accurate account of the various events and conversations that have taken place here. What interested me most were all the letters, especially those from abroad, sympathising with my letter to Pobedonostsev and the three Metropolitans. None of Lev Nikolaevich's manuscripts has received such wide or speedy distribution as this letter of mine, and it has been translated into all the foreign languages. I was delighted, but it did *not* make me conceited, thank God! I dashed it off spontaneously, passionately. It was God's will, not mine, that I should do it.[21]

An important event today: Lev Nikolaevich has sent a letter 'To the Tsar and His Assistants'. What will come of it! I would not want us to be exiled from Russia in our old age.[22]

Another event for me was my concert in aid of the orphanage. Some very pleasant people took part, and this lent the concert an exceptionally decorous, elegant and respectable tone. The young ladies selling programmes all wore white dresses, and there were baskets of fresh flowers on the tables. Few of the performances received encores, but Mikhail Aleksandrovich Stakhovich did a fine rendering of an excerpt from L.N.'s 'Who is Right?', and I was not disgraced before all these people whose opinion I esteem. We did not make much for the orphanage, only 1,307 rubles.[23] Lev Nikolaevich's health has improved, apart from the pains in his arms. This public affair seems to have given him a new lease of energy and strength. He is being affectionate and passionate with me again. The two generally go together, alas!

I have started fasting. I am knitting hats for the orphanage and today I sewed a black skirt for Varechka Nagornova, L.N.'s dear helpless niece. She is 50 years old, yet there is still something so childlike about her. We play a lot of duets together. Yesterday we did a Beethoven symphony.

I had a rather unpleasant scene with Sasha on Palm Sunday. I called her to go to vespers with me and she refused, saying she had lost her faith. I told her that if she wanted to follow her father's path she must go the whole way, like him: he was extremely orthodox for many years – long after he got married too – then he renounced the Church in the name of pure Christianity, and also renounced all earthly blessings. Sasha, like so many of my children, was of course simply jumping at the easiest solution – in this case not going to church. I burst into tears, she went to ask her father for advice and he told her:'Of course you must go – you mustn't distress your mother.'

So she came to the orphanage church and attended vespers, and now she is going to fast with me. (I did not fast in fact.)*

It said in the newspaper today that Vannovskii had been appointed Minister of Education, which is good.

It is fine, although there's a lot of snow around. The temperature has been between 2 and 5 degrees.

March 27 The other day I received Metropolitan Antonii's reply to my letter. His completely failed to move me – it was all perfectly correct but

*This sentence added later.

completely soulless.[24] I wrote mine in the heat of the moment, it has gone round the entire world and has simply *infected* people with its sincerity. But all this has now receded into the background and life goes on, remorseless, complicated and difficult as ever . . .

These public events have exhausted me, and I have turned to introspection; but my inner life is tense and joyless too.

March 30 Things have gone from bad to worse with Sasha. She would not fast with me: first she pleaded a sore leg, then she refused outright. Yet another worsening in our relations.

I received the Eucharist today. I have found it very difficult to fast; there are such vast contradictions between what is genuine – the Church's *true* foundations – and all these rituals, the wild shrieks of the deacon and so on, that it is very hard to persevere and one sometimes feels like giving up altogether. This is what disgusts young people so much.

I was standing in the church today and the invisible choir was singing so beautifully, and I thought: the simple people go to church rather as we go to a good symphony concert. At home there is poverty, darkness and endless, backbreaking toil. They come to church and there is light, singing, a performance . . . There is both art and music here, and what is more, there is a spiritual justification for all this entertainment, since religion is approved of, even considered good and necessary. How could one possibly live without it?

I fasted without much conviction, but went about it in a serious and sensible way, and was glad to exert myself both physically and spiritually – to get up early, stand for a long time in church praying and reflecting upon my spiritual life.

It was all very tiresome at home today, with Sulerzhitskii's singing, Seryozha's noisy accompaniment, Bulygin's painfully loud voice and senseless giggling from Sasha, Yulia Ivanovna and Maria Vasilevna – utterly frightful!

Andryusha has arrived. How sad that his only interests in life are horses, dogs, provincial friends, and that he has absolutely no intellectual life whatsoever.

We had a quiet day yesterday, and a pleasant evening with Repin. He said there were two demonstrations at the Wanderers' Exhibition in Petersburg, where he had shown his portrait of Lev Nikolaevich (bought by the Alexander III Museum). In the first one a small group of people gathered in the large exhibition hall. Then a student stood on a chair, decked the frame surrounding Lev Nikolaevich's portrait with flowers and delivered a laudatory speech; there were shouts of 'Hurrah!' and a mass of flowers showered down from the gallery. The result of all this was that they removed the portrait from the exhibition, and now it won't even be shown in Moscow, let alone in the provinces, which is a great pity indeed![25]

May 1901 My happiest times recently were two evenings, on May 3 and 5, when Sergei Ivanovich played for us. He played extraordinarily well too – a Mozart rondo, a Schumann sonata, Schubert's 'At the Spinning-Wheel', a Mendelssohn duetto and the overture to *Der Freischütz*. Even Tanya and Lev Nikolaevich were enchanted. The following day he and Goldenweiser played his fourth quartet as a duet.

May 18 We have been in Yasnaya Polyana for ten days now. We travelled with P.A. Boulanger in a well-appointed private carriage, and L.N. had a very comfortable journey. I warmed him up some precooked porridge, boiled him an egg and made coffee, then he ate some asparagus and went to sleep on a splendid bed. We were seen off in Moscow by Uncle Kostya Islavin, Dunaev, Fyodor Ivanovich Maslov and his sister Varvara Ivanovna, as well as some young people we had never met before – technical students I think they were – who shouted 'Hurrah!' and drew pictures of Lev Nikolaevich. It was all very moving.

Masha and Kolya are here, and Lyova and Dora too, and we all had a cheerful dinner together today. An American is visiting from Boston; he needs to study Russia – and Tolstoy, of course – for some lectures he is giving. It is a lovely lush spring. The lilac, the apple trees and the lilies-of-the-valley are all in bloom, the green is so fresh, the nightingales are singing – it's the same every spring, yet one revels in it as in any other pleasure, no matter how often it is repeated.

But now, having suffered so much, and with Lev Nikolaevich's life and energy ebbing away and my own emotional life becoming increasingly complicated, everything bears the imprint of grief and dejection, as though something were coming to an end. Then there is this feeling of spiritual disharmony, stemming from an excess of physical energy, my constant need to look ahead, to be active, to move about and seek new experiences.

Everything flares up and dies, everything rises and falls . . . Lev Nikolaevich's infirmity drags me with it, and I *ought* to grow old with him, yet I cannot and could not if I wanted to . . .

I am going to Moscow on Monday . . .

June 6 I have been to Moscow. I did my business there and lived alone with the maid in my big empty house. I visited Vanechka's and Alyosha's graves and went to see my living grandson, Seryozha's little boy. He's a splendid child, serene and straightforward. I saw Misha and Lina, who always make an excellent impression, and I saw a lot of the Maslovs. I also saw Sergei Ivanovich. There has been a cooling in our relations recently, and I have neither the energy nor the inclination to maintain our former friendship. Besides, he really isn't the sort of person one can be friends with. Like all gifted people he is always seeking new experiences and he looks for other people to provide them, while giving almost nothing of himself.

It is hot, stuffy, lazy weather.

L.N. is taking salt baths and drinking Kronenquelle. He is fairly cheerful, and it is a pleasure to look after him now after a winter of illnesses. Pasternak is staying here; he wants to paint a group portrait of L.N., Tanya and me for the Musée de Luxembourg, and is doing rough sketches for it at the moment.[26] Chernogubov is here too, sorting and copying Fet's letters to Lev Nikolaevich and me.[27] Miss Welsh has arrived and is keeping Sasha busy.

June 14 My goodness what a lovely summer! Through my window I can see the moon in the clear sky. It is still and silent, and the air is caressing and delightfully warm. I have been spending almost all my time outside with nature; I go swimming and in the evenings I water the flowers and go for walks. My beloved Tanya is staying here with her husband, with whom I am becoming reconciled since she loves him so. He has a sweet nature but is terribly selfish, which makes me fear for Tanya.

Pasternak the artist has been here and has drawn both me, Lev Nikolaevich and Tanya in a variety of poses and angles. He is planning to do a genre painting of our family for the Luxembourg.

We also have staying here a sculptor named Aronson, a poor Jew who has spent the last eight years in Paris turning himself into an accomplished sculptor. He is doing busts of Lev Nikolaevich and me, and a bas-relief of Tanya – they're not too bad either.

He hasn't made me look as hideous as all the artists have done.[28] I don't know why it is that although people generally find me quite pretty, all the portraits, photographs and busts of me are really very ugly. They say one can never really catch the expression in a face, the sparkle in the eyes, the colour of the skin and the irregularity of the features.

Lyova, Dora and Pavlik have left for Sweden. It was terribly painful to part with them. I have a special place in my heart for them. I feel with them and in all their griefs and joys – although they have not had many joys this year! They lead such irreproachable, Christian lives, with the very finest ideals and intentions. They have nothing to hide, one could safely look into the depths of their souls and find nothing there but purity and goodness. At 5 in the morning poor little Dora ran to Levushka's grave to say goodbye to her darling baby; I wanted to sob, I was suffering with her so in her maternal anguish.

Lev Nikolaevich still complains of pains in his arms and legs, and is very weak and thin. My heart is in my mouth when I see how he is ageing, and how close he is to that great inner change for which neither he nor I – however hard we may try – are yet prepared.

This morning L.N. was walking by the house and said, 'It's so sad without the children here – one minute there were two perambulators outside, now they're gone.' (We have just had Pavlik and Andryusha's daughter Sonyushka staying here.)

June 20 I went to Moscow to negotiate the sale of Sasha's land; another frightful waste of time and energy. It was hot, I spent two nights on the train, talked to the barrister, did some shopping and so on. My house was very cosy, though, the garden was looking lovely, and the whole place contains such good memories.

When I returned exhausted next morning, they hadn't sent any horses, so I had to walk back from Kozlovka; I was in a thoroughly bad temper, the heat was insufferable and the house was crowded with good-for-nothings – Alyosha Dyakov, Goldenweiser, some sculptor, the Sukhotins. Tanya is the only one of them I care about. I long again for peace and quiet and some sort of creative intellectual activity.

A rainy and windy day. I go in to see L.N. and inquire about his health and find we are separated by a wall which I am trying to beat down. This has happened to me so often, and it is always so painful!

I had suggested, amongst other things, that he write to Andryusha and urge him to treat his wife a little better.

'Why should you order me what to do!' he said angrily. I said I wasn't *ordering* him, just *asking* him to stand up for Olga and advise Andryusha to be a bit kinder and more restrained to his wife – only because I knew he would do it much more intelligently than I or anyone else. 'Well, if I'm so much cleverer then there's no reason to tell me what to do, is there,' he said.[29]

July 3 Something frightful is drawing near, and although everyone anticipates it yet it is utterly unexpected when it comes – it is death, and the death of someone whose life means far more to me than my own, because I have lived exclusively through Lyovochka and the children he has given me.

I still cannot understand the state of my heart; it has turned to stone; I *mustn't* listen to it, as I need all my strength and energy now to look after him.

Lev Nikolaevich fell ill on the night of June 27–28. He felt generally wretched, could not sleep and had difficulty in breathing. Sasha and I had planned to visit my son Seryozha on the 28th, his name-day and birthday, and Tanya, Sonya and the children and Varya Nagornova were coming too, and I was so looking forward to seeing them all and giving Seryozha a nice day, but I wasn't sure whether I could leave Lev Nikolaevich. In the end, though, we did go, at 8 that morning. When I had left he got up and went for a walk, but that evening his temperature went up to 38.5. He slept well that night apparently, but the following day he set off for a walk and could hardly manage it, he was so weak; it was an enormous effort for him to get home, he had a long way to walk and got terribly tired. The pain in his chest grew worse, but they put a hot blanket on it and that eased it somewhat. He again had a fever on the evening of the 29th when I returned, having beeen reassured by a telegram on the 28th assuring me that he was well. No one had looked after him properly while I was away! It broke my heart to see him and his chest was terribly painful all that night. It must he his heart, I told him. The following morning we conferred as to which doctor to call. Eventually we decided on Dreyer from Tula, who discovered that he had a high fever and a dangerously high pulse of 150 per minute. He prescribed 10 grains of quinine a day, and caffeine and strophanthus for the heart. But when his temperature fell, to 35.9 °, his pulse was still 150.

So then we wired Doctor Dubenskii in Kaluga. (He is the chief doctor at the town hospital and a good friend of ours.) Dubenskii was amazed by his pulse and said it was the pulse of the death agony. But he had his doubts about the fever, and felt it was not a stomach or bowel disorder. After several doses of quinine the fever passed and for two days running now his temperature has been normal, 36.2 °. But he has just had another two sleepless nights, with a slight chill, a fever and profuse sweating, and he is now feeling absolutely exhausted, and what is much more serious, his heart has been considerably weakened.

The children have all arrived – apart from Lyova, who is in Sweden, and Tanya. Ilya's children are here too. Yesterday he invited his three grandsons and Annochka his granddaughter into his room, gave them all chocolates out of a box, made four-year-old Ilyusha tell him about the time he almost drowned in a rain-water tub, and asked Annochka about her hoarseness. Then he said: 'Off you go now, I'll call you again when I'm next feeling bored.' And when they had gone out he kept saying: 'What marvellous children.'

Yesterday morning I was putting a hot compress on his stomach when he suddenly gazed intently at me and began to weep, saying: 'Thank you Sonya. You mustn't imagine that I am not grateful to you or that I don't love you . . . ' And his voice broke with emotion and I kissed his dear, familiar hands, telling him what pleasure it gave me to look after him, and how guilty I felt when I could not make him completely happy, and begging him to forgive me for being unable to do so. Then we both wept and embraced. For such a long time my soul has yearned for this – a deep and serious recognition of our closeness over the thirty-nine years we have lived together . . . The things that have occasionally happened to destroy this were a mere external delusion and never altered the powerful inner love that has bound us together all this time.

Today he said to me: 'I am now at a crossroads. I would just as soon go forwards (to death) as backwards (to life). If this passes now, it will just be a respite.'* Then he reflected a little and added: 'But there's still so much I want to tell people!'

Today when Masha brought Lev Nikolaevich his latest article which N.N. Gué had just copied out for him, he was as happy to see her as a mother greeting her beloved sick child who is brought to her bed, and he at once asked Gué to make various corrections and asked me to collect all the rough copies of the article downstairs in his study, tie them all together and write on them: 'Rough copies of the last article.' Which I did.[30]

Yesterday he was anxiously enquiring about some peasant victims of a recent fire in a far-away village, to whom he had asked me to give 35 rubles; he wanted to know if any of them had arrived at our house, and asked us to tell him if any of them came asking him for anything.

He had a terrible night last night, July 2–3; I was with him from two to seven in the morning. He didn't sleep a wink, and his stomach was aching. Later his chest started hurting, so I massaged it with spirit of camphor and made a cotton-wool compress, which eased the pain a bit. Then he started having pains in the legs and they grew cold, so I massaged them too with spirit of camphor and wrapped them up in a warm blanket. He began to feel a little better then, and I was so happy to be able to relieve his suffering. But then he began to feel very low and miserable, so I took his temperature. It was up again – from 36.2 ° to 37.3 ° – and he remained feverish for three hours. Then he went to sleep, and I went off to bed as I was dropping with exhaustion. First Gué took my place, then Masha.

Our son Misha came. L.N. had a talk with him, asked after his wife and said what a great joy it was to him that all his daughters-in-law were not only such fine but such lovely women. Seryozha was saying to him: 'You know, Papa, Misha can do anything,' to which L.N. replied: 'Well thank goodness for that – that *will* be useful for him.' Then he asked: 'Has he finished that vile military service of his?' And Misha said he had 'served his time now, thank God'.

I was sitting in his room today reading the Gospels, in which L.N. has marked the passages he considers especially important, and he said to me: 'Look how the words accumulate. In the first Gospel it says that Christ was simply christened. In the second it has been expanded to: "And he saw the skies open," and the third makes the further addition: "He heard the words, 'Sit down and eat, my son,'" and so on.'[31]

Now my Lyovochka is sleeping. He is still alive, I can see him, hear him speak, look after him . . . What will happen next? My God, what unendurable grief, what horror to live without him, without the familiar support of his love, his encouragement, his intelligence, his enthusiasm for all the finest things in life.

*The sentence beginning 'If this passes . . . ' is entered between the lines and was probably written later.

I don't know if I shall be in any condition to write. But I do so want to write down everything that happens to him; everyone, everyone needs him and loves him. Help me, Lord, it is so unbearably painful . . . !

July 14 I cannot remember now everything that has happened: Tanya came with her husband, Doctor Shurovskii arrived from Moscow, a lot of our friends visited. Telegrams, letters, a great crush of children, grandchildren and acquaintances, one anxiety after another . . . Eventually I fell ill too. I had a high fever all night, my heart-beat was weak, my pulse was 52, and I had to stay in bed for two days, unable to move. I am better now. We have a young doctor here called Vitt Nikolaevich Savvin who takes L.N.'s pulse, which goes up to 90 the moment he gets tired. He went downstairs today, and took a walk round the house looking at the flowers; he is now sleeping on a couch under the maple tree.

All the doctors were of the opinion that his illness and weak heart had been caused by the presence of the malarial poison in his organism. They gave him quinine and suggested arsenic injections, which L.N. stubbornly refused, I regret to say. He is now very thin and weak, but has a good appetite, is sleeping well and is out of pain; he works every morning on his article about the labour question.[32]

Thank God, thank God, for yet another reprieve! I wonder how much longer we will live together! For the first time in my life I clearly realised that I might lose my precious husband, and my heart was gripped with a sorrow which has not passed and I don't think ever will. I take one look at Lyovochka's sunken face, his white hair and beard and his emaciated body, and the persistent ache in my heart, which will not go away, becomes unbearable and I feel as though my life were at an end and I had lost all my interests and energy. But how long did I have anyway? Will I ever pick myself up again?

Yes, a phase of my life has just come to an end. A sharp line has been drawn between that period when life *went on*, and now, when my life has simply *stopped*.

I kept thinking: 'Salt baths will help, he'll gradually get better, he'll live another ten years; Ems water will repair his digestion, and the warmth of summer and lots of rest will restore his strength . . . '

But now suddenly it is the *end*. No health, no strength, nothing to restore, nothing to repair – there's so little left of Lyovochka now, too little to repair. And what a giant he used to be!

It's sad to hear him berating the doctors and me for treating him. As soon as he feels better he always comes out with a stream of accusations. Yet when he is ill he always lets himself be treated.

July 22 Lev Nikolaevich is on the mend now. He is taking long walks through the forest and eating and sleeping well. Thank God!

We received letters from well-wishers in Tula yesterday evening, and Kolya Obolenskii read them out to us. They all expressed sympathy and joy at L.N.'s recovery. He listened, then burst out laughing and said: 'Well, next time I start dying I shall have to do so in earnest, I really mustn't joke about it any more. I'd be ashamed to make people go through all that again, with everyone gathering round, the journalists arriving, the letters and telegrams – and all for nothing. No, it's quite impossible – why it's positively indecent.'

We had a delightful letter from Queen Elizabeth of Romania today. She has sent L.N. a brochure she has written, and writes how happy she will be if '*la main du maître*' lies for a moment on her little book.[33]

A hot, dry, dusty day. The oats are being harvested. Bright, sunny days, moonlit nights; it's so beautiful, one longs to make better use of this lovely summer.

Yesterday, when L.N. said that decency demanded that he should die when next he falls ill, I replied: 'Yes, life is depressing when one is old. I too would like to die soon.' At this he suddenly came to life and burst out with passionate indignation: 'No, one must live! Life is beautiful!' It's wonderful to have this energy at the age of 73, and it's this that will save both of us. But my daughter Tanya writes to me today that we her parents want never to grow old, and this is pointless, she says. Who knows what is best?[34]

July 30 L.N. was poorly again yesterday evening. He had a bad attack of indigestion, an accumulation of bile and a fever: at 11 p.m. yesterday the thermometer showed a temperature of 37.8 ° and his pulse was around 90 all day.

And up till now he has been making such a rapid recovery! He was eating well, joking and chatting happily with us in the evenings, and we took such a cheerful walk round the Zakaz forest the other day with Fyodor Ivanovich Maslov, our daughter Masha, Kolya, Sasha and Yulia Ivanovna.

It is hot again today and there is a smell of burning, as though there were smoke in the air. It's impossible to see anything, and the sun has turned into a tiny red ball.

I lead a dreary life, sitting all day by my sick husband's door and knitting caps for the orphanage. All the life and energy in me has died.

I received a letter from Countess Panina offering us her dacha, Gaspra, in the Crimea, and we are planning to go, although I don't want to leave before September.

August 3 Lev Nikolaevich's latest illness has robbed him of even more of his strength, although he is a little better today. Terrible heat, very dry again, I swim every day. We were visited this morning by the Myasoedovo villagers who were burnt out in the fire, and we gave them all 7 rubles in the courtyard. There have been so many fires this summer, and so many people to be helped!

Then another visitor we didn't know, called Falz-Fein, who has just lost his young wife and has been left with three young children, desperate and ill with grief. L.N. took him out for a walk and talked to him.

I sight-read various pieces of music: a concerto by Hummel, some Mozart and some Weber. I also copied out Weber's A Minor Sonata for myself. Music is the best occupation in the world. I took some photographs with Masha, studied a little Italian, did some housekeeping.

But I am haunted by the terrible feeling that everything is coming to an *end*. Something must *end*. L.N. and I have lived together for a whole era – thirty-nine years of our life. And now all these changes: we're leaving for the Crimea, and L.N. is weak and depressed, although he keeps to his usual regime, writing in the morning, taking short walks in the garden or the nearby wood, sitting with us in the evening . . . Will all this last? *How* will my life turn out? I can't predict anything, I don't know . . . 'Thy will be done.'

August 26 We're leaving for the Crimea on September 5. I went to Moscow on business and shall go again before we leave, probably on the 1st.

Cold, windy, damp and vile.

L.N.'s sister, Maria Nikolaevna, is here, and Varya Nagornova; Lyova has arrived from Sweden, my son Seryozha is with us, and many others. My sister Tanya came, which gave me great joy.

L.N. was again feeling unwell, but he takes such bad care of himself. Doctor Dubenskii came yesterday and said that his condition was satisfactory.

This life is not to my liking at all – housekeeping, bills, taxes, packing, endless practical tasks . . . No walks, no music, nothing but boredom and low spirits. It seems we will be staying in the Crimea for the winter, and this makes me terribly sad! Well, whatever God ordains. The line has been drawn now and a new phase in our life is starting. Just so long as Lev Nikolaevich is alive and well.

December 2 (Gaspra, the Crimea) We have been living here since September 8 for the sake of Lev Nikolaevich's health; he is making a slow recovery. You have only one life, he was 73 in August, and he has aged and grown very much weaker this year.

I have not been writing my diary; it has taken me such a long time to get used to the new living conditions and emotional deprivations I have to endure here. But I am now used to it, helped by the knowledge that I am fulfilling my stern duty and my wifely obligations.

Last night I wrote letters to our four absent sons[35] (Andryusha has just arrived), and was then kept awake all night by a mass of tormenting memories of my children's early years, my passionate anxious relationship with them, the unwitting mistakes I made in their education and my relationship with them now they are *grown-up*. Then my thoughts turned to my dead children. I saw with agonising clarity first Alyosha, then Vanechka, at various moments of their lives. I had a particularly vivid vision of Vanechka, thin and ill in bed, when after his prayers, which he almost invariably said in my presence, he would curl up into a cosy little ball and go off to sleep. I remember how it broke my heart to see his little back and to feel his tiny bones under my hand.

And as for the spiritual and physical solitude I experienced last night! Things have happened exactly as I imagined they would. Now that physical infirmity has forced Lev Nikolaevich to abandon amorous relations with his wife (this was not so long ago), instead of that peaceful affectionate friendship which I have longed for in vain all my life, there remains nothing but complete emptiness.

Morning and evening he greets me and leaves me with a cold and formal kiss. He calmly accepts my anxieties about him as his due, he frequently loses his temper and tends to regard the world about him with utter indifference, and there are now only two things that excite, interest and torment him in the material and intellectual realms – death and his work.

I think more and more of death, I imagine with a calm joy that place where my infants have gone and where I feel I will have more peace of mind. There can be no peace in *this* life; once one *strives* for it, and tries to *elaborate* a wise and accepting attitude to life, a religious resignation and lucidity, then one's life is already over. Life is energy and struggle, constantly changing feelings, the ebb and flow of good and evil – life is life, there's no stopping it. Besides, one would not want deliberately to stop it. Although when the time comes for it to stop naturally, we must greet the end calmly and joyfully; then, contemplating God and submitting to His will, we shall be spiritually reunited with Him and physically reunited with Nature. And there can be nothing but good there.

December 3 A hot day. I went to Yalta and sent a letter to Seryozha authorising him to buy 46¼ *desyatins** of land in Telyatinki to add to the Yasnaya property. I received and remitted money – oh, this endless unbearable business, which is all so completely unnecessary to me! I felt tired then, wandered round the town on my own and went to Chukurlar, where I met a consumptive young man begging for a living. Everything here is so dreary and chaotic. And there's more to come. Lev Nikolaevich rode over to Alupka, then played chess all evening with Sukhotin. His sons Ilya and Andryusha, who have just arrived, were playing cards, to my great

*Roughly 150 acres.

displeasure, with Sasha, Natasha Obolenskaya, Klassen and Olga. I sat sewing silently on my own, then studied some Italian.

December 4 Another hot day, brighter and lovelier than yesterday. The sun is as hot as summer. What a strange changeable climate here, and one's moods are equally changeable. Lev Nikolaevich, Sukhotin with his son and tutor, Natasha Obolenskaya and I walked over to Orianda. The walk tired us a little but the 'Horizontal Path' was very lovely. We drove home with Sonyusha and Olga, and the sea and sunset were quite magical. I was afraid that Lev Nikolaevich would be chilled and exhausted. The others rode on to Uchan-Su, and Ilyusha came back very excited about some photographs he had taken. Today was Varvara's name-day, and I remembered my visits last year with Marusya to see Varya Nagornova and the Maslovs. What a happy, hospitable time we had at the Maslovs! I wonder what they are doing today – how strange to think it's winter there now, with snow and sledges!

December 7 I have just said goodbye to Andryusha and my good-natured, eternally childish Ilya. Lev Nikolaevich will accompany them to Yalta and spend the night there with Masha, which he has wanted to do for a long time. Either the arsenic or simply the good weather has had an excellent effect on him, and he is feeling much more fit and energetic now. And this bustling activity shows how delighted he is to be better. First he walked with us to Orianda, from where we drove home. The following day he rode over to Simeiz and back. Yesterday he was on his feet from morning to night, and that evening he walked to the hospital, marvelling at the view in the moonlight. Today he got ready to leave for Yalta.

I wanted to help him pack so he wouldn't exert himself too much, but he snapped at me so peevishly that I almost burst into tears, and went off without saying another word.

I had a letter from Countess Aleksandra Aleksandrovna Tolstaya today. What a delightful woman, and what exceptional spiritual harmony! She has so much genuine love and sympathy to offer people.[36]

I incline more and more to the view that every kind of sectarianism, including my husband's teachings, tends to dry people's hearts and make them proud. Two women whom I know well, Lev Nikolaevich's sister, Mashenka the nun, and the afore-mentioned Aleksandra Aleksandrovna, have both become better, nobler people without leaving the Church.

We have had four days of extraordinary summer weather: the windows are open, we walk about in light summer dresses, and even then we are too hot. This evening it was 12 °.

My poor Tanya gave birth to another dead baby, a boy, on November 12. She is even more devoted to her frivolous selfish husband. There is nothing left of her now, she has been completely absorbed by him; he *allows* himself to be loved, and loves her very little himself. Well, thank God if that is to her liking! We women are able to live for love alone, even when it's not reciprocated. And even then one can live a full and active life!

Various pieces of news from Moscow – none of which gives me particular pleasure – and from Yasnaya too. Our affairs are being neglected, our friends are forgetting us; I am tantalised by all those wonderful recitals and symphony concerts, but it's no use, I just have to sit here and mope.

Duty, duty, all my energy is exhausted in fulfilling my duty, and in suppressing my own personality.

After I had seen Lev Nikolaevich off to Yalta I went to mass; the girls sang beautifully and I was in a peaceful, prayerful mood.

December 8 Lev Nikolaevich did not return from Yalta today. Sasha came back alone and told us that the Obolenskiis and the doctor had persuaded him to stay another night.

When I saw him off yesterday I suddenly felt very depressed that I no longer had anything to live for. Today I felt better and went for a walk on my own in a happy sober mood. It is unusually warm, 12 ° in the shade, and the sky is all pink from the sun, which is hidden behind the clouds. It is beautifully secluded in the park. It grieves my heart that my husband and I should be living here like two strangers!

Sasha said he wrote 8 pages of something in Yalta today, and was weak and exhausted.

December 9 It's just as I thought – Lev Nikolaevich has been taken ill in Yalta and his heart-beat is irregular again. I have just spoken to him on the telephone; he sounded quite cheerful, and said it was again his stomach that was bad. The long ride over to Simeiz and back irritated his intestines. It must be the hundredth time he has done this. Just before he left he wolfed down some treats we had got for little Andryusha's sixth birthday – some dumplings and grapes, a pear and some chocolate. And now look what happens. The moment he gets a little better he undoes everything with his immoderate appetite and excessive activity. Then he takes fright, is treated, gets better, then ruins everything again . . . And so it goes, like a vicious circle.

I went to mass. The girls sang beautifully. I am in a happy, calm, familiar state of mind. Unlike other people I am not bothered by foolishness like 'with ranks of angels bearing spears', 'at the right hand of the Father' and so on. Above and beyond all this is the Church – the place which reminds us of God, the place where many millions of people have brought their noble religious sentiments and their faith, the place where we bring all our griefs and joys, at every moment in our fickle fate.

December 13 When I last wrote my diary I was at first reassured, then worried about the state of Lyovochka's health when I spoke to him on the telephone, and I decided to leave immediately after dinner for Yalta. I found him quite cheerful when I arrived, but lying in bed. Apparently even the doctor had been worried. His heart palpitations had been quite bad, and he was prescribed camphor injections, although this wasn't actually necessary, as all the symptoms were related to the stomach and intestines.

Liza Obolenskaya and I took him back to Gaspra with us today.

At first, after drinking some coffee with milk, he was very lively, and this evening he played two games of chess with Sukhotin; but then he felt weak and eventually took to his bed. We had been urging him to go to bed all along, as the doctor had ordered, but he wouldn't listen.

The Sukhotins have had some bad news. Their Seryozha has fallen ill with typhus at the Naval School, and they have been informed by telegram that his condition is serious. Tanya is wretched and has been weeping. She takes such a childish view of her fate; she thinks someone is forever out to hurt her.

We heard to our great joy today that a son, Ivan, had been born to Misha and Lina on the 10th. May my Vanechka invest this little boy with his soul and pray for him to grow up to be a fine, happy, healthy child. I would dearly love to see this new Vanechka.

Today I feel deeply and humbly sorry for Lev Nikolaevich, and cannot look at him without sorrow. I am pleased by this feeling; for at times I am overwhelmed with irritation at him for wasting his energy and shortening his life, which we all value *so much* that we all sacrifice our *own* lives in its service. I remember how my sister used to scold her children when they fell and hurt themselves, and I realised that she was blaming them for making her feel so sorry for them. And I am just the same: I sometimes blame Lev Nikolaevich (usually silently, in my heart) for the fact that his infirmities cause me such unbearable suffering.

December 14 Lev Nikolaevich moved downstairs yesterday so as not to have to climb the stairs. His room next to mine is empty and there is something ominous and poignant about the deathly silence upstairs. I no longer have to put the wash basin down quietly on the marble table, and tiptoe around, and refrain from moving chairs.

Liza Obolenskaya (his niece) is sleeping downstairs next to his room at present, and he gratefully accepts her help and is glad not to have to bother me.

December 15 Lyovochka has completely recovered now and we have all cheered up. He is in good spirits, his heart is quite better (though his stomach hasn't quite recovered) and the fever has passed. He had dinner with us and walked as far as the gates of the estate, although he was very tired when he got back.

He had a call from Doctor Altschuler, who is treating him here, a pleasant, clever Jew, not at all like most Jews, whom Lev Nikolaevich trusts, listens to and even likes. He was given his thirtieth arsenic injection today, and took five grains of quinine.

We have here a Czech called Doctor Makovitsky, whom we have already met,[37] accompanied by some sort of Georgian called Evg. Iv. Popov, who is apparently a Tolstoyan. We spent the evening much as usual – chess, newspapers, letters and work.

I went for a walk on my own today; it was warm outside and very beautiful. Then I played the piano for over two hours, and enjoyed myself with a Weber sonata and a Chopin impromptu. When I read the newspapers I was enticed by all the concerts I saw advertised and was especially sorry to have missed a series of recitals by M. Pauer, who was playing *all* the Beethoven sonatas.

December 16 A dreary day. I have seen almost nothing of Lev Nikolaevich. The hateful Popov and Makovitsky are with him at the moment. Boulanger came.

December 23 Lev Nikolaevich is fully recovered; he went for a long walk today, and looked in on Maxim Gorky – or rather Aleksei Maksimovich Peshkov;[38] I do dislike it when people write under assumed names. Lev Nikolaevich, Olga, Boulanger and I all came home in the carriage. It is fine, windy and warm – 6 °. Lev Nikolaevich brought a large mauve-pink wild flower into the house and it has blossomed again. The almond tree is also trying hard to come into blossom and the white snowdrops are in flower. So beautiful! I am beginning to love the Crimea. My depression has lifted, thank God, mainly because Lev Nikolaevich is so much better now. Long may this last!

The Sukhotins left yesterday and Andryusha arrived, unwell but affable, although unpleasantly reserved, especially with his wife.

December 24 Seryozha and Goldenweiser have come. Misha Vsevolozhskii came to visit. This evening Lev Nikolaevich played vint with his children and Klassen (the German bailiff here). They all shouted and got very worked up over a grand slam no trumps – I always find this excitement over card games quite incomprehensible, shouting a lot of nonsense as though they have all suddenly lost their reason.

Lev Nikolaevich is suffering from bad pains in his arms, although he is taking better care of himself now that the days are warmer. Life seems to have lost all its taste, and I am no longer looking forward to my trip to Moscow. I don't want to go – it will be dreary and cold there, and it's a great nuisance. What sort of pleasure can it possibly be?

December 25 We have had a festive Christmas. Lev Nikolaevich is better – his fever has passed and his legs and arms aren't hurting him.

December 26 Boulanger has left. It's such lovely weather, everyone is going out for walks and drives. Lev Nikolaevich is in good health. I cut out some clothes, developed photographs, did some sewing and this evening I looked at my Italian grammar. I am preparing anxiously for my trip to Moscow. I am sorry to have to leave Lev Nikolaevich, and make this long journey on my own. We spent the evening at Klassen's – German conversation, strange people and sweet food – not at all to my liking.

December 27 The Chetverikovs and the Volkovs were here this evening. A discussion about music with Eshelmann. Goldenweiser played. Lev Nikolaevich is taking walks again, writing about freedom of conscience and making more revisions on his article 'On Religion'. When he was going to bed this evening he asked me for some warm milk – which he drinks a great deal of now – and while it was being heated up and I was saying goodbye to our tedious guests he suddenly appeared at the door in nothing but his underclothes and querulously asked me where his milk was.

Sasha started bustling about, and just as I was taking the warm milk off the oil stove and was about to take it to his room, he irritably jumped out of bed and again appeared at the door.

December 29 The Tartars had a festival today; they were seeing a Mullah off to Mecca for three months and had prepared a dinner for him, and the streets of Koreiz and Gaspra were crowded with cheerful people of all nationalities, all in their best clothes. The Turks danced in a circle, looking very picturesque and characteristic. I tried to take a photograph of them, but they were moving too fast and it came out badly. Lev Nikolaevich walked off on his own to Ai-Todor. He was gentle and kind today, and we are getting on well together – what a joy! I am dissatisfied with my day: I took photographs, did some sewing, and that was all.

December 30 A very mixed lot of people came to see Lev Nikolaevich today – three revolutionary workers filled with hatred for the rich and dissatisfaction with the present social arrangements, then six sectarians who have lapsed from the Church, three of whom are true Christians, in that they lead a moral life and love their neighbour. The other three were originally Molokans and are still sympathetic to their beliefs. I did not hear their discussion with Lev Nikolaevich – he doesn't like to be disturbed – but he told me later that one or two of them had spoken with great intelligence and passion. There was also an old man, better off and more intelligent than the rest, who apparently wants to go to the Caucasus and found a monastery by the sea-shore based on new principles. He wants all the brothers to be highly educated, so that this monastery could be a sort of centre of learning and civilisation; furthermore, the monks would work the land and support themselves through their own labour. A difficult venture, but a worthy one.

This evening we went to the public library, where a dance had been organised. The music was provided by three travelling Czech musicians and a young man on a big harmonium, and chambermaids, and craftsmen's wives and daughters all danced waltzes, polkas and *pas de quatre* with men from various social classes. Two Tartars did some Tartar dances, two Georgians did a *lezginka* with a dagger, and a lot of people – including Volkov the *zemstvo* doctor, a highly capable and energetic man – danced the *trepak*, squatting and leaping Russian-style. These popular dance-parties are a fine thing and provide much innocent fun and excitement. We all went to watch, even Lev Nikolaevich.

December 31 So another year has gone by. The last day of a difficult year! Will the new one be any better? Life seems to be getting worse and worse, and I don't seem to be getting any better either.

I seem to have wasted the whole of today rushing around – this invariably happens when the Obolenskiis arrive in the middle of the day.

Lev Nikolaevich walked over to see M. Gorky and returned with Goldenweiser, who is staying with us.

I have copied out the first chapter of 'On Religion', and so far I don't particularly like it. He says little that is new, and it seems somewhat insubstantial. We shall see how it goes on! I did not at all like the way L.N. compared people's abandoned faith in religion with an outworn appendix.

We have Popov and Makovitsky here. A charming letter from Dora and an interesting one from Muromtseva. I went with Sasha to Koreiz to buy wine, oranges and refreshments for the servants' New Year party. We are having a party too, although I don't much like these *semi*-celebrations. People just sit around and eat, then at midnight something is suddenly supposed to *happen*.

· 1902 ·

April – young student shoots dead Minister of Interior. July – worker shoots governor of Kharkov. Waves of peasant riots in the countryside; some ninety estates plundered, with the help of Socialist Revolutionary 'expropriators'.

June – Tolstoys leave the Crimea. Tolstoy works on two plays, The Light Shines Even in Darkness *and* The Living Corpse, *a few short stories, an essay on Shakespeare and a popular anthology,* Thoughts of the Wise Men For Every Day. *Sofia works on the eleventh edition of his* Complete Works.

January 1 We had a quiet family New Year party yesterday. (Lev Nikolaevich had to go to bed early, as he felt ill after his bath.) Klassen came this morning with some lovely violets.

I am copying Lev Nikolaevich's article 'On Religion', a little at a time, but it lacks something – it needs more passion, more conviction.

I took a walk to the Yusupovs' Park and the sea with Olga and Tanya. It was a warm and summery day, and by the sea we met Gorky and his wife. Then Altschuler called. Our servants all came in dressed as mummers and stamped and danced about; it was terribly tedious – I am really much too old for that sort of thing.

Lev Nikolaevich, Goldenweiser, Seryozha and Klassen the German bailiff played vint. I wrote five letters, finished knitting a scarf, and gave presents to Ilya Vasilevich and the cook. I received charming letters from Sonya and Lina,[1] and felt so pleased that somewhere far away at least two of my children, Ilya and Misha, are happily married. What will this new infant Vanechka Tolstoy be like? He couldn't possibly be anything like the first one! But how delighted he would have been to know that his darling brother Misha also had a Vanechka.

It's terribly windy outside, quite unbearable, and I fear for Lev Nikolaevich's health.

It was a warm day; Tanya, Olga and I went out for a walk together, and drove home.

January 4 For the past three nights I have been sleeping on the leather sofa in the drawing-room, or rather not sleeping but listening out all night for Lev Nikolaevich next door, and worrying about his heart. He has been ill for three days now – his heart has been very irregular. Yesterday and today he got up and came down to dinner, but he grew dreadfully weak afterwards and today we felt so worried about him that we summoned Tikhonov, the Grand Duke's doctor, from Dülber. He has just been. He said there was no immediate danger, but like all the other doctors he warned of dire consequences if Lev Nikolaevich continued to lead this reckless life, over-tiring himself and over-eating. His temperature is normal but his pulse is irregular.

Seven inches of snow fell in the night, and it is still on the ground. Yesterday there was a north wind and 3 degrees of frost; today it is half a degree above freezing, with no wind. I knew this weather would have a bad effect on Lev Nikolaevich. It always does.

We have not managed to speak to Altschuler on the telephone, and I am looking after Lev Nikolaevich all on my own. Everyone keeps offering to help, but as long as I don't actually collapse, I love to look after him on my own – although his obstinacy, his tyrannical behaviour and his complete ignorance of hygiene and medical matters makes this terribly hard, even unbearable at times. For instance, the doctors order him to eat caviare, fish and bouillon, but he will not because he is a vegetarian – it will be the ruin of him.

I have been reading an extraordinary little book, a translation of Giuseppe Mazzini's *On Human Duty*. What marvellous ideas and language – simple, concise, full of power and conviction.[2] I copied out some more of 'On Religion' and cut out a bodice for myself. I don't go anywhere, as I am afraid to leave Lev Nikolaevich, even for half an hour.

January 5 Lev Nikolaevich was very poorly all yesterday evening and last night: palpitations, difficulty in breathing, insomnia, general misery. Several times during the night I got up and went to him. He drank some milk with a spoonful of cognac, took some strophanthus (which he asked for himself), and managed towards morning to get a little sleep. Doctor Tikhonov called yesterday evening and again today, and said there was an infiltration of the liver, a weakness of the heart and a disorder of the intestines. These complaints appeared long ago, but are now following their course in a more pronounced and malignant fashion, and manifest their ominous symptoms yet more frequently and painfully.

L.N. himself is very dejected, and keeps us all at a distance, calling us only if he needs something. He sits in a chair, reads or goes to bed. He slept very little again today.

There is snow on the ground and the temperature is at freezing-point. A terrible wind has been howling all day. The whole place seems so cheerless and desolate. My head is heavy. I received a telegram from Sukhotin to say that they will be spending the winter in the Crimea. I am so glad that Tanya will be staying with us for a bit, I am glad that Sasha will have a friend here, and darling little Dorik too, and I have even grown to love Alya. If only Lev Nikolaevich would get better! I have put all thoughts of Moscow out of my mind for now – I was worried enough about the trip as it was. Although it's absolutely essential that I go!

I sit at home all day sewing and ruining my eyes; I am sunk in torpor, as I used to be in my youth at Yasnaya Polyana, when I lived this kind of unexciting, uneventful life for years on end. But then I had the children . . . !

January 8 The last few days of Lev Nikolaevich's illness have been extremely difficult. His pulse is still quick and feeble. Doctor Altschuler and Doctor Tikhonov came yesterday and prescribed a twice-weekly dose of extract of buckthorn (the plant), in tablet form, and five drops of strophanthus, three times a day, for six days. But Lev Nikolaevich has suddenly rebelled and refuses to take anything. I am tired of this forty-year struggle, I am tired of having to employ tricks and stratagems to make him take this or that medicine and generally help him get better. I no longer have the strength to struggle. There are times when I long to get away from everyone and withdraw into myself, if only briefly.

I have now formed a clear picture of L.N.'s illness: a disorder of the intestines, liver and stomach, and complete atony. Who knows how much longer he will be strong enough to survive these regular bouts of illness?

Last night, the 6th–7th, there were 8 degrees of frost and a terrible wind. Today it is 4 degrees, but grey, dismal and overcast.

Yesterday they all went off to a recital given by Goldenweiser. Olga and I stayed behind. I sat alone in the drawing-room all evening, sewing, writing and ruining my eyes, until I eventually fell asleep on the sofa. (L.N. had already been asleep for a long time.) The family returned at around 2 a.m.

All this morning I was copying out Lev Nikolaevich's 'On Religion'. This is more of a socialist work than a religious one.

I told Lev Nikolaevich this yesterday. A religious work should be poetic and exalted, I said his 'On Religion' was very logical but it did not capture the imagination or elevate the soul. He replied that it needed only to be logical, a lot of poetry and lofty obscurity would just confuse the issue.

I was thinking about my trip to Moscow again, and caught myself thinking that I would like to go.

January 10 The atmosphere here is so gloomy at times. I am sitting alone after dinner sewing in the dark drawing-room. Lev Nikolaevich is next door in his room. Tanya is rapidly tapping away on the Remington on the other side, Seryozha is silently reading the newspapers in the dining-room, and Olga is upstairs with Sonyusha. There is dead silence in the house, broken at times by terrible gusts of wind, which howls and groans and stalks about the house, filling it with cold.

I have no life here, just the undoubtedly good and necessary task of looking after Lev Nikolaevich. He is so weak at present that he often calls me simply to cover him with a rug or adjust his blanket. I have to make sure that he doesn't overeat, or that people don't make a noise when he is trying to sleep, or that there aren't any draughts. I have just put a compress on his stomach. He drinks Ems water twice a day.

January 11 I went to Yalta with Tanya to do some business and shopping, and I bought her a hat for her name-day. Masha was looking very thin and wretched.

Poor Olga's baby has stopped moving inside her in her sixth month. I feel so sorry for her. I brought Sasha home; yesterday she rode her horse over to Gurzuf, and today she attended a rehearsal of *It's not All*

Cream for the Cat, in which she plays Fiona. I have now finished copying 'On Religion', which I began to like better towards the end. I liked what he wrote about the freedom of a man's soul illuminated by religious feeling – but that is not new. Yasinskii has just published Lyova's novel; I am afraid to read it.[3]

January 12 The whole day was absorbed by small chores and family worries. First I played with my granddaughter, then I comforted poor Olga who was weeping for her baby; then I washed and mended Seryozha's cap; then I gave Sasha some advice about her theatrical costume; then the doctor came to see Olga; then this evening I prepared an enema for Lev Nikolaevich; then I put a compress on his stomach and brought him some wine, and he drank some coffee which had been heated up for him. Everything makes him nervous at present. He had an irregular pulse again this evening, and gave himself some strophanthus. Then he started to flag, went to bed, had some coffee to drink and became very gloomy. Yet his face is so fresh, and he does not *look* ill. He took a two-hour walk today – the doctor said he was *never* to walk for more than an hour. Oh, how awkward he is! And he will go to his grave with this senseless attitude to hygiene and health matters.

Tanya's name-day. She has arrived from Yalta and is in a melancholy mood. Andryusha too is sad and quiet: his marriage is in difficulties and I feel very sorry for him. Seryozha has just left for Yalta intending to celebrate the first day of the Moscow University year. He has spent the last few days playing the piano on his own in the side wing. I have been deprived of even that pleasure now! I cannot leave the house, I cannot leave Lev Nikolaevich or Olga with anyone. My old age is turning into a sad time. Yet that storm of desires and aspirations for something loftier, for a more spiritual, more significant life, has not been extinguished in my soul. When will it? In the other world I suppose.

January 14 How time flies . . . There is no winter here and no certainty about the time. There is nothing to rejoice about either. Lev Nikolaevich's health is not improving. He needs a complete change of diet, but he is so stubborn and self-willed; with great respect, this great man has a dreadfully obstinate nature which simply will not agree to the diet of fish and chicken which has been recommended, but insists on eating carrots and red cabbage, as he did today, and then suffering for it.

I sat by his room until half-past three in the morning yesterday, waiting for Andryusha and Seryozha to return from an evening of cards. Lev Nikolaevich slept well. At the moment I am copying out his letter to the Tsar. I fear the Tsar will be angered by the cruel unadorned truth of his words.

January 15 Lev Nikolaevich has a fever of 37.7. Altschuler called. The doctors cannot understand it at all. It's a bad business. I am very worried.

January 16 A terrible night. L.N.'s temperature went up to 38. I spent the whole night in the drawing-room next to his bedroom and had no sleep at all. Towards morning he began to sweat, his temperature went down to 36.1 and his left side started aching. Both yesterday and today we rubbed him with iodine and applied a compress. He had five grains of quinine at 2 in the afternoon and has been taking 5 drops of strophanthus twice a day. Despite all this he got up, did some writing and played vint with Klassen, Kolya Obolenskii and his sons. Tanya copies out his letter to Tsar Nicholas II, sealed it and sent it off to the Grand Duke Nikolai Mikhailovich, who has undertaken to give it to the Tsar if convenient. The tone of this letter is extremely harsh, and I am very much afraid that it will anger the Tsar.[4]

Tanya keeps planning to leave and then postponing it. Now she will probably go tomorrow.

Sasha, Olga, Natasha and I drove to a pine copse in the mountains. It was a lovely warm day and the views on all sides were delightful. On the table in my room I have some beautiful fresh flowers – they're snowdrops but they look like orange-blossom.

I sewed all day and all evening with a sad, anxious, stupefied feeling, as though something were about to happen.

January 17 The same as yesterday, the same medicine, the same pain in his side, although he himself is a little more cheerful. Chekhov called,[5] and Altschuler. The weather is warm and fine. Tanya has left to see her husband in the country. I have just copied out L.N.'s letter to the Tsar – an angry insulting letter, abusing everything on earth and giving him the most absurd advice on how to run the country. I do hope Grand Duke Mikhailovich understands that this letter is the product of a sick liver and stomach and does not give it to the Tsar, for if he does, it will infuriate him and he may take some action against us.

January 18 Lev Nikolaevich is a little better today, although his stomach has not fully recovered yet, his side is still aching and he had a fever of 36.3 this morning and 37 this evening. He has been reading all day and has written some letters; this evening he played vint with Klassen, Obolenskii and his sons.

I put my husband to bed every evening like a child. I bind his stomach with a compress of spirit of camphor mixed with water, I put out a glass of milk, a clock and a little bell, and I undress him and tuck him up; then I sit next door in the drawing-room reading the newspapers until he goes to sleep. I have summoned up all my patience and am doing my utmost to help him endure his illness.

January 20 I went to see Sasha in the role of Fiona the old housekeeper in *It's not All Cream for the Cat*, which is being performed in the local public library. It was Sasha's first acting attempt and she wasn't at all bad. The cast was a strange mixture of people – a doctor's wife, a blacksmith, a nurse, a stone-mason and a countess. This is all to the good.

Lev Nikolaevich is better, the pain in his side is not so bad, his stomach is not hurting and his temperature was 36.3 this morning and 36.9 this evening, as it was yesterday. He took some strophanthus, but refused to take quinine. We didn't apply a compress today. I spent the night in the room next to his; he slept well and woke up in a more cheerful mood.

There has been a thick fall of wet snow, and I feel better – I had been feeling a little unwell.

January 21 A day and night of waiting, anxiety, dull despair and an oppressive nervous drowsiness, all caused by Lev Nikolaevich's deteriorating condition. His side has been aching and his temperature has gone up to 38. The two doctors, Elpatevskii and Altschuler, were here and diagnosed a return of the fever, a disorder of the intestines and an attack of neuralgia.

There is snow on the ground and it is freezing.

January 23 Doctor Bertenson (a distinguished physician-in-ordinary) arrived from St Petersburg yesterday evening. He is an intelligent, straightforward man, and obviously an experienced and capable doctor.

Today clever Doctor Shchurovskii came from Moscow and the two of them had a serious consultation with Altschuler. I shall note down their recommendations on the following page.

Much talk about Amfiteatrov's feuilleton in the newspaper *Russia*; this contains references to the Tsar and the royal family, mentions the deportation of the author of this article (or rather fairy-story)[6] to Irkutsk, and describes the gluttony, stupidity and brazen audacity of Minister Sipyagin. Bertenson told us a great many things about St Petersburg high society and the Grand Dukes, and Shchurovskii told us about his trips to the Caucasus. It was an exhausting day. Gorky came with Sulerzhitskii. Bertenson was determined to visit Gorky and went off to see him. Shchurovskii is going to Yalta tomorrow to see Chekhov.

All interests in life have paled in the face of L.N.'s illness. I received a letter yesterday from Sergei Ivanovich urging me to come and hear an extraordinary singer called Olenina d'Ahlheim.[7] But I have been feeling so uninterested in everything, so exhausted! Oh I am tired of life! I have done absolutely *nothing* today but look after Lev Nikolaevich. My eyes are so bad, I cannot even see to read. And there's only one thing that matters to me now, only one thing that is necessary to my happiness, and that is being close to L.N.!

Here then are the doctors' recommendations:

Regime:

1 Avoid all exertion, physical as well as emotional (excessive . . . * and so on).

2 Not to go for long walks, to be mindful of his diminished strength and not to set out to increase it through activity. Horse-riding and climbing strictly forbidden.

3 To rest for 1 to 1½ hours every day, taking off his clothes and going to bed.

4 To have three meals a day, and eat no peas, lentils or *red cabbage*. To drink no less than four glasses of coffee with milk every day (¼ coffee to ¾ milk). If milk is drunk on its own, it must be taken with salt (¼ teaspoonful per glass).

Wine may sometimes be replaced by porter (no more than two madeira glassfuls per day).

5 To take a bath every two weeks. The water to be 28 degrees and the soap (half a pound of it) to be dissolved into it. To sit in the bath for five minutes and sponge himself with clean water of the same temperature. The bath to be taken during the day.

In the interval between baths to rub the body with a solution of half soap spirit and half eau-de-cologne.

Treatment:

1 A twice-weekly enema made from 1 pound of oil slightly warmed, to be administered at night.

For the other days, 1–5 pills, depending on their effectiveness, to be taken at night. If the pills prove ineffective, to administer a water enema in the morning.

2 ⅓ glass of Karlsbad Mühlbrun, slightly warmed, to be drunk three times a day for one month, half an hour before morning coffee, lunch and dinner.

3 Three camomile capsules a day for three days; repeat after two days, and so on.

4 Should heart medication (strophanthus) be required, this must be administered by a doctor.

5 In the eventuality of a bad nervous illness, capsules (+Coff) should be taken for the pain.

If the doctor considers it necessary to give quinine under the prescribed regime, this must not be obstructed.

Lev Nikolaevich's diet must consist of: four glasses of milk and coffee a day.

Gruels: buckwheat porridge and gruel, rice, oats, *smolensk* and semolina with milk.

*Omitted in the original.

Eggs: fried, whisked raw, in aspic, scrambled with asparagus.

Vegetables: carrots, turnips, celery, Brussels sprouts, baked potatoes, potato purée, pickled cabbage chopped up fine(?),* lettuce scalded in hot water.

Fruits: sieved baked apples, stewed fruit, raw apples chopped up small; all oranges to be sucked.

All sorts of jellies and creams are good; meringues.

Written later, the evening of the 23rd Lev Nikolaevich had a terrifying attack of angina pectoris and his temperature went up to 39 °.

January 24 The doctor listened to his heart this evening and diagnosed pleurisy in the left lung. Shurovskii has now returned to us and is treating him.

January 25 They have decided that it is pneumonia of the left lung, which subsequently spread to the right one too. His heart has been bad all this time too.

January 26 I do not know why I am writing – this is a conversation with my soul. My Lyovochka is dying . . . And I know now that my life cannot go on without him. I have lived with him for forty years. For others he is a celebrity, for me he is my whole existence. We have become part of one another's lives, and my God what a lot of guilt and remorse has accumulated over the years . . . But it is all over now, we won't get it back. Help me, Lord. I have given him so much love and tenderness, yet my many weaknesses have grieved him so! Forgive me, Lord! I ask for neither strength from God nor consolation, I ask for faith and religion, God's spiritual support, which has recently helped my precious husband to live. The other day he read somewhere: 'The old woman groans, the old woman coughs, it's time the old woman prepared her shroud.' He was referring to himself when he repeated this to us, and he wept. My God! Then he added: 'I'm not crying because it's time for *me* to die, but because it's such a beautiful verse.'[8]

January 29 I would like to record everything concerning my dear Lyovochka, but I cannot; I am suffocated by tears and crushed by the weight of my grief . . . Yesterday Shchurovskii suggested that Lyovochka inhale some oxygen, and he said: 'Wait a bit, first it's camphor, then it's oxygen, next it'll be the coffin and the grave.'

Today I went up to him, kissed his forehead and asked him: 'Is it hard for you?' And he said: 'No, I feel calm.' Masha asked him: 'Is it horrible,

*Sofia Tolstaya's question mark.

Papa?' And he replied: 'Physically, yes, but emotionally I feel happy, so very happy.' This morning I was sitting beside him and he was groaning in his sleep, when he called out suddenly in a loud voice: 'Sonya!' I jumped up and bent over him and he looked at me and said: 'I dreamt that you were in bed somewhere . . . ' Then the dear man asked about me, asked whether I had slept and eaten . . . This is the first time *anyone* has asked about me! Oh Lord, help me to live with Thee and not expect anything from people, but be grateful for everything that I may receive from them. For I have received so much from God and am so grateful to Him for everything.

Often, when I thought my Lyovochka was dying I have been almost vexed with him and have almost wanted to do the impossible – to stop loving him before he is taken from me.

His pleurisy is pursuing its terrifying course, his heart is growing weaker, his pulse is quick, his breathing is short . . . He groans day and night. These groans carve deep scars into my brain and heart – I shall hear them for the rest of my life. He often talks at length about what has been preoccupying him lately: his letter to the Tsar and other letters he has written.

I once heard him say: 'I was wrong,' and then 'I didn't understand.'

He is generous and affectionate with everyone around him, and is evidently well pleased with the treatment he is receiving. 'That's wonderful,' he keeps saying.

No, I cannot write, he is groaning downstairs. He has had several injections of camphor and morphine.

Tanya is arriving tomorrow. Lyova has just left for St Petersburg. If only he lives long enough to say goodbye to all his children.

It is now 5 in the afternoon. His temperature is going up and he has been delirious for some time. But in the brief moments when he regains consciousness he drinks some milk or takes his medicine.

He once said in his delirium: 'Sevastopol is burning.' And then he called out to me again: 'Sonya what are you doing? Are you writing?'

Several times he asked: 'When is Tanya coming?' And I told him today that Lyova had left too. He gazed at me, then asked: 'What time is it?' He asked what the date was, and whether today was the 27th.

January 28 Tanya, the Sukhotins and Ilya have come, bringing a lot of noise and worries about food and accommodation. How frightful it all is: the painful struggle of a great soul in its passage to eternity and oneness with God, whom he has served – and all these base earthly cares here in the house.

It is so hard for him, the dear, wise man . . . Yesterday he said to Seryozha: 'I thought it was easy to die, but it isn't, it's terribly hard.'

And he said to Doctor Altschuler: 'In the Lord's Prayer there are various ways of interpreting the words "Give us our daily bread." It is an appeal to

God for spiritual nourishment every day. But then look at you doctors ministering to the sick every day – that's good too, especially when it is disinterested.'

Lev Nikolaevich had a slightly better day today; he was in less pain, slept for an hour and a half during the day and was able to talk to us. But his strength is failing, and, more importantly, his heart is in a bad way. But I mustn't allow myself to think about it, I must keep my spirits up and look after him. I try to bury deep in my heart the despair which assails me every so often.

He has just called Tanya in to see him. He was so happy when she arrived. He was also pleased to get a telegram from Grand Duke Nikolai Mikhailovich, saying he had personally handed his letter to the Tsar.[9] He had been waiting for both these things to happen.

He has had another camphor injection, and is being given digitalis, milk with cognac, Ems water and champagne. They put a plaster on his left side (that was three days ago).

Doctor Volkov is on duty one night, Altschuler the next and Elpatevskii the third; Shchurovskii is here all day.

January 29 9 o'clock in the morning. They insisted that I go upstairs and get some sleep, but having spent the past hour sobbing I now feel like writing some more. My Lyovochka (although he is not mine now but God's) had a terrible night. The moment he dropped off to sleep he started choking and shrieking and could not sleep. First he asked Seryozha and me to sit him up in bed, then he drank some milk, followed by half a glass of champagne and some water. He never complained but he was tossing about and suffering terribly.

I too have a spasm in my chest every time he groans. How can I not suffer too, when it is my other half that is suffering?

Every loved person's passage to eternity enlightens the souls of those who tenderly bid him farewell. Oh Lord, help my soul to remain to the end of my life in this lofty enlightened state which I experience increasingly these days! He has just gone to sleep and Liza Obolenskaya (his niece) and Masha have taken my place. I sat with him and attended to him until 4 in the morning.

January 30 Yesterday morning he was feeling so well that shortly before 1 he sent for his daughter Masha and dictated into his notebook roughly the following words: 'The wisdom of old age is like carat diamonds: the older they are the more valuable they are, and must be given away to others.'[10]

Then he asked for his article on freedom of conscience and began to dictate various corrections to that.[11]

His temperature was normal all day, he was in good spirits and we all cheered up. This evening I took up my nightly vigil by his bed; I sat with him until four in the morning, listening to his breathing, and all was well.

Lyova arrived yesterday evening; I always love to see him, and pity him so. Misha too came this evening, bubbling with life as usual.

This morning I went to take a nap and when I returned I discovered to my horror that his temperature had gone up to 37.6 again. My heart sank. The doctors say that his lungs are getting back to normal, that there is no danger, and that his heart is in a quite satisfactory state.

But are they to be believed? I long to be deceived; I haven't the strength to suffer any more.

Today he asked what was in the post, then asked for some illustrated newspapers to read and for the *New Times* and the *Russian Gazette*. We did not give him the two journals, for fear of tiring him.

At about three he began choking and tossing, then he went to sleep. They have been giving him digitalis, first every four hours, then every two hours. He has coffee with milk, milk with Ems water, raw eggs and wine with Ems water; and they dilute the digitalis in champagne.

It is now eight o'clock in the evening and he is sleeping peacefully.

He generally calls for Andryusha when it is time for him to change position, and he eats most happily from Masha's hand. My suffering for him is involuntarily communicated to him, he often strokes my hand and tries to spare my strength – and he will accept only the lightest personal attentions from me now.

January 31 He had a bad night. He tossed and gasped until 4 a.m., called twice for Seryozha and asked him to sit him up in bed.

Yesterday he said to Tanya: 'What was it they said about Adam Vasilevich (Count Olsufiev)? That he had an easy death?[12] Well it's not at all easy to die, it's hard, very hard, to cast off this familiar skin,' he said, pointing to his emaciated body.

Lyovochka was better today and called for Dunaev and Misha; every new arrival delights him. Ilya's wife, Sonya, also arrived today. It's noisy and crowded here, but still the death of this great man, my beloved husband, pursues its natural course. I certainly don't believe in a complete recovery – I can barely believe in a temporary respite . . .

He has been dictating notes for his notebook again, as well as for some articles which he has already started.[13] He looks so peaceful and serious in bed. He dictated a long telegram to his brother Sergei.[14]

February 1 He has had a terrible night. He was awake until seven in the morning, he had a stomach-ache and he was gasping for breath. I massaged his stomach several times, but it did not help. Once he fell asleep for ten minutes while I was massaging, and I stopped rubbing and froze, kneeling on the floor, with my hand on his left side. I thought he would take a nap, but he soon woke up and started groaning again. At five in the morning I went out and Liza and Seryozha took my place. At seven o'clock we woke up Doctor Shurovskii, who gave him a morphine injection. Doctor Elpatevskii also kept watch over him, but by then he was so exhausted that he went to sleep. He had a fairly peaceful day, and Shchurovskii put another plaster on his left side.

He dictated some notes to Masha for his notebook.[15]

February 2 Ilya's wife, Sonya, came yesterday evening, as well as old Uncle Kostya and Varya Nagornova. Lev Nikolaevich is obviously delighted to have visitors.

Last night started badly again. After Boulanger and I lifted him up in bed and I had been attending to him for some time, he said to me, 'Darling, I have exhausted you.'

At three in the morning he had a small morphine injection (a sixth of a grain), and ten minutes later fell asleep and slept till morning. Today for the first time his temperature was 35.9 instead of 36.9. He tucked into an egg and some tapioca with milk, and is looking forward to a meringue for dinner – the doctor has allowed this.

He dictated to Masha some corrections to his article 'On Freedom of Conscience'.

Yesterday all the children and I had our photograph taken – in memory of a sad but important time.

February 3 Last night I was again plunged into despair. His temperature went up to 37.8. It was a terrible night; at three in the morning he had another morphine injection, but it did not relieve his agony and insomnia. I was alone with him till five. Seryozha and Doctor Altschuler came in twice.

After I had lifted Lyovochka up in the bed and had attended to him all night without once sitting down, he squeezed my hands and stroked them tenderly, saying: 'Many thanks, darling,' and 'Sonya, I have exhausted you.' And I kissed his forehead and hands and said it gave me great pleasure to look after him, if only to relieve his sufferings a little.

He had a bad chest again and was gasping for breath; he drank a little wine and champagne mixed with water.

His temperature was 37.2 or .4 this morning, yet he was dictating in his weak voice still more corrections to his article. He takes an interest in the letters, of which we give him an abbreviated account.

The *Russian Gazette* has at last published news today of Lev Nikolaevich's illness.

Yesterday morning Lyova left for St Petersburg.

L.N. has just taken a little soup, an egg and a meringue. He asked Sonya, 'Where did you bury your mother last year?' 'We took her body to

Paniki, at my brother's request.' 'How senseless,' said L.N. 'What's the point of moving a dead body?'

February 4 Last night L.N. had a morphine injection and slept quite peacefully. This morning he was more cheerful than he has been for a long time; his temperature was 36.7, rising again to 37.7 towards evening.

Shchurovskii has left for St Petersburg, and Misha and Ilya also left today. When he was saying goodbye to them he told them that he might well die, but that he would die with the same faith with which he had lived for the last 25 years. 'Let my family ask me, when I am on the point of death, whether my faith was good and true and whether it helped me in the final moment, and I shall nod my head in a sign of assent.'

Ilyusha wept when saying goodbye to him.[16] Lyovochka called out to me twice today, and once he asked: 'Why are you so quiet, are you asleep?' I had been sitting alone feeling lonely and sad, and he had *sensed* this.

February 5 The situation is unchanged. A night under morphine – they gave him an injection of ⅛ of a grain. Temperature 36.7 in the morning, rising to 37.4 towards six in the evening. He is calm and silent; he drinks champagne and milk with Ems water, and eats purèed oat soup, eggs and gruel. We applied a compress today. I am sitting here exhausted and numb; it has all been too much for my heart, I have thought so much, felt so much – and now I have just slumped, waiting.

February 6 9 in the evening. A sleepless night, two injections of morphine, nothing helped. At 5 o'clock I went off to bed, exhausted. A morning of anxieties. He felt chilled all day, then suddenly ran a high fever and his temperature went up to 38.7. Chest pains.

Elpatevskii and Altschuler came. They say this is the crisis. The pneumonia has suddenly started to clear from both lungs. But what will happen when his temperature falls – what if his strength suddenly fails him too? We are all living in terror. I lay down for a couple of hours like a corpse, my strength suddenly gone. How shall I endure the night? None of us will sleep in anticipation of the crisis. 'Everything is in the balance,' said Lev Nikolaevich today to his niece Varenka. He is taking his own pulse and temperature and is very frightened; we are forced to deceive him and reduce the degrees.

The cold and wind make matters worse.

February 7 The situation is almost, one might say totally, hopeless. His pulse was inaudible all morning. He had two camphor injections. A sleepless night. Pain in the liver. Suffering. Unnatural agitation due to all the valerian drops, champagne and so on. Until 5 o'clock I was doing everything I could to relieve his suffering. The only time my darling

Lyovochka dropped off was when I lightly massaged his stomach and liver. He thanked me and said: 'Darling, you must be exhausted.'

Olga's pains began this morning, and at seven she gave birth to a dead baby boy.

Today Lev Nikolaevich said: 'There, you've arranged everything perfectly, give me a camphor injection and I'll die.'

Another time he said: 'Don't try to predict what will happen. I can't foresee anything.'

He asked for the medical notes on the progression of his illness – his temperature chart, medicines, diet and so on – and read it closely. Then he asked Masha what she had felt during the crisis in her typhus attack. Poor, poor man, he so wants to go on living, yet his life is slipping away . . .

This morning his temperature was 36.2 and now, at seven in the evening, it is 36.7. He won't eat anything unless we make him. And when we told him that his temperature was 36.6 he said in despair: 'And afterwards it will go up to 37, then 37.5, and so on.'

There is thick snow on the ground and a strong wind. Oh this hateful Crimea!

Tonight there were eight degrees of frost.

February 8 Lev Nikolaevich spent a slightly more comfortable night, although he woke up several times. But he did get some sleep. And he slept this morning too. His temperature was 36.4, and 36.7 this evening. It is now 7 p.m.; he is weak and dozing, but all is well, and his pulse is regular and his pneumonia is clearing.

He called Masha today and dictated a page of ideas to her – all against war and 'fratricide', as he calls it.[17]

I sat with him until five in the morning; I turned him over with the help of Pavl. Aleks. Boulanger, changed his soaking underwear and gave him his medicine (digitalis), and some champagne and milk.

When I examine my soul I realise that my entire being aspires only to nurse this beloved man back to life. But when I'm sitting with my eyes closed all sort of dreams suddenly creep up on me, and plans for the most diverse, varied and improbable life . . . Then I come back to reality and my heart aches again for the death of this man who has become so much part of my life that I could not now imagine myself without him.

A strange double life. The cause, I explain to myself, is my own indestructible health, my enormous energy, which demands an outlet and finds nourishment only in those difficult moments when it is really necessary to *do* something – feeding, washing, turning over and attending to the patient. And not to sleep – and that is the hardest thing of all. But as soon as there is nothing to do, in all those hours spent sitting beside the patient, then the life of the imagination sets to work.

If it weren't for my failing sight, I should read; what a good diversion and use of the time that would be!

February 9 Another sleepless night of toil and anxiety and suffering! His liver and stomach were aching.

When he asked to be propped up in bed last night and asked me to sit beside him and support him, it broke my heart to feel the pitiful bones of my powerful giant, once so hearty and strong, now so sick and suffering. None of the people looking after him can possibly feel what I feel. Quite apart from the emotional pain, I always feel as though something were being torn from me when he suffers.

The other day he said: 'It keeps hurting, the machine has broken down. Pull the nose and the tail gets stuck, pull the tail and the nose gets stuck.' And this morning he was exhausted and said: 'How hard it is to die when you're neither dying nor getting any better.' Oh, what will happen?

Yesterday was a fine day, and he was better. It is snowing again today, and it is dark, overcast and freezing; yesterday there were 3 degrees of frost.

Yesterday evening L.N. again dictated some thoughts to Pavel Aleksandrovich Boulanger.[18]

February 10 Another fine day – it was 3 degrees; our dear invalid had a good night and was in less pain during the day, although he is still dreadfully weak and he had a temperature of 36.3. He hasn't said a word all day, nothing interests him, he just lies there quietly; he had three small drinks of coffee, asked once for some champagne and was given two camphor injections. He is peaceful and I too feel fairly calm.

I am re-reading Lev Nikolaevich's work *The Christian Doctrine*. I feel as though I have known it all for a long, long time, as though I have known it since childhood and thought about it twenty times.

'The purpose of human life consists in the desire for happiness, one's own and every living creature's. Only if people join together is it possible to attain this . . .'[19]

And which of us in their earliest childhood did not experience this longing for *everyone* to be happy and well? Maman is happy, Papa is laughing, Nurse has been given a dress, the dog has been fed, I've made peace with Misha – all is right with the world because *everyone* is happy.

But when you get a bit older and grow up you realise that there is suffering everywhere, and *everyone is unhappy*. The other day I was looking through the newspaper: an earthquake in Shemakha in Azerbaijan, thousands perish in terrible agony . . . Some English soldiers have made a living rampart out of women and children and protect themselves with them while they shoot the Boers, in other words these same women's husbands, brothers and sons.

And it's hard to believe that one's ardent childish desire for universal happiness has any meaning at all, and one loses heart. Although of course it does not prevent one's soul from aspiring to this, and love, and God.
Evening L.N. has been asleep almost all day. This evening he called Masha and me and told us to write to Lyova, who was terribly distressed at having upset his father with his novel, and the announcement by the journal's editor that it was written against the Tolstoyans, and this is what he said: 'I very much regret that I said something which offended you. It is not right for two people to be estranged, especially when they are as closely connected as we are. There can be no question of forgiving what was said of course . . .'[20]

My little soul was excited by various announcements of concerts, and the performance of some of Sergei Ivanovich's works, and like a starving man seeking food I suddenly had a passionate desire for music, especially the music of Taneev, which has always had such a profound and powerful effect on me.

February 12 L.N. has been very weak and drowsy lately, and hardly speaks at all. Yesterday he asked Doctor Volkov how the common people cured old men like him – did they give them camphor injections? Who lifted them up in bed? What did they give them to eat? Volkov answered all his questions, saying they treated them just the same, but that it was generally the family or the neighbours who attended to them, lifted them up and helped them.

Shchurovskii has returned, bringing his daughter with him.

Sasha is ill. It is a little warmer.

I am physically and emotionally exhausted, but God gives me strength and I thank Him for that.

February 13 He had another bad night. Yesterday his temperature stayed at around 37 all day. Today it has been 36.5. But there was this terrible weakness and drowsiness all day; he did not even wash himself and was too sleepy to take more than two tiny cups of coffee, two eggs and one small glass of milk. I slept this morning and spent the whole day sitting with Lyovochka, sewing pillow-cases, cushion-covers and so on.

Today I finished reading Lyovochka's *Christian Doctrine*. It is very good on prayer and the after-life.[21]

February 14 An anxious night. It's a long time since I felt so weak and exhausted as I do today. My heart is weak again and I am short of breath.

I read my unfinished children's story 'Skeletons' to the children, Varya Nagornova and some young ladies, and they seemed to like it.[22]

As for Lyovochka, I simply don't know what to think: he eats less and less, his nights are worse and worse, he talks more and more quietly. I don't know whether this weakness is temporary or terminal. I keep hoping, but today matters have again taken a gloomy turn.

How I should love to look after him patiently and gently to the end, and forget all the old heartaches he has caused me. But instead I cried bitterly today for the way he persistently scorns all my love and concern for him. He asked for some sieved porridge, so I ran off to the kitchen and ordered it, then came back and sat beside him. He dozed off, the porridge came and when he awoke I quietly put it on a plate and offered it to him. He then grew furious and said that he would ask for it himself, and that throughout his illness he had always taken his food, medicines and drinks from other people, not me. (Although when someone has to lift him up, go without sleep, attend to him in the most intimate ways and apply his compresses, it is, of course, me whom he forces mercilessly to help him.) With the porridge, however, I decided to employ a little cunning, so I called Liza to him and sat down in the next room; and the moment I had gone out he asked for the porridge, and I began weeping.

This little episode summarises my whole difficult life with him. This difficulty consists of one long struggle with his *contrary spirit*. My most reasonable and gentle advice to him has always met with protest.

February 15 For the past three days Lyovochka has been getting weaker and refusing to eat. Today matters were complicated by a bad pain in his gall bladder. Masha and I applied an oil and chloroform compress and he is now a little better. But his arms and legs are cold . . . The doctors say there is still hope, but his heart pains are insufferable and there seems little cause for it . . . He slept quite well last night and I sat up with him until five in the morning, when Liza took my place. Once, when Lyovochka was gripped with an agonising pain in his right side, I bent over him, kissed his forehead and hands and said how sorry for him I was, and how I hated to see him in such pain again. He looked weakly at me, his eyes full of tears, and said quietly: 'It doesn't matter, darling, it's all for the best.'

And today for the first time I was pleased to see in him a calm resignation, instead of that mournful desire to get better. Help him, oh Lord, then it will be easier for him to suffer and die.

Sasha is ill. I have now started worrying about her too. My God, what a dismal winter we are having! Two stillborn grandchildren, Lev Nikolaevich gravely ill – I wonder what else lies in store for us! Today L.N. had a temperature of 36.2 and his pulse was 100. They gave him another camphor injection.

Evening I received a letter from the St Petersburg Metropolitan Antonii exhorting me to persuade Lev Nikolaevich to return to the faith and make his peace with the Church, and help him to die like a Christian. I told Lyovochka about this letter and he told me I should write to Antonii that his business was now with God, and should tell him that his last prayer had been: 'I left Thee. Now I am coming to Thee. Thy will be done.' And when I said that if God sent death then one should reconcile oneself in death to everything on earth, including the Church, L.N. said: 'There can be no question of reconciliation. I am dying without anger or enmity in my heart, but what is the Church? What sort of reconciliation could there be with something so undefined?' Then he sent Tanya to tell me not to write anything to Antonii.[23]

The pains in his right side are now much worse; his lungs are still inflamed and tomorrow they are going to apply a plaster.

It's foggy and cool. There is a steamer in the sea beyond Gaspra, and its sirens are hooting mournfully. The steamers are all at anchor at the moment; I suppose they are afraid to move in this fog.

February 16 Lev Nikolaevich is a little better today: he is not in pain and is lying quietly; he slept much better too, both last night and today. But I am afraid to rejoice. Shchurovskii has left and Slivitskii is coming; he is a former *zemstvo* doctor who attends the Sukhotins, an excellent man, no longer young. The weather was bright and warm this morning, but now it has clouded over again.

I sat beside Lev Nikolaevich while he was asleep and read a book about the last years of Byron's life. There are a great many unfamiliar names and episodes in it, and a great deal of *specialist* information, but it was all very interesting. What a powerful, important man and poet he was. And what a fine attitude he took to so many questions which even now have not been properly aired in public. Both he and his friend Shelley met sad ends: Shelley was drowned in the sea, and he died in Greece trying to achieve a general armistice.

It is extraordinary how selfless these doctors are: neither Shurovskii nor Altschuler nor the *zemstvo* doctor Volkov, the poorest but kindest of them all, will accept any money; they are all so generous with their time, and never begrudge the labour, the financial loss or the sleepless nights. They put a plaster on his right side today.

The back of my head was aching this evening, and my head felt as though it would burst, so I lay down on the divan in Lev Nikolaevich's room. He called out to me. I got up and went in to him. 'Why are you lying down?' he said. 'I can't call you if you do that.'

'The back of my head is aching,' I said. 'What do you mean, you can't call me? You call me at night.' And I sat down on a chair. He then called to me again: 'Go into the other room and lie down. Why are you sitting up?' 'But I can't leave – there's no one here,' I said. I was terribly agitated, and I was almost hysterical I was so tired. Then Masha came in and I left, but then urgent tasks awaited me on all sides – business documents from the accountant in Moscow, summonses and translations, and everything had to be entered into the book, signed and sent off. Then Sasha had to have a compress, the washerwoman and the cook had to be paid, the notes had to be sent off to Yalta . . .

February 19 I have not written my diary for several days: the nursing is very hard work and leaves me with so little time – barely enough for housework and essential letters and business.

My poor Lyovochka is still very weak, languishing with this long illness of his. Doctor Slivitskii arrived on the evening of the 17th and will be staying with us for the time being. Volkov and Altschuler come every day to administer his daily camphor injection and give him his Nux Vomica. L.N. has been very thirsty, and today he drank as many as four half-bottles of *kefir*. The doctors say the pneumonia is making very slow progress in clearing from the right lung. But I am more worried about this daily fever. This morning he had a temperature of 36.1, and by six this evening it was 37.5. This is what it was both yesterday and today.

Tatarin came to give his regards and wish us health, bringing a fez and a yashmak as presents; L.N. tried on the fez too. Two nights ago he called Boulanger again and dictated his thoughts to him.[24] What a need he has for intellectual work!

Liza Obolenskaya has decided not to leave but to stay here and look after Lev Nikolaevich, which I find most touching.

February 20 He was better yesterday; his temperature was only 37.1 and he was much more cheerful. 'I see I shall now have to live again,' he said to Doctor Volkov.

'Are you bored then?' I asked him, and he said with sudden animation: 'Bored? How could I be? On the contrary, everything is splendid.' This evening he was concerned that I might be tired, and squeezed my hand, looked at me tenderly and said: 'Thank you, darling, that's wonderful.'

February 22 Lev Nikolaevich is much better; his temperature was 36.1 this morning and 36.6 this evening. They are still giving him camphor injections, and arsenic every other morning. Boulanger reluctantly returned to his family today. What a grief it must be to have a family one doesn't love – none of the rewards and all the difficulties.

I still stay with him every day until 5 a.m., and am then too exhausted to sleep. I sit sewing all day in the room of an invalid who is irritated by the slightest rustle. The housekeeping is very tedious and difficult because everything is so expensive. I wrote a few words in response to Metropolitan Antonii's letter.[25] Sasha is still ill with a bad attack of membranous colitis, and her ear and teeth ache too. It is cold and snowing.

I received a letter from Butyonev suggesting that I resign as guardian of the orphans' home as I am away and cannot be useful to them.[26] We shall see whom they choose in my place and how they run their affairs.

February 23 Another bad night. Towards evening his temperature rose to 37.4, and his pulse was 107, although it soon dropped to 88, and then 89.

At night he called out to me: 'Sonya?' I went in to him. 'I was just dreaming that you and I were driving to Nikolskoe in a sledge together.'

This morning he told me how well I had looked after him in the night.

February 25 The first day of Lent. I yearn for the mood of peace, prayer and self-denial, the anticipation of spring and all the childhood memories which assail me in Moscow and Yasnaya with the approach of Lent.

But everything is so alien here, so indiscriminate.

Lev Nikolaevich's condition is almost exactly the same. He is more cheerful in himself, and for the first time last night he slept from 12 to 3 without once waking up; at 5 a.m. I went off to take a sleep and he was awake the rest of the night. This morning he read the papers and took an interest in his letters, although the letters themselves weren't at all interesting. Two exhort him to return to the Church and receive the Eucharist – there have been others like this – two beg him to send his works as a gift, and two foreigners express feelings of rapture and reverence. I too received a letter, from Princess Maria Dondukova-Korsakova, saying I should draw L.N. back to the Church and give him the Eucharist.[27]

These spiritual sovereigns expel L.N. from the Church and help him to leave – then call on me to draw him back to it! How absurd!

It is grey, cold and windy. The whole of February has been quite appalling: this climate is vile and most unhealthy. Sasha is better.

February 27 I did not write anything yesterday. I noticed a deterioration in Lev Nikolaevich's condition this morning. He had slept badly the night before and had eaten almost nothing all that day; in the middle of the day his temperature went up to 37.5, and towards night it was 38.3. And again I was thrown into a state of terror. When I counted his frighteningly fast and irregular pulse of 108 per minute, I almost became ill myself with the emotional *angoisse* which I have experienced so often this winter.

But L.N. did not sleep badly that night, towards three this morning his temperature went down to 37.5, and later this morning it was 36.1. His energy and appetite returned, he even read the newspaper, eagerly drank *kefir* again and he ate three small meals.

Seryozha looked after his father all night with extraordinary energy, gentleness and care. 'How astonishing,' Lev Nikolaevich said to me. 'I never expected Seryozha to be so sensitive and attentive,' and his voice was trembling with tears.

Today he said to me: 'I have now decided to expect nothing more; I kept expecting to recover, but now what will be will be and it's no use trying to anticipate the future.' He himself now reminds me to give him his digitalis, or asks for the thermometer to take his temperature. He is drinking champagne again and lets them give him camphor injections.

February 28 It is now 10.30 at night. Lev Nikolaevich has a temperature of 38 again and his pulse is weak and irregular and is causing great alarm. Today he said to Tanya: 'A long illness is a good thing, for it gives one time to prepare for death.'

And he also said to her today: 'I am ready for anything; I am ready to live and ready to die.'

This evening he stroked my hands and thanked me. But when I changed his bedclothes he suddenly lost his temper because he felt cold. Then of course he felt sorry for me.

This morning he had something to eat and looked through the newspaper, and by this evening he was feeling very weak.

A terrible blizzard with one degree of frost; the wind is howling, shaking and banging the window frames.

I spilt some ink and got it all over everything.

March 4 Lev Nikolaevich is steadily improving from one day to the next. The doctors listened to his heart and said there was still a lot of wheezing. Yesterday evening he dictated to me a letter in reply to Bertenson,[28] and every day Boulanger sends off open letters to various people at his dictation.[29] This Boulanger is a splendid man, and he looked after L.N. like a son, yet I have a slight feeling of distaste for him, amounting almost to physical disgust. But then so few men are at all likeable.

March 5 Lev Nikolaevich is better; his temperature was 35.7 this morning and 36.7 this evening. The doctors say there is still some wheezing, but apart from that everything is quite normal. He has such a huge appetite that he cannot wait for his dinner and lunch, and he has drunk three bottles of *kefir* in the past twenty-four hours. Today he asked for his bed to be moved to the window so that he could look out at the sea. He is still very weak and thin, he sleeps badly at night and is very demanding. He once called out five times in one hour – first he wanted his pillow adjusted, then he needed his leg covered up, then the clock was in the wrong place, then he wanted some *kefir*, then he wanted his back sponged, then I had to sit with him and hold his hands . . . And the moment one lies down he calls out again.

We have had a fine day and the nights are moonlit, but I feel dead, dead as the rocky landscape and the dull sea. The birds have been singing outside and for some reason neither the birds, nor the fly buzzing by the window, nor the moon seem to belong to the Crimea, but keep reminding me of spring-time in Yasnaya Polyana or Moscow. So the fly takes me back to a hot summer at harvest time, and the moon evokes memories of our garden in Khamovniki Street, and returning home from concerts . . .

March 6 Last night was frightful. Agony in his body, his legs, his soul – it was all too much for him, and what grieved me most was that he let slip how bad he felt and cursed the fact that he had got better. 'I can't imagine why I recovered, I wish I'd died.'

He was sunk in apathy all day. I sat with him as usual, but slipped off to the side wing for the first time to play a few of my favourite pieces . . . But now I mustn't even do this.

March 7 We were absolutely terrified – in the middle of the day his pulse suddenly started pounding at 108 per minute, yet Lev Nikolaevich himself had been utterly apathetic all day, wouldn't sit up or wash himself, and had almost no dinner – although he ate well this morning. His temperature did not go above 36.8, and this evening it was even lower. His liver ached and we put compresses on both his stomach and his lungs.

The weather has been fine these past three days, but *le fond de l'air* has been cold. This morning it was 4–5 degrees and windy, but the sun is blazing, the buds are bursting and the birds are singing.

March 8 I felt quite ill when I got up this morning: I had aches in the pit of my stomach and back, even though L.N. had a very good night and slept better than he has done for a long time.

I had a nasty scene with Seryozha. He has an insufferable character – argumentative, strident and constantly spoiling for *une querelle.* This morning I had to take my coffee into the drawing-room, where I collapsed in hysterics. This happened the other day too, when Seryozha shouted at a servant and provoked him beyond endurance. This time it was all because of Lev Nikolaevich's new armchair: Seryozha said we should wire Odessa about it, but he had absolutely no idea where or whom. I said we should first decide what kind of armchair was needed, then send a detailed letter to Moscow about it. This made him lose his temper completely and he began shouting.

March 10 I went out for my first walk today and was astonished to see that spring was here. The grass is like the grass at home in Russia during May, various coloured primulas are in flower and there are dandelions and dead-nettles all over the place. The sun is bright, the sea and sky are blue and the birds, sweet creatures, are singing.

Lev Nikolaevich has made a marked improvement in this fine weather – his temperature was 35.9 today and his pulse was 88. He has a huge appetite, he drinks *kefir* day and night with great relish and reads the papers and letters. But he doesn't seem very cheerful.

Liza Obolenskaya and Doctor Slivitskii left yesterday. An Armenian doctor (in exile)[30] spent the night with L.N. and I was with him again until 4.30, when Tanya came.

March 11 Lev Nikolaevich is getting better. I went to Yalta, it was a lovely day, the sea and sky were blue, the birds were singing, the grass was springing up everywhere. The trees are still bare, but here and there the odd almond tree is in flower. This evening I was sitting with L.N. and he said: 'I've made up some verses, or rather paraphrased the one that goes:
"Everything is mine, said gold." And I've said:
"I'll break everything, said strength,
"I'll grow everything, said thought."'[31]

We rubbed him all over with spirit and warm water, and at ten o'clock we put him to bed.

March 12 Lev Nikolaevich is slowly but surely getting better. Today he read the *Herald of Europe* and the newspapers, and took an interest in the latest Moscow news from Lyova Sukhotin, who has just come from there. Doctor Altschuler was here and is considering whether to apply another plaster.

I resolutely stayed at home all day and sewed, getting up only to attend to Lev Nikolaevich. I always wash him myself every morning, give him breakfast and brush his hair. His temperature went up to 36.8 this evening, but he ate well and went off to sleep quickly. He is certainly recovering now, but his pulse is still somewhere between 88–89 and 92.

March 13 It is warmer – 13 degrees in the shade – and there was a warm rain. Lev Nikolaevich continues to improve. I am still sitting with him until 5 in the morning; Sasha took my place yesterday and Tanya will do so today.

Late yesterday evening I read a translation of an essay by Emerson called 'The Over-Soul'. I could find little new in it: it was all said long ago and much better by the ancient philosophers – amongst other things, the statement that every *genius* is more closely connected to the dead philosophers than to the living members of his family circle. It is rather a naïve conclusion.[32] Of course it's true that when their material earthly life has fallen away, there remains nothing of these dead philosophers but their written thoughts. So that not only geniuses but we simple mortals, when we read their thoughts, can come into much closer contact with these dead philosophers than with geniuses, even living ones. For living geniuses, until they have thrown off their mortal envelope and passed into history with their works, are created to consume the entire existence of the apparently uncomprehending members of their family circle.

For a *genius* one has to create a peaceful, cheerful, comfortable home; a *genius* must be fed, washed and dressed, must have his works copied out innumerable times, must be loved and spared all cause for jealousy, so that he can be calm; then one must feed and educate the innumerable children fathered by this genius, whom he cannot be bothered to care for himself, as he has to commune with all the Epictetuses, Socrateses and Buddhas, and aspire to be like them himself.

And when the members of his family circle have sacrificed their youth, beauty – everything – to serve this genius, they are then blamed for *not understanding* geniuses properly – and they never get a word of thanks from the geniuses themselves of course, for sacrificing their pure young lives to him, and atrophying all their spiritual and intellectual capacities, which they are unable to nourish and develop due to a lack of peace, leisure and energy.

I have served a *genius* for almost forty years. Hundreds of times I have felt my intellectual energy stir within me, and all sorts of desires – a longing for education, a love of music and the arts . . . And time and again I have crushed and smothered all these longings, and now and to the end of my life I shall somehow or other continue to serve my *genius*.

Everyone asks: 'But why should a worthless woman like you need an intellectual or artistic life?' To this question I can only reply: 'I don't know, but eternally suppressing it to serve a genius is a great misfortune.' However much one loves this man whom people regard as a *genius*, to do nothing but bear and feed his children, sew, order dinner, apply compresses and enemas and silently sit there dully awaiting his demands for one's services, is sheer torture. And there is never anything in *return* for it either, not even simple gratitude, and there's always such a lot to grumble about instead. I have borne this burden for too long, and I am worn out.

This tirade about the way geniuses are misunderstood by their families was provoked by my anger at Emerson and all those who have written and spoken about this question since the days of Socrates and Xantippe.

When genuine love exists between a genius and his wife, as there used to be between Lev Nikolaevich and me, she does not need a great mind to understand him, she needs only her loving feelings and the instincts of her heart, and everything will be clear and they will both be happy, as we used to be. I never minded spending my entire life labouring and serving my genius husband, until I read his diaries and saw that he had always blamed *me* for his being so famous. (He had somehow to justify his life of comparative luxury with me.) This happened in the year of my Vanechka's death, when I clung to my husband with my grief-stricken soul – and was cruelly disappointed in my feelings for him.

March 15 L.N. was awake all last night with terrible pains in the legs and stomach. This morning he had a temperature of 36.1, and this evening it was 36.5. He was very listless all day; he looked through the letters and papers, dictated a letter to Liza Obolenskaya[33] and hardly spoke a word.

I drove back from the sea with Masha and Kolya. (I had walked there earlier on with Yulia Ivanovna.) Waves, breakers, shades of green – I am feeling so gloomy, nothing touches me. It doesn't feel as though spring were here. Not at all like our triumphant Russian spring, with the snow and ice shifting, the rivers bursting their banks, the torrents flooding, the birds arriving, and as if by a miracle everything turning green, flourishing, coming to life . . . Here it's a little warmer, the parks are slightly green, but it's just the same old rocks, the same crooked trees, lifeless earth and tossing sea.

I did a lot of sewing today.

March 19 Life here is so monotonous, there's nothing to write about. L.N.'s illness has almost run its course; he is just very weak now and occasionally his temperature goes up to 37 degrees. His pulse is 80 in the morning, 92–6 after he has eaten. He has a good appetite, but his nights are disturbed.

As for his state of mind I can see only that he is depressed and silent. Whenever I come into his room he is intently counting his pulse beats. Today he was looking through the window at the sun, poor man, and he begged me to open the door of the terrace for a moment. But I simply did not dare to.

April 5 A lot of time has passed and little has happened. Tanya left on March 30 with her family and Andryusha arrived on the 24th. L.N.'s health is almost the same, but his pulse has been much faster these past few days. His various treatments continue – he has been having arsenic injections since April 2, and today they gave him electrical treatment for his stomach; he was taking Nux Vomica but is now taking magnesium, and at night he has bismuth with codeine and ether-valerian drops. His nights are very disturbed and his legs and stomach ache, so his legs have to be massaged, which I find very tiring: my back aches, the blood rushes to my head and I feel quite hysterical. He rejected all such things, of course, when his health was good, but with the onset of his first serious illness every conceivable treatment is set in motion. Three doctors visit practically every day; nursing him is extremely hard work, there are a lot of us here, we are all tired and overworked, and our personal lives have been completely eaten up by his illness. Lev Nikolaevich is first and foremost a writer and expounder of ideas: in reality and in his life he is a weak man, much weaker than us simple mortals. I could not endure the thought of writing and saying one thing and living and acting another, but it doesn't seem to bother him especially, just so long as he doesn't suffer, so long as he lives and gets better . . . What a lot of attention he devotes to himself these days, taking his medicines and having his compresses changed, and what a lot of effort he takes to feed himself, sleep and lessen the pain.

L.N. has been very upset by news of the assassination of Sipyagin, Minister of Internal Affairs.[34] Evil begets evil – it is truly terrible. He spent a long time today on a letter to Grand Duke Nikolai Mikhailovich, expounding to him, as he had done in his letter to the Tsar, his views on land ownership according to the system of Henry George. He wrote also that Sipyagin's murder might well unleash further evils, and that in order to put a stop to this it was necessary to change the system of government in Russia.[35]

Yesterday and today I played the piano in the side wing for over two hours on my own, which was very pleasant.

The weather has been quite appalling – a blizzard and a cold wind. It has been 4 degrees for the past few days, although today it was 7 degrees. I don't leave the house any more and just stay here sewing and reading. My eyes are bad.

April 13 Saturday, the evening before Easter Sunday, and my God, the depression is unbearable! I am sitting all on my own upstairs in the bedroom, with my granddaughter Sonyushka sleeping beside me, while downstairs in the dining-room there is the most vile heathen commotion going on. They are all playing vint, they have wheeled Lev Nikolaevich's armchair in there, and he is enthusiastically following Sasha's game.

I am feeling very lonely. My children are even more despotic, rude and demanding than their father. And their father is so good at arguing irresistibly in paradoxes and false ideas that I, who lack both his mind and his prestige, am completely powerless to make any demands. His present state grieves me terribly. All morning, all day and all night, hour after hour, he looks after, attends to and cares for his body, and I can detect absolutely no spiritual feelings in him whatsoever. He used to talk about death, his attitude to God and eternal life. When I observe him now I realise to my horror that there is not a trace of religion left in him. With me he is rude and demanding, and if I do something carelessly out of sheer exhaustion he shouts at me peevishly.

May 11 I am ashamed of all the unkind things I wrote in my diary last time about Lyovochka and my family. I was angry about their attitude to Holy Week, and instead of being mindful of my own sinfulness, I transferred my anger to my nearest and dearest. 'Grant me to see my own sins and not judge my brother . . . '

What a long time has passed since then, and what a ghastly time we are going through once again!

L.N. was at last beginning to recover from the pneumonia; he was walking about the house with a stick, eating well and digesting his food.

15 Moscow, 1896. At the back, Sofia Tolstaya and Sergei Taneev. At the front, left to right, Maria Tolstaya, Tatiana Tolstaya, Konstantin Nikolaevich Igumnov

16 Above: Vladimir Chertkov with colleagues at the Free Word publishing house in Christchurch, England, *c.*1901

17 Below: Gaspra, Crimea, 1901. Left to right, Anton Chekhov, Sofia Tolstaya, Lev Tolstoy and their daughter Maria

Masha then suggested that I attend to my business in Yasnaya and Moscow, for this really was very necessary. After turning it over in my mind I decided to go, for as short a time as possible, and on the morning of April 22 I left.

My trip was very pleasant and successful. I spent a day at Yasnaya Polyana, where Andryusha joined me. The weather was delightful; I adore the early spring, with its soft green hues and its fresh hopes for a new and better life . . . I busied myself with the accounts and bills, toured the apple orchards with the instructor, inspected the cattle and walked over to Chepyzh as the sun was setting. The lungwort and violets were blooming, the birds were singing, the sun was setting over the felled forest, and this pure natural beauty, free of all human cares, filled me with joy.

In Moscow I was delighted by the way people treated me. Everyone was so friendly and cheerful, as though they were all my friends. Even people in the shops and banks welcomed me back most warmly after my long absence.

I dealt successfully with my business; visited the Wanderers' Exhibition[36] and the exhibition of St Petersburg artists; went to an examination performance of Mozart's cheerful opera *Cosi Fan Tutti* [*sic*]; saw a lot of friends, and on Sunday invited a group of my closest friends to the house – Marusya, the Maklakovs, Uncle Kostya, Misha Sukhotin and Sergei Ivanovich, who played me some of Arenskii's lesser-known pieces, a Schumann sonata and his own charming symphony, which gave me more pleasure than anything else.

Soothed and satisfied, I set off for Gaspra, assuming from the daily telegrams that everything there was in order; I looked forward to spending the month of May in Gaspra, and having the pleasure of seeing L.N. recover. But on my return to Gaspra on the evening of May 1 I discover that L.N. has had a fever for the past two or three evenings, and has deteriorated daily. He had a high temperature every day, and eventually typhoid fever was diagnosed. These past days and nights have been sheer agony and terror for all of us. And last night, between 10 and 11 o'clock, with a temperature which had earlier been as high as 39 degrees, and today was down to 38.6, his pulse suddenly started to waver, constantly stopping and starting, and it was so weak and inaudible that we could not count the beats. I sat by Lyovochka's bed all night, and Kolechka Gué came and went, although he declined to take his pulse, saying he didn't know how to. At two in the morning I called Doctor Nikitin who is staying here with us, and he administered some strophanthus, stayed a while, then went off to bed. At four in the morning I felt his pulse again and there was no improvement, so I gave him some coffee with two teaspoonsful of cognac, and he had a camphor injection. Towards morning his pulse improved, I sponged him down and his temperature went down to 36.7.

Lev Nikolaevich is now lying quietly in the large gloomy Gaspra drawing-room and I am writing at the table. The house is gloomy, silent and ominous.

L.N. is in a tearful depressed state of mind, but he dreads the idea of dying. Yet when I asked him about his emotional state yesterday he replied, 'Tired, terribly tired, and I want to die.' But he is looking after himself assiduously, taking responsibility for his own pulse and treatment. In the mornings, when he is better, he catches up with the newspapers, looks through the post and peruses the books people send him.

Today Doctor Shchurovskii is coming from Moscow, and Tanya, Seryozha, Gué, Igumnova, Natasha Obolenskaya and Sasha have all arrived from Kochety to look after the invalid. Seryozha is being harsh and unpleasant to me.

May 13 Lev Nikolaevich is better, thank God. His temperature is falling steadily and his pulse has improved. Shchurovskii left yesterday. Today P.A. Boulanger and my son Ilya came. Kolechka Gué is going tomorrow. All this coming and going is rather tiresome. Seryozha is being insufferable and keeps finding new reasons for being angry with me: he had decided beforehand to reproach me for wanting to take his father to Moscow this *winter*! How foolish, spiteful and unreasonable of him! L.N. hasn't even recovered from his serious illness and Seryozha is already imagining what will happen in the autumn. But what *do* I want? I just don't know. Sensitivity, a clear, bright understanding of life, the desire for peace and happiness – I have a heightened sense of all these things at present. But life brings one nothing but suffering – and one simply submits to it.

I live only for *today*, and it's enough for me if everything is all right. I played the piano alone for two hours in the wing while L.N. slept.

May 15 This unpleasantness with Seryozha has taken its toll. Yesterday I had such terrible pains all over my body that I thought I was dying. I am better today though. L.N.'s typhus is passing; his temperature was 36.5 after his bed-bath this evening, and his pulse was 80; his maximum temperature today was 37.3. But he is weak and terribly wretched. I was told not to go downstairs, but I couldn't resist going to visit him. It is cold, 11 degrees.

May 16 Lev Nikolaevich is much better and his temperature is down to 37, not even that. He is very bored, poor man. I should think so too! He has been ill for almost 5 months now.

Today he received a reply from Grand Duke Nikolai Mikhailovich.[37] He is still dictating ideas about the unequal distribution of the land and the injustice of land ownership; this is his major preoccupation at the moment.[38]

I am ill and weak and my pulse is 52. Yulia Ivanovna is also ill. Life here has become even harder and more fraught since my visit to Moscow; I feel I am about to break. If only I could leave!

May 22 Lev Nikolaevich is gradually recovering: his temperature is back to normal, no higher than 36.5, and his pulse is 80, even less. He is upstairs at present as the downstairs rooms are being cleaned and aired. The weather is cool and rainy. Everyone in the house has become terribly homesick all of a sudden, and even L.N. is in low spirits, despite his recovery. We are all longing to be back in Yasnaya. Tanya is missing her husband, and Ilyusha his family. To be perfectly frank, all of us are feeling the need for some sort of personal life again, now that the danger is past. Poor Sasha, it's quite reasonable for her to want that at her age.

Yesterday and today I played the piano on my own in the wing, which was most enjoyable. I am assiduously practising that very difficult Chopin scherzo (the second, in five flats). What a lovely piece it is, and how it harmonises with my present mood! Then I sight-read that Mozart rondo (the second, the minor), such an elegant, gracious work.

I was lying in bed today wondering why a husband and wife so often find a certain estrangement creeping into their relations, and why relations with outsiders are often so much more pleasant. And I realised that this was because married couples know *every single aspect of one another*, both the good and the bad. And as one grows older, one becomes wiser and sees everything more clearly. We do not like people to see our *bad* side, we carefully conceal our bad traits from others and show ourselves off to our best advantage, and the cleverer and more adroit a person is the more able he is to present his best qualities. With a husband or wife, though, this is not possible, for everything is so transparently visible. One can see all the lies and all the masks – and it's not at all pleasant.

I dreamed of Vanechka last night; he was so affectionate to me, and solemnly blessed me with his pale little hand. I woke in tears. Yet seven years has passed since his death. The greatest joy of my entire life was his love for me – and in general all *young* children's love for me.

I am reading Fielding's *The Soul of a People*, translated from the English. It is quite delightful. It contains a wonderful chapter called 'On Happiness'. How much better Buddhism is than our Orthodoxy, and what a marvellous people these Burmese are.[39]

May 29 I have not written for a whole week. On Saturday the 25th Tanya went home to Kochety. On the 26th Lev Nikolaevich was carried downstairs and taken outside to the terrace, where he sat in his armchair. He has been outside every day since then, and has been speedily regaining strength. Yesterday he even took a spin in the carriage with Ilyusha. Professor Lamanskii was here yesterday, and some peculiar fellow who talked about the low cultural level of the peasants and the necessity to do something about it. He kept saying 'pardon' in French, and deliberately didn't pronounce his 'r's'. Lev Nikolaevich got very angry with him, but when I sent him away to take L.N.'s pulse – which was 94 per minute – he angrily shouted at me in the presence of Lamanskii: 'Oh, I'm so tired of you!' which hurt me deeply.

Ilyusha left today, happy to have been useful and good company for his father.

I went to Yalta and tired myself out; I had gone there to look at the steamer in view of our imminent departure. When I got back I sat with Lev Nikolaevich and sewed in silence. I thought about Nirvana, about peace, and about the book I had just read. How good to be mild and forgiving like the Burmese people, and to love and respect everyone.

The lovely white magnolias and lilies have come into flower.

June 5 (Gaspra) Still in the Crimea. The time has passed so quickly, we have all been very busy and no longer miss home so desperately. It is very pleasant here at the moment; the days are so hot and fine and the moonlit nights are so beautiful; I am sitting upstairs, admiring the reflection of the moon in the sea. Lev Nikolaevich is walking about with a stick now and seems well, although he is still very thin and weak. It distresses me deeply to see him like this, especially when he is being meek and gentle, as he has been recently. He only lost his temper once with me yesterday, when I cut and washed his hair. He writes every morning – a proclamation to the working people, I think, and also something or other about the ownership of the land – and at times he overexerts himself.[40]

Doctor Bertenson came on June 3 and found Lev Nikolaevich in a good state, apart from his bowels.

June 11 Today L.N. went for a drive with Doctor Volkov to the Yusupovs' Park, in Ai-Todor, which he enjoyed very much. Altschuler's wife visited, as well as Sonya Tatarinova, the Volkov family and Elpatevskii with his son. A large crowd of strangers came and peered through the window at Lev Nikolaevich.

We have been enjoying life here, the weather has been fine and L.N.'s convalescence is progressing well. I went riding twice, once to Orianda with Klassen and once to Alupka with him and Sasha. It was most enjoyable. I play the piano, sew and take photographs. Lev Nikolaevich is writing an appeal to the working people, 'On the Ownership of the Land', in which he says much the same thing as he wrote to the Tsar. We are planning to leave on the 13th, and I am apprehensive but happy. I have started packing.

June 13 Yet again it looks as though we won't be leaving Gaspra for a while: in Russia it's damp, raining and very cold – only 12 degrees. And

Lev Nikolaevich has an upset stomach. He has grown so terribly weak.

Poor man, I cannot bear to look at him, this world-famous person who in real life is such a thin, pathetic old man. He never stops working and is still writing his proclamation to the workers. I copied the whole thing out for him today. Much of it is illogical, impractical and unclear. Either it will be very bad or he will have to do a lot more work on it. The fact that the land is owned by the rich, and the great suffering this imposes on the peasants, is indeed a crying unjustice. But this matter will not be resolved in a hurry.

June 15 Seryozha and Boulanger came yesterday. I spent the morning copying out Lev Nikolaevich's article for him. He went for a walk this morning and is feeling much better.

June 17 This notebook is coming to an end, and so too, I hope, is our life in the Crimea. Once again we did not leave, as Sasha fell ill with influenza; today she is better. Lev Nikolaevich took a drive to Orianda with Klassen in the Yusupovs' rubber-tyred carriage. This evening he played vint with Seryozha, Boulanger and Klassen. His knee is hurting and his stomach is bad.

Bad news about Masha – yet another baby has died inside her! This is the seventh. What a tragedy. Trouble with the Bashkirs.[41] Numerous visitors milling around all day.

June 26 Yesterday we finally left Gaspra. As a result of living in the Crimea, Sasha has been very ill with a fever for the past two weeks, and Lev Nikolaevich has still not fully recovered.

Yesterday's steamer trip (the first in my life) was beautiful and comfortable. We are now in the train, travelling in a special luxurious carriage fitted with a saloon. Sasha and L.N. have taken to their beds, exhausted by the journey. Tomorrow we will be home, thank God. L.N.'s stomach and legs ache and we have applied compresses. It is hard to write as the train is jolting.

We left for the Crimea on September 4, 1901, and returned to Yasnaya Polyana on June 27, 1902. My diary for the Crimea is a special notebook. I am now resuming my old book, and my old life. I thank God that He has granted us to take Lev Nikolaevich home once more! I pray he never has to leave again!

June 27 (Yasnaya Polyana) Today we returned home from the Crimea. We rode to Yalta on horseback, with the invalids, Lev Nikolaevich and Sasha, travelling in the Yusupovs' rubber-tyred carriage. There were Lev Nikolaevich, Sasha, I, my son Seryozha, Boulanger, Yu. I. Igumnova and Doctor Nikitin in our party. In Yalta we boarded the steamer *Aleksei*. Ladies, bouquets, crowds of people waving farewell . . . On the steamer

L.N. sat on deck, ate in the public dining-room and felt extremely well . . . In Sevastopol we disembarked on to a skiff and sailed round the harbour to the station; the sun was bright and it was all so beautiful. A specially large comfortable carriage with a saloon had been set aside for L.N. Sasha was ill and miserable and still had an upset stomach. At the Kharkov station people – mostly women – welcomed him with ovations. Plevako met us there and gave us all sorts of interesting news. At the Kursk station there were crowds of people who had just been to an exhibition on popular education. The police pushed them back, and deputations of men and women teachers and students boarded the train – Misha Stakhovich, Dolgorukov, Gorbunov and Lodyzhenskii, amongst others. Plevako and Stakhovich had a lot of interesting things to tell us.

It was a joy to get back to Yasnaya, but our joy was short-lived; that evening Masha began to have pains, and soon afterwards she gave birth to a dead baby boy.

June 30 Lev Nikolaevich had a temperature of 37.8 this evening and we were all very anxious about him. I sat with Masha all morning. It is cold and raining. The saffron milk-caps* are out.

July 1 I collected the mail. It is raining. D.D. Obolenskii and Salomon came, and we had interesting talks. L.N. joined in eagerly. He is better today; his temperature was 37 this evening, and he had 5 grains of quinine.

July 2 Lev Nikolaevich drinks a lot of *kumis*, walks about the house energetically and does a lot of writing in the morning, but has not gone out yet; it is still damp and cool. Sasha is better.

July 3 Vasya Maklakov and Maria Aleksandrovna came and have already left. Seryozha and Salomon left this morning. Lev Nikolaevich walked to the side wing to see Masha, and this afternoon he played Haydn's second symphony as a duet with Vasya Maklakov. Sasha brought in some saffron milk-caps; there are such a lot of them.

July 4 Lev Nikolaevich is well; he went to the side wing and back. This afternoon he had a long talk with Doctor Nikitin about psychiatrists, whom he was criticising.

July 23 The time is passing terribly fast. On July 5 I went to see Ilyusha at Mansurovo, his estate in the province of Kaluga, and spent a delightful two days with him, Sonya and my grandchildren. We went for walks and drives through the lovely woods and countryside and had long heart-to-heart talks.

*A small, yellowish mushroom.

On July 7 I went to Begichevka to see Misha and my delightful, lovable little grandson Vanechka. Lina is a sensitive, serious, loving woman. Misha is young and arrogant, but this will pass. I feel happy about them at present anyway, thank God. On the night of the 8th I returned to Yasnaya with Misha. Lev Nikolaevich is well but weak. Sasha had a nervous attack on the 10th.

On July 11 Sasha and I went to Taptykovo to visit Olga on her name-day. We had a pleasant day, and returned home late that night after a heavy downpour of rain.

Mikhail Sergeevich Sukhotin is gravely ill with a suppurative inflammation of the lung. I felt so anxious, and so sorry for poor Tanya, and on the evening of July 16 I finally set off for Kochety. The atmosphere there was cold and depressing. Mikhail Sergeevich looked thin and wretched, and Tanya, who had been sitting up with him every night and had had no sleep, was tense and exhausted. I spent four days there and returned on the morning of the 21st.

It is still cool, and yesterday it poured with rain. The rye still hasn't been sheaved and the oats aren't cut. It is afternoon now, and only 10 degrees. Before it rained yesterday I took a drive round Yasnaya Polyana and the plantations and had such an enjoyable time. How wonderfully beautiful it all is!

Sasha's health is improving, but L.N. still complains of a bad stomach-ache. The *kumis* does no good, merely upsets his stomach. His digestion would improve if the weather were warmer.

Looking after him gets harder and harder because of his attitude to us. One goes into his room to attend to him and it is quite clear from the look on his face that one is disturbing him and he is merely waiting for one to leave. As though we were to blame for his weak and sickly state! And however patiently and attentively I look after him, I never get a word of affection or gratitude, nothing but complaints. With outsiders like Yulia Ivanovna or the doctors he is all courtesy and appreciation, but with me he is peevish and bad-tempered.

July 26 A full and happy day. Ilya's family came, with Annochka and the grandsons, and we took a walk with Zosya Stakhovich and Sasha. This evening Goldenweiser played, beautifully, a Schumann sonata and a Chopin ballade. Then we talked about poets and Lev Nikolaevich recalled a Baratynskii poem called 'On Death'. We straightaway got out the book and Zosya read us this lovely poem, written in such an exalted style. Then she declaimed some verses by Fet on death. Lev Nikolaevich said that Baratynskii had the proper Christian attitude to death, whereas poets like Fet, Turgenev and Vasilii Botkin merely took an epicurean approach to it.[42]

On the 22nd a son was born to Lev and Dora; we had a telegram from them today.

Lev Nikolaevich is well, despite the fact that it is damp, rainy outside, and only 12 degrees. He played vint all evening and enjoyed the music. In the mornings he writes his novel *Hadji Murat*, to my great delight.[43]

July 27 Music continues to have its usual healing effect on me. This evening Goldenweiser played, excellently, the Chopin sonata with the funeral march. L.N. was sitting near me and the whole hall was filled with my nearest and dearest – Ilyusha, Andryusha, Sonya, Olga, Annochka, Zosya Stakhovich and Maria Aleksandrovna. And moved by the music, I felt a quiet joy creep into my heart and fill it with gratitude to God for bringing us all together once more, happy and loving, and for allowing Lev Nikolaevich to be with us still, alive and comparatively well . . . And I felt ashamed of my weaknesses and resentments and all the evil that spoils this good life of mine . . .

I love having Ilya, Sonya and my grandchildren here. Zosya Stakhovich has left. Such a clever, profound, sincere girl. Andryusha has just arrived with Olga and A.D. Dyakov.

I walked to the end of the village today with L.N., Zosya, my grandchildren and Yulia Ivanovna; L.N. and Misha walked on to Yasenki and back. It was a most enjoyable day, and so warm and bright too.

August 9 What a long time it is since I wrote my diary! The past month has been filled with anxieties about Sukhotin's health; he is now worse again. My poor darling Tanya. She loves him too much, and is finding it so very hard; nursing him is difficult enough as it is. I went to Moscow on the 2nd and was extremely busy, checking accounts, attending to business, and ordering the new edition.[44] I dined with Dunaev, a kind, hospitable man, although I still find him a complete stanger. I returned home on the 3rd; sister Masha had come to visit from the convent. On the 4th I went to see the Maslovs. What good, kind people. Terribly shocked by the idiot boy in their house. Sergei Ivanovich is immersed in work on a musical textbook, which he wants to finish before leaving for Moscow.[45] I asked him to play something but he adamantly refused, and was stern, unapproachable and even rather unpleasant. There is something sad and serious about him nowadays; he has aged and changed, and this makes me very sad. I was happy to get home. The only pleasant thing at the Maslovs' was our drive through the woods. Lina came yesterday with little Vanechka, and this morning Misha arrived. The whole family is utterly charming in every respect. Glebova came yesterday with her daughter Lyuba. My nephew Sasha Behrs is here, and Annochka and Maude,[46] and Liza Obolenskaya has also arrived. A lot of commotion, but most enjoyable. Today we all took a lovely drive in the carriage to Grumond, then got out and walked a long way. Lev Nikolaevich has had a stomach-ache all day, and has been in low spirits. I went in to see him several times, and he admitted me coldly, even grudgingly. Later on he cheered up, played a game of vint and even asked for something to eat. He is still writing his story *Hadji Murat*, and today his work evidently went badly, as he played patience for a long time – a sure sign that his mind is working particularly hard and he cannot work out something he needs to understand. The priests keep sending me religious books which curse Lev Nikolaevich.[47] Neither he nor they are in the right; all extremes lack the *wisdom* and *goodness* of inner tranquillity. Lev Nikolaevich is remarkably indifferent to everyone and everything at present, and how hard that is! Why must people erect a wall in front of themselves, as L.N. and Sergei Ivanovich do? Do their intellectual, artistic and musical labours really demand this kind of barrier, this complete lack of involvement with others? Meanwhile we simple mortals beat our fists against these barriers and pine away from loneliness, and from our love for those who defend themselves against us. A hard and undeserved role . . .

A grey day, but no wind. A bright sunset and a moonlit night.

August 11 Misha's family left yestereday, and Olga arrived with Sonyushka. What a sweet, affectionate, clever little girl she is! I love her so much. Liza Obolenskaya left, Sasha Behrs and Stasov arrived, and also Ginzburg,[48] who has sculpted a bas relief of Sasha which is very bad and not at all like her. I have now learnt how to do this myself and would very much like to attempt a medallion of L.N. and me.

Stasov is huge and very noisy; he is 78½ and has developed the habit of saying pleasant things to everyone. But he knows a great deal and is an interesting and intelligent old man.

We all went to pick saffron milk-caps yesterday; I left the others and had a lovely time wandering through the forest on my own. The old fire in my heart is extinguished and I am obviously growing old. Lev Nikolaevich's illness and debilitated state have curbed all my spontaneous energy and liveliness, and I feel so dreadfully weary! L.N. had a stomach-ache again today, but has been very lively and talkative. He told us that when he was in Sevastopol he had asked to be assigned a *post*, and they had sent him and the artillery to the fourth bastion. But he was removed from there on the Tsar's orders, after Nicholas I sent Gorchakov a message saying: 'Remove Tolstoy from the fourth bastion and spare his life, for he is worth something.'[49]

He also told us that Leskov had once taken a subject of his for a story, distorted it and published it. Lev Nikolaevich's story went as follows: 'A certain young girl was once asked to describe the most important person, the most momentous period and the most necessary activity. And she thought a bit, then said: the most important person was the one whom you were with at the time, the most momentous period was the one in which you lived, and the most necessary activity was to do good to every person you met at any given moment.[50]

Rain all day; the oats are still in the field; 13 degrees.

August 28 Lev Nikolaevich's 74th birthday. We went out to meet him on his way back from his walk. He had gone a long way but had kept stopping to rest. Four of our sons have come; the fifth, Lyova, is in Sweden, and my poor darling Tanya could not be here either, as her husband is still ill. We celebrated my great husband's birthday in the most banal fashion: dinner for twenty-four ill-assorted people, with champagne and fruit, and a game of vint afterwards, just like any other day. Lev Nikolaevich simply cannot wait for evening, when he can sit down to a hand of vint. And they have now dragged Sasha into their games, which greatly distresses me. The nicest of our guests, apart from my children, was Misha Stakhovich – and Marusya Maklakova.

We had two very pleasant weeks here with Lev Nikolaevich's sister, Maria Nikolaevna. We discussed religion and had a lovely time playing duet arrangements of symphonies by Haydn, Mozart and Beethoven. I love her so much and feel very sad now that she has left. Lev Nikolaevich still complains of his stomach; Doctor Nikitin, who is staying here with us, massaged it for him in the evening, which he likes very much. He is working hard on *Hadji Murat*.

September 2 On August 31 two doctors arrived from Moscow for a consultation – that capable, energetic, lively, clever Shchurovskii, and P. Usov, a dear cautious man who has treated L.N. before. They both decided that it would be best to spend the winter here in Yasnaya, which is far more to my liking than the idea of them having to travel here, there and everywhere. Life is *genuine* here at home. There wasn't any *life* in the Crimea, and it's insufferable if there's no *fun*. I personally find it much easier in Moscow; there are a lot of people I love there, and a lot of music and serious innocent entertainments – exhibitions, concerts, lectures, contact with interesting people, social life and so on. With my bad eyesight it will be hard for me to fill the long evenings here, and it is going to be very tedious in the country. But I realise that Lev Nikolaevich finds Moscow *insufferable*, with all the visitors and the noise, so I shall gladly live in my dear Yasnaya and shall visit Moscow only when I feel exhausted here.

Meanwhile life is very eventful, time speeds past, I am kept busy all day long, and there isn't even any music, or a chance to rest. These guests can be very tiresome at times – the entire Halperin family was here, for instance. I have started to sculpt a medallion of L.N.'s and my profiles. I am very nervous and find it terribly hard, as I haven't really learnt how to do it and have never attempted such a thing before – I'm in despair that I won't be able to finish it but I do so want to; I occasionally sit up all night, as late as 5 a.m., straining my eyes.

October 10 I haven't written for so long – the time has flown. On September 18 I saw my Tanya and her family off to Montreux in Switzerland. My heart ached to see her, wretched, pale and thin, bustling about on the Smolensk station with all the luggage and her sick husband. But we have just had good news from her, thank God.

I spent my name-day in Moscow too. I invited a lot of guests, who came to say goodbye to the Sukhotins, and Sergei Ivanovich too, whom I had run into on the street and invited. He was so solemn and austere; something in him has changed, he has become even more impenetrable than before.

At 11 o'clock on September 11 we had a fire in the attic and four beams were burnt. By a sheer stroke of luck I had gone up to inspect the attic and noticed the fire. If I had not, the whole house would have burnt down and the ceiling could easily have collapsed on top of Lev Nikolaevich, who was asleep in the room directly below the burning attic. I was led by the hand of God, and I thank Him for it.

We have all been living peacefully and happily together. After the various repairs had been done to the house I cleaned and tidied up, life resumed its normal course and all went well. Lev Nikolaevich's health was good; he went horse-riding, worked on *Hadji Murat*, which he has now finished,[51] and started on a proclamation to the clergy. Yesterday he said: 'How hard it is, one must expose evil, yet I don't want to write unkind things as I don't want to arouse bad feelings.'[52]

But our peaceful life here and our good relations with our daughter Masha and her shadow – her husband Kolya – have now been disrupted. It is a long story.

When the family divided up the property, at Lev Nikolaevich's wish and insistence,[53] our daughter Masha, who had already reached the age of consent, refused to partake of her parents' inheritance, then or in the future. As I did not believe her at the time, I took her share in my name and wrote my will, leaving this capital to her. But I did not die, and then Masha got married to Obolenskii and took her share, as she had to support both herself and him.

But as she did not have any rights in the future she decided for some reason, without telling me, to copy out of her father's diary for 1895 a whole series of his wishes after his death. Amongst other things, he had written that it made him unhappy that his works should be sold, and that he would prefer his family not to sell them after his death. When L.N. was dangerously ill last July, Masha, without telling anyone, asked her father to sign this paper which she had copied out of his diary, and the poor man did so.[54]

This was all exceedingly unpleasant for me, when quite by chance I found out about it. To make L.N.'s works *common* property would be utterly senseless and wicked in my opinion. I love my family and want the best for its welfare; by making his works public property we only line the pockets of the rich publishing companies like Marx, Zetlin and so on. I told L.N. that if he died before me I would *not* carry out his wishes and would *not* renounce the copyright on his works; and if I thought that was the right and proper thing to do, I would give him the pleasure of renouncing it *during his lifetime*, but there was no point at all in doing so after his death.

Now that I have taken over responsibility for publishing Lev Nikolaevich's works and have at his request kept hold of the copyright and not sold it to anyone else, despite the huge sums that have been offered,[55] it is most unpleasant for me that Masha should have got possession of this bit of paper, signed by Lev Nikolaevich, saying that he does not want his works to be sold after his death. As I did not know the exact contents of this piece of paper, I asked Lev Nikolaevich to give it to me, after he had taken it from Masha.

He readily agreed, and handed it over to me. Then something completely unexpected happened: Masha flew into a rage. Yesterday her husband was shouting God knows what nonsense, saying that they had planned to make this bit of paper 'public property' after Lev Nikolaevich's death, so that as many people as possible would know that he had not wanted to sell his works, but that his wife had made him do so.

So the upshot of this whole episode is that Masha and Kolya Obolenskii will now be leaving Yasnaya.

October 23 Masha and I have made it up; she has stayed on in the side wing at Yasnaya, and I am very glad. Things have been very peaceful and happy again. I went through a difficult time from October 11–22, when L.N. was ill with bad pains in the liver, and we all lived in fear lest this turn into a serious bilious attack; but it did not, thank God. Nikitin, his doctor, treated him very wisely, gave him a bath and kept his stomach warm, and yesterday he started getting much better.

I was even more worried about Dora in St Petersburg, who had an attack of nephritis. But she too is better now.

An unbearably muddy, cold, damp autumn. It snowed today.

Lev Nikolaevich has finished *Hadji Murat* and we read it today; the strictly epic character of the story has been very well sustained and there is much artistic merit in it, but it does not move one. We have only read half of it, though, and will finish it tomorrow.

I tidied up and Abrikosov and I entered the books into the catalogue. I am very tired.

November 4 All would be well if it weren't for Lev Nikolaevich's illness. His voice was so weak today, and he has been particularly despondent recently. This liver disorder of his, which started on October 11 and first got worse, then better, simply will not go away. I am feeling very sad and anxious about him today. This great man whom I love so much is in real life such a pitiful, frail, debilitated old man.

It is very frosty; last night it was 15 degrees below freezing and there has been almost no snow. The little girls – Sasha, Natasha Obolenskaya and their young pupils – cleared the skating-rink today and went skating. We have had two young doctors here, our Nikitin and Arsenevskii, who is visiting. The sun is bright, the sky is blue . . . I don't feel like skating or doing anything at present, I just worry constantly about L.N.'s health.

I was coming up the avenue to the house today when I had a sudden vivid memory of the distant past, and I recalled walking up this same road from the skating-rink carrying a baby on one arm, shielding him from the wind and closing his little mouth, while the other arm dragged another child along in a sledge, and behind us and before us were happy, laughing, red-cheeked children, and life was so full and I loved them so passionately . . . And Lev Nikolaevich came out to meet us, looking so healthy and cheerful too, having spent such a long time writing that it was now too late for him to go skating . . .

Where are they now, those little children who were reared with such love? And where is that giant – my strong, cheerful Lyovochka? And where am I, as I was in those days? It is sad here on the ruins of our vanished happiness! It would not be so hard if I felt old, but I still have my health and energy, and all the old agonising sensitivity which has carved such deep furrows into my memories of the past. If only I could live a little better and not store up so much *guilt* towards people, especially my family.

November 8 We lead a quiet and profoundly monotonous existence. Life no longer seizes one and *forces* one to be active, one has to fill the time, find things to *occupy* one. Before, there was never enough time for all the urgent things that had to be done. But that's all changed now! Here in the country one's life and mood is so affected by the weather. Yesterday the sun shone, we were all in high spirits and I went skating with the little girls – Sasha, Natasha Obolenskaya and their young pupils. We all had a fine time on the ice, even P.A. Boulanger. The exaggerated rapture and movement of this physically weak but energetic man – and especially the sight of his back – aroused a slight feeling of disgust in me. I do not much care for men on the whole, I have always found them somewhat alien and physically repellent, and I have to love a man's soul and talent for a long time before I can love and appreciate him fully. There have been three such men in all the fifty-eight years of my life, the main one being my husband, of course.

But even him . . . ! Today we had a discussion about divorce, provoked by Paul Margueritte's novel. Lev Nikolaevich said: 'What do the French need to get divorced for? It's not as though they're so fastidious in their everyday life after all.' I said that divorce was sometimes necessary, and cited the case of L.A. Golitsyna, whose husband abandoned her three weeks after the wedding for a dancing-girl, whom he told quite cynically that he had only *married* in order to have her as his mistress, otherwise he would never have managed to get her.

Lev Nikolaevich replied that marriage was merely the Church's seal of approval on adultery. I retorted that this was only the case with bad people. He then snapped back in the most unpleasant way that it was so for *everyone*. 'What about in reality?' I said. To which he replied, 'The moment I took a woman for the first time and went with her, that was marriage.'

And I had a sudden painful insight into our marriage as Lev Nikolaevich saw it. This naked, unadorned, uncommitted sexual coupling of a man and a woman – this is what he calls marriage, and after that coupling it doesn't matter to him whom he has just gone with.

And when he started saying that one should only get married once, to the first woman one fell with, I grew extremely angry.

It is snowing, and there seems to be a path forming in the snow. I looked through the proofs of *The Cossacks*.[56] What a well-written story, what brilliance, what talent. A man of genius is always so much better in his works than in his life!

Lev Nikolaevich has just been writing an article called 'To the Clergy'. I haven't read it yet, but he finished it today and is sending it to Chertkov in England.[57] He is now playing vint with the doctors, Masha and Kolya Obolenskii.

November 25 I feel more and more lonely here in the company of those members of my family whom I still have with me. Today I returned from Moscow to find that Dr Elpatevskii had just arrived from the Crimea, and this evening L.N. read him a legend he has just written, about devils.[58]

This work is imbued with the most truly negative, malicious, diabolical spirit, and sets out to mock everything on earth, starting with the Church. The supposedly Christian feelings which L.N. puts into these negative discussions amongst the devils are presented with such coarse cynicism that it made me sick with rage to hear him read it: I became quite feverish, and felt like weeping and shouting and stretching out my hands to ward off the devils.

And I told him in no uncertain terms, how angry it had made me. If the ideas in this legend are true, why do they have to be dressed up as devils, with ears and tails and black bodies? Would it not be more fitting for an old man of seventy-five, whom the whole world respects, to do like the Apostle John, who when he was too weak and debilitated to speak, simply announced, 'Children, love one another!' Neither Socrates, Marcus Aurelius, Plato nor Epicurus had any need to attach ears and devils' tails to the truths they wanted to pronounce. But then maybe contemporary man, whom L.N. is so clever at pleasing, needs this sort of thing.

And my children too – Sasha, who is too young to know better, and Masha, who is a complete stranger to me – both imitated their father's gloating laugh with their own hellish laughter after he had finished reading his devilish legend, and I felt like sobbing. Did he have to go on living just to do work like this! God grant that this is not the last thing he does, and that his heart is softened.

December 7 My soul is again filled with despair and the terror of losing my beloved husband! Help me, Lord . . . Lev Nikolaevich has a fever – 39 this morning – his pulse is bad, his strength is failing . . . The only doctor who has seen him cannot understand what is wrong.

We have summoned Dreyer from Tula and Shchurovskii from Moscow and are expecting them here today. We have wired our sons too, but none of them has arrived yet.

While there is still hope and I still have the strength, I shall write down everything that has happened.

On the morning of December 4 there was a north wind and 9 degrees of frost, rising to 13 degrees. Lev Nikolaevich got up as usual, did some work and drank some coffee. I wanted to send a telegram to Varvara Ivanovna Maslova on her name-day and went in to ask L.N. if he needed to be taken to Kozlovka. 'I'll go there myself,' he said. 'But that's out of the question,' I said. 'It's terribly cold today and you've just had pneumonia.' 'No, no, I'm going,' he insisted. 'Well I'll send the telegram with the coachman anyway, so you won't feel you have to go all the way just for the telegram if you get tired,' I said, and went out. He shouted at me as I was leaving the room that he was going to Kozlovka anyway, but I sent the coachman off.

Later, when Lev Nikolaevich was having lunch, I came in and sat with him. He ate porridge and semolina with milk, and he asked for some curd pancakes from our lunch, which he ate with the semolina. I remarked that these pancakes were a little heavy for him while he was drinking Karlsbad – which he has been taking for four weeks now – but he wouldn't listen.

After lunch he set off for a walk on his own, and asked to be driven to the highway. I assumed he would take his usual walk along the main road, but without saying a word he set out for Kozlovka, turned off into Zaseka – 6 *versts* in all – and came out on to the highway; then he put on a frozen fur coat over his sheepskin jacket and drove home, flushed and exhausted, in a cold north wind and 15 degrees of frost.

Towards evening he began to look tired. Mirolyubov, editor of the *Journal for All*, came and asked him to join a committee set up to commemorate the 200th anniversary of the establishment of the press. Lev Nikolaevich declined, but had a long talk with him. He slept well that night.

The following morning, December 5, at 12 o'clock or just before, he began to feel chilled and wrapped himself up in his dressing-gown, but remained at his desk with all his papers all morning and ate nothing. He went to bed in the afternoon and his temperature went up to 38.8. That night he started having bad stomach pains; I stayed with him all night and kept his stomach warm. That evening he had a temperature of 39.4, but then Masha suddenly ran in, beside herself, and said, 'His temperature is 40.9!' We all looked at the thermometer, and sure enough it was – although I am still not sure whether there wasn't something wrong with the mercury. We were all utterly distraught; we sponged him down with alcohol and water, and when we took his temperature again it was 39.3 again.

But all last night he was burning, tossing, groaning and unable to sleep. Doctor Nikitin and I were with him and put a compress of alcohol and water on his stomach, but it did nothing to ease the pain. His weak, sad eyes, those dear, beloved intelligent eyes gazing at me with such suffering, and I can do nothing to help, although I would gladly give my own life for him to be well again and live!

I am haunted by the thought that God did not want to prolong his life after he wrote that legend about the devils. What will happen! My God! I have not eaten or slept for three days; my chest has swollen and hardened. I must be strong to look after him, I want to be there with him and care for him . . . We have lived together for forty years, and whatever I may have done in my life, I can truly say that Lyovochka has always been in the forefront of my mind, he has always been the dearest person in my life . . . Although Vanechka perhaps . . . But that was quite a different emotion . . . He was a child!

I am going in to Lyovochka again – oh, those groans, how I suffer for him . . . Forgive me, my darling, God bless you!

December 8 His temperature has gone down now and the fever has passed in a profuse sweat. But his heart is still weak. The doctors have diagnosed influenza and now fear these bacteria may lead to pneumonia.

We had a visit this morning from those two dear selfless doctors, always so bright and kind – warm-hearted Pav. Serg. Usov and cheerful Vlad. Andr. Shchurovskii. Doctor Chekan from Tula stayed the night here and our own Doctor Nikitin has been very kind, sensible and diligent.

Seryozha, Andryusha and his wife and Liza Obolenskaya arrived yesterday and Ilya arrived today. Pav. Aleks. Boulanger also came today.

I looked after Lev Nikolaevich until five this morning, when Seryozha took my place. The doctors also took turns – first Nikitin, then Chekan.

Today I had an unpleasant feeling of regret for all my wasted labours caring for Lev Nikolaevich. You give so much love, attention and time, you devote every moment of your life to saving Lev Nikolaevich's. And then all that tender loving care is greeted with an angry sullen protest, as happened on the 4th, as though I had done something wrong, as though he were being deprived of his freedom. So this means yet more wasted efforts, and yet another step closer to death. Why? It's not as though he welcomed death, he hates the idea of dying. And his bad state of mind saddens me too – it is not at all spiritual.

December 12 It is now six in the morning of December 12. I have spent yet another night sitting beside Lyovochka's bed and I can see him slipping away. His pulse is uneven and quick, 120 beats a minute and more . . . Ah how pathetic he is, when he sits there hanging his thin grey head, and one realises that all are equal in the face of suffering and death. To think that the whole world loves, bows before this pathetic head which I hold in my hands and kiss, as I say farewell to one who has meant more to me than my own life.

A cheerless life looms ahead – soon there will no longer be anyone for me to hurry in to see in the morning, putting on my dressing-gown the moment I wake up to find out what has happened in the night while I was asleep, how he is, whether he slept well and walked about and what sort of mood he is in. He always seems glad to see me, asks about me, asks how I am, then goes on writing.

When my mind has been set at rest, I can go about my business . . .

Today he said to me for the first time, with such sincere sadness, 'I can truly say that I should like to die.' 'Why?' I asked. 'Are you tired? Are you bored with living?' 'Yes, I am bored with everything,' he said.

No sleep . . . No life . . . Long sleepless nights, with a heart full of anguish, a terror of life and a dread of living without Lyovochka. We have lived together for forty years! Almost my *entire* conscious life! But I must not let myself regret or blame myself for anything, or I might go out of my mind.

As I was leaving the room just now he said, 'Goodbye, Sonya!' in such a distinct and significant tone of voice. And I kissed his hand and said 'Goodbye' to him too. He thinks I might be asleep when he dies . . . No, he doesn't think anything of the sort, he understands *everything*, and it's so hard for him . . .

God grant that his soul may be enlightened . . . He is much better and calmer today, and is evidently thinking more of death than of life . . .

December 13, evening But Lyovochka has come back to life again, and is now much better – his pulse, temperature and appetite have improved and everything is gradually settling down. I wonder how long it will last. Boulanger was reading Kropotkin's *Notes* to him.[59]

Today the following announcement from Lev Nikolaevich appeared in the *Russian Gazette*:

We have received this letter from Count Lev Nikolaevich Tolstoy:

'Dear Sir, Most Honoured Editor,

Due to my extreme age and the various illnesses which have taken their toll, I am obviously not in particularly good health, and this deterioration in my condition will naturally continue. Detailed information about this deterioration may be of interest to some people – and in completely opposite senses too – but I find the publication of this information most unpleasant. I would therefore ask all newspaper editors not to print information about my illness.

Lev Tolstoy, December 9, 1902'[60]

I fully understand Lev Nikolaevich's feelings about this matter and I myself only gave this information about him to avoid all the tedious hard work involved in replying to countless letters, inquiries and telegrams asking about his health.

I have been feeling ill and disgracefully sorry for myself today. I have given so much of my strength, energy and health to look after L.N., who out of sheer stubbornness and some strange spirit of contrariness insists on walking four miles through the snow or stuffing himself with curd pancakes, then suffers for it and makes all of us suffer too . . .

It is Nikish's second concert in Moscow today – it was my fondest dream to attend both of these concerts, but I was deprived of this innocent pleasure as usual, and am now feeling sad and angry at my fate.

It still torments me to remember my last painful conversation with Sergei Ivanovich, exactly a month ago. There is so much to explain, yet never any opportunity to do so . . .

December 18 Lev Nikolaevich is still in bed. He sits up, reads and takes notes, but is still very weak . . .

I have been reading Hauptmann's *The Weavers*: all we rich people, landowners and manfuacturers live such extraordinarily luxurious lives, I thought; I often don't go into the village simply to avoid the awkwardness and shame I feel for my own wealthy, privileged life and their poverty. And yet I am constantly astonished at how meek and gentle they are with us.

Then I read some of A. Khomyakov's poems. There is so much genuine poetry and feeling in them, despite everything. How good 'Dawn' is, for instance, and 'Stars', 'Inspiration', 'To Children' and 'To approaching sleep' . . . 'To Children' simply pours out of his heart, honest and passionate. If one has never had children, one could not possibly understand the feelings of a parent, especially a mother.

You go into the nursery at night and look at the three or four little cots with such a feeling of fullness, richness and pride . . . You bend over each one of them, look into those lovely innocent little faces which breathe such purity, holiness and hope. And you make the sign of the cross over them or bless them in your heart, then pray for them and leave the room, your soul filled with love and tenderness, and you ask nothing of God, for life is full.

And now they have all grown up and gone away . . . And it's not the empty cots that fill one with sadness, it's one's disappointment in those beloved children's characters and fates. For a long time we try to avoid seeing or believing these things. And we never ask our children to pray for us, but we pray constantly for them, longing for them to be happy and for their souls to be enlightened.

Today is the last Hoffmann concert. I did so want to hear him – but I was destined not to. I am about to leave for Moscow on business. I wonder if I shall go today?

These past few days I have been copying portraits of Lev Nikolaevich's father in water-colour. I never learnt to paint in water-colour so I have had to work hard at it and the results were mediocre, but it was great fun and very interesting to teach myself *how* to do it.

December 27 It is again a long time since I have written. I spent three days in Moscow – the 19th, 20th and 21st; I got the accounts for the book sales from the accountant, did some shopping and got presents for the children, servants and so on, which gave them enormous pleasure.

I spent an evening with Muromtseva, who has just returned from Paris; Marusya Maklakova was there, as well as my two eldest sons, F.I. Maslov and S.I. Taneev. Relations with him were cold, strained and formal.

Lev Nikolaevich improved greatly while I was away and got up, went into the next room and worked. Then on Christmas Day he suddenly got worse. He had stomach and liver pains from six that morning, his stomach swelled up and his heart-beat was weak and irregular, 130 per minute. He ate nothing, was given strophanthus and caffeine, and the doctor was evidently nonplussed. Yesterday he was much better again.

When Lev Nikolaevich was so ill on Christmas Day, he said half-jokingly to Masha, 'The Angel of Death came for me but God called him away to other work. Now that he has finished he has come for me again.'

Every deterioration in Lev Nikolaevich's condition causes me greater and greater suffering and I become more and more terrified of losing him. In Gaspra I did not feel nearly so much pain and tenderness for Lyovochka as I do now. What agony it is to see him suffering and sinking, weak and stricken in mind and body!

I take his head or his thin hands in both my hands and kiss him with such tender love and solicitude, and he looks at me so blankly.

What is happening to him? What is he thinking?

Andryusha came with his family. Darling little Sonyusha took Lev Nikolaevich's hand when she was saying goodbye to him, and said: 'Goodbye, Grandpapa!' I was pleased to see them, especially as it was the holidays, and especially as I was feeling so sad.

December 29 First Lev Nikolaevich gets better, then he gets worse. Today he said to me: 'I am afraid I shall be exhausting you for a long time.' He probably thinks he won't recover from his liver illness now, but that it will drag on and gradually carry him off. I think this too, more and more frequently, and it is an agonising thought. He called Pavel Aleksandrovich Boulanger into his room today and told him how marvellous Baron Taube's book was; he said there were many Christian ideas in it, and he praised the conclusion, in which Taube says that the Boer and Chinese wars have demonstrated that we have now entered a new period of barbarism.[61] And L.N. said that his own view was that only religion, and specifically the Christian religion, could lead people out of their present primitive, barbaric state.

We also talked about the English. Two Englishmen from some spiritual society walked to London dressed only in jackets and open shirts, and from there they travelled to Russia without so much as a kopeck, with the sole purpose of seeing Tolstoy and asking him to clear up all their religious doubts. They stayed with Dunaev, and we sent a couple of L.N.'s fur coats and caps over to them so they wouldn't freeze.[62]

December 30 I sit day and night with L.N. and review my entire life. And it has suddenly occurred to me that I have lived it almost completely *unconsciously*. I don't know if it has always been so. I have no time to work things out sensibly *in advance*, and no time to consider them *afterwards* either. I have been swept along in life's current, merely submitting to events, acting not from my own choice or free will but from force of circumstance (*par la force des choses*).

I have never been able to resist – I never had the strength. How could I, with my husband and the life I lead? My husband's intellect, age and property have always given him authority over me . . . And forty years have passed in this way . . . There have been so many shortcomings in our life; well, there's no point in weeping about it now . . . Thank God for everything that has happened.

· 1903 ·

Riots in the countryside continue. April 6, Easter Day – massacre of Jews in Kishinev, Bessarabia. (Tolstoy writes to governor of Kishinev to protest.) May – railway worker blows up governor of Ufa with high explosives. June 17–30 – 2nd RSDLP congress: split between Bolsheviks and Mensheviks. August – another great pogrom in Gomel, White Russia. First Factory Act making employers liable to pay compensation in cases of industrial industry.

Tolstoy visited by increasing numbers of radical students and revolutionaries. Eleventh edition of his Complete Works *published.*

January 1 A sad start to the new year. We had a letter from Tanya yesterday saying that her baby has stopped moving again and she is in utter despair . . . [1] L.N. read her letter first and when I went in to see him this morning he said to me, 'It's all over for Tanya now, you know.' His mouth trembled, he burst into sobs and his thin sick face was filled with grief.

I feel desperately sorry for Tanya, and it is torture to see Lyovochka slipping away from life. These are the two people I love best in my family.

Then today a poor peasant woman called Domna came from the village to beg a bottle of milk to feed her twin baby daughters.

We saw in the New Year yesterday. My two daughters-in-law, Olga and Sonya, are here with the children. Ilyusha and Andryusha arrived last night. There are a lot of people here – nineteen in all, including the servants. Two more Englishmen have come, some sort of crazy spiritualists from the partly educated working class. They took L.N. by the arm and suggested praying for his recovery; they are quite convinced that this will save him.[2]

I stayed up with Lev Nikolaevich until half past four in the morning. He did not sleep all night and was in constant pain. I rubbed his feet, soothed him and tried to reassure him, but to no avail. He would be calm for a moment and thank me, then start tossing again. His pulse was bad this morning and very irregular; he had a morphine injection and has been asleep all day.

At five this morning I went into my bedroom, raised the blind and opened the ventilation window. The white moonlight streamed over the countryside, poured over the linden avenues and into my room. Then the cocks started crowing in the village – such an eerie sound! Today I went for a long walk through the woods, along the path to the swimming pool and back. Silence, solitude, nature – wonderful! Goldenweiser played beautifully for us this evening.

January 2 News from Tanya: she gave birth to two dead baby boys yesterday! We are all feeling utterly crushed, but at least the birth was not too difficult, thank God. Heaven knows what will happen now.

L.N. slept well and his pulse is steady, but he has been very weak and listless all day. It is overcast and 12 degrees below freezing.

January 19 I returned today from Moscow, where I placed a new order with another printer. There is not a single copy of the *Complete Works* for sale at the moment, and not one copy of *War and Peace* either.

I heard a lot of music in Moscow: Arenskii played his study with Ziloti, and conducted his musical poem to the words of 'The Goblet'[3] – it was utterly delightful.

I had a most disturbing conversation yesterday with Sergei Ivanovich, which made me realise just why I had always loved and appreciated him so much. He is an extraordinarily good and noble man.

Goldenweiser has insinuated himself into our private family life in the most loathsome fashion. L.N. is completely better now, thank God. He is busy selecting philosophical thoughts for the calendar he is compiling.[4] He started on this when he was ill and couldn't write anything serious.

The weather is still and warm, 1 degree below freezing. The silence of nature is so good, for God is there. How I long to merge with nature and join God. Instead of reading proofs I just sit here and cry all day. Help me, Lord!

January 21 Seryozha was rude to me the other day because I spoke to Sasha while they were playing vint and interrupted their game. I burst into tears, went to my room and lay down on the bed. After a little while, when I had comforted myself with the thought that it is better to be hurt than to hurt others, L.N. came in leaning on his stick, still looking very weak and thin, and he was so kind and understanding and told me he had reprimanded Seryozha.

I was very touched by this, and I felt such tenderness and reverence for him that I started sobbing again, kissing his hands with that involuntary sense of guilt which has lately been leading me down some fateful path I know not where.

Evening L.N. went outside for the first time today – twice. He overtired himself of course. His pulse is weak and irregular. He had a dose of strophanthus this evening.

It is freezing and windy; it may be that the weather affects the nerves, and the nerves affect the heart.

January 24 L.N. became very poorly after his walk; his temperature went up to 38.2, his stomach ached and he had a mild attack of influenza.

January 28 My Dunyasha often says, 'The Lord is merciful, He knows what He is doing.' And he has indeed been very merciful to me. My inner torment reached a pitch of suffering and guilt and I longed to see and talk to the man I love. I was taken ill, and felt very bad; then I fell down and could not stand up all evening. They put ice on my head and I lay there with it on all night, tense and overwrought; my body simply stopped living. But today, three days later, I am feeling emotionally much better, for the illness put a stop to all my anguish and emotional torment. And once again I beg God to help me in my moments of weakness, or lead me without sin or disgrace to the land where 'the dead have no shame'. For at present I feel this shame before myself, God and my conscience.

As long as I can endure this storm in my soul and stand firm in my actions, as I have done up till now . . .

February 9 I went to Moscow again. There was a chamber music recital at which they played Taneev's quartet (I saw him briefly), the Mozart clarinet quintet (delightful, it gave me enormous pleasure) and Tchaikovsky's sextet (*Memories of Florence*). I felt so calm and happy afterwards. The old ladies, Uncle Kostya and Sergei Ivanovich all came to see me the following day and we read Lev Nikolaevich's 'Destruction and Reconstruction of Hell' (about the devils). This again had the most unpleasant effect on me, and on the other listeners too. Ek. Iv. Baratynskaya attacked Sergei Ivanovich most provocatively, defending the article against his logical and intelligent arguments. He was in a very lively mood and I found him quite charming. I went to the Hoffmann concert, at which he played the wonderful Chopin piano concerto. I also had a lot of work to do – finding a proof-reader, publishing, binding and so on – and I left much of it unfinished. I also attended to Sasha's financial affairs . . . It is all so emotionally exhausting and such a waste! My letter to the *New Times* in response to Buryonin's article against Andreev was published on February 7, 1903.[5]

February 20 Lev Nikolaevich has an old man sitting with him, a soldier from the days of Nicholas I who fought in the Caucasus and is now relating his memories.[6] L.N. went for a drive through the woods yesterday, and this morning he sat outside on the upper balcony. He is healthy and calm. I did a little work on his correspondence today – mostly begging letters and notes asking him for his autograph.

What has happened recently? 1) A son, Ilya, was born to Andryusha on the night of February 3–4. I went to see him and to congratulate Olga. 2) Masha and Kolya have gone abroad. The house seems very empty without them, but I feel relieved – they were almost daily guests here. N.V. Davydov visited over Shrovetide and read us an extract from his story. Boulanger and Dunaev visited too, and Zosya Stakhovich came to stay. A clever lively girl, but I am slightly worried that I might have been too open with her.

Sasha went to St Petersburg and distressed me with her news of Dora's continuing bad health and Lyova's nerves.

There are not many of us here at the moment – just Sasha, Yulia Ivanovna, Doctor Hedgoft and Natasha Obolenskaya.

A warm, damp winter: it is still 2 degrees above freezing, the hollows are filled with water, the sun is shining and there's almost no snow at all. It was slightly colder today – 2 degrees below freezing and cloudy.

We lead such a secluded existence, and I am happy to be going to Moscow again. Our landowning life is so unnatural – just a few individuals living here amongst the rural population, with absolutely no contact with the people. And it would be quite unnatural, anyway, to make contact with a class that has not been educated to our level.

I receive many letters concerning mine to the *New Times*. Many condemn Lev Nikolaevich as the instigator of sordid literature, with his *Resurrection*, 'The Power of Darkness' and *The Kreutzer Sonata*.[7]

But this is a misunderstanding, mere foolishness. Many people are overjoyed, and thank me for my letter – mainly because I wrote it as a mother. But Andreev too has his defenders. All this makes me feel as though I had scattered Persian powder on some bedbugs, which were now all scuttling away in every direction. I write one letter to the newspaper, and it provokes countless letters, articles, notices and caricatures. Our untalented press was delighted by the scandal and poured forth all sorts of rubbish about it.

I am bored, and have lately been feeling vey depressed.

Music is one consolation, and the other is knowing that I am doing my duty looking after Lev Nikolaevich and easing his suffering.

February 22 A daughter, Tanya, has been born to Misha.

March 6 I went to Moscow – to see Andryusha, who is very ill, check the book sales, have my teeth filled, go shopping, place some orders and go to concerts: Taneev's cantata and various other pieces, performed by the philharmonic orchestra, a symphony concert, the *Manfred* overture, *Der Freischütz* and so on, some Beethoven and Mozart quartets, and the pianist Buyukli played Chopin's A Major Polonaise.

I then went to St Petersburg. Lyova and Dora were so sweet, and so were their dear little boys; my sister Tanya was wretchedly short of money; my brother Vyacheslav was there with his ugly wife and was so kind and sensitive. I spent one day there, two nights on the train, then it was Moscow again and a lot of dashing around, entertaining guests, visiting sick Andryusha – and all this anxious, senseless waste of physical and emotional energy gave me such a sense of powerlessness, dissatisfaction and depression.

It is better in Yasnaya. The beauty of the bright days, the sun shining on the smooth glassy expanse of frozen water, the blue sky, the stillness of nature and the twittering birds are all a premonition of spring.

We went for a drive through the woods and L.N. came too. He was so tenderly concerned about me, making sure that I was all right and enjoying the drive. We went in three sledges, and as we were driving along he made us stop, got out of his sledge, came up to me and asked me so kindly, 'Well, are you enjoying it?' And when I said that I was, 'very much indeed', he said he was so happy. When I tucked him up and said goodnight to him this evening, he tenderly stroked my cheek, like a child, and I was delighted by his fatherly love . . .

Those dull, ugly Rozanovs were here . . . [8]

I have finished the proofs of *Anna Karenina*. By following the state of her soul, step by step, I grew to understand myself and was terrified . . . But people do not take their lives to *avenge themselves* on someone; no, they take their lives because they *no longer have the strength to live* . . . At first it is struggle, then prayer, then reconciliation, then despair – and finally powerlessness and death.

And I had a sudden clear vision of Lev Nikolaevich weeping his old man's tears and saying that no one had ever seen what was taking place within my soul, no one had ever helped me . . .

How could they have helped me? To allow Sergei Ivanovich to be invited here again and help me restore our old peaceful friendly relations. And to forgive me for my feelings, so that I needn't feel guilty about them any more.

March 10 Lev Nikolaevich is well. We went for a lovely drive today along the forest paths through Zaseka, although the thaw has already started. L.N. sat with Sasha, I sat with Lyova and the doctor with Natasha and Yulia Ivanovna. Then I sat with Lev Nikolaevich. My heart leapt for joy to see him looking so well and driving the sledge; so many times I have thought his life was over, and now here he is, returned to us again! Yet even the joy of seeing him better does not cure my sick heart; when I go into my room I am overwhelmed by the evil mystery of my emotional state, and I want to weep, I want to see that man who is now at the centre of my disgraceful, untimely madness – but let no one raise their hand to me because I have already endured such torment and am so afraid for myself. I must *live*, I must think of my husband and children, I must not betray my madness, I must not see the person I love to distraction . . .

And all I can do is pray to be cured of this sickness . . .

March 18 I often think how little my children have to reproach me with – I have loved them too much, and their criticisms and occasional rudeness have a devastatingly painful effect on my soul.

When I went into the library today to fetch a book I found Lyova asleep in there, and I was moved to tears of tenderness by the sight of his thin body, his small balding head with its thin black hair, and his slightly open lips. I felt so sorry for him, trying so hard to be brave about his life – which has just separated him from his dear sick wife and two little boys. Heaven knows how Dora's illness will end! And then I look with such tenderness at Seryozha, always so gloomy and preoccupied, and at Ilyusha, my confused grown-up child, and at my irresponsible, affectionate Andryusha, who closes his eyes to anything serious, and beloved Tanya, and sick Masha, and

Misha, who is happy at present but still so unaware, and Sasha, who is the same.

And I want just one thing – for them to be happy, morally good people.

I am leaving for Moscow today, which worries me, and rather frightens me too!

We have had a whole month of sunny weather. L.N. is well and everyone here is happy, but I am in a state of emotional turmoil; I pray constantly, especially at night, kneeling before the old icon, and wishing so much that the Saviour would raise his outstretched arm to me in blessing, and grant my soul some peace.

July 1 I have written nothing all spring and summer and have spent the whole time outside with nature, taking advantage of the delightful weather. I cannot remember such an utterly beautiful summer or such a dazzling spring. I did not want to think or write or examine my soul. What would be the point? 'You stir up still waters when you seethe . . . '[9] We have been living peacefully and quietly, even happily together.

There was a hateful conversation at dinner today. L.N., in front of large numbers of people and with a naive grin on his face, began cursing doctors and medicine in his usual way. I found this quite insufferable now that he is well; after those nine doctors in the Crimea had worked so selflessly, intelligently and disinterestedly to restore his health, I felt that no honourable man should regard those who save his life in this way. I would have kept quiet, had not L.N. then added that according to Rousseau all doctors were in league with women – so that meant I was in league with the doctors. At that I simply could not contain my rage. I am sick and tired of eternally acting as a screen for my husband to hide behind. If he did not trust the way these doctors treated him, why did he summon them in the first place, and then submit to their diagnoses?

Our painful conversation of July 1, 1903 is no mere chance event, it is a result of the solitude and the general dishonesty of my life.

My husband blames me for everything: his works are sold against his will, Yasnaya Polyana is kept and managed against his will, the servants serve against his will, the doctors are summoned against his will . . . There is no end to it . . . And meanwhile I work like a slave for everyone and my life is simply not my own.

So now I keep my distance from everything, for I am exhausted by the never-ending hard work and reproaches. L.N. can live the rest of his life in accordance with his convictions and his wishes. I am tired of acting as his screen and must escape from this role that has been foisted on me.

July 5 There is something in my husband that is quite beyond my own possibly feeble comprehension. I must *understand* and *remember* that his purpose in life is to *teach* people, to *write* and to *preach*. His life, our life, the lives of everyone in his family, must serve this purpose, which means that his life must be arranged exactly right. One simply has to close one's eyes to all the compromises, discrepancies and contradictions, and see Lev Nikolaevich as a great writer, preacher and teacher.

July 9 The children have returned from abroad – Masha and Kolya Obolenskii on the 6th, Andryusha on the 7th and Lyova on the 8th. Andryusha looks so thin, weak and wretched, but he is being very agreeable. Poor Lyova is in a state of emotional turmoil; he is so pathetic, and so very dear to me. Masha has recovered and is as much a stranger as ever.

L.N. had difficulty in breathing today; his pulse was 78 before lunch, quite normal, but after eating some potatoes and a slice of bread and honey, he began gasping for breath and his pulse became quick and irregular. Yesterday and for the past few days he has been complaining of weakness, and he had a bad night last night. I was so worried about him, and terrified at the prospect of my empty life if he should go before I do.

July 10 L.N. was much better yesterday evening. He has overexerted himself recently, riding, walking and eating a lot of heavy food. A young officer of the household cavalry called Adlerberg came here this evening with his immensely fat wife. L.N. invited him into his room and questioned him closely about all is military activities: 'What do you do when you troop the colours? When does the Tsar get on his horse to review the troops? Who leads the horse?' and so on and so on. He is studying the history of Nicholas I's reign at present, and is collecting and reading a lot of material about it. All this is for *Hadji Murat*.[10]

July 12 I wanted to write something good today, but instead I became engrossed in reading, and now I am too tired. Yesterday I went to Taptykovo to see Olga on her name-day. Andryusha is sick and exceedingly thin and I feel so sorry for him. I find Olga quite incomprehensible. What exactly does she live for, I wonder? I went there with Lyova, and this son brings me no joy either. His wife is dying of nephritis in Sweden, and he is making plans, says he wants to enrol in the medical faculty and live in Moscow; there is a terrible restlessness about him. Lev Nikolaevich is not very well: he still has difficulty in breathing and an irregular pulse. The weather has turned – it is terribly windy and only 11 degrees. This evening L.N. played a lively game of vint with Masha, Kolya, Sasha and Nikitin.

I spend a lot of time sitting on my own in my room. Boulanger says that my room is like that of a young girl. How strange that now that I live alone, untouched by a man's gaze or caress, I often have a quite virginal sense of purity, an ability to pray for a long time on my knees before the large icon of the Saviour or the small one of the Mother of God, with which Tatiana Aleksandrovna blessed Lev Nikolaevich when he went off to war. And sometimes my dreams are not the dreams of a woman, but pure as those of a young girl . . .

July 13 Great commotion all day. First two Italians came to see L.N. One was an abbot, more interested in the Russian way of life – particularly our life – than in conversation. The other was a professor of theology, a man of ideas, who energetically defended his convictions to L.N.; broadly these were that one had to preach those truths which one discovered in religion and morality, without destroying forthwith all existing forms of worship. L.N. said that these forms were simply not necessary, '*la réligion c'est la verité*', and the Church and the forms were just a lie, which confused people and obscured the great truths of Christianity.

I was very interested to hear what they had to say.[11] But then my sons Lyova and Andryusha came. Later on Stakhovich came with his daughter, and my son Misha arrived.

The discussions continued, the children shouted, food and drink had to be served – it was all terribly tiring. Then we had a visit from an old man and his wife who had been arrested for blaspheming against Athanasius; they were very pathetic but it seems impossible to do anything for them. L.N. sent a letter to the Tsar via Count Aleksandr Vasilevich Olsufiev, making enquiries about this Athanasius.[12]

Masha and Kolya have left, and their departure, like their arrival, made almost no impression at all on our household.

August 10 It is generally said that no one but God can ever judge a husband's treatment of his wife. So let this letter which I am copying here not provide grounds for judging anyone. But it has disrupted my life in many ways, and has shaken my trusting, loving attitude to my husband – not the letter, that is, but the reasons which made me write it.

It was in the year of my beloved little son Vanechka's death. He died on February 23, 1895, at just seven years of age, and his death was the greatest tragedy of my entire life. At that time I clung with all my soul to Lev Nikolaevich, in whom I sought comfort and some purpose in life, and I worked for him and wrote for him. Once, when he went to Tula, I found that his room had not been properly cleaned, so I went in to tidy it up.

The following explains everything . . .

How many tears I shed as I wrote this letter.

Here it is; I found it today, August 10, amongst my papers. It is a rough draft.

October 12, 1895

These past few days I have been walking about with a great weight on my heart, but I have been unable to talk to you about it, not wanting to upset you or to remind myself of that state I was in just before Vanechka's death, when we were in Moscow.

But I cannot forebear from telling you (for the last time . . . I shall try to make this for the last time) what is making me suffer so.

Why do you always refer to me so spitefully in your diaries, whenever you mention my name? Why do you want future generations to abuse me as your *evil, frivolous* wife, who made you so unhappy? It would be incomparably kinder if you simply cursed me or hit me for all the things you found so bad in me, for that is over quickly.

After Vanechka's death – remember his words: 'Papa, don't ever hurt my Maman' – you promised me to cross those angry words out of your diary. But you did not do so: on the contrary.

Perhaps you are afraid that your posthumous fame will be less if you don't represent me as the tormentor and you as the martyr?

Forgive me if I have been so base as to read your diaries; it was chance that prompted me to do so. I was tidying your room and dusting a cobweb off your writing desk, from which fell a key. The temptation to look into your soul was too great . . .

And then I came across the words (roughly: I was too upset to remember them precisely):

'S. came back from Moscow. Butted into my conversation with Bool. Pushed herself forward. She has become even more frivolous since Vanechka's death. One must bear one's cross to the end. Help me Lord . . . ' And so on.

When we are gone, anybody will be able to interpret this 'frivolousness' just as they see fit; anybody can throw *your* mud at *your* wife because this is what you wished, and what you write actually encourages people to do so.

And all because I have lived my entire life for you and your children, because I have loved you alone, more than anyone else in the whole world (apart from Vanechka), because I have *not* behaved 'frivolously' (as your diaries inform future generations that I have), and because I belong to you, body and soul, and shall die as *your* wife . . .

I try to rise above the suffering which torments me now; I try to stand facing God and my conscience, and to reconcile myself to the hatred of the man I love, and whatever may happen, the remain constantly in communion with God; to 'love our enemies', 'as we forgive them their trespasses against us', and 'to see our own sins and not condemn our brother.' And God grant that I may attain this lofty state.

But if it is not very hard for you to do so, then please delete those angry words against me from your diaries – for this is the *Christian* thing to do, after all. I cannot beg you to love me, but please spare my name; do this, if it is not too hard for you. If not then God be with you. This is simply one more appeal to your heart.

I am writing this with grief and tears; I would never be able to say all these things to you. Forgive me; every time I go away I cannot help wondering if we shall see one another again. Forgive me if you can.

S. Tolstaya.[13]

At the time we did manage to reach some sort of agreement, and L.N. crossed out one or two things in his diary. But I was not seeking love and comfort from him then, and my heart never again turned to my husband with that spontaneous love and trust which had once been there. It closed for ever then, painfully and irrevocably.

November 17 I go into Lev Nikolaevich's room this evening as he is getting ready for bed, and I realise that I *never* hear a single word of comfort or kindness from him nowadays.

What I predicted has indeed come true: my *passionate* husband has died, and since he was never a friend to me, how could he be one to me now?

Happy are the wives who live to the end of their days with their husbands on warm and friendly terms! And wretched and lonely are the wives of egoists, those great men whose wives the next generation will turn into the Xantippes of the future!!

This life is not for me. There is nowhere for me to put all my energy and passion for life, no contact with people, no art, no work – nothing but total loneliness all day while L.N. writes, and games of vint all evening for L.N.'s recreation. Oh, those hateful shrieks of 'Little slam in spades! No threes! Why did they get rid of their spade, we'll have to do a revoke! How d'you like that, you took that grand slam very neatly . . . !'

It's like the ravings of lunatics, and I simply cannot get used to it. I have tried taking part in this madness myself, so as not to have to sit on my own, but whenever I played I always found myself feeling utterly ashamed of myself, and even more depressed than before.

Doctor Berkenheim saw how depressed I was and looked at me sympathetically, without saying a word, and he now reads aloud to me in the evenings. We have just read some Chekhov, which was very pleasant.

· 1904 ·

January – Russia declares war on Japan. Temporary halt to unrest, with new mood of conciliation between liberals and government. But a series of disastrous defeats for Russia unleashes more demonstrations, riots and strikes. June – Russian governor of Poland assassinated. July – Minister of the Interior, V. K. Plehve, blown up. August – Plehve succeeded by more liberal Svyatopolk-Mirskii, who repeals some harsh laws (including local courts' power to administer floggings), pardons some political exiles and proclaims the 'dictatorship of the heart'. This lifting of restrictions gives the impetus to the gathering revolution. Summer – south and west Russia see a horrendous wave of pogroms. October – liberal Union of Liberation formed by liberal zemstvo *landowners. December – Port Arthur, Russia's stronghold in the far east, surrenders to Japan.*

January – Tolstoy starts on the Circle of Reading. *August – Andrei Tolstoy joins the army. Pavel Biryukov, released from exile, settles at Yasnaya Polyana where he writes biography of Tolstoy. August 23 – Tolstoy's brother Sergei dies. Sofia writes a short story, 'Groans', under the pseudonym 'A Tired Woman' and starts work on* My Life. *She becomes increasingly distant from Taneev.*

January 18 Life flies past so terribly quickly. From December 6 to 27 my Tanya stayed here with her family. The elections, the Christmas party and the holidays were so exhausting that there was simply no time to rejoice. An attack of influenza has left me feeling very weak. L.N. fell ill just before the New Year, and we had a sad New Year's party with Seryozha, Andryusha, Annochka, Sasha and the Sukhotin boys. Then my sister Tanya came to stay, happy and irresponsible as ever; but she has been broken by life, and this is what has taught her that peculiar *manner* of hers. There was an unpleasant scene over the vint, and I felt ill with the chagrin. On January 8 three students from the St Petersburg Mining Institute arrived here with a letter. I had a long talk with them; they were very intelligent,[1] but like all young people nowadays they do not know where to put their energy. That evening we all left for Moscow, where I stayed until the evening of the 15th. I went twice to Arenskii's opera *Nal and Damayanti*, a melodious and graceful piece, although not a work of great power. But what a delightful image of modern woman this poem contains!

I took Sasha everywhere with me. We also went to a symphony concert at which Chaliapin performed. He is the most intelligent, talented singer I have ever heard in my life. We went to a Goldenweiser concert too – he played with much more spirit than usual – then a rehearsal of Chekhov's *The Cherry Orchard*, which gave me immense pleasure. Sensitive and intelligent, humour alternating with a genuine sense of the tragedy of the situation – just right.[2]

But my main business in Moscow was to transport nine boxes containing Lev Nikolaevich's manuscripts and works from the Rumyantsev to the Historical Museum. They had asked me to remove these boxes from the Rumyantsev Museum because they were repairing the building. But it seemed rather strange to me that there should have been nowhere in the whole building to store nine boxes, 28 inches long. I asked to speak to the Museum director, a former professor called Tsvetaev. He made me wait for half an hour, then did not even apologise and addressed me rather rudely:

'You see, we are putting up new shelves in the room where those boxes were kept. And we now need the space for *more valuable manuscripts*,' he said, amongst other things.

That made me very angry. 'What sort of rubbish could be more important than Tolstoy's manuscripts and the diaries for his whole life?' I said. 'I suppose you follow the views of the *Moscow Gazette*?'

My anger disarmed the loathsome, uneducated Tsvetaev, and when I said that I hoped to get a better place for the various busts, portraits, and other things relating to Lev Nikolaevich's life, he became quite upset and even apologised and tried to flatter me, saying that although he had not known me before he would now do everything he could. As I was leaving I added that the reason I was angry was because I valued everything that concerned Lev Nikolaevich so highly, and that as the wife of Lev* I too was a lioness who could show her claws if need be.

After this I left for the Historical Museum to see eighty-year-old Zabelin. A white-haired old man with kind eyes and a red face came out to see me, barely able to move his legs. When I asked if he could take and store Lev Nikolaevich's manuscripts in the Historical Museum, he took my hands and kissed them, saying in a sweet voice: 'Can we take them? But of course we can, bring them immediately! Oh, what a joy! My dear lady, this is history, you know!'

The next day I went to visit Prince Shcherbatov, who also said how pleased he was that I had decided to store Tolstoy's manuscripts and things at the Historical Museum; I also met his dear wife Princess Sofia Aleksandrovna (née Princess Apraksina) and his lovely little girl, Marusya. The following day we went to inspect the place where the manuscripts were to be stored – they are giving me two rooms directly opposite Dostoevsky's rooms.

The staff of the Historical Museum – Stankevich the librarian, his assistant Kuzminskii, Prince Shcherbatov and his wife – all treated me with the respect and esteem due me as Lev Nikolaevich's representative.

Only Georgievskii was there in the manuscript department of the Rumyantsev Museum when the four of us arrived – Kuzminskii, assistant librarian at the Historical Museum, Rumyantsev my accountant, a soldier and I. We took the boxes, carried them safely to the Historical Museum and put them in the tower. I am now consumed with anxiety about all Lev Nikolaevich's other things and manuscripts, which must be brought there too so as to save them as far as possible from the mindless plundering of his children and grandchildren.

L.N. and I are good friends at the moment. Indeed, whenever we are on our own, all the old trust and affection between us is restored; the presence of the four eldest children does nothing to disrupt this either – it is

*'Lion' in Russian.

destroyed only by the presence of my daughter Masha, my sister Tanya and certain friends and acquaintances.

L.N. has been in very good spirits recently, working hard and eagerly compiling his new book of wise thoughts; he thought he might even include short stories and a whole series of readings, with one theme for every day in the year.[3] 'Of course I shan't have time to do anything with my life now,' he says sadly.

One day he rode between ten and sixteen *versts* on his horse, and the next day he went for an equally long walk. Today he was feeling unwell; this evening he was sneezing and could not drink his tea.

In Moscow I discovered that the March issue of the *Journal for All* is to print my prose poem 'Groans', which will appear under the pseudonym 'A Tired Woman.'[4]

February 3 A dreadful man came to see us yesterday, a Cossack officer named Beletskii. He used to be in the army, but then renounced war and finished his university course as a law student. Talking to him gave me a somewhat clearer understanding of my attitude to my husband's ideas. If we were in complete *disagreement*, then we should not love one another. What I loved in Lev Nikolaevich, I realised, was all the *positive* side of his beliefs; I have never been able to endure the *negative* side, which arises from that part of his nature which has to be forever *protesting* against something.

L.N. is well. One day he goes for a walk, the next day he goes horse-riding. Three days ago he was out for an extremely long time. He appeared at almost six and we discovered that he had ridden over to Tula and back to buy the last telegraph for the latest news about the war with the Japanese.[5] This war has stirred us all up, even here in the peaceful countryside. The mood of elation here and the general sympathy with the Tsar are astounding. This is because the Japanese attack was so utterly brazen and unexpected. As far as Russia was concerned, neither the Tsar nor anyone else had the slightest desire for war. This war was simply *forced* on us.

Another warm winter: today and yesterday it was 2 degrees above freezing, although it is now 2 degrees below and windy.

L.N. is busy with some fiction; he is working on his story 'The Forged Coupon.'[6]

I have had the audacious idea of trying to copy an oil painting, even though I have never in my life turned my hand to oils before.

My Dream of February 3

I am going to see the Maslovs; I have a bunch of faded mauve and yellow flowers in my hand. I desperately long to brighten my flowers with some red or pink ones and some greenery, and search for some by the windows. Then I look wistfully at my withered flowers and leave the house. At the lintel of the hall door stands my mother, her hands clasped behind her back. I shout with joy, but am not at all surprised to see her. I ask her what she is doing there. 'I have come for you,' she replies. 'Well, let's go to the Maslovs first, and I'll introduce you to them,' I say. 'They are my best friends,' I say. My mother agrees, and we go up the stairs together to see them. 'This is my mother,' I announce with pride and joy to each of the Maslovs, and they all greet her. Then we go into the huge drawing-room where there is a long tea-table and Varvara Ivanovna is sitting at the samovar. After that we leave. My mother says she is hurrying to catch a ship which is about to set sail, and we walk there together. We get on to the ship, and I see all my children there. The ship leaves, and we see a lot of other ships, sailboats and steamers in the ocean. Suddenly we stop; something in the ship has broken. I want to go to my children, but suddenly I see before me a deep hollow made of wooden boards. It is impossible to cross it. 'But how did my children get across?' I ask. They are young, they jumped, they say. I see my Tanya in the distance, happily buying candied-fruit jelly from a buffet where various sweet things are being sold behind a glass window; she smiles and waves at me. Lyova, thin, small and black-haired, is begging her to give him a kopeck for sweets.

At this point someone suddenly rolls a great empty barrel across the bottom of the hollow, and when I ask what this is for they reply that they are mending the ship with it. And we set off again . . .

An interpretation: the withered flowers are the faded joys of life. Looking for red flowers – the search for new joys: looking for green leaves – the search for hope. My mother comes to take me away. The ship and the journey are the passage to death. The boarded hollow is the coffin and the grave. My inability to follow my children across it is my inability to continue living with them. We sail on – into a new life beyond the grave, eternity . . .

May 26 Lev Nikolaevich told us the story of how he entered military service.

Today Sasha and I were sorting through the things which Countess Aleksandra Andreevna Tolstaya left her goddaughter Sasha after her recent death. (There were also a few little things for me, Tanya, Seryozha and Lev Nikolaevich.) Amongst her possessions were three portraits, one of her father, Count Andrei Andreevich Tolstoy, and two of her brothers, Konstantin, who died young, and Ilya Andreevich, who was already an old man when he died.

It was *à propos* of these portraits that L.N. related the following story to Misha, Lina and me:

Once, after he had lost badly at cards in Moscow and squandered a lot of money, he decided to go to the Caucasus to see his brother Nikolai Nikolaevich, who was serving there. At the time he had absolutely no intention of serving in the army; he went to the Caucasus in his own civilian coat, and when he went on a raid for the first time he wore the same coat and a service cap with a great peak. He stayed with Nikolai Nikolaevich in Stary Yurt (known as Hot Springs, as there were sulphur springs there), and from there they went on a raid on Groznaya. (Lev Nikolaevich has described this raid elsewhere.)

Once L.N. rode over to Khasav Yurt with an old Cossack to visit some acquaintances; the old Cossack had a falcon on his arm. On the road, which was thought to be very dangerous, they met Count Ilya Andreevich Tolstoy, driving along in his carriage, surrounded by Cossacks.

Count Ilya Andreevich invited L.N. to go with him to see Baryatinskii, and Baryatinskii praised Lev Nikolaevich for the calm and courage he had displayed during the raid, and urged him to join the army. Count Ilya Andreevich joined Baryatinskii in urging L.N. to apply, and this is what L.N. did: he applied to the brigade commander and entered the artillery as a cadet. He remained a cadet for two years without being promoted, although he took part in several dangerous operations. His late aunt, Pelageya Ilinichna, told me that his promotion was held up because various documents of his got lost and had to be replaced. And Baryatinskii, who had promised so much, simply forgot all about him.

It was only after two years that he was transferred to the ensigns. When war with Turkey broke out, Lev Nikolaevich applied to enter the Danubian army under Gorchakov, and then applied to go to Sevastopol, where the military operations commenced.[7]

August 8 On August 5, just three days ago, I saw off to war my sweet, devoted, loving son Andryusha (even though he has lived badly.) I want now to describe his departure with the staff of the 6 Kromsk Infantry Regiment from Tambov. He enlisted in this regiment as a non-commissioned officer, a senior cavalry orderly. He went to war voluntarily. He had just left his wife and children, having fallen in love with Anna Leonidovna Tolmacheva, the daughter of General Sobolev, a weak, empty-headed woman who none the less knew how to be tender and loving. I shall not judge either my son or my pretty, virtuous, intelligent daughter-in-law. Only God can judge a husband and wife. But I suffered and struggled with myself for a long time before I finally decided to petition for Andryusha to be taken into the army. He convinced me by saying that it was all the same to him whether they took him or whether he went without my help – only that way would be much harder for him. And indeed if anywhere is the right place for him at present, it is certainly the regiment. His warm, open charm makes him universally liked, and the regimental commander told me that 'Andrei Lvovich had so far given full satisfaction'. But my maternal feelings make me digress from my story.

Having made all the necessary purchases for Andryusha in Moscow and completed my own financial transactions, I went with Lyova to Tambov, where Misha, Ilya and his wife Sonya had all gathered. We stayed in the Evropeiskii Hotel, which by Tambov standards was quite magnificent. I was feeling very ill, did not sleep all night and got up early. That morning I set off for the camp with Andryusha, and he took me to the stables, where we met his fellow orderlies. Like all my children Andryusha loves horses, and he showed me his mare, the best horse in the whole regiment, which he had bought from Mary Boldyreva (née Cherkasskaya). The twelve orderlies, Andryusha's comrades, were running about the stables, their red shirts flashing; I had bought these shirts for Andryusha's comrades and they had immediately put them on with great excitement. Andryusha introduced me to an adjutant of their regiment, a very decent man called Nikolai Ivanovich Ruzhentsov, and we walked around the square, chatting and waiting for the horses to be harnessed to the military carts. We were also approached by the company commander, an unpleasant thickset man accompanied by his elderly mother, who looked like a common merchant's wife. She was bitterly lamenting her fate, sobbing that her last and only remaining son was going to war and leaving her completely alone in the world. She wept uncontrollably, and I tried to comfort her, inviting her to join me in my cab and to follow the officers and soldiers as they left the camp. She was delighted to accept, and said that God had sent me to her to help her endure the parting in better spirits. Yet despite all this, that unhappy mother is now completely alone in the world!

When she and I got into the cab, we saw a crowd of people approaching in the distance. These were the soldiers, accompanied by all their relatives and loved ones. There was something so melancholy about the distant music and drumbeats. The old soldier's wife (her husband had been a home guardsman at Sevastopol) heard the music and immediately burst into tears again. The orderlies were riding along with them, and my Andryusha, in his sand-coloured shirt and cap, led them all on his lovely mare. It is all etched so vividly in my memory: the mare's legs bound with some sort of white bandage, Andryusha looking so handsome seated on his horse, and the old woman's words: 'Oh, how your son rides that horse – what a picture he makes, just like the one in the study at home.'

The soldiers stopped at the well and some women started to pump water, drawing it up in buckets and giving it to them to drink. It was a hot morning and the wind stirred up the dust, scattering it everywhere. Then the officers shouted something and they all moved off again towards the trains. The crowds of friends and relatives kept getting larger and accompanied the soldiers to the waiting train not far from the station.

The wives, mothers, fathers and little children were all carrying things –

parcels and bundles of ring-shaped rolls. Not far from me stood a young soldier boy with his wife and mother. The old woman suddenly stopped and said in a heart-broken voice: 'I can't go any further!' The soldier embraced her, kissed her and ran off to catch up his regiment. His wife followed him, but his mother stood there as if turned to stone.

When they reached the train they were given the order 'Stand at ease!' The soldiers loosened their uniforms and began to load the horses. Andryusha helped and gave orders. The crowd milled around the carriages. The soldiers left their things with their relatives, who sat on what they could find or on the ground. Some started eating, some soothed their children, some cried. Almost no one was drunk. The task of loading the horses and vehicles on to the train was completed quickly and efficiently. They had a long struggle with one bay horse, however, which eventually had to be dragged on by force. By four o'clock everything had been loaded and there remained only the bales of hay and a huge pile of loaves. I took Andryusha back to the hotel for dinner. He was tired but cheerful and we took care not to make one another cry. We were soon joined by the others, who had come to see him off – Ilya and his wife, Misha, Lyova, Nikolai Maklakov and two Tambov landowners called Shulgin and Rtishchev. After dinner we went back to the train with Andryusha and the others.

By now the crowd around the train was even denser. The soldiers were getting into their compartments and the wives and relatives were handing them their things and food for the journey. One soldier leaned out and shouted to his four-year-old son: 'Don't cry, Lyonka, I'll bring you some chocolate when I get back!' Another soldier, whose hair was already grey, lay down, tipped back his head so his cap fell off, raised his legs in the air, closed his eyes and sobbed with such despair that it broke my heart. A pale young ensign stood on the platform, his eyes dull and his white face tinged with yellow, like a wax doll. He did not say a word. A few soldiers were weeping discreetly. I went up to the regimental commander and thanked him for being so good to Andryusha, and he said it was a 'great pleasure to have him in the regiment'. I was then introduced to the head of the division – Lieutenant-General Klaver, I think it was. He kissed my hands and said: 'We certainly live through some extraordinary moments in our life.'

Andryusha took us to the first-class compartment to which he had been assigned, thanks to his influential patrons. He had a folding seat by the door. It will be so hard for him, spoilt and ill as he is, to endure all the discomforts of the journey and army life – it distresses me to think of it.

Eventually the third and final whistle went, there was a flourish of music and everyone wept. I kissed Andryusha, made the sign of the cross over him and could look at no one else. His flushed, distraught face, wet with tears, nodded to us out of the window. What was he experiencing in those moments . . . ? Further and further away, then he disappeared completely, and for a moment I lost all consciousness of life and its meaning. I felt something similar to this, only much more intensely, when I left Vanechka's funeral. Only mothers will know what I mean.

However hard one searched for some sign of patriotic, military elation amongst these soldiers, officers and generals – and particularly amongst those seeing them off – there was simply not a trace of it to be found. Everyone was suffering, everyone was leaving against his will, bewildered and unhappy. General Klaver did shout out to the soldiers as they said goodbye to him from the train: 'Give them hell!' But his words sounded vile, inappropriate and absurd. It was as if he had suddenly realised that he was supposed to encourage the departing soldiers, but knew how utterly pointless this was.

Yet again something has broken in my heart. Seeing my son and all the other soldiers off to war, and the terrible impression this made on me, marks the end of one whole phase in my life and the beginning of an important new one. What is war? Is one foolish man, Nicholas II – who is not really so wicked and himself deplores what is happening – really capable of creating so much evil?

It suddenly occurred to me that war was like a thunder-storm – an elemental force; it is just that we do not see the evil power which mercilessly and inexorably crushes so many human beings to death. When someone pokes an anthill with a stick and destroys the ants, they drag out their eggs and litter and see neither the stick nor the hand nor the man who is destroying them. Likewise, we do not see the power which has caused the murderous destruction of war.

August 17 When you live through terrible experiences life goes on through sheer inertia and you have no emotional energy for anything else. When I saw Andryusha off to war I suddenly felt connected with everyone else grieving over the fate of their children, husbands, brothers and loved ones. I lost all pleasure in life, I was terrified for my son, and all the horror of war, which had lain buried for so long in the depths of my soul, suddenly surfaced with terrible power and clarity and would not let go of me.

Andryusha sent a bright and cheerful letter from Ufa, where the train had stopped. But he says nothing of the future . . . [8] His poor wife Olga and the children are staying here with me, and it breaks my heart to see them. Sonyusha is such a sad and touching sight, with her dimpled cheeks and her sensitive, sick little soul.

But Misha's family is a joy. What charming children – what cheerful, lovable warm-hearted little mites; it's a pleasure to be with them. And Misha's wife, what a lovely, warm, intelligent woman she is. I sometimes long to hug her and tell her how much I love her and how terribly sorry I would be if she were ever unhappy. My dear friend Varya Nagornova is here too. I went for a swim today; it was cold and windy and the water was 14 degrees. I need to refresh my body and my soul.

L.N. has been staying in Pirogovo with Masha for the past week. He actually went there to see his brother Sergei Nikolaevich, who is dying of cancer of the face, eyes and jaw. The poor man is suffering very much, but his emotional state is far worse; no patience, no faith, no love of people . . . Save us from such an end.[9]

Varya Nagornova and my son Lyova are playing Mozart quintets as duets; I should like to play too, and it is hard to write while the music is going on.

· 1905 ·

Sunday, January 9 – thousands of workers assemble outside the Tsar's palace to present their petition for a constitution. Cossacks fire on the peaceful crowd and many hundreds killed. Bloody Sunday is the start of Russia's first revolution. Waves of strikes follow, the countryside is ablaze with riots, and hundreds of estates are looted and burnt. February – Russian army defeated at Mukden. The Tsar publishes a manifesto rallying his citizens to the throne, while announcing the formation of a new consultative assembly, or Duma, *whose unequal franchise is universally derided. May – Russian fleet annihilated in the Tsushima Straits. As riots continue, extreme right-wing organisations unleash a wave of pogroms. Summer – general strike in Odessa, supported by the battleship* Potemkin. *August – Treaty of Portsmouth ends war; law giving autonomy to universities, whose halls become forums for great protest meetings. September to October – general strike in Moscow. October 17 – Tsar issues manifesto promising more freedom and the formation of a Council of Ministers. Workers' councils (*soviets*) formed in St Petersburg and elsewhere. November – St Petersburg* soviet *delegates arrested. Moscow* soviet *organises armed uprising in protest. Troops sent into Moscow; hundreds killed.*

January – Andrei Tolstoy discharged from army with nervous disorder. Tolstoy writes 'On the Social Movement in Russia' and letters and articles condemning violence. His influence on the revolution is in decline. November – Tanya Sukhotina gives birth to a daughter, Tanya (Tanechka, Tanyushka).

January 14 I want to leave this diary to the Rumyantsev Museum for safekeeping, but I should like to write some more now that we have started the new year.

I went in to see Lev Nikolaevich on the morning of January 1, kissed him and wished him a happy new year. He was writing his diary but he stopped when I came in and stared at me. 'I feel so sorry for you, Sonya,' he said. 'You did so want to play that violin sonata, but you weren't able to.' (I wasn't able to because both he and the children opposed the idea; I had been very upset about this the previous day.) 'Why are you sorry for me?' I asked. 'Well, they wouldn't let that violinist play yesterday, and you are always so unhappy and I feel so sorry for you.' And at that he suddenly burst into tears, caressed me and started telling me how much he loved me and how happy he had been with me all his life. Then I began to cry too; I told him that if I was not very happy sometimes it was my own fault, and I asked him to forgive me for my unstable state of mind.

L.N. always weighs up his life at the beginning of every year. And just before this new year Pavel Ivanych Biryukov, who was recently released from exile in Switzerland,[1] was reading L.N.'s diaries and his letters to me. L.N. glanced at these from time to time and read through one or two passages, and his whole life seemed to flash before him, and he said to Pavel Ivanych, who is writing a biography of him,[2] that he could not dream of any greater family happiness, that I had given him everything, that he could never love anyone so much . . . It made me so happy when Pavel Ivanych told me that.

On the night of January 10–11 our son Andryusha returned from war, thank God. He has been given a year's leave. His head is sick and his nerves are shattered. He is as childish as ever, but the war has left its mark, and he seems to have changed for the better. The cruelty of war is quite atrocious. Simple shooting aside, people are punished like martyrs: they are beaten with sabres and bayonets, then cast aside, before receiving the final blow, to die in frightful agony; they are tied up and burnt alive on fires; they are thrown into wolf-holes with a stake at the bottom . . . And so on. To think that human beings could do such things . . . ! It is quite beyond my understanding. It makes me suffer terribly to hear of people's brutalisation and this endless war.

Lev Nikolaevich is writing an article saying that the government must act, and voicing the demands for a constitution and an assembly of the *zemstvo*.[3] Yesterday he rode over to Tula and returned by sledge, and the dear man seems none the worse for it.

Dreadful news from St Petersburg. 160 thousand workers came out on strike, the troops were called in, and it is said that 3,000 people were killed.[4]

(1906 – Events prove the freedoms promised in the Tsar's October manifesto to be a fraud, and his Council of Ministers a fiction. January – first congress of the new Constitutional Democrat (Cadet) Party, which supports a constitutional monarchy. April 27 – opening of the First State Duma. *All its demands for reforms rejected by the Tsar. July 9 –* Duma *dissolved. Strikes and riots continue, but with less intensity than the previous year.*

Mikhail Sukhotin elected to the Duma. *Sofia prepares twelfth edition of Tolstoy's* Complete Works. *Tolstoy writes 'On the Significance of the Russian*

18 Above: Tula schoolchildren visiting Lev Tolstoy at Yasnaya Polyana, 1907

19 Below: Sofia and Lev Tolstoy during his illness at Gaspra, 1901

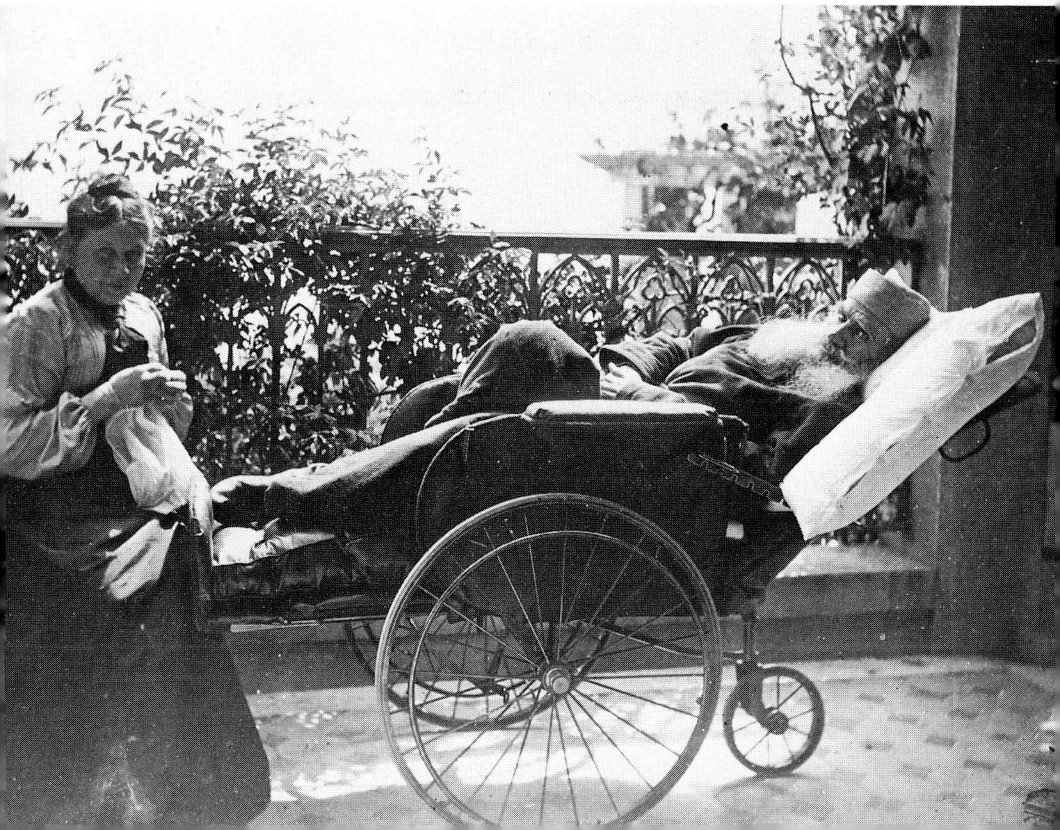

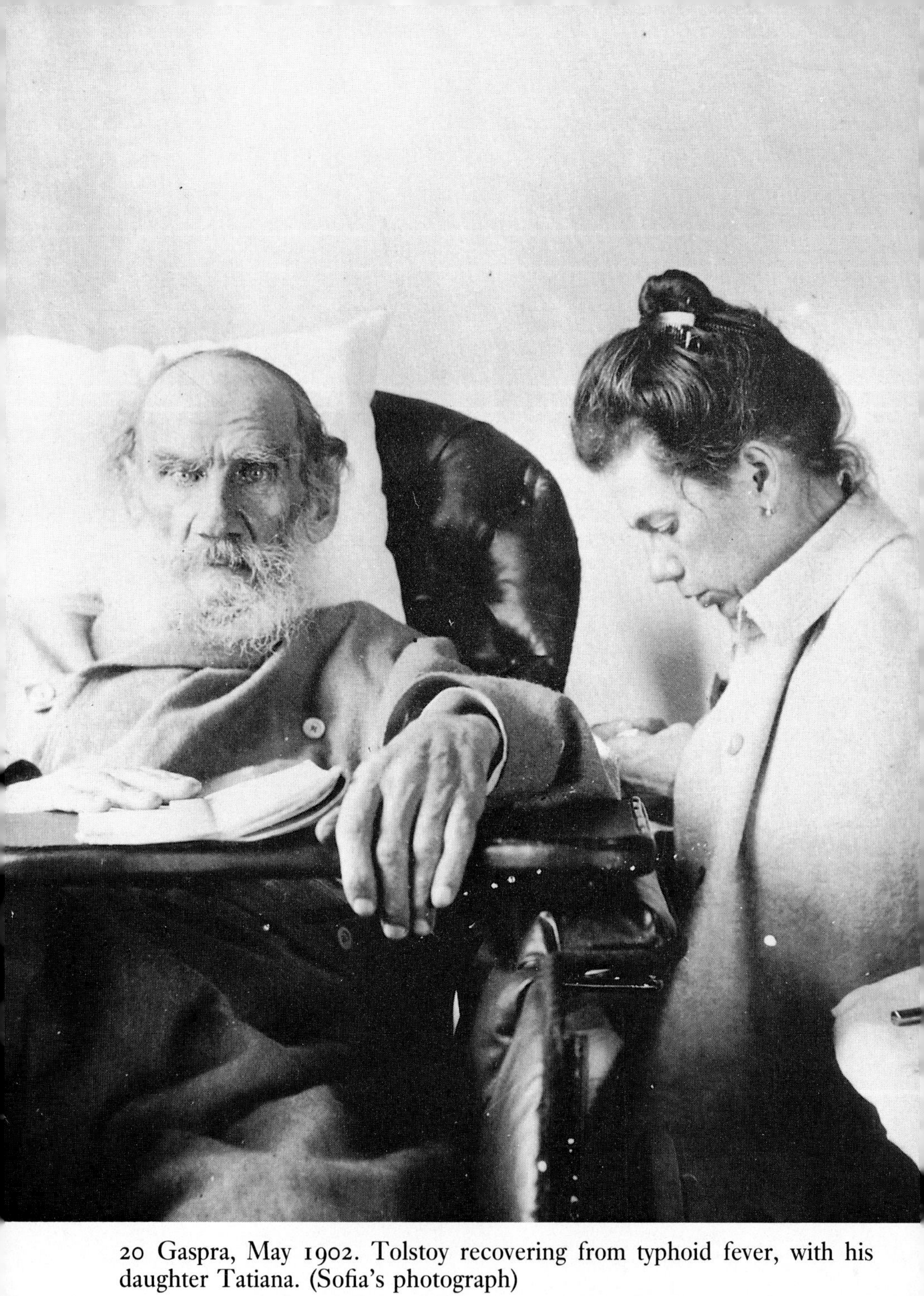

20 Gaspra, May 1902. Tolstoy recovering from typhoid fever, with his daughter Tatiana. (Sofia's photograph)

Revolution' and 'Two Roads', and starts on 'The Children's Law of God'. June – peasants steal wood from the Yasnaya estate, and Sofia calls police, which provokes bitter arguments with Tolstoy. August – Sofia critically ill with peritonitis, and has operation to remove fibroma of the womb. November 26 – Masha Tolstaya dies of double pneumonia.

1907 – Some 2,500 terrorist murders in this year. Members of the security police infiltrate terrorist group of Socialist Revolutionary Party, murdering two Cadet Duma *deputies and making two attempts to kill Count Witte, President of the Council of Ministers. Terrorist campaign reaches climax, then collapses, with hundreds of terrorists in prison, emigration and exile. June 3 – second* Duma *dissolved as too radical, and Social Democrat deputies arrested and imprisoned. July – announcement of Russo-Japanese reconciliation. August – Anglo-Russian entente. November – third* Duma, *dominated by conservatives, completes its full term (until June 1912).*

May 19 – Sofia's brother Vyacheslav murdered by terrorists. Marauders break into the Yasnaya Polyana estate, and Sofia applies to police for guards to protect the property. (The occasion for more bitter arguments with Tolstoy.) September – Tolstoy receives a telegram from an extreme right-wing organisation threatening his life. October – his secretary, Nikolai Gusev, arrested for 'revolutionary propaganda', and exiled for two years to the Urals. November – Andrei Tolstoy marries his second wife, Ekaterina Artsimovich. Tolstoy starts evening class for peasant children, and writes a Children's Circle of Reading *and 'Thou Shalt Not Kill'. Winter – he has several strokes and memory losses. Chertkov returns to Russia from exile in England, and takes control of Tolstoy's diaries. Sofia continues work on* My Life *(referred to in this period as her* autobiography*).)*

· 1908 ·

Spring – revolution defeated, reaction once more triumphant, most revolutonaries in exile, emigration or prison. Under the patronage of Nicholas II, ultra-conservative organisations multiply. Large numbers of people move to Siberia to colonise its barren wastes.

Tolstoy writes 'I Cannot Be Silent', a manifesto to the Tsar begging for an end to the carnage. It is banned, but circulates none the less (those found reading it being punished heavily). Sofia working on My Life, *and a series of short stories for her grandchildren. Summer – Chertkov buys estate near Yasnaya Polyana and is a constant visitor. Sofia's battles with him begin in earnest. September – Tolstoy's eightieth birthday celebrated in grand style. He suffers more strokes and phlebitis. Violent quarrels with Sofia over the copyright to his post-1881 works.*

September 7 It is a very long time since I have written my diary. I have come in my old age to where two paths lie before me: I can either raise myself spiritually and strive for self-perfection, or I can seek pleasure in food, peace and quiet and various pleasures like music, books and the company of others. This last frightens me. My life is set in such a narrow frame; it is a constant effort looking after Lev Nikolaevich, whose health is becoming visibly weaker. When he gets worse I am horrified by the prospect of my pointless, empty life without him. When he gets better I feel as though I must prepare myself for this, and assure myself that I shall then be free to serve him – to which end I am at present putting all his manuscripts in order and copying out all his diaries, notebooks and everything else relating to his creative work.

He has recently been confined to his wheelchair again, as he has to keep his leg up. It's slightly swollen, although there is no inflammation or pain. He is feeling generally rather weak.

Living here in Yasnaya at present are Lev Nikolaevich and I, our daughter Sasha, the Czech Doctor Makovitsky, Sasha's friend and assistant Varv. Mikh. Feokritova, and Lev Nikolaevich's secretary N.N. Gusev, to whom he dictates corrections and new ideas every morning for the new edition of his *Circle of Reading.*[1]

We have recently celebrated Lev Nikolaevich's so-called eightieth jubilee. What an enormous amount of love and respect people have for him. This was evident from all the articles, the letters and especially the telegrams – of which we received some 2,000. I am collecting everything and shall send it all to the Historical Museum in Moscow, which is going to open a 'Jubilee Archive'.

There were some very touching presents too: the first was from waiters at St Petersburg's Bouffe Theatre, and was accompanied by a charming letter. The present was a nickel-plated samovar with engraved inscriptions which read: 'Not in God our Strength but in Truth', 'The Kingdom of God is Within You', and 72 signatures.[2] Some artists sent a lovely album of water-colours,[3] and there were numerous portraits of Lev Nikolaevich, one embroidered on silk, and another done from tiny words taken from a short story of his.[4] There was a beautiful embroidered red cushion from some craftsmen; the Borman bakery sent four and a half *poods** chocolate, of which 100 boxes were given away to the Yasnaya village children; someone else sent 100 scythes for our peasants; there were 20 bottles of St Raphael wine for Lev Nikolaevich's stomach, and from the Ottoman factory a box of cigars, which Lev Nikolaevich returned with a letter of thanks, saying that he was against tobacco and smoking.[5]

There were also a number of malicious presents, letters and telegrams. For instance, there was a box containing some string and a letter, signed 'A

*162 lb.

Mother', saying: 'Since Tolstoy has no reason to think that the government will hang him, he had better do it himself.'[6]

This mother probably had a child who died in the revolution, and she blames its propaganda on Tolstoy.

The following people gathered at the table for Lev Nikolaevich's birthday party: L.N. himself, four of our sons – Seryozha, Ilya, Andryusha and Misha (Lyova is in Sweden awaiting his wife's confinement) – and I. Of our daughters only Sasha was here; Tanya had visited shortly before the 28th. She came for my birthday but could not bear to leave her little daughter a second time. Then there were Mikhail Sergeevich Sukhotin, Mikhail Aleksandrovich Stakhovich, the Goldenweisers, the Chertkovs (father and son), Maria Aleksandrovna Schmidt, Ivan Ivanovich Gorbunov, an Englishman called Mr Wright, who brought a letter from some English writers,[7] Mitya Kuzminskii, my sons' wives, Masha (Zubova) and Sonya (Filosofova), and Andryusha's second wife, Katya, who came that evening. Then Galya Chertkova arrived, and the Nikolaevs. Everyone was calm, quiet and very moved, not least Lev Nikolaevich himself, who had only recently recovered from his illness and attended the dinner in his wheelchair. There was such a sense of love, both from the world outside and in the hearts of all those present on that day. When Lev Nikolaevich went to bed that evening and I tucked the warm blanket I had knitted round his shoulders, he said: 'Ah, how good that was, how good! As long as it doesn't all end in some disaster . . . !' But so far God has been merciful.

Lev Nikolaevich felt fairly well today, although he was again confined to his wheelchair with his slightly swollen leg stretched out in front of him. He ate a hearty lunch with us, and told us he had just received a letter from some colonel he had never met, who asked him the name of the horse on which he had galloped away from the Chechens when he was in the Caucasus.[8]

The story went like this:

An 'exploration party', as it was then called in the Caucasus, had been organised, and they all set off in carriages and on horseback, accompanied by soldiers. Three of them, wanting to prance about and show off their horses, detached themselves from the main party and galloped on ahead – these three being Lev Nikolaevich, Sado his '*kunak*' (or friend) and Poltoratskii. Lev Nikolaevich was on a large, very beautiful grey horse, which had cost a great deal of money and had a lovely gait, but was very heavy, in other words a dawdler. His dear Sado suggested that they change horses, so that Lev Nikolaevich could experience the speed of his own Nogai horse. They had just done so when some armed Chechens suddenly appeared from under the brow of the hill, advancing towards them. Neither Lev Nikolaevich nor Poltoratskii had a gun. Poltoratskii was on a slow artillery pony and fell behind; they shot at him, attacked his horse and slashed him with their sabres on the spot, but they did not kill him. While

Sado was brandishing his rifle and shouting something in Chechen to his fellow tribesmen, Lev Nikolaevich managed to gallop away on his '*kunak*'s' fleet-footed little Nogai horse.[9] So yet again Tolstoy's life was saved by a sheer lucky chance.

After dinner Lev Nikolaevich played chess with Goldenweiser, then listened to him play Chopin's third scherzo, a sketch by Arensky and two Chopin ballades, the second of which he played marvellously well, with an inspiration that he managed to communicate to everyone.

My life is entirely reduced to material cares. The contractor came and drew up estimates for rebuilding the floor in Sasha's room, repairing the bath-house and the coach-house, building a poultry-yard and so on. I don't even have the chance to take a walk: first I sit with Lev Nikolaevich, then there are things to be done in the house. But I do adore nature – I look at the reddening maples and I long to paint them. And I love art too – I walk across the field repeating Tyutchev's verses: 'There is in early autumn a short but glorious time . . . ' I listen to Goldenweiser playing and I long with my whole being to study music . . .

Indeed my entire life has been one of unsatisfied longings and the stern call of duty. But now these longings are abating: I am no longer confronted by that wall, the barrier to this earthly life, which puts a stop to all human desires and the creative fever. 'It will pass. Soon there will be an end to everything.' Only prayer remains, but even prayer grows cold in the face of hard, everyday material life. Abandon it, abandon it . . . But to whom?

September 8 I got up late and went to see how Lev Nikolaevich was; he had had a bad attack of heartburn during the night. I went to close the netting door of the balcony leading from Lev Nikolaevich's study, and when he saw me he joyfully shouted out, 'Ah, it's you, Sonya!' which pleased me so much.

Today he and Gusev were composing a letter of thanks to everyone who had honoured him on his eightieth birthday. Gusev read it out to me this evening, and I made one or two corrections and suggestions, with which both Gusev and Lev Nikolaevich agreed.

Sasha has gone to a concert in Tula with Varvara Mikhailovna. N.V. Davydov came and we spent a very pleasant day with him. We had a long talk about literature and everyone deplored the pornography, the lack of talent and the crude audacity of our modern writers. We discussed the death sentence, and Davydov said how utterly senseless and ineffective he thought it was. And we discussed many more things besides with him, Lev Nikolaevich, Khiryakov and Nikolaev. The days simply fly past – and so fruitlessly that it makes me wretched; I feel as though I was losing something very precious, and that is time, the last years of my life and the lives of those closest to me.

September 10 I am completely taken up by the estate. I gave orders today for the potatoes to be dug up; I go to the field and find that they have all gone to dinner and there is no one there but a puny lad of fourteen, 'guarding' the potatoes and the field from thieves. 'What are you sitting there for?' I say to him. 'Why don't you dig some potatoes?' So he and I pick up some sacks and set to work digging potatoes and putting them in sacks until the rest of the labourers return. It is so much more enjoyable to work than to be a housewife and make others work. My taking part seemed to infuse the others with energy, and on that day they dug a great many potatoes. We then sorted them out and carried them to the cellar, with me supervising and helping. The guards looked at me in amazement.

Lev Nikolaevich is much better; the swelling on his leg has gone down and he was walking about on his own today; he is much more cheerful too. He worked for a long time on his *Circle of Reading*, then listened to some music, and played vint all evening with Sasha, Varvara Mikhailovna and his niece Liza Obolenskaya, who arrived today. It is 10 degrees outside and very still; everything is still so green, and there are some lovely phlox just outside my window – and all over the garden too.

September 13 Reading the newspapers in search of any mention of Lev Nikolaevich's name takes a great deal of my time and has a very depressing effect on me. As I read them the whole sad story of Russian life passes before me; you feel as though you're doing something and learning something, but in fact it's all to no purpose. I make cuttings and paste them into a book. On August 28 I collected seventy-five newspapers, and some journals too. People have so much love for Lev Nikolaevich, and so little real understanding of him. Today I made some final revisions to his letter to the newspaper thanking everyone who had honoured him on August 28.[10] It is a clear, bright, fresh day, and this evening it was 3 degrees. As I walked around the estate attending to various things I recalled some verses which Fet sent me once with the message: 'Here, for your name-day, I am sending you my last autumn flower. I fear your refined and penetrating taste.' The verses begin with the words: 'Again the autumn lustre of dawn . . . ' And these lines are particularly good:

> The heart is glad to ache again
> With yet more sweet and bitter pain . . . [11]

There's a truly *autumnal* atmosphere about that.

Some red-headed barefoot peasant came to see Lev Nikolaevich and they had a long talk together about religion. Chertkov had brought him, saying what a good influence he had on all those around him, despite his poverty. I wanted to listen to their conversation, but whenever I stay in the room when Lev Nikolaevich has guests he gives me a questioning glance which tells me he does not wish to be disturbed, so I am forced to leave.

Seryozha's crops have been set on fire and he has lost some 1,000 rubles' worth of wheat. L.N. sat out on the balcony for breakfast, and this evening he played chess with Chertkov and chatted with Nikolaev. His health is better, and he seems pleased and even touched by all the love and devotion people showed him on his birthday.

September 14 This morning I decided to pay off all the Yasnaya day-labourers. The girls and young men all gathered at the office, Varvara Mikhailovna came to give me a hand, and later on my Sasha came with Nadya Ivanovna. We all worked away, checking their tickets, noting them down and then paying them. The girls broke into song and cracked jokes, and the children ran about gleefully. I paid out 400 rubles in all. I went on working at it in the house too, and stamped 'paid' in their books. It has been a still grey day – 8 degrees towards evening. Sasha has picked a few large honey agarics and saffron milk-caps.

L.N. was inundated by guests all day. A Russian visitor from America (Bianco I think his name was), who is married to a grand-niece of Dickens, asked Lev Nikolaevich for a portrait to take back to America, where there are now some three thousand Molokans, who have named their school after Tolstoy.

Then came eight young revolutionaries who recently published a proclamation urging people to rise up and kill the landowners. L.N. had sent for these young men himself after learning about them from others in their group, and he tried to make them see reason and inspire them with good Christian feelings.[12] God alone knows what this will lead to.

Then I found a young man sitting with L.N. and weeping piteously. It transpired that he had been ordered to do his military service, and this was abhorrent to him; first he wanted to refuse, then he weakened, now he weeps incessantly and still cannot decide what to do.[13] Then a simple old fellow came for a chat. Two soldiers who came with a civilian were not allowed in, but were given some books.

L.N. sat out on the balcony during the day.

I am reading the papers and making cuttings about Tolstoy. Today I found a good one for September 12 in *New Russia*.

September 16 After two months sitting at home, L.N. went out for the first time with Gusev in the carriage. He himself drove, and they went to see Chertkov in Telyatinki. His appetite is good and he seems to be making an excellent recovery.

There is always some domestic problem to be dealt with, which weighs on one and obscures the real problems of life and one's thoughts of imminent death.

It is as though everyone here were preparing for something; we're merely *preparing* ourselves for life – for it does not really exist: there is no real peace, no leisure, no time for all the activities one so longs to be involved in. This is why L.N.'s life has been such a wise and happy one: he has always worked from choice, never from obligation. If he felt like writing, he wrote, and if he felt like sowing, he sowed. He took it into his head to make boots – so he stubbornly went off and made boots. He thought he might like to teach children – so he taught children for a while. And when he got bored he would give it up. Could I try to live like that, I wonder? What would happen to L.N. and the children if I did?

September 17 My name-day. I went for a walk with Varya Nagornova, and was enchanted by the hot, youthful beauty of the autumn countryside. The bright, infinitely varied tints of the forest were like an endless series of marvellous paintings, and I longed desperately to reproduce it in oils. In the flower-bed in front of the house one rose is still flowering, and once again I kept thinking of that verse which goes: 'You alone, princess rose, are fragrant and lush . . .'[14]

I also took a walk with Andryusha and his wife. Maria Aleksandrovna Schmidt came too, and it was almost as though we were 'celebrating' my name-day. I do not usually like 'celebrations', but today was most enjoyable. This evening, L.N., Sasha, Andryusha and Varvara Mikhailovna all played vint, while I did more newspaper cuttings. L.N. went for a drive with Sasha today in the rubber-tyred carriage, with Chertkov riding on the box. He went for a drive yesterday too. Late this evening he began talking about his *Circle of Reading*, and read us some of his own sayings and those of other writers. He is very absorbed in this work at present, and obviously loves it. He said that human happiness consists in universal love, constant communion with God and the aspiration to experience and fulfil God's will throughout one's life. He has never clearly defined exactly *what* he means by God's will, however, or how to apply this to one's life. 'Through love,' he replies when one asks him. But this is not clear either. Everyone experiences and understands God in his own way; and the deeper that understanding is, the firmer and better it will be, and the less need there will be to talk about it.

L.N. has aged greatly over the past year; he has now passed over to the last stage. But he has aged well. His spiritual life evidently predominates now. He likes to go for drives, he likes good food and a glass of the wine which the St Raphael wine company sent him for his jubilee, and he also likes a game of vint or chess, but his body seems to live a separate life, and his spirit exists on an altogether higher plane, independent of his body and indifferent to the earthly life. A change seemed to take place in him after his illness; one senses a certain distance in him now, and I sometimes feel intensely sad about all the things that have been lost, both in his life and in his relations with me and those around him. Do others see this?

September 30 I am completely absorbed in estate matters. But it is possible for me only because it brings me into contact with nature and I can admire it to my heart's content. (By nature I also mean the working people.) Today I went to the apple orchards, where forty peasants were clearing the moss, cutting away the dead wood and smearing the tree-trunks with a compound of clay, lime and cow dung. What a beautiful sight the bright figures of the girls made against the background of the dazzling green grass, the blue sky and the yellow, red and brown trees. I stood there admiring one Oporto apple tree in particular. It would have been hard to reproduce these soft yellows, pinks and bright greens; the whole shape of the tree was utterly charming.

Then I walked on to see how they were progressing with the dam and the slope on the lower pond.

I also picked a bunch of flowers in the garden for Lev Nikolaevich, but he didn't want it. It seems he has no need of anyone any more. I don't know whether it's this illness, which has kept him at home and had such a depressing effect on him, or whether it's old age, or whether it's this wall of Tolstoyans – mainly Chertkov, who has practically moved in with us and almost never leaves Lev Nikolaevich alone – but he has become not merely distant but even bad-tempered with me, and with everyone else as well. Yesterday we had a letter from his sister Maria Nikolaevna, a delightful letter full of warmth – and L.N. didn't even bother to read it.[15]

The *Circle of Reading* has been crossed out, corrected and revised yet again, and poor Sasha has to copy it out yet again on the typewriter. It's a good thing I got Varvara Mikhailovna here to help her, otherwise her nerves and eyesight would be ruined.

I am copying out the catalogues in our library, as they are about to collapse. It is a tedious and difficult task, but a necessary one. I am also altering some winter dresses. I feel so bored – I am not writing my 'Life' or doing anything creative. I often long to play the piano, but both the grand pianos are in the drawing-room and one can never play there . . . Either people are eating or Lev Nikolaevich is working or asleep . . .

I have recently been reading articles about Lev Nikolaevich and the rest of us in every language. No one knows or understands him; no one knows the essence of his character and mind as I do. But I shan't be believed whatever I write. L.N. is a person of enormous intellect and talent, a person of extraordinary imagination, sensitivity and refinement, but without any heart or real goodness. His goodness is all a matter of *principle*, and never *spontaneous*.

Heavenly weather. A bright sun, 11 degrees in the shade, the leaves have not fallen yet and the birches in front of our windows, bright yellow against the blue sky, are truly astonishing.

My heart is heavy, I feel lonely, no one loves me – I evidently don't deserve it. I have a lot of passion and spontaneous sympathy for people, but I too have little real goodness. My best qualities are my maternal feelings and my sense of duty.

The day before yesterday we had a visit from a former revolutionary called N.A. Morozov, who was in prison for twenty-eight years, first in Schlüsselburg, then in the Peter and Paul Fortress. I longed to hear him talk about his psychological state during his imprisonment, but he talked more about the way they had deliberately starved them with bad food which gave them scurvy. They would cure the scurvy and then starve them again with bad and inadequate food, so that of eleven prisoners in the fortress at the same time only three lived out their term, and eight died.

Morozov still looks very fit, though, and he got married last year. His voice is somewhat muted, but he is full of life and absorbed in his passion for astronomy. He has already written and published a book about the Apocalypse,[16] and his work now consists in discovering references to astronomy in the old sacred texts.

Morozov came with an old woman called Lebedeva, an old friend of his, and they stayed the whole evening.[17]

December 8 I want to write down something I happened to overhear yesterday evening. Chertkov, who visits us every day, was in Lev Nikolaevich's room and was talking to him about the sign of the cross. And I could not help hearing their conversation from the hall. L.N. said he made the sign of the cross sometimes from habit, as though even if his soul was not praying at that moment, his body was making the sign of prayer. Chertkov replied that it was very possible that he might make the sign of the cross when he was dying or in great pain, and that those with him might think that he had converted to Orthodoxy, or wanted to do so; so in order that people should think no such thing, Chertkov would make a note in his notebook of what Lev Nikolaevich had said.

What a narrow-minded individual this Chertkov is, what an unimaginative view he takes of everything! He is not even interested in the psychology of Lev Nikolaevich's soul at that moment when, alone before God, he blesses himself with the sign of the cross, as he himself was blessed by his mother, his grandmother, his father, his aunts and his little daughter Tanya, who used to bless her father every evening when she said goodnight to him, quickly moving her little hand over him and saying, 'Bless Papa!' All Chertkov ever does is to *collect information, make notes* and *take photographs*.

He told us an interesting story of two peasants who came and asked him to make them members of any 'party' he wanted, saying they would sign anything he wanted, with whatever he wanted – ink, blood, they didn't mind, just so long as they were paid for it.

This happened because of all the appalling characters who have gathered in Chertkov's house. There are thirty-two people living and eating there at present; the house is a large one and it is completely full. Among those living there are four young Yasenki peasants, comrades of his son Dima, who do absolutely nothing, eat with their masters, collect 15 rubles a month each and are the envy of all the others. Also living there with their mother are my poor little grandchildren Sonyushka and Ilyushok. It grieves me so to see them.

All the locks have been broken in the side wing, the windows have been smashed and the honey has been stolen from the hives. I hate the peasants, and having to live under the constant threat of being robbed by them. I hate both capital punishment and the precariousness of this government.

· 1909 ·

Russia drops claims to Straits of Constantinople and recognises Austria's annexation of Bosnia-Hercegovina, which arouses deep hatred in Russia for Vienna and Berlin.

March – Tolstoy ill again. Chertkov expelled from his estate for 'subversive activities', and moves to Kryokshina, near Moscow. October – Chertkov and Aleksandra Tolstaya prevail upon Tolstoy secretly to draw up a new will bequeathing all his post-1881 works to Tanya, Aleksandra and Sergei Tolstoy, and making Chertkov sole heir to his literary estate. Sofia driven nearly mad by suspicion.

January 14 Today I resumed my old work – I have been copying out a new fictional work by Lev Nikolaevich which he has just completed.[1]

The subject is revolutionaries, punishments and where all this springs from. It may be interesting. But it's still the same old themes, and the same old descriptions of peasant life. He relishes that peasant wench with her strong female body and her sunburnt legs, she allures him just as powerfully now as she did all those years ago: the same Aksinya with the flashing eyes, almost unrecognisable at the age of eighty, has risen from the depths of the memories and sensations of his past. Aksinya was a Yasnaya peasant girl, Lev Nikolaevich's last mistress before his marriage, and she still lives in the village. It all had rather a depressing effect on me. And I suppose later on there will be a poetic depiction of the revolution – for however much he takes refuge in Christianity, L.N. is certainly in sympathy with it; he hates all authority, and everything which fate has placed in a position of power.

But I shall copy some more and we shall see what happens further on in this story. He did not want to give it to me to copy at first, as though he was embarrassed about it. And indeed if he had slightly more sensitivity he would not call his peasant heroines Aksinya. And then there is his peasant hero, who is meant to be so sympathetic, with his smile and his accordion, but who then goes astray and becomes a revolutionary. Maybe I shall change my mind, but so far I do not like it at all.

Wanda Landowska came today and performed for us. She played a Chopin mazurka and a Mozart sonata to perfection, bending low over the keys as though forcing them to reveal the meaning of the music to her. The refinement and expressiveness of her playing were taken to the very extremes of beauty. She played some early music too – a bourrée, a dance, pieces for old people, young people and servants – and it was all very interesting and performed astonishingly well. Apart from our family the Chertkovs, father and son, were here, and my daughter-in-law Olga.[2] Marusya Maklakova has just left.

· 1910 ·

June – law allowing communal village land to pass to individual peasant ownership. Law empowering Russian legislature to pass all laws affecting Finland. Students riot over flouting of autonomy (granted to universities in 1905). Strike movement slumps.

*Furious arguments between the Tolstoys over possession of his diaries and the copyright to his works. January – Tolstoy writes 'On Suicide' (later titled 'On Madness'). Summer – Tolstoy rewrites his will, leaving everything to his daughter Tanya, should Aleksandra die before him, and giving Chertkov sole power to change or publish anything after his death. His sons Andrei and Sergei contemplate certifying him to invalidate will. July – Tolstoy calls in psychiatrist to examine Sofia. Diagnosis: paranoia and hysteria. A mounting crescendo of reproaches and recriminations. October 28 – Tolstoy leaves home with his daughter Aleksandra and his doctor. November 7 – Tolstoy dies at Astapovo station. His death touches off student riots in many towns of Russia.**

June 26[1] Lev Nikolaevich, my husband, has given all his diaries since the year 1900 to Vl. Gr. Chertkov, and has started writing a new diary at Chertkov's house, where he has been staying since June 12.[2]

*For introductions to the years 1911 to 1919, see relevant sections of Daily Diaries.

In this diary, which he started at Chertkov's and which he gave me to read, he says amongst other things: 'I must try to *fight* Sonya with love and kindness,'[3] Fight?! What is there to fight, when I love him so passionately and intensely, when my one concern is that he should be happy? But to Chertkov, and to future generations who will read his diaries, he must present himself as unhappy and magnanimous, 'fighting' some sort of imaginary evil.

My life with Lev Nik. becomes more intolerable each day because of his heartlessness and cruelty to me. And it is Chertkov who has brought all this about, gradually and quite consistently. He has done everything in his power to take control of this unfortunate old man, he has separated us, he has killed the creative spark in L.N. and has kindled all the protest, castigation and hatred that one senses in these recent articles which his stupid evil genius has reduced him to writing.

Yes, if one believes in the devil, he has been embodied in Chertkov and has destroyed our life.

I have been ill these past few days. I am tired and depressed by life, I am exhausted by an endless variety of tasks; I live alone, without help,without love, and I pray for death – it is probably not too far off now. Lev Nikol. is an intelligent man, he knows the best way to get rid of me, and with the help of his friend Chertkov he has been killing me gradually; soon it will be all over for me.

I fell ill all of a sudden. I was living here at Yasnaya on my own with Varvara Mikhailovna, as Lev. Nikol., Sasha and the whole retinue – his doctor, his secretary and his servant – had left for Meshcherskoe to see the Chertkovs. For the sake of Sasha's health (she has been ill) I had to make sure everything was clean, and to destroy the dust and germs I was obliged to paint the house and repair the floors. I hired some workmen, and with the help of good Varvara Mikhailovna I moved out all the furniture, pictures and so forth myself. There were also a lot of proofs to read, and things to attend to on the estate. All this exhausted me, and the separation from L.N. was becoming oppressive; eventually I had a nervous attack which was so bad that Varvara Mikhailovna sent Lev Nikol. a telegram saying: 'Bad nervous attack, pulse over a hundred, weeping in bed, insomnia.'[4] He referred to this telegram in his diary: 'Received telegram from Yasnaya. Distressing.'[5] And he did not send one word in reply, nor of course did he come.

By that evening I was feeling very bad indeed, and the spasms in my heart, my aching head and unbearable feelings of despair were making me shudder all over; my teeth were chattering, I was choking and sobbing, I thought I was dying. I cannot remember ever in my whole life being in such a frightful emotional state. I was terrified, and in a desperate attempt to save myself I naturally threw myself at the mercy of the man I love, and I myself sent him a second telegram: 'Implore you come tomorrow, 23rd.'[6]

But on the morning of the 23rd, instead of taking the 11 a.m. train and coming to my help, he sent a telegram which said: '*More convenient* return morning 24th. If necessary, will take night train.'[7]

I detected the cold style of the hard-hearted despot Chertkov in that 'more convenient'. My despair, my nervous anguish and the pains in my head and heart reached the limits of endurance.

At the Chertkovs they had all assumed that I wouldn't have had time both to receive and reply to the telegram. But I had calculated on their cunning, and we sent a telegram, in Varvara Mikhailovna's name this time, which read, 'I think necessary', and we wired it express.

The violinist Erdenko and his wife had come to visit the Chertkovs that day and naturally Chertkov had urged Lev. Nikol. that it would be tactless of him to leave. And though of course he didn't say so in so many words, he contrived to make the violinist mean more to him than his sick wife, and prevented him from leaving. And L.N. was only too happy at this opportunity to spend just one more day with his wonderful, beloved idol.

On the evening of the 23rd Lev Nik. returned – with his hangers-on – in a disgruntled and unfriendly mood. For while I regard *Chertkov* as having come between *us*, both Lev Nik. and Chertkov regard *me* as having come between *them*.

We had a painful talk, and I said everything that was on my mind. Lev Nik. sat on a stool looking hunched and wretched, and said almost nothing. What could he have said? There were moments when I felt dreadfully sorry for him. The only reason I didn't poison myself that time is that I am such a *coward*. But there were good reasons for doing so, and I hope the Lord will take me free of a sinful suicide.

While we were having our painful talk a wild beast suddenly leapt out of Lev Nik., his eyes blazed with rage and he said something so cutting that at that moment I hated him and said: 'Ah, so that is what you are really like!' And he grew quiet immediately.

The next morning my undying love for him got the better of me, and when he came into the room I threw myself into his arms asking him to forgive me, take pity on me and be nice to me; he embraced me and wept, and we both decided that henceforth everything would be different, and we would love and cherish one another. I wonder how long this will last.

But then I couldn't bear to tear myself away from him; I wanted to be close to him, to be one with him. I asked him to go to Ovsyannikovo with me, as I wanted to be with him, and he made a great effort to please me and agreed to go, although he obviously didn't want to. Then on the road he kept trying to get away from me and getting out and walking, and I began weeping again, as there seemed no point in going if I was just going to drive along in the carriage on my own.

But we arrived together and I became calmer – there was some small ray of happiness in just being *together*.

Today I read Lev Nik.'s diary which he gave me, and I was again chilled and shocked to learn that he had given Chertkov *all* his diaries since 1900, so that he could copy out extracts from them; the cunning Sergeenko's son is working with Chertkov, and in all probability he is copying the whole thing for his future advantage. Lev Nik. has always deliberately represented me in his diaries – as he does now – as his tormentor, someone he has to fight and not succumb to, while himself he presents as a great and magnanimous man, religious and loving . . .

I must try to reach a higher spiritual plane, and see how petty, in the face of death and eternity, are all Chertkov's intrigues and L.N.'s attempts to abase and destroy me.

Thou knowest, Lord – if indeed there is a God – how my soul hates lies, and that my love of goodness and people come from my heart, not my mind.

Evening Yet another conversation, yet more anguish and heartache. No, it is impossible, I must do away with myself. When I asked Lev Nik. why he wanted to fight me he replied: 'Because you and I are in constant disagreement, about the land question, the religious question, everything.' 'But the land isn't mine,' I say. 'I consider that it belongs to all of us, to the family.' 'But you could give away *your* land,' he says. 'But why aren't you bothered by Chertkov's million rubles and all his land?' I ask. 'Oh, I'm not going to talk to you any more, leave me alone . . . !' First he shouted, then he withdrew into angry silence.

At first, when I asked him where his diaries since 1900 were, Lev Nik. replied quickly that *he* had them. But when I asked him to show them to me, he mumbled something and admitted that Chertkov had them. Then I asked him again: 'So where are your diaries? Are they with Chertkov? What if his house is searched and they're taken? Anyway I need to refer to them for my "Notes".' 'He has taken all the necessary measures,' replied L.N. 'They are in the bank.' 'Which bank? Where?' 'Why do you want to know?' 'Because I am your wife, the person closest to you.' 'Chertkov is the person who is closest to me, and I don't know where my diaries are. Anyway what does it matter?'

Is Lev Nikolaevich speaking the truth? Who knows? Everything is so sly, secretive and dishonest these days. Everything is a plot against me. It has already been going on for so long, and it will end only with the death of this poor old man, who has been led astray by the devil Chertkov.

I thought I had made up my mind what to do. Just before Lev Nik. left to visit Chertkov the other day, he was angrily criticising the life we led, and when I asked: 'But what is to be done?' he cried out indignantly: 'Leave here, abandon everything, not live in Yasnaya Polyana, not see the beggars, the Circassian guard, the servants waiting at table, the petitioners, the visitors – it's all utterly loathsome to me!'

'Where can we old people go then?' I asked. 'Wherever you want – Paris, Yalta, Odoev. And of course I'll go with you.'

I listened to his angry words, then took 30 rubles and went out, intending to go to Odoev and settle down there.

It was terribly hot; I ran to the highway, gasping with agitation and exhaustion, and lay down in a ditch by the side of the road, beside a field of rye.

Then I heard the coachman approaching in the cabriolet, and I got in, defeated, and returned home. Lev Nikolaevich had been having palpitations while I was away. What was to be done? Where could we go? What should we decide? This was the first real cut in our relations.

So now I have returned home, back to the old life and its burdens. My husband keeps a sullen silence, and there are the proofs, the painters, the bailiff, the guests and the housekeeping to see to . . . I am answerable to everyone, I have to satisfy everyone. My head aches, it feels large and swollen, as though about to burst, and something is straining and crushing my heart too.

And then this evening, pacing the avenues in the park for the tenth time, I made up my mind: without any arguments or discussions I would abandon all my old responsibilities, my old life and rent a small corner in someone's hut and settle there, a poor old woman living in a hut with some children, whom I would love. That is what I must try to do.

But when I told Lev Nikolaevich that not only was I ready to adopt a more simple life with him, I regarded this as a happy idyll, and asked him just to tell me exactly *where* he wanted to go, he initially replied: 'To the south, the Crimea or the Caucasus,' then said: 'All right, let's go, but first . . . ' And then he started telling me that the main thing was human *goodness*.

Of course he won't go anywhere as long as Chertkov is here, and he won't go to Nikolskoe to see Seryozha either, as he promised. '*Goodness*'! When, for the first time in 20 years, he could perhaps have shown *me* a little kindness for a change, when I *begged* him to come back, he and Chertkov wrote a telegram saying it was 'more convenient' not to. 'Who composed and wrote that telegram?' I asked him. 'I think it was Bulgakov and I,' he replied quickly. 'But I really don't remember.'

I asked Bulgakov about this, and he said he had had nothing to do with it and hadn't even known about the telegram. It has to be said, though, that it bears Chertkov's style; Lev Nik. evidently wanted to protect him, and I realised to my horror that he had simply told me an outright lie.

It is night, and I am writing on my own in the drawing-room. Dawn is breaking, the birds are singing and the canaries are stirring in their cages.

I shall surely die from all the suffering I have endured.

Lev Nik. accused me today of disagreeing with him about *everything*. About what? I asked. The land question, the religious question, everything . . . But that is not true. It's simply that I don't understand Henry George's ideas on the land question; and I consider it utterly unjust to give away land and deprive my children. It's the same with the religious question. We both believe in God, in goodness, and in submitting to God's will. We both hate war and capital punishment. We both love and live in the country. We both dislike luxury. The only thing that I don't like is Chertkov, and I love Lev Nik. And he does not love me, but loves his idol.

June 30 Lev Nik., Sasha, I, Dushan Petrovich and N.N. Gué all left for Nikolskoe on the 28th to see Seryozha on his birthday. We all got up early and I went in to Lev Nikol. to say that if he felt ill he shouldn't go, and Gué and I would go together instead. He said he would think about it. (Earlier on he had given me his word that he would go.) But then he must have felt ashamed, for he did decide to go.

I was still feeling very ill, and the previous evening I had decided not to go. I was sitting there watching Lev Nik. play chess with Goldenweiser, when Bulgakov came in and said that Chertkov had now left exile and was going to stay with his mother in Telyatinki.[8] I jumped up as if bitten, the blood rushed to my head and heart and I immediately made up my mind to go and see Seryozha, come what may. I packed quickly and then could not sleep all night. That morning Lev Nik. said he would go ahead on foot, and I could catch him up in the carriage. But then Chertkov arrived, Lev Nikolaevich lost his head and instead of walking to Zaseka he went in the direction of Yasenki. Then he suddenly realised where he was, took fright and hurried to the stable on the hill. From there he and Chertkov caught up with me in Chertkov's trap, but he got down some way away, then walked to my carriage, got in and we travelled on together.

Some horses were supposed to be waiting for us at Bastyevo, the stopping place, but when we got there we found that they hadn't sent any. Sasha and Gué got out at Chern and went by troika to Nikolskoe, where it transpired that they had not received our telegram, which had been held up and had not been sent from Bastyevo. It's a long time since I felt so melancholy as I did in those three hours waiting in that dirty, crowded, inhospitable station.

Lev Nik. went on ahead again and took a wrong turning, and again we had to go looking for him in the trap, when it eventually arrived from Nikolskoe. It was a good thing I had brought some boiled porridge, coffee and milk with me, so I could give him something to eat; I never think about myself, and had nothing all day but one egg and a glass of disgusting tea.

At Nikolskoe we were met by our daughter Tanya, the Orlovs, Gayarinov, Tanya Behrs – and dear, dear Varechka Nagornova. We took some lovely walks, but I found it all a great strain. Talking to Tanya upset me even more; she said so many cruel and critical things, and ruthlessly imposed so many impossible demands on me that I felt even worse than before. Varechka, on the other hand, was warm, affectionate and sensible about my sufferings.

The last walk absolutely exhausted me, but on the whole I was glad we went, for it meant I was close to my Lyovochka for two days. When we disembarked at Zaseka last night he insisted on holding my arm, and when we left the station he was so touchingly concerned that I might be cold, as no warm clothes had been sent for me and I was wearing just a dress, that he went to the carriage to ask whether there was something warm for me to put on. Gué brought his rug and put it over my shoulders.

A train had stopped by the bridge at Zaseka, and it was such a tight squeeze between the railings and the train that it was almost impossible for us to pass; if the train had moved, the carriages might well have pushed us off.

I felt very concerned about Lev Nik.'s health this morning. Still the same drowsiness and lack of appetite, plus his old stomach condition, and his pulse is over 80. He spent almost the whole day in bed, where he received Sutkovoi, Goldenweiser and Chertkov. I overheard his conversation with Sutkovoi, to whom he said, amongst other things, 'I made a great mistake in getting married . . . ' A mistake?

He considers it a 'mistake' because his married life interferes with his spiritual life.

Later on that evening he got up, played chess with Goldenweiser and corrected the proofs of *The Power of Darkness*.[9] We had a quiet, happy, peaceful evening – without Chertkov.

July 1, evening I spent the whole day correcting the proofs for the new edition of *The Fruits of Enlightenment*,[10] and felt utterly wretched about everything. Lev Nikolaevich did not like my letter to Chertkov.[11] But what could I do? One should always write the truth, and never mind the consequences, and I sent the letter all the same. Then this evening Lev Nik., Sasha and Chertkov all retired behind closed doors for some secret conversation, of which I overheard very little, apart from frequent mention of my name. Sasha came outside to check whether I was listening to them, and when she saw me she ran back to tell the others that I had probably heard their conversation – or confabulation – from the balcony. And again my heart froze and I felt unbearably hurt and sad. I then went quite openly into the room where they were all sitting, faced Chertkov and said to him: 'What, another plot against me?' At which they all looked embarrassed, and L.N. and Chertkov both started talking at once about the diaries, but in such an incoherent and unclear fashion that I never did find out what they had been discussing, and Sasha simply went straight out of the room.

I then had a painful confrontation with Chertkov. (Lev Nikol. went out to greet Misha, who had just arrived.) I repeated what I had written in the above letter and asked him to tell me *how many* of the diaries he had, *where* they were and *when* he had taken them. At this Chertkov flew into a rage and said that since Lev Nikol. had trusted him he did not have to answer to him or anyone else. And that Lev. Nik. had given him the diaries so that he could cross out any unpleasant intimate details.

He soon calmed down and suggested that we should work together to love and care for Lev Nikolaevich, and that we should both devote ourselves to his life and work. As if this wasn't what I had done for almost my entire life – for the past 48 years in fact! But no one came between us then, we lived one life. Chertkov then announced that he was Lev Nikol.'s 'spiritual confessor'(?), and that I should eventually have to reconcile myself to this.

During our conversation the crudest words and thoughts kept breaking into Chertkov's speech. For instance at one point he shouted: 'You're afraid I shall use the diaries to unmask you! If I really wanted to I could really *drag you and your family through the mud*! (a fine expression for a supposedly decent man!). I have enough connections to do so. The only thing that has stopped me is my affection for Lev Nikolaevich.' And to show just what was possible, he cited the example of Carlyle, who had a friend who 'unmasked' his wife and showed her in the worst possible light.

What a vile way Chertkov's mind works! What do I care if some stupid retired officer 'unmasks' me after my death to various ill-intentioned gentlemen? My business in life and the state of my soul concern me and God alone. I have devoted my entire life on this earth to such passionate, self-sacrificing love for Lev Nikolaevich that no mere Chertkov could possibly wipe out the past, the half-century of my life which I have given to my husband.

Chertkov also shouted that if he had such a wife as I he would have shot himself or run off to America long ago. Then as he was coming down the stairs with my son Lyova I heard him say angrily: 'I can't understand a woman like that, who spends her *entire life* murdering her husband.'

Well, this murder is certainly a slow business, considering that my husband has already lived to be 82. But he has now put this idea into Lev Nik.'s head, and that is why we are so unhappy in our old age . . .

What is to be done now? Alas, I shall have to dissimulate if Lev Nikolaevich is not to be taken away from me entirely. I must be sweet and kind to Chertkov and his family this month, although knowing what he thinks of me and me of him, I shall find this intolerably difficult. I must visit him more often and do my utmost not to upset Lev Nikolaevich, seeing that he has been coerced, controlled and enslaved by Chertkov. I have lost his love for ever if the Lord does not see my plight. And I feel so sorry for Lev Nikolaevich! He is so unhappy under the tyrannical Chertkov's yoke – and he was happy when he was with me.

After the business with the stolen diaries I managed to get Chertkov to write a note undertaking to finish his work on them as soon as possible and to give them straight back to L.N.[12] And Lev Nikolaevich has given a verbal undertaking to give them to *me*. He too was going to put this in writing for me, but then he got worried and went back on his word. 'I'm not signing bits of paper for my *wife* – that's ridiculous!' he said. 'I've promised to give them to you and I shall.'

But I know that all these notes and promises are merely a trick. (And sure enough, Lev Nik. did *not* give me the diaries but deposited them in the bank at Tula.)*[13] Since Chertkov knows perfectly well that Lev Nikolaevich has not much longer to live now, he will drag out his invented work on the diaries and won't hand them over to anyone.

This is the true reason for my grief in these last years of my life. I shall write my diary every day from now on.

This evening I drove to Zaseka station to sign some pages of proofs, as I had forgotten to do so yesterday evening.

Nikolaev has come and my son Misha is paying a short visit. He is as calm, affable and inscrutable as ever; when I told him about our recent painful experiences, his attitude to it was one of calm indifference. I find Sasha's behaviour to me very painful. My daughter is a traitor. If someone urged her to draw her father away from me, telling her this was for the sake of his peace of mind, she would do so at once. Today she shocked me by holding a secret whispered conversation with her father and Chertkov, constantly looking over her shoulder and running out of the room to see whether I had heard what they were saying about me. They have surrounded me with a mentally impenetrable wall: I sit and pine in my solitary confinement and take this as a punishment 'for my sins', the cross I must bear.

July 2 I have been quite incapable of doing anything, I have been far too upset by my recent discussions with Sasha. What spite, what coldness, what injustice! We are growing more and more estranged. How sad that is! Wise, impartial old Maria Aleksandrovna Schmidt talked to me, which I found a great help, She urged me to rise above all Chertkov's criticisms, cavils and curses; and she said that when my daughters pestered me to go and live 'elsewhere' with Lev Nikolaevich, since he obviously finds it intolerable now in Yasnaya, they were talking utter rubbish, as the visitors and petitioners would find him wherever he went; it would not make matters any easier anyway, and it was sheer folly to disrupt one's life in one's old age.

I went to visit the Goldenweisers. Aleksandr Borisovich had just left for Moscow, but his wife, his brother and his sister-in-law were most agreeable. Meanwhile Lev Nikolaevich rode over to visit the Chertkovs, and was evidently exhausted by the heat.

*Added later.

A crowd of people arrived after dinner and my son Lyova got here in time for dinner, in a lively, happy mood. He is delighted to be back in Russia and to see Yasnaya Polyana and his family again.[14]

We had a discussion on the terrace about some followers of Dobrolyubov[15] living in the Samara province. Sutkovoi was here with his sister, also Kartushin, M.A. Schmidt, Lev Nikolaevich, I.I. Gorbunov, Lyova and I.

Sutkovoi told us that these 'Dobrolyubovtsy' all sit down together in complete silence, and then some sort of secret spiritual communion takes place between them. Lev Nikol. made some retort to this, but unfortunately I do not remember what he said and I would not want to misrepresent his ideas.

Chertkov's mother came. She is a very good-looking woman, extremely aged, very agitated and not quite normal. She is a 'Redstockist', a kind of sectarian, and believes in redemption; she believes too that Christ dwells within her and that religion is a kind of inspiration.[16] But this poor *mother* has lost two sons. She talked at great length about the death of her youngest, 8-year-old Misha. 35 years have passed since then, yet the pain of this loss is still fresh, and her heart is still torn with grief, for the death of her young Misha brought an end to all the joy in her life. Thank God she has found comfort in religion.

Lev Nik. had a bath today; his stomach has been upset, but in general his health is not too bad, thank God!

July 3 Before I had even got dressed this morning I learnt that there had been a fire on Tanya's estate at Ovsyannikovo.[17] The house where the Gorbunovs are living was burnt down, as was M.A. Schmidt's cottage. She had spent the night with us, and they had set fire to it while she was away. Everything in it was burnt, and what distressed her most was that her trunkful of manuscripts was lost. She had copied out everything that Lev Nik. had ever written and stored it in her trunk, along with 30 letters to her from Lev Nik.[18]

It breaks my heart when I remember her rushing up to me, throwing her arms round my neck and sobbing in despair. How could I comfort her? I could only sympathise with all my heart. All day I have been sadly recalling her last words to me: 'Darling, we have such a heavenly life in Ovsyannikovo.' She called her cottage her 'palace', and she grieved too for her old three-legged mongrel dog who was burnt to death under the stove.

Tomorrow Sasha is going to Tula to buy various things for her immediate needs. We shall provide her with clothes and furniture as best we can, but as to *where* she will live I have simply no idea. She does not want to live with us, for she is used to her independence, her cows and her dogs, her own kitchen-garden and strawberry-bed.

Lev Nikolaevich rode over to Ovsyannikovo with Lyova after the fire, and kept saying, 'M.A. is doing very well,' by which he meant that she was bearing her misfortune bravely. This is all very well, but something for her to wear, eat and drink *now* has to be found, for she has nothing.

Thank God the Gorbunovs managed to drag their possessions out of the house, and will not abandon a helpless old woman.

It is terribly hot and they are making slow progress with the hay harvest, which is rather annoying. My health has improved. I went for a swim today. Goldenweiser and Chertkov came this evening, and Lev Nik. played chess with Goldenweiser while Chertkov sat there looking haughty and unpleasant. Lyova is being so sweet and sympathetic and gives me a lot of encouragement, yet I still feel so sad!

I have corrected a lot of proofs and am now going to send them off.

July 4 I wrote a description of our journey to Moscow and to the Chertkovs',[19] then read Maude's biography of Lev Nik. in English. It is not very good; he puts too much of himself into it, advertising his own translations (on art) and other things.

Lyova said that yesterday he had glimpsed such a lovely expression on Lev Nikolaevich's face; it was the expression of someone not of this world, he said, and he had longed to capture this look in a sculpture. I, of course, with my wretched shortsightedness, can never catch the expression on people's faces.

Yes, Lev Nikol. has already half left us despicable worldlings behind, and one must be constantly aware of this. How I long to be close to him, to grow old with him, to calm my passionate turbulent soul with him and discover with him the vanity of all earthly things!

Somewhere in the depths of my soul I have already experienced this state; I discovered the path to it when Vanechka died, and I shall try to find it again in my lifetime, or more importantly while my husband Lyovochka is alive. It is so hard to sustain that state when one has to shoulder the entire burden of worldly cares – housekeeping, publishing, servants, relations with outsiders and their spitefulness, relations with the children – and when I hold in my hands that vile instrument *money*!

Sasha and Varvara Mikhailovna bought Maria Aleksandrovna enough things for her immediate needs, and I began making some things for her this evening. Absolutely everything she had was burnt, and we must set her up again and give her new clothes. So this is yet another worry!

Chertkov came over this evening with some stereoscopic photographs which were taken in Meshcherskoe while Lev Nik. was staying with him. And Lev Nik. was as pleased as a child, pointing himself out in all of them. Goldenweiser played for us, and Lyova burst into nervous tears. It is cool, 12 degs., and there is a north wind.

July 5 This is no life. Lev Nikolaevich's heart is as cold as ice, Chertkov has taken complete control of him. This morning Lev Nik. went over to see him, and this evening Chertkov came to see us. Lev Nik. was sitting on a low sofa and Chertkov was sitting very close to him and I was beside myself with rage and jealousy.

Then they embarked on a conversation about madness and suicide. I left the room three times, but I wanted to stay and drink tea with the others. And as soon as I came back Lev Nikol., turning his back on me and facing his idol, again started talking about suicide and madness, cold-bloodedly discussing it from every angle,[20] accurately and calculatedly analysing this condition in terms of my present suffering. This evening he cynically told me that he had forgotten everything, everything he had ever written. 'And what about your old life?' I asked. 'And your old relations with those close to you? I suppose now you live only for the present?' 'Well yes, I do live only for the present now,' replied Lev Nik. This had a terrible effect on me! I truly believe that a heartbreaking physical death, with our former love intact to the end of our days, would be preferable to this misery.

Something is hanging over me in this house, some great weight which is crushing me and destroying me.

I was determined to be calm, and to be on good terms with Chertkov, but it was no good; still the same icy relations with Lev Nikol., still the same adoration of that idiot.

I called on his mother today, to return her visit, and saw my grandchildren.[21] She is a harmless old woman; I was particularly struck by her large ears and the quantities of food she ate in my presence – sour milk, berries, bread, she simply never stopped.

I sewed some shirts for Maria Aleksandrovna, made her a skirt on the machine and cut out some handkerchiefs. I had a headache.

Bulygin, N.N. Gué and Goldenweiser came. Oh, what a strain it all is. I feel so ill, I pray constantly for death. Will this never be settled? Will Chertkov be allowed to stay in Telyatinki?

Woe is me! I would dearly love to read L.N.'s diary, but now everything of his has been locked up or given to Chertkov.

And we've never in all our life hidden anything from one another. We have always read *all* one another's letters, *all* one another's diaries, *all* that Lev Nikolaevich has written. No one will ever understand my suffering, for only death can put an end to this agony.

July 6 I didn't sleep all night. I kept seeing the hateful Chertkov before my eyes, sitting very close to Lev Nik.

I went for a swim on my own this morning, praying as I went. I prayed for this delusion to go away, somehow or other. If it doesn't, I nurture the idea as I walk to the river every day, of committing suicide by drowning myself in my beloved Voronka. Today I was remembering that time long ago when Lev Nik. came to the river where I was swimming alone . . . All that is forgotten now, that is no longer what is needed; what is needed now is quiet, affectionate friendship, sympathy and closeness . . .

When I got back Lev Nik. spoke to me very warmly and I at once grew calm and cheerful. He then rode off somewhere, I don't know where, with Dushan Petrovich.

My son Lyova is being so touchingly kind to me; he came down to the river to see how I was. And I determined to be calm and to see Chertkov as little as possible.

I went to see Zvegintseva, who was delighted to see me; we chatted about women's matters, but we both agreed absolutely on one thing – our opinion of Chertkov.

I was late for dinner. Lev Nik. had not wanted to eat, but when I asked him to sit down with us at least, he readily ate his way through the entire dinner, which had been prepared especially to suit his stomach – puréed soup, rice, eggs and bilberries on bread soaked in almond milk.

This afternoon I sewed a skirt for Maria Aleksandrovna; then Chertkov arrived, Sutkovoi and Nikolaev walked here and finally Goldenweiser came and played Beethoven's Sonata Opus 90, a Brahms rhapsody and a heavenly Chopin ballade.

Lev Nik. and Sutkovoi had a discussion about the Dobrolyubovtsy sect in Samara, which moved on to a discussion of religion in general. Lev Nik. said that first of all one had to know God in oneself, and not seek all sorts of forms and artificial complications like miracles, sacraments, unnatural silence or some sort of imaginary communion with some mystical world. Instead one should eliminate everything superfluous, everything that hindered one's communion with God. And to achieve this one needed to make enormous *efforts*. Lev Nik. has just written a little book on this subject which he is very pleased with; he finished correcting it today and sent it off to Gorbunov for publication.[22]

I am feeling less agitated today, and seem to have regained my self-control, although I cannot forgive Chertkov for threatening to 'drag me through the mud'. It's so odd! So many idle discussions and so little real understanding of what is important in life.

I remember during my operation I fell into an abyss of suffering, etherised sleep and impending death – and before my inner eye flashed with terrifying speed innumerable images of everyday bustle, mainly in the city. And how strange and unnecessary these cities appeared to me, with their theatres, trams, shops and factories – all such insubstantial rubbish in the face of imminent death. What was the purpose of it all? I couldn't help wondering. Where were all these activities and aspirations leading to? What was important in life, what was necessary? And the answer came to me, clear and certain: 'If we are destined to live out our lives here on earth according to God's will, then undoubtedly *the best thing people can do is to help one another*. It doesn't matter what form this mutual aid takes, whether it is feeding, curing or comforting, just so long as we help one another and relieve one another's suffering.'

So that if Lev Nik., instead of a lot of speeches, had come to me instead of delaying when I wrote 'I implore you to come', he would have *helped* me to live, helped me in my sufferings, and that would have been far more valuable than all his cold sermons. Thus whatever we do we must always *help one another to live out our lives on earth.* For this is consistent with Christianity.

July 7, morning Rain, wind and damp. I have proof-read *The Fruits of Enlightenment* and finished sewing Maria Aleksandrovna's skirt. I took the proofs of *Resurrection* from Lev Nik.'s divan, before Chertkov sniffed them out and took them away.[23] Lev Nik. went to see his idol today, despite the weather. I realised today that although his last diaries are very interesting, they have all been *composed* for Chertkov and those to whom it pleases Mr Chertkov to show them! And now Lev Nikol. never *dares* to write a word of love for me in them, for they all go straight to Chertkov and he would not like this. What made them valuable in my hands was their sincerity, their power of thought and feeling.

I have guarded Lev Nik.'s manuscripts very badly. But he never gave them to me – before he used to keep them with him, in the drawers of his divan, and never allowed anyone to touch them. When I decided to move them to the museum[24] we were not living in Moscow, so I could only move them, and could not sort them out. And when we were living in Moscow I was dreadfully preoccupied with my large family and various other matters which simply could not be ignored, as they were our daily bread.

Lyova also quarrelled with that rude uncouth idiot Chertkov yesterday.

It is pouring with rain, but despite this Lev Nikol. rode over to Chertkov's, and I waited for him in despair on the porch, worrying and cursing our proximity to Chertkov.

Evening No, Lev Nik. hasn't been taken from me yet, thank God! The sheer force of my suffering and my passionate love for him has broken the ice which has recently separated us. Nothing can resist the power of this emotional bond – we are joined by our long life together and our great love for one another. I went into his room as he was going to bed and said: 'Promise me you won't ever leave me on the sly, without telling me.' And he replied: 'I wouldn't ever do such a thing – I promise I shall never leave you. I love you,' and his voice trembled. I burst into tears and embraced him, saying how afraid I was of losing him, that I loved him so much, and that despite some innocent and foolish passions in the past I had never stopped loving him for a moment, and still in my old age loved him more than anyone else in the world. Lev Nik. said that he felt exactly the same, that I had nothing to fear, that the bond between us was far too strong for anyone to destroy, and I realised that this was true, and I felt so happy. I went into my room, but returned a moment later and thanked him for taking this great weight off my heart.

I said goodnight to him then, and went off to my room, but after a little while the door opened and Lev Nik. came in.

'Don't say anything,' he said. 'I just want to tell you that our conversation this evening made me so happy too, so very happy . . . ' And he burst into tears again, embraced me and kissed me . . . 'Mine! Mine!' I said in my heart. I shall be much calmer now, I shall come to my senses, I shall be kinder to everyone, I shall try to get on better with Chertkov.

He wrote me a letter trying to justify his behaviour to me.[25] I invited him here today for a reconciliation, and told him that as a decent man he must at least apologise to me for those two appalling things he had said: 1) 'If I really wanted to I could *drag you and your children through the mud.* I have enough connections to do so. The only thing that has stopped me is my affection for Lev Nikol–ch.' And 2) 'If I had such a wife as you, I would have shot myself or run off to America long ago.' But he wouldn't apologise for anything, and said that I had misinterpreted his words, and so on.

But what could be clearer? He is a proud, spiteful and very stupid man! Where are these supposedly Christian principles of love, humility and non-resistance? It's all nothing but hypocrisy and lies. He simply has no breeding.

But when he was going downstairs he said he thought he probably should not have made that second remark, and that if his letter did not satisfy me, then he was prepared to express his *regret*, in order to remain on good terms with me. The letter was nothing but cunning and hypocrisy.

But I don't mind any more. Lev Nikolaevich has shown me his heart, shown me that he loves me, and that has given me strength and I am happy. I despise everything else now, for I am invulnerable.

The cocks are crowing, dawn is breaking. Night . . . The trains rumble and the wind rustles the leaves on the trees.

July 8 My husband's kind words soothed me, and this is the first day I have spent in a normal state of mind. I went for a walk, picked a large bunch of wild flowers for Lev Nikolaevich and copied out my old letters to my husband, which I found amongst his papers.[26]

The same people here as usual – Chertkov, Goldenweiser, Nikolaev and Sutkovoi. It has been cool, windy and raining. The fallow field is being double-sowed and the roofs are being painted. Sasha is in low spirits, has a bad cold and is sulking at me. Lev Nikol. read us a lovely French short story by a new writer called Mille. He enjoyed a story by him yesterday too, called '*La Biche écrasée*'.[27]

He would be quite healthy if it weren't for his constipation.

July 9 Lord! When will these vile episodes and intrigues end! My daughter-in-law Olga arrived, and there was yet another conversation about my relations with Chertkov. He was rude to me again and I didn't say one impolite word to him – and they all go into corners and pick over my bones, gossip about me and accuse me of I know not what. I simply cannot get used to the fact that some people simply *lie* – I find it quite astonishing. Sometimes one is horrified and tries naïvely to establish the truth, to remind them or explain . . . But all such attempts are quite unnecessary; people often *simply do not want the truth*, for it is neither necessary nor to their advantage. This has been the case in this Chertkov business. But I shall say no more about it, I have quite enough worries as it is. Today Lev Nikol. and Lyova went for a ride through the woods. There was a large black rain-cloud ahead, but they rode straight into it; they had not taken anything with them, and Lev Nikol. had nothing but a thin white shirt on, while Lyova was wearing just a jacket. I always beg Lev Nik. to tell me which route he is taking, so that I can send on warm clothes or a carriage for him, but he will never hear of it. Eventually the storm burst, it poured with rain, and for 1½ hours I was running around the terrace in a terrible state of anxiety. My heart contracted painfully, the blood rushed to my head, my mouth was dry and my heart was filled with despair.

They arrived home soaked to the skin. I wanted to rub Lev Nikolaevich's back, chest, arms and legs with spirit of camphor, but he angrily rejected my help and in the end he only grudgingly agreed to let his valet Ilya Vasilevich give him a massage.

Olga got angry for some reason and took her children away without staying for dinner.

My head was aching for the rest of the day and I felt quite ill. I had a slight temperature (37.5) and could not do a thing, although I had a lot of work to do, especially on the new edition, which has now come to a complete stop. I was feeling quite debilitated this afternoon, and went to my room, where I fell asleep and unfortunately slept on and off all evening.

Chertkov and Goldenweiser came, and Nikolaev, who evidently infuriates Lev Nik. with his talk. L.N. played chess with Goldenweiser, who then played the piano for a little while. That heavenly Chopin mazurka transported my soul! My son Lyova is very worried about his foreign passport; they would not give him one in Tula, demanding evidence from the police that he was free to leave Russia, and Lyova is under arrest for publishing two pamphlets in 1905 called 'What is the Solution?' and 'The Construction of Hell'.[28] It's a very worrying business.

12 degs., damp and unpleasant. Sasha has a harsh, rasping cough, and this is also very worrying.

And then something is drawing to an *end*. Is it my life, or that of someone in my family, I wonder?

Chertkov brought me an album of photographs of Lev Nikolaevich (not the complete album, however, as he had promised), some of which were delightful, and his mother sent me a booklet called 'Misha', about her dead boy.

I read it and was very touched, but there is a lot of artificiality which I cannot understand in her relations with God, Jesus, and even her child.

July 10 Lev Nikolaevich naturally did not *dare* write in his diary how he came into my room late at night, wept, embraced me and said how happy he was that we had reached some understanding and closeness together. Instead he writes: 'I must restrain myself' everywhere. What does this mean? No one could possibly love or care for him as I do, no one could desire his happiness as I do. Yet he gives his diaries to Chertkov, who will publish them and repeat to the whole world what he said to me – that a wife like me would make one want to shoot oneself or run off to America.

L.N. rode with Chertkov into the forest today, where they had some sort of discussion. They gave Bulgakov a horse too, but they made sure he kept his distance, as they did not want him to disturb their privacy. It is *I* who have to 'restrain myself' every day at the sight of that odious figure.

In the forest they dismounted twice for some reason, and in the gulley Chertkov pointed his camera at Lev Nik. and took his photograph. As they were riding back, Chertkov noticed that he had lost his watch, and he deliberately got as far as the balcony before telling Lev Nik. where he thought he had lost it. And L.N., looking so pathetic and submissive, promised to go to the gulley after dinner *to look for Mr Chertkov's watch*.

We had some very pleasant guests to dinner – N.V. Davydov, M. Salomon and N.N. Gué. Davydov brought me *Resurrection*, which he had read for the new edition, but I still have a great deal of work to do on it.[29] My son Seryozha is also working on it.

I thought Lev Nik. would be embarrassed to drag a lot of respectable people off to the gulley in search of Mr Chertkov's watch. But he lives in such fear of him that even the thought of being made to look foolish – *ridicule* – did not deter him from taking a crowd of 8 people out to the forest. We all stamped around in the wet hay, but did not find the watch – heaven knows where that absent-minded idiot lost it! Why did he have to take a photograph in the soft wet hay anyway? Then for the first time this summer Lev Nik. asked me out for a walk with him, and I was overjoyed, and waited anxiously to get away from the gulley and the watch. But I was wrong, of course. The following morning Lev Nik. got up early, went to the village, summoned some peasant lads, went off to the gulley again and found the watch.

This evening Mr Salomon read us a boring French allegory about the prodigal son,[30] then we read a light-hearted story by Mille, and another also by him.[31]

Davydov left, and I told Lev Nik. how annoyed and embarrassed I had felt when instead of taking everyone out for a walk he had taken them to the gulley to look for Chertkov's watch; he grew angry, of course, there was another quarrel, and I saw the same cruelty and coldness in him, the same desire to shield Chertkov. I felt quite ill and was thrown into another sudden fit of despair. I lay down on the bare boards of the balcony and remembered how it was on that same balcony, 48 years ago, when I was still a girl, that I first became aware of my love for Lev Nikolaevich. It was a cold night and I liked the idea that I should find my death where I had found his love. But I had evidently not earned this yet.

Lev Nikolaevich heard a rustle, came out on to the balcony and stood there shouting at me to go away, as I was preventing him from sleeping. I then went into the garden, and lay on the damp ground for two hours in a thin dress. I was chilled through, but I longed to die – and I still do.

They raised the alarm, and Dushan Petrovich, N.N. Gué and Lyova came and shouted at me and helped me up off the ground. I was shaking all over from cold and nerves.

If only those foreigners could have seen to what state Lev Tolstoy had reduced his wife, lying on the wet ground at two or three in the morning, numbed and in the throes of despair, how astonished those good people would have been! When I thought this I did not want to leave the wet earth, the grass, the dew and the moon, appearing and vanishing in the sky. I did not want to leave until my husband came out and took me home, because it was he who had driven me out. He did come out eventually – only after my son Lyova shouted at him and demanded that he do so – and he and Lyova took me home. It was now three in the morning, and neither he nor I could sleep. We could not come to any agreement, and I was unable to extract a drop of love or pity from him.

Well, what now! What is to be done! I cannot live without his love and tenderness, and he cannot give it to me. 4 in the morning . . .

I had already told Davydov, Salomon and Nikolaeva about Chertkov's malicious intrigues against me, and they were all sincerely horrified. They were astonished that my husband could tolerate these insults to his wife, and they all unanimously spoke of their dislike for that spiteful, proud fool Chertkov. Davydov was particularly incensed that Chertkov had stolen all Lev Nik.'s diaries since the year 1900.

'But these should belong to you and your family,' raged dear Davydov. 'And that letter Chertkov wrote to the newspapers when Lev Nik. was staying with him was really the height of stupidity and insensitivity.'[32]

All this seems quite clear to everyone else – but what about my poor husband . . . ?

It was already light now, and we were still sitting opposite one another in my bedroom, not knowing what to say. When has that happened before?! I longed to go back to the garden and lie down under the oak; it would have been so much easier there than in my room. Eventually I took Lev Nik. by the arm, begged him to go to bed and we both went into his bedroom. I returned to my room, but then I longed to see him and went back to his room. He looked so old and sad, lying with his face to the wall, wrapped up in the blanket with the Greek design that I had knitted for him, and a desperate feeling of pity and tenderness awoke within me; I kissed the dear, familiar palm of his hand, begging him to forgive me, and the ice melted. We both wept again, and I finally felt his love for me again.

I prayed to God to help us live the last years of our life in peace and happiness, as before.

July 11 I slept only from 4 to 7.30 a.m. Lev Nik. also slept very little. I am ill and exhausted, but my soul is happy. Relations with Lev Nik. are friendly and straightforward again, just as they used to be. I love him so intensely, and so foolishly. And so clumsily! He needs me to make concessions and heroic sacrifices, but I am incapable of doing this, especially now at my age.

Seryozha came this morning. Sasha and her shadow, Varvara Mikhailovna, are cross with me – as if I *cared*! Lyova is being very sweet to me, and the clever fellow has started working on a sculpture of me.

Lev Nik. went for a ride with the doctor. This evening Iv. Iv. Gorbunov came, and Lev Nik. had a long talk with him about the new kopeck booklets. We all took a stroll around the park; Lev Nik. was looking very tired, but he spent the evening talking quietly, playing chess and listening to dear Mr Salomon's stories.

We all went to bed early. L.N. himself asked Chertkov not to come this evening. Thank God! Just to breathe freely for one day is such a rest for one's soul.

July 12 Today I posed for Lyova; he has been sculpting a bust of me, and today it began to look quite lifelike. What a talented, clever, good person he is. And alas, what a contrast with Sasha!

Lev Nik. waited in for Goldenweiser, as he wanted to go for a ride with him, but he didn't appear. So he sent Filka to Telyatinki, and Filka invited Chertkov by mistake, instead of Goldenweiser. I did not know about this, but L.N. eventually decided not to wait any longer for Goldenweiser and went to the stable to saddle his horse (which he has never done before), so as to ride out to meet Goldenweiser. I thought that if Lev Nik. did not find him he would be all on his own in this fierce heat, and might well get sunstroke again, so I ran to the stable and asked Lev Nik. where he was going and whether he was meeting anyone. Lev Nik. was trying to hurry up the coachman, and the doctor was there too. So I said, 'Look, why doesn't Dushan Petrovich go with you?' and Lev Nik. agreed. But as soon as he had left the stable I saw the odious figure of Chertkov, approaching from under the hill on his white horse. I groaned and shrieked that I had been deceived again, that they were trying to hoodwink me, that they had lied about Goldenweiser and had invited Chertkov instead, and I had a hysterical attack right there, in front of all the servants, and ran off home. Lev Nik. told Chertkov that he would not ride with him, Chertkov went home and L.N. rode on with the doctor.

Fortunately it turned out that there had been no plot, merely that Filka had been half asleep, had forgotten where he had been told to go, and by mistake had invited Chertkov to see L.N. instead of Goldenweiser. But I am in such a state of torment that the merest mention of Chertkov, and especially the sight of him, drives me into a state of frenzied agitation. When he arrived this evening I left the room and shook like a wretch for a whole hour. Goldenweiser and his wife were here, and were both very agreeable. Salomon has just left; he is such a splendid, lively, clever, sympathetic man. Lyova is being so touchingly kind to me. Lev Nikol. is much gentler now, but he evidently did not belong to himself this evening; he waited for Chertkov a long time, and when he didn't come he eventually went off and wrote him a letter explaining why he had not come to see them.[33] Very important work! I am sure he has written something bad about me in this letter. He promised to show it to me, but yet again the conspiracy was not revealed to me. I am surrounded by lies and secrets.

Tanya and Mikhail Sergeevich Sukhotin have come. More painful discussions. Tanya and Sasha believe only what they want to of what I tell them; despite the truth of my words they will accept only what serves their purpose in abusing and condemning me.

It will surely kill me, one way or another; and it makes me happy to think that I shall not survive Lev Nikolaevich. What a joy to be rid of all these sufferings!

Chertkov's mother, Elizaveta Ivanovna, wrote inviting me to call on her today. Two preachers have come to visit her; one is called Fetler, and the other was some Irish professor whom I could barely understand, but who ate very heartily and occasionally made religious pronouncements in a mechanical sort of way. But Fetler was a man of principle and very fluent; he spoke beautifully and tried assiduously to convert me to his faith – in Redemption. I argued with him only when he insisted on material redemption, the shedding of blood, and the suffering and death of Christ's *body*. I said there was no need to bring material things into religious matters, since Christ's teaching and divinity lived in the spirit, not the body. This did not please Fetler at all, and he got down on his knees and started praying for me, for Lev Nikolaevich, for the peace and happiness of our souls, and so on. It was a beautiful prayer, but it was all so strange! Elizaveta Ivanovna was there all this time, and at one point she called me over to ask me why I hated her son. I told her all about the diaries, and explained that her son had taken my beloved husband from me. To which she replied: 'And I have been so unhappy because your husband has taken my son from me!' And she is quite right.

Three o'clock in the morning. A lovely moon is shining through my window, and my soul is so sad, so sad. There is nothing left now but the morbid joy that breathing and sleeping near me is my Lyovochka, who has not yet been completely taken from me . . .

July 13 After sending Chertkov away yesterday for my sake while he was out riding, Lev Nik. spent the whole evening waiting for him to come so he could explain the reason. Chertkov did not come for a long time. Sensitive to my husband's moods, I saw him anxiously looking about him, waiting like a lover, becoming more and more agitated, and sitting out on the balcony downstairs staring at the road. Eventually he wrote a letter, which I begged him to show me. Sasha brought it, and soon I had it in my hands. It was 'dear friend', of course, and endless endearments . . . and I am once again in a frenzy of despair. None the less he gave this letter to Chertkov when he arrived. I took it under the pretext of reading it, and then burnt it.[34] He never writes me tender letters, I am becoming more wicked and unhappy, and even closer to my end. But I am a *coward*. I did not want to go swimming yesterday, because I was afraid of *drowning*. I need only *one moment* of determination, and I have been incapable of even that.

I spent a long time posing for Lyova. Lev Nik. went for a ride with Goldenweiser and the Sukhotins, and I looked for Lev Nik.'s last diary but could not find it. He realised that I had found a way of reading it, and hid it in another place. But I shall find out where he has hidden it, unless it's with Chertkov, Sasha or the doctor.

We are like two silent enemies, constantly suspecting, spying and sneaking up on one another! We hide, or rather Lev Nik. hides everything he can from me, by giving it to that 'spiteful pharisee', as one close friend – N.N. Gué, the son – called him. Maybe he gave his last diary to Chertkov yesterday.

Lord take pity on me, people are so evil, they won't spare me . . . Take pity on me and save me from sin . . . !

Night of July 13–14 Let us assume that I have gone mad, and my 'fixation' is that Lev Nik. should get his diaries back and not allow Chertkov to keep them. Two families have been thrown into confusion, there have been painful arguments – not to mention the fact that I have suffered to the very limits of my endurance. (I have not eaten a thing all day.) Everyone is depressed, and my tormented appearance annoys everyone like a bothersome fly.

What can be done to make everyone happy again, and put an end to my sufferings?

Get the diaries back from Chertkov, all those little black oilcloth notebooks, and put them back on the desk, letting him have them, one at a time, to make excerpts. That's all!

If I do eventually manage to overcome my cowardice and summon up the courage to kill myself, everyone will see, on looking back, how easy it would have been to grant my wish; they will realise that it really was not worth cruelly and stubbornly refusing my request and tormenting me to death.

When they explain my death to the world they won't give the real reason. They'll say it was hysteria, nerves and my wicked nature – and when they look at my dead body, killed by my husband, no one will *dare* say that the *only* thing which could have *saved* me was the one simple expedient of returning those four or five oilcloth notebooks to my husband's desk. (There were seven of them.)*

Where is their Christianity? Where is their love? Where is their 'non-resistance'? Nothing but lies, deception and cruelty.

Those two stubborn men, Chertkov and my husband, have joined forces and are crushing me, destroying me. And I am so afraid of them; their iron hands crush my heart, and I long to tear myself from their grip and escape. But I am still so afraid . . .

We speak of a person's 'right' to do something, and of course it is Lev Nik.'s 'right' to torment me by refusing to take *his* diaries from Chertkov. But does he have the 'right' to do this to his wife, with whom he has lived for half a century? And is it also his 'right' when it is a matter of life and death, of maintaining the peace and good relations with people, of love and happiness, people's health and tranquillity – and finally the 'non-resistance' L.N. is so enamoured of? What about that?

L.N. will probably visit Chertkov tomorrow, Tanya and her husband are going to Tula, and I – I shall be free, and if not God then some other force will help me to take my leave not only of this house but of this life . . .

I am telling them how to *save* me – get back the diaries. And if they don't want to they can strike a bargain: Chertkov can have the 'rights' to the diaries, and I shall have the 'right' to life and death.

The thought of suicide is growing stronger all the time. Thank God my sufferings will soon be over!

What a terrible wind! It would be good to go now . . . I must try once more to save myself . . . for the last time. If they *refuse*, it will be even more painful, and even easier to deliver myself from suffering; I should hate to keep making threats, then pester with my presence all the people whose lives I have made such a misery . . . But I should love to come back to life so that I could see my husband carrying out my wishes, and see that gleam of love which has warmed and saved me so many times in my life, but which Chertkov now seems to have stifled for ever. Without that love my life is over.

'A drowning man grasps at a straw . . . ' I would dearly love my husband to see all the things that are passing through my soul, but the thought that

*Added later.

this will only arouse his wrath, and then he will really kill me, drives me into a frenzy of anxiety, fear and depression . . .

Oh, what suffering, what hell, what pain in all my being! I long to shout 'Help!' But it would be lost in this evil chaos of life and earthly vanity, where help and love are only words found in books, and where in real life all is coldness and cruelty . . .

Just as before, the one and only time in all these decades I begged him to come home, when my nerves were disordered and I felt so ill, Lev Nik. made my sick condition worse with his cold and unfriendly response; so now this indifference to my wants, and this stubborn resistance to my sick entreaties, may have the worst possible consequences . . . And then it will be too late . . . But what does he care!! He has Chertkov . . . or wishes he did. But Chertkov has the diaries and must hand them back . . .

July 14 I have not slept all night and was within a hair's-breadth of suicide. These expressions of my suffering, however extreme, could not possibly do them justice. Lev Nikol. came in, and I told him in a terrible state of agitation that everything lay in the balance: it was either the diaries or my life, he could choose. And he did choose, I am thankful to say, and he got the diaries back from Chertkov. In my nervousness I have made a bad job of pasting into this diary the letter he gave me this morning;[35] I am very sorry about this, but there are several copies, including the one I made for the collection of Lev Nikolaevich's letters to me,[36] and the one that our daughter Tanya has.

Sasha drove over to Chertkov's to fetch the diaries and give him a letter from Lev Nikolaevich.[37] But my soul is still grieving, and the thought of suicide, clear and firm, will always be with me the moment they open the wounds in my heart again.

So this is the end of my long and once happy marriage . . . ! But it is not quite the end yet; Lev Nik.'s letter to me today is a scrap of the old happiness, although such a small and shabby scrap!

My daughter Tanya has sealed up the diaries, and tomorrow she and her husband will take them to the bank in Tula. They will fill out a receipt for them in the name of Lev Nik. and his heirs, and will give this receipt to L.N. I hope to God they do not deceive me, and that Jesuit Chertkov doesn't wheedle the diaries out of Lev Nik. on the sly!

Not a thing has passed my lips for three days now, and this has worried everyone terribly for some reason. But this is the least of it . . . It's all a matter of passion and the force of grief.

I bitterly regret that I have made my children Lyova and Tanya suffer, especially Tanya; she is being so sweet, kind and compassionate to me again! I love her so much. Chertkov must be allowed to come here, although this is very, very difficult and unpleasant for me. If I do not let them meet, there will be page upon page of secret, tender letters, and that would be much worse.

July 15 I did not sleep all night; I kept thinking that if it was so easy for Lev Nik. in his letter to break his promise not to leave me, then it would be equally easy for him to break all his promises, and where would all his 'true and honest' words be then? I have good reason to worry! First he promised me in front of Chertkov that he would give *me* his diaries, then he deceived me by putting them in the bank. How can one keep calm and well when one lives under the constant threat of 'I'll leave, I'll leave!'

I have such a strange headache – at the back of my head. Could it be a nervous attack, I wonder? That would be good – as long as it is fatal. My soul is sick, for my husband is trying to kill me. This morning, after a sleepless night, I asked Lev Nik. to give me the receipt for the diaries which are being taken to the bank tomorrow, so as to set my mind at rest that he will not break his word again and give them to Chertkov, as he did so easily once before (break his word, I mean).

This made him terribly angry. 'No, absolutely not, not for anything!' he said, and ran out of the room. I had another frightful nervous attack and longed to drink opium but again lacked the courage to do so, and instead told Lev Nik. a wicked lie and said that I had taken it. I confessed immediately, and wept and sobbed, but I made a great effort and managed to regain my self-control. How ashamed and wretched I feel, but . . . no, I shall say no more: I am sick and exhausted.

My son Lyova and I went in the cabriolet to look at a house in Rudakovo to replace Tanya's house in Ovsyannikovo.[38] Lev Nik. went for a ride with the doctor. I thought we were going together, but L.N. deliberately went in the opposite direction. I shall go along the highway, he said, and home via Ovsyannikovo. He then went a completely different way, turning off just before Ovsyannikovo, as though quite by chance. But I notice everything, remember everything, and suffer deeply.

I forced myself to let Chertkov visit us and behaved *correctly* with him, but I suffered terribly as I watched their every movement and glance. They were very cautious. How I loathe that man! His presence causes me such suffering, but I must endure it so as to see them together before my eyes, not somewhere else, plotting some long correspondence instead of meeting.

Chertkov's son was here too, a sweet, straightforward boy accompanied by his English friend who drives motor-cars. Another Englishman from South America came, a dull, stupid, tedious man.[39] The papers have published a short article by L.N. called 'From My Diary', about his conversation with a peasant.[40]

Today Lev N.'s diaries were sealed up, all 7 notebooks of them, and tomorrow Tanya and I are taking them to the bank for safekeeping. At the moment they are in Tula with Doctor Grushetskii, which worries me. We were going to take them to the bank today, but everything in Tula was closed as they were holding a public service for the cholera epidemic, so we shall have to collect them from Grushetskii and deposit them at the bank tomorrow. This is a new and unpleasant trait in Lev Nik. Why in the bank? Why not keep them at home or leave them at the Historical Museum, where all his other diaries are? And why am I not allowed to read *these* diaries? Everyone will be able to read them after Lev Nik.'s death, but God forbid his *wife* should read them *now*! It never used to be like this! It hurts my soul so! And this is all Chertkov's influence. 'Of course you feel hurt, I understand,' said Sukhotin. 'I don't like Chertkov either.'

A mass of dull people here: the Englishman, Dima and his comrade (they are not so bad), the monotonous, tedious Nikolaev, Goldenweiser and Chertkov. And since none of these gentlemen had anything to talk about, they played the gramophone. I tried to read some proofs – but couldn't. Lyova is sculpting me; I feel much calmer with him. He understands everything and loves and pities me.

Taking these diaries from Chertkov has cost me dear, but I would do it all over again if I had to; I would gladly give the rest of my life to ensure that they never went back to Chertkov again, and I do not regret all the health and strength I have lost in rescuing them. This must now lie on the conscience of Chertkov and my husband, who clung to them so stubbornly.

They will be deposited in Lev Nik.'s name, and he will have the sole right to take them out. What an insensitive, distrustful attitude – and how unkind to his wife!

I received a letter from A.I. Maslova, and it made me yearn for their kind, friendly, honest little world, without all these plots and painful complications; maybe Sergei Ivanovich[41] is there too, and I could rest my soul with them, soothed by the music which soothed my grief in the past. I am so tired of problems, plots, secrets, cruelty – and my husband's acknowledged 'growing indifference' to me! Why should I be perpetually in a *fever*, loving him to distraction? My heart too can change and cool towards a man who does all he can to let me know of his indifference. If one has to live, and not kill oneself, one has to find some comfort and happiness in life. 'I cannot live like this,' I shall say. 'You give me your cold heart, and Chertkov your passion.'

July 16 Now that they have discovered I am keeping a diary every day, they have all started scribbling *their* diaries.[42] They are all out to attack me, condemn me and bring all sorts of malicious evidence against me for daring to defend my conjugal rights and asking for a little more love and trust from my husband, and for the diaries to be taken away from Chertkov.

God be with them all: I need my husband, while I am still not completely frozen by his coldness; I need justice and a clear conscience, not the judgements of others.

I went to Tula with Tanya and we deposited Lev Nikolaevich's seven notebooks in the State Bank.[43] This is a half-measure, i.e. a partial concession to me. They have been removed from Chertkov, thank God, but now I shall never be able to see or read them in Lev Nik.'s lifetime. This is my husband's revenge on me. When they were brought back from Chertkov's I took them frantically and leafed through them to see what he had written (even though I had already read most of them before), and I felt exactly as though my beloved lost child had just been returned to me and was about to be taken away again. I can imagine how furious Chertkov must be with me! This evening he visited us again. I am still tormented by hatred and jealousy of him. A mother whose child is lured away by the gipsies, and then returned to her, must feel exactly what I felt today.

The diaries were deposited in Lev Nik.'s name alone, without Sukhotin's, so they can be taken out only by him, or by power of attorney.

Chertkov was here this evening, as well as Bulgakov and M.A. Schmidt, and that insufferable alien Englishman is still lounging around the house. Goldenweiser came too and played some Chopin mazurkas beautifully.

Lev Nik. is being much nicer to me than before, and it makes me so happy when I catch his friendly glance and return it with love. He and Bulgakov went for a ride in the woods without us today. He is not complaining about his health. I know hardly anything about his work; at night I got into the so-called 'office', where Sasha and Varvara Mikhailovna are copying for him, and look through all his papers.

There are various letters there, an introduction to the kopeck booklets, an article about suicide, several beginnings, but nothing important or serious.[44]

There has been the most terrible thunder-storm all evening, and it is now pouring with rain. I am very worried about Tanya's departure, especially as her husband, who left to see their daughter in Pirogovo, was going to go to Lazarevo station tomorrow, but now the road is so bad that it will be difficult for him to get there. And Tanya is feeling anxious here without her husband or daughter, and I am feeling so sorry for her – even though she often made me very unhappy with the harsh and critical things she said to me in defence of her father.

Lord, what rain! The noise of the storm, the wind and the leaves on the trees make it impossible to sleep . . .

July 17 My daughter Tanya left this morning. The storm has passed. I went to bed late and slept till 12; I got up feeling utterly exhausted and my first thought was of Lev Nikolaevich's diaries. Last night I read Tanya my letter to Chertkov, which is affixed to this diary,[45] and I thought: if Chertkov really loved Lev Nik. he would have given me the diaries when I asked him to, seeing what a desperate state I was in, instead of letting us all be so unhappy all this time. Any good and decent man, I thought, would have had the sensitivity (which is something he completely lacks) to bring them back and give them not to me but to Lev Nikolaevich, to whom they belong, and then take them, one notebook at a time, for his own work, returning them to Lev Nikolaevich when he had finished. But oh no, *having these precious notebooks in his possession* obviously meant more to him than L.N.'s peace of mind, and it was only when L.N. ordered him to do so that the dolt gave them back.

So are things better now? This business has brought grief to our entire family for the past two weeks; the diaries are completely inaccessible now, and Lev Nik. has offered *never* to see Chertkov again if I wish. Chertkov is now openly at war with me. I am winning so far, but I confess quite honestly that I have paid for those diaries with my life, I know there is more of the same to come, and this has made me develop a deep hatred for Chertkov. Lev Nik–ch. was worried today because Chertkov, Goldenweiser and Bulgakov went out in that terrible storm last night, fell out of the cart, broke it, and had to unharness the horse and walk home. Observing his anxiety, I forestalled him, saying: 'I expect you're riding over to Chertkov's?' To this he replied: 'I won't if you don't want me to.' But however hard it may be for me, I would not want to distress my dear old man for anything, and I urged him to go; he went alone, and of course Chertkov the collector, who is only interested in photographs and manuscripts, immediately took a colour photograph of Lev N. Later, when Lev N. told me that Chertkov was coming this evening too, I protested with all my strength, then eventually became reconciled to the idea. But then Lev Nik. himself asked Varvara Mikhailovna to drive over to Chertkov's and tell him not to come.[46] This evening I went for a peaceful walk with Liza Obolenskaya and Verochka Tolstaya, who had just arrived. Lev Nik. played chess with Goldenweiser, then took a stroll, drank tea and went to bed early. I posed for a long time for my bust; Lyova is working with a will and making good progress.

Lev Nikolaevich told me today that his diaries had first been hidden with our daughter Sasha, and that Sasha, at Chertkov's insistence, had given them to young Sergeenko, who had taken them to Chertkov behind my back on November 26, 1909.

What vile, secretive behaviour! What a web of plots and intrigues against me! Lies! Isn't my daughter Sasha a traitor? What a sham that was, when I asked Lev Nikol. 'Where are the diaries?' and he took my arm and led me to Sasha, as though he didn't know, but she might know where they were. And Sasha too said she didn't know, and she too was lying. Though Lev Nikol. had probably forgotten that he had given them to Chertkov.

All these people surrounding Lev Nik. have grown so skilled in lying, cheating, justifiying themselves and planning endless conspiracies! I hate lies; it's not for nothing they say the devil is the father of lies. It was never like this before in our bright, honest family atmosphere; it has only started since Chertkov's devilish influence has been in this house. For good reason their surname derives from 'devil'.*

A list of people who do not like Chertkov and have told me so: M.A. Schmidt, N.V. Davydov, M.S. Sukhotin, N.N. Gué, I.I. Gorbunov, Mister Maude, E.F. Yunge, all my sons and I, P.I. Biryukov, Zosya Stakhovich, and probably many others whom I do not know.

Today Lyova told me that when Chertkov was coming down the stairs, he said, in front of everyone: 'What sort of woman spends her entire life *murdering* her husband?' It is he who has filled our house with this stench which is choking us all, and this gentleman, in the face of simple justice and the opinion of the world, which respects my love and concern for my husband's life, none the less accuses me of 'murdering' him. He is now fuming because I have seen through him, and know just what a Pharisee he is, and he wants his revenge. But this does not frighten me.

July 18 I have been very sick, sad and gloomy all day, and I felt like weeping. I thought that if Lev Nik. went to such pains to hide his diaries from me – something he has never in his life done before – there must be something in them which had to be kept from me; which was why they were hidden with Sasha and Chertkov, and are now imprisoned in the bank. After a whole day and night tormented with doubts and suspicions, I spoke my mind to Lev Nik. and voiced my suspicion that he had betrayed me one way or another, and put this into his diaries, which was why he was now concealing them. He assured me that this was not the case and that he had never betrayed me. But then why hide them? Out of sheer spite and stubbornness? Surely if they contained a lot of good thoughts they could only be of benefit to me . . . But no, if he hides them it *must* be because there is something bad in them. I hide *nothing*, neither my diaries nor my 'Notes' – they are for the whole world to read and judge. What do I care for people's judgements? I know my own life has been pure, I know that I can now read my husband's character like a book, all his sensations and experiences and the very essence of his nature, and it saddens and horrifies me! But I am still *devoted* to him, unfortunately. When I reminded Lev Nik. that after Chertkov had written a note undertaking to give the diaries back to him after they had finished working on them,[47] he too had been about to promise in writing to give them to me, but had then had second thoughts, and said: 'Why should I sign bits of paper for my *wife* – I've promised to give them to you and I shall.' He made a spiteful face and said: 'I never said that.' 'Oh yes you did,' said I. 'It's recorded in my diary on July 1, and Chertkov was a witness.'

*'Devil' – 'chert' in Russian.

Then L.N. changed the subject and shouted: 'I have given everything away, my property and my works; I have only my diaries left, and now I have to give them away too . . . I wrote to you saying I would leave, and I shall leave if you go on tormenting me.'

What does 'I have given everything away' mean? He has not given away his copyright, but has made his wife bear on her back the *running* of his property and the organisation of his life, from which he derives far more benefit than I; I have nothing but perpetual backbreaking work. But the whole point is that it's not necessary to *give* me the diaries; let Lev Nik. keep them to the end of his life. I am merely hurt that they are being concealed from me and given instead to Sasha, Sergeenko, Chertkov – to everyone and anyone, but *God forbid* that his *wife* should catch sight of them . . .

Lev Nik., Dunaev, who had just arrived, Lyova, Lizonka and I all walked over to the fir plantation after dinner. Masses of small Boletus luteus. Fierce heat all day. I wrote letters to E.F. Yunge, Maslova, Katya and Belskaya, and sent the accountant a letter and 195-ruble money order.

Nikolaeva walked over to see us, and Chertkov arrived with Goldenweiser, and we all drank tea on the balcony. I read Lizonka various passages from L.N.'s old diaries; the depravity of his youth horrified her at her tender age, and she was very distressed by the things I revealed to her about her grandfather, whom she had always regarded as a saint.

Lev Nikol. hates me for growing wise to so many things, and obstinately taking his diaries like this is a ready weapon to wound and punish me. Oh, this sham Christianity, founded on hatred for one's family, rather than simple kindness and fearless honesty!

July 19 They break my heart and torture me, and now they call for the doctors – Nikitin and Rossolimo. Poor men! They do not know how to cure someone who has had wounds inflicted on her from all sides! The chance reading of a page from his old diary disturbed my soul and my tranquillity, opened my eyes to his present infatuation with Chertkov and irrevocably poisoned my heart.[48] First they suggest the following remedy: that Lev N. should live in one place, and I in another, he would go to Tanya's and I would go who knows where. When I realised that everyone around me was intent on separating me from Lev Nikolaevich, I burst into tears and refused. Then seeing how weak I was the doctors began prescribing baths, walks, no excitement . . . It was so absurd! Nikitin was amazed to see how thin I had become. It is all because of my grief and my wounded loving heart – and all they can say is leave him! Which would be more painful than anything else.

I drove to the river for a swim, and felt even worse. The water is very low in the Voronka, like my life, and it would be hard to drown in it at present; I went there mainly to estimate how much deeper it might get.

I washed Lev Nik.'s cap. He went over to Ovsyannikovo in the heat of the day and ate no dinner. He now looks very tired. No wonder! 14 miles on horseback in 36 degrees, in the glare of the sun! This evening he played chess with Goldenweiser. I did not say a word to him all day, as I am afraid to upset him, and myself too. I posed for Lyova; I always enjoy being with him. I then corrected some proofs, but still have not sent them off – I cannot work . . . It is late now and I must go to bed, although I am not sleepy.

July 20 We have now had two quiet peaceful days without Chertkov. The doctors left earlier on. I suppose they were asked here merely to testify that I am mad, just in case. Their visit was completely pointless. I would be quite well if every day was like the past few days.

Lev Nik. went for a ride with Filka, our stupid, good-natured stable-boy, then sat on the balcony outside his room all evening, quietly writing, reading and resting. Goldenweiser came and they had a quiet game of chess, then we all drank tea on the balcony together. I feel so sorry for my son Lyova. He has been sad and preoccupied all day. Has he suddenly recalled some painful experience in Paris, or is he worried because they won't give him the necessary document for a foreign passport, or are all the painful problems of our life here too much for his nerves . . . ?

I went swimming with Liza Obolenskaya, Sasha and Varvara Mikhailovna, and we drove home. Insufferable heat, a lot of white mushrooms, the rye is being harvested . . .

I read some proofs – the new edition of the *Collected Works* in Russian, and Maude's biography of Lev Nik. in English – and posed for Lyova.

July 21 I am writing this in a terribly anxious state; Lev Nik. has a bad pain in his liver, his stomach is not working properly and the bile is not flowing. But the main reason I feel so tormented is that it is my fault that he is not getting better. Chertkov came again this evening with his son. I heard this morning that he was coming and felt distraught all day. But I drove to the river for a swim, finished correcting the proofs of Maude's English biography of L.N., posed twice for Lyova and was glad to be able to keep calm.

Lev Nik. went for another ride in this terrible heat, this time with the doctor; he looked very tired afterwards and did not want to come down for dinner, but eventually he did and ate a lot of boiled peas, even though his liver has recently been aching and enlarged. This evening he played chess with Goldenweiser on the balcony upstairs. Then Chertkov came. The moment I heard his cabriolet approaching I began trembling all over. Earlier on I had walked around the garden for an hour and a half trying to regain my self-control. I cannot bear that man and only let him into the house for Lev Nikolaevich's sake.

But then they all sat out on the terrace together, and Maria Aleksandrovna too, and I felt so wretched that everyone but me was enjoying Lev Nik.'s company, and here we were, coming to the end of our life together on earth, and I could not even be with him. Three times I tried to go out on to the terrace to drink tea with the others, and when I eventually did summon up the courage to go, what happened? I was so agitated that the blood rushed to my head, my pulse was barely perceptible, I could hardly stand and I simply could not see Chertkov. I tried to say something, and it was as though my voice were not mine but that of some wild creature. Everyone stared at me. I struggled desperately to be calm, merely in order to avoid creating a scandal and distressing Lev Nikolaevich, but with little success. Lord help me! I desire this more than anything! I feel so ill and wretched. Yet I would gladly suffer a thousand times more, just so long as my Lyovochka recovers and is not angry with me . . . None of this might have happened had they given in before to my legitimate (although partly morbid) wishes.

I keep hearing those words: 'Not for anything! Absolutely not!' Are things any better now, I wonder? Everyone is unhappy and it is all my fault. Lev Nik. is ill, Chertkov is banished from his good favours, the diaries are imprisoned . . . Well, enough of this. How *terribly* sad and painful it all is!

July 22* First thing this morning the doctor applied leeches to the small of my back to stop the blood rushes to my head. I got up, reeling after a night without sleep. Lev Nik. had gone for a ride with Goldenweiser, Sasha and Varvara Mikhailovna; Olga, who had just arrived, had gone off with her children and the Finnish girl to pick mushrooms and take a swim. I stayed behind on my own and worked on the proofs and the new edition, then sent off some proofs and L.N.'s foreword to La Bruyère and others.[50] Lyova has set off in the carriage for Chifirovka to see Misha and his family.

Lev Nik. again lost his temper with me at dinner today, after I had voiced my chagrin and bewilderment at never being shown any copies of his latest works to read, since Chertkov immediately takes away all his manuscripts. I again burst into tears, left the table and went upstairs to my room. He thought better of it and came after me, but our conversation soon turned acrimonious again. Eventually, though, he invited me to take a stroll around the garden with him, which I always appreciate so much, and all our resentment seemed to pass.

Chertkov came after receiving a note from me to say that he could visit Lev Nikolaevich if he wished; I do want to be magnanimous to him, despite his rude and unpleasant behaviour. I managed to conquer my feelings and sat down to a game of draughts with my granddaughter Sonya, which distracted me from thinking about Chertkov.

*July 22 was the day on which L.N. wrote his will in the forest,[49] unknown to me. (Sofia Tolstaya's note.)

Lev Nik. is listless, his liver is aching, he has no appetite and his pulse is quick. But he will not do anything about it. I implored him to take some rhubarb and apply a compress, as he normally does in these cases, but he became irritable and stubbornly refused to do so; and the doctor went to bed without examining him, although I had begged him to be a little more attentive to Lev Nikolaevich. I am partly to blame for his illness, but it is partly this terrible heat – 29 degrees in the shade. We are both afflicted with these liver complaints.

July 23 Lev Nik. was much worse this morning. His temperature was 37.4, his pulse was racing, his condition was listless and his liver and stomach were bad, as I knew they would be.

Whatever I say, whatever I recommend, however loving I am, he sullenly rejects all my attempts to help him. This has again been the case ever since he stayed at Chertkov's. This evening he came again; Lev Nik. asked Sasha to invite him here when she went to Telyatinki, and Goldenweiser too to keep him entertained. But I went to Lev Nik.'s room and stubbornly sat there, preventing them from having a *tête à tête*, until Chertkov, seeing that I had no intention of going or leaving them alone together, eventually left, telling Lev Nik. that he had only come to take a last look at him while he was still alive. 'Before I murder him,' I added, referring to that remark of his: 'I cannot understand how a woman can spend her entire life *murdering* her husband.'

But I did have one great joy today – my darling grandchildren came: first Sonyushka and Ilyushok arrived with their mother, then Lyova, Lina and Misha came from Chifirovka with Vanechka and Tanechka. They are all such sweet, lovable children. But as I was looking after Lev Nik., watching over him and listening out for his call, I could not spend much time with them, which made me very sad.

When I discovered that Chertkov was coming here again, I burst into tears and started trembling all over. And Sasha virtually spat in my face as she went past, shouting, 'Oh, what the devil is it now! I'm so bored with all these scenes!'

What a horribly rude creature. It is simply beyond my understanding how she could insult her mother so, when I have not done her any harm or said a single word to her. And what a terrible, wicked expression she had on her face when she said that.

Oh, how one longs for death in the midst of all this evil, deception and hatred, this lack of common courtesy for their own kin who have done them no harm.

I read a little two-act play which Lev Nik. wrote in Kochety after learning that Dima and his peasant pals had put on his play *The First Distiller*, and wanted him to write something else for them. He just scribbled it down, and there are plenty of mistakes; for instance the young peasant woman says: 'I bake and I cook . . . ' whereas it's always the old woman in the play who is at work by the stove. Then the young woman hides her money and her purchases in the storeroom, and it later appears on the window, whence it is stolen. This little play is just raw material so far,[51] but he has thought it all out and in parts it is very good. I kept being reminded of *The Power of Darkness*.

In the past, when I used to copy everything for Lev Nikol., I used to point out to him all the mistakes and clumsy bits, and we would correct them together. Nowadays the others do all his copying for him, very accurately, but like machines.

July 24 Chertkov came again this evening, and I overheard Lev Nik. whispering to him: 'Do you agree with what I wrote?' And the other replied: 'Of course I agree!'[52] Yet another plot! Lord have mercy on us!

When I asked Lev Nik. with tears in my eyes to tell me what 'agreement' they were talking about, he made a sullen, spiteful face and stubbornly refused to tell me anything. He is unrecognisable! And once more I am in the throes of despair. There is a phial of opium on my table, and the only reason I have not drunk it is because I don't want to give them all, including Sasha, the satisfaction of seeing me dead. But how they persecute me! Lev Nik.'s health is much better now and he will certainly do everything he can to survive me so as to continue his life with Chertkov. I long to drink that phial and leave a note for Lev Nik. saying, 'Now you are free.'

This evening he said to me spitefully: 'I have decided today that I want to be free, so I am not going to pay attention to anything any more.' We shall see who will be the winner if he does declare open war on me. My weapon and my revenge is death, and it will be his and Chertkov's disgrace if they kill me. 'She is mad!' they will say. Yet who was it who drove me mad?

Misha's family has just left, but Olga and her children are still here. Save me, Lord, I think I have made up my mind . . . But I feel so sorry for my old, loving Lyovochka . . . And now I am crying . . .

And he *dares* to write about love, when he tortures the person closest to him – his wife!

He is my husband, he could save me, but he does not want to . . .

July 25 The discovery that Lev Nik. and Chertkov had come to some secret agreement and plotted some business against me and my children (I had been quite sure all along that this was happening) naturally made me desperately unhappy. Never in my whole life have I kept any secrets from my husband – all these secrets, *apartés* and plots are bound to hurt a loving wife . . . In any case Lev Nikolaevich's present instructions are causing fierce battles between his children and that sly Pharisee Chertkov, and how sad that is! Why is Lev Nik. making this posthumous memory for himself and creating such bad feelings? He keeps writing and talking about 'love' of one kind or another, and throughout his life he has always denounced documents, saying he would never write such things. But all these denunciations have been mere words. Documents . . . ! He *wrote* to the newspapers renouncing all his works written since 1881,[53] and he has now given his diary to the State Bank, which has given him a *written receipt* for them; he has been *writing* something with Chertkov – and Bulgakov too, I think – and today he gave him some large pieces of paper, probably a new will depriving his family of his works after his death. He has renounced money, yet he always has several hundred rubles on his desk to give away. He has renounced *travelling*, yet he has already made three journeys this summer, he has visited his daughter Tanya in Kochety twice this year, he has been to see Chertkov in Kryokshina and Meshcherskoe, and his son Seryozha with me – and now he wants to go to Kochety again.

On the evening of the 24th I sat down at my writing desk in a state of great agitation, and stayed there *all night long* in just a light summer dress, without once closing my eyes. How many painful, bitter thoughts passed through my mind that night! At five in the morning I had such a headache and my heart and chest felt so constricted that I decided to go outside for some fresh air, even though it was extremely cold and pouring with rain. But then my daughter-in-law Olga (Andryusha's former wife) ran out of the room next door, grabbed me with a strong arm and said: 'Now where are you going? I know you're about to do something silly and I'm going to stay with you!' And that dear, sweet, kind woman sat up with me all night, without sleeping a wink, poor thing, and tried to comfort me . . . Stiff with cold, I moved to a stool and dozed off. (Olga told me that I moaned pitifully in my sleep.) The next morning I decided to leave, if only for a short time; in the first place so as not to have to see Chertkov, suffer his vileness and be constantly distressed by his presence and all the secrets and plots; in the second place, simply to get some rest and give Lev Nikolaevich a rest from my presence and my suffering soul. I still had not decided where I would settle, but I packed my case, took some money, some writing work and my permit and decided either to move into a hotel in Tula or to my house in Moscow.

I drove to Tula in the trap which was being sent to collect Andryusha and his family. I met him at the station and decided that after seeing them off to Yasnaya I would go on to Moscow that evening. But Andryusha immediately sensed my state of mind and firmly announced that he would not leave me on my own for a moment. There was nothing to be done, and I agreed to return to Yasnaya with him, although all the way back I was shuddering at the memory of my recent experiences and the thought that the same thing would simply happen all over again when I returned.

I was exhausted by all the agitation, and the journey there and back, and barely managing to climb the stairs I straightaway lay down on my bed, for fear of meeting my husband and being the butt of his jibes. But in fact, to my great joy, it all turned out quite differently. He entered my room with tears in his eyes and thanked me tenderly for returning: 'I realised that I simply could not live without you,' he said weeping. 'I felt shattered, I went to pieces . . . We are so close, we have grown so used to one another . . . I am so grateful to you for coming back, darling, thank you . . . '

And he embraced me and kissed me, clasping me to his thin chest, and I cried too and told him I loved him just as passionately and intensely as when I was a girl, and that it was a joy to cling to him and be one with him again; and I begged him to be more open and straightforward with me, and not to give me occasion to be suspicious and anxious . . . But the moment I broached the subject of his conspiracy with Chertkov, he closed up and would not talk about it, although he did not deny that they had conspired together in secret. He has been so strange lately: he often does not immediately understand what is being said to him, and he takes fright at the mere mention of Chertkov's name.

But thank God I have felt his heart and his love again. His children, not I, will defend my rights after my dear husband's death.

We had a peaceful, friendly evening with the family – and without Chertkov, thank God. Both Lev Nik. and I are in poor health.

July 26 Sad news this morning from Tanya, who is ill in bed. She begs Lev Nikolaevich (but not me) to go to Kochety, and I am terribly afraid he will, although if he does, I shall too. Our doctor says that dysentery is infectious, and I am worried that Lev Nik., with his weakened system and disordered stomach and liver, will catch it from Tanya.

My sons have been splendid, and have united to defend me. Sasha looks maliciously at me, like all guilty people. Having insulted me and spat in my face, she is now sulking and unconsciously wants to take her father away from me; but of course for his sake I would abandon everything and leave here.

I posed a long time for my bust, and Lyova is making good progress. It is a warm damp day, with a lot of little clouds but no rain. They are cutting the oats now, although the rye has still not been sheaved and some of it has been stolen.

I am affixing here this letter which I wrote to my husband before I went away, as well as an article to the newspapers which I wrote but did not send.[54]

July 27, morning Another sleepless night, anxiety is gnawing at my heart, I cannot bear not knowing about this conspiracy with Chertkov and that piece of paper Lev Nik. has just signed. (This was evidently a supplement to his will, drafted by Chertkov and signed by Lev Nik.*) That document is

*Added later.

his revenge on me for the diaries and for Chertkov. Poor old man! What sort of memories will he leave behind after his death?! His heirs will yield *nothing* to Chertkov and will contest *everything*, because they all hate Chertkov and his sly, spiteful influence. 'Non-resistance' has proved to be a mere empty phrase, as one might have expected.

This evening, July 27, Bulgakov denied that he had had any part in Lev Nikolaevich's documents and signed statements.[55] This may well be so, but one cannot make sense of anything here! When I asked my daughter Sasha what she knew about her father's will and the document about which Lev Nik. has been having all these secret discussions with Chertkov, she replied in her usual rude and bad-tempered manner that she did not want to talk about it. What an insult to his *wife* that he makes secrets with his daughter and Chertkov, and hides everything from me!

The moment I got up this morning I took Vanechka's basket and wandered off into the woods. And whom should I see there but L.N., sitting on his shooting-stick and scribbling something. He seemed very taken aback to see me, and hurriedly covered up his piece of paper. I suspect that he was writing to Chertkov.

I was out for two and a half hours, and it was so good to be with nature, far away from cunning, spiteful people. That silly little Parasha, who is watching over our calves, is such a happy, kind-hearted creature; she had picked some inedible mushrooms which she gave me, but with such good nature! Two shepherds greeted me amiably as they drove our cattle past. I gazed into the cows' eyes and realised that they were only *nature*, and had no soul.

The boys were out picking mushrooms, such cheerful, artless fellows . . . In the barn the men who guard our orchards and the girl labourers (who have come from far away) were all sitting down on the threshing floor to their dinner. They all looked so bright and cheerful; not one of them had ulterior motives, or was drawing up plots and documents with sly fools like Chertkov. Everything is simple and honest with them! We should learn to merge with nature and the common people; our lives would be so much simpler without the stench of false non-resistance.

Lev Nik. is being cold and taciturn again. I went to bed before dinner and slept for 1½ hours. My head cleared somewhat, and I was able to do a little work on the new edition after dinner. I sent some articles and a letter off to Stakhovich,[56] and wrote to the printers, then I posed for Lyova. There has been a heavy thunder-storm and it poured with rain; the crops will be ruined. L.N. went for a ride with Dushan Petrovich and they got caught in the rain, then he played chess with Goldenweiser; later on he listened to our son Seryozha, who has just arrived, play a Chopin polonaise, something by Schumann, some Scottish songs and a Chopin mazurka. We had such a pleasant evening. I see almost nothing of Sasha; she spends most of her time sitting alone in her room, slandering me to all and sundry from her own malevolent perspective, and in the evenings she writes her diary, from the same biased point of view.

At midnight Seryozha and I were still sitting alone together, and I told him all about our recent experiences. Like the rest of them he kept trying to put the blame on me; one dog snaps at someone's heels and the whole pack follows suit, tearing their victim to pieces. So it is with me; they all want to separate me from Lev Nikolaevich. But they won't succeed in *that*!

July 28 Zosya Stakhovich has come; she badly wanted me to tell her everything that has happened, so I gave her all the details. She criticised me for demanding Lev N.'s diaries so implacably, but then despite being very intelligent she is only a girl after all, and could never understand the bond that grows between a husband and wife in 48 years of marriage.

Chattering away without any work to do is very tedious, and posing for Lyova is even more tedious. He is always terribly nervous. 'Be quiet, be quiet!' he shouts the moment I open my mouth. This endless posing has begun to exhaust me – today I *stood* for almost an hour and a half. I now like a quiet friendly life filled with useful work and not too many guests, just the occasional very close and dear friend who visits us purely out of love, not with some purpose in mind.

This evening, after playing chess with Goldenweiser and drinking tea with honey, Lev Nik. went to his room, and I thought he seemed sad. So I went to him and said that if he was unhappy because he had not seen Chertkov, I was very sorry and he should invite him here.

And he said to me with such evident sincerity: 'I am not unhappy about that, I do assure you! I feel so calm and happy now that I don't need Chertkov – just so long as we love one another and you are calm.'

And I was so happy to have had this doubt removed from my mind, to know that I was not the cause of Lyovochka's separation from Chertkov and that he himself seemed glad to have freed himself from Chertkov's odious authority. And we embraced with such love and friendship, just like in the old days, and I left him with joy in my heart.

Now it is night, and he is asleep. I should so like to see again that dear old face which I have loved all these years and have grown to know so intimately; but we now have separate rooms across the corridor from one another, and I spend the whole night listening out for him.

No, Mr Chertkov, I shall not let Lev Nik. out of my hands again, I shall not give him up. I shall do all I can to make him sick of Chertkov so that that man never enters my house again.

This evening Lev Nikol. read us a witty little story by Mille called '*Le Repos hébdomadaire*', which he liked very much, and the beginning of another story called '*Le Secret*'.

July 29 We have regained our old calm existence again, and life has returned to normal. Thank God! Chertkov has not visited us for five days now, nor Lev Nik. him. But at the mere memory of him, and the possibility of their renewed intimacy, something rises from the depths of my soul and seethes away, tormenting me. Well at least it's a rest!

Zosya Stakhovich has cheered us all up and is such pleasant company. Lev Nik. went out for a ride, even though it is still pouring with rain. I have been working on the proofs and was delighted by *The Cossacks*.[57] How weak his later stories are by comparison!

I wrote to my daughter Tanya and to my nieces Liza Obolenskaya, Varya Nagornova and Marusya Maklakova. Nikolaev came after dinner and Lev Nik. talked to him about Henry George and 'justice'. I heard snatches of their conversation, which evidently exhausted L.N. Zosya Stakhovich talked animatedly about Pushkin, whom she has just been reading, and recited some poems. Then they organised a game of vint; Sasha wanted to exclude me, and when I firmly took a card she pulled a face and left the room, whereupon Lev Nik. and I cheerfully took a grand slam no-trumps. I don't really like cards, but it is so depressing sitting on my own when all my family are enjoying themselves at the card table. The day passed quietly, without Chertkov. Lev Nik. was in better health and spirits today.

July 30 I have been unable to do a thing all day: nothing but humdrum tasks, tedious worries about food, making the guests comfortable, supervising the rye harvest and the repairs to the store-room, and so on and so on, and nothing in return but endless criticisms and homilies about my 'materialism'.

I posed for Lyova for an hour, then went out on my own for about two hours to pick mushrooms; I didn't find any but I enjoyed being alone with nature.

P.I. Biryukov's family have come to visit, all five of them, and the children are evidently going to be a great burden as they are very noisy and not at all attractive. I already had a bad headache, but the noise, the shouts, the gramophone, the barking poodle and Sasha's loud laughter made it even worse. This evening they all sat down to a game of cards, and this would have been a rest for my poor eyes and head, but they excluded me as usual. So I poured tea for them all, like some sort of hanger-on. But it is Varvara Mikhailovna who is the hanger-on here, and this outsider, who is very young, of course, calmly took her seat at the card table, to Sasha's great delight. But sensitive Lev Nik. realised how hurt I felt, and when I had left the room so as to avoid bursting into tears, he asked: 'Where are you going?' And I said: 'To my room.'

Yes, too often in my life I have stepped aside for others, and now I am going to take a different line: I don't want to be unhappy any more, I want to enjoy life to the full, taking drives, playing cards and going everywhere Lev Nik. goes.

Zosya Stakhovich has left. My present feelings about guests are: away with them all! I am tired and ill, I am bored with serving everyone and worrying about everyone, with never anything in return but endless criticisms. Zosya is better than most: at least she cheers one up and takes part in everything.

Lev Nik. rode over to Ovsyannikovo to take Iv. Iv. Gorbunov the proofs of the little kopeck booklets.[58] It is cool – 6 degs. this evening.

July 31 How hard it is to move from reading proofs to ordering dinner to buying rye to reading Lev Nik.'s letters – and finally to writing my diary. How fortunate are those people who have leisure, and can spend their entire lives concentrating on one abstract topic.

While I was reading through L.N.'s letters to various people I was struck by his insincerity. For instance he writes frequently and with apparent affection to a Jew named Molochnikov – a carpenter from Nizhnii Novgorod. Yet Katya and I were remembering just today that Lev Nik. once said: 'I am always particularly careful to be friendly to Molochnikov; this is particularly hard for me, as I find him rather distasteful, so I have to make great efforts to behave well to him.' L.N. also writes to his wife, whom he has never met.[59] And all this because Molochnikov was sent to prison, apparently for distributing Tolstoy's books – although I am told that he is simply an embittered revolutionary.

I was also struck by his frequent laments in these letters that 'it is hard to live in luxury as I do, against my will . . . ' Yet who but he needs this luxury? There are doctors for his health, two typewriters and two copiers for his writings, Bulgakov for his correspondence, Ilya Vasilevich, the valet, to look after a weak old man, and a good cook for his weak stomach.

And the entire burden of finding the money for this, supervising the estate and getting his books published rests on my shoulders, in order that Lev Nik. can have the peace, comfort and leisure he needs for his work. If anyone took the trouble to examine *my* life, any honest person would realise that I personally need nothing. I eat once a day, I go nowhere, I have just one maid, a girl of eighteen, and I now dress quite shabbily. Where is all this luxury I am supposed to have forced on him? How cruelly unjust people can be! May the sacred truth contained in this diary survive to cast light on all these matters which have been obscured.

The Lodyzhenskiis came, bringing with them the Russian Consul to India.[60] He had little of interest to offer, but the Lodyzhenskiis have both travelled widely, have been to India and Egypt and studied religion, and are interesting, lively people.

I corrected the proofs of the forewords,[61] posed, and did a little work on the new edition. Andryusha has left. My husband and I are on friendly terms, and this morning he was being very affectionate. Sasha and Varvara Mikhailovna are sulking in the most odious fashion. Varvara Mikhailovna clings to Sasha and gives herself such airs – she won't even pour the tea and always leaves me to do it. I really should dismiss her and take on a more useful assistant, someone who would read aloud to me. Changeable weather, 9 degrees this evening.

August 1 I have felt very ill all day; again everything torments and worries me. Lev Nik. is being cold and withdrawn and is evidently pining for his idol. I am trying to work out in my mind whether I can bear the sight of Chertkov – and I realise that I cannot, I cannot . . .

I have been sorting through some Russian and foreign books and newspapers, but the blood keeps rushing to my head in the most distressing way . . .

I did some good work with Biryukov on the new edition, and I found his advice and recommendations most helpful.[62] This evening I read my children's stories to the Biryukov children.[63]

Three villagers came to visit Lev Nik.; we had asked them for the names of our poorest peasants so we could buy rye seeds for them with the money Maude sent us in aid of the starving. The peasants had a talk with Lev Nik. and promised to make a list of the poorest peasants. He told me the names of two of them, but not the third – it must be Timofei, his son by that peasant woman.[64] (In fact it was Aleksei Zhidkov.)*

I told fortunes with the cards tonight. For Lev Nikolaev. I drew that he would live with a young woman (Sasha) and the King of Diamonds (Chertkov), and that he would have love, marriage and happiness (all hearts). I simply drew death (the Ace of Spades and the Nine); for the heart I drew an old man (the King of Spades) or a villain; then I drew all four tens, which means that my wish will be granted, and my wish is to die, although I should hate to yield Lev Nikolaevich up to Chertkov when I do. And how they would all gloat and rejoice after my death! The first blow against me was well aimed, and has done its work. *It is these sufferings that will bring about my death.*

August 2 Writing his diaries has lost all meaning for Lev Nikolaevich now. His life and his diaries – with their revelations of both the good and bad impulses of his soul – have become two completely separate things. His diaries are now composed for Mr Chertkov, whom he does not see, although from the evidence I assume that they are in correspondence, and that their letters are passed on by Bulgakov and Goldenweiser, who come here every day.

The last time Chertkov was here Lev Nikol. asked him if he '*received his letter, and whether he agreed with it*'.[65] To what new abomination has Mr Chertkov given his approval now? If his visits would put a stop to this

*Added later.

clandestine correspondence, then let him visit here by all means; but they continue to correspond even when they are meeting, so it's better that they don't see one another – they only have their letters now, and no meetings. L.N.'s love for Chertkov intensified after he stayed with him this summer without me, and it weakens with distance and time.

Lev Nik. rode *alone* to Kolpna today to inspect the rye which we are buying for the peasants. I could not do a thing; my heart was pounding wildly, my head was aching and I was terrified lest he had arranged to meet Chertkov somewhere and they would go there together. Eventually I ordered the cabriolet to be harnessed and drove out to meet him. He was alone, thank God, followed, it so happened, by a peasant of ours called Danila Kozlov.

I have such a lot of work to do and proofs to read, but I can do nothing while Chertkov is in the neighbourhood, and am afraid of getting things in a muddle. I forced myself to go to dinner, but immediately afterwards I felt so ill and had such a bad headache that I had to go to my room and lie down. Lotions and mustard plasters on my head eased the pain, and I eventually dropped off to sleep.

Lev Nik. was kind and solicitous. But later on, when I heard that Bulgakov had come with some mail, and I asked: 'Is there a letter from Chertkov?', he grew furious, and said: 'I think I have the right to correspond with whomever I please . . . ' (I hadn't said one word about 'rights'.) 'He and I have a vast amount of business connected with the printing of my works and various writings . . . '

Ah yes, but if it was only *that* sort of business, then there wouldn't be any of this *secret* correspondence. When things are secret there is bound to be something bad hidden away there. Christ, Socrates – none of the ancient philosophers did things in secret; they preached openly on the squares before the people, fearing nothing and no one. And they were killed for it too – but then they joined the gods.

But criminals – conspirators, libertines, thieves and suchlike – always do things in secret. And Chertkov has inveigled poor saintly Tolstoy into this situation which is so alien to his nature.

If Lev Nik. and Chertkov need to conceal everything, it means they are bound to be hiding something bad or evil; I am convinced of this and it makes me deeply unhappy.

August 3 When Lev Nikol. learnt that Mr Maude had revealed in his biography of him various loathsome things about Chertkov (even though he did not name him and merely referred to him as 'X'), he stooped so low as to write to Maude, on July 23, begging him to delete these vile truths and to remove an excerpt from a letter written by our late daughter Masha, which refers contemptuously to Chertkov. I received two letters from Maude today, one to me, the other to Lev Nikolaevich.[66] What a terrible thing it is that L.N. should love Chertkov so much that to protect him he is prepared to humiliate himself to the point of lying or keeping silent.

The passage that Lev Nik. asked Maude to delete was a derogatory reference to Chertkov in a letter written by our daughter Masha. L.N. was very hurt by this attack on Chertkov, especially coming from his beloved Masha, who always seemed such good friends with Chertkov; but even she saw through him in the end.

I received a letter today from E.I. Chertkova, filled with reproaches.[67] I quite understand her feelings as a mother: she idealises her son and does not know him. I replied to her in restrained, courteous and somewhat proud tones; but I shall not seek a reconciliation.[68]

I wanted to explain to Lev Nik. the source of my jealousy of Chertkov, so I showed him that page of his old diary, for 1851, in which he writes that he has never fallen in love with a woman but has frequently fallen in love with men.[69] I thought that like Biryukov and Doctor Makovitsky he would understand my jealousy and reassure me, but instead he turned white and flew into a terrible rage such as I have not seen for a long, long time. 'Get out! Get out!' he shouted. 'I said I would leave you and I will . . . !' He rushed from room to room and I followed him horrified and bewildered. Then he went to his room, slammed the door and locked me out. I stood there stunned. Where was his love? His non-resistance? His Christianity? And where, finally, was his justice and compassion? Does old age really harden a man's heart like this? What had I done? Why had this happened? It chills my heart to remember that shout and the fury on his face.

I went out to the bath-house, and Lev Nik. came into the drawing-room just as though nothing had happened, drank tea with great gusto and listened to Dushan Petrovich read something about Pyotr Chelčický, translating from the Slavonic as he went.[70]

When the others had gone to bed, Lev Nik. came to my room and said he had come to apologise. I trembled for joy. But when I followed him out and suggested that we should try to live out the end of our lives in a more friendly fashion, and then mentioned something else too, he refused to listen and said that if I didn't go away he would regret coming in to see me. What is one to make of him!

August 4 Today passed without any reference to Chertkov, thank God! Things have become slightly easier and the air has cleared somewhat. I am so grateful to my dear Lyovochka for taking pity on me. If everything started all over again I do not think I would have the strength to endure it. I do hope that everyone will leave Telyatinki soon, so I can stop living in terror of their secret meetings, and trembling with anxiety every time Lev Nikol. goes out for a ride.

I am ill, my head feels strange, I hardly sleep at all and I cannot concentrate. I often lie in bed unable to sleep and wild fantasies pass through my head, and I fear I am going mad.

The Biryukovs have left. The weather is brighter, and some mushrooms have appeared. Sasha went to Tula to see the doctor, but he did not prescribe anything. Tanya is better, thank God. I posed for Lyova, corrected the proofs of 'Art' and inserted some passages that had been omitted, which was slow and difficult work.[71]

Lev Nik. rode over to Basovo to see Lodyzhenskii, which tired him out. I met him on his way back, on what we call our 'prospect'. I was wondering why I could not reconcile myself to Chertkov. I do want to be charitable, 'as we forgive them that trespass against us', and I can imagine myself no longer hating him. But at the thought of actually *seeing* that figure again, and seeing Lev Nikol.'s face light up with joy, the old suffering rises in my soul and I want to weep, and I cry out desperately: 'No, not for anything! I want no more of that agonising misery!' I feel I am completely in my husband's power, and if he does not stand firm, everything is lost!

There is an evil spirit in Chertkov; that is why he frightens and disturbs me so.

August 5 I spent a terrible night re-living the whole of my recent ordeal. How insulting that my husband did not even stand up for me when Chertkov was so rude to me. How he fears him! How he has subjugated himself to him! The shame and the pity of it!

I tried to work on some proofs but could not. I keep choking, my head aches and my heart trembles; I went for a walk and was out for almost three hours. The cabriolet came to take me to the main road. Lev Nik. went for a ride with Dushan Petrovich. I met Lyova on his way back from Telyatinki, and he said he had seen Chertkov from a distance. I wonder if he was riding out to meet Lev Nik.?

I heard today that there are 30 people at Telyatinki furiously copying something. What can it be? Didn't Lev Nikol. take his diaries back yesterday? It's impossible to discover what is happening! With sly, malicious obstinacy Lev Nikolaevich hides *everything* from me, and we are like two strangers.

I am to blame for a great deal, of course. But then I have suffered such remorse that a *kind* husband would forgive me the wrongs I have done him,* and now that we are at the end and near to death he would draw me closer to him, if only because I have returned to him with such ardent, passionate love in my heart, and because I have never betrayed him.

How happy I should be if he would only draw me closer to him and say nice things to me. But this will never happen – even if Chertkov is kept away from him!

*Especially in my present sick and hysterical state. (Added later.)

Lev Nik. was cold and distant again today. So depressing!

I read some terrible articles by Vl. Korolenko about capital punishment and people who have been sentenced to it,[72] then looked through a novel by Rosny.[73] This evening Goldenweiser performed that astonishing Chopin sonata with the funeral march. But he played rather lifelessly. The weather is changeable, and it has rained 3 times today.

Night . . . I cannot sleep. I prayed for a long time on my knees, and asked God to return me my husband's heart from Chertkov and melt his coldness towards me. I pray every day, and I often remember Aunt Tatiana Aleksandrovna in my prayers and beg her to pray for me. I am sure she would understand and take pity on me.

August 6 A sleepless night, like every other night recently. Each morning I wake up in terror at what the day will bring. And this is what happened today. I looked into Lev Nikolaevich's room at 10 o'clock and he was not there, as he had gone out for his walk. I dressed hurriedly and ran to the fir plantation, where he usually takes his morning walk, and while I was running I thought: 'What if he is there with Chertkov?' But there he was, that dear, calm old man walking all on his own. Although Chertkov might have already left, of course. I met some village children and asked them: 'Have you seen the old Count, my little ones?' 'Yes, we saw him sitting on the bench.' 'Alone?' 'Yes, alone.' I then began to take myself in hand and calmed down a little. The children were so sweet, and seeing that I could not find any mushrooms – for I certainly couldn't! – they gave me five browncaps, saying pityingly: 'You can't see a thing, can you! You're completely blind!' Lyova came into the fir plantation – I don't know whether he was looking for me or if it was by chance; and a little later he met me again on horseback, by the swimming pool.

I stayed out for four hours and gradually grew a little calmer. The house has been invaded by the apple merchant, the guards, bearing apples and bowing – and later on the baker. Lev Nik. is being cold and severe, and when I see him so cold I keep hearing that cruel cry: 'Chertkov is the *person closest to me*!' (And not his wife!) Well, at least Chertkov isn't closest to him *physically*. I hope to God that they leave soon. I am sure his old mother is staying on here deliberately to spite me. She was going to leave before the 6th to visit her sister.

Lev Nik. and Bulgakov went out for a ride and got lost at Zaseka, but they were not back late. More proofs of *Art*. V.G. Korolenko walked here today from Zaseka station and spent the evening with us talking endlessly about the most fascinating things: about various sectarians who all assembled at a holy lake in the Makarevskii district, about monasteries, tortures, prisons, his first acquaintance with Gorky, Repin's paintings, and so on and so on. It was a pity we could not write it all down.[74] Korolenko talks so well, he is both pithy and eloquent. We sent for Goldenweiser, who played chess with Lev Nik. and was utterly fascinated by Korolenko. Sasha went to Provaly with Olga, the children and the Goldenweisers. It is still raining and they all got wet.

August 7 Still the same weight hanging over us, the same gloomy atmosphere in the house. The rain pours incessantly and has beaten down the oats in the field which have sprouted. Our peasants came and we distributed Maude's money amongst the households. It came to 5 rubles, 50 kopecks per household – 410 rubles, 50 kopecks in all. Korolenko left. I posed for Lyova and sat with our guest, then sent Part XV to the printers to be set. I shall not write about the most painful thing in the world, which gnaws at my heart day and night – Lev N.'s coldness and cruelty to me. He has not so much as said hello to me today – he doesn't say a word all day and is sullen and angry; he behaves as though I interfere with his life, as though I am a burden to him. And all because for my sake he has stopped seeing Chertkov.

So Lev Nik. has decided not to speak, to sulk all day in silence – a stubborn, spiteful silence. For someone with my lively, open nature this silence is quite unbearable. He wants to torment me, and he is going about it very successfully too.

I did not forbid Chertkov to come here, either in words or in writing. L.N. or Lyova may have written something to him – I don't know;[75] everything is a secret with them. And I have no idea whether the Chertkovs will go soon either, or whether L.N. wants to see him again. He says nothing and he does nothing. What is going on in his soul? Who knows? Anger and grief are written all over his face. Oh, to melt the ice in his heart!

We lived quite happily without Chertkov for several decades. And what now? We are the same people, but now sisters quarrel with their brothers, the father is ill-disposed towards his sons, the daughters towards their mother, the husband hates his wife, his wife hates Chertkov, and all because of that gross, stupid, corpulent figure who has insinuated himself into our family, ensnared the old man, and is now destroying my life and happiness . . .

I shall now pray again. The moment I think of prayer I become easier in my mind; it is such a joy to be able to kneel down here and enter into communion with God, for He will comfort me, calm my fears, heal my sorrowing soul and soften my husband's stony heart.

August 8 And that is exactly what happened: God answered my prayer astonishingly quickly. Today my Lyovochka's heart melted and he was kind and affectionate to me – even tender. I thank Thee, Lord! I can endure endless physical suffering, just so long as that lifelong emotional bond with Lyovochka endures, and there is no more of that coldness which destroys me. Another sleepless night; I kept thinking that I should suggest to Lev Nikol. that he sees Chertkov again. So when he got up this morning I said this to him. He waved his arm, said that he would discuss it later and went out for his walk. At 9 o'clock I went out too, wandered all over the woods and parks of Yasnaya and tripped and fell flat on my face, scattering all my mushrooms; I then gathered a big bundle of oak branches and grass, laid them on the birch bench and lay down, weeping and exhausted, until I eventually dozed off into some fantastic dreams The oak branches were wet from the rain and I was completely soaked, but I lay there in the silence, gazing at the pine trees, for more than an hour. I was out for more than 4 hours altogether – without eating anything, of course.

When I got back, Lev Nik. called me into his room and said (and by then I was so happy to hear his voice): 'You suggest that I see Chertkov again, but I don't want to. What I want more than anything is to live out the end of my life as calmly and peacefully as possible. I cannot be calm if you are agitated. So I think it would be best if I were to visit Tanya just for a week and for us to part for a little while, so as to give us both a chance to calm down.'

At first the idea of another parting seemed unbearable to me. But after a while I realised that Lev N.'s separation from Chertkov was the best possible alternative, and I realised what a good idea it was, for it would give both of us a rest from this emotional aggravation. My Lyovochka assured me that my peace of mind was so precious to him that it destroyed him to see me in such an anxious and depressed state, and he was prepared to do anything to help me and comfort me. And his concern was the best possible remedy for my ailments.

Today he wrote down on a piece of paper an appeal to young people wanting to refuse military service.[76] It was very good, and Sasha has already copied it out, but where has the original gone? Can they have given it to Chertkov again?

I did some work on the new edition, wrote to Maude about the peasants' money, and wrote to the accountant. This afternoon I went to sleep. Goldenweiser played a Beethoven sonata,[77] which I did not hear unfortunately; but I did hear him perform a Chopin waltz and mazurka, and he played beautifully.

I have a pain in the pit of my stomach and am not digesting my food properly; my whole system has broken down. There was another brief shower today. The oats have sprouted and there are some white mushrooms, and various other kinds too.

August 9 I have been sewing things for Lyovochka all day; first I altered his shirt, then his white cap, and I found it so soothing. I deliberately did no other work today, so as to give my nerves a rest. It would all be perfect if it weren't for these extraordinary outbursts of vile rudeness from Sasha.

She keeps going to see the Chertkovs, and they do all in their power to turn her against me for making my husband sever connections with the Telyatinki clique. I could never have imagined it possible that my daughter would dare to treat her mother like this – not to mention her emotional attitude to me. When I told her father about her intolerable rudeness, he said sadly: 'Yes, it is a great shame, but this rudeness is in her nature. I shall speak to her about it.'

He went to see Gorbunov at Ovsyannikovo today and was disappointed not to find him in, as he had brought him the proofs of the kopeck booklets, on which he has been so busy lately.

He looked very gloomy when he came down to dinner today, and again I felt a pang in my heart. I went to him and asked why he was so sad, and first he said he just felt a little low, then he told me that he did not feel gloomy, merely 'serious'. What sort of mood is this, when 'all the conversations seem so tedious and unnecessary, and everything is so pointless'. Naturally the conversations were dull and irrelevant today, for we had our neighbour V. YU. Feret here, the vice-governor of Smolensk and an old acquaintance whom we have not seen for five years. He is kind and good-natured, loves music and played duets with Lyova, but he is a commonplace sort of man.

Later on the Goldenweisers came, things cheered up as the evening went on and Lev Nik. became less gloomy. We are on good terms at present, thank God, but I still worry – I am terrified of losing his good feelings towards me. We are expecting Tanya at 3.30 a.m.

August 10 Tanya arrived at four a.m. today. I was listening out for her all night but did not hear her arrive. This morning I had another long talk with her about the same thing, and I became so upset that we eventually agreed not to talk any more about this subject which so torments us all.

I posed for Lyova, and when I got up, I suddenly felt faint, went to the window and lost consciousness. I came to with a bad pain in my leg, and Lyova struggling to lift me up. 'Poor woman!' he said, for I had cut and bruised my leg quite badly as I fell. Lev Nikol. was so sweet and concerned when he heard about my fall. But how sad and silent he is still – he is obviously still pining! I am sure he would never admit that he is missing Chertkov, for fear of distressing me. Yet the more he pines the less desire I have to renew relations with Chertkov and once again to have to endure the ordeal of their intimacy and that hateful man's visits here. I learnt today that they are not leaving until September 1, which is another reason why I ought to welcome Lev Nik.'s planned visit to Tanya's. Yet I find the thought of another parting with him quite unbearable! We have been apart so much this summer, and we don't have much longer of our lives left now! But then Lev Nik. is evidently bored with life here in Yasnaya Polyana. It's always the same, day after day, and he now likes all sorts of diversions. He takes his morning walk, always to the same places, then he works, then he has lunch, then he goes for a ride with Dushan Petrovich, then he has a nap, then dinner – and then a lonely sad evening sitting in his room; or better, Goldenweiser comes and they play an almost daily game of chess. Sometimes Goldenweiser plays the piano too, and that gives us all pleasure.

Some soldiers came today to Yasnaya to see us for some reason. They dispersed through the village, and four of them managed to slip into the house to see Lev Nik., although I never did discover what he discussed with them. He has such a strange attitude to my presence on such occasions. If I am interested in what he is talking about and go into his room, he looks at me angrily, as though I were in the way. And if I do not go in and seem uninterested, he takes this as a sign of indifference and even outright disagreement. So I often don't know what to do. Whenever I am forced by the circumstances of my life to take some decision, they regard this as despotism; no one wants to make any decisions themselves and they all wait for me to do so instead, so they can then criticise, contradict and condemn me

The wind is blowing again, my head aches, my heart pines. Lyovochka is leaving on Saturday to see Tanya in Kochety. What shall I do! I am already worrying in advance about what will become of me. How am I supposed to get better here when everyone is leaving me?

I read *Christianity and Patriotism* for the new edition, and regretfully deleted some passages which had not yet been censored. I find all this so hard to understand![78]

August 11 I feel somewhat easier in my mind today, despite new anxieties about Lev Nikolaevich's health. He is very hoarse and has a bad cold, and he feels chilled; as long as he can bear to sit quietly at home and look after himself, then, God willing, it will pass.

Bulygin, Gué and Salomon's nephew have come for a short visit. The others all drove to Tikhvinskoe to look at a house, and then to Ovsyannikovo; I went there with Tanya later on.

It made me so happy today when Lev Nik. dictated a letter to me, and I sat writing in his room for quite a long time.[79] This evening I did a little work on the new edition, then we played vint. Lev Nik. stayed at home all day; his cough worries me, although I hope it will soon pass.

August 12 No sooner do I grow a little calmer and begin to live normally, without any particular worries, when yet another anxiety arrives. Lev Nik. has had a bad cough but is none the less *determined* to go to Kochety. He is sure to catch a chill on top of it, and pneumonia is so dangerous at his age. We are both keeping silent about this journey, but he only wants to go in order to distress me. This is yet another attempt to get rid of me; but I will not and cannot be parted from him again, and three days from now I shall be going there with him. Everyone around me is desperately trying to separate us, but they won't succeed.

I was out picking mushrooms for 3½ hours today with Ekaterina Vasilevna.[80] It was so delightful in the fir plantation, with the red saffron milk-caps nestling amongst the green moss, and everything so fresh, peaceful and secluded. Then I posed and worked on the new edition. What hard work it is!

N.N. Gué and Goldenweiser came, then Nikolaev arrived. Endless talk. L.N. played a game of chess. He has not left the house all day, apart from a short stroll this morning. He had lunch in his room; the influenza has left him very listless, and he complains of lumbago in the back and weakness.

This evening Tanya made a number of painful accusations against me, almost all of which were unfounded, and I detected Sasha's suspicions and lies there, for she is trying to slander me in every way she can, turn everyone against me and separate me from her father. She is the greatest cross I have to bear. Such a daughter is worse than all the Chertkovs in the world; she can't be sent away, and no one will marry her with her frightful character. I often come in through the courtyard merely to avoid having to see her, for I never know if she is going to spit in my face again, or viciously attack me with a choice selection of oaths and lies. What a grief in one's old age! How has it happened?

I have just read through my diary and was horrified – alas! – by both myself and my husband. No, it is almost impossible to go on living like this.

August 13 I feel even more agitated, and my heart is trembling. But I did have a happy day today. Lev Nik. stayed at home all day, just going on to the terrace this morning. His health is much better now, and he has only a slight cough. He is in good spirits too, and is not being hard and angry with me. Thank God for that. He wrote yet more letters, mainly replies to enquiries.[81] Tanya was so sweet to me, and told me with tears in her eyes that she would always love me, care for me and have compassion for me. We played vint with Boulanger; Goldenweiser played the piano a little; Maria Aleksandrovna came. It has been *pouring* with rain all day, and this evening there was a real summer storm, with thunder and brief lightning flashes.

I entered some books into the library catalogues and cut out a dress for Maria Aleksandrovna. I have done no work today; my head is not fresh and my heart is not calm. I wrote to Buturlin, Torba, Seryozha, Biryukov, Davydov and the accountant (with the translation).

August 14 Agitation much worse, pounding heart all day, blood rushes. The thought of parting from Lev Nik. is unbearable. I hesitated all day between staying in Yasnaya or going with him to see Tanya in Kochety, and I eventually decided on the latter and hastily packed. I am very sorry to be leaving Lyova, who is awaiting trial in St Petersburg for the pamphlet he published in 1905, *The Construction of Hell*;[82] they will not give him a foreign passport as he is under arrest. I am also sorry to be leaving Katya and Mashenka too, and abandoning my work. But I simply will not be parted from my husband again, I cannot bear it.

I went to the fir plantation with Katya, but the saffron milk-caps had all been picked. Lev Nik. wrapped up warmly and went for a two-hour ride through Zaseka with Dushan. He is much better.

This evening Goldenweiser performed Beethoven's 'Sonata Quasi una Fantasia', but his playing was cold and lifeless. He also played two Chopin pieces, excellently, and Schumann's 'Carnaval', which was not bad technically, although he quite failed to convey the different character of each separate piece.

I felt so ill all day that I went without dinner. A lot of people came – Dima Chertkov (the son), a gentle, simple, good-natured lad, quite unlike his father; Nikolaeva, Goldenweiser and his wife. Maria Aleksandrovna, and a stranger called Yazykova. I finished packing and went to bed late.

August 15(Kochety) We got up early and drove to Zaseka, seen off by a great many people including Lyova; then we set off for Kochety with Tanya. It was a long and difficult journey, and we had to change trains at Oryol for the Blagodatnaya line. Lev Nik. slept most of the way, hardly ate a thing and seemed very weak. But this evening in Kochety he played vint with great enthusiasm until midnight – then complained of feeling weak.

Our little granddaughter Tanechka met us so touchingly in Kochety. What a sweet, adorable, loving child! How affectionately she kissed and caressed me – at least someone was pleased to see me! That sacred innocence is always so moving in a child. So unlike us adults! When I went to say goodnight to my husband today he was asking Sasha (in my presence, it so happened) for his notebook; she mumbled something, and I realised that there was yet another plot afoot. 'What are you asking for?' I said. Lev Nik. realised that I had guessed something and told me the truth, thank God, otherwise I would have been terribly upset. 'I am asking Sasha for my diary,' he said. 'I give it to her to hide, and she copies my thoughts out of it.'[83]

They are *hiding it from me*, of course, *copying out his thoughts for Chertkov*. L.N.'s present diaries, as I said before, are simply composed for Mr Chertkov, so there can be no sincerity in them. Well, God be with them and all their secrets and subterfuges. Everything will become clear in time. I am their *conscience*, which hates anything secret, and they cannot bear that. In Yasnaya I had already discovered their secret hiding place for Lev Nik.'s diaries in Sasha's room, and this is why I have recently been so upset. (Although they still thought they had *hidden* them from me.) I then asked Lev Nik.: 'And does Sasha read your diaries?'

'I don't know,' he replied. 'She copies my thoughts out of them . . . ' What does 'I don't know' mean, if she *copies* them? More lies! But I didn't say anything.

It's merely an excuse, of course. It does not worry me if he hides the diaries; that is quite reasonable and understandable, although if he does, he should hide them from *everyone*. No, what worries me is that he lets both *Chertkov* and *Sasha* read them, but not *me, his wife*. So he rails against me and leaves me to the mercy of Sasha and Chertkov. And that is cruel and wicked of him.

There are crowds of people here; they are all so good-natured and not at all spiteful or secretive, as in our family *hell*. I think my husband's treacherous behaviour has weakened my love for him. I can see it in his face, his eyes and his whole mien, that spite which he vents on me all the time; and that spite is so unattractive and uncalled-for in an old man, especially when to the rest of the world he keeps preaching about 'love'. He knows he is tormenting me with those diaries, he is doing so on purpose; I pray to God to help me disentangle myself from this insane attachment to him. How much freer and easier my life would be if I could! Sasha and Chertkov could then cast evil spells with him to their hearts' content!

Dear Tanya unselfishly gave me her room, which makes me feel so *guilty*; I shall worry about it all the time now.

August 16 How can there be any joy or happiness in life when Lev Nik., and Sasha, at his wishes, are taking such enormous pains to hide something in his diaries from me; while I of course make equally great and cunning efforts to find them and read what is being concealed from me, and what they are saying about me to Chertkov – and through him to the entire world. I did not sleep all night, my heart was pounding, and I kept devising new ways of reading what L.N. is so frantic to hide from me. If there is nothing there, wouldn't it be much simpler to say: 'There, take them, read them and calm down.' But he would die rather than do that, because that is his nature.

He complained of feeling drowsy and weak today, lay in his room, then went for a walk. I saw him for a moment, though, and handed him a scrap of paper on which I had written that I considered it quite fair and reasonable to hide his diaries from *everyone*, and not let *anyone* read them. But to give them to Sasha to read and copy for Chertkov, and then furtively hide them away in cupboards and desks from *me*, his *wife*, was hurtful and insulting. 'Let God be your judge,' I ended my note, and I shall say no more about it.[84]

Yesterday evening after our journey, L.N. was playing vint enthusiastically until midnight, and this morning he was feeling quite well. But now I expect he is angry with me for criticising him. What is to be done! We exasperate one another. An 'enemy' has come between us, as the peasants would say – i.e. an evil spirit. Help us, Lord! I pray for a long time every evening, I pray when I go out for a walk on my own, I pray, as now, when my soul aches . . .

Evening In the middle of the day Lev Nik. called me into his room and said: 'Are you offended again?' 'Of course I am,' I said. 'Did you read my note?' 'Yes,' he said, 'but I just want to tell you that Sasha does not read my diaries; at the end of each day I have in them a section devoted to thoughts, and Sasha is copying these out for Chertkov to add to the previous ones. But the diaries stay with me and I don't give them to anyone.'

This comforted me somewhat – so long as it isn't yet another deception – and I found it easier to get through the day. I played with darling little Tanechka and Mikushka, and Tanyushka said: 'I love Granny more than anyone else in the world!' We went out to pick mushrooms and found some saffron milk-caps and other kinds. I had such fun with the children.

There are crowds of people here; it is all rather tiring, but such a relief not to have any responsibilities for the housework. It is hard work for poor Tanya, though, and I feel badly that the four of us have come when she already has her own large family to look after. This evening we all played vint, and I was so grateful just to be able to spend an evening with my husband. He is a keen player and is always scolding me for playing so badly, and trying to exclude me from the game. But yesterday I beat them all.

Poor Sukhotin is very depressed about this rain, which has ruined his oats and must have cost him some three thousand rubles. And Tanya's luggage has been lost – they probably didn't put it on the train at Oryol. I ate my dinner with the children and their nurse today. The children were overjoyed – and I was overjoyed when Lev Nik. got up from the table to come and look at me. How foolishly infatuated with him I still am!

August 17 I spent the whole day hard at work correcting the proofs of *Childhood.*[85] It is astonishing to see exactly the same traits of character in his youth as in his old age – his worship of beauty (Seryozha Ivin), for instance, the way he suffers such agony from his own ugliness and longs to be beautiful in exchange for being a *good, clever* boy. The chapter 'Grisha' has an extraordinary passage in the manuscript version, omitted from the book: that sensual scene in the store-room with Katenka directly after they witness Grisha, the holy fool, alone in his room in a state of tender, exalted religious ecstasy.

Beauty, sensuality, sudden changes of emotion, the eternal search for religion and truth – that is my husband through and through. He tells me that his growing indifference to me is due to my 'lack of understanding'. But I know that what he actually dislikes is that I suddenly understand him all too well, and see all too clearly things that I hadn't seen before.

He went for a walk round the park, and was visited by a *skopets*,*[86] with

*A member of the *skoptsy*, a sect practising castration.

whom he talked for more than two hours. I do not generally like sectarians, especially the *skoptsy*, but this one seemed intelligent enough, even though he boasted disagreeably of his time in exile.

Lev Nikolaevich seemed sad and distant again today. I expect he is pining for Chertkov, his idol. I should remind him of the wise words: 'Thou shalt not make graven images'. But there's nothing you can do with a person's heart if they love someone intensely.

What grey dreary weather! But everyone here is so kind and simple – not to mention my daughter Tanya, who is so concerned about everyone. Mikhail Sergeevich is totally absorbed in the estate, and it doesn't worry Lev Nikolaevich a bit; he actually warms to this familiar old-fashioned landowning life. In Yasnaya he has to renounce everything and *suffer* all the time, and so many things are spoilt for him by bad memories. He long ago loaded all the problems of life on to *me*, and of course he must feel very guilty about this. When I think of our life at Yasnaya recently I don't want to go back there. I want a *new* life, new people, new conditions. Everything about our life there is so painful! And it has been like that for such a long time too!

I spent a listless, weary evening; the only enjoyable thing was when we played with the children. What little darlings they both are! Later Lev Nik. played vint with great enthusiasm until midnight. He then asked Tanya for a light French novel to read. He is so *bored* with being a religious thinker and teacher – he is *tired* of all that! He needs pleasant diversions now, like card games, or playing 'opinions' with the children. He longs for a rest from his role as religious teacher, but he does not want me to see this, which was why he did all he could to dissuade me from coming to Kochety. I remember with an aching heart that when I asked him if he would spend our birthdays in Kochety or return to Yasnaya (on the 22nd or the 28th), he said: 'But that's just a few days away. Why don't *you* stay in Yasnaya and come to Kochety on the 28th for my birthday?'

I burst into tears of grief and rage. What do I need to celebrate his birthday for, if he is so anxious to get away from me! And it was there and then that I decided to go to Kochety too; there at least I would have my two darling Tanyas. Since I have a lot of work to do on the new edition at the moment, I asked Lev Nik. how long he thought we would be staying there, and he rudely said: 'I'm not a soldier, I won't be told how much leave I can take!' How can one live with such a man! I am afraid that in his usual treacherous fashion he will stay on here for several months,[87] knowing how *essential* it is for me to get back.

But even so I shan't leave here for anything; I shall abandon my work, forget it! I wonder which of us will come off best in the end? To think that two people who once loved one another so deeply could have started up this vicious battle. Or is it just old age? Or the influence of outsiders? Sometimes I look at him and feel as though everything alive, kind, perceptive, sympathetic, honest and loving in him has perished, killed by that dry, heartless sectarian Chertkov.

August 18 I read some terrible news in the papers today: the government has given Chertkov permission to stay in Telyatinki![88] Lev Nikolaevich has immediately cheered up; he looks years younger and his gait is brisk and sprightly. But I am aching with unbearable anguish, my heart-beat is 140 a minute, and my head and chest are aching.

This cross I have to bear is God's will; it was sent to me by His hand, and he has chosen Chertkov and Lev Nikolaevich as the instruments of my death. Maybe the sight of me lying there dead will open L.N.'s eyes to my enemy and murderer, and he will grow to hate him and repent of his sinful infatuation with the man.

And how his behaviour to me changed all of a sudden! Suddenly it is all tenderness and concern. Perhaps she'll make the peace with Chertkov now, he thinks, and it will be like old times again. But that will *never* happen, I will never have Chertkov in my house again. The old wounds are too painful and too deep, and they have broken my heart. It is impossible for me to forgive Chertkov for being so rude to me, and for suggesting to Lev Nikolaevich that I *spent my entire life murdering* him.

I did some work on the new edition but I could not concentrate; then I went out to pick mushrooms with Tanyushka. I wrote to Lyova and drafted a rough letter to Stolypin asking him to remove Chertkov from our neighbourhood, although I did not send it, as Stolypin has just left for Siberia. Sukhotin advises me not to send it at all; I shall talk it over with Lyova, and with Dm. A. Olsufiev, who arrived here today with Seryozha. Poor Tanya is exhausted by all her guests.

Tanechka's nurse has been a marvellous comfort to me. 'Pray to your guardian angel to soothe and calm your heart,' she said firmly, 'and everything will turn out for the best. You must take care of yourself,' she added.

We went to the village school, where the peasant children were performing *The Screw* by Chekhov, adapted from a short story of his;[89] it was stuffy and tedious.

August 19 I awoke very early and at the thought of Chertkov living there so close to Yasnaya all the old suffering started up all over again. But then my husband managed to console me. He came into my room before I got up and asked me how I had slept and how my health was; and he did not ask in his usual cold manner, but with genuine concern. Then he repeated his promise:

1) *Never to see Chertkov again,*
2) *To give his diaries to no one,*
3) *To let neither Chertkov nor Tapsel take his photograph*. This was at my

request. I found it most distasteful that his idol should photograph him in forests and gulleys like some old coquette, despotically dragging the old man here, there and everywhere merely so that he could build up a collection of photographs to add to his manuscripts.

'But I shall remain in correspondence with Chertkov,' he added, 'because that is essential for my work.'

I hope that this will indeed be a correspondence about *business*, rather than something else. But never mind, I am grateful to him for saying that.

I received a letter from Lyova, who writes that he will be tried in St Petersburg on September 13 for publishing his pamphlet *The Construction of Hell* in 1905. This is bad news. He will be leaving Yasnaya Polyana on the 10th.[90] When I asked Lev Nik. if we would be leaving here before then, he hastily replied that he didn't know, and could not possibly decide so far in advance. I can already foresee new anxieties; he is probably planning something, and of course he knows perfectly well what he wants to do, but his love of vagueness and his lifelong delight in tormenting me with it have now become a habit that he cannot give up.

I went with Tanya to pick mushrooms, of which there were masses, then I played with the children and cut out paper dolls for them. I cannot work, my heart is *physically* aching, and the blood keeps rushing to my head. L.N. and Chertkov between them have half killed me already – another two or three heart spasms like the one yesterday will finish me off. Or I shall have a nervous attack. That would be good! They will *certainly* torment me to death at this rate – I do not want to kill myself and yield Lev Nik. to Chertkov.

Things have turned out in such a strange and even absurd way. Chertkov said I was killing my husband, whereas in fact it is quite the opposite: L.N. and Chertkov have already half murdered me. Everyone is astonished by how thin I am and how altered my appearance is – not from illness, but from all the emotional suffering!

Lev N. went off for a ride with Dushan Petrovich; I was very worried about him, as he does not know this area. This evening I told D.A. Olsufiev about the whole sad business with Chertkov, and he advised me to wait before writing to Stolypin[91] about Chertkov's removal from the neighbourhood. Now is clearly not the time to do this, as he has only just been sent back. If Chertkov starts engaging in some sort of propaganda, and involves Lev Nik. in this too, or if Lev Nik. resumes his intimate relations with him, then it would be better if I were to talk to Stolypin about it in person. But all that is in the future. We must just live in the present.

Lev Nik. played vint for three hours non-stop today. How sad to see all these weaknesses appearing at his age, when the spiritual life should be taking precedence! But I try to close my eyes to all his failings; I must turn my heart away from him and seek elsewhere for the light, for I can no longer find it in the darkness that has enveloped our family.

August 20 Two bulky parcels were posted this afternoon addressed to Bulgakov – i.e. for Mr Chertkov.[92] Having given up all meetings with him for my sake, Lev Nikol. is now consoling his idol with all sorts of papers for his collection, and is sending these to him via Bulgakov. Lev Nik. took a long ride through the forest to Lomtsy today; this evening he played vint but was very sleepy.

Olsufiev and our son Seryozha left here this morning. I have been working hard on *Childhood* for the new edition. I am trying to be calm and to immerse myself in work, but I cannot quite do so; the merest mention of Chertkov (today it was his photograph) drives me into a frenzy, the blood rushes to my head and heart, and my soul is in despair. No, there will be no more joy in our house now; I shall either have to accept this or seek happiness in others! Abrikosov has come.

The photograph they took at Kochety this summer while I was not there showed everyone seated at the table, and Chertkov sitting *very, very* close to Lev Nikolaevich. How it made my blood boil again! I wrote to Maslova and Eliz . . .

August 21 Another night without sleep, more palpitations of the heart. I want to weep, I don't want to live. Why, *why*, did my eyes have to be opened to these things? And why do I so passionately crave my husband's love, affection and former trust? He has turned the key on his diaries and locked them away from me. If this was from *everyone*, well and good, but it is only *me* he is hiding them from! I was telling Abrikosov about it all today. 'God knows what they think about my jealousy of Lev N. and Chertkov,' I said. 'But I simply feel as though he has stolen my husband's *soul.*' 'It's quite true, he has,' said Mikhail Sergeevich. 'But now it's too late, his soul was stolen long ago; we have realised it all too late . . . ' So it is irreparable. I feel this too; I am to blame and shall have retribution, and shall ask for deliverance not from people but from God! This will probably come to pass only with my death . . . ! My heart is sick, very sick.

Today was hot and bright – summer is back again. I went for a walk in the forest with Tanya, Lyolya and the children, and I now feel very tired. Lev Nik. went out on his own. This afternoon he again played chess, and a lively game of vint. I was feeling very ill and spent most of the afternoon in bed. He came in to see me and was pleased that I was lying quietly in bed; I thought I detected a faint note of sympathy in his voice. How eagerly one grasps at these rare notes of kindness these days!

Lev Nikolaevich is exhausted by all the years he has spent renouncing worldly things, and now *il se ratrappe*,* enjoying all the worldly blessings he possibly can. At Yasnaya he won't have endless games of vint and a lot of simple, ordinary people to talk to; he is bored there and isn't in a hurry to return. I wrote to Katya, Andryusha and my sister Tanya.

*'He is catching up.'

Childhood is now ready for the printers. I re-read the chapter 'The Ivins' and was struck by the words: 'Seryozha made a great impression on me the moment I saw him. His unusual beauty astonished me and captivated me. I felt irresistibly attracted to him . . . ' And further on: 'Just the sight of him was enough to make me happy, and at one time the whole strength of my soul was focused on that desire. If by chance I did not see that lovely little face for three or four days I would fret and become sad and cry. All my dreams were of him . . . ' And so on.[93]

Night . . . I cannot sleep. I prayed and wept for a long time, and realised that what I am going through now must be the means by which I appeal to God and repent of my sins – maybe too it spells the return of *happiness* or inner peace . . .

August 22 My 66th birthday; I still have all my old energy and passion, the same acute sensitivity and, I am told, the same youthful appearance. But these past two months have aged me considerably and, God willing, have brought me closer to my end. I got up exhausted after a sleepless night and went for a walk round the park. It was utterly delightful: the old avenues of various trees, the wild flowers which had just come into bloom, the saffron milk-caps and other mushrooms, the silence, the solitude. Alone with God, I walked and prayed. I prayed for reconciliation, prayed that I might with God's help stop suffering so – I even prayed that He might return my husband's love to me before we died. And I believe that through my prayers and all the tears and faith I put into them, I shall recover his love.

Lyolya and the darling children came in to greet me this morning, and Lev Nik. came out twice while I was walking to ask how I was. (Propriety demands, after all, that one greet one's wife on her birthday.) I looked into his eyes, trying to glimpse a flicker of the old love and trust. Perhaps when I can return this love I shall be able to reconcile myself to Chertkov. But it's all so hard! Exactly the same thing will happen all over again.

Lev Nik. rode a long way off to see that eunuch who was here previously, and had earlier on visited Chertkov while Lev Nikolaevich was there. He played vint again this evening. I played at the other table with Lyolya Sukhotina, who had asked me to teach her the game. My eyes were exhausted after a whole day spent reading the proofs that had been sent to me, so playing cards was a rest for them.

The proofs were of the 'Tales of War'.[94] What beauty there was in the Sevastopol tales! I was in raptures – what a delight they were to read. Yes, he is an artist of genius, this husband of mine! If it weren't for Chertkov, hounding him to turn out pamphlets like 'The One Thing Necessary', Lev Tolstoy's writing over the past few years would have been quite different. I am feeling a little less agitated now, although my heart is aching and I live in constant fear of fresh attacks and spasms.

I cannot imagine how things will be resolved between us. After Lev Nik.'s birthday I shall go to Yasnaya, and then probably on to Moscow. And after that . . . ?

August 23 I had a calm day, but do not feel at all well. I cannot rid myself of my *idée fixe* – about Lev Nik.'s intimacy with Chertkov.

My heart is aching physically from all the emotional strain. God knows what thoughts are passing through my mind. The right side of my head is aching . . . My end is near. But it would be too painful for me to leave my husband – to Chertkov!

I received a letter and some articles from Biryukov for the new edition;[95] I should work, but I lack the energy and my mind is not fresh. Today I mentioned my departure, just to see how Lev Nikolaevich would respond. He seemed only too happy at the prospect, and his happiness made me terribly sad! I am sad to have to leave too.

I went for a walk and worked on *Childhood*; I am preoccupied with the problem of *how* to publish Volume I.[96] Lev Nik. also went for a walk on his own, wrote a letter to some revolutionary in Siberia,[97] and said he was feeling quite well. After he came back from his walk he called out to me through the open window, which filled my soul with the most absurd joy! Ah, if only he really did love me once more! I read to my darling little Tanyushka.

It is now 11 in the evening. L.N. plays cards every evening with great enthusiasm, and he is still playing.

August 24 Oh, the agony of these sleepless nights! Yesterday evening I prayed and wept for a long, long time. My most earnest prayer is for the evil spirit to be driven from our house and from my relations with my husband.

There are two infants in the Sukhotin household, and these little angels make life happy. At Yasnaya Polyana, however, even if Chertkov himself is not there, it will take a very long time for his phantom to disappear from its walls and my imagination, for I shall be haunted wherever I go by that huge, hateful figure, carrying that vast bag he always brings with him, in which he slyly and deliberately hides all Lev Nikolaevich's manuscripts.

I worked on the proofs of 'What Then Must We Do?'[98] and *Childhood* for the new edition. Tanya, Sasha and I called on a neighbour, Princess Golitsyna, a most agreeable, intelligent, resolute woman. Staying with her are her brother-in-law, her niece and a highly original old woman called Matsneva. She is about 80 years old, very lively and interested in everything – but she seems to be spiritually dead, and to have stopped meditating upon spiritual matters.

We spent a quiet evening sitting in our own rooms, with no chess or vint. Time flies, I don't feel like doing any practical work; I don't want to leave for Yasnaya and Moscow to work. I am tired!

August 25 This morning I had the unexpected joy of seeing Lev Nikolaevich at my door. I could not go to him at once, as I was washing, but I hastily flung a dressing gown over my wet shoulders and ran up to him. 'What is it, Lyovochka dear?' I asked. 'Nothing, I just came to ask how you slept and how you were feeling,' he said. I told him and he left. But a few moments later he was back again. 'I wanted to tell you that at midnight last night I kept thinking about you and wanted to come in and see you,' he said. 'I thought you might be lonely on your own at night, I wondered what you were doing – and I felt so sorry for you . . . ' At this the tears came into his eyes and he began to weep. I was overcome with joy, and this sustained me through the day, even though I have been feeling far from well, and my imminent departure for Yasnaya and Moscow fills me with alarm.

I spent the whole day working on *Resurrection* for the new edition. Some uncensored passages have to be deleted, some omitted passages have to be inserted – all very important and responsible work. Davydov and Seryozha have made some recommendations and have been a great help. But the actual work of *inserting* the passages is something only I can do.[99]

I enjoy myself with Tanyushka, take walks and grieve for my daughters' unjust attitude to me and their partiality for Chertkov. I had a long talk with Tanya yesterday evening, but we did not manage to change one another's minds. I have endured *too much* these past two months not to realise that there must be a reason for it. There has indeed been a good reason for it, and a terrible one too! But I pray continuously, and yesterday I wept hot, bitter tears as I prayed for my husband's heart to be returned to me. And what an astonishing coincidence! At precisely 12 o'clock that night, while I was on my knees in tears, appealing to God, my husband was thinking about me with compassion in his heart! How could one not believe in prayer after that? No, the power of sincere, *passionate* prayer, the prayer for heartfelt love, can never be in vain, for there is no doubting it!

I wrote to Vanya Erdeli and my grandson Seryozha.

August 26 Although I have partly regained my self-control and try to be wise and spiritually independent of other people, and piously to preserve that prayerful mood, there are none the less times when I forget myself and am tormented with anxiety.

My conversation with Tanya last night cleared up a great many things for me. She, Sasha and Lev Nikolaevich all have a business correspondence with Chertkov. They are so terrified that I shall read something they write (although I have never had this vile habit of hiding letters), that in Yasnaya their letters are passed on to Chertkov only by people who are close to them, and here they either put them in the mail bag at the last moment and carefully close it up, or write to him via Goldenweiser or Bulgakov.

L.N. is also careful to lock away his diary so I cannot see it; but when he is at home there is always the possibility that his diary will fall into my hands in one way or another. Now, however, it is not in his diary that he is weaving this web of treacherous and cruel slanders against me (under the guise of 'Christian reconciliation', of course), but in his correspondence with Mr Chertkov. It was this thought that kept me awake all last night. L.N. has assumed the role of Christ, and has assigned to Chertkov the role of His beloved apostle. I have not read any of L.N.'s letters to Chertkov, or from Chertkov to him, but I can deduce everything written in them from the way he refers to me: 'S.A. (Sofia Andreevna) is very pathetic, I try to stand my ground and remember the role I have been called on to fulfil . . . More than ever before I realise how spiritually close to you I am . . . I think of you constantly, I should like to see you . . . but this is not necessary if we know that our souls are in communion and that we both serve the Father . . . I pray God for patience, I kiss you . . . ' and other tender words of this pharisaical nature, in which, with the genius of a writer, he laments the suffering he has to endure from his wicked wife. And this correspondence between him and Chertkov, based entirely on that theme, will be carefully preserved for future generations to read . . .

God knows how I try to cultivate the wisdom to help me withstand my husband's hatred for me and his love for Chertkov, and to instil in me a calm indifference to all these subterfuges which have been laid, for earthly incentives, by my family (my daughters), my husband and that 'evil Pharisee', as N.N. Gué calls Chertkov. But sometimes I feel so sad.

Whatever I may have done, no one could possibly have given my husband more than I have. I have loved him passionately, selflessly, honestly and considerately, I have surrounded him with care, I have guarded him, I have helped him as best I could, I have not betrayed him with so much as a word or a gesture – what more can a woman give than this most intense love? I am 16 years younger than my husband, and have always looked 10 years younger than my age, but I have given my passion, love, health and energy to him and to no one else. I now realise that my husband's sacred philosophy of life is only in books; he needs a comfortable, settled existence for his work, and has lived all his life in these conditions – as though it were for *my* sake! God be with him, and Lord help me! Help people to discover the *truth* and see through this Phariseeism! For whatever they may plot against me, Lev N.'s love for me pervades everything he does, and everyone must ask themselves: if two people live together and love one another for 48 years, must there not have been *some reason* for this love?

Now they all treat me as though I were *ab*normal, hysterical and even mad, and so everything I do is attributed to my morbid condition. But other people, and the Lord above, will judge for themselves.

Evening I spent the rest of the day patiently, although not entirely calmly. I did a lot of work on *Resurrection* for the new edition. I do not like this work; it contains a lot of hypocrisy and covert hatred of people. I told the children a story I had made up, then read to them; I wandered about the park, praying as I went, and spent the evening playing vint with Lev Nik. and the Sukhotin brothers. Lev Nik. pretended that he was not averse to playing with me, but I know he would have preferred to play with his daughters. Why must I be continually spurned like this, why must I spend my whole life fretting and yielding to others? I have lived such a self-sacrificing life, and now look what I have come to! I've had enough!

Lev Nikol. drove in the trap with Mikhail Sergeevich today to Trekhanetovo, where there is a large apple orchard, and returned on foot. He corrected the proofs of the kopeck booklets which Gorbunov sent him, and spent the evening chatting to a peasant from Saratov.[100] He complained of feeling weak, but this hot, heavy, stuffy air is having a bad effect on everyone's health, and none of us has any energy.

We live for today, no one knows what tomorrow will bring. I wrote to Vanechka Erdeli and N.B. Nordman about Chertkov.

August 27, morning My jealousy for Chertkov is a living wound! Why did it please God to open my eyes to these things?!

I again woke up sobbing this morning from an agonising dream – I was awakened by my own sobs!

I dreamt Lev Nik. was sitting there wearing a new fur jacket with a hood at the back, and a tall sheepskin hat, and he had such an unpleasant, aggressive look on his face. 'Where are you going?' I asked. 'To see Chertkov and Goldenweiser,' he said in an offhand manner. 'I have to look through an article with them and clear up a few things.'

I was in despair that Lev Nik. should have broken his promise, and I burst into agonising sobs which woke me up. And now I can hardly write, my heart and hand are trembling so.

Evening I took a walk on my own in a state of great agitation, praying and weeping as I went. I am terrified of the future. Lev Nik. has promised never to see Chertkov, to have his photograph taken at his bidding or to give him his diaries. But he now has a new excuse which he uses whenever he wants and whenever it suits him. He merely says, 'I forgot', or 'I never said that', or 'I take back my promise'. So that one is now afraid to believe a word he says.

I have done a lot of work on the proofs. I have been correcting *On Art*, 'On the Census' and *Resurrection*.[101] Mine is a hard task! I have such a terrible headache – and oh, the depression, the depression!

When I said goodnight to Lev Nik. I told him everything that was on my mind: I told him that I knew he was writing letters to Chertkov addressed to Bulgakov, Goldenweiser and all the other spies, I said I hoped he would not go back on his promises behind my back, and I asked him whether he wrote to Chertkov every day. He told me he had written to him twice, once in a note he had added to a letter of Sasha's and once on his own. That is still two letters since August 14.[102]

August 28 Lev Nikolaevich's 82nd birthday. A marvellous, bright summer day. I got up feeling very anxious after another sleepless night, and felt even more so after going in to greet him. I wished him a long life, without secrets, tricks or plots – and said I hoped he would soon be completely *at peace with himself*, now that he is reaching the end of his life.

At this he pulled an angry face: the poor man is possessed – he considers that he and Chertkov have already reached the pinnacle of spiritual perfection. Poor, blind, proud man! How much more spiritually exalted he was a few years ago! How sincerely he aspired to live simply, to sacrifice all luxuries, and to be good, honest, open and spiritually pure! Now he enjoys himself quite openly, loves good food, a good horse, cards, music, chess, cheerful company and having hundreds of photographs taken of himself.

He is kind to people only if they flatter him, look after him and indulge his weaknesses. All his old responsiveness has gone. Is it merely his age?

Varya Nagornova and my daughter-in-law Masha have arrived, and I was delighted to see them. But I feel that everyone now regards me as sick, if not mad, which means they all keep their distance from me. And that is very hard!

If only I knew what terrible *crime* I had committed against my family, I should try to mend my ways.

Chertkov abuses me, my husband no longer loves me, everyone hides everything from me and they all criticise me – but how am I supposed to start mending my ways? Grow fond of Chertkov all of a sudden? It's unthinkable! The injury he has done me hurts and torments me continuously!

Lev Nik. said today that the Christian ideal was celibacy and total chastity. I retorted that the two sexes were created by God, that was His will, so why did one have to go against Him and the laws of nature. L.N. said that besides being an animal man also had reason, and this reason must be inspired and must not be preoccupied about the perpetuation of the human race; for that is what distinguished us from the animals. All well and good, if L.N. was a monk and an ascetic and lived a celibate life. But meanwhile at my husband's wishes I have conceived 16 times by him, 13 living babies and 3 stillborn.

I now stand before him after 48 years of marriage and feel as though *I* were to blame for all his demands on me – as though he were now prepared to hate me for *this*, to renounce everything he has lived for and instead form the sort of 'spiritual union' which involves Mr Chertkov in removing all his papers, taking hundreds of photographs of him and whispering endless secrets to him.

Evening I feel more and more crushed by the problems of my life. *How* will it all be resolved? God knows, and He alone can help. This is what happened: we all went this evening to watch the children having their bath, and when we got back I sat down with my knitting and thought a while. Then I spoke to Lev Nik. He had talked about total chastity as the ideal, I said, but if this ideal was really and truly achieved there would be no children at all, and without children there would be no heavenly kingdom on earth. For some reason this made him absolutely furious, and he started shouting at me. (Mikhail Sergeevich later told me that he was just about to lose his third game of chess to him.) L.N. said that an ideal meant the *desire* to achieve it. I said: but if you reject the ultimate aim, i.e. having children, that desire makes no sense at all. What is the point of it? 'You don't even try to understand! You won't listen!' he shouted in a rage.[103]

I with my sick soul could not sit there calmly and be spoken to in that tone of voice, and bursting into tears I went off to my room. After he had finished his game of chess he came in to see me and said: 'Why are you so upset?' What was there to explain? I said that he never spoke to me, but whenever he did he was invariably unfair and spiteful and lost his temper. The conversation gradually turned acrimonious – I became bitter and Lev Nikolaevich became extremely angry. All the old reproaches were brought up: to my sick entreaty as to *how* we might be better friends, he pointed furiously to the table where the proofs lay and said: 'Give away the copyright, give away the land, live in a hut!' 'All right,' I said, 'just so long as we can live without outside people and influences; we'll live alone with the peasants, just the two of us . . . ' But the moment I agreed with him he rushed to the door and said in a desperate voice: 'Oh, my God, let me go, I'm leaving . . . ' and so on. 'How can one be happy if one hates half the human race as you do . . . ,' he said. Then he gave himself away. 'No, I was wrong when I said half the human race.' 'So whom do I hate?' I asked. 'You hate *Chertkov and me*,' he said. 'Yes, Chertkov I hate, but I cannot and will not link your name with his.' And it pierced my heart again, his insane love for his idol, whom he simply cannot tear himself away from, this Mr Chertkov, who represents half of humanity for him. I grew even more firmly resolved never on any account to let him into the house or see him again, and to do everything I possibly could to ensure that L.N. broke with him; and if that cannot be done, then Chertkov will have to be killed, come what may. What does it matter now anyway, if life is such hell?

Varenka understood everything, but Masha has a very limited view of things and fortunately for her there is a lot she simply does not know about or understand. It would be good to open her eyes to Lev Nik.'s love for Chertkov. Perhaps she would understand my sufferings and where they come from if I read her the page glued to the end of this notebook.[104]

Live in a hut! When he was out walking today, L.N. gave apples to all the village children, this evening he spent two hours or more playing chess, and another two hours playing vint. He soon grows bored without all these entertainments, and all this talk about a hut, and living in a hut, is merely an excuse to rage at me, so that with his usual writer's skill, he can describe his disagreements with his wife in such a way as to present himself in the role of a martyr and a saint.

No wonder that legend about Xantippe exists: stupid people will ascribe that role to me, but intelligent people will investigate more closely and will understand.

I want to leave here, if only for a short while, just to be alone for a bit and escape this persecution. My room is constantly filled with people and noise, and everyone thinks badly of me for *daring* to suffer so in soul and body.

August 29 Lev N.'s anger yesterday affected me so badly that I did not sleep a wink; I prayed and cried all night, and first thing this morning I went out to wander about the park and the wood. Then I called on a dear young nurse called Anna Ivanovna, and she and her sweet sympathetic mother comforted me. L.N. had been searching everywhere for me. I went in to see him when I got back and he reiterated his promises: 1) Not to see Chertkov, 2) Not to give him his diaries, and 3) Not to let him take his photograph. But once again he made the stipulation – he wanted a quiet life. It was he who had lost his temper and shouted, but of course once again it was all *my* fault. He will seize on any opportunity he can to see Chertkov, and will deliberately upset me and break his promise. This is what terrifies me so. But in that case I shall *definitely* leave. It is unthinkable that I could ever go through all this suffering again.

I received a telegram from Lyova saying that his trial had been fixed for September the 3rd, not the 13th, and that he was leaving on August 31. I was glad of the excuse to leave, and I badly wanted to see my son, say goodbye to him and give him some encouragement. So Sasha and I travelled to Oryol on the Blagodatnaya line, and from there we went on to Yasnaya. L.N. and I bade each other a tender and loving farewell, and we both cried and asked one another's forgiveness. But the tears and the farewell were like the end of our former happiness and love; as though our love, like a beloved child, was reawakened and then buried for ever, injured, killed and killing us both with grief. For now it has disappeared and has been transferred to another. My Lyovochka and I mourned its death in each other's arms, kissing one another and weeping, but knowing that it was irrevocable! He *could not* stop loving Chertkov, and this tormented him too!

I was sleepy and exhausted on the train – I felt shattered. It was terribly cold, only 2 degrees, and Sasha and I were shivering and yawning all the way. We arrived home at five in the morning.

August 30 I am home now – it is so good to be back, much better than being away. It was a fresh, bright, sunny day, and I went for a walk with my son Lyova and my daughter-in-law Katya. Bulgakov, Bulygin and Maria Aleksandrovna were here when we got back, and I told Bulygin in great agitation the whole sad story about Chertkov. It seemed as though he understood everything but did not want to admit it. I wandered around the house and went into Lev Nikolaevich's rooms, and everything looked so different, as though something had been buried for good. And now things will indeed be quite different from the way they were before. But *what* will happen? I do not know and cannot imagine.

Sasha and Varvara Mikhailovna went to see Chertkov. They say he is very cheerful and lively. I can just imagine his idiotic laugh. How loathsome!

The September issue of the New York magazine *The World's Work* has arrived containing a very flattering article about me and some biographical information about Lev Nik. Amongst other things, they say that I have been Lev N.'s 'confident and counseller [*sic*]'* throughout my life, that I have given him 'the strength of her body, mend [*sic*] and spirit',* and many other things, all very flattering to me.[105] No wonder I feel so crushed, now that this role of 'confident and counseller' has been taken from me and given to Chertkov! No wonder I am so thin and weep all the time!

The moulders cast Lyova's busts today, and it is plain to see that they are extremely good and very talented.[106] M.I. Agafin is an old acquaintance, and had previously cast Lev N.'s busts and various others.

I reluctantly attended to some housekeeping, some papers and some business, sent for the painters and the shoemaker and clarified various matters – but my head is not fresh and I cannot make sense of anything.

August 31 I received letters from Tanya and Lev Nikolaevich. At first I was delighted, then I wept. 'How good it would be for you, and for me, if you could just *control yourself*,' writes my husband.[107] He has one aim and one wish, and that is for me to 'control' my feelings and accept his intimacy with Chertkov. But for me this is out of the question.

It is a bright and beautiful day, but cold and sad, for I have just seen Lyova off to St Petersburg for his trial. I went for a walk with Katya and Varvara Mikhailovna, but felt too tired to go on, and my stomach and legs were aching. This afternoon I worked hard on the proofs, and before that I copied out some letters. I am so dreadfully tired! What a great load of different tasks I have! I sleep very little and eat almost nothing.

September 1 Katerina Vasilevna and her little daughter left this morning, and I miss them. Bulgakov and Maria Aleksandrovna were here for lunch, as well as Liza Rizkina (née Zinger) with her two boys. She is well educated and is no fool, but I find her erudition and her materialism

*In English in the original.

rather alien. Nadya Ivanovna came this evening. I did not go for a walk today; I did not want to wash with my tears and darken with my sorrow my favourite haunts at Yasnaya, where for most of my life I have darted about with a light step and a light heart, conscious of nothing but the beauties of nature and my own joy! And now too it is all extraordinarily beautiful, and the days are clear and brilliant, but my soul is sad, so sad!

I did a lot of work on the proofs[108] and various other things connected with the edition, and I gave some orders around the estate. But nothing is going well; I was intending to go to Moscow, but I have no energy and have not prepared anything, and it all seems so futile and unimportant.

There was an unpleasant scene with that coarse Sasha. She came into the drawing-room as I was telling Maria Aleksandrovna how L.N., at Chertkov's insistence, had forced all of us – Davydov, Salomon, me and various others – to go out to the gulley in search of Chertkov's watch, which he had lost there when they had got off their horses for some reason and Chertkov had taken Lev Nikolaevich's photograph; and I told her how ashamed and embarrassed and annoyed we had felt at Lev Nik.'s humiliation and our humiliation on his account.

I was just coming to the end of the story when Sasha came in for tea, but she immediately started screaming at me for talking about Chertkov again. I was unfortunately infected by her bad temper and lost mine, and we had a most distressing altercation, which I now very much regret. But do I really have to ask my daughter's permission as to what I may and may not talk about with my friends? So the day ended badly, and I am now feeling even iller and sadder. I wrote to my husband.[109]

September 2 I worked all day on *Resurrection* for the new edition. Today I sent for the priest, who performed a service with holy water.[110] The prayers were lovely, apart from the last one: 'Victory to the Lord our emperor,' and so on. After all those prayers about the softening of hearts and the deliverance from griefs and troubles, it seemed utterly inappropriate to pray for victory, i.e. the murder of people.

Nikolaev came this evening and told me heatedly what a worthless person Chertkov was, and urged me not to lower myself to his level, or to say that he had taken my place beside Lev Nik. 'It is simply that Chertkov has made extremely efficient arrangements for copying out Lev Nik.'s writings, and Lev Nik. is grateful to him for this,' he said. Both he and Maria Aleksandrovna Schmidt evidently dislike Chertkov heartily.

In Lev Nik.'s room I managed to find Chertkov's letter to the Tsar begging to be allowed to return to Telyatinki; it is a truly pharisaical letter, but what struck me most about it was his desire to be close to Lev Nikolaevich.[111] What has happened, though, is that the Tsar allowed him to return, but now Tolstoy's *wife* has driven him away. '*Femme veut, Dieu* *le veut.*'* He must be furious with me! And I am delighted!

Still the same enchanting weather – bright days, cool nights and a dazzling variety of greens on the leaves, bushes and trees. The potatoes are being dug now, the painters are finishing work on the roofs and the outhouses, the earth is being removed from the hothouses, and here and there in the woods there are still a few mushrooms.

I feel much calmer and happier after attending the service and staying at home all day. I chatted to the priest and he was horrified, as is everyone, by Chertkov's coarse behaviour. But enough of him – I shall draw a veil over that man and his vileness.

September 3 I marvel at the beauty of nature and the dazzling autumn days, yet I am still sad! I received a kind letter from my husband.[112] and now feel so happy that I long to merge my life with his once again, as in the old days, and forget all the anger and disagreements. But a letter is not *life*! I wrote to him too, a nice enough letter I think, which Sasha took with her when she left today for Kochety. I shall go there myself the day after tomorrow. It is as God wills, but I should dearly love to return home with Lyovochka on Wednesday. Work on the new edition has come to a complete halt. I must go on with it; it is a duty both to my own conscience and to the public who read and love Tolstoy.

Nikolaeva came this evening. Her life is not an easy one either, with a *principled* husband (who is none the less a very good man), *five* children and no servants.

September 4 I am becoming increasingly impatient to see my husband, and shall go to Kochety tomorrow without fail. Today I went for a walk on my own, feeling sad at heart; I received a sweet letter from Lyova saying that his trial would be on the 13th. I worked on *Resurrection* with Varvara Mikhailovna, and took a stroll round the estate. It is warm, with a light breeze and little clouds in the sky, with wild flowers everywhere and the most marvellous garden flowers, and such bright coloured leaves – how good it all is! But how sad to be alone! I do not like solitude, I like people and movement and life . . . That is why it is better at the Sukhotins', where there are a lot of people and life is so much simpler, without endless ideas and renunciations. Lev Nik. is more cheerful there too; he plays chess for a couple of hours after dinner with Sukhotin or the local doctor, then takes a walk, reads letters, goes into the dining-room, asks where everyone is and for the table to be laid as soon as possible. Then he plays a game of vint, and that goes on in the most lively fashion for about three hours, until 11.30 p.m. He does not have to strike any attitudes, since none are expected of him; there are no petitioners, no beggars, no responsibilities – he just lives, writes, plays, talks, sleeps, eats and drinks . . .

*'What woman wants God wants.'

I am very much afraid that he will miss all this in Yasnaya Polyana. I shall try to make sure that there are more people here. But we have managed to drive everyone away from our house, and now I have driven away Chertkov and Co.

September 5 (Kochety) I am writing this later, as I did not write my diary yesterday. I left for Kochety early on the morning of the 5th, travelling via Mtsensk. Deep in my heart I hoped that Lev Nik. would return to Yasnaya with me, as I am tied to this essential work on the new edition and must stay close to Moscow, where I have all the books and materials to hand.

I travelled the 35 *versts* from Mtsensk in a strong wind and driving rain, and the muddy road, the ferry crossing and the agitation left me completely exhausted.

I had a cold reception in Kochety from both my husband and my daughter. Lev Nik. realised that I wanted him to come home and he had no desire to leave his cheerful life in Kochety, with all the card games and the company. He had just ridden over to visit the *skopets*, 16 miles there and back, and in this appalling weather!

But then how warmly I was met by the two little five-year-olds, my granddaughter Tanechka and her little friend Mikushka Sukhotin!

September 6 Lev Nik.'s big toe is red and swollen after yesterday's ride, and he keeps saying: 'This is senile gangrene and I shall surely die.' He felt ill all day, stayed in bed until evening and would not eat a thing.

Drankov has arrived and this evening he gave us a cinematographic presentation. Lev Nik. got up and watched too, although he was very tired. They showed Yasnaya in winter, amongst other things, with all of us standing there. Drankov made me a present of the film, which I am giving to the Historical Museum in Moscow to keep.[113]

September 7 Lev Nik. is much better, had dinner with the rest of us and played a game of chess. Afterwards we all went to watch the cinematograph, which was being shown to the whole village. Then Zosya Stakhovich, who had just arrived, read us all the preface to the works of Bordeaux, called *Peur de la mort*.[114]

Relations are strained. We all cling jealously to Lev Nik., while he merely decides where he wants to stay, completely ignoring my desperate, passionate wish that he return to Yasnaya with me.

September 8 I felt so much calmer when I arrived in Kochety, but now it has all started up again. I did not sleep all night and got up early. Drankov filmed us all again for the cinematograph, then filmed a village wedding which they had put on specially for his benefit.

When I eventually plucked up the courage to ask Lev Nik. when he was returning home, he grew furious, shouting angrily about his 'freedom', waving his hands around and making the most unattractive gestures. Then to cap it all he said he regretted his promise to me never to see Chertkov.

I realised that this regret expressed everything. He is avenging himself on me for his promise, and he will stubbornly continue to do so for a long time to come. My crime this time was merely that I asked L.N. for an *approximate* date as to when he would be returning home.

I had no dinner, of course, and lay in bed sobbing all day; I eventually decided to leave, so as not to foist myself on the Sukhotins in this wretched state.

But when I thought how pitilessly and deliberately Lev Nik. had exacerbated my nervous illness and hastened my fast-approaching death, I was plunged into despair. I wanted only to take my heart and my love away from my husband so as not to suffer so.

I received a letter from Chertkov – a lying pharisaical letter in which he asked for a reconciliation with the evident desire that I should let him into the house again.[115]

September 9 I wept and sobbed all day; I ache all over, my head, my heart and my stomach hurt, and my soul is torn apart by suffering![116] Lev Nik. did *try* to be a little kinder to me, but his egoism and malevolence won't let him concede to me in anything – *not for anything* will he tell me if he is planning to return to Yasnaya, and if so, when.[117]

I wrote a letter to Chertkov, but I have not posted it yet.[118] This man is the cause of all my sufferings, and I cannot reconcile myself to him.

September 10 I stayed in bed all morning, then took a long walk round the garden. Lev Nik. flew into a rage with me again today, and said: 'I shall never give in to you on anything ever again! I bitterly regret my promise never to see Chertkov, it was a terrible mistake!'

His shouting and anger crushed me once and for all, and I lay down on the sofa in his room in a state of helpless despair. Meanwhile he sat at his desk and started writing something. Then he got up, and taking both my hands in his, he stared at me, smiled so sweetly, then suddenly burst into tears. 'Thank God!' I said to myself. 'He still has a glimmer of love for me in his soul!'

In the middle of the day I called on the mother of Putilina the nurse, a dear, pious old woman. She comforted me and advised me to trust in God's charity and pray – which I do without cease, night and day.

September 11 I keep waiting for something to happen, my head is heavy, my heart and stomach ache. I forced myself to take a walk with Tanya and the children and grew terribly tired. I cannot eat a thing. After dinner Lev

Nik. made a great effort and asked me to join in their game of cards. I sat down and played with them for a while, but my head was spinning and I eventually had to lie down. I have decided to leave tomorrow. Despite feeling so ill and unhappy, I have been reading proofs and booklets for the new edition all this time.

September 12 I felt terribly agitated again this morning; I wept bitter tears of anguish and despair, and my head felt as though it were about to fall off. Then I took myself in hand and did some proofs. I avoided meeting Lev Nik. all day. His stubborn refusal to tell me *approximately* when he might be leaving has made me feel quite desperate. His heart has turned to stone! By the time I left I had suffered so deeply from his coldness, and was sobbing so wildly, that the servant who was seeing me off started crying too. I did not even look at my husband, my daughter and the others. But then Lev Nik. suddenly came round to the other side of the trap, and said to me with tears in his eyes: 'Well give me another kiss then, and I'll be back very, very soon . . . ' But he did not keep his promise, and stayed another ten days in Kochety.* I sobbed all the way home. Tanya, Tanechka and Mika got in beside me and travelled part of the way with me.

I reached Yasnaya that night and was met by Varvara Mikhailovna and Bulgakov. How terribly empty and lonely the house seemed! Just before I left I had written Lev Nik. a letter which Sukhotin had given him. It was filled with tenderness and suffering[119] – but it's impossible to break the ice in Lev Nik.'s heart. (I copied this letter into the notebook which contains all my letters to my husband.)

Lev Nik. wrote a brief, cold reply,[120] and we did not write to one another for ten days, something which has never happened in all the 48 years of our marriage.†

Tired and exhausted, I was simply reeling by the time I arrived home. But I am still alive – it's as though nothing can destroy me. But I am growing so thin, and I feel that these troubles are hastening my death. And thank God for that!

September 13 I have been working hard on the proofs, and have tried to be calm and to remind myself of Lev Nik.'s words: 'I'll be back very, very soon.' For this has been my only consolation. Annenkova and Klechkovskii came to visit me.

It is so hard to talk to anyone, for they all consider me abnormal and think I am being unjust to my husband. But I only write true facts in my diary. People can draw their own conclusions from them. I am tormented by life and material concerns.

*This sentence added later.

†This sentence added later.

September 14 Natalya Alekseevna Almedingen came to collect Lyova's bust of me. She is a lively and highly intelligent woman, and my loneliness and depression made me tell her the whole story about Chertkov.

I learnt that Lyova's trial for publishing his pamphlet, *The Construction of Hell*, in 1905, has been postponed until September 20.

September 15 Yet another depressing day. No letters, no news, I went for a walk on my own, picked flowers, wept – silence, solitude! None the less I have been working hard on the proofs.

September 16 The same.

September 17 My dream that my husband would return for my name-day has been dashed; he has not even written, nor have any of the rest of them from Kochety – apart from my dear granddaughter Tanechka, who sent me a greetings card. The others just sent me a lifeless collective telegram![121]

My name-day was the day when Lev Nik. proposed to me. What did he do to that eighteen-year-old Sonechka Behrs, who gave him her whole life, her love and her trust? He has been torturing me with his coldness, his cruelty and his extreme egotism.

I went to Taptykovo with Varvara Mikhailovna. Olga (my son Andryusha's first wife) and her children, Ilyushok and my granddaughter and name-sake Sofia Andreevna, were very sweet to me, and I would have enjoyed my name-day were it not for this weight on my heart.

September 18 I returned to Yasnaya this morning. I have been crying continuously all day, and am unbearably unhappy. I received a great many letters of greeting, but not one from my husband or children. This empty house is unspeakably depressing! I read proofs and strained my eyes from concentration and tears. At times I am overcome by anger at that man who has so calmly persecuted me for hating his idol, Chertkov.

September 19 (Moscow) I corrected proofs, packed my suitcase and left this afternoon for Moscow on business. In Tula I met my son Seryozha, to my great joy, and he said his wife and sons were travelling to Moscow in the same train carriage, which was very pleasant for me.

September 21 I was preoccupied with business in Moscow on the 20th and 21st. I also paid a visit to Taneev's old nurse to find out how he was. He was still in the country. I should love to see him and hear him play. This good, calm man was such a help to me after Vanechka's death, and gave me such spiritual consolation.

But this is not possible now; I no longer love him as I did, we do not see one another any more for some reason, and I have done nothing at all for a very long time to bring this about. I heard about the Maslovs too.

September 22 I arrived back in Yasnaya this morning. It is a bright frosty day, and my soul is a hell of grief and despair. I went round the garden, wept myself senseless, and now have a terrible headache. Yet I am still alive, walking, breathing and eating – although I cannot sleep. The frost has withered the flowers, like my life. It all looks so desolate now, and my soul is desolate too. Will the spark of joy and happiness be rekindled in our lives?

I do not think it will ever happen as long as Chertkov is living here!

Not a word from Lev Nik.[122] He could not give me one day of his epicurean life at the Sukhotins', with his daily games of chess and vint, and I was already waiting for him without quite as much love as before. So that when he, Sasha and the doctor all arrived here tonight I met him with reproaches instead of joy, burst into tears, then went off to my room so as to let him rest after the journey.

September 23 Our wedding anniversary. I stayed in my room for a long time this morning, weeping on my own. I wanted to go in to my husband, but opening the door to his room I heard him dictating something to Bulgakov, and I went off to wander about Yasnaya Polyana, recalling the happy times – what few of them there were – of my 48-year marriage.

I then asked Lev Nik. if we could have our photograph taken together. He agreed, but the photograph did not come out, as Bulgakov is inexperienced and did not know how to do it.

L.N. was a little nicer to me this evening, and I felt easier in my mind. It was a comfort to feel that I really had found my 'other half' again.

September 24 Lev Nikol.'s kindness to me did not last long, and he shouted at me again today. The Dieterichs' former French governess had told me in Taptykovo that they had read a tale by L.N. called 'Childhood Wisdom' at the Chertkovs',[123] so I asked him to let me read it too. When it transpired that there wasn't a copy of it in the house, even in Lev Nik.'s personal possession, I was annoyed and aggrieved, and said that of course Chertkov had been in a hurry to take the manuscript, since he was nothing but a *collector*. This made Lev Nikol. frightfully angry and he shouted at me so that I started crying inconsolably. I went off to the fir plantation, where I sawed some branches, then I developed some photographs and read some proofs, and saw almost nothing of my husband for the rest of the day.

September 25 I am so happy that my husband is actually *here* with me, and I am beginning to feel calmer. But his soul is so distant! I love him more than he loves me.

He is reading Malinovskii's *Blood Revenge*[124] with great interest at the moment; he went for a ride today.

September 26 We had a peaceful happy morning. Sasha and Varvara Mikhailovna went off to Taptykovo to see Olga, Maria Aleksandrovna stayed the night with us, and I developed some photographs. As I was passing Lev N.'s study today I saw that Chertkov's portrait, which I had removed to the far wall while L.N. was away, and replaced with a portrait of his father, was again hanging in its former place above the armchair in which L.N. always sits.

I could not bear seeing that hateful man's face hanging above Lev Nik. every morning when I went in to see him.

The fact that he had put it back drove me to despair – he can't bear to part with it now that he is not seeing Chertkov every day – so I took it down, tore it into little pieces and threw it down the lavatory. Lev Nik. was furious of course, and quite rightly accused me of denying him his freedom. He is possessed by the idea at present, although never in his life has he bothered about it before – he never even gave it a thought. What did he need his 'freedom' for when we always loved one another and tried to make one another happy?

Once again I was reduced to utter despair, and consumed with burning jealousy for Chertkov; I wept myself into a state of exhaustion, my head was aching, I considered suicide, and thought I should remove myself from Lev Nik.'s life and give him his longed-for freedom. I went to my room, found a toy pistol and tried to fire it, thinking that I would buy myself a real one. I fired it a second time when Lev Nik. returned from his ride, but he didn't hear.

Maria Aleksandrovna, thinking that I was planning to shoot myself in earnest, without finding out what was really happening, wrote to Sasha in Taptykovo begging her to come home, as her mother had shot herself – or some such story.

I knew nothing about all this until that night, when I heard a carriage approaching the house and someone knocking at the door. It was very dark and I could not imagine who it might be. I went downstairs and to my amazement I saw Sasha and Varvara Mikhailovna standing there. 'What has happened?' I asked. And all of a sudden two voices were showering me with such angry words and foul names that for a while I was simply stunned. Then I went upstairs, followed by Sasha and Varvara Mikhailovna, still shouting at me. Eventually I lost my temper with them and became terribly angry. What had I ever done to those two? Why was I to blame?

Unfortunately I started shouting too – I said that I would throw them both out of the house tomorrow, and dismiss Varvara Mikhailovna, who merely lived off us and licked Sasha's boots. Maria Aleksandrovna, realising her mistake, began to cry and begged the two loudmouths to leave her room.

But those shrews were not in any hurry to calm down, and the next morning they packed their things, took a couple of horses, the dogs and the parrot, and set off for Sasha's house at Telyatinki. It is they who are in the wrong; they lost their tempers and acted disgracefully.

September 27 We old people are all on our own here now. Lev Nik. went for a ride along the highway on his own, and I followed him in the cabriolet. Looking behind him every so often, he kept riding farther and farther ahead, evidently assuming that I would soon feel cold (for I was thinly dressed) and turn back for home. But I did not; even though I was chilled through and later caught a bad cold, I returned with him, by which time we had covered 15 miles. He slept until 7.30 and we had dinner at 8.

This evening Lev Nik. played chess with Khiryakov. He is listless and sleepy and has a stomach-ache; evidently the ride in the cold affected him badly.

Despite all the unpleasantness I did a lot of work on the new edition and the proofs.

September 28 I work on in solitude with this heavy weight on my heart. Not only do they not help me to recover, they do all they can to make me worse! Even chance is against me! Lev Nik. rode over to Ovsyannikovo to see Maria Aleksandrovna and met Chertkov, who was going to visit Olga in Taptykovo. My heart ached to think of their joy at seeing one another. But Lev Nik. did not get off his horse, they did not talk for long, and there was no *aparté* as Dima and Rostovtsev were there too. L.N. has eaten very little all day. He has a slight cough and has started a cold. Of course yesterday's ride is now taking its toll, and it was a long ride over to Ovsyannikovo too, and very cold. These trips of his to Ovsyannikovo never pass without consequence.

September 29 Relations with Lev Nik. are calm and friendly, and I am happy! I sat with him after he had had his lunch today, and I ate something too – pancakes with curd cheese, I think. It was wonderful to see the joy on his face when after asking who the pancakes were for I said, 'For myself.' 'Ah, how glad I am that you are eating again at last!' he said. Then he brought me a pear and tenderly begged me to eat it without fail. When other people are not here he is generally kind and affectionate to me, just as he used to be, and I feel he is *mine* again. But he has not been very cheerful lately, and this worries me. I have been very active all day: I sawed some dry branches off the young fir trees, then drove to Kolpna to buy rye and flour. A lovely bright frosty autumn day.

September 30 Lev Nik. has had bad heartburn all day. This is always a bad sign, and I feel particularly anxious, as he has been in such low spirits recently. Sasha's departure was a new and unexpected blow for him. Is she really so thick-skinned that she doesn't mind making her old father unhappy by running away from home? Despite his physical weakness Lev Nik. went for a long ride with stupid Dushan through the forests and gulleys. I say 'stupid' because the other doctors insist that he take care of L.N. and make sure he doesn't do anything rash, and there is a freezing wind again, although it is sunny. I have a cold and my soul is low. I glued newspaper cuttings into the scrapbook, sorted out magazines and made various arrangements for the estate and the new edition, but I have neither the health, the energy nor my former capacity for work. I shall soon die.

October 1 Goldenweiser came this morning, and played chess with Lev N. this afternoon. Sasha arrived too, and took Goldenweiser back to the Chertkovs. I was going to suggest that L.N. went there too, but the moment it occurred to me and I mentioned the idea to my husband I started choking back the tears and shaking with agitation; the blood rushed to my head and I felt as though I were being flayed alive – especially when I saw the joy on Lev N.'s face at the prospect of seeing Chertkov again. I felt utterly desperate, and went off to my room to cry. But my dear husband did not visit Chertkov, bless him, and instead took another ride through the wood and gulleys, and exhausted himself. I finished work on *Childhood* and read the proofs of 'On Money'.[125] It is windy and pouring with rain.

October 2 This morning dear P.I. Biryukov arrived; he is always so kind, gentle, intelligent and understanding, and I wept as I told him of my grief. He dislikes Chertkov too, and understood me completely. Lev Nik. was worse today; he had a stomach upset, ate nothing, did not leave the house and slept all day. After dinner we had a good talk, my son Seryozha arrived and everyone played chess.

October 3 Lev Nik. took a walk this morning, then went for a short ride and returned stiff with cold; his legs went numb and he felt so weak that he collapsed on to the bed and fell asleep without even taking off his cold boots. He was so late for dinner that I grew worried and went to see him. He looked vacant, kept picking up the clock and checking the time, talking about dinner, then falling into a doze. Then to my horror he started to rave, and things soon went from bad to worse! Convulsions in the face, terrible shuddering in the legs, unconscious, delirious, raving. Two or three men could not hold down his legs, they were thrashing so violently. But I did not lose my composure, thank God; I filled hot-water bottles at desperate speed, put mustard plasters on his calves, and wiped his face with eau de cologne. Tanya gave him smelling-salts to sniff, we wrapped his cold legs up in a warm blanket and brought him rum and coffee to drink, but the paroxysms continued and he had five more convulsions. As I was clasping my husband's feet I felt acute despair at the thought of losing him. My whole being was overcome with remorse, pangs of guilt, prayer and the most desperate love for him – I would do anything for him, anything, just so long as he lived and got better, so that I would not have to live with this gnawing guilt for all the anxieties which my own anxious state and morbid fears have caused him.

I also brought the little icon with which Aunt Tatiana Aleksandrovna blessed her Lyovochka when he went off to war, and attached it to his bed. He regained consciousness during the night, but could remember absolutely nothing of what had happened to him. His head and limbs ached, and his temperature was 37.7 at first, then 36.7.

All night I sat beside my patient on a chair and prayed for him. He slept quite well, groaning occasionally, but the shuddering stopped. My daughter Tanya arrived during the night.

October 4 Tanya's birthday; we all celebrated. The others went off to visit the Chertkovs. Lev Nik. is much better, although he has not left his bed. He has regained consciousness and has his memory back now, although he keeps asking what happened to him and what he said. His tongue is coated, his liver hurts slightly and he has eaten nothing. We wrote to Tula summoning Doctor Shcheglov, who gave him Vichy water and rhubarb with soda; I made him a vodka compress for the night.

Sasha and I had a moving and heartfelt reconciliation, and we decided to forget our quarrel and both work instead to make Lev Nik.'s life as peaceful and happy as possible. But my God! How hard this will be for me if it means resuming relations with Chertkov. It is utterly impossible, I am afraid – this sacrifice would be quite beyond me. Well, everything is in God's hands! Meanwhile the joy of Lev Nik.'s recovery has made us all much calmer and kinder to one another.

October 5 Lev N. has been better today. He ate some rusks and a whole gingerbread, and drank so much coffee and milk that I grew quite alarmed. He took some Vichy water, then had dinner with the rest of us. Seryozha left this morning, and Tanya spent the day at Ovsyannikovo. Sasha and Varvara Mikhailovna have returned, and life is now much more cheerful. Tanya is being very harsh; she keeps scolding and threatening us, then assuring us that she really wants to help us make the peace. I feel shattered; the left side of my stomach is hurting and I have a headache.

Sergeenko came. I do not like him; he is a hypocrite and exploits us for all we are worth; he is full of flattery when he needs something, and makes sweet speeches if he thinks it is to his advantage to do so.

Lev Nik. has been very kind to me since his illness; he saw how hard I took it, how much I felt for him, how selflessly and efficiently I looked after him and how sorry I was not to have taken better care of him before!

October 6 Lev Nik. is better, but he is still very weak, and says he has bad heartburn and an aching liver. He got out of bed this morning and was going out for a walk later in the day, but he hankered after his daily ride, and rode off to Bulgakov without telling me, which upset me terribly.

We had visitors – Bulygin, Boulanger and Strakhov with his daughter. It is better when there are guests, it isn't so depressing then. I asked them for some advice on the new edition. We spent the evening chatting quietly. Sasha went to see Chertkov during the day, and with my consent she invited him to come and visit Lev Nikol. Chertkov wrote a mean and characteristically unclear letter – and did not come.[126] I don't know whether L.N. felt very aggrieved about this. I expect he did. But thank God for at least one day without that loathsome man!

October 7 There was yet another discussion about Chertkov's visit, then Tanya and Sasha went to see him and he promised to come at 8 this evening. But I arranged with the doctor that he would order Lev Nik. to take a bath this evening – for this would be good for his liver and would shorten Chertkov's visit.

So that is what happened. I spent the whole day preparing myself for this dreaded visit, worrying and unable to concentrate on anything, and when I heard the sound of the sprung carriage through the ventilation window I had such terrible palpitations that I thought I would die. I ran to the glass door to see what happened at their meeting, but L.N. had just drawn the curtain. I rushed into his room, drew back the curtain and took out the binoculars, straining to catch any special expressions of joy. But L.N., realising that I was watching, merely shook Chertkov's hand with a blank expression. Then they had a long talk about something and Chertkov leant closer to L.N. and showed him something. Meanwhile I started his bath and sent Ilya Vasilevich to tell him that the water was ready and would get cold if he didn't hurry. Chertkov then stood up, they said goodbye and he left.

I felt terribly shaken all that evening. I did not cry, I just felt I was about to die. Lev Nik. kept taunting and tormenting me, saying that Chertkov was the 'person closest to him', until I put my hands over my ears and shrieked, 'I can't listen any more! I've heard that twenty times already – that's enough!'

He went out of the room and my soul was groaning in torment. Oh, the agony! I could never have foreseen anything like this – I would never have imagined it possible. Eventually, reduced to the depths of misery, I went to sleep exhausted.

What an effort it cost me to let that idiot into the house, and how I struggled to control my feelings! It's quite impossible, I simply cannot endure him, he is the devil incarnate! L.N. is gloomy again; I feel sorry for him and worry about him, but his suffering is as nothing compared to mine.

I did almost no work today, and did not go out for a walk, just sat at home all day. The double windows have been put in and it is an extraordinarily beautiful, bright, sunny, calm day. Lev Nik. went off for a fairly long ride at midday, and I was amazed to see how briskly he swung into the saddle. But towards evening his gait became tired and listless, and he is evidently very angry with me for taking Chertkov's visit so hard.

I sadly said goodbye to Tanya, who is leaving tomorrow; it distresses me that I have worried both her and Sasha by my attitude to Chertkov, who so loves their father and hates their mother! But what can one do? God will decide, one way or another. The best thing would be if Chertkov went away. The next best would be either his death or mine. The worst thing would be L.N.'s death. But I shall try to steep myself in prayer. 'Thy Will be Done!' I shall not kill myself now, or leave, or freeze myself to death, or starve, or destroy myself with tears. I am in such a bad way physically and emotionally that I am fast approaching my death without having to do violence to my organism, which, I am quite convinced, can never be killed *voluntarily*.

October 8 I got up early to see my daughter Tanya off, then went back to bed feeling ill and utterly exhausted. When I had got up, Lev Nikolaevich came in to see me, and as I was already dressed I followed him out. He was very flustered and evidently displeased about something. He asked me to listen to him in silence, but I could not help interrupting him several times. What he had to say, of course, concerned my jealous, hostile behaviour to Chertkov. He put it to me, in an extremely agitated and angry manner, that I had made a complete fool of myself, and that I must now stop it, that he did not love Chertkov *exclusively*,[127] and there were various other people who were much closer to him in every way, such as Leonid Semyonov, for instance, and some complete stranger called Nikolaev, who has just sent him a book and lives in Nice.[128] This of course is simply not true. I have now released him from his promise not to see Chertkov again; but he saw what his meeting with that repulsive idiot cost me yesterday, and he reproached me for never giving him any peace of mind because he had my disapproving attitude to Chertkov constantly hanging over his head like the sword of Damocles. But why do they have to meet anyway?

L.N.'s health is better, thank God, and he ate such a large and hearty dinner today that I was quite worried about him. But he took it very well, and this evening he ate a water-melon, drank some tea and went to bed feeling calm and well-disposed towards me. How happy I am when I don't have to worry about the next meeting with Chertkov, and we are alone together writing, working and on good terms with one another!

If we could live like this for just a month I would soon recover my health and composure. At the moment the thought that Lev Nik. is about to go off and see Chertkov fills me with dread, and my insides hurt, and there is no life or joy!

Lev Nik. went for a ride with the doctor today, and I went out to the woods to saw some branches off the firs and oaks. L.N. read Nikolaev's book; I read 'The End of an Epoch'[129] for the new edition, corrected proofs and entered some books into the library catalogues. We have accumulated such a lot of books, and I still have a lot more work to do on them. There is a lot of work to be done in general, but I simply don't have enough energy or peace of mind!

October 9 A quiet, quiet day, thank God! No visitors, no reproaches, no acrimonious discussions. But there is something oppressing us all here, and everyone is sad and sleepy. Lev Nik. walked to the village to visit the peasants' library, as he was curious to see what they were reading. From there he went for a ride with the doctor through Baburino and Zaseka. I was terrified he was going to visit the Chertkovs. He read for a long time this evening, then wrote his diary, as he always does before going to bed, and I looked through the balcony door, gazing at his serious face with boundless love and the persistent fear that he would leave me, as he has so often threatened to do lately. It's only this year that he started locking his diary away from me. Yes, all my misfortunes started with his visit to Chertkov's this summer.

I tidied up the books – a dull chore! – and was so tired that I spent the whole afternoon asleep, or rather in bed. I read a small part of the book by this unknown Nikolaev from Nice, and liked it very much. It is logical and well thought-out – what a pity L.N. does not have more people like that around him.

Lev N. and I have lived lives of such moral and physical purity! And now he has revealed the most intimate details of our life in his diaries and letters to Chertkov and Co., and this repulsive man draws his own conclusions and observations from these letters and diaries, which are often written merely to please him – and often in his tone of voice too – and then he writes to Lev N. about it, for instance:

October 1, 1909

> I am particularly anxious to collect all such letters relevant to your life, so that I may in due course provide an *explanation* of your position for the benefit of those who have been seduced by hearsay and rumour . . .[130]

I can well imagine the sort of 'explanation' this spiteful, loathsome man will provide, and what sort of 'selection' he will make when he launches his attack on L.N.'s family – concentrating especially on the moments of struggle . . .

October 10 I have been a little calmer today; there was no mention of Chertkov all day, and Lev Nik. still has not been to visit him. This morning I finished entering the books in the library catalogues, then my daughter-in-law Sonya arrived with my granddaughter Verochka; I was delighted to see them both. L.N. went for quite a long walk on his own this morning, and later in the day too, and I was in agony imagining that he had gone to meet Chertkov. I am still tormented by curiosity about his diary, and long to read it. What can he have written in it?

I worked for a while on the new edition, and decided how to arrange the articles. It's such hard work! Boulanger and Nazhivin came. Life is easier with other people here, and Lev Nikol. has cheered up.

It was overcast this morning and there were 2 degs. of frost, but towards evening it became sunny and calm and much warmer. Relations with Lev N. are not particularly close at present, but he is being slightly more gentle and considerate towards me. And I live *only* for him.

October 11 Yesterday I did not give Lev N. those excerpts from Chertkov's letter to him last year, but today I put them on his desk with my comments attacking the hypocrisy of Chertkov's 'spiritual' union with him. Lev Nik. must surely realise his mistake and see just what a stupid vulgar idiot the man is. But of course he doesn't want to abandon his dream, the idealisation of his idol, for in his place there would be nothing but emptiness.

I did not sleep all night and felt very bad all day. I went out to the fir plantation and sawed some branches, then sat down exhausted on the bench and listened to the silence. How I love my plantation! I used to come and sit here with Vanechka. I have done very little work; I am in too much physical and emotional pain.

Lev Nik. went for a ride with Dushan Petrovich, and told me that he had wanted to meet me at the firs, but I had already left. Then he brought me a pear and was so sweet to me. I told him he ought to go and see Galya Chertkova, who, according to him, was very upset that he had broken off relations with them. But he did not want to go, although he said he might tomorrow; meanwhile I shan't stop worrying until he does. Galya of course is merely a pretext for him to see her hateful husband.

My daughter-in-law Sonya has left. She too has suffered a lot with her husband, poor woman, for Ilya has fallen in love with someone else and ruined himself – and he has 7 children too! We had a good talk to one another as two wives and mothers, and understood one another perfectly. Nazhivin too has left. I told him about everything I had endured with Chertkov, my husband and my daughters.

This evening we looked through an academic book about Pushkin's library.[131] He built it up and chose all the books *himself*. Our library here, however, is completely random: people send us books from all corners of the earth, and some of the books are very good and some are utter rubbish! Lev Nik. has almost never bought any books *himself*, most of them have been sent, and our library has grown up, without any shape, form or guiding principles.

Bulgakov has returned. he is going to Moscow tomorrow, as he wants to leave the university and then refuse his military service. Poor man!

October 12 I keep discovering more and more vile things that Chertkov has done. He has now persuaded Lev N. to give instructions that the copyright should not go to his children after his death, but should be made common property,[132] as are his last works. And when L.N. said he would talk to his family about it, Chertkov was *hurt*, and would not let him! Scoundrel and despot! He has taken this poor old man in his dirty hands and forced him into these despicable deeds. But if I live, I shall have my revenge, and he won't be able to do any such thing. He has stolen my husband's heart from me and stolen the bread from my children's and grandchildren's mouths,[133] while his son has millions of stray rubles in an English bank, quite apart from the fact that those rubles were partly earned by me, because of all the help I gave L.N. Today I told Lev Nikol. that I knew about these instructions of his, and he looked sad and guilty but said nothing. I said it was a mean trick, that he was plotting strife and discord and that his children would not give up their rights without a struggle. It makes me very sad to think that over the grave of this dear man there will be such a lot of anger, reproaches and painful scenes! Yes, an evil spirit has guided this Chertkov's hand – it is no coincidence that his name derives from the word 'devil', and that Lev Nik. wrote in his diary:

'Chertkov has drawn me into a struggle. And this struggle is painful and hateful to me.'[134]

I have also discovered just how much Lev Nikol. dislikes me at present. He has forgotten everything – forgotten the time when he wrote in his diary: 'If she refuses me, I shall shoot myself.'[135] Whereas of course not only did I not refuse him, I lived with him for 48 years and never for one moment stopped loving him.

I am in a hurry to publish the new edition before Lev Nik. does something desperate, since he is capable of anything in his present grim mood. He rode out to meet Sasha but she was late and he missed her. He went to sleep when he came back, and had dinner on his own at 7 o'clock.

He is writing to Tanya.[136] He loves his daughters but does not care for his sons – some of them he actually hates. They are not vile, like Chertkov.

This evening I showed Lev Nik. his diary which I had copied out for 1862, when he fell in love with me and proposed to me. He seemed astonished, then said, 'How painful!'

But I now have one consolation, and that is my past! He of course finds this painful. He has replaced a life that was pure, honest and happy for one that is false, secretive, impure, evil – and weak. He suffers terribly, loads everything on to me, and just as I predicted, he casts me in the role of Xantippe, which is very easy for him thanks to his popularity. But how will he answer to God, his conscience, his children and his grandchildren? We all have to die, and my enemy too will breathe his last, but what will we experience in our last moments? Shall I too be able to forgive my enemy?

I cannot regard myself as guilty, for I feel with all my being that by keeping Lev Nikolaevich away from Chertkov I am saving him from the enemy – the devil. I pray to God that the heavenly kingdom may enter our house once more. 'May *Thy* kingdom come' – not that of the enemy . . .

October 13 Thoughts of suicide are growing again, with greater strength than before. But now I nurture them in silence. Today I read in the newspapers about a little girl of fifteen who took an overdose of opium and died quite easily – she just fell asleep. I looked at my big phial – but still lacked the courage.

Life is becoming unbearable. It has been like living under bombardment from Mr Chertkov ever since Lev Nik. visited him in June and completely succumbed to his influence. '*Il est despote, il est vrai*,' his mother once said to me.

And so a poor old man has been enslaved by this despotism. It is just the same now as when he was very young and wrote in his diary that when he fell in love with his friend he wanted above all to *please* him and not hurt him, and that in order to do so he once spent 8 months of his life in St Petersburg . . . So now too he has to *please* this idiot and do everything he says.

It all started when this despot took all Lev Nik.'s manuscripts with him to England.[137] Then he took his diaries (which are at the moment in the bank), and which I recovered at the cost of my life. Then he kept Lev Nik. himself with him as long as he could, and slandered me viciously both to my face and behind my back, such as telling my son Lyova that I had spent my entire life murdering my husband.

Eventually he persuaded and helped Lev N. to draft an official renunciation of the copyright, after his death probably (I don't know exactly in what form it was written), thereby stealing the last crust of bread from the mouths of his children and grandchildren who survive him. But the children and I, if I live, will defend his rights.

Monster! What business has he to interfere in our family affairs?

He is sure to think up something else, this wicked Pharisee who deceived me once before with his assurances that he was our 'closest family friend'.

This morning I went out and I walked around Yasnaya Polyana. It was frosty, bright and astonishingly beautiful! But for me there is nothing sweeter than the thought of death. I must put an end to this agony. Otherwise Mr Chertkov will next order *me*, not the manuscripts, to be taken away and put in the insane asylum, and Lev Nik., weakened by old age and wanting to *please* him, will do so, thus isolating me from the whole world and depriving me of the chance of ending it all with my death. Or else, enraged with me for *unmasking* him, Chertkov will persuade my husband to go away with him somewhere. But then there is always a way out – opium, or the pond, or the river in Tula, or a branch in Chepyzh. Opium is the safest and easiest. And then I won't have to suffer any horrifying arguments, dissensions and quarrels with our enemy over the grave of my once beloved husband, and I won't have to live with this constant sense of poisonous resentment, which exhausts my heart, torments my soul and forces me constantly to devise the most complicated and terrible ways to avoid seeing the evil deliberately perpetrated by the father and grandfather of our large family under the influence of the despotic Chertkov.

When I suggested to Lev Nik. that it was wicked and unkind of him to give instructions for his copyright to be given after his death to the world, rather than to his own family, he merely kept an obstinate silence, and his general attitude was: 'You are sick, I must endure this in silence, but in my soul I shall hate you.'

Lev N. has been infected by Chertkov's vile suggestion that my main motivation was *self-interest*. What 'self-interest' could there possibly be in a sick old woman of 66, who has both a house, and land, and forest, and capital – not to mention my 'Notes', my diaries and my letters, all of which I can publish?!

I am hurt by Chertkov's evil *influence*, hurt by all their endless secrets, hurt that Lev N.'s 'will' is going to give rise to a lot of anger, arguments, judgements and newspaper gossip over the grave of an old man who enjoyed life to the full while he was alive, but deprived his numerous direct descendants of everything after his death.

Urged on by Chertkov, he curses the government in the coarsest possible terms in all his writings; they then hide behind the law and the government with their vile deeds, giving the diaries to the *State* Bank and drawing up a *legal* will, which they want that same government to ratify.[138]

In some fairy-story I remember reading to the children, there was a wicked little girl who lived with the robbers and whose favourite game was to terrify her animals – a horse, a deer and a donkey – by passing a knife in front of their nose and throat and taunting them that she was about to plunge it into them. This is how I feel now, and it is my husband who is brandishing the knife. He has threatened me with everything: giving away the copyright on his works, secretly running away from me, and countless other spiteful threats too . . . We talk about the weather, about books, about all the dead bees in the honey – but as for what is in our souls, at first we don't talk about it, but it gradually burns our hearts, shortens our lives and lessens our love for one another.

I am now so terrified of my husband's shouting and anger – which he imagines makes me calmer and better – that I am afraid to say anything to him.

I went for a long walk – 4 degs. below freezing – then drove to Yasenki to the post.

October 14 I woke up early and straightaway sat down and wrote my husband a letter.[139]

When I timidly opened the door into his study he said, 'Can't you leave me in peace?' I said nothing, closed the door and did not go in to see him again. He came to see me later, but there were yet more reproaches, a blank refusal to answer my questions, and such hatred![140]

Lodyzhenskaya came, and I told her much more than I should have done – but I simply had to express these groans in my soul. Lev Nik. went for a ride and called in at Zaseka station to find out whether I had gone there as I had planned to, which pleased me. He was worn out by the time he returned and his eyes were glassy; he had completely forgotten about the Lodyzhenskiis, and just greeted her and went off to bed. Gorbunov came to dinner and L.N. became more cheerful. He is reading Dostoyevsky's *Karamazovs* at present, and says it is no good; the descriptions are excellent, he says, but the dialogue is very bad – it is always Dostoyevsky speaking, rather than the individual characters, and their words are simply not characteristic of them.

I have done a lot of work on the new edition, but I am feeling weak, my head is aching and I keep falling asleep over my books and papers. Yesterday evening I wrote to Andryusha. Magnificent weather – clear, starry, frosty and bright – but I did not go out.

October 15 M.A. Stakhovich came this morning. Dolgorukov arrived from Seropolko to look over the peasants' library,[141] and this evening Seryozha arrived. I told Stakhovich everything, and he tried to explain it away, as though it were all quite simple and there was nothing to worry about. But mere words won't console me. The fact that Lev Nikol. has not visited Chertkov is some comfort. But he is weak and sad. He went for a ride with Dushan Petrovich today; his horse did not want to jump the brook, and when she did Lev N. was shaken so badly that he had a violent stomach-ache and heartburn all evening. The day passed in conversation – life is much easier with guests here. Tonight I read more proofs. We all worked in the library with our guests. Still the same frosty, clear, dry weather.

October 16 I woke up early and could not get back to sleep for worrying about how to get Lev Nik.'s diaries out of the Tula State Bank. I got up feeling calm but not at all well, went down to breakfast, and Lev Nik. suddenly announced that he was off to see Chertkov. That sly Galya had sent for Dushan Petrovich, claiming to have neuralgia, and L.N. had seized on this as an excuse to visit her, saying that he also had to see Chertkov about some letters; it's only a pretext of course.[142]

I cannot express what I felt! It was as though all my insides were falling out! This was the threat I had been living under all this time! But I merely said quietly, 'This is only the second day in which I've started to get a little better,' and went off to my room. I got dressed and went outside, then came back in, took my husband aside and said to him quietly and tenderly, almost in a whisper, 'Please wait a bit before going to see Chertkov if you can, Lyovochka. It's so terribly hard for me!'

At first he did not lose his temper, merely said that he would not promise anything and wanted only to do what was best. But when I repeated my entreaty, beside myself with anguish by now, he repeated in a rage that he had promised nothing. Then I ran out to the woods and clambered into some gulleys where it would have been extremely hard to find me had I been taken ill. Then I came out into the field, and from there I raced to Telyatinki (carrying the binoculars, so as to be able to see everything from a long way off). When I got to Telyatinki I lay in the ditch near the gates leading to the Chertkov's house and waited for Lev N. to arrive. I don't know what I would have done if he had – I kept imagining that I would lie down on the bridge across the ditch and let his horse trample over my body.

Fortunately, though, he did not come. I saw young Sergeenko and Pyotr, who had gone to fetch water.[143] (Chertkov, in the name of some sort of Christian unity, has recruited various young people to work for him, as our servants work for us.)

At 5 o'clock I wandered off again. I entered our grounds as it was growing dark, went to the lower pond and lay down for a long time on the bench under the large fir tree there. I was going through such agony at the thought of Lev Nikolaevich's exclusive love for Chertkov, and a resumption of their relations. I could just imagine them locked away together in some room with their endless *secrets*, and these frightful imaginings turned my thoughts to the pond, in whose icy water I could that very moment have found total oblivion and eternal deliverance from my tormenting jealousy and despair! But again I was too much of a coward to kill myself. Eventually I wandered back to the house, although I don't remember which path I took. I did not go in, though, as I was too afraid, and sat down on the bench under the fir tree. Then I lay down on the ground and dozed off.

When it was completely dark and I could see Lev N.'s light through the windows (which meant he had woken up), they came out in search of me with lanterns. Aleksei the yardkeeper found me, and I got up and saw

Varvara Mikhailovna standing there. I was beside myself with cold, exhaustion and my recent harrowing experiences.

I arrived home numb with cold and utterly insensible; I sat down on the bed without undressing and stayed there like a mummy, without having any dinner or taking off my hat, jacket, or galoshes. This is how you kill people – without weapons but with perfect aim!

It transpired that Lev Nik., having tortured me and promised me nothing, had gone not to Chertkov's but to Zaseka, and had sent Dushan Petrovich to tell me this. But Dushan Petrovich could not find me, as I had already left for Telyatinki.

When I asked L.N. this evening why he had made me so unhappy, and whether he would be going to see Chertkov later, he would not tell me, then started shouting in a rage: 'I want my freedom, I won't submit to your whims and fancies, I'm 82 years old, not a little boy, I won't be tied to my wife's apron strings . . . ' and many more harsh and hurtful things besides, which made me suffer terribly. Then I said to him: 'But that's not the point, that's not what you're always saying. According to you, man's loftiest achievement is to sacrifice his own happiness to deliver the person closest to him from suffering.' He did not like that at all, and merely shouted: 'I take back all my promises, I promise nothing, I shall do whatever I want . . . ' and so on.

He cannot live without seeing Chertkov, of course, and this is why he gets so angry with me: because I simply *cannot* force myself to endure a resumption of relations with that scoundrel.

I went in to see Lev Nik. twice during the night, in an utterly desperate state, and tried somehow to repair our relations. I managed with great difficulty to do so, and we forgave one another, kissed and said goodnight. He said, amongst other things, that he would do all he could not to grieve me and to make me happy. I wonder what tomorrow will bring?

No sooner had we embarked on a new peaceful life than it was again overshadowed with grief; I shall grow weak and ill again for an even longer time; Lev Nik. has damaged his health again and can do no work. And all because of this *idée fixe* of his about being 'free' (how is he not free, apart from his attachment to Chertkov?), and his passionate longing to see that man.

October 17 A quiet, happy day. I managed to do a lot of work on the proofs and the new edition. Lev Nikolaevich, in his Gospel for children, writes among other things about anger (quoting from the Gospel): 'If you think your brother has done you a wrong choose a time and a place to talk to him eye to eye, then go to him and tell him *briefly* about your grievance. If he listens to you, then instead of being your enemy he will be your friend for life. If he does not listen, then take pity on him and *have nothing more to do with him*.'[144]

This is exactly what I want from Chertkov – I want nothing more to do with him, and an end to our relations.

Dear I.I. Gorbunov has left. Yakubovskii was here, a most sympathetic man, and some loathsome Jew who publishes a vegetarian journal – Perker I think his name was. It is snowing heavily, just like winter.

I am so physically and emotionally exhausted that my mind is blank and I don't feel like writing. I would desperately like to know what my husband is writing in his diary. His present diaries are like works of literature, from which people will extract the ideas and draw their own conclusions. Mine are a genuine cry from the heart, and a true description of everything that happens to us. Sasha too is writing a diary. What with her hatred of me and her bad temper I can well imagine how she will go out of her way to attack me and give her own interpretation of my words and feelings! But God knows! At times I feel such tenderness and pity for her. But at the moment she is being her usual coarse, sharp, intolerant self, and I long to get away from her. She serves her father diligently enough, and threatens me with her diaries. God be with her!

I have decided not to go anywhere, neither to Moscow nor to concerts. I now treasure every moment of my life with Lev Nik. I love him as intensely, as though it was all starting anew, like the last flame of a dying fire, and I could not possibly leave him. Maybe if I am gentle with him he will grow more fond of me too, and will not want to leave me. God knows! He has very much changed for the worse, and is now more prone to anger than to spontaneous kindness. Despite my jealousy of Chertkov, I surround him with love, care and tenderness, and anyone else would appreciate this. But he has been spoilt by the rest of the world, which judges him by his books (and his words), rather than his life and deeds. Just as well!

October 18 I got up late feeling shattered, sick and unhappy, haunted by my usual fears of some quarrel or unpleasantness. When I look back on the past four months of my ordeal, and Lev Nik.'s treatment of me, I am reminded of the cat and mouse game. It tortured me that his seven notebooks were with Chertkov, and I begged him to get them back. But he kept refusing to do so, and went on torturing me like this for two or three weeks, by which time he had driven me to despair, then he took them back, only to deposit them in the bank. I had fallen ill with a nervous disorder long before this episode with the diaries – he had delayed his return and had come back only after this delay had seriously worsened my condition.

He deliberately stayed on in Kochety because he *knew* that I had to be near Moscow for the new edition. The separation and the worry about him was utter agony for me, yet he stubbornly stayed on and would not return to Yasnaya. And when, at the end of my stay there, I begged him with tears in my eyes to tell me *roughly* when he might return, even if only for my name-day, he grew furious and stubbornly refused to.

When I asked him about the document or will that he had just given to Chertkov, he again grew furious and refused to tell me.

I live in constant fear of some new rebuff, and the endless anticipation of something unpleasant, or some new decision about his manuscripts, diaries and will, makes my life anxious, painful and quite intolerable.

Yet today, when he woke up before dinner and was listless and would not eat, I was consumed with anxiety about him and would have made any sacrifice for him, even to the extent of letting him see the Chertkovs again, who are even greater enemies to me now than they were three months ago, when he went to stay with them. And he does seem to have come to his senses since then, and grown closer to me and Sasha, who has devoted her entire life to serving her father, her only joys in life being her horses and her little property at Telyatinki.

I did almost no work today. I feel very disturbed, both physically and emotionally. I have even become lax about saying my prayers. This afternoon, after a sleep, I pasted newspaper cuttings, wrote letters, then did more cuttings. Terrible weather – a driving blizzard and thick snow; by this evening it was completely white and 6 degs. of frost.

October 19 E.V. Molostvova came to visit. She has made a study of various religious sects and is writing something about them. She is a sensitive intelligent woman, and understands a great deal. I told her about my woes, and she dismissed much of what I said, insisting that besides me, Lev Nik.'s wife, Chertkov represented such an insignificant figure that I demeaned myself by imagining that he could ever occupy *my* place in his relations with Lev Nik. But I was not at all convinced, and am still terrified that they may resume their friendship.

We all took walks on our own, including Lev Nik. This evening he was reading Dostoyevsky's *The Brothers Karamazov* with great delight, and said: 'Today I realised why people love Dostoyevsky so much – he has some wonderful ideas.' But then he started criticising him, saying again that all the characters speak in Dostoyevsky's voice, and they all speak at far too great length too.

Last night I got very anxious when I saw that Lev Nikol.'s diary had disappeared from the table where it invariably lies in a locked attaché case. And when he woke up in the middle of the night I went into his room to ask him whether he had given Chertkov the diary. 'The diary is with Sasha,' he said, and I grew a little calmer, although I was hurt that it was not with me. Sasha copies the *thoughts* out of his diary, obviously for the hateful Chertkov, who could not possibly have any good or pure thoughts of his *own*.

Clear, frosty weather; it is now 8 degs. below freezing, and starry and silent. Everyone is asleep.

October 20 Yesterday Molostvova was telling me that when she stayed with the Chertkovs last summer her husband, a good, artless man, a nobleman of the old school, well-disposed towards everyone, none the less could not wait to get away; they all seemed crushed by some terrible burden, and everyone seemed perpetually unhappy, dissatisfied and gloomy. I write this because here we have just had such a calm, happy, untroubled day that it actually makes me want to live again. Sasha was busy looking after her sick horses and writing for her father; she also went to a meeting in our village to talk to the local peasants about the consumers' store in Yasnaya Polyana.

Lev Nikol. worked on his writing and played patience, rode over to Zaseka, came into my room several times and spoke kindly to me. Some peasants came to see him – Novikov, a clever peasant who writes articles,[145] and some of our villagers, one of whom went to prison for two years for being a revolutionary.[146]

It was icy this morning, 12 degrees of frost, but bright and calm; it grew warmer this afternoon, but now it is windy and overcast. I am still working on the new edition and pasting cuttings into the scrapbook. How avidly Lev Nik. reads everything about himself in the newspapers! He obviously couldn't do without this now!

October 21 Today I saw in the newspaper *Sparks* the photograph taken of Lev N. and me on our last wedding anniversary. More than a hundred thousand people can see us there together, hand in hand, as we have lived all our lives. I had a long talk with Sasha today. She knows nothing of life and people, and there is an enormous amount she simply does not understand. Telyatinki is her entire world; there she has her beloved little home, and nearby live the tedious dull-witted Chertkovs.

I am continuing to read Lev Nik.'s pamphlets for the new edition, and find them terribly monotonous. I warmly sympathise with his denunciation of war, violence, punishments and murders, but I do not understand his denunciation of governments. People *need* leaders, masters and rulers; any sort of human organisation is unthinkable without them. It is essential, however, that the ruler is wise, just and self-sacrificing in the interest of his subjects.

Lev Nik. complains of slight pains in his liver, and this is probably why he is so gloomy. But maybe he is sad at not seeing Chertkov; although today Sasha told me that it did not grieve her father *not to see him*, what grieved him was my hatred for this gentleman and the restriction of his freedom, since the possibility of their meeting made me so unhappy. Every day I think: 'Well thank God for another day in which Lev Nik. hasn't been to see Chertkov.'

I pray fervently that God may remove this infatuation from my husband's heart and return his love to me, his wife.

That loudmouthed but pleasant Dunaev came. The weather is terrible – 2–4 degs. below freezing, a howling gale and icy snow driving against the windows. Nadya Ivanovna came too. I wrote to the printers.

October 22 Another sleepless night tormented by the diaries in the bank and by the idea of L.N. renewing his relations with Chertkov; I tried to decide whether I could endure this, but try as I might I simply cannot accept the idea.

While preaching 'universal love', he has created for himself this 'person closest to him' – in other words his *idol*, and by doing so he has insulted me, wounded me and broken my heart, so that I am utterly unable to reconcile myself to a meeting with this 'person closest to him'. Now of course they do not have the direct intimacy of meetings and this spiritual intimacy is all very intangible, and could not possibly be sustained for long with that fool. When Chertkov started publishing L.N.'s works abroad again, that was an excuse to contact him, but now there is nothing to sustain this 'spiritual communion' of theirs.

I spoke to Dunaev and met the same blank incomprehension, the same suggestion that I go abroad, and the conviction – which I fully share – that I should remember L.N.'s age and his closeness to death, and indulge him and yield to him whenever possible. But if I yielded to him at the cost of my life – or at least of my leaving home – would that really be easier for Lev Nik. than if he did not see Chertkov in the first place?

I still cannot answer for myself. *I do not know* how I would react to this, but *I feel* as though I simply could not endure L.N.'s renewed intimacy with Chertkov – ever.

Bulgakov arrived with yet another of those unfortunate young men who have fallen into Chertkov's net. Nadya Ivanovna is also here. I read some proofs, did almost no work, and have been feeling most unwell, both physically and mentally. Lev Nik. was more cheerful today, ate well, went for a walk in the garden and seemed to be resting well. He played chess with the young man, who played badly, so Lev N. did not enjoy playing with him and beat him twice. It is thawing outside, but the ground is covered with ice and completely impassable.

October 23 Now that he lacks Chertkov's *intimacy*, Lev Nikol. seems to have grown closer to me. He occasionally talks to me, and today I had two joys – my dear husband, the *old* Lyovochka, noticed my existence *twice*. Early this morning when Nadya Ivanovna was leaving and there was a great deal of bustle and commotion, Lyovochka thought it was me walking about, and came and told me how worried he had been. Later on he ate a delicious pear and brought one for me to share with him.

How long will things remain as calm and happy as they were today, I wonder? He and Dushan Petrovich rode to Zaseka, where some soldiers were chasing a fox; this morning, as always, he worked. Recently he has been busy writing something, but he seems very dissatisfied with it. He has started on something about socialism, something about suicide, and something about madness.[147] What he was working on this morning I do not know.[148] This evening he was frantically sorting out his kopeck booklets for distribution, and subdividing them into good, middling and bad, as well as deciding which ones were for the most intelligent and which were for the less educated.

I took the dogs Belka and Marquise for a walk to Zakaz, following the horses' hoofprints in the direction where Lev Nik. and the doctor had ridden. The autumn depresses me! I don't like it at all! My walk soon upset me, and all my old *idées fixes* flared up again to torment me.

Thawing, no roads, grey and windy.

I have done a lot of reading for the new edition. My eyes are bad, I soon grow tired and I am terribly worried about the uncensored state[149] of Lev Nikolaevich's later works.

October 24 We had a visit from a young lady called Natalya Alekseevna Almedingen, who edits children's magazines. Also Gastev, a long-standing Tolstoyan who lives in the Caucasus, and Bulgakov. I missed our time alone yesterday; today I was not so aware of Lev Nikolaevich's presence. Although this morning he greeted Natalya Alekseevna who was passing, and by mistake said: 'Ah, Sofia Andreevna,' and then 'Hello Sonya!', and I was so pleased to be remembered like this. He went out for a terribly long ride with Bulgakov along a frightfully icy road, and returned home exhausted at 5 o'clock. But this evening he was cheerful and talked a lot about books and about the present tendency of the Intermediary, which he said was becoming increasingly monotonous. Gastev talked very interestingly about a sectarian called V.K. Syutaev, whom Lev Nikol. had known in 1881, and had been a favourite disciple of his, and Lev Nik. enjoyed hearing about him.[150]

I went for a walk today with the young lady, and suddenly on the hillock in front of the swimming pool we saw two riders, Lev Nikol. and Bulgakov. I was delighted to see L.N. as I had been thinking about him, wondering if he would go home without me, and worrying lest he had an accident on the slippery road.

Towards evening it poured with rain and grew warmer. There was no mention of Chertkov today, but every day when L.N. sets off for his walk I wait in trepidation and terror for him to return, in case he has gone to see him, and I fret and cannot work, and calm down only when I see him approaching from the other direction, and then I am happy for the rest of the day. We haven't had any conversations about Chertkov either, and things are quiet, peaceful and happy. Lord, how long will it last! God save us!

October 25 I got up early, spent the morning with Almedingen and read six pages of proofs. Then I went to our village school, where one young and inexperienced teacher is in charge of 84 girls and boys. This evening our son Seryozha came; he played chess with his father, then played the piano. Seryozha's visits are always a pleasure. I read Almedingen the 'Notes' I wrote about my girlhood and marriage,[151] and she seemed to like them.

Lev Nik. exchanged letters with Galya Chertkova today.[152] I asked what they were about, and he made another excuse and pretended to have forgotten. I asked to see Galya's letter, and he said he did not know where it was, which was not true either. Why not just say, 'I don't want to show it to you'? But recently it's been nothing but endless excuses, lies and evasions . . . How morally weak he has become! Where is his kindness, his clarity, his honesty?! It's so sad, so terribly, depressingly sad! He has closed his heart again, and again there is something ominous in his eyes.[153] My heart aches and I am in agony – I don't want to live, I have given up . . .

An evil spirit rules our house and my husband's heart.

'May God resurrect him and drive away his enemies!'

I am coming to the end of this terrible diary, the history of all my sad sufferings, and I shall seal it up for a long, long time!

Curses on Chertkov, curses on the person who was the cause of it all! Forgive me, Lord.

November 7 On November 7, at 6 o'clock in the morning, Lev Nikol. died.

November 9 I have not recorded the events of the 26th and the 27th, but on October 28, at 5 in the morning, Lev Nik. slipped out of the house with D.P. Makovitsky. His excuse for leaving was that I had been rummaging through his papers the previous night. I had gone into his study for a moment, but I did not touch one paper – indeed there *weren't* any papers on his desk. In his letter to me (written for the entire world) the pretext he gave was our luxurious life and his desire to be alone and to live in a hut, like the peasants.[154] But then why did he have to write telling Sasha to come with her hanger-on, Varvara Mikhailovna?

When I learnt from Sasha and the letter about L.N.'s flight, I jumped into the pond in despair. Sasha and Bulgakov got me out, alas![155] Then nothing passed my lips for the next five days, and on October 31 at 7.30 a.m. I received a telegram from the editors of *Russian Word*: 'Lev Nikolaevich in Astapovo, temperature 40 °.' Andrei, Tanya and I travelled by special train from Tula to Astapovo. They did not let me in to see Lev Nik. They held me by force, they locked the door, they tormented my heart.[156] On November 7, at 6 in the morning, Lev Nik. died. On November 9 he was buried at Yasnaya Polyana.

II

DAILY DIARY 1905–7 AND 1909–19

· 1905 ·

January 1 Yesterday we saw in the New Year in splendid style. Good resolutions were made by all. Lev Nikolaevich went for a ride.

3 I worked on the portrait again, still no good. Copied out my letters to L.N. this evening. What a lot of work I have done in my life! Lev Nikolaevich is not well. Biryukov left. Bulygin arrived with 2 ladies.

12 Worked on the portrait, then took photographs of Andryusha and of Lev Nikolaevich first standing with his horse then in the saddle. He drove to Tula. Strumenskii[1] and Puzin came.

17 Spent the day looking through Lev Nikolaevich's papers in the Historical Museum. Pav. Iv. Biryukov was there too, reading documents for his biography of Lev Nikolaevich.[2]

21 Spent the morning at home attending to business. Mr Davitt[3] came. Went to the Museum, then on to attend the elections to the Assembly of Nobles. This evening the opera – Chaliapin singing *Boris Godunov*. Left the theatre for Yasnaya.

22 Travelled home with Biryukov. The snow was falling heavily and was thick on the ground. Orlov is here, Prince Tenishev has just left. I played the piano for a while, then copied out Lev Nikolaevich's article about the disorders in St Petersburg.[4]

24 Sasha has left for St Petersburg. I went as far as Tula with her. I paid for the books and received some money from Stasyulevich, played the piano a little and made some mittens for Lev Nikolaevich. He took a walk in Zaseka, and Biryukov brought him back in the sledge. We looked at portraits of the Decembrists, about whom Lev Nikolaevich is now reading.[5]

25 Spent the day tidying up the books and entering them into the library catalogues. Lev Nikolaevich has started on a new article called 'On Religion'.[6] He went for a ride.

27 Biryukov has left. I tidied up. Lev Nikolaevich dictated to me a piece about *Hadji Murat*, to be read at the charity concert on February 8 in aid of soldiers leaving hospital.

28 Visited the bank, went shopping, dined with the Gagarins. We read Lev Nikolaevich's latest article, about the present situation and the ways one can help.[8] This evening a philharmonic concert; Goldenweiser played a Rachmaninov concerto and Chaliapin sang.

February 1 Returned to Yasnaya this morning. Spent the whole day on the library again. Accounts, bills, the estate, endless unpleasant scenes with the servants – oh, I'm so bored with it all! Lev Nikolaevich went out on his own in the sledge to see Maria Aleksandrovna.

2 Finished tidying up the books and played the piano for a long time – 2 sonatas by Beethoven, 2 by Weber, 2 nocturnes and a rondo by Chopin. I was in the right mood and didn't play too badly. I went to look at Orlov's painting. There are a lot of faults in the perspective and alignment, but it may be all right.[9]

6 Iv. Iv. Gorbunov arrived with the proofs of Lev Nikolaevich's compilation of philosophical sayings.[10] Lev Nikolaevich rode all the way to Basov.

7 The correspondent for *Le Matin* came.[11]

8 I started on an oil painting of 'that house', and made prints of my photographs. Sergeenko came. My eyes are aching, I am out of sorts.

9 Worked on my landscape outside. Read Sergeenko my autobiography and Vera Kuzminskaya my prose poems, published last March in the *Journal for All*.[12] L.N. walked to Ovsyannikovo, and returned with Sergeenko.

14 Glebova's disgraceful charity concert at which excerpts from *Hadji Murat* and *War and Peace* were read.[13] A pointless exercise, a chilling failure, complete indifference from the audience.

18 L.N.'s name-day. Gorbunov and Nikolaev came. Lev Nikolaevich read us his new article.[14]

I am still unwell – I feel asleep, half dead. Still tormented by this sense of something irreconcilable, unfinished and wrong.

24 An American correspondent came.[15] The pain is still there, and I am in bed. I did another painting of some flowers. I am learning about perspective from a book, but finding it hard to understand. Lev Nikolaevich is lethargic; he has been writing about Pascal.[16]

March 4 Copied out my letters to L.N. Went for my first walk of the year.

5 We went for a lovely drive through the woods; Zosya sat with Lev Nikolaevich, I with Misha, and Lina with Sasha. This evening we read L. Avilova's story 'The First Grief'.[17]

6 We had a visit from the sculptor Andreev, who is sculpting Lev Nikolaevich's head. I drew Sasha – badly.

7 I drew Sasha again, somewhat better this time. I did some sewing, and copied out my letters. Lev Nikolaevich's bust is no good – very clumsy and not at all lifelike.[18] L.N. himself is not entirely well.

10 Went for a walk this morning and did a little painting, then packed for Moscow. Lev Nikolaevich rode to Tula and back. He was horrified by the town – the state monopoly, the churches and the police.

17 Arrived back in Yasnaya today. Lev Nikolaevich is well; he is writing his article and reading about the reign of Elizaveta Petrovna.[19]

18 I wrote a letter stating my views on war and peace, and sent it to Chertkov to publish.[20]

25 Goldenweiser and Sibor came and gave us a magnificent concert. They played 3 sonatas by Weber, 2 by Beethoven (including the 'Kreutzer'), 1 by Schubert and various other minor pieces. Sibor has now left.

April 10 Lyova and Misha Stakhovich arrived. Interesting talks.

14 The first thunder-storm. I went for a walk with Tanya and Marusya, and worked in the garden. It rained all day. It was quiet and melancholy outside, but so good! I love spring. 'Thou art so tender, thou hast promised me joy on this vain earth . . . '[21]

15 Lev Nikolaevich is unwell – his liver is aching. My daughters are in low spirits. Barkov, a correspondent for the *Stock Exchange Gazette*, visited.

16 Spent the whole day outside. Went for a walk with Tanya and Yulia Ivanovna. Then walked round the estate with the bailiff and on my own. L.N. is unwell, but went for a long ride all the same. I read an article by Sergei Ivanovich on Rimsky-Korsakov's dismissal. Very dry and logical.[22]

17 Bright Easter Sunday. I.K. Dieterichs came, and Maria Aleksandrovna. They took photographs of me in a chair, of Lev Nikolaevich and the others. L.N. is better.

18 Outside all day, took a walk with Marusya, this evening listened to her singing. Cleared the front garden of 'that house'. I sewed, while the others played vint and roared with laughter. Earlier on I developed some photographs. Lev Nikolaevich went for a ride; this evening he read about the life of Henry George[23] and listened to Marusya Maklakova singing.

22 Chertkov has sent me the translation of my letter to *The Times* about the war, and I am delighted. I played the piano for a while. The weather has been fine for a week now. The yellow lungworts are in flower. They have brought morels back to the house three times. Here and there the leaves are coming out.

27 (Moscow) Shopping, business, Wanderers' Exhibition. I am fascinated by art at present.[24] I left for St Petersburg this evening.

28 Stayed in St Petersburg with my sister Tanya. Went to see Lyova – his children are Swedish, alas! and very foreign. Dora and I went to the portrait exhibition at the Tauride Palace. Splendid![25]

May 1 Returned to Yasnaya at about eight in the evening and was met by Sasha and Andryusha. The house is quiet, the nightingales are singing and everything is green, but cloudy and lifeless. Andryusha is a pitiful sight. I have influenza.

7 We went out to the forest to look at the Round Birchwoods. I am tired and unwell. Lev Nikolaevich touchingly came to meet me in the carriage.

12 (Moscow) Business with the accountant all morning. Paid 10,159 rubles to the Kushneryov printing works and for Howard's paper. Boulanger came, and we went to the Historical Museum together. Then shopping and business. This evening I visited the graves of my little ones, and I planted flowers. Some lads have broken the angel off them.

13 Returned to Yasnaya this morning. Cool and overcast, rumbling thunder, warmer later on. A Belgian called Sarolia came,[26] and Davydov. Nadya Ivanova is here. Walked round the estate, sorted out documents and bills from Moscow.

15 A hot day. I wandered about the park delighting in nature, the flowers and the beauties of spring. Lev Nikolaevich, Andryusha and I considered how to put up a wire fence. Anna Alekseevna and I read a short story by Lev Nikolaevich called 'Prayer'.[27]

16 Hard at work all day sorting out all the books and letters sent to Lev Nikolaevich, so as to take them to the Historical Museum in Moscow. I am exhausted, L.N. is not well.

22 Sorted out the letters and made a note of them. Drove along the highway with Lev Nikolaevich, who picked some cornflowers and lilies-of-the-valley.

25 Lev Nikolaevich went for a ride but was back before the storm. Gusev, Dunaev and Goldenweiser came. L.N. is not well. I spent a long time taking notes of the letters and packing them up.

27 Drove to Kozlovka with Yulia Ivanovna and sent all Lev Nikolaevich's letters to the Historical Museum. L.N. is not well. This evening I played the piano a little; my fingers were stiff, but Chertkov praised my playing.

30 I chatted with my sister Tanya and copied some of the letters Lyovochka sent her when she was young. Seryozha played the piano and Tanya sang. The correspondent of *Holy Russia* came, and Andreev the sculptor.[28]

June 2 (Moscow) Marusya came this morning. She and I sorted letters at the Historical Museum. This evening I left for home.

3 I returned to Yasnaya this morning. Crowds of people – Masha Erdeli, Tanya Sukhotina's family, Chertkov's friends and various others. I lay on the chaise longue all day feeling ill.

4 Lay on the chaise longue again all day. Chertkov,[29] Briks, Zosya, Andreev the sculptor, Yusha Obolenskii and his wife and the others have all left. The Biryukovs arrived from Switzerland.

7 Tsurikov came with his son, and Gorbov, and Annochka with Kristy the French girl. We read aloud the introduction to Chekhov's 'Darling',[30] and various letters.

9 Lev Nikolaevich rode over to Taptykovo and back. This evening he told Biryukov about his visits to the Optyna Pustyn monastery,[31] and about his defence of the soldier.[32] He read us 'Mikula Selyaninovich', one of the fables from his *ABC*, and told us how he had come to write them.[33]

13 Professor Snegiryov came to see me this morning, with Aleksei Mitrofanovich. Misha Romanovskii and Goldenweiser came, and later Seryozha arrived. Lev Nikolaevich read us his story 'Berries'.[34]

16 I did some work on the story of my life and stayed in bed most of the day, but got up before dinner to play the piano. Gorbunov, Nikolaev, Kruse and Biryukov came. Pokhitonov is doing a lovely drawing of the entrance to the estate. Lev Nikolaevich is unwell. He went for a ride on the horse he has bought from the Glebovs.

21 Bad pains all morning, stayed in bed all day. A telegram from Snegiryov, to say he is coming tomorrow. My Lyova came, to my great joy. Lev Nikolaevich is better and rode over to Tula.

23 I stayed in bed all day. Lev Nikolaevich rode over to visit Jones and Goldenweiser, then went for a swim.

27 Spent the day reading the letters I wrote to my sister Tanya in the 60s. Zavalishina, the Decembrist's daughter, was here.[35]

July 7 The plasterers finished work at four this afternoon. I did not sleep all last night. Lev Nikolaevich went swimming, and I went for my first swim this evening. I printed some photographs. I entered the negatives into the catalogue. We read aloud a short story by Gorky.[36]

8 Sorted out books, went swimming with Olga. Lev Nikolaevich rode to Taptykovo. Attempt on Pobedonostsev's life.[37]

18 L.N. went for a walk and a swim. In the evenings he dictates his memoirs to Sasha for Biryukov's biography of him, while Biryukov takes notes.[38] I copied out my letters to L.N. and finished selecting those for the years of famine.[39]

20 Ilya's name-day. I went to Ovsyannikovo with Maria Nikolaevna and we brought M.A. Schmidt back with us. Then Lebrun came, and

Boulanger. I copied out my letters, went for a swim and did nothing else all day.

Lev Nikolaevich read us some philosophical sayings from his book this evening.[40]

21 Went out looking for mushrooms and round by the swimming pool. Went for a swim. Cut down some acacias this afternoon to make room for Vanechka's little oak trees. F.A. Strakhov arrived, and the Goldenweisers came for the evening. Lev Nikolaevich rode through the woods, played chess with Goldenweiser and did some writing.

27 Generals Bestuzhev and Kuhn were here. Lev Nikolaevich had an argument with Bestuzhev about revolution and religious tolerance.

29 The Goldenweisers, Lebrun and some student came to see Lev Nikolaevich. These guests prevent me from doing any real work. Lev Nikolaevich read us some Herzen this evening.[41]

August 3 (Moscow) Another morning spent doing accounts, talking to Panchenko, ordering paper and organising the publication of Volume II and *Childhood*. The *ABC* has left the printers. At 5 in the afternoon I left for Yasnaya; I arrived at midnight and worked till 4 this morning. Lev Nikolaevich has gone to Pirogovo with Sasha and the doctor.

8 Went to lunch with Masha in Pirogovo, then returned to Yasnaya with Lev Nikolaevich and the doctor. This afternoon Annenkova and M.A. Schmidt came, and a teacher with 10 pounds of honey from Butkevich. I played a Haydn symphony as a duet. L.N. approved.

9 A painful discussion this afternoon with L.N., full of anger and unjust accusations, and life is depressing again – too much commotion and too little leisure.[42] Nikolaev and Lebrun came. Sasha left for Taptykovo. Endless visitors – the Swedish woman, villagers fleeing the fire, beggars, factory-workers, dark ones . . .

10 This evening I sorted old photographs; Lev Nikolaevich was delighted with them and was reminded of old times. We have made up our quarrel.

12 The Kuzminskiis and the Yazykovs visited. Snegiryov came. A day of guests. This afternoon Lev Nikolaevich played chess with Olsufiev and Goldenweiser, who then played some études, a barcarolle and various other Chopin pieces. Later on Lev Nikolaevich read us more Herzen.

14 This evening Goldenweiser and his wife played a Haydn symphony as a duet; Lev Nikolaevich was in raptures. He played chess, then read us a little Herzen. The day went well and we are both in good health.

15 A clever, lively Frenchman called Joseph Reinack came for the day. Lev Nikolaevich went for a ride with him and Olsufiev, and had a long talk with him.

16 I went out into the garden this morning with some black glass, looking for a lovely view to paint in oils, but I got carried away chopping down some branches and shrubs. An American came to see L.N.; he drove off with this man to Ovsyannikovo, and came back on foot, exhausted. I copied out my letters. Goldenweiser came. L.N. played chess all evening.

22 My 61st birthday, but I simply don't feel old. The Kuzminskiis, Erdeli and Maria Aleksandrovna came, and today I was glad to see them all. There are times when I am carried back to the past, and all the things that have hurt me in recent years imperceptibly go out of my head.

26 Endless anxieties all day about our guests on the 28th. All very tedious and difficult. Lev Nikolaevich is better. He did not like my children's story, which upset me.

27 Lev Nikolaevich is quite cheerful; he read us a short story by Herzen.

28 Lev Nikolaevich's 77th birthday. A magnificent summer day dancing with spiders' webs. Our guests were: Tanya, Misha and Mikhail Sergeevich Sukhotin, Ilya, Sonya and Annochka, Maria Aleksandrovna, Konshin, Gorbunov, Goldenweiser, Bulygin, Princess Volkhonskaya, Prince and Princess Cherkasskii, Boldyryov, my sister Tanya with her husband and son, Dunaev and others. Vint, singing, talking. Exhausting.

30 I did an oil painting of some mushrooms, then went to see Zvegintseva and read her L.N.'s story 'After the Ball'.[43] Shtange came.

31 Salomon came to visit, and Biryukov with his son. Lev Nikolaevich read us his article 'The End of the Century'.[44] He is well and cheerful, and went for a ride.

I painted the white mushrooms by the oak tree, then did a rough pencil sketch of my portrait. I want to do so many different things, but haven't the time or leisure.

September 4 I did some work on my life story, then played a Haydn symphony as a duet with Sonya Mamonova. Lev Nikolaevich rode to Yasenki for the post; he was complaining about his age this afternoon.

7 We called the doctor for Masha. Lev Nikolaevich is still working on his article 'The End of the Century'. He has also just received the proofs of his philosophical sayings and of 'Berries', and is very busy. He went for a ride. I painted a view of the pond. It kept changing all the time. Very difficult. I copied letters, knitted, dug up bushes. News that Sergei Ivanovich has left the conservatoire.[45]

12 I copied out Lev Nikolaevich's letters to Tanya Kuzminskaya. Neuralgia pains down the right side of my face.

We read aloud Lev Nikolaevich's 'Reminiscences', about his father and his aunt, Tatiana Aleksandrovna Ergolskaya. A marvellous work, full of artistry and feeling; I wept, and felt as though I were re-encountering my beloved husband as he used to be – as an artist.[46]

13 We read aloud again from Lev Nikolaevich's 'Biography'; parts of it are weak, but the extracts from his diaries and letters are good.

I read through my letters this afternoon, and copied out some excerpts. L.N. went for a ride through the woods, then played vint all evening.

14 Sergeenko has left. I was annoyed by Biryukov's biography of L.N., and L.N. too is dissatisfied with it. So tactless of him to include those letters of his to V.V. Arseneva.[47]

19 This evening Lev Nikolaevich read a passage from Taine,[48] and Nadya Ivanova and I played two Mozart quintets arranged as duets.

23 Our 43rd wedding anniversary. The day did not go as I would have wished. I was busy organising the photographs of Lev Nikolaevich and me. Guests all evening and for dinner.

24 It is pouring, the roads are a quagmire, the potatoes aren't dug – we have been cursed. I painted some fly agarics, and went out twice to look at them. Then I printed photographs. This evening I copied out my letters, and we all took turns to read Lev Nikolaevich's article 'The End of the Century'. A German theology professor called Andreas was here, and Stefanovich,[49] and a German woman.

25 A terrible gale all yesterday and today. I worked all day on my oil painting of the fly agarics. Lev Nikolaevich went for a ride and played chess with Sukhotin. He said he was very pleased with his article 'The End of the Century'.

30 (Moscow) I finished my business early this morning, came home, strolled round the garden, had a sleep, and at 5 o'clock Sergei Ivanovich came. We drank tea together, then spent two hours correcting a letter to Gr. Duke Konstantin Konstantinovich about the state of the conservatoires.[50] It explained the past: 'I inclined to your view, but I had such a high opinion of Nikish and Tchaikovsky', and it was friendly and well-written. I left for home.

October 1 Back in Yasnaya. All very cheerful here. Lev Nikolaevich is well and in good spirits; he played vint and walked through the woods. We read aloud his story 'Kornei Vasilev'.[51]

3 Buturlin, Nikitin and Berkenheim came. I went for a walk. The lower pond is being drained, and they are dragging L.N.'s felled trees across it. I wish they hadn't cut them down. Lev Nikolaevich is reading about the reign of Alexander I, and plans to write something about it.[52]

4 Tanya's birthday. Lev Nikolaevich read us a short story by Gorky this evening – very poor.[53] Then some Herzen – what a brilliant style, his thoughts simply take wing. I painted the fly agarics on to canvas.

6 Rain again all day, 2–4 degrees. I sewed sheets on the machine. I worked on my life story first thing this morning, before getting dressed. A young lady has arrived with a Remington to copy my letters to my sister Tanya. Lev Nikolaevich is reading about the reign of Alexander I and Paul.[54] He called on Maria Aleksandrovna, then played vint.

7 I went out to pick saffron milk-caps with Parasha Gué; we collected 2 large basketsful and got soaked. Buturlin, Nikitin and Berkenheim have left. Lev Nikolaevich is in high spirits and has been telling marvellous stories. He recalled that in Kazan they had lived opposite the jail, and he had thought how interesting it would be to explore the life of each one of the inmates.

9 Sasha, Verochka, Parasha Gué and I went to the crown forest to pick milk-caps; we picked a lot and enjoyed ourselves immensely. Lev Nikolaevich is unwell. I sewed all evening, and listened to the others reading a tale by Kuprin called 'The Duel'.[55] Recollections of thinning hair and the joys of intimacy (the story, I mean).

11 The strike on the railways is continuing. I worked well on my autobiography, and managed to write 26 pages. This evening we read Kuprin's 'The Duel'.

12 The strike continues. The Kursk train has stopped at Kozlovka-Zaseka, with 110 passengers on board; they are being fed and are sleeping either in the carriages or on the station. I worked hard on my autobiography. This evening Seryozha and Lev Nikolaevich read us Kuprin's 'The Duel'. We are all unwell. I have lost my voice.

13 The typhus epidemic in Yasnaya continues. Another peasant woman has died, the 5th. 60 people have been affected so far.

I did some writing and played a sonata by Weber; we finished reading 'The Duel'.

17 A tense mood of anticipation here – for Tanya's labour to start and for the strike to finish and the trains to move. Lev Nikolaevich is ill. He had a bad fall on the kitchen porch with a bucket. Misha has come from Tula with news of total revolution there, in Moscow and in Petersburg.[56]

19 Typhus is still raging in the village, with yet more victims. Lev Nikolaevich rode to Basov and brought back news about the manifesto (a constitution).[57] Sasha went to Tula. There was music, singing, crowds chanting 'Hurrah!' and all the workers were let out for 4 days. Flags and celebrations.

22 Read Mikh. Serg. Sukhotin the story of my life, and he praised it. Played some Beethoven sonatas again, and this evening I copied out my letters to Lev Nikolaevich. L.N. rode to the gates of Tula; it was all quiet there today. This evening he read us Herzen on revolution – so intelligent and always so timely.[58]

24 Spent the day sorting through my letters to my sister Tanya; a young lady called Lyutetskaya is copying them out on the Remington as material for Lev Nikolaevich's biography.[59]

31 Shcherbakov, Zvegintseva and Korvet came. Lev Nikolaevich played vint with his guests until 1 in the morning. He is finishing and revising his article 'The End of the Century'.

November 2 I was most upset by an article about L.N. in the *Moscow Gazette*. I wrote a little article about it but have not yet sent it off to the printers.[60]

3 Sorted some letters, read through others, copied out others. Did some sewing. Unpleasant discussion with L.N. concerning Biryukov's letter about the Arseneva letters. We are all secretive sometimes, but this I simply cannot endure.[61]

6 At midday today Tanya was safely delivered of a baby daughter.[62]

7 Tanya and her daughter are doing well. Lev Nikolaevich complained this evening of feeling weak. He is correcting 'The Human and the Divine'.

8 I read some touching letters from my father to me and Lev Nikolaevich, as material for my autobiography. I feel ill and weak, and have a bad cough. L.N. too is unwell, but he went for a long walk along the highway none the less. He is hard at work correcting the galley-proofs of 'The Human and the Divine'.

10 This evening I copied some letters, then played the piano for a long time and with great pleasure – 2 Beethoven sonatas and some Chopin. Everything is going well at present. Lev Nikolaevich is in good health; he is reading about the murder of Paul I,[63] and is still writing 'The Human and the Divine' for Chertkov.[64]

22 We had a visit from a German newspaper correspondent called Hess.

23 Spent a long time writing my notes; Gudim Levkovich, Gusev and Postupaev came.[65]

26 I slept late this morning, then painted my landscape. Sulerzhitskii has arrived with an actor from the Arts Theatre.[66]

27 We had a visit from one Yuvachov, who has spent one and a half years in solitary confinement and 8 years in Sakhalin.[67] I worked on my landscape.

29 A pile of newspapers has arrived. The situation in Russia is very bad indeed. They are robbing the banks and looting the landowners, the soldiers and sailors are mutinying, there is no government.

December 1 I did an oil painting of some mushrooms for my sister Tanya, copied out my letters to L.N., and am now about to leave for Moscow. Lev Nikolaevich is writing 'Freedoms and Freedom' and various other minor articles.[68]

3 (Moscow) Discussions with Makarenko about the books and the new editions of *Childhood* and *War and Peace*.

4 Spent the morning at the Tretyakov Gallery – a lot of it rather disturbing. Then a chamber concert – a trio by Saint–Saëns and a

Rachmaninov cello sonata. Went on to visit Olenina and my grandchildren, dined with the Maslovs, and this evening read them 'Kornei Vasilev'.

5 More shopping and business. Copied out papers in the Historical Museum, and left this evening for Yasnaya.

6 Back in Yasnaya. The Goldenweisers, Nikolaev, the Obolenskiis and the Sukhotins are here. Andryusha has returned and Seryozha came with me. It is very crowded – too crowded. There were 18 for dinner. The Goldenweisers played.

15 I tidied books, sewed underwear on the machine, read, copied, and did a little of everything. There have been barricades and shooting in Moscow. The post and railways are on strike.[69] Lev Nikolaevich was very ill last night and this morning, but was better this evening.

16 Lev Nikolaevich walked to Kozlovka and drove back. I finished copying my letters to him. I sewed and listened to him reading Herzen.

17 Andryusha has arrived in Krapivna – he has been discharged from the army. I have started on a self-portrait. I cannot rid myself of this depression, although it's a sin to be so downcast. Lev Nikolaevich was better today. We read more Herzen.

27 I worked on my portrait and sat with the guests. Sasha decorated a Christmas tree for the servants' children, and they all put on fancy dress. Lev Nikolaevich is unwell; he played chess.

29 Worked on my portrait again. We read Taine on the Jacobins.[70]

31 Worked on my portrait: first I spoil it, then I correct it, then I spoil it again. Lev Nikolaevich is writing an article about the government, revolution and so on.[71] He went for a ride today, and I walked out to meet him. Tanyushka is much better now; she sleeps more, screams less, and smiles. The end of a hard year of war, revolution and strife.

· 1906 ·

January 9 Walked to Zakaz with Lev Nikolaevich and the Goldenweisers. Sasha, Kolya and the Sukhotins attended the Assembly of Nobles in Tula. I started on an evening landscape and made a nightshirt.

Goldenweiser played this evening, marvellously: Schumann's 'Davidsbündlertänze' and a ballade and nocturne by Chopin. He and his wife have now left for Moscow.

10 I worked on my evening landscape and this evening I sewed – nothing else. Lev Nikolaevich travelled round the villages visiting peasants of his acquaintance and finding out what they needed.[1] 7 degrees below freezing and still, with a hoar-frost. I went out this evening to check that the tone of my little painting was true to nature.

11 I spent the whole day tidying up last year's journals and books. Lev Nikolaevich is unwell, but rode over to Kozlovka none the less.

13 Sasha, Masha, Kolya, Mikhail Sergeevich Sukhotin and Doctor Grushetskii have gone abroad.

15 (Moscow) I went to Kerzin's concert[2] – songs by Taneev – and dined with Taneev at the Kerzins', where we read Lev Nikolaevich's article 'Government, Revolutionaries and People'.[3] I read it this evening too at the Maslovs'.

16 I gave Davydov Lev Nikolaevich's article 'Government, Revolutionaries and People' to publish in *Russian Thought* or somewhere else, as well as an announcement to the newspapers telling all publishers of L.N.'s works to apply directly to Chertkov.[4]

I visited Lina and my twin grandchildren, went to see Yunge, and on to the Bolshoi Theatre. They were doing 2 musical pictures by Rachmaninov, 'The Miserly Knight' and 'Francesca da Rimini'.

18 Historical Museum, shopping, dinner with the Glebovs.

Davydov was here this evening; this morning Kerzina came, and we read each other our notes – hers about Stasov and the musical circles,[5] mine about my life.

I left this evening for Yasnaya.

21 Worked on my portrait all morning. Took a walk after dinner with Tanya, Yulia Ivanovna, Natasha and Dorik. I played some Mozart quintets arranged as duets, first with Natasha, then with Lev Nikolaevich.

29 Printed photographs of Tanyushka and pasted them into the album. Went for a walk with Boulanger.

We had an Englishman named C . . . here,[6] a young lady named Zubrilova, and Bulygin and Boulanger.

L.N. went for a ride and played vint. The other day he wrote a legend.[7]

February 1 I am in Moscow. I dined at home with Seryozha, and spent the evening with the Glebovs, Misha, Lina and my darling grandchildren. Then on to the Maslovs, where we read 'Berries', 'Kornei Vasilev', The Foreword to Chekhov's 'Darling'[8] and L.N.'s legend. P.I. Yakobi, S.I. Taneev and Skuratov were there, as well as our hosts.

3 Worked all morning in the museum with Boulanger's brother, listing all the boxes and putting them all in order. Then shopping, dinner with my brother Sasha and Goldenweiser's concert.

6 At Yasnaya. 10 degrees below freezing, sunny. Worked on my portrait, tidied up, did the accounts. Went to the side wing to make things ready for the guests. Drove to the woods to collect Lev Nikolaevich.

8 Nikolaev and Nazhivin came. Sergei Ivanovich Taneev arrived this evening.

I started copying another of Pokhitonov's landscapes.[9]

11 Worked on my landscape again. Took photographs. We all walked to the well. We read aloud Kuzminskii's account of the disorders in Baku.[10] Sergei Ivanovich and Goldenweiser played me a duet arrangement of Taneev's symphony. This evening they played Beethoven's 9th Symphony on 2 pianos, and Arenskii's suite again.

13 Andryusha has returned. A frightful blizzard all day, 14 degs. below freezing. I printed my photographs of Taneev and Goldenweiser – very bad – and wrote my 'Memoirs'.

Lev Nikolaevich stayed at home most of the day and read; he told us about a Japanese novel someone had sent him in English.[11]

This evening we played Mozart's 2nd Symphony as a duet, as well as a Haydn trio. Then I did a little sewing.

14 I spent the whole day printing my photographs. My little granddaughter Tanyushka is turning into a lovely happy little girl. A professor from Warsaw came, and my son Ilya. He read us his love story.[12]

I am in low spirits. Lev Nikolaevich has been for a ride; he is now reading his Japanese novel and a book about Paul I.

15 I printed photographs and walked to Chepyzh to photograph some more views.

We read aloud 'The Death of Emperor Paul I' in French.[13]

16 More photographs for Sergei Ivanovich and Goldenweiser. Sewed some underwear on the machine. Took photographs of the house and the Kuzminskiis' wing.

Lev Nikolaevich went for a ride through the woods; this evening he read us Poroshin's 'Notes' about the childhood of Paul I.[14]

23 Worked on the story of Vanechka's and my life, initialled towels and stockings, played some Mendelssohn overtures, some Mozart and various other things as duets with Natasha.

24 I worked diligently all day on my autobiography and am pleased with the results.

25 Worked badly on my writing. Got up early and took a walk on my own through the forest to Zakaz. Sewed underwear until late at night.

Lev Nikolaevich finished his story 'For What?',[15] wrote letters, went for a walk and spent the evening playing vint with Tanya, Andryusha and Sukhotin.

26 Walked to the well again this morning, then wrote for a long time – badly. Read Lev Nikolaevich's story 'For What?', which he has just finished; it's very good. Played the piano for an hour.

Sewed all evening while the family played vint.

28 Cold and windy, everyone is ill. It has been snowing a blizzard. Tanya drove to Ovsyannikovo with Yulia Ivanovna. Lev Nikolaevich rode there through the woods. I spent the whole day sewing. Natasha and I played Schubert's C Major Symphony as a duet. This evening we read 'The Schlüsselburg Fortress' and 'Monastery Prisons' by Yuvachov. Excellent.[16]

On February 24 Lev Nikolaevich said: 'I dislike them selling my "Notes for Soldiers" on the streets. I would prefer them to take my ideas as a whole, rather than using them for goals that are alien to me.'[17]

March 1 There is a wind again; it becomes quite strong towards evening. It has been snowing and it is now 4 degrees below freezing. I worked on the story of my life, and Natasha and I played a Schubert symphony and a Mozart quintet as a duet. Then I sewed while Lev Nikolaevich read me something by Veresaev about war.[18]

4 I copied out Lev Nikolaevich's new story 'For What?' before dinner. Then I felt ill and lay down.

7 We had visitors – Marusya Maklakova, E.F. Yunge and her son, Salomon and Carbonel,[19] Aleksandri and two young men. My health is better. I have done nothing all day.

9 I finished painting a copy of a Crimean landscape[20] and read E.F. Yunge my 'Memoirs'; she approved. I spent the evening sewing again.

Lev Nikolaevich went for a ride, played chess with Sukhotin, and read us his 'Thoughts of the Philosophers'.

It is most unpleasant that this fellow Askarkhanov is now publishing all his previously banned works.[21]

11 Sergeenko came with his daughter and read me some passages from his biography of Lev Nikolaevich, including various things about me. It's fairly accurate and not too bad.[22] I left for Moscow this evening.

14 **(Moscow)** Sergeenko came and we discussed the publication of L.N.'s banned works.[23] In the museum he kept harassing me with requests for material. A concert in memory of Arenskii. S.I. Taneev played.

15 Spent the morning copying excerpts from Lev Nikolaevich's letters to Countess A.A. Tolstaya. Dinner with the Maslovs, then on to visit Aunt. Read Lev Nikolaevich's story 'For What?'.

17 From 11–3 in the museum. Commissioned Makarenko to look through the previously banned works.

18 From 12–2.30 in the museum. Dinner at home, conversation with I.I. Gorbunov about the new edition.

24 Fine days. Worked hard on my autobiography and wrote a lot. Very difficult!

27 Heard that M.S. Sukhotin had been elected to the Duma.[24]

We had a visit from someone collecting money for the wounded and disabled in the name of the Empress, but Lev Nikolaevich didn't give him any. I developed photographs. Lev Nikolaevich rode over to Tula.

28 Spent the whole day printing photographs and pasting them into the book. Lev Nikolaevich went for a walk; he is fascinated by his reading about Catherine II and Paul I.[25]

29 Another fine day. I wrote a lot of my autobiography – rather dull. L.N. went for a walk, wrote and read. This evening we had Prince G.E.

Lvov, N.S. Lopukhin, F.I. Gayarin and F.E. Arbuzov here – people like us. Very agreeable.

30 M.A. Stakhovich arrived with Vladimirov. I read Stakhovich the story of my life. I sewed, and took photographs of Lev Nikolaevich with Stakhovich and Sukhotin, then of Tanyushka with her father and grandfather.

April 6 D.D. Obolenskii, P.A. Sergeenko and I.K. Dieterichs have come. Sergeenko read his *Biography*.

15 Heavenly spring weather. Lev Nikolaevich has not been well lately, but was better today. He played vint and felt sleepy. He is writing an article inspired by his reading of D.A. Khomyakov's book *Autocracy*.[26]

19 I packed away the winter things, went for a little walk and did a lot of sewing. Astonishingly warm weather – 12 degs. at night; the cuckoos and the nightingales are singing.

Andryusha has returned. Lev Nikolaevich gave Sasha his article on Khomyakov's *Autocracy* to copy out. He went for a long walk.

27 Did a lot of sewing for L.N., went for a little walk, tidied up the Kuzminskiis' wing for Lyova's family and the pavilion for Seryozha. Klechkovskii the musician[27] was here, and two strangers came to see Lev Nikolaevich.

30 My son Seryozha has come. I played some Mozart quintets as duets with N. Ivanova. Thunder-storm and rain. It has grown cooler, but the nightingales are still singing, the apple trees are coming into blossom, and the ground is covered with white petals.

Lev Nikolaevich has been planting orange pips in boxes and to his delight some shoots have now appeared.

May 1 Thunder-storm. It is cooler now – 5 degs. at night. Nazhivin, Lebrun and my son Ilya came. Arguments between father and sons.[28]

10 Maude and Shanks came. Very hot; I went swimming with the young ladies and came home on foot. L.N. rode down to the river for a swim.

21 Whit Sunday. Spent the morning with my grandchildren, then watched the peasant women singing and dancing.

My son Misha came, and the sculptor Andreev. This evening more songs, games, dances and youthful fun.

23 It has brightened up again, the sun is shining, the sky is blue and the air is fresh. We all went swimming. Lev Nikolaevich took his grandsons Palya and Nikita out with Tanya Denisenko and sat them all one by one on his horse.

Poets and lovers can discover and bring out the best qualities of the person they love.

24 Lev Nikolaevich constantly compares the present situation with the French revolution as described by Taine.[29]

25 A hot day; I went swimming with Dora and the grandchildren, and Tanya came too. Lev Nikolaevich planted some orange and lemon pips, and from the shoots now appearing he has constructed a whole theory of human and universal life.

I admire nature, flowers and children, but am stupid and lazy.

27 I got up late, went for a swim and walked over to the felled plantation. The flowers were exquisite. A heavy thunder-storm; it hailed and poured. Lev Nikolaevich went swimming, then read us Rousseau's *Confessions d'un Vicaire Savoyard* and excerpts from an English book on revolution.[30]

31 (L.N.) is still writing his article 'On Autocracy', prompted by Khomyakov's article.

June 1 An overcast day. Went swimming, sewed, did a lot of housework and gave various orders around the estate.

Lev Nikolaevich says that progress and civilisation through industry (i.e. machines) is possible only by force and slavery to capital, and is incompatible with a Christian life, which must be based on mutual aid.

6 Belyaev, a correspondent from *New Times*, was here.[31] It's quite impossible to write my memoirs, work on my oil painting, play the piano or do anything – one's whole life is held up by this crowd of useless people. Belyaev has left.

7 It has turned cold and we've all been sitting at home. I played with my grandchildren; my writing went well and I made some useful corrections to my autobiography.

12 It has become cooler. We drove with the Stakhoviches to Grumond and the surrounding countryside. I added to my catalogue of photographs. Lev Nikolaevich has been correcting the proofs of Yur.

Belyaev's article for *New Times*, concerning their discussion about politics and land ownership.[32]

17 I am kept busy with housework and trifles and simply have no time for anything. A real Japanese has come, a writer.[33]

19 I did some hurried work on my autobiography; Lev Nikolaevich had reminded me of a few things for it.

20 This evening Lev Nikolaevich read us his article; it takes a negative attitude to current political affairs, and advises the people not to submit to *any* authority. I do not like this article: I find it naïve, idealistic and insincere.[34]

22 Lev Nikolaevich was ill all day. Temperature 38.2.

24 Doctor Berkenheim came this morning. Frightful heat. We all cheerfully went off for a swim. At dinner we congratulated Seryozha and his bride-to-be, Masha Zubova. This evening we had singing, guitars, balalaikas, and Andryusha danced.

29 I packed for Moscow and left with Sasha for Seryozha's wedding.

30 We were delayed and arrived late in Moscow. Andryusha and Ilya said the wedding was at 12 o'clock, so we hurried to the house and got dressed. Then Marusya arrived, and we all went off to our Church of the Revelation in Zubovo. A cheerful wedding, followed by dinner at the Zubovs'. Dear Count Aleksandr Vasilevich Olsufiev was there. We went to the station and saw Seryozha and Masha off on their foreign travels.

July 6 It is very cold, with a north wind. The rye has been stooked, here and there the oats are being cut, and there are some mushrooms out.

I worked well on my 'Memoirs', and have got as far as 1870.

7 Andryusha is very ill, with a temperature of 38.8: Doctor Afanasiev came. Our guests today were Goldenweiser and his wife, 2 Japanese men,[35] Volodya Kristy, and some other companion of Felten's. Exhausting! I went for a swim and entered books in the catalogue.

9 All very depressing. Petya is worse and Doctor Sukhinin called. I wrote my 'Memoirs'. The Yasnaya Polyana estate is deteriorating and is increasingly unprofitable; I cannot do it and hate it. Lebrun came. L.N. is listless and gloomy.

16 Petya is worse and has a fever again; everyone here at Yasnaya is in a melancholy mood, and I feel like crying all day. Lyova is terribly agitated and anxious about his son. It is warm and fine. I have been making shirts for tramps and wandering about in a state of depression. Lev Nikolaevich looks quite shrunken; but he is working and I cannot.

19 Sewed shirts for the tramps. We had a visit from some woman called Nikolskaya, who wanted Lev Nikolaevich's advice. He has been correcting the proofs of the *Circle of Reading*.

21 Andryusha left this evening for Tambov. I made some apple jam this morning. N.V. Davydov came – it was so pleasant to see him. This evening Goldenweiser played for us – a Beethoven sonata, a polonaise and various other Chopin pieces. I sewed shirts.

Lev Nikolaevich went for a swim, and chatted with Dobrolyubov. Two young peasant revolutionaries came to see him.

23 Unpleasant scenes regarding the oak trees which have been stolen by the peasants. Sergeenko and Chertkov have come. Lev Nikolaevich has upset me greatly.[36]

27 Got up early and said goodbye to Lyova and his family who are off to Sweden. Felt very sad but managed to restrain myself.

I wrote my 'Memoirs', and played the piano for two and a half hours – a Weber sonata, a Chopin nocturne and one of Mendelssohn's 'Songs Without Words'. I tidied up in 'that house' and this evening I did some sewing.

30 I drove to Kozlovka to see the Sanftlebens, went on to Ovsyannikovo to visit the Gorbunovs and brought Ivan Ivanovich back with me. After dinner all four Goldenweisers came and Lev Nikolaevich read us his article 'Two Roads', with its dreams of universal peasant life. As usual the negative side is strong, while the positive is weak. Leroy-Beaulieu said of the Russian revolution, when he stayed with us: '*Vous en avez pour 50 ans*,'*[37] yet Lev Nikolaevich wants to stop it with an article on anarchy and universal love.

August 1 Rain and thunder all day; and I have been writing my 'Memoirs'. Lev Nikolaevich rode to Yasenki to enquire about the widow.[38] Sasha went off for her music lesson. Lev Nikolaevich keeps working away at his (in my opinion) unsuccessful article 'Two Roads'.

*'You have enough to last you for 50 years.'

3 I went out for a swim and to pick mushrooms, drove to the Goldenweisers', sewed. Lev Nikolaevich also went swimming, then read a lot of newspapers and the *Review of Reviews*. He is appalled by recent events and all the bombs. He said that if Herzen had not been exiled, the young people would have followed him, and he would have led them in the proper direction, towards the goals he himself reached towards the end of his life. He was also talking about his dislike for Chernyshevskii[39] and Spencer.[40]

5 I ran to the Voronka for a swim first thing this morning. They are cutting the buckwheat, sowing the rye and picking the apples. Tanya arrived, to our delight, followed by Mikhail Sergeevich.

7 Everyone has left: Tanya and her husband returned home this morning, and Lev Nikolaevich, Chertkov, Sasha and Doctor Makovitsky have gone to Pirogovo and I am alone here with Lebrun.

10 I went for a swim as soon as I got up. There was a north wind, but it was very pleasant. I met I.K. Dieterichs with a priest who had come to see Lev Nikolaevich – a lively, intelligent man.

The others have all returned from Pirogovo, where my sister Mashenka was visiting from the convent. I did a lot of writing on my life story. Goldenweiser was here and another priest.

11 M.O. Menshikov came and had some very unpleasant discussions with Lev Nikolaevich.[41] Chertkov has left for England.

13 I have been busy with estate affairs all day. I printed some photographs of L.N. Lev Nikolaevich is still correcting the *Circle of Reading* proofs.

15 The news in the papers has cast a shadow over the day. Lev Nikolaevich read us some Anatole France this evening, about the war with the yellow race.[42] I spent the day making a quilted dress for Maria Aleksandrovna.

16 Prince Dmitrii Dmitrevich Obolenskii came. Discussions about hunting, and yet more talk about Henry George's theories on the land. Lev Nikolaevich has been writing his article for seven months now. First it was called 'Two Roads', now it has another title. He went for a ride.

19 Lev Nikolaevich was sick today. Pav. Iv. Biryukov has come; we discussed his *Biography* of Lev Nikolaevich together, and I gave him some information.[43]

20 Mikh. Serge. Sukhotin came, and Mikh. Vas. Nesterov the artist, who has been sketching Lev Nikolaevich in his album.[44] I.A. Ilin, recently offered a place at the university, came too, and the Goldenweisers.

Lev Nikolaevich was a little better this evening.

22 At four a.m. I was overcome by excruciating pains in the left side of my stomach.

My 62nd birthday – I cannot believe I am so old.

29 I cannot remember a thing – frightful pains.

31* The onset of peritonitis, unbearable pain, we wired Snegiryov.

September 1* I confessed, took communion and bade a tender farewell to the family and the servants. All the children came except Lyova. I saw death at close quarters. My love for L.N. and the children overwhelmed me with its power.

2* Snegiryov operated.[45] Lev Nikolaevich went to the woods at Chepyzh while it was going on, and asked them to ring once if it was successful, several times if it was unsuccessful.

4* I have had the doctors with me, the children were kept away, Lev Nikolaevich was allowed in once a day. Endless pain.

20 Doctor Gaichman has left. I got up and walked about the bedroom. Berkenheim has arrived.

23 I was helped downstairs to the hall for our 44th wedding anniversary.

28 Snegiryov and Polilov arrived. They are trying to make me travel to some warm place – the very thought makes me anxious.[46]

30 Four weeks since my operation. I feel much better but very weak. Everything is dismal, I walk with a stick.

October 6 I went out on to the balcony for the first time. Tanya and Sasha went to Tula and sold some land to the peasants.

7 Tanya and Sasha visited Tula again. Lev Nikolaevich went to Sudakovo to petition for the peasants who were burnt to death by a passing train.[47]

I did not sleep last night.

*Added later (Sofia Tolstaya).

11 A heavy fall of snow – it's thick on the ground. Basilevskii came and played us his works.

Vl. Vas. Stasov died today. We have lost a good, serious person and a dear friend.

16 Still the same gloomy weather; the snow is melting. Lev Nikolaevich rode to Yasenki and brought me back a letter from Chertkov.[48] I played the piano a little. My soul is depressed. Little Volodya is very touching.

23 I played with my granddaughter Tanyushka, played the piano for a long time on my own and walked around the garden with Dorik and Volodya. Lev Nikolaevich rode to Yasenki. This evening we read about the women of the French Revolution.[49]

24 I played a Weber sonata and sewed. This evening we read about French women in the Revolution, and Lev Nikolaevich listened. He went for a long ride today, and worked, as always, all morning.

28 I went through a drawer of books and manuscripts. We are looking for an excerpt from one of Lev Nikolaevich's works to read at a charity evening in Tula, for which he has promised to give us something.[50]

November 4 Cold and windy. I am in low spirits. I sewed, catalogued books and played two Beethoven sonatas. An American was here with his Jewish wife.[51] Lev Nikolaevich is well.

7 Windy; 2 ° this morning, 1 ° below freezing this evening. The snow has all gone. I have started copying a landscape by Pokhitonov (of Fanfaronova Hill).[52]

8 I painted my landscape, coached Dorik, and spent the evening with Tanya in the Kuzminskiis' wing. Lev Nikolaevich is writing a letter in French to Sabatier about his book;[53] he went for a ride and is well.

10 Sat with Tanya again and walked around the park with Anna Ivanovna. My son Seryozha came, as well as Zhozya Dieterichs and the American, who was with a Jewish woman translator.[54] Anna Ivanovna and the American have now left.

13 The snow has turned to mud and it has been raining; it is 4 °. I painted my landscape and this evening I sight-read some concertos – by Weber, Hummel and Mozart. [L.N.'s] article about Shakespeare appeared in the *Russian Word* today. It was translated from the English.[55]

15 Rain, impassable mud, 4 °. I wrote, drew pictures for Tanyushka and coloured them, then Natasha and I played two Haydn trios arranged as duets. Lev Nikolaevich is unwell; he is reading Montaigne.[56] He has heard that Verigin (the Dukhobor) is leaving Canada for Russia.[57]

17 Mr Salomon came. My son Lyova has arrived.

It snowed last night and thawed again today; it is slippery outside and the road is impassable. My eyes are aching – I haven't done a thing all day.

19 Andryusha has returned, having done all my errands for me. We all took a walk to the young fir trees, where Masha and Andryusha saw the vixen. Masha fell ill this evening, and was shaking and shivering; I am very anxious about her.

20 Masha is very poorly; her temperature was 40.8 this evening. My heart is like lead; I feel so sorry and afraid for her. The house is sad and silent.

21 Masha is very ill, day and night her temperature is 41.3. Doctor Afanasiev came.

23 Masha has a fever of 40.7, and has difficulty speaking. I am terrified, I don't sleep at night, my soul is oppressed.

Lina and Misha came for dinner and it became a little more cheerful; there are still plenty of people to love, so long as I have my grandchildren.

24 Masha is still very ill. V.A. Shchurovskii and Vl. Alekseevich Afanasiev came. There is an inflammation of the left lung and pleurisy.

Lina and Misha have left, Ilya came – wanting money as usual. 1 ° of frost, snowing. We can think of nothing but Masha's illness.

25 Masha is in a frightful state – groaning, tossing and delirious. I was sitting with her and it was unbearable to see her. I walked along the avenue and thought: *why* do people so value their own lives and those of their loved ones? We are all tense with anticipation.

27 Masha died quietly at twenty to one this morning. Lev Nikolaevich was sitting beside her, holding her hand. She sat propped up on the pillows, and we were all with her (in the room under the arches). I kissed her forehead and stood beside L.N. Kolya kept weeping and kissing her hands even after she had fallen quiet. A terrible wind was howling and tearing at the house. I cannot believe Masha is gone; it is very painful.

28 Sasha Dolinino-Ivanskaya came. Masha has been laid in her coffin, and Marfa Kub[asova], Olga Ershova, Matryosha and her mother are all sitting with her. Lev Nikolaevich, Kolya and Tanya went in to see her and the funeral service has been performed. I have been with Kolya and Andryusha, who is making all the arrangements.

29 We buried Masha.

30 I do nothing all day, life has stopped. I went to the side wing to see Tanyushka, who is utterly adorable.

December 6 4 Dukhobors came this evening with 2 young girls.[58] Goldenweiser arrived, Sonya Mamonova left.

9 I wrote letters on the Remington; Verigin and the Dukhobors came and sang a hymn. Extraordinarily beautiful! My soul is melancholy, everything is hopeless.

10 Lev Nikolaevich rode to Yasenki on Raven, and spent the evening writing letters. The Dukhobors have left.

13 I read Zosya my autobiography, visited the Kuzminskiis' wing and spent the evening sewing shirts for the poor. Lev Nikolaevich took Dorik and the village lads into his study and read them the thoughts of Epictetus; he is trying to make his *Circle of Reading* accessible to everyone.[59]

14 The boys came in to see Lev Nikolaevich again, and he read and explained to them the sayings from his *Circle of Reading*. I worked a little on my autobiography and did some sewing.

28 I wrote my autobiography again. Makovitsky said to my great alarm that Lev Nikolaevich had become much thinner, and that the wheezing in his lungs has worsened. I am feeling very anxious.

31 27 degrees below freezing, although warmer towards evening – 14 degrees below – with snow and a wind.

Lev Nikolaevich still has a cough, and his cold is worse, but he continues to write. Yesterday he entered 11 or 12 pages from his notebook into his diary.[60] He has grown thinner and older over the past month.

We saw in the New Year with the Sukhotins. A rather sad occasion, not surprisingly, considering how many of us are absent, dead, ill or unhappy! When I kissed Tanya she burst into tears.

· 1907 ·

January 1 'Weak, headache, wrote letters to Stakhovich (very heartfelt) and Olga.'*[1] This morning I sorted out and read Lev Nikolaevich's letter to Tanya, then wrote my autobiography. I was most alarmed about L.N.'s health this evening.

3 I am terribly worried about Lev Nikolaevich's health. His cough is worse and his general condition has deteriorated. Went out to take photographs of Tanyushka, sewed, looked after L.N. Depression, endless grief, no life.

8 Read Sukhotin my memoirs.[2]

12 Did some good work on my memoirs and took some bad photographs. Little Tanyushka was brought in to see us. Mar. Aleksand. Schmidt came. Lev Nikolaevich is much better. Learnt that Sergei Ivanovich had typhus.

13 Did a lot of work on my autobiography. Printed some bad photographs. Coached Dorik. Lev Nikolaevich is still weak and is staying at home. He is reading Socrates[3] and has finished an English novel.[4] He is compiling a simplified version of the *Circle of Reading*.

15 I read Lev Nikolaevich my autobiography for 1877 and '8 today. He added one or two things and praised it, which delighted me. We had little Tanyushka here, and she went out for a walk. Lev Nikolaevich also went out today for the first time – on two separate occasions.

18 My daughter and granddaughter, the two Tanyas, have influenza and a high fever. Lev Nikolaevich's cough is worse. Iv. Iv. Gorbunov came. I did a little writing and coached Dorik, but I cannot get a grip on anything. I am frightened for everyone, my soul is weary.

19 The two Tanyas are much better, thank God, and the fever has passed. I wrote my autobiography and read part of it to Mikh. Serg. Sukhotin. He thought it was very interesting and well written. I devote a lot of time to Tanyushka. My soul is anxious and depressed. Lev Nikolaevich went out for a walk and a drive, and he is reading a lot. Today he read Montaigne.

20 Lev Nikolaevich went for a ride through the woods again today. We had a visit from two astronomers called Ganskii and Stefanik, who

*Added by L.N. Tolstoy.

told us some fascinating things. I coached Dorik and worked on my memoirs.

23 I have been rather inactive these past two days. I went for a walk and admired the beauty of the sun and the hoar-frost. Yesterday and today we read aloud the memoirs of Morozov (the revolutionary).[5] We also read an article by Menshikov about Nesterov's painting *Holy Russia*; Lev Nikolaevich liked it very much and wrote Menshikov a letter about it.[6] The invalids are all better now; I am leaving for Moscow.

28 (Moscow) Spent the morning at the Wanderers' Exhibition. Some lovely landscapes by E. Volkov and Dubovskoi – Kiselev's were not so good. Vl. Makovskii's *Two Mothers* and especially his *Huntsmen* were lovely.[7]

29 Went to the museum this morning and read Strakhov's letters. This evening a recital by some musicians from Paris playing ancient instruments – a harpsichord, a viol and a bass. They played beautifully – some Bruni, an andante, some sonatas, a bourrée by Bach and a gavotte by Handel. I didn't get home until late this evening.

30 Back in Yasnaya, with darling little Tanyushka and her toys. It's nice to be home.

31 I slept badly and got up late. I read some of Strakhov's letters, which Tanya had hidden away. They were interesting, but did not contain much material for my memoirs. I went to visit my granddaughter Tanyushka; an extraordinarily sweet child.

Lev Nikolaevich went for a walk; he is reading a lot and is in good health. He played chess with Sukhotin. He receives such a lot of interesting letters. A young man arrived yesterday asking L.N. to give him some money by way of an 'expropriation'. L.N. tried in vain to teach him the error of his ways – a stubborn, stupid young fellow.

February 1 I made prints of Lev Nikolaevich's Crimean photographs for Countess Geiden, then played Chopin for about two hours. Lev Nikolaevich went for a ride through the woods; he is compiling a moral reader for children.[8]

2 I wrote my autobiography all day. Lev Nikolaevich praises and encourages my work, and I read it to him. I went to the wing and played with Tanyushka, while L.N. went for a walk through the woods. He was telling us about an article he had read which exposed the spiritualists and their tricks.

4 Wrote my autobiography all day. Spent the evening making a felt hat for a poor boy who lives in Ovsyannikovo. Lev Nikolaevich has a slight cough but went for a walk. This evening he listened to Tregubov's 'Appeal' to the revolutionaries.

5 Tanyushka is ill with a high fever. Andryusha and Nazhivin came, and Misha visited for a couple of hours. Nazhivin is going to Moscow tomorrow to speak about Tolstoy to some workers, at their request.[9] I had an argument with him about the Church and the marriage service.

8 Tanyushka is better, her temperature is back to normal. Lev Nikolaevich went for a quiet walk and then sat down; he still has difficulty breathing. We read Flammarion's piece about spiritualism.[10]

9 I have been writing my book; I am annoyed that there is so little material – I just use whatever I can find. Lev Nikolaevich is reading Renan's *Saint Paul*,[11] and is still writing his book for children; he is writing letters and his diary too; he seems better. I read *My Reminiscences* by Fet – poorly written, over-detailed and of little interest.[12]

11 Konshin came with Gorbunov, and my son Andryusha. I sorted through some letters. Makovitsky is not at all happy about Lev Nikolaevich's heart – but I don't trust him. He went for a ride, and is now working on his anthology of wise sayings for children.[13]

13 Lev Nikolaevich went for a ride and spent the evening with the peasant boys, testing out on them his book of moral precepts for children.

14 The peasant boys came to see Lev Nikolaevich this afternoon and he spent some time with them. This evening Mikhail Sergeevich read us some stories by Kuprin, including 'Allez'.

15 I printed some photographs for Countess Geiden and myself, then coached Dorik. This evening Natasha and I played a Haydn symphony and Mozart's 5th quintet as duets. The peasant boys came in to listen; they had just been with Lev Nikolaevich, who had been explaining the Gospel to them. Lev Nikolaevich was wheeled around the park in his wheelchair. He complains of feeling weak.

16 I wrote 34 pages of my memoirs and coached Dorik. I am alarmed by Lev Nikolaevich's weak state. Dmitriev and Kartushin came to visit – idealistic young men.

17 B.N. Leontiev was here. Lev Nikolaevich is still weak and his heartbeat is irregular.

22(Moscow) Went to the museum this morning and stayed there until 3. An all-Schubert chamber recital this evening.

25 Spent the day dashing from one exhibition to another – first the Union of Russian Artists, then Borisov-Musatov, finally Nesterov. The last one was the best of all. Musatov is horribly decadent. The Russian artists have taken a false path and are of little interest. Nesterov himself came with me and to his exhibition, and talked so interestingly about his paintings. This evening I went to a concert – a Haydn trio, a Schumann quintet and Nezhdanova, who sang beautifully.

26 Worked hard in the museum all morning. Finished my shopping and business, spent the evening with my family and left late at night for Yasnaya.

March 7 Misha's family has left. Tanyushka was brought in to see us, and this evening I went to see her. The peasant boys came to see Lev Nikolaevich every evening and he has been reading them various stories which he is planning to rewrite.[14] The bailiff has asked me to be godmother to his baby so I sewed my little godson a shirt. I did quite a lot of writing.

8 Bodyanskii, Uspenskii and Mazaev the Molokan* came.[15] Andryusha and I went to the christening of Alyosha the bailiff's son. I worked hard on my autobiography.

9 I worked hard on my memoirs and read them to Mikh. Serg. Sukhotin; Lev Nikolaevich listened to some of it and praised my writing, which pleases me.

14 Some rowdy peasant lads came to visit Lev Nikolaevich and exhausted him.

15 I coached Dorik, worked on my memoirs and tacked some trousers for Lev Nikolaevich. He read the village lads Semyonov's story 'The Night Before Christmas', grew over-excited and lost his voice.[16]

17 Lev Nikolaevich went for a ride, then taught the boys in the second class.[17] He is well.

*Member of a milk-drinking religious sect, mainly south Russian peasants.

18 N.F. Nazhivin came; I read him my 'Autobiography', and he praised it. I sewed for Lev Nikolaevich all day. He went for a ride, taught the senior boys and read them the Sermon on the Mount.

19 We read a review of Lyova's play *Landowning Brothers* in the *New Times* – very flattering.[18]

20 I wrote my memoirs and coached Dorik. Lev Nikolaevich and I spent the evening with Tanya. I read a little about Nik. Nik. Gué from my 'Memoirs' and everyone approved.[19]

23 Read the old 'Postbox' all day.

26 Busy with estate and money matters all morning, then worked on my autobiography. Went in to see Tanya and read her old diaries, from which I took a few notes.[20] L.N. is feeling weak, but he went for a ride none the less and worked with the boys.

27 Spent the day taking notes from various documents for my book. After dinner I played with Tanyushka and sewed. We read aloud Menshikov's article about the apostles and prophets.[21] Lev Nikolaevich went for a ride and worked with the boys.

29 Lev Nikolaevich has a heavy cold. We all went into Tanya's wing, where he read us Chekhov's story 'The Butterfly'; it was very good.[22] I did a lot of writing on my memoirs and sewed.

April 1 Lev Nikolaevich is still staying at home. He played literary lotto with the village boys, and I helped. Most unsuccessful.

9 (Moscow) I hired a new accountant and set him to work. Endless affairs to see to – ordering books, taking stock of sales, checking things. I sat in the museum all morning.

10 Returned to Yasnaya this morning. Tanyushka shines like a light. My son Andryusha arrived with Sutkovoi, and I read him my 'Memoirs'.

13 I read the diaries of Varya Tolstaya (Nagornova) both to myself and aloud to Lev Nikolaevich. They're very good.[23] I took some notes. This afternoon I played the piano. Lev Nikolaevich went to visit Maria Aleksandrovna. We had crowds of beggars and petitioners here.

14 I spent the whole day making notes from all the material I have gathered for my 'Memoirs'. My soul is sad and terribly melancholy.

Timber is stolen from the forest, then the wretched peasant petitioners, then the dear, sad little orphans. L.N. played literary lotto with the village lads.

16 I started writing, and intended to write all day, but everyone kept disturbing me. I enjoyed myself enormously this afternoon playing Beethoven sonatas. [L.N.] went for a ride. He read us Leskov's story about the robbers.[24]

17 The first warm day of summer. The house is being cleaned and tidied; I wasted the whole day on trifles. This evening I played some Beethoven sonatas and we read aloud Menshikov's article[25] and Lyova's comedy.[26]

19 I painted the garden seat, coached Dorik and read Lyova's play *Landowning Brothers*. It isn't bad and it's theatrical and lively, but it's contemporary, and that's always a mistake. One should write about things that are eternal and universal, not merely incidental. L.N. rode to Tula.

22 I sorted out some old photographs – so many people have been so long gone!

24 There's a rumour going around St Petersburg and elsewhere that L.N. is dead, and Andryusha galloped over here from Tula. This evening we all gathered in my room and had a good talk.[27]

25 I worked on my 'Memoirs'. Lev Nikolaevich was spiteful and unpleasant to me in a discussion about the estate.[28]

29 I read my 'Memoirs' to Dunaev and Strakhov. They approved. Lev Nikolaevich worked with the boys and went for a ride.

May 1 They're hard at work ploughing and sowing the oats. The birches are in leaf, the cowslips are out. Iv. Iv. Gorbunov came, the Nikolaevs visited the village. I worked hard on my 'Memoirs', then I went to watch them sowing the oats and ploughing. Lev Nikolaevich walked 9 *versts* and then worked with the boys. He told Tanya and me that people had lost all religious feeling, and that it was as impossible to live without religion as without air.

3 Spent the day in Moscow. Left this evening for St Petersburg.

4 Stayed with my sister Tanya in St Petersburg and visited Lyova. Dora and the children are very sweet, and they lead a good life. To the theatre this evening for a performance of Hamsun's *Drama of Life*.[29]

6 Visited Krivoshein to intercede for Ilya. Spent an hour and a half at the Alexander III Museum looking at paintings.

7 I went to the Duma with Zosya Stakhovich and was horrified by the nonsense she talked. I dined at home and was then taken to the station in Sanya's motor car. I left for home.

12 I attended to the estate; the potatoes are being cut for planting and the oats are being sown. I spent the morning and evening revising my autobiography and dividing it into chapters. Lev Nikolaevich and Varya listened to me reading it aloud, and were delighted with it.

16 Attended to numerous estate matters and had the roofer, 2 painters and an upholsterer here. I revised my memoirs. Lev Nikolaevich still has a cough. He has been writing an article about the holy apostle Paul, prompted by his reading of Renan's *St Paul*.[30] The village boys came to see him.

18 I worked hard today on my autobiography – for the year 1884. Very hard! And so little material. This evening we read aloud Pobedonostsev's letters to Tyutchev about the assassination of Tsar Alexander II.[31]

19 Lev Nikolaevich is very hoarse and has been staying at home in his dressing-gown; he is still working with the village boys. Tormenting depression all day.

20 At last an explanation of my depression: it was a premonition of evil. Ghastly news that my brother Vyacheslav was murdered yesterday by workers.[32]

21 I worked a lot on my autobiography today. I am drowning my depression in work.

23 I worked hard on my autobiography and wrote well. Then suddenly during dinner I heard from Makovitsky that L.N. had a fever. I ran in to see him, and discovered that he had a temperature of 39.4. I nearly fainted. But I took strenuous measures and by midnight it was down to 37.9. I sat with him till four in the morning.

24 Sasha and Doctor Nikitin arrived this morning. Lev Nikolaevich is better. Berkenheim came. I sat beside Lev Nikolaevich all day and sewed.

26 Lev Nikolaevich was 36.6 this morning, 38 at 6 this evening, and 37.6 at midnight. I feel sad, depressed and anxious. Gorbunov and Maria Aleksandrovna came too. Some peasants, women teachers and schoolchildren from some workers' union came to shake Lev Nikolaevich's hand, and two of them stayed to talk with him. Even they are affected by the revolutionary mood. There were also a couple of Jews here.

31 L.N.'s fever has passed. I finished my memoirs for 1884 and packed them up. This evening I left for Moscow with Olga on business.

June 3 (Moscow) The Duma has been dissolved – a manifesto was issued this evening.[33] I drove to my children's graves today and planted flowers. Later on I left for Yasnaya.

4 Unpleasant domestic matters to attend to all day at Yasnaya. L.N. is weak but well. Goldenweiser came, and Nikolaev walked over to see us.

10 Whit Sunday. I have been very busy with my autobiography; I read a lot of old letters and grew very agitated. Zvegintseva, Volkov, Mikhailov and the three Goldenweisers were here.

11 The whole village came here, and there was singing and dancing. Nikolaev and Mikhailov visited, and there were the usual endless tedious discussions about Henry George. Lev Nikolaevich went for a ride, worked with the boys and wrote his children's *Circle of Reading*.

12 Did a lot of writing. Lev Nikolaevich went for a ride around Zaseka; this evening he asked me to find him his books by Vauvenargues.[34] Then he worked with the boys.

19 The Chertkovs arrived this evening on the fast train.

22 I wrote quite a lot. Lev Nikolaevich walked over to Ovsyannikovo, and drove back. The doctor came to see our patient, and young Semyonov (Leonid).[35]

24 More unpleasant scenes with the haymakers – they wouldn't go out to mow, and refused to let anyone else go. I had to settle the whole thing myself – the bailiff is quite useless. L.N. went swimming for the second time in two days, and took a walk. Nesterov has started on his portrait.[36] Lev Nikolaevich read the village lads his new story about Palechek the clown.[37] Marusya sang for us; she has now left. Galya sang too. Goldenweiser and Nikolaev were here.

26 850 children with their teachers travelled here from Tula to take a walk round Yasnaya. They went swimming with L.N., sang, danced and drank tea, and we took their photographs. Then they arranged a solemn and splendid procession with flags.[38]

27 It poured with rain again, and the hay was ruined. We went swimming and I wrote my memoirs; I have now finished 1885. I played duets with Nadya Ivanova – two Haydn symphonies and a Mozart quintet. Then I stayed up till 3 a.m. developing my photographs of the children who came yesterday. The Chertkovs were here. L.N. played chess while Nesterov painted his portrait. There's something not quite right about it. We've just heard that Sasha Behrs is seriously ill.

July 2 Discussed land with the Yasnaya peasants this morning. Agreed terms.[39]

7 Worked for about three hours on my memoirs and went swimming. Then three Americans arrived, two women and a man, a Mr Barrow, the husband of one of them.[40] Spent the rest of the day with them. Sutkovoi and the Chertkovs came. L.N. is well; he drove over to see Galya Chertkova.

8 Chertkov, Nikolaev and Sutkovoi were here. Pav. Iv. Biryukov arrived, followed this evening by Nikitin. I immersed myself in letters for the year 1886, which I am reading for my autobiography. Lev Nikolaevich is well; he has stopped teaching the children and says he is now bored with it.[41]

14 This afternoon a whole crowd of people, including Orlov the artist, arrived to take a look at Tolstoy – children, teachers, schoolmistresses, the Nikolaevs, Goldenweiser, Chertkov and various others. I find them all so alien, apart from Nikolaev's wife.

19 Lev Nikolaevich read us his article 'Thou Shalt Not Kill Anyone' this evening.[42] Goldenweiser and the Chertkovs were here.

22 I checked the accounts book before dinner, read Lev Nikolaevich's article 'Thou Shalt Not Kill Anyone' and made some pencil notes on a piece of paper. L.N. agreed with them. Zosya Stakhovich came, and my son Lyova, and a lady who distributes L.N.'s works,[43] and was accompanied by some simple woman. Chertkov was here.

26 Went for a walk with Zosya and read the proofs of *Anna Karenina*. Lyova has left for St Petersburg. After dinner we read the revised version of Lev Nikolaevich's article 'Thou Shalt Not Kill Anyone'. Crowds of people here – the epileptic student,[44] mad Silchevskii the writer, Kuzmin, the Chertkovs, Dosev, Apollov, Gusev and others. Goldenweiser played beautifully – a polonaise, ballade and étude of Chopin.

27 Zosya Stakhovich has left. I read her my autobiography. This evening I sewed myself some underwear and quarrelled with Nikolaev about Syutaev and Lev Nikolaevich.[45] The same people here – young Sergeenko, the epileptic student and the Chertkovs.

28 Our visitors today were the Chertkovs, the Goldenweisers, Nikolaeva and some stranger called Kulakov. Lev Nikolaevich is still working on 'Thou Shalt Not Kill Anyone', and visits the Chertkovs almost every day.

30 I visited the Goldenweisers to read them my autobiography.

August 3 Goldenweiser, Dima Chertkov, some young officer and the Khiryakovs came. Lev Nikolaevich visits the Chertkovs every day and endlessly revises his article 'Thou Shalt Not Kill Anyone'.

4 Seryozha has come with his wife and son. I have been busy checking the bailiff's accounts. A journalist called Kenchitskii came.[46] Goldenweiser played the Chopin sonata with the 'Marche funèbre', and two other pieces. I have been reading Repin's book about art.[47]

6 Lev Nikolaevich read 'Palachek' and some parables with the boys.

8 Aleksei the yard-keeper told us a strange tale of how some hooligans had questioned him about our house and offered him a hundred rubles if he collaborated. We have all been terribly frightened and cannot sleep. I wrote to the governor and sent someone to buy a gun. Mikh. Serg. Sukhotin came. We read Tanya's splendid article about the fire, and were very moved.[48]

9 Four policemen were sent over here with an officer. Nothing has happened, although yesterday some tramps ordered Aleksei to bring them some bread.

A Czech journalist was here.

10 Some Jewish journalist came,[49] and Chertkov. We also had an insurance agent called Ivanov here, and I insured the hay, the threshing barn and the grain. I played the piano a little and badly. I corrected the fourth part of my autobiography.

13 I revised my memoirs. Yet more people here – the two Chertkovs, Khiryakov, Varvara Mikhailovna, Sulerzhitskii, Nikolaev. Suler sang and danced and told stories. What energy!

14 A crowd of people here this evening – the two Chertkovs, Ginzburg, Suler, Nikolaev, Dorik and Dashkevich, the Goldenweisers. He played Schumann's 'Davidsbündlertänze' and some Chopin. Suler and Ginzburg did comic acts.

16 Spent the whole day with my brother Petya, and read him my autobiography. Chertkov visited with young Kramorev. My brother Petya and his son have left. Lev Nikolaevich rode over to Ovsyannikovo.

18 I wanted to visit Zvegintseva and the Chertkovs, but was prevented from leaving by that uncouth General Ilinskii.[50] He ruined the entire day. Gorbunov arrived this evening, accompanied by Benevskii, Shatskii and Izyumenko – all dark ones. Izyumenko told an interesting story about prisons, Siberia and the disciplinary battalion.

19 A tragic accident! A 7-year-old boy has drowned in the middle pond; his 16-year-old sister waded in to save him and was also drowned. The poor mother! She is the sister of Varya, our washerwoman. Lev Nikolaevich and I went to visit the Chertkovs. Endless talk and crowds of young people, mainly peasants. He preached – utter hypocrisy. Abrikosov came, and two schoolmistresses from Kazan.

22 My 63rd birthday, I cannot believe I'm so old. The Chertkov family was here, the Goldenweisers, Maria Aleksandrovna, Rostovtsova and Abrikosov. I thought of my children and longed to see them. I played the piano for a long time during the day, and this evening I read Zosya Stakhovich my memoirs. Lev Nikolaevich visits the Chertkovs almost every day.

23 Lev Nikolaevich drove through Zaseka to Provaly with Zosya Stakhovich, then wrote a little article rather like a catechism, which I copied on the Remington.

24 I went to the young fir saplings looking for mushrooms but there were almost none to be found; autumn is in the air. I played the piano a lot today, both alone (Chopin) and with Nadya Ivanova (some Beethoven and Mozart overtures). Chertkov, young Sergeenko, Kartushin, Dosev, Perna and Kuzmin came. L.N. chatted with them, then rode over to Chertkov's house.

26 Lev Nikolaevich walked to Ovsyannikovo and drove back. He has eaten nothing all day. He is reading the memoirs of Izyumenko and Drozhin, both of whom refused to do military service.[51]

28 Lev Nikolaevich's 79th birthday. Our guests were: Seryozha and his wife, Vas. Al. Maklakov, my granddaughter Annochka, Natasha Sukhotina, the Chertkovs, Maria Aleksandrovna, Nikolaeva, the Goldenweisers, Kuzmin, Perna, Dosev, young Sergeenko and Kartushin.

September 3 Mitya Kuzminskii, Kolya Obolenskii and Andryusha came, and Sytin, Ertel, Goldenweiser and the Chertkovs were here too. I did almost no housework; I visited the Nikolaevs, read the proofs of *The Cossacks* and wrote to the governor about the shootings.[52]

4 Andryusha visited the governor to complain about the shootings. Nikolaev, the Chertkovs and the Goldenweisers were here. He played Beethoven's 'Appassionata' extraordinarily well. Lev Nikolaevich wept as he listened to the music.

5 Today we had the Chertkovs, the Nikolaevs, Zvegintseva, Volkhonskaya Goldenweiser, Perna, and Genr. Osip. Klepatskii, a correspondent for *Voice of Moscow*. They have sent us 7 guards, a police officer and a sergeant. Arrests and searches in the village. So distressing![53]

6 Zhozya Dieterichs and Malevannyi the sectarian came. Lev Nikolaevich rode over to visit the Chertkovs. He is writing his children's *Circle of Reading* at present. I copied extracts from his diary for 1895 and '96. One of the three tramps has been shooting in the woods again.

7 Governor Kobeko came this morning with Skablanovich and Smirnov. Crowds of police officers, guards and carriages. They have left me 2 guards. Andryusha has come. The Chertkovs, Rostovtsov and the Goldenweisers were here. He played his usual pieces – an étude, a ballade and a nocturne by Chopin. Lev Nikolaevich went to visit Zvegintseva. I took notes from L.N.'s diary.

8 Up till late last night copying excerpts from L.N.'s diary. Finished the notebook for 1895–7. Painful memories! No guests today, apart from some sick hysterical woman we had never met.

9 I called on Zvegintseva and the Chertkovs. We were visited by a doctor from Siberia,[54] a priest from Tula and a former prisoner.[55]

11 (Moscow) I took my memoirs to the museum, and did a little work.

13 I worked in the museum from 11 to 3, but I did very little and was annoyed that I had to leave without accomplishing anything. More shopping. This evening I left for home.

14 Unpleasant news about the theft of yet more of our oaks, and an unpleasant conversation with Lev Nikolaevich about the guards.[56]

16 A whole day spent worrying about the costumes for *The Power of Darkness*, to be performed at the Yavorskii Theatre in Tiflis.[57] The peasants have been pleading with us over the stolen timber. All very distressing. They have been taken away and thrown into jail.[58] Zosya has left for Tiflis with the costumes.

18 I tidied up the Kuzminskiis' wing for Repin and walked over the estate. M.S. Sukhotin came, and Leonid Semyonov. Then I wrote to the chairman of the *zemstvo* and the member for this district, to complain about the peasants.

19 I played with Tanyushka and spent the rest of the day tidying up the books in the library. I am re-reading Turgenev's *Notes of a Huntsman*.

20 Seryozha is visiting, to my great joy. Lev Nikolaevich went for a ride today; he is working hard on his new *Circle of Reading*.[59] I sent another appeal to the chairman of the *zemstvo*.

21 Repin starting sketching a portrait of Lev Nikolaevich this morning, and spent the rest of the day working on one of me.[60] I read Repin and Nordman my memoirs.

23 Our 45th wedding anniversary. I.E. Repin started painting my portrait in oils. Then Lev Nikolaevich, Repin and I had our photograph taken together.

24 Took a walk with Natalya Borisovna Nordman, played with Tanyushka and printed photographs. This evening I read my memoirs to Repin, Nordman and Biryukov. Repin worked on Lev Nikolaevich's portrait today, and went for a ride with him.

25 I read Pavel Ivanovich Biryukov my memoirs. (He left today.) Then I posed for Repin. This evening we played a Beethoven septet and *Der Freischütz* overture arranged for 8 hands. Lev Nikolaevich read us a translated story by An. France called 'Crainquebille', and a Chekhov story about Pasha.[61]

26 I posed again today. I got up late and wandered happily around the park. We played the Beethoven septet again. This evening Lev Nikolaevich read us Kuprin's 'Night Shift' and 'Allez'.[62]

27 Lev Nikolaevich made some unpleasant remarks about the guards this morning, and we had a distressing conversation. Then I played with darling Tanyushka and posed for my portrait. This evening we played the Beethoven septet again – Lev Nikolaevich with Sasha, and I with Tanya. The *Freischütz* overture went badly.

28 Repin finished our portraits today and went for a ride with Lev Nikolaevich. Sasha rode with Seryozha Sukhotin and Tanya drove in the charabanc with N.B. Nordman. I took photographs all day – Sasha and L.N. playing the piano, Natalya Borisovna, and L.N. and me.

29 Repin and Nordman have left. My sister Tanya Kuzminskaya came this evening, and Seryozha Sukhotin left. I printed photographs and went for a walk. Gorbunov and Gusev came to visit.

30 I read sister Tanya my memoirs. Relations with L.N. are cool: he is angry about the guards and the harsh treatment meted out for the theft of the trees.

October 3 I read my sister my memoirs; parts of it are rather bad!

4 Tanya's birthday; how sad that her little girl is still ill and feverish. My sister sang. I did a little oil painting on a stone.

5 Tanyushka is still ill. It grieves my heart to see her. And she is so sweet to me. I have been looking after her. I painted some pansies on a stone for my daughter Tanya, and read sister Tanya my 'Memoirs'. A threatening telegram from a certain 'Goncharov' in Podolsk, saying: 'Expect a guest'.

7 Lev Nikolaevich rode into the woods and through the gulleys and cuttings at Zaseka. He's still working on the *Circle of Reading*. I read my memoirs aloud. Pav. Iv. Biryukov came with his son Borya. I have started painting a landscape on stone (the entrance to the estate with the towers).

9 I did another painting on stone for my sister – of a rose. This evening I read aloud a play by Loyson called *Le Droit de vierge*. Lev Nikolaevich and Tanya read it too.[63] My sister sang a little. I read aloud my memoirs again.

13 I walked round the estate, read my memoirs to sister Tanya and played with Tanyushka. This evening an Italian correspondent called Arlotta came, and we talked to him.[64] Then the three old women, Tanya, Liza and I, sat down together like good friends and laughed and chatted. Lev Nikolaevich is busy with his correspondence and his *Circle of Reading*: he rode over to Zaseka.

14 Games of vint and discussions of death, man's spirituality and his relationship with the world. Another threatening telegram from 'Goncharov', saying 'Expect me!'[65]

16 Spent the whole day painting a book for little Tanyushka to take on the journey. Sutkovoi was here; he is going to Kazan and Samara to distribute money to the hungry. Gusev was here with some young man who wants to refuse military service.[66]

18 (Moscow) Went to the theatre this evening to see Lyova's play *My Country*; unsatisfactory and overstated.[67]

20 Went this morning to the clinic, then to the museum for an hour for some information about Turgenev, and made some corrections. Then shopping, dinner with my brother, and this evening a symphony concert in the Hall of Columns. Met Lavrovskaya, Sergei Ivanovich and the musicians . . . No news from home, which worries me.

22 Returned to Yasnaya Polyana this morning. Everyone well.

23 Gusev arrested. Lev Nikolaevich again busy with the village boys every evening.

25 Count Dm. Al. Olsufiev came to see us. The boys visit L.N. every day. He is no longer compiling this *Circle of Reading* for children, as I had assumed. L.N.'s memory is evidently failing, and this saddens me.

26 Lev Nikolaevich visited Gusev, who is being taken to Krapivna. He has been jailed for inserting the words 'the brainless tsar' into L.N.'s article 'Where Is the Solution?', and also for not having a passport.[68]

28 I sewed this evening while Lev Nikolaevich read us Nazhivin's story 'The Golden Squadron'.[69] Then he played chess with Count Olsufiev.

29 I spent the whole day checking ghastly estate accounts and the day-labourers' work tickets. Andryusha came wanting the impossible – our sympathy for his marriage to Artsimovich.[70]

30 L.N. and Mikhail Sergeevich read us something about the Buddha.

November 1 The village lads visited L.N. this evening for their lesson. I typed on the Remington a complaint against the Grumond peasants. Lev Nikolaevich went to Tula alone in the sledge and interceded with Lopukhin for Gusev.[71]

2 I made a shirt for Lev Nikolaevich. He went for a ride and wrote letters all evening. He is still busy with the *Circle of Reading*.

4 Lev Nikolaevich has gone to Krapivna to visit N.N. Gusev, who is under arrest there.

5 I printed some photographs this morning. Lev Nikolaevich has returned from Krapivna, where he saw Gusev and Bulygin; he is well and cheerful.

18 Nik. Grig. Sutkovoi has come. Arrears are being collected in the village; the peasants cannot pay and are selling off their cattle.

19 There's been a blizzard blowing day and night, so eerie and depressing. Sutkovoi came – and has left. A young Irishman called Lesley came to visit with a lot of lofty plans for living with the poor.

21 I walked around the estate; the weather is fine, 5 degrees of frost. I played some Beethoven sonatas and Chopin waltzes, checked the day-labourers' work tickets, and this evening did some embroidery. Lev Nikolaevich rode to Zaseka and met 3 suspicious-looking tramps in the forest. Today he said he had finished his *Circle of Reading*.[72] He is weak and listless.

22 This morning I prepared a canvas and traced on to it Repin's portraits of us. I played the piano for a long time, and practised some Chopin, then this evening Nadya and I played Mozart duets. L.N. wrote to Andryusha and wept.[73]

24 I worked on the portraits again – badly; I am beginning to despair. The newspapers are all filled with the attempt on the Moscow Governor-General's life.[74] Situation very tense elsewhere too. Lev Nikolaevich went for a ride and wrote letters. He is well.

26 I am in a hurry to finish the portraits; today I painted a bunch of flowers. Lev Nikolaevich read us something about Buddhism. He has taken a walk and is well and cheerful.

27 The anniversary of our daughter Masha's death. Exactly one year. How sad and strange it is now she is gone. Our life is so dreary, quiet and lonely now. I have developed a passion for painting portraits, which is a great waste of concentration and energy. Lev Nikolaevich goes riding and muddles up his *Circle of Reading*: it's like Penelope's labours – one day he works, the next day he does it all over again.

29 Worked again on my portrait, and on Lev Nikolaevich's pillow-slips. He is cheerful and well, and has been for a ride. Apart from the *Circle of Reading*, he is interested in the idea of a 'Geography' which would describe every nation's life and habits.[75] He is tormented by humanity's lack of religion.

30 At about 5 this evening, as Lev Nikolaevich was returning home, he fell over the head of his horse, who had stumbled in a rut, and hurt his left arm, his shoulder and shoulder-blade.

December 1 Lev Nikolaevich did not sleep all night. The doctors say his liver has been shaken. He is very lethargic, and has been groaning and dozing, but nothing serious so far. I worked on the portrait and spoilt it; then I took a photograph of it, which I developed this evening.

2 Dushan Petrovich drove to Tula to fetch Doctor Chekan, as he thought Lev Nikolaevich had dislocated something, but it turns out that he hasn't. I painted portraits and printed photographs again all day. L.N. was reading indoors all day but was in good spirits.

3 I painted portraits all day. Lev Nikolaevich read us some of Herzen's thoughts this afternoon – what a lucid mind.

6 Andryusha came with his new wife – today is her 30th birthday. I cannot understand her; how can one be happy after abandoning a splendid husband and 6 children? I painted a portrait and did some embroidery. Lev Nikolaevich read us an Anatole France story called 'Oui Monsieur', and Sasha and Andryusha sang. I wrote to the accountant and the American woman, and sent the translations to the prison.

12 (Moscow) Went to the Historical Museum, the bank and the shops. Visited E.F. Yunge, who is sick.[76]

14 Worked hard in the museum until 3 o'clock, then visited E.F. Yunge.

15 Went to an exhibition of paintings with Masha. Sverchkov's huge painting *Kholstomer and the Herd* is there; it costs 6,000 rubles and nobody wants to buy it.[77]

17 I am back in Yasnaya. I looked at the portrait I copied – my face is atrociously painted. I have tried to correct it, but cannot, I lack the skill. Lev Nikolaevich is busy and well. What a good face he has.

19 Gorbunov, Maria Aleksandrovna and young Bulygin came. Lev Nikolaevich read us some letters he had received and was moved to tears by these simple people who read his books and change their lives in accordance with them.[78]

21 Gusev is back. He and Lev Nikolaevich read us Arapova's memoirs of her mother, Pushkina-Lanskaya, in *New Times*.[79]

23 Marusya Maklakova came this morning and Wanda Landowska arrived this evening with her husband and her clavecin. A most sympathetic woman, sensitive to everything; she obviously has the soul of an artist.

24 Spent the whole day with the Landowskis. Her playing, on both the piano and the harpsichord, was quite astonishing – gentle, measured, elegant and exquisitely expressive. Everyone, including Lev Nikolaevich, was in ecstasies.[80]

25 The young folk ran riot all day; even I danced – with Sasha and with Landowska's husband, while she played. I took a photograph of her with Lev Nikolaevich. A fierce blizzard, 3 ° below freezing, everyone went out for a walk or a drive, but had to return. Landowska played beautifully again. The Goldenweisers have left.

29 More photographs. Lev Nikolaevich took a walk, then went out in the sledge. It's difficult to walk and impossible to drive. He is still writing his *Circle of Reading*.

31 The end of the year, and that much nearer the end of my life, and of those dear to me. Andryusha and his wife came, and Maria Aleksandrovna Schmidt, and we had quite a festive New Year's party.

· 1909 ·

An alarming start to the year. Andryusha's wife arrived here, distraught, with her 10-month-old baby daughter. There was a fire on their estate today. Then someone saw a glow at Telyatinki, and feared it might be Sasha's house and that of the Chertkovs. (It turned out to be some peasant's barn.) Sasha decorated a Christmas tree for 115 village boys. Lev Nikolaevich was delighted to see the children but was very anxious. But everything went splendidly, and everyone was well pleased.

January 3 I copied *Hadji Murat*. Both L.N. and I wrote to Tanya.[1]

5 Lev Nikolaevich wrote something in the form of a play. He keeps searching for the right tone, but cannot find it. He has already made various starts on some work of fiction.[2] He went for a ride and is well.

10 I copied *Hadji Murat* and found some old manuscripts in Lev Nikolaevich's sofa. The proofs of *Resurrection* were there, and various other papers. Goldenweiser came and played Chopin, beautifully.

11 Goldenweiser played Chopin this evening – a polonaise, a sonata, a waltz, a nocturne and a mazurka. He played very well – quite sensitively at times. The family all went off to Tula for a concert given by the gipsy Varya Panina. L.N. rode over to see Chertkov, who read him a paper on village games. The Goldenweisers have left.

15 Spent the day with the Landowskis.[3] Andryusha and his wife, Chertkov and Strakhov came. I finished my copying for Lev Nikolaevich. We all went to visit the Chertkovs. Immense pleasure from Landowska's playing again this evening. So simple and original, such rhythm and expressiveness. Exquisite! They have now left.

16 I have done absolutely nothing but copy out *Hadji Murat*. It's so good! I simply couldn't tear myself away from it.

A certain landowner who has given his land to the peasants came to see Lev Nikolaevich with his son. His name is Scheierman.[4] Mitya Kuzminskii and Chelishchev have arrived.

18 I went through Aunt Tatiana Ergolskaya's workbox and sorted out her letters and papers, as well as those of Lev Nikolaevich's parents. I have copied it all out and am taking it to the museum. I also looked through the rough drafts of *Hadji Murat*, and am taking them to the museum too.

Scheierman and Chertkov were here. Lev Nikolaevich is better today.

20 Bishop Parfenii of Tula was here with a spiritual moderator, our priest and a retinue of 6 people, including the police. Everyone liked the bishop; he is an intelligent, simple, good man. Lev Nikolaevich thanked him with tears in his eyes for coming, and for his courage in coming to visit us.[5]

Sewed the sleeves for a dress, and sat up late copying out Lev Nikolaevich's letters for 1854 and 1856.

23 Am leaving for Moscow. Have sorted out my papers and all I need for my various errands. Have started copying *Father Sergei*.

Lev Nikolaevich groans, yawns and sighs all day. Weakness and heartburn. He read, and was delighted by a letter of sympathy from a Little-Russian peasant.[6]

27 **(Moscow)** Worked in the museum with Stakhovich's young ladies, who are copying an inventory of the museum out of a book.

31 Spent a tedious day altering and mending a jersey for Lev Nikolaevich. If it wasn't for him I would never have wasted my time on such a thing and would have written my memoirs or copied *Father Sergei* instead. This evening Lev Nikolaevich read us a story by Novikov about soldiers going to war, called 'The Reservists', I think. Very good.[7]

February 2 Lev Nikolaevich is not well – he has not eaten all day and just sleeps. I am unwell too. I copied *Father Sergei*, looked through material for *My Life* and want to write more.

5 I have almost finished copying *Father Sergei*. I sorted and annotated my letters. The Gayarin brothers came and played violin duets; very cheerful and high spirited. Lev Nikolaevich enjoyed the music and is much better. Berkenheim has left.

6 Chertkov and M.A. Schmidt came. I sorted letters and finished *Father Sergei*. Lev Nikolaevich walked around the house. He is interested in everything; he said today that God was love, and there could be no other God.

14 Unwell, got up late, worked on *Hadji Murat*, checking over what I had copied, then on some material for my 'Memoirs'. Zosya Stakhovich came. This evening I did some more on Maria Aleksandrovna's dress. We read aloud an article about Karakozov's execution in *Russian Antiquity*.[8]

16 Sewed Maria Aleksandrovna's dress, then worked on my memoirs and copied extracts from some documents. I very much want to write more.

Maria Aleksandrovna and the two Strakhov brothers came. The younger one sang Mephistopheles and Faust in his pleasant bass, as well as an aria from *Demon*, then told comic stories and read some Chekhov. I can never laugh. Chertkov was here too. The *Russian Gazette* published a summary of L.N.'s article 'The Law of Violence and the Law of Love'.[9]

17 A mass of guests – poor Bulygin, whose wife has just died, his son Seryozha, Kartushin, Dosev and various other Tolstoyans, and Maria Aleksandrovna. Endless discussions. Lev Nikolaevich also had some Jewish writer from Kiev to see him.[10] When they had all gone Lev Nikolaevich cried: 'The Numidian cavalry charge!' and raising his arm he began to prance around the table. This, in old Yasnaya Polyana jargon, means relief at getting rid of unwanted guests.

19 Guests all day – Lina and her sister, Lyuba Golitsyna, Ogaryova, my son Misha, Chertkov. Lev Nikolaevich is writing an article called 'An Issue of a Newspaper'.[11] He went for a ride, with Zosya and Filka following in the carriage.

20 I was planning to go to Moscow, but am still here. It's all very annoying and depressing – I have bronchitis and a bad cough. I spent the whole day correcting Molostvov's biography, written from Sergeenko's notes. Very badly written.[12] Ogaryova has left.

21 Finished correcting the chapter in Molostvov's biography entitled 'Countess S.A. Tolstaya', and sent it off to him with a letter. Tried to write my memoirs but couldn't.

23 I am still unwell. I played a Beethoven sonata, but became feverish and lay down. I spent the whole evening writing *My Life*, and it went well. Lev Nikolaevich went for a ride; he cannot work. This evening he, Felten and Chertkov read aloud various letters, including a few from some prison inmates.

25 I wrote again all day and corrected the proofs of *Childhood*. L.N. is well; he went for a walk and wrote.

26 Lev Nikolaevich has been ill all day. Felten came, and the Strakhovs, and Chertkov. I worked on my book. Lev Nikolaevich dictated letters in the form of articles to Gusev, who has just returned; yesterday he wrote quantities of letters.[13]

27 L.N. is slightly weak. He wrote to Minister Timiryazev, who has promised Andryusha a position.[14]

28 Wrote, then corrected the proofs of the illustrated *Childhood*.[15] What a *chef d'oeuvre*! Lev Nikolaevich, Gusev, Varvara Mikhailovna and Dushan Petrovich called on the Chertkovs. There was a woman traveller there who gave a talk about various nationalities and showed coloured pictures on a screen. Lev Nikolaevich enjoyed it immensely.[16]

March 1 Lev Nikolaevich has a bright red swelling on his leg, and we have persuaded him to stay in bed all day. Chertkov came, and Olga, and two ladies with a photographer, who show scenes of India through a magic lantern.

5 I have finished my memoirs for 1891: they cost me a great effort. I sat all day with Lev Nikolaevich. He has to sit quite still with his leg up, but in general he is much better. I stamped the library books with my grandchildren.

6 Distressing news about Chertkov's deportation from the province of Tula.[17] Everyone wept. Sasha, Dima and Olga have all been crying, Lev Nikolaevich is distraught, and so is our entire household. The villagers and the servants are outraged: 'As if they hadn't killed enough of them – they have no respect for good people.' Chertkov is ill. Lev Nikolaevich has a swollen leg. So depressing! I have written an angry letter to the papers, but haven't yet sent it.[18]

8 The Chertkovs visited, and Novikov the peasant read Lev Nikolaevich his works.[19] I copied out L.N.'s letters. He is a bit better today. An Englishman was here too. I rewrote my letter.

9 I walked round the estate today. Very tedious and difficult. I copied extracts from various letters for my book (*My Life*). Lev Nikolaevich is better. Yesterday I wrote a letter to Tanya enclosing my article.

11 General bewilderment in the newspapers over Chertkov's deportation.

12 Lev Nikolaevich is ill. Fever of 37.6. Lying in bed. I sat at home taking extracts from some letters for my work. The newspapers have printed my letter about Chertkov's deportation.[20]

13 Lev Nikolaevich is a little better. I packed and left this evening for Moscow. Nikitin stayed behind.

16 (Moscow) Nikitin arrived in Moscow and alarmed me by saying that L.N.'s heart was in a bad way. I hurriedly wound up my affairs, handed some telegrams and letters over to the museum, and left this evening for home.

17 Back in Yasnaya. Heart in anguish. Lev Nikolaevich was better this morning, but this evening he was 37.3 and much worse, and my journey was for nothing – I'd intended to finish my affairs and go to the Kerzin concert.

18 Sat at work all day, and initialled Lev Nikolaevich some handkerchiefs in satin stitch. He is better, and is lively again and even cheerful. But my heart is filled with blank despair. Why is this? Chertkov was here, and Biryukov visited and told us at great length about the Tolstoy exhibition in St Petersburg.[21]

20 Lev Nikolaevich is much better, thank God. He is fascinated by a book called *Krishna*.[22]

22 Lev Nikolaevich sat out on the balcony; he is much better, but is still being careful. We read Kuprin's story 'The Reluctant Actor'.[23]

23 Tanyushka is sick. Dreadful anxiety. I have done nothing, I am in a fever, I make clothes for her doll and my soul is in despair. We are reading Kuprin's 'Small Fry'.

31 Today was my poor dead Vanechka's birthday. I took Tanyushka on to the balcony and the verandah; the sun was blazing and it was very pleasant. Then I assiduously sorted through Aunt Tatiana Ergolskaya's old papers. What a fine, pious woman she was. I copied out three of Lev Nikolaevich's letters to her – one from Kazan, another from Sevastopol and one about a bear hunt![24] – and shall take the originals to the museum. Bulygin came, and my son Andryusha. This evening a correspondent from *Russian Word* arrived.

Lev Nikolaevich played vint with the children. He has been talking a lot about the blessings of old age, and has a rather squeamish attitude to youth, especially the sexual side. How often he has returned to this question throughout his life, and how preoccupied he is with this side of life.

April 5 An anxious day: Lev Nikolaevich stayed in bed all day, ate nothing and was weak and sleepy, and again my soul is heavy with fear and anticipation.

6 This morning I got up early to see how Lev Nikolaevich was, and he said, 'Much better – I'm just having some coffee.' Then he said, 'I'm so fortunate, and so happy!' 'Why? Because everyone loves you?' I asked. 'No, it's you,' he said, 'I'm so happy with you,' and he burst into tears. It was all so unexpected – why did he say that? I read through some letters for my memoirs. Then we read aloud Yuvachov's story 'Heavenly Judgment'.

7 I spent the evening sewing and looking through a vast quantity of newspapers. They have sent me the French paper containing my letter about Chertkov. Lev Nikolaevich is well again, and is busy reading about the Chinese and their ancient laws and statutes.[25] He played vint.

10 Lev Nikolaevich is better. He is delighted by the letters he has been receiving: today he had one from a carpenter who has left the Church and now considers that the only thing necessary for one's soul is to do good to others.[26] Nikolaev came. I wrote to Nordman and the printers.

14 Sewed and read four proof pages of the illustrated *Childhood* and *Boyhood.* Some Telyatinki peasants came; they have taken 13 *desyatins* of land to grow oats on metayage. Lev Nikolaevich is weak and his leg hurts. All very depressing. He is quiet and melancholy. This evening he played vint.

16 Nothing but practical and estate matters – tedious and inescapable. I sorted out the provisions from Eliseev, cleaned and tidied the larder, nailed veneer on to the chairs and read the proofs of *Boyhood.* It's so easy now to see what fruits these seeds would later bear in Lev Nikolaevich's spiritual life.

17 The same as before: estate matters, games and walks with Tanyushka, work. I played the piano – badly and clumsily: I don't have the technique. Lev Nikolaevich said, 'I'm always tired these days.' He is writing his article on violence.[27]

18 Lev Nikolaevich went for a drive on his own in the carriage, and this evening played vint. He picked a nasty quarrel with me about doctors, and said I needn't have had the operation; I am always so distressed by these conversations. I read some proofs and diligently tidied and catalogued the books.

20 I have finished entering the new books into the catalogue. My son Seryozha came, and a Frenchman called Mr Mazon.[28] Tanya talked interestingly about Italy this evening and L.N. listened eagerly, lying on the sofa.

22 Sukhotin has returned. Lev Nikolaevich read him his letter to Bulgakov about upbringing and education, and I listened. Very good.[29]

24(Moscow) Spent the morning in the Historical Museum taking notes and working hard. Then shopping. This evening a concert exhibition by Deisha-Sionitskaya.

27 A Gogol meeting at the conservatoire, and this evening a Gogol concert. Saw the Gogol monument – hideous.

28 In Yasnaya Polyana. Lev Nikolaevich is poorly.

29 Lev Nikolaevich is much better. I have seen almost nothing of him today; he is very busy with his writing and letters.

30 L.N. rode over to the Chertkovs, I took a walk with our guests – Pasternak the artist with his wife, and Mogilevskii the violinist. This evening he played us a Bach sonata, Beethoven's 8th violin sonata, two movements from a Mozart sonata, a Mozart minuet and a Bach aria.[30]

May 3 Tanya has returned from St Petersburg, where she has been pleading Chertkov's case with Stolypin. I cannot make out whether they will send him back or not. Molochnikov has left. (L.N.) went for a ride during the day. He is writing an article about education; it is being written mainly in the form of letters in answer to questions . . .

6 Out in the garden all day painting benches and pillars. We had a visit from an officer of the Semyonovskii regiment called Nazimov,[31] and from a certain Uspenskii.[32] Lev Nikolaevich is well; he chatted with our guests, went for a ride and read. He is writing a lot of letters and is fascinated by the Chinese.[33] An Armenian newspaper editor came to visit.

7 This evening we read aloud Kuprin's story 'The Pit', about prostitutes; what a loathsome picture of their life.[34]

9 Strakhov, Nikolaev and Tregubov came, and some stranger, a former deacon. News of the minister's official refusal to allow Chertkov to return home. Lev Nikolaevich rode over to see his family.[35]

11 Lev Nikolaevich rode over to the Chertkovs. Unpleasant news in the papers about the trial of Felten, and a provocative letter from L.N. to the prosecutor.[36] Read 'The Devil', a most disagreeable work by L.N. which he has been hiding from me.

12 This evening we read aloud Dostoyevsky's description of death in a penal colony.[37]

18 Tanyushka is better; I wrote to her and Tanya. Lev Nikolaevich drove to Zaseka and consulted Doctor Grushetskii about her. He came back and said the immediate danger was over, but they were now afraid of paralysis. There was a telegram: 'Improvement continues'.

I met a beggar who said: 'Nikolai Veryovkin . . . '[38]

20 Our doctor has returned from the Sukhotins; Tanyushka is much better, thank God! My grandsons have come too. Lev Nikolaevich had a visit from a *Russian Word* correspondent called Spiro,[39] and from a peasant who talked of the common people's need for a spiritual life.[40]

22 (Moscow) I worked in the museum for about three hours. I was very vexed by the loss of 2 keys, to boxes 7 and 10.

28 A quiet, grey, warm day. Lev Nikolaevich is rather poorly. Lyova has started work on a magnificent bust of his father. I have been busy with my memoirs.

29 Walked with Lyova and my grandson Seryozha to the swimming pool. Sorted out material for my memoirs. Gorbunov, Nikolaev, Ivanovna and the Goldenweisers came, and we chattered the whole evening away. Lev Nikolaevich is cheerful and well; he rode to Kolpna to make enquiries at the district government offices about the widows.

30 Mechnikov came with his wife and I spent a very pleasant day with them. Such simple cultured people – and such easy company. Some photographers and correspondents came, and I took photographs too. Goldenweiser played this afternoon – a ballade, an étude and a mazurka by Chopin, and something by Schumann. Lovely. Lev Nikolaevich is well. He liked Mechnikov, and went for a drive with him to Telyatinki. The Mechnikovs left this evening.[41]

June 1 I went for a walk with Olga and my grandchildren, Sonyushka and Ilyushok, and read them my children's story 'Skeletons'.[42] Lev Nikolaevich rode to Zaseka. Today he said: 'I have left all my old patriotism behind; I'm no longer interested in purely Russian matters but in universal questions concerning the whole of humanity.'

2 I worked hard taking notes for my memoirs, then developed photographs of Lyova's bust and of Mechnikov with Lev Nikolaevich. Only one was successful. I pasted in newspaper cuttings. Goldenweiser came.

5 I tried to work on my memoirs, but it was quite impossible. We had a visit from Henry George's son (also called Henry George) and his friend, a Mr Moore.[43] Then Tikhomirov, founder of the League of Sobriety, arrived, followed by Olga and the vast colony of Chertkovs. Then our servants all came to hear Troyanovskii playing the balalaika. He plays extraordinarily well, and L.N. was in ecstasies,[44] despite being unwell.

7 We are going to Kochety, even though the weather is changeable and rainy. I shall miss Lyova terribly – he is staying on in Yasnaya. I love him so much; he and Tanya are much closer to me than the others.

8 We got up early and left for Zaseka. It was a long and difficult journey. Lev Nikolaevich quarrelled with a landowner,[45] fussed and took an interest in everything, while I was anxious all the way. Kochety is so comfortable and welcoming. The two Tanyas are a delight. L.N. is tired but tolerably well.

10 (Kochety) Life is calm and untroubled. Walks with Tanyushka, work, evenings spent talking. Lev Nikolaevich went for quite a long ride: he has spent too long sitting at home in Yasnaya, and is now delighted by every new face, place and situation.

11 Took a very pleasant walk round the park with the two Tanyas. Very hot. Then some drawing and painting. Lev Nikolaevich is enthusiastic about everything, and is taking a rest from his everyday life, with its beggars, petitioners and endless guests. He went for a ride, played vint, watched the tennis and listened to the singing.[46]

12 This evening we read aloud some prose poems by Turgenev. Then there was a discussion about old age, and Lev Nikolaevich said: 'I don't know about the *external* changes an old man goes through, but in my inner life I'm exactly the same Lyovochka as I was at his age,' and he pointed at 13½-year-old Dorik.

14 Lev Nikolaevich was telling us this evening about punishments in the reign of Catherine II, which was very interesting. He leads his usual life and is well.

16 We bustled about all morning preparing to leave; Lev Nikolaevich was not well. I left for Blagodatnaya with Dorik, and arrived at Zaseka at 4 in the morning.

20 I wrote to Lev Nikolaevich this morning, and to Tanya this evening.[47] I went with Olga to visit the Chertkovs and the Goldenweisers. This

evening Lyova and I had another talk together; he works all day on his sculptures of Sasha and Lev Nikolaevich.[48] I played some Weber, and some Beethoven sonatas.

21 I did a little work on my memoirs, then spent the rest of the day with the Goldenweisers. I read them 'After the Ball' and the passage from my memoirs describing my meeting with the Tsar.[49] I received a second letter from Lev Nikolaevich.[50] He is having a very worldly time in Kochety, and is quite happy. He is bored with the life of solitude and sermonising that he has created for himself. He doesn't say a word about his return home, and I feel angry for some reason, although I try not to.

25 Feeling very depressed. Lev Nikolaevich is not coming home, and Lyova is leaving tonight for Sweden via Riga; I printed some photographs of his father for him. The artist Ivan Kirillovich Parkhomenko came, wanting to paint Lev Nikolaevich's portrait.

27 Gusev has appeared promising that Lev Nikolaevich will arrive tomorrow. I worked on my memoirs, attended to the estate, sewed and swam.

29 The sad news is that Lev Nikolaevich will not be coming for another 4 days. Chertkov went to meet him in Oryol province, 3 miles from Kochety. I printed photographs of Andryusha and his children, went for a swim and tried to paint some rose bushes in oils.

July 1 Got carried away painting the roses, but there's nothing to show for it. I received payment for the hay – the peasants' money burns my hands.

3 Painted my roses – badly. This evening Lev Nikolaevich returned with Doctor D.P. Makovitsky and Ilya Vasilevich the servant. Life is easier. Spent the whole day dashing about the meadows trying to reconcile the quarrellers and make concessions, and doing all I could to make the peace, but there's still such a lot of envy, spite and robbery.

4 Lev Nikolaevich went to say goodbye to Galya Chertkova this morning. He wrote,[51] and is energetic and even cheerful.

5 Lev Nikolaevich was a little weaker today; he went for a walk and talked at length to a strange peasant from the Vladimir province, who says that all labour is harmful and unnecessary.[52] An unpleasant visit from the district police officer concerning Sasha's defence of a drunken peasant; the guard wanted to beat him but she gave him a good reference.

6 I have bad neuralgia in my right arm and shoulder.

8 I am in terrible suffering. This was exacerbated by the nervous shock of learning that Lev Nikolaevich had suddenly decided to go off to Stockholm for the Peace Congress.[53] Lord save us from such a thing!

12 My arm is better, but I am feverish and depressed and my mind is unhinged. It has all been a bad shock to my entire nervous system. L.N. is well, cheerful and carefree; picks flowers and eats berries. He visited the Chertkov colony this afternoon with Sasha, and read them his letter.[54]

13 In bad health – fever of 37.8, my arm is better, I eat nothing. Lev Nikolaevich rejoices in the flowers, and brings great bunches of them in from the fields and the garden.

15 I struggle against illness but still feel very bad. I have a fever and my heart is weak. Lev Nikolaevich is out of sorts but says nothing. Today he rode along the highway on his own. He was chatting to Iv. Iv. Gorbunov this evening, and to Denisenko. The *Circle of Reading* is his favourite child – he is always reading passages to us.

16 My health is better. Lev Nikolaevich went for a ride with Onisim Denisenko, and this afternoon he read a lot of letters. Some student came to see him. He is well.

17 I am still ill. Dushan Petrovich has found an infiltration and a slight inflammation of the left lung.

We read aloud Mechnikov's book. [L.N.] didn't like it at all; he said Mechnikov was completely alien to him, and his views were diametrically opposed to his.[55]

18 I asked Lev Nikolaevich formally to grant me the copyright to his works to make it easier for me to publish his works and conduct his affairs. He refused – emphatically, sharply and unpleasantly. I flew into a passion, but then the result was so painful that we made it up. L.N. was both materially and morally right to refuse. But how hard it is for a person to renounce property, despite what he preaches!

19 The artist Parkhomenko came and started on a portrait of Lev Nikolaevich. All the young people from some school arrived from Moscow; they took photographs of themselves with Lev Nikolaevich and called out for me too, as they wanted to see me.

20 Health bad – weakness, depression, fever. Parkhomenko's portrait of L.N. is good, but there is no real *spiritual* resemblance.[56] Lev Nikolaevich is stern and distant. He intends to go to the Peace Congress in Sweden, and it torments me; we had a painful discussion.

21 I told L.N. how worried I was about his trip to Sweden, then did not sleep all night. I am alone amidst these dark ones who encircle Lev Nikolaevich, they are all against me, and I work for them all. Then there's Molochnikov's vile treatment of B.A. Vasilchikov, repeating to him various remarks Lev Nikolaevich made under the influence of Molochnikov's own false evidence.[57]

I have summoned Andryusha to comfort me and defend me against the dark ones; he has been so helpful and reassuring.

22 My daughter Tanya arrived to my great joy, although I feel badly to have called for her. She is so kind and comforting, and I feel that she too is a supportive friend. Lev Nikolaevich is unfriendly, cold and aloof, and I cannot help remembering that 'a husband loves a healthy wife' – and I am always sick. I again had a fever and crepitation in my left lung and a weak heart.

24 My daughter Tanya left this morning, and I felt sad again. I read my *Life* to Posse, Ginzburg and Denisenko, and they praised it excessively. The guests have left.

26 I cannot remember anything. I remember that when Buturlin and Seryozha came Lev Nikolaevich again said he intended to go to Stockholm for the Congress of the League of Peace, thus breaking the promise he made to me not to go if I found it so painful.

I was terribly shaken, worse than before. I decided to die. I suffered such agony, both physical and mental, during this time.

30 I did a little work on my children's stories – I want to publish them.[58] Spiro, a correspondent on the *Russian Word*, was here.[59]

August 1 I checked the proofs of Molostvov's biography of Lev Nikolaevich and tidied the books. Lev Nikolaevich is being rather sullen, and is angry with me for opposing his trip to Sweden.

2 I finished the proofs of Molostvov's biography of Lev Nikolaevich, and wrote him a letter.[60] Goldenweiser played a Schubert impromptu, and an étude and a beautiful sonata by Chopin.

Today I told Lev Nikolaevich that I would go to Sweden with him, but the idea appalls me![61]

200 foresters came, and one of them made a speech to Lev Nikolaevich.[62]

4 This evening the district police-officer and his assistant arrived, with a jingling of bells, and told Gusev that he was to leave with them within the hour, that he was under arrest and was being exiled to the province of Perm.[63] It was a terrible shock to all of us, and there was general rage and indignation at the government as we bade Gusev a sad farewell. Lev Nikolaevich was very brave and tried to be cheerful, but he was terribly agitated.

7 Lev Nikolaevich went for a ride on his own. Sasha and Marusya went to Tula, where Marusya visited the governor and asked him to allow Gusev to travel on the train, rather than on the convict route.

8 I tidied the books. Lev Nikolaevich read out his statement about Gusev's exile with tears in his eyes and great agitation, then went for a ride with Sasha. He is sad and gloomy.

9 I tidied library books. Then Gusev arrived in a distraught state with the village policeman and the guard: the only people he was allowed to meet were Sasha, Maria Aleksandrovna and Makovitsky. I felt outraged. So I can't even go into my own rooms in my own house now! What, is the village policeman going to throw me out? It is all frightful and depressing. Lev Nikolaevich is shattered and the rest of us are frantic.

11 I had a letter from the editors of *Le Matin* in Paris, enquiring about Gusev's arrest. Lev Nikolaevich rode to Yasenki on his own and took the reply in person. Goldenweiser and Nikolaeva came, and some peasant from Moscow who has refused military service.[64] This evening we read aloud a story by Chertkov about his years as a young man in government service.[65]

12 Lev Nikolaevich's statement about Gusev's exile appeared in the *Russian Gazette* on August 11. There's a small article there too.[66]

14 This evening we read something about Gogol; much of it was new to me, and very interesting.[67]

19 I wrote to Zosya Stakhovich, Maude and Yunge, then read the proofs of Maude's English biography of Lev Nikolaevich.[68]

21 Spent the morning with Botkin, then took excerpts from some letters for my memoirs. Feverish again, went to bed and dozed, then made a

shirt. Goldenweiser came. Lev Nikolaevich went for a ride on his own, played chess, read letters and sent a telegram to Berlin giving them permission to read the article on peace which he wrote for the Stockholm Congress.[69]

27 I tried to paint some illustrations for my children's stories.[70] I want to be able to do everything, but I can't do anything. L.N. drove out to meet Boulanger.

28 Lev Nikolaevich's 81st birthday. He is in good spirits, and went for a ride with V.A. Maklakov. He has received a copy of his book of readings for every day of the year, and is well pleased with his work.[71] 20 people came to dinner – Seryozha, Zinger, Semyonov, Andryusha and his wife, Tanya, Maria Aleksandrovna, Gorbunov, the Goldenweisers and others. It wasn't very cheerful but no matter – it was calm and not too gloomy. Goldenweiser played delightfully – a Chopin scherzo and polonaise, and a study by Arenskii.

31 This morning we had a visit from a 30-year-old Romanian who had castrated himself at the age of 18 after reading *The Kreutzer Sonata*.[72] He then took to working on the land – just 19 acres – and was terribly disillusioned today to see that Tolstoy writes one thing but lives in luxury. He was obviously very hurt, said he wanted to cry, kept repeating, 'My God, my God! How can this be? What shall I tell them at home?' and questioned everyone, seeking an explanation of this contradiction. Then a rich deaf-mute arrived from Kiev with his friend, a barber, especially to make Tolstoy's acquaintance.[73] Goldenweiser came and played chess with L.N.

September 2 Lev Nikolaevich's preparations to visit Chertkov are very painful for me. I corrected the proofs of Maude's English biography of him and drew some illustrations. Our visitors today were the Nikolaevs, Goldenweiser, Kalachyov, the deaf-mute and some cinematographers from Paris.[74]

3 A sad farewell and departure. Lev Nikolaevich left today for Chertkov's with Sasha. With them went Dima Chertkov, Goldenweiser, Dushan Petrovich, Ilya the servant and some friends of Dima's.

5 Maria Nikolaevna and Liza have left for the convent; a sad parting. The Goldenweisers were here, and Aleksandr Borisovich told us how Lev Nikolaevich could listen to a musical instrument in Moscow and then reproduce the piano style of all the famous performers; how he would walk

down the Kuznetskii Most, fascinated by everything he saw; and how the public would greet him at the station.[75]

8 (Moscow) Spent the morning in Moscow, then packed and left for Kryokshina to visit the Chertkovs. Everyone there, including Lev Nikolaevich, welcomed me most warmly. It was all very friendly, gracious and comfortable. He played *Mignon*.

10 Visited the banks in Moscow. This evening all the directors of the paper factory and the printing press came. I ordered books from them and we drew up a sales account.

11 I went to the museum where I did a lot of interesting work on Lev Nikolaevich's manuscripts and handed in some things. This evening the artists Kasatkin and Moravov came to talk about my illustrations.

13 Sonya and I have arrived in Kryokshina. They all greeted me – Lev Nikolaevich, Olga and the grandchildren, Chertkov, the steward with a bunch of flowers and the others. This evening Goldenweiser, Sibor and Mogilevskii played trios by Arenskii, Haydn and Mozart.

15 We are all staying at the Chertkovs'. We had a visit from a woman called Lineva who collects songs.

16 Lev Nikolaevich is well and is living his normal life, chatting with peasants, correspondents and teachers.

18 Chertkov wrote to the newspaper announcing the time of Lev Nikolaevich's departure from Moscow. We packed and left for Moscow, and rapturous crowds greeted Lev Nikolaevich at the station. In Khamovniki we were met by Seryozha and his wife, Dunaev, Buturlin, the Chertkovs, Marusya, Chesnokov, Semyonov, Konisi and others. Lev Nikolaevich went out with the others this evening to watch the cinematograph, and came back tired and dissatisfied.

19 (Moscow) We left on the fast train. Thousands of people (5,000) greeted Lev Nikolaevich at the station, shouting 'Hurrah!' over and over again, and almost crushing us. There were multitudes of guards. At home in Yasnaya Lev Nikolaevich fainted twice, to our great alarm. Berkenheim helped us bring him round.

20 We spent an anxious night, no one slept. But Lev Nikolaevich is much better. He went for a walk, wrote, read letters, ate, and we felt very relieved. Everything is normal and happy here.

21 I am reading the proofs of the English biography of Lev Nikolaevich, which Maude sent me. Nikolaev, Aleksandri, the cinematographers[76] and the doctor came, and a young farmer called Novikov.

24 Spent the morning with Maude, and together we looked through my corrections of his biography of Lev Nikolaevich.[77] This evening the whole village gathered here and we had a showing of the cinematograph.[78] L.N. is well, and keeps writing his letter-articles.

26 P.I. Biryukov came, and this evening Doctor Nikitin arrived. Lev Nikolaevich is worried about a scratch on his leg. He took a walk and wrote letters. I worked on the accounts, copied Lev Nikolaevich's letters for 1852 and pasted newspaper cuttings.

October 1 I walked around the estate, and spent the rest of the day giving Biryukov material for his biography of L.N. We read and took notes, and this evening I read a story by Ek. Very poor.[79]

8 I sewed all day, rested my leg and didn't go out. Lev Nikolaevich walked along the highway to meet Sasha on her way back from Tula, and drove home with her. He was brighter today. Mikh. Dm. Chelyshchev, a *Duma* member, arrived from Samara. A large, loud, clever man, he has devoted his life's work to the abolition of vodka. L.N. enthused to him about the theories of Henry George.[80]

10 Lev Nikolaevich is not very well. He walked about five *versts* along the highway to meet Sasha and Varvara Mikhailovna on their way back from Tula, where they had gone to pay the taxes for Yasnaya Polyana and to get a passport for Dima Chertkov. I did a lot of sewing, pasted newspaper cuttings and supervised the installation of the double windows.

12 Lev Nikolaevich was brighter today. He went for a ride and wrote to various foreigners. Some German had asked him his views on capital punishment.[81] He is still reading Andreev, whom he considers very talented.

13 I tidied the house and my room, sewed, and read Lev Nikolaevich a story by Andreev about a town.[82]

15 The same activities – taking notes from Mengden's diary,[83] embroidering and so on. I haven't been out, I don't feel well. Lev Nikolaevich took a walk today and wrote letters. He is studying oriental literature and history – Buddha, the Indians and so forth.[84]

16 We had a visit from a Polish woman doctor from Paris called Mel. Andr. Lipinska, and also from Semyonov (a peasant writer). Lev Nikolaevich rode to the district government offices to attend a trial, but missed it.[85] He is pursuing his interest in oriental literature.

17 A crowd of people arrived with a gramophone on which various scribblers, poetasters and so forth have recorded their voices.[86] Insufferable and very awkward. L.N. was exhausted this evening; earlier on he had gone for a ride and spoken to Olga on the telephone.

19 This evening L.N. was reading *Russian Thought*, which contained Sologub's short story 'The Silver Birch Tree' and some verses of his, and he was horrified by this nonsense and the large sums of money that were paid for it per line, and said that modern writing was nothing but a lunatic asylum.

24 (Moscow) I visited the city's governor, Adrianov, to urge him to release the 1,600 seized copies of Biryukov's Biography of Lev Nikolaevich – and I succeeded.[87]

25 Attended a historic concert – Mozart and Beethoven. The fifth concerto was delightful. I dined with the Maslovs. Sergei Ivanovich was there, and was simple and pleasant. Left this evening for Yasnaya.

26 Arrived home this morning. Lev Nikolaevich is well. Sasha is being nice and more reasonable, thank God! Lev Nikolaevich is preoccupied with his personal life, as usual, and scarcely notices anything else. He has not long to live, and is in a hurry to do as much work as he can.

28 Mikhail Sergeevich Sukhotin has arrived. Leonid Semyonov came, but I didn't see him. Lev Nikolaevich rode to Ovsyannikovo with Dushan Petrovich to see Maria Aleksandrovna; he slept from 5 to 9 this evening, and had several more memory lapses.

29 Lev Nikolaevich played chess with Sukhotin and read aloud L. Andreev's story 'Christians'.[88]

30 I played the piano for a long time – I cannot get that Chopin piano concerto out of my head. Then I corrected the proofs of my short stories. Lev Nikolaevich rode over to Novaya Kolpna to attend the district court.[89]

31 Zosya Stakhovich has come, and this evening everyone played vint with Lev Nikolaevich. He laughed and was cheerful.

That strange Leonid Semyonov is here. He has completed studies at two separate faculties, yet goes about in birch-bark sandals, works with the peasants, and has walked here from the province of Ryazan without a kopeck in his pocket.

November 3 Moravov is drawing and painting a portrait of L.N.;[90] he behaves very modestly.

8 I wrote my last will and testament today, but so far it's only a scribbled version and is unwitnessed. Then I finished taking notes for my memoirs. My right eye is almost blind, and it terrifies me. The artist Moravov has left.

9 I wrote a lot for the year 1892. Ilya's Annochka has had a son – so now we have a great-grandchild. Lev Nikolaevich rode to Telyatinki. He is reading Gorky[91] and writing various articles; he is quiet and lethargic.

11 A cut version of Lev Nikolaevich's article 'On Science' (a reply to a peasant) has appeared in *Russian Gazette*.[92] I did almost no work today because I felt ill and feverish.

12 Tanya has come and we are all happy. She played vint with her papa. Everyone is cheerful and well.

14 I catalogued books and arranged catalogue cards. Lev Nikolaevich was sleepy and weak all day and didn't leave the house. He is preoccupied with all these printed extracts everywhere from his article 'On Science'.[93] Sasha was rude to me and upset me. This afternoon I did a sketch of Ilyushok.

15 Andryusha came today; he burst into tears when he read my will. I wrote a lot of *My Life*. Two rich peasants, Tolstoyans, arrived from the South to see Lev Nikolaevich.[94]

19 **(Moscow)** Business, shopping, wrote my will, consulted the notary. Olenina d'Ahlheim's concert. She sang beautifully. Worked in the museum.

20 I have been trying to place some orphans in orphanages, at Lev Nikolaevich's request.[95] My will is written.

21 I visited the eye doctor and the surgeon. The right eye is almost blind, and the left one is bad too.

23 I deposited my will at the State Bank* and rushed about shopping all day. Hoffmann's concert this evening, then straight on to the train.

29 Lev Nikolaevich is in good spirits; he showed me his pamphlet *On Reason and Faith* today, which states that Christ is not God, and so on, and costs only one or half a kopeck. The censor has evidently gone through it.[96] Exquisite hoar-frost, sunny, 4 degrees below, everyone out skating. L.N. and the doctor went to visit a sick man in Kryltsovo, but he was already in his death agony; L.N. wept as he told us about it.[97]

30 Lev Nikolaevich went to Kolpna for some information about the cattle and goods that were sold for taxes.[98]

December 1 Spent the day making myself a dress. Wrote for little Tanechka and drew for my grandsons. Lev Nikolaevich keeps revising his *Circle of Reading* – he has rewritten the preface several times.[99] Iv. Iv. Gorbunov is here.

2 Boulanger and the Gorbunovs were here. They played vint this evening and L.N. was very cheerful. He said that an artist like himself could turn into a ladder, and either raise himself spiritually to great heights or sink very low; this was why he understood others so well. He is still busy with his preface to the *Circle of Reading*. I pasted newspaper cuttings; Olga is helping me to make myself a dress.

4 I printed photographs of Lev Nikolaevich for the artist Moravov all morning.

7 Lev Nikolaevich has overtired himself again. He has been working very hard recently, he went to Ovsyannikovo again in the sledge, and all this made him very sleepy. He slept for five hours, had no dinner, had forgotten a lot when he woke and had difficulty remembering again. He then kept dozing off.

9 I wrote a lot of my *Life*, and wrote to Drankov the cinematographer.[100]

12 **(Moscow)** I took the jubilee telegrams and the 3rd book of cuttings to the museum.

13 This morning I visited the orphanage to ask them to accept the boy from Yasnaya. On to a historic concert with Wanda Landowska playing Haydn's piano concerto, delightfully, and the harpsichord. Then a

*I subsequently withdrew it and wrote another, which was kept at home. (S.A. Tolstaya's note.)

dreadful telegram from Sasha saying Lev Nikolaevich had a fever of 40.4 and was chilled through. I didn't undress or sleep all night. The trains had all left.

14 Took the fast train to Yasnaya with Nikitin. This morning there was a much more reassuring telegram – 37.4 ° – and I found Lev Nikolaevich in a far better state.

16 I cannot remember a thing. I sat at home with Lev Nikolaevich, he got better, and this evening I again left for Moscow to finish my business and publish my children's book in time for the holidays.

18 Still in Moscow, doing the holiday shopping. Went this evening to the Landowska concert, and left immediately afterwards for Yasnaya.

23 Wrote my memoirs and finished 1892. Played the piano for a long time. Lev Nikolaevich rode over to Demyonka to visit a poor soldier's wife.[101] He is writing 'A Dream'. Bulgakov the student came.

26 Lev Nikolaevich was talking about his 'Dream'. He wanted to do scenes and dialogue, but he has turned it into a speech about the ownership of the land, as he wants it to be clear and powerful.[102]

29 Lev Nikolaevich went for a ride with Dima Chertkov and is feeling much better. Wanda Landowska played the harpsichord for us all evening – Rameau, Couperin, Bach and Scarlatti. Wonderful! I wrote to Drankov.

31 I tried to write my memoirs, but was interrupted by Wanda. I am growing weary of guests. This evening Wanda played several pieces on the harpsichord and a Mozart sonata on the piano; beautiful. Mitya Olsufiev came this evening and we all saw in the New Year together.

·1910·

January 1 New Year. The Landowskis have left. Lev Nikolaevich rode over to Ovsyannikovo. He is writing three things – 'A Dream', 'Vagrants' and something else, as yet without a title.[1] It is windless and warm – 2 °. I sent telegrams to Goldenweiser and Andryusha.

2 Learnt of my brother Styopa's death; his children have gone to the funeral.[2] Marusya Maklakova has left. A *Figaro* correspondent called Marchand came;[3] I entertained him and did some embroidery. I wrote to

Gradovskii,[4] Yulia Ivanovna, Denisenko, Loyson, Varya Nagornova and Lanin. It is warm – 4°; this morning there was a frost.

3 I decorated a second Christmas tree with my little grandchildren. The Sukhotins (the two Tanyas and Mikhail Sergeevich) arrived by the fast train. We were delighted to see one another and everyone was cheerful and contented. I went to bed late.

4 Unpleasant scenes this morning, with the bailiff telling tales against the Circassian guard, and the guard telling tales against the bailiff. Then more Christmas tree decorations, and this evening a masquerade. Everyone dressed up, even me (as a witch), and danced. The children had a wonderful time. Nadya Ivanova came and everyone played vint with Lev Nikolaevich. A warm, fine morning, windy towards evening.

5 Decorated the Christmas tree and sat with the children. Nikolaev and Abrikosov came. This evening a party round the Christmas tree, everyone danced. Little Tanechka was charming, so graceful and light-footed. Then a noisy game of vint; I sat doing nothing and resting my eyes. My leg is very painful. I am exhausted but cheerful. A warm day, with snow.

6 It is warm – zero degrees. My son Seryozha has left. The whole day was devoted to cinematography. Drankov photographed us all this morning, and this evening they showed us the film of our journey, first to see Chertkov in Kryokshina, then to Moscow, with the crowds of people at Kursk Station.[5]

An unpleasant incident with Sasha's horse, which very nearly crushed me, and more importantly little Tanechka, to death; I managed to drag her away in the snow just in time. Boulanger came – more vint.

7 These guests make any serious work impossible. I played a Schubert trio arranged as a duet with Nadya Ivanova; the first part is splendid. Lev Nikolaevich went for a ride with Dushan Petrovich. I played with Tanyushka, and the whole evening was taken up with cinematography. We watched our departure from Kryokshina to Moscow, then Drankov presented me with the whole film. Masha, Mitya Olsufiev, Seryozha, Drankov, Yuzhin[6] and Nadya Ivanova have left. Bulygin has arrived. I read Sukhotin and Olsufiev my autobiography, and they praised it. 1 degree above freezing, no wind.

9 Tanechka's nurse is unwell, and I spent the whole day with her; I took my three grandchildren out for a walk and we made a little house and some fir-trees in the snow; the children had a marvellous time. This

evening I made some dolls for the Christmas tree. A lovely fine day, no wind – beautiful: dazzling whiteness and the solemn splendour of the winter countryside.

10 I stayed at home all day, busy with estate matters. When the others went out I played a little of a Beethoven sonata. This evening Tanya felt very ill; her head and chest were aching and she had to lie down. I have hired a new bailiff.

12 Two name-days – the two Tanyas, mother and daughter. The mother is ill, the daughter jubilant. Nazhivin, Boulanger and Maria Aleksandrovna came. Olga and I tidied up some of the books. My eyes ache and I have to wear dark glasses. So depressing!

13 2 ° of frost and windy. Sasha has an intestinal disorder; she has just driven Maria Aleksandrovna back to Ovsyannikovo. Tanya is better. I am doing nothing – I have to rest my eyes; I play with the children and tidy a few things. Lev Nikolaevich took a ride in the woods, and this evening he read us a letter from Persia about the followers of Babism, expounding their faith.[7] I wrote a letter about the newspaper *New Russia*.[8]

14 I wrote to my daughter-in-law Sonya. Bulygin came with his son. The laborious change-over from one bailiff to another is in progress, and I do nothing but sit here in my dark glasses. All very difficult! There's a mass of things to be done, and I do love to work. I am very worried about Lyova, after hearing about the flood in Paris.[9] It is windy and warm here, 2 degrees above freezing. Lev Nikolaevich read us Gusev's letter about a converted revolutionary.[10] He played vint. Earlier on he went out for a ride.

15 I wrote off for spring seeds and catalogued library books. It is raining and windy, 1½ ° above freezing. Tanya went to Tula. Lev Nikolaevich went for a ride through the woods, and this evening he played chess with Mikhail Sergeevich, then vint. He writes endless letters and works on his new *Circle of Reading*.

16 Lev Nikolaevich went off to Tula with the doctor this morning to attend the trial of some peasants accused of robbing the post.[11] They were acquitted, so his journey was rewarded. It is warm – zero degrees – and windless. I played Beethoven's 4th sonata; the end is charming, and Lev Nikolaevich liked it very much. This evening I played vint with Tanya, Lev Nikolaevich and Varvara Mikhailovna. Lev Nikolaevich was overjoyed by the arrival of the *Circle of Reading* from the *Odessa Leaflet* publishing house. It's a good edition.[12]

17 I wrote to Lyova and Masha Tolstaya, looked through some Haydn sonatas and played a Chopin nocturne, then sat with Tanyushka. The others went out for a drive in 2 sledges – Lev Nikolaevich went on horseback. Boulanger and Maria Aleksandrovna came, and Bulgakov, who will help Lev Nikolaevich compile his new *Circle of Reading* for children and peasants.[13] They noisily played vint, while I spent the evening all on my own, sewing. 4 degs. below freezing, no wind.

18 Got up late and did a little work on my memoirs for 1892. Prevented from working by estate matters, the children and my desire to be with my family. Sat down this evening for a game of vint; one could grow fond of the game – at the cost of one's mental capacities. There is a wind, and the barometer is at zero. Lev Nikolaevich complained of feeling weak. He went for a short walk. He gave me the finished version of his 'Dream' today and *

19 I worked on the letters and read various materials for my memoirs. But I felt sick from the charcoal fumes and went into the wing to see Olga; then I went out for a long walk. Lev Nikolaevich, Tanya, Sasha and the grandchildren took a drive through the woods and enjoyed themselves, and I felt very envious, but I am afraid to go for a drive with my bad leg. It is warm – zero degrees. This evening I read more letters. Misha Sukhotin came. Lev Nikolaevich is completely absorbed with his new *Circle of Reading*.

21 Lev Nikolaevich slept till late this morning and when he woke up he couldn't remember a thing; he didn't recognise Ilyushok, and he came into my room and told me he couldn't remember whether I was at home or in Moscow. He ate nothing, spent the day in bed and slept all evening too; he was very weak and his temperature was 37.2, falling to 36.9. Boulanger, Bulgakov and the Bulygins were here. I worked on my memoirs all day. A fine day, clouding over towards evening; 6 ° below freezing this morning, 6 ° above in the sun.

22 Lev Nikolaevich got up feeling quite fresh and had a good day. He took some herbs and two rhubarb tablets. He is still constipated. Then he played vint. I worked on my memoirs all day, which plunged me into depression.

23 Still working on my memoirs. Took a bath. Neuralgia in the temple, the eye and over the right eyebrow. I am afraid of going blind. I played a Mozart duet. Lev Nikolaevich went for a walk and wrote a great many letters. He has become interested in cooperatives, and wrote replies on this

*Sentence unfinished.

subject to Totamyanets and Prince A.V. Golitsyn.[14] I wrote to Lyova, Maslova and the accountant. Dorik and Nadya Ivanova came.

24 I have done only practical things, sorting and tidying the papers and accounts. My temple and eye ache. My son Ilya arrived this evening looking saddened and aged. He has a disorder of the throat and his affairs are going badly. 11½ degrees of frost all morning. Lev Nikolaevich is well. Outwardly his life is the same as before, but his inner life is laborious and difficult.

25 I spent a lot of time on the bills, papers and documents, and am preparing to leave for Moscow. Seryozha came after dinner. They all cheerfully played vint – apart from me; I don't like cards and cannot play.

26 Seryozha left this morning, and Olga and the children went to Tula. It is 2 ° below freezing and windy. My son Andryusha and his wife Katya arrived at 2 this afternoon, and later on Sergeenko came with a gramophone. This was a gift from the 'Gramophone' company, for whom Lev Nikolaevich had spoken in 4 languages on to a record.[15] I do not like gramophones.

27 I have decided to go to Moscow. I spent a lazy day playing with Tanyushka and listening to the gramophone. I went for a walk with the two Tanyas; 2 ° and windy. They have brought the ice. Good news from Lyova. Lev Nikolaevich went for a long ride with the coachman, played chess with Mikhail Sergeevich and listened to the gramophone. Sergeenko has left.

28 I packed and left this evening for Moscow.

29 (Moscow) This morning I summoned some businessmen here, then drove to three banks to attend to my financial affairs. This evening Landowska's concert and the Glebovs' ball. Old friends were most affable. I am exhausted. I also went to the Glebovs' during the day to see my grandchildren, Misha's children. Utterly adorable.

30 More business today, but mainly shopping. Dined with the Glebovs and saw my darling grandchildren again; they danced with me and were so simple and sweet. This evening a tedious symphony concert with a dull Berlioz symphony; only the *Egmont* was any good.[16]

31 I accompanied the Orlovs to two exhibitions, the Wanderers' and the 'Union'. At the Wanderers' I saw Repin's portrait of Lev Nikolaevich in an armchair, and Moravov's of him writing in a corner of his study. They weren't too bad.[17] In Repin's portrait there is a morbid, sad, perplexed expression in the eyes and even the whole face.

This evening I went to the Hoffmann concert. He played a Chopin sonata and ballade rather lifelessly.

February 1 I have finished my shopping and business in Moscow. This morning I worked in the museum with Pavel Ivanovich Biryukov, who dined with us, and this afternoon I stayed at home. Prince Pavel Dmitrievich has opened a peasant library in Yasnaya Polyana.[18]

2 This morning I attended to business, then I went to a Kerzin concert, and later on I paid some calls – Glebova, Ermolova and Maslova. This evening Torba came and I worked with him on the new editions. Later I left for Yasnaya Polyana.

3 I am back in Yasnaya and am happy to be home. Staying here is Sonya Mamonova, with whom I have spent most of the day. We spent the evening drawing and engraving profiles, and listening to the gramophone. Dorik Sukhotin has caught the measles. Lev Nikolaevich rode a long way to visit the orphans.[19]

4 I wrote letters to Molostvova, S.A. Stakhovich, Nyuta Behrs and Lyova. Sonya Mamonova and Tanya have gone to Tula. It is 8 ° below freezing. One of the orphans came; I am placing her and her brother in orphanages in Moscow. Lev Nikolaevich went for a ride; he is still revising his new *Circle of Reading*. This evening he played vint.

5 Lev Nikolaevich is better; he went for a walk and returned home in the sledge. Everyone went for a drive, while I spent the day making a dress for the orphan girl, and cut out some other things this morning. The weather is fine and much warmer. My grandchildren have been playing happily in my room.

6 I received the Chopin Impromptu in the post. It's a pity I play so little, my fingers are so stiff. I worked on the orphan's dress. Tanya, Sasha, and the children all went for a drive through the woods, with Lev Nikolaevich on horseback. It is warm – 3 ° below freezing – and still. This evening I played vint with the others so as to give my eyes a rest. Olga and Mikhail Sergeevich went to Tula. A great to-do in the courtyard over a stolen cockerel. I wrote to Molostvova and Marusya.

7 I went to the recently opened library – which I can hardly believe will be successful. The village lads all crowd in, but there isn't a single adult there. I played with the children, listened to the gramophone and did absolutely no work. My eyes ache, I have had a temperature for three days. Rumours about the attempted theft of some hay. Lev Nikolaevich is furious with the court and most upset about the letters from Felten and Molochnikov.[20]

8 I wrote to Andryusha and my sister Tanya. I worked quite hard all day on my memoirs. Lev Nikolaevich was distressed by the appearance of an article entitled 'The Last Phase of My Life' in three newspapers, *Morning of Russia, New Times* and the *Voice of Moscow*. The ideas could have been his, but not the style.[21] I am still feverish, but less so.

9 Yesterday and today my grandchildren set me to work making egg-shell baskets. When the others had gone for a walk I wrote my *Life*, and made a little progress.

Every evening we have the drone of the gramophone and later on it's spades, hearts, slam, and all the other senseless things people say when they play vint. Boulanger and Bulgakov were here. A quiet moonlit night, 3 ° below freezing. What a lovely winter! Dorik is worse; he has a fever of 38.7.

10 Olga and the children went to Tula, then on to Taptykovo. Tanyushka is ill with a temperature of 38.6, Sasha has a cough and a temperature of 38.1, and Dorik's is 39. It's all so depressing, I worry about all of them. I wrote a little of my *Life* and stitched a cap for a poor peasant boy. It is a clear, cold day, 10 degrees of frost day and night.

12 (Moscow) I went to the Council of Orphanages this morning with Olga and the little boy, and Olga then took him to the orphanage, where he was given new clothes and then left. I felt so sorry for him. Then I went to two banks and did some shopping. This evening a recital of Beethoven quartets,[22] played by some Czechs. Beautiful!

13 I left the house early this morning for a rehearsal of the philharmonic concert, where I talked to Ziloti and Rachmaninov.[23] From there I went to the museum, where I did a little work. Then business, and this evening the philharmonic concert. Rachmaninov did a beautiful performance of his piano concerto with the orchestra.

14 N.O. Torba came to the house and gave me the accounts for my errands and transactions. I went to the Kerzins' concert; the Czechs played again, excellently. This evening I went to the Mozart Requiem.

15 I have finished my affairs. There was a telegram from home to say that both Sasha and Tanechka had measles; everything is proceeding normally, they both have temperatures of just over 39. I wanted to leave but Berkenheim reassured me that it wasn't serious, so I went to the museum, where I worked for over 3 hours. I dined with the Maslovs and read them 'The Devil',[24] went to a recital given by the Czechs, then left for home. Sergei Ivanovich was at the Maslovs'.

16 Things are bad here. Sasha has a temperature of 40.4 during the day, she has a bad attack of measles and a nasty cough. They have written to ask Nikitin and Parasha Gué to come. Everyone is in low spirits; I am tired, my heart is exhausted, and Lev Nikolaevich weeps constantly. Tanechka has only a mild attack of measles, and I have been sitting with her.

17 Nikitin arrived, followed by Olga Konstantinovna, Nadya Ivanova and Meyer for the cinematograph.[25] I do no work, just fritter away the days on trifles. Sasha was choking today; they gave her a steam inhalation and she improved. Her temperature was around 39, but towards evening it went down a little. Wrote to Chertkov[26] and Stasyulevich. Took a bath.

19 Sasha was better this morning, and her temperature was down, but she now has an ear-ache. And towards evening her temperature was 38.5 again. Nikitin left yesterday evening. Prince Dmitrii Dmitrievich Obolenskii visited. It is warm – zero degrees. Misha Sukhotin (the son) has left. I have been working on the new edition. Lev Nikolaevich has heartburn and feels perpetually depressed about Sasha. But he manages to work, and today he went for a long ride to Ovsyannikovo and the environs. Tanya and her husband went to Rudakovo.

20 I am permanently busy with the books for the new edition. Two Jews arrived from Tula, a lawyer called Goldenblatt with his two children, and a Jew from Norway who is a Russian correspondent.[27] Sasha is better; her temperature is down to 37.4 now. I wrote letters to Katya, Lyova, Liza, Masha and Lina.

21 Books again. Sasha is still better; her temperature is 37. These endless guests prevent one from working; today it was the Molostvovs, husband and wife. It is warm – 4°. Lev Nikolaevich went for a ride, but is rather weak at present and is eating very little. He played chess with Molostvov.

22 I entertained our guests (the Molostvovs) all day, and made a puppet theatre for my grandchildren. Lev Nikolaevich rode 13 miles through the woods at a walking pace. He is still writing his *Circle of Reading*, and frequently talks of death. Sasha has had a bad cough and a toothache all day, and her temperature is 37.8 again. She is worn out, poor thing!

23 The Molostvovs left this morning. I spent the day tidying up the books and am now utterly exhausted. Sasha is better. Lev Nikolaevich went to visit Maria Aleksandrovna Schmidt, who is in poor health; he has tired himself out and hurt his leg. This evening Lev Nikolaevich, Mikhail Sergeevich and Tanya read aloud some reviews of Paul Bourget's *Barricade*, sent by Halpérine-Kaminskii in Paris.[28] Lovely fine weather.

25 Books again, then worked on the puppet theatre for my grandchildren. Olga came with her children. Snow thawing, no wind. Lev Nikolaevich did not go out, but his leg is better. Sasha has neuralgia in the forehead. My legs ache and my soul is melancholy.

26 I showed my puppet theatre at last this evening, with great success. Lev Nikolaevich felt ill this morning and didn't eat a thing until six o'clock, but he did a lot of writing. This evening he was better. Nadya Ivanova came. Sasha has got up.

27 Lev Nikolaevich is a little better and Sasha is up, although she is so weak her head is spinning. Cold, wind, sun. I finished recording the books and wrote letters to Yunge, the accountant, the translator, Molostvov and Liza Obolenskaya. Then I played two Haydn symphonies as duets with Nadya Ivanova. Bulgakov sang in a crude, monotonous style, although he has a great voice.

28 A warm bright day. I went for a long walk, first around the estate, which is a great burden to me, then to the peasant library. Today there were 69 people there, but there have been as many as 80. This evening I played some Mozart overtures and trios as duets with Nadya Ivanova. Tanechka touchingly asked me to be with her and stopped me doing any work. Everyone is well, thank God. Dorik has gone to Tula. Unpleasant business with some lost money.

March 1 Spent the whole day ill in bed.

2 Felt better today and got up. Worked on the accounts and read the 2nd instalment of Molostvov's biography of Lev Nikolaevich.[29] Very bad. And the drawings are appalling! A scientist called Lev Isaakovich Shestov came,[30] a Jew by all appearances. Lev Nikolaevich took him off to his room as usual for a talk. A warm day, with snow. I wrote to A.I. Maslova and Olga, and to Bulygin about the firewood.

3 I still feel unwell. I worked on the new edition again. Boulanger came and this evening they all played vint while I sewed. It is warm, springlike weather. The rooks have arrived.

4 I feel even iller today. Bright and sunny this morning, then misty, 10 ° in the sun. Lev Nikolaevich and Goldenweiser, who had just arrived, drove to Ovsyannikovo to see Maria Aleksandrovna. This evening Goldenweiser played beautifully. Everyone recalled Sergei Ivanovich's playing and I longed to hear him again. Lev Nikolaevich read us a Buddhist's view of Europeans, translated from the German. Very powerful and true.[31]

5 2 degs. and windy. Lev Nikolaevich went to Telyatinki with a peasant from Tambov province. I corrected the proofs of the appendix of *War and Peace*,[32] and this evening did some more work on the books and articles for the new edition. I am still ill. This evening I corrected the whole of the *Kreutzer Sonata*.

6 I wrote to the *Russian Word* and sent them Lev Nikolaevich's article 'On Suicide',[33] which I like very much and consider very relevant to our times. Dorik returned, and this evening Tanya and Mikhail Sergeevich left for Moscow. Mikhail Aleksandrovich Stakhovich arrived and everyone played vint. Sasha, little Tanechka, Varvara Mikhailovna and the nurse all went to Ovsyannikovo. Impenetrable fog, 5 °, no wind.

8 I looked after Tanyushka again. M.A. Stakhovich left; Boulanger, Nikolaev and Gorbunov came. Lev Nikolaevich complained that his visitors exhausted him. I too am tired and dream of being left alone to work. I took a bath. I still feel ill. It rained and the snow thawed rapidly. 3 °. Varvara Mikhailovna and I have started reading aloud Lev Nikolaevich's banned works.[34]

9 I do not work and waste the whole day on petty anxieties about everything and everyone. Zosya Stakhovich came, and Ivan Ivanovich Gorbunov, who made various helpful suggestions about the new edition.

Lev Nikolaevich is preoccupied with a plan to compile an encyclopaedic dictionary for peasant libraries. Someone has bequeathed 15,000 rubles to a good cause, and they have asked Lev Nikolaevich's advice as to *which* good cause, so he suggested this dictionary.[35] I wrote to Lyova.

10 I try very hard to work, but simply cannot find the time. I played the piano a little today, and this evening my son Misha arrived. They all played vint and started up the gramophone; then Misha played the piano and danced with Tanya – such a cheerful lad. The Sukhotins have

returned from Moscow. Today's papers contained Lev Nikolaevich's article 'On Suicide' and my letter.

11 I wrote my *Life*, then Varvara Mikhailovna and I checked the 4th volume of Lev Nikolaevich's works, preparing it for the printers and amplifying it. Later Zosya read aloud Lev Nikolaevich's letters to the late Countess Aleksandra Andreevna Tolstaya.[36] They are beautiful letters, in which Lev Nikolaevich flirted with her and flaunted his best, artistic side to her. Zero degrees, a quiet, moonlit night.

12 I wrote a lot of my *Life* today, and this evening Zosya read us more of Lev Nikolaevich's fascinating letters to Countess Aleksandra Andreevna Tolstaya. 3 °, the snow is slowly thawing. The artist Meshkov arrived, and is sketching Lev Nikolaevich.[37]

13 I wrote to Lyova. Magnificent weather, with a light frost towards evening, and a brilliant red sunset. I went for a walk; it still looks very wintry with plenty of snow about. I wrote my *Life* and read parts of it aloud to Zosya Stakhovich. This evening we had another reading of Lev Nikolaevich's letters to Countess Tolstaya. Dorik arrived. Meshkov sketched Lev Nikolaevich all morning and evening.

14 I wrote to sister Tanya, finished my memoirs for 1893 and tried to play some Chopin, but was so agitated that I had to stop. Al. Al. Stakhovich came. This evening we read aloud more of Lev Nikolaevich's letters to Countess Tolstaya. They tell a fascinating story of his life – although a one-sided one. In them he parades all the *best* aspects of himself, his thoughts and feelings. 2 ° below freezing.

18 Zosya Stakhovich left this evening. During the day everyone drove off to various different places, while I wrote letters – to Marusya Maklakova, Kerzina, Sonya Tolstaya and some woman called Linda – sent off proofs and so on. Lev Nikolaevich has a cold. He went for a drive in the sledge and wrote a lot of letters, including one to Gusev.[38]

20 Lev Nikolaevich has developed a bad cough; he has been sitting at home drinking Ober-Salzbrunn with milk and doing a lot of work. I am still resting my eyes. I have done nothing, apart from unstitching a dress. Olga came with Sonyushka and Ilyushok. It is warm – 5 ° – but the countryside and the roads are still very wintry. Dorik Sukhotin walked here from his boarding school in Tula.

21 Our guests today were Bulgakov, Dima Chertkov and Ernefeldt,[39] with his son and daughter – 17 to dinner. I spent the whole day

entertaining our guests. Lev Nikolaevich is better; he is coughing less and is much brighter in himself. Sasha was not well though. A fine day; 10–12 in the sun, 3 degrees of frost towards evening. My eyes are a bit better.

22 I took it into my head to copy a portrait of myself which I started in 1906 and abandoned.[40] No good, I can't do anything properly. Lev Nikolaevich is better. Bulygin, Dima Chertkov and the Ernefeldts were here again. The weather is delightful – sunny with a light frost. I have not been out, I'm too busy.

23 I got carried away again by my portrait. But it's no good, it won't do. A young man arrived with some cymbals which he played for us.[41] He gave us no pleasure – an uneducated musician, although talented. A fine day, 1½ ° this evening. Lev Nikolaevich still has a cough and is staying inside.

25 Lady Day. I went for a walk with the two Tanyas, Mikhail Sergeevich and Dunaev, who had just arrived. Your feet get stuck wherever you walk, in the snow or the mud. Later it grew misty, and this evening it was 2 °. I stupidly tried to correct my portrait by candlelight, and only made it worse. Lev Nikolaevich said he felt depressed. There's so much evil in the world, and it torments him. Sasha still has bronchitis.

26 An empty day. I mended Lev Nikolaevich's jersey and played with Tanyushka. There is a slight frost. Lev Nikolaevich is still writing and correcting the preface to the new *Circle of Reading*.

27 Lev Nikolaevich did not go for a walk or a drive all day, and ate no dinner, but he was in good spirits. I did a lot of sewing, and read 'The Kingdom of God' with Varvara Mikhailovna. I doubt they will allow this to be included in the new edition.[42] There is a slight frost, 2 ° at night, a sunny day. The roads are frightful – some go out in the sledge, some in the cart. I wrote to Andryusha, Denisenko, Lyova, Zosya and Maria Nikolaevna (Zubova).

28 The Circassian guard came to see me, and so did Anisya the laundress. I sewed all morning, then walked round the estate giving various instructions. Stakhovich and his sister Rydzevskaya came. The roads are terrible, mud and snow everywhere. Chertkov and Bulgakov came. Lev Nikolaevich is still not very well, but he went out for a ride none the less.

29 We went for a long walk, broke the ice in the streams and made outlets for the water. There is still a lot of snow and travelling is terrible, but at least it's on wheels now. I read my *Life* to Stakhovich and Sukhotin, who liked it. Stakhovich has now left. Mazaryk and Strakhov have come. A lovely fine day.

30 I worked at home, sat with our guests and packed. Strakhov has left with Mazaryk, who contributed nothing of interest, a most uncommunicative person. Lev Nikolaevich enjoyed his company very much, though.[43]

31 (Moscow) Manya Rydzevskaya and I left for Moscow via Tula on the fast train, sharing a compartment with a garrulous lady from Yalta. In Moscow I hurriedly changed my dress and went to a lecture about Lev Tolstoy delivered by Stakhovich in the Tolstoy house-museum. In the course of it he referred to my own small services to L.N., and at the mention of my name the whole artistic company in the hall stood up and there was long, loud, unanimous applause.[44] I stood up bowing first to the lecturer and then to the audience in a state of terrible confusion. Today is Vanechka's birthday. He would have been 22.

April 1 I went to the museum, where I met Biryukov and Stakhovich, and sorted out some letters for Stakhovich's anthology for the Tolstoy Museum journal.[45] Then at five o'clock Stakhovich, Biryukov, Buturlin, Gorbunov and Seryozha met at the house and discussed the new edition from the point of view of the censors. Spent the evening at home adding up accounts for the book sales over the past two months.

2 Sat up until late last night correcting the proofs of the English biography of Lev Nikolaevich which Maude sent me.[46] Went to the Peasant Bank this morning, then worked in the museum until 3. M.A. Stakhovich came to the museum. Shopping, rushing here and there, utter exhaustion. Spent the evening with Ekaterina Fyodorovna Yunge. A reassuring telegram from home.

3 All morning in the museum, then shopping. Saw the director of the printshop at 5, dined at home, spent the evening with the Maslovs. Then sorted out *Boyhood* and put the pages in order. Very tired, things are progressing slowly.

4 Went at 8.30 to a rehearsal of the philharmonic concert of Rachmaninov's works, at which Rachmaninov himself performed. Hard to understand at first, but interesting. Drank coffee in Loskutnaya and visited an exhibition of St Petersburg painters. Interesting. K. Makovskii's large paintings were bad. Those of Welz, Ignatovich and so on were good. Then

I read 'After the Ball' aloud to Kerzina.[47] We left this evening for Yasnaya. It was pouring with rain.

5 At home. A delightful sunny spring day, with a thunder-storm this evening. I ran about the garden delighting in the spring. The white crocuses are out in the meadow, and some small yellow wild flowers, and Tanya found a little lungwort already in flower. There was a brief shower. They have sowed some oats, but only on the hillock. I am exhausted.

7 Moscow accounts, business records, letters – to Molostvova, Zosya Stakhovich, Chefranov, Gradovskii[48] and someone else. Sasha is in bed with bronchitis. A southeast wind. Some yellow flowers and lungworts are out. Vladimir Vladimirovich Filosofov came, and Bulgakov and Belinkii walked over here. We are all angry that Lev Nikolaevich has been refused permission to visit a murderer in prison[49] – he needs to do this for his writing. In a letter to Maria Arkadevna Ofrosimova I added that the government did not have much faith in Tolstoy.

8 I finished the proofs of Maude's English biography of Tolstoy, and went for a walk with Tanyushka. A warm strong wind. Sasha is still in bed. Lev Nikolaevich went for a ride and did a lot of work. I wrote to Maude and Nordman.

9 Anxiety about Sasha. She has such a bad cough. We sent some mucus off for investigation, and by looking through a powerful microscope they discovered several tuberculosis bacilli. We are preparing to leave for the Crimea. Rain, a south wind. I went for a walk with Tanechka and we picked yellow flowers and lungworts. Tanya went to Tula. Lev Nikolaevich went for a ride and worked on *Thoughts for Every Day* and the preface. I carefully went through the manuscript of *Childhood*.[50]

11 Went for a long walk with Tanechka and Tanya; my granddaughter put a bunch of pansies in her button-hole. A fresh day, but no wind. Dima Chertkov came, and Olga with her children, Sonya and Ilyushok. I did a little work on my new edition. Lev Nikolaevich went for a ride and said he couldn't write. 'My swimming days are over,' he says. (The title of a story by his brother Sergei about an old servant.)[51]

12 I walked about the estate for a long time on my own. Extraordinarily beautiful days and nights. Ilya's children Misha and Ilyusha are here; Ilyusha is very sweet. Bulygin, Belinkii and Nadya Ivanova came to visit. I am working enthusiastically on *Childhood*.

13 A wonderful, bright spring day. Went for a long walk with Olga and Anna Alekseevna Goldenweiser. Lungworts, yellow flowers, swelling buds, fleecy clouds in the sky, rain in the evenings. The fields are being ploughed and sowed with oats. Sasha and Varvara Mikhailovna have left for the Crimea; Sasha still has a bad cough. Gorbunov, Maria Aleksandrovna and the Goldenweisers came. He played, to Lev Nikolaevich's delight. I have done nothing all day, I keep being disturbed – first the melancholy business of Sasha's departure, then guests. Ilya's children are here. I wrote to Lyova, Marusya, Yunge, Glebova, Misha's children and Lina.

14 Lev Nikolaevich was depressed last night and could not sleep. Some photographers arrived from Mey's photographic firm, and photographed Lev Nikolaevich on his own, then the two Tanyas and me,[52] then little Tanya and me, then me alone. A fine day with a southeast wind; 7° towards evening. I tidied the books and newspapers; impossible to do any real work. Lev Nikolaevich is reading the thoughts of Leskov, which enchant him.[53] He rode to Ovsyannikovo today. Nikolaev came. I wrote to Zosya, Sasha, Kerzina, Ilya's children and my sister Tanya.

15 Tanya and Olga went to Tula. I took my grandchildren for a walk and we sawed branches and picked flowers. Heavenly summer weather – we're hot even in summer dresses. The scented violets are in flower. I did a little work on *Childhood*, and this evening I played duets with Olga – two Mozart overtures and a Haydn trio. There are leaves on the raspberry bushes. Lev Nikolaevich is still writing *For Every Day* and has been out for a ride. His health is better. I wrote to Biryukov.

16 I wrote to Andryusha, my sister-in-law Masha and Denisenko, and wasted the whole day tidying up and marvelling at this utterly delightful spring. Sasha is the only worry on my mind at the moment, I think constantly of her. Lev Nikolaevich rode to Telyatinki to see Dima Chertkov. He is trying to write a play for them to put on for the peasants.[54] Tanya, Olga and the children went to Ovsyannikovo to see the Gorbunovs. Dima Chertkov came with Lev Nikolaevich. I wrote to Sasha.

17 As soon as I got up I walked along the ravine with Tanechka and Ilyushok to Zakaz, looking for scented violets. We were caught in the rain, and then there was a thunder-storm. We all spent the day happily painting eggs, and this evening I sat with Tanya and Seryozha. I saw almost nothing of Lev Nikolaevich all day, apart from briefly this evening; he had visitors with him. I wrote to A.A. Behrs, and Seryozha wrote to Biryukov. A quiet starry night. The bells are ringing for matins.

18 Easter Sunday. A medallioned officer came with some defamatory verses about Lev Nikolaevich.[55] Very remorseful. We rolled eggs on the balcony with the children. A warm summery day, 18 ° in the shade. The birches are delightful with their soft green leaves. The cheerful sounds of humming bees and singing birds. Clear, bright days, intermittent rumbling of thunder, peasants singing in the village. Seryozha has left; he played the piano a little, his own works too, which were lovely. This evening Nikolaeva came to visit. Endless talk, they all prevented me from doing any work today.

19 There are some lovely bulbs out in the meadow – and marguerites and violets. Still the same heavenly fine weather – it could be June. We had dinner on the verandah, and rolled eggs there. Two real Japanese men visited;[56] one owns a lot of schools in Japan, the other is a student in Moscow. Maria Aleksandrovna came, and Gorbunov. Then Mezhekova the typist arrived with her little girl. After mass they played the gramophone at the village library, and a lot of people came to listen. Lev Nikolaevich talked to the peasants; some of them asked him about the comet, and others about the construction of the gramophone. Tanya is packing – unfortunately: I shall miss Tanechka. I played 'opinions' with the children. Tanechka thought and thought, then said, 'Granny is an angel.'

20 My two darling Tanechkas, mother and daughter, left this morning. I worked hard on the proofs of *Childhood.* I miss my daughters and worry about Sasha. This evening I sat down to play the piano – the whole of Beethoven's 'Pathétique', and another sonata of his. Lev Nikolaevich listened happily.[57]

21 The writer L. Andreev came to visit,[58] and Lev Nikolaevich took him out for a walk. There was a sudden thunder-storm, wind, hail and pouring rain, and we were all very worried. But Lev Nikolaevich and Andreev were just by the side wing. Misha came, and this evening Dima Chertkov arrived. I read 'After the Ball' to Andreev. Distressing news from Sasha – she has tuberculosis in the apex of both lungs. Lev Nikolaevich is crushed, I have a great weight on my heart.

22 The Goldenweisers came this evening. He played Beethoven's sonata 'Quasi una Fantasia', a Chopin ballade and various minor pieces. I walked round the plantations with Lev Nikolaevich, the children and the Goldenweisers. Beautiful weather. It keeps raining off and on, there are some alarming thunder-storms. Our guests this evening were Boulanger, Nikolaeva, Nadya Ivanova, the Gorbunovs and so on. I wrote to Tanya and my daughter-in-law Sonya.

23 At Lev Nikolaevich's request I wrote to Dolgorukov about the cheap booklets in the Yasnaya Polyana library, to the Swiss Society about the translation of some folk-tales into French for their peasants over there,[59] to Onechka and to the Discount Bank. Changeable weather, it has turned cool. The oak is in leaf, the cowslips are out. I went to the meadow and cut the grass around the bulbs – there are such a lot of them. Then I sent Sasha a telegram. This evening Sibor and Goldenweiser played a lovely Mozart violin sonata, some early pieces and Beethoven's 'Kreutzer Sonata'.[60]

24 Lev Nikolaevich ate nothing all morning, complained of feeling weak and having a bad taste in his mouth, and just slept and dozed. I spent the day editing *Childhood* for the complete collection of his works. Olga went with her children to Ovsyannikovo and Taptykovo. Cool, cloudy and rainy. Lev Nikolaevich has ordered his horse Délire to be unshod, as he feels it makes the peasants jealous that he has such a good horse.

25 I wrote to Lyova and Sasha. It rained the entire day, but it's not cold. The oaks are in leaf, and this evening the nightingale sang for the first time. Lev Nikolaevich is better; he had dinner and later took a bath. I edited *Boyhood* all day, and typed out the first page on the Remington. The new edition is making no progress, and I am very worried.

26 Terrible anxiety, choking, keep wanting to cry. I have too many different jobs to do. Lev Nikolaevich is better, thank God; he took a long walk with Olga and the children, and they drove home. I keep working at the new edition, but it's hard work. I am going to Moscow.

28 (Moscow) Set off this morning to work in the museum, then to the shops and the bank, to withdraw the interest. Spent the afternoon at home, then off to the Maslovs'.

29 Visited Ekaterina Fyodorovna Yunge after finishing work in the museum. She is very ill; thought sadly of her immense energy, her creativeness and people's love for her. Everything is gradually dying in her wasted exhausted organism. Spent the evening at the Davydovs' for their '*jour fixe*'.*

30 Went to the museum again and painfully read and took notes for the period covering Vanechka's death. Finished my business, dined with the Maslovs, visited old Praskovya Vasilevna and saw Sergei Ivanovich. He too was delighted to see me. This evening left for home.

*'At home'.

May 1 Arrived back in Yasnaya. Lev Nikolaevich met me, and I was overjoyed to see him. He plans to leave for Kochety to see Tanya, and I was hurt that he wasn't prepared to wait one day for me. 20 technical students came[61] and Lev Nikolaevich presented them all with autographed booklets. Nikolaev, Dima Chertkov, Maria Aleksandrovna and an Englishman were here. Lev Nikolaevich is packing. Olga and the children have left for Taptykovo.

2 Lev Nikolaevich left this morning to visit the Sukhotins in Kochety, with Doctor Makovitsky and Bulgakov his secretary. The same magnificent weather; the apple trees are covered in blossom and are an enchanting sight. Dorik, Maria Aleksandrovna, Nikolaeva and a Kiev psychiatrist called Petrovskii were here. Nikolaeva read her high-flown stories. I tidied up the Kuzminskiis' wing and cut the grass.

3 Alone in the house all day with Maria Aleksandrovna, correcting the proofs of the newly printed articles and checking the text of *Boyhood.* Played some Beethoven sonatas and Chopin nocturnes this evening, and strolled around the apple orchard. Wrote to Lev Nikolaevich,[62] Varya Nagornova, Lyova and others.

5 Spent the day with Andryusha's family; this evening finished my business, posted letters, corrected proofs. Went to bed at 3 a.m. Raining, cool.

6 Poured with rain all day. 4½° earlier on, 2° this evening. Cleared up later, cold, moonlit night. Andryusha and I sorted and copied various fascinating articles relating to Lev Nikolaevich's youth which still haven't seen the light of day.[63] I sent a telegram to Kochety saying I wasn't coming, and posted a book.

7 I have again deferred my visit to Kochety on account of the terrible weather and my ill health. I am very busy sorting and copying Lev Nikolaevich's manuscripts with Andryusha. Cold dreary weather. It's so depressing to see Andryusha with his new family and his financial worries.

9 (Kochety) Andryusha and I left Zaseka for Blagodatnaya early this morning. Very cold, a north wind. I travelled from Oryol with an old Polish woman and a most agreeable lady called Sudbinina. I was met in Kochety by my two dear Tanyas, Bulgakov and the doctors; Mikhail Sergeevich seems to have lost some of his good humour. Lev Nikolaevich looks well. Vladimir Grigorevich Chertkov is here; that was why Lev Nikolaevich was in such a hurry to leave.

10 Spent the day with my granddaughter Tanechka – we love one another very much. It is so simple, peaceful and happy here, although the weather is cold and overcast. Lev Nikolaevich went for another ride, and covered about 18 miles looking for some peasant dissenter.[64]

11 (Kochety) Played with Tanechka and went for a walk with her and Tanya. Cool, light showers. The Abrikosovs came, father and son. Took notes all evening from my letters to Tanya.

12 Spent the morning with my granddaughter Tanya, then took notes from my letters to my daughter Tanya, and painfully re-lived all the sufferings of 1894 and 1895. This evening I read, slept and talked about Vanechka. He is constantly alive in my heart. Lev Nikolaevich is cheerful and well. He drinks bilberry juice but won't take soup. 11 ° and still cool.

13 Went for a walk with Tanyushka this morning, then took notes from my letters to Tanya; interesting, and sad too! The two Sukhotin sons have come, Lyova with his wife and child, and Seryozha. So many people, and so much work for Tanya. Lev Nikolaevich is very happy; he is taken good care of, and has his whole retinue here – Chertkov, Bulgakov and Makovitsky. It is still cool – 11 ° during the day.

14 A fine bright day, cool in the morning. Lev Nikolaevich is well, and is still rewriting his preface to the *Circle of Reading*.[65] Bulgakov has copied it out so many times already. Little Tanya and Mika are delightful. I wrote to Marusya and Lyova, and took the little ones for a long walk. Lev Nikolaevich walked to a nearby village and talked to the peasants.[66] Tanya followed him in the carriage. A cool bright day. The Gorbovs came.

15 I have left the Sukhotins; Lev Nikolaevich is staying behind with his retinue. Tanya took me to the Abrikosovs' wretched little house. Their parents were staying and their children were there: such a sympathetic household. The elder Abrikosovs travelled with me to Zaseka, where I got off. I was terribly tired. The house seemed so empty, there was a mass of things to do. Katya and Maria Aleksandrovna were there.

16 Another terribly busy day – correcting proofs, copying out Lev Nikolaevich's old manuscripts, dividing up the separate volumes, seeing to the estate. By this evening I was senseless with exhaustion, but I left for Zaseka all the same, and then Moscow. (I forgot my keys and had to go back.) I took the boy to the orphanage.[67]

17 (Moscow) To the museum, the bank and the shops; Olga and I were driving around in our cab from 11 o'clock onwards. I got a lot done, but am now exhausted. I have handed Volumes IV, XI and XII of the new edition over to the printers.[68]

19 Andryusha arrived in Yasnaya this evening, and I got back this morning. Katya has been staying here with her little girl. I feel too tired and ill to do any real work. I sewed some oilcloth covers for the tables, and Andryusha and I upholstered the sofa in the drawing-room. I went to bed late.

20 I walked around Yasnaya Polyana for three hours, picking flowers and admiring the sky and the spring – it was lovely. But our beautiful flourishing garden has been attacked by weevil, the rye is scanty, the earth is poor, there are constant battles with the peasants over the trees and their cattle, which trample all over our meadows, and the whole estate is nothing but a torment. Lev Nikolaevich, Makovitsky and Bulgakov have returned from Kochety. Lev Nikolaevich is safe and well. This morning my grandson Sergei Sergeevich arrived with his tutor.[69] Andryusha has left for Moscow. I wrote to Tanya, Sasha and Lyova.

21 My son Seryozha came, followed by Maria Aleksandrovna Schmidt, and life is more cheerful. I worked on the new edition, distributing the articles throughout the various volumes, then I pasted in newspaper cuttings. I discussed with the bailiff the question of giving away some land. This evening they played the gramophone, then Seryozha played the piano, which was much more pleasant.

I have too much to do, and am also ill.

Delightful weather, a beautiful spring. Sad news of my brother Petya's death.

22 I wrote to Felten and Krashennikov the house-painter. I grieve constantly for my dead brother Petya, that good, honest person. Andryusha has returned, the Gorbunov couple have come. I walked to the swimming pool with her, Seryozha and his tutor, but it's not ready yet. A hot, fine day, the nightingales are singing. Lev Nikolaevich is well; he revised his play for the peasant theatre, and went for a ride with Bulgakov. He took a walk this morning and got lost, coming out of the forest at the crown nurseries. I am very busy with the new edition, the estate, the house, tidying up the books and so on, and feel wretched.

23 Terrible depression all day, there's no point in anything, I'm sick to death of it all. Lev Nikolaevich is like wood – he never speaks, never says a kind word, never takes an interest in anything; that's why I am so unhappy. I made him a waistcoat and some trousers. A mass of people here

– Bulygin, Nikolaev, Mitasha Obolenskii, Dima Chertkov, Sergeenko and some dark one.[70] Very warm – quite hot during the day.

24 Spent the entire day tidying and cataloguing library books. A hot day and a warm night. Dry. Took a short walk round the park. Lev Nikolaevich rode to Krivy, played chess with Goldenweiser and read a lot. Sergeenko came, and some dark one.

25 Lev Nikolaevich has been getting up early every morning and bringing back bunches of wild flowers. He is writing something for the kopeck booklets, which interest him very much. He and Bulgakov went to Ovsyannikovo to talk to Gorbunov about it.[71] I have finished tidying the books. I still feel unwell and have no energy for work, so I mended stockings and went for a walk. Nikolaeva came. It has clouded over.

26 Andryusha and his family have left for Tambov. Goldenweiser was here. Sasha and Varvara Mikhailovna are leaving the Crimea tonight. I worked on the new edition, and made Lev Nikolaevich a cap. This evening I took my grandson Seryozha out to pick night violets. It is cooler – 8 ° towards evening.

27 Sasha and Varvara Mikhailovna got back this evening. N.N. Gué and Bulygin came. I worked on the new edition, made Lev Nikolaevich three caps and altered his waistcoat. He went for a ride through the woods and was very excited by a letter from Chertkov, who wrote about an actor called Orlyonov and his scheme to put on plays for the peasants.[72] It is cool – 9 ° – and very dry.

28 A lazy morning, then I proof-read the pedagogical articles for Volume IV of the *Complete Collected Works*, sewed Lev Nikolaevich's waistcoat and scythed the nettles around the flowerbeds for some exercise. Bulygin and the Goldenweisers were here. A hot day, 7 ° at night, with the threat of a drought. Bulgakov has left; earlier he went for a ride through the woods with Lev Nikolaevich. I wrote to Gradovskii, Tanya, Soikin. My leg is hurting.

29 Painful discussion with Lev Nikolaevich (Odoev, Paris). Reproaches flung at me for our privileged life, after I complained about the difficulties of running the estate. He wants to drive me out of Yasnaya to live in Odoev or Paris or some other place. I went out (of the house), terrible heat, aching leg, wild pulse, lay down in a ditch and stayed there, they sent a horse for me.[73] Stayed in bed all day, wept, did not eat. Paolo Trubetskoi came with his wife.

30 Crowds of people here – the Trubetskois, Nadya Ivanova, Gorbunov, N.N. Gué, Nikolaeva. Zosya Stakhovich came for dinner. Unpleasant business with the theft of three horses from our herd; I sent the governor a written statement. Then a disagreeable note from Shchelkan (Taneeva), to which I replied today.[74] Warm and dry. So much to do, so little time. Sasha still has a cough – most alarming.

31 Endless bustle, impossible to do anything. Went to Ovsyannikovo to see Maria Aleksandrovna and the Gorbunovs. The children were there. My grandson Seryozha and N.N. Gué went with me. Trubetskoi is still doing sketches of Lev Nikolaevich and the rest of us. He is very gifted, and loves art.[75] Zosya Stakhovich and Kolechka Gué have left. Goldenweiser was here. A hot day, drought. Lev Nikolaevich went for a ride with Trubetskoi. He is revising his 2-act comedy and working on the kopeck booklets.

A stolen horse has been found in Tula. I wrote to Glebova and the governor. The plasterers have started work on the outside of the house, and the roofer is installing a hood in the laundry.

June 1 I finished Lev Nikolaevich's waistcoat and wrote to my son Ilya. I have a bad stomach – it was ruptured by the operation. Another hot day and warm night. L.N. went for a ride with Trubetskoi both yesterday and today. Sasha is copying his play for him.[76]

2 Went for the first swim of the year. The Trubetskois went swimming on their own; husband and wife jumped straight into the river, to our great astonishment. I took unsuccessful photographs of Trubetskoi and Lev Nikolaevich, and this evening developed these and my photographs of Andryusha's family. Another hot day; I mowed hay for silage. Lidia Aleks. Ivanova – a very lively women – came from Tatev, and this evening my daughter Tanya arrived. An artist with his wife, a lunatic with a persecution mania, beggars – endless visitors all day.

3 We all cheerfully walked down to the river for a swim – Tanya, Masha Zubova (who has just arrived), Varvara Mikhailovna, Sasha (who is forbidden to swim) and I. She is guarding her health and looks well – but who knows for how long? Very hot. Trubetskoi is sculpting a small figure of Lev Nikolaevich on his horse.[77] I printed photographs and pasted them into the album.

4 I went for a swim and did one or two jobs, but didn't manage to do any real work – too hot, too many visitors. Dima Chertkov, O.K. Klodt, Bulgakov and Boulanger came. Lev Nikolaevich is distraught because the

Circassian guard has brought Prokofii in for stealing a beam; and he is an old man who once worked with him.[78] Oh, I've had enough of the estate!

5 I corrected the proofs of the first article in Volume XII,[79] and went swimming with Masha. The water is cool, and the air was 10 ° this evening. Lev Nikolaevich posed on his horse for Trubetskoi, who has been sculpting with great enthusiasm. Our Tanya left this morning, and I saw her off. Semyonov the peasant writer has turned up.[80] I took more photographs.

6, Whit Sunday Fine and dry, cool at night. I wrote to Lyova, Liza Obolenskaya, Molostvova, Chertkov and the proof-reader. A large number of peasants arrived from the three villages of Yasnaya, Telyatinki and Grumond, with drums, balalaikas, the harmonium, the gramophone, singing and dancing. Sasha and Masha handed out sweets to the children and I gave the women money. Lev Nik. talked to them at great length about land ownership, religion and so on. Goldenweiser, Klodt, Nikolaeva and Semyonov were here. I corrected proofs.

7, Whit Monday More unpleasant recriminations against me this morning for keeping on the Circassian guard; it *looks* so bad for Tolstoy to employ a mounted guard on his estate.[81] I said no wood had been stolen since he arrived, and everything had been quiet with no police or criminal proceedings. It turned into another painful conversation, with yet more recriminations; I was in tears almost all day, went to bed for the whole afternoon and couldn't do a thing. Lev Nik. is in a terrible state: he torments both himself and me. Seryozha has left. It is cold, dry and cloudy, with a north wind. Nikolaev visited and was insufferably quarrelsome with L.N. I wrote to Lyova and Soikin.

8 Lev Nik. is ill. When he woke up this morning, having slept longer than usual, he couldn't remember a thing. His temperature was 37, and rose to 37.2, although by this evening it was 36.6. It's probably his enlarged liver. He is in a difficult mood, constantly losing his temper and refusing to be treated. Still cold and very dry, with a north wind. Nikitin and Nadya Ivanovna came to visit, and Dima Chertkov, Bulygin and the actor Orlyonov arrived. I finished reading the proofs of Maude's English biography of L.N.,[82] mended stockings and moped.

9 I wrote to Biryukov, Rundaltsev, Landowska and my daughter Tanya. Lev Nik. was much better and had dinner with us, although he felt weak and stayed at home all day. He has again written a letter to the newspapers asking people not to demand money from him, as he hasn't got any, but they

haven't printed it.[83] A cold day, 10 °. Nikitin has left. I worked hard dividing up the separate volumes for the new edition.[84] The grass in the garden has been cut. I have a bad stomach.

10 Rain, 5 ° this evening, still a north wind. Lev Nik. has recovered, and even went for a ride with Bulgakov. Some Czech has arrived, a pedagogue.[85] I played my two favourite Beethoven sonatas, then developed photographs of L.N. on his horse, and Trubetskoi with his statuette. I wrote to Chefranov and the printers. The wells have been cleared and the courtyard walls are being plastered.

11 I worked hard on the proofs. A Japanese man called Konisi came, and some Jewish Czech pedagogue. Cold and dry; the grass in the garden is being cut. Preparations are being made to visit the Chertkovs. Sasha is not well and is not sure about going, but of course her father won't wait for anyone in the world.

12 Lev Nikol. and Sasha have left for the Chertkovs', along with L.N.'s retinue – the doctor, Bulgakov his secretary and Ilya Vasilevich the servant. There was a north wind all morning, then it grew warmer. I took a walk with N.N. Gué and Varvara Mikhailovna. They're raking the hay in the garden. The Trubetskois have left – he has finished his statuette of Lev Nik. and a ploughing peasant.[86] I wrote to Maslova and the house-painter, and sent off the proofs of the *ABC* and of 'Forty Years'.[87]

13, All Saints' Day Got up late feeling ill. N. N. Gué and Varvara Mikhailovna went off to Kryltsovo and Khatunka to visit Bulygin. I sat working from one to six, and corrected the proofs of *The Power of Darkness* and *The Kreutzer Sonata*.[88] What a terrible message these two pieces contain, especially the second. I had dinner all on my own and walked round the farm and the estate for two hours. This evening my son Ilya arrived. He was born 44 years ago today, on All Saints' Day. I wrote to Lyova and Tanya.

15 To my great delight I received a letter from Lev Nikol. at the Chertkovs'.[89] I sent Sasha a letter and L.N. a short note,[90] wrote to Chefranov and Pilkov and sent Volume XIII to the printers. Intense heat and strong wind all morning. Thunder-storm and slight rain this evening. The first berries have been picked.

More work on the new edition. More instructions about the plastering and painting work around the house. Stored furniture.

16 Spent the whole day in Tula. Had my teeth seen to, consulted a woman doctor called Kidanova, visited the bank, went shopping with

Varvara Mikhailovna and felt exhausted for some reason. Complete chaos at home: the painters and plasterers have been working here. A hot day and a cool night, windy. Another affectionate letter from my daughter Tanya.[91] Nikolaeva and the Goldenweisers came.

17 It rained all day, I worked hard on the proofs. Unbearable mess and bother with the repairs. The carpenters came. An alarming telegram from a St Petersburg newspaper enquiring about Lev N.'s health. I sent off a telegram and two letters.[92] I also wrote to congratulate Sasha and Tanya. I sat on my own all evening feeling vacant and distraught.

18 Sasha's 26th birthday. I couldn't sleep all night, as I was waiting for the telegrams. This morning Lev Nikolaevich replied that all was well, and that my question had surprised him.[93]

I went for a swim with Olga, Sonechka and Ilyushok. Yesterday Maria Aleksandrovna and the Goldenweisers came. A terrible thunder-storm this evening, and heavy rain. We let the Goldenweisers stay the night – I myself urged them to. I wrote to Lev Nik.[94] and Lyova.

20 I live on my own here with nature, the flowers and my thoughts. I went swimming with Varvara Mikhailovna before dinner, and read proofs this morning. This evening I walked over to the Nikolaevs. Their children were there. A warm day, no wind; the hay is being gathered; it is night now, and I can hear them singing in the village.

Lev Nik. says nothing about his return. I am no longer necessary to him. The Chertkovs have priority now; I must create my *own* personal life – or my own *personal death*.

21 Printed photographs all day; I want to give my son Seryozha an album of my pictures for his birthday. A lovely hot day and a quiet night. I drove to the river in the trap with Varvara Mikhailovna, Verochka Sidorkova and Tanya Nikolaeva, and we had a swim. This evening I tidied Lev Nik.'s room and rinsed the photographs, then we all drank tea on the balcony. Everything is so charming here – and so empty. Lev Nikolaevich's present state has brought me – and himself – a painful old age. 'Everything is sad!' as Vanechka used to say.

October 26 I got up early and went for a long walk through the fir saplings, gathering dry branches as I went. Then I took my oil paints and covered a long branch with designs. A warm day, the snow has vanished. I finished reading the articles for the new edition. My son Andryusha came and I was delighted to see him. He is mine, wholeheartedly *mine*, unlike Sasha. Lev Nik. rode to Ovsyannikovo to see Maria Aleksandrovna, returned exhausted and slept till 7. We were all very anxious about him. He dined on his own. A worrying telegram this evening from Masha about Seryozha's duel.[95]

Andryusha went to Tula. My soul is uneasy. What will happen?

27 A quiet, busy day. All is well with Seryozha, who is now in Moscow; but poor Andryusha must be exhausted. What a good person. I did not sleep last night, and got up this morning feeling very agitated. I was also hurt by L.N.'s cold, spiteful 'principled' behaviour over Chertkov's letter – instead of *kind* reassurance.[96] He went for a ride with Dushan, did a lot of writing, and read.[97] It snowed.

28 Lev Nik. has left! My God! He left a letter telling me not to look for him as he had gone for good, to live out his old age in peace. The moment I read those words I rushed outside in a frenzy of despair and jumped into the middle pond, where I swallowed a lot of water; Sasha and Bulgakov dragged me out with the help of Vanya Shuraev.[98] Utter despair. Why did they save me?

29 All the children have come, apart from Lyova.[99] They are so kind and attentive but they are unable to help or comfort me. Mitasha Obolenskii has come,[100] Seryozha, Ilya and Misha have left. Vanya discovered that L. Nik. had gone to Belev – maybe to see his sister Maria Nikolaevna?[101]

30 I cry day and night and suffer dreadfully. It is more painful and terrible than anything I could have imagined. Lev Nik. did visit his sister in Shamordino, then travelled on beyond Gorbachevo – who knows where.[102] What unspeakable cruelty!

31 I haven't eaten or drunk anything for four days now, I ache all over, my heart is bad. Why? What is happening? Nothing to write about – nothing but groans and tears. Berkenheim came with some stupid doctor called Rastorguev and a young lady fresh from medical school.[103] These outsiders make it all much more difficult, but the children don't want to take *responsibility*. What for? My life? I just want to leave the dreadful agony of this life . . . I can see no hope, even if L.N. does at some point return. Things will never be as they were, after all he has made me suffer. We can never be straightforward with one another again, we can never love one another, we shall always *fear* one another now. And I fear for his health and strength too.

November 1 I am growing weak; I have eaten nothing for five days now, and have just drunk a little water. Today I feel slightly better, and am not such a prey to my passionate love for L.N. which has so tormented my heart, and is now so poisoned. I received the eucharist, talked with the priest and decided to take a little food, for fear of not being strong enough to go to Lev Nik. should he fall ill. My son Misha arrived. I did a little work.

2 I received a telegram from the *Russian Word* first thing this morning: 'Lev Nik. ill in Astapovo. Temperature 40.' Tanya, Andryusha, the nurse and I all left Tula for Astapovo on a special train.

3* (Astapovo) Doctor Nikitin arrived, then Berkenheim. Lev Nikolaevich has pneumonia in the left lung. They will not let me see him.[104] Seryozha is here, and Tanya. Lev Nik. wired for Chertkov in person.[105]

4* Lev Nik. is worse. I wait in agony outside the little house where he is lying. We are sleeping in the train.

5* Shchurovskii and Usov have come. There is evidently little hope. I am tormented by remorse, the painful anticipation of his end, and the impossibility of seeing my beloved husband.

6* Dreadful atmosphere of anticipation, I can't remember anything very clearly.

7* At 6 o'clock in the morning Lev Nikol. died. I was allowed in only as he drew his last breath. They would not even let me take leave of my husband. Cruel people.[106]

8* We are leaving with the body. They have lent us the carriage in which we were staying.

9* Back in Yasnaya. Crowds of people at Zaseka. We lowered the coffin on to the station and they came to pay their last respects. Masses of young people and delegations. They all followed the coffin from Zaseka to Yasnaya Polyana. We buried Lev Nikolaevich.

10* I am ill with a cough and a fever of 40.4 – I cannot remember a thing. Varya Nagornova and my sister Tatiana Andreevna are here with me. It's good to be with them. Sasha left this morning for Telyatinki.

11* I am ill, they have hired a nurse, Ekat. Fyod. Terskaya.

*All written much later. (Added by Sofia Tolstaya.)

12 Ill.

13–15 Ill. My sons were here.

16–18 Ill in bed. Many letters and telegrams.

19–21 Ill in bed.

22–4 Ill.

25 Better, but still in bed. Terrible sleepless nights!

26 Tormenting neuralgia night and day.

27 Got up, but still have neuralgia. Bulygin, Posha Biryukov, the Sukhotins and various others came. They brought my granddaughter Sonechka here.

28 Health better. Anna Iv. Maslova came, and Drankov the cinematographer and Spiro the journalist. All very painful, but it's a little easier with other people. What will happen when I am alone? Terrible! No future.

29 Unbearable depression, pangs of remorse, weakness and painful feelings of pity for my late husband's sufferings – what he must have endured at the end! . . . I cannot go on living. A. Iv. Maslova has left. My sister Tatiana Andreevna has a sore throat.

30 Sasha has arrived with Maria Aleksandrovna and Vaka Filosofov. Tanya is better. Mikhail Sergeevich has left for Pirogovo. Zero degrees, a damp overcast November, with almost no snow. A dismal, frightening life ahead – and in a few days' time I shall be all alone.

December 1 The same thing, day after day, endless depression, I haven't written a thing.

2 Everyone is still here, thank God. What will happen afterwards? Sasha arrived with Varvara Mikhailovna.

4 Mikh. Serg. Sukhotin has left for Moscow. A correspondent of the *New Times* has arrived – a certain Ksyunin.[107] Seryozha Sukhotin arrived this evening. Windy and overcast, no snow. I haven't done a thing. A lot of chatter on all sides.

5 Sergeenko, Seryozha and others came. We show Lev Nik.'s room to visitors.

6 More people came to visit the grave with Al. Vas. Zinger. A dear man. I showed them the rooms. Bulgakov was here. I read him my memoirs. My two darling Tanechkas have left. It's even more sad and difficult.

7 Deep unbearable despair all day. I didn't sleep all night and wept all morning. My daughter-in-law Sonya came, Ilya arrived for dinner, and things become slightly more cheerful. Bulgakov and Belinkii came. Still zero degrees.

8 Sister Tanya left this morning, and I wept terribly. The loneliness is agony, no one to care for, no one to talk to. I don't remember what I did. I wrote something and went to L.N.'s grave with Sonya.

9 I translated some letters from French and copied them out for the new edition.[108] Proofs. The artist Rossinskii came.[109] My daughter-in-law Sonya left this evening.

10 Read proofs all day. The artist Rossinskii is still here. My son Misha arrived for dinner and left at eight to see Sasha, whence he will return to his estate in Chifirovka. I took a bath. A wind has blown up. I wrote to Maslova, Taneev,[110] Lyova and Andryusha.

11 Lebrun's wife, Yuliana Semyonovna, was here. Ilya Vasilevich and I tidied up Lev Nikolaevich's things to save them from moths and depredation. It was terribly painful – life in general is torture. I wrote to Tanya and E. Fyod. Yunge. I went to sleep this afternoon to the sounds of a terrible gale. Loneliness, remorse, despair!

12 Read proofs, walked to the village with the nurse and felt even more depressed. Everyone weeps when they see me. I sorted through the newspapers. Dushan Petrovich has left to see Misha; his son Petya has pneumonia. Some publisher called Lenkovskii was here. This evening there was a telegram announcing Seryozha's arrival.

13 I didn't sleep a wink last night. Oh, these ghastly sleepless nights, alone with my thoughts, my agonising conscience, the darkness of the winter night and the darkness in my soul! Two ladies from St Petersburg came with a letter from M.A. Stakhovich – one was called Elena Iv. Timrot. N.N. Gué, Dm. Vas. Nikitin and my son Seryozha came too. Life is easier with them here. But soon there'll be loneliness again!

14 My guests haven't left yet, and I am so glad! I didn't sleep last night, wept and suffered all day and visited the grave. There I found an artist and the village policeman – most unpleasant. I catalogued library books, most of them Lev Nikolaevich's. What a warm winter! It's 2 ° today. I wrote to Lyova.

15 Seryozha, Maria Aleksandrovna, Bulygin and Gué spent the day with me. Sasha came – all very affable. I weep incessantly, tormented by my eternal separation from Lev Nik. My one consolation is that I too have not long to live. Nikitin has left. I have done a little work on the proofs and am feeling very unwell.

16 All the villagers from Yasnaya Polyana – peasants, women and children – gathered today, 40 days after his death, at Lev Nikolaevich's grave, which they tidied and laid with branches and fir wreaths. They knelt on the ground three times, took off their caps and sang 'Eternal Memory!' I cried and suffered deeply, but felt so moved by the peasants' love for him. At that moment we were all experiencing the same thing together. And they were so sweet to me too. I wrote to my sister Tanya and my daughter Tanya, Ilya and Andryusha. So sad and lonely!

17 I took a sleeping powder and slept, but waking was frightful! Yet more visitors from far-off places, both to see the grave and visit the house. Proofs, newspapers – such a lot to be done. I live here with the nurse, Ekat. Fyod. Terskaya. Proofs, copying and depression day and night. It sometimes feels as though all this is temporary, and things will soon return to normal.

18 Terribly depressed all day. I went out and walked around the garden in the heavy snow, then visited Lyovochka's grave. I feel so puzzled whenever I go there – can that really be my beloved Lyovochka, lying there under the ground? And every time I cry and cry until my chest aches. I copied his articles and read proofs. Oh, the loneliness! 52 girl students from St Petersburg came to visit the grave and look around the house.

19 I copied out a play by L.N., then walked to the village to find out about the taxes, and to ask who was selling what to pay them. Biryukov visited briefly, a correspondent from *Russian Word* was here, and there were yet more visitors. They come from all corners of the world. There were four Slavs from Austria the day before yesterday, a man from the Caucasus and another Mohammedan who brought a wreath. A lot of snow, it's all white, quiet and beautiful. 5 ° below freezing. But where is *He*? Where?

20 Sasha, Varvara Mikhailovna, Khiryakov and his wife, Pav Iv. Biryukov and Sytin all paid brief visits. Also some Jews from Tula called the

Varshavers came to look at L.N.'s room and his grave. I didn't sleep last night, wept all morning and did almost no work, just a little copying and proof-reading. Snow, silence, whiteness, 5–6 ° below freezing, like yesterday. And it's all so pointless, tedious, empty and unnecessary!

21 Spent the day with Mikh. Al. Stakhovich,[111] which was very pleasant. He has read a great deal about Lev Nik. We went to the grave together.

22 Got up late. Proofs. Andryusha came, then Ilya. I am delighted to see them, but they are both sad and preoccupied with money worries. I did a little copying, went to bed late. Visited L.N.'s grave with Andryusha. Wept. Painful discussions with my sons about their father's inheritance.

23 Ilya has left. He visited Sasha and Chertkov, about whom we are discovering more and more bad things. A sly, malicious man. I went to photograph the grave, weeping as I did so. What a delightful, fine, bright day it was, with the white hoar-frost and the blue sky. But the beauty made me even sadder! 13–17 ° below freezing. I wrote to Marusya, Bulygin and Tanyushka. This afternoon I developed my photographs of Lev Nik.'s grave.

24 Another sleepless night – torture! I was woken by a mouse. This morning I printed the photographs of L.N.'s grave. Then I wrote letters to sister Tanya, Chefranov, the accountant, the editors of *Herald of Europe* and *Russian Wealth*, the stationmaster and Sergeenko, plus a letter to Razumovskaya enclosing 10 rubles 50 kopecks. This evening I copied out L.N.'s manuscript of *The Light Shines Even in Darkness*.[112] A rough draft, and not very good. Andryusha is a little calmer, but still irritable.

25 A painfully sad Christmas! I was pleased to have Andryusha here, but he left at three. I visited L.N.'s grave with the nurse, and decorated it with white and pink hyacinths, leaves, primulas, and some other little flower. I wept bitterly. The beauty of nature and the light of the sun were quite astonishing. Dushan Petrovich, the nurse and I wrote quietly for a long time in the drawing-room together. 15 ° below freezing.

26 Slept badly, as depressed as ever. Wrote all day. Yu. Iv. Igumnova came to visit. Kind, red-cheeked and energetic as ever. Another beautiful day, hoar-frost, sun and ice. Didn't leave the house. Wrote letters to Stakhovich, Maslova and sister Tanya, and two business replies.

27 Took some veronal for my insomnia and slept till 12. Felt quite dazed, but it's better like this – the suffering is less acute, as the body loses the capacity to respond to spiritual pain. But where is the soul then? I did a lot of copying and wrote to Lina, Vanya and Tanya, Sonya and Ilyushok, plus two business letters. 15 ° below freezing as before, and windy.

28 It is two months today since Lev Nik. left. I went to the grave; life is just as unbearably painful. I wrote to my daughter Tanya in Rome and sent her a photograph of the grave. 10 ° below freezing; windy and not quite so beautiful outside. I am copying out some manuscripts. My daughter Sasha came, and Andryusha with his wife and daughter. There have been a lot of visitors to Lev Nik.'s grave and his rooms.

29 I wrote all day and corrected proofs – there were a lot to do. Andryusha is a sorry sight with his unstable nerves. We're all like that now! And so depressed. The weather is warmer; I didn't go out. I copied out a very good excerpt from a work of Lev Nikolaevich's about God.[113] He wrote well, but what did he *do*?

30 My son Ilya arrived with his wife and three eldest boys. Andryusha is a little better today, but still very anxious. Windy, 6 ° below freezing. I had a sleepless night, slightly feverish all day, didn't leave the house. I'm glad my sons are here, I don't feel so lonely now. Read a lot of proofs, and copied a lot of Lev Nik.'s story 'What I Dreamed About'.[114]

31 This morning I read proofs, copied *Father Sergii* and played for a while with my granddaughter Mashenka. My son Seryozha arrived before dinner, and Vaka Filosofov came this evening. When the clock struck 12 we all gathered in the drawing-room and talked about Lev N.'s last days. Then we went into the big dining-room and drank tea. There was a cake, fruit and fruit juice for the children. The atmosphere was sad but very touching. I am so grateful to all the people who came to comfort me – Seryozha, Ilya, Sonya and the three grandsons, Andryusha and his wife, Vaka Filosofov, Yulia Ivanovna, Terskaya the nurse and Dushan Petrovich. Ilya told me an interesting thing that old Professor Snegiryov had told him about Lev Nikol.'s death. Apparently there's a certain kind of pneumonia which starts as an unnatural excitement of the brain, and the patient, infected by this poison, rushes out of the house, goes off he knows not where and roams around. Just like Lev Nik., first leaving the house, then visiting Shamordino, then rushing off he knew not where. He bought tickets that were valid for three months.[115] Snegiryov assumes that Lev Nik. was already ill when he left Yasnaya Polyana.

· 1911 ·

January to February – student riots, followed by arrests, dismissals and deportations; 125 professors resign. Universities come under police control. Jews disenfranchised from zemstvo. *Arrest of Mendel Beilis, a poor Jew accused of the ritual murder of a gentile boy (trial in 1913). September – Stolypin, recently appointed President of Council of Ministers, assassinated by agent of security police. Ascendancy at court of the monk Rasputin and his increasing influence on ministerial decisions and appointments. Summer – Germany sends warship to Agadir to protect German interests in Morocco and France, backed by Spain, sends troops to the capital, Fez, to defend it. The start of a series of wars in the Balkans for control of the Ottoman Empire, with Russia pursuing a vacillating and contradictory policy.*

Battle over Tolstoy's manuscripts begins, with Sofia and her sons against Chertkov and Sasha (who issues injunction forbidding her mother access to her room at the Historical Museum and halting publication of her editions). Government declines to buy Yasnaya Polyana, so as not to honour Tolstoy's memory, but the Tsar provides his widow with a fairly generous pension. Mikhail Kuzminskii and Sofia's sons Lev, Mikhail, Andrei and Ilya negotiate with American businessmen against her will, over the possible purchase of Yasnaya (it comes to nothing). March – official opening of the Moscow Society of the Tolstoy Museum. Sofia starts work on an edition of Tolstoy's letters to her.

January 1 Made a copy of Lev Nikol.'s diary for July and August to give to Lyova. Ilya, Andryusha and Vaka Filosofov left this afternoon to visit Maria Nikolaevna in the convent at Shamordino. Lovely weather, 5°, moonlit nights and oh, such sadness! My children, grandchildren, guests and people in general are no real consolation, only a diversion. I even love my sadness, as the final contact with my Lyovochka. The tears are still there, every moment of the day, but I try to restrain myself and now fear them. Seryozha is closest to me, for we both grieve more than the others.

2 Proofs all morning. Took fresh flowers to the grave and scattered seeds to the birds. Wept bitterly; inconsolable, irreparable grief. Prayer is no comfort. My three grandsons have left. Andryusha returned from the convent and told me a great deal; it was so painful to hear of L.N.'s fears that I might chase after him, and his tears and sobs when they told him I had tried to drown myself.[1]

4 A brief snow-storm this morning. The artist N.V. Orlov has arrived, my son Seryozha has left. I tidied up the books again – so tedious! This evening my sons Ilya, Andrei and Misha rushed in and demanded 1,500 rubles to send Ilya off to America in order to sell Yasnaya Polyana. I find this most distasteful and sad and not at all to my liking.[2] I should like to see Yasnaya Polyana in Russian hands, as public property.

5 A lot of proofs, all to no purpose, it seems. There's no spiritual centre to the world now, no lofty, abstract life in this house – and it is very sad! There's no love either – although I was robbed of that long ago, the expression of it anyway, if not my place in Lev Nik.'s heart.

6 Dushan Petr. Makovitsky left here for good today. I wept; one more link with Lev Nik. is now broken. I corrected some proof pages of Volume XX[3] and wrote Tanya a postcard. Then I tidied up some books, although there are still a lot of new ones from Dushan Petrovich to be sorted. This evening I pasted cuttings into the album and wrote to Halpérine-Kaminskii in Paris.

8 I sketched a calender for Andryusha today and didn't weep once, thank God! Then I pasted newspaper cuttings, trying not to read them, as it is all so endlessly painful. I am tormented by these discussions with my sons about the sale of Yasnaya Polyana, and by Andryusha's attempt to contest the will. I can sympathise with one aspect of this, however: his desire to disinherit the hateful Chertkov.

11–15 **(Moscow)** Sasha has again fallen under the same influence that destroyed both Lev Nik. and me – Chertkov. He has set her on to me, and now, through Muravyov her attorney, she has issued a legal injunction barring me from my room in the Historical Museum, halting the publication of my edition at the press, and other similarly despicable acts.[4] And she has found yet another ally in her persecution of me – Al. Bor. Goldenweiser. I visited the Historical Museum, talked to the administrators and gave them a document in response to Sasha's,[5] also forbidding anyone to enter my room or have access to the things and manuscripts there. Sasha has threatened to damage my edition in every way possible – let her! I left this evening for Yasnaya Polyana, without having come to any agreement with her. How her late father would have grieved at her behaviour.

19 Spent the morning reading proofs, and was about to go to the grave when my son Misha arrived from Moscow. Long discussions about how to defend ourselves against Chertkov's and Sasha's malevolence. Terribly painful and nerve-racking! Were it not for my impoverished sons I would have given up. Busy pasting newspaper cuttings again, then P.A. Sergeenko arrived and again interrupted my work. More painful discussions about the manuscripts and the new edition. How tired I am.

20 Wrote to Kuzminskii, Ksyunin and Ezhov, went to the grave, wept bitterly and prayed. Proofs, newspaper cuttings, painful discussions

with Andryusha: 'If there's no money I'll shoot myself!' How terrible to think like that! Wrote also to Bazhyonov. My God, how wearisome! The newspapers and lawyers have stood up for my rights.[6] But how much better it would be to have peace and friendly agreement.

21 Very depressed, especially so today, and the tears keep coming to my eyes. Did the same things as usual – reading proofs and pasting in newspaper cuttings. Hypocritical feuilleton by Mr Chertkov in all the papers.[7] The more I think about it, the more clearly I realise that Lev Nik. preferred Chertkov at the end of his life, and the more sad and painful that is. Very frosty, −20°. Everything is bright and beautiful; how white and pure it all is, and how black *we* all are . . .

22 Read 3 pages of proofs and marvelled at the artistry of Lev Nik.'s writings.

23 Read probably the *last* proofs of *Youth* I shall ever read. A telegram from Spiro telling me to prepare a reply to a letter from Chertkov in today's papers, which I don't yet have.

24 Wrote to Ksyunin and the State Bank. Most unpleasant to read Sasha's letter next to Chertkov's in all the newspapers.[8] The persecution continues. How will it all end! At times like these one longs and prays for death. The articles in the papers are all so unpleasant too; they have cheapened my beloved Lyovochka's name, and this is unbearably painful. S.P. Spiro, a collaborator on *Russian Word*, came to visit. I begged him not to publish anything on my behalf. Cold, −16°, wind. I stay at home all day. Such depression!

25 Pasted cuttings all day, and wept bitterly for my Lyovochka as he was before the influence of Chertkov and his love for him. They have sent an enlarged portrait of Lev Nikol.; how sad and serious he looks! My son Seryozha came, and was reading his father's diaries from 1846 to 1862. Andryusha is making prints of all the photographs and putting things in order.

26 Seryozha spent the day with me. Also P.I. Biryukov with an offer from Sytin to buy the *Complete Collected Works* from me, and Zinger with an offer from Davydov to help me with the inheritance and ownership of Lev Nik.'s manuscripts. Distressing conversations, my head started to ache. I have to defend the inviolability of the manuscripts and place them permanently in the museum. Sasha and Chertkov are doing all they can to ensure that Sasha gains custody of them. I shall not yield to them on any account.

30 This evening I cut out 'For Every Day' from *New Russia*; I had been collecting newspapers at Lev Nik.'s wishes.[9] Later on I re-read my old daily diaries and Lev Nik.'s old diaries.

February 4 Oh, what sadness! The wind has howled all day. I copied out some interesting pages from Lev Nik.'s notebooks – material for an unwritten work about the Peter the Great period. Fascinating.[10]

I received a letter from Tanya containing both advice and criticisms – unconvincing.[11] I heard that Sasha had returned to Telyatinki.

7 Walked around the garden, sawed off branches, prayed, invoked the soul of Lyovochka and begged him to forgive me. Copied some pages from his notebook. Read about Lev Nikolaevich in *Herald of Europe*.[12]

8 Copied the letters I wrote to Lev Nik. after he left home.

9 Copied my letter to Koni.[13] Initialled handkerchiefs. Went to Lev Nik.'s grave and wept and prayed, begging him to forgive me for being unable to make him happier at the end of his life. I should have accepted the fact that he preferred Chertkov, but I could not. I pasted newspaper cuttings and grieved all day.

10 Wrote to Ksyunin and E.F. Yunge. Terrible snow-storm this morning Copied out the diary L.N. kept when he wooed and married me.[14] Did a little sewing. I'm depressed and afraid of going to Moscow – although I must; I have to clear up various things for future generations.

11 Andryusha and Ilya came. (Ilya has already left.) I am again planning to leave for St Petersburg to sell Yasnaya Polyana. With an aching heart I copied out Lev Nikolaevich's last letters to me and his little diary.[15] It's all so unbearably painful – and he *isn't here*. Where has my loving, beloved Lyovochka disappeared to?

12 Misha called in briefly and Mr Salomon came. Did absolutely nothing all day. Received a telegram saying the new edition was ready.

13 (Moscow) Sasha came, fat and red-cheeked, as stubborn, secretive, uncommunicative and spiteful as ever. Painful discussion. What a cross this daughter of mine is. Then a lot of tedious business and bustle. The new edition has appeared in 20 volumes.

16 We are hurrying to sell and distribute the new edition.

17 Went to the warehouse this morning to give various instructions, then to the bank and to Howard's to ask about the account and the cheques. Learnt that Volumes 16, 19 and 20 of the *Complete Collected Works* had been seized.[16] This complicates everything. Home this evening.

18 Went to the Maslovs' to discuss the seizure of the volumes, but didn't find Fyodor Ivanovich in. Talked to dear, sympathetic Yulia Afan. Yurasova though. Read, mourned – everything is so complicated. Salomon and Buturlin dined here. I am listless and sleepy. I found out the cost of the new edition – 77,000 rubles so far.

19 Stakhovich came and wrote me a letter to give to the Court Minister about L.N.'s letters to the Tsar in Volume XX of the new edition.[17] Had dinner with the Maslovs and spent the evening there. Read them L.N.'s first and last diaries about our life together. So sad! And how uncertain and menacing everything is now!

20 Maklakov and Stakhovich came. They recommend that Sasha and I go to a court of arbitration. All courts are so painful. Ilya and Andryusha came, and briefly Misha. I went to see him and his family off from Paveletskii station. Endless partings – life is so lonely! Things aren't going well – endless problems. I wrote to the Court Minister about L.N.'s letters to Nicholas II.*

21 Worked frantically on the sale of the new edition all morning. Paid Howard 20,000 rubles for paper and the Kushneryov printers over 15,300. Went to the bank to see Dunaev. Did some shopping, went about mainly on foot. Thawing snow and terrible mud in Moscow. Spent the evening quietly at home. Torba came. Depression.

22 Went to the bank, and met M.N. Ermolova. Visited the museum and talked to Prince Shcherbatov about the manuscripts; he is going to St Petersburg.[18] Wrote to Minister Kasso about the same thing.[19] Some artists came this evening – Moravov and a Polish academician. They want to sketch some views of Yasnaya. Torba was here. The police sealed up Vols. XVI, XIX and XX in the warehouse today.

23 I went to the warehouse early this morning to ask the police-officer not to spoil the books when they're sealing them up, then walked to the mushroom market with Verochka. Thawing. Went home, copied out my summer diary and painfully re-lived it all over again. Went to church.

*It was not given to him as the minister had gone away. (Sofia Tolstaya's note.)

Today is the day of my Vanechka's death. May the Lord reunite me soon with my Lyovochka and Vanechka.

24 Delivered the newspaper announcements about the publication of the new edition of Lev Nik.'s works.[20] Although people are hardly going to buy it minus three volumes. How difficult it all is! D.A. Olsufiev was here and urged me to go to St Petersburg and sort it out there.

26 I painfully re-lived past sadness while copying out my diaries; I feel I am unwittingly to blame for so much.

27 A.I. Maslova and S.I. Taneev visited me. Such a pleasure!

March 2 Spent the whole day copying out the sad story of my life during the summer of 1910. I weep for things that can never be put right. Yet it was all fore-ordained. Stakhovich was here. Negotiations are starting today between him, Belgard and Stepanov (procurator of the Palace of Justice). Tomorrow they will be summoning me too.

3 Misha Stakhovich came this morning, and Aleksei Valer. Belgard, chief press censor, a most sympathetic man. They are defending my interests over the seizure of the 3 volumes of the *Complete Collected Works*. I am so grateful to them. But then one *has* to take L.N. Tolstoy's widow's wishes into account; one could hardly put her in prison or lock her up in a fortress. I stayed indoors all day and talked to Count M. Fyod. Geiden.

4 My negotiations over the seizure of the 3 volumes are going badly. I shall have to reprint two volumes at least – that's the best that can happen. At worst they can throw me into the fortress and put me on trial. I spent the day copying and weeping.

5 This morning I made a selection from Sergeenko's letters to replace parts of Volume 20.[21]

6 Copied all morning. Then called on Ek. Fyod. Yunge, who was so kind and sympathetic. Talked to Seryozha and Chefranov this evening about reprinting the censored volumes and about putting an announcement in the newspapers.

7 Visited the editorial boards with an announcement of the sale of Lev Nik.'s works. Sat up late copying and did 4 pages – 90 more to go. Telephone conversation with my brother about Prince Shcherbatov.

8 Prince Shcherbatov told me on the telephone that he would be visiting me at 5 in the evening on Wednesday, and said that he had good news for me from St Petersburg. We shall see! Copied at home all day. Very cold, 10 to 12 ° of frost, unusually bright stars. A.E. Yunge came, and Orlov with his son. Mourned deeply and silently all day.

9 Prince Shcherbatov called on me and stayed a long time, telling me how I could get the manuscripts back, although he said they hadn't come to any agreement and everything was exactly as it was before. He advised me to write to Kasso and take up the matter in St Petersburg, and if I didn't achieve any results with the ministers to go and see the Tsar himself. I stayed at home all day and copied.

10 I wrote two letters to Kasso, Minister of Education, one asking them to return everything of mine to me (diaries, letters and so on), the other asking to be allowed to use various documents for my memoirs. I also prepared to leave for St Petersburg. Sonya Mamonova, Misha Olsufiev and Count Geiden dined with us, which was very pleasant. I visited the Rumyantsev Museum and the Historical Museum, asked for copies of the paintings and visited the exhibition.

11 I copied my diary all day. I want to leave it to a museum, the Rumyantsev maybe, if they won't let me into my room at the Historical Museum. I had a visit today from Georgievskii, keeper of manuscripts at the Rumyantsev, who brought a copy of the receipt for everything I gave the museum in 1894. Spent the evening with E.F. Yunge.

12 I worked all morning and late into the night and finished copying my diary from June to October, when Lev Nik. left. This evening I went to vespers at the Palace Church in the Kremlin, where L.N. and I were married. The service was very crude, the deacon and the singers had the most disagreeable bass voices, the church was empty and dark, and the whole thing had a dismal effect on me. Maslova and Prince and Princess Odoevskii came to pay their respects and compliments.

14 Took my last diary to the Historical Museum, as well as three notebooks containing Lev Nik.'s first and last diaries, and copies of various letters of his; I shall receive a receipt for all these tomorrow. Then I rushed around the town – I am planning to leave for Yasnaya tomorrow. A wonderful spring day, the sun is shining, the streams are thawing – and everything is so melancholy! I long for home and the grave.

15 I wrote to my daughter Tanya in Vichy (?) and Andryusha in Tambov, packed, received my receipt from the Historical Museum for the

notebooks, said goodbye to the Maslovs and took back a book from S. Iv. Taneev. He is *weeping* for his nurse, I am weeping for my husband, and we had a good heart-to-heart talk about it. This evening I left for Yasnaya.

16 I got back to Yasnaya; I cried as I approached the house, cried when I went to the grave and cried when I went into Lev Nikol.'s room. It is just as though he were still here – as though he was just about to come in and I was going to tell him something. Yulia Ivanovna and the artist Orlov are staying. Old Dunyasha and Nurse are quietly living out their last days here. All so empty and so sad! Nothing but bills, housekeeping and business at present!

21 Copied out the diaries. What a lot of careful, conscientious background work on his books he put into those diaries!

23 I have finished copying Lev Nik.'s notebook – to my great sorrow! Now I have nothing of his to work on! Endless sadness, I just sit here at home on my own all day! I have hung the large portraits of Lev Nik. on the walls. But they don't speak to me. There are so many of them – they're everywhere!

24 Today I have been vividly recalling the events surrounding Lev Nik.'s last days, and despite all the anguish I feel that it *could not* have been otherwise – it was fore-ordained.

25 Dm. Vas. Nikitin came to pay us all a visit. He had been to see Sasha. We talked about the disputed manuscripts. There was a letter from Kasso, Minister of Education. He has refused all my requests and I am distraught.[22] I copied out my daily diaries. I have no energy for anything.

27 Went to Lev Nik.'s grave and wept inconsolably. I thought about my daughter Sasha. She must be so lonely amongst all those strangers, poor thing. She has left her mother, her brothers don't love her – even her dogs come to see me, especially Belka, but she never pays her grieving mother a visit.

28 This evening Nik. Vas. Orlov read us a critical article about Lev Nik.'s religious search for God, then some short stories by Chekhov. I can never laugh, so I took little pleasure in them.

April 4 We read aloud my son Lyova's letters from America.[23] I went to bed, then got up and talked to Halpérine, and read some of his article about Lev Nik.'s departure.[24]

7 I carefully wrote my will[25] and had it signed by Orlov and Volkov. Every night I read from the Gospels and the *Circle of Reading*, which is a comfort.

9 Deep sadness all day, tormented as always by guilt at my inability to make Lev Nik.'s last days happier for him.

10 A warm, windy day; I went out for the first time – to Lev Nikolaevich's grave, of course. In the distance they were energetically ringing the church bells, and 'Christ is Risen!' rang out over the whole of Russia. But in the forest and beside the grave there was utter silence, and the wind shook the withered wreaths as I prayed and wept. Then I sat in silence for a long time on a board that had been laid on the top of a tree-stump. Did Christ rise in my beloved late husband's heart when he cruelly left me and his home and disinherited his poor sons and their families? May the Lord forgive him!

14 Tanya arrived at 5 this morning, full of energy, common sense and sympathy as always. She has gone off to see Sasha in Telyatinki. I have finished my copy and will correct it as soon as it dries.

16 My son Seryozha arrived. I had such a good day resting my soul with people I love; and my health seems better too. We had a cosy evening together – Seryozha, Tanya, Maria Aleksandrovna, Yulia Ivanovna, Andryusha, Katya and I. We drank tea and chatted amicably. I feel rather excited by my copy of Pokhitonov's landscape, and am painting a second one.

18 My eldest children, Tanya and Seryozha, have left, and once again I am alone with Yulia Ivanovna. The artist Orlov is staying, and is copying Repin's portrait of Lev Nikol. I went out with Mashenka for my first walk. Marvellous spring day. Melancholy!

19 I am reading Chirikov's novel *Youth*.[26] What a narrow vision of life! I worked on my copy of Pokhitonov's landscape. Pouring rain all day. This evening Orlov read us some Chekhov short stories.

20 How uninteresting my life is! I went out twice to visit the grave and could not find the fence – they've broken the lock again. I painted a view of the grave and read some Chekhov – very clever, but he sneers a lot and I don't like that.

A fine morning, then a thunder-storm and a short, fierce shower. I haven't been crying recently – I've grown cold, my life is merely a matter of *patience*. 'To *live* means to *submit*!', as Fet said.[27]

21 I read some unpleasant news in the papers today: the Palace of Justice has decided to destroy Volumes XVI, XIX and XX of my edition. This is extremely annoying, and means huge financial losses.[28]

25 (Moscow) I went to the Palace of Justice and asked Stepanov the procurator to speed up the decision on my case concerning the seizure of the 3 volumes of the new edition;[29] he promised to send the decision to Al. Al. Sidorov, the chief censor. I then went to the Censorship Committee, where Sidorov promised to remove the ban the moment he received the court's decision.

26 I went to the Pokhitonov exhibition – paintings of the house, grounds and entrance to Yasnaya Polyana, and some very bad portraits of Lev Nikolaevich.[30]

27 Visited the censorship inspector at Chernyshevskii Street, then on to the Censorship Committee. They are all doing all they can, and the ban on the books will be lifted tomorrow;[31] Chefranov was here and I have assigned him to reprint the three volumes. This evening I went to the Maslovs but no one was in. I worked on Volume XX until 2 in the morning.

29 (St Petersburg) I was met by Andryusha and my sister Tanya. Everything's so friendly and informal here at the Kuzminskiis'. I wrote to Countess Geiden, a maid-of-honour, about gaining an audience with the Empress, Maria Fyodorovna.

30 Countess Geiden visited. The Empress has refused me an audience.[32] Halpérine came with his daughter.

May 1 A crowd of visitors – Yazykova, Vera Meshcherinova, Misha Islavin with his wife, Natasha Dehn with her husband, and so on and so on. I had dinner with Stakhovich – a wonderful old man. This evening was the first meeting of the Society of the Tolstoy Museum.[33] My son Seryozha came too; he is president, I am an honorary member. A lot of dull speeches. Zosya took me in her carriage. I wrote to Naryshkina and Minister Shcheglovitov.[34]

2 Went to Lyova's bookshop on Basseiny Street. Guests this evening – Repin, Nordman, M. Stakhovich, Dm. Ad. Olsufiev, the Halpérine family and Minister Shcheglovitov, who was extremely affable and promised to help me with the manuscripts. Earlier on I visited Naryshkina in the Winter Palace and asked her to arrange an audience with the Tsar. She promised rather feebly.

3 Spent the morning at home, then visited Minister P.A. Stolypin; sister Tanya came too. Like Naryshkina, he fully understands the advantage and necessity of buying Yasnaya Polyana and giving me the manuscripts, but is afraid to announce this to the Tsar, especially now, what with this new 'religious' spirit at court. Everyone is very friendly, but the matter is making no progress at all. My family and I dined with Lenochka Fuks, which was very pleasant.

5 A lot of guests; Arabazhin, who read a charming article he wrote about me,[35] Dina Ogaryova and Zosya Stakhovich, N.A. Zinoviev and his wife, N.A. Almedingen, Meshcherinov and various others. This evening the Auerbachs came, and my brother Vyacheslav's children. At 8.30 this evening I visited Minister Kokovtsov about the purchase of Yasnaya Polyana; he was dry, sober, businesslike and somewhat distracted, but promised to cooperate.[36]

6 Visited Shubinskii the lawyer this morning, who promised both to help and defend me if Sasha should take the matter to court. I am writing to Naryshkina about an audience in Tsarskoe Selo, and also to Stolypin and the Tsar explaining the main points of my case. I cannot bear the idea of losing Yasnaya Polyana!

7 Stayed at home and wrote to the Tsar and Minister Stolypin. Drove around town with Tanya. I'm being pestered by journalists; I miss home and long to get back and see the grave again. The sale of Yasnaya Polyana is beginning to torment me.

8 My trip to Tsarskoe Selo didn't take place; Naryshkina wrote to say that it had to be cancelled because of the arrival of Grand Duchess Elizaveta Fyodorovna, and that she had arranged a meeting for Tuesday in the Winter Palace. So annoying! I want to go home as soon as possible. Mitya Olsufiev was here, and S.P. Auerbach. I mended some sheets for Tanya and am staying at home.

9 I was visited by E.A. Naryshkina and Academician A.A. Shakhmatov.[37] I didn't sleep last night – such depression and so many failures.

10 Went to the Winter Palace to see Naryshkina. She was most affable, gave me a copy of her memoirs,[38] and undertook to give the Tsar my letter.[39] I left for Moscow this evening.

12 (Moscow) I gave the printers all the material for the reprinting of the 3 banned volumes.[40]

13 Visited the Duma and talked to Guchkov about the sale of my Moscow house.[41] It breaks my heart to destroy all my nests, which contain so many memories of a full and happy life. I visited Ek. Fyod. Yunge; she isn't at all downcast, even though she too is alone now, and has suffered a lot.

15 I wrote to Al. Mikh. Kuzminskii with copies of my letters to Kasso and of his to me.[42] I also wrote to Ilya and Misha about the document for the Historical Museum. I didn't go to the grave – there were so many visitors, and Lyovochka and I need to be alone together.

16 Went to the grave, laid a bunch of wild flowers on it and sat for a long time weeping and praying. My life is over, I am numb and indifferent to everything, my soul is heavy with suffering. I wandered over to Chepyzh, walked around the house, picked some flowers – it's all so pointless! Corrected the English proofs of Maude's chapter on Lev Nik.'s end, and felt more upset than ever.[43]

17 I read about my Lyovochka in the books by Bulgakov, Lazurskii, Rolland, Maude and the others. It's all wrong, it's all wrong![44]

18 My son Misha came. I walked in the rain to Lyovochka's grave, picked some wild flowers and put them there – someone had already adorned it with lilies-of-the-valley, wreaths and forget-me-nots. I prayed and wept. Korotnyov in Tula has copied Seryozha's plans of Yasnaya Polyana.[45]

20 Printed photographs for the album. My son Ilya has come for a short visit. Wrote to Stolypin about an incorrect measurement of the land here.[46] Am reading Bulgakov's and Rolland's books about Lev Nik. What a difference between Bulgakov's style and that of the cultured Frenchman.

24 Still working on my photographs. Very tired. Visited the grave. Every time I go there I weep bitterly, as though I were responsible for my husband's death. But how passionately I loved my Lyovochka – to the very last moment of his life! What happened is a complete mystery, we will never know. A wonderful warm day. No flowers anywhere, they've all been destroyed by frost. I am reading articles by Roche, Rion and so on about Tolstoy in the journal *Foi et vie*.[47]

25 Worked hard finishing my photographs; tomorrow morning I shall have done them all, and shall send them to Moscow to be turned into an album of phototypes.[48]

28 Photography all morning. Vas. Nik. Goryainov came, and P.I. Biryukov. Then this afternoon my son Seryozha arrived with

Bogdanov, secretary of the Tolstoy Society in Moscow. Later on Seryozha played some Chopin and Schumann beautifully. Tormenting memories of L.N. – how he loved music and how he loved listening to these pieces in particular. But I love it too, and find music a great consolation. There is an announcement in the papers – or rather in *Russian Word* – that the Council of Ministers has decided to buy Yasnaya Polyana for 500,000 rubles.[49]

30 Had a visit this morning from Spiro of the *Russian Word.* A lot of visitors to the grave and the estate. Seryozha has left. I printed 14 photographs of Yasnaya Polyana for him. This evening I knitted, listened with an aching heart to the gramophone and read about Belinskii.[50]

31 Read a lot about Belinskii, sat for a long time by the grave; a lot of strangers were there, and I wasted a lot of time talking to them. I spent all day waiting for Tanya, but she didn't come, to my great distress. I wandered on my own about the estate and grieved over the sale of Yasnaya Polyana to the government.

June 2 The Prishvins, mother and son, came to see Lyovochka's grave and his study.[51] I did almost nothing all day. Tanya drove to Ovsyannikovo with Makovitsky, who arrived with her; she saw Sasha there, who is pining away from loneliness. A terrible wind, rain all evening. I wrote some letters – to Lyova and Bulgakov.

5 My Tanya and the artist Vinogradov left today, and the house is empty again.

6 Read an old French book called *De l'Amour*[52] – naïve and insubstantial but the language is beautiful. Copied my daily diaries.

9 (Moscow) Dined at the 'Praga'. A pleasant conversation with the artist Nesterov,[53] and a friendly meeting with Aleksei Maklakov. This evening Biryukov visited.

10 Went shopping, finished my business in Moscow, looked at a little house I might buy after selling this one, and went to the archives to talk things over with Kovalevskii. A hot, bright day. Left this evening for Yasnaya. I gave photographs to Mey for his album.

11 Got back this morning, then Andryusha came. Painfully sad homecoming to deserted Yasnaya Polyana. I tidied up, had a sleep and went to the grave. A nasty scene with the Circassian guard, who robbed a woman in the village of her grass; I ordered him to give it all back.

13 Didn't sleep last night. My son Misha came and asked me for 1,600 rubles. I gave it to him, although I hate the way all my children – apart from my daughters – constantly demand money from me. I have started on another copy in oils – a portrait of Lev Nik. by Repin. It's not going at all well. Heard that a member of the Peasant Bank had arrived to discuss the sale of Yasnaya Polyana. So sad and painful!

15 Some valuers came to look over the estate today – Trukhachov from Tula, and Ivan Lvovich and Aleks. Aleksandrovich Nikiforov from St Petersburg. Endless bustle all day. All my sons came – apart from Lyova. I worked a little on my copy – nothing else. The plan is for me to move to the Kuzminskiis' wing; everything is different, life is in decline and it's all very hard.[54]

16 Seryozha, Misha and Ilya left, and Lyova unexpectedly arrived. I have done nothing all day; endless discussions about this nightmarish sale of Yasnaya Polyana, inventories, and all the other things concerning that dear, beloved man. I put a brave face on it, but it is so hard! There was a distant thunder-storm and a brief shower, and they have already picked the first berries, white mushrooms and milk-caps. Later this evening there was a heavy thunder-storm and it poured with rain.

17 I have made a list of all the things in the bedroom, and am giving almost all of it to the government, care of the museum. All very sad, yet I know it must be done. I worked a little on my copy, and after dinner I walked to the grave. I spent a long time there weeping and praying, in spiritual communion with my Lyovochka. Ilya and Misha have come again. Andrei left feeling very irritated. A warm day, no rain. They have started mowing the hay.

18 Today is Sasha's 27th birthday. I thought about her all day. Poor girl! It must be so sad for her to be alienated from her family – her beloved father's family too. Misha and Lyova left, and so did Nikiforov. It has been raining and thundering off and on all day. I did some work on my copy, it's a bit better now. I looked through the inventory.

19 I wrote to Torba, Ksyunin and the stockbrokers' office. About 125 people visited the grave and house today. I received the guests – although not all of them – with Yulia Ivanovna. Trukhachov has left. A hot, still day. They're singing in the village – but my soul is sad, so sad! I am growing used to being alone, and think constantly of death. I am copying my portrait. Very bad!

20 O.V. Friederichs came with his son, his daughter and his friend, Maria Vasilevna. I took a walk with my Lyova and we had a long talk. There are no happy people in this world! It was very hot today; they have been gathering the hay and picking berries and white mushrooms.

21 The same – I painted my copy, it rained, I read Naryshkina's fascinating reminiscences. A brilliant courtly life but an intelligent one too – quite unlike my own naïve memoirs about my commonplace life as a mother.

23 I have started copying a view of Chepyzh by Pokhitonov – I'm letting my copy of the portrait dry. Andryusha is back. it rained all day. Lyova is tense and nervous and his plans are erratic. I live only for today with the one happy certainty that every day brings me closer to death.

24 I wrote to Torba and the Russian Photographic Society. Drove with Dush. Petr. Makovitsky to Ovsyannikovo to visit Maria Aleksandrovna and the Gorbunovs, which was very pleasant. No rain today, very warm, the brown hay is still lying on the ground. I did some painting in oils and am very dissatisfied with the results. One cannot get far if one has no training and is almost blind. A lot of pointless and painful discussions about making money.

25 I finished copying my landscape and ruined the portrait. I visited the grave with a great bunch of flowers and wept. Andryusha upset me terribly at dinner.

A wonderful evening – the light, the sunset, the fresh green, the flowers . . . and the more beautiful it is the sadder I feel . . . At the grave I met some young people who had come to pay their respects; I asked them not to touch my flowers and roses.

27 I decided to finish my copy and stop working on it; I am not up to it. I finished reading Naryshkina's reminiscences. Zvegintseva, Count and Countess Lanskii (brother and sister), young Prince Cherkasskii and some other gentlemen all came to visit today. They all went to the grave and looked over the house. Exactly one year ago my darling Lyovochka and I were setting off to visit our son Seryozha. He didn't want to go, but did so for my sake.

28 My son Seryozha's birthday today – he is 48 already. I was going to visit him but didn't. Who needs me there? I thought. And here Mashenka will be on her own, Katya is going to meet her father, I am loath to leave Lyova, as he won't be here much longer, and I am feeling so ill! I read a lot of newspaper and journal articles about Lev Nik., catalogued

books and visited the grave with some roses and other flowers. I sobbed as I recalled our trip last year to see Seryozha, and his birth 48 years ago. I was just 18.

29 It rained all yesterday; in the evening it was 8 °. Today is fine and cool. I tried very hard to stifle my grief – mowed hay, pumped water and took a long walk with Yulia Ivanovna to the plot of land I have just bought in Telyatinki; there's a birch grove there. I spent the evening with my sons. None of them is happy – and that's so sad! It's not real life, just dreams of some undefined life of happiness.

30 I photographed Lev Nik.'s personal diary. Sun and rain in quick succession. The hay is ruined. A cold night. Misha looked in for a moment with Kulishov. I wrote to A.I. Mey and Tanya. Katya and Andryusha have returned. Dushan Petrovich paid a brief visit. Sorted stamps with Mashenka all evening. Later I re-read some of Lev Nikolaevich's letters to me and was disturbed by memories of our life and love.

July 1 Wrote to Dm. Al. Matryoninskii asking to see the conductor. Didn't go out – legs and eyes aching. Developed my photographs of L.N.'s diary. Andryusha and Lyova went to Tula. This evening we read aloud L.N.'s letters to me for 1871, '72, '76 and '78. Andryusha was very moved. Cold and rain. The mown hay has been left lying on the ground. Iv. Iv. Ozolin arrived from Astapovo station with his son.

2 Printed photographs all morning and took more photographs of the diary. The two Trepov sisters – one of them is a Gall by marriage – came to look at Lev Nikol.'s rooms and grave; they are the daughters of Dmitrii Fyodorovich. The land surveyor came; he is drawing up plans for Gretsovka, the land by the Kuzminskiis' wing and the servants' cottages. How strange it will be to start life in a new place, and how tedious to have to rearrange everything all over again! I visited the grave with some flowers. This evening I read L.N.'s letters to me for the years 1879, '80, '81 and '82.

4 Worked hard all day photographing Lev Nik.'s personal diary. It makes sad and painful reading! My poor darling Lyovochka, we were so completely estranged by the end! I feel it was my fault, yet I was so unhappy myself! And so ill too. I took a long walk after dinner with Andryusha, Katya and Yulia Ivanovna. Mown hay lying everywhere. We walked across the meadow and along the Voronka, returned by the swimming pool path and visited the grave. My eye is aching. I knitted all evening. A fine bright day, only 8 °. Painful discussions about the will. There is no more intellectual or spiritual life in this house, and that's very hard! It's badly missed!

5 I worked hard all day and have now finished my photographs. This evening I went out to pick flowers and took a large bunch to Lyovochka's grave. Lyova is a little calmer now; he spent a long time playing our piano, which he praised highly, although his playing, like his thoughts, constantly jumps from one tune to another. He could play so well too, but he just fritters away all his talents.

6 Today P.I. Biryukov brought two hundred (200) peasant teachers, men and women, to look round the house, the estate and Lev Nikolaevich's grave. I helped and talked to a lot of them, and met with a great deal of sympathy. This evening I newspaper pasted cuttings. Another insufferable polemic inspired by an article of Chertkov's![55] The rain has ruined the hay.

8 I have felt ill all day and my eyes are aching. My son Lyova has left for St Petersburg. Very depressed, choking back the tears, heart aching. If only he had been happy this would never have happened! I wrote to Mey about the album and sent him some sample photographs. Raining again all day. I wrote to Yunge, Tanya and Natalya Abrikosova. I read *From My Memoirs* by Yunge and 'Youth' by Chirikov.

9 Andryusha is back and Count D.A. Olsufiev has arrived. I have started painting Lyovochka's grave in oils.[56] A lot of discussions and painful memories today about his departure and his state of mind in those last days. That wasn't *my* Lyovochka!

10 There were about 140 visitors to the house today, and even more at the grave. I took some of them round the house myself. I read the second notebook of Lev Nik.'s letters to me. It's sad to recall the past, but sometimes it's good too. I continued painting the grave in oils; it's very hard, I can hardly do it. I wrote to Torba, it's pouring with rain. This evening I had a good talk about the past with Olsufiev. He is a dear man.

12 Did almost nothing all day. This evening read Makovitsky's notes about Lev Nik. and our life. Turgid, like Makovitsky himself.[57]

15 Went to the grave with a large bunch of flowers, and for some reason I wept especially bitterly today, and longed for death. This evening Sasha and Dushan Petrovich took our nun, Maria Nikolaevna, to Telyatinki. I haven't seen her yet.

16 Couldn't sleep last night, took some veronal and got up late. Went to Sasha's house in Telyatinki to see my sister-in-law Maria Nikolaevna. Many discussions and many tears. I didn't learn anything new, apart from the fact that a chapter in *Resurrection* called 'The Liturgy' had been published abroad.[58] Lev Nik. had promised his sister not to publish this part, but Chertkov has already done so.

17 A very busy day. Crowds of visitors to the grave and house. Artists taking photographs for Merkurov the sculptor, who has been commissioned to produce a relief-map of Yasnaya Polyana.[59] Katerina Vasilevna is ill.

19 Our dear nun, Maria Nikolaevna, came for the day. I have been choking back the tears all day – the number of times I have started to weep! Discussions, memories . . . I have seen my daughter Sasha twice now, and we are getting on well together.

21 Endless bustle all day, but I am free of it. My grief at losing Lev Nikolaevich is so splendid, so solemn and profound, that nothing else seems important.

24 What turmoil. My son Ilya, his wife Sonya and Sanya Kuzminskii paid a brief visit, our dear nun, Maria Nikolaevna, came, and some Serbian doctor, an acquaintance of Dushan Petrovich. I was flustered by domestic worries and the desire to see everyone. Then came Gusev, who has just returned from exile.[60] There were 15 for dinner.

26 Maria Nikolaevna came to visit; she said Chertkov had taken six photographs of her, and on every occasion he too had been in the group, and Sasha too. How unpleasant! More gales, thunder-storms and rain. A dry branch has broken over the grave. Such a lot happening, impossible to do any work.

29 Our former governor Zinoviev came, with his daughter Nadya Feret. I took a walk with them and we visited the grave. I read them and the Goryainovs my memoirs. Later this evening I drove to Telyatinki, had a talk with Maria Nikolaevna and returned home with Varya.

30 I painted the grave in oils; Varya Nagornova accompanied me. A lot of visitors, mainly young people. I wrote to my sister Tanya and sent her a little book and wrote Salomon a letter.[61]

31 Iv. Vas. Denisenko came with his wife Lenochka, and Zosya Stakhovich. All these visits are completely lacking in soul, love or joy

for anyone. It makes me sad; I have given so much love to other people and have met with so much injustice, immorality, coldness and censure. I evidently didn't deserve any better. And then the contrast between me and my dead Lyovochka is so vast! He *knew* how to win people's love, I never did. I made another attempt to paint the grave, but was thwarted by the rain. There were a lot of visitors today. It was a fine, warm day, apart from some slight rain and a little cloud. Varya Nagornova has returned to her mother's in Telyatinki.

August 2 I went to the grave to finish my painting, but was prevented from doing so by a thunder-storm. I ruined it and went home. My son Seryozha and the Sukhotins arrived unexpectedly during dinner and I was delighted to see them. Then Raevskii came with his wife and her sister (a Filosofova). She sang for us to Seryozha's accompaniment and we had a very pleasant evening.

4 Katya is much worse, and we are all terribly anxious! I visited Lev Nikol.'s grave with Varya Nagornova. With this new anxiety my inconsolable grief flared up again with all its old power. I have been remembering my darling Lyovochka all day, and the tears are choking me.

5 Mashenka came with Sasha. Tanya and her husband have left. Katya is still ill, and a heavy weight lies on all of us. I went to the grave with Varya Nagornova and wept. I remembered so painfully clearly how unhappy my beloved Lyovochka was at the end, and how I was partly to blame for it all – even though unwittingly!

6 Went to Telyatinki to see Sasha and had a talk with my sister-in-law Maria Nikolaevna the nun. I was particularly struck by something she said about Lyovochka, who before he died kept repeating: 'What is to be done? What should I do now?' And he spoke with such anguish and despair. I feel so desperately sorry for him! His soul was not at peace before his death. In Telyatinki Olga made a spiteful remark and Sasha ostentatiously left the room.

10 Had a visit from Spiro, correspondent of *Russian Word*.

11 Busy tidying up again. Went to the grave, took flowers, wept and talked to my Lyovochka's soul. Where is he? Tormenting, unanswerable question. Left this evening for Moscow.

12 (Moscow) Went to the town Duma this morning and delivered an application for the sale of our house in Khamovniki Street.[62] Everything there is just as it was in the old days, and it's just like a grave! Where is Vanechka? Where is Masha? Where is Lyovochka? They all lived there once, but now . . . It's frightful! I wept terribly! I have signed the contract for my photograph album. This evening Torba came and we agreed to sell the *ABC* and various other books at half price.[63]

13 More discussions this morning about the album; I rather fear that we shall have to ask a high price for it; it will cost such a lot to produce. Did some shopping, and this afternoon went to the cinematograph for Verochka's sake. Most depressing! Stupid subjects for an uncultured audience. We couldn't leave Moscow this afternoon as there were such crowds at the station, so we returned to Khamovniki Street.

14 We left Moscow this morning and arrived back in Yasnaya this afternoon. Sadness everywhere! Everything is being divided up; Katya, sick and smiling, Andryusha, nervous and exhausted, Yulia Ivanovna, who has recently grown very stout, and Mashenka, gentle and affectionate. On the train I read 'Does Woman Represent God'.*

16 I printed some photographs and sent them to Mey, then made some jam – apple and peach – and marinated some red plums. A lot of bustle, and all for what? Eating is the only sweet and purposeless activity. A widow visited today with her 2 little mites, and how they grabbed at the white bread! I gave her 4 rubles. N.N. Gusev came. Is he sincere, I wonder? I wrote to sister Mashenka about the portable chairs.

19 My cousin A.A. Behrs and his daughter have left. I dreamt of Lyovochka last night; he was lying there with his eyes open. I felt so frightful today, so sad! I couldn't stay indoors and kept wandering around the house and looking at the side wing, my future lair. I wrote to Guchkov.[64]

20 Khris. Nik. Abrikosov came. I painted the grave again in oils. This evening I copied out a little of my daily diary for 1910. What sad memories it holds!

21 I went with Abrikosov to Ovsyannikovo to visit M.A. Schmidt, who was looking very thin and poorly. Then I pasted in some newspaper cuttings and photographs. I spent the afternoon in bed. I have a sore throat and my eyes are aching again. It's so tedious to be unable to read or write. What is there to live for? Nothing but thoughts. But I'm not like my Lyovochka. I'm a weak character and need intellectual help.

*English in original; not attributed (and no question mark).

22 My 67th birthday. Why was I born? Who needed it? Surely my wretched life must soon end. I printed photographs, but was hindered all day by the rain.

25 Even colder – 4 ° – although the night was bright and moonlit. I wrote to Sasha; she is also ill with a cough and a touch of pleurisy, and I am worried about her. She sent me some plums and I gave her a striking clock and a barometer, which she liked. I tidied both Lyovochka's rooms today with love and sadness. Poor man! I suppose he didn't like his little nest – that's why he left. I painted the grave and rested my eyes; I do almost nothing.

26 I didn't sleep all night and did almost nothing all day, as my eyes were aching. I visited the grave. Baturin is doing a lovely painting of it without the fence, which is far nicer. This evening he told me the sad story of his marriage. I read the memoirs of Ek. Fyod. Yunge.[65] So well written – they make me ashamed of my own memoirs.

28 Lev Nikolaevich's birthday. About 300 visitors came to the house and many more to the grave. I didn't go: I cannot bear to see so many policemen, and there's so little real feeling for Lev Nik. too.[66]

My son Seryozha came, and my grandson Seryozha with his teacher Mr Kuez. A crowd of guests – the Biryukov family, Gorbunov and his wife, Lineva, some Czechs and so on. Spent the whole day with them. Princess Cherkasskaya was here too. My soul is sombre and sad but my head is a fog. Spiro was here.

30 I went to the grave and got soaked in the rain. Chatted to Taras Fokanov. Worked hard taking notes for *My Life*, and suddenly rediscovered my interest in my old work. My eyes were better today. This evening I read a little of E.F. Yunge's *From My Memoirs*. Prince Dolgorukov came to talk about the peasants' library.[67]

31 I worked on my memoirs. Long and difficult work. One has to read so much! Cold, a north wind, I didn't go out. Depression, no energy for work, no energy for life – what do I need it for! The image of my Lyovochka is before me day and night. There's no bringing him back! And without him my whole life is over. Where is he? Where is Vanechka, Masha, my mother . . . I have been re-reading her letters . . . there are so many of them, so many. I too shall soon discover that mystery. But why do one's loved ones' deaths bring so much misery? Who needs it?

September 3 Worked very hard on my memoirs, and read some sad family letters written in 1894, when Lyova was so ill. Then wandered sadly about the garden. What a hard life! Rain all day, a burning red sunset and a starry night. Copied out my sad daily diary for last year. News of an attempt on Stolypin's life.[68]

4 I couldn't sleep last night, and when I did doze off I kept dreaming of my husband – not happy but wretched and spiteful. This morning I felt very melancholy, and picked some flowers and visited the grave. At home I talked to Taras Fokanov and we recalled the old days. I tried to work on my *Life*, but became too depressed and had to abandon it. I spent the evening with Baturin, we looked at old photographs and I knitted.

7 A delightful warm bright day, but the leaves have already taken their autumn colouring. I couldn't stay indoors – too sad! – and went out to saw some dead wood off the apple trees. Then I had to tidy up the cellar and boil the jam again. I sat in the barn and thought intensely about eternal life. *Where* do we all go? Where has my Lyovochka gone? This evening I copied out my daily diary for 1910.

8 Zvegintseva came, and M.A. Schmidt. I had a really good talk with her, heart-to-heart, about Lev Nikolaev. Nothing to be done today. I couldn't help celebrating the holiday. Fine, 14 to 16 ° in the shade, with a south wind. Copied a little of my daily diary for that sad, sad time. So painful!

11 I walked to the fir plantation, and Biryukov and El. Vl. Molostvova, who had just arrived, came out to look for me. I was so pleased to see them. My Sasha was here too with a visitor, the Frolov boy. She and I are friends, thank God.

12 I didn't sleep last night and felt so wretched this morning that I got up early and went out to Lev Nik.'s grave. On the way I found some mushrooms – honey agarics and milk-caps – and picked a whole basketful. At the grave I wept and prayed as usual, and spoke to L.N. No one was there for a change. I spent the whole day painting the autumn leaves in water-colour and wandering around Yasnaya Polyana.

13 Vlad. Aleksandr. Posse came and asked me all about Lev Nik. and his last days.[69] I sorted out old letters and grew agitated. So many people have died!

14 Rain all day. I went to see Zvegintseva – very tedious! This afternoon I read aloud Vetrinskii's little book about Lev Nikolaevich; concise and well written.[70]

19 I wrote to Minister Kokovtsov about the sale of Yasnaya Polyana,[71] painted and sat with N.A. Almedingen. Life is dull and tedious these days, and my soul is unbearably sad.

20 I wrote to the Moscow Duma about the sale of the house,[72] and let Kulishov, Bibikov and their party look round all the rooms. I did some drawing, my eyes ached, and I couldn't take a walk as there was a frightful wind. I am afraid of losing my sight. This afternoon Sonya Bibikova arrived.

21 I got up late, did another water-colour of the autumn leaves, then picked some flowers and went to the field to look for cornflowers. The village girls, the peasants, the horses, the potatoes being ploughed under . . . everywhere life goes on, but my soul is dead. I visited the grave; no one was there and I cried especially bitterly. In the gulley an old woman and her grandchildren were picking honey agarics. This evening I copied and read.

22 I painted, copied, knitted and didn't leave the house. News of Liza Obolenskaya's arrival. I am so pleased. How good Socrates' last discussion with his pupils was.[73] So good to re-read it. One *must* believe in *eternal* life, otherwise it would be impossible to go on.

23 Our wedding anniversary! The grief was so intense, yet there was so much joy too! When I got up I picked some white flowers and some roses – the emblem of my vanished youth – and took them to the grave. There I stood alone and wept. Where are you, my bridegroom, my beloved husband? Liza Obolenskaya came, and my son Ilya paid a brief visit. Then dear Maria Aleksandrovna arrived. This evening we read aloud *The Living Corpse*.[74] Not very good.

25 There were guests. I visited the grave with Lizanka Obolenskaya, and we walked back through the fir plantation and Chepyzh. The tears were choking me and kept welling into my eyes, but I managed to restrain myself, for they will ruin my eyes – although if you don't cry you merely ache inside. This evening I read aloud some of Turgenev's letters to Mme Viardot.[75] I did another painting of a leaf and knitted. A blizzard tonight, and rain.

26 Dushan Petrovich, Sasha and Stakhovich came; my eyes were aching, so I did nothing, just a little painting. I gave Stakhovich some large photographs and my own little ones for the exhibition.[76]

28 Spent the whole day copying for my son Seryozha, and sent him various documents.[77]

29 An actor, an artist and a photographer arrived from the Arts Theatre to measure and photograph Lev Nikol.'s study and bedroom.[78] Then Sergeenko's son-in-law, also a photographer, came. I sorted my letters for the whole year and made a note of them. I sent postcards and some documents to Tanya and Seryozha.

30 Pasted newspaper cuttings and plans. Read about Nekrasov. Val. Fyod. Bulgakov came – such a good man. Baturin has returned. Liza Obolenskaya left this morning, unfortunately.

October 1 Dm. Dm. Obolenskii came with two engineers from St Petersburg who have come to inspect the Belgian factories at Kosaya Gora, (Sudakovo). Andryusha has returned from Krapivna. He was unanimously voted a town councillor of the Krapivna district.

2 I played the piano for a long time – sonatas by Beethoven and Weber. I wanted to forget myself but couldn't, and felt even more wretched.

Then I copied out my daily diary, painted an autumn leaf and read various articles about *The Living Corpse.* Frightful weather, 2 ° below freezing, dark sky. It distresses me that I haven't visited the grave for so long. I have been unwell.

3 My soul is filled with material things. Sasha wrote to me about referring the manuscripts to a court of arbitration, when she had previously refused any such idea. I sent her a copy of *The Living Corpse.*[79] She is leaving today for the Crimea.

4 Tanya's 47th birthday. Already! How vividly I remember her birth. Lev Nik. had a broken arm, and how he sobbed with emotion when his first daughter was born, and how he loved me! I visited the grave for a long time. Gusev and Belinkii came and I gave them 'Tikhon and Malanya' and 'Idyll' to copy for Sasha's edition.[80] Terribly cold, more snow has fallen.

5 Painted, wandered sadly around the garden; desolate autumn, desolate soul. This evening I played the piano; my eyes and hands are so bad now. I am 68! Everyone here has influenza. Gusev came and took more notebooks of 'Tikhon and Malanya'.

6 Painted, wanted to work on my memoirs but grew very melancholy and went to the grave instead. Talked there to the Maklakovs, women from our village. After dinner I played songs from *A Life for the Tsar,* my

mother's favourite opera, and thought of her. This evening I read aloud Sergeenko's book *Tolstoy and His Contemporaries*.[81] Some interesting things about Turgenev.

7 A messenger from Stakhovich came to collect the suitcase for the Tolstoy exhibition.[82] I wrote to Stakhovich and Prince Shcherbatov about the table.[83] They are putting in the double windows – I did my own. This evening I again read aloud Sergeenko's 'Tolstoy and Turgenev'. It's not badly written. It has been warm, overcast and windless. Andryusha returned this evening.

8 Lovely weather. Clear, still, 7 °. I went to the grave and talked to Taras Fokanov, who loved Lev Nikol. and now guards his grave. This evening I finished reading aloud 'Tolstoy and Turgenev'. I have tried to work on my memoirs but still haven't written anything. My spiritual life is sober, severe and contemplative. I must be brave! But it's so lonely and hard!

9 Baturin has left. Not many visitors today – eight in all. Andryusha, Yulia Ivanovna and I visited the grave. Taras, Ivan (Drozd) and I measured the space for the wrought-iron fence. I don't like their plans. I worked hard on my memoirs for 1894. Life was hard then, but it got worse.

10 They only finished installing the double windows yesterday. I did some oil painting and ruined the view of the grave. I wrote *My Life* and this evening I read it aloud. Everyone approved. Dushan Petrovich came. He is also writing his memoirs about Lev Nikolaevich. I sent a telegram giving my permission to take the glass case full of things from the Historical Museum to use at the exhibition. I have already given the desk.

12 Vas. Nik. Goryainov came, and the editor of *Sun of Russia*, Aleks. Ed. Kogan, accompanied by a photographer. A lazy, wasted, idle day! Grey, damp and warm – 7 °; I don't like autumn! I wrote my life story tonight.

13 Goryainov has left; the editor of the *Sun of Russia* was very tiresome and kept demanding things – photographs, my memoirs, my portrait. I went to the grave and to my great annoyance found the editor there, with the photographer.[84] I played the piano a little, read a little of a French religious book written in 1817 and wrote a little.

15 I visited the grave; a splendid, warm, bright day, 8 ° in the shade. Then I did some drawing. I looked sadly at the birch grove as I walked past, and remembered Lev Nik. helping two-year-old Tanya to plant

birches there, saying: 'You'll be able to pick mushrooms here later.' This evening I pasted newspaper cuttings. Felten came.

16 Andryusha returned from Moscow and told us about *The Living Corpse* and the Tolstoy exhibition.[85] He understands a lot. Dushan Petrovich and Felten were here. I spent the whole day drawing autumn leaves; I didn't feel disposed to write. A warm wind. The workmen have arrived to mend the path by the grave and dig ditches.

17 I again painted a water-colour and wrote a lot of my life story. Andryusha went to Tula to discuss the purchase of Taptykovo. It's painful writing my memoirs and reliving all my memories. But then *everything* is painful! Life is not easy.

18 At 7.20 this morning M.A. Schmidt died in Ovsyannikovo. Yet another dear, close friend is no more – yet again my heart is like lead! She died suddenly, as she lived, without bothering anyone, all alone with her maid. I went to Ovsyannikovo to look at her stern, yellow face and say goodbye to my dear friend. A fine sunny day, with a freezing northern wind. Before going to Ovsyannikovo I visited the grave; the workmen are there mending the ditches and the road, and it's seething with activity.

19 I went to the grave; they were all hard at work there, as they were yesterday. Then I went to the barn and the threshing machine. There they all were, peasants and young folk, laughing and joking and threshing – life goes on around me, but my heart is sad and silent. As silent as the small, thin, dead figure of Maria Aleksandrovna in her coffin. Baturin has returned. A warm windy day, with fleecy clouds in the sky. I drew and wrote.

20 We buried Mar. Al. Schmidt today. Biryukov and Bulygin came and I was pleased to see them. I attended to business documents: I have neglected a great many things in the course of this sad year, and now that the house is to be sold it all has to be seen to. Andryusha and Katya are packing up and preparing for a new life in Taptykovo. A still day, 5 °, and a starry, moonlit night. It's good to be with nature, even though it's autumn.

21 This morning I went to the grave. Yesterday and today they've been destroying it and putting up another sort of fence. There are a lot of workmen there.

23 I wept bitter, painful tears as I walked back from the grave and recalled Lyovochka's tortured state of mind at the end of his life, and I am still weeping now. Visitors arrived from Moscow and I showed them everything. I attended to the day-labourers' records and accounts, and packed my bag for Moscow.

25 (Moscow) Went to the banks and delivered the album and *Skeleton Dolls*.[86] Everyone was very pleasant. Had dinner and spent a pleasant evening with Seryozha and Masha, and my grandson Seryozha and Tat. Vas. Olsufieva. Later I received an account of the book sales from Torba, and gave him some instructions.

26 Business all morning, dinner with my brother Sasha, evening with the Biryukovs. All the children are so pleasant. I paid Chefranov for Kushneryov, Howard for the paper and Mey for the album.

27 Shopping and business all morning, dined with Seryozha again. Saw my grandchildren, Misha's children, and was very, very happy.

28 It was on this day that Lev Nikol. left Yasnaya Polyana. Spent the morning at the Tolstoy Exhibition. Various gentlemen kept following me around so I had to force myself not to cry, and it was very distressing, although interesting![87] I saw Misha's family again and had a long talk with Lina. Dined and spent the evening with the Maslovs, then left for Yasnaya. Poor Jacobi was at the Maslovs. He is sick and has just buried his wife.

29 Back at Yasnaya. The moon was shining at 7 this morning. The house is silent, sad and empty. Andryusha's family left for Taptykovo while I was away. I visited the grave and planted some fir trees there, then settled some accounts. All so pointless! This evening I felt exhausted and had a sleep on my sofa. Oh, the loneliness! No one has any reason to visit me now.

31 I have started copying Repin's portrait of Lev Nik. – very hard. This evening I read Arabazhin's book about Lev Nikolaevich; very well written.[88] A grey, windy day. I took a bath. Lev Nik. lives for ever in my heart, as though I were carrying him within me like a pregnant woman with her baby. And I'm forever thinking, according to old habit: 'Oh, I'll tell Lyovochka that, I must show him that . . . ' But then he was so utterly indifferent last year to everything that concerned my life. He lived only for Chertkov. It's painful to remember it! It was on this day that he stopped at Astapovo. My despair then was too terrible to recall! But I lived through it and, alas, I am still alive!

November 1 I wrote letters to sister Tanya, Marusya Maklakova, Lyova and my daughter-in-law Katya. Also about the waltz and the poems.[89] I worked on my copy of Lev Nik.'s portrait, and went to the grave; they're finishing the work on the fence and the paths. This afternoon I wrote a letter.

2 Spent the whole day painting my portrait again. I gaze into his face and eyes and search for the loving expression of my Lyovochka as he used to be in the old days, and I am in agony, for it's not right, not right . . . Then I did another drawing of a leaf, and this evening I pasted in some newspaper cuttings and read some verses dedicated to the memory of Lev Nikol. I am so unhappy; I had a dream about my Lyovochka, but it wasn't a good one.

3 This morning I worked on my portrait. The Sukhotins came for dinner – Tanya, Mikhail Sergeevich and Tanyushka – and I spent the evening with them. Dushan Petrovich came too. An announcement in the *Russian Gazette* that the government has revoked its decision to buy Yasnaya Polyana.[90]

4 I visited the grave with Tanya, Tanyushka and Yulia Ivanovna; a quiet, grey, warm day, 5 °. Then I drew and played with Tanyushka. Posha Biryukov came with an offer from Sytin to buy *all* the books from me.[91] The *Voice of Moscow* correspondent was here, and Dushan Petrovich came. My eyes are aching; I wasted the whole evening talking.

5 Drove to Tula with Tanya to visit my sister Liza, and we had a most enjoyable time.

7 A sad day. A year ago today Lev Nikolaevich died. All my sons came, apart from Lyova, and a crowd of correspondents and members of the Tolstoy Society – about 500 visitors in all. Our peasants followed me to the grave and sang 'Eternal Memory'. My granddaughter Tanyushka Sukhotina was with me. Endless bustle, long discussions about the sale of Yasnaya Polyana and sadness in my heart.

8 I played with Tanyushka and read a lot – a great many newspaper articles about Lev Nikolaevich. Seryozha came this evening with a lot of newspapers, and we read them aloud. Makovitsky was here too. Few of the articles were any good. Some were crude lies, others were sweetly hypocritical. I hated the way they mistakenly attributed to me the name 'Levushka' for my husband;[92] I never called him that, either to his face or behind his back.

11 The Sukhotins, Yulia Ivanovna, Verochka and I are all in Moscow. We are staying for the last time in my house in Khamovniki Street, and are happy to be here. Sukhotin and Makovitsky stayed with my son Seryozha in Staro-Konyushenny Street.

12 I visited the *Duma* to discuss the sale of my house to the city of Moscow.

14 Sytin has now refused to buy all my editions off me, and has taken back his offer.[93]

15 N.V. Davydov visited Seryozha one evening recently with some advice about the letter I should write to the Tsar about Yasnaya Polyana.[94]

16 I saw Tanya, Tanyushka, Mikhail Sergeevich, the nurse and the woman doctor off on their foreign travels. I was sad to see them go. My son Ilya has arrived, and I feel even sadder.

17 Ilya complains about his affairs and says: 'I'll shoot myself.' I have been visiting Speshnev the notary about the sale of the house.[95] Dzhunkovskii the governor came to give me some advice about my letter to the Tsar. I wrote him a letter about the sale of Yasnaya Polyana, and Ilya and I decided to send it straight to Livadia with my son Misha. I still don't know whether it has been sent.[96]

20 (Moscow) The Moscow Art Theatre gave me a ticket for a box to see *The Living Corpse.*

21 I went to see the Dunaevs and the Gorbunovs and we read an extraordinary article by Fyodor Strakhov about the drawing up of Lev Nikolaevich's will.[97] I dined with the Maslovs.

22 I delivered the Album and an announcement to the editorial office of the *Russian Gazette*, then had dinner at Seryozha's with Kolomzin. This evening we went to the Art Theatre and sat in the director's box with Zosya and old Aleksandr Aleksandrovich Stakhovich. *The Living Corpse* is remarkable more for the performance of the actors (and often in a bad sense, as in the part of Fedya) than for its literary merits.[98] It's better to read it.

23 Spent the morning at the Merchant Bank and the *Duma.* I received 125,000 rubles for the house and sent off 60,000 rubles of this to my 6 children; Sasha is so rich now, but she is all alone.

24 I went to see Golovin the eye doctor – my eyes aren't too bad. This morning the inspector from the *Duma* took possession of my property. So sad! Ilya came, Misha has returned from the Crimea. Drentlen has given my letter to the Tsar, at Misha's request. I had dinner with Seryozha

and Masha, and this evening I read *Days of Our Grief*[99] and corrected various inaccuracies.

26 I tidied up my old house in Khamovniki Street and choked back the tears as I said farewell to the past. Yet one more thing has been torn from my heart. I dined with Seryozha; he then left for the English Club, and this evening I set off home for Yasnaya.

27 I am back again; the house is cold and empty. The artist N.V. Orlov is here. I went to bed and slept till one, then drank some coffee and went to the grave. The grey sky looming overhead, the forest silence, our peasants chopping brushwood in the gulley – everything's so sombre and severe here in the country. Letters from Lyova, tender but sad.

28 I got up late feeling rested but very sad and lonely. I had letters from the children, which was a great consolation – Andryusha's was very affectionate, Tanya's was long and kind, and there was one from Liza Obolenskaya too. I replied to Andryusha and Lyova, and spent the whole day working on newspaper cuttings; I didn't go out at all. I was told that Sasha had walked over to the house and hadn't come in! What a strange creature!

30 I went to the village and took over the peasants' library from Maria Valentinovna, who is leaving. The villagers take out books and don't return them, which is most annoying. The library will have to be closed down, and that'll be the end of it. Our peasants are still so uncultured. I worked on the newspaper cuttings until late tonight, and pasted them in. Unbearable depression!

December 1 I went to the grave again; there were a lot of little birds there, and they seemed to recognise me. 5 ° and no wind. I walked for a long time, read and pasted in the newspaper cuttings about Lev Nikol.'s posthumous works which have recently been published.[100]

2 I wrote to sister Tanya and Varya Nagornova, visited the grave, wept and prayed. Life is so hard and lonely! I am melancholy these days. I finished pasting in the newspaper cuttings which had accumulated in my absence. 7 ° below freezing, no wind, a golden sunset. I played some Beethoven and Weber sonatas and a Chopin nocturne for two hours today, and corrected *Days of Our Grief*.

4 I wrote a reply to Shcherbatov at the Historical Museum,[101] and to the *Petersburg Gazette*, No 305 of which was sent to Seryozha and Salomon.[102] I lead a sad and lonely life.

5 I went to Taptykovo with Verochka to visit my son Andryusha. The road was terrible! Not much snow, frozen mud, potholes and unbearably bumpy. They were all touchingly pleased to see me, and I was glad I went; Katya, Andryusha and little Mashenka warmed me with their love. I looked round their comfortable house.

6 Andryusha's 34th birthday; we spent the whole day together.

7 We spent the morning together again, and Katya and Andryusha touchingly thanked me for coming. A strong wind, a terrible road, 2½ ° below freezing. I was utterly exhausted and fell asleep on the sofa in the drawing-room. This evening I read Countess Aleksandra Tolstaya's 'Reminiscences', which I found fascinating, and also her correspondence with Lev Nik., published in a splendid Tolstoy Museum edition.[103]

8 I read all the newspapers – a lot in them about the Tolstoy exhibition. This afternoon Orlov read me Aleksandra Tolstaya's memoirs.

9 Newspaper cuttings all morning. Then I took the library books back from the peasant children and entered them into the catalogue. I wrote to Torba and Princess P.D. Dolgorukova. This evening Orlov again read from Aleksandra Tolstaya's memoirs. Then I read and corrected *Days of Our Grief*, and wept bitterly.

10 How strange it is to feel the dying of the flame which burnt within me all my life and kept me alive. Old age! But it's not peaceful! Andryusha came – he had to talk to his former wife about the sale of Taptykovo. I spent a sad and empty day. This evening I sewed a shirt while Orlov read from Lev Nik.'s correspondence with A. Tolstaya. He wrote fine phrases and toyed with fine feelings to save himself from his coarse liaison with the peasant woman. I can see all this now. Yet there was still the same seeking after God, the same religious aspirations, and that was good.

12 I took the library books back from the peasant children – some were lost, some were torn and filthy. Then I drew up a contents table for my memoirs. I didn't go out all day. There was a heavy fall of snow. I re-live my whole life when I read my memoirs.

15 Wanda Landowska and her husband arrived here from Sasha's. Their talk upset me. Before they came I went to the grave and fed the birds again: silent forest, hoar-frost, 5° below freezing. This evening Orlov read aloud Lev Nik.'s correspondence with A. Tolstaya.

17 Nyuta Behrs and I went to the grave and again fed the birds. Then we wandered around our garden and I remembered trying to drown myself in the pond – and not succeeding! It was extraordinarily still and white after last night's snow. This evening Nyuta and I played a duet version of a Mozart serenade, and his 2nd Symphony. It went badly but was pleasant none the less.

18 I walked to the grave again with Nyuta Behrs, then on through the forest to the river. I was glad to be alone in the forest with nature, but painfully sad that I would never, ever see or hear my Lyovochka again – I still remember him so vividly! This evening Orlov read aloud from Lev Nik.'s correspondence with Aleksandra Andreevna, and also a story by Kuprin called 'The Garnet Bracelet'.

19 We played a Mozart quintet and sonata arranged for four hands, and this evening we read aloud an article about Lev Nikolaevich by M.S. Sukhotin, called 'The Kiev Highway'.[104] Nyuta and I went for a fairly long walk through the new snow, which exhausted us, then we read the end of Kuprin's story 'The Garnet Bracelet'. Not bad, but too wordy.

21 Went to the grave with Nyuta and Yulia Ivanovna; a blizzard and strong wind, but warm. Orlov and Yulia Ivanovna are doing a portrait in oils of Nyuta. She has such an interesting face. Orlov read aloud some Kuprin stories – not good. I again attended to the affairs of the peasant library.

22 Unwell, stayed at home. The house was cleaned and I tidied up my Lyovochka's rooms myself. He is always in my thoughts, and I like being able to live on in this big house, just as though he were still here. Nyuta and I played Haydn's 20th Symphony and his 'Abschiedssymphonie'; I used to play these with Lyovochka. I painted the 'wooden company' of dolls for my grandchildren, who will soon be here.

24 Orlov left yesterday evening, and today we saw Nyuta off to Moscow. 27–30 ° of frost; 18 ° by this evening, but windy. I did some copying on the Remington for my daughter Tanya – my correspondence with Shcherbatov and Kasso about the manuscripts in the Historical Museum. I also wrote her a letter. Then I read 'The Forged Coupon'.[105] What a lot of murders! It is painful to read.

25 Christmas. Alone with Yulia Ivanovna. I walked on my own to the grave, weeping and praying incessantly. I entered the library books into the catalogue (the returned ones), gave the peasants generous presents, and worked hard on my memoirs for 1895, the year of Vanechka's death.

It's strange, when I go back to the past, even the painful times, I stop living in the present and live entirely in my memories – they're so vivid, they're almost real.

26 Dushan Petrovich was here; he noticed some note Lev Nik. had made in his French Gospel and in various other books.[106] I worked all day on my memoirs; at the moment I am preparing material for each month. I sent Tanya another letter of Shcherbatov's about the manuscripts, along with my reply.[107] 13 ° of frost, slight snow. They're doing a performance in Telyatinki of *Poverty's No Sin*, and everyone is hurrying over there.

27 While copying out my painful memoirs of Vanechka's death, and all the sad arguments over 'Master and Man' that preceded it,[108] I was able to do a lot of work on my memoirs for that period. This evening I played some sonatas by Haydn and Weber.

28 My daughter-in-law Sonya came this morning with my grandchildren Volodya, Vera and Kirill. We visited the grave and fed the birds, then played and decorated the Christmas tree. My sons Ilya and Andryusha came for dinner. Painful discussions with Ilya about financial matters and the sale of Yasnaya Polyana. Andryusha left late this evening.

29 I spend time with Ilya and my grandchildren, have intimate conversations with my daughter-in-law, sit and sew – and nothing else. We are decorating the Christmas tree and listening to the gramophone, which I dislike so much.

31 I was busy with the children and the Christmas tree, and talked to Ilya. This too has been a depressing year for me – yet I'm still alive! I wrote to Torba and Pr. Cherkasskaya. Cold, strong wind and a blizzard, so Sonyushka and Ilyushok couldn't come and see the Christmas tree. Ilya's elder sons didn't come either, and the Christmas tree and the New Year's party were dreadfully unexciting. But I'm glad Ilya and his family came, otherwise things would have been very lonely! Even so the tears kept coming to my eyes. So much sadness – not to speak of Sasha's estrangement; she must be so lonely surrounded by strangers. Sonya went to visit her in Telyatinki.

· 1912 ·

An increasing number of strikes, including large one at Lena goldfields, in which workers are shot. June – establishment of sickness fund, from contributions from workers and employers. October 8 – Montenegro, Serbia and Greece join forces in military action against Turkey. Tsar persuaded by his Foreign Minister that his ambitions for world domination via the Black Sea and the Dardanelles would be unrealisable without a world war, for which Russia is unprepared.

Aleksandra Tolstaya receives 120,000 rubles for the copyright on Tolstoy's posthumous works and 28,000 rubles for the exclusive licence to publish complete edition of his works. More conflicts with Sofia (who has already produced eight editions of Tolstoy's works). The Moscow house is sold to the municipal government, for 125,000 rubles, with the request that it be used as a Tolstoy museum and library. Excerpts from My Life *(covering the years 1862 to 1901) published.*

January 2 The two Ilyas, my son and grandson, have left, and 33 women students arrived from St Petersburg; I myself showed them around the house, 11 young ladies at a time. Then I worked on my 'Memoirs' (*My Life*). For the time being I am still collecting material. This evening I pasted in newspaper cuttings and read.

4 I worked hard on my Memoirs and finished the material for 1895. This evening I made notes of all the books that had been returned to the peasant library. The whole business has become disastrously muddled. Silence, nobody here.

7 I diligently wrote my 'Life' for 1895. I kept having to stop and weep as I described Vanechka's illness and death, his life, and indeed all the terrible things I experienced at that time.

9 Every grief should be assuaged in the place in which it arose, and I am re-living mine painfully here in Yasnaya as I write about my former life. It's both good and painful – so many memories, as though I were seeing them all.

14 (Moscow) P.I. Biryukov visited this morning, then I paid off Mey and Kushneryov and Co.[1] My sister Tanya came to see me; we had a talk, then went to the Wanderers' Art Show[2] and looked in on the church of Vasilii the Blessed. What an astonishing old building.

16 Spent the evening with E.F. Yunge, read her my memoirs.

19 Went to the Tolstoy Museum, where there were some *English guests.* Prince Dolgorukov gave a speech and an Englishman replied beautifully in French.[3] The young lady typist came and I dictated my memoirs to her.

20 Endless commotion all day - Sytin with an offer to buy some books, Prince Dolgorukov about the village library, the lady copyist; I dined hurriedly with my brother Sasha, then saw Sytin and Levitskii again about the sale of the books.[4] This evening a recital by the Czechs, with S.I. Taneev's quintet, difficult but good. Andryusha and Katya came, which was a joy, and Misha too.

21 This morning my son Ilya came, wretched and penniless. I went to an exhibition by the Union.[5] A lot of bad decadence. Then I dictated my memoirs to the girl copyist.

24 Ilya came, I gave him 1,000 rubles. He is pathetically poor, and what is so bad is that he blames everyone else for his poverty. I wrote to V.N. Kokovtsov thanking the Tsar for my pension.[6]

29 More negotiations with Levitskii about the sale of the editions to Sytin. He hopes to win Sasha and Chertkov over, but I don't think he will, for they are devising all sorts of traps to make me recognise Sasha as the heir to all her father's writings – even those in the Historical Museum.[7] I dictated to the copyist again.

February 7–13 We are exhausted by all these promises to buy my edition and bring Sasha to some agreement with Sytin or Marx, or both of them together! They turn everything into a secret; you can't understand what is happening. And of course Chertkov spitefully interferes with everything. I read three books, two French and one Russian – Fonvizin's *Two Lives*, which wasn't bad.[8] I went to three art shows and three concerts: two were recitals by the Czechs, who played magnificently, especially the Beethoven quartets. Taneev's quintet was also very good, but hard to understand at once. He played himself. I also went to Wanda Landowska's concert. She played marvellously, both the harpsichord and the piano. I am indifferent to everything, I died with my Lyovochka! But it seems I shall have to bear my healthy body for a long time yet! And I'm sad and I don't want to live.

March 10 I copied Tanya's proposed letter to the newspapers.[9]

11 I printed photographs of the grave and my own youthful portrait, at An. Iv. Maslova's request, and sent them to her. I sent Tanya her article and my letter to Ginzburg. I copied Tanya's article on the typewriter – she has now decided not to send it.[10] I am reading more of the Gospels, and have just read Vetrinskii's book about the famine, based on Lev Nikol.'s memories.[11]

15 I did a lot of work on the village library. It's hard to put it all in order, and I got Vasilii Orekhov from the village to help me. What an extraordinarily backward young lad! Dushan Petrovich came and checked his memoirs from my notes.

18 I read Countess Al. An. Tolstaya's letters to Lev Nik., which for some reason she wanted me to have after her death. Why didn't they go to Lev Nik.?[12] This evening I played some Haydn sonatas and various pieces by Chopin. Haydn does not touch me for some reason.

21 Posha Biryukov came and I gave him *Childhood* and *Boyhood* to copy.[13]

23 I copied Lev Nik.'s notebook for 1908. I endlessly re-live the past, there is no present, nothing excites me, nothing consoles me. It's a most unpleasant spring. Fog all morning, then it cleared, but the wind was terrible, a real tempest. The barometer is at zero. I read nothing but the Gospels these days.

24 I have finished copying Lev Nik.'s notebooks and have put down in ink everything that he wrote in pencil. I am reading Semyonov's *Retribution*.[14]

27 A large crowd of strangers unexpectedly arrived to see the grave and take a look at the house and Lev Nikol.'s rooms. I showed them round myself and talked to them.[15] Some of them were from the Chertkovs, and heard some bitter truths from me. I went to the grave and decorated it with roses, primulas, stocks and hyacinths – it looked beautiful. I read a lot about Herzen today. Yulia Ivanovna has left for Moscow and I am completely alone here at Yasnaya. I worked again on my memoirs for 1896, but there is very little material and I remember almost nothing.

28 I read letters from my children for 1896 as material for my memoirs. My son Andryusha unexpectedly arrived; I was delighted to see him and spent the rest of the day with him. It is sad to realise that *not one* of my children is happy and they are all short of money.

29 Andryusha left this morning. I worked again on my letters, as material for *My Life*. I live in the past, I have no life in the present, utter loneliness! But re-living the past is often very, very painful! There were some workers from the Brashnin factory, some women teachers and various other visitors. Their attitude to L.N.'s memory and to me was very touching. I stayed up late writing *My Life*. I am sitting all on my own here, with a frightful wind howling outside.

30 Yulia Ivanovna is back. I worked on my memoirs all day. It's all so difficult! The things that are interesting and precious to me are of little interest to the public. Work on *My Life* does drown a little of the sorrow that eats at my heart, and it's good to live in the past, even though it's irrevocable.

April 1 Misha left this morning. Magnificent weather; frosty nights, gradual thaw during the day. I worked on my writing. Dushan Petrovich came; he is reading my daily diary for his memoirs of Lev Nik. I mourned him so bitterly today, and felt his loss so keenly! Where are you, my beloved Lyovochka!

4 Went with some workmen to the forest to visit the grave, and had a very pleasant talk with them. This evening I played the piano and wrote a little.

6 News of the death of Lev Nik.'s sister Maria Nikolaevna. How sad! I wrote to Varya and Liza, Tanya and Lyova. I have finished working on 1896. It was painful to write about it. Last night I dreamt of Lev Nikol.; he was walking along the street straight towards me, gazing seriously into the distance, and as he got closer he melted away.

9 I gave 77 Yasnaya Polyana schoolchildren 3 yards of calico, which I received from Dm. Gen. Burylin in Ivanovo-Voznesensk. It was a joy to see so many children and I wanted to love them and make much of them.

10 I took fresh flowers to the grave and decorated it again, then I read an article about my sister-in-law Maria Nikolaevna. It was well written and affectionate.[16] She had prayed away all her sins, lucky woman!

11 I went to Tula, and saw my three sons Ilya, Misha and Seryozha in the Chernyshevskii Hotel; they are all wretchedly poor. They told me about Maria Nikolaevna's touching death and funeral.[17]

13 I want to read, write, and think. Dushan Petrovich has come and I am glad to see him; he is much better now than he used to be – good-natured, simple, and always calm and happy.

14 Misha looked in and I gave him 3,000 rubles. I sent Yurgenson Lev Nikolaevich's autograph.[18] Dushan Petrovich is staying with us. I re-read my memoirs and started working on an article for September 23, my wedding anniversary, either for the newspapers or for a journal.[19] I read them to Saltanov, to test public response.

17 A telegram from Zhdanov, appealing for an end to the business over the books sales. I spent the day writing my article for September 23, re-living the past and weeping. I drew some flowers.

21 (Moscow) The Sukhotins left early this morning, and I finished my business with Sytin; I received 100,000 rubles for the books,[20] sent my sons some money, and took out a bank-note of 20,000 for Tanya. I stayed with my brother Sasha and my sister Liza. I left for St Petersburg this evening.

22 (St Petersburg) I was met in St Petersburg by my son Lyova, who took me to his house on Tavricheskaya. The darling children were there, and I had a delightful time with them all. I was glad to see my sister and her husband too, and Masha Erdeli.

25 I visited Kasso to discuss the manuscripts in the Moscow Historical Museum. He refused to return them and advised me to lodge a complaint against him with the First Department of the Senate.[21] What a stupid creature! Had dinner and spent the evening with my sister Tanya. Enjoyed her singing.

26 Wrote to Kasso, Minister of Education, about the manuscripts.[22]

28 Half the day in the train, the other half at home in Yasnaya, where I arrived at 8 this evening. Two artists are here, Orlov and Saltanov, and Yulia Iv. Igumnova.

May 3 I read the Gospels every evening and think a lot: what troubles me most is that 'it's easier for a camel to pass through the eye of a needle than for a rich man to enter the Kingdom of Heaven'. I am reading L.N.'s 'Fyodor Kuzmich'.[23]

5 Spent the whole day copying my 50th wedding anniversary article on the Remington. I had a worrying letter from my sister, who wants to spend the summer with me in Yasnaya.

8 Went to Tula with Yulia Ivanovna. Witnessed the documents (copies) for the Senate case concerning the manuscripts, saw Andryusha, and spent the evening finishing my 50th wedding anniversary article.

10 Painful discussion this evening with Orlov about Chertkov and Lev Nik.'s relations with him. I missed him painfully all day.

15 (Moscow) Andryusha and I tidied up the Khamovniki house, decided what things were to go to the Stupin warehouse, what was to be sold and what was to go to Yasnaya. How sad that everything is being destroyed and everything is coming to an end – the beautiful old life has died, and it will not be continued by the children.

21 80 women students came with assistant-professor Valentin Nik. Bochkaryov. They took an interest in everything, walked to the grave, then all went off to Telyatinki. I too went to the grave this afternoon and planted it with forget-me-nots and other flowers. This evening I copied some documents to send to the Senate.

27 A mass of visitors all day. Unpleasantnesses with the gardener, the assistants and the visitors. Pav. Iv. Biryukov came and I gave him *Youth*, the notes for *Youth* and the end of *Boyhood*.[24] The artist Saltanov came this morning.

June 2 I am re-reading the *Pensées de Pascal*.[25] Books and ideas like these are good, for they help to explain our inner spiritual life.

5 Went to the grave. Some young people there. Showed them Lev Nik.'s rooms. Simple folk.

7 Read aloud some passages from Bourdon's book *En Écoutant Tolstoi*.[26]

9 We all went to the grave. I put a large bunch of flowers in water. My son Seryozha has come and we're all very glad to see him. Sister Tanya sang for us this evening – she still has a fine voice – Seryozha played the piano beautifully for us all, and Yasnaya Polyana came to life again. But there is no soul to it any more – it has gone.

11 Seryozha has left. We took a long walk through the plantation to the grave and back again. It's so good with nature! I looked through the prayer-book of Lev Nikolaevich's mother; it was in French and was dated 1731.

16 Sasha arrived with Varvara Mikhailovna. We have made friends again, thank God!

22 Korotnyov brought an estimate for the forest and a proposed plan for the parts of Yasnaya Polyana that will be left after the sale.[27]

28 (Nikolskoe) Seryozha's name-day and 49th birthday. My daughter Tanya came too, and my daughter-in-law Sofia Nikolaevna, and Varya Nagornova with her son, daughter and grandson. Sonya and Tanya sang, then everyone sang together, then Tanya danced with Orlov the artist. His whole family was here, and we had a good-natured, even cheerful time. We all went for a walk. The day was marred only by a distressing discussion with Sonya about money.

July 1 I wanted to rest my eyes and went out to cut the nettles by the house; Musya Erdeli joined me, and we then both made up bunches of flowers for Lyovochka's and Vanechka's portraits. I did a drawing of some flowers and looked through my memoirs and the *Tolstoy Museum News*.[28]

2 My sons Andryusha and Misha came this evening; then Sasha arrived to discuss the sale of Yasnaya Polyana, which I always find very painful.

5 Distressing discussions this afternoon about Lev Nik.'s flight and his relations with Chertkov. Aleksandr Mikhailovich is very wise and sympathetic in his judgements; I wish I could say the same for my sister Tanya Andreevna. She is much changed.

6 The peasants from the new settlements came here: 23 households were burnt to the ground. I gave 10 rubles to every family and waived their rent for the rest of the year.

8 This morning I received various visitors who had come to see Lev Nikol.'s rooms, and wasted time chatting. This evening the Kuzminskiis and I read aloud Vl. Fed. Snegiryov's letter to me of April 19, 1911.[29]

13 Stayed in bed all day reading and got up this afternoon. Sasha came with Nadya Ivanova and Bulygin, and we spent a very pleasant evening. I wrote to M.A. Stakhovich asking him to vouch for L.N.'s words about the manuscripts and my rights to them.[30]

16 Went to the grave; a lot of young people on bicycles there. I read, and finished the article 'Tolstoy and Rousseau' in the *Herald of Europe*.[31] He expounds his ideas in a very muddled, unclear fashion.

17 Gusev and Dm. Vas. Nikitin came and spent the whole day with me. I read them my account of my wedding, Snegiryov's letter and my daughter Tanya's article.[32]

18 I am reading another article on Rousseau and Tolstoy, but this is a French booklet which I have just received from the author; it's better than the Russian article.[33]

19 I am copying Pascal's *Pensées*; there's a strange essay by him called 'Passion et l'amour'.[34] I took a great bunch of flowers to the grave this evening. There were some white lilies there which someone had brought. And there are always visitors. Late this evening I copied my article for September 23, 1912.[35]

29 I finished my drawing of the flowers. Biryukov and Bulgakov were here. The same conversations for two years now about Lev Nik., his flight, the will and so on. And the same thing again this evening with Kuzminskii. Aleksandr Mikhailovich is an extraordinarily good and logical person. Tanya is quite the opposite. She shouts, loses her temper, puts wholly unjustified nuances of criticism into everything. How she has changed! What a shame it is!

30 I had a letter from Mikh. Al. Stakhovich and copied it out,[36] then did a little drawing.

August 3 The whole Denisenko family came and were very pleasant company. My brother Sasha arrived too, and we were delighted to see him. I went to the grave with the Denisenkos; we took some flowers and were given a bunch by a stranger who was passing through Zaseka and had been at the fourth bastion in Sevastopol.

4 The Gorbunov-Posadovs came. They're dear people, I love them both. We all visited the grave.

5 My brother Sasha and Sasha Kuzminskii read my article about my wedding and praised it highly.

6 I copied out Lyovochka's sad diary on the typewriter.[37] What happened? It's incomprehensible! A lot of it is very unjust. My soul is in mourning.

9 My granddaughter Annochka came with my darling little great-grandson Seryozha. Annochka and my sister sang some duets very prettily and my son Seryozha played the piano. Dushan Petrovich visited and I spent the whole day with guests; a lot of commotion, but it is pleasant that Yasnaya Polyana is again becoming a place where people gather. Tears in my throat all day.

14 I went to the grave as soon as I got up and decorated it with flowers. And I felt so sad, so hopeless! Then I went to the village library. About 175 books have been appropriated and torn by the peasants and I find this so depressing that I no longer feel like working on it. I am reading a series

21 On previous page: Sofia Tolstaya in the park at Yasnaya Polyana, 1903. (Sofia's photograph)

22 Above: Yasnaya Polyana, 1904. The Tolstoys' eldest sons, left to right, Lev, Ilya, Sergei, Andrei and Mikhail. (Sofia's photograph)

23 Below: Sofia Tolstaya at the window of the stationmaster's house at Astapovo station, where Tolstoy was dying, November 1910

of articles called 'On Tolstoy's Religion',[38] and for a rest I read Potapenko's 'The Janitors of Fame'.[39] This evening I read biographies of various people from portraits published by Grand Duke Nikolai Mikhailovich.[40]

19 This morning I sat with my sister while she read me her notes about our genealogy; it's not badly written.[41] Biryukov came, visitors came to see the study and N.N. Gusev came asking for money for the consumers' shop. I read him my memoirs (or rather excerpts from them), and he approved. This evening Zvegintseva and Cherkasskaya visited. Bulgakov came and took away three books of poems.

22 My 68th birthday. I had a very, very pleasant day. Andryusha's family came, then my sons Ilya and Seryozha. We went to the grave with my granddaughter Masha. Then the Sukhotins came. There were 19 people to dinner. Yasnaya Polyana came to life again! This evening we sang and danced. It was all so cheerful that I wanted to weep with emotion, and a bitter sense of loss. I am even closer to the children now, thank God!

25 I went to the grave and prayed there for a long time, begging Lyovochka to forgive me for all the ways in which I hurt him. Then I decorated the grave with flowers. It was so good that no one else was there at that time. The others had all gone off to see Sasha, who drove back with Parasha Gué. I enjoy the company of my family.

27 Sasha asked if she could spend the winter in the Kuzminskiis' wing; she wants to extricate herself from the hateful Chertkov.

28 Lyovochka's birthday – the late Lyovochka. I went to the grave with my little granddaughter Tanechka Sukhotina. That was the best moment of the day. This evening there was a lot of singing, noise, uproar and dancing, and I felt sadder and sadder. Hofstetter and Bulgakov came too.

September 1 This evening I read Varya Nagornova letters from Snegiryov, Maria Nikolaevna and her mother, as well as Tanya's article and Lyovochka's diary.

4 I read Vetrinskii's book on Herzen.[42] Lev Nik. loved Herzen very much. I spent the whole day copying on the Remington.

8 Spent the whole day copying Lev Nik.'s diary on the typewriter. Busy all evening sorting out papers for Moscow. Ilya has left; I feel dreadfully sorry for him!

9 I packed and went to the grave to say goodbye to Lyovochka. It is all very sad! Bulgakov came, then Martynov the artist, who asked in a very familiar manner where he and his wife could stay.

12 **(Moscow)** To the editorial offices of the *Russian Word* about my article[43] and my grandchildren's portraits,[44] then to the banks.

13 More business. Went to the Historical Museum and corrected some mistakes in an earlier copy of Lev Nik.'s diary.

17 My name-day. I have never enjoyed *celebrations*, even as a child. But I was very glad that Sasha, Dushan Petrovich and Varvara Mikhailovna came, and poor Katya, Andryusha's wife, who is still in a very distressed state. My sister sang. I went to the grave, and took two magnificent roses there.

18 Have started on an article about *The Power of Darkness* for the *Tolstoy Museum News*, at the request of young Sergeenko.[45] A cool day, I have a cold and did not leave the house. I received a copy of *Spark*, with portraits of my 20 grandchildren, and sent it to Naryshkina.[46]

23 My wedding anniversary; 50 years have passed since I married the man who is no longer with me. I try to fight off the sadness that clings to me so tenaciously. My heart has suffered terribly these past two years! At night I hear strange rattling sounds. Andryusha's wife, Katya, is here, and Baturin the artist. I took flowers to the grave and wept.

24 The Gruzinskiis have left.[47] They printed my article very prominently on the front page in yesterday's issue.[48]

25 I have no *real work* to do in my life. I am waiting until I am completely alone to copy and edit Lev Nik.'s letters to me. I have received several letters applauding my article.[49]

26 I have written to the *Russian Word* reprimanding them for not sending me the promised issues. I also wrote to Gautier's about the novel *Les Dieux ont soif.*[50]

28 It poured with rain all day. I did a little work and felt very melancholy. Lev Nik.'s old black cap fell to pieces in my hand, and I suddenly saw before me his old head, which I loved so much.

29 I copied my first letter to sister Tanya after my marriage,[51] I wrote to Bykhanova about the 85 rubles and to Mikh. Serg. Sukhotin about his splendid response to my article in the *Russian Word* of September 23 of this year. Andryusha and Katya came.

30 I went to the grave and took more flowers – the last of the year. A clear day with an icy wind. I copied some material for 1897, but there isn't enough; I don't know whether it will be possible to put something together. Martynov the artist came, and I spent the whole evening chatting to him. I feel tired and depressed.

October 1 The artist Martynov is here again. Linev came too (a member of the Tolstoy Museum), and took away all the photographs of the estate. I do almost no work, merely squander my energy on trifles and feel constantly ill. My daughter Sasha came. We are on friendly terms.

2 Sister Tanya and Vanechka Erdeli have left. I forced myself not to cry and wandered about the house for a long time in a deep depression. Then I worked on an excerpt from my memoirs, 'The First Performance of *The Fruits of Enlightenment*'. I finished writing it, then copied it out on the typewriter for the *Sun of Russia*.[52]

7 Dushan Petrovich came to visit me, and this evening I read his interesting memoirs about Lev Nikolaevich and had another conversation with him.[53]

8 I received a charming letter from El. Alekseevna Naryshkina regarding my article about my wedding.[54]

10 No news from any of the children; only my darling Tanechka doesn't forget me. I read. Various sounds in the silence of the house. Are the dead coming back to me?

12 Andryusha came to visit and took 2,000 rubles from me; we talked about the sale of Yasnaya Polyana and how they had chosen him as an elector. I wrote to Kuzminskii, who wants me to visit St Petersburg to petition for a cinematographic lampoon about me to be banned.[55]

13 My health is so much worse that I wrote to Makovitsky asking for his help. I am very listless; I feel as though I were half asleep, and don't want to do anything, particularly after this distressing news from Petersburg about the cinematograph. I read Makovitsky's memoirs to Yulia Ivanovna.

15 Sasha sent Mikh. Pavl. Popov the valuer to see me, with his assistant, and we looked at the plan. Then Dushan Petrovich came and we discussed his memoirs, which I read again to Yulia Ivanovna this evening. Sasha has bought a house in Moscow across the Moscow river.

19 (Moscow) I visited the town governor to discuss the cinematograph, which has now been banned.[56]

20 (St Petersburg) I have arrived in St Petersburg and have asked the ministers for a meeting.

22 I was received by the Minister of Justice, and gave him my complaint (a copy), which I had sent to the Senate.[57] Shcheglovitov seems well-disposed towards me and my campaign over Lev Nik.'s manuscripts.

23 Today I visited the Minister of Internal Affairs, Makarov, about the cinematographic lampoon against me, and he promised to ban it throughout Russia. But we still have to write to Poland, Finland and the Caucasus.[58]

24 I wrote registered letters to Zein, Skalon and Count Vorontsov-Dashkov about the cinematograph; I dined at home with the Kuzminskiis, saw Lyova, then left for Yasnaya Polyana. My sister Tatiana Andreevna saw me off.

25 I was happy to get home to Yasnaya Polyana. Dushan Petrovich was here.

27 This evening I read Chirikov's 'Banishment' aloud to Yulia Ivanovna. Lightly written, little content.[59]

28 Painful memories of Lev Nikolaevich's flight two years ago today; I got up with an aching heart. After dinner I read Chirikov's 'Banishment', then sewed under the lamp – the first lamp in our house, which my Lyovochka lovingly brought for me.

31 It's so sad that I cannot work on my memoirs; when I read papers and letters I become upset and cry. It's a wearisome life. I cannot move with all the work I have to do. I wrote to Varya Nagornova, to Gorbunov about the Crimean photographs and to the Italian woman about the translation of the article.

November 1 A photographer arrived this morning from Pathé. I didn't leave the house. I wrote a reply to Strumenskii's questions about the group and about Il. And. Tolstoy. I am reading Anatole France's *Les Dieux ont soif.*

2 A correspondent from the *Russian Word* was here about the Yasnaya Polyana schools in 1862. I worked on 1897 again. It's hard to re-live the past, and to live with the guilt of having made that beloved man so unhappy.

3 The artist Saltanov visited and my daughter Sasha came to say goodbye. She is moving to Moscow to live in the house she has bought, and I worry about her.

6 I wrote a lot with a heavy heart about the time when Lev Nikol. was so jealous of Taneev and me, and suffered such torments, poor man. I wrote all day, and this evening read Chirikov's 'Banishment' aloud.

7 The anniversary of Lev Nikolaevich's death. All sorts of visitors to the house and the grave all morning – police, cinematographers, correspondents, the general public. Andryusha came, and Seryozha arrived shortly afterwards. This afternoon when the visitors had all left, I went to the grave with Andryusha. Seryozha went on his own. Dushan Petrovich came for the evening.

9 This evening Saltanov read aloud Chirikov's 'Banishment'. I read a great many articles about Lev Nikol. in the newspapers, and a spiteful note by Chertkov in *Speech*.[60]

10 I went to the grave as soon as I got up. Whenever I am there on my own I weep and talk to Lyovochka and pray. I scattered crumbs to the birds, and a flock of them flew up and chirped cheerfully at me. I went back and wrote a lot of *My Life*, and this evening I played both pianos and read a French article about Rod.[61] We read many articles about Lev Nik., and Yulia Ivanovna cuts them out and pastes them into the book.

12 I have finished writing 1897. This evening I read some articles about Lev Nik. in the *Sun of Russia* for November 7,[62] and a spiteful article by Menshikov in *New Times*,[63] and Saltanov read aloud Makovitsky's memoirs.

13 I have started copying out 1897 on the typewriter. Such a colourless depiction of that time, and so sad!

16 A sleepless night. Writing my memoirs upsets me terribly – so many memories and so much sadness!

19 I rose early and went to the grave, where I chatted there to some peasants I had never met before, who were carrying logs. Then I wrote and wrote all day. An unpleasant article about the manuscripts in the *Russian Gazette*.[64]

December 1 I catalogued the library books. They are all either by L.N. Tolstoy or about him. I live only for him and everything that concerns him.

3 I again worked on the papers for my last edition. V.F. Bulgakov has come to study our library.[65]

4 I copied extracts from Lev Nik.'s diaries for my son Seryozha, and sent them to him.[66] I have been looking through my memoirs for something Denisenko can read.

7 I took myself in hand and wrote 'Lev Nik.'s Four Visits to Optina Pustyn' for Denisenko to read at the Tolstoy evening in Novocherkassk.[67] This evening I read it to Yulia Ivanovna, Korotnyov and Saltanov, and they approved. Then I read aloud from Chirikov's 'Banishment'.

11 I read all day and finished two French books. Bulgakov came to work on the library, and Gusev came; he seems embarrassed to see me after his lecture.[68]

12 Today a young priest I have never met before held a funeral service – at his own request – over Lev Nikolaevich's grave then performed a requiem mass in his bedroom. He left this evening. An energetic, intelligent man, just 27. Bulgakov, Yulia Ivanovna, Verochka and I attended the funeral service, and Nurse and Semyon the cook came for the requiem.[69]

13 I started on some difficult work today, copying and editing all my late husband Lyovochka's letters to me.[70] That's a job I won't finish in a hurry. I shall re-live the whole of my married life as I read them. It will be very hard at times.

14 The same work – and it will go on for a long time to come – copying out Lev Nik.'s letters; it both delights and saddens me. We are all busy here – Bulgakov in the library, Saltanov with his paintings and Yulia Ivanovna with her sewing.

16 I managed to copy a few letters today. All those memories of our young life and my love for L.N. came back to me so vividly.

21 I ordered a book of articles about *War and Peace* from the Clan publishing-house.[71] This evening I played the piano a little, then copied a great many of Lev Nik.'s letters to me from the '60s.

22 I wrote an article for *Russian Word* in reply to Pankratov's lying article about the priest's visit.[72] I also wrote to sister Tanya, and to the editors of the Clan publishing house about the *Illustrated Anthology on 'War and Peace'*, which has been banned by the censors.[73]

24 I stood for a long time today at the grave in spiritual communion with my husband Lyovochka. This evening I copied and read aloud to Yulia Ivanovna and Bulgakov Lev Nik.'s letters from the Samara steppes, written in 1871.

25 Went to L.N.'s grave as soon as I got up, taking fresh flowers and seeds for the birds. Taras was there. On the way back I met the village policeman and the guard – not a pleasant experience. I spent the day with outsiders – Yulia Ivanovna, Bulgakov, Saltanov. This evening an Englishwoman travelling around here on foot arrived with some Jew. I copied out some of L.N.'s letters and one from N.N. Strakhov, which I sent to *Contemporary World*.[74]

29 I spent the day with Liza Obolenskaya. We checked the years and dates on L.N.'s letters to me and recalled many happy times from the past.

30 I went to the grave with Lizanka Obolenskaya; there were a lot of visitors there today, in troikas and on skis. I walked round the grounds with her. It was so still in the garden and the forest, and only 4 ° of frost. Liza left this evening. She told Bulgakov and Saltanov a lot.

31 I worked on the letters a little this morning, and Andryusha and Katya came for dinner. We spent a pleasant day together, and saw in the New Year in such a nice friendly fashion. Dushan Petrovich also paid a brief visit.

· 1913 ·

March 8 – huge Women's Day demonstrations, under auspices of Bolsheviks and Mensheviks, in Moscow, St Petersburg and other towns. May – armistice signed with Turkey. Divisions emerge within anti-Turkish coalition over spoils, and Bulgaria attacks Serbia, Romania and Greece. August – new peace treaty signed. Tsar Nicholas urged by many in his government to take Straits of Constantinople.

February 26 – Aleksandra Tolstaya buys Yasnaya Polyana from her mother and brothers for 40,000 rubles, which Sofia divides between her thirty-eight dependants. March 26 – over two-thirds of Yasnaya Polyana's land, including forests, is transferred to peasants (according to conditions of Tolstoy's will), while Sofia retains rest of estate, including house and orchard. She starts work on edition of Tolstoy's diaries. More excerpts from My Life *published.*

January 4 Despite the cold and my cough, I visited the grave, then went for a long walk. I love these bright, frosty, sunny days, and the dazzling white snow. I took some roses and white hyacinths to the grave, scattered crumbs to the birds, prayed and wept. For the rest of the day I copied Lyovochka's letters for 1882. He loved me then! Bulgakov is ill.

7 Sasha and Varvara Mikhailovna came; we drank tea, talked and parted on friendly terms. I collected some books to be bound, wrote to *Russian Word* about No 45 of *Spark*, which is missing, and to the *Sun of Russia* about the same thing.[1] I spent the rest of the day copying my late husband's letters, which I enjoyed.

10 I write and write, and copy out the past, and am carried back so vividly into my memories. And I rejoice at everything that happened, and I weep . . . I keep thinking and worrying about Ilya. What will he do!

12 I want only to write and write Lyovochka's letters to me and re-live the distant past. But what of the children? Are any of them happy? There are so few happy people in this world.

13 Zhdanov the barrister arrived this evening with Miller his assistant. I chattered away for far too long and didn't write enough. Belinkii came and asked for the banned volumes,[2] but I don't have any.

15 Bulgakov has returned. It's as if I had no children, and that makes me sad. None of them write, they've all forgotten about me – and I think so much about them.

17 This evening Bulgakov and I read aloud the letters of Lev Nikol. and N.N. Strakhov.[3] At nights I am reading the novels of the French writer Prévost.[4]

18 I copied out a lot of Lev Nikol.'s letters, and I often seem to hear his voice speaking to me. It's so quiet here. Bulgakov is busy in the library, and in the evenings we read aloud from the correspondence between N.

Strakhov and Lev Nikolaevich. Bulgakov is a pleasant, cultured person to talk to.

19 I am reading an anthology of articles entitled *War and Peace*, in memory of L. Tolstoy.[5]

20 I had a visit from my son Andryusha, still unwell, and Ilya; I lent him (supposedly) 6,000 rubles and he cheered up immediately. But will it last? The visitors arrived and looked around the house. I did more copying. This evening I read Andreev's story 'He'.[6]

22 Heard of the death of Ek. Fyod. Yunge. How sad! One less friend. Did a lot of copying and started on the 3rd book.

26 I copied all morning, and spent the rest of the day pleasantly with Dushan Petrovich. He read me remarks of Lev Nik.'s which he had noted down,[7] and I read him Lev Nik.'s letters to me. Later we read Baryatinskii's book about Fyodor Kuzmich, which claimed that he was the Emperor Alexander I.[8]

31 I am reading nothing but French books. I have never read Zola's *Fécondité* and am curious to do so. More unpleasantness with Sasha; she wants to gain possession of the property and the Yasnaya Polyana library. What will this strange – to say the least – girl think up next? More threats and blackmail!

February 2 Our Seryozha left this morning; we had a friendly talk together about business and the family's ownership of the grave, and he livened up the house with his music and stories. Varechka Nagornova came and I was delighted to see her.

4 I went to the grave with Varechka. Korotnyov came to draw up a plan of the two acres of land, including the grave, which is to remain family property. I wrote to Seryozha, Tanya and Andryusha saying that one acre would be quite enough. After dinner Bulgakov and Korotnyov sang duets. Both Varya and I accompanied them.

7 Andryusha came – I'm always so pleased to see him! More discussions about the grave, the forest, the sale of Yasnaya Polyana and so on.

8 Dreadfully upset by news in the papers about the Senate's decision on the manuscripts; it seems they'll refuse again, the cowards![9]

12 I visited the grave with Varechka and decorated it with flowers. A fine day, but a cold north wind. I copied, and read Varya and Bulgakov a story I wrote long ago.[10]

13 I spend most of the time with Varya, copy out Lev Nik.'s letters, and the more I do the more my heart suffers at our gradually dwindling happiness. My daughter Sasha visited briefly – a stranger, alas! This evening I played a Mozart quintet and symphony as a duet with Varya.

15 Dushan Petrovich came to see us and we talked about Lev Nik.'s letters to me, his memoirs and his life.

16 Varechka Nagornova left this morning and my son Lyova came to dinner. I'm very glad to see him. But he is not in a happy state: he's exhausted by St Petersburg and his family, and sees and feels everything much too keenly.

18 Gruzinskii came for dinner, and afterwards we discussed the editing of Lev Nik.'s letters to me.[11]

19 I took counsel with Gruzinskii about the publication of Lev Nik.'s letters to me. He has undertaken to edit them for 500 rubles. Lyova has returned from seeing Andryusha, he is anxious and perpetually dissatisfied, and it makes him wretched.

21 Did a lot of copying. Read Ilya's moving article in the *Russian Word* about Saltanov's exhibition, based on childhood memories of Yasnaya Polyana.[12] Read N.N. Strakhov's letters to Lev Nikolaevich.

23 Yesterday evening I finished copying all of Lev Nik.'s letters to me. It was terribly hard to do the last ones! My son Ilya has arrived, cheerful and full of energy. P.I. Biryukov came, evidently to get material for his biography of L.N., which I gave him.[13]

24 Various people arrived early this morning to look at the study – Academician Sreznevskii, Shokhor-Trotskii, some dentist and a member of the Tolstoy Museum. We visited the grave with Pav. Iv. Biryukov, took flowers and were again surrounded by a flock of hungry birds. I spent the rest of the day embroidering underwear, and gave Biryukov a lot of material for his biography of Lev Nik.

25 Biryukov has left. I did some embroidery, and numbered L.N.'s letters to me; there are 638.[14]

26 Went to Tula this morning to discuss the buying and selling of Yasnaya Polyana.[15] I was joined by Ilya and Sonya, Andryusha, Misha, Sasha (in another hotel), Vaka Filosofov and many friends. Painful, tedious business discussions, visit to the notary, exhaustion. The streets are rivers and the sun is shining, but the countryside is still plunged in grim winter.

28 Gusev, Dushan Petrovich and Belinkii have come. I gave Gusev some information about Lev Nikolaevich's diaries, which he is editing.[16]

March 2 Worked hard on the photographs, printed photographs of Repin's portrait of Lev Nik. and me for Zhdanov and Miller the barristers.[17]

3 Printed photographs all day. Ilya visited. He keeps coming up with plans to make enough money to live on. He doesn't have any of his Yasnaya Polyana money left. He took my memoirs to use them to write his reminiscences of his father.[18]

4 I printed photographs and we took one of the bust of Aleks. Petrovich for Ilya. He left at 5. He gets carried away by all sorts of plans, none of which ever comes to anything. I played a Mozart fantasie, some Beethoven variations and various other things – all badly, all so difficult! I read Bernstein's *Leo Tolstoy*.[19]

5 I copied out on the typewriter a letter from the Academy of Sciences and one from Koni about Lev Nikol.'s death. Then I drafted letters to Snegiryov and Koni, asking for permission to publish their letters.[20] Andryusha came with a financial account for Yasnaya Polyana.

10 Yulia Ivanovna and I left by express train for the Crimea, via Tula. We were given a lovely large compartment just for the two of us.

11 (Yalta) We arrived in Yalta by automobile, after various adventures with a burst tyre and so on, at 5.30 in the evening. The Sukhotins welcomed us warmly, especially little Tanechka. It's a pity my room is downstairs and theirs is up on the 4th floor.

14 Tanya, Tanyushka and I visited my mother's grave, high on a hill with a view of the sea and mountains. Painful memories of Mother's suffering and death, followed by the murder of her son Vyacheslav, still in deep mourning at the time.[21]

17 We went to visit the Tatarinovs, and this evening I read Mertvago's fascinating memoirs.[22]

22 I went to Gaspra with Yulia Ivanovna. It was so pleasant, even the memories of Lev Nikol.'s illness, because we, his *family*, looked after him with love when he was ill, and he was *mine*, not Chertkov's! And how beautiful it was!

28 We travelled by sea to Sevastopol, where we went for a walk. Mikhail Sergeevich went with Yulia Ivanovna to see the Malakhov burial-mound, and this evening we returned home by train. I had a pleasant journey with the Sukhotins in a spacious international carriage. The weather was fine, and we were so comfortable.

30 This morning we said goodbye to the Sukhotins, who are staying in Oryol. My heart ached at the parting, but it was good to get home. Dear Bulgakov was happy to see us, and the servants seemed so too. I went to L.N.'s grave and decorated it with Crimean flowers.

31 I tidied up my papers and threw out a lot of things. Mikh. Vas. Bulygin came. I'm always glad to see him – he's a good and honest man. Late this evening I read some of N.N. Strakhov's letters, and one from Lev Nikolaev. Magnificent early spring weather; the lungworts are in flower, and there are snowdrops and crocuses in the meadow. The bees are active and buzzing, spring is here and it's all so good.

April 3 Endless bustle all day. Korotnyov came to discuss the boundaries of my property at Yasnaya Polyana. Ganeev called about the workmen who are digging the ditch and the dam. Some people arrived from Belobrodov regarding my sons' payment for the trees.[23] I printed photographs of Lev Nik. and the grave, visited the grave, and this evening read Andreev's 'He'. Rubbish.

4 Most upset this morning by Sasha's article in the newspapers about her right to the manuscripts.[24] Yet more vileness: she says *I* refused to go to a court of arbitration, without mentioning that *she* was the one who *first* refused to go.

5 After dinner Yulia Ivanovna and I went to inspect the new boundaries. Korotnyov came and started work. I learnt that the Senate had referred the matter of the manuscripts to a general session of the senators.[25]

9 I went to church again and was distressed by the way the deacons shouted instead of praying. One cannot understand *a single word* they are reading. It's outrageous! And people are surprised at the impoverishment of the faith amongst the common people!

12 Kolechka Gué came, followed by Misha Bulygin. I sat with Gué almost until dinner, and read him the letters I received after Lev Nik.'s death.

13 Al. Ed. Yunge came and I went with him to the grave; we took flowers, then had a long talk about his late mother and about Lev Nikolaevich.

14 Dushan Petrovich came, and he, Yunge and I read some selected passages from the diaries published in *Russian Word*.[26] We took flowers and removed yesterday's bunch. Sasha and Varvara Mikhailovna came and we got on well.

16 Yunge left yesterday evening. There were a lot of visitors to L.N.'s rooms today, and even more at the grave. I did some typing for N.N. Gué.

18 Bulygin and Gué have left. I copied Tanya's article on the typewriter for N.N. Gué.[27]

20 I wandered about Yasnaya Polyana for a long time, then sat down on the bench in the fir plantation, where Lev Nik. used to sit so often, and where I once lay down and sobbed for several hours, not noticing the rain or damp. I cried today too, and prayed. Then I went back and worked on L.N.'s letters to me, and this evening I read an article by Mikulich about her friendship with our family.[28]

21 A visit from Nordman (the woman who lives with Repin) and her secretary. I went to the grave, then wandered about. Nordman has read a lot, and I liked her today, for she understands a lot and has spiritual aspirations. She has now left. I played Beethoven sonatas and read Rousseau.

May 1 (Moscow) I went to Moscow with Verochka, dined with Seryozha and spent the evening with him. On the train I read Pascal.

3 I went to the warehouses, paid Stupin for storing our furniture and things,[29] and collected the books from the late Kokoryov's warehouse on the embankment across the Moscow River. I dined with the Maslovs.

4 Finished my business and left this evening for St Petersburg.

7 Spent a very pleasant day with Lyova, Dora and their delightful children. Yesterday the chief procurator of the Senate, N.A. Dobrovolskii,

called on the Kuzminskiis – and me, and promised that my case would be successful in the Senate. This evening I left for Moscow.

9 (Moscow) Verochka and I went to the Pokrovksoe-Glebovo cemetery in Nikolskoe to visit the graves of my boys Alyosha and Vanechka; we planted some flowers – pansies, forget-me-nots and so on. Both tombstones have been broken – the cross on one and the praying angel on the other.

11 I left Moscow for Yasnaya this morning – a hot day. Saltanov the artist is here.

15 I walked to the Voronka this morning with Lyova and my grandchildren to see where we should put the new dam. A hot, sunny day; later it rained and grew cooler. Tanya has come, and my daughter Sasha. We spent a pleasant day together and I felt relieved of my anxieties. We all walked to the grave after dinner.

19 I worked all day on Lev Nik.'s letters to me. So painful and so sad! And so irreparable! I long helplessly to see the people I loved so much like Vanechka and Lyovochka!

21 I was storing Lev Nik.'s things from the moth, and it tore my heart to hold in my hands all his clothes, his underwear, his shirts and so on. How I loved him – and love him still! I went to inspect the building work, watered the flowers and read some letters. I'm very tired.

26 My grandson Seryozha arrived with his Russian teacher this morning. There were a lot of visitors, including three Japanese men and two of their wives. Unfortunately I was still in my room and didn't see them. This evening M.V. Bulygin came, and N.N. Gué.

29 Gué and Bulygin have left. Dushan Petrovich came and he too has left, leaving me his memoirs. I have read them and there are a lot of mistakes, inaccuracies and longueurs in them.[30]

30 I have finished reading Dushan Petrovich's memoir, which he left me. There is evidence throughout of a rather shaky knowledge of the Russian language, and a certain insensitivity. I was soaked by the rain on my way to the grave; I took a bunch of peonies, blue columbines and double white eglantines. This evening my grandson Seryozha and I had a discussion about philosophy and religion.

June 4 I am reading the letters of N.N. Strakhov and Lev Nikolaevich in *Contemporary World*. A lot of Lev Nikol.'s letters have been lost.

5 I was reading the letters again, and it occurred to me that the lost ones may be with Chertkov, who took them to copy and probably kept most of them.[31]

6 Reading Lev Nik.'s letters to Strakhov gave me less pleasure than I had anticipated. They're so studiously abstract – and there's such a lot of flattery. I feel as lifeless as ever, and so is work. I played the piano for a long time after dinner – the *Freischütz* overture and a Beethoven sonata.

11 I sewed, and worked on a preface to Lev Nikol.'s letters.[32] A.E. Gruzinskii came; I shall start working with him tomorrow.

12 A German baron visited. He has been round the world and was terribly talkative. I spent the whole morning with him, then talked to Gruzinskii about the publication of the letters. I sawed dead wood, chopped and mowed. A fine day. This evening Gruzinskii played the piano.

13 This evening I copied all of Lev Nikol.'s letters that were missing from the first copy.[33]

14 I copied Lev Nikol.'s letters to me, then wrote to Lyova, to a Frenchman about aristocratic families in Europe, to Krapivna about the Circassian guard,[34] and to Shenshin about the books.

15 A hot fine day, everything is more cheerful. This morning I did some sewing, then sorted letters with Gruzinskii. Then I picked a huge bunch of mixed flowers, which I took to the grave after dinner. It was so quiet, and there was a lovely sunset. I prayed and mourned; all my family has dispersed – it's as though I have no one left!

17 My son Andryusha came; I'm always glad to see him, although I disapprove of much of what he does, and grieve for him. The police came, after hearing of Vas. Konyshev's threats to beat the bailiff to death. So unpleasant! It's raining again. I am writing to the newspapers about badly behaved visitors.[35]

22 I copied *my* letters to Lev Nik., to add to his letters to me, and I wept.[36] The wound has not healed and is still very painful. I wrote to Chefranov about the edition.[37]

23 A.E. Gruzinskii has left and my son Ilya has arrived. We spent the day reading his memoirs of his father and our old family life.[38] I live entirely in the past now. The hay is being gathered, and the white mushrooms and saffron milk-caps are out. There are a lot of berries.

25 My son Ilya arrived last night. A great many visitors today – 11 men on bicycles from St Petersburg, an American from New York, and a husband and wife from Siberia. Then Bulygin came to give advice on the construction of the dam. A lovely hot day! I drew some mushrooms.

27 Bulgakov and I went to visit Seryozha in Nikolskoe. We travelled from Cherni by cab, and I greatly enjoyed our drive through the fields and country lanes. We spent a quiet family evening chatting together. I love Nikolskoe, and always remember my youth there whenever I go there.

28 My son Seryozha's birthday – he is 50 already. I congratulated him and gave him 100 golden rubles. Old Countess Zubova was there too, a dear old woman. Varya Nagornova then came with Ada, and their arrival was followed by such a heavy shower that we didn't expect to see Tanya Sukhotina and her husband – but shortly afterwards they too arrived. We had a very happy day. Bulgakov sang all evening, and Seryozha played beautifully.

29 The Sukhotins left at 12, followed by Varya. We went for a walk, then visited the colony – 30 boys and three teachers. The boys performed a bad play and sang badly for us – earlier on they had been playing ball. What sad little city starvelings these boys are.

30 Bulgakov and I left Nikolskoe today. On the journey I re-read Seryozha's guide to Yasnaya Polyana, which he gave me. A few things need to be added.[39]

July 2 I copied Seryozha's guide to Yasnaya Polyana and added my own observations and corrections. Bulgakov left.

4 I wrote to Posse about an article in *Life for All*, which contained some false information about Agafya Mikhailovna.[40] I wrote to Sasha and Ilya about the plans for Yasnaya Polyana, and to Zhdanov about the same thing. I visited the grave.

9 I had a visit from Vengerov, who is preparing Tolstoy's works and a biography for the firm of Brockhaus and Efron. I devoted the whole day to him and gave him various pieces of information.[41] This morning I visited

the grave and left flowers. I saw Lev Nikolaevich vividly in a dream, and that made me very happy. Vengerov arrived with Bulgakov.

12 A great many visitors – the Volkhonskiis (husband, wife and daughter), Kaufmann, the wife of the former minister of communications – and we all went to the grave together. Later this evening, 15 young people came – cadets, young girls and so on. After dinner I went to visit Sasha with Verochka. She has a lovely little place.[42] I am glad we are now on good terms.

20 I helped Bulgakov with his work on the library, showed the rooms to 30 waiters from vegetarian canteens in Moscow and read about suicide and spiritualism.

29 Osman the Circassian is wretched. They have refused to allow him and his brother to go home to their native country. The poor old man was sobbing and in a state of despair – I wanted to cry too.[43]

30 My son Lyova has come, to my great joy. He wants to stay with us for a while.

August 3 Spiro came and insisted that I give him something for the *Argus*.[44]

6 Pav. Iv. Biryukov came for the day and we inserted dates and years into his biography of Lev Nikol.

11 I picked flowers, walked to the grave and decorated it, talking loudly to my dead Lyovochka as I did so; we haven't been completely separated – I always feel his presence here in Yasnaya. He is *not* happy and *not* at peace, and I pray for his soul. Sasha was here, I'm happy to say, and explained a great deal to me.

12 I sent a telegram to Spiro refusing to give him an article.

13 Boris Petr. Brio, a correspondent for the *Russian Word*, came asking for information about Turgenev.[45]

18 I wrote an application for Osman to return to the Caucasus.[46] I started work on my *Autobiography*.[47]

20 I spent all morning and afternoon writing a short *Autobiography* for Vengerov.

21 Lena Feret visited with her friend, a young girl of 16 or 17. Then Lopukhin the governor arrived with an official and some guards. Then an official called Pav. Il. Popov came about some statistics. I was busy all day.

22 My 69th birthday today – I feel so old! It poured with rain all morning. Dushan Petrovich came for dinner, and Sasha arrived late with Onechka Denisenko.

24 Sonya Bibikova brought a priest's daughter here, and I have taken her on as my companion;[48] she is very sympathetic.

26 I worked on my *Autobiography*, then played Weber sonatas for a long time. Lyova, Bulgakov and I had long conversations about war, the social order and so on.

28 Lev Nik.'s birthday. The Gorbunovs came, and Sasha, Dima Chertkov, Boulanger, all the Yasnaya peasants and various Telyatinki types all went to the grave. The peasants sang 'Eternal Memory' and everyone prostrated themselves three times. I dined with Zvegintseva and Princess Cherkasskaya, who were with an officer I didn't know. I am reading La Bruyère. I have finished a rough draft of my *Autobiography*.

September 1 Some peasant victims of a fire in Telyatinki arrived and I gave them just 10 rubles. Dushan Petrovich visited briefly and took the *Complete Collected Works*. This evening I read some interesting memoirs of Guy de Maupassant by a woman.[49]

2 I went to the grave with some flowers, packed my bag and prepared to leave for Moscow; I put flowers before all the portraits. Lyova is sculpting an excellent bust of Bulgakov.[50] He has completely recovered his health.

3 I have been sent the finished copies of *L.N. Tolstoy's Letters to His Wife*. I bade Lyova a tender farewell and left for Moscow.

4 (Moscow) Attended to various business matters this morning. Took an announcement to the newspapers, paid Levenson 1,000 rubles for the book.[51] Petitioned the administrators about Skosyryov, the Zaseka stationmaster.

14 Worked on my *Autobiography* until almost two in the morning, then read Landau's *Moses*.[52]

15 Read my *Autobiography* to Bulgakov, Medvedev and Saltanov. A telegram from some Germans about the translation of Lev Nik.'s letters to me.[53] A visit this morning from six intellectuals.

17 Didn't fall asleep until 6 this morning. My name-day. My guests were Ilya and Sonya, Salomon, Garin the writer, Sonya Bibikova, Zvegintseva and Prince and Princess Cherkasskii. Sonya and Bibikov sang one or two things excellently. I read aloud my *Autobiography*, and they all criticised it as too personal and intimate.

19 I wrote various documents about the translation of Lev Nik.'s letters to me. Despite the book's great success, I now feel sad that I've thrown my holy of holies to the crowd.

22 I sent the manuscript about Lev Nik.'s visits to Optyna Pustyn to the Petersburg Tolstoy Museum;[54] I spent the whole evening copying it out. I sorted out some photographs and put papers in order.

25 (Kochety) Did a little work on my *Autobiography*. It's going badly. Very hard.

26 I wrote a lot of my *Autobiography*, played wooden dolls with the children and watched a game of charades.

27 Last night I wrote my *Autobiography* until 3.30 a.m., and today I read it to Tanya and Sukhotin.[55] I try to be honest, and to write in an interesting, compressed style, and it's very hard. Little Tanya and Mika played charades; they're so sweet. I am very happy here.

28 I have looked through my *Autobiography* again, and am disturbed by the words 'close person'.[56]

October 1 I read and corrected Lev Nikol.'s letters to me. Reading them makes me both agitated and happy. There was a frost this evening, and I worry about how I shall get home.

2 Still in Kochety, re-reading my husband's letters and revising them for a second edition.[57] I sit with Tanyushka and her parents.

4 My daughter Tanya's birthday. We all took a walk together. A very cold wind, but fine. I'm sad to be leaving for home. Who will meet me there. . . ? I have no one!

5 I returned to Yasnaya. Two outsiders, Saltanov and Bulgakov, warmly welcomed me home and I'm grateful even for them. The journey to Mtsensk was frightful – frost, mud, snow, frozen roads, unbearably bumpy. It was sad parting with the two Tanyas.

6 Antonina Tikhonovna, my new companion, has arrived. She read aloud L.N.'s letters to Strakhov and various articles.

7 I spent the whole day outside; cold and bright, with a north wind. I went to the grave with a bunch of chrysanthemums, which are blooming in the drawing-room. Then I helped the workmen tidy up the barn and the firewood. This evening I sorted out some French newspaper cuttings from the *Argus de la Presse*,[58] from the time of Lev Nik.'s departure and death. I sent Nikitin *L.N.'s Letters to His Wife.*

8 Spent the evening with Saltanov, pasting in foreign newspaper cuttings from 1910 about L.N.'s death. I am reading Landau's booklets. Very bad![59]

16 Copied and corrected my *Autobiography* all morning, then coached the little girl, then copied and corrected again till 2 in the morning. I'm pining away without my children's love, or any news from them. I should have died long ago.

18 Went to the grave with some lovely chrysanthemums and leaves. Had a talk with Taras about the vexing problem of the peasants, and how to allot the firewood – to each soul or each stove. I urged the latter, and this was what was finally agreed. I sawed some bushes, corrected the proofs of my article on Lev Nik.'s four visits to Optyna Pustyn,[60] and copied. Sad and lonely!

21 Read N.V. Davydov's *From the Past.*[61] Visitors arrived to see the rooms – Baron Wrangel with some children and young people.

22 I am reading Davydov's book and one or two other things – some poems by Khomyakov and Aksakov, an English novel and so on.

25 This evening I read Davydov's *From the Past.* I find his description of Chertkov most unpleasant, and much of it is quite inaccurate.[62] It's not written from the viewpoint of the truth, but from his own personal attitude to everything and everyone.

26 All evening I read Davydov's *From the Past.* A lot of it is close to me, and very interesting.

27 Tonight it will be three years since Lev Nik. left. It's not surprising I feel so depressed every autumn. Today I copied one or two more things into my *Autobiography*, and this evening Antonina Tikhonovna read Davydov's memoirs to me, which I found most interesting.

28 Cheerless weather, rain and wind. This life is very depressing, however brave one tries to be. A little letter from Lyova – he loves me, and so I think does Tanya, and this is the only light in my life. I wrote to Davydov about his book, which we are reading aloud.[63]

29 Zosya Stakhovich came, lively, intelligent and kind as ever. I read her my *Autobiography* and she criticised the ending.

30 Sasha and Dushan Petrovich came, Zosya Stakhovich left. I sorted library books and entered them in the catalogue. I am reading an English novel in translation; they write better than the Russians. A great fuss in the newspapers about the acquittal of Beilis.[64]

November 1 Cold, wind, rain. Went to the grave with Sonya, Kiryusha and Nina. Discussed my *Autobiography* with Sonya; we decided that I should try to restrain my personal anger, so as not to give rise to polemics from the opposing side.

2 Sonya and Kiryusha left, and Andryusha arrived for dinner. I wrote to Minister Krivoshein at his request, and sent him the book of *Letters*. I also wrote to Shamin about the house,[65] and gave my permission for visitors to come and inspect the house and L.N.'s rooms.

3 I spent the whole day writing a new version of my *Autobiography*; this was very hard. Antonina Tikhonovna read *From the Past* to me.

4 Prince Nakashidze came this morning with his 9-year-old nephew, a typical little Georgian, and Dosev, whom I received most coldly after the letter he wrote while L.N. was still alive, about his desire to leave.[66] I finished looking through the *Letters*; then sorted out some Georgian newspaper cuttings.

5 This evening I read Nik. Nik. Strakhov's correspondence with L.N. Tolstoy; Strakhov always delves so deeply into his own inner life. I pasted Russian newspaper cuttings into a new book.

7 The third anniversary of Lev Nikolaevich's death – three years have passed, yet it's still very painful! I spent the day well. I went to the grave as soon as I got up – there were already various visitors there. Then about a

hundred people came to the house, mostly young people. My four sons came, Seryozha, Ilya, Andryusha and Misha. Then two ladies came, the daughter of N.I. Storozhenko and her friend. Seryozha played, Bulgakov sang, good discussions. Andryusha and Misha have now left.

8 Everyone left this morning – Seryozha, Ilya and the two ladies. I have hired a new Circassian, after successfully petitioning for our Osman to return to his own country. I did some sewing, and this evening I copied various writers' autographs and dedications to Lev Nik–ch from various foreign books here.

9 I have settled into a routine of work and silence. I coached the little girl, read a lot of articles about Lev Nik.'s death, and sent a correction to *Russian Word* – the word 'stoves' instead of 'children'.[67]

10 I did a great deal of typing today, and am still busy with my *Autobiography*. Seryozha took it away to make some corrections to it.

12 Sasha came, talked to the peasants about their affairs, had dinner and is staying the night here.

18 I coached the little girl, and spent the rest of the day copying my *Autobiography* on the typewriter, making corrections as I went along. Solemnly said goodbye to the Circassians, and took visitors around Lev Nik.'s rooms.

23 **(Moscow)** Went out on business this morning with Nina; the manager of Levenson's came to visit, and said that my book, *Letters to His Wife*, had almost sold out.

24 Spent the morning at home, wrote to Bulgakov and sat with Mikhail Sergeevich, who has a bad leg. (He is staying in the room next to mine in the Slavonic Bazaar.) I invited some people here for a reading of my *Autobiography* – Buturlin, Nikitin, Berkenheim, Sukhotin and Molostvova. They discussed it and all decided that I should not offend Chertkov. My son Ilya also came to see me. I dined with Sasha.

26 Mikh. Al. Stakhovich was here and I read him my *Autobiography*; everyone advises me against publishing the ending, but I've already softened it so much.

28 I drove to the Maslovs' for dinner and read them my *Autobiography*. Everyone I read it to makes their own suggestions, and I now feel thoroughly confused.

29 I packed and left for Yasnaya Polyana. Everything is all right here; Bulgakov was happy to see us.

30 I went to the grave. The same silent, sombre, hopeless little hillock, inducing such depression and such sad memories. I read various articles – sister Tanya's about Maria Nikolaevna,[68] Lev Nik.'s letter to S.A. Rachinskii, and so on.[69]

December 1 I wrote to Vengerov, Varya Nagornova and Golubyov about the three volumes.[70] Then I tidied books, sorted out business papers and letters and read an article about Lev Nik. and his correspondence with Strakhov.

3 I read Dostoyevsky's *The Possessed* again after dinner, then sight-read a little of Gluck's *Orpheus* and Mozart's *Don Giovanni*. I sat and talked about books with Bulgakov.

4 I am working hard on all sorts of things. After dinner we read *The Possessed* again and before dinner I played some Beethoven sonatas. I am reading L.N. Tolstoy's correspondence with Strakhov, but there are very few letters from L.N.; Chertkov had them, and he stole the best and longest of them.[71]

5 The same as usual: coached the bailiff's little girl, sewed and played the piano for a long time this evening trying to forget myself, and stop myself grieving and worrying. Bulgakov read me today's instalment of Ilya's memoirs,[72] which wasn't very good.

6 St Nicholas' Day, a church holiday and Andryusha's birthday. Poor fellow, what a weak-willed eternal sufferer he is! This evening Bulgakov read me an article by Rozanov about Strakhov and others.[73] Very bad!

7 I revised my *Autobiography*, and at 4 o'clock Andryusha arrived; he has grown very sickly, and I always feel so sorry for him for some reason. I was glad to see him; he never forgets me and always livens up my loneliness.

11 We read in *Speech* about the drawing up of Lev Nik.'s will, and the old pain flared up in my heart once again.[74] Distressing conversation with Bulgakov.

12 I copied and revised yet again my *Autobiography*, then read Ilya's memoirs. Tomorrow is the Senate's decision on the fate of the manuscripts in the Historical Museum, and I'm not really very worried!

13 I sent 25 rubles to the priest who performed the funeral service for Lev Nik.[75] We are still reading *The Possessed.*

14 Did a lot of typing – finished copying my *Autobiography*. We read *The Possessed.* Nothing has been decided in the Senate; there was one vote too few in my favour.[76]

15 Nina and I checked my *Autobiography* against the rough draft. I am tired of it, it has brought back so many painful memories. I played part of a Weber sonata; Lev Nik. loved these sonatas once, and used himself to practise them diligently.

17 We have started reading Dostoyevsky's *The Idiot.*

19 Bulgakov's guests have left. A German came with his Russian wife, and we discussed a German translation of L.N.'s letters to me. I shall lose my exclusive rights to them if I don't publish them in a book and keep the rights. We read *The Idiot.*

21 I read *The Idiot*. Bulgakov left. Dostoyevsky is so coarse; I don't like him.

22 I went at last to the grave; the weather was most unpleasant and my soul was desolate. I prayed all the way. Young G.V. Serov came and took away his father's portrait of me for an exhibition.[77] This evening we gilded nuts for the Christmas tree.

23 The pre-Christmas commotion is quite unbearable because it's so joyless. Bulgakov came, and has left for Moscow. This evening we read Gruzinskii's article about Tolstoy's letters,[78] then some Dostoyevsky.

27 I copied Lev Nik.'s diaries, then played for a long time this evening to soften the painful impression Lev Nik.'s last diary made on me.

28 My daughter-in-law Masha came, with Seryozha my grandson and his English tutor. My son Seryozha arrived via Nikolskoe. I have now finished copying Lev Nik.'s first and last diaries, starting from when we got married.

30 I spent the morning completely alone, but had some delightful letters from various grandchildren. This evening I lit up the Christmas tree for all the servants' children. They recited poems, and we played the gramophone, and I think everyone had a good time. Sonya Bibikova came,

and Nina's sister. Medvedev and Lyova Sergeenko came to see Bulgakov, and I invited them upstairs.

31 Seryozha, Andryusha and his wife came; Sasha too was here, and we had a nice New Year's party, without much merriment but very amicable. I was grateful to them for not letting me pine away here on my own. After supper Sasha suddenly appeared again with Varvara Mikhailovna. Bulgakov sang and Seryozha played – very well too. A sunny day, a brilliant sunset, a quiet moonlit night. That strange but pathetic Sonya Bibikova visited.

· 1914 ·

Summer – strike movement reaches its highest point since 1904–6 and violent demonstrations greet President Poincaré of France when he visits St Petersburg. June 28 – Archduke Ferdinand of Austria assassinated in Sarajevo. July 28 – Austria declares war on Serbia and Belgrade bombarded. Tsar Nicholas II orders mobilisation. August 2 – Russia enters war (to protect Serbia). August 4 – England declares war on Germany. Waves of patriotism sweep Russia and there is a lull in strikes and demonstrations. August 17 – Russian 'steamroller' invades East Prussia. By mid-September some 50,000 Russians killed. Growing discontent at home. September 5 – anti-German alliance formalised, binding France, Russia and Great Britain not to conclude separate peace and to reach preliminary agreement as to its terms.

March – legal dispute over manuscripts finally settled in Sofia's favour. Summer – Yasnaya Polyana empties as peasants conscripted. Sofia, horrified by the war, is dismayed when her son Andrei enlists and her daughter Aleksandra enrols as a nurse at the Turkish front, and finds her ideas becoming closer to her husband's. October – police visit Yasnaya Polyana at night, search it and arrest Tolstoy's former secretary Valentin Bulgakov. Sofia finishes work on My Life.

January 1 The start of another year, and I am still alive. Andryusha and Katya have left. Sasha came with Mansfeld. I read him my autobiography, and at the end he began to cry. Seryozha played beautifully all evening – Beethoven sonatas and other things.

4 Nik. Nik. Bogdanov, treasurer of the Moscow Tolstoy Museum, came with his wife. Nina has returned. I spent the whole day sorting and tidying journals, books and newspapers.

5 Worked all day with Nina sorting and tidying books, journals and newspapers. I am reading Pankratov's article about L.N.; very poor.[1]

6 Tidied, catalogued and stamped the books in the library. I had a visit from V.I. Alekseev, who used to be my children's teacher,[2] and it was so pleasant to remember happier times with him. This evening I read Dostoyevsky. A terrible earthquake in Japan. It's quite unbelievable, like a fairy-story.

9 Today I started copying out my letters to my husband, a long and difficult task as all the years and dates are muddled up.[3] We read Dostoyevsky's *The Idiot* aloud. There were several visitors to Lev Nikolaevich's grave and rooms.

10 I copied my letters and finished reading *The Idiot*. I shall now read Chirikov's novel and Yakubovskii's book *Positive Peasant Characters in the Work of Tolstoy*.[4]

11 I took some flowers to the grave and cleared the snow from the hillock where lies the man I once loved so long and passionately. I fed the birds again, prayed and wept. It is now four years since Lyovochka died, and I feel just the same. Did a lot of copying. Dushan Petrovich came.

12 Spent the day with Dushan Petrovich. In many ways I find him very alien – there's something obtuse about him – but I like him none the less, maybe because he loved Lev Nikol., and I am always sad when he leaves. I copied my letters to my husband and played the piano.

13 I am copying my letters to my husband – 15 pages a day is my quota. I am reading Chirikov's *Return*;[5] he writes well. Nina has returned with her brother, Dushan Petrovich has left.

14 Bulgakov returned and started working on the library again. I wrote to my daughter-in-law Sonya, and to the Piccadilly Club about the book of letters.[6]

16 My son Ilya came to dinner with my grandson Andryusha and his teacher, Nik. Vlad. Vavilov, expelled from the fourth year of the natural history faculty when Moscow University was turned upside down by that scoundrel Kasso.[7]

19 I wrote a little and read Timkovskii's book *The Soul of Tolstoy*.[8] Ilya is making a copy, and is writing an article about Déroulède's visit to Yasnaya Polyana.[9]

28 Did some copying, coached the little girl, played both pianos, and this evening sorted out letters with Bulgakov. Gruzinskii has edited them so

badly, and we have to put them right.[10] Lev Nik.'s letters and mine evoked such a lot of memories; it's both cheering and depressing to recall my undoubted happiness.

February 1 These past few evenings I've been reading, or rather looking through the *Pensées de Pascal* and the *Circle of Reading*. The Chertkovs have been searched by the police.[11] I am interested in the new change of ministers.

2 I can hardly get up in the mornings when I realise how useless my life is. I did a lot of copying and embroidering, and this evening Nina read me a pamphlet, sent to me by a certain Golubkov, called 'L.N. Tolstoy as God-Seeker'.[12] Not bad.

3 I read Andreev's story about a dead aviator – very artificial.[13] I feel terribly agitated.

4 This evening Nina read me Turgenev's *Faust*, which I had forgotten, then we corrected *Tolstoy's Letters to His Wife*. And so it goes every day. It's as though life had frozen. I think a lot and grieve that I see so little of my children and grandchildren, but I have neither the physical nor spiritual strength to raise myself up.

7 My son Lyova arrived – an unexpected pleasure; also the artist Saltanov.

8 Delightful weather: the earth is covered in last night's snow, and the whiteness is enchanting. I went to the grave with Lyova; we took flowers, and food for the birds, although there weren't any today. Silence, the barometer is at zero. Saltanov has left: Lyova played the piano for a long time, then played chess with Saltanov. I did a little copying.

13 Dushan Petrovich came; he will be in Kochety until May. I am reading Chirikov's *Return*, and *Mont-Oriol* in French.[14] Bulgakov and I have finished correcting the letters.

14 40 students from Shanyavskii University came to visit the grave and the house. There were some women with them too. I chattered on for far too long about Sasha and Chertkov. Then I copied out 28 pages of my letters. I have finished reading Turgenev's *The Calm*.

22 We read some Turgenev this evening. I am reading Strakhov's old article 'Rumours about Tolstoy';[15] I sorted out, copied and arranged

chronologically my letters to L.N. It's painful to re-live all our old sufferings and arguments in them. I played a Mozart concerto.

23 The anniversary of Vanechka's death. I went to the grave – there's water everywhere. Then I read and knitted and read aloud some silly stories in *The Contemporary*. A German was here with his wife; they want to translate *L.N. Tolstoy's Letters to His Wife*.[16]

24 My son Ilya came, energetic and good-natured as always, bringing me oranges and candied fruit. He corrected the copy of Repin's portrait of Lev Nik. He is reading Lev Nik.'s old diaries (up to 1861), which I copied out long ago.

25 I got up late; Ilya had just started work on his copy, which was looking much better by this evening. Ilyusha is such pleasant company when he is in good spirits. Someone has suggested that he should travel around the cities of Russia giving lectures about his father.[17]

March 6 (St Petersburg) I visited Lyova and dined with them; the children were adorable. I talked on the telephone with N.A. Dobrovolskii about my case in the Senate concerning the manuscripts. He said: 'I simply cannot understand why they're dragging out this business so long.'[18]

10 (St Petersburg) This morning Dora and I went to the Wanderers' Exhibition. It was very weak in subject-matter, and even technique; Repin's *The Duel*, or rather *Single Combat*, is so much worse than his earlier works.[19]

11 I returned to Yasnaya via Tula – a frosty, overcast day. I found Varya Nagornova at home with her daughter Ada. My lodgers Bulgakov and Nina are also very pleasant. This evening we read aloud 'Lermontov and Tolstoy'.[20]

12 I wrote a letter to the Tsar, asking for a place for Andryusha. I find this most difficult and disagreeable, but Andryusha is so ill and anxious that I was afraid to refuse him. I have sent him the letter to read through.[21] My guests and servants all had a lively evening: Bulgakov sang, Sonya Bibikova accompanied him and they laughed and played cards all evening. I have a great many household matters to see to.

13 I worked on some material for the new chapter I have been asked to write for my *Autobiography*.[22] Sonya Bibikova came and we played

duets – Weber's 'Invitation to the Waltz', Mozart's Jupiter Symphony and a quintet also by him.

17 A rude outburst from Bulgakov,[23] very distressed and couldn't do any work – apart from copying out my letters to my husband. Varya and I read L.N.'s last little diary, which made me terribly sad![24] We played a Mozart symphony as a duet, and this evening we read aloud 'Lermontov and Tolstoy'. Very poor.

18 Slight frost, everything covered with a light layer of snow, fine weather, dazzling stars, a bright moon. I coached the little girl, worked hard on my new chapter, and this evening we again read aloud 'Lermontov and Tolstoy'. A letter from Kuzminskii about the favourable outcome of my case in the Senate concerning the manuscripts.[25]

24 I sent off the new chapter from my *Autobiography* to Vengerov.[26]

26 Bulgakov has left for Moscow to give a lecture about the library at Yasnaya Polyana.[27]

27 Copied; this evening we read 'Tolstoy and Turgenev', then I read my 'Groans', from the *Journal for All*, March 1904. Varenka and Nina very much liked these prose poems of mine.

30 Nina and I started fasting today, and we went to church. This great mass of people – i.e. the peasants – is still so foreign to me, even though I have lived with them for almost 52 years. There's something wild and incomprehensible about them.

April 10 25 visitors came to the house and the grave, then all our peasants arrived to invite me to the grave. But alas, I was still ill!

16 Nina and I read my daughter Tanya's book about Maria Montessori, the Italian who practises free educational methods.[28]

20 I went for my first walk of the year. It was so good – spring is really here! But with none of the old joys of spring. I picked lungworts, blue snowdrops and yellow and violet-coloured flowers for Lyovochka's and Vanechka's portraits. Where are they, my dear ones . . .

25 A former priest named G.S. Petrov came to visit; he went to the grave with his companion, Marchenko, and they both drank coffee with me. We all roundly reviled Kasso and Chertkov. This evening we read aloud Lermontov's 'Masquerade'.

May 8 (Moscow) Polyonov the artist came with his daughter. He's still a very lively old man and loves all art, but he has grown very garrulous. I visited the Tolstoy Museum – it made a sad impression!

10 Visited the grave and took flowers. I met three village children there and took them home, where I gave them sweets and played them the gramophone. But they didn't seem to enjoy themselves particularly. I am reading the letters of the Prelate Feofan.[29]

11 I made an inventory of the things on Lev Nik.'s desk and on the table in his room.

13 Today's guests were Dm. Kulishov, Princess Shakhovskaya and a young lady named Tulubeva. Bulgakov left for Siberia and bade us a touching farewell. Ilya Vasilevich and his wife have suddenly decided to leave, which makes me very sad. They're tired of serving and have had enough. Quite understandably! I visited the grave and decorated it beautifully with flowers. This evening I read Feofan's letters about the spiritual life.[30]

15 (Ascension Day) We didn't count the visitors, but I think there must have been about 150. Antonina Tikhonovna and I let them in. I copied the list of all the things in Lev Nik.'s rooms and felt so sad!

18 My son Andryusha came. There was an excursion of 62 young girls here, and various other visitors as well, and I showed them round Lev Nik.'s rooms. Towards 8 this evening my son Lyova came with his two sons Kita and Petya. My sons told me many interesting things, and I loved seeing them! But I am not myself.

20 Lyova's 45th birthday. We had an unexpected visit from Vl. Mikh. Doroshevich, one of the main contributors to the *Russian Word*. We went to the grave twice and took flowers. Sasha and Varvara Mikhailovna came.

23 This evening I sewed up parcels of photographs of the Moscow houses, which I shall send to the Moscow and Petersburg Museums.[31]

26 I am still not used to the children's noise, though it's nice to have some life around me again. I did a little copying, and this evening I played some Weber violin sonatas; I wanted to play them again with the Frenchwoman who came with Lyova. Then I discussed Lev Nik.'s diaries with Lyova and Dora.

31 I copied, visited the grave and went for a long walk. (My eyes are aching with neuralgia, which is a nuisance, and I am resting them.) I am so sad to hear that my sons have started playing cards. Dora says Lyova has lost about 50 thousand. Poor, pregnant, considerate Dora! Lev Nik. was a thousand times right to give his money to the peasants, rather than to his sons. It would only have gone on cards and carousing. It's disgusting, sad and pathetic! And it will be even worse after my death! A hot fine day. Nature is delightful, but my soul is depressed. I didn't sleep all night. Lyova returned on the morning of June 1.*

June 1 I had a visit from Serg. Step. Ermolaev, director of the Levenson printworks, a relative of his called Yurii Venyaminovich, and a Czech photographer called Wiedmann who made prints of my negatives to make them into postcards. I spent the evening with the children.

13 We all drove to the river for a swim, just like in the old days, in two separate trips, with the children and governesses, and Lyova's three boys, who drove with their father. It was very hot – 24 ° in the shade. They've started mowing the old orchard. When we got home I read *Evgenii Onegin* to the boys.

19 I was engrossed all morning in Pushkin's stories; I haven't looked at them for such a long time.

25 We all go swimming and love it. I did a lot of copying this morning and finished the 5th book of my letters to my husband. My daughter Tanya has returned from Tula and Andryusha came to dinner. We spent the second part of the day very pleasantly and went to bed late. Andryusha has left.

30 I spent the whole day copying out my letters, and felt so sad. It's all too late! I wrote to Zhdanov regarding the money left after Lev Nik.'s death, and to whom it should be sent.[32]

July 2 I read the newspapers and short stories, and have neither the leisure nor the inclination for any serious reading. All the papers are filled with news of Rasputin's murder.[33]

5 Today I visited the grave with flowers and prayed. There was no one there, which was good. I copied a rough version of the letter I wrote to Chertkov in 1910.[34] I endlessly re-live the past, and it's very painful. It's a joy to watch the children's young lives at close quarters, even though one

*Added later.

doesn't take an active part in them. But it's saddening to see their mother, with all her illnesses and her worries.

16 I copied and read the papers with alarm – is it really war?

18 Depressed all morning – life is so pointless. I wrote Lyova a postcard and am sending him his manuscript from the editorial offices of the *New Times*.[35] I read aloud a story in the *Herald of Europe* called 'The Lucky Woman'. Very bad.[36]

19 This ghastly war will lead to great misery in Russia. Everyone is despondent. People who are being torn from their land and their families are talking of a strike: 'We won't go to war!' they say. From here they've taken the bailiff, seven horses, the coachman and two workers! And meanwhile Russia is starving! What will happen!

20 This morning I sat down to copy my letters. What a lot of suffering I've had in my life! I copied up to December 1900, when little Levushka died.[37] Tanya gave birth to a dead baby girl and so on. And I was with them all, and wept with them all.

21 I have a heavy weight on my heart. My son Misha has been conscripted and sent off to Bryansk. They've also taken Karing, our bailiff, and our peasants and horses. Tears and terror on all sides – and all in the name of what? I shall never understand war!

27 I wandered around Yasnaya Polyana all day with an aching heart, waiting for Andryusha who is ill; he wrote that Misha would be in Tula on Tuesday, and that I should go there and give him 1,000 rubles. They are enlisting him in the *active* regiments – the cavalry – and that is yet another blow for me. Sasha was here, and is going off to be a nurse. We tenderly said goodbye to one another. It's all terrible! Here in the country it's sunny, still and warm.

28 The news is all terrible: Lyova has sent his family off to Sweden and is leaving with N.S. Guchkov for the Polish frontier as a Red Cross representative. Magnificent hot weather, a lot of mushrooms – and on all sides there are groans and tears. A group of 20 women visitors came to see the grave and the house.

29 So much suffering – yet one continues to live and endure it! I said goodbye today to my son Misha who is off to war! I forced myself not to cry, and it was terribly hard! Andryusha is no cause for joy either: he's having difficulties with his wife, he has a limp, bad intestines and bronchitis, poor fellow, and is very thin. I am utterly exhausted in body and soul!

31 I walked through the forest with Nina but didn't find any mushrooms: the villagers pick a lot of the white ones. I see to the housework and the estate – all in a dream. I spent the whole evening alone. I shall never get used to this painful solitude, yet to go away and leave Yasnaya Polyana, the bailiff, the servants and all my things, would be unthinkable. My soul is in the same state as it was that October when Lev Nikolaevich left – it's as though everything has changed – nature, people, everything. I have the same ache in the pit of my stomach on the left side, the same sense of hopelessness. I worry terribly about Misha, God save him! I'm afraid for Lyova and Sasha too, although they're both doing peaceful work with the Red Cross. And I feel so sorry for Andryusha, ill and unhappy. There's no happiness anywhere, in fact!

August 1 I didn't sleep last night, and this morning I went to Mass with Nurse.[38] The church was filled with women – there were almost no men. The deacon shrieked some incomprehensible words, and it was all very sad! My alienation from the people is sad too; I am the *only lady* amidst this peasant population, and the children regard me as something strange and foreign.

2 I walked with Nina to the grave, then to the woods. Bulgakov has returned from Siberia, and I am very happy to see him.

3 Nadechka Ivanova came, then Sonya, Ilya's wife, and she and I had good talk about everyday and spiritual matters. Bad news from Tanya – Sukhotin had a stroke while staying at the Abrikosovs', but since the 1st has been getting better.

4 Bulgakov has left for Chertkov's house. I wandered about the estate. Memories everywhere, but no life, just melancholy. This evening Nina read me Turgenev's *Rudin* as a diversion, but I found it dull and dated. I also am too old for novels now.

5 I cannot do anything sensible or intelligent – I'm overwhelmed by dull grief! I have made everything ready for the Kuzminskiis' arrival. I read the papers almost every day. This evening I was shocked by the sad news that Mikh. Serg. Sukhotin had had a second stroke. My poor Tanechkas!

8 An eclipse of the sun. Varya Nagornova came and I was very pleased to see her. This evening we glued together some booklets from proof

pages to give to the guards in the orchard to read.[39] Bad news from Tanya. Her letter tormented my already aching heart.

9 I received a telegram announcing the death of M.S. Sukhotin. I packed hurriedly and prepared to leave for Kochety. My heart was filled with such grief and despair, yet I had to see to everything at home before I left. My poor, sad, wretched Tanya!

10 I went by coach to Kochety. They have brought Sukhotin's body home from the Abrikosovs'. Tanya is trying to keep cheerful and is organising everything, but she looks so thin, tense and anxious, it breaks my heart to see her. God help her!

11 Tanya, little Tanya and I all went for a walk, then sat together. The four sons have arrived to bury their father. My Sasha is here too, and Liza Obolenskaya and our Seryozha. There will be a requiem mass.

13 The Kochety house is empty now. Tanya is being very brave and is not letting herself go, but it's very hard for her, for she loved her sick old man; her life will be quite different now and it won't be easy! And what about the war? We are all gripped with terror by the events of this ghastly war!

14 After our walk today Tanya read us her work *Tanya Tolstoy's Childhood*.[40] It's excellent, and most movingly written. Even we shed a few tears as we listened to her reading it. She and her daughter are planning to spend the winter with me. How good that will be. I can hardly believe it!

15 We went for another walk, and again listened to Tanya reading her work. We saw Dorik and Seryozha Sukhotin off to their regiment – Dorik as a volunteer and Seryozha as an officer. The elder Sukhotin, Lev, is distraught, and we are all very sad. I have packed and shall leave tomorrow.

16 Varya and I got up very early, and at 7 we left Kochety in the Sukhotins' troika for Mtsensk. There we met Liza Obolenskaya. They wouldn't give us tickets, as there were no seats, but we begged the stationmaster, and eventually he allowed us on to the train, where we sat on our suitcases. The talk everywhere is of the war, everyone has their sorrow. At home everything was as usual.

22 My sister Tanya Kuzminskaya came this morning, and her husband Aleks. Mikh. came for dinner. Today is my birthday; I am 70.

25 I read the Kuzminskiis my autobiography; everyone praises it highly.

28 We read the newspapers and suffer for our loved ones at war.

29 Varya Nagornova has left, D.P. Makovitsky has arrived.

September 5 Drove to the swimming pool in the carriage with Nina and the Kuzminskiis, then back through Zaseka, and coming out on to the highway. We all marvelled at the warmth, the autumn tints and the picturesqueness of the road. When we got home I set to work raking leaves into piles. I received an account of Sukhotin's death from my daughter Tanya, and a beautiful letter from his son Alya.

7 I wandered about aimlessly; I can't do anything with this frightful war on, and with grief and worry for Tanya, fear for my sons and anxiety about Dora, who should be giving birth any day. I raked up piles of leaves for cattle bedding, gave the day-labourers their receipts and spent the evening doing accounts with Nina. Dushan Petrovich and I then had tea with the Kuzminskiis in their wing.

11 I go out and work in the garden raking dead leaves until I'm exhausted; I want to forget myself, escape these persistent thoughts about the war, my children and grandchildren. I read the papers, throw them aside, pick them up again – and oh, the sadness, the sadness! I am reading 'What Is the Spiritual Life?' by Feofan.

17 My name-day, a day full of memories. I picked flowers, went to the grave and decorated it. It was drizzling quietly. I received a lot of telegrams, one from Lyova to say he would be arriving tonight. This evening Tanya and Bulgakov sang, and Mikulich read us a short story. But my soul has no need of songs.

25 My Andryusha came, bringing Ilya's wife Sonya with him. Later on Bulgakov went to collect Andryusha and Olga's daughter Sonya, and we all spent a pleasant evening together. I read Ilya's article from the war.[41]

26 This evening my sister Tanya read me her memoirs, which I found very interesting.[42]

27 My sister is distraught because her son Mitya has also volunteered for the war, as an orderly. Incomprehensible hypnotism! We read aloud Makovitsky's memoirs.

29 I picked a beautiful bunch of fresh flowers, and walked with my sister to the grave, then on to the river, to the place where in the old days we had our swimming pool. It was good to walk with Tanya, but sad to see them chopping down the trees, and to realise that now they were no longer ours. A bright frosty day. I read a lovely article by Leroy-Beaulieu about Lev Nikolaevich in the *Revue des deux Mondes*, of December 15, 1910.[43] Tregubov came.

30 I did some typing for my sister. This evening Bulgakov read us his article protesting against the war; it was very good.[44]

October 1 I showed various visitors around Lev Nik.'s rooms and the drawing-room – some officers who had been to the war, two army doctors, Al. Serg. Levitskii and a lady. They were touchingly interested in everything.

2 Sister Tanya has left. A beautiful still bright day. I went out and wandered around the estate; they've planted some apple trees, gathered up the brushwood and raked the dead leaves, and I too swept some up into four piles. We read the papers. There were 6 visitors today – some officers, some army doctors and two women. They looked round the drawing-room and Lev Nik.'s rooms.

4 My Tanya's birthday. I went to Tula with Nina, and there I saw Grisha Tolstoy, Sergei Nikolaevich's son. He has received another post. On the way back I met an entire battery of soldiers and officers, who had been to Yasnaya Polyana; I am very sorry that I didn't see them and receive them personally. I sent Lyova 1,000 rubles.

6 I had a letter from Tanya saying that she would arrive here on the 8th or 9th. We read aloud two articles by Kropotkin.[45]

8 I revised *L.N. Tolstoy's Letters to His Wife*, then played the piano for a long time – a Weber sonata, a Mendelssohn 'Song Without Words' and so on. I feel starved of music.

9 I had intended to work on revising the letters this morning, but I was drawn instead to the piano and played for a long time, trying to pass the time before Tanya's arrival. Then they all arrived – the two Tanechkas, Miss Welsh, S.I. Lavrentieva and Ganya the maid. My granddaughter Tanechka is delightful, and Tanya is so close and dear to me. This evening we had a good talk.

11 I did some more writing, then talked to my granddaughter and showed her her mother's childhood paintings. This evening I catalogued books.

12 Unpleasant news in yesterday's *Russian Gazette* about the Senate's refusal to award me the manuscripts.[46]

13 This evening Tanya read us her beautifully written memoirs of her childhood.[47]

15 This evening Tanya read us the story about an old Swedish man who arrived here during the famine, in 1891 or '2, I don't exactly remember.[48]

16 This evening we read aloud *The Kolychev Patrimony*.[49]

18 The American consulate has informed me that my grandson Misha has been taken prisoner in Milevič, in Bohemia.[50]

21 I received a letter from Al. Mikh. Kuzminskii telling me that I had won my case in the Senate,[51] and giving me some sad family news: Masha is ill, Mitya is off to war, three more sons are already at war and my grandson is wounded.

23 This evening my daughter Tanya read a little from *War and Peace*, then Bulgakov sang.

26 I drew and played Mischief with Tanechka. The police burst in during the night and questioned Bulgakov about his appeal against the war.[52] I was extremely angry and wrote to Dzhunkovskii.

27 I have sent my article[53] about the police visit to three newspapers and my sister Tanya. My son Seryozha came for dinner; he played the piano for a long time, and Bulgakov sang. Painful memories. In a few hours it will be 28 October, four years since the night when Lev Nikolaevich left home.

28 A sad date – it was four years ago today that Lev Nikolaevich left home. A large number of policemen came and arrested V.F. Bulgakov, taking him away and charging him with distributing harmful leaflets. I was distraught, and angrily drafted a harsh letter to Dzhunkovskii about Bulgakov.[54]

29 My son Seryozha left this morning, having corrected my letter to Dzhunkovskii for me; I have copied it out and shall now send it off.

November 3 I received a disagreeable telegram from Dzhunkovskii. These gentlemen make me nervous – one is found guilty without having done anything wrong.[55]

7 The anniversary of Lev Nikolaevich's death. This morning six members of the Tolstoy Museum came – Merkurov the artist, three students, Aivazov, Burdzhalov, Amosova, and various others. What pathetic representatives of the Tolstoy Society they were! I was delighted by the arrival of my son Seryozha. Later on all the Yasnaya peasants came and we went to the grave with them and recited 'Our Father' and 'Eternal Memory'. I went with Tanechka; Tanya came too, and my daughter-in-law Sonya with her son Kiryusha, and Seryozha, and it was so good. But the weather and the roads are terrible. It's 2 degrees and there was a fall of wet snow. This evening Sonya sang and Seryozha played.

9 Once again I spent the day revising *Letters to His Wife* for the second edition, and I finished it. I am reading *Chopin and George Sand*.[56]

13 I went to Tula with Nina and visited Bulgakov; he is being very brave but has lost a lot of weight and evidently has no idea what to expect. Tanya read us some verses by Fet this evening.

14 This evening Tanya read aloud some poems by Tyutchev, and I read various sayings from my little red book.

18 I typed out a copy of Lev Nik.'s will to be checked in Moscow. Then I copied some letters of his which I want to add to the new edition.[57]

25 I had an argument with Tanya about the Church. She repeats her father's words and denounces the Church, forgetting that for more than two years he was a passionate churchgoer. This evening Andryusha came; he always cheers us up.

27 Left for Moscow this morning. The train was packed. Austrian prisoners-of-war at Tula.

28 (Moscow) All morning in the banks. Paid the Stupin warehouse up to May 1915. Dined and spent the evening with Seryozha. Dunaev was there. The roads were mud, travelled by cab.

December 2 Saw Sasha in Moscow; on the 10th she is leaving with a detachment as a nurse.

3 Went to the Polyonov exhibition with Nina. Excellent![58]

4 Returned to Yasnaya Polyana. It's most unpleasant, the gendarmes are drawing up a statement against Seryozha for saying that that captain was wasting his time in the police force.[59]

5 I dismissed the workers, made a note of the bills, gave some household instructions and worked. I am reading M.S. Gromeka's analysis of *Anna Karenina*. I had read it before but forgotten it![60]

6 I wrote to Misha and Levenson. I am annoyed by their refusal to print postcards of my photographs. I had a letter from Grand Duke Konstantin Konstantinovich about the manuscripts and meant to reply to it today, but became muddled.[61]

11 Went to Tula with Tanya and made the Kuzminskiis' wing hers for life. Received my pension. Saw Bulgakov at the police station.

12 Life passes quietly. The war and Bulgakov's foolish deed are a great weight on my heart. Dushan Petrovich, who also signed his appeal, has also been summoned to Tula by the police.[62]

19 I keep myself busy, but cannot apply myself to anything serious while this war is on. Dreadful sadness in my soul. Of my children I know nothing, and it breaks my heart to see my daughter Tanya; she is chronically ill with something.

20 My son Lyova came for dinner. A lot of talk, and it's all war, war, war.

31 Decorated the Christmas tree as usual. Seryozha came to dinner, and Tanya, Lyova, Andryusha, little Tanya, Antonina Tikhonovna, Dushan Petrovich and I all saw in the New Year enjoyably together. My nerves are shattered. I want to weep all the time. It is astonishing that three of my children are here with me; I am sad to have no news about Seryozha, who promised to come, and I worry about Andryusha, who is ill.

· 1915 ·

Russia driven out of Serbia, and discontent spreads. At the front whole regiments are surrendering and there is open talk of revolution. Russian defeat seems beyond question. Russian forces inferior in every way to those of enemy. At home the economic situation deteriorates, with soaring living costs, declining wages, amid rampant speculation and administrative chaos. Strikes and demonstrations increase and women's 'food riots' sweep the country. August 4 – Warsaw falls to Germans, followed by fortresses of Brest Litovsk and Kovno. September 18 – Germans advance to gates of Riga. Enemy well within Russian borders, civilian inhabitants ordered to evacuate war zones and their homes and crops set on fire. Two and a half million registered refugees. Tsar Nicholas assumes supreme command of army.

Summer – Aleksandra Tolstaya returns briefly to Yasnaya Polyana to recuperate from malaria. June 6 Taneev dies; Sofia does not attend his funeral.

January 8 I sat down with Seryozha and Bulygin this morning and we discussed the manuscripts with reference to making copies of them and continuing our negotiations with the academies and museums.[1] Seryozha has now left.

10 I received a telegram from Prince Shcherbatov, saying that the whole of my archives in the Historical Museum was being returned to me.[2]

11 I read Lev Nik.'s letters to Prince S.S. Urusov, and Ovsyaniko-Kulikovskii's note about Tolstoy.[3]

13 Ilya came, said a great many interesting things and this evening went away again. The Senate has issued an edict about the manuscripts – everything has been awarded to me.[4]

14 The two Tanyas, Liza Obolenskaya, Varya Nagornova and I went to the grave; we took some flowers and scattered seeds for the birds. I am sadly preparing to leave for Moscow, in order to transfer the manuscripts there.

18 I read three proof pages of the *Letters*, took stock of the expenses from the shopping books, then with the bailiff's wife I added up the money spent and received and made a note of it. I read Tanya and Varya my diary.

19 We're all terribly upset – Dushan Petrovich has been arrested and imprisoned for signing Bulgakov's appeal.[5]

22 (Moscow) Went to the State and Merchant Banks, then on to the Rumyantsev Museum, where I had a long discussion with the keeper of the manuscripts, Gr. Petr. Georgievskii. They are giving me a good room for the manuscripts, but there is a dreadfully steep cast-iron

24 Above: Tolstoy's sons carrying his coffin, November 8, 1910, at Astapovo station

25 Below: Sofia Tolstaya by Tolstoy's grave at Yasnaya Polyana, 1912

26 Over page: Sofia Tolstaya and her granddaughter Tanya, 1917

spiral staircase up to it. Dined and spent the evening with Seryozha and Masha. Seryozha, Pol and Shore played some Beethoven trios and so on.

23 I went to two exhibitions with Nina, the Union and the Wanderers'.[6] Exhibitions are so bad nowadays, not at all what they used to be. There's such a lot of decadent daubing. This evening Nina's brother came, we drank tea and I corrected three proof pages of *L.N. Tolstoy's Letters to His Wife*. I saw Iv. Iv. Gorbunov and Dima Chertkov in the vegetarian canteen where we were dining.

27 Spent the evening at the Maslovs'; Taneev and Marusya Maklakova were there. Georgievskii came to discuss the transfer of the objects and manuscripts from the Historical to the Rumyantsev Museum.

February 4 I pasted in a large allegorical painting which I found in the library, and yesterday a plan of Yasnaya Polyana when the Tolstoys were young. Varya and I went to the grave with a potted hyacinth. This evening we read about the Peter the Great period by a gentleman-of-the-bedchamber called Bergholz.[7]

5 I corrected three proof pages of *L.N. Tolstoy's Letters to His Wife*, coached the little girls and added up the expense and income books. Tanya and Varya Nagornova went to Tula; they weren't allowed into the prison to see either Bulgakov or Makovitsky.

7 I wrote an article about the Turkish War of 1877 and Lev Nik.'s attitude to it, and sent it off to Ilya for his paper.[8] I listened to a reading of the book *Everyday Russian Life*.[9]

10 E.A. Shchelkan came. This evening I read *Day of the Press* – a lot of articles in it about the war.[10]

15 P.A. Sergeenko came. I do not like him, but even he is a diversion when one is alone. He told me a few things about Chertkov and about Lev Nik.'s last diaries.

19 I often think sadly of poor Dushan Petrovich. It is hard for me to protest – my health is poor, I have no energy and my strength has gone. I listened to a reading of Leskov's *No Way Out*.

21 I read with an aching heart some extracts from Lev Nik.'s last diaries and letters in Mirolyubov's new journal.[11]

25 I read Lev Nik.'s letters to Prince L.D. Urusov in the *Herald of Europe*, and a stupid article about him by Ovsyaniko-Kulikovskii;[12] an unsuccessful comparison of Urusov with Oblonskii from *Anna Karenina*.

March 1 Spent all the day picking out sister Tanya Kuzminskaya's letters from all those received. After dinner I sewed a shirt and read Nikiforov's letters from Lev Nik.'s diaries and letters in Mirolyubov's journal.[13]

4 Sorted letters again. Seryozha was here, and Bulygin, a handsome and high-principled fellow whose beliefs will be the death of him. Bad news about the fate of Bulgakov and Dushan.[14]

5 Tanya went to Tula and saw Bulgakov and Dushan Petrovich.

11 I am reading *Romain Rolland and Tolstoy*.[15]

17 My daughter Tanya has returned from Moscow and St Petersburg, where she visited 4 ministers and pleaded for Dushan. He will be tried in a civil court.

23 I showed some officers from the war around Lev Nikolaevich's rooms. P.A. Boulanger arrived this morning.

26 I visited the grave with my daughter-in-law Sonya and her son Andryusha, who has just gone off to war again. Gr. Petr. Georgievskii, keeper of manuscripts at the Rumyantsev Museum, came for dinner, with an architect called Vikt. A. Visnev. We showed them and told them everything, and they showed us their plans for a Tolstoy study which they're constructing.[16] Sonya's sad account about her Kiryusha's death.

30 This evening I read Aldanov's *Tolstoy and Rolland*. I find it interesting, but Tanya says it's stupid.

April 3 Everything is so sad that I cannot do anything. A letter from Misha about the illness and death of his son; a letter from Sasha filled with a spirit of youthful merriment – and she is at war! I simply cannot make her out.

6 Misha arrived looking fresh, cheerful and even handsome. He has come to say goodbye, for he is off to war again, this time in the staff of the Khan of Nakhichevan. It was painful to part with him yet again, and painful too to hear about his son's death.

8 The Lord has sent me a joyless old age! Everything is melancholy! My heart aches constantly for Tanya and Lyova, and I worry about the others too. I finished arranging and cataloguing the books on the 24th shelf, on the top. Then I cleaned the balcony and took a walk across the meadow with Tanyushka, who delighted in the new flowers. Distressing letter from Lyova – my heart aches constantly for him.

12 I spent the day copying Strakhov's article about Lev Nik.'s will for Mr Maude.[17] My heart is heavy, I am alone in the world. Tanechka is a delight.

15 I read Turgenev's letters to Countess Lambert.[18]

16 I read Lev Nikolaevich's letters to Rusanov, and their constant references to *death* made a dismal impression. God knows whether he had prepared himself for it, or whether he feared it! Ovsyanikov-Kulikovskii's spurious arguments.[19]

19 Today I had visitors from Tula – the teachers and headmistress of the Arsenev High School. Sympathetic people. Some peasants came wanting money for their shop. Seryozha Bulygin came for the evening and is staying the night. I visited the grave with the two Tanyas, and we decorated it with flowers.

27 Bad news from the war; they're firing on Liepaja, the Germans have taken five provinces and sunk a private English steamer. Tanya is worse again. I was overwhelmed with such melancholy that I could do nothing all day but wander about Yasnaya Polyana. I corrected the proofs of the *Letters*.

30 I showed Lev Nikolaev.'s rooms to a great many visitors – including some revolutionary workers. I went to the grave and planted flowers there – violets, daisies and cowslips.

May 1 A lot of visitors – some girls just out of secondary school and a lot of schoolboys and young people. I showed them round Lev Nikolaevich's rooms and told them about him. I wrote to Kostsov about 'The Three Elders'.[20]

10 Andryusha came with Baranov, and they visited the grave. The public behaved outrageously; I have asked the police to come tomorrow. There were 55 visitors or more.

13 I find this solitude very hard, despite the delights of spring and nature. I corrected proofs, read Romain Rolland's *Vie de Tolstoi*, wandered around the grounds, and didn't find pleasure in any of it. Proof-reading L.N.'s letters upsets me terribly.

15 Antonina Tikhonovna and I went to Tula and managed to obtain permission from the police-general to visit Dushan Petrovich and Bulgakov. They were touchingly pleased to see me and asked about everything. Police General Volskii gave us the permit. I sent 700 rubles to my son Andryusha and attended to a lot of business in Tula.

16 I have finished reading the proofs of L.N.'s heart-rending *Letters to His Wife*, and sent off the last pages.

20 Visited the grave with Nina, and took a large bunch of wild flowers. I have regained my ability to marvel at nature, but my soul is still sad. Today is my son Lyova's birthday; what a poor fellow he is! And what about Tanya, Ilya, Misha, Andryusha and Sasha! With Seryozha there's less to worry about. This evening I read an article by Ovsyanikov-Kulikovskii about the value of life.[21]

21 Ovsyanikov-Kulikovskii's article again this evening. I don't like it – or don't understand it.

27 Spent the morning alone. First did some drawing, then played a lot of Chopin and practised the 2nd Scherzo; but it is very hard and I can't master it. Read several interesting articles in the *Voice of the Past*. Visited the grave with Nina, and after dinner I walked to the fir plantation. We read an article by N. Morozov,[22] then the newspapers.

28 I corrected the index to the letters.[23] It was very hard and I had to abandon it – I shall have to employ a proof-reader. A lot of visitors arrived today, including V. Mamontov, who came with a general. There were some children too.

31 Yasnaya Polyana is full of visitors and ramblers. Two people were working on an article about *War and Peace*. One of them was a student from Kiev University called Apostolov.[24] We went to the grave; there were a lot of people there and they had piled it with branches and grass. Havoc in Moscow – this business with the Germans. I shall write to Maklakov about it tomorrow.

June 2 I went to Tula and visited the notary to make some changes in my will. I wrote to Maklakov about these foolish rumours and the threat of pogroms.[25]

4 I set to work compiling an index to *L.N. Tolstoy's Letters to His Wife*. The proof-reader has refused. It's very hard work.

7 I am deeply shaken by the sad news of Sergei Iv. Taneev's death on the 6th.

11 More visitors. I worked on the index and went out to watch the hay being harvested. Very hot, with the threat of drought. I feel S.I. Taneev's death more deeply and painfully than ever. I read about his magnificent and well-attended funeral. He was truly appreciated.

13 I typed a copy of the completed index. After dinner I visited the grave with Nina and decorated it with flowers. Apart from the wild flowers there are many garden flowers in bloom – jasmine, sweetbriar and some magnificent roses. I grieve constantly for Sergei Ivanovich.

20 A very hot day, with distant rumblings of thunder. I did a drawing of a difficult and original flower which I had never come across before, and after dinner I took a splendid bunch of flowers to the grave. This evening I read a very good story in the *Herald of Europe* called 'At Sunset'.[26] It is about the psychology of our age, and describes the attitude of an old man of 70 toward children.

21 I don't want to do anything. I don't want to live. Apart from personal griefs, this war kills everything with a slow fire. I re-upholstered the moth-eaten bench in Lev Nik.'s bedroom, went for a little walk and did a little drawing. A hot dry day. Visitors – three Belgians full of French compliments.

23 I am reading Romain Rolland's *Le Temps viendra*.

28 I left this morning for Taptykovo to visit Andryusha and Katya. Her legs are aching, and they are both miserable. We went for a walk and watched a beautiful foal being driven round in circles. They have four haystacks this year, the estate is doing well, yet their life seems wretched and precarious; Mashenka is sickly and strange.

July 9 We sat on the balcony this afternoon sewing respirators for the army and drinking tea. I am reading the Gospels all the way through. Every age in life has its own viewpoint.

11 This evening Tanya read us something about Chekhov.

12 Guests all day. The Gorbunovs arrived – seven people for lunch; we had difficulty feeding them. Varvara Mikhailovna arrived during dinner with her sister and read a heartbreaking letter from Sasha about Turkish women refugees and their children, suffering and dying. I did a little sewing on some respirators.

19 I am rapidly losing interest in life. Bad news from the war. Life here is frightening, with no guards and no dogs.

22 A man named Darskii visited, asking for information about Fet. I have nothing – all the letters are in the museum.[27]

24 The whole house has been plunged in gloom by news of the German capture of Warsaw. I never believed in a Russian victory from the start, and now things are going from bad to worse.

August 7 I tidied up Lev Nik.'s rooms. I spend the day doing trivial tasks while my soul aches for the war, the poor wretches who have died, and our losses.

8 Dreadful news from the war: Kovno, Novogeorgievskii[28] and various other places have been taken, Riga is being evacuated and there's fighting in the Gulf of Riga.

10 I have started cataloguing the books and pamphlets on *my* shelf.

11 This evening I catalogued Tolstoy's books.

14 Completely alone until dinner. Entered Lev Nik.'s pamphlets and letters into the new catalogue. All these are either printed, copied or typed. The original manuscripts are all with Chertkov, alas![29]

17 I tidied up and made a note of the Jubilee newspapers for August 28, 1908.

18 Went to visit An. Evg. Zvegintseva. My son Misha and his wife arrived during dinner, to my great joy. He is off to war again, which is very sad. This evening we all had a good talk. My Misha has grown very thin.

22 I am 71 today; I cannot believe I am so old. I spent the whole day on my own – apart from Nina and her vast family, who are always visiting her. I didn't go out and spent the whole day reading my daughter Tanya's

letters to me. She has had a lot of grief in her life too – if only from the operation on her nose and forehead.[30]

23 My daughter Sasha has returned, cheerful, full of experiences and stories, and much thinner.

28 Lev Nikolaevich's birthday. A wet, overcast morning, but then it brightened up. I went to the grave and prayed for the souls of Lev Nik. and the parents who bore him. It's strange how quickly Tolstoy has been forgotten. There was *no one* here today, neither friends nor outsiders.

30 I was delighted to see Andryusha, Katya and Mashenka today, but they didn't stay long. Some refugees from Courland managed to get here; they looked round L.N.'s rooms, walked about the grounds and were in ecstasies over the place. There were about 50 visitors today. I get very tired without Nina.

September 1 Just after dinner this evening my Seryozha arrived here on foot from Zaseka; I was delighted to see him and love him very much. He brought a new promissory note regarding his debt.

8 I wrote to Minister Krivoshein yesterday about the threatened closure of the Duma.

10 They sent a workman from the Tolstoy Museum to collect the wreaths from Lev Nikolaev.'s funeral.

14 I showed some Latvian refugees around Lev Nik.'s rooms. There were more than 40 of them.

16 I took fresh flowers to the grave. It was 52 (fifty-two) years ago today, the day before my name-day, that Lev Nik. gave me the letter containing his proposal.[31]

17 I spent my name-day very happily. Andryusha came with his wife and little daughter, and Sasha with her woman doctor friend, and my grandchildren played and enjoyed themselves all day long.

21 I wrote to the editors of the *Stock Exchange Gazette* about Sergeenko's article.[32]

October 10 I went to the grave this morning with some chrysanthemums and fir branches, scattering the path with sand as I went and spiritually communing with Lev Nik. But oh, the endless melancholy! When I got back I sorted books with Nina, a hard and interminable job!

22 I wrote two articles about Lev Nikolaevich for Denisenko;[33] he had asked me for something to read somewhere in Novocherkassk on the anniversary of Lev Nik.'s death.

28 A sad day – today it is five years since Lev Nikolaevich left. It is still just as painful, even though five years have passed! The village policeman was here and wrote an application for me to be sent a guard.

November 8 I finished cataloguing the books, had a long chat with Bulygin and unburdened my heart by railing against Chertkov. More and more vile things are revealed about him all the time.

11 We read aloud 'The Polonetskiis', and tonight I read a biography of Mazzini.[34]

17 I worked hard taking notes for *My Life* – at present I'm doing 1898. The village policeman was here with a document about the hiring of the guard.

18 I am sewing a blanket for the refugees. Tanya went to Zaseka and came back with a terrible account of their poverty; the children go to school barefoot, many of the women have nothing but light blouses over their shoulders, and short little skirts. I again took notes for *My Life*. It's so hard sometimes to re-live the old life!

19 I devoted the entire day to finishing my notes for 1898. This evening Nina read me a critical article about Sienkiewicz, and the beginning of his *Quo Vadis*.[35]

21 I started work on my autobiography, but it didn't go at all well – there isn't enough material, I have lost my memory, and I don't have what is needed for inspired writing. And I am constantly being dragged away from my work by mundane domestic matters.

24 (Moscow) I left for Moscow. Problems with the tickets – they had trouble finding me a seat. I travelled with some officers and an army doctor who were home on leave. I am staying at the Slavonic Bazaar on Nikolskaya Street. This evening I went to a quartet recital in memory of Sergei Ivan. Taneev.

26 Businessmen here all morning, then a visit from Prince V.D. Golitsyn, Director of the Rumyantsev Museum, and Georgievskii, keeper of manuscripts; I gave them my diary and Lev Nik.'s little one.[36] Dinner with Seryozha, and this evening a recital held in Taneev's memory of quartets by the Duke of Mecklenburg.

27 At 11 this morning I went straight to the Rumyantsev Museum. Prince Golitsyn took me around with Georgievskii, and showed me the new reading-room. I worked there until nearly 4, dined with Misha and Lina and spent the evening with the Maslovs. They showed me a great many portraits of Taneev and Fyodor Ivanovich.

28 I started the day with a visit to the art gallery at the Rumyantsev Museum. Very dismal – almost no paintings there at all. Then I worked on the manuscripts until nearly 4. I dined with my brother, spent the evening at the Slavonic Bazaar and drank tea with V.F. Bulgakov.[37]

December 2 I left this morning in an excellent compartment, comfortable and spacious. I found both Tanyas in good health and spirits, and am overjoyed to be back.

5 I read the *Turgenev Anthology*. Much of it jarred on me. Is it really necessary to turn the whole of people's intimate life inside out?[38]

7 Dush. Petr. Makovitsky has arrived here from the prison,[39] and K.A. Salomon from Paris. He had his passport stolen on the journey, as well as various essential documents and 200 rubles in a wallet.

10 I read the *Turgenev Anthology* all day and all evening. It's very interesting, although much of it is untrue – for instance that Tolstoy's two letters to Turgenev were sent together.[40]

17 I wasted the whole day searching for Gradovskii's letters to me, which I want to send to the Commission for Poor Writers for an anthology in memory of him. I sent 17 letters to Kaufmann.[41]

18 This evening we read aloud Sienkiewicz's *Quo Vadis*, and some verses dedicated to the memory of L.N.

19 I read in the papers about the newly published thoughts from L.N.'s diaries.[42]

22 My son Lyova arrived early this morning. He rails against himself for gambling and living such a disorderly life, but it doesn't make things any easier! Yet he has so many good qualities! This evening we read his play.[43] Gloomy, but clever.

29 Late yesterday I read some crude articles about Lev Nikol. by Amfiteatrov. This failed writer and priest's son has now revealed himself as a thorough scoundrel.[44]

31 My son and grandson Sergei arrived late this morning after their train was delayed. We all went in to see Tanya and decorated the Christmas tree. Andryusha arrived from Tula with Nina in time for dinner. I am very glad my sons have come to see in the New Year with us. I have not long to live and I love my children, although they worry me terribly with their gambling, their marital problems and so on. The last day of 1915. What will the new year bring? If only the war would end! Bless us, Lord!

· 1916 ·

Lull in fighting until March, while arms supply improved. June – new offensive launched along Austrian front which gains only some 100,000 miles and forces Austria to abandon offensive in Italy, but involves some two million Russian deaths and injuries. Mobilisation creates havoc in agriculture, industry and transport.

Andrei Tolstoy dies of pleurisy. Yasnaya Polyana, like other large estates, deteriorates. Ilya Tolstoy leaves his wife and emigrates to the United States.

January 1 Seryozha, Andryusha, Lyova and my grandson Sergei have cheered us up. We worked on the Christmas tree all day, and this evening the servants' children came – 20 of them – and they sang, played games, danced and received their presents. Everyone seemed to enjoy themselves. Later on we had a family discussion about Lev Nik.'s will and last wishes.

9 Wrote to the editorial board of *New Times* and to the Tolstoy Museum in St Petersburg.[1] Worked all day on my memoirs. It's hard to find a connection for everything and to get all the right dates (*les dates*).

16 We all drank tea with Tanya in the Kuzminskiis' wing, and she read us a sketch she has written called 'Kurzik'.[2] Not bad.

17 Sasha arrived this morning accompanied by Maria Alekseevna, her woman doctor friend. We were all glad to see her and we had a happy day. There were 14 visitors. I looked through Vol. I of *Tolstoy's Diary*, edited by Chertkov. It's just extracts and thoughts, not the whole diary.[3]

19 My son Ilya came with two people who want to make a cinematographic film of the story 'What People Live For'.[4] One appears to be a Jew, the other is a boy of 16. I walked to the grave today and felt a little calmer.

20 Ilya and the visitors walked around the estate taking photographs for the cinematographic film of 'What People Live For'. One of them, an actor playing an angel, stood naked in the snow!

23 There is almost no material for 1899, so work is not progressing well. This evening Nina read me Sienkiewicz's *Without Dogma.*

24 We drank tea with Tanya, who read us her diary.[5] and a children's play she has written.[6] We had a long talk.

30 I had a visit from P.I. Raevskii, now a military doctor at the Tula infirmary. A pleasant, friendly man. Tregubov appeared too, with a Pole, and visited the grave. Several people came to see Lev Nik.'s rooms; one was from the island of Sakhalin.

February 2 This evening my daughter Tanya read aloud some short stories by Sleptsov, then Lyova read passages from L.N.'s 'Kingdom of Heaven' and excerpts from Maupassant and Rod.

5 Misha arrived from Goryachkino with Kulishov. It broke my heart to say goodbye to him. His face bears signs of great unhappiness, although he tries to be brave.

10 I have finished writing 1899; it was very thin in ideas and events.

11 Dreadfully worried by news of Andryusha, who is ill and has a high fever. The days pass quickly and uneventfully. Bulgakov is leaving for Gusev's tonight with Dushan Petrovich's memoirs.[7] It would be better to post it.

14 Re-read until dinner time various letters from the 1900s. Very little material there for my memoirs. Spent the evening with Tanya and read Salomon's letter about the death of his nephew at war.[8]

17* There are no trains from Tula to Moscow this week, as they're letting a military cargo through. I am planning to leave for Petersburg with Lyova and am packing my bags. Andryusha begged Katya to ask me to go there. He is evidently very ill!

*From February 17 to 28: I wrote this later. (Sofia Tolstaya's note.)

18 Lyova and I left for Petrograd, via Tula. Unimaginably crowded trains. We were given two first-class tickets (apparently by mistake), and we managed to squeeze ourselves into the compartment of two men who turned out to be extremely courteous and obliging. At 8 a.m. we were given our own compartment, and we slept until morning. I stayed with the Kuzminskiis, Lyova with his family. Andryusha looks very ill to me, and I am dreadfully worried.

19 The doctors keep repeating the same senseless words: 'It's a serious illness but there's no danger at present.' And they continue saying so to the end. Andryusha has pleurisy and a bad liver. His breathing is laboured, he is a greenish-yellow colour all over, he shrieks and groans continuously. His temperature goes as high as 42 °, and three or four times a day he is racked by a fierce, agonising chill.

22 I suggested that Andryusha should receive the Eucharist. He calmly consented, and when the priest came he confessed in a loud voice, repeating the responses and kissing everyone who came to greet him. Then he grew tired, and towards evening he started shivering again and his temperature went up to 41 °. Everyone is astonished that his heart is still holding out.

23 Andryusha has been unconscious almost all day, his breathing is agonisingly laboured and he groans. And so it has continued until late in the night. I had to stop up my ears and run away in despair. My darling, loving, generous, happy, honest Andryusha. I pray endlessly to God to deliver me from this unspeakable suffering. His wife Katya has been at his bedside, as well as her sister Jenny, Masha Erdeli, Liza Obolenskaya, the nurse, Lyova and I.

24 Andryusha died at 10 minutes past one in the morning of the 23rd to 24th. It was on the 23rd that Vanechka died. The funeral service, the people – it's all so immaterial! Andryusha's children Sonya and Ilyushok came with their mother Olga. My son Ilya came. Katya and Lyova went to buy two plots at the cemetery of the Aleksandr Nevskii Monastery (at Nikolskoe), and he will be buried there. My God! How can we go on living without Andryusha! I have only just realised how hard it will be!

26 Andryusha's funeral. How frightful that he is gone and we shall never see him again! A splendid, brilliant funeral. Masses of wreathes, a crowded church. It was all like a dream. Seryozha arrived late. We buried Andryusha at the Nikolskoe cemetery of the Aleksandr Nevskii Monastery.

29 The train was late, and we didn't reach Yasnaya until this evening. Everyone is glad that I'm back, and so am I.

March 6 I got up feeling shattered, and aching all over; I lay down on my own in the drawing-room and thought about Andryusha and how loving he always was to me. I have been sorting through my letters for 1915 to 1916, and Andryusha's are the most affectionate. This evening we all played with the pictures in the secretaire with Tanyushka. Interesting philosophical discussions later on with Lyova and Bulgakov. Lyova has developed a passion for Confucius and is studying his father.

7 My heart is racked with grief for the death of my darling, loving Andryusha. At times I long to cry out, as Dora cried out after the death of her Levushka: 'It cannot be!' Is he really gone for ever? Today Nina and I checked over my memoirs together, which she has copied, and I read Turgenev's tedious *On the Eve.*

9 There has been a strong wind all day, and it makes my heart even heavier. Where is my Andryusha now! Once when I was ill he said to me, 'We shouldn't attach any great significance to anything.' But what great significance his death has had for me! I took notes from my letters for my work.

13 I worked on my autobiography. This evening Bulgakov left for good.[9] He and Makovitsky are to be tried on the 21st.

15 This morning I re-read my letters as material for my memoirs. This evening I read aloud an American book in translation called *To Life.*[10]

20 I looked through several documents and pamphlets concerning Lev Nik., in search of material. After dinner Lyova read us his article; there are some good ideas in it, but on the whole it is muddled and incoherent.[11]

23 It is very sad that Lyova's family life has broken down, yet for me it's much more pleasant to have him living here than to be on my own, especially now that my daughter Tanya has left for the trial.[12]

26 They have written to us from Krapivna ordering us to take in three prisoners of war. I sent for them, and added my signature to those of the other women protesting against the sinking of the *Portugal.*[13]

27 I sent for the prisoners of war, four Rumanians, who arrived on government horses. I finished writing 1901 today. Very scanty and

incoherent, not enough material. This evening I read aloud something by Ertel.

29 I coloured my children's drawings again. I sit here in silence for hours on end, my heart aching for Andryusha. I weep endlessly now. I shall never again hear his voice downstairs, greeting me affectionately as he comes in the door.

30 I'm reading Timkovskii's *The Soul of Tolstoy*. Much of it is very true. I heard today that the two Tanechkas wouldn't be coming for another month, and that all the Tolstoyans, apart from Seryozha Popov, had been acquitted.[14]

April 5 This evening Lyova read us a lot of dull verbiage from an article by Menshikov.[15]

16 This evening my son Misha arrived, looking cheerful and well. He is leaving again for this cursed war on the 25th.

17 I copied Lyova's article on the typewriter; it's not bad and it's sincerely written, but there's a lot of repetition and it will need to be corrected.[16]

25 I read an article in a supplement to the *New Times* by my sister Tanya and, it appears, Varya. Very bad, and immodest.[17]

30 I wrote to Tanya criticising one or two things in her *New Times* article. I'm afraid she'll take offence.[18]

May 6 I read some memoirs of Lev Nik. by a former servant of ours called Ustyusha. It's mostly pure invention.[19]

9 However heavy my heart, I never lose my love and appreciation for nature. I marvel at the flowers, the sky, the fresh green leaves on the trees and the thick green grass. I did a lot of copying, and after dinner I took a walk with Nina. I think a lot about my loved ones who are dead, and grieve for those who are alive. Dushan Petrovich fainted today.

10 This afternoon I invited a Molokan to tea – an interesting old man who used to visit Lev Nik.[20]

11 I read Lyova's story – terribly gloomy but not at all bad.[21] I also tried to read some stories by Dmitrieva. Unbelievably bad!

14 There were a lot of visitors – three officers and 28 common folk from the Co-operative society.

15 I read the conclusion to the article about my sister Tanya, published under Varya Nagornova's name.

16 I finished copying Lyova's article 'The Vanity of Mankind'.[22]

17 I corrected my copy of Lyova's article. Bulgakov and my daughter Tanya have been working together on an account of his appeal against the war, Tanya's intercession and the trial.[23]

21 A certain Vlad. Mikh. Popov arrived from the Academy of Sciences to make enquiries about L.N.'s manuscripts.[24]

23 My grandson Andryusha Ilich came. He has two George Crosses from the war.

24 The Kuzminskiis, my sister and her husband, arrived today. Interesting discussions about history with my daughter Tanya over evening tea.

26 News of 30,000 soldiers taken prisoner, and a battle in which *all* of our officers were killed.

29 A vast number of visitors – workers from a metal factory, a great many soldiers with their officer and his wife.

June 3 This evening we read Nazhivin's stories about Tolstoy. Very bad.[25] Both Tanyas, my sister and daughter, are being rather hostile to me, and this makes me very sad. What is the reason for it? Lyova is being very kind though.

4 I copied out Lyova's novel for him.[26] In the war, 165,000 prisoners have been taken, but an entire regiment of ours has been drowned in the river.

6 I visited the grave with Nina, and we decorated it beautifully with flowers. I no longer feel that agonising grief which I used to feel at the grave, and which I now experience from Andryusha's death.

16 We read some excerpts from Sergeenko, and some letters written by Lev Nik. and me after his departure. It upset me dreadfully.

18 Sasha's birthday. Where is she now, I wonder? I wrote down some information about the beginning and end of my marriage to Lev Nikolaevich, and became dreadfully agitated.

22 I had a letter from my daughter Sasha. I'm so worried about her – she's so close to danger, and might easily fall under enemy fire.

30 We had a visit during dinner from V.I. Sreznevskii and A.L. Boehm, both from the Academy. We showed them around and told them about everything.

July 7 Today, July 7, is a great day – my daughter Sasha returned from the war. She looked cheerful, healthy and plump, thank God, and we listened to her stories all evening.

10 My son Seryozha came and we were overjoyed to see him. This evening he suggested that each person present perform something. He played, Tanya read, Bulgakov and Dushan Petrovich sang, Nina, Mitya Kuzminskii and little Marina danced, Lyova played one of his own compositions, my sister Tanya sang, and everyone enjoyed themselves immensely. I read some of my own verses.[27]

18 My daughter Sasha has gone off to war again. It was very painful to see her go. Worse than before. During the day I corrected a sad tale by Lyova about his own life, written in the form of a novel.

24 Today is the Kuzminskiis' 49th wedding anniversary. They've never been very happy together! My sister was telling me only recently that she had never truly loved him.

August 6 I had a visit this evening from my grandson Ilya Ilich Tolstoy, who has just finished at the Naval Academy. Such a nice young fellow.

9 Spent the whole day in Tula with Nina and wrote a new will.[28] It breaks my heart to see the soldiers and hear them singing.

14 Lyova had a sudden attack of anxiety and a desire to travel, so off he went to Taptykovo. I feel both sorry for him and worried about his instability. This evening we read my story aloud.

27 I spent the day weaving wreaths for Lev Nik.'s grave. Tomorrow is his birthday. With the white flowers I made a cross to cover the whole grave, and with the others I made garlands.

28 I copied out Prince Abamelek-Lazarev's article about Lev Nikolaevich,[29] and waited for guests to arrive. *No one* came – it was really rather depressing. I visited the grave with Nina and we covered it with the floral cross. Fresh flowers had been placed all around it and someone had also left two plaited wreaths of wild flowers. We spent the evening talking and reading. My sister read us passages from Mulford's book *To Life*. A beautiful, fine, still day.

29 I copied out Abamelek's article 'Memories of Lev Nikolaevich'; very badly written.[30] This evening Lyova read us Chekhov's 'The Bear'.

September 6 We had a visit from two Japanese men, a journalist and an artist; they had lunch with us, looked around the house with great interest and asked a great many questions. One of them spoke Russian, the other a little French. Lyova has written a memorandum for the Tsar called 'On Fixed Prices', and wants to go and give it to him.[31]

11 Today was a happy day. First my two Tanechkas came, then Seryozha arrived with Orlov. Fascinating conversations, then Seryozha played some Indian songs and an Arabian dance.

12 I copied out my sister Tanya's memoirs for her.[32]

October 3 I copied Lyova's story.[33]

9 I discussed the museum's affairs with Seryozha. They need some articles for the *Tolstoy Yearbook*, and Seryozha is looking through Lev Nik.'s papers for something to publish.[34] I also discussed the variants of *Hadji Murat* with Tanya. Seryozha and Lyova played a Mozart quintet as a duet, then some of Brahms' Hungarian Dances.

11 I finished copying my son Lyova's story-article.[35]

16 Learnt of Iv. Vas. Denisenko's death.

19 Lyova has left for Moscow. The house feels empty and sad without him, although his state of mind has been causing me great anguish.

22 33 tourists, final-year students from Malakhovka, came to visit. I showed them Lev Nik.'s rooms, and my daughter Tanya gave them tea and something to eat in the wing. Then they all went out to the meadow, played games, sang songs and visited the grave.

26 Tanya read us her reminiscences of Agafya Mikhailovna this evening.[36] Then we read Goncharov's *The Precipice*.

28 The sad anniversary of Lev Nikolaevich's departure from this house.

31 I read a pamphlet which was sent to me called 'Truth and Falsehood About Tolstoy'.[37] What a strange attitude all the critics have towards me – 'earthbound' indeed! Why, I longed all my life to take flight, but life *tied my wings*.

November 1 I finished reading the pamphlet by Glinka (Volzhskii). He described Chertkov very well,[38] but his style is strange.

3 Lyova has returned with new plans to travel to India and China and to give lectures. Ilya has just gone off to America with the same thing in mind.[39] I have a lot of grief in store – if I don't die soon.

4 We discussed Lyova's lecture about his father, and got him some books and photographs. I shall worry about him terribly, yet I can never refuse him money however much it irks me to give it to him.

5 I am living through my last days with Lyova before his latest mad scheme – a journey through China and India. Everything seems dreary and indifferent – as if everything was over. Today there is to be a Tolstoy evening in Moscow, organised by my daughter Tanya in aid of the Tolstoy Museum,[40] and on the 7th there will be another evening to commemorate Lev Nik.'s death.[41]

6 Today Varya and I played Schubert's Tragic Symphony as a duet, and I loved it. I was interested to read the article about the Tolstoy evening organised by the Tolstoy Society.[42] Tomorrow is the anniversary of his death; it's sad to recall all the tragic events of that period.

7 I visited the grave first thing this morning, and took some chrysanthemums and primulas. Our visitors today were an old woman and two young Slavs. Every city in Russia is organising evenings in memory of L.N. Tolstoy.

8 Varya and I played Mozart's Eighth Symphony as a duet, followed by Haydn's Twelfth. They're both lovely. I read Rolland's *Vie de Tolstoi* and did some newspaper cuttings.

9 Distressing conversations and memories this evening about Lev Nik. at the end of his life.

10 My son Lyova's departure is painfully close now, and it is very sad. He has been staying with me for 11 months now. What's to be done? This evening he read us L. Tolstoy's 'Albert', and became very agitated.

11 I felt unbearably sad parting with Lyova today. He has brought so much to our lives – music, ideas and a good, gentle attitude to life. How talented he is and what a good disposition he has! Yet he's so wretched and unstable.

16 Life has become like a dream – I've lost all my energy and interest in things. What is the reason for this deathly state? And then every sad or joyful experience becomes so intensified and torments me so – the day-labourers' music, *The Precipice*, work and reading (Izmailov's 'Memories of Tolstoy').[43]

25 I received the Yasnaya Polyana booklets, and sorted and catalogued them. This evening I read some excerpts from my autobiography to Varya and Dushan Petrovich, and they both approved and praised my work.

December 2 I finished *An Ordinary Story* by Goncharov today. This evening I read the newspapers and copied Tanya's story about Maria Aleks. Schmidt.[44]

4 N.N. Apostolov visited from Kiev today with some young lady. I have been collecting information about how *War and Peace* was written, copying out the passages marked by Lev Nik. in the *Mémoires de Ste Hélène*.[45] I am still copying Tanya's article on M.A. Schmidt.

6 Today is my late son Andryusha's birthday. What a short life he had! I have been thinking about him all day.

21 I am engrossed in the newspapers. The war, the murder of Rasputin, the chaos in the government – it all fascinates and even disturbs me.

29 Visitors to Lev Nikolaevich's rooms all morning. It must be so pleasant to feel this deep love for him – especially if one is young. People are always astonished at the simplicity of our life here.

31 We all saw in the New Year together, and I think everyone enjoyed themselves. But my heart was grieving for my sons – Ilya in America, Lyova on his way to Japan, Sasha at war, and Misha about to leave any day now. And Andryusha is no more – how sad! Thank God I still have Seryozha, Tanya and my darling grandchildren. The end of the sad year of 1916 is over!

· 1917 ·

March 8, Women's Day – women demonstrate in their thousands on streets of newly renamed Petrograd. Strikes, demonstrations and 'food riots' become more violent, and some buildings set on fire. March 16 – Tsar abdicates, his government is toppled and a new 'Provisional' Government is formed, composed of liberal landowners. The Soviet is resurrected and challenges the power of the Provisional Government. Spring – revolutionaries amnestied and many (including Lenin) return to Russia. Bolsheviks' popularity increases. June – Provisional Government urges on Russian soldiers against Germans; strikes and demonstrations in the towns reach massive proportions. July – unsuccessful attempt by soldiers, sailors and workers to seize power. September – Bolsheviks plan to take power, and October 25 to 26, at the Second All-Russian Congress of Soviets, they do so and declare an end to war, with no annexations or indemnities. December – armistice signed with Germany, while Trotsky and others attempt to persuade German High Command at Brest Litovsk to accept Bolshevik peace terms. France, Britain, Japan and the United States prepare to attack Soviet Russia.

Angry peasants return from front and loot and burn estates near Yasnaya Polyana. Summer – approaching band of looters driven off by staff brandishing pickaxes, scythes and hatchets, and Sofia Tolstaya applies to Provisional Government for armed protection. One hundred men despatched to protect property, and Governor of Tula requested to pay special attention to her needs. Tanya Sukhotina's husband dies, and she and her young daughter move in to Yasnaya. Sergei Tolstoy gives a series of concerts, which receive good reviews. Tolstoy Museum agrees to bring out new Complete Collected Works, *edited by his children Aleksandra and Sergei Tolstoy, and others.*

January 1 Seryozha's wife came with their son and his friend Chicherin, and after dinner Tanya and the children put on a play she had written.[1]

5 I looked through my memoirs for Academician Sreznevskii, who wanted me to check the dates of my children's births and deaths; I felt so melancholy as I read through them.[2]

10 I checked the sales of books published by the Tolstoy Museum. Dushan Petrovich is back from Moscow.

13 I received a book about Gradovskii containing an account of his visit to Yasnaya Polyana; a most flattering description of me.[3]

19 Our old nurse, A.S. Sukolyonova, died at midnight last night, and the nuns are now reading the psalter over her body. What grief! I had lived with her for 35 years, and it was time for her to leave this life – she was 88. I coached my darling Tanyushka; I am reading a lot. The supplement to *Life for All* contains an interesting account of the various religions. This was Lev Nik.'s idea – a popular exposition of all the religions.[4]

20 I looked through the letters again. How affectionate and solicitous my dear dead Andryusha's were! And how pathetic Masha was!

21 We buried our nurse Anna Stepanovna today; the little place by the window where she always used to sit and greet me is now empty, and I feel so sad.

I looked through and sorted letters until I collapsed with exhaustion. My memories are so painful, and I don't have many friends left now.

23 I cannot rid my heart of these nagging anxieties about my children, especially Lyova, who is the most unstable and therefore the most unhappy.

24 I have finished reading *Religion*; it was extraordinarily interesting. Dushan Petrovich has left for Moscow to see Gusev, and will not be home until February 4. (He and Gusev are to revise his memoirs together.)[5]

25 Tanya read aloud Pushkin's *Boris Godunov*. It's so much better than *Prince Serebriany*,* which I am still reading. Important news in the papers that America has broken off relations with Germany.

February 2 I paid the workmen's salaries. I often feel very sorry for the working people, and would love to feed and clothe them better and show them some affection – especially the children. I finished Romm's article about Turgenev and Viardot; very vividly written.

3 Workers at the Tula ordnance factory are on strike. They have to stand in queues to buy anything, and when they're late for work they're fined. Where's the justice in that?

5 Everyone from the Kuzminskiis' wing dined with me today, as well as Dushan Petrovich and his nephew – who is called Zdeno Osipovich! My Tanya read us *The Fruits of Enlightenment*.

13 I read Sulerzhitskii's book on the Dukhobors; very well written.[6]

*By Aleksei Konstantinovich Tolstoy (1817–75), a distant cousin of L.N. Tolstoy.

17 Terribly upset by Tanya's story about Lyova's gambling losses in Moscow before leaving for Japan. How dreadful! A new weight on my heart.

19 Tanya read us *Poverty is No Sin*,[7] and before dinner she read us Lev Nik.'s *Childhood*. What freshness of feeling! Although there are some weak parts in it too.

20 I have been copying out on the typewriter some of Lev Nik.'s letters from 1900 which were found recently at Tanya's, and I am pasting them into my book of *Letters to His Wife*. In time they'll all be put together in the proper place.[8]

21 I copied L.N.'s letters to me again, and pasted them into the book. We have found more too, which will need to be copied.

23 The anniversary of Vanechka's death, and at midnight on the 24th, that of my Andryusha. Oh, how weary my soul is. Tanya went to Tula and returned in low spirits. Everyone there is talking of revolution, it's impossible to buy anything, there's no bread or kerosene to be found, and all the shops are closing.

March 1 An unexpected visit from Seryozha Popov, who was tried along with Bulgakov and Dushan Petrovich. An interesting circular from the Duma distributed by all the railways: a new Provisional Government has been established. Frightful news of 8,000 people killed in Petrograd when they rioted for bread. Rodzyanko is head of the new *Duma*.

3 I read the paper carefully to find out about the change of government and the authority of the new State Duma. Everyone is in a tense and expectant mood.

5 An important day for Yasnaya Polyana. Workers from the Kosaya Gora cast-iron foundry arrived with red flags and badges to pay their respects to Tolstoy's house and widow. Bearing portraits of Lev Nik., they all tramped through deep snow and in a biting wind to the grave. My two Tatianas went too. The workers sang and made speeches – all about 'freedom' – and I replied with a short speech about L.N.'s legacy. Then everyone sang 'Eternal Memory' and took photographs.

6 I sent *Russian Word* my article about the workers' demonstration yesterday.[9]

7 A little soldier boy was sent here by Sasha to collect four copies of the *Complete Collected Works of L.N. Tolstoy*. The new freedom doesn't make me happy for some reason – everything frightens me.

11 I was shocked to receive a letter from my sister Tanya informing me that Al. Mikh. Kuzminskii had died.[10] He had already embraced death long ago, with his quiet, mild, affectionate attitude to all those around him. My sister was not with him at the time – she had gone to a sanatorium.

20 Dushan Petrovich read us Lev Nik.'s 'Our Revolution' this evening.[11]

26 My life is not at all interesting. As soon as I got up today I went out to the verandah, where 63 girls and boys from our school were gathered, plus 20 non-school children. Amongst the schoolchildren we distributed some lengths of calico, sent to us by Burylin. Ghastly news from the war! Hundreds of thousands killed. I woke up with tears in my eyes, haunted by all the dead.

27 This evening Dushan Petrovich read us Bienstock's book of L.N.'s thoughts and sayings,[12] then Manya read me a novel by Wells.

29 Dushan Petrovich read me some passages from Fet's *Memoirs*.[13]

April 4 There were a great many visitors to the house and Lev Nik.'s rooms. One militiaman dictated to me a letter applying for a militiaman to protect me. Dushan Petrovich's relatives came to visit him. We now have some Slovak prisoners here.

5 I conscientiously read all the newspapers. Everything is so frightening – the war and the famine; there's menace in the air.

10 I cannot rid myself of this gnawing anguish. Nothing can awaken my soul now or call it back to life – neither the spring, nor my former happiness, nor music, nor art. My only pleasure now is having my two Tanyas living with me, but they'll be leaving any day now for their home in Ovsyannikovo.

12 Sasha and Varvara Mikhailovna have arrived. Sasha is just the same, thank God, plump and blooming, with the same loud, cheerful laugh. I am delighted she came, but also wish she hadn't, since she'll be here for only two days, and we have waited and worried about her for so long.

15 Sasha went off to the front again with Varvara Mikhailovna; she was full of energy and high spirits, and I had to force myself not to cry.

16 A person's life is like a leaf: first the bud, then the fresh little green leaf, then the full-blown leaf, then it fades, life dies away, and the leaf turns dry and yellow and falls off. My brain and capacities are all withering and dying away now in the same way. I can see it and sense it, yet I know it's impossible to halt this process of death.

18 Some professional and industrial workers from Kosaya Gora came to visit. They brought a wreath tied with a red ribbon from some soldiers, they carried some magnificent red flags embroidered in gold and silver, and they played music which the entire crowd could understand. It is strange to hear the 'Marseillaise' played here in Russia. They made speeches, then they all went off to the grave and there were more speeches – from a schoolboy, an Italian and a Czech.

19 16 soldiers came to see the house and visit the grave. An engineer from Kosaya Gora called Al. Nik. Parshin visited with books for the library.

20 We tried to read some Chekhov this evening, but I always find him so tedious; I can never laugh, that is my great failing. Then Dushan Petrovich read us some books by Nikolaev.

23 Life is dull and pointless and there's little joy – apart from my two Tanechkas of course. The moment I got up today I had to deal with an endless series of demands: the day-labourers' wages, the widows' pensions, visitors, students, soldiers, officers, a certain woman. The officers were most sympathetic, and said that people visited Yasnaya Polyana as Christians visited Jerusalem and Mohammedans Mecca – to pay their respects to a sacred place. Terrible news about a peasant murdered by Austrian prisoners.

26 My son Misha has arrived. He told me a lot of interesting things. The lack of discipline in the troops is terrible. And the general situation is terrible.

27 A mass of visitors. Forty-five schoolboys, five women, four soldiers and several other gentlemen. It has grown warmer, and the nightingale is singing; we all had dinner on the verandah together, although everyone had their own food.

30 An enormous number of visitors to the house and the grave, all of them soldiers. They were fascinated by everything, and were most sympathetic to my daughter Tanya and me. There is no cattle fodder and this worries me. Our provisions too are running low.

May 7 This evening Dushan Petrovich read me something about Crosby, an American who once visited us in Yasnaya Polyana.[14] I wrote to Kolupaev, a soldier who had asked me for some books. There were ten officers here, and I chattered away to them about nothing. But they were good people.

16 I.E. Erdeli came. He has been at the war, where he was made a general at the age of 47, but he is as lively and cheerful as ever; he played *pas-de-géant* with the children, and this evening he played the piano.

21 My son Seryozha arrived, to everyone's joy, and played superbly. A vast number and a variety of visitors – soldiers, officers, young girls, children. Tanya, Dushan Petrovich and I showed them round L.N.'s rooms.

22 My son Seryozha has left for Moscow. When he was sitting downstairs in the dining-room of the Kuzminskiis' wing, he looked so sad, and so preoccupied with present events, that it made my heart tremble to look at him. May God keep yet another of my children from death. I went to the grave with my grandchildren and planted forget-me-nots there. Numerous visitors.

28 I showed some officers and soldiers round Lev Nikolaevich's rooms – more than thirty of them. This evening my sister Tanya read aloud Sienkiewicz's *The Deluge* and my daughter Tanya read us Turgenev's *The Calm*.

30 200 soldiers came on foot to the house, and Ivanov, commander of the regiment, drove up later with his little girl. The soldiers were marching to music, and they played very well too, first the 'Marseillaise', and at the grave the Funeral March. There were a lot of discussions – about Lev Nik., about the royal family and about Chertkov. I invited the commander to dinner, but he declined.

June 3 I received thanks from Moscow University for donating the *Complete Collected Works* to them, and they praised my edition as 'the best'.[15]

8 I showed a great many visitors around the house – about 70, most of them very young. I am exhausted. It's all quite beyond me now.

12 I spent the day searching through the journals *All the World* and *Flame* for some articles by Lyova[16] which I wanted to send him in America, but I couldn't find them. Sister Tanya helped me. After dinner we visited the grave.

13 I selected some books off the shelves to send to Lyova in America. There weren't very many.

17 400 soldiers arrived this morning with their colonel. They marched into the village last night playing music, and today they came to see us. I showed L.N.'s rooms to more than 62 of them.

18 More visitors to Lev Nik–ch's rooms – soldiers, Jews, 100 children from Kosaya Gora and several schoolboys.

19 Sister Tanya, Varya and I all visited the grave together, and I plaited some white wild flowers into a garland. We read aloud *The Peasant* by Polents;[17] what astonishing knowledge of the characters and their way of life.

21 I spend days idly and to no purpose. I am too old to run the estate; my strength is waning and my consciousness of earthly life is becoming more and more worthless. The news in the papers is of battles, and 10,000 taken prisoner, but it doesn't bring me any joy, it torments me that people should suffer so.

25 I played a Mozart sonata as a duet with my granddaughter Annochka, then we did Beethoven's 1st Symphony and Weber's 'Invitation to the Waltz'. Several guests – ladies, soldiers with their officer and so on. Then the Deputy Minister for Communications, Georgii Step. Takhtamyshev, arrived. We gave them tea and berries, and showed them the rooms. The minister had his two sons with him and some friends.

29 I spent the day with Seryozha and Masha, and was very pleased they came. This evening Seryozha, sister Tanya, Dushan Petrovich and I all went for a walk; a beautiful sunset, a prisoner was scything the timothy-grass. Seryozha left for Moscow later on with Dushan Vladimirovich, Dushan Petrovich's nephew. Seryozha's state of mind alarms and grieves me. The raids on the land and property at Nikolskoe are taking on a threatening character.

July 6 I have finished putting in order (partially, anyway) various letters. This evening sister Tanya and I read the *Early Morning* newspaper. Frightful occurrences in Petrograd: shooting, killing of our own people, looting, rioting. And these bandits are our leaders![18] My sister takes it all passionately to heart and follows everything with great interest; I merely suffer deeply. Sister Tanya is still so young – why she's even carried away by French novels!

8 I read Dushan Petrovich's memoirs. Much of it is very interesting, but there's much too that is superfluous and inaccurate.

10 We had visitors – a military doctor with some nurses, then a Japanese man serving with the Japanese embassy.

16 A party of students arrived, 40 of them, and I showed them Lev Nikolaevich's rooms in groups of ten; there were some other visitors too.

19 This evening I received visitors, young men and girls. I read Alphonse Karr's *Clothilde*, in Russian translation unfortunately.[19]

20 More guests; I showed them Lev Nikolaevich's rooms. This evening we read Loyson's play.[20]

21 Loyson arrived this evening with his secretary, who is also his interpreter.

22 I listened to Mr Loyson talking for a long time, but couldn't follow it all – his speech is so fast and complicated. Tanya took him out to visit the peasants, but almost none of them were in. Loyson's friend, Mikhail Aleksandr. Boguslavskii, an emigré, has now left.

25 I have finished a crayon drawing of a thistle (a large burdock). It was very difficult. There is a reference to this thistle in Lev Nik.'s story *Hadji Murat*.

August 1 I spent some of the time before dinner with my daughter Sasha, and the rest copying out Tanya's letters. I visited the grave and dug into the ground a vase filled with water, in which I put a great bunch of flowers. This evening sister Tanya read aloud from Danilevskii's memoirs of Tolstoy.[21]

2 My daughter Tanya went to Basovo; she is interested in village politics. I am copying letters.

6 The peasants are celebrating a double holiday; they're all singing in the village, even the two soldiers sent here to defend us. A lot of loathsome visitors.

12 N.N.Gusev has arrived.

13 There were a lot of visitors from the Shanyavskii University in Moscow, and another group with the director of the Tula High School. I was on duty from 12.30 to 4, showing them round the rooms and explaining everything.

14 I did a little copying, then at 8 o'clock I went out with my daughter Tanya to buy provisions. We visited eight shops, including four consumers' cooperatives, and we found absolutely nothing apart from ten lettuces and a loaf of rye bread. Famine looms. Dushan Petrovich's nephew went to Tula, and there too there was nothing to buy. I chattered away to Gusev, and now wish I hadn't.

17 Splendid clear summer days and moonlit nights. When Lev Nikol. visited Glebova-Streshner, my parents' house in Nikolskoe, for a month or so, the nights were just like these and he called them 'mad nights'. There were a great many visitors, a lot of them children.

20 Reading the papers takes a lot of time and induces a feeling of horror. I read the Gospels every evening; earlier on my sister and I were reading *The Black Year.*[22]

22 Today I am 73 years old. What a terrible anniversary to be alive for! Where are my unfortunate children and what are they all doing? And what about my countless grandchildren? My heart aches with the tormenting prospect of famine. I was notified today by the Committee of Enquiry that ten armed mounted soldiers would be arriving tomorrow with two officials.

25 It is sad that relations with my sister are so bad. She flies into a rage at the slightest thing, is always losing her temper with me and calling me a holy fool because I appear to take things so calmly. But no one sees what takes place in my soul.

27 I spent the day making garlands of fresh flowers and a monogram for L.N.'s grave. Tomorrow is his birthday.

28 As soon as I got up this morning I went with little Varya Eliseevna and my granddaughter Tanyushka to the grave. I put the flowers there and we swept it clean and tidied it. Then the ten mounted soldiers arrived with their two commanders. We read Danilevskii's *The Ninth Wave.*

29 We read *Communist Ideas*, collected by Posse as a supplement to *Life for All.* Most interesting![23]

30 We read the paper avidly this evening, and with great sorrow. Internecine war threatens; Kerenskii and Kornilov will not yield power. I do not wish to judge them, but this new government has done absolutely nothing for Russia.

September 1 Dreadful rumours on all sides. It's impossible to get hold of bread anywhere, all the ministries have collapsed, the best ministers have left, the best generals have been arrested. I fear that Kerenskii will turn out to be mentally ill, with delusions of grandeur.

2 I was terribly cheered by my son Misha's arrival from the Caucasus, where he wants to take his family for the winter. He was in very low spirits and I wept when he left.

5 I went out to the field and picked nine baskets full of potatoes.

11 Incomprehensible manoeuvres in government circles! Kerenskii will evidently soon fall; there are so many intrigues and failures, so much love of power and so little understanding of what is important for the country and the people!

18 I copied out Tanya's letters to me and talked to Val. Fyod. Bulgakov, who arrived this morning.[24] I am very happy to see him again; we are bound by so many memories.

20 My son Ilyusha arrived this morning, looking thin and old and wretched. He left this evening, and it was sad having to part so soon.

23 Today is my wedding anniversary. I was married to Lev Nikol. on September 23, 1862. I picked a bunch of flowers and tidied the grave, then wandered alone around the garden, recalling my youth.

27 Pyotr Aleks. Sergeenko came, saying he had been sent by Minister Nikitin to find out about the disturbances in Yasnaya Polyana.[25]

28 This evening sister Tanya and I read Danilevskii's novel *The War of 1812*. Sergeenko called some peasants in and made some suggestions to them about the defence of Yasnaya Polyana.

29 Sergeenko has gone off to a meeting.

30 I read a book of Lev Nik.'s thoughts, published by Bulgakov.[26]

October 1 A party of young girls and boys arrived from a Moscow high school where they are all taught together.

2 I have been grieving particularly for my dead ones; as though this bright weather and strong wind carry their souls to me and my love to them.

3 I wrote to Bondarchuk about the translation of Tolstoy into Ukrainian.

11 The two Tanyas read aloud L.N.'s play *The Light Shines Even in Darkness*.[27] Sergeenko is with us again.

12 N.N. Apostolov came to collect some information about *War and Peace* for his lecture.[28]

13 I read my sister an extremely intelligent article (or letter) by Prince Kropotkin.[29]

17 An agronomist called Dm. Nikit. Volkov drove here from Tula in a motor car. They have brought 12 or 10 soldiers – I can't remember how many – to protect us, and we have managed somehow to accommodate them all.[30] The entire southern part of the Krapivna district has been set on fire.

23 There is a rumour that we're to be raided, and some militiamen have come for the night to keep guard over us. None of us slept – we didn't even take off our clothes.

November 4 Captain Lyzlov and another officer came to say goodbye. The cavalry left today, and tomorrow a hundred infantrymen will be leaving. Life in the country is becoming more and more frightening, but there's nowhere else to go now.

5 The hundred infantry soldiers left today, thank God. This evening a senior militiaman arrived from Kosaya Gora with an engineer and four other men from there. It turns out that they are going to keep guard over everything, both the house and the books; they have spent the past three nights here already. This is most reassuring.[31]

7 Today is the anniversary of Lev Nikolaevich's death – seven years have passed and I am still alive! I visited the grave. There were only four visitors – two peasant intellectuals from a distant district and two Tula men.

16 My sister and I have had the idea of reading something to the village boys, but it's hard to know what. Our peasants came here this evening and held elections to the Committee. None of this is very clear to me. They started talking about an armistice, then read my story about Vanechka.[32] and Sergeenko's children's story.

19 This evening Sergeenko read us his story 'The Nurse'; it wasn't bad. Then he invited in all the soldiers and servants and first read them 'God Sees the Truth But Does Not Speak Quickly',[33] then played the gramophone.

23 This evening I was notified in a telephone call to the chief forester that we will be receiving our food from the Sergievskii Rationing Committee. I read Bulgakov's *Ethics*.

December 1 Butovich came to visit and I showed him round Lev Nik.'s rooms; he is very interested in all forms of visual art.

4 I am living in a dream and in a state of terrible turmoil. I feel so sorry for Tanya. Crowds of idle people mill around all day – apart from Tanya and me, of course, who are immersed in worries, mainly about food – and the presence of all these useless people prevents me from applying myself to anything. My daughter Sasha has arrived at last with Varvara Mikhailovna. I am so pleased to see them, despite all the difficulties we have had in the past – although even then there was a lot of closeness between us. Sasha and my sister sang beautifully this evening.

10 Alek. Nik. Parshin, the factory director, came from Kosaya Gora and told us a lot about the Urals and the factories and land there. We all spent the evening together, and Tanya read us Al. Tolstoy's poem 'The Sinner' and various verses by other poets.

11 Lidia Georgievna Parshina visited this evening and sang for us with Sasha and sister Tanya. My sister still has a lovely timbre to her voice. We read Danilevskii's 'Fugitives in New Russia'.

18 Time flies, war continues, famine looms ever closer. Sergeenko helps us to get the things we need – rye, macaroni, beans and rice.[34]

19 Endless noise and turmoil . . . I'm so happy to have my two daughters and my granddaughter here – my life depends on it. My heart aches for my absent sons.

25 Tanya read us *Evgenii Onegin*. Delightful.

26 Tanya finished reading *Evgenii Onegin* today. What a marvellous speech that is of Tatiana's rebuking Onegin! I hadn't read the work for a long time – one should always re-read old things.

27 I copied out Lyova's sad and illegible letters for 1894,[35] sewed handkerchiefs, glued some little boxes and played patience. I yearn for my dead Andryusha and absent Lyova.

28 Yet more visitors to Lev Nik.'s rooms – the officer of a sappers' regiment, called Avenarius, with his comrade and a pretty young girl. There were more soldiers here too – ours – with a guest of theirs.

31 The last day of a difficult year. This evening Tanya read us 'What People Live For'.[36] We didn't see in the New Year, but everyone had dinner with us – 12 of us in all – and just as the New Year was about to begin Sergeenko read us some short stories by Chekhov. When I was alone in my room my heart started aching for my sons. Where are Lyova and Ilya? Are Seryozha and Misha still alive? What about their families? And what about Dora and her eight children? My soul grieves for them all.

· 1918 ·

February – first allied landings in North Russia. Germany resumes invasion. March 3 – the Bolsheviks, after long and bitter arguments amonst themselves, finally agree to sign Brest Litovsk peace treaty with Germany, which grants their aggressor a large percentage of Russia's coalfields, industrial centres and farming land. May – Civil War begins in earnest, when Czech prisoners of war, backed by France and Britain, rise up against Bolshevik government. This signals a wave of revolts, financed by Britain, France, America and Japan, and led by former tsarist generals and admirals (Kolchak, Denikin, Yudenich, and others) known as White Guards. Anticipating an invasion of Moscow, the Bolsheviks move the capital to Petrograd. Summer – Bolsheviks' fortunes at their lowest ebb.

April – official opening of Yasnaya Polyana Society in Tula, which takes control of estate. Tanya Sukhotina becomes caretaker of the Yasnaya Polyana Museum. Food in short supply and life is hard. Tanya knits scarves to sell in the market to support her sister, mother and daughter. May – Bolshevkik commissars visit Yasnaya Polyana. November – Tanya Sukhotina replaces secretary of Yasnaya Polyana Society and takes control of the house. Lev Tolstoy leaves Russia with his wife and children to live in Sweden.

January 1 This evening we lit the candles on the Christmas tree, invited 20 children in and gave them all something. After the Christmas tree we had a 'democratic ball', as Sergeenko put it, and everyone danced – soldiers and prisoners, our servants and maids and the two Tanyas.

3 Tanya read us Leskov's 'The Wild Beast' this evening, and another story. Then Sergeenko read us 'The Old Genius'.

4 Sergeenko went to Tula for kerosene – we sit her with one lamp and a wax candle. For just one *pood** of bad kerosene we now pay 60 rubles.

5 During the recent storm the roof was broken and blown off, and L.N.'s room was flooded with melting snow.

6 My daughter Tanya read aloud an excerpt from *War and Peace*. How good it is, and how profound in places.

7 We were all shocked to hear that the Constituent Assembly had been dissolved and that Shingarev and Kokoshkin had been murdered by two sailors.[1] Some peasants came to visit, and Sergeenko and my daughter Tanya talked to them. This evening we read aloud some more Leskov. I don't like him, although my sister reads him very well.

14 I am handing over the management of Yasnaya Polyana to my daughter Tanya, and shall hire a steward. I missed my sons terribly today, especially Lyova and Andryusha. Is Lyova still alive, I wonder?!

18 I spoke on the telephone to the manager of a sugar factory and asked him to let me have some; I am getting ten pounds. Then I asked Volkov for some iron from the *zemstvo* to mend the roofs, and they agreed to give me seven sheets but refused to give me anything else. This evening Tanya read aloud some Turgenev prose poems.

21 Vysokomirnyi came and introduced some discipline amongst the soldiers;[2] he is a most agreeable man, also a soldier at present.

23 Tanya went to Kolpna for a committee meeting. They are taking our forest away from us.[3]

26 Alarming rumours of a pogrom of the young villagers. Distressing discussions with Tanya about Sergeenko, who has returned from Tula infected with delusions of power and keeps interfering with her instructions. Her unkind attitude to me almost made me weep.

*About 4 gallons.

February 2 This evening Tanya read aloud *The Power of Darkness.*[4]

4 I worked hard on the library all morning. Some visitors came to see the house, the grave and Lev Nik.'s rooms.

5 I wrote to Meyer and a peasant telling them where to get hold of a copy of *A Collation of the Four Gospels*, and I sent the letter on to the Intermediary company.[5] This evening my sister read us 'Daisy', an extremely bad short story by Sergeenko.[6]

6 Went to Lev Nikolaevich's grave with Manya. We cleared a little snow and scattered oats for the birds.

14 Sasha arrived for dinner with a scheme to publish a new edition of the *Complete Collected Works of L.N. Tolstoy.*[7]

15 News that the Germans have seized Petersburg;[8] the situation in Russia is becoming increasingly desperate. My daughters and I sorted through various manuscripts and documents concerning Lev Nik–ch.

16 Sasha and I spent the morning transferring the rights to the manuscripts to her and Seryozha, photographing them and deciding which works should be annotated and issued separately.

17 It's a sad life. We are seeing Sasha off to Moscow again, and it is particularly hard to part with her this time for some reason. I found her a little food to take, as she'll be arriving there during the night. My daughter Tanya read us 'Lucerne'[9] and a letter from Salomon about his murdered nephew.[10]

19 I've had a sudden passionate desire to paint a portrait of Lev Nik. – a copy from Repin: there is one by him which he did not complete and I want to finish it. I have collected everything I need, although I don't know whether the paints will do – they may have dried out.

23 The anniversary of Vanechka's death, and the day before Andryusha's. Where are they now, my beloved boys? My daughter Tanya is my chief consolation now. If only she were happy – as it is, I feel so sorry for her.

25 I did a lot of writing. Everyone had dinner with me. Politics are an incomprehensible muddle. Vysokomirnyi came from Tula. He serves on the Committee of Enquiry (there, I think).[11]

26 I set Vysokomirnyi various tasks – the album, the flower and mushroom drawings, cataloguing books and so on. I did almost no writing at all, just a mournful account of the death of Liza Olsufieva.[12] Dushan Petrovich and Sergeenko have gone off to an arbitration court at Kosaya Gora, and Vysokomirnyi has left.

March 2 I did some copying, then got everything ready to correct my copy of Lev Nik.'s portrait. I fear I am no longer capable of working in oils. Vanya Erdeli played various pieces beautifully on the piano. Bad news from Moscow; they're not issuing any money.

3 I've started correcting my copy of Repin's portrait of Lev Nik–ch. My work is hampered chiefly by the unsteadiness of my hand: try as one might to draw a straight line, it comes out crooked. My soul is melancholy. Maria Mikhailovna, Sergei Nikolaevich's widow, has just died.[13]

5 I copied L.N.'s portrait again, and again it was no good. This evening I looked through *My Life* and on reading it became very agitated.

8 They have refused me a pension, and have promised me 300 rubles instead of 800.[14]

15 After dinner I looked through my memoirs (*My Life*) for Misha Sergeenko, who is taking notes in the room where Lev Nik. used to write.

17 My daughter read aloud some stories by Victor Hugo after dinner, then Mitya read us various documents published in *The Past* about Lev Nik.'s supposed death and funeral in Yalta.[15] Painful and pointless political arguments between Kolya Obolenskii, Mitya Kuzminskii and sister Tanya. Exhausting too.

20 I copied out Tanya's letters and compiled an inventory of Dushan Petrovich's room, which is still in exactly the same state as it was after Lev Nik.'s death.

21 I went with Manya to three consumers' cooperatives and two shops, where I found some bad brown macaroni, some stale Greek nuts, some matches and some chicory coffee.

24 I wrote an inventory of the two libraries and Lev Nik.'s bedroom.

25 I inventoried the main things in Lev Nik–ch's rooms all morning. Then I wrote to my son Seryozha about the impossibility of taking photographic copies of Lev Nik.'s manuscripts, and to Georgievskii saying the same thing.[16]

26 Busy all day sorting out and taking notes from my letters of 1917 and the first part of 1918.

29 I worked on *My Life*, entering the dates on to the pages; I had not done so before for some reason.

30 An unexpected joy – my son Misha spoke to me on the telephone and promised to visit tomorrow. I worked hard on *My Life*.

31 This morning I worked on my memoirs and read the papers. Horrors!
My son Misha arrived; he is much changed, and I feel so sorry for him with his worries and his indecisiveness. But he's a splendid fellow – energetic, intelligent and agreeable.

April 1 I spent the day with my beloved Misha, who has now left for Tula. He is cheerful and energetic. Lord help him!

3 Tanya invented a game for us to play: she brought in several pictures and asked each of us to choose one and write something about it. I wrote a story yesterday evening, and today I copied it out.[17] Our visitors were a delegate from the Swedish embassy, with Countess Douglas and a translator.

4 There was an unpleasant scene with P.A. Sergeenko today. He was rude to me, and I told him that if Lev Nik. could have heard a complete outsider insulting his wife in this way he would have thrown him out of the window.

5 It was very disagreeable having to see Sergeenko this morning, despite all the help he has given me in the past. 'He is not a gentleman,' Miss Welsh once said of him.* He is not an educated or a good person, and he has something on his mind concerning Yasnaya Polyana.

7 Two agronomists, Dmitr. Nik. Volkov and Serg. Georg. Bogoyavlenskii, arrived from Tula today to discuss Yasnaya Polyana. They want to repair the garden and set it to rights. The spring brings me little joy; I suffer too much from thoughts of those going hungry in Russia and in our house.

*In English in the original.

10 I am very depressed at having lost my six-page inventory of things on the top floor. I've looked absolutely everywhere, and nowhere can I find my six pages. Two hungry girl students came from Moscow to look round the house.

12 A great many visitors came to look round the house and Lev Nikol–ch's rooms. This took up the whole of my day. After dinner I read some Russian journals, and this morning before coffee I walked to the grave with Misha Sergeenko, and silently begged Lyovochka's forgiveness before the fast.

15 Our young peasants came here this evening, saying they wanted to take all my land away.[18]

24 I copied out Tanya's letters. Then the whole village came and invited me to accompany them to Lev Nik.'s grave. Naturally I went – relations are good. Everyone knelt, and everyone sang 'Eternal Memory' three times.[19]

27 A Frenchman called M. Vauchet came with a young translator from *L'Illustration*.

28 I spent the day with the Frenchman, Robert Vauchet, correspondent for *L'Illustration* and *Petit Paris*, and his translator.

29 A great crowd of people of every class gathered at the grave today: smart ladies and little girls, children and young people. (There were very few real peasants – they were all in Tula.) Vakulenko the photographer took a photograph of the whole groups. What was it all for, and for whose benefit? It's a complete mystery. Then he photographed me and a group of people standing by the house. All so distressing and pointless.

30 The two Frenchmen left yesterday evening, and Goldenblatt and Vysokomirnyi dined with us.

May 6 Spent the morning copying, then visited the grave with my sister's maid; there were some young people there. Before dinner the war commissar, Bor. Iv. Kalinin, came with two young people and three women.[20]

8 Sorted out papers and destroyed some of them.

9 The religious holiday of Nicholas the Miracle-Worker, which the peasants celebrated in their usual coarse fashion. I did some writing and

Sergeenko came in for a talk. It's terribly difficult to communicate with him – one moment he's being sentimental, the next he's impossibly rude. But he has been such an enormous help that one has to simply put up with it. Several visitors – teachers from the railway – and I had my photograph taken with them.

12 I received some books from Bulgakov[21] and Nelyubin about Grand Duke Konstantin Konstantinovich.[22]

13 I had a visit from the Tula land committee, all from the common people but not disagreeable.

15 I read Bulgakov's *The Last Year of L.N. Tolstoy's Life*. It makes painful reading. There are a lot of assumptions, evasions and half-truths in it. For instance, he doesn't mention the fact that on the evening of October 28 Lev Nik.'s pulse was 96, and he was ill when he left.

17 I started the day by tidying up Lev Nikolaevich's rooms. Then some rather pleasant visitors came to see L.N.'s rooms. After dinner D. Nikit. Volkov came with a Latvian friend of his called Iv. Iv. Ritten.

20 My sister and I have been sorting out papers and putting them in order. Sergeenko is going off tomorrow to buy bread, potatoes and bran.

23 My son Seryozha has asked me to copy out the years and dates of the entries in Lev Nikolaevich's diaries, and I have been working on this all day.[23]

24 I continued the work on Lev Nik.'s diaries which Seryozha had asked me to do, I said goodbye to my sister Tanya: she is leaving for Petersburg.

28 I worked on various manuscripts, papers and other things concerning Lev Nik., and started compiling a catalogue. E.V. Tolstoya arrived this evening.

June 2 Still the same work sorting out the manuscripts (although now there are more printed documents of Lev Nik.'s).

3 An unpleasant telegram from Sergeenko saying he is stuck in Kazan and doesn't think he'll be able to find any provisions. A huge party of young people here – all Jews. I showed 82 of them around the rooms and am now exhausted. I visited the grave.

6 Misha Sergeenko has been reading me Bulgakov's book about Lev Nik. every evening.

7 Some visitors came to see Lev Nik.'s rooms and grave and stayed in Zaseka – pupils and a teacher from Kashira technical school; then two doctors, three women and two other men arrived from Kolpna; then some sort of clerk and four other men. All very exhausting, but solitude is also hard.

8 A happy telegram from Lyova in Petrograd, of June 20/7.[24]*

9 I decided to clean and tidy the pavilion. The soldiers mowed the grass around the house and chopped off dead branches, and I helped. Count Dmitrii Georg. Tolstoy came to visit accompanied by two artists; one was an academician with a grade-one diploma.

14 Spent most of the day reading Bulgakov's *Lev Tolstoy in the Last Year of His Life*. It was such a sad time, and so painful to read about and remember. I made a few corrections to my inventory of the house.

16 Tikh. Iv. Polner arrived with my daughter Sasha. She is full of energy; she and Seryozha are apparently making an excellent job of the manuscripts, and sorting out everything in the Rumyantsev Museum. She is just the same plump jolly Sasha with her love of gipsy songs – and just as incomprehensible to me as ever.

18 I corrected some mistakes in Bulgakov's book, talked to Polner and read him excerpts from *My Life*, which he praised.[25]

19 I corrected Bulgakov's book and sorted out my manuscripts. I have to make a table of contents for *My Life*.

25 I am reading V.F. Bulgakov's *Diary* – the further I read the worse it gets. Boasting flattery, subservience to Chertkov, occasional departures from the truth, spiteful silence about various things, and tactless disclosures of things that should not have been mentioned at all.

29 I had a visit from the grandchildren of Sergei Nikolaevich Tolstoy. Sergei Grigorevich is a good, naïve boy.

July 2 I read Lev Nik.'s *Circle of Reading*.

*After the October revolution the Bolshevik government adopted the modern Julian calendar, 13 days in advance of the old Gregorian calendar. Hence the two dates.

4 Unpleasant discussions with Sergeenko about the suitcases full of L.N.'s manuscripts and things in the Tula archive.[26]

7 I read the *Circle of Reading* a little at a time. Sergeenko brought an assistant commissar here this evening to discuss the ownership of the land, and I showed him round the rooms.

14 I have finished listing all the books in Lev Nik.'s rooms. It came to 16 half-sheets of paper.

15 This morning I chopped the dead branches off the linden trees and showed visitors around Lev Nikolaevich's rooms. Al. Al. Saburov, director of the State Bank, arrived with his two daughters and Seryozha Tolstoy.

16 I am slowly reading through the *Circle of Reading*. A surveyor called Vekshin called with an assistant to draw up plans for a path from the highway to the grave.[27]

20 I got carried away by a copy of my own painting of the pond. Tanya read us 'Polikushka'.[28]

22 Some commissars and various other gentlemen arrived from Tula – twenty in all – and looked at Lev Nik.'s rooms.

30 I wandered about the estate all day, my heart heavy with the woes of Russia. An architect-academician came with plans for constructing a school. This evening we read aloud some Fet and Salias.[29]

August 5 This evening my daughter Tanya read us various poems.

8 This evening Sergeenko read us *Woe from Wit*, and later we all had a discussion about literature.

9 My son Seryozha came – I was intensely glad to see him. 'My dearest eldest children,' as Lev Nik. said to Seryozha and Tanya just before his death. This evening Seryozha played the piano and little Tanya beat the drum in time to him. My 55-year-old Seryozha has grown very thin, and this is very sad for his mother.

10 I sat and talked to Seryozha all morning; Sasha arrived earlier on. I love seeing my children, but it's sad to have to part with them, and annoying to be unable to give them any *treats*. Seryozha played the piano long and beautifully this evening.

11 Seryozha went out for a walk looking sad and thin. This evening he played marvellously two Beethoven sonatas and some other pieces: music is a source of such pleasure, and also such sadness. I have grown to understand it better now.

17 I visited the grave with my granddaughter Sonechka, and from there we took a long walk through the wood and the felled sapling plantation. I remember when Lev Nik. and I cheerfully planted these trees together – they weren't even allowed to grow! I read an article about current events in the *Herald of Europe*.[30]

26 Count Dmitrii Adam. Olsufiev arrived this morning with Nikol. Evgen. Felten. We spent the evening talking, the guests looked through my memoirs and albums and were fascinated by everything.

27 This morning I picked a meagre bunch of flowers and made garlands for Lev Nik.'s grave for his birthday tomorrow. We then took the flowers to the grave.

28 My son Misha arrived this morning, and P.A. Sergeenko. I am oppressed by the worry of finding food for everyone – there were twelve of us here for dinner today. Some of our peasants came and invited me to accompany them to the grave, and we all went and sang 'Eternal Memory' three times.

29 My son Misha and Count Dm. Adam. Olsufiev have left for Kiev and beyond. May God keep them safe. Misha's family is in Zheleznovodsk.

September 3 I wrote a new will to include Sasha amongst my heirs: she had been cut out for her outrageous behaviour to me after her father's death, but now I have forgiven her.[31]

13 Some technicians arrived late this evening to draw up an estimate and a plan for a water-pipe.

October 7 A rushed and exhausting day. Dehring came from the Rationing Committee with three comrades – a Jew, a Latvian and a Russian called Stepanov. We drank tea and visited the grave, then a party of about fifty people came – adult horticultural students. I showed them Lev Nik.'s rooms in four groups

8 Alya Sukhotin read us *An Ordinary Story*.[32]

12 My daughter-in-law S.N.Tolstaya came this morning. I was pleased to see her, for she reminds me of old times, although many things about her are very foreign to me now. She finds life easier than most because she is a theosophist; she sings too, and she and Sasha organise singing evenings together.

13 I swept up piles of dead leaves for some exercise. I love work of every kind – intellectual, artistic and physical.

14 After dinner Tanya read us Pushkin's *Dubrovskii*. It's a long time since I last read it; it's interestingly written.

17 This evening we read aloud Turgenev's *Nest of the Gentry*. Obolenskii was reading.

19 Life is sorrow. I could be happy with my two Tanyas, though. But I am estranged from my sister – we're so different in everything.

23 I visited Tula with Manya and Misha, collected my pension and went to the State Bank to negotiate a bank-note for 65,000 rubles. A festival of freedom is being organised in the town.

24 A lady called Anna Mitrof. Golenko arrived from the Board of Administrators to inventory all the valuables at Yasnaya Polyana.[33]

25 Seryozha and Sasha arrived this evening and brightened up our lives.

26 How happy I am to have my children here! I particularly love my Seryozha. Tanya is so severe with me, but Seryozha is especially sweet and gentle.

28 The anniversary of Lev Nikolaevich's departure from the house. This evening Seryozha and Sasha read aloud Seryozha's splendid article about Turgenev's visit to Yasnaya Polyana.[34]

November 2 We finished *Evgenii Onegin* and started on *Poltava*.

4 My daughter Tanya read us Pushkin's *Queen of Spades* and later on Misha Sergeenko and my sister read us a biography of Pushkin.

7 The two Tanyas, Miss Welsh, Misha Sergeenko and Verochka Sidorkova went to Tula for an evening organised to commemorate Lev Nik.'s death. Our peasants called at the house and invited me to L.N.'s grave. I went, and we all sang 'Eternal Memory' three times. This evening we read the Pushkin biography.

8 Everyone returned from Tula, where they had attended an evening commemorating Lev Nik.'s death. I did a lot of copying and read a biography of N.A. Nekrasov. What a terrible childhood, and what a monster of a father! And his poor beloved mother!

10 I did some copying and read a biography of the unfortunate poet Nekrasov. Then we read aloud Ostrovskii's *The Marriage of Balzaminov.*

11 The little girls sang with Tatiana Andreevna, whose tender, mellifluous voice always touches me deeply.

21 Pav. Iv. Biryukov and Varv. Mikh. Feokritova came. This evening Pavel Ivanovich read the third part of his biography of Lev Nikol–ch.[35]

23 We read Lev Nik.'s biography again this evening. From it I realised that for him Chertkov was a *repository of ideas*, expressed in all the letters and articles he sent. For Chertkov, of course, these were a valuable *repository of manuscripts*, which he then took to England.[36]

24 Pavel. Iv. Biryukov and V. Mikh. Feokritova left for Moscow. I coached Tanyushka and worked. This evening Sergeenko read beautifully from Gogol's *Dead Souls*, and later my son Ilya's three boys arrived from the station – Misha, who has just spent four years as a prisoner of war, Andryusha with his St George Cross, and Volodya.

25 Two groups of visitors arrived from Tula to look round L.N.'s rooms.

27 My grandsons Andryusha, Misha and Volodya left early this morning and I did some copying. This evening Tanya read a little, then Dushan Petrovich read us his reminiscences of Lev Nik.

December 3 I am mourning the death of my brother Sasha. He had been in poor health for some time.

10 Sergeenko came and brought an architect to design a model school for the peasants. Nothing will come of it; it's an enormous enterprise.

11 This evening Sergeenko read us some Ovid and Socrates from the *Circle of Reading*.[37]

21 My daughter Sasha arrived late this evening, with Zosya Stakhovich and my grandson Ilyushok. They are all hungry, but Sasha always laughs about everything.

22 I talked to Zosya about her research on *War and Peace*. She is evidently approaching it very intelligently. This evening she read us some excerpts from it.[38]

29 At N.V. Davydov's request I copied a letter to him and an excerpt from my notes containing information about the comedy *The Nihilist, or The Infected Family*.[39]

30 Where am I? Where is my love for the arts, nature and people? I had an argument with my beloved daughter Tanya about all these outsiders here – then there's the trouble with the servants and people's constant dissatisfaction with everyone and everything, despite my attempts to please them all.

31 Tanya arranged a completely unexpected New Year's party at my grandson Ilyusha's request. We were all delighted and went into her wing, where we happily saw in the New Year together.

· 1919 ·

July to August – Crimea falls to Whites. September – Ukraine evacuated as Whites invade, then Bolsheviks' fortunes improve. October – Yudenich's White Army beaten back from Petrograd. November – Denikin's White Army in headlong retreat. December – Bolshevik government introduces 'militarisation of labour'.

March – at the request of Sofia Tolstaya and Tanya Sukhotina, the Yasnaya Polyana Society takes over their portion of the land and uses it as farm. July – Sofia writes farewell note and distributes valuables amongst her loved ones. September – Red Guards quartered in village of Yasnaya Polyana. October – guards moved to nearby village after protests from Yasnaya Polyana Society. November – Sofia Tolstaya catches chill. November 4 – she dies of pneumonia. Buried beside her daughter Masha in Kochaki cemetery. Shortly afterwards her son Mikhail emigrates to France.

January 2 We read *Dead Souls* this evening.[1] I do not like these false-comic characters and situations, but there are some lovely lyrical passages and descriptions of nature. I haven't read it for a long time.

3 Dm. Nik. Volkov came with his daughter and had a discussion with Tanya about the fate of the neglected Yasnaya Polyana apple orchard and various other estate matters. This evening Tanya read us Vasilii Morozov's memoirs about the school, Lev Nik., and their journey to the *kumis* cure. It's very cleverly written.[2]

4 I miss my children dreadfully. It's so hard for Seryozha, who is no longer young, to go hungry and cold! Where is Misha's family, and what are they doing? Where is Ilya? Where is Lyova and his family?! I added some explanations and notes to *Letters to His Wife*.[3]

7 I spent most of the day writing my notes, and this evening Pyotr Alekseevich read one or two comic passages from Ilya's memoirs.[4] Earlier this evening we read Gogol's tedious *Dead Souls*.

9 I read Lev Nik.'s pamphlet 'To Political Activists'.[5]

12 I did a lot of writing – typing and making notes for my book of Lev Nik.'s letters to me.

16 I finished one book of notes, and I will start on another tomorrow.

20 Various guests – Yak. Iv. Butovich the millionaire, Dmitrii Nikit. Volkov to talk about the land and the estate, and B.I. Denisenko about another matter.

21 Sergeenko sneaked in and choked me with talk for an hour and a half. What a tiresome man. He said some people had arrived from some sort of committee for the defence of the children of Krapivna; they wanted to evict everyone but me from the two houses, he said, in order to build a home for twelve orphans, and I would be given two rooms to live in. I don't believe a word of it, but one feels constantly alarmed.[6]

26 I wrote letters, and made copies of them, to the sales department of Kushneryov and Co., asking them to give me back my book *L.N. Tolstoy's Letters To His Wife*.[7]

27 Arsenev, Vysokomirnyi, Goldenblatt, Mikh. Al. Yusov the foreman, headstrong young Varshaver, Sergeenko and my daughter Tanya all held a conference on Yasnaya Polyana affairs. I have little confidence in their plans. This evening my daughter Tanya arrived with Felten.

30 Al. Nik. Arsenev arrived from Tula with two other men. Tanya wants to hand the estate over to the Society for the Protection of Yasnaya

Polyana.[8] I do not understand how this could be done, and I cannot believe it would be successful. This evening I entered a lot of my new notes into *L.N. Tolstoy's Letters to His Wife.* Then at 11 o'clock P.A. Sergeenko arrived and showered me with coarse, spiteful criticisms, blaming me for driving L.N. out of the house. What business is it of his? How *dare* anyone judge a man and wife? Especially a diabolical, spiteful, uneducated boor like him. I was so stunned I couldn't even reply.

31 I made a lot of notes. To do this I have to re-read the whole of *L.N. Tolstoy's Letters to His Wife.* How much love there is in those letters! How could everything have changed so suddenly? This evening Tanya came. She's always pleasant company and often very interesting. What about my other unfortunate children? It's terrible to imagine them freezing and starving.

February 1 I sat at my desk all day making notes to *Letters to His Wife.* I was tormented with sadness as I read some of his letters to me, in which one could sense how much suffering I caused him with my criticisms, my demands that he live with me and so on. But my desire not to be parted from him sprang from my love for him! I loved him so deeply, to the end of his life.

3 I visited the grave and felt a little less dismal; Tanya and the children gave me a ride home. I had a letter from Felten, saying that the present government had allowed me, as an exception, to take possession of my books of *Count L.N. Tolstoy's Letters to His Wife*, and that they would buy them from me for 8,000 rubles.

5 I have started copying Tanya's letters again. Reading them carries me back painfully to the past. How far we were then from what is happening now.

8 Verochka Sidorkova came, bearing unpleasant news: apparently there are only 8 copies of *L.N. Tolstoy's Letters to His Wife* at the Kushneryov works. What can have happened to the other 4,432?

9 My sister and I sat together at the large round table in the drawing-room, and recalled all the people who had sat at that table in the past. We never thought then that most of them would leave, and it breaks my heart to think that those who are still alive are cold, hungry and at war.

18 I signed a document handing over the Yasnaya Polyana estate to Kolya Obolenskii.

23 P.A. Sergeenko and Kolya Obolenskii have left for a 'conference' of the Tolstoy Society. I have no faith in the successful management of the Society.

24 Kolya Obolenskii and P.A. Sergeenko gave me to understand in a brief conversation on their return that there were disagreements within the Tolstoy Society. As far as I can understand, they want to raise a large loan on the dilapidated Yasnaya Polyana estate – but who will pay for it no-one knows. There is no landlord, no bailiff and no workers.[9]

Tanya said a lot of cruel things to me today. If only she could understand how unhappy she makes me! She has taken on the running of the estate, hasn't made a success of it, and now suffers for it and attacks me, although I cannot imagine why. And there's no one in the world I love more than her!

28 My daughter Tanya has gone to Tula for a meeting of the Tolstoy Society this evening. Kolya Obolenskii went too.

March 1 P.A. Sergeenko read us *Madame Bovary* – unfortunately in a Russian translation.[10]

2 Two members of the Tolstoy Society, Serebrovskii and Chenkov, arrived from Tula. A lot of talk, but I still don't know how this business of the estate is to be settled.

3 Five Bolsheviks came here with Goldenblatt, and for some unknown reason they brought us some white flour, cheese, coffee and tea.

5 Obolenskii went to Tula for a meeting of the Tolstoy Educational Society. I have no confidence in their efficiency or value.

7 I copied letters and read a book of Kuprin stories[11] which I took from Lev Nik.'s shelves – very dull and often very improper.

8 I have recently had a sense of Lev Nik.'s presence, and there was a quiet, affectionate tenderness about his behaviour to me. Where is he now? And where are all those who have left and whom I used to love? How much longer will I languish on this earth? But it is all in God's hands!

11 I finished copying Tanya's letters to me for 1905. The Clan publishing house has taken her Memoirs and will pay her for them.[12] Poor Tanya, she has to earn a living for herself and her little girl! Vysokomirnyi came this evening. He has some job on the Investigating Committee – a most sympathetic man, but already worn out by his work. Everyone here has

such a strange attitude to me – it's as if they merely *tolerate* me, listening patronisingly to what I have to say, and hurrying away. I have evidently become *superfluous*.

13 Vysokomirnyi left this morning for Tula, well pleased with his visit to Yasnaya Polyana.

16 Serebrovskii, B. Os. Goldenblatt and Al. Nik. Gassilovskii came to discuss the running of the estate and the repairs, and they stayed for tea and dinner.

20 I did some sewing, poured coffee for Dushan Petrovich, then went into the Kuzminskiis' wing and stayed a long time there with Tanya. She always makes me feel happier, stronger and easier in my mind.

21 Spent the time before dinner sorting through papers and entering them into my notebook. What an enormous variety: sheet music, paintings, records of the mowing and the village economy, inventories, visiting cards, open letters – impossible to name it all. I tried to read a little: I wanted to re-read Doroshevich's article about the time after Lev Nik.'s departure, called 'Sofia Andreevna', but I couldn't – my sight is too bad.[13]

April 28 My daughter Tanya set us a competition – we all had to write an essay called 'The Dream'. I have already written mine.[14]

29 This evening P.A. Sergeenko read aloud Pushkin's *Mozart and Salieri*.

May 1 I visited the grave. Magnificent weather, a beautiful spring day. My sister and I picked some lungworts and other forest flowers, and took them there. This evening Dushan Petrovich read us 'Johannes Damascenus'.[15]

8 I carefully tidied and cleaned Lev Nik–ch's rooms and my own. I was visited this evening by two engineers who are going to build a road to Yasnaya Polyana, and I chatted idly to one of them, who had known Andryusha as a child. His name is Kalita.

19 A large party of 79 young people came. They visited the grave with P.A. Sergeenko and sang 'Eternal Memory' to Lev Nik–ch three times. The Seryozha business (they were threatening to throw him out of his flat) has now been settled and they have left him in peace.

25 A vast number of people came to look round Lev Nik.'s rooms – children, high-school boys, young girls and members of some tribunal or other.

30 A mass of visitors this morning. Some young girls sang in a choir, went for a walk, then ate their own lunch in the village – bread, eggs and milk. After we had had our dinner they sang again and drank tea with us; then my sister Tatiana Andreevna sang beautifully – first with a small choir, with my little granddaughter Tanechka joining in, then on her own – and everyone was enchanted by her voice. There were more than 200 people here in all.

June 3 I visited the grave with the engineer to show him where to lay the footpath (or pavement) to the grave. Sergeenko's plan is quite unsuitable.

4 At four o'clock today my son Seryozha arrived and I came to life, got up and had dinner with the others.

5 This morning I checked Lev Nik.'s diaries with Seryozha.[16] It's very painful to read what he wrote about me. A party of 80 young girls and boys arrived.

6 I checked Lev Nikolaevich's diaries with Seryozha, and gave him his father's service-list[17] and our marriage licence to copy. It's so pleasant to have Seryozha here. As I listened to him play I vividly recalled Lev Nikolaevich, his eyes filled with tears and an expression of anguish on his face.

7 Seryozha played beautifully this evening – first some Grieg, then a brilliant performance of a Weber sonata which Lev Nikolaevich loved and played many times himself. A disagreeable conversation with Obolenskii about the estate. He loves to throw money around and lord it over us.

8 Whit Sunday! Beautiful weather, the lilacs and lilies-of-the-valley are all flowering profusely. There are grass snakes and patches of dry moss on the apple trees. Sasha and my granddaughter Annochka arrived from the station, and everyone was delighted to see them. Lots of singing and dancing.

9 Delightful weather, magnificent lilacs, nightingales, a mass of lilies-of-the-valley. We have everything here, and my 'beloved' eldest children, as their father called them, are with me – yet a terrible sadness gnaws at my

heart; I have so little love for people, I only love my *own* children and my little Tanechka. Annochka, another granddaughter, has come, and I am happy to see her.

11 I visited the grave with Seryozha Obolenskii, and imagined with agonising clarity the face of my beloved husband lying beneath the earth. I was thinking about Seryozha, and realising that the reason I have such a special relationship with him and Tanya is because they are both a link with my past happiness.

14 Endless worries about the estate and keeping things in order. I sorted through books and journals, then copied Tanya's letters to me. How much love there used to be between us! And now? People merely tolerate me, they don't love me. But I love my children, come what may.

18 Copied Tanya's letters all morning, then took excerpts from my memoirs for Tanya's literary work.

19 Tidied Lev Nik.'s rooms. 120 visitors, all boys.

21 Sasha came this morning, accompanied by a certain pedagogue called Maksin, with whom my daughter Tanya had a long talk. We all walked to the Voronka, past the grave, and it was sad to see for the first time the old forest devastated by felling.

22 We had a great many visitors today and I am exhausted. Another meeting of the Tolstoy Society – all words and no action. More visitors this evening from the Rationing Committee. One of them was nothing but a dreamer.

23 A party of children and schoolboys came from Tula, and Tanya showed them round Lev Nik.'s rooms. I plaited a garland of daisies, picked some wild flowers and covered the whole grave with them.

27 Yesterday I took some of our stamped library books from Dushan Petrovich.

July 5 I copied letters. Various rumours about Denikin's victories, the capture and burning of Elets, the entrenchments at Kosaya Gora and so on.

9 The air was very stormy again this morning, and I again started choking and had to lie down. Interesting discussions and recollections on the verandah this evening of various Russian writers.

13 I again spent the morning and part of the day in bed, gasping for breath. Various parties of people walked and drove over here to see our house and visit the grave. Tanya bought me a big bouquet of wild flowers and a bunch of sweet late berries. I wept when she left. I have never loved anyone so much as I love her, but it seems I have grieved her deeply!

14 Rumours that General Denikin is marching on Tula with his troops. Unrest in Tula; people have been marching with white flags and putting them up over the post-office building. What will come of it? The artist Yuon paid me a visit and praised my flower drawings. I wrote a letter to be opened after my death, bidding farewell to my family and begging forgiveness from those I am abandoning.[18] My grandson Ilya came, and certain gentlemen arrived from Tula with splendid horses and carriages to inspect the site for a school.

15 I felt so unwell these past few days that I thought my death was near. So I summoned my two darling Tanyas, who have been living with me for three years, and the three of us went through my few valuable possessions together. I considered it only fair to give my best things to my daughter and granddaughter. They have lived with me through the most difficult time in my life and have always been such a comfort to me. To my granddaughter I gave my gold watch and chain, which Lev Nik. gave me, and a large diamond brooch which was a present from him when we were engaged to be married; to my daughter I gave my mother's bracelet (gold) and a ring with two diamonds and a ruby, a present from Lev Nik. for all my help and labours when he was writing *Anna Karenina*. (This ring was in fact called *Anna Karenina*.)

19 Rumours that Denikin is marching here with his troops to fight the 'Bolsheviks', but whether that will be any better God knows! The Bolsheviks give us everything we need and do not insult us. P.A. Sergeenko read to us this evening from his *Tolstoy Almanac*.[19] It was very interesting; I had forgotten so much, and it was good to be reminded of it.

20 I gave Tanya the will I made in her favour.[20] A worrying letter from my son Seryozha. Where are my sons and their families!!! My soul is sad.

26 Alarming rumours that Denikin's troops are marching on Tula, and are going to plunder us.

August 1 Nik. Nik. Gusev came. Vysokomirnyi is still here, and the Pyatnitskii family has settled in the village. (He is a dentist.)

6 I tidied Lev Nik.'s rooms, which was very difficult with my bad leg. Every time I go into his room I recall my dead husband's image, and it makes me so sad! I read a little book by Dickens that I came across called *A Christmas Carol.* I love Dickens.

11 My mind is weakening. 'The road ran up to the mountain,' as Turgenev said.

14 Rumours that the Bolsheviks' power is collapsing. Everyone here is rejoicing, but I am grateful to them for their constant help and attention.

17 My daughter-in-law Olga Konstantinovna came with her children and niece, as well as a Georgian who heads some government commission. Later this evening Val. Fyod. Bulgakov appeared. We were delighted to see one another again, and had a long conversation about Tolstoy affairs.

18 Bulgakov is a good and intelligent man, and a pleasure to be with.

20 Tanya, Bulgakov and I were hosts to a meeting about the renovation of the Khamovniki house, but I don't believe anything will come of it.

24 Tanya has started talking more and more about leaving Yasnaya Polyana. She hates Sergeenko-*père*, she feels overwhelmed by the Obolenskii family, the noise of the children, the worries about food, the loneliness and so on – it is all a great burden to her and I quite understand. But life without my two Tatianas is a sad and lonely prospect.

27 P.A. Sergeenko read us *Father Sergii.*[21] What a lovely work of art this is! I live here with my sister and find myself more and more estranged from her. I expect I am to blame, and this is very painful.

28 Bulgakov has left for Tula to give a lecture about Tolstoy. My life is sad and lonely. My daughter Tanya is cold and distant with me, and this is very hard. I have never loved anyone so much.

September 1 There are rumours that some Red Guards are being stationed in our village to fight Denikin.[22]

5 Alarming news this evening that soldiers have been quartered in peasant huts with their regimental commander. Also that some soldiers have been dispatched from Tula to guard our apple orchard.

6 They have sent us a large number of soldiers. Some are being lodged in the village to do various jobs of work, and some are guarding the orchard. How terrible to think that armed people are living on the land where Tolstoy was born!

10 Lev Nikol–ch's birthday. I made a wreath from white and pink phlox and yellow marguerites, and added some wild flowers. I visited his grave and stayed there for a long time, then wandered through the woods and even got a little lost.

12 Serg. Andr. Dehring came with the aeronautical artillerymen – in a motor car.

29 After lunch I visited the grave and met one or two people on the way. I sat on the grave for a long time, then wandered about conversing silently with my dead Lyovochka – as he was when we loved one another.

30 My name-day. How many memories are associated with this day! Life is so terrible now: a whole regiment has been stationed in the village, with its headquarters in our house, and they're threatening to fight a battle in Yasnaya Polyana the moment Denikin arrives. What has life come to! They say the shells can kill us all and destroy our house. Goldenblatt arrived with Serg. Mitr. Serebrovskii to discuss the affairs of the Tolstoy Museum. They talk a lot, but matters are not progressing at all.

October 1 Goldenblatt spent the night in Tanya's wing. Negotiations are going on about the removal of the soldiers and the inviolability of Yasnaya Polyana and Lev Nik.'s grave. God knows how it will all end!

5 Vysokomirnyi came; they're planning to visit Moscow to ask the authorities to remove the military guard and the billeted soldiers from Yasnaya Polyana.[23]

6 My wedding anniversary; 57 years ago I was married to Lev Nikolaevich in Moscow, in the Palace Church of the Virgin Birth. It's a fine warm day, with a slight wind. I dressed all in white and went to the grave, having picked a few flowers with which to decorate it. We had visitors – 10 men from a medical detachment who stopped at Zaseka station (now named Yasnaya Polyana).

7 Something sinister and terrible is approaching. A lot of bulls and horses and 4 vans have been driven here from Kursk. Kursk has been routed, and the Jews there were slaughtered.[24] A very agitated Volkov dashed in briefly to visit us this evening. He is responsible for sorting out the cattle

that were driven over here (for some reason) from Kursk. I have had a bad cough and have been staying at home. I wrote a letter to Davydov in reply to his about 'Polikushka'.[25] I washed the floors and took the window frames out to the verandah. Something terrible is approaching. Rumours that Denikin is in Mtsensk, or very near to it.

9 A great quantity and variety of complete strangers here to visit Lev Nik–ch's rooms. A certain Levitskii told me that some Red Army troops had marched to Tula in the night; he said that there would be a battle not far from Tula, and that they were cutting up barbed-wire entanglements.

12 I looked through my memoirs to find some information for Denisenko, who wanted to know about the times when Lev Nik. came into collision with the legal world (refusing to take the oath, the bull that gored the cattleyard worker, and so on). This is a difficult task, but I shall attempt to do it. The weather is brighter and finer but my health is worse – I am terrified that I may have paralysis of the throat, like my father. My Tanya is even more precious to me than ever – and she has grown prettier recently too.

13 I wrote a long letter to Davydov in answer to his question about Lev Nik. and the lawyers,[26] and took notes from my letters and memoirs. This evening Sergeenko read us some of Lev Nik.'s letters to Countess Aleks. Andr. Tolstaya. A beautiful poetic correspondence.

14 I did some writing and pasted in some of Lev Nik.'s letters to me which had been omitted.

16 All the soldiers of the 21st Cavalry Regiment have now left. The younger ones turned out to be good lads, and the older ones were thoroughly decent people.

17 My daughter Tanya's birthday. I went into her wing to greet her and gave her a little porcelain cup – my mother's last present to me – containing a gold 10-ruble piece. I want to give everything away before my death, which will be very soon now. My choking cough is turning into something like whooping cough – this is my 3rd attack of whooping cough. Relations between Sergeenko and Obolenskii have become very strained. Sergeenko is a spiteful and dangerous man.[27] The weather is overcast and cold – 5 °. And it's cold in the house too; the winter glazing hasn't been put in and the stoves haven't been mended. We're threatened with war and a battle near Yasnaya Polyana.[28]

18 My granddaughter Annochka (Ilinichna) came, and my daughter Sasha. I was glad to see them. This evening B.O. Goldenblatt and Alya Sukhotin arrived. A fresh day; I didn't go out, my soul is sick. We keep waiting for something.

19 There was a meeting to decide how best to defend Yasnaya Polyana against pillaging.[29] Nothing has yet been decided. Carts, oxen and people are streaming down the highway to Tula. They say these are refugees from Oryol and the south.

III

Appendices

· *Our Trip to Troitsa* ·

June 14, 1860 We left at four in the morning, half asleep and in a bad mood. Lyuba[1] and I took our seats inside the charabanc, Maman[2] sat with the driver, and the two Lizas[3] and Sasha[4] travelled in the cart. We dozed all the way and didn't talk, although the monotony of the journey was broken once by a burst of laughter from the cart, where Sasha had woken up. When we got to Mytishchi a crowd of peasant women ran out to greet us as usual, offering us tea in the shade of the birch-trees and urging us not to leave without trying some of their Mytishchi water. We arrived at Bratovshchina at 9 that morning as planned, and went to the best inn. The moment we arrived we set to work on our food parcels and in no time at all we had finished off a whole mushroom pie. Then the samovar was brought in. Meanwhile I was examining the pictures on the walls. There were portraits of the Tsar, the Tsarina and the Metropolitan. There were also two paintings with French inscriptions and two depicting religious themes. Sasha lies down and reads his *Comic Calendar*, Lyuba and Petersburg Liza bustle about clearing up, Maman washes the dishes and our Liza gets in everyone's way, acting up, begging for food and trying to steal caramels out of the bag. After we'd had tea, Lyuba and I went outside to ask a peasant about a chapel that was standing there. He took us into his hut and embarked on a long story about how in 1812 the old church had been moved to another place, as they wanted to build a tavern there, but the priest and the church elder had reported this to the head of the Church, i.e. the Metropolitan, who had forbidden it and ordered them to build a chapel where the old church had stood. We then pester them to let us go swimming. It's eventually agreed that we will be taken down to the River Skalda by the innkeeper's daughter, a girl of 17, about whom her father, a garrulous peasant, enters into a long philosophical discussion. It was so hard to marry off one's daughters, he said, and so difficult to get to know people and they were all so dishonest. He spoke with real Russian good sense. He said it was their custom to pay the father for his daughter when she married, and the father in his turn had to supply the dowry. We are now going to have a rest, but I don't expect we'll sleep. Afterwards we'll go swimming and have some dinner, and at 4 p.m. we'll drive off. All this time I had been hoping we would meet some other travellers. And my wish was granted. On the other side of the thin wooden partition there were some other people having tea – a fat gentleman, a lady of equal proportions, an old woman and a thin fair little girl. They were terribly quiet, our neighbours weren't at all cheerful. I was greatly amused to see them getting out of their trap. A bench was brought along to help them, and one by one, groaning and stumbling, they disembarked from the carriage. I am already bored with the place and feel like moving. I'm out of sorts. Nothing cheers me up as it used to. I try to think of other things, but my head keeps swarming with horrible thoughts.

It all went according to plan. We left Bratovshchina at four. Lyuba, Sasha and I went in the cart, while the others sat in the charabanc. On the way we had a rather cheerful, or rather a pleasant, conversation. We stopped at the chapel, where we ate pancakes and chatted to the village girls, who crowded around us in large numbers. They asked us what relation we all were to one another, whether any of us were married and when we would be coming back, and when we left they showered us with blessings and good wishes, saying they had rarely seen such unaffected gentlefolk.

At nine that evening we arrived in Troitsa, where we were given a nice good-sized room overlooking the whole monastery. The weather was beautiful, still and warm, and inclined one somehow to meditate. The Troitsa-Sergievskaya Monastery made a strange impression on me during our trip. I had never before driven up to it with such a feeling of awe and veneration. This is what it means to suffer great sorrow. I believe that when I pray all my cares and griefs will fly away, and that it's quite true that 'faith saves'. These ideas of mine may seem absurd, but what can I do when my only hope and my only salvation lie in faith and prayer? I have put my trust in God, closed my eyes tight and shall now follow my life's path under His authority and His blessing. Life is hard – I don't know how to guide myself. How many times have I made some good resolution, how many times have I reached some firm decision – only to find that my resolve weakens and I reluctantly foreswear my promises. But I'm day-dreaming. I've got such an odd, silly nature. The others are all bustling about, we've just had tea and now we're making up the beds. Lyuba has made up two beds next to each other for the two of us. The things are all packed up and we shall soon go to sleep.

I keep remembering a young woman I saw standing on the porch of the hotel. She was in deep mourning and was holding a newborn baby girl in her arms – her daughter most likely, as they were as like as two peas. I immediately assumed that this lady had just lost her husband, I don't know why. She was dark and very beautiful – exactly my taste – but she looked so wretchedly unhappy that I felt sorry for her. But then I'm always feeling sad these days and being sorry for people and thinking melancholy thoughts, and I can't get rid of them. I am going to bed now. Lyuba is calling me.

June 15, 1860 We got up at 7, and Maman had a struggle to get me and

Lyuba out of bed. We had made up a double bed for ourselves and slept together, and everyone teased us and said we were like a married couple. I called Lyuba my husband and we kept kissing one another.

We got up, drank tea and went to mass. Then we took a walk and looked around the monastery, showing our cousins all the remarkable churches and buildings. We attended mass at the church of St Sergei. The choir was excellent and one of the monks preached rather a sensible sermon on faith and piety. There we met Golovin, who accompanied us for a stroll. We walked around the place, went everywhere worth going to and bought lots of icons, toys and presents to take home. Then we went swimming in the pond, where the theological students had a bathing cabin; but the water was filthy. It's now half-past-two and we're about to have dinner. At around four we'll be setting out for home. I don't know whether to be glad or sad about going home; I feel so utterly bored and wretched that everything seems bad at present.

Evening of June 15, 1860 We're on our way home again. We left Troitsa, seen off by Golovin, who was really very nice and friendly to us. We stopped near the village of Talitsa and took a stroll round the caves there. They were damp and cold, with very low ceilings, and I kept wishing I hadn't gone. Then we set off again and I sat on the box and drove the horses all by myself, which greatly amused all the pedestrians and travellers we passed. When we reached Bratovshchina again we called on our previous hosts and invited a huge party of village boys and girls and made them sing for us.

We had a lot of fun with them and they even made me laugh. I was just sorry that when we gave the boys money they went straight off with it to play pitch-and-toss. This passion for gambling starts far too early. Then they were all made to sing again for some gentleman lodging at the next inn.

After tea Lyuba and I took a walk down the road. You always see a lot in the country. The innkeeper's brother-in-law drove past us drunk, on his way to the inn. And the innkeeper himself, also dead drunk, was staggering around in front of the house, cursing and talking nonsense. The women just weep and complain, but the older ones are so used to it by now that they bear it in silence.

Our innkeeper's sister-in-law says you don't find many sober husbands these days. And as there's both an inn and a tavern in the village, it's hard for them not to go. I was talking to her sitting on a bench behind the gate and playing with her little girl, a pretty, fair-haired child of four called Tanya. She was such a clever lively little thing and I made her say some words in French, which she pronounced very comically. I'm going to bed now. Liza, Mother, Lyuba and the other Liza are already in bed. It's 10 o'clock. We shall be starting out at 2 in the morning (in the night rather).

Sasha is snoring behind the wall and Maman envies him. Lyuba is asleep too. The three of us, i.e. Lyuba, Petersburg Liza and I, have spread out some hay on the floor to sleep on, and covered it with sheets and a carpet.

On the way home we'll stop at Mytischchi for tea, at about 8 or 9 in the morning. I'm not at all pleased to be going home now, it's all the same to me. I'd far rather just go off somewhere, or even disappear and die, anything not to have to remember the past. I used to be such a happy, cheerful person, but it didn't last long, and now life is so hard. I daren't live on memories, it's too frightening. I try instead to forget, but I don't have the strength to forget. What's to be done? How should I live? I don't know, and I dart here and there like a bird in a cage, beating its wings against the sides.

This may be the place to quote some verses of Lermontov:

I am lonely and sad
With no one to take my hand . . .

If only someone would stretch out a hand to me, and offer me some sensible advice, how eagerly I would listen!

We arrived at Mytishchi at 6 and had tea and coffee there. Now at last we're home again and I'm glad to be back; we found everyone here cheerful and well.

· *L.N. Tolstoy's Marriage* ·

Our Trip to Ivitsy and Yasnaya Polyana

At the beginning of August 1862, Maman told me and my two sisters, to our great joy, that she had decided to drive us three little girls and our brother Volodya to the estate of her father and our grandfather, Aleksandr Mikhailovich Islenev,[1] in an Annenskii coach (still in use at the time).

Our grandfather (who appears in Lev Nikolaevich's *Childhood* as 'Papa'), was then living in the Odoevskii district on his estate at Ivitsy, which was all that remained of what had been a large fortune – and even this had been bought in the name of his second wife, my mother's stepmother. This woman, née Zhdanova, appears in Lev Nikolaevich's *Childhood* as '*la belle Flamande*'.

The three daughters of my grandfather's second marriage[2] were young girls at that time, and I was very friendly with the second one.

My grandfather's estate was some 50 *versts* from Yasnaya Polyana, where Lev Nikolaevich's sister Maria had been living ever since she returned from Algeria,[3] and as my mother and she had been close childhood friends and they were naturally anxious to see one another again, my mother, who hadn't visited Yasnaya Polyana since she was a child, decided we would call in there on our way. We were in ecstasies at the news, and Tanya and I were especially pleased, like all young people eager for change and movement. We cheeerfully prepared for the journey. Smart new dresses were made, we packed our bags and waited impatiently to leave.

I don't remember anything about the day we left, and my memories of the journey itself are very vague – just the stopping places, the changing of horses, the rushed meals and the exhaustion from all the unaccustomed travelling. We went to Tula to visit my mother's sister Nadezhda Aleksandrovna Karnovich, who was married to the Tula Marshal of the Nobility, and took a look round Tula, which struck me as a very dull, dirty, uninteresting place. But we were determined not to *miss anything* and to pay careful attention to everything during our trip.

After dinner we drove on to Yasnaya Polyana. It was already evening by then, but the weather was magnificent. The highway through Zaseka[4] was so picturesque, and this wild expanse of nature was a new experience for us city girls.

Maria Nikolaevna and Lev Nikolaevich gave us a noisy and joyful welcome. Aunt Tatiana Aleksandrovna Ergolskaya, reserved and pleasant greeted us affably in polite French, while old Natalya Petrovna,[5] her companion, silently stroked my shoulder and winked in a most beguiling way at my younger sister Tanya, then just 15.

They gave us a large vaulted room downstairs, not only modestly but even poorly furnished. All round the room there were sofas, which were painted white, with very hard cushions at the backs and hard seats covered in blue-and-white striped ticking. There was a chaise-longue too, similarly upholstered and also painted white, and there was a rough birchwood table made by the local joiner. Set into the vaulted ceiling were iron rings from which gammons, saddles and so on used to hang in the days when the house belonged to Lev Nikolaevich's grandfather, Prince Volkonskii, and this room was used as a store-room[6]

The days were growing shorter now, for it was already the beginning of August. After we had run all round the garden, Natalya Petrovna took us to the raspberry bushes. This was the first time we had eaten raspberries straight from the bush, rather than from the little baskets which were brought to our dacha when we were making jam. There weren't many berries left now, but I loved the beauty of the red fruit against the green leaves, and enjoyed their fresh taste.

The Night and the Chair

When it began to grow dark, Maman sent me down to unpack the bags and make up the beds. Aunt's maid Dunyasha[7] and I were just getting the beds ready when Lev Nikolaevich suddenly walked in. Dunyasha told him she had made up three beds on the sofas but didn't know where to put a fourth one.

'What about the chair?' said Lev Nikolaevich moving out the chaise-longue and pushing a broad square stool against it.

'I'll sleep on the chair,' I said.

'Well, I'll make up your bed for you,' said Lev Nikolaevich, clumsily unfolding a sheet. I felt embarrassed, but there was also something lovely and intimate about making up the beds together.

When it was all ready we went upstairs and found Tanya curled up fast asleep on a little sofa in Aunt's room. Volodya had been put to bed too. Maman was chatting away to Maria Nikolaevna and Aunt about the old days. Liza stared at us inquisitively. I vividly remember every moment of that evening.

In the dining-room, with its large French windows, Aleksei Stepanovich,[8] the little cross-eyed butler, was laying the table for supper with the help of the stately, rather beautiful Dunyasha (daughter of old Nikolai,[9] who appeared in *Childhood*). In the middle of one wall was a door which opened on to a little sitting-room with an antique rosewood clavichord, and this sitting-room had the same sort of French windows, leading out to a little balcony, which had the most lovely view. It has given me pleasure all my life, and I love it to this day.

I took a chair and going out on to the balcony alone sat down to admire the view. I shall never forget that mood I was in - although I'd never be able to describe it. I don't know if it was the effect of nature, real untamed nature and wide open spaces; or a premonition of what would happen a month and a half later when I entered this house as its mistress; perhaps it was simply a farewell to my girlhood freedom; perhaps it was all these things, I don't know. But there was something so significant about my mood that evening, and I felt such happiness and such an extraordinary sense of boundlessness. The others were all going in to supper and Lev Nikolaevich came out to call me too.

'No thank you, I don't want anything,' I said. 'It's so lovely out here.'

From the dining-room I could hear my sister Tanya showing off, joking and being naughty – everyone spoilt her and she was quite used to it. Lev Nikolaevich went back to the dining-room, but returned to the balcony to see me without finishing his supper. I don't remember exactly what we talked about, I just remember him saying to me: 'How simple and serene you are,' which pleased me very much.

I had such a good sleep in the long chair which Lev Nikolaevich had made up for me. I tossed about a bit at first, for the arms at the side made it rather narrow and uncomfortable, but my heart was singing with joy as I remembered Lev Nikolaevich arranging my bed for me, and I fell asleep with a new feeling of joy in my young soul.

The Picnic at Yasnaya Polyana

Waking up next morning was a joyful experience too. I longed to run everywhere, look at everything, chatter away to everyone. How light and airy it was at Yasnaya, even then! Lev Nikolaevich was determined that we should enjoy ourselves, and Maria Nikolaevna helped to ensure we did. They harnessed the so-called '*katki*' – a long carriage more like a wagonette – and put Baraban the chestnut in the shafts, and Strelka in the traces. Then the bay Belogubka was harnessed up with an old-fashioned lady's saddle, a magnificent grey was saddled up for Lev Nikolaevich, and we all got ready for our picnic.

More guests arrived – Gromova, the wife of a Tula architect, and Sonechka Fyodorovna Bergholz, niece of Yulia Fyodorovna Auerbach, the headmistress of Tula high school for girls. Maria Nikolaevna was overjoyed to have her two best friends there – my mother and Gromova – and was in a particularly playful, cheerful mood, laughing, telling jokes and keeping us all amused. Lev Nikolaevich suggested that I ride Belogubka, which I was very keen to do.

'But I can't, I don't have a riding-habit,' I said, looking at my yellow dress with its black velvet buttons and belt.

'That doesn't matter,' said Lev Nikolaevich, smiling. 'There are no dachas here, and no one but the forests to see you.' And he helped me mount Belogubka.

I was the happiest person in the world as I galloped beside Lev Nikolaevich down the road to Zaseka, our first stopping place. In those days it was all unbroken forest. Later I would drive to those places again and again, yet they never seemed quite the same. Then everything seemed different – it all seemed magically beautiful, as it never is in everyday life, but only in certain moods of spiritual elation. We rode up to a little clearing where there was a haystack. Over the years we would have many picnics in that clearing in Zaseka with Tanya's children and mine, but on that day it was a different clearing, and I saw it with different eyes.

Maria Nikolaevna invited us all to scramble on to the haystack and roll down, and we all agreed with alacrity. And it was a thoroughly cheerful noisy afternoon.

The following morning we drove off to the village of Krasnoe, which used to belong to my grandfather Islenev.[10] My grandmother[11] was buried there, and Maman was very keen to visit the place where she was born and had grown up, and to kneel at her mother's grave by the church. They didn't want us to leave Yasnaya, and Maman had to give her solemn word of honour that we would call in on our way back, even if only for a day, at Yasnaya Polyana.

Krasnoe Village

Maria Nikolaevna had lent us a carriage for the journey to Krasnoe, and we hired the horses. We didn't spend long there.

I remember the church and the tombstone, with its inscription: 'Princess Sofia Petrovna Kozlovskaya, born Countess Zavadskaya.' I vividly pictured my grandmother's life: what misery she must have endured with her first husband Kozlovskii, a drunkard, to whom she was married against her will, then with her unlawful second husband, Aleksandr Mikhailovich Islenev, my grandfather, living in this country place, bearing an endless annual succession of children,[12] and worrying constantly lest my grandfather in the grip of his gambling mania lose his entire fortune and be forced to leave the estate – which is exactly what happened to him at the end of his life. The old priest and Fetis the deacon both remembered Sofia Petrovna well and spoke about her with great warmth. 'I committed the sin of marrying them in secret,' the old priest told us. 'She begged me to do so: "I want to be Aleksandr Mikhailovich's wife in the eyes of God, even if not in the eyes of men," she said.'

Fetis the deacon, we were told, had died and was in his coffin, and had suddenly come to life just as they were burying him, and had jumped up out of his grave and walked home. To this day I can see his withered little figure, his sparse hair plaited into a grey pigtail at the back of his head. I had never seen a deacon with a pigtail in Moscow, but nothing surprised me any longer. Everything seemed fantastic, full of beauty and magic.

Ivitsy

When the horses had been fed we left Krasnoe in the same carriage and drove to my grandfather's estate of Ivitsy. We were given a solemn and joyous reception. Grandfather moved rapidly – he seemed to slide across the floor in his soft ankle boots. He kept teasing us, and calling us 'the young ladies of Moscow', and he had a habit of pinching our cheeks with his middle and forefinger and winking when he said something funny, then screwing up his humorous little eyes. I can still see his powerful figure, the little black skull-cap on his bald head, his large aquiline nose and his ruddy clean-shaven face.

Sofia Aleksandrovna, his second wife, always used to astound us by smoking a long pipe, her lower lip sagging; all that remained of her former beauty were her sparkling, expressive, black eyes.

Their second daughter, the lovely Olga, who looked so cool and imperturbable, took us upstairs to the room which had been prepared for us. My bed was behind a cupboard, with just a plain wooden chair instead of a table.

Next day we were taken to visit some neighbours of theirs, and were introduced to some young ladies who were very friendly but utterly different from us. They were real young ladies from the country, like those in Turgenev's stories. In those days the landowners' whole way of life was still steeped in serfdom. They lived very simply; they had no railways and were content to restrict their interests to their immediate environment – farming matters, neighbours, hunting with hounds and borzois, women's handicrafts, and the occasional unpretentious, cheerful family celebration or church holiday.

Our arrival in the Odoevskii district created much excitement. A lot of people came over to look at us, and picnics, dances and drives were organised for us.

The day after we arrived in Ivitsy, Lev Nikolaevich suddenly turned up on his grey horse. He had covered fifty *versts* and was in cheerful high spirits. My grandfather, who loved Lev Nikolaevich and the whole Tolstoy family – for he had been friends with Count Nikolai Ilich – was delighted to see him and greeted him most warmly.

There were quite a number of visitors that day, as the young folk had organised an evening dance after the day's drive. Some officers came, some local young landowners and a lot of ladies and young girls. They were all perfect strangers and we found them a little odd, but what did we care? We had great fun, that was all that mattered. Various people took turns to play dance tunes on the piano.

'How smart you all look!' said Lev Nikolaevich, looking at my white-and-mauve dress with lilac ribbons fluttering from the shoulders. (This was the current fashion, known as '*suivez-moi*'.) 'I wish Aunt had seen you in that smart dress,' he said smiling.

'But why aren't you dancing?' I asked.

'Oh, I'm too old for that,' he said.

Some ladies and old men had been playing cards at two tables and these were left open after all the visitors had left. The candles were burning down but we didn't go to bed and Lev Nikolaevich kept us up with his lively talk. Then Maman said it was time for us to go to bed and firmly ordered us upstairs. We dared not disobey. But just as I was going out of the door Lev Nikolaevich called to me:

'Wait a moment, Sofia Andreevna!'

'What is it?'

'Will you read what I'm going to write?'

'Very well.'

'I'm only going to write the initials – you must guess the words.'

'How can I do that – it's impossible! Oh well, go on!'

He brushed the games scores off the card table, took a piece of chalk and began writing. We were both very serious and excited. I followed his big red hand, and could feel all my powers of concentration and feeling focus on that bit of chalk and the hand that held it. We said nothing.

What the Chalk Wrote

'Y.y.&.n.f.h.t.v.r.m.o.m.a.&.i.f.h.'

'Your youth and need for happiness too vividly remind me of my age and incapacity for happiness,' I read out.

My heart was pounding, my temples were throbbing, my face was flushed – I was beyond all sense of time and reality; at that moment I felt capable of anything, of understanding everything, imagining the unimaginable.

'Well let's go on,' said Lev Nikolaevich and began to write once more:

'Y.f.h.t.w.i.a.m.&.y.s.L.Y.&.y.s.T.m.p.m.'

'Your family has the wrong idea about me and your sister Liza. You and your sister Tanechka must protect me.' I read the initials rapidly, without a second's hesitation.

Lev Nikolaevich wasn't even surprised; it all seemed quite natural somehow. Our elation was such that we soared high above the world and nothing could possibly surprise us.

Then we heard Maman crossly summoning me to bed. We hurriedly said goodnight, extinguished the candles and went out. Behind my cupboard upstairs I lighted the stump of a candle, sat down on the floor, put my notebook on the wooden chair and began to write my diary. I wrote down the words to which Lev Nikolaevich had given me the initials, and grew vaguely aware that something of great significance had occurred between us – something we were now unable to stop. But for various reasons I curbed my thoughts and dreams, as though I were locking up for a while everything that had taken place that evening, keeping back things that were not yet ready to see the light.

When we left Ivitsy we called in on Yasnaya Polyana for the day. But we didn't have such fun this time. Maria Nikolaevna was leaving with us for Moscow, and from there she was going abroad, where she had left her children, and Aunt Tatiana Aleksandrovna, who adored her, was sad and silent. It was always hard for her to part with her Mashenka, whom she had brought up from childhood and loved like her own daughter, and who had been so unhappily married to her nephew, Count Valerian Petrovich

Tolstoy, the son of her sister Elizaveta Aleksandrovna.[13] I was embarrassed by Lev Nikolaevich's attitude to me, and the suspicious looks from my sisters and the others. Maman seemed worried about something too, and Tanya and little Volodya were tired of travelling and longing to get home.

The Journey in the Annenskii Coach

We ordered a large Annenskii coach (named after its owner) from Tula. There were two seats at the back, rather like those of a covered cab, and four seats inside. We older girls were sorry to be leaving Yasnaya. We said goodbye to Aunt and Natalya Petrovna and looked for Lev Nikolaevich to say goodbye to him too.

'I'm coming with you,' he said cheerfully. 'How could I stay in Yasnaya now? It'll be so dull and miserable.'

I didn't ask myself why I suddenly felt so happy, why everything was suddenly shining with joy. I ran off to announce the news to my mother and sisters, and it was decided that Lev Nikolaevich would travel the whole way on one of the outside seats at the back, and that my sister Liza and I would take turns on the other; she would sit outside till the first stop, then I would take her place, and so on until Moscow.

We drove and we drove . . . Towards evening I remember I began to get terribly sleepy. I was cold and wrapped myself up, blissfully happy to be sitting there next to this old family friend whom I had loved since childhood, the beloved author of *Childhood*, who was now being so nice to me and whom I now liked even better. He told me wonderful long stories about the Caucasus, of his life there, the beautiful mountains, the wild scenery and his own exploits. I loved listening to his steady voice, full of tender emotion and somewhat hoarse, as though coming from somewhere far away. I would nod off to sleep for a moment and wake to the sound of the same voice telling its lovely poetic Caucasian tales. I felt ashamed of being so sleepy, but I was still so young, and although I regretted missing Lev Nikolaevich's stories I couldn't help dozing off sometimes. We travelled all night. Everyone in the coach was asleep, although occasionally Maman and Maria Nikolaevna would speak to one another or little Volodya would squeak in his sleep.

At last we were approaching Moscow. At the final staging-post it was again my turn to take my place on the back seat with Lev Nikolaevich. When we stopped Liza came up to me and begged me to let her sit outside.

'Sonya, would you mind letting me sit outside? It's so stuffy in the coach!' she said.

We came out of the station and everyone took their seats. I climbed inside.

'Sofia Andreevna!' cried Lev Nikolaevich. 'It's your turn to sit at the back!'

'I know, but I'm cold,' I said evasively. And the carriage door slammed shut behind me.

Lev Nikolaevich stood and pondered for a moment, then climbed on to the box.

The next day Maria Nikolaevna went abroad and we returned to our dacha in Pokrovskoe, where my father and brothers were waiting for us.

The Last Days of Girlhood and the Story

My entire life was different now. The surroundings were the same, the people were the same, I was the same – superficially. But I seemed to have lost all sense of who I was – I was still in the grip of those feelings that had overwhelmed me at Yasnaya Polyana. My personal 'I' was consumed in a limitless sense of space, free, all-powerful and unchecked. Those last days of my girlhood were extraordinarily intense, lit by a dazzling brightness and a sudden awakening of the soul. I have had this same sense of spiritual elation on two other occasions in my life, and it was these rare and extraordinary awakenings of the soul that have done more than anything else to convince me that the soul has an independent life of its own – that it is immortal, and that it is when the body dies and the soul is liberated, that it finds its freedom.

Having driven with us to Moscow from Yasnaya Polyana, Lev Nikolaevich rented an apartment in the house of some German shoemaker and moved in there. At that time he was very involved with his school work[14] and with a magazine entitled *Yasnaya Polyana*, an educational publication primarily intended for use in peasant schools. It lasted only one year.[15]

Lev Nikolaevich visited us nearly every day in Pokrovskoe. Sometimes he would be brought back by my father, who often went to Moscow in connection with his work. I remember Lev Nikolaevich once telling us that he had visited the Petrovskii Park and called in at the royal palace, where he had handed the aide-de-camp on duty a letter to Tsar Alexander II describing the insult he had suffered from the police, who had made a completely unwarranted search of Yasnaya Polyana.[16] This was on August 23, 1862. Tsar Alexander II was then in Moscow for the manoeuvres on the Khodynka Field, and was staying in the Petrovskii Palace.

Lev Nikolaevich and I had long walks and talks together, and he once asked me if I kept a diary. I told him I had kept one for a long time, ever since I was eleven, and that last summer when I was sixteen I had also written a long story.

'Let me read your diaries,' Lev Nikolaevich said.

'No, I couldn't do that.'

'Well, let me see your story then.'

So I gave him the story. The following morning I asked him if he had read it. He replied casually that he had just glanced through it. But later I read in his diary the following entry about my story: 'She gave me her story to read. What a powerful sense of truth and simplicity!'[17] Later he also told me that he hadn't slept all that night, and had been very disturbed by my verdict on the main character, Prince Dublitskii, in whom he had recognised himself, and of whom I had written: 'The Prince was extraordinarily unattractive in appearance, and was always changing his opinions.'

I remember we were once feeling very happy and playful, and I kept repeating the same foolish sentence: 'When I am Tsarina I'll do such and such,' or 'When I am Tsarina I'll order such and such.' Just beneath the balcony stood my father's cabriolet, from which the horse had been unharnessed. I hopped inside and shouted, 'When I am Tsarina I'll drive around in a cabriolet like this!'

Lev Nikolaevich immediately stepped into the horse's place, seized the shafts and pulled me along at a brisk trot. 'And I'm going to take my Tsarina for a drive!' he said. This episode illustrates just how strong and healthy he was.

'Do stop, please! It's much too heavy for you!' I cried, but I was loving it, and was delighted to see how strong Lev Nikolaevich was, and to have him pull me around.

What heavenly moonlit evenings and nights that year! I can still see the little glade bathed in moonlight, and the moon reflected in the nearby pond. There was something steely, fresh and bracing about those August nights . . . 'Mad nights!' Lev Nikolaevich would say as we all sat on the balcony or strolled about the garden. There were no romantic scenes or confessions. We had known each other for so long. Our friendship was so simple and easy. And I was in a hurry to end my wonderful, free, serene, uncomplicated girlhood. Everything was wonderfully simple, I had no ambitions, no desires for the future.

And Lev Nikolaevich kept coming to visit us. Sometimes when he stayed late my parents would make him spend the night with us. Once at the beginning of September we went to see him off, and when it was time to say goodbye my sister Liza asked me to invite him to her name-day party on September 5. 'Why does it have to be the 5th?' he said, and I didn't dare tell him, as I had been told not to mention the name-day.

But Lev Nikolaevich promised to come, and to our great joy he kept his word. Things were always so jolly and interesting when he was there.

At first I didn't think his visits had anything to do with me. But gradually I began to realise that my feelings for him were growing serious. I remember I once ran upstairs in a state of great agitation to our bedroom, with its French window overlooking the pond and beyond it the church and all the things I had known and loved all my life (for I was born at Pokrovskoe). And as I stood at the window, my heart pounding, my sister Tanya came in and immediately realised how agitated I was.

'What is it, Sonya?' she asked solicitously.

'*Je crains d'aimer le comte*,'* I said abruptly.[18]

'Really?' Tanya was astonished, for she had had no suspicion of my feelings. She was even a little sad too, for she knew my character. For me '*aimer*' never meant playing with feelings. Both then and later it was something closer to suffering.

In Moscow

Between the 5th and 16th of September our whole family returned to Moscow. As usual Moscow at first felt cramped, dull and stuffy to me after our country dacha, and this had a very depressing effect on me. Before we left Pokrovskoe we always used to say goodbye to our favourite places and pay a brief visit to as many of them as possible. But that autumn I was really saying goodbye for the last time to Pokrovskoe, and to my own girlhood as well.

In Moscow Lev Nikolaevich started his almost daily visits again. One evening I tiptoed into my mother's bedroom and slipped round the screen to her bed. Whenever we came home from a party or theatre, Maman would always cheerfully say, 'Well, dear, what happened?' And I would give her a detailed account of everything that had happened that evening or act out what I had seen at the theatre. But this time both of us were rather glum.

'What is it, Sonya?' Maman asked.

'Well you see, Maman, everyone thinks Lev Nikolaevich will marry someone else, not me, but I'm sure it's me he loves,' I said shyly.

For some reason Maman was furious and scolded me roundly.

'She's always thinking people are in love with her!' she raged. 'Be off with you and stop thinking a lot of nonsense!'

My mother's response to my candid confession hurt me deeply, and I never mentioned Lev Nikolaevich again. My father was angry too that Lev Nikolaevich should visit us so often without proposing to the eldest daughter, as Russian tradition demanded, and he was cold to him and unkind to me. The atmosphere in our house became strained and awkward, especially for me.

On September 14, Lev Nikolaevich said he had something very

*'I am afraid I love the Count.'

important to tell me, but he didn't manage to say what. It wasn't hard to guess. He spoke to me at length that evening. I was playing the piano in the drawing-room while he leaned against the stove, crying, 'Go on playing! Go on playing!' the moment I stopped. The music prevented the others from hearing what he said, and my hands trembled with excitement and my fingers stumbled over the keys as I played for practically the tenth time the same waltz, '*Il Bacio*', which I had learned by heart to accompany Tanya's singing.

Lev Nikolaevich didn't actually propose then, and I don't remember now exactly what he said. The gist of it, though, was that he loved me and wanted to marry me. It was all hints and allusions. But in his diary he wrote:

> **September** 12, 1862 I love her as I never thought it possible to love anyone. I'm mad, I'll shoot myself if it goes on much longer. They had a party. She is utterly enchanting . . .
>
> **September** 13 The minute I get up tomorrow I'll go there and tell her everything. Otherwise I'll shoot myself. It's almost 4 a.m. I've written her a letter and I'll give it to her tomorrow, i.e. today, the 14th. My God, I'm terrified of dying! God help me![19]

Another day passed, and on Saturday, September 16, my brother Sasha and his cadet friends arrived. We were having tea in the dining-room and feeding the hungry cadets. Lev Nikolaevich spent the whole day with us, and choosing a moment when no one's eyes were on us, he called me into my mother's room, which was empty at the time, and said:

'I wanted to say something to you, but I haven't been able to, so here is a letter which I've been carrying around in my pocket for several days now. Please read it, and I'll wait here for your answer.'

The Proposal

I seized the letter and tore downstairs into the girls' bedroom, which I shared with my two sisters. This is what the letter said:

> Sofia Andreevna, I can bear it no longer. Every day for the past three weeks I've been saying to myself: 'Today I'll tell her everything,' yet I always leave with the same feelings of sadness, remorse, fear and joy in my heart. And every night, as now, I re-live what has happened and torture myself – why didn't I speak to you? And if I had what would I have said? I am taking this letter with me in case it's again impossible for

me to speak to you, or my courage fails me. *Your family has the wrong idea about me* – I think they imagine that I am in love with your sister Liza. They are wrong. *I cannot get your story out of my head*, because when I read it I clearly realised that I, like Prince Dublitskii, had no business to be dreaming about happiness, that you need an *exceptional*, poetic kind of love. I am not jealous and shall not be jealous of the man you fall in love with. I thought I could love all of you, like children. At Ivitsy I wrote: '*Your presence reminds me too vividly of my old age.*' But then as now I was lying to myself. Then I might still have been able to tear myself away and return to the monastery of solitary labour and interesting work. But now I can do nothing, for I feel I have created havoc in your household and have forfeited the simple straightforward feelings of friendship you once felt for me as a good and honest man. I cannot leave and I dare not stay. You are an honest person. With your hand on your heart and without hurrying (for God's sake don't hurry!) tell me what to do. There's no laughter without pain. I would have laughed myself sick a month ago if I'd been told one could suffer as I have been suffering, gladly, this past month. Tell me, as an *honest person*, do you want to be my wife? If you can say *yes* with your whole heart, *boldly*, then say yes. Otherwise, if you have the faintest shadow of doubt in your heart, it's best to say no. For God's sake think about it carefully. I am terrified of hearing a 'no', but I am quite prepared for it and shall have the strength to endure it. What terrifies me much more is the idea that I shall not be loved as much as I love you![20]

I didn't read the letter all the way through, I merely skimmed through it to the words: 'Do you want to be my wife?' I was just on my way upstairs to say yes to Lev Nikolaevich when I ran into my sister Liza in the doorway, who asked me: 'Well, what happened?'

'*Le comte m'a fait la proposition*,'* I answered hurriedly. Then my mother came in and realised at once what had happened. Taking me firmly by the shoulders she turned me towards the door and said: 'Go to him and give him your answer.'

I flew up the stairs on wings, tore past the dining-room and drawing-room and rushed into my mother's bedroom. Lev Nikolaevich stood in the corner, leaning against the wall, waiting for me. I went up to him and he seized both my hands.

'Well, what's the answer?' he asked.

'Yes – of course,' I replied.

Within a few moments everyone in the house knew what had happened and was coming in to congratulate us.

*'The Count has proposed to me.'

My Name-day and Engagement

The next day, September 17, was my name-day and that of my mother, Lyubov Aleksandrovna. All our Moscow friends and relatives came to congratulate us and were told of our engagement. When the old university professor who came to teach my sisters and me French heard that I and not Liza was going to marry Lev Nikolaevich, he said naïvely: '*C'est dommage que cela ne fût Mlle Lise; elle a si bien étudié*,'*

But little Katya Obolenskaya threw her arms around me and said: 'I'm so glad you're going to marry such a splendid man and writer.'

My betrothal lasted for only a week, from September 16 to 23. During that time I was taken round the shops, where I unenthusiastically tried on dresses, underwear and hats. Lev Nikolaevich visited every day, and one day he brought me his diaries. I remember how shattered I was by these diaries, which out of an excess of honesty he made me read before our wedding. It was very wrong of him to do this; I wept when I saw what his past had been.

I remember one evening when Maman and my sisters had gone to the theatre to see *Othello*, played by a famous tragedian of the day called Aldridge. My mother sent a carriage for us so that we could go too. I remember that I was a bit afraid of Lev Nikolaevich then, afraid that he'd soon be disillusioned by a silly insignificant little girl like me. And we drove almost the whole way there in silence.

Another time he arrived during the day and found me sitting by the window in the drawing-room with my friend Olga Z.,[21] who was weeping bitterly.

Lev Nikolaevich looked very surprised.

'Why, it looks as though you're burying her,' he said.

'It's the end of everything, you'll take her away and we'll never see her again,' she said in French, unable to stop crying.

The week passed like a bad dream. For many people my wedding was a sad event, and Lev Nikolaevich was in a terrible hurry to get it over. Maman said she would have to have at least some essential garments made before the wedding, if not the whole trousseau.

'She's got enough clothes,' said Lev Nikolaevich. 'And looks very smart too.'

She managed to get one or two things hastily made for me, including the outfit for my wedding, which was set for September 23 at 7 in the evening, at the Palace Church. At our house everyone was rushing about getting ready for it, but Lev Nikolaevich had to rush about seeing to things too. He bought a magnificent *dormeuse*,† ordered photographs to be taken of everyone in my family and presented me with a diamond brooch. He also

*'It's a pity it was not Mlle Lise; she has studied so well.'

†Large sleeping carriage.

had his own photograph taken, which I had begged to him to have fitted into a gold bracelet my father had given me. He also had a lot of trouble and inconvenience from a certain Mr Stellovskii[22] to whom Lev Nikolaevich had just sold his works. But I didn't get a great deal of pleasure from the dresses or presents – I just wasn't interested, I was too wrapped up in my love for Lev Nikolaevich and the fear of losing him. These fears have never left me; they have remained in my heart throughout my life, although thank God we have kept our love for one another intact throughout 48 years of marriage.

When we discussed our future together, Lev Nikolaevich said I should choose where I would like to live after the wedding – we could stay on with my parents in Moscow for a bit, we could go abroad, or we could go straight to Yasnaya Polyana. I said I wanted to go to Yasnaya Polyana, so as to start a proper family life *at home* straightaway. And I could see that Lev Nikolaevich liked this very much.

The Wedding

It was September 23 at last, the day of the wedding. I didn't see Lev Nikolaevich all day, but he dropped in for a moment. We sat down together on our valises and he started tormenting me, questioning me and doubting my love for him. The thought occurred to me that he wanted to run away, and that he might have sudden fears of marriage.[23] I started to cry. At that moment my mother came in and pounced on Lev Nikolaevich: 'Well, you've chosen a fine time to make her cry,' she said. 'Today is her wedding-day, it's hard enough for her as it is, and she's got a long journey ahead of her, and look at her crying her eyes out.' Lev Nikolaevich looked very penitent. He soon went off to dine with Vasilii Stepanovich and Praskovia Fyodorovna Perfilev, his wedding sponsors, who would bless him and take him to the church. He had asked Timiryazev to be his best man, as his brother Sergei Nikolaevich Tolstoy had gone to Yasnaya Polyana to get things ready and would be meeting us there.

Also from Lev Nikolaevich's side of the family was his aunt Pelageya Ilinichna Yushkova. She was to drive to the church with me and my little brother Volodya, who carried the icon.

Just before seven that evening, my sisters and friends began to dress me. I begged them not to call the hairdresser, as I wanted to do my own hair, and the girls pinned on the flowers and the long tulle veil. The dress was also tulle, and in the current fashion – very open at the neck and shoulders. It was so thin, light and airy, it seemed to envelop me like a cloud. My thin, childish unformed arms and shoulders looked pitifully bony. I was soon ready, and we now had to wait for the best man to come and tell us that the bridegroom was in the church. An hour or more passed, and no one came.

It flashed through my mind that he had run away – he had been so odd that morning, after all. But then who should appear instead of the best man but cross-eyed little Aleksei Stepanovich, Lev Nikolaevich's valet, who rushed in looking very agitated and asked us to open up the suitcase immediately and get out a clean shirt. In all the preparations for the wedding and the journey they had apparently forgotten to leave out a clean shirt! Someone had been sent to buy one, but it was Sunday and all the shops were closed. Another age elapsed while they took the shirt back to the bridegroom and he put it on and got to the church. Then began the farewells, the tears and the sobs, and I felt utterly distraught.

'However will we manage without our little countess!' my old nurse kept saying over and over again. (She always called me that, probably in memory of my grandmother, Countess Sofia Petrovna Zavadskaya, after whom I had been named.)

'I'll die of grief without you,' my sister Tanya said.

My little brother Petya just gazed at me despairingly with his sad black eyes. Maman avoided me and bustled about preparing the wedding supper. Everyone was plunged in gloom by the impending separation.

Father was not well. I went to say goodbye to him in his study, and he seemed deeply touched. They prepared bread and salt, Maman took down the icon of St Sofia the martyr, and with her brother, my uncle Mikhail Aleksandrovich Islenev, standing beside her, she blessed me with it.

We all drove in solemn silence to the church, which was just a moment away from our house.[24] I was sobbing all the way. The winter garden and the Palace Church of the Virgin Birth were magnificently lit up. Lev Nikolaevich met me in the winter palace garden, took me by the hand and walked me to the doors of the church, where we were met by the priest. He took both our hands in his and led us to the lectern. The palace choir was singing, two priests conducted the service, and everything was very solemn and splendid. All the guests were assembled in the church, and there were a great many complete strangers, palace employees mostly. They all remarked on my extreme youth and my tear-stained eyes.

Lev Nikolaevich has described our wedding beautifully in his account of Levin and Kitty's wedding in his novel *Anna Karenina*.[25] Not only did he paint a brilliantly imaginative picture of the ceremony, he also described the whole psychological process taking place in Levin's mind. As for me, I had already had so much excitement over the past few days that I experienced absolutely nothing as I stood there at the altar. I just felt as though something obvious and inevitable was happening. As though it couldn't be otherwise, and there was no point in questioning it.

My best men were my brother Sasha and his friend P.,[26] a former Guards officer with him.

The ceremony ended, everyone congratulated us, and then Lev Nikolaevich and I drove home together, just the two of us. He was being very affectionate to me and seemed happy . . . At home in the Kremlin they had prepared the usual wedding feast – champagne, fruit, sweets and so on. There were a few guests – just close friends and relatives.

Then I had to change into my travelling dress. Our old chambermaid Varvara, whom my father's great friend the waggish Doctor Anke had named the 'Oyster', was coming with me, and was now bustling about with Lev Nikolaevich's valet, finishing the packing.

The Departure and Send-off

The postilion brought round six mail horses, which were harnessed to the brand new *dormeuse* which Lev Nikolaevich had bought, gleaming black trunks were buckled and strapped to the top of the carriage, and Lev Nikolaevich grew impatient to be off.

I had an agonising lump in my throat and was choking with misery. For the first time I suddenly realised that I was actually leaving my family and everyone I had ever loved in my life *for ever*. But I struggled to control my tears and my sorrow. Then the farewells started. It was frightful! I broke down and sobbed when I said goodbye to my sick father. When I kissed Liza goodbye I stared into her eyes and she too was in tears. Tanya burst into loud sobs, like a child, and so did Petya, who explained that he had drunk too much champagne in order to dull the sadness, and had to be taken off to bed. I then went downstairs and made the sign of the cross over my two-year-old little brother Vyacheslav, who was sound asleep, and said goodbye to my nurse, Vera Ivanovna, who sobbed and hugged me, kissing my face and shoulders, then kissing me all over. Stepanida Trifonovna, a reserved old lady who had lived with us for over thirty-five years, politely wished me much happiness.[27]

These were the last moments now. I had deliberately kept the final farewell with my mother to the very end, and just before getting into the carriage I flung myself into her arms and we both sobbed. Those tears, parting tears, expressed our mutual gratitude for all the love and kindness we had given one another, forgiveness for the pain we had unwittingly caused, my sorrow at parting with my beloved mother, and her motherly wish that I should be happy.

At last I managed to tear myself away from her and took my seat in the carriage without looking back. I shall never forget the piercing cry she uttered then, for it seemed to have been torn from her heart.

The autumn rain was pouring down, and the puddles reflected the dull glow of the street lights and carriage lamps, which had just been lit. The horses were stamping impatiently and the ones in front with the postilion were straining to be off. Lev Nikolaevich slammed the carriage door shut. Aleksei Stepanovich jumped on to the back seat, and old Varvara the

'Oyster' got up beside him. The horses' hooves splashed through the puddles, and we were off. I sat crouched in one corner, wretched and exhausted, and wept uncontrollably. Lev Nikolaevich seemed puzzled and dismayed. He had never had a real family and had grown up without a father or mother, and as a man he couldn't have understood what I was feeling anyway. He said he could see I didn't love him very much if it hurt me so to leave my family. What he didn't realise then was that if I was capable of such passionate love for my family, I would later transfer this love to him and to our children. Which is exactly what happened.

We left the city of Moscow and it became dark and frightening. I had never travelled anywhere in autumn or winter before, and I found the darkness and the absence of street-lamps terribly dispiriting. We barely spoke a word to one another until we reached the first stop, Birulevo I think it was. I remember Lev Nikolaevich was particularly gentle and considerate to me. When we arrived at Birulevo, a young couple, and titled at that, in a brand new *dormeuse* driven by six horses, we were given the royal suite. The rooms were large, bare and cheerless, with red damask furniture. They brought in the samovar and made tea. I huddled in a corner of the sofa and sat there silently, as though condemned to death.

'Come now, you must be mistress and pour out the tea,' said Lev Nikolaevich.

I obeyed and we had tea, and I felt terribly bashful and nervous. I simply couldn't bring myself to change to the 'thou' form, as he had done, and avoided calling Lev Nikolaevich anything at all; I called him 'you' for a long time afterwards too.

Our Arrival at Yasnaya Polyana

The journey from Moscow to Yasnaya Polyana took just under twenty-four hours, and we reached our home the following evening, to my great joy. It felt so strange – here I was, *at home*, yet home was now at Yasnaya Polyana.

The first thing I saw as I went up the steps of the house where I was destined to spend the next half-century of my life was Aunt Tatiana Aleksandrovna, holding up the icon of the Blessed Virgin Mary, and Sergei Nikolaevich, my brother-in-law, standing beside her with the bread and salt. I bowed to their feet, made the sign of the cross and kissed first the icon then Aunt Tatiana. Lev Nikolaevich did likewise. Then we went into her room, where we met Natalya Petrovna. That day was the start of my life in Yasnaya Polyana, where I lived almost uninterruptedly for the first eighteen years of my marriage.[28]

Lev Nikolaevich wrote in his dairy: '*September 25, 1862.* Unbelievable happiness! Is it possible that this will last all our lives?'[29]

· *Various Notes for Future Reference* ·

Yasnaya Polyana, February 14, 1870 The other day I was reading a biography of Pushkin[1] and it occurred to me that I could be of some service to future generations if I recorded some details of Lyovochka's life – not so much his everyday activities as his intellectual life – so far as I am capable of understanding it. I have often thought of doing this before, but so far I haven't had time.

Now is a good time to start. *War and Peace* is finished and no major new work has been embarked upon yet. He spent the whole of last summer reading and studying philosophy; he was captivated by Schopenhauer,[2] and thought Hegel merely a collection of empty phrases.[3] He engaged in long and painful meditation, he often said his brain was hurting him and was working too hard, that he was finished and it was time for him to die, and so on. Later on his gloom passed. He began to read Russian folk-stories and epics and this gave him the idea of writing children's books for four different ages, starting with an *ABC*.[4] He was enchanted by these tales and epics. The epic of Danila Lavchanin gave him the idea for a play, and the stories and characters – Ilya Muromets, Alyosha Popovich and all the others – inspired him with the idea of a novel based on old Russian folk heroes. He particularly liked Ilya Muromets and said he wanted to describe him as an educated and very intelligent man from the peasantry, who had studied at university. I can't describe the character as he sketched him out for me, but I know that it was absolutely splendid.[5]

After all these folk-tales and fables he then read a mass of dramatic works – Molière, Shakespeare and Pushkin's *Boris Godunov* (which he doesn't think much of)[6] – and he now plans to write a comedy. He has actually made a start on this, and was telling me of a rather foolish subject, but I am sure this is not his real work. He himself said the other day: 'No, once one has attempted the epic genre (i.e. *War and Peace*) it's hard to write drama, and not worth it either.' But I can see he is quite determined to try his hand at a comedy, and he is directing all his energy at the dramatic genre.[7]

February 15 Last night Lyovochka was talking about Shakespeare at great length and with great enthusiasm; he regards Shakespeare as a very great dramatic talent.[8] Goethe, he said, was an aesthete, elegant and well-proportioned, but without dramatic talent. He said he kept meaning to discuss Goethe with Fet, who was a great admirer of his. He also said that Goethe was truly great only when he argued and philosophised.

I was passing L.'s study this morning and he called me in to give me a long talk about various Russian historical characters. I found him reading Ustryalov's history of Peter the Great.[9]

He is fascinated by the characters of Peter and Menshikov. Menshikov he said was a strong character, very Russian, a type found only amongst the peasantry. Peter the Great he described as an instrument of his age; he had the agonising task of bringing Russia into contact with Europe, for this was his destiny. He is searching history for a suitable subject for a play, and taking notes on anything he considers suitable. Today he was taking notes on the story of Mirovich, who tried to release Prince Ioann Antonovich from the fortress. Yesterday he told me he had again given up the idea of comedy and was now thinking of drama. 'Such a lot of work to do!' he keeps saying.[10]

He and I have just been out skating together. He likes to try all sorts of tricks, skating on one leg, then on two, skating backwards, going round in circles, and so on. He enjoys himself like a little boy.

February 24 Today, after many doubts and hesitations, L. has at last got down to work. Yesterday he said that after serious consideration he had realised that it was the epic genre which suited him best at present.

The other day he went to see Fet, who told him that drama wasn't his strong point, and he now seems to have abandoned his ideas about comedy and drama.

This morning he covered a whole sheet of paper with his close handwriting. The action begins in a monastery, with a large crowd of people, including all the main characters.[11]

Yesterday afternoon he told me he had had the idea of writing about a married woman of noble birth who ruined herself. He said his purpose was to make this woman pitiful, not guilty, and he told me that no sooner had he imagined this character clearly than the men and the other characters he had thought up all found their place in the story.[12] 'It's suddenly become clear to me,' he said. He decided yesterday that the educated peasant he had thought up would be a bailiff.

'I am accused of fatalism,' he says, 'yet no one could be a truer believer than I. Fatalism is merely an excuse for wrongdoing – I believe in God and in that phrase from the Gospels that even the very hairs on your head are numbered, I believe that everything is preordained.'

We get neither papers nor journals. L. says he doesn't want to read the critics. 'The critics always infuriated Pushkin,' he said. 'It's better not to read them at all.' We are sent free copies of the *Dawn*, however, in which Strakhov praises L.'s talents to the skies.[13] This delights him. And then Ries sends us a German paper.[14] And that's that. Apart from our subscription to the *Revue des deux mondes*.

December 9 Today he seems at last to have begun writing in earnest. I cannot describe what he went through all that time he was unable to work. He had an idea about a man's travels around Russia, and an idea about an educated man of peasant origins. The beginning of this story, which he has just read to me, tells of a proud man of extraordinary brilliance who sincerely desires to be useful to others and to teach people, but who, after spending some time travelling around Russia and meeting many simple and genuinely useful people, struggles with his conscience and eventually comes to the conclusion that his idea of helping others is fruitless, and so he learns peace of mind, humility, a simpler, more genuine life, and ultimately – death.[15]

That's how I understand it anyway, from what L. has just told me.

He is in the drawing-room with a theological student at present, having his first Greek lesson. He suddenly decided he wanted to learn Greek.

All this inactivity (mental rest I'd call it) has been a great strain for him. He said he was ashamed of his laziness not only in front of me but the servants too and everyone else.[16] There were moments when he thought his inspiration was returning and that made him happy.

Sometimes (but only when he is away from his home and his family) he imagines that he is going mad, and so great is his fear of madness that I feel terrified whenever he talks about it.

He came back from Moscow[17] three days ago. He bought us dolls, decorations for the Christmas tree, some material and various other things. 'What a joy to be home! What a joy to see the children!' he kept saying on his return. 'How I love being with them!' He is giving Seryozha mathematics lessons. He sometimes loses his temper[18] with him, but always begs him to stop him when he gets too angry.

March 27, 1871 He has been persevering with his Greek since December. He sits immersed in it day and night, and nothing delights or interests him more than to learn some new Greek word or phrase. At first he read Xenophon, but now it's Plato, and he is reading the *Odyssey* and the *Iliad*, which he absolutely adores. He likes me to hear him do his oral translation and to correct it against Gnedich's, which he considers an excellent and thorough work. His progress in Greek, compared even to those who have studied it at school and university, seems almost incredible.

When I correct his translation I sometimes find as few as two or three mistakes in as many pages.[19]

He wants to do some writing, and often says so. He dreams of a book that would be as pure, elegant and devoid of excess as classical Greek literature, or Greek art . . . I can't explain it very well, but I understand exactly what he has in mind. He says it isn't hard to write something, what's hard is *not* to write. By which he means it's hard to avoid verbiage – something almost no writer manages to resist.

He would dearly like to write something about life in ancient Russia. He is reading the *Cheti-Minei*, the lives of the saints, and says this is the genuine poetry of Russia. He is in poor health and has been unwell all winter. He has had a terrible pain in his knee and a fever, which he now admits was mainly a result of over-exerting himself at his Greek; he has now developed a dry rasping cough, but he refuses to admit it and gets furious whenever I mention it to him. 'Nothing of the sort!' he always says, and that distresses me more than anything.

January 16, 1873 I have broken the resolution I made to keep a note of everything L. was doing and working on. He has compiled four children's books.[20] He worked on these with pride, confidence and the firm conviction that he was doing good and useful work. This *ABC* of his has been a terrible failure and he was terribly angry and upset about this at first. Fortunately it didn't stop him working, though. Yesterday he said: 'If my novel had been such a failure I would readily have believed them and simply accepted that it was no good. But I feel quite convinced that my *ABC* is unusually good and they just didn't understand it.'[21]

At present he is reading material about the Peter the Great period.[22] He had a sudden wild impulse to make this the subject of his next book. It just came over him, almost imperceptibly. He jots down in various little notebooks anything that might come in useful for an accurate description of the manners, customs, clothes, houses and the general way of life in this period – particularly that of the peasants and those far from the court and the Tsar. Elsewhere he jots down any ideas he may have about the characters, plot, poetic passages and so on. It's like a mosaic. He is so immersed in the details that he came back especially early from hunting yesterday, as he wanted to go through various documents to find out whether one writer was correct in saying that they wore high collars with the short kaftan in the days of Peter the Great. L. thinks these were worn only with the long coats, particularly amongst the lower orders. This evening we read aloud some notes about Russian marriage customs and peasant traditions in the days of Aleksei Mikhailovich.[23] Lyovochka has a very high opinion of Ustryalov's history and regards it as an absolutely meticulous piece of work.

January 31 He is still reading documents, and one by one the characters are all coming to life before his eyes.

He has written about ten different opening chapters, but isn't happy with any of them. Yesterday he said: 'The machine is all ready, now it must be made to work.'[24]

March 19 Last night L. suddenly said to me: 'I have written a page and a half, and it seems good.' I assumed this was yet another attempt to write about the Peter the Great period, and didn't pay much attention. But then I realised that he had in fact embarked on a novel about the private lives of present-day people. So strange, the way he just pitched straight into it. Seryozha had kept aski-g me to give him something to read aloud to his old aunt, so I gave him Pushkin's *Tales of Belkin*. But it turned out that Aunt had already fallen asleep, and as I couldn't be bothered to go downstairs and take the book back to the library, I left it lying on the drawing-room window. While L. was having coffee next morning he picked it up, glanced through it and went into ecstasies. At the beginning of the volume (the Annenkov edition) he found some critical notes. 'I have always learned so much from Pushkin!' he said. 'He is my father, and one must always be guided by him.' He then read me some passages about the old days, about how the landowners used to live and travel about,[25] and this book cleared up much that had baffled him about the life of the gentry in the Peter the Great period; this evening he read various other excerpts from the book, and under Pushkin's influence he sat down to write. He went on with his writing today, and said he was well pleased with it.[26]

At the moment he is out looking at the fox with his two sons, their tutor Fyodor Fyodorovich and Uncle Kostya.[27] This fox runs past the bridge near our house every day.

The weather is lovely and fine, with bright sun by day and brilliant stars and a sharp sickle moon by night.

October 4 *Anna Karenina* was started this spring, and at the same time L. wrote a summary of the whole work. Throughout the summer, which we spent in the province of Samara,[28] L. did no writing, but he is now polishing, revising and continuing with the novel.[29]

Kramskoi is doing two portraits of L., and this tends to prevent him working. But to make up for it there are long discussions and arguments about art every day.[30]

Yesterday we both drove to Shakovskoe to visit the Obolenskiis. He was coughing, and I was worried about him. He went on as he wanted to go hunting, but I returned home. (It was Tanya's ninth birthday.)

November 20 L.N. has just been describing to me the way he got some of the ideas for his novel:

'I was sitting downstairs in my study and examining the white silk embroidery on the sleeve of my dressing-gown, and I thought how beautiful it was. And then I wondered how it occurred to people to invent all these designs and decorations and embroideries, and I realised there was a whole world of fashions and ideas and hard work which make up women's lives. All this must be very jolly, I thought, I can understand why women are so fascinated by it. So all this naturally led my thoughts (thoughts about the novel, that is) to Anna . . . And suddenly this piece of embroidery on my sleeve suggested a whole chapter to me. Anna is cut off from all the joys of this side of a woman's life, for she is alone, other women spurn her, and she has no one to talk to about all the ordinary, everyday things that interest women.'

All this autumn he kept saying, 'My brain is asleep.' But suddenly, about a week ago, something within him seemed to blossom and he started working cheerfully again – and he seems quite satisfied with his efforts too. He silently sat down at his desk this morning, without even drinking his coffee, and wrote and wrote for more than an hour, revising the chapter dealing with Anna's arrival in St Petersburg and Aleks. Aleks.'s relations with Lidia Ivanovna.[31]

Notes on Remarks Made by L.N. Tolstoy on His Writing

November 21, 1876 He came up to me and said: 'This bit of writing is so tedious!'

'Why?' I asked.

'Well, you see, I've said that Vronskii and Anna were staying in the same hotel room, but that's not possible. In St Petersburg at least, they'd have to take rooms on different floors. So as you see, this means that all the scenes and conversations will have to take place in two separate places, and all the various visitors will have to see them separately. So it will all have to be altered.'

March 3, 1877 Yesterday L.N. went to his table, pointed at his notebook of writing and said: 'Oh, how I long to finish this novel (i.e. *Anna Karenina*) and start something new. My ideas are quite clear now. If a work is to be really good there must be one fundamental idea in it which one loves. So in *Anna Karenina*, say, I love the idea of the *family*; in *War and Peace* I loved the idea of the *people*, because of the 1812 war; and now I see very clearly that in my new book I shall love the idea of the Russian people's *powers of expansion*.' These powers are demonstrated for Lev Nikolaevich by the constant migration of Russians to new areas of South-Eastern Siberia, the new lands of Southern Russia, the Belaya River region, Tashkent, and so on.

One hears a great deal about these migrants at present. Last summer, for instance, when we were staying in Samara, the two of us drove out to a Cossack settlement some twenty *versts* from the farm where we were staying, and on the way we passed a whole string of carts with several families and numerous children and old men, all looking very cheerful. We stopped and asked them where they were going. 'We are travelling from Voronezh to the new lands,' they said. 'Our people went out to the Amur region some time back, and now they have written telling us to join them there.'

Lev Nikolaevich was fascinated by this. And just the other day at the railway station he heard yet another story, of a hundred or more Tambov peasants leaving to settle in Siberia on their own initiative. They crossed the steppe and finally reached the Irtysh River. There they were told that the land belonged to the Kirghiz people, and that they couldn't settle there, so they went on a little further.

This is the idea for his next book, as I understand it anyway, and around this main idea he is gathering new facts and characters, many of which are still quite unclear, even to him.[32]

When L.N. came back from his morning walk today, he said, 'How happy I am!'

'What makes you happy?' I asked him.

'First of all you do, and secondly my religion. Neither Bobrinskii[33] nor Al. Andr. Tolstaya have converted me to their brand of Christianity, but Doctor Zakharin the materialist and Levitskii (our guest yesterday) have. Zakharin with his genuine desire to be religious, and Levitskii with those stories he read us, which deal with Russian history in such a splendidly original and *religious* manner!

Levitskii relates all historical events to the fact that in the old days, when the Russians were not Christians and lived merely for their own needs, God punished them for it, and that later on, when they became Christians, they began to live for their souls . . . L.N. was very touched by these stories, and he said today that he couldn't endure much more of this terrible religious conflict with which he has been struggling these past two years, and hoped the time was near when he could become a thoroughly religious man and not . . . [34] (I was interrupted, and have forgotten what I wanted to say.)

August 25 L.N. has gone to Moscow to find a Russian tutor for the children.[35] His religious faith is becoming more firmly established with every day that passes. He says his prayers every day now as he did when he was a child, and on every holy day he goes to matins, where all the peasants immediately crowd round him and question him about the war;[36] on Wednesdays and Fridays he fasts, he speaks constantly of the spirit of humility and won't let anyone speak ill of others, stopping them half-jokingly if they do. On July 26 he visited the Optina Pustyn Monastery and was much impressed by the monks' wisdom, culture and way of life.[37]

Yesterday he said: 'My mental valve has been unblocked, but I now have a terrible headache.' He is very upset about all our reverses in the war with Turkey and the situation at home, and he spent all yesterday morning writing about it. That evening he told me he knew that the best way to express his ideas would be in a letter to the Tsar.[38] By all means let him write it, but it's a risky way to express oneself and he mustn't send it.

September 12 L.N. says: 'I can't write anything while there's a war going on – just as when there's a fire in town you can't keep away and can think of nothing else.' He took his borzois out hunting today, then he's leaving from Lazarevo station for his property at Nikolskoe, where he has to attend to the estate.

October 25 L.N. has gone out hunting with the hounds, but all morning he was telling me how he was gradually putting together the ideas for his new book. I still don't understand exactly *what* he is going to write, and he doesn't seem very clear about it himself, but so far as I can understand it the main theme seems to be the power of the peasants, which is revealed exclusively in agriculture. Today he said to me, 'I very much like that proverb I read yesterday: "*One son is no son, two sons are half a son, but three sons are a son.*" That will be the opening epigraph. I'll have an old man with three sons – the eldest is sent off to the army, the second doesn't do much and lives at home, and the third, his father's favourite, learns to read and write and longs to get away from the peasantry, which hurts the old man. So it will start with this family drama, as perceived by a well-to-do peasant.' The clever son later comes into conflict with people of a different, more educated world, and a whole series of events ensues. In the second part, according to L.N., there'll be a settler, a sort of Russian Robinson Crusoe, who emigrates to the new lands (the Samara steppes) and makes a new life for himself there, based on the most primitive and essential human needs.

'Peasant life is always very difficult and interesting for me – when I'm describing our own life I feel quite at home,' L.N. says.

Anna Karenina is now being printed, and is shortly to appear in a separate edition.[39] Today L.N. was saying: 'In the new book too the main idea will be treated very consistently . . . ' But what idea?

December 26 At three in the morning on December 6 our son Andrei was born. This seemed to release L.N.'s mind from its mental shackles, and a week ago he started writing some new religious-philosophical work in a large bound volume. I haven't read it yet, but today he was saying to my brother Styopa: 'The purpose of the work I'm writing in the large book is to demonstrate the absolute necessity for religion.'[40]

I like the argument he puts forward in favour of Christianity and against all the socialists and communists, who believe that social laws are higher than Christian laws, and so I am going to record it. It goes like this:

'If it had not been for the teachings of Christianity, which over the centuries have taken root within us and have laid the basis of our entire social life, there would have been no laws of morality and honour, no desire for equality, goodness and a fairer distribution of the earth's blessings, which is what these people live for.'

L.N.'s mood has changed greatly over the years. After a long struggle between lack of faith and the longing for faith, he has suddenly become much calmer. Ever since the autumn he has been observing the fasts, going to church and saying his prayers. And when asked why he has chosen these ceremonies to express his beliefs, he replies: 'I want eventually to obey all the commands of the Church, but for the time being I shall merely observe as many of them as I can.' And he is constantly questioning us: 'Will you go to confession?'

'Yes.'

'The priest will ask if you have been keeping the fast.'

'I know.'

'Well you must either do so or lie to him.'

L.N.'s character too keeps changing. Although he has always been very modest and undemanding in all his habits and needs, he is becoming even more modest, tolerant and humble. The perpetual struggle for self-perfection, which he began when he was young, is now being crowned with success.

January 8, 1878 'I am now experiencing something rather similar to what happened when I wrote *War and Peace*,' L.N. said to me today with a slight smile, half happy and half nervous about the words he had just spoken. 'Then too, as I started writing about some Decembrist returning from Siberia, I had to go back to December 14 and the whole period of the revolt, then I went back to the childhood and youth of the men involved in this revolt, then I became fascinated by the war of 1812, and as this war was all bound up with the war of 1805 the whole book eventually started with that.' L.N. has recently developed an interest in the period of Nicholas I, and particularly in the Turkish war of 1829. He has begun to study this period now, and while doing so he has become interested in the accession of Nikolai Pavlovich and the December 14 revolt.

Another thing he said to me was: 'I'm going to set the whole thing on Mount Olympus, with Nicholas I and his noble company as Jupiter and the gods, while somewhere down below in Irkutsk or Samara the peasants are migrating. One of those involved in the December revolt falls in with these migrants, and the "simple life meets the noble life".'[41]

He then said that just as a pattern needed a background, he too needed a background, and this would be his present religious ideas. 'How will that be?' I asked.

'If only I knew – there wouldn't be anything to think about then,' he said. But then he added: 'Well, for instance one should observe the December 14 revolt without condemning anyone – neither Nicholas I nor the conspirators – simply describing everything and understanding everyone.'

March 1 L.N. has been busily reading up on Nikolai Pavlovich. He is fascinated mainly by the history of the Decembrists, and is totally immersed in his studies. He went to Moscow and brought back a huge pile of books and he is frequently moved to tears by these memoirs.[42] He has gone to Sergievskoe today to help organise compensation for soldiers' families.

December 18, 1879 He is writing about religion – an interpretation of the Gospels and of the conflict between 'Church and Christianity'.[43] He reads for days on end, and fasts every Wednesday and Friday; Zakharin won't hear of him observing a full fast because of his headaches, which are probably related to his stomach.

All his conversation is steeped in Christ's teachings.

He is in a calm, earnest state of mind. He has put the Decembrists behind him now, and all his other former endeavours too, although he sometimes says: 'If I do write anything again, it will be something quite different. So far all my writings have been mere exercises.'[44]

January 31, 1881 Yuriev, the editor of *Russian Thought*, came to see us. When he and I were alone together – Lev Nikolaevich having returned to his study with a glass of tea to work (as is his wont, between lunch and dinner, from 12 to 5) – Yuriev asked me why L.N. had abandoned work on *The Decembrists*. I myself had never thought through very clearly why this had happened, but after some reflection I cast my mind back to that time and gave Yuriev a lively account of what had happened. He responded most enthusiastically. 'That's a valuable story you have just told me,' he said. 'You must write it down without fail.'

So I am taking his advice and am writing it down.

It's only during the winter that L.N. works hard. He had researched all the documentary material and started a few rough drafts of *The Decembrists*, but he still hadn't managed to write anything important by the summer. In order to use his time profitably and benefit his health he started taking long walks along the Kiev highway, which runs near our house, two *versts* away, where in the summer one meets a large number of pilgrims, coming from all corners of Russia and Siberia and making pilgrimages to Kiev, Voronezh, Troitsa and elsewhere.

Feeling that his knowledge of the Russian language was far from perfect, L.N. decided this summer to set himself the task of studying the language of the people. He had long talks with pilgrims, holy wanderers and other people he met on the highway, and jotted down in his notebook all the popular words, proverbs and ideas he was hearing for the first time. But it had some quite unexpected results.

Until about 1877 L.N.'s religious feelings were vague, or rather indifferent. He was never an outright unbeliever, but nor was he a very *committed* believer. This caused L.N. terrible anxieties (he actually wrote a religious confession at the beginning of his new work).

But from this close contact with the people, the holy wanderers and pilgrims, he was deeply impressed by their lucid, unshakable faith, and terrified by his own lack of it. And suddenly he resolved wholeheartedly to follow the same path as the people. He started going to church, keeping the fasts, saying his prayers and observing all the laws of the Church. This continued for some time.

But soon L.N. came to see that the source of all this goodness, patience and love that he had witnessed in the people was not the Church and its teachings: as he himself said, having seen the *rays* he followed them to the *light*, and discovered that this was Christianity itself, through the Gospels. He persistently denies any other influence. I shall quote his own words on this: 'Christianity lives unconsciously but securely in the spirit and traditions of the people.' That is what he says.

Then, little by little, L.N. saw to his horror what a discrepancy there was between Christianity and the Church. He saw that the Church, hand in hand with the Government, had conspired against Christianity. The Church thanks God for the men killed in battle and prays for military victories, yet in the Old Testament it says: 'Thou shalt not kill,' and in the Gospels: 'Love they neighbour as thyself.' The Church enforces an oath of allegiance, yet Christ said: 'Do not swear.' The Church has given people a lot of rites and rituals which are supposed to assure their salvation, but have been an obstacle to Christianity; its true teachings about God's kingdom on earth have been obscured because people have been forced to believe that they will be saved by baptism, communion, fasting and the like.

This is L.N.'s current preoccupation. He has begun to study, translate and interpret the Gospels.[45] He has been working on this for two years now, and it seems to be only half-finished. But his soul is now happy, he says. He has seen the *light* (in his words), and this light has illuminated his whole view of the world. His attitude to people has changed too, according to him, for whereas before he had just a small circle of *intimates*, people like *him*, he now has millions of men as his brothers. Before, his wealth and his estate were his *own* – now if a poor man asks for something he must have it.

He sits down at his work every day, surrounded by books, and toils away until dinner-time. His health is deteriorating, he suffers from headaches, his hair is turning grey, and he lost a lot of weight over the winter.

He does not appear to be as happy as I should wish, and has become quiet, meditative and taciturn. We almost never see those cheerful exuberant moods of his now, which used to enchant us all so much. I put all this down to excessive overwork and exhaustion. How unlike the old days, when he was writing about the hunt and the ball in *War and Peace*, and looked as joyful and excited as though he himself were joining in the fun. His soul is undoubtedly in a state of calm clarity, but he suffers deeply for all the human misery and poverty he sees about him, for all those in jail, for all the hatred, injustice and oppression in the world – and this deeply affects his impressionable soul and undermines his life.

Why Anna Karenina was called 'Anna', and What Suggested the Idea of Her Suicide

We have a neighbour here, a man of about 50, neither rich nor educated. His name is A.N. Bibikov. He had living with him a distant cousin of his late wife, an unmarried woman of about 35 who looked after the house and was his mistress. One day Bibikov hired a new governess for his son and niece, a beautiful German woman, with whom he soon fell in love, and to whom before very long he had proposed marriage. His former mistress, whose name was *Anna* Stepanovna, left the house to visit Tula for the day, saying she was going to see her mother, but she returned from there with a bundle of clothes under her arm (containing nothing but a change of clothes and some underwear), to Yasenki, the nearest railway station, and there she jumped on to the tracks and threw herself under a goods train. Then there was a post mortem. Lev Nikolaevich attended, and saw her lying there at the Yasenki barracks, her skull smashed in and her naked body frightfully mutilated. It had the most terrible effect on him. Anna Stepanovna was a tall, plump woman with a typically Russian temperament and appearance. She had dark hair and grey eyes, and although she wasn't beautiful she was very pleasant-looking.[46]

1877
L.N. Tolstoy's Quarrel with I.S. Turgenev

In the early days of Lev Nikolaevich's literary career in St Petersburg, his relations with Turgenev were very friendly. Turgenev saw that he had a great talent and wrote the most flattering letters about him to L.N.'s sister, Maria Nikolaevna. They saw a lot of one another and were evidently good friends, despite the fact that Turgenev was 10 years older and, it seemed, couldn't help seeing Tolstoy as a literary rival.[47]

One day Turgenev and Tolstoy met at Stepanovka, Fet's estate in the district of Mtsensk, in the Oryol province. There was a conversation about charity work, in which Turgenev said that his daughter, who had been educated abroad, did a lot of good work helping the poor. L.N. said he hated the kind of charity which imitated the English, who chose 'their own poor' (my poors)* to whom they automatically handed out a tiny fraction of

*English in the original.

their income. Real charity came from the heart, he said; it meant doing good spontaneously, abandoning oneself to one's feelings.

Turgenev then said, 'So you think I'm bringing up my daughter badly, do you?' To which L.N. replied that he had merely spoken his mind and hadn't meant to be personal. Turgenev got even angrier, and suddenly said, 'If you go on talking like that I'll punch your face.'[48]

L.N. got up and drove to Bogoslov, a station situated half-way between our estate at Nikolskoe and Fet's at Stepanovka. From there he sent for his gun and some bullets, and sent Turgenev a letter challenging him to a duel for insulting him. In this letter he told Turgenev that he didn't want one of those vulgar duels in which two literary men meet a third literary man somewhere, they all take out their pistols and the whole thing ends with champagne – he wanted a real duel, he said, and asked Turgenev to meet him at the edge of the Bogoslov forest and to bring his pistols with him.

Lev Nikolaevich waited up for him all night. In the morning a letter came from Turgenev saying he could not possibly agree to Tolstoy's conditions and that he wanted this duel to be conducted according to the established rules. Lev Nikolaevich wrote back saying: 'You are afraid of me. I despise you and refuse to have anything more to do with you.'

Some time passed, and Lev Nikolaevich, who was then living in Moscow, had a sudden characteristic change of heart and longed to be good and to make others happy. In this wonderful mood of goodness, love and humility, the idea of having an enemy was unbearable to him, and he wrote to Turgenev regretting that they had fallen out: 'Forgive me if I have offended you,' he said. 'It is unbearably sad for me to think I may have an enemy.' He sent this letter to him in St Petersburg, care of Davydov, a bookseller with whom Turgenev had had dealings. But it did not reach Turgenev, who wrote Lev Nikolaevich an angry letter from Paris:

'You are telling everyone that I am a coward and would not fight with you. For this I now demand satisfaction, and shall fight you on my return to Russia' (that would have been in about 8 months' time).

Lev Nikolaevich replied that he found it utterly absurd that Turgenev should challenge him to a duel in 8 months' time, that he treated this letter with as much contempt as the last one, and that if Turgenev really needed to justify himself in public, he would send him another letter, which he could show to anyone he liked. In this letter Lev Nikolaevich wrote: 'You said you would punch my face, but I refused to fight you.'

The idea behind this letter was that if Turgenev had no personal sense of decency, merely a public code of honour, he could satisfy the public with this letter, but that Lev Nikolaevich was above such things and despised public opinion. And this time too Turgenev revealed his weakness of character, and replied that he now considered himself fully satisfied.[49] It is not clear whether or not he ever got the letter sent to him via Davydov the bookseller. Here the quarrel ended, but the two enemies remained unreconciled, unfortunately, until . . . [50]

This was taken from Lev Nikolaevich's own words on January 23, 1877.

Lev Nikolaevich Tolstoy's Reconciliation with Ivan Sergeevich Turgenev

Written on August 12, 1878 As he became increasingly religious, it made Lev Nikolaevich sad to think that he might have an enemy, so in the spring he wrote to Turgenev in Paris begging him to forget any enmity there might once have been between them, and to remember their old friendship when L.N. had first embarked on his literary career and had loved Turgenev so sincerely. He even wrote: 'Forgive me for all the wrong I have done you.' Turgenev responded with an equally affectionate letter: 'I will eagerly shake the hand you offer me . . . ' and promised to visit us when he was next in Russia.[51]

Last week, on August 6, just after we had returned from Samara, we received a telegram from Turgenev announcing that he would be with us on the 8th.[52] Lev Nikolaevich went to meet him at Tula, and I don't know what happened when they met. Turgenev, a gentle man with grey hair, enchanted us with the eloquent and picturesque way he described both the simplest and the most sublime of subjects. He first described Antokolskii's statue of Christ[53] in such a way as to bring it to life before our eyes, and then told us about his beloved dog Pegasus with exactly the same descriptive mastery. It is only too obvious what a weak character Turgenev has, a naïve, childlike weakness. But he is obviously gentle and kind too. It seem to me that this weakness of his was the whole cause of his quarrel with Lev Nikolaevich.

He naïvely admits to be utterly terrified of cholera, for instance. And then there were thirteen of us at the table and we were joking about this and wondering who was fated to die first and who was afraid of death. Turgenev put up his hand and said with a laugh: '*Que celui qui craint la mort lève la main.*'*

As no one else put up their hand, L.N. did so to be polite, and said: '*Eh bien, moi aussi je ne veux pas mourir.*'†[54]

Turgenev spent two days with us. There was no mention of the past; they had a lot of abstract discussions and arguments, and I felt that L.N. was being slightly stiff, very friendly and anxious not to overstep the limits. As Turgenev was leaving he said to me: '*Au revoir.* I have had such a delightful time here with you.'

He kept his word too; *au revoir* it was, for he came again at the beginning of September.[55]

*'Let anyone who is afraid of death raise his hand.'

†'Well yes, I don't want to die either.'

· *The Death of Vanechka*[1] ·

A few days before Vanechka's death he astonished me by beginning to give away all his things. He put little labels on everything, which he addressed in his own hand: 'With love to Masha from Vanya,' or 'To Simeon Nikolaevich our cook, from Vanya,' and so on. Then he took all the little framed pictures off the walls of his nursery and took them into his brother Misha's room; he had always been terribly fond of Misha. Then he asked me for a hammer and nails, and hung up all his pictures in his brother's room. He was so fond of Misha that if they had a quarrel and Misha would not make it up with him immediately he would be desperately unhappy and weep bitterly. Whether Misha loved him as much I don't know, but he did call his eldest son after him later.

Shortly before he died Vanechka was looking out of the window, when he suddenly looked very thoughtful: 'Maman, is Alyosha (my little son who died) an angel now?' he asked.

'Why yes,' I told him. 'It's said that children who die before they are seven turn into angels.'

To which he replied: 'Well, I too had better die, Maman, before I am seven. It will be my seventh birthday soon, but I may still be an angel yet. And if I don't, dear, dear Maman, please will you let me fast so I shan't have any sins?'

Those words of his painfully engraved themselves in my mind. On February 20 my daughter Masha and Nurse suggested taking Vanechka to the clinic, where they had made an appointment with Professor Filatov. They all looked so cheerful and excited when they got back, and Vanechka told me with great glee that he had been told he might eat whatever he wanted and could go out walking and even driving. After lunch he took a walk with Sasha, and afterwards he ate a hearty dinner. We had all been through such agony while Vanechka was ill, and now the whole house cheered up again. Tanya and Masha, who had no children of their own, lavished all their maternal affection on their little brother.

On the evening of the 20th Sasha and Vanechka asked their sister Masha to read them the children's version of Dickens' *Great Expectations*, which was called *The Convict's Daughter.*[2] When it was time to go to bed Vanechka came to say goodnight to me. I was touched by the sad weary look in his eyes and asked him about the book Masha had been reading to them.

'Oh, don't talk about it, Maman. It was all so sad! You see Estella doesn't marry Pip in the end!'

We went downstairs to the nursery together and he yawned, then with tears in his eyes he said sadly: 'Oh, Maman, it's back again, that, that . . . temperature.'

I took his temperature and it was 38.5 °. He said his eyes were aching and I thought it must be an attack of measles. When I realised Vanechka was ill again I burst into tears, and seeing me cry he said: 'Don't cry, Maman, don't cry. It's God's will.'

Not long before this he had asked me to explain the Lord's Prayer to him, and I had explained 'Thy Will Be Done' with special feeling.

Then he asked me to finish reading a Grimm's story we hadn't finished – the one about the crow as far as I recall. I did as he asked. Then Misha came into the nursery, and I went off to my bedroom. I later discovered that Vanechka had said to Misha, 'I know that I am dying now.'

He was very feverish all night but managed to sleep through it. The next morning we sent for Doctor Filatov, who said straightaway that Vanechka had scarlet fever. His temperature rose to 40 ° and he had pains in his stomach and violent diarrhoea. (Scarlet fever is often complicated by a distemper of the bowels.)

At 3 in the morning Vanechka woke up, looked at me and said: 'Forgive me, dear Maman, for keeping you awake.'

'I have had my sleep, darling,' I said. 'We're all taking it in turns to sit with you.'

'Whose turn is it next, Tanya's?'

'No dear, it's Masha's.'

'Call Masha then, and go to bed.'

How lovingly my darling little boy sent me away. He hugged me to him tightly and pressed his dry little lips to mine, tenderly kissing me again and again.

'Is anything hurting you?' I asked him.

'No, nothing's hurting,' he said.

'Just miserable?'

'Yes, just miserable.'

He never regained consciousness properly after that. The next day his temperature went up to 42 °. Filatov wrapped him in blankets soaked with mustard water, and laid him in a warm bath – but it was no good, his little head hung helplessly to one side as if he were dead, then his little hands and feet grew cold; he opened his eyes once more, with a look of pure astonishment, then grew still. It was 11 at night on February the 23rd.

My husband Lyovochka led me into Tanya's room and we both sat down on the couch together. I leant my head on his chest and lost consciousness. We were both half-dead with grief.

My daughter Masha and Maria Nikolaevna the nun were with Vanechka during the final moments and were praying for him constantly. I was later told that Nurse, like me maddened with grief, just lay on her bed sobbing. Tanya kept running in and out of the nursery.

When Vanechka had been dressed in his little white shirt and his long, fair curly hair had been brushed, Lyovochka and I plucked up the courage to go back into the nursery. Vanechka was lying on the couch. I laid an icon on his little chest, and someone else lit a wax candle and put it at his head.

Everyone had loved our Vanechka, and before long news of his death had spread to our friends and relatives. They all sent masses of flowers and wreaths and the nursery soon looked like a garden. No one worried about the risk of infection. Dear kind Sapho Martynova, who had four children of her own, came straightaway and wept passionately with us and grieved with us. And we all seemed to cling together in our love for our poor Vanechka. Maria Nikolaevna stayed with us and gave us heart-felt religious consolation, and Lev Nikolaevich's diary records the cry of his heart: '**February 26.** We have buried Vanechka. It's frightful! No, not frightful, a great spiritual experience. I thank Thee, Father.'[3]

On the third day, February 25, Vanechka's funeral service was held, the lid of his little coffin was hammered down, and at twelve o'clock his father, his brothers and Pavel Ivanovich Biryukov carried it out of the house and set it on our large four-seated sledge. My husband and I sat facing one another and we slowly moved off, accompanied by our friends.

I later described Vanechka's death and funeral in a letter to my sister: 'And you know Tanya, all through Vanechka's funeral service I didn't shed a single tear, just held his cold little head between my hands and tried to warm his little cheeks with my lips. I don't know now why I didn't die of sorrow. But although I am weeping as I write to you I shall go on living, and for a long time too I expect, with this stone on my heart.'[4]

Lyovochka and I silently bore off our beloved youngest child, our one bright hope, to be buried. And as we approached the Pokrovskoe cemetery, near the village of Nikolskoe, where Vanechka was to buried alongside his little brother Alyosha,[5] Lyovochka recalled how he used to drive along that road to our dacha in Pokrovskoe after he had first fallen in love with me. He wept and caressed me and spoke so tenderly, and his love meant so much to me.

The Burial

We found crowds of people at the cemetery, both villagers and people who had travelled there to attend the funeral. It was a Sunday and the schoolchildren were walking around the village, admiring all the wreaths and flowers.

The little coffin was again lifted from the slege by Lev Nikolaevich and our sons. Everyone wept to see the father, so old, bent and bowed with grief. Many of our friends came to the funeral, as well as members of our own family – there were Manya Rachinskaya, Sonya Mamonova, Kolya

Obolenskii, Sapho Martynova, Vera Severtseva, Vera Tolstaya and many more. They all sobbed loudly.

When they lowered the coffin into the grave I again lost consciousness, as if I too were disappearing into the earth. They told me afterwards that Ilyusha had tried to shield me from that dreadful pit, and that someone else had held my arms. Lyovochka embraced me and held me to him, and I stood there with him for a long time in a stunned state.

I was brought back to my senses by the happy shouts of the village children, to whom I had asked Nurse to hand out sweets and cakes. The children were laughing, dropping gingerbread on the ground and picking it up again. Then I remembered how Vanechka had loved to celebrate and hand out sweets, and I burst into tears for the first time since his death.

Immediately after the funeral, when everyone had left, Kasatkin the artist arrived and made two sketches of the fresh grave.[6] He offered one to me and the other to Tanya, and attached to them a most moving and poetic letter expressing his love for Vanechka, whom he described as 'transparent'.[7]

We returned, bereft, to our deserted house, and I remember Lev Nikolaevich sitting down on the sofa in the dining-room downstairs (where it had been put for our son Lyova, who had been ill), and bursting into tears, saying: 'I had always thought that of all my sons Vanechka alone would carry on my good work on earth after I died.'

And a little later he said almost the same thing: 'And I had dreamed of Vanechka carrying on God's work after me. Well, there's nothing to be done about it now.'

The sight of Lyovochka's suffering was even more painful to me than my own. I wrote about him to my sister Tanya: 'Lyovochka has grown bent and old; he wanders sadly about the house, his eyes bright with tears, and it's as though the last bright ray of sunshine of his old age has been extinguished. Two days after Vanechka's death he sat down and sobbed: "For the first time in my life I have lost hope."'[8]

Of all our children Vanechka looked most like him, with the same bright, penetrating eyes, the same earnest, searching mind. Once I was combing his curly hair in front of the mirror and he turned his little face to me and said with a smile: 'Maman, I really do look like Papa, don't I!'

After the Funeral

The first night after Vanechka's death I jumped out of bed in terror, hallucinating the most fearful smell. It pursued me for a long time afterwards too, even though my husband, who was sleeping with me at the time, assured me that there was no smell and I had just imagined it. Then I would suddenly hear Vanechka's dear gentle voice. He and I used to say our prayers together and make the sign of the cross over one another. 'Kiss me hard, Maman,' he would say. 'Put your head beside mine, and breathe on my chest so I can fall asleep with your warm breath on me.'

There is no love so strong, so pure or so good as the love of a mother and child. With Vanechka's death the dear little nursery world in our house came to an end. Sasha was inconsolable without her playmate and wandered sadly about the house on her own. She was wild and unsociable by nature, whereas Vanechka loved people, he loved writing letters and giving presents, he loved organising treats and celebrations, and how many people loved him!

Even cold Menshikov wrote: 'When I saw your little son I was sure he would either die or live to be an even greater genius than his father.'[9]

I had many, many wonderful letters of sympathy from people who wrote to sympathise or to remember Vanechka. N.N. Strakhov wrote to Lev Nikolaevich: 'He promised much – maybe he would have inherited not only your name but your fame. What a lovely child – words cannot describe him.'[10]

A writer called Zhirkevich wrote: 'Without knowing either you, Lev Nikolaevich or Vanechka, a St Petersburg writer is writing a passionate article about this wonderful little creature who offered us all so much hope. Mothers and fathers everywhere share your grief, and my voice is drowned in a chorus of condolences.'[11]

Mikh. Al. Stakhovich wrote: 'I feel sorry for Vanechka himself too. What a fascinating, lovable, touching child. I saw him only a few times, but I shall always remember him because he was so different from other children, with his earnest, determined expression and the clever things he did and said.'[12]

Olga Andreevna Golokhvastova wrote: 'Sweet, clever, sensitive little Vanechka.'[13]

Sofia Alekseevna Filosova wrote to console me and to assure me that people still loved and needed me: 'You will do even more good now, with your serene, sincere and suffering soul.'[14]

Anna Grigorevna Dostoyevskaya hardly knew Vanechka at all, yet she wrote: 'He was a highly gifted person with a tender and responsive heart.'[15]

Peshkova-Toliverova, who had published Vanechka's story in *The Toy*,[16] wrote: 'He stands before me now, a pale modest little boy with enquiring eyes.'[17] Our old friend Prince S.S. Urusov soothed me with his comforting assurances about the blessed state of Vanechka's soul in paradise. And he believed this so earnestly himself, for he was a very religious and orthodox man, that I found his faith infectious.

Many people prayed for Vanechka and for us two, in churches and homes. Many parents sympathised with us, particularly those who had lost children of their own, such as Aleksandra Alekseevna Chicherina (née Countess Kapnist), who had lost her only little girl; Baroness Mengden, whose two grown-up sons had died, and others.

I wrote to my sister at this time: 'I try to console myself with the thought that my sufferings are necessary if I am to pass into eternity, purify my soul and be united with God and Vanechka, who was all joy and love. "Thy will be done!" I cry. If this will bring me closer to eternity, so be it. Yet despite these lofty spiritual aspirations, and my sincere and heartfelt desire to submit to God's will, there's no consolation for me in this or anything else.'[18]

For some reason Lev Nikolaevich refused to believe in my religious activities. It annoyed him that I kept visiting churches, monasteries and cathedrals. I remember spending nine hours once in the Arkhangelskii Cathedral during Lent, standing up during the services and then sitting on the steps with the pilgrims and old women. There was another educated woman there too, who had just lost her grown-up son, and like me was seeking comfort in prayer in the house of God.

Returning from the Kremlin one day to Khamovniki Street, I got soaked in the rain, caught a bad chill and was ill in bed for a long time. Before this Sasha and I had been fasting, and all this was evidently not to Lev Nikolaevich's liking. He wrote in his diary: '*March 27, 1985*. Sonya is suffering as much as before, and is incapable of rising to a religious level. The reason is that she has put all her spiritual energies into her animal love for her child.'[19]

Why *animal* love? I have had many children, but my feelings for Vanechka, and our love for one another, was fundamentally spiritual in nature. We lived in spiritual communion with one another, we always understood one another, and despite the difference in our ages we always spoke on such a lofty, abstract plane.

But he was very sweet to me then.[20] I remember he once asked me if I would go and visit his sister Mashenka on her name-day, March 25, and we both tried to decide what to give her as a present. I remembered that she had said she would like an alarm-clock, to wake her up for church services, so we both went and bought one, and she was delighted with it, as with our visit.

Another time, I remember, Lev Nikolaevich invited me out to the market to buy flowers for Palm Saturday, pretending he wanted to buy some books to take to the prison. He thought this would divert me. I bought a lot of artificial white flowers and a branch of white lilac, which I have kept to this day and which now hangs over the big portrait of Vanechka.

After visiting his sister Maria Nikolaevna, Lev Nikolaevich wrote in his diary: 'Mashenka has become so much kinder since being in the monastery. What does this mean? How can one reconcile paganism with Christianity? I cannot properly explain this to myself . . .'[21] He considered me a pagan too, simply because I, like Mashenka, had not rejected the Church. Yet I have always believed that it is a bad faith which puts too much store by forms and ceremonies. Besides, how can my faith be obstructed by a place where people have gathered in God's name over the centuries to preserve the idea of the deity; they have brought to his temples all their griefs, joys, hopes, fears and feelings – all the things that mankind has ever lived for.

IV

References

Abbreviations

The following abbreviations are used in the Notes for books, journals, institutions, etc. which occur frequently.

Bulgakov	V. Bulgakov, *L. N. Tolstoy v poslednii god ego zhizni*, Goslitizdat, Moscow, 1960.
DST	*Dnevniki S. A. Tolstoi* (Diaries of S. Tolstaya), 4 vols, Moscow, 1928–36 (earlier edition of present volumes).
GM	*Golos minuvshego* (Voice of the Past). Journal.
GMT	Gosudarstvennyi muzei L. N. Tolstogo (State Museum of L. N. Tolstoy).
Goldenweiser	A. B. Goldenweiser, *Vblizi Tolstogo* (Near Tolstoy), Moscow, 1923.
GTG	Gosudarstvennaya Tretyakovskaya Galereya (State Tretyakov Gallery).
Gusev	N. N. Gusev, *Dva goda s L. N. Tolstym* (Two Years with L. N. Tolstoy), Khudozhestvennaya Literatura, Moscow, 1973.
Gusev, *Materialy*	N. N. Gusev, *Lev Nikolaevich Tolstoi. Materialy k biografii* (Material for a Biography), Academy of Sciences, Moscow: vol. 1: *1828–1855, 1954*; vol. 2: *1855–1869, 1957*; vol. 3: *1870–1881, 1963*; vol. 4: *1881–1885, 1970*.
IRLI	*Institut Russkoi Literatury (Institute of Russian Literature). Pushkin House.*
IV	*Istoricheskii vestnik* (Historical Herald). Journal.
Kuzminskaya	Tatiana A. Kuzminskaya, *Moya zhizn i doma i v Yasnoi Polyane* (My Life at Home and at Yasnaya Polyana), Tula, 1973.
KN	*Knizhki nedeli* (Books of the Week). Journal.
Letopisi	*Letopisi Gosudarstvennogo Literaturnogo Muzeya* (Annals of the State Museum of Literature).
LN	*Literaturnoe nasledstvo* (Literary Heritage). Journal.
MZh	Sofia Tolstaya, *Moya zhizn* (My Life), typescript in the GMT.
NV	*Novoe vremya* (New Times). Journal.
PS	*Perepiska L. N. Tolstogo s N. N. Strakhovym* (Correspondence between L. N. Tolstoy and N. N. Strakhov), Society of the Tolstoy Museum, St Petersburg, 1914.

PSS	L. N. Tolstoy, *Polnoe sobranie sochinenii v 90 tomakh* (Complete Collected Works in 90 vols), Goslitizdat, Moscow, 1928–58.
PST	S. A. Tolstaya. *Pisma k L. N. Tolstomu, 1862–1910* (Letters to L. N. Tolstoy, 1862–1910), Akademiya, Moscow/Leningrad, 1936.
PTG	*L. N. Tolstoi i N. N. Gué. Perepiska* (L. N. Tolstoy and N. N. Gué. Correspondence), Akademiya, Moscow/Leningrad, 1930.
RB	*Russkoe bogatstvo* (Russian Wealth). Journal.
Re	*Rech* (Speech). Journal.
RM	*Russkaya mysl* (Russian Thought). Journal.
RO	*Russkoe obozrenie* (Russian Review). Journal.
RS	*Russkoe slovo* (Russian Word). Journal.
RV	*Russkie vedomosti* (Russian Gazette). Journal.
Sergeenko	P. A. Sergeenko, *Tolstoi i ego sovremenniki* (Tolstoy and His Contemporaries), Moscow, 1911.
Stasov	*Lev Tolstoi i V. V. Stasov. Perepiska, 1878–1906* (Lev Tolstoy and V. V. Stasov. Correspondence, 1878–1906), Leningrad, 1929.
T. L. Sukhotina	T. L. Sukhotina-Tolstaya, *Vospominaniya* (Memoirs), Khudozhestvennaya Literatura, Moscow, 1976.
SV	*Severnii vestnik* (Northern Herald). Journal.
TE	*Tolstovskii ezhegodnik* (Tolstoy Yearbook).
I. L. Tolstoy	Ilya L. Tolstoy, *Moi vospominaniya* (My Memoirs), Khudozhestvennaya Literatura, Moscow, 1969.
S. L. Tolstoy	Sergei L. Tolstoy, *Ocherki bylogo* (Notes From the Past), Tula, 1975.
Tolstoi v vosp.	*L. N. Tolstoy v vospominaniyakh sovremennikov* (L. N. Tolstoy in the Memories of His Contemporaries), 2 vols, Goslitizdat, Moscow, 1960.
Tolstoi. Perepiska	*L. N. Tolstoi. Perepiska s russkimi pisatelyami* (L. N. Tolstoy. Correspondence with Russian Writers), Khudozhestvennaya Literatura, Moscow, 1962.
Turgenev, *Pisma*	I. S. Turgenev, *Polnoe sobranie sochinenii i pisem v 28 tomakh* (Complete Collected Works and Letters in 28 volumes), Academy of Sciences, Moscow.
VE	*Vestnik Evropy* (Herald of Europe). Journal.
VFP	*Voprosi filosofii i psikhologii* (Questions of Philosophy and Psychology). Journal.
YaPL	Yasnaya Polyana Library.
Yasn. Sb.	*Yasnopolyanskii sbornik* (Yasnaya Polyana Anthology), Tula.
YaZ	D. P. Makovitsky, *Yasnopolyanskie zapiski* (Yasnaya Polyana Notes), manuscript, GMT.
YaZ, I, II	D. P. Makovitsky, *Yasnopolyanskie zapiski* (Yasnaya Polyana Notes), Zadruga, Moscow, 1922, 1923.
ZV	*Zhurnal dlya vsekh* (Journal for All). Journal.

Notes

DIARY 1862–1910

1862

1 'P' is M.A. Polivanov. He was in love with Sofia Behrs, and evidently intended to marry her. (See Kuzminskaya, pp. 65–74; 133–6.)

2 Before Tolstoy's marriage he gave his fiancée his old diaries to read, as he did not want to conceal anything of his past from her. Reading them made a terrible impresssion on the 17-year-old Sofia Behrs. (See Appendix: 'L.N. Tolstoy's Marriage', pp. 826–43.)

3 A.M. Islenev, Sofia Tolstaya's grandfather, visited Yasnaya Polyana at this time with his daughter Olga.

4 G.S. Tolstoy, the son of S.N. Tolstoy and M.M. Shishkina, was regarded as illegitimate, as his parents were not married. The wedding did not take place until June 7, 1867.

5 T.A. Ergolskaya.

6 Sofia Tolstaya is evidently either quoting from a letter from her father which has not been kept, or quoting not entirely accurately from his letter to her of October 5, 1862: 'Life would have been very hard for you had you not found a husband who loves you so tenderly and will always be a faithful support to you' (GMT).

7 Nikolskoe-Vyazemskoe was the Tolstoys' estate in the Chern district of Tula province. It belonged to the eldest Tolstoy brother, Nikolai Nikolaevich Tolstoy, on whose death it passed to Lev Tolstoy.

8 Sofia Tolstaya was friendly with Olga Isleneva, but in a letter to her sister Tatiana Behrs of October 5, 1862, she confessed: 'You know how jealous I have always been. Well, everything makes me angry: the fact that she plays with him, and that he likes her. You must understand that I could never imagine that he doesn't love me, but it's so unpleasant. I'm glad she's leaving on Sunday' (GMT).

9 This entry reveals her attitude to Tolstoy's 'educational activities', and his relations with the peasants. In her view, the new conditions of family life should have banished all other interests but practical family matters. Tolstoy wrote in his diary: 'All this time I have been busy with nothing but practical matters. But I now find this idleness oppressive. I cannot respect myself. And this makes me dissatisfied with myself and confused in my relations with others. I have decided to finish with my diary, and, I think, with the schools too. I am constantly angry, with my life, and sometimes even with her' (*PSS*, vol. 48, p. 47). But Tolstoy himself always described this time as a very 'happy time in my life' (see *PSS*, vol. 54, p. 94).

10 The students and teachers at the Yasnaya Polyana school and the other schools opened by Tolstoy in the Krapivna district.

11 N.P. Okhotnitskaya.

12 This entry echoes a letter from Tolstoy to Tatiana Behrs of March 23, 1863, in which he describes his wife turning into a 'cold porcelain doll' (see *PSS*, vol. 61, pp. 10–13). Sofia Tolstaya's diary entry and Tolstoy's letter reflect their emotional state in the first months of their marriage. For more detail about this see V.A. Zhdanov, *Lyubov v zhizni Lva Tolstogo* (Love in the life of L.N. Tolstoy), vol. I, Moscow, 1928, pp. 98–106.

13 Evidently Sofia Tolstaya had either been re-reading or was recalling Tolstoy's reference in his diary, on May 13, 1858, to the Yasnaya Polyana peasant woman Aksinya Aleksandrovna

Bazykina: 'I am in love, as never before' (*PSS*, vol. 48, p. 15). Tolstoy portrayed her in his stories 'Idilliya' (Idyll) and 'Tikhon i Malanya' (Tikhon and Malanya) (*PSS*, vol. 7), and in the long story 'Dyavol' (Devil) (*PSS*, vol. 27).

1863

1 Sofia Tolstaya is evidently referring to harsh words spoken to her in a quarrel the day before. Tolstoy referred to it in an entry of January 8: 'This morning it was her dress. She called for me, wanting me to criticise it, which I did – and then there were tears and trite explanations' (*PSS*, vol. 48, p. 49).

2 G.A. Auerbach, an acquaintance of the Tolstoys, lived near Tula on his estate at Goryachkino. In the 1860s he frequently visited Yasnaya Polyana with his wife. 'I was afraid of them and avoided them,' recalled Sofia Tolstaya, 'for they were very clever' (*MZh*, book 2, pp. 21–2).

3 Tatiana Andreevna Behrs.

4 Aleksander Andreevich Behrs.

5 On December 23, 1862, the Tolstoys went to Moscow. They took rooms in the Hotel Chevriet, on Gazetnyi Street, and stayed there until February 8, 1863. During their visit to Moscow they paid almost daily visits to the Kremlin to see the Behrs.

6 Aksinya Aleksandrovna Bazykina (see this Diary, 1862, note 13).

7 Tolstoy referred in his diary to this quarrel on January 15: 'The last argument left (imperceptible) traces [. . .] Every such argument, however insignificant, is a cut in our love' (*PSS*, vol. 48, p. 50).

8 Sofia Tolstaya was reading Tolstoy's diary from January 3 to March 3, 1863. On February 23 he noted: 'I love her more and more' (*PSS*, vol. 48, p. 52).

9 Sofia Tolstaya was reading Tolstoy's letters to V.V. Arseneva, whom he was planning to marry between 1856 and 1857. In his letters to her he depicted in detail their future family life together, and he called himself Khrapovitskii and her Dembitskaya. (See letters for November 12–13 and 19, 1856. *PSS*, vol. 60, pp. 108–10 and 114–20.) This love affair was reflected in the story 'Family Happiness'. (See P.A. Zhurov's article 'L.N. Tolstoy i V.V. Arseneva' (L.N. Tolstoy and V.V. Arseneva), in *Yasn. Sb.*, 1976, pp. 119–35.)

10 At this time Tolstoy was intending to build a distillery with his neighbour, a landowner named A.N. Bibikov, who owned the estate at Telyatinki. In May 1863 a small distillery started operating, but it only existed for eighteen months.

11 In a letter to her sister of February 13, 1863, Sofia Tolstaya wrote: 'We are turning into complete landowners: we buy cattle and poultry, pigs and calves. Come here and I'll show you. We're buying bees from the Islenevs. You can eat the honey, I don't like it' (*Yasn. Sb.*, 1976, p. 158).

12 The identity of 'V.V.' has not been established.

13 Avdotya Ivanovna Bannikova, Sofia Tolstaya's chambermaid.

14 Tatiana Andreevna Behrs, Aleksandr Andreevich Behrs, Aleksandr Mikhailovich Kuzminskii and Anatolii Lvovich Shostak.

15 Sofia and Lev Tolstoy feared that Tatiana Behrs was in love with Shostak, whom she had met in St Petersburg in the spring of 1863. The Tolstoys made some excuse and sent the young man away from Yasnaya Polyana. (See Kuzminskaya, pp. 205–13.)

16 Aleksandr Behrs and Aleksandr Kuzminskii.

17 On June 28, 1863, the Tolstoys' son Sergei was born. 'I suffered for a whole day, it was terrible,' recalled Sofia Tolstaya. 'Lyovochka was with me all the time, and I could see he felt very sorry for me; he was so loving, and his eyes shone with tears, and he kept wiping my forehead with a handkerchief dipped in eau-de-cologne [. . .] There was another hour of agony, and at 2 in the morning of June 28 I was delivered of my first-born. Lev Nikolaevich sobbed loudly, clasping my head and kissing me' (*MZh*, book 2, pp. 88, 89–90). Tolstoy

attempted to describe what he had experienced in his diary on August 5, 1863, but the entry was not finished. (See *PSS*, vol. 48, pp. 55–6.) It found expression partly in the description of Kitty's labour in *Anna Karenina*, book 7, ch. XV.

18 On June 18, 1863, Tolstoy wrote in his diary: 'I am petty and worthless. And I have been so ever since I married the woman I love [. . .] I have irrevocably destroyed, in an orgy of farming, the last nine months, which might have been the best but which I myself made some of the worst of my entire life [. . .] How frightful, terrible and senseless, to link one's happiness with material things – wife, children, health, riches' (*PSS*, vol. 48, pp. 54, 55).

19 Sofia Tolstaya's mother came to stay with her before her confinement.

20 Because Sofia Tolstaya was ill, a wet-nurse was brought into the house, and this aroused Tolstoy's fury.

21 Subsequently recalling this time, Sofia Tolstaya wrote: 'He was very bitter with me, would go out of the house and leave me alone for days on end, without help, and everything made him angry' (*MZh*, book 2, p. 93). Tolstoy himself wrote angrily in his diary that his wife's character was 'deteriorating every day' (*PSS*, vol. 48, p. 56; see also p. 54). It was only two months later that he felt calm and happy again, immersed in work on his new novel. 'October 6,' he wrote. 'It has all passed and it's all untrue. I'm happy with her.' And here too he wrote: 'There's no need to choose. The choice was made long ago. Literature means art, teaching and family' (*PSS*, vol. 48, p. 57).

22 This was what the Behrs family called Tolstoy before his marriage to Sofia.

23 The Behrs had supposed that Tolstoy would marry their eldest daughter, Elizaveta. See Appendix: 'L.N. Tolstoy's Marriage'.

24 Tolstoy was jealous of his wife's relations with A.A. Erlenwein, a teacher at the school organised by Tolstoy in the village of Baburino. On June 18, 1863 he noted in his diary: 'Her evident happiness today to chat and attract his attention [. . .] I should read this and admit: yes, I know, it's jealousy!' (*PSS*, vol. 48, p. 54).

25 Natalya Kazakova, the wet-nurse of the Tolstoys' son Sergei.

26 This is the only known reference to Tolstoy's desire to go to war (the war to crush the Caucasus had not yet ended). Tolstoy evidently did not pursue it.

27 Valerian Petrovich Tolstoy, the husband of Maria Nikolaevna Tolstaya.

28 See entry in Tolstoy's diary for March 3, 1863: 'Today she feels bored and cramped. A madman seeks a whirlwind – but this is youth, not madness. And I fear this mood more than anything in the world' (*PSS*, vol. 48, p. 52). These moods are present in Sofia Tolstaya's diary entries for December 19 and 24.

29 'Alexandrine' was Aleksandra Andreevna Tolstaya, Tolstoy's cousin once removed. Tolstoy first became friendly with her in 1853; their affectionate correspondence over forty-seven years is exceptionally interesting because of the variety of its content and the openness with which Tolstoy expressed his views, his literary plans and his emotional upsets. Tolstoy himself described this correspondence as his best autobiography. Re-reading copies of these letters in the last year of his life, he said: 'When I look back on my long, dark life, the memory of Alexandrine is always a ray of brightness in it' (*Perepiska L.N. Tolstogo s gr. A.A. Tolstoi*' (L.N. Tolstoy's correspondence with Countess A.A. Tolstaya), St Petersburg, edited by the Tolstoy Museum, 1911, p. vi).

30 In a letter which he began on October 17, 1863, Tolstoy wrote to A.A. Tolstaya: 'Lying here are 4 pages of a letter I started writing to you, but I'm not going to send it' (*PSS*, vol. 61, p. 23). The letter is unknown, but it is plain that Tolstoy had written very openly about his family life, which explains why Sofia Tolstaya was so disturbed by it. In the letter he did send (of October 17–31, 1863), he wrote: 'I am a calm and happy husband and father, with nothing to hide from anyone, and no desire but that everything should continue like this' (ibid., p. 24).

31 Evidently a reference to one of the drafts for the beginning of *War and Peace*.

32 A reference to the love affair between Tatiana Behrs and Sergei Nikolaevich Tolstoy, which

lasted from the summer of 1863 to June 1865. See Kuzminskaya, pp. 218–30; 299–304; 351–66.

33 Sergei Nikolaevich Tolstoy visited Yasnaya Polyana from his estate at Pirogovo; in 1863 he was 37.

34 When this love affair started Maria Shishkina had already been his common-law wife for fifteen years, and they had several children.

1864

1 'Grandmother' was what Tolstoy jokingly called Aleksandra Tolstaya, even though she was only eleven years older than he. Their affection was mutual. In 1857 Tolstoy was sincerely enamoured of her, as evidenced by his diary entries for May 11 and October 22, 1857: 'I am so disposed to fall in love that I am appalled. If only Alexandrine were 10 years younger. A splendid nature.' And: 'Alexandrine is a delight, a joy and a consolation. And I haven't met one woman to match her' (*PSS*, vol. 47, pp. 127, 160).

2 Sofia Tolstaya is referring to her younger sister Tatiana Behrs, who was 17 in October 1863, and to her 9-month-old son Sergei.

3 Sofia Tolstaya's mood was induced by Tolstoy's departure to Nikolskoe-Vyazemskoe, stopping off on the way at Pirogovo to see his brother Sergei.

4 On October 4, 1864, the Tolstoys' daughter Tatiana was born.

5 On September 26, 1864, Tolstoy fell off his horse while hunting and dislocated his right arm. The Tula doctors set the arm, but unsuccessfully, so on November 21 Tolstoy went to Moscow for a consultation with some doctors who, on November 28, carried out another operation.

1865

1 Evdokia Nikolaevna Bannikova (married name Orekhova), a chambermaid at the Tolstoys' house.

2 Aksinya Aleksandrovna Bazykina (see this Diary, 1862, note 13).

3 Tatiana Aleksandrovna Ergolskaya, Tolstoy's aunt and governess, was staying with Tolstoy's sister Maria in Pirogovo.

4 Letter of March 8, 1865 (GMT; referred to in *PSS*, vol. 61, p. 76).

5 Sofia Tolstaya confessed that she 'had no special liking for Mashenka' (see the Tolstoys' letter to Tatiana Behrs of March 24, 1865 – *PSS*, vol. 61, pp. 77–8).

6 'Zefirots' was the family name for Liza and Varya, the daughters of Tolstoy's sister Maria, who stayed at Yasnaya Polyana for much of the time between 1864 and 1866. For the origin of this name see *PSS*, vol. 83, p. 39.

7 On March 15, 1865 Sergei Tolstoy's son Nikolai (born in 1863) died; Tolstoy went to the funeral.

8 Tolstoy's story *The Cossacks* was published in *RV* in 1863 (no. 1). Sofia Tolstaya was probably reading E. Markov's article in *Otechestvennye zapiski* (Notes of the fatherland) (nos 1–2, 1865), entitled 'Narodnye tipy v nashei literature' (National types in our literature), or D.I. Pisarev's article in *RS* (no. 3, 1865), entitled 'Progulka po sadam rossisskoi literatury' (A walk through the gardens of Old Russian literature). 'Markov's is a bad article,' noted Tolstoy in his diary that day (*PSS*, vol. 48, p. 61).

9 The first part of *War and Peace*, entitled *1805*, was published in *RV* in 1865 (nos 1–2). The second part was finished only in November that year.

10 Sofia Tolstaya had evidently read the notes in Tolstoy's diary referring to the memoirs of Auguste Frédéric Louis de Marmont, a Napoleonic marshal (see *PSS*, vol. 48, pp. 60–2): *Mémoires du Maréchal Marmont, duc de Raguse, de 1792 à 1832*, vols I–IX, Paris, 1856–7 (YaPL). This work served as one of Tolstoy's sources for *War and Peace* (see *PSS*, vol. 16, pp. 69, 145).

11 The wedding was set for June 29. See note 13.
12 Sergei Tolstoy left for Pirogovo with his son Grisha and the boy's tutor, Gustav Keller.
13 Sergei Tolstoy abruptly stopped visiting Yasnaya Polyana and explained to Tolstoy in a letter that he could not leave Maria Shishkina and their children: 'Throughout these ten miserable days I have been lying, believing that I was telling the truth, but when I saw I must finally break with Masha I realised this was completely impossible' (GMT). Tatiana herself refused him when she discovered this. She wrote to inform her parents: 'Do not be surprised or grieved; I could not have done otherwise and would always have had it on my conscience. All may now be for the best.' (Quoted in Kuzminskaya, pp. 354–5.) Tolstoy described this letter as 'wonderful' and her behaviour as 'noble' and 'splendid' (*PSS*, vol. 61, p. 87).
14 Tolstoy shared Sofia's feelings about his brother, and wrote to him: 'I cannot convey to you the hell in which you have placed not only Tanya but our entire family, including me' (*PSS*, vol. 61, p. 86).
15 Maria Nikolaevna Tolstaya with Varya and Liza.
16 Maria Afanasievna Arbuzova.
17 Tatiana Aleksandrovna Ergolskaya.

1866

1 The Tolstoys arrived in Moscow on January 21, 1866. Sofia Tolstaya wanted to 'show the children to her parents' and Tolstoy wanted to 'revive memories of people and society' (see his letter to Aleksandra Tolstaya ('Alexandrine'), *PSS*, vol. 61, p. 128). At first they lived with the Behrs family, but on February 3 they moved into a separate apartment in Khludov's house on Bolshaya Dmitrovka Street (now 7 Pushkin Street), where they stayed until March 6.
2 Sofia Tolstaya evidently means Mitrofan Andreevich Polivanov, whom she met during this visit to Moscow. 'My God, what a scene Lev Nikolaevich made about my somewhat tactless behaviour towards this person,' she wrote later. 'I was simply being rather affected, as I felt awkward with him and was insanely frightened of Lev Nikolaevich's jealousy' (*MZh*, book 2, pp. 200–1).
3 During this visit Tolstoy worked in libraries and attended the School of Art, Sculpture and Architecture, where he took sculpture lessons with N.A. Ramazanov.
4 Pyotr Andreevich Behrs, Sofia's brother.
5 'In the summer of 1866,' recalled Sofia Tolstaya, 'Lev Nikolaevich hired a certain impoverished young nobleman and former cadet as estate-manager. He had a smart, pretty wife, a crop-haired nihilist, who loved to talk and philosophise. I don't remember their surname, but she was called Maria Ivanovna' (*MZh*, book 2, pp. 211–12).
6 Tolstoy involved himself in the fate of the soldier Vasilii Shibunin, who slapped his company commander's face because of his cruelty and was court-martialled. Tolstoy was a defence witness at the trial, and through Aleksandra Tolstaya he interceded with Tsar Alexander II for Shibunin's pardon. His petition was not successful, however, and Shibunin was executed on August 9, 1866.

In 1908, at the request of P.I. Biryukov, his biographer, Tolstoy described his memories of the soldier's trial in the form of a letter to Biryukov (*PSS*, vol. 37, pp. 67–75). He began his letter by confessing that this had had a far greater influence on his life 'than all the other apparently more important events of life'.
7 Konstantsia Lvovna, the daughter of Sofia Tolstaya's midwife, M.I. Abramovich.
8 The wing which housed the school from 1859–1865; subsequently it was called 'the Kuzminskiis' wing'.
9 Tolstoy was in Moscow between November 10 and 18. In his letters to Sofia Tolstaya from there he described his activities in detail: reading Masonic manuscripts in the Rumyantsev

Museum, discussing the illustrations for *War and Peace* with the artist M.S. Bashilov, and arranging with Katkov's publishing house for a separate edition of *1805*; he also wrote of his visits to Poiret's gymnasium. (See *PSS*, vol. 83, pp. 114–31.)

10 In the winter of 1866–7 Tatiana Behrs was gravely ill (consumption was suspected). Her trip abroad was delayed because of the death of Dyakov's wife. She eventually left with Dyakov's family in April 1867.

11 September 17 was Sofia Tolstaya's name-day. As a surprise, Tolstoy had invited a military band from Yasenki, where a regiment was stationed, and organised a dance; the regimental commander P. Yunosha visited the Tolstoys that day, as well as his officers. (See Kuzminskaya, pp. 411–13.)

12 Sofia Tolstaya copied out most of the manuscript of *War and Peace.*

1867

1 Hannah Tracey, the English governess, arrived at Yasnaya Polyana on November 12, 1866. The cause of their initial awkwardness, according to a letter Sofia Tolstaya wrote to her husband in Moscow, was their 'ignorance of one another's languages' (see *PST*, p. 67). Everyone soon grew to love her, however, and her pupil Tanya Tolstaya wrote many years later of the devotion she still felt for her (see T.L. Sukhotina, p. 43).

2 In a letter to M. Bashilov dated January 8, 1867, Tolstoy wrote: 'My work is going well and progressing quite rapidly – so rapidly, in fact, that I have finished three parts in rough (one part – the one for which you are doing the pictures – has been printed, and the other two are in manuscript), and have started on the fourth and final one. Unless I am delayed by some unexpected disaster, I expect to be ready with the whole novel by autumn' (*PSS*, vol. 61, p. 155). The novel was not finished by the autumn of 1867 – correcting the original rough version demanded almost three more years of intense labour.

3 See this Diary, 1866, note 11.

1870

1 Lev Lvovich Tolstoy was born on May 20, 1869 in Yasnaya Polyana. In the Tolstoys' home he was known as Lyolya or Lyova.

1871

1 Aleksandr Mikhailovich Kuzminskii, the husband of Sofia Tolstaya's sister Tanya, was appointed public prosecutor in Kutaisi. Sofia took her sister's departure very hard.

2 Tolstoy left for Moscow on June 9, 1871, and on June 11 travelled on from there with Sofia's brother Stepan to the village of Karalyk, near Buzuluk, in the province of Samara. He stayed there for six weeks, returning to Yasnaya Polyana on August 2. For a description of Tolstoy's visit to Samara see Stepan A. Behrs, *Vospominaniya o gr. L.N. Tolstom* (Memories of Count L.N. Tolstoy), Smolensk, 1893, pp. 52–7.

1872

1 Tolstoy left for Moscow on March 28. Moscow life filled him with such 'revulsion for all that idle luxury, and for all the things men and women acquire so dishonestly', that he decided 'never to go there again'. (See his letter to Aleksandra Tolstaya of March 31, 1872–*PSS*, vol. 61, p. 281.)

2 Mitrofan Nikolaevich Bannikov, the horse-trainer.

3 The proofs were sent back to F. Ries' printing-house in Moscow, where at the end of December 1871 the manuscript of the *ABC* had been sent for printing.

4 In a letter to Aleksandra Tolstaya, Tolstoy declared that he would have to live '10 people's lives, for a 100 years', in order to do 'what had to be done', and that 'the *ABC* alone could provide work for a 100 years' (*PSS*, vol. 61, p. 283).
5 Nikolai Mikhailovich Nagornov married Maria Tolstaya's elder daughter Varya in the summer of 1872.
6 The only reference to this trip of Tolstoy's.
7 Maria Lvovna Tolstaya, the Tolstoys' year-old daughter.
8 Stepan Andreevich Behrs, Sofia's brother.
9 Tolstoy's letter (which has not been kept) was addressed to his lawyer in Moscow, by means of whom he got the original of the *ABC* back from Ries and 'stopped publication'. (See his letter to N. Strakhov of May 27, 1872 – *PSS*, vol. 61, p. 289.) It was decided to print the *ABC* in Petersburg and Tolstoy asked Strakhov to be responsible for its publication (see ibid., pp. 287–90). The *ABC* was printed at Zamyslovskii's printing-house and came out in early November 1872.
10 The letter was not kept. In *DST*, vol. 1, p. 104 this phrase was mistakenly read as 'Today he wrote to Lieven *and* Sasha', which gave grounds for referring in the *PSS* (vol. 61, p. 384) to two unfinished letters: to the publisher Lieven and to Sofia's brother Aleksandr Behrs.

1873

1 Tolstoy went to Moscow for discussions with M.N. Katkov's printing-house about the publication of a third edition of his collected works. He returned to Yasnaya Polyana on February 16 or 17. *Sochineniya L.N. Tolstogo* (The works of L.N. Tolstoy), in 8 vols, 3rd edn, came out in November 1873.
2 Pyotr Lvovich Tolstoy was born June 13, 1872.
3 Fyodor Fyodorovich Kaufman, Tolstoy's sons' tutor. Seryozha Tolstoy recalled him thus: 'He was an ill-educated but decent and kindly man of about thirty-five' (S.L. Tolstoy, p. 35).
4 The governess Emily Tabor arrived at the Tolstoys' on February 11.
5 'His throat swelled up and he could not breathe,' Tolstoy wrote to his brother Sergei on November 10, 'it was what they call croup' (*PSS*, vol. 62, p. 52). This was the first death in the Tolstoy family for eleven years, and it was a very great blow for everyone. Tolstoy wrote to Aleksandr Kuzminskii that 'the house seemed so empty' (ibid., p. 56).

1875

1 Pelageya Ilinichna Tolstaya, Tolstoy's aunt.
2 In letters to Afanasii Fet and Nikolai Nikolaevich Strakhov, which he wrote on October 26, 1875, Tolstoy explained that the cause of this state was his own ill health, the 'ill health of his family' and the fact that he had 'thrown himself from one piece of work into another, but had accomplished practically nothing' (*PSS*, vol. 62, pp. 208, 210). Later, in his *Confession*, Tolstoy wrote: 'I began to be afflicted at first with moments of despair, when life stopped and I no longer knew how I should live or what I should do' (*PSS*, vol. 23, p. 494). These moods of his are connected with his religious quest at the end of the 1870s (see note 34 to the Appendices: 'Various Notes for Future Reference').

1876

1 On September 3, Tolstoy and his nephew Nikolai Valerianovich Tolstoy left Yasnaya Polyana. They arrived at Samara on September 7, and on the same day Tolstoy travelled by train to Orenburg to buy horses for the stud farm he intended to set up. In the telegram he

sent from Orenburg on September 12 he announced that he was well and finding it 'very interesting' (*PSS*, vol. 83, p. 231).

2 Stepan Andreevich Behrs.

3 On October 24, 1876, Sofia Tolstaya began to write Tolstoy's biography. This work continued, with interruptions, until the end of 1878. See this Diary, February 1877, and October to November 1878. The rough draft was published by E.S. Serebrovskaya as: *Tri biograficheskikh ocherka Tolstogo. Ocherki, sostavlennye Sofiei Andreevno so slov Tolstogo i im vypravlennye* (Three biographical sketches of Tolstoy, compiled by Sofia Andreevna from Tolstoy's own words, and corrected by him) (*LN*, vol. 69, book 1, pp. 497–516). See this Diary, 1878, note 37.

4 In the summer of 1876 Ippolit Mikhailovich Nagornov stayed at Yasnaya Polyana.

5 The telegram is dated September 17 (*PSS*, vol. 83, p. 231). On September 20 Tolstoy returned to Yasnaya Polyana. His journey was 'very enjoyable' and 'very interesting', as he wrote to Strakhov and Fet on his return (*PSS*, vol. 62, pp. 286, 287).

6 Ilya Tolstoy remembered Jules Rey as a 'crude and stupid man' (I.L. Tolstoy, p. 66).

1877

1 See this Diary, September 17, 1876, and note 3.

2 Chapters XIII to XXIX of book six of *Anna Karenina* appeared in *RV*, no. 2, 1877.

3 Sofia Tolstaya wrote to Tanya Kuzminskaya on February 25: 'Lyovochka went skiing and [. . .] fell and hit his head on a tree, and it was such a powerful blow that it stunned him and he had a lump and a scar. Since then his head has ached continuously and he has had bad blood rushes, and his condition worries me. Maybe it's not even the result of his injury, but of the pressure of writing – or simply his nerves – but I begged him nevertheless to go and see Zakharin, and he did so and promised to take his health seriously' (GMT).

1878

1 Nikolai Valerianovich Tolstoy came with his fiancée Nadezhda Fyodorovna Gromova.

2 Tolstoy was at that time observing all the church rituals very punctiliously.

3 Annie was the governess Anna Phillips.

4 Leonid Dmitrievich Urusov was an old friend of the Tolstoy family; from 1876 to 1885 he was Vice-Governor of Tula. 'Urusov has again become a frequent visitor,' Sofia Tolstaya wrote to Tanya Kuzminskaya on October 3, 1878. 'Lyovochka is always pleased to see him. They went out hunting together on Sunday, then played chess, and had the most interesting discussions all day' (GMT).

5 O. Feuillet, *Le Journal d'une femme*, Paris, 1878. Tolstoy considered Feuillet 'a great talent' (see *PSS*, vol. 48, p. 21).

6 Aleksandr Grigorevich Michurin, the music teacher.

7 Vasilii Ivanovich Alekseev, teacher of the older Tolstoy children from 1877 to 1881.

8 Liza Malikova, Alekseev's 10-year-old adopted daughter.

9 This draft of *The Decembrists* begins with the words: 'On January 23, 1824, at a general meeting of the Department of Religious and Civil Affairs of the State Council, was heard the case of . . . ' (published in *PSS*, vol. 17, pp. 288–91).

10 In the autumn of 1871 Tolstoy bought 2,500 *desyatinas* of land from N.P. Tuchkov, in the Buzuluka district in the province of Samara. In April 1878 he added to this an adjacent plot of 4,022 *desyatinas*, bought from R.G. Bistrom. A.A. Bibikov was manager of Tolstoy's estate from 1878 to 1884.

11 A. Dumas, *Les Trois Mousquetaires*, nouvelle édition, Paris, 1875 (YaPL). Sergei Tolstoy recalled: 'In the evenings father sometimes read Dumas' *The Three Musketeers* to us in

French, leaving out the parts that were unsuitable for children. We listened avidly' (S.L. Tolstoy, p. 53).

12 Tolstoy wrote to Nikolai Strakhov on October 27, 1878: 'Everything is going well here. My wife and I are on good terms, as we always are when we lead a proper life . . . ' (*PSS*, vol. 62, p. 445).

13 This work continued until the end of November. See note 37.

14 The books have been kept in the YaPL: M.Yu. Lermontov, *Demon, Angel, Rusalka, &c. A portrait, a biography*; Belinskii on Lermontov's poetry, 'Russkaya Biblioteka' (Russian Library), series II, St Petersburg, 1874, and A.S. Pushkin, *Sochineniya, s prilozheniem materialov dlya ego biografii* (Works, with supplementary biographical material), vol. I, ed. P.B. Annenkov, St Petersburg, 1855.

15 The book referred to is probably P. Kulish, *Zapiski o zhizni N.V. Gogolya sostavlennye iz vospominanii ego druzei i znakomykh, i iz ego sobstvennykh pisem* (Notes on the life of N.V. Gogol, compiled from memories of his friends and acquaintances and from his own letters), 2 vols, St Petersburg, 1856; or, also by Kulish, *Opyt biografii N.V. Gogolya so vklyucheniem do soroka ego pisem* (An attempted biography of N.V. Gogol, with the inclusion of forty of his letters), St Petersburg, 1854.

16 V. Cherbuliez. *L'Idée de Jean Têterol*, Paris, 1878. Tolstoy praised the works of Cherbuliez very highly (see *PSS*, vol. 62, p. 18).

17 This entry, and those for October 21–4, 27 and 29, 1878, refer to his work on *The Decembrists*. On October 31 Tolstoy started on a new opening scene – see entry for November 1.

18 '*Levashniki*' – a special cake made by the Yasnaya Polyana cook, M.N. Rumyantsev. (See I.L. Tolstoy, p. 49.)

19 L. Tolstoy, *The Cossacks: a Tale of the Caucasus in 1852*. Translated from the Russian by Eugene Schuyler, London, 1878 (YaPL). Tolstoy wrote to Turgenev about this edition: '. . . very well translated' (*PSS*, vol. 62, p. 446).

20 In a letter to Afanasii Fet of October 27, 1878, Tolstoy referred thus to Aleksandr Navrotskii: 'He seems a decent sort of fellow, but his head is of course filled with the usual total confusion' (*PSS*, vol. 62, p. 450).

21 'Kolpik' – the name of the horse. Levin, in *Anna Karenina*, has a horse called Kolpik, 'a good-natured little bay' (part 2, ch. XIII).

22 See *PSS*, vol. 62, pp. 445–7, which has the definitive date of October 27.

23 Charles Dickens, *The Life and Adventures of Martin Chuzzlewit, his Relatives, Friends and Enemies*. In two volumes, Leipzig, 1844 (YaPL).

24 See Tolstoy's letter to Aleksandra Tolstaya about the children, dated October 26, 1872 (*PSS*, vol. 61, pp. 332–5).

25 See note 37.

26 Praskovia Nikolaevna Kryukova, daughter of the cook Rumyantsev.

27 There are two versions of the new beginning to *The Decembrists*: version one, *PSS*, vol. 17, pp. 291–7; version two, ibid., pp. 47–55. Both editions refer to the future Decembrist Zakhar Grigorevich Chernyshev.

28 Maria Dmitrievna Dyakova.

29 A. Theuriet, *La Maison des deux barbeaux*, in *Revue des deux mondes*, April 15 and May 1, 1878. In a letter to L.P. Nikiforov of July 20–1, 1890, Tolstoy recommended Theuriet amongst various other authors whose works would be 'suitable for *Posrednik* [The Intermediary]', a publishing house (*PSS*, vol. 65, p. 130).

30 Charles Dickens, *Dealings with the Firm Dombey and Son; Wholesale, Retail and for Exportation*. In three volumes, vol. 1, Leipzig, 1847 (YaPL).

31 F. Fabre, *Le Roman d'un peintre*, in *Revue des deux mondes*, June 1 and 15, July 1, 1878.

32 Akulka – the granddaughter of Maria Afanasieva Arbuzova. Uncle Sergei – Sergei Petrovich Arbuzov, one of the Tolstoys' servants.

33 Sollogub's vaudeville, *Masterskaya russkogo zhivopistsa* (The Russian painter's studio) is in Vladimir Sollogub, *Sochineniya* (Works), vol. IV, Moscow, 1856, pp. 123–71.

34 D.D. Obolenskii went into business building sugar factories during the Russo–Turkish War and was ruined. In 1878 he was arrested for embezzlement. He was acquitted, but declared insolvent, and the case dragged on for many years.

35 'Alexander II was travelling on the Moscow–Kursk line. Because it was feared an attempt would be made on his life there were three separate royal trains, and it was not known in which one the Tsar was travelling' (*DST*, I, p. 198).

36 Grigorii – the butler, serving temporarily at Yasnaya Polyana; his surname is not known.

37 Tolstoy also considered that Sofia Tolstaya's biography was unsuitably long, although he did describe it as 'excellent' (in a letter to Nikolai Strakhov dated November 23, 1878 – *PSS*, vol. 62, p. 454). Tolstoy shortened it and on November 28 it was sent off to Strakhov (ibid., pp. 455–7). It was printed, after more additions had been made to it, as issue no. IX in the 'Russkaya Biblioteka' (Russian Library) series, publisher M.M. Stasyulevich, St Petersburg, 1879.

1879

1 In other words the fourth edition of *Sochineniya L.N. Tolstogo* (The works of L.N. Tolstoy) in 11 volumes, published by the brothers Salaev, 1880.

1882

1 In September 1881 the Tolstoys moved to Moscow to be with their eldest son, who was starting at the university. They rented an apartment in Volkonskii's house on Denezhnyi (now Malyi Levshinskii) Lane, where they lived during the winter of 1881–2.

2 Sergei Tolstoy entered the natural sciences department of the university; Tanya Tolstaya was accepted at the School of Art, Sculpture and Architecture. Ilya and Lev attended Lev Polivanov's private high school on Prechistenka (now Kropotkin Street).

3 Tolstoy was oppressed by city life. On October 5, 1881 he noted in his diary: 'The past month has been the most agonising period of my entire life. The move to Moscow [. . .] Stench, jewels, luxury, poverty. Depravity. Criminals have gathered here to rob the people, then have assembled various soldiers and judges to guard their orgies while they feast' (*PSS*, vol. 49, p. 58). Sofia Tolstaya wrote to her sister Tanya Kuzminskaya about Tolstoy's state of mind, in a letter dated October 14, 1881: 'Lyovochka has sunk into something far worse than depression – it's a sort of hopeless apathy. He cannot sleep or eat, he often cries – *à la lettre* – and at times I think I shall go mad' (GMT).

4 Tolstoy's differences with his family became more acute during their visit to Moscow. Tolstoy felt isolated in his spiritual search. He described this state in a letter to N.N. Strakhov in March 1882: 'I have become frightfully tired and weak. This past winter has been completely fruitless. It appears that people do not in fact need the things I believe in. At times I long to die' (*PSS*, vol. 63, p. 94). Sofia Tolstaya felt equally lonely, without the spiritual unity she was used to with her husband. 'You do not tell me in your letter what is in your heart and what you are thinking about, what makes you happy and what makes you sad, what bores you and what pleases you,' she reproached him in a letter of September 17, 1882 (*PST*, p. 202). To Tatiana Kuzminskaya she wrote that Tolstoy was 'very advanced in his views; he leads the crowd and shows people which path they should take', whereas she '*was* the crowd, and went with the common flow'; she saw the light which Tolstoy carried but could 'go no faster' for she was 'weighed down by the crowd, by home and custom' (letter of January 30, 1883, GMT).

5 The Tolstoys' 10-month-old son.

6 Tatiana Kuzminskaya's husband, Aleksandr Mikhailovich Kuzminskii, was then president of the St Petersburg regional court.
7 Tolstoy went to Moscow to supervise building work and repairs on a house he bought in the summer of 1882 from I.A. Arnautov in Dolgo-Khamovniki Street (now Lev Tolstoy Street). On October 8 the whole family moved to Moscow, and spent their winters there until 1901.

883

1 From the end of 1882 to January 1884 Tolstoy worked on a tract entitled 'What I Believe' (*PSS*, vol. 23). The first edition (in 1884) was seized and banned, and it was only in 1906, after the first Russian revolution, that it was published the first time in Russia (in *Vsemirnyi vestnik* (World Herald), no. 2, and separately by *Vsemirnyi vestnik* and the Intermediary.

885

1 Tolstoy and L.D. Urusov travelled to the Crimean coast for two weeks starting on March 11, 1885 (see Tolstoy's letters to Sofia Tolstaya for March 1885 – *PSS*, vol. 83, pp. 492–502).
2 Tolstoy was in Sevastopol during the Crimean War, from November 7, 1854 to the middle of November 1855.

886

1 At the beginning of August 1886, Tolstoy hurt his leg while working in the fields; it turned into periostitis, which lasted until October. 'I can now walk again, although with a slight limp,' he wrote to N. N. Gué at the beginning of November (*PSS*, vol. 63, p. 403).
2 Sergei Tolstoy wrote, à propos of this entry: 'One reason for the discord between Lev Nikolaevich and Sofia Andreevna was the undefined nature of the demands he made on her. L.N. demanded that their life should be simplified but gave no limits for this simplification and rarely gave any concrete advice as to what should be done. Questions as to where and how his family should live, what should be done with the estates, how the children should be educated, and so on, remained unanswered' (*DST*, I, p. 200).
3 Konstantin Nikolaevich Zyabrev, a very poor peasant at Yasnaya Polyana.
4 A penurious peasant-woman at Yasnaya Polyana.
5 Aleksandr Petrovich Ivanov, one of Tolstoy's secretaries, who suffered from alcoholism.
6 From October to November 1886 Tolstoy was writing his play *The Power of Darkness*, inspired by a story related to him by N. V. Davydov. Tolstoy was 'very absorbed' in this work (see his letter to N.N. Gué, *PSS*, vol. 63, p. 403). The play was sent to the typesetters on November 25 and Tolstoy corrected the proofs in December 1886. The play was first published by the Intermediary publishing house in February 1887, under the title *Vlast tmy, ili kogotok uvyza – vsei ptichke propast* (The power of darkness, or If a claw is caught the bird is lost) (*PSS*, vol. 26).
7 L. Diogène, *La Vie des plus illustres philosophes de l'antiquité. . .* , Paris, 1841 (YaPL, Tolstoy's notes).
8 Sofia Tolstaya wrote in *MZh* that she and Urusov had in common their 'love for Lev Nikolaevich and his interest in religious writings'; with her he was 'gallant, affable, occasionally somewhat exalted. Never, in so much as a word or gesture was there any romance between us' (*MZh*, book 3, pp. 552, 554).
9 Tolstoy's work 'Issledovanie dogmaticheskogo bogosloviya' (An investigation into dogmatic theology) (*PSS*, vol. 23), on which he was working from 1879 to 1884; it was banned in

Russia and was first published in Geneva in the Elpidine edition (part 1 – 1891; part 2 – 1896) under the title 'Kritika dogmaticheskogo bogosloviya' (A critique of dogmatic theology).

10 Ilya Tolstoy was in love with Sofia Nikolaevna Filosofova, whom he married in February 1888. Tolstoy regarded this marriage with 'both joy and fear' (*PSS*, vol. 64, p. 117).

11 See note 6 to this Diary, 1887.

12 *Rodnik* (The Source), an illustrated monthly children's magazine, St Petersburg 1882–94 (YaPL).

13 *Rodnye otgoloski* (Echoes of the homeland) – an anthology of verses by Russian poets with drawings by I. Panov and engravings by Pannemaker. Paris–St Petersburg, edited by P. Polevoi, 1875 (YaPL).

14 A Yasnaya Polyana peasant-woman.

15 L.B. Feinerman, a young teacher, settled in the village of Yasnaya Polyana in the summer of 1885. According to Ilya Tolstoy he was a 'sincere follower of my father, a convinced and selfless idealist. He lived in the village, worked for the peasants without demanding any payment apart from the simplest and roughest food, and dreamed of establishing a peasant commune' (I.L. Tolstoy, p. 196). Later Feinerman wrote several highly unreliable books about Tolstoy, under the pseudonym 'Teneremo'.

16 N.N. Gué's letters to Maria and Tatiana Tolstaya were written in September and October 1886 (see *PTG*, pp. 75–8 and 80–1). Tolstoy wrote to Nikolai Gué: 'We received your letters yesterday, my dear friend. Thank you for writing to my girls . . . ' (*PSS*, vol. 63, p. 399).

1887

1 On March 1, 1887 the police arrested five students (Osipanov, Generalov, Andreyushkin, Kanger and Volokhov), for taking part in the attempt on Alexander III's life. The following day they arrested Lenin's elder brother, Aleksandr Ulyanov, and others involved in the plot. In April five of them, including Aleksandr Ulyanov, were tried and sentenced to death, and were executed on May 8, 1887.

2 On February 3, 1887, A.A. Stakhovich wrote to Sofia Tolstaya that he was reading *The Power of Darkness* in St Petersburg and trying to familiarise a large number of influential people with the work in order to exert pressure on the censor. On January 27 he read the play in the presence of Alexander III, who found it a 'marvellous piece' and recommended that it be staged at the imperial theatres. (See A.A. Stakhovich, 'Klochki vospominanii ("Vlast Tmy", drama L.N. Tolstogo)' (Fragments of memories: *The Power of Darkness* by L.N. Tolstoy), *TE*, Moscow, 1912, pp. 27–47.) Tolstoy wrote to Stakhovich: 'I am delighted you are taking such an interest in the play, but utterly, utterly indifferent to the consequences' (*PSS*, vol. 64, p. 9).

3 At the beginning of November 1886 Sofia Tolstaya went to visit her dying mother in Yalta. After her death she returned to Moscow.

4 From the end of 1886 until June 1887 Tolstoy was working, on and off, on a story called 'Khodite v svete, poka est svet. Povest iz vremyon drevnikh Khristian' (Walk in the light while there is light. A tale of the ancient Christians) and on an introduction to it entitled 'Beseda dosuzhnykh lyudei' (Idle chatter) (*PSS*, vol. 26). It was first published by M.K. Elpidine in Geneva in 1892, and in Russia in 1893, in an anthology called *Put-doroga. Nauchno-literaturnyi sbornik v polzu obshchestva dlya vspomoshchestvovaniya nuzhdayushchimsya pereselentsam* (The pathway. A literary-scientific anthology in aid of the Society for Aiding Needy Migrants), St Petersburg, edited by Sibiryakov.

Tolstoy was dissatisfied with this work. 'There are some good ideas in it,' he wrote to Chertkov, 'but it's not artistically written – it's too cold' (*PSS*, vol. 86, p. 49).

5 This was Tolstoy's first title for his tract *O zhizni* (On life) (*PSS*, vol. 26). A long letter of Tolstoy's to A.K. Dieterichs on life and death, written at the end of September 1886, served

as the beginning of the work (see *PSS*, vol. 85, pp. 392–6). He continued working on it throughout the whole of 1887.

Tolstoy was carried away by the work: 'For one and a half months now I have thought of nothing else, day and night,' he wrote to Chertkov on April 2, 1887 (*PSS*, vol. 86, p. 42). In reply to V.V. Mainov, who asked him which of his works he thought the most serious he wrote on October 17, 1889: 'Either 'What I Believe' or *On Life*, I cannot decide which' (*PSS*, vol. 64, p. 317). A separate edition of the book in 1888 was banned and destroyed by the censor. The book first appeared, edited by M.K. Elpidin, in 1891 in Geneva.

6 She is referring to the sixth edition of *Sochineniya L.N. Tolstogo* (The works of L.N. Tolstoy), vols. I–XII, Moscow, published by the heirs to the brothers Salaev. It came out shortly after the fifth edition, which appeared in the same year.

7 Sergei Tolstoy was then a member of the Tula department of the *zemstvo* peasant bank.

8 Chertkov's letter to Tolstoy was dated February 18–20, 1887 (*PSS*, vol. 86, p. 33).

9 Sofia Tolstaya is referring to the Intermediary publishing house, founded by Tolstoy, Chertkov and Biryukov in 1884 to publish literary and popular scientific works for a popular audience. Chertkov wrote to Tolstoy on February 25, 1887, with various questions about the publication of his works by the Intermediary (*PSS*, vol. 86, pp. 36–7).

10 On March 14, 1887, at a meeting of the Moscow Psychological Society, Tolstoy gave a paper on 'The Understanding of Life' – a short resumé of his book *On Life*. In it he criticised prevailing ideas on religion and morality and formulated his own new world outlook (see *PSS*, vol. 26, pp. 753–4). Tolstoy's paper was published in *RV*, 1887, no. 78, March 21.

11 Sergei Tolstoy wrote in his memoirs: 'He became especially committed to vegetarianism after his acquaintance with the positivist and vegetarian William Fry, who visited him in the autumn of 1885. My sisters Tanya and Masha were also converted at that time to "food without killing". My mother thought vegetarianism was harmful and she was wrong: when my father had liver problems it was of undoubted benefit to him. And it never did my sisters any harm' (S.L. Tolstoy, p. 145).

12 Probably *Sochineniya Grafa L.N. Tolstogo* (The works of Count L.N. Tolstoy), vols. I–XI (vol. XII separately), Moscow, 1886, sixth edn.

13 There was an announcement in *Moskovskie vedomosti* (Moscow Gazette), December 12, 1869, no. 270: '*War and Peace* is for sale. *The Works of Count L.N. Tolstoy*, 2nd edition, Moscow 1868–9. The price for all six volumes is 10 silver rubles, including postage.'

14 In a letter of February 18–20, 1887, Chertkov wrote to Tolstoy: 'I am inexpressibly grateful to God for granting me the blessing of being at one with my wife. This always makes me mindful of those for whom this spiritual communion with their wives is not possible and who, it would appear, deserve this happiness far, far more than I' (*PSS*, vol. 86, p. 33).

15 Ilya Tolstoy was serving in the volunteer regiment of the Suma dragoons, stationed in the Khamovniki barracks.

16 See note 10. N.N. Gué, son of the artist Gué, was then living in the wing of the Tolstoys' Khamovniki Street house, and helping Sofia Tolstaya to edit Tolstoy's works.

17 At the end of 1886 M.G. Savina, an actress at the Aleksandrovskii Theatre, asked Tolstoy's permission to put on a benefit performance of *The Power of Darkness*. Having received his permission, she visited Tolstoy in Moscow at the beginning of 1887 to get his instructions on how to stage the play. In February 1887 rehearsals started at the Aleksandrovskii Theatre. In a letter to Sofia Tolstaya of March 12, 1887, A.A. Potekhin (director since 1882 of the casts of the Aleksandrovskii Theatre in St Petersburg, and of the Maly Theatre in Moscow) wrote that 'in order to learn about this type of peasant and the details of their homes and surroundings, and to find the characteristic local costumes for those acting in the play, two specialists were sent off to the province of Tula, to the environs of Yasnaya Polyana itself' (GMT). Evidently the person to whom Sofia Tolstaya refers is one of these specialists. We have no other information about him.

18 Initially Alexander III gave permission for the play to be performed but K.P. Pobedonostsev wrote the Tsar a letter sharply condemning the play, and he succeeded in having the permission withdrawn. After the seventeenth rehearsal, on March 22, 1887, Savina told A.A. Stakhovich that 'the dress rehearsal, due to take place today, was cancelled and *The Power of Darkness* has been indefinitely postponed'. (See 'K istorii zapreshcheniya postanovki "Vlasti Tmy". Pisma k A.A. Stakhovich' (A brief history of the banning of the Power of Darkness. Letters to A.A. Stakhovich, *Letopisi*, book 2, Moscow, 1938, pp. 226–7.) On the same day A.A. Potekhin informed Sofia Tolstaya of this in a letter of March 22 (GMT), and on March 31 he wrote to Tolstoy himself (see *Tolstoi. Perepiska*, pp. 508–9). It was only on October 18, 1895, that *The Power of Darkness* was staged at the Aleksandrovskii Theatre, with Savina in the role of Akulina.

19 Grigorii was a servant in the Tolstoys' home.

20 See note 12.

21 Sofia Tolstaya is referring to Tolstoy's letter to M.A. Engelhardt (December 1882–January 1883) in which he wrote: 'You probably do not realise this, but you cannot imagine how lonely I am and how much the real "I" is despised by those around me' (*PSS*, vol. 63, p. 112). On March 21, 1909, Sofia Tolstaya confessed that she was 'terribly hurt by this letter' (Gusev, p. 244).

22 Sofia Tolstaya had evidently seen Tolstoy's letter to N.L. Ozmidov of June 12, 1887 (*PSS*, vol. 64, pp. 51–3). For details about Ozmidov see *PSS*, vol. 63, pp. 310–11.

23 'Dark ones' was Sofia Tolstaya's name for those who shared Tolstoy's views.

24 It has not been possible to discover the man's name.

25 The American traveller and writer George Kennan visited Tolstoy on June 17, 1886; he told him about the life of political exiles in Siberia and talked to Tolstoy about the study of non-resistance to the evil of violence. His memoirs were published as 'A Visit to Count Tolstoi', in *The Century*, no. 34, New York, 1887.

26 The Suma regiment of dragoons was then stationed in the village of Vladykino, near Moscow.

27 Sofia Tolstaya is referring to V.M. Florinskii's book *Domashnyaya meditsina. Lechebnik dlya narodnogo upotrebleniya* (Home medicine. A medical guide for popular use). It went through five editions between 1881 and 1892.

28 The actor V.N. Andreev-Burlak visited Tolstoy on June 20, 1887. About his story, which served as the inspiration for *The Kreutzer Sonata*, see this Diary, December 28, 1890.

29 Tolstoy had been acquainted with I.F. Gorbunov, the well-known actor, writer and raconteur, since the 1850s, and on March 28, 1886 Gorbunov had visited the Tolstoys at Khamovniki Street and 'talked about many things' (see I.F. Gorbunov, *Sochineniya* (Works) vol. III, St Petersburg, 1907, p. 460).

30 N. Strakhov, *O vechnykh istinakh. Moi spor s spiritualizmom*) (The eternal truths. My argument with Spiritualism), St Petersburg, 1887 (YaPL, with a dedication). Tolstoy approved of this book. (See his letter to Strakhov of March 3, 1887: *PSS*, vol. 64, p. 23.)

31 N.N. Strakhov stayed at Yasnaya Polyana from June 26 to July 2.

32 His tract *On Life*. See note 5.

33 Sergei Tolstoy visited the Tolstoys' Samara estate in order to put the running of it in order (see S.L. Tolstoy, pp. 158–61).

34 P.I. Biryukov stayed 'four days' in Yasnaya Polyana, and Tolstoy was 'delighted with him – more and more delighted' (*PSS*, vol. 86, p. 68).

35 The adopted daughter of P.D. and O.A. Golokhvastov, Varvara (Arochka).

36 The teacher's surname has not been established.

37 Tolstoy and Aleksandra Tolstaya were well pleased with this meeting, despite the serious religious differences between them at the time. 'Tolstoy behaved very mildly throughout my stay in Yasnaya Polyana,' wrote Aleksandra Tolstaya, 'although we had quite a few discussions' (Perepiska L.N. Tolstogo s gr. A.A. Tolstoi (L.N.'s correspondence with

Countess A.A. Tolstaya), St Petersburg, published by the Tolstoy Museum, 1911, p. 33). 'We spent ten days together without, thank God, any arguments,' Tolstoy wrote to Chertkov. 'We parted equally amicably' (*PSS*, vol. 86, p. 70).

38 The final text of the treatise *On Life* was dated by Tolstoy 'August 3, 1887'. Concerning this change in the title, Tolstoy wrote to Chertkov, August 4, 1887: 'Dear Pavel Ivanovich set off yesterday to take the article *On Life* to the printers. I had started writing about life and death, but when I finished it was obvious that the second part of the title would have to be deleted since for me, at least, this word had completely lost all the meaning I had given it in the title' (*PSS*, vol. 86, p. 70).

39 The first portrait, given to Sofia Tolstaya – *L.N. Tolstoy at his Desk* – is at Yasnaya Polyana; the second – *L.N. Tolstoy in an Armchair, with a Book in his Hand*, dated by Repin '1887, August 13–15. Yasnaya Polyana' – is in the GTG. Tatiana Tolstaya wrote to Elizaveta Olsufieva à propos of this portrait: 'On the first day of his visit here Repin sketched Papa in various poses, in his album, in order to familiarise himself with him, and yesterday he started on his large portrait in oils. By today he had already finished the whole head and it is marvellous, in both the execution and the expression. He managed to capture that good sweet expression on Papa's face, which neither Gué nor Kramskoi was able to convey' (GMT).

40 Stepan Andreevich Behrs and Maria Petrovna Behrs.

41 Tolstoy considered the first part of *Dead Souls* to be a 'very fine work' (*PSS*, vol. 38, p. 50), and declared that Gogol had 'enormous talent' (ibid.).

42 Sofia Tolstaya decided to store Tolstoy's manuscripts in one of the Moscow archives. On September 1, 1887, with Tolstoy's agreement, she deposited them at the Rumyantsev Museum in Moscow (now the Lenin State Library of the USSR). See V.A. Zhdanov's introductory article in *Opisanie rukopisei khudozhestvennykh proizvedenii L.N. Tolstogo* (A catalogue of the manuscripts of L.N. Tolstoy's literary works), Moscow, 1955, pp. 5–17.

43 A dried flower is pasted into the diary.

1890

1 Masha Tolstaya was very close to her father. Ilya Tolstoy recalled: 'She identified closely with her father's loneliness, was the first of us all to renounce her peers, and imperceptibly but determinedly went over to his side' (I.L. Tolstoy, p. 195).

2 On November 26, 1890 Tolstoy went to Krapivna to attend a session of the Tula magistrate's court where four Yasnaya Polyana peasants were being tried for killing when drunk a horse-thief from the village, Gaviril Balkhin.

Before the trial Tolstoy visited the peasants in jail. The trial he regarded as a 'shameful comedy' (*PSS*, vol. 51, p. 11). Tolstoy's presence there influenced the sentence. 'One was completely acquitted, and the other three received lenient sentences,' Tolstoy wrote to A.V. Alekhin, December 2, 1890 (*PSS*, vol. 65, p. 197).

The story about the murder of the horse-thief probably served as the basis for the description of the peasant Ivan Mironov's murder in the story 'Falshivyi kupon' (The forged coupon) (part I, ch. XIV–XV).

3 Ovsyannikovo was Tatiana Tolstaya's estate, five *versts* from Yasnaya Polyana. Sofia Tolstaya was involved in a legal dispute with the priest of the village of Ovsyannikovo.

4 Vanechka was the Tolstoys' 2-year-old son.

5 Nikolai Leskov's story 'Chas voli bozhei' (The hour of God's will) was first published in *RO*, no. 11, 1890, pp. 115–40. Leskov borrowed the subject of the story from Tolstoy (see the note in Tolstoy's diary, June 12, 1898; *PSS*, vol. 53, p. 198). After reading the story Tolstoy wrote to Leskov that he had 'liked the tone and the extraordinary mastery of language', but found 'much of it excessive and disproportionate' (*PSS*, vol. 65, p. 198).

6 Tolstoy's *Dnevnik molodosti* (Diary of youth) was first published, in abridged form, by

Chertkov (Moscow, 1917). It was published in full in *PSS* (vol. 46, 1847–1854; and vol. 47, 1854–1857).

7 Biryukov wanted to marry Masha Tolstaya. Sofia Tolstaya was against the marriage.

8 Seryozha Tolstoy writes in his memoirs: 'My father's way of life throughout the 1880s, and especially at the beginning of 1884, gradually changed. In Moscow he began to get up early, tidy his own room, saw and chop wood, draw water from the well in the courtyard outside, and drag it to the house in a large tub on a sledge. Then he learnt from a shoemaker how to make boots, and started sewing them in the little room next to his study' (S.L. Tolstoy, p. 145).

9 Tolstoy noted in his diary, December 15, 1890: 'When I went out of the house this morning Ilya Bolkhin came up to me pleading for a pardon: they have been sent to jail for six weeks. I feel exceedingly depressed, and my heart has been heavy all day [. . .] I must leave' (*PSS*, vol. 51, p. 111).

10 In 1897 Masha Tolstaya married Nikolai Leonidovich Obolenskii, and in 1899 Tatiana married Mikhail Sergeevich Sukhotin. Lev and Sofia Tolstoy were not in favour of these marriages.

11 Diary for October 19, 1852 (*PSS*, vol. 46, p. 146).

12 Sasha was the Tolstoys' 6-year-old daughter.

13 In a letter to Tatiana Kuzminskaya, of December 14, 1890, Sofia Tolstaya wrote: 'We have staying with us an Englishman named Dillon, who translated Lyovochka's story "Walk in the Light While There is Light", then gave it to Chertkov, unfinished and badly translated. On account of this translation, *Le Figaro* published an article (in the November issue, number 21) which was very offensive to me, and as I have no one to defend me, I want the enclosed letter to be printed, and beg Sasha to ask M. Villot to correct it and send it to some French newspaper which is as widely circulated as *Le Figaro*' (see this Diary, January 9, 1891).

14 Seryozha Tolstoy comments thus on the episode: 'It is doubtful that Lev Nikolaevich would have advised her to "give the peasants a fright", as she writes. Any such activity in defence of property which still formally belonged to him was extremely distasteful' (*DST*, I, pp. 208–9).

15 The eighth edition of *Sochineniya L.N. Tolstogo* (The works of L.N. Tolstoy) in 11 vols, Moscow, 1889. Vol. 12 was published separately – *Proizvedeniya poslednikh godov* (The works of the last years), Moscow, 1889, also vol. 13 – *Proizvedeniya poslednikh godov* (The works of the last years), Moscow, 1890. In the middle of December 1890, when Sofia Tolstaya received the proofs for vol. 13, the censors had not yet banned *The Kreutzer Sonata* from this volume. For the subsequent fate of *The Kreutzer Sonata* and the history of its publication see this Diary, notes for February to June 1891.

16 There is a note in Tolstoy's diary about this nocturnal discussion: 'I went to bed yesterday but could not sleep. I was sick at heart [. . .] I got out of bed at two and walked about the drawing-room. She got up too, and we talked until gone four [. . .] I told her something of my feelings. I think I should announce to the government that I do not recognise my property or rights, and let them do whatever they want about it' (*PSS*, vol. 51, p. 113).

17 In the testament which Tolstoy wrote in his diary on March 27, 1895, he wrote: 'I ask that the diaries of my former unmarried life – after extracting the little that is good in them – be destroyed [. . .] I ask that these diaries of my unmarried life be destroyed not because I want to conceal my evil life from the world: I've led the same sort of shabby life [. . .] as all young men without principles, but because I wrote them only when my conscience was tormented by guilt. They give a false impression and represent [. . .] Anyway, let us leave my diaries alone. One can at least see from them that despite all that was base and shabby in my youth, I was not abandoned by God, and have at last in my old age begun to understand and love him a little' (*PSS*, vol. 53, p. 15). See note 6.

18 The term 'dark ones' had become current in the Tolstoy house and not only Sofia Tolstaya used it, but Tolstoy too. On December 18, 1890 he wrote to Nikolai Gué (the son): 'We

have had dark ones staying with us all this time: Butkevich, Posha, Rusanov, Boulanger, Popov, Khokhlov. They are still here' (*PSS*, vol. 65, p. 209). Sofia Tolstaya called Evgenii Ivanovich Popov an 'Oriental' as he was Georgian by birth.

19 A.M. Novikov was Andrei and Mikhail Tolstoy's teacher from 1889 to 1892.

20 Fillip Rodionovich Egorov.

21 Natalya Nikolaevna Filosofova (married name Dehn) was the sister of Sofia Nikolaevna Tolstaya.

22 At this time Tolstoy was working on his treatise *Tsarstvo bozhie vnutri nas* (The kingdom of God is within us) (*PSS*, vol. 28). In June 1890 he started on the introduction to his *Katekhizis neprotivleniya* (Catechism of non-resistance) for Adin Balle (see Tolstoy's letter to Adin Balle, dated June 30, 1890 – *PSS*, vol. 65, pp. 113–14). The introduction gradually expanded; Tolstoy wanted 'briefly and clearly to express the meaning of Christian non-resistance' (see *PSS*, vol. 65, p. 166). The article, 'On Resistance to Evil, the Church, and Military Service' (ibid., p. 189) grew into a book of social criticism, which was published abroad in 1893. The treatise was banned in Russia and first published there in 1906, by *RSS*.

23 A son, Nikolai, was born to Ilya and Sofia Tolstoy, on December 20, 1890; he died in 1893.

24 The letter from Fet to Sofia Tolstaya, dated December 21, 1890, which begins with the words: 'Dear Countess, it is not my fault that I am a poet – you are my shining ideal. Let the matter be tried before the court of Heaven, and if the word poet means fool I willingly submit to this. It is not a matter of intellect but of happiness. And to bear in our heart people that are dear to us is a great happiness' (GMT). Sofia Tolstaya's sharp words here about Fet are uncharacteristic: she was always very warmly disposed towards him, visited him in the months of his fatal illness (from September to November 1892), and talked of him in great detail in *MZh* (book 6).

25 Tolstoy disapproved of Masha Kuzminskaya's forthcoming marriage. On January 9, 1891 he wrote to her mother: 'Your Masha is a darling, but she is afraid: afraid of staking her whole life on one card, as she is doing now. I have told her this' (*PSS*, vol. 65, p. 218). The wedding took place on August 25, 1891.

26 E. Rod's book *Le Sens de la vie* (Lausanne, 1889) was sent to Tolstoy by the author in February 1889, and he was 'transported' by the 'sincerity and power of the writing' (see *PSS*, vol. 64, p. 230). He described the chapters on war and government as 'staggering' and 'extraordinary' (*PSS*, vol. 51, p. 35). In October 1890 Tolstoy translated Rod's pronouncements in his book on war, and included them, along with statements by Maupassant and Vogué, in chapter 6 of his tract *The Kingdom of God Is Within Us* (*PSS*, vol. 28, pp. 122–4).

27 Leonid Dmitrievich Urusov, who died in 1885.

28 It has not been possible to establish which corrections Sofia Tolstaya made for Aleksandra Tolstaya.

29 See note 28 to the Diary for 1887. Begun in 1887, *The Kreutzer Sonata* (*PSS*, vol. 27) was finished in 1889. It was first published in November 1890 in Geneva, edited by M.K. Elpidine. It was published in Russia in 1891. See note 15.

30 Sofia Alekseevna Filosofova, mother of Ilya Tolstoy's wife.

1891

1 Tolstoy read excerpts from the first three chapters of the tract *The Kingdom of God is Within Us* (*PSS*, vol. 28, pp. 1–67).

2 On that day, January 7, 1891, Tolstoy wrote a letter to Biryukov expressing the hope that Sofia Tolstaya's agitation would soon pass, and that 'when she realises there has been no change in either Masha, you, or me, she will once again see things as she did' (*PSS*, vol. 65, p. 214).

3 With M.F. Egorov.
4 A separate vol. 13 of *The Works of L.N. Tolstoy* (of 1890) included *The Kreutzer Sonata*, the comedy *The Fruits of Enlightenment*, the articles *On the Moscow Census* and *What Must We Do?* and several other works.
5 P.V. Zasodimskii sent his story, in fact called 'Before the Dying Hearth' (*SV*, no. 1, 1891, pp. 247–79), to Tolstoy, and in a letter dated December 28, 1890 asked if he thought such a story 'might in a small way guide man away from evil' (*Tolstoi. Perepiska*, p. 657). Tolstoy liked the story, which he read 'once to myself and a second time to the servants' (letter to P.V. Zasodimskii of January 13, 1891 – *PSS*, vol. 65, p. 219).
6 See note 13 to this Diary for 1890, and *RV*, no. 8, January 9, 1891.
7 Vladimir Sergeevich Solovyov, 'O liricheskoi poezii. Po povodu poslednikh stikhotvorenii Feta i Polonskogo' (On lyrical poetry. An account of the late works of Fet and Polonskii), *RO*, no. 12, 1890, pp. 626–54 (YaPL).
8 Nikolai Gué, son of the painter, arrived at Yasnaya Polyana on January 1.
9 Aleksei Mitrofanovich Novikov.
10 In the autumn of 1884 Tolstoy renounced the ownership of his land, property and literary rights. He entrusted Sofia Tolstaya to conduct his affairs and be responsible for all his works published before 1881.
11 I.M. Klopskii (or Klobskii) first visited Tolstoy on January 1, 1889, together with Fyodor Alekseevich Strakhov. He had lived in Tolstoyan agricultural communities. Gorky refers to him in *My Universities*. On January 23, 1891, Tolstoy wrote to Nikolai Gué (the son): 'After you came Klobskii. He has become a very, very good person, you know. I was so glad to see him, especially as he is now' (*PSS*, vol. 65, p. 226). See also the entry in Tolstoy's diary for January 15, 1891 (*PSS*, vol. 52, p. 4).
12 Pyotr Vasilevich was the Tolstoys' cook.
13 Maria Nikolaevna Zinovieva, the younger daughter of Nikolai Alekseevich Zinoviev.
14 In a letter written in Moscow to Tolstoy on January 11, 1891, Baroness Varvara Ikskul asked for permission to publish 'Tolstoy's stories' "Kholstomer" and "Polikushka", in a series of books for popular reading under the heading *Pravda*' (Truth). On the following day she wrote to Sofia Tolstaya about the same thing (GMT). It is possibly in connection with this that Tolstoy noted in his diary, on January 15: 'I have been worrying that Sonya may not give permission for my works to be published' (*PSS*, vol. 52, p. 4).
15 Ilya Tolstoy asked Sofia Tolstaya to 'purchase for him and his family the property of Grinevka, adjacent to Nikolskoe' (*MZh*, book 6, p. 6). The Grinevka estate (a hundred *versts* from Yasnaya Polyana, in the Chern district of the Tula province) passed to Ilya Tolstoy in 1892, after the land was apportioned.
16 Possibly Sofia Tolstoy was reading Spinoza's book *Ethics, Expounded by Geometrical Method and Divided into Five Parts*, translated from the Latin by V.I. Modestov, St Petersburg, 1886. The fourth edition is in the YaPL (St Petersburg, 1904).
17 See note 3 to this Diary for 1890.
18 Sofia Tolstaya was reading the proofs for vol. 13 of *The Works of L.N. Tolstoy*, which included *The Kreutzer Sonata* and the Afterword to *The Kreutzer Sonata*. The volume was compiled without the censors' permission and was banned. See this Diary for February 28, and note 38.
19 N.N. Gué's letter is not known. Tolstoy's reply, dated January 29, is in *PSS*, vol. 65, p. 233.
20 Lyova Tolstoy's story 'Montecristo' was published in *Rodnik* (The Source), no. 4, 1891, the story 'Love' in *KN*, March 1891, under the pseudonym L. Lvov. Tolstoy wrote to his son, November 30, 1891, about these stories: 'You have, I think, what they call talent, which is very common and of no value – that is, the capacity to see, observe and describe. But there is no evidence in these stories of that deep heartfelt need to *express* something [. . .] In both these stories you cling to subjects that are too large, and are beyond your power and

experience [. . .] Try to take a subject that is less broad, less obvious, and try to elaborate it at a more profound level where you might express more simple, childish, youthful feelings and experiences (*PSS*, vol. 65, p. 195).

21 The village custom of 'tobogganing on benches' meant turning benches upside-down so that the upturned seat served as the runner.

22 Tolstoy noted in his diary for January 25, 1891: '[. . .] began to think how good it would be to write a novel "*de longue haleine*", and illuminate it with my present view of things. And I was thinking that I could include in it all the plans which I have not, to my regret, fulfilled – all, that is, except Alexander I and the soldier: I could include "the robber", and "Konevskaya", and "Father Sergei", and even "the migrants" and *The Kreutzer Sonata*, and "education". And "Mitasha", and "Notes of a Madman" and "the nihilists" ' (*PSS*, vol. 52, pp. 5–6). This scheme was partly realised in the novel *Resurrection*. The other subjects are used in *The Posthumous Notes of Old Fyodor Kuzmich*, *The Forged Coupon*, and *Mother*. See N.N. Gusev, 'Nezavershennye khudozhestvennye zamysly Tolstogo' (Tolstoy's Uncompleted Literary Projects), in *Sbornik Gosudarstvennogo Tolstovstogo muzeya* (Anthology of the State Tolstoy Museum), Moscow, 1937.

23 Tatiana Tolstaya recalls this reading in a letter to Elizaveta Olsufieva of February 14, 1891: 'Papa and Maman are both very cheerful and are trying to amuse us, Maman with all kinds of things to eat and drink, and Papa with readings from *Don Carlos* – which, by the way, we didn't like' (GMT). Possibly Tatiana read the play in the 1840 edition: Friedrich Schiller, *Sämtliche Werke in einem Bande*, Stuttgart u. Tübingen (YaPL).

24 Paul Bourget, *La Physiologie de l'amour moderne*, Paris, 1891 (YaPL).

25 A.N. Beketov, 'Pitanie cheloveka v nastoyashchem i budushchem' (The present and future nourishment of man), St Petersburg, 1879. Tolstoy advised Chertkov to publish this article in the Intermediary. 'This is absolutely necessary,' he wrote to him on May 16, 1891 (*PSS*, vol. 87, p. 92). In 1893 the pamphlet was published by the Intermediary publishing house in a series entitled 'For Intelligent Readers'.

26 Tolstoy's diaries for 1854–7 (*PSS*, vol. 47), copied out by Sofia Tolstaya, are kept in the GMT. Recalling this work later, she wrote: 'I copied out Lev Nikolaevich's old diaries so that there would be two copies of them [. . .] I was filled with the idea that everything that came from Lev Nikolaevich's pen must be preserved, and that there must therefore be two copies' (*MZh*, book 6, p. 19).

27 In the 1890s Masha and Tatiana Tolstaya organised a school in a little stone house near the entrance to the Yasnaya Polyana estate. The school had not been officially permitted and was closed on the information of the priest. Lessons continued in 'that house', i.e. the left wing of the main house.

28 Tolstoy noted in his diary, on February 14, 1891: 'Today, like every other day, I have sat over notebooks of works I have started – on science, art and non-resistance to evil – and I cannot get down to them' (*PSS*, vol. 52, p. 8).

29 Tolstoy made a note of this in his diary, on February 11, 1891: 'There was an article in *Open Court* about Buts and me, as examples of Phariseeism [. . .] It was very painful to read, and it is still painful as I write now. It need not be painful, and I can place myself in a position where it is not; but that is very hard' (*PSS*, vol. 52, pp. 6–7).

30 Tolstoy noted in his diary on February 14, 1891: '[. . .] started re-reading my diary, which Sonya is copying out. And it was so painful. I spoke irritably to her and infected her with my irritation. She lost her temper and said some cruel things. It didn't last longer than an hour. Then I stopped thinking of myself and thought of her instead, and we affectionately made it up' (*PSS*, vol. 52, p. 7).

31 See this Diary for 1890, note 29.

32 Sofia Tolstaya was evidently referring to the puerperal fever which set in immediately after the birth and continued in an extremely serious form for a month. Sofia Tolstaya's relationship with Masha was complicated and erratic. Masha's desire to serve the simple

people sometimes far exceeded her strength, for she was not in good health, and provoked her mother's irritation. She did not always believe in the sincerity of her daughter's intentions, and considered that she was 'constantly thinking up some new venture which was beyond her strength, and bound to make her suffer' (*MZ*, 1893, book 6, pp. 16–17). Sofia Tolstaya did not encourage her fascination with medicine, which prompted her visits to the hospital. Masha's inclinations and her passionate temperament also provoked her mother. Masha realised this and suffered much, always trying to yield to her mother and mollify her.

33 The letter of February 12, 1891, in which Tolstoy described his state of mind: 'Recently', he wrote, 'my thoughts have borne fruit in a more optimistic view of life and people. Everyone seems good to me now, it would have been impossible for me to think like this before, and it is a very pleasant feeling. It seems to me that this, like everything else in the world, depends on the state of one's own mind and soul' (GMT). Aleksandra Tolstaya's letter of February 11, 1891 (GMT) is in response to a note which Tolstoy added to a letter from Tatiana Tolstaya, of January 20, 1891 (*PSS*, vol. 65, pp. 224–5). Tolstoy noted his impressions of this letter, and the feelings they inspired, in his diary, on February 14 (*PSS*, vol. 52, pp. 7–8).

34 In his letter to Sofia Tolstaya of February 13, 1891 (GMT), M. Stakhovich wrote about the duel between two guards officers named Vadbolskii and Lomonosov (the latter was fatally wounded).

35 Nikolai Gué visited Yasnaya Polyana on his way to St Petersburg, where he was taking his latest picture, entitled *Conscience*, to the nineteenth Wanderers' Exhibition. (The picture was originally entitled *Judas* or *The Traitor*.) 'It is good and heartfelt, but not so powerful or important as *What Is Truth?*' Tolstoy wrote to Pavel Biryukov on February 21, 1891 (*PSS*, vol. 65, p. 255).

36 This is a story called 'The Thief', by P.E. Nakhronin (in *KN*, December 1890). Chertkov sent it to Tolstoy in January 1891. Having read it, Tolstoy wrote to Chertkov on January 15: 'It is excellent. Artistically good and very touching. Who is the author? It would be better to call it "The Clock" (*PSS*, vol. 87, pp. 68–9). The Intermediary published it in 1892 under the title 'The Clock' ('Chasy').

37 Yakov Petrovich Polonskii sent Tolstoy a collection of his poems entitled *Vechernyi zvon. Stikhi 1887–1890* (Evening chimes. Verses 1887–1890), St Petersburg, 1890 (YaPL). In a letter of February 16 he wrote: 'I recently published a small collection of my verses, and for all my desire to send it to you, I hesitated. How can I send him my *Evening Chimes*, I thought, when I know he regards the writing of poetry as the emptiest of pursuits' (quoted in *Letopisi*, book 12, Moscow 1948, p. 217. Collated with an autograph, GMT.) On February 26 Tolstoy replied to Polonskii: 'I have read the book through, and more than anything I liked the first verse, "Childhood". It is true that I see poetry rather differently now, differently from the way most people see it too; but I can still see it with my former eye' (*PSS*, vol. 65, p. 259).

38 On February 25, 1891, volume 13 of *The Works of Count L.N. Tolstoy* was seized. *Works of the Last Years* (Moscow, 1891) included *The Kreutzer Sonata*, which was first published in June 1891 on the orders of Alexander III, who permitted publication of *The Kreutzer Sonata* in *The Collected Works of L.N. Tolstoy* but forbade it to be published elsewhere. (See this Diary, April 22, 'My Visit to St Petersburg'.)

39 F.D. Nefedov, 'Evlampeeva doch' (Daughter of Eulampius), in the book *V pamyat S.A. Yureva. Sbornik, izdannyi druzyami pokoinogo* (In memory of S.A. Yurev. An anthology written and published by the friends of the lamented), Moscow, 1891, pp. 312–96 (YaPL).

40 A forest lodge five *versts* from Yasnaya Polyana.

41 The article 'On Non-Resistance', which later grew into the tract, *The Kingdom of God Is Within Us*. In 1894 the tract was first brought out in Russian in Berlin, by the publishing

house of A. Deibner (see *PSS*, vol. 28).

42 Tolstoy wrote also to Sergei about the sick peasant from the village of Telyatinki. In a letter to him of April 1, 1891 he wrote: 'Have just received Sergievskii's reply about the sick peasant: it is accepted that it is terminal, if not chronic, and I have therefore decided to take him to Tula. Rudnyov has promised to take care of him there' (*PSS*, vol. 84, p. 71). On April 11, 1891 the patient died of gangrene of the leg.

43 A.A. Smirnov, 'Na zakate (rasskaz)', (At sunset (a short story)), *RO*, no. 1, 1891.

44 Spinoza, *Oeuvres*, Paris, 3 vols (no date). Vol. 1: 'Introduction Critique'; vol. 2: 'Vie de Spinoza. Notice Bibliographique. Traité théologo-politique. Traité politique'; vol. 3: 'Ethique. De la réforme de l'entendement. Lettres' (YaPL). Sofia Tolstaya recalls her reading of Spinoza in *MZh*: 'At that time I began again to read and study the philosophy of Spinoza. I even had a chart, given to me long ago by Prince Urusov, which enabled one by means of geometry to understand more clearly the theory of this philosophy. But it was not then within my intellectual powers, and I could make nothing of it. The first part, on the history of the Jewish people, seemed dull to me. But his description of the concept of God satisfied me completely. The second part, *Ethics*, I found deeply interesting, and I was especially struck by his discussion of power and miracles [. . .] Yet I could not grow to like Spinoza, and only with difficulty did I finish it – although I was interested more than anything else in the abstract ideas of the philosophers, rather than in analyses and criticisms of their works' (*MZh*, book 6, pp. 7–8).

45 See this Diary, February 4, and note 20.

46 M. de Vogué, 'On "The Kreutzer Sonata" ', *RO*, no. 12, 1890 (YaPL).

47 *KN*, nos 3–5, 1891.

48 Vyacheslav Andreevich Behrs.

49 Tolstoy was visited by James Creelman, who had come to Russia to study the Slavs. In a letter to Leonila Fominichna Annenkova of March 12, 1891, Tolstoy wrote: '[. . .] I am terribly tired of his presence: you have to speak in a language you speak with difficulty, and this man and his worldly view of things is of little interest to me. Yet I would feel guilty about going out and leaving him alone, when he has no one to talk to and came here especially to do so. Sonya and Tanya are helping me' (*PSS*, vol. 65, pp. 267). For more details of Creelman's visits to Tolstoy (in 1891 and 1903) see *LN*, vol. 75, book 1, pp. 427–34.

50 Sofia Andreevna wanted an audience with the Tsar, because of the banned volume XIII, and asked Aleksandra Tolstaya to discover whether this would be possible. Aleksandra Tolstaya replied in a letter dated March 12, 1891 (GMT).

51 After her return from Moscow, Sofia Tolstaya wrote to Sergei, in a letter of March 17: 'I returned today from Moscow where I had hurried off for a couple of days to find out about the banned Volume Thirteen. It is a bad business: 18,000 copies printed, and it's not known what will happen to them. All the articles in Volume Twelve have been banned. I have arranged that the other twelve volumes will go on sale with a slip of paper inside on which I have written: "Due to circumstances beyond the Publisher's control, Volume Thirteen cannot be released" ' (GMT).

52 'Schopenhauer's Ideas on Writing', from *Parerga und Paralipomena*, under the signature L. *RV*, no. 30, March 23, 1891.

53 From March 21 to 29, the 19th Exhibition of Paintings of the Fellowship of Wandering Artists took place on the premises of the Tula Assembly of the Nobility.

54 It was L.N. Tolstoy's renunciation of his property that led to its division amongst members of his family. In a letter to Tatiana Kuzminskaya of April 21, Sofia Tolstaya wrote: 'We have been discussing the division of the property all this time, and we still haven't decided how to share it out. There is something sad and improper about the way this division affects the father. Well it's not my business, I didn't plan it' (GMT). Tolstoy expressed his own attitude to it in a letter to N.N. Gué (the son), dated April 17, 1891: 'I am having to sign a

document, a deed of settlement, which releases me from the property, and the very signature of which means a retreat from principle. Yet I shall sign it, for if I don't I shall arouse great anger' (*PSS*, vol. 65, p. 289). Tolstoy signed the deed of settlement on April 17, 1891. In July 1892 the division was complete. The deed is in the Tolstoy Museum.

55 Seryozha Tolstoy served as a leading *zemstvo* official in the Chern district in the province of Tula. He recalled his service thus: 'I did not agree with the reactionary laws concerning *zemstvo* officials, and I later recognised that it was a mistake for me to have served in this position. I did so because I wanted to be independent, I was interested in the life of the peasants, and I thought that since recognised laws and government were needed in the countryside, I could do a certain amount of good, acting as independently of the provincial authorities as I could, while not actually changing or palliating the odious clauses of the new law' (S.L. Tolstoy, p. 180).

56 Tolstoy was working on his article 'On Non-Resistance' at the time (see note 41). In a letter of April 17, 1891 to N.N. Gué (the son), he wrote: 'I am writing strenuously but it is moving very slowly; I don't know whether it's because the subject isn't important, whether I am demanding too much of myself or whether my powers are weakening, but I am working very slowly. I have a lot more patience and stubbornness, though, and copy everything out 20 times' (*PSS*, vol. 65, p. 289).

57 His tract *On Life*, published as a separate booklet, was banned on the orders of the Synod on April 8, 1888, on the grounds that it expressed doubts about the divinity of Christ and the dogmas of Christianity. His article 'What Then Must We Do?', written for *RM*, no. 1, was banned by the censors in 1885. The chapters from *On Life* to which Sofia Tolstaya referred were published in *Nedelya* (The Week), nos. 1–4, 6, 1889.

58 *NV*, no. 5432, April 12, 1891.

59 The nineteenth Exhibition of Paintings of the Fellowship of Wandering Artists, and the Annual Exhibition of the Academy of Arts.

60 Mikhail Aleksandrovich Novoselov, a student at Moscow University and a disciple of Tolstoy's, illegally printed Tolstoy's article 'Nikolai Palkin' on a hectograph, and circulated it. He wrote to Tolstoy at the end of 1887: 'I have spent the whole summer in a village in the Tver province, ploughing, scything and reaping [. . .] and at home I've mainly been busy copying out and checking the Gospels, and publishing your "Nikolai Palkin" (I didn't ask your permission, as I've always heard that you have nothing against all your works being distributed)' (GMT). At the end of December 1887, Novoselov's flat was searched by the police, the article was discovered and Novoselov and several of his friends were arrested. When Tolstoy heard about this he actively petitioned for his release, 'pointing out the illegality of their arrest, when he, the chief culprit, remained at liberty'. (For more detail on this, see P.I. Biryukov, 'Moi dva grekha' (My two sins), in the book *Tolstoi. Pamyatniki tvorchestva i zhizni* (Tolstoy. A commemoration of his art and life), Moscow, 1923, pp. 51–3; L.P. Nikiforov, 'Vospominaniya o Tolstom' (Memories of Tolstoy), in *Tolstoi v vosp.*, vol. 1, p. 328.

61 The reference is to the Intermediary publishing house. For this see V.K. Lebedev's article 'Knigoizdatelstvo "Posrednik" i tsenzura (1885–1889)' (The Intermediary and the censors (1885–1889)), in *Russkaya literatura* (Russian Literature), no. 2, 1968, pp. 163–70.

62 Tolstoy wrote in his diary, on April 18: 'Sonya arrived about three days ago. I find it most unpleasant that she has been ingratiating herself with the Tsar and complaining to him about people stealing my manuscripts. I couldn't control myself and said some harsh things to her, but it has passed' (*PSS*, vol. 52, p. 27).

63 P.A. Gaideburov, editor and publisher of *Nedelya* (The Week) and *KN*, wrote to Sofia Tolstaya on April 21, 1891, asking if he might publicise in his newspaper a readers' poll on the new edition of Tolstoy's works. Sofia Tolstaya's reply is not known.

64 Her letter to Durnovo is dated April 27 (rough copy in GMT). See this Diary, May 15, 1891.

65 Lyova Tolstoy was a student for a year at the medical faculty of Moscow University, then transferred to the first year of the philological faculty. In the spring, illness forced him to leave the university. In a letter to Sofia Tolstaya dated April 26, he wrote that he could no longer endure the examination procedures at the university, and could not submit to 'having a lot of names, figures and Slavonic grammar stuffed down my throat [. . .] What am I going to do then?' he wrote. 'Well, first of all, I've never done anything up to now anyway, so at least it will be no worse. Secondly, I have a year of military service. And after that who knows? It's too early to tell [. . .] ' (GMT).

66 P. Enfantin, *La Vie éternelle, passée, présente, future*, Paris, no date. L.P. Nikiforov, who sent Tolstoy this book on April 25, 1891, wrote to him: 'As to *The Eternal Life*, I should be very, very grateful to you if as you read it, you would mark the good and the bad places, and make your own observations on it too. If you think it deserves to be translated, then I shall try to finish it, although it is hardly likely that the censors will permit it. I am very interested to know what you think about it in general. I love the book' (GMT).

67 From July 1890 to May 1893, Tolstoy was working on his tract *The Kingdom of God Is Within Us*. See this Diary for March 2, and note 41.

68 Vladimir Fyodorovich Orlov was a teacher at a railway school near Moscow. His letter was brought to Tolstoy by a friend of his called A. Kosterev, and in his letter he wrote that Kosterev had very much wanted to see Tolstoy and talk to him. In his diary Tolstoy referred to him as 'a gentleman who has no need of me, and I no need of him. How sad that one cannot be more loving' (*PSS*, vol. 52, p. 29).

69 Tolstoy's article 'Dlya chego lyudi odurmanivayutsya?' (Why are people being stupefied?), which contains these phrases, appeared in volume XIII, for which Sofia Tolstaya was pleading with the censors. The article had already been published as the preface to P.S. Alekseev's book *O pyanstve* (On drunkenness), Moscow, 1891, published by *RM*.

70 Durnovo's letter to Sofia Tolstaya is dated May 6 (GMT).

71 His letter to Alekhin, dated May 14, 1891 (*PSS*, vol. 65, pp. 296–300), is in reply to a letter to him from Alekhin.

72 On May 22 Tolstoy noted in his diary: 'I dictated to Tanya the beginning of "Notes of a Mother". A lot of pages, but it's no good. One should write about oneself, otherwise it's just clumsy' (*PSS*, vol. 52, p. 32).

73 Fet and his wife stayed two days (May 20 and 21) at Yasnaya Polyana. On his return to Vorobevka Fet wrote to Sofia Tolstaya: 'I bore away with me, as always, an impression of the count's mighty fingers, and I would wear a veil over my face, like Moses, rather than let the crowd drain me with their eyes of the powers he has bestowed on me. I thank you for your magnificent hospitality, and must observe that "man shall not live by bread alone". You and the lovely Tatiana Andreevna once more force me loudly to proclaim this simple truth by which I have always unconsciously lived my life [. . .] It would be nothing new for me or anyone else to say that you and Tatiana Andreevna are truly "*femmes du foyer*" (generous hostesses), but I am always so happy when I hear the silvery tones of your poetic little hearts. I grow young when I am with you both, my old age seems but a dream and I become active, i.e. perpetually young' (*Russkaya literatura*, no. 3, 1971, p. 99).

74 The editor of the newspaper *Kurskii listok* (Kursk Leaflet) was named S.A. Fesenko.

75 Leonila Fominichna Annenkova's husband was Konstantin Nikiforovich Annenkov.

76 Evidently the sculptor Leopold Bernstamm, about whom A.S. Suvorin wrote to Tolstoy on November 21, 1889: 'There is a Russian sculptor in Paris called Bernstamm, a talented man who has done various things, including busts of Renan and others. He wrote saying that he would like to do a bust of you, and is prepared to leave Paris to visit you. He is held back only by his doubts as to whether you will agree to pose a few times for him' (GMT). Tolstoy

replied to Suvorin on November 27, 1889: 'If you can release me from this sculptor then please do so' (*PSS*, vol. 64, p. 335).

77 Richard Deirenfurt had probably been sent by Loewenfeld to take Tolstoy the proofs of his book *Leo Tolstoi. Sein Leben, seine Werke, seine Weltanschauung*, Berlin, 1892. On June 2 Tolstoy wrote in his diary: 'We've had a German visiting, from Loewenfeld. Very tedious' (*PSS*, vol. 52, p. 36). About the reading of these proofs, see ibid., p. 38.

78 See this Diary, note 84.

79 *The Kingdom of God Is Within Us.*

80 *SV*, no. 6, 1891, published a story by M. Maikov, called 'Istoriya odnogo braka' (The story of one marriage). No. 5 contained part of a story by M. Albov, 'V tikhikh vodakh' (In quiet waters). It has not been possible to establish which story Sofia Tolstaya was reading.

81 See this Diary, note 77.

82 L.N. Tolstoy, *Vtoraya russkaya kniga dlya chteniya* (The second Russian reader), 18th edn, Moscow, 1891.

83 The pavilion was what they called the little wooden house with the tiled roof, built in the park at Yasnaya Polyana in 1888. Masha Tolstaya and some local doctors ran a surgery for peasants in it. It was later used to accommodate guests in the summer months. In 1808 and 1809 Nikolai Gusev lived there.

84 In April 1891 Tolstoy received a book from Chertkov entitled *The Ethics of Diet*, by Howard Williams, London, 1883 (YaPL). On April 11 he wrote to his wife: 'I have just been reading a wonderful book, a history of the ancients' attitude to vegetarianism' (*PSS*, vol. 84, p. 78). As he continued reading this 'wonderful and necessary book', he wrote to Chertkov about his desire to write a preface to it (*PSS*, vol. 87, p. 84), and in a letter to him of May 6 he wrote: 'The people at home here have started translating it, and I have been helping' (ibid., p. 85). Sofia, Tatiana and Masha Tolstaya all worked on the translation of this book (see *PSS*, vol. 84, p. 79), and others helped to finish it. 'For the preface' (*PSS*, vol. 87, p. 95) Tolstoy visited a slaughter-house, on June 7. The preface he embarked on then evolved into an article, 'Pervaya stupen' (The first step) (*PSS*, vol. 29). In 1893 the Intermediary (in the series 'For Intelligent Readers') brought out a Russian translation of the book *Howard Williams. Etika pishchi, ili nravstvennye osnovy bezboinogo pitaniya dlya cheloveka, so vstupitelnoi statei 'Pervaya stupen' L.N. Tolstogo* (The ethics of diet, or the moral basis for a non-violent diet for man, with an introductory article by L.N. Tolstoy: 'The First Step') (YaPL, notes).

85 Ilya Repin's drawing is called 'Sofia Tolstaya with her two youngest children Sasha and Vanechka' (GMT). Sergei Tolstoy wrote: 'This picture bears so little resemblance to the originals that if there hadn't been an inscription on it I would never have recognised my mother, brother and sister' (S.L. Tolstoy, p. 327).

86 See notes 38 and 51 to this Diary. This was probably a supplementary edition.

87 The French Trade Fair (with a large art section) opened in Moscow in the spring of 1891.

88 In a letter of July 11, Tolstoy sent his wife the draft of an announcement to the newspapers, written in either his name or hers, renouncing the copyright on all the works which he had written since the 1880s, and which had appeared in volumes XII and XIII (*PSS*, vol. 84, pp. 81–2). After a discussion with his wife about this, he noted in his diary on July 14: 'She cannot understand, nor can the children, as they go on spending money, that every ruble which my books earn and which they live on causes me suffering and shame. The shame doesn't matter. But why should they weaken this action of mine, which might have had some power to preach the truth. Well, the truth will do its work without me' (*PSS*, vol. 52, p. 4).

89 Ilya Efimovich Repin stayed in Yasnaya Polyana between 26 June and 16 July. In this time he did a bust of Tolstoy (GMT) and two portraits: a sketch, 'Tolstoy Praying' (GTG) and 'Tolstoy Working In His Study Under the Arches' (IRLI). He also did various other sketches. According to Seryozha Tolstoy, these were less successful than Repin's previous works, and he felt that this was because the painter was then under the influence of Impressionism.

Repin, as he put it, was 'embellishing reality with his own imagination' (S.L. Tolstoy, pp. 327–8).

90 Sofia Tolstaya later wrote: 'If people want to put up a monument to Lev Nikolaevich, not one of the sculptures representing him has managed to convey his true appearance. The best one is the small bust with folded arms by Trubetskoi (*MZh*, book 6, p. 114).

91 In a letter to the editors of *RV* and *NV* of September 16, Tolstoy wrote: 'I hereby offer anybody who wants to the chance to publish, without payment, in Russia and abroad, in Russian and in translations, and also to put on the stage, all those works which I wrote since *1881*, and which were published in 1886, in Volume XII of my *Complete Collected Works*, and in Volume XIII, published in this year of 1891, as well as all my works which are as yet unpublished in Russia, and have been allowed to appear only since the publication of this recent volume' (*PSS*, vol. 66, p. 47). Published on September 19 in *RV* (no. 258) and *NV* (no. 5588).

92 The Yasnaya Polyana Library contains the following works (including Lermontov's play *A Strange Man*): M.Yu. Lermontov *Sochineniya* (Works), published by Glazunov, 5th edn, corrected and supplemented by P.A. Efremov, St Petersburg, 1882, vols 1 and 2; M.Yu. Lermontov, *Polnoe sob. soch.* (Complete collected works), moderately priced edition published by F.I. Anskii, Moscow, 1891.

93 Tolstoy's *Novaya azbuka* (New ABC), published first in 1875, had been republished many times. Sofia Tolstaya worked on the next edition, the seventeenth, published in 1891.

94 Tolstoy's story 'Lipinyushka' was taken from an anthology edited by F.A. Khudyakov, *Velikorusskie skazki* (Great-Russian Tales), 2nd edn, Moscow, 1861. It was shortened, stylistically reworked, and first published in *Pervaya russkaya kniga dlya chteniya* (First Russian Reader), Moscow, 1875 (see *PSS*, vol. 21, pp. 120–1; 630).

95 'I haven't seen her – she is with Masha at present,' Sofia Tolstaya wrote to her daughter Tatiana on July 29 (GMT). In his diary Tolstoy noted on July 31: 'Larionova was here, a student from Kazan, whom I had the pleasure of helping' (*PSS*, vol. 52, p. 47). In a letter to Tolstoy the following day, Larionova wrote: 'I didn't manage yesterday to tell you how grateful I was. Thank you! It was the old story: before I came to see you I didn't care whether I lived or died. I was just trying to find a way out of this brutal life – and I didn't succeed either. Now I've come to life again! [. . .] Yesterday I wanted not only to shake your hand passionately and say 'thank you!' – I wanted to cry with love for you' (GMT).

96 The psychologist Charles Richet and the writer Octave Gudail visited Tolstoy. For an account of their visit to Yasnaya Polyana see *Vestnik inostrannoi literatury* (Herald of Foreign Literature), December 1891, pp. 318–22 (Gudail), and a paragraph in *Nedelya* (The Week), no. 36, 1891, by Richet. On August 27, Tolstoy noted in his diary: 'Of little interest' (*PSS*, vol. 52, p. 50).

97 On June 20, 1891, as the famine in Russia was intensifying, Nikolai Leskov asked Tolstoy in a letter: 'What do you think about this disaster – should we poke our nose in? What is the decent thing for us to do? Maybe I could be useful in some way, but I have lost faith in all the so-called "good works" of public charity, and I don't know if one doesn't actually do more harm than good by meddling in something which only results in more idleness. But it's also hard to do nothing. Please tell me what you think one should do' (*Tolstoy. Perepiska*, p. 540). Replying to Leskov on July 4, Tolstoy wrote that 'there is one thing we can do to fight this famine, and that is for us all to do as many good works as we possibly can [. . .] You ask me precisely what can you do? My reply to you is to appeal to people's love for one another; not only their love in time of famine, but always and everywhere' (*PSS*, vol. 66, p. 12).

98 E. Rod, *Les Trois Coeurs*, Paris, 1890 (YaPL).

99 Sofia Tolstaya's story 'On *The Kreutzer Sonata*' (GMT). She recalled: 'When I was doing the proofs for *The Kreutzer Sonata*, which I had never liked, because of Lev Nikolaevich's coarse attitudes to women in it, I suddenly had the idea of writing a novel myself, about *The*

Kreutzer Sonata. This idea kept returning to me, and took such a hold of me that I couldn't control myself, and so I wrote this story, which has never seen the light and which is now kept with my papers' (*MZh*, book 6, p. 8).

100 She is referring to Tolstoy's letters to Vasilii Petrovich Zolotaryov, Mikhail Aleksandrovich Novoselov, Evgenii Ivanovich Popov and Pyotr Galaktionovich Khokhlov, all dated October 8, 1891 (*PSS*, vol. 68, pp. 50–5).

101 Tolstoy and his daughter left for Pirogovo on September 17. Between the 18th and the 22nd, they visited villages in the Krapivna, Bogoroditskii and Efremovskii districts of Tula province. Concerning Tolstoy's famine relief work, see his articles in *PSS*, vol. 29. (See also: T.L. Sukhotina, pp. 201–16.)

102 Probably a woman landowner named Byrdina (or Burdina).

103 On October 15, Tolstoy sent Nikolai Grot his article 'On the famine', for publication in *VFP*. The November issue of the journal, in which this article appeared, was seized, and the article was sent to the Chief Department of Press Affairs. It was published, greatly abbreviated, in *KN* in January 1892, under the title 'Pomoshch golodnym' (Aid to the hungry).

104 Sofia Tolstaya's request was granted. For her letter, dated October 15, and for Vorontsov-Dashkov's reply, see *Letopisi*, vol. 12, Moscow, 1948, 2, pp. 106–7. The money from the performance of Tolstoy's plays went to charity.

105 A.N. Kanevskii worked in Tolstoyan agricultural communes. He had set out on foot for the 'Krinitsa' colony in the Caucasus, and on the way had visited Yasnaya Polyana. On October 24, 1891, Tolstoy wrote in his diary: 'Kanevskii has just left. He is touchingly simple and self-sacrificing. He came from Moscow without a kopeck. I sent him off to his father with 4 rubles. He spent two nights here' (*PSS*, vol. 52, p. 56).

106 Lev Lvovich Tolstoy could not apply in Samara the famine relief measures which his father had applied. He was forced to distribute supplies to the peasants individually, which did not combat starvation as effectively as canteens would have done. Tolstoy was dissatisfied with this decision, and wrote to his son, on December 23, 1891: 'The main thing to realise is that you are not called upon to feed 5,000 or 6,000 or x number of souls, you are called upon to distribute the aid which has come into your hands in the best possible way. In all good conscience, is this really what you are doing?' (*PSS*, vol. 66, p. 120). In *MZh* Sofia Tolstaya quotes excerpts from various unpublished letters from Lyova to his father about the conditions of work in the Samara province: 'Why talk of canteens?' he wrote; 'when there isn't so much as a crust of bread [. . .] We could open canteens, I quite agree, they would be far more effective than merely distributing the food, but first give us an army of 100 bakers, 10 wagon-loads of supplies and a whole crowd of people [. . .]' (*MZh*, book 6, p. 196). Afterwards Tolstoy regretted that he had been so sharp about his son's activities, and told his son so in a letter (no longer extant). In a letter to Sofia Tolstaya of January 10, 1892, Lyova Tolstoy referred to his father's 'heated' letter, which made him scrutinise his own activities yet more closely' (GMT). See also Lev Lvovich Tolstoy, *V golodnye goda. Zapiski i stati* (In the years of famine. Notes and articles), Moscow, 1900.

107 *RV*, no. 303, November 3, 1891.

108 *RV*, no. 306, November 6, 1891, published Tolstoy's article 'Strashnyi Vopros' (A terrible question). The reactionary *Moskovskie vedomosti* (Moscow Gazette) (nos. 308, 310, 312, November 7, 9 and 11) then published various articles condemning Tolstoy and his family for giving aid to the starving.

1892

1 Tolstoy's article 'On the Famine' (*PSS*, vol. 29), which he sent to *VFP*, was banned by the censors. Tolstoy then sent it to Edward Dillon, correspondent for the London *Daily Telegraph*. The article was translated by Dillon and published in several issues of the paper

between 12 and 30 January, in the form of a series of letters entitled 'Why Are the Russian Peasants Starving?' *Moskovskie vedomosti* (Moscow Gazette) (no. 22, January 22) cited one of these 'letters' (the end of Chapter 4 and the beginning of Chapter 5), inaccurately translated back from the English, in a lead article entitled 'Gr. Lev Tolstoi o golodayushchikh krestyanakh' (Count Lev Tolstoy on the starving peasants). According to them, Tolstoy's 'letters' were 'open propaganda for the overthrow of the whole social and economic structure of the entire world'. On January 23, Sofia Tolstaya sent a 'Letter to the Editors of the *Moscow Gazette*', to refute this, but it was not published.

2 Ivan Ivanovich Raevskii, Tolstoy's friend and assistant during the famine, died on November 26, 1891. On November 28, Tolstoy wrote an obituary article, 'Pamyati I.I. Raevskogo' (Memories of I.I. Raevskii) (*PSS*, vol. 29), and on November 29 he wrote to his daughter: 'I am suffering a great grief – my friend has died, one of the best people I have ever known. He was ill for a week with influenza and died in my arms. He and I worked together and had grown to love one another even more than before' (*PSS*, vol. 66, p. 100).

3 Vera Mikhailovna Velichkina, a doctor and revolutionary. She had got to know Tolstoy in January 1892 and had worked with him during the famine. (See Vera Velichkina, 'V golodnyi god s Lvom Tolstym' (The year of famine with Lev Tolstoy), in *Tolstoi v vosp.*, vol. 1, pp. 500–6.

4 Sofia Tolstaya's letters to Durnovo, Sheremeteva, Aleksandr Kuzminskii and Tatiana Kuzminskaya, in *Pravitelstvennyi vestnik* (Government Herald), were written on February 8. Replying to her in a letter dated February 13, Durnovo wrote: 'Despite my great desire to grant your request, I find it difficult to agree to the promulgation of the denial you have sent me, since by its very nature it is bound to evoke further denunciations, which will undoubtedly occasion yet more polemics, which are extremely undesirable in view of the present social climate' (GMT). The other replies to her letters are also stored in the Tolstoy Museum.

5 Tolstoy's letter to *Pravitelstvennyi vestnik* (Government Herald) on February 12, written at Sofia Tolstaya's insistence (*PSS*, vol. 66, pp. 160–2), was not published, on the pretext that polemics could not be engaged in on the pages of this paper. On the advice of Nikolai Grot, Sofia Tolstaya had 100 copies of this letter hectographed and sent to various periodicals, government figures and individuals (*MZh*, book 6, p. 230). *S. Peterburghskie vedomosti* (St Petersburg Gazette) published it on March 8 (no. 66), as did *Russkaya zhizn* (Russian Life) (no. 66, March 8), *NV* (no. 5757, March 9), *Novosti* (News) (no. 67, March 9), *Moskovskii listok* (Moscow Leaflet) (no. 69, March 10). See also Tolstoy's letters to Edward Dillon, of January 29 (*PSS*, vol. 66, pp. 144–5), and to Sofia Tolstaya, of February 9 and 28 (*PSS*, vol. 84, pp. 117, 128–9).

6 See this diary, September 21, 1891, and note 99.

1893

1 Vladimir Grigorevich Chertkov at one point stored some of Tolstoy's manuscripts with a former fellow-soldier in the household cavalry, D. Trepov. Sofia Tolstaya wrote in *MZh* (book 6, p. 41): 'In that year (1893), Chertkov, knowing that he might be searched, gave Lev Nikolaevich's banned works and manuscripts to his friend Trepov for safekeeping. When he took them back I do not know. This was the beginning of Chertkov's despotic, yet excessively reverential and loving relationship with Lev Nikolaevich.' After Chertkov was exiled in 1897, the manuscripts of all Tolstoy's works written after 1880 were sent, with Tolstoy's permission, to Chertkov's home in England, where they were stored in a special reinforced concrete vault, built near Christchurch, Hampshire. In 1913 these manuscripts were sent to the Academy of Sciences Library in St Petersburg, and in 1926 they were removed to the Tolstoy Museum in Moscow.

2 Sofia Tolstaya explained this 'insane' page in her diary, in *MZh* (book 6, pp. 54–5): 'Lev

Nikolaevich was at that time writing his article "On Religion"; someone had copied it out for P.A. Boulanger, and Lev Nikolaevich and Masha were staying on at Yasnaya Polyana as though they had no intention of ever leaving for Moscow. I took a very dim view of their sojourn in the country, because I was feeling very miserable without my husband. Of course most people would find it quite reasonable and natural that Lev Nikolaevich should seek peace and solitude to pursue his literary labours, but this didn't make it any easier for me. I did, however, try not to let Lev Nikolaevich see how dissatisfied and impatient I was [. . .] But I couldn't help it; my overwrought state turned to malevolence, and it suddenly seemed to me that the devil had possessed Lev Nikolaevich, and had frozen his heart.'

1894

1 On March 2 and 14, Sofia Tolstaya wrote to Tanya and Lyova Tolstoy: 'Papa and Dunaev went to the mushroom market by the river. They bought some dried mushrooms for the Pirogovo Tolstoys, and some for themselves, then had a little picnic. There were a great many people there, a lot of peasants from other parts, and Papa was absolutely fascinated by this market' (GMT).

2 Sofia Tolstaya was publishing the 9th edition of Tolstoy's works.

3 Mrs Humphrey Ward, *Marcella*, New York, 1894.

1895

1 Jules Verne, *Vingt milles lieues sous les mers, 1 et 2. parties*, Paris, 1870. In 1873 and 1874 Tolstoy read these and other novels by Verne to his older children (I.L. Tolstoy, pp. 91–2).

2 S.I. Fonvizin, 'Spletnya' (Gossip), *VE*, nos 1 and 2, 1895.

3 Tolstoy's brother Sergei Tolstoy was living with his family in Moscow at the time.

4 In the middle of December 1894 Sofia Tolstaya received a telegram from Yasnaya Polyana to say that thieves had broken into the house through a window, 'breaking into trunks and cupboards, opening up everything, throwing things around and stealing clothes, bedding, an overcoat, and various other things' (*MZh*, book 6, pp. 77–8). Several days later she left for Yasnaya Polyana.

5 The brothers Grimm, *Skazki* (Fairy-stories), published by A.F. Marks, St Petersburg, 1893 (YaPL).

6 Lidia Ivanovna Veselitskaya (Mikulich) arrived from Moscow to see Tolstoy without notifying him in advance of her arrival. Since he was not there, she spent several days with Masha and Sofia Tolstaya before leaving for home. (See V. Mikulich, *Vstrechi s pisatelyami* (Meetings with writers), Leningrad, 1929, pp. 83–5.)

7 At the end of December 1894, Tolstoy was persuaded by Chertkov to have his photograph taken by Mey, with Chertkov, Biryukov, Gorbunov-Posadov, Tregubov and Popov. Tolstoy noted in his diary, on December 31, 1894: 'Chertkov was here. There was a very unpleasant argument over the portrait. Sonya was as decisive as ever, but rash and spiteful too' (*PSS*, vol. 52, p. 157).

8 The letter was from Nikolskoe-Obolyanovo, and was written on January 8 or 9 (*PSS*, vol. 84, pp. 234–5).

9 Evidently Sofia Tolstaya read through these letters while preparing to send his manuscripts to the Rumyantsev Museum. See also this Diary for April 10, 1863, and note 9.

10 Tolstoy had become friendly with Boris Nikolaevich Chicherin in the winter of 1856–7. They were especially close in 1858. In his memoirs Chicherin wrote: 'We were soul-mates. Even now I cannot read his old letters to me without feeling deeply moved. They breathe youth, sincerity and freshness; they depict him so well in that early period when his talent was just beginning to develop, and they take me back so vividly to those distant times [. . .] However, even in those days there was already evidence of that tendency to philosophise

which would later prove so fatal to him. His solitary life in the country gave even greater scope to this disease. He was preoccupied by lofty questions of existence, but there was never any basis for their resolution. Instead he gave himself up to his own private train of thought, mixed with large amounts of fantasy' (B.N. Chicherin, in *Tolstoi v vosp.* vol. 1, pp. 83–4). Fourteen letters from Tolstoy to Chicherin have been published, as have thirty letters from Chicherin to Tolstoy. (See *Pisma Tolstogo i k Tolstomu* (Letters from and to Tolstoy), Moscow, 1928. Also *PSS*, vols 60, 62, 65 and 68, for letters from Tolstoy to Chicherin.)

11 Aleksandr Behrs and his wife Anna Aleksandrovna (née Mitrofanova).

12 Alphonse Daudet, *Les Rois en éxil* (1879). It is not known what edition of the book she was reading.

13 An ariston was a mechanical musical instrument rather like a musical box.

14 Tolstoy and his daughter Tanya stayed with Adam Vasilevich Olsufiev and his wife from January 1 to 18, in their estate at Nikolskoe-Obolyanovo. Tolstoy worked on his story 'Master and Man', took long walks around the neighbouring countryside, met the artist R.S. Levitskii, and the Apraksins (at their estate in Olgovo) and the whole trip had a beneficial effect on Tolstoy's physical and mental state. (See: P.I. Neradovskii, 'Vstrechi s Tolstym' (Meetings with Tolstoy) in *LN*, vol. 69, book 2, pp. 130–8); M.F. Meiendorf, 'Stranichki vospominanii o Lve Nikolaeviche Tolstom' (Pages of memories about Lev Nikolaevich Tolstoy) in *Tolstoi v vosp.*, vol. 2, pp. 63–6.

15 The *zemstvo* representatives of Tver, and various other regions, sent petitions to Tsar Nicholas II expressing their willingness to participate in the internal government of Russia. In response, the Tsar gave an audience to the *zemstvo* representatives on January 17, 1895, and dismissed their wishes as 'senseless dreams'. Tolstoy responded to this with an article, 'Bessmyslennye mechtaniya' (Senseless dreams) (*PSS*, vol. 31, pp. 185–92). Tolstoy also refused to sign a petition on the freedom of the press, drawn up by the Tsar's government representatives in Moscow and St Petersburg.

16 Tolstoy took part in a congress called by representatives of the liberal intelligentsia in order to organise a protest against the Tsar's speech. This congress was organised by D.I. Shakhovskoi and took place in the apartment of N.F. Mikhailov, publisher of *Vestnik vospitaniya* (Herald of Education). Those present failed to make any practical decisions. 'A complete waste of time,' Tolstoy wrote in his diary on January 29. 'All very stupid, and quite obvious that the organisation was only parading the strength of the individuals present' (*PSS*, vol. 53, p. 4).

17 Boris Chicherin, 'Prostranstvo i vremya' (On space and time) in *VFP*, vol. XXVI, 1895.

18 This was probably a reply which has not been kept to a letter from P.P. Kandidov (tutor of the Tolstoy boys Andryusha and Misha), dated January 29, 1895; in it he described his life with his mother in the town of Elatma, in the province of Tambov, where he had gone from Moscow the previous month. At the end of the letter he asked Sofia Tolstaya to tell him all about her family.

19 'Smert Ivana Ilicha' (The death of Ivan Ilich) (*PSS*, vol. 26), written between 1884 and 1886, was first published in *Sochineniya Gr. L.N. Tolstogo* (The works of Count L.N. Tolstoy), vol. 12, Moscow, 1886.

20 In this note Sofia Tolstaya is describing two separate visits by Turgenev to Yasnaya Polyana. The episode in the snipe-shooting party took place in the beginning of May 1880 (see I.L. Tolstoy, pp. 153–5; T.L. Sukhotina, pp. 248–9) The episode with the dancing was in August 1881 (see I.L. Tolstoy, pp. 151–2; T.L. Sukhotina, pp. 249–51).

21 *SV*, no. 22, 1894, published Tolstoy's translation from the English of 'Karma', a story by the American writer Paul Karus, with an introduction by Tolstoy, and in 1895 (no. 1), they published his article 'Religiya i nravstvennost' (Religion and morality) under the title 'Protivorechiya empiricheskoi nravstvennosti' (Contradictions of empirical morality).

22 Tolstoy referred to this painful argument between them in a letter to Nikolai Strakhov of

February 14: 'My story has brought me much grief. Sofia Andreevna was very distressed that I had given it for nothing to the *Northern Herald*, and there ensued an insane bout of jealousy (without any basis in reality), provoked by her feelings for Gurevich [. . .] She was close to suicide, and it is only now, two days later, that she has gained control of herself and come to her senses' (*PSS*, vol. 68, pp. 32–3). Further on Tolstoy begged Strakhov to 'put the word out' that the story would be published not only in the *Northern Herald* but also in Sofia Tolstaya's edition and in The Intermediary, and that he considered this to be the right thing to do. The experiences of these days are reflected in detail in Tolstoy's diary, February 7, 15 and 21 (*PSS*, vol. 53, pp. 4, 7, 8–9).

23 Later recalling her mental state at that time, Sofia Tolstaya wrote: 'With time I realised that the real cause of my utter despair at that time was my premonition of Vanechka's imminent death, which happened at the end of February. I fell into exactly the same despairing state in the summer just before Lev Nikolaevich's death. Such times are beyond our powers of endurance. There are always plenty of opportunities for grief in our life. The question is whether we have the strength to survive them and control ourselves' (*MZh*, book 7, p. 18).

24 Lyova Tolstoy was sent to the hospital for nervous diseases established by Doctor M.P. Ogranovich near Zvenigorod, just outside Moscow. On February 21 Tolstoy wrote in his diary: 'Yesterday Ogranovich helped me to understand Lyova a little better. He explained that he had some latent form of malaria. And I suddenly began to understand his condition and felt sorry for him, although I still cannot summon up any genuine feeling of love for him' (*PSS*, vol. 53, p. 10).

25 The story 'Master and Man' appeared simultaneously in three editions: The Intermediary, *The Works of Count L.N. Tolstoy*, 9th edition (Appendix to vol. XIII), and *SV*, no. 3. 1895.

26 In these difficult times for the Tolstoy family, Masha Tolstaya wrote to A.N. Dunaev: 'Maman is terrible in her grief. Her whole life had been with him, she had given him all her love. Papa alone can help her, though he cannot do so alone. But he too is suffering terribly and cries all the time' (letter written at the end of February–early March; GMT). For more details see: T.L. Sukhotina, pp. 400–4; I.L. Tolstoy, pp. 216–18. See also the appendix to this book, 'The Death of Vanechka.'

1897

1 Maria Lvovna Tolstaya married Nikolai Leonidovich Obolenskii on June 2, 1897. Referring to her parents' attitude to the marriage, she wrote to Leonila Fominichna Annenkova, on May 8, 1897: 'Maman was at first opposed to my marriage, since he is very poor, that's to say he has nothing and is slightly younger than me; Papa likes my future husband very much, however, and thinks he is the best person I could have chosen. But he pities me and feels wretched for me, although he will never say what's on his mind, never gives me any advice, and just avoids me. I am delighted that he likes Kolya, and more importantly, believes in him, but of course the prospect of parting with him is dreadfully painful for me . . .' (GMT).

2 *Sochineniya gr. L.N. Tolstogo* (The works of Count L.N. Tolstoy), vols I–XIV, 10th edn, Moscow, 1897.

3 In January 1897, Tolstoy began work on his tract *What Is Art?* Completed in 1898, it was first published in *VFP* (chapters 1–5 in November–December 1897, chapters 6–20 in January–February 1898. The first separate edition appeared in volume XV of *Soch. Tolstogo*, Moscow, 1898, and was also published by the Intermediary in the same year. Large cuts were made by the censors in all editions. The first uncensored edition appeared in 1898 in London, translated into English by Aylmer Maude, with an introduction by Tolstoy.

4 Sofia Tolstaya was probably referring to the notes in Tolstoy's diary which refer to the period of her friendship with Sergei Ivanovich Taneev, after the death of her youngest son

Vanechka. Tolstoy noted in his diary, on February 4, 1897: 'Sonya read this diary without telling me, and was aggrieved that people might *later* infer from it that she had not been a virtuous wife. I tried to soothe her – all our life and my attitude to her recently will show what kind of wife she has been. If she looks at this diary again let her do what she wants with it; I cannot always write with a view to what she or later readers will make of it, or turn it into a sort of character witness for her' (*PSS*, vol. 53, p. 133). See also this Diary, December 14, 1890, and note 11, 1890.

5 This was possibly a letter from Evgenii Schmidt, which has not been kept in the archive, but to which Tolstoy replied on June 11, 1897 (*PSS*, vol. 70, p. 94).

6 Sofia Tolstaya described her relationship with Sergei Ivanovich Taneev in *MZh* (book 3, pp. 556, 560, 561): 'After the death of my little son Vanechka, I was in a state of utter despair, such as one experiences only once in a lifetime. Such grief usually kills one, but if it does not, then one's heart is incapable of suffering so deeply again. But I survived, and I owe this to fate and to one strange thing – music [. . .] Once I had been intoxicated by music and had learnt how to listen to it, I could no longer live without it [. . .] But it was Taneev's music that affected me more powerfully than any other; it was he who first taught me, with his beautiful playing, how to listen to and love music [. . .] Sometimes I had only to meet Sergei Ivanovich and hear his calm, soothing voice to feel comforted [. . .] I was in a distressed state, and this also coincided with my critical period. In the mood I was in at the time, I didn't think very much about Taneev's personality. To all appearances he was not very interesting, always equable, extremely reticent, and a complete stranger to me to the very end.'

7 *The Power of Darkness* appeared in volume XII of the 10th edn of *Sochineniya L.N. Tolstogo* (The works of L.N. Tolstoy), 1897.

8 In accordance with the division of the property between the Tolstoy children (in 1891), the part belonging to Maria Tolstaya was worth 57,000 rubles. At first she refused this, but after her marriage she decided to accept her share. Her brother Sergei was to pay her this money from the mortgage on the Nikolskoe-Vyazemskii estate. Before this, however, Sofia Tolstaya had taken this money, assuming that her daughter would later accept her share, and Sergei gave an undertaking to pay the money to his mother. Sofia Tolstaya now had to hand over to Maria the money Sergei had given her, and transfer to her name the remainder of the sum which he owed her.

9 It has not been possible to discover who this visitor was.

10 On June 19, 1897, Nikolai Aleksandrovich Chudov visited Yasnaya Polyana. Tolstoy described him as 'a [. . .] clever, passionate man, and a good writer, for which he has suffered much and continues to suffer' (*PSS*, vol. 72, p. 179). Chudov was harassed for his banned poetry, which was hectographed and illegally distributed. He wrote a poem about the Khodynka catastrophe called 'To Nicholas II, in Memory of his Coronation', which included these verses:

> Evil conscience, you aren't disturbed
> In your secret private palaces
> Or can it be that you did not see
> Those hundred thousand corpses?
>
> You did not see them buried in the earth,
> But grieve, and always remember
> That *you* it was who murdered them,
> Those thousands of innocent men.

Chudov immediately wrote an account of his visit to Tolstoy, and sent it to him in a letter of June 25: 'The attached article was already typed and slashed by the censor, when I asked myself: "Am I doing the right thing?" If you want to forbid its publication, don't hesitate to write to the Sunday issue, No . . .' (GMT). Tolstoy's reply has not been kept, but he evidently had no objections. The article was published in *Orlovskii vestnik* (Oryol Herald), no. 171, June 29, 1897, under the title 'Den v Yasnoi Polyane' (A day at Yasnaya Polyana). During his exile in the province of Vologda (from 1899 to 1900), Chudov appealed to Tolstoy for help (see *PSS*, pp. 72, 179, 180, 547).

11 Maria Mikhailovna Kholevinskaya, a *zemstvo* doctor in the Krapivna district of the province of Tula, was arrested in Tula in March 1896 and sent to prison for distributing the banned works of Tolstoy. She was arrested after a search had revealed Tatiana Tolstoy's visiting card, with the message: 'Give Tolstoy's "What I Believe" to a man you don't know, who is none the less reliable.' This work Tolstoy had intended to give to a worker in Tula called I.P. Novikov. Since he had no copy of his own to give him, Tolstoy asked Tatiana to help him grant Novikov's request. Tatiana, remembering that Kholevinskaya had a copy in Tula, sent Novikov her card with a request to Kholevinskaya to give the book to its bearer. Tolstoy worked passionately for Kholevinskaya's release. In April 1896 he sent letters to the Minister of Justice, N.K. Muravyov, and the Minister of Internal Affairs, I.L. Goremykin, containing a statement about the case (*PSS*, vol. 69, pp. 83–7). On March 28, 1896 he appealed to A.F. Koni for help: 'If you can, please assist our poor dear friend, a woman doctor [. . .] I suppose one should be used to Russian lawlessness and cruelty, but one is constantly struck by new and unexpected examples of it, ever more senseless and fantastic' (ibid., vol. 69, p. 78). At the beginning of April that year, Kholevinskaya was released from prison and exiled to Astrakhan. In a letter to Sofia Tolstaya of May 30, 1897 Kholevinskaya said she was in bad health, and begged Sofia Tolstaya to 'do her utmost to see that the punishment meted out to her was alleviated' (GMT). What was 'unpleasant' about this letter was evidently the fact that Kholevinskaya referred several times to being unjustly punished on account of 'Tatiana Lvovna's ill-considered action'.

12 Romain Coolus, *L'Enfant malade. Pièce en 4 actes dont un prologue. Acte 1'ère, Revue blanche*, no. 97, June 15, 1897 (YaPL).

13 Chertkov reproached Tolstoy in a letter of June 19 for not replying to several letters of his. On June 20 Tolstoy sent Chertkov a telegram apologising for the delay in writing, and on that same day Chertkov's letter of June 19 arrived (*PSS*, vol. 88, pp. 30–4).

14 In a letter to Sofia Tolstaya of June 16, 1897, V.V. Stasov thanked her for her invitation to visit Yasnaya Polyana. Enclosed in the letter was a photograph of Ginzburg's bust of Tolstoy, then being shown at an art exhibition in Venice. (See 'Neopublikovannye pisma V.V. Stasova' (Unpublished letters of V.V. Stasov) in *Isskustvo* (Art), no. 10, 1958, p. 65.)

15 N.A. Belogolovnyi, 'Tri vstrechi s Gertsenom' (Three meetings with Herzen), in *RV*, nos. 167 and 171, from June 19 to 22, 1897.

16 Gué's painting *The Crucifixion* (started in 1884 and finished in 1894) was shown at the Wanderers' Exhibition in St Petersburg in 1891, and immediately provoked many arguments and discussions. On the orders of Alexander II, who apparently said of it 'It's a slaughter-house', the painting was removed from the exhibition and banned. On March 14, 1894, Tolstoy wrote to the artist: 'The fact that the painting was removed, and the things people are saying about it, is all very good and instructive. Especially that word "slaughter-house" [. . .] Its removal is your victory. The first time I saw it I was sure it would be banned and now that I can so vividly imagine the exhibition, with all its usual splendour and grandiosity, with its women, landscapes and "nature-morts", it seems almost ludicrous that it was ever shown in the first place' (*PSS*, vol. 67, pp. 81–2). Tatiana Tolstaya wrote about the painting in her diary, on February 17, 1894: '*The Crucifixion* is making an enormous impression on everyone [. . .] It depicts the very moment of Christ's death [. . .] Both the crucified men are standing on the ground. The robber is not nailed to the cross, but bound. It is very well painted, but I must confess I wasn't greatly impressed by it. I am sorry about this; there's a lack of freshness and spiritual sensitivity about it' (T.L. Sukhotina, pp. 222–3).

17 Louis Pierre, *Aphrodite*, Paris, 1894 (YaPL). For Tolstoy's negative opinion of this book, see his *What is Art?* (*PSS*, vol. 30, p. 89).
18 Marcel Prévost, *Les Demi-vierges*, Paris, 1894 (YaPL).
19 J.J. Rousseau, *Oeuvres*, vol. 9, Paris, 1822 (YaPL).
20 Possibly N. Ezhov's story 'Svidanie' (Meeting) in *NV*, no. 7665, July 1897.
21 Stepan Vasilevich Shidlovskii, a peasant Stundist, living in the village of Kishentsa in the Uman district of Kiev province. (The Stundists were an evangelical, communistically inclined sect, living in communes mainly in the South of Russia.) In a letter to P.I. Biryukov, of July 14, Tolstoy wrote: 'New friends have appeared in the province of Kiev. One of them, Shidlovskii, has been staying with us. I liked him very much' (*PSS*, vol. 70, p. 104).
22 It has not been possible to discover who this was.
23 Anton Rubinstein, *Muzyka i ee predstaviteli. Razgovor o muzyke* (Music and its practitioners. A discussion about music), Moscow, 1891.
24 V.V. Longinov, later rector of the Kharkov ecclesiastical seminary.
25 Gustave Guiches, *Snob* (Acts I and II), in *Revue blanche*, no. 99, July 15, 1897 (YaPL).
26 A plaster model of the statuette is in the GMT.
27 I.e. Akim Lvovich Flekser (pseudonym A. Volynskii).
28 She is referring to *What Is Art?*
29 Ginzburg could not initially bring himself to ask Tolstoy to pose for him, and sculpted the statuette from photographs which Sofia Tolstaya took for him. When he had seen the sculptor's work, Tolstoy agreed to pose. As Ginzburg wrote in his memoirs: 'Lev Nikolaevich willingly posed for me because he had a love of art and artists, and this attitude is crucial to the success of one's work for it encourages the artist and raises his spirits. By no means everyone who poses has this attitude to artists and their work' (*Skulptor Ilya Ginzburg. Vospominaniya, stati, pisma* (The sculptor Ilya Ginzburg. Memoirs, articles and letters), Leningrad, 1964, p. 61). A facsimile of the statuette (in bronze) is in the GMT.
30 Pyotr Alekseevich Bulakhov, a former Old Believer. According to Tolstoy, a man of 'Herculean strength, both morally and intellectually' (*PSS*, vol. 53, p. 149). Tolstoy wrote to Chertkov about him on March 22, 1897: 'I have just been [. . .] to see Bulakhov, that clever factory-worker I told you about' (*PSS*, vol. 88, p. 19).
31 See note 42 to the Diary for 1887. Between 1888 and 1889 Sofia Tolstaya gave Tolstoy's manuscripts and letters to the Rumyantsev Museum for safekeeping. In 1904 she had to store them elsewhere, so she transferred them to the Historical Museum. In 1915 they were returned to the Rumyantsev Museum once more and remained there until 1939, when they were transferred to the GMT.
32 Tolstoy noted in his diary on August 7: 'A silly, naive little Frenchman' (*PSS*, vol. 53, p. 149). There is no other information about him.
33 Lyubov Yakovlevna Gurevich's letter to Sofia Tolstaya is dated August 3, 1898 (GMT).
34 Nikolai Alekseevich Kasatkin stayed at Yasnaya Polyana, at Sofia Tolstaya's invitation, from August 4 to 7. He attended Ginzburg's sessions, and painted a study in oils of the studio with Ginzburg at work and Tatiana Tolstaya posing for a bas-relief (GMT).
35 Tolstoy noted in his diary, on August 15: 'Lombroso came, a naive and narrow-minded old man' (*PSS*, vol. 53, p. 150). Lombroso wrote his memoirs of this visit to Yasnaya Polyana: *Moe poseshchenie Tolstogo* (My visit to Tolstoy), Geneva, published by Elpidine. An extract from this was published in *Tolstoi v vosp.*, vol. 2, pp. 99–100.
36 Tolstoy's critique of late nineteenth-century art is in chapter 10 of *What is Art?* (see *PSS*, vol. 30).
37 H. Taine, *Philosophie de l'art*, vol. 1, 6th edn, Paris, 1893. Notes in Sofia Tolstaya's hand; vol. II, 7th edn, 1895 (YaPL).
38 In a letter of August 8, Chertkov wrote to Tolstoy: '[. . .] the recoupment of the funds spent on publication is directly dependent on the success of the English editions of your

writings. And this success is largely dependent on us being the *first* to publish your latest works, which means preventing any other translators from acquiring by devious means a Russian transcript of your writings, either before us or simultaneously with us [. . .] It is most important for us to have a transcript of every new work of yours, if possible three weeks before it is distributed in manuscript form in Russia' (GMT). On August 8 Tolstoy replied to Chertkov: 'There need be no doubt that all my writings will go to you before anyone else, and that you will make arrangements for their translation and publication' (*PSS*, vol. 88, p. 46).

39 Tolstoy read Taine's *Philosophie de l'art* while working on *What is Art?*, in which he quotes Taine's concept of beauty (*PSS*, vol. 30, p. 52), and conducts a polemic against him on the definition of art.

40 *Notes sur la philosophie critique* by André Spire, translated from the French by N.A. Braker, and incuding a brief biography of him by the translator, was published by the Intermediary in 1901 (YaPL).

41 On August 29, 1897 (the date of the authorised copy at the GMT) Tolstoy wrote an open letter to the Swedish newspaper *Stokholm Tagblatt* refusing the Nobel Prize. Tolstoy felt that the prize should be awarded to the Dukhobors. In October 1897 the paper published Tolstoy's letter. It was published in Russian in the journal *Svobodnaya mysl* (Free Thought), no. 4, 1899, (Geneva) (*PSS*, vol. 70, pp. 148–54). Sofia Tolstaya, in referring to Nobel as a 'kerosene merchant', was confusing the Swedish engineer Alfred Nobel with L.E. Nobel, the well-known oil magnate.

42 There is no information about this visitor.

43 Tolstoy's friends and co-thinkers, Biryukov, Tregubov, and Chertkov, were exiled for 'propaganda and illegal interference in the trial of the sectarians' and for distributing a proclamation, 'Help!', signed by them and Tolstoy, appealing for support for the Dukhobors (*PSS*, vol. 39, pp. 192–6). Chertkov was deported to England, Biryukov and Tregubov to the province of Courland.

44 See this Diary, August 31, and note 41.

45 Arthur St John, formerly an officer in the Indian Army, left the army under Tolstoy's influence and settled in a farming colony in the south of England. In September 1897 he travelled to Russia on Chertkov's instructions to give the Dukhobors some money collected by English Quakers. As he wanted to be more closely acquainted with the Dukhobors he went to the Caucasus, and there he was arrested and banished from Russia.

46 Pavel Aleksandrovich Boulanger was deported from Russia for his dealings with the Dukhobors in the Caucasus. His article about the position of these Dukhobors, based on material collected by L.A. Sulerzhitskii and F.Kh. Grauberger, was published in I.I. Yasinskii's article 'Sekta, o kotoroi govoryat' ('The sect everyone is talking about'), for the *Birzhevye vedomosti* (Stock Exchange Gazette), no. 213, August 6, 1897 (morning edition). In October 1897 Boulanger left for England.

47 She is probably referring to her story 'Pesnya bez slov' (Song without words) (GMT). It was written between 1895 and 1898, and dealt with the period after the death of her son Vanechka, when she developed her passion for music and her friendship with S.I. Taneev.

48 The monument to Nikolai Pirogov, by the sculptor V.O. Sherwood, was erected outside the clinic in his name in 1897.

49 On September 18, 1897, some Molokans visited Tolstoy from Samara begging him to use his influence to get their children returned to them. Their first visit to Tolstoy was in May that year. Tolstoy did everything in his power to help them. He wrote two letters to the Tsar and to a large number of influential people and friends. It was only in February 1898 that the children were eventually returned, thanks to the efforts of Tatiana Tolstaya, who had visited K.P. Pobedonostsev in January with that specific purpose. (See *PSS*, vol. 70, pp. 72–5, 140–1, and also T.L. Sukhotina, pp. 229–33.)

50 See this Diary for August 31, and note 41.

51 On August 12, *RV*, no. 221 carried a report from Kazan of the third All-Russian Conference of Missionaries, at which it was proposed to petition for a law which would remove sectarians' children from their parents and educate them in diocesan schools. *NV* no. 7748, September 22, refuted this report. Tolstoy then wrote a letter, on September 26, to the editors of *RV*, describing in detail all the facts he knew about the forcible removal of the Molokans' children (*PSS*, vol. 70, pp. 154–5). Tolstoy's letter was not published. See also note 49 to this Diary, September 22.

52 Tolstoy gave the Molokans who visited in May a letter he wrote on May 10 to the Tsar, as well as letters for A.K. Koni, A.V. Olsufiev, A.S. Taneev, K.O. Khis and A.A. Tolstaya, asking them to help the Molokans, and above all to forward his letter to the Tsar (*PSS*, vol. 70, pp. 76–80). The Molokans destroyed the letters for fear of reprisals. On May 18 Tolstoy again wrote to the above-mentioned people, and gave these letters to Boulanger (ibid., vol. 70, pp. 83–5). Sofia Tolstaya learnt that the case of the Molokans' children was being taken up in the Senate from Koni's letter of reply to Tolstoy of September 25 (GMT).

53 M.O. Menshikov's article 'O polovoi lyubvi' (On sexual love) (*KN*, no. 9, 1897), was part of a larger article by him entitled 'Elementy romana' (Elements of romance) (*KN*, nos 6–12, 1897).

54 Prince Leonid Dmitrievich Urusov.

55 See note 51. Tolstoy changed his mind and wrote a separate letter (*PSS*, vol. 84, p. 293), on October 6, to the editor of the *S. Peterburgskie vedomosti* (St Petersburg Gazette), which was published in no. 282 of that paper, on October 15 (*PSS*, vol 70, pp. 162–3).

56 Ludwig Nohl, *Beethovens Leben*, 1867, translated into Russian as *Betkhoven, ego zhizn i tvoreniya* (Beethoven, his life and works), 1893, 3 vols. Sofia Tolstaya referred to this book in a letter to Tolstoy of November 10, 1897: 'It is extremely interesting, it has taught me so much and given me so many new ideas. It will be so much more interesting for me now to listen to his music' (*PST*, p. 684).

57 It has not been possible to establish which work on Mendelssohn Sofia Tolstaya was reading.

58 Letter of November 8, 1897 (*PSS*, vol. 84, pp. 299–300).

59 Letter of November 11, 1897 (*PSS*, vol. 84, pp. 300–1).

60 Evidently Chekhov's story 'V rodnom uglu' (In their native village) (*RV*, no. 317, November 16, 1897). Sofia Tolstaya wrote to Tatiana Tolstaya on November 17: 'Dunaev read me the new Chekhov story' (GMT).

61 Letter of 17 or 18 November, 1897 (*PSS*, vol. 84, p. 302).

62 In 1898 Misha Tolstoy left the lycée and enlisted.

63 It has not been possible to find any information about this article.

64 Sofia Tolstaya wrote to Tolstoy on November 25: 'I thought, Lyovochka, that you would come here with Tanya, but you are evidently so loath to do so that you are delaying your visit for as long as possible. Tanya told me that you had even gone so far as to say that living in Moscow would be "suicide" for you. Since you feel you are only coming here for my sake, this is not suicide, I am killing you. So I am now hastening to write and tell you: for God's sake, don't come! This visit, which is such agony for you, will only deprive us both of our peace of mind and freedom. You will feel you are gradually being "murdered" [. . .] Let us not kill one another with demands and reproaches, let us write to one another as friends, and I shall visit you when my nerves are calmer' (*PST*, pp. 690–1). Tolstoy referred to this in his diary: 'An aggrieved letter from Sonya. I shouldn't have said it, but Tanya shouldn't have repeated it' (*PSS*, vol. 53, p. 166).

65 See this Diary, September 12, and note 47.

66 In *Sénèque le philosophe* . . ., vol. 1, Paris, 1860, pp. 83–145 (YaPL).

67 Letter of November 26 (*PSS*, vol. 84, pp. 304–6).

68 On November 28, Dushan Petrovich Makovitsky, who had set up a Slovak branch of the

Intermediary publishing house in Hungary, made a second visit to Yasnaya Polyana (the first was in August 1894). His visit was probably in connection with publishing matters. On that day Tolstoy noted in his diary: 'This morning Makovitsky came, a sweet, pure, mild man' (*PSS*, vol. 53, p. 166). On November 30 Makovitsky visited Sofia Tolstaya in Moscow and told her that Tolstoy had sent the *SV* his preface to a translated article by Edward Carpenter, 'Modern science'. A few days later, at the insistence of his wife, Tolstoy took his preface back. Two months later, however, Sofia Tolstaya gave her consent to its publication in this journal (*SV*, no. 3, 1898, pp. 199–206).

69 See this Diary, February 21, 1895.

70 Tolstoy's telegram of December 6 read: 'Wanted to go, but feel weak. Please come home at once, no cause for suffering. Reply' (*PSS*, vol. 84, p. 306).

71 Tolstoy noted, on December 7: 'Yesterday we talked and talked, and I heard something from Sonya that I have never heard before: an acknowledgment of her crime. This was a great joy [. . .] No matter what the future holds, it has happened and it is very good' (*PSS*, vol. 53, p. 169).

72 A.I. Sumbatov-Yuzhin's comedy *Dzhentlmen* (The gentleman).

73 André Beaunier, a French critic and journalist, visited Tolstoy to make his acquaintance and find out about his life and teachings, and to write about it in the pages of his newspaper *Le Temps*. He spent several days with Tolstoy, subsequently writing a series of essays under the general title 'A Week in Moscow. Near to Tolstoy', published in *Le Temps* in January 1898. On the eve of his visit to Yasnaya Polyana, Beaunier wrote to Tolstoy, on December 7, 1897: 'In France, especially amongst the young, you have a large number of admirers who not only love your literary genius, but passionately seek in your works an indication of how best to organise their lives. I too am one of these' (translated into Russian from the French, GMT). For more details of Beaunier's visit to Yasnaya Polyana see V.Ya. Lakshin's 'Vblizi Tolstogo' (Near Tolstoy) in *LN*, vol. 75, book 2, pp. 79–97.

74 Tolstoy wrote to A.L. Flekser on December 5 about his refusal to publish the preface (*PSS*, vol. 70, p. 208). According to Gurevich, this would arouse the distrust of her subscribers, who would 'attribute it to Lev Nikolaevich's dissatisfaction with the journal or its editorial board'. In a letter of December 14, Gurevich begged Sofia Tolstaya to ask Tolstoy to send the journal some other work, 'which would show that it was merely chance factors that had prevented him from sending the preface' (GMT). See also note 68 to this Diary, November 30.

75 Tolstoy's story *Hadji Murat*.

76 Tolstoy's story is recounted in greater detail in Zinger's memoirs: *Nenapisannyi rasskaz Tolstogo* (An unwritten story by Tolstoy), in *Tolstoi v vosp.* , vol. 2, pp. 143–6.

77 L. Bukh, 'Zhizn' (Life), St Petersburg, 1898 (YaPL).

78 Probably in connection with his work on the tract *What is Art?* (see *PSS*, vol. 30, chapter 10 and Appendix 1).

79 On December 10 Tolstoy sent a letter off to Aylmer Maude (*PSS*, vol. 70, pp. 217–18), and on December 20 a telegram to Chertkov (*PSS*, vol. 88, p. 69). There is no record of Maude's telegram.

80 Gurevich's letter to Tatiana Tolstaya of December 20 (GMT). See also notes 68 and 74 to this Diary, November 30 and December 14.

81 The letter is in the GMT. Tolstoy wrote in his diary on December 21: 'Received an anonymous letter yesterday threatening to kill me if I didn't mend my ways by 1898. 1898, no longer. It's both frightening and good' (*PSS*, vol. 53, p. 172).

82 Taneev went to work at the Monastery of Gethsemane, near the Troitsa-Sergievskaya Monastery (now Zagorsk), just outside Moscow.

1898

1 V.V. Stasov wrote to Alfred Lyudvigovich Boehm, on January 9, 1898: 'I too am in indescribable ecstasy over that marvellous article "What is Art?", despite the fact that I do not agree with everything in it. We had a huge argument there, in fact, about Richard Wagner (about whom Lev writes very clumsily in this article).' See *Zabytym byt ne mozhet* (He cannot be forgotten), compiled by N. Chernikov, ed. by A. Plyushch, Moscow, 1963, p. 175.

2 See this Diary, February 21, 1895.

3 See this Diary, November 30 and December 21, 1897.

4 Rimsky-Korsakov's opera *Sadko* was performed at the private Moscow opera house of S.I. Mamontov.

5 According to Stasov's eye-witness account, the engraver Vasilii Vasilevich Mathieu brought Tolstoy, as a present, an album of his engravings, amongst which were portraits of Tolstoy from paintings by Repin. (See V.V. Stasov, *Pisma k rodnym* (Letters to relatives), vol. 3, part 1, Moscow 1962, p. 202.)

6 Tolstoy's acquaintance with Rimsky-Korsakov was initiated by Stasov, who came to the première of *Sadko*.

7 Tolstoy's views on beauty are expounded in chapters 2 to 7 of *What is Art?* (*PSS*, vol. 30, pp. 32–80).

8 Tolstoy made the acquaintance of the pianist, composer and music critic Vladimir Ivanovich Pol in December 1897, and discussed art with him on two occasions. See V. Pol, 'Vstrechi s Tolstym' (Meetings with Tolstoy), in *Novy mir* (New World), no. 12, 1960, pp. 244–7.

9 In this period Tolstoy was continuing to work on his story *Hadji Murat*. On January 13, he noted in his diary: 'Still attempting to find a satisfactory form for *Hadji Murat*, and still cannot' (*PSS*, vol. 53, p. 176).

10 On February 3 Tolstoy recommended to Repin – through S.A. Stakhovich – the following subject for a painting: 'It's the moment when the Decembrists are being led out to the gallows. Young Bestuzhev-Ryumin, who is utterly besotted by Muravyov-Apostol (his personality, rather than his ideas), and has been as one with him in everything, weakens only before the gallows and weeps. Muravyov embraces him and they walk together to the gallows' (T.L. Sukhotina, p. 229). Repin did a sketch for *The Decembrists*.

11 Nikolai Dmitrievich Kashkin, ' "Sadko", an Opera-Fable in Seven Tableaux, by Rimsky-Korsakov', signed 'N. K——in' (*RV*, no. 7, January 7, 1898).

12 The 17th Annual Exhibition of the Society of Art-Lovers, at the Historical Museum.

13 Tolstoy wrote to Lyova and Dora Tolstoy, on January 20 (?), 1898: 'Our life here is bad only because of this city bustle. I often think of the solitude, and the clean snow and the sky [. . .] I simply cannot summon up the energy to work' (*PSS*, vol. 71, p. 260).

14 Alfred Dreyfus was a French officer in the General Staff, convicted of spying for Germany. The Dreyfus trial lasted from 1894 to 1906 and ended with his acquittal.

15 In January 1898 a number of newspapers reprinted from *VFP* various excerpts from the first chapters of *What is Art?* accompanied by critical comments.

16 *Sochineniya L.N. Tolstogo* (The works of L.N. Tolstoy), vols I–XVI, 10th edn, Moscow, 1897–8; vol. 1. Sofia Tolstaya set about preparing and publishing this edition in 1897, and corrected the proofs in 1898.

17 There is no information about this 'village newspaper'.

18 See this Diary, December 25, 1897.

19 The letter is from Z.S. Sokolova, from the village of Nikolskoe, Voronezh province. Tolstoy wrote a letter to the editors of *RV* on February 4, 1898, naming several other districts in which the peasants were starving and appealing for help (*PSS*, vol. 71, pp. 270–1). Tolstoy's letter was published along with Sokolova's in *RV*, no. 39, February 8, 1898.

20 Pavel Biryukov, deported in 1897 to Bauska in Latvia for his part in helping the Dukhobors (see note 43 to this Diary, 1897), received permission to go abroad in January

1898. Tolstoy evidently sent him a letter (undated) via E.I. Popov, as well as a 'photograph of some Japanese people' which he had received for Biryukov (*PSS*, vol. 71, p. 262). There is no information about the Japanese.

21 Tolstoy addressed a petition to the Tsar in the name of one of these visiting Molokans – F.I. Samoshkin – and asked Tanya Tolstaya, who was in St Petersburg at the time, to support their campaign. (See his letter to Tanya Tolstaya of January 25, and the text of the petition, *PSS*, vol. 71, pp. 263–4.) He also wrote to A.F. Koni requesting his support for the Molokans (ibid., p. 265).

22 Elizaveta Behrs' articles 'Differentsialnyi tarif' (Differential tariff), 'Arifmetika differentsialnykh tarifov' (The arithmetic of differential tariffs) and 'Velikorusskaya obshchina' (The Great-Russian community) appeared in her book *O prichinakh razoreniya zemledelcheskoi Rossii* (The causes of the collapse of agricultural Russia), St Petersburg, 1899 (YaPL).

23 To be published in *VFP*, vol. 1, 1898.

24 *Le Désastre*, a novel by the brothers Paul and Victor Margueritte, Paris, 1897. The book was sent to Tolstoy by the authors with a dedication: 'To Mr Lev Tolstoy, with respect from his admirers, Paul and Victor Margueritte' (YaPL).

25 Tanya Tolstaya went to St Petersburg to enquire about the sales of the album she had compiled, *Kartinnaya galereya 'Posrednik': 'Poslednii luch'* (The Intermediary Picture-Gallery: 'The Last Ray') by G. Breton, and other paintings by French artists, Moscow 1898. (The album contained 12 reproductions.) She had also prepared an album of German paintings which she did not manage to publish.

26 For more details about this see T.L. Sukhotina, pp. 229–33. At the end of February 1898 the Molokans' children were returned to their parents.

27 Evidently S.I. Taneev was correcting his opera *Oresteia* (1895) for a second edition (it was republished in 1900 by M.P. Belyaev), and was probably referring to his fourth string quartet, on which he began work in July 1898.

28 In *Rodnik* (The Source), nos. 1–4, 1898 (reprints of it have been kept at the Yasnaya Polyana Library).

29 See this Diary, April 22, 1891 and note 54.

30 I.N. Kramskoi's painting *Vstrecha voisk* (Meeting of the troops), 1879 (Ivanovo City Art Museum).

31 Sofia Tolstaya is relating the contents of Victor Hugo's *Les Misérables*, which Tolstoy reworked for his *Circle of Reading*. See the book *Tolstoi – Redaktor* (Tolstoy as editor), ed. by E. Zaidenschnur, Moscow, 1965, pp. 268–73.

32 *Princesse M. Ouroussoff. Histoire d'une âme. Souvenirs recueillis par sa mère*. Paris, 1904. Tolstoy probably read it in manuscript.

33 Maria Leonidovna Obolenskaya's letter is dated January 30, and Tolstoy's is dated January 31.

34 Apart from the guests mentioned by Sofia Tolstaya there were N.Ya. Trovatyi, M.F. Gulenko and L.A. Sulerzhitskii (*PSS*, vol. 53, p. 178).

35 She is referring to the notebook containing his diary jottings from October 28, 1895 to December 17, 1897 (*PSS*, vol. 53). Sofia Tolstaya was against this diary being handed over to Chertkov to be copied, as she did not want outsiders to read and copy it. Sofia Tolstaya later gave this diary, along with Tolstoy's manuscripts, to the Rumyantsev Museum for safekeeping (see note 42 to this Diary, 1887).

36 Having read Nohl's book (see this Diary, 1897, note 56), Sofia Tolstaya wrote to Tolstoy in Yasnaya Polyana, on November 19: 'Reading Beethoven's biography has opened my eyes to the fact that people who serve humanity and receive in return the highest gift – fame – become unable to resist this temptation, setting aside everything that stands in the way of this fame and hindering their service to it' (*PST*, p. 688). Tolstoy replied to his wife on November 26, 1897: 'Your view [. . .] that fame is the goal of all my activities is unjust. Fame may be the goal of a young or empty-headed man [. . .] A slightly older and wiser

man – such as I consider myself – cannot fail to see that the only blessing approved by one's conscience is to work at the thing I know best, and which I consider useful to others [. . .] I wish you too could do something like this [. . .] Merely playing the piano and going to concerts is certainly no sort of work for you' (*PSS*, vol. 84, p. 304–5).

37 J. Tissot, *La Vie de Notre Seigneur Jésus-Christ*, Tours, 1896–7.

38 In September 1882 Sofia Tolstaya read (in French) *Oeuvres complètes de Sénèque*, trans. by Y. Baillard, vol. 2, Paris, 1860–1 (YaPL, with Tolstoy's notes). Tolstoy valued Seneca as a representative of stoicism, and repeatedly referred to him in his letters and works. He included some sayings of Seneca in his *Circle of Reading* (*PSS*, vols 41–2).

39 At the time of writing his article *What is Art?* Tolstoy wrote a preface to an article by Edward Carpenter called 'Modern Science', translated by his son Seryozha. Tolstoy confessed that this article 'explained' his own 'work on art' to him (*PSS*, vol. 71, p. 274).

40 Ivan Petrovich Brashnin.

41 See this Diary, October 1878.

42 Tolstoy's article *What is Art?* was published, in Maude's translation, in three instalments as a supplement to the journal *The New Order*. The first (in January 1898) contained chapters 1–9; the second (March 1898), chapters 10–14; and the third (May 1898), chapters 15–20.

43 While working on *What is Art?* Tolstoy re-read various world classics, including the plays of Schiller. V.F. Lazurskii noted on February 13, 1898: 'At tea today he [Tolstoy] was full of this new aesthetic work of his, and said he was picking up from works of world literature examples of what he considered to be sincere art'; 'Dnevnik V.F. Lazurskogo' (The diary of V.F. Lazurskii), *LN*, vols 37–8, p. 495.

44 In this black oilcloth notebook, on pages 1–8, there was a rough draft of his article 'Gde Vykhod?' (Where is the solution?), dated by the author 'May 17, 1897, Yas. Pol.' (*PSS*, vol. 34). Further on there are sketches for the fifth edition of *Hadji Murat* (January 1898).

45 Tolstoy observed in his diary on February 19, 1898: 'Recently I have been doing nothing but revise and amplify and spoil the final chapters of "On Art" ' (*PSS*, vol. 53, p. 182).

46 Pyotr Alekseevich Sergeenko was starting a book called 'Kak zhivet i rabotaet gr. L.N. Tolstoi' (How Count L.N. Tolstoy lives and works).

47 Edward Carpenter's article 'Modern Science' was published, along with Tolstoy's introduction, in *SV*, no. 3, 1898. See also note 39.

48 The play was called *Sandra*, and was not published (GMT).

49 The house was sold by Tolstoy in the autumn of 1854. Sergeenko's book *How Count L.N. Tolstoy Lives and Works* (see note 46 (Moscow, 1898) contains photographic reproductions of this house and of several rooms, taken by the photographer P. Preobrazhenskii. Tolstoy's sketch is in the GMT, and published in *LN*, vol. 69, book 1, p. 505.

50 S.I. Taneev, *The Sunrise*, to a poem by F.I. Tyutchev, 'The East hesitantly falls silent . . .' (1865).

51 The lines are in fact from *Pushkin*'s poem, 'I wander along the noisy streets . . .' (1829).

52 Tolstoy replied to this letter on February 25, 1898 (*PSS*, vol. 71, p. 293).

53 On February 25, 1898 Tolstoy noted in his diary: 'I can't write although I can't stop thinking about "Hadji Murat" ' (*PSS*, vol. 53, p. 184).

54 See this Diary, 1897, note 45.

55 On this day Tolstoy wrote ten letters (*PSS*, vol. 71, pp. 286–96; vol. 88, p. 79), to P.I. Biryukov, his brother Sergei and S.O. Krasovskii, amongst others.

56 'Polchasa u grafa L.N. Tolstogo' (Half an hour with Count L.N. Tolstoy), *Russkii listok* (Russian Leaflet) no. 57, February 26, 1898. For Tanya Tolstaya's visit to Pobedonostsev, see this Diary, January 29, 1898. For Tolstoy's views on the Dreyfus affair see his article 'O Shekspire i o drame' (On Shakespeare and drama) (*PSS*, vol. 35, pp. 260–1).

57 Tolstoy wrote on February 28, 1898 to A.V. and A.M. Olsufiev: '[. . .] I cannot stop crying when I write and think about that dear, dear, extraordinarily dear girl, your Liza, whom I

loved with such unostentatious tenderness' (*PSS*, vol. 71, p. 297).

58 Tolstoy made revisions and corrections to the proofs of vol. 15 of *Sochineniya L.N. Tolstogo* (The works of L.N. Tolstoy) (10th edn). These were not made for the version of the article which appeared in the journal.

59 Tolstoy told Grot about this in a letter of March 3, 1898 (GMT). See note 61.

60 Taneev's note of March 7, 1898 (GMT).

61 The censors made large cuts in chapters 6 to 20 of *What is Art?*, and altered the text in a way that distorted Tolstoy's ideas. Tolstoy considered the article 'mutilated' (letter to Chertkov, March 17, 1898; *PSS*, vol. 88, p. 84). Chapters 6 to 20 were published in vol. 1 of *VFP*, 1898.

62 Tolstoy's letter to J. Gibson, a member of the Christian Commonwealth, was dated March 11, 1898 (*PSS*, vol. 71, pp. 306–10).

63 See this Diary, December 16, 1897.

64 See this Diary, April 2.

65 The Dukhobors, having received permission from the Russian government to emigrate, appealed to Tolstoy for help. On March 17 he wrote a letter to the editor of the *St Petersburg Gazette* appealing for public support for the Dukhobors, and he also wrote to E.E. Ukhtomskii, the paper's editor (*PSS*, vol. 71, pp. 314–18). The appeal was not published. Sofia Tolstaya's copy is kept amongst the rough drafts of Tolstoy's letters (*PSS*, vol. 71, p. 317).

66 After his meeting and talk with Tolstoy, M.M. Antokolskii published an article, 'Po povodu knigi grafa L.N. Tolstogo ob iskusstve' (Count L.N. Tolstoy's books on art), for the journal *Isskusstvo i khudozhestvennaya promyshlennost* (The Arts and the Art Trade), nos. 1 and 2, October–November 1898.

67 On March 30, 1898, the Dukhobors P.V. Planidin and D. Chernov visited Tolstoy to ask his advice about their planned emigration. The editor of the *St Petersburg Gazette*, E.E. Ukhtomskii, sympathised with the Dukhobors and suggested a plan for them to emigrate to Turkestan. The Dukhobors did not like the plan.

68 See *PSS*, vol. 71, pp. 345–7. The petition was not submitted. See this Diary, August 26, 27, and note 125.

69 *Sochineniya grafa L.N. Tolstogo* (Works of Count L.N. Tolstoy), vol. 15, 1st edn, 1898. A notice about the book's publication appeared in *RV*, no. 94, April 5, 1898.

70 It seems that at the paper's editorial office Tolstoy was handed some donations in aid of the emigrating Dukhobors. See this Diary, April 7, and note 73.

71 See this Diary, April 20, and note 80.

72 Letter from M.O. Menshikov, April 6, 1898 (GMT).

73 *RV*, no. 93, April 4, 1898 contained an announcement about the donations received for the Dukhobors. On the orders of the police-chief, Trepov, the collection was stopped. On April 21, 1898 the paper was closed down for two months.

74 Her story 'Pesnya bez slov' (Song without words) (GMT).

75 Koni read his lecture on the poet Odoevskii at the Historical Museum. See *RV*, no. 100, April 13, 1898.

76 The 26th exhibition of paintings by the Fellowship of Wandering Artists.

77 The sixth exhibition of paintings by the St Petersburg Society of Artists. G.I. Semiradskii's painting *Neron i Khristianskaya Tsirtseya* (Nero and Circe the Christian).

78 At Taneev's suggestion, Seryozha Tolstoy was translating from the English Ebenezer Prout's book *Musical Form*, Moscow–Leipzig, 1900 (YaPL). (See S.L. Tolstoy, p. 383.)

79 After the division of the property between Sofia Tolstaya and the children in 1891, the Tolstoys' Moscow house belonged to Lyova Tolstoy. See this Diary, April 22, 1891.

80 At the end of March or the beginning of April 1898, Tolstoy received from the publishers of the journals *La Vita internazionale* (Milan) and *L'Humanité nouvelle* (Paris) a questionnaire on his attitude to war and militarism. In reply Tolstoy started writing an article, which he

entitled 'Carthago delenda est', and which he finished on April 23, 1898. It was translated into Italian and published in *La Vita internazionale*, September 20, 1898.

81 This is probably a reference to an article by I.S. Listovskii, 'Biografiya grafa P.V. Zavadovskogo' (A biography of Count P.V. Zavadovskii), in vol. 2, 1883.

82 A plaster copy of Trubetskoi's bust of Tolstoy is at the GMT.

83 Tolstoy stayed in Grinevka from April 24 to May 27. His son Ilya, who accompanied him on his trips around the region, later wrote that when making these enquiries, 'Father almost always did the hardest work himself – that is, finding out how many mouths there were to feed in each peasant family. He often used to travel round the villages for days at a time, often until late at night' (I.L. Tolstoy, p. 226). In all twenty canteens were opened. Tolstoy wrote about his work helping the starving in 1898, in his article 'Golod ili ne golod?' (Famine or no famine?) (*PSS*, vol. 29).

84 On April 27, 1898, the day of his wife's departure, Tolstoy noted in his diary: 'I am happy. Slightly unwell. Sonya left this morning – sad and distraught. It is very hard for her. And I am very sorry for her and cannot help her' (*PSS*, vol. 53, p. 191).

85 Sonya Tolstaya's letter, April 29, 1898 (GMT).

86 Letters of April 29, 30 and May 1, 1898 (*PSS*, vol. 84, pp. 308–11).

87 Letter of May 3, 1898 (*PSS*, vol. 84, pp. 311–12).

88 Letter of May 9, 1898 (*PST*, pp. 701–2).

89 Tolstoy asked for an assistant in a letter of May 6, 1898 (*PSS*, vol. 84, p. 315), and E.P. Muravskaya, a mathematics student, arrived at Grinevka.

90 Chertkov's letter of May 2, 1898. It contains no mention of Shkarvan in it.

91 Chertkov begged Tanya Sukhotina for a loan in two letters to her from England, dated May 8 and 9 (GMT). On July 14 Tolstoy informed Anna Konstantinovna Chertkova (Chertkov's wife) that his son Lyova Tolstoy had agreed to loan Chertkov the required sum (*PSS*, vol. 88, pp. 108–9).

92 Weber's opera *Der Freischütz*.

93 In April 1898 A.N. Trubnikov, the governor of Oryol, gave Ilya Tolstoy permission to open one canteen for needy peasants. At the same time he sent the Mtsensk district police-officer a secret instruction to keep the canteen under surveillance. In his reports the police-officer, A.A. Ivanov, kept Trubnikov informed of Ilya and Lev Nikolaevich Tolstoy's activities in helping the peasants, and wrote that the landowners were worried about this and confirmed that there was no famine in these areas. See *Novy mir* (New World), no. 7, 1956, pp. 275–6. On May 19, 1898 Trubnikov sent a letter to Ilya Tolstoy with a request not to open any more canteens (*PSS*, vol. 84, pp. 319–20. See also I.L. Tolstoy, pp. 224–7).

94 See this Diary, June 26.

95 Sofia Tolstaya wrote on May 20, 1898: 'Dearest Lyovochka, I think constantly about your health, and it is agony for me not to know anything about you [. . .] How is your work with the canteens? [. . .] After staying with you for a while I have become so involved in all your interests' (GMT).

96 Sofia Tolstaya was probably reading A.M. Kalmykova's book *Grecheskii uchitel Sokrat* (Socrates the Greek teacher), Moscow, Intermediary, 1886 (YaPL). (2nd edn, 1891.) In 1885 the book was edited by Tolstoy and Chapter 7 was entirely written by him (*PSS*, vol. 25, pp. 429–61).

97 On May 27, 1898, Tolstoy and Ilya's wife Sonya left Grinevka for the district of Efremov, to examine the crops. On this day Tolstoy wrote to his wife: 'I have decided that it is necessary to do this in order to dispose of the money I receive in the best possible way' (*PSS*, vol. 84, p. 323). He fell ill with dysentery on the way, and was forced to stay with a landowner of his acquaintance, P.I. Levitskii, at his estate in Alekseevskoe. Sofia Tolstaya was sent two telegrams from there on May 30 (*PSS*, vol. 84, p. 323).

98 S.I. Taneev stayed at Yasnaya Polyana in the summers of 1895 and 1896.

99 Tolstoy wrote to Sergei and Ilya Tolstoy, on June 7 (10?) 1898: 'Please continue the work as

it was started and extend it if this is genuinely needed. I can send another 30 rubles [. . .] Please, Ilyusha, send me an accurate estimate of how much more money is needed, so that the newspapers can be informed' (*PSS*, vol. 71, p. 376).

100 *NV*, nos. 7996, 8002 and 8009, June 3, 9 and 16, 1898. Tolstoy considered the story 'stupid and untalented' (*PSS*, vol.53, p. 199).

101 The French philologist and psychologist Charles Richet visited Yasnaya Polyana on August 20, 1891.

102 Concerning this episode Tolstoy wrote a 'Letter to the editor' (*PSS*, vol. 90, p. 138).

103 The 9th edn of Tolstoy's works, vols 1–13, Moscow 1893. In 1898 Sofia Tolstaya published an additional volume (vol. 14, not 15) to this edition. This contained works written between 1897 and 1898, not in any strict chronological sequence.

104 On this day Tolstoy noted in his diary: 'I fell seriously ill on the 16th. I have never felt so weak and close to death. I feel ashamed to exploit the attention everyone here lavishes on me. I can do nothing' (*PSS*, vol. 53, p. 199).

105 As a result of this court case the land remained with the Tolstoys (*PST*, p. 683).

106 Letter unknown.

107 The exact text of Tolstoy's entry in his notebook, in April 1898, was: 'A woman can only be liberated if she is a Christian. A liberated woman who is not a Christian is a wild beast' (*PSS*, vol. 53, p. 331).

108 See note 42.

109 Rafael Loewenfeld was working on the 2nd edn (not the 2nd volume) of a book entitled *Lev N. Tolstoi, ego zhizn, proizvedeniya, mirosozertsanie* (Lev Tolstoy: his life, works and world view), Berlin, 1892. In a letter to Sofia Tolstaya of June 11, 1898, he wrote: 'I should like to make use of your help and that of the censors' (GMT).

110 Probably a reference to *Sandra*, the play which Tanya Tolstaya wrote with Sergeenko.

111 In *Rus* (Holy Russia), nos 4 and 5, July 2 and 3, 1898 (see note 83).

112 See Tolstoy's letter to Chertkov (*PSS*, vol. 88, pp. 109–10), and his diary for July 17, 1898 (*PSS*, vol. 53, p. 203).

113 In June 1898 Tolstoy resumed work on his story *Otets Sergii* (Father Sergii), which he had started in 1890, but after returning to Yasnaya Polyana he did no work on it and it was not published in his lifetime (*PSS*, vol. 31).

114 Tolstoy had intended to publish three works which were still unfinished and needed to be revised: *Father Sergii*, 'The Devil', and *Resurrection*. But he then concentrated all his attention on *Resurrection*, on which he worked until the end of 1899.

115 Two Dukhobors, P.V. Planidin and S.Z. Postnikov, who arrived at Yasnaya Polyana on August 3, had no passports and were hiding from the authorities.

116 The article was 'Dve voiny' (Two wars) (*PSS*, vol. 31). It was first published in England by V.G. Chertkov in the journal *Listki svobodnogo slova* (Leaflets of the Free Word), no. 1, 1898.

117 This refers to vol. XIV of the 9th edition of Tolstoy's works. See this Diary, June 21. The book came out in 1898.

118 See this Diary, December 19.

119 R.V. Loewenfeld, who stayed in Yasnaya Polyana on July 1 and 2, 1898 (see note 109), sent Sofia Tolstaya his article about the visit. On August 25, 1898, he wrote to her: 'I beg you to read this and delete whatever you feel you need to' (GMT). It was published in Russian as 'U grafa Tolstogo' (At Count Tolstoy's), in *RV*, no. 244, September 10, 1898.

120 At the beginning of August 1898 Tolstoy sent letters to five wealthy Muscovites, L.I. Brodskii, V.A. Morozova, S.T. Morozov, A.M. Sibiryakov and K.T. Soldatenkov, asking them to contribute to the Dukhobors' emigration fund (*PSS*, vol. 71, pp. 417–24).

121 Tolstoy wrote short stories on these subjects – 'Zapiski materi' (Notes of a mother) (*PSS*, vol. 29), started in 1891; 'Falshivyi kupon' (The forged coupon) (*PSS*, vol. 36), started in the 1880s; and 'Posmertnye zapiski startsa Fyodora Kuzmicha' (The posthumous notes of old Fyodor Kuzmich) (*PSS*, vol. 36), started in 1905. All these stories remained unfinished.

122 The New York paper *The Sunday World* sent Tolstoy a telegram on August 19, 1898 in connection with the Russian government's appeal to the other powers to meet for a peace conference at The Hague. Tolstoy replied on August 20–22 (?) (*PSS*, vol. 71, p. 210).

123 His name is not known. On that day Tolstoy wrote in his diary: 'The Bavarian talked about their life over there. It boasts a great degree of freedom but they also have compulsory religious instruction of a crude Catholic variety. This is the most ghastly despotism' (*PSS*, vol. 53, p. 210).

124 V.G. Chertkov was a member of a committee formed by English Quakers in London to help the Dukhobors. At Tolstoy's suggestion two Dukhobors, N.S. Zibarov and I.P. Obrosimov, visited Chertkov in England on August 29, 1898 to clarify the terms of the emigration to Canada and work out how much the journey would cost.

125 See Tolstoy's letter to the Dukhobors of August 27, 1898 (*PSS*, vol. 71, pp. 433–4). He promised in this letter to do all he could to submit to the Tsar the petition he had written earlier (see this Diary, April 2, and note 68).

126 The first completed edition (1899) of the novel ended with Nekhlyudov's marriage to Katyusha and their departure to London (*PSS*, vol. 33, pp. 93–4).

127 The article was published in *Rus* (Holy Russia), nos 4 and 5, July 2 and 3, 1898, after which the editors were given a preliminary warning by the Minister of Internal Affairs.

128 See this Diary, August 24.

129 Sofia Tolstaya's letter of August 27, 1898 (GMT).

130 Tolstoy gave his son a detailed list of instructions to give to Chertkov (*PSS*, vol. 88, pp. 120–1). Besides this Sergei Tolstoy had to find out how much money could be got for published translations of *Resurrection* (*PSS*, vol. 71, p. 439).

131 See this Diary, September 19, 1891.

132 For his subsequent negotiations with A.F. Marx see this Diary, October 6, and note 140.

133 D.E. Troitskii.

134 On August 6 and 7 Tolstoy read *Resurrection* to friends and relatives at Yasnaya Polyana.

135 Maria Nikolaevna's letter of September 17, 1898 (GMT).

136 See this Diary, January 8, 1899.

137 After being refused permission to inspect Tula prison Tolstoy travelled to Oryol, where he was allowed to visit the prison after M.A. Stakhovich ahd interceded for him (Gusev, p. 88).

138 Probably the editor of the Paris weekly *Le Monde illustré*, with his wife. Tolstoy consulted them about payment for the French translation of *Resurrection*. (See Tolstoy's letter to Chertkov, *PSS*, vol. 88, p. 130.)

139 Leonid Osipovich Pasternak spent several days at Yasnaya Polyana. He later recalled that he did not want simply to 'illustrate certain passages [. . .] but to do a powerful artistic rendering of the Russian life Tolstoy was describing in his portraits of various layers of society'. See L.O. Pasternak, *Zapiski raznykh let* (A record of several years), Moscow, 1975, p. 194. The novel was published in the French paper *Echo de Paris* in 1899.

140 It was Marx's deputy, Yu.U. Grunberg, who visited Yasnaya Polyana. The final agreement of the contract was postponed at Tolstoy's request. On October 12, 1898 he wrote to Marx that he was willing to give his novel to *Niva* (The Cornfield) with royalties of 1,000 rubles per quire, with an advance of 12,000 rubles, not 20,000, as he had previously asked for (*PSS*, vol. 71, pp. 466–7).

141 The story was published in *RM*, vol. 13, 1898.

142 Letter of October 19, 1898 (*PSS*, vol. 84, p. 329).

143 Letter of October 21, 1898 (*PST*, pp. 711–12).

144 Lev Lvovich Tolstoy's letter from Yasnaya Polyana, undated (GMT). Tolstoy was working on *Resurrection*.

145 Sergei Tolstoy tried to persuade his mother to renounce the right to the royalties on all Tolstoy's works written before 1881, and to allow them to be published for nothing. For Tolstoy's renunciation of the copyright see this Diary, September 19, 1891.

146 P.A. Sergeenko, 'Dezi' (Daisy), Moscow, 1899.
147 S. Maksimov, *Sibir i katorga* (Siberia and hard labour), St Petersburg, 1891, in 3 vols (YaPL).
148 M.L. Obolenskaya's letter of October 29, 1898 (GMT), and Tolstoy's of October 30, 1898 (*PSS*, vol. 84, pp. 330–1).
149 Tatiana Tolstaya sent an extract from the unfinished story 'History of a Mother' (*PSS*, vol. 29, pp. 251–9, under the title 'Mother'). On November 3, 1898 she wrote: 'Dearest Maman [. . .] We spent the whole evening copying out this excerpt I am sending you for the "Tolstoy Evening" [. . .] Papa wants Vladimir Nemirovich-Danchenko to read it – he heard him read once and liked it' (GMT). Nemirovich-Danchenko agreed to read it on December 19, 1898 at the concert at the Korsh Theatre.
150 S.I. Taneev, 'My restless heart is beating . . .', a song to words by N.A. Nekrasov.
151 Letter of November 2, 1898 (*PSS*, vol. 84, pp. 333–4).
152 The play was performed on the stage of the Moscow Public Art Theatre.
153 D.A. Khomyakov, 'Graf L.N. Tolstoi. Predislovie k rasskazam Mopassana' (Count L.N. Tolstoy. His preface to the stories of Maupassant), no. 11, 1898.
154 'Ostrov Sakhalin' (The Island of Sakhalin), *RM*, nos. 10–12, 1893; nos 2–7, 1894.
155 The director of the Katkovskii lycée was L.A. Georgievskii.
156 A reference to an excerpt from Tolstoy's 'Vstuplenie k istorii materi' (Introduction to the story of a mother). See this Diary, November 6 and note 149. For more detail see I.A. Pokrovskii, 'Sudba dvukh proizvedenii' (The fate of two works), in *Oktyabr* (October), no. 2, 1978.
157 See this Diary, February 17 and note 46.
158 Letter of November 17, 1898 (*PSS*, vol. 84, pp. 334–5).
159 Letter of November 18, 1898 (*PSS*, vol. 84, pp. 335–6).
160 Letter of November 19, 1898 (*PST*, pp. 717–8).
161 On November 25, 1898 the Private Moscow Opera House staged the première of Rimsky-Korsakov's opera *Mozart and Salieri*. The part of Salieri was sung by Chaliapin. Gluck's *Orpheus and Eurydice* was performed on the same night.
162 Letter of November 25, 1898 (*PSS*, vol. 84, p. 337).
163 Sofia Tolstaya's letter to Tatiana Tolstaya of November 23, 1898 (GMT).
164 Taneev's 'From land to land, from town to town'. For two choirs for mixed voices, set to words by F.I. Tyutchev (1899).
165 Letter of November 27, 1898 (*PSS*, vol. 84, p. 338).
166 Tolstoy's telegram of December 1, 1898 to Sofia Nikolaevna Tolstaya (Ilya's wife) (*PSS*, vol. 71, p. 496).
167 Letter of December 1, 1898 (*PSS*, vol. 84, pp. 338–9).
168 D. Chernov was sent by Seryozha Tolstoy. Tolstoy produced his reasons against settling in Arkansas in a letter to Seryozha of December 5, 1898 (*PSS*, vol. 71, pp. 498–9).
169 See this Diary, April 29.
170 E.K. Gureli was not fatally wounded, and died in 1900.
171 C. Fielding, *The Soul of a People*. The American writer Ernest Crosby sent Tolstoy this book in November 1898. It was later translated into Russian on Tolstoy's initiative, and published as *Dusha odnogo naroda. Rasskaz angliiskogo ofitsera Fildinga o zhizni ego v Birme* (The soul of a people. The story of the English officer Fielding and his life in Burma), Moscow, Intermediary edn, 1902. The Yasnaya Polyana Library contains a copy with the dedication: 'To dear Lev Nikolaevich Tolstoy, from his grateful and devoted translator, April 13, 1902, Moscow, P. Boulanger.'
172 Seryozha Tolstoy's letter and telegram are unknown. For more details see L.A. Sulerzhitskii, *V Ameriku s Dukhoborami* (To America with the Dukhobors), Moscow, Intermediary edn, 1905 and S.L. Tolstoy, pp. 184–203.

1899

1 Letter to Seryozha Tolstoy of January 5, 1899 (GMT).
2 M.O. Menshikov, 'Nachalo zhizni. Deti' (The origins of life. Children), *KN*, no. 2, 1898.
3 Andrei Tolstoy married Olga Konstantinovna Dieterichs. Tolstoy referred to them on January 12, 1899 in a letter to A.K. and V.G. Chertkov: 'I saw the young people on their wedding-day. God be with them. They were both sweet, especially Olga' (*PSS*, vol. 88, p. 150).
4 H. Sudermann, *Das Glück im Winkel*, 1896, translated from the German by I. Vladimirov, Moscow, 1898.
5 Ten of Tolstoy's letters of January 12 have been kept (*PSS*, vol. 72, pp. 17–34, 149–50). Tolstoy was at the time revising his reply to M.P. Shalaginov's letter of December 18, 1898, asking whether Christianity was compatible with war (*PSS*, vol. 72, pp. 37–42). The final version of this letter was published as an article under the title 'Pismo k feldfebelyu' (Letter to a sergeant-major) (*PSS*, vol. 90). Tolstoy was also busy editing his reply to the Group of Swedish Intellectuals (*PSS*, vol. 72, pp. 9–17). The final version of this was also published as an article, under the title 'Po povodu Kongressa o mire. Pismo Shvedam' (Regarding the Peace Congress. A letter to the Swedes) (*PSS*, vol. 90, pp. 60–6).
6 A.P. Chekhov's story 'Dushechka' (Darling), in the journal *Semya* (Family), no. 1, 1899. 'It's a pearl, a genuine pearl of art,' said Tolstoy when he had read it. (See Sergeenko, pp. 227–8.) 'Darling', edited by Tolstoy (*PSS*, vol. 42, p. 610) and with an afterword by him, was included in the *Circle of Reading* (*PSS*, vol. 41). The second story, 'Po delam sluzhby' (On matters of service), was in *KN*, no. 1, 1899.
7 Maria Yakovlevna Shanks and Natalya Aleksandrovna Jenkin.
8 'We discussed my stay in the monastery,' wrote Taneev in his diary on January 15, 1899 (manuscript at the Tchaikovsky House Museum). Taneev often went to work at a monastic retreat near the Troitsa-Sergievskaya Monastery, just outside Moscow.
9 N.N. Myasoedov (see *DST*, II, p. 273).
10 I.M. Vinogradov, inspector of the Butyrki convict prison in Moscow, was invited by Tolstoy to look over the proofs of *Resurrection* for him. Tolstoy noted down his observations and made use of them in his subsequent work on the novel. See also I.M. Vinogradov, 'K istorii sozdaniya "Voskreseniya" ', *Tolstoi i o Tolstom* ('An account of how "Resurrection" was written' in *Tolstoy and about Tolstoy*), 3rd edn, Moscow, 1927, pp. 48–53.
11 The 18th annual art exhibition of the Moscow Society of Art-Lovers.
12 The Belgian art exhibition opened in Moscow on January 10, 1899 in the Stroganovskii Educational Institute.
13 Andryusha and Olga's letter to Sofia Tolstaya was dated January 19, 1899 (GMT).
14 Chekhov's play *The Seagull* was performed at the Moscow Public Art Theatre (now the Moscow Arts Theatre).
15 Sofia Tolstaya sent Marx a text of the epigraphs, along with a letter, on January 27, 1899; *Sbornik Pushkinskogo doma na 1923 god* (Pushkin House Anthology for 1923), Petrograd, 1922, p. 305.
16 While he was working on *Resurrection*, Tolstoy repeatedly appealed to his old friend, the lawyer Vasilii Alekseevich Maklakov, for information. See 'Zapiski P.A. Sergeenko' (Notes of P.A. Sergeenko), *LN*, vol. 37–8, p. 539, and Maklakov's letter to Tolstoy of September 15, 1898 (*GM*, no 4–6, 1918, p. 295).
17 Sergei Tolstoy's song 'We met again . . .' was set to words by A.A. Fet; Tolstoy considered it 'sincere' (S.L. Tolstoy, p. 416).
18 See Tolstoy's letter to K.T. Soldatenkov of August 5, 1898 (*PSS*, vol. 71, pp. 423–4).
19 Chapters 17–20 of the tract 'What Then Must We Do?' (*PSS*, vol. 25, pp. 247–81), were published separately under the title 'Dengi' (Money), Geneva, Elpidine edn, 1890.
20 Letter to P.I. Tchaikovsky of December 19–21, 1876 (*PSS*, vol. 62, p. 297).
21 'Famine or No Famine?' (See this Diary, April 29, 1898, and note 83.)

22 The first symphonic meeting of the Moscow branch of the Russian Musical Society, under the conductorship of Rubinstein, took place on November 22, 1860.
23 See Tolstoy's letter to Savva Morozov of August 5, 1898 (*PSS*, vol. 71, pp. 420–1).
24 See this Diary, February 7–27.
25 Sofia Tolstaya was probably reading the memoirs in manuscript. They were published later: V. Mikulich, *Vstrecha s znamenitostyu* (A meeting with a celebrity), Moscow, Intermediary, 1903.
26 *Izobrazheniya iz sv. Evangeliya i Psaltyrya v svobodnykh podrazheniyakh drevneishim istochnikam* (Illustrations to the Holy Gospels and Psalter, in free imitations of the ancient sources), St Petersburg, 1884.
27 Sofia Tolstaya left for Kiev on February 8, 1899. In reply to a letter from his wife informing him of Tatiana Kuzminskaya's almost hopeless condition, Tolstoy wrote, on February 11–12: 'I know that we all die and that there's nothing bad about death, but it is still very painful. I love her very much' (*PST*, pp. 723–4; *PSS*, vol. 84, p. 340).
28 The musical evening at the Tolstoy house took place on February 7, 1899. 'Lev Nikolaevich, as always, took a lively interest in the musicians.' See *Dnevnik V.F. Lazurskogo* (Diary of V.F. Lazurskii) (*LN*, vol. 37–8, p. 496).
29 Sergei Tolstoy's letter to Sofia Tolstaya of January 26–February 7, 1899 (GMT).
30 Eduard Sinet, an artist who had refused military service on religious grounds. He was in correspondence with Tolstoy throughout 1899 and 1900. 'An interesting and lively Frenchman called Sinet is staying here. He's the first religious Frenchman I've met,' Tolstoy wrote in his diary on February 21, 1899 (*PSS*, vol. 53, p. 219).
31 Trubetskoi did several sculptures of Tolstoy on horseback. The Tolstoy Museum contains a bronze sculpture (1904) and a bust (plaster covered in bronze 1900) by Trubetskoi, which Sofia Tolstaya considered the best of all his sculptures (*MZh*, 1899).
32 In a letter to A.S. Prugavin of March 10, 1899 Tolstoy refers only to Yu.M. Komarova, who subsequently also worked on the famine in the Samara province (*PSS*, vol. 72, p. 91).
33 Tolstoy informed Chertkov about this money in a letter of March 2–9, 1899 (*PSS*, vol. 88, pp. 159, 160–1). A party of Dukhobors, who had earlier emigrated to the island of Cyprus, set off for Canada in May 1899.
34 Sergei Tolstoy returned to Moscow on April 4, 1899.
35 The note which Tolstoy referred to in his letter to his wife of May 19, 1899, was evidently destroyed (*PSS*, vol. 84, pp. 285–8). See also Tolstoy's diary, May 16–17, 1899 (*PSS*, vol. 53, pp. 145–7).
36 Tatiana Tolstaya's letter to Sofia Tolstaya of October 1899 (GMT).
37 The artist N.E. Sverchkov presented Tolstoy with his water-colour paintings *Kholstomer in His Youth* and *Kholstomer in Old Age* (1887) (GMT). The whereabouts of Sofia Tolstaya's copies are unknown.
38 See this Diary, 1897, note 47.

1900

1 Tolstoy worked on his play *Zhivoi trup* (The living corpse). (originally titled *Trup* (The corpse)) from the beginning of January to November 1900. The play remained unfinished and was not published in Tolstoy's lifetime (*PSS*, vol. 34).
2 Pavel Aleksandrovich Boulanger had had the idea of publishing a weekly, illustrated, literary-political and scientific journal called *Utro* (Morning). When they heard about Tolstoy's proposed participation in the scheme, the Chief Department for Press Affairs forbade the journal to be published. See: 'Sudba ezhenedelnika *Utro*' (The fate of the weekly *Morning*), *GM*, nos 4–6, 1918, pp. 300–3.
3 A.N. Koreshchenko's opera *Ledyanoi dom* (The ice house), libretto by Modest Tchaikovsky after the novel by I.I. Lazhechnikov, was performed in 1900 in the Bolshoi Theatre.

4 See A.B. Goldenweiser, *Vblizi Tolstogo* (Near Tolstoy), Moscow, 1959, pp. 77–8 (note for November 9, 1900).
5 See this Diary, October 16, 1891, and note 104.
6 From January 1900 to February 1902 Sofia Tolstaya was a guardian at an orphanage.
7 See Goldenweiser, *Vblizi Tolstogo*, p. 78 (note for November 10, 1900).
8 A reference to the biblical Martha, entirely consumed by everyday cares (Luke 10: 40–2).
9 On November 12, 1900 Tolstoy set out in his diary his understanding of Confucius' 'Teachings of the middle way' (*PSS*, vol. 54, pp. 57–62).
10 On November 19, 1900 Tolstoy was visited by a Dutchman called Engelberg, who had an administrative post on the island of Java, and arrived with his friend, whose name has not been ascertained. They visited Tolstoy once again on December 5. 'I liked Engelberg very much,' Tolstoy wrote to Biryukov on December 6, 1900 (*PSS*, vol. 72, p. 509). For more details about Engelberg and his meeting with Tolstoy see *PSS*, vol. 72, p. 507.
11 S.I. Taneev. Two choral works and a 'capella' for four mixed voices. No. 1, 'Zvezdy' (Stars), 'V chas polnochnyi' (At the midnight hour), words by A.S. Khomyakov; no. 2, 'Alpy' (Alps), 'Skvoz lazurnyi sumrak nochi' (Through the azure gloom of night), words by F.I. Tyutchev.
12 Probably a reference to a musical evening at Professor S.S. Korsakov's psychiatric clinic.
13 The children's home of which Sofia Tolstaya was a guardian was supported by charity, and she wanted to organise a literary musical evening to raise money for it. See this Diary, March 26, 1901.
14 On November 27, 1900 Tolstoy read the manuscript of M.P. Novikov's article 'Golos krestyanina' (Voice of a peasant) and wrote in his diary: '[. . .] it made a strong impression on me. I remembered things I had forgotten – the peasants' lives, their poverty and degradation, our sins' (*PSS*, vol. 54, p. 65). The article was published anonymously abroad in *SS*, no. 86, 1904.
15 From 1900 to 1908 Sergei Tolstoy served on Moscow City *Duma*.
16 See this Diary, November 20 and note 9.
17 A.N. Bodyanskii, who was living with the Dukhobors in Canada, wrote to Tolstoy telling him that several of the Dukhobors' wives wished to return to Russia, to the Yakutsk region. On December 7 Tolstoy appealed to the Tsar to allow them to do so, enclosing Bodyanskii's letter in his own (*PSS*, vol. 72, pp. 514–20). See also notes in Tolstoy's diary for December 8 to 15 (*PSS*, vol. 54, pp. 69, 71) and Tolstoy's letter to Bodyanskii of December 6 (*PSS*, vol. 72, p. 510).
18 Tolstoy contributed an excerpt from an unfinished story called 'Kto prav?' (Who is right?) (*PSS*, vol. 29, pp. 264–7). See this Diary, March 26, 1901.

901

1 Lyova Tolstoy's letter to Sofia Tolstaya of December 24, 1900 (GMT).
2 Tatiana Sukhotina's letter to Sofia Tolstaya of December 27, 1900, sent from Kochety to Yasnaya Polyana (GMT).
3 Nikolai Nikolaevich Chernogubov, who was 'collecting and reworking material for a biography' of A.A. Fet, asked Sofia Tolstaya in a letter of June 7, 1900 whether he could look at Fet's letters to her and to Tolstoy (GMT). See this Diary, June 6.
4 Letter of January 8, 1901 (*Stasov*, p. 256).
5 Sofia Tolstaya was accidentally mixing up two comedies, *Zarazhyonnoe semeistvo* (The infected family) (1863–4) and *Nigilist* (The nihilist) (1866). She evidently took from the Rumyantsev Museum the first extant manuscript of *The Nihilist*, on the cover of which was written, in her hand: 'A continuation of the comedy "The Nihilist".' See *Opisanie rukopisei khudozhestvennykh proizvedenii L.N. Tolstogo* (Catalogue of manuscripts of L.N. Tolstoy's artistic works), no. 1, Moscow, 1955, p. 92.
6 V.M.Doroshevich, 'Za den' (In a day), *Rossia* (Russia), no. 608, January 4, 1901.

7 According to Tatiana Sukhotina's memoirs, Tolstoy saw Labiche's play in the Maly Theatre. 'During the interval he met a certain professor he knew in the foyer [. . .] "So you too have come to watch this rubbish, Lev Nikolaevich," he said with a sneer. "I have always dreamed of writing something like this," said Father. "But I don't have the talent" ' (T.L. Sukhotina, p. 441).

8 The twentieth annual exhibition of paintings of the Moscow Society of Art-Lovers.

9 According to V.F. Lazurskii, Tolstoy found Jan Styka's panorama 'interesting, although the faces are banal' (*Dnevnik V.F. Lazurskogo* (Diary of V.F. Lazurskii), *LN*, vol. 37–8, p. 501.

10 This extract from Tolstoy's story, which was selected to be read aloud at the concert, was submitted beforehand to the censors, as the authorities feared that Tolstoy would be noisily applauded. 'Police-chief Trepov,' she wrote, 'questioned me as to whether I could pacify the public if there was noise and disorder' (*MZh*, 1901). See this Diary, March 26.

11 Sofia Tolstaya's letter of December 7, 1864 (*PST*, pp. 49–51).

12 Sofia Tolstaya's letter of January 21, 1901, in *Stasov*, pp. 257–8.

13 Masha Obolenskaya's letter to Tolstoy of January 26, 1901 (GMT). For Tolstoy's letters to her of the end of January and February 15, see *PSS*, vol 73, pp. 30, 35. See also this Diary, February 12.

14 See this Diary, November 30, 1900, and note 14.

15 See this Diary, March 26.

16 I.I. Yanzhul visited Tolstoy on February 10. The following day Tolstoy observed in his diary: 'I asked him his thoughts on death, whether he believed in the process of destruction or not. He does not understand' (*PSS*, vol. 54, p. 89). See also Yanzhul's article 'Strakh smerti: razgovor s L.N. Tolstym' (The fear of death: a conversation with L.N. Tolstoy), in *Russkaya starina* (Russian antiquity), no. 12, 1910, pp. xv–xvi.

17 G. Ohnet, *La Ténébreuse*, Paris, 1901 (YaPL).

18 On February 24, 1901, issue no. 8 of the *Tserkovnye vedomosti* (Church Gazette) published an announcement from the Holy Synod about Tolstoy, dated February 20–2, which said: 'The Church does not consider him a member as long as he does not repent and does not restore his links with it.' On February 25 this document appeared in the newspapers. This was Tolstoy's official excommunication from the Church. The newspaper cutting is pasted into the diary.

19 On February 26, 1901 Sofia Tolstaya sent a letter to the chief procurator of the Synod, K.P. Pobedonostsev, and to the metropolitans who had signed the excommunication. Learning of its contents, Tolstoy said, 'There have been so many books written on the subject that you couldn't even fit them into this house – and you want to teach them what to do with your letter' (*MZh*, 1901). Sofia Tolstaya's letter was printed on March 24, 1901 in a supplement to no. 17 of the unofficial part of the *Church Gazette*, along with Metropolitan Antonii's reply of March 16, 1901. Sofia Tolstaya pasted a cutting of this letter into her diary, with her own comments in the margin. '[. . .] There are no limits to my sad indignation,' she wrote, 'And not because my husband will be spiritually destroyed by this document: this is not men's business, it is God's. The religious life of a human soul is known to none but God, and mercifully it is not answerable to anyone. But as for the Church to which I belong and which I shall never renounce, which was created by Christ to bless in God's name all the significant moments of life – births, weddings, deaths, human joys and griefs – from the point of view of this Church, then, the Synod's instructions are utterly incomprehensible to me. It provokes not sympathy (save from the *Moscow Gazette*), but anger, and great love and compassion for Lev Nikolaevich. We are already receiving expressions of this – and there will be no end to them – from all over the world.'

20 183 students were drafted into the army for participating in the student uprisings that took place in Kiev University in January 1901. This provoked students in St Petersburg and elsewhere to come out in support of them. On February 25 there was a demonstration of students and workers in Moscow.

1 Sofia Tolstaya's letter was published only in the foreign newspapers. It was distributed in Russia only in hectographed form, as the Moscow censorship committee had been sent a circular forbidding them to publish telegrams and other material 'expressing sympathy' with Tolstoy.

2 Tolstoy's proclamation 'To the Tsar and His Assistants' (*PSS*, vol. 34) was a response to the government's persecution of students who had taken part in the demonstrations (see note 20). It was sent to the Tsar, with a letter addressed to him, on March 26, 1901 (*PSS*, vol. 73, p. 55), and was also sent to the Grand Dukes and all the Ministers.

3 The concert took place on March 17, 1901. The programme of the concert has been sewn into the Diary.

4 Metropolitan Antonii wrote to Sofia Tolstaya on March 16, 1901: '[. . .] It is not the Synod which has acted cruelly, in announcing your husband's lapse from the Church, it is he himself who has acted cruelly in renouncing his faith in Jesus Christ, son of the living God, our saviour and expiator. This renunciation should have provoked your grief and anger long ago. And your husband will not of course perish from a scrap of printed paper, but from the fact that he has turned aside from the source of life eternal [. . .] You receive expressions of sympathy from the entire world. This does not surprise me, but I do not think this is any cause for consolation. There is human glory, and there is the glory of God [. . .]' (GMT).

5 The 21st Wanderers' Exhibition in St Petersburg exhibited Repin's painting *Na molitve* (At Prayer). Visitors to this exhibition on March 25 sent Tolstoy a telegram with 398 signatures, a letter and 25 rubles collected for the poor. The telegram never reached Tolstoy; it had been forbidden to send him telegrams of sympathy. In a letter to O.I. Ivanova, dated April 20, 1901, Tolstoy thanked everyone for the money and the 'kind [. . .] thoughts' (*PSS*, vol. 73, p. 61).

6 L.O. Pasternak stayed in Yasnaya Polyana from 2 to 4 June 1901 and did a series of sketches from life for his painting *Tolstoy with His Family*. The Musée de Luxembourg in Paris 'suggested to five Russian artists that [. . .] they each do one painting about Russian life for the museum,' wrote Pasternak. 'As the most interesting Russian subject I chose Tolstoy at home with his family and executed it in pastels, in an artificial evening light' (L.O. Pasternak, *Zapiski raznykh let* (Memoirs of various years), Moscow, 1975, p. 206). The painting is in the Russian Museum.

27 See this Diary, January 6 and note 3.

28 Apart from the works mentioned, the sculptor N.L. Aronson did two pencil portraits of Tolstoy in this time, and some eighty sketches (five are in the GMT). The busts – Tolstoy's in bronze and Sofia Tolstaya's in plaster – are in the GMT.

29 Tolstoy wrote later to Andrei – on August 22–3 – about his way of life (*PSS*, vol. 73, pp. 129–31).

30 The article 'Edinstvennoe sredstvo' (The only way) (*PSS*, p. 34).

31 *Evangelie* (The Gospels), St Petersburg, 1894. The title page bears a note by Sofia Tolstaya: 'The passages marked by Count Lev Nikol. Tolstoy are considered by him to be the most important in the Gospels. Countess S. Tolstaya' (GMT).

32 'The only way.'

33 Letter from Queen Elisabeth (pseudonym Carmen Silva) of July 16/29 (GMT. On July 28/August 10 Tolstoy thanked her for her letter and told her he had not received the work she sent (*PSS*, vol. 73, pp. 106–7). It is not in the YaPL.

34 Tatiana Sukhotina's letter to Sofia Tolstaya of July 19, 1901 (GMT).

35 The GMT contains only her letter to Sergei Tolstoy, of July 19, 1901.

36 Letter to Sofia Tolstaya of December 3, 1901 (GMT).

37 Doctor D.P. Makovitsky had visited Yasnaya Polyana twice before: in 1894 and 1897.

38 A.M. Gorky was staying at a dacha in Oleiza (about a mile from Gaspra). On December 23–30, 1901 he wrote to K.P. Pyatnitskii: '[. . .] Tolstoy came here [. . .] He praised Leonid (Andreev) and me to the skies for the first half of *The Three*, but of the second half

he said: "This is anarchy, cruel and vicious" ' (M. Gorky, *Collected Works in 30 vols*, vol. 28, Moscow, 1954, p. 210).

1902

1 Letters from Sofia Nikolaevna Tolstaya of December 10, 1901, and from Aleksandra Vladimirovna Tolstaya (née Glebova) of December 19, 1901 (GMT).
2 Giuseppe Mazzini, *Ob obyazannostyakh cheloveka* (On human duties), Moscow, 1902 (YaPL). Tolstoy considered the book 'excellent' (*PSS*, vol. 54, p. 118). See also Tolstoy's letter to Mazzini's son, Luciano, of March 7, 1905 (*PSS*, vol. 75, p. 233).
3 Lev Lvovich Tolstoy, *Poiski i primirenie* (Search and reconciliation), in *Ezhemesyachnye sochineniya* (Monthly works), nos. 1–12, 1902 (the journal was edited by I.I. Yasinskii). Tolstoy's followers served as the prototypes for several of the negative characters in the novel, and this possibly disturbed Sofia Tolstaya. (See this Diary, February 10.)
4 Tolstoy's letter to Tsar Nicholas II, in which he spoke of the sad plight of the peasants and the need to abolish the 'shameful, unjust system of land distribution', was started on December 26, 1901. He finished it on January 19, 1902 (*PSS*, vol. 73, pp. 184–91). Tolstoy asked Grand Duke Nikolai Mikhailovich to give it to the Tsar. Having received the Grand Duke's consent, he sent him the unpublished letter with a request to read it and 'decide once more whether it was suitable' to give it to him. This covering letter was written on January 16 (*PSS*, vol. 73, pp. 183–4). Nikolai Mikhailovich did as Tolstoy requested. See Tolstoy's letter to him of April 5, 1902 (*PSS*, vol. 73, pp. 228–30).
5 Anton Chekhov, who was living in Yalta, visited Tolstoy soon after his arrival in the Crimea, and had several meetings with him.
6 A.V. Amfiteatrov's satirical sketch 'Gospoda obmanovy' (The lords of deception'), a pun on Saltykov-Shchedrin's *Gospoda Golovlyovy* (The Golovlyovs) was written about the royal family. *Rossia* (Russia), no. 974, January 12, 1902. The author was exiled to Minusinsk and the paper closed.
7 S.I. Taneev's letter of January 18, 1902 (GMT).
8 In V.P. Buryonin's humorous article 'Kriticheskie ocherki. Razgovor s razocharovanym. Razgovor tretii' (Critical sketches. Conversations with a disillusioned man. The third conversation), *NV*, no. 9294, January 18, 1902. Tolstoy read out the following quatrain from a popular song:

> The old woman did groan,
> The old woman did cough.
> Time for the old woman to make her shroud,
> Make her shroud and lie in the grave.

On January 23, 1902, Tolstoy copied these 'wonderful verses' into his diary and observed: 'What a delight popular speech is. Picturesque, touching and serious' (*PSS*, vol. 54, pp. 119–20).
9 See note 4.
10 The following words appear in Tolstoy's diary, written in the hand of Masha Obolenskaya: 'The wisdom of old age increases its value in carats, like diamonds: it is most valuable at the end, just before death. It must be treasured and given away in the service of others' (*PSS*, vol. 54, pp. 120–1).
11 Tolstoy was continuing work on 'O veroterpimosti' (On religious tolerance).
12 Apropos of the death of A.V. Olsufiev, a friend of the Tolstoy family who died on September 9, 1901 of diabetes, Tolstoy wrote to his brother Sergei, on November 6, 1901: '[. . .] he was walking about in the morning, talked for 10 minutes, realised he was dying, said goodbye to everyone, gave advice to his children and kept repeating: "I never thought dying would be so easy" ' (*PSS*, vol. 73, p. 158).

3 The entry in his notebook for January 31, 1902 is in P.A. Boulanger's hand (*PSS*, vol. 54, p. 267). Tolstoy was also dictating insertions for articles 'On religious tolerance' and 'Chto takoe religiya i v chem sushchnost ee?' (What is religion and what is its essence?).

4 His telegram to Sergei Tolstoy, of January 31, 1902, on the state of his health (*PSS*, vol. 73, p. 206).

5 His diary entry for February 1, 1902 was made by Maria Obolenskaya, 'not under dictation but from memory' (*PSS*, vol. 54, p. 123).

6 For Ilya Tolstoy's stay in Gaspra see I.L. Tolstoy, pp. 227–9.

7 Evidently the first version of the Preface to 'Soldatskaya pamyatka' (Notes for soldiers) and 'Ofitserskaya pamyatka' (Notes for officers). The text was written in Masha Obolenskaya's hand, and dated February 8 (unpublished, GMT).

8 Probably the second version of the Preface – see note 17 (*PSS*, vol. 34, pp. 278–9).

9 The article 'Khristianskoe uchenie' (The Christian doctrine), chapters 7 and 9 (*PSS*, vol. 39, pp. 125, 127).

0 The publication of Lyova Tolstoy's novel *Search and Reconciliation* (see note 3) was preceded by a publicity announcement in *Birzhevye vedomosti* (Stock Exchange Gazette), nos. 343 and 346, December 16 and 19, 1901, which said that this novel by 'Lev Tolstoy's son' portrayed 'Tolstoyanism'. On Tolstoy's attitude to his son's work, Olga Konstaninovna Tolstaya wrote from Gaspra to Anna Konstantinovna Chertkova on December 3, 1901: 'Yesterday evening Lev Nikolaevich was terribly grieved and upset by Lyova's writings, his lack of sensitivity and talent and his arrogance' (GMT). On January 29, 1902 Lyova Tolstoy visited Gaspra for several days. After he had left he wrote to Sofia Tolstaya, on February 5, 1902: 'Tell him that I love him and kiss his hand, and ask him to forgive me for offending him' (GMT). The reply which Tolstoy dictated to him was written down in Maria Obolenskaya's hand in his notebook (*PSS*, vol. 54, p. 263; vol. 73, p. 207).

1 His long article 'The Christian Doctrine', chapters 60 and 64 (*PSS*, vol. 39, pp. 184–5, 190–1).

2 The short story 'Kukolki-skeletsy' (Skeleton dolls), final title, appeared in a book: S.A. Tolstaya, *Kukolki-skeletsy i drugie rasskazy* (Skeleton dolls and other stories), Moscow, 1910 (YaPL).

3 On February 21, 1902, Sergei Tolstoy replied to Metropolitan Antonii's letter to Sofia Tolstaya of February 11, 1902: 'Your Holiness, my father, Lev Nikolaevich Tolstoy, has entrusted me to write and implore you to leave him and his wife – my mother – in peace, as all that can be said on the matter by you and other representatives of the Orthodox Church has already been said, and there is nothing left now to discuss. For my own part I should like to add that the doctors have prescribed total mental rest for my father; to disturb this would seriously influence the course of his recovery' (GMT).

4 Possibly he was dictating corrections to his Preface (see note 17), which were written in the margins of the manuscript.

5 The letter was not sent (rough draft at the GMT). See this Diary for November 12, 1900.

6 K.A. Khreptovich-Butyonev's letter of February 16, 1902 (GMT). See this Diary, February 12, and note 23.

7 M.M. Dondukova-Korsakova's letter to Sofia Tolstaya of February 19, 1902 (GMT).

8 Tolstoy's letter to his doctor, L.B. Bertenson, of March 3, 1902 (*PSS*, vol. 73, pp. 211–12).

9 P.A. Boulanger stayed in Gaspra from January 30 to February 22, 1902, and looked after Tolstoy. See his memoirs 'Bolezn L.N. Tolstogo v 1901–1902' (Tolstoy's illness in 1901–2), in *Minuvshie gody* (Years past), no. 9, 1908. After his departure Tolstoy wrote to him almost every day - there are known to be seventeen letters to Boulanger, written under dictation, from February 23 to March 27 (*PSS*, vol. 73, pp. 208–27).

0 A.O. Ogandjanyan.

1 Tolstoy was paraphrasing Pushkin's poem 'Zoloto i bulat' (The gold and the sword).

2 R.W. Emerson, *Vysshaya Dusha* (The Over-Soul), Intermediary edition, Moscow, 1902 (YaPL).

33 Letter to E.V. Obolenskaya of March 15, 1902 (*PSS*, vol. 73, p. 218).
34 D.S. Sipyagin was assassinated by S.V. Balmashev on April 2, 1902.
35 Letter to Grand Duke Nikolai Mikhailovich of April 5, 1902 (*PSS*, vol. 73, pp. 228–30).
36 Thirtieth exhibition of paintings by the Fellowship of Wandering Artists.
37 Letter from Grand Duke Nikolai Mikhailovich of May 11, 1902 (*LN*, vol. 37–8, pp. 308–9), in reply to Tolstoy's letter of April 25–May 1, 1902 about the ownership of the land and the system of Henry George (*PSS*, vol. 73, pp. 236–40).
38 The contents of this dictated text relates to his article 'K rabochemu narodu' (To the working people) (*PSS*, vol. 35).
39 See this Diary, December 24, 1898, note 171.
40 Tolstoy was continuing work on his article 'To the Working People'.
41 This relates to Tolstoy's disagreement with Sofia Tolstaya as to whether some Bashkirs should be invited to Yasnaya Polyana: Tolstoy was strongly urged by his doctors to drink *kumis* (see Tolstoy's letter to P.A. Boulanger of May 22 and to Maria Obolenskaya of June 11, 1902 – *PSS*, vol. 73, pp. 245, 256–7).
42 E.A. Baratynskii's poem 'Smert' (Death), 1828, was included by Tolstoy in the first edition of his *Krug chtenya* (Circle of Reading), Moscow, Intermediary, vol. 2, 1906, pp. 193–4. Sofia Aleksandrovna Stakhovich probably read one of three of Fet's poems: 'Smert' (Death), written in 1856 or 7, 1878 and 1884.
43 Tolstoy resumed work on *Hadji Murat* on June 24, 1902. 'I looked through "Hadji Murat",' he noted on that day in his table diary (*PSS*, vol. 54, p. 308).
44 Sofia Tolstaya had embarked on the preparation of the eleventh edition of *Sochineniya gr. L.N. Tolstogo* (The works of Count L.N. Tolstoy), vols 1–14. This came out in Moscow in 1903.
45 S.I. Taneev finished his work *Podvizhnoi kontrapunkt starogo pisma* (Mobile counterpoint on old notation) in 1908 and published it in 1909 (YaPL with a dedication).
46 Aylmer Maude visited Yasnaya Polyana from July 9 to 13 in connection with his biography of Tolstoy.
47 It has not been established which leaflet was sent to Sofia Tolstaya. On August 8, 1902 Tolstoy observed in his diary: 'Leaflet from a priest – very painful. Why do they hate me?' (*PSS*, vol. 54, p. 136).
48 V.V. Stasov and I.Ya. Ginzburg stayed in Yasnaya from August 10 to 14 at Sofia and L.N. Tolstoy's invitation (Stasov, pp. 275–6). Tolstoy asked Stasov during this visit to send him material for his work on *Hadji Murat*, and gave him a list of things he needed (*PSS*, vol. 73, pp. 276–7).
49 This episode (at the end of 1855) is referred to in several biographies written during Tolstoy's lifetime. Tolstoy's last biographer, N.N. Gusev, having checked all the facts, states that it cannot be 'definitely established who initiated this transfer' (Gusev, *Materialy*, I, pp. 560–1).
50 Tolstoy drafted a rough sketch of a story on this subject (untitled) in a letter to Chertkov (*PSS*, vol. 86, pp. 62–3), and published it under the title 'Mudraya devitsa' (The wise virgin) (*PSS*, vol. 26). Tolstoy suggested this subject to Leskov (see Goldenweiser, p. 133), who then wrote the story 'Chas voli bozhiei' (The hour of God's will), *RO*, no. 11, 1890. Tolstoy expounded his views of this story in a letter to Leskov of December 3, 1890 (*PSS*, vol. 65, p. 198). His rough draft of 'The Wise Virgin' subsequently served Tolstoy as the canvas for a story entitled 'Tri voprosa' (Three questions) (1903) (*PSS*, vol. 34).
51 On October 11, 1902 Tolstoy wrote to Chertkov: 'I have finished "Hadji Murat", which I have put aside in an unfinished state and shall not publish in my lifetime' (*PSS*, vol. 88, p. 278). He none the less continued working on the story until 1905.
52 Tolstoy began work on his article 'K dukhovenstvu' (To the clergy) (*PSS*, vol. 34).
53 See this Diary, April 22, 1891 and note 54.
54 Tolstoy wrote his first will in his diary on March 27, 1895 (*PSS*, vol. 53, pp. 14–16). Maria

Obolenskaya copied it out, and in August 1901 she gave it to her father to sign. Tolstoy signed it and asked his daughter to keep the document in her possession. (For more details see *PSS*, vol. 54, pp. 640–4.)

5 On July 13, 1902 N.S. Zetlin, owner of the publishing house Prosveshchenie (Enlightenment), visited Sofia Tolstaya 'offering to buy the permanent rights to the edition for a million rubles'. Sofia Tolstaya did not agree. See Daily Diary, July 13, 1902.

6 See note 44.

7 The author's final date on this manuscript is November 1. The article appeared in *Svobodnoe Slovo* (Free word) in 1903.

8 The legend 'Razrushenie ada i vosstanovlenie ego' (Destruction and Reconstruction of Hell), on which Tolstoy worked from November 1902 to the end of that year, was thought up as an illustration to his article 'To the Clergy'. S.Ya. Elpatevskii did not like it. (See S. Elpatevskii, *Literaturnye vospominaniya* (Literary memoirs), Moscow (n.d.), p. 48.)

9 P.A. Kropotkin, *Zapiski revolyutsionera* (Notes of a revolutionary), London, 1902. On Tolstoy's admission, 'reading Kropotkin's splendid memoirs' helped him to consider writing his own memoirs, and he started doing so in January 1903 (see his letter to Chertkov, January 11, 1903 – *PSS*, vol. 88, pp. 284–5).

0 Tolstoy's letter was published in *RV*, no. 343, December 12, 1902 (*PSS*, vol. 73, p. 341). The papers continued to print bulletins on his health, despite its publication.

1 M. Taube, *Istoriya zarozhdeniya sovremennogo mezhdunarodnogo prava* (History of the conception of contemporary international law), vols 1–3, St Petersburg, 1894–1902. The third volume appeared under the title *Mezhdunarodnyi stroi srednevekovoi Evropy vo vremya mira* (The international system in medieval Europe in peacetime), St Petersburg, 1902 (YaPL, with Tolstoy's notes).

2 See this Diary, January 1, 1903, and note 2.

1903

1 Tatiana Sukhotina's letter to Sofia Tolstaya of December 23, 1902 (GMT). See Tolstoy's letter to Tatiana Sukhotina of January 9, 1903 (*PSS*, vol. 74, p. 11).

2 Tom Ferris and Bert Toy visited Russia in order to meet Tolstoy and discuss spiritualism with him. They visited Yasnaya Polyana, but their conversation with Tolstoy was a brief one because he was ill.

3 A.S. Arenskii, 'Kubok' (The goblet), a ballade for solo voice, choir and orchestra, opus 61, to words by Schiller, translated by V.A. Zhukovskii.

4 In December 1902 Tolstoy had the idea of compiling a calendar in which the days of the year would be accompanied by philosophical sayings. 'Just think,' he said to Kh.N. Abrikosov, 'people will be able to read the pronouncements of the great philosophers, instead of a lot of rubbish' (Kh.N. Abrikosov, 'Dvenadtsat let okolo Tolstogo' (Twelve years with Tolstoy), *Letopisi*, book 12, pp. 439–40. In early January 1903 Tolstoy started compiling a selection of aphorisms (for a list of sources see *PSS*, vol. 40, pp. 479–80). This work was finished on January 23, 1903. The anthology was published by the Intermediary on August 28, 1903 under the title *Mysli mudrykh lyudei na kazhdyi den* (Thoughts of the wise men for every day) (*PSS*, vol. 40).

5 *NV*, no. 9673, February 7, 1903, published Sofia Tolstaya's letter expressing her negative opinion of Andreev's short story 'Bezdna' (The abyss), and her support for Buryonin's review of it (*NV*, no. 9666, January 31, 1903).

6 Tolstoy needed information about the Nicholas I period and the war in the Caucasus for his work on *Hadji Murat*.

7 Ivanov wrote about this from Odessa, in a letter of February 8, 1903 (GMT).

8 The literary critic V.V. Rozanov and his wife came to make the Tolstoy's acquaintance and talk to them. Tolstoy 'was astonished [. . .] by Rozanov's lack of education', and found him

'of little interest' (letter to Sergei Nikolaevich Tolstoy of March 10, 1903 – *PSS*, vol. 74, p. 67). See also Lyova Tolstoy, *Iz dnevnika* – 'Stolitsa i usadba' (From my diary – 'The capital and the estate'), no. 4, 1914, pp. 4–5.

9 A line from Tyutchev's poem 'Silentium!' (1830).

10 Tolstoy wrote to Biryukov, on June 3, 1903: 'I am now struggling with the chapter on Nikolai Pavlovich, which [. . .] I feel is very important, as it serves as an illustration of my understanding of power' (*PSS*, vol. 74, p. 140). He was reading a book by N.K. Schilder at the time, called *Imperator Nikolai I, ego zhizn i tsarstvovanie* (Emperor Nicholas I, his life and reign), St Petersburg, 1903 (YaPL), in which he found 'much of interest' (*PSS*, vol. 54, p. 177).

11 Father Semeri and a professor of theology called Monocci visited Yasnaya Polyana on their way from Rome to Manchuria.

12 The peasant A.A. Ageev was sentenced to exile in Siberia, in January 1903, for blasphemy. Tolstoy tried to help him and his family and took an active part in their case. He begged N. Davydov to make an application for mercy, and in a letter of April 7, 1903 Tolstoy asked A.V. Olsufiev to pass this application to the Tsar (*PSS*, vol. 74, pp. 103–4). The application was rejected by the Minister of Justice, N.K. Muravyov, and on August 29, 1903 Ageev was sent to Siberia.

13 There exist four versions of this letter. The final version, different from the one published in the Diary, is published in *PST*, pp. 617–18. The note in Tolstoy's diary, quoted in this letter, is from October 6, 1895. Seventeen lines are deleted in the original (*PSS*, vol. 53, p. 59).

1904

1 A delegation of students from the St Petersburg Mining Institute brought Tolstoy a letter expressing their deep love and admiration (GMT); they wanted to discuss the agrarian question and the student revolutionary movement with him. See the memoirs of A.N. Tikhonov, who was a member of this delegation in N. Serebrov, *Vremya i lyudi* (Time and people), Moscow, 1955, pp. 227–49.

2 Rehearsals of Chekhov's *The Cherry Orchard* were going on at the Moscow Public Art Theatre.

3 In January 1904 Tolstoy started work on compiling his *Circle of Reading*.

4 The verses were published in *ZV*, no. 3, 1904.

5 The Russo-Japanese War started on January 27, 1904, and every day from then on notes appeared in Tolstoy's diary about this 'terrible deed', as he called the war (*PSS*, vol. 55, pp. 10–11).

6 'The Forged Coupon' was started in the second half of the 1880s. Tolstoy repeatedly returned to this story, and worked most intensively on it from October 1902 to February 1904. It remained unfinished, and was not published in Tolstoy's lifetime.

7 In May 1851 Tolstoy and his elder brother Nikolai left for the Caucasus, where Nikolai was serving. In June Tolstoy took part in a raid, as a volunteer, and he described this in his story 'The Raid' (*PSS*, vol. 3). On January 3, 1852 he joined the artillery as a cadet, in January 1854 he was made an ensign and transferred at his own request to the Danubian army, and in November of that year he moved to Sevastopol, where he stayed until the end of the siege.

8 A.L. Tolstoy's letter to Sofia Tolstaya of August 10, 1904 (GMT).

9 On August 11, 1904 Tolstoy went to Pirogovo, where he stayed until August 21. 'I think I might be able to help him in the most important thing, his spiritual state,' he wrote to his wife at the time (*PSS*, vol. 84, pp. 366–7). Sergei Nikolaevich Tolstoy died on August 23, 1904.

1905

1 P.I. Biryukov was deported from Russia in 1897 for giving aid to the Dukhobors. He received permission to return from emigration after the manifesto of August 11, 1904. He went to Yasnaya Polyana on December 24, 1904 and stayed there until January 3, 1905.

2 Biryukov started compiling material for a biography of Tolstoy in 1901. The first volume was published in 1906 by the Intermediary, under the title *Lev Tolstoi: Biografiya.*

3 In January 1905 Tolstoy wrote an article entitled 'Ob obshchestvennom dvizhenii v Rossii' (On the social movement in Russia), last version dated February 2 (*PSS*, vol. 36). It was a reply to the innumerable letters begging Tolstoy to speak out about the *zemstvo*'s agitation for a limitation of the autocracy and the introduction of a representative system of government, and about the massacre of peaceful demonstrators in St Petersburg on January 9, 1905 (Bloody Sunday). The article was published in England by Chertkov in *Svobodnoe slovo* (Free Word), no. 92, 1905.

4 Those in Yasnaya Polyana learnt about the events of January 9, 1905 in St Petersburg from the newspapers of January 11, and from the account of P.A. Boulanger, who visited shortly afterwards (*YaZ*, I, pp. 81–4).

1908

1 Tolstoy was continuing with the revision, started in August 1907, of a second edition of the *Circle of Reading.*

2 In a rough version of a letter to those institutions and people who had sent him greetings on his birthday, Tolstoy wrote: 'I thank all who have written to me, and those dear people who have touched me so much with their presents – the St Petersburg waiters who gave me a lovely inscribed samovar, various workers, and many others' (*PSS*, vol. 78, p. 242).

3 An album of drawings by N.A. Kasatkin, A.M. Vasnetsov, Baturin, L.O. Pasternak and others (water-colours, pastels and pencil drawings) was sent to Tolstoy by the Moscow Society of Art-Lovers (it is now at the Yasnaya Polyana Estate Museum).

4 E. Cherchopova sent a satin-stitch embroidery of Tolstoy in the fields. The portrait was sent by the artist Gusikyan.

5 The letter to the Ottoman tobacco factory (in St Petersburg) was written on September 3, 1908 (*PSS*, vol. 87, pp. 224–5).

6 This parcel arrived in Yasnaya Polyana on September 1, 1908. A detachable coupon showed a Moscow address and the surname of the sender, O.A. Markova. Tolstoy replied to O.A. Markova on September 3, 1908: 'You would make me very happy if you would explain to me the reasons for your ill feelings' (*PSS*, vol. 78, p. 223). Later N.N. Gusev established that there was no O.A. Markova living at this address. For more details see Gusev, p. 201–2.

7 Charles Hagberg Wright, a librarian at the British Museum, came to Yasnaya Polyana on August 28, 1908 and brought Tolstoy a letter of greetings from English admirers which said: 'The whole world loves you for the boldness and sincerity with which you have presented humanity with lofty new ideals' (GMT). It was signed by artists, actors, musicians, public figures and writers, including George Bernard Shaw.

8 G.Ya. Politkovskii's letter of September 5, 1908 (GMT). Gusev replied to it on September 13, 1908, at Tolstoy's request (*PSS*, vol. 78, p. 358).

9 This happened on June 13, 1853. Some details of this episode were later used by Tolstoy in his story 'Kavkazskii plennik' (The prisoner of the Caucasus) (*PSS*, vol. 21, pp. 304–6).

10 There exist five rough versions of this letter, the first of September 8, the last dated October 5. It was published on October 8, 1908 in several newspapers (*PSS*, vol. 78, pp. 239–42).

11 This poem was sent by Fet to Sofia Tolstaya with a letter, on September 14, 1891 (GMT).

12 This proclamation was issued by the Socialist Revolutionaries in Tula. Four (not eight) Tula printers who were members of the party visited Tolstoy at his invitation. For a detailed

account of their conversation see N.N. Gusev, *Lev Tolstoi protiv gosudarstva i tserkvi* (Lev Tolstoy against the State and the Church), Berlin, 1913, pp. 42–55. See also Tolstoy's letter to the Tula workers, dated September 15, 1908 (*PSS*, vol. 78, pp. 229–30).

13 The visitor's name is not known. After his meeting with him Tolstoy wrote in his diary, on September 14, 1908: 'He made a sad impression' (*PSS*, vol. 56, p. 151).

14 An inaccurate quote from Fet's poem 'Osennyaya roza' (Autumn rose) (1886).

15 Letter dated September 6, 1908 (GMT).

16 In April 1907 Tolstoy received N.A. Morozov's book *Otkrovenie v groze i bure. Istoriya vozniknoveniya Apokalipsa* (Revelation in storm and tempest. A history of the origins of the Apocalypse) (St Petersburg, 1907), with a dedication: 'To Lev Nikolaevich Tolstoy, as a mark of the author's deep esteem, March 31, N. Morozov' (YaPL). He told Morozov of his response to the book in a letter of April 6–11 (*PSS*, vol. 77, p. 78).

17 V.D. Lebedeva recalled: 'All evening the Count [. . .] questioned Morozov about life in the fortress.' And as they were saying goodbye he said 'he hoped Morozov would come again and would spend several days there [. . .] He said this was the first time in his life that he had met a man who had spent 20 years in prison' (Vera L., 'Vstrechi s L.N. Tolstym' (Meetings with L.N. Tolstoy), *Sovremennik* (The Contemporary), no. 4, 1912.

1909

1 Sofia Tolstaya was copying the rough drafts of the story 'Kto ubiitsy? Pavel Kudryash' (Who are the murderers? Pavel Kudryash), on which Tolstoy worked from December 1908 to February 1909. The work remained unfinished and was not published in Tolstoy's lifetime (*PSS*, vol. 37).

2 This was the second time the harpsichordist Wanda Landowska visited Yasnaya Polyana. Tolstoy wrote of her playing this time: '[. . .] she plays pleasantly and charmingly, but does not transport one's soul, and I love that experience, however painful it may be' (from a letter to M.S. Sukhotin of January 15, 1909 – *PSS*, vol. 79, p. 31).

1910

1 Sofia Tolstaya did not keep a diary for the first half of 1910. This was the first entry.

2 Tolstoy's diary for 1910 was written in two notebooks. He started the second of these on June 14 in Otradnoe (see *PSS*, vol. 58, P. 65). Seven notebooks, from May 19, 1900 to June 13, 1910, were kept with Chertkov.

3 Tolstoy wrote: 'I must try to fight Sonya consciously, with love and kindness' (*PSS*, vol. 58, p. 67, entry for June 20).

4 On June 22 there was a sharp deterioration in Sofia Tolstaya's hysterical condition, and at her insistence a telegram was sent to Tolstoy saying: 'Sofia Andreevna's nerves in bad state, insomnia, weeping, pulse a hundred, please telegraph, Varya.' (See *PSS*, vol. 84, p. 398.) Varvara Feokritova testified that this telegram was dictated by Sofia Tolstaya.

5 Entry for June 22 (*PSS*, vol. 58, p. 68).

6 Cf. *PSS*, vol. 82, p. 59.

7 Cf. *PSS*, vol. 84, p. 398.

8 Chertkov received permission to live in Telyatinki while his mother was staying there. He arrived on June 27.

9 This was included in vol. XII of the 1910–11 edition.

10 This was included in vol. XII of the 1910–11 edition.

11 In this letter of July 1, Sofia Tolstaya explained the reasons for her change of attitude to Chertkov, chief of which was his possession of Tolstoy's diaries: 'If you have any feelings for me and for Lev Nikolaevich's peace of mind, which will be fully restored if you and I can make friends in the last years of his life, then I beg you, with an aching heart and a readiness

to love and appreciate you even more – give me Lev Nikolaevich's diaries! [. . .] If you do carry out my request then we shall be friends, more so than before. If not, it will be painful for Lev Nikolaevich to see our relations; I am incapable of forcing my feelings in another direction – I have been too shocked by the disappearance of the diaries.' (The letter was inserted into the text of her diary, and published in *DST*, IV, pp. 258–9.)

2 In a note to Tolstoy Chertkov wrote: 'Dear L.N., In view of your wife's desire that I give her back your diaries, which you gave me to delete the passages you indicated, I shall make haste to finish this work and shall return the notebooks as soon as I have done so. July 1, 1910, V. Chertkov' (quoted in *DST*, IV, p. 305).

3 Aleksandra Tolstaya noted in her diary: 'It was decided to extract the passages we didn't want to give Sofia Andreevna, cut out those pages and give her the rest' (GMT).

4 Lyova Tolstoy arrived from Paris on July 2 and stayed in Yasnaya Polyana until September 1.

5 Followers of the poet and religious preacher A.M. Dobrolyubov, who called on people to work in the fields and live simply.

6 E.I. Chertkova was a follower of the English preacher Grenville Redstock: according to his interpretation of the Gospels, man would acquire salvation from sin through faith in the redemption of the human race, brought about by Christ's death.

7 The fire was in the village that belonged to Tatiana Sukhotina. There were suspicions that it might be arson, started either by V.A. Repin, who was mentally ill, or by a village youth who had been given shelter by Maria Aleksandrovna Schmidt.

8 *PSS* published twenty-one letters from Tolstoy to M.A. Schmidt, written before the fire. Apart from one, dated August 3, 1887, they were all taken from copies kept by Chertkov. He also kept copies that M.A. Schmidt had made of 'Investigations into Dogmatic Theology', the final version of the story 'Rabotnik Emelyan' (Emelyan the worker) and various other works.

9 'Istoriya poezdki Lva Nikolaevicha k Chertkovu v sentyabre 1909 g. v Kryokshino' (The story of Lev Nikolaevich's visit to Chertkov in Kryokshino in 1909) (GMT).

20 In Otradnoe Tolstoy resumed work on his article 'On Suicide', which he had started in March and which was now given the title 'On Madness', later 'O bezumii' (On insanity). It remained unfinished. See *PSS*, vol. 38.

21 Sofia and Ilya, Andrei Tolstoy's children from his first marriage to Olga Konstantinovna Dieterichs, who lived at Telyatinki with Chertkov.

22 The pamphlet 'Usilie' (Effort) formed the twentieth chapter of the anthology *Put zhizni* (The path of life) (Moscow, 1910), compiled from various different publications and booklets (*PSS*, vol. 45).

23 Tolstoy had kept the proofs of *Resurrection*, with his corrections. As a rule duplicates with the author's corrections copied on to them were sent to *The Cornfield*, where the novel was being published, but Sofia Tolstaya needed the proofs, as she was preparing the text of the novel for her own edition. See note 29.

24 See this Diary, 1887, note 42.

25 Chertkov, wishing to put an end to this conflict between them, wrote in his letter: 'My remark that I could "drag you through the mud if I wished" was provoked by the distrust and suspicion you showed towards me before, by assuming, without the slightest justification, that I wished to come between L.N. and you, to take possession of various documents and generally to abuse L.N.'s trust in me and my close relations with your family [. . .] I have already indicated to you that hitherto I have never abused the intimate knowledge of your family life which force of circumstances has given me, that I have never committed any "indiscrétions" on the subject, and that I shall never do so in the future, *despite the fact* that I have for a long time possessed sufficient material to harm you should I want to. But because you were in such an agitated state at the time, and because you did not let me finish speaking and did not pay attention to the real meaning of my words, you

grasped at separate remarks I made and gave them a threatening sense, which was very far from my mind' (quoted in *DST*, IV, p. 307). Chertkov did not keep his word and published a series of biased reports about Tolstoy's family drama.

26 Sofia Tolstaya made copies of her letters to Tolstoy; she intended some of these to be included in an anthology entitled *Pisma L.N. Tolstogo k zhene* (L.N. Tolstoy's letters to his wife).

27 Tolstoy was reading a collection of stories by Pierre Mille called *La Biche écrasée*, Paris, 1909 (YaPL), which the author sent him on April 13, along with a letter. (The text of the letter is in *PSS*, vol. 58, pp. 442–3.) Tolstoy found the story 'La Biche écrasée' 'charming' (ibid., p. 77), and he liked the other stories in the collection too (ibid.).

28 See note 82.

29 At Sofia Tolstaya's request, N.V. Davydov helped prepare the text of *Resurrection* for her edition. On June 27 he wrote to her: 'I have finished the task I have undertaken, and now that I have read it through in Chertkov's foreign edition I have jotted down in a separate notebook everything that I think should definitely be omitted so as not to subject the work to the risk of confiscation and the publisher to punishment. I should like to suggest that I visit you in Yasnaya Polyana on the 9th or 10th of June, with the book and my notebook' (GMT).

30 This refers to André Gide's book *Le Retour de l'enfant prodigue*, Paris, 1909 (YaPL), which Charles Salomon took to Tolstoy at the author's request. He did not like it. (See *PSS*, vol. 58, pp. 47, 445.)

31 Charles Salomon recalled in a letter to Chertkov of April 4, 1932: ' "La Biche écrasée" was very successful, especially one place which Tolstoy made me read again and again, three days running, in front of various guests.' (Quoted in *PSS*, vol. 58, p. 444.)

32 On June 18, shortly after Tolstoy's arrival at Otradnoe, the following letter from Chertkov appeared in many major newspapers, dated June 13: 'In view of the fact that various announcements have appeared in the press regarding Lev N.—ch Tolstoy's visit to my house, I consider it necessary to warn any persons who might wish to visit him here that on those occasions when L.N. leaves Yasnaya Polyana he is in need of rest and seeks as much privacy as possible. For those who value his health and tranquillity, therefore, the best way to show their good wishes towards him is to refrain from visiting him on these occasions [. . .] I am making this announcement with L.N.'s consent, in the full confidence that those who wish him well will respect the feelings that have inspired this appeal, and will act in accordance with it.'

33 Letter of July 12 – see *PSS*, vol. 89, p. 192.

34 This letter of July 12 was brought from Telyatinki by Goldenweiser, and according to him 'Sofia Andreevna did not return it to Chertkov, saying she had lost it' (Goldenweiser, II, p. 116). It was published in a version copied by P.A. Sergeenko.

35 The letter, written on the morning of July 14, in which Tolstoy announced his decision: '1) I shall give no one my present diary, and shall keep it with me. 2) I shall take my earlier diaries back from Chertkov and shall keep them myself, probably in the bank.' Tolstoy also explained in this letter the reasons for his estrangement from his wife and suggested 'terms for a good and peaceful life'. If these were not accepted, he wrote, he would 'leave' Yasnaya Polyana. (See *PSS*, vol. 84, pp. 398–401.)

36 Sofia Tolstaya is referring to the book containing her own handwritten copies of Tolstoy's letters to her.

37 Tolstoy's letter of July 14 asking for the seven notebooks, which Goldenweiser had brought from Moscow on July 3, to be given back to him, via Aleksandra Tolstaya (*PSS*, vol. 89, p. 193).

38 Sofia Tolstaya was intending to buy the Rudakov house to remove and erect in Ovsyannikovo, in place of the house belonging to Tatiana Sukhotina, which was burnt down. See this Diary for July 3.

39 Matthew Herring, an American and a Master of Law from Edinburgh University.

40 'Blagodarnaya pochva. (Iz dnevnika)' (The grateful earth. (From My Diary)), published on July 14 in *Re*, *RV* and *Utro Rossii* (Morning of Russia) under the title 'From My Diary' (*PSS*, vol. 38).

41 S.I. Taneev.

42 In 1910 Aleksandra Tolstaya, Varvara Feokritova, V.F. Bulgakov, D.P. Makovitsky and A.B. Goldenweiser all kept diaries. Tolstoy's family drama and Sofia Andreevna's conduct were described in great detail by all the memoirists. Those of Aleksandra Tolstaya, Varvara Feokritova ('Poslednii god zhizni L.N. Tolstogo' (The last year of L.N. Tolstoy's life)) – both unpublished and in the Tolstoy Museum – and Goldenweiser (*Vblizi Tolstogo* (Near Tolstoy)) are especially biased and hostile to Sofia Tolstaya.

43 The end of the Daily Diary for 1910 contains a catalogue of the seven notebooks, compiled by Sofia Tolstaya, and about the eighth she wrote: 'It's with Lev Nik. for now. He writes it and carefully conceals it from me. October 1910' (GMT).

44 Tolstoy started various works in 1910, including 'Tri dnya v derevne' (Three days in the country), 'Net v mire vinovatykh' (There are no guilty people in the world), 'Khodynka' (Khodynka) and the article 'O bezumii' (On Madness).

45 Letter of July 1, see note 11.

46 On this day Tolstoy went himself to see Chertkov. It was his last visit to Telyatinki.

47 See note 12.

48 Sofia Tolstaya was referring to a note written by Tolstoy on November 20, 1851 on a separate piece of paper (*PSS*, vol. 46, pp. 237–8), which she prejudged and misinterpreted.

49 On July 22 Tolstoy signed a will drawn up by the lawyer N.K. Muravyov, according to which all his literary works, published and unpublished, finished and unfinished, all his manuscripts, and everything he had ever written would become the 'exclusive property of Aleksandra Lvovna Tolstaya'. Tolstoy was obliged to name someone as his heir, otherwise the will would have been legally invalid. The writer's real wish, that 'all his works [. . .] and all his writings' should not belong 'to any private individual' and should be 'published and reprinted by anyone who wished', was expressed in an 'Explanatory Note' written by Chertkov as a supplement to the will. Chertkov was granted the right to supervise and publish the writer's manuscripts after his death (*PSS*, vol. 82, pp. 227–30).

50 The proofs of vol. XVII, published 1910–11, which contained Tolstoy's prefaces to the works of various authors included in Tolstoy's anthologies of sayings (for instance the Preface to the anthology *The Collected Thoughts of La Bruyère, with the Addition of Selected Aphorisms and Maxims of La Rochefoucauld, Vauvenargues and Montesquieu*) (*PSS*, vol. 40).

51 She is referring to the unfinished play *Ot nei vse kachestva* (She has all the qualities) (*PSS*, vol. 38). Possibly the remark 'I bake and I cook' was intended by Tolstoy to summarise the character. The accusations of inaccuracy are unfounded, as there is no indication in the author's stage directions as to where the purchase was put.

52 This refers to the corrections Tolstoy made to the text of the 'Explanatory Note'. See note 49.

53 See this Diary, 1891, notes 88 and 91.

54 See *PST*, p. 789. The letter, dated 'The night of July 24 to 25' is copied into her diary below this entry. She has attached here a note which was not sent to the newspapers, saying, 'The facts can be checked on the spot.' See *DST*, IV, p. 130.

55 V.F. Bulgakov in fact played no part in the drafting and writing of the will. (See Bulgakov, p. 307.) The witnesses were A.D. Radynskii and A.P. Sergeenko. A.B. Goldenweiser was there at the signing.

56 At Sofia Tolstaya's request M.A. Stakhovich read Tolstoy's recent journalistic works to help her decide whether or not they could be included in the new edition under the existing censorship laws, and he consulted the president of the Censorship Committee A.V. Belgard. Referring to *The Kingdom of God . . .*, 'Letter to the Liberals' and *On Religious Tolerance* he wrote to Sofia Tolstaya on July 20: 'I have read them through

carefully, consulted with Belgard on the doubtful passages, and we both consider that none of these works could possibly subject the new edition to the threat of arrest' (GMT). Sofia Tolstaya also sent him 'Christianity and patriotism', 'To the Tsar and his assistants' and Tolstoy's letters to Nicholas II, with the same purpose. Sofia Tolstaya's letter is not extant.

57 *The Cossacks* appeared in vol. II of the 1910–11 edition.

58 Tolstoy did not reach Ovsyannikovo, as he met Gorbunov on the way and rode back to Yasnaya Polyana with him. Tolstoy was working on the proofs of the booklets 'Zhizn v nastoyashchem' (Life in the present), 'Slovo' (The Word), 'Smirenie' (Resignation), and 'Smert' (Death) from the anthology. *The Path of Life* (*PSS*, vol. 45).

59 V.A. Molochnikov, a follower of Tolstoy's, was twice brought to court, in 1908 and in 1910, for harbouring and distributing banned works by Tolstoy. He made Tolstoy's acquaintance in 1907 and was in correspondence with him from 1906. Tolstoy treated him very warmly and conducted a wide-ranging correspondence with him (there are known to be more than forty letters). See Daily Diary for 1910, note 20.

60 S.V. Chirkin.

61 Vol. XVII of the 1910–11 edition. See note 50.

62 Biryukov was looking through various recent journalistic works of Tolstoy's to decide whether they could be included in the 1910–11 edition under the existing censorship regulations. 'I have received from Seryozha a list of works which I have undertaken to read, and I shall start doing so in a few days' time,' Biryukov wrote to Sofia Tolstaya on April 24 (GMT). Biryukov was also helping to choose the text to be published, as many works of Tolstoy's were published in Russia with censorship cuts, whereas they appeared abroad in *Svobodnoe slovo* (Free Word) uncut.

63 Probably the stories from the collection *Skeleton Dolls* (Moscow, 1910).

64 Aylmer Maude sent Tolstoy part of the money he received for his English translation of *Resurrection*. Tolstoy decided to use this money to buy rye seeds and give these to the neediest peasants. Apart from Aleksei Zhidkov, Tolstoy was visited by Taras Fokanov and Danila Kozlov (*YaZ*, August 1).

65 See this Diary, July 24, and note 52.

66 Aylmer Maude sent Sofia Tolstaya a copy of a letter Tolstoy wrote to him on July 23 and his reply. Tolstoy expressed his dissatisfaction that in the second volume of his biography of him Maude had described his daughter Masha's relation with Chertkov as 'not good', and he asked Maude to delete this passage. 'I very much regret your unfriendly attitude to Chertkov, as such an attitude is both unsuitable and incorrect in a biographer, and can only mislead the reader,' Tolstoy wrote to him. And in conclusion he asked him to 'take these remarks into consideration'. (See *PSS*, vol. 82, p. 82.) Maude replied: 'I shall delete this passage according to your wishes, but allow me to say that I bear your friend no ill will [. . .] I think you know that however strong your attachment to him may be you should be impartial in your judgements of both him and me. But in any case it's your business, and it's not for me to judge.' (Quoted in *DST*, IV, p. 320. The English text is pasted into the notebook after the diary entry.)

67 Letter of August 3. (See *DST*, IV, pp. 320–1.)

68 In her letter Sofia Tolstaya accused Chertkov of exercising a 'despotic influence' on her husband, of setting him against her, of collecting manuscripts and photographs, and so on. 'Yes, I am wildly jealous of Lev Nikolaevich and shall not give him up, even if it costs me my life,' she wrote. 'And I consider that Vladimir Grigorevich has had a harmful influence on our life' (*DST*, IV, pp. 321–2).

69 See note 48.

70 On that day Makovitsky noted in his diary: 'I read aloud from the Czech journal *Vaše doba* [Your Time], May 1910, a poem by I.S. Makhar called "Chelčicky". L.N. listened attentively, but said nothing' (*YaZ*, August 3).

71 Sofia Tolstaya was working on the proofs of *What is Art?* (vol. XVII, 1910–11 edition).

Starting from the text of the first edition (*L.N. Tolstoy Collected Works*, vol. XI, Moscow, 1898), she checked these against the manuscripts and proofs and inserted a number of omissions and passages deleted by the censor.

72 V.G. Korolenko, 'Bytovoe yavlenie (Zametki publitsista o smertnoi kazni)' (An everyday occurrence. A journalist's observations on capital punishment), in *RB*, nos. 3 and 4, 1910.

73 Three novels by the French writer J.H. Rosny have been kept (YaPL, with a dedication).

74 Aleksandra Tolstaya noted down Tolstoy's conversation with Korolenko in her diary, as did Bulgakov (see Bulgakov, pp. 320–5).

75 See Tolstoy's letter to Chertkov of August 7, in which he wrote: '[. . .] I have felt guilty, ridiculous and sad to have avoided you all this time, but I cannot do anything else. I feel very sorry for her, and she is doubtless even sorrier for me, so that I should feel very bad, pitying her as I do, to increase her sufferings' (*PSS*, vol. 89, p. 201). On July 23 Goldenweiser noted: 'Chertkov told me that Lev Nikolaevich had written him a letter advising him not to go to Yasnaya or attempt to clarify his relations with Sofia Andreevna' (Goldenweiser, II, p. 159).

76 On that day Tolstoy was to receive five young peasant recruits intending to refuse military service. Tolstoy wrote an appeal for them, 'Neizvestnym' (To the Unknown Ones) (*PSS*, vol. 82, pp. 100–1).

77 On that day Goldenweiser played for Tolstoy Beethoven's *Appassionata* (Goldenweiser, II, p. 223).

78 The treatise 'Christianity and Patriotism' was banned in Russia and distributed illegally. In a letter of August 7 Stakhovich told Sofia Tolstaya that he had found 'dubious' and 'indisputably dangerous passages' in all the books she sent him, including this work. The treatise was published in vol. XVIII of the 1910–11 edition with extensive cuts.

79 In her Daily Diary for this day she noted: 'This morning he dictated to me a letter he had written to a peasant about faith' (*DST*, IV, p. 153). This letter was to A. Mirov (see *PSS*, vol. 82, pp. 106–7).

80 Ekaterina Vasilevna Tolstaya, Andrei Tolstoy's wife.

81 On that day Tolstoy wrote letters to V.I. Ermolov Ermokhin, N. Petrov, I.M. Shekhovtsev and Sri Paramakhams; the last had written enquiring about the possibility of visiting Yasnaya Polyana (*PSS*, vol. 82, pp. 108–10).

82 The trial took place on November 20. L.L. Tolstoy was acquitted.

83 Aleksandra Tolstaya, at her father's request, was copying the thoughts contained in the notebook section of his diary (see *PSS*, vol. 58, note of August 7).

84 À propos of this, Tatiana Sukhotina wrote to Chertkov on August 16: 'There was nothing but grief and distress when she [Sofia Tolstaya] caught L.N. going into Sasha's room this evening for his diary. And today she wrote him a note about this. But later on I asked her not to say any more about it and she agreed, saying she would try to control herself' (*DST*, IV, p. 327).

85 In her Preface to vol. 1, Sofia Tolstaya wrote that Tolstoy's letter to his brother Sergei expressing his irritation at the censors' interference with the publication of *Childhood* in *Sovremennik* (The Contemporary) (*PSS*, vol. 59, p. 217), had made her 'read through all the manuscripts concerning the work and reconstruct the story from them, without all the "trite and stupid" passages to which Lev Nikolaevich referred. [. . .] As I felt that the publication of *Childhood* in the manuscript version, written entirely by Lev Nikolaevich, without any interference from the publishers or cuts from the censors, would be of great interest, I decided to print the manuscript text for the new edition.' She did not, according to her, have at her disposal the manuscript 'from which *Childhood* was printed' (*Works of Count L.N. Tolstoy*, vol. 1, Moscow, 1911, pp. 5–6). She therefore took as her basis the manuscript of the third, incomplete version, supplemented it with passages from the fourth version, and thus created a corrupted text.

86 V.Ya. Grigoriev.

87 Goldenweiser noted in August 15: 'Aleksandra Lvovna told me that L.N. packed things he never normally took when he went away. He evidently anticipates the possibility of not returning for a very long time – perhaps not at all' (Goldenweiser, II, p. 264).
88 On August 14 Chertkov received official notification that the government had lifted the ban against his living anywhere in the province of Tula, and particularly in the village of Telyatinki. This information appeared in many newspapers on August 18.
89 A dramatisation of the story 'Zloumyshlennik' (The malefactor). 'Went to a performance in a school. Very good,' wrote Tolstoy (*PSS*, vol. 58, p. 94).
90 See note 82.
91 'Sofia Andreevna's letter to Stolypin was written when she was half out of her mind and was not sent,' wrote Tatiana Sukhotina to Chertkov. 'The following day she came to her senses' (GMT).
92 Bulgakov was sent three letters which Tolstoy had received, with his notes and a request for an answer (see *PSS*, vol. 82, pp. 261–2), as well as a letter from Aleksandra Tolstaya containing a list of books which were to be sent to the addresses indicated (see Bulgakov, p. 334), and one letter for Chertkov (*PSS*, vol. 89, p. 207).
93 Quotations from the 3rd edition of *Childhood* (part I, 1910–11 edn, p. 91).
94 The proofs of vol. II of the 1910–11 edition, which included 'The Raid', the Sevastopol tales, 'The Felling of the Forest', *The Cossacks* and 'Morning of a Landowner'.
95 As well as a letter of August 18, Biryukov sent by parcel post some articles by Tolstoy: 'The One Thing Necessary', *On Life*, and others, which were to be included in the new edition. In the first he had indicated the 'passages safe from censorship'.
96 See note 85.
97 Letter to V.F. Krasnov (*PSS*, vol. 82, pp. 118–19).
98 Included in vol. XV of the 1910–11 edition.
99 See note 29. On July 27 Sofia Tolstaya wrote to M.A. Stakhovich: 'Nik. Vas. Davydov has already brought me *Resurrection*, which he has been correcting, but there is still a lot of work to be done on it, and Seryozha is busy with this at the moment' (GMT). As a result of all this preliminary work, various passages that had been deleted when it was first published in *The Cornfield* were restored, and those lines and chapters which could not be published under the existing censorship laws were marked by asterisks (vol. XVIII of the 1910–11 edition).
100 Tolstoy was talking to Ivan Chepurin, who had brought with him a manuscript of his autobiographical work.
101 Sofia Tolstaya was busy preparing vols XIII, XV and XVIII of the 1910–11 edition.
102 Tolstoy wrote to Chertkov on August 14 (two letters), 20, 24 (a note added to a letter from Aleksandra) and 25 (see *PSS*, vol. 89, pp. 204–8).
103 On this day Tolstoy wrote in his 'Diary for Myself Alone': 'Things getting worse and worse with Sofia Andreevna. No love, just the demand for love, which is closer to hatred and is turning into hatred [. . .] The children have saved her – an animal love, but selfless none the less. But when that ends there'll be nothing left but the most frightful egoism. And that egoism is an abnormal condition – madness' (*PSS*, vol. 58, p. 135).
104 An excerpt from Tolstoy's diary of November 29, 1851. (See entry for July 19 in this Diary, and note 48.)
105 *The World's Work*, vol. XVI, no. 94, September, 1910, with photographs (YaPL).
106 Lyova Tolstoy had finished the bust of Sofia Tolstaya which he had started on July 11; it is now at the Yasnaya Polyana Estate Museum.
107 Letter of August 29. Tolstoy wrote: 'How good it would be if you could just control – I don't know what to call it – the feelings in you which are making you so unhappy. How good it would be for you, and for me' (*PSS*, vol. 84, p. 401).
108 For vol. XVII Sofia Tolstaya was reading the proofs of various articles; Tolstoy's Preface (written in the form of a letter to the editor) to L.D. Semyonov's short story 'Smertnaya

kazn' (The death sentence), 'O lozhnoi nauke' (On false science), 'Otvet krestyaninu' (Reply to a peasant) and others.

09 Letter of September 1, sent with Aleksandra Tolstaya (see *PST*, p. 792).

10 Sofia Tolstaya invited a priest called T.A. Kudryavtsev to the house to perform a service with holy water exorcising the spirit of Chertkov. When he heard about this, Tolstoy wrote on September 3–4 in his 'Diary for Myself Alone': 'She burns his pictures and has a service performed in the house [. . .] I must try to remember that she is ill' (*PSS*, vol. 58, p. 136).

11 This refers to Chertkov's letter of March 1910 to the Tsar begging him to revoke his exile from Tula province. Chertkov rewrote and abbreviated the first version of the letter at Tolstoy's suggestion (see *PSS*, vol. 89, p. 177).

12 Letter of September 1 (see *PSS*, vol. 84, p. 401–2).

13 The film was made that winter in Yasnaya Polyana. See Daily Diary, January 6, 1910 and note 5.

14 Henry Bordeaux's book was in fact called *La Peur de vivre* (Paris, 1901).

15 A letter of September 6 in which Chertkov attempted to give a detailed explanation of his relations with Tolstoy, and to persuade Sofia Tolstaya not to feel such 'bitter enmity' for him. 'In any case none of you has the slightest cause to *fear* my influence on Lev Nikolaevich, for I repeat, mine is merely an executive role,' Chertkov assured her. 'I merely fulfil Lev Nikolaevich's wishes and instructions regarding his writings.' At the end of his long missive he appealed to Sofia Tolstaya: 'For the sake of Lev Nikolaevich, who has been so debilitated by all that has happened [. . .] to restore the positive aspects of our mutual relations over these past few years' (see *DST*, IV, pp. 332–6).

16 Tolstoy noted in his 'Diary for Myself Alone': 'She spent the whole of yesterday the 9th in hysterics, ate nothing, wept. She was very pathetic' (*PSS*, vol. 58, p. 136).

17 'Painful discussion about my departure. I stood up for my freedom. I shall go when *I* want,' Tolstoy noted on that day in his diary (*PSS*, vol. 58, p. 101).

18 On September 9 Sofia Tolstaya sent Chertkov a note: 'I have received your letter and shall reply in detail when I feel better and my head is clearer. I shall write from Yasnaya Polyana when I return there with Lev Nikolaevich.' (Quoted in Goldenweiser, II, p. 286.) In a letter of September 11–18 Sofia Tolstaya set out in detail the causes for her enmity towards Chertkov (see *DST*, IV, pp. 337–9).

19 Her letter of September 11, in which she wrote: 'I beg you to understand that all my wishes – not my *demands* as you put it – have but one source: my love for you, my desire to be parted from you as little as possible, and my mortification at this intruder whose influence on our long, loving, intimate marital life has had such a malign effect on me. If this influence is removed – although I realise that unfortunately you would be very loath to see this happen – I shall be eternally grateful for your great sacrifice, which will give me back my life and happiness, and I swear to you that I shall do all I can to surround you with love and happiness, and look after you physically and spiritually.' She also admitted that her 'means to achieve this [. . .] were wicked, clumsy and malicious,' and 'agonising for both of them' (*PST*, p. 793).

20 There is only one known letter from Tolstoy in Kochety; brief and restrained, without salutation, it was dated September 14 and was received on the 15th. See a note in the Daily Diary: 'Received chilling letter from L.N.' (*DST*, IV, p. 195). Tolstoy wrote to his wife: 'I do not wish to speak about our relations, I shall merely try to improve them and am quite sure that with your help I shall manage to do so' (*PSS*, vol. 84, p. 403).

21 See *PSS*, vol. 84, p. 403.

22 On September 22 a telegram was sent from Kochety to Yasnaya Polyana announcing Tolstoy's arrival, but it was evidently delayed (see *PSS*, vol. 84, p. 403).

23 'Detskaya mudrost' (Childhood wisdom) was a journalistic work consisting of 21 dialogues between children and adults (see *PSS*, vol. 37).

24 She is referring to I.A. Malinovskii's book *Krovavaya mest i smertnaya kazn* (Blood

revenge and the death sentence), Tomsk, 1910, sent to Tolstoy by the author with a dedication: 'To Lev Nikolaevich Tolstoy, who exposes all violence, and especially the great evil known as capital punishment' (YaPL). Tolstoy found 'much good and useful material' in this book (*PSS*, vol. 58, p. 107).

125 She is referring to the tract 'What Then Must We Do?', included in vol. XV of the 1910–11 edition. Sofia Tolstaya is using one of Tolstoy's working titles for the piece. 'I am completely occupied with the article "What Is To Be Done?", which is all about money,' he had written at the beginning of April 1885 to Chertkov (*PSS*, vol. 85, p. 160).

126 On October 6 Chertkov wrote Tolstoy two letters. In the first of these he wrote: '[. . .] I think that both in order to give Sofia Andreevna the opportunity to adopt a more loving attitude to you, and to enable you to derive full benefit from the relief that this change will bring, it would be most unwise, while Sofia Andreevna's condition continues to improve, to mention me, under any pretext whatsoever' (quoted in *DST*, IV, p. 350). In the second letter Chertkov accepted an invitation to visit Tolstoy at Yasnaya Polyana, on condition that 'Sofia Andreevna is not there' (GMT).

127 In his 'Diary for Myself Alone' Tolstoy wrote: 'I told her everything I thought necessary. She answered back and I lost my temper' (*PSS*, vol. 58, p. 140).

128 P.P. Nikolaev sent Tolstoy his book *Ponyatie o boge kak sovershennoi osnove zhizni (dukhovno-monistichesckoe mirovozrenie)* (The conception of God as a complete basis of life. (The Spiritual-Monist world view)), vol. I, Geneva, 1907. Vol. II was sent in proofs. (It was published in Geneva in 1910.)

129 The article was intended for vol. XIX of the 1910–11 edition.

130 In this diary entry Sofia Tolstaya inserted an extract from a letter from Chertkov of September 21, 1909, with her own extensive comments, and later supplemented it with a letter from Chertkov to Tolstoy of October 1, 1909 (see *DST*, IV, pp. 217–18).

131 She is referring to an article by B.L. Modzalevskii called 'Biblioteka Pushkina (bibliograficheskoe opisanie)' (Pushkin's library, a bibliographical guide) in the anthology *Pushkin i ego sovremenniki. Materialy i issledovaniya* (Pushkin and his contemporaries. Material and research), issues 9–10, St Petersburg, 1909.

132 It is possible that Sofia Tolstaya had read a long letter from Chertkov of August 11, to which he had affixed an excerpt from his diary of December 4, 1908. In this he sets out in detail the story of the drafting of Tolstoy's will, refers to the mercenary intentions of his family, who, he claimed, were going to appropriate the rights to his literary inheritance, and demonstrates the necessity of a legal will. (See Goldenweiser, II, pp. 230–42).

133 Sofia Tolstaya had found Tolstoy's 'Diary for Myself Alone', which he had scrupulously concealed from her, and in which she learnt (in an entry of July 29 – see *PSS*, vol. 58, p. 129) about the existence of a secret will. See note 49.

134 Entry for July 30 in 'Diary for Myself Alone' (see *PSS*, vol. 58, p. 129).

135 She is referring to Tolstoy's note of September 12, 1862: 'I am mad, I shall shoot myself if this goes on much longer' (*PSS*, vol. 48, p. 44). See Appendices, 'L.N. Tolstoy's Marriage'.

136 Letter of October 12 (*PSS*, vol. 82, pp. 188–9).

137 Tolstoy sent the manuscripts of his works to Chertkov in England to keep for him, and also to publish, as under the existing censorship laws many of them could not be published in Russia. In 1913, after Tolstoy's death, the manuscripts were brought back to Russia and Chertkov gave them to the Academy of Sciences. See Daily Diary, 1915, note 29.

138 The Tula circuit court ratified Tolstoy's will in a public meeting of November 16, 1910.

139 The letter, of October 14, was pasted to the manuscript of the diary (*PST*, pp. 794–5).

140 Tolstoy noted in his diary on that day: 'On my desk was a letter from Sofia Andreevna, filled with accusations [. . .] When she came in I asked her to leave me in peace. She went out. I had difficulty breathing and my pulse was over 90' (*PSS*, vol. 58, p. 118).

141 See Daily Diary, February 1, 1910, note 18.

42 A.K. Chertkova was indeed ill, as Makovitsky informed Tolstoy (*YaZ*, October 16).

43 This meeting with Sofia Tolstaya was described by Sergeenko. (See Goldenweiser, II, pp. 319–20.)

44 A quote from the article 'Uchenie Khrista, izlozhennoe dlya detei' (Christ's teachings explained for children) (see *PSS*, vol. 37, p. 116). This appeared in vol. XIV of the 1910–11 edition.

45 M.P. Novikov described his meeting with Tolstoy in an account entitled 'Moe poslednee svidanie' (My last meeting), published in the journals *Golos Tolstogo i edinenie* (Unity and the voice of Tolstoy) and in *Istinnaya svoboda* (True freedom), no. 7, 1922. Tolstoy told Novikov about his intention to 'leave' Yasnaya Polyana. 'I want to die in peace, I want to be with God,' he told him; 'here they're all wondering what I am worth [. . .] I shall leave, I shall certainly leave' (p. 12). On October 24 Tolstoy wrote Novikov a letter with a request: 'Do you think you could find me a hut in your village, no matter how small, just so long as it's warm and secluded?' Novikov delayed in replying, and spent 'whole days and nights pondering how [. . .] best to dissuade him from leaving Yasnaya Polyana' (pp. 12–13). His letter was eventually brought to Tolstoy at Astapovo.

46 'Perevoznikov came too, and Tito's son, a revolutionary,' noted Tolstoy (*PSS*, vol. 58, p. 121). 'Tito's son' was M.Y. Polin, who had just left prison for participating in the revolutionary movement. Perevoznikov, a metal-worker and a member of a workers' circle, lived with Chertkov.

47 Tolstoy was at the time busy revising his article 'O sotsializme' (On Socialism). See also note 20.

48 Tolstoy was making new corrections to his article 'On Socialism'.

49 Sofia Tolstaya was busy on a compilation of the last works of his life, which included his late journalistic pieces, many of which were banned in Russian and confiscated.

50 On Tolstoy's advice P.N. Gastev wrote down his memories of V.K. Syutaev, whom he had met in 1890 in a commune in Novosele, in the Tver district. See *Vegetarianskoe obozrenie* (Vegetarian review), nos 1–2, 1912.

51 Sofia Tolstaya was reading the first part of her memoirs (*MZh*) (GMT).

52 His only known letter to A.K. Chertkova is dated October 23 (see *PSS*, vol. 89, p. 229).

53 Sofia Tolstaya later added this observation here: 'At that moment he was probably planning his escape, for I sensed the approach of something terrible.'

54 In his farewell letter to his wife Tolstoy wrote: 'I cannot go on living in the luxury which has always surrounded me here, and I am doing what most old men of my age do: leaving this worldly life in order to spend my last days in solitude and silence. Please understand this, I beg you, and do not come to fetch me, even if you should discover where I am' (*PSS*, vol. 84, p. 404).

55 According to Bulgakov, A.K. Chertkova told Goldenweiser on October 29: 'Sofia Andreevna has been in a state of great agitation. She has attempted to kill herself by various methods' (Goldenweiser, II, p. 335).

56 The only members of Tolstoy's family who were with him were his daughters Tanya and Sasha and his son Sergei. The 'Medical findings on the illness and death of L.N. Tolstoy', dated November 9 and signed by D.P. Makovitsky, D.V. Nikitin and G.M. Berkenheim, gave the following explanation for this: 'It was decided at a family council in accordance with the doctors' proposal, that no other members of his family should be allowed in to see L.N., as there was good reason to believe that he would grow extremely agitated at the appearance of any new faces, and this might have dire consequences for his life, which was hanging on a thread.' (Quoted in V.A. Gotvalt, *Poslednie dni Lva Nikolaevicha Tolstogo* (The lst days of Lev Nikolaevich Tolstoy), Moscow, 1911, p. 39.)

DAILY DIARY 1905–7 AND 1909–19

1905

1 The lawyer S.E. Strumenskii had a talk with Tolstoy about the current political movement in Russia, and the events in St Petersburg of January 9, 1905. For more details see *YaZ*, I, pp. 82–6.
2 See this Diary, January 14, 1905.
3 M. Davitt, an Irish political activist, visited Yasnaya Polyana twice. On January 19, 1905, he and a journalist called McKenna visited 'as representatives of ten American newspapers', in order to discover Tolstoy's attitude to the situation in Russia and the events of January 9. On February 3 (new style) Davitt's interview with Tolstoy was published in the newspaper the *Standard*, and McKenna's with him was published in the *New York World*. See also *YaZ*, I, pp. 94–5.
4 Tolstoy worked on his article 'Ob obshchestvennom dvizhenii v Rossii' (On the social movement in Russia) (*PSS*, vol. 36) from 13 to 22 January, and on January 23 he sent it off to Chertkov to publish in England. It came out in 1905 in the Free Word edition.
5 On January 23, 1905 Biryukov brought Tolstoy various documents from Stasov referring to the Decembrist affair: '[. . .] papers, notes, statements [. . .] of the Decembrists.' On March 2, 1905 Tolstoy wrote to V.V. Stasov: 'I received the notes on the Decembrist affair, and have read them with excitement, joy and some quite inappropriate ideas for one of my age.' Later in the letter he asked Stasov to send him some more material (*PSS*, vol. 75, p. 226).
6 The article was called 'Edinoe na potrebu. O gosudarstvennoi vlasti' (The one thing necessary. On government power) (*PSS*, vol. 36). At this time Tolstoy decided to join it to the article 'Kamen glavy ugla' (The corner-stone) (on the meaning of religion), on which he had been working since December 1903.
7 This charity concert was organised by S.N. Glebova. At her request (to give 'just one page to be read aloud') Tolstoy dictated to her an excerpt from *Hadji Murat*. (This did not go into the definitive text, which was published in *PSS*, vol. 35, p. 556.) At this concert, on February 14, A.I. Yuzhina also read an excerpt from *War and Peace*, included in the programme with Sofia Tolstaya's consent.
8 'On the social movement in Russia.' See Daily Diary, January 22 and note 4.
9 At Yasnaya Polyana, in what had once been Tanya Tolstaya's studio, there was a painting by N.V. Orlov called *Before the Flogging* (1904). (It is now in the Museum of the Revolution.) It was reproduced in the album *Russkie muzhiki. Kartiny khudozhnika N. Orlova s predisloviem L.N. Tolstogo* (Russian peasants. Paintings by the artist N. Orlov with an introduction by L.N. Tolstoy), St Petersburg, 1909, here entitled *The Flogging*.
10 The proofs of the *Circle of Reading*. This was subjected to major revisions in the proof stage, and new stories were written and inserted into it. Work on this continued until the end of 1905.
11 Tolstoy's conversation with the correspondent (whose name is not known) of the French newspaper *Le Matin* concerned the internal political situation in Russia (*YaZ*, II, pp. 31–2).
12 See Diary, January 18, 1904.
13 See Daily Diary, January 27 and note 7.
14 The article 'The One Thing Necessary'.
15 The name of this correspondent has not been established. Tolstoy said of him: 'A correspondent from the *Northamerican* [*sic*] came to see me, dressed up to the nines in a waistcoat, ring and chain! An obtuse, uneducated man, doesn't understand a thing.' Tolstoy evidently meant the *North American Newspaper* (*YaZ*, II, p. 64).
16 Tolstoy asked Nikolai Obolenskii to compile a biographical sketch of Pascal. He then totally

reworked the text and wrote an introduction and conclusion. Signed 'L.N. Tolstoy', it was published in the *Circle of Reading*, vol. II, Moscow, Intermediary, 1906 (*PSS*, vol. 41).

17 L.A. Avilova sent Tolstoy her story 'Pervoe gore' (The first grief), at his request (published in *RB*, no. 8, 1900). The story was edited twice by Tolstoy, with Avilova's consent (*PSS*, vol. 75, p. 236) and published in the *Circle of Reading*, vol. II.

18 N.A. Andreev's bust, *Tolstoy at Work*, 1905, in plaster, is at the GMT.

19 K. Waliszewskii, *La Dernière des Romanoff. Elisabeth I*, 3rd edn, Paris, 1902. V.V. Stasov was asked by Tolstoy to send him this book (*PSS*, vol. 75, p. 194).

20 Sofia Tolstaya wrote an open letter stating her views on the war after an article by Lyova Tolstoy, 'Mysli i zhizn' (Thoughts and life) appeared in *NV* (no. 10,414, March 3, 1905), supporting the continuation of the Russo-Japanese War. She sent this letter off to Chertkov in England for publication on March 18, 1905, along with a letter in which she said that she was doing so 'with the approval of Lev Nikolaevich and the others' (GMT). On March 23 Sofia Tolstaya wrote to her son: '[. . .] I hear rumours on all sides that it was Lev Lvovich's mother who inspired him with these views, and that his mother preaches war, in opposition to Lev Nikolaevich. As this is untrue, I wanted to state the facts and publish to the whole world my *own* views on the war' (GMT). See Daily Diary, April 22.

21 Lines from Fet's poem 'Maiskaya noch' (May Night) (1870).

22 S.I. Taneev's article 'Po povodu postanovleniya direktsii imperatorskogo Russkogo muzykalnogo obshchestva ot 19 Marta 1905' (On the decision taken by the Imperial Russian Musical Society on March 19, 1905), (*Rus* (Holy Russia), no. 93, April 11, 1905), in which he attacked the unlawful decision to dismiss Rimsky-Korsakov from the conservatory without the knowledge of the Artistic Council.

23 The Book *Izbrannye rechi i stati Genri Dzhordzha* (Selected speeches and articles by Henry George), tr. S.D. Nikolaev (Moscow, Intermediary, 1905, YaPL), contained a biography of Henry George written by the translator. Tolstoy was again 'in raptures' (*PSS*, vol. 55, p. 134).

24 The 33rd exhibition of paintings by the Fellowship of Wandering Artists was opened in the School of Art, Sculpture and Architecture.

25 On March 7, 1905 an exhibition of Russian portraits opened in the halls of the Tauride Palace, organised by L. Bakst, I. Bilibin and S. Diaghilev. Some 3,000 portraits by Russian artists were exhibited, including one of Tanya Tolstaya by I.E. Repin (oils, 1893), which belonged to Tolstoy.

26 Charles Sarolia, professor of French literature at Edinburgh University. He describes his meeting with Tolstoy in his article 'Tolstoy kak reformator' (Tolstoy as reformer), in *Mezhdunarodnyi Tolstovskii Almanakh* (International Tolstoy Almanac), Moscow, 1909.

27 Tolstoy's story 'Molitva' (Prayer), written from late April to early May 1905 and published in the *Circle of Reading*, vol. I, Moscow, Intermediary, 1906 (*PSS*, vol. 41).

28 Andreev was working on a second bust of Tolstoy at Yasnaya Polyana (1905, plaster, GMT).

29 After Chertkov had left, Tolstoy wrote in his diary: 'It was very good with him, even better than I expected' (*PSS*, vol. 55, p. 144).

30 Tolstoy wrote the Afterword (not the Foreword) to Chekhov's 'Darling' in January–February 1905, and it was published in the *Circle of Reading*, vol. I. See also Diary, January 14, 1899 and note 6.

31 Tolstoy visited the Optyna Pustyn Monastery three times before 1905 – in 1877, 1881 and 1890. This probably refers to his visits in 1877 and 1881, as Biryukov includes a description of these in his two-volume *L.N. Tolstoi Biografiya* (L.N. Tolstoy. A biography), Moscow, Intermediary, 1908, chapters XII and XVIII, devoted to Tolstoy's life in the years 1862–84.

32 For Tolstoy's part in the defence of the soldier V. Shibunin, see Diary, August 10, 1866, and note 6. A description of this episode was included in Biryukov's biography (vol. II, ch. 5).

33 For a description of Tolstoy's work on the fables see Appendices: 'Various Notes for Future Reference', February 14, 1870, and note 5. The fable 'Mikulushka Selyaninovich' was in book IV of the *ABC*, Moscow, 1872, pp. 92–6 (*PSS*, vol. 22).

34 According to Tolstoy, his story 'Yagody' (Berries) was written 'in two days' (June 10 and 11), and was 'not bad' (*PSS*, vol. 55, p. 146). Published in *Circle of Reading*, vol. 1.

35 M.D. Zavalishina brought Tolstoy her father's book *Zapiski dekabrista* (Notes of a Decembrist), vols 1–2, Munich, 1904 (YaPL). Tolstoy had been personally acquainted with D. Zavalishin, and in the early 1880s had offered to publish his memoirs in Russia at his own expense, but Zavalishin had not wanted them to be published, as he feared major deletions by the censors.

36 Gorky's story 'Tyurma' (Prison) in the *Sbornik tovarishchestva Znanie za 1904* (Anthology of the Knowledge Fellowship for 1904), book 4, St Petersburg, 1905.

37 The newspaper *Slovo* (Word), no. 200, July 7, 1905, announced that there had been an attempt on Pobedonostsev's life. A denial of this was published in *NV* on July 9 (no. 10,542).

38 In July 1905 Tolstoy looked through the typed manuscript of the first volume of Biryukov's biography of him, and made various corrections and additions to it. On that day Tolstoy dictated to Biryukov an abbreviated version of his childhood reminiscences (*PSS*, vol. 34, pp. 401–3).

39 In other words the years 1891–2, when Tolstoy and his family worked together to help the starving peasants of the Ryazan and Tula provinces. On July 18, 1905 Sofia Tolstaya wrote to her daughter Tatiana Sukhotina: 'And today I have been sorting through [. . .] the letters from the famine years. That too was an important and sad time. But it's good to work as we worked then' (GMT).

40 Probably sayings from his book *Mysli mudrykh lyudei na kazhdyi den, sobrannye L.N. Tolstym* (Thoughts of the wise men for every day, collected by L.N. Tolstoy), Moscow, Intermediary, 1903 (YaPL), which Tolstoy was constantly re-reading. See Diary, 1903, note 4.

41 A.I. Herzen's story 'Dolg prezhde vsego' (Duty before everything) (*YaZ*, July 27).

42 The cause of this discussion was that Tolstoy's latest articles had been taken by I.I. Gorbunov-Posadov, and Sofia Tolstaya considered that both he and I.D. Sytin were 'making money from Tolstoy's works' (*YaZ*, August 9). On August 10 Tolstoy noted in his diary: 'Yesterday I sinned and lost my temper over my works and their publication' (*PSS*, vol. 55, p. 157).

43 Tolstoy's story 'Posle bala' (After the ball) was written in 1903 but was not properly finished, and was not published in his lifetime (*PSS*, vol. 34).

44 This article was inspired by the defeat of the Russians at Tsushima on May 14, 1905. Tolstoy remarked in his diary: 'This latest crushing blow to the fleet evokes a number of thoughts which must be expressed' (*PSS*, vol. 55, p. 140). He began the work in June 1905 and finished it in December. The article was published in the Free Word edition in London, in 1905 (*PSS*, vol. 36).

45 On September 4, 1905, no. 240 of *RV* published a letter from Taneev about his departure from the conservatoire. Taneev took this decision because of a conflict that arose between him and the director, S.I. Safonov, who particularly condemned him for publishing a letter in defence of Rimsky-Korsakov. See an excerpt from Taneev's diary in the book *P.I. Chaikovskii, S.I. Taneev. Pisma.* (P.I. Tchaikovsky, S.I. Taneev, letters), Moscow, 1951, p. 526. See Daily Diary, April 16.

46 These chapters of his 'Reminiscences' about his father (chapter III) and Tatiana Ergolskaya (chapter VI) (*PSS*, vol. 34, pp. 355–8, 364–70) were written by Tolstoy in January–February 1903 and included in vol. I of Biryukov's biography, which Tolstoy was looking through at this time.

47 Biryukov, with Tolstoy's permission, had included in chapter 10 of the first volume of his biography, his letters to V.V. Arseneva (see Diary, 1863 and note 9). At Sofia Tolstaya's request these letters were excluded and Biryukov simply wrote a brief summary of them.

They were published in the third edition of Biryukov's biography, vol. I, Moscow/Petersburg, 1923. See also Daily Diary, November 3.

48 H. Taine, *L'Ancien Régime et la révolution*.

49 It was Lepsius, not Andreas, who came with A.I. Stefanovich to see Tolstoy (*YaZ*, September 24).

50 In the letter which Sofia Tolstaya wrote on September 30, 1905, with the collaboration of Taneev and Goldenweiser (and in another letter of September 10), she addressed Grand Duke K.K. Romanov, the vice-president of the Russian Musical Society, about the extremely unsatisfactory situation in the Moscow and St Petersburg conservatoires, which had come about after the constitution of the RMS was abolished by its directors, and which was largely due to the rude and autocratic behaviour of Safonov. She expressed her unease that the 'St Petersburg conservatoire was now without Rimsky-Korsakov, Lyadov and Glazunov, and Moscow was without Ziloti and Taneev' (GMT).

51 Tolstoy worked on this story from February to May 1905, and published it in the *Circle of Reading*, vol. I, Moscow, Intermediary, 1906 (*PSS*, vol. 41).

52 From September 27 to October 6, 1905 Tolstoy was reading N.K. Schilder's book *Imperator Aleksandr Pervyi, ego zhizn i tsarstvovanie* (Emperor Alexander I, his life and reign), vols. 1–4, 2nd edn, St Petersburg, 1904–5. His notes are on all the volumes. See *Biblioteka L.N. Tolstogo v Yasnoi Polyane* (L.N. Tolstoy's library at Yasnaya Polyana), vol. 2, Moscow, 1975, pp. 467–8. Tolstoy had for many years been interested by the legend according to which Alexander I did not die at Taganrog but assumed the name Fyodor Kuzmich and ended his life in Siberia. On October 6, 1905 he noted in his diary: '[. . .] read and made notes on Alexander I. What a weak and confused creature. I don't know whether I shall write anything about him' (*PSS*, vol. 55, p. 164). But a week later he remarked: 'Fyodor Kuzmich fascinates me more and more' (*PSS*, vol. 55, p. 165), and in the beginning of November he started work on his story 'Posmertnye zapiski startsa Fyodora Kuzmicha, umershego 20 yanvarya 1864 g. v Sibiri, bliz goroda Tomska v zaimke kuptsa Khromova' (The posthumous notes of old Fyodor Kuzmich, who died on January 20, 1864 in Siberia, near the town of Tomsk, in the village of the merchant Khromov) (*PSS*, vol. 55, pp. 170, 36). The story remained unfinished and was not published in Tolstoy's lifetime.

53 They were probably re-reading Gorky's story 'Tyurma' (Prison) (*YaZ*, *GM*, no. 3, 1923, p. 12).

54 Tolstoy was at the time reading N.K. Schilder's study *Imperator Pavel I* (Emperor Paul I) (St Petersburg, 1901) and S.A. Poroshin's *Zapiski, sluzhashchie k istorii Pavla Petrovicha* (Notes for a history of Paul I), 2nd edn, St Petersburg, 1881. For more details see *YaZ*, *GM*, no. 3, 1923, pp. 5, 7–10, 13.

55 Kuprin's tale 'Poedinok' (The duel) in *Sbornik tovarishchestva Znanie za 1905* (Anthology of the Knowledge Fellowship for 1905, book 6, St Petersburg, 1905). They began reading it on October 8, and after hearing the first chapters, Tolstoy observed: 'What audacity! How did it get past the censors!' After reading chapters XII to XV of the work he said of Kuprin: 'He gives a vivid picture of army life.' For more details see *YaZ*; *GM*, no. 3, 1923, pp. 12, 14–15.

56 This was the October All-Russian political strike.

57 On October 17, 1905, under pressure from the revolutionary movement, Nicholas II granted a manifesto which promised people 'the firm foundations of civil freedom: personal immunity, freedom of conscience, speech, assembly and union'. A State Duma (Parliament) was convened. Telling his family about the manifesto, Tolstoy said, 'There's nothing bad in it.' But on October 23, having read this manifesto, he said: 'There's nothing in it for the people' (*YaZ* and *GM*, no. 3, 1923, pp. 20–1, 27).

58 A.I. Herzen, *Pisma iz Frantsii (pismo odinadtsatoe)* (Letters from France, the eleventh letter), *YaZ* and *GM*, no. 3, 1923, p. 25.

59 Tolstoy informed Biryukov, in a letter of October 18, 1905, that Sofia Tolstaya was copying out his letters to Tatiana Kuzminskaya at his request, and would give them to Biryukov, as they contained an 'exceedingly detailed description of all the events of our marriage' (*PSS*, vol. 76, p. 44).

60 *Moskovskii vedomosti* (Moscow Gazette), nos 285–6, October 27–8, 1905 published an article by Ya.G. Bulanov entitled 'L.N. Tolstoi i "osvoboditelnoe dvizhenie"' (L.N. Tolstoy and the 'liberation movement'). The author accused Tolstoy of promoting the development of the revolutionary movement throughout the country with his works, which were 'directed at the radical abolition of the bases of religion, autocracy, government and law'. The GMT contains a rough draft of Sofia Tolstaya's article. It is not known whether it was published or not.

61 In a letter to Sofia Tolstaya of November 10, Biryukov wrote that he assumed that she would not consider it possible to publish Tolstoy's letters to V.V. Arseneva, as they had not got permission from Arseneva herself, and begged her to help him obtain this from her. After a discussion with his wife, Tolstoy wrote to Biryukov, on November 11, 1905: 'I am very sad that your dear, kind letter was taken so badly' (*PSS*, vol. 76, p. 48).

62 A daughter, Tatiana, was born to Tanya and Mikhail Sergeevich Sukhotin.

63 At Tolstoy's request (*PSS*, vol. 76, p. 45), V.V. Stasov had sent him some books about the murder of Paul I: Brückner, *Kaiser Paul's Ende*, Stuttgart, 1897; A. Czartoryski, *Mémoires*, London, 1888, 2 vols.

64 The story 'Bozheskoe i chelovecheskoe' (The human and the divine), on which Tolstoy had been working since 1903, was being prepared by Chertkov for publication in the Free Word edition and for translation into English. In October 1905 he sent the proofs of the story from England. Tolstoy looked through them, decided that 'the major part, Svetlogub's last hours, are disgustingly bad' (*PSS*, vol. 89, p. 25), and set to work rewriting the story. For more details see V.A. Zhdanov, *Poslednie knigi L.N. Tolstogo* (L.N. Tolstoy's last books), Moscow, 1971, pp. 217–42. On December 3, 1905 the story was sent off to Chertkov (*PSS*, vol. 89, p. 29), but was not published. It was first published in the *Circle of Reading*, vol. II.

65 The subject of Tolstoy's discussion with Gusev and the self-educated poet F.E. Postupaev was the second congress of the All-Russian Peasant Assembly, held in Moscow from November 6 to 10, 1905. They also discussed the poetry of V.Ya. Bryusov. See Postupaev's memoirs *U L.N. Tolstogo* (With L.N. Tolstoy), Jubilee Anthology, Moscow/Leningrad, 1928, p. 240.

66 L.A. Sulerzhitskii and V.E. Meyerhold arrived in Yasnaya Polyana (*YaZ*, November 26).

67 I.P. Yuvachov (Mirolyubov) on several occasions sent his books and reprints of his articles to Tolstoy. Several of them contain a dedication. See *Biblioteka L.N. Tolstogo v Yasnoi Polyane*, vol. 2.

68 On November 30 Tolstoy made the final corrections to a small article 'Pismo L.N. Tolstogo k krestyaninu o zemle (O proekte Genri Dzhordzha)' (L.N. Tolstoy's letter to a peasant about the land (on the Henry George plan)), (*PSS*, vol. 90). Tolstoy also made some additions to his article 'Konets veka' (The end of the century) (*PSS*, vol. 89, p. 29) and continued writing his article 'Svobody i svoboda' (Freedoms and freedom), which later formed chapter XII of the article 'The end of the century' (*PSS*, vol. 36, pp. 267–75).

69 A reference to the armed uprising in Moscow in December 1905.

70 See note 48.

71 In the middle of December 1905 Tolstoy started work on his article 'Pravitelstvo, revolyutsionery, narod' (Government revolutionaries and people) (final title: 'Obrashchenie k russkim lyudyam. K pravitelstvu, revolyutsioneram i narodu' (An appeal to the Russian people. To the government, revolutionaries and people) (*PSS*, vol. 36). Later he told Chertkov that 'despite my distance from the centre of struggle, I was carried along in the wave and wrote my article under the influence of that struggle' (*PSS*, vol. 89, p. 36).

1906

1 Tolstoy was collecting information about peasant families in need of help, in order to distribute amongst them the money he had received from various people in aid of those stricken by the bad harvest.

2 She is referring to a concert at the Circle of Russian Music-Lovers (1896–1912) organised in Moscow by the lawyer A.M. Kerzin.

3 This was not published in *RM*, as Tolstoy thought it would be (see his letter to Chertkov of January 14, 1906 – *PSS*, vol. 89, p. 34). The article, entitled 'An Appeal to the Russian People. To the Government, Revolutionaries and People', appeared as a separate pamphlet in the Free Word edition, 1906.

4 November 22, 1905 saw the publication of the 'Temporary Rules for the Press', announcing the abolition of preliminary censorship for periodical publications. After this some editors announced the publication in journals and supplements of previously banned works by Tolstoy. On January 14, 1906 Tolstoy, on the advice of Chertkov, wrote a letter to editors recommending that in order to avoid publishing inaccurate texts they should 'apply for the originals [. . .] to [. . .] Chertkov, who has the most complete collection' (*PSS*, vol. 76, p. 81). This was published on January 18 in *RV*, no. 17, and *NV*, no. 10, 721, and was reprinted in other papers.

5 The manuscript of M.S. Kerzina's unpublished works *Moi vospominaniya o kruzhke lyubitelei russkoi muzyki* (My memoirs of the Circle of Russian Music-Lovers) is now at the Glinka State Museum of Musical Culture in Moscow.

6 A correspondent of the London newspaper *Tribune*, a physician named Cunard, visited Yasnaya Polyana (*YaZ*, January 29).

7 Sofia Tolstaya may have had in mind the unfinished story 'The Posthumous Notes of old Fyodor Kuzmich . . .'. which was based on the legend about the death of Alexander I. Tolstoy worked on this throughout December 1905. See Daily Diary, 1905, note 52.

8 All these stories were published in the *Circle of Reading*, vol. 1.

9 Sofia Tolstaya told Tanya Kuzminskaya, in a letter of March 27, 1906, that she was copying a landscape of Pokhitonov's called *Oaks in Chepyzh*. Copy in oils at the GMT.

10 In 1905 Aleksander Mikhailovich Kuzminskii made a senatorial tour of inspection of Baku in connection with the Armenian-Azerbaijani nationalist upheavals. He told Sofia Tolstaya, in a letter of February 5, 1906, that he had sent an account of the tour to Yasnaya Polyana (GMT).

11 The Japanese writer Kenziro Tokutomi (pseudonym Tokutomi Roka) sent Tolstoy his novel, *Tokutomi. Nami-Ko* (Boston, 1904) (YaPL) with a dedication. A Russian translation is contained in *Mir Bozhii* (God's World), nos. 1–4, 1905.

12 Ilya Tolstoy's story 'Slishkom pozdno' (Too late), published in *VE*, no. 4, 1904.

13 The chapter 'Mort de Paul' is from A. Sorel's book *L'Europe et la Révolution française*, vol. 6, Paris, 1903, pp. 118–38.

14 S.A. Poroshin, *Zapiski, sluzhashchie k istorii Pavla Petrovicha* (Notes for a history of Paul I), 2nd edn, St Petersburg, 1881 (YaPL).

15 Tolstoy worked on his story 'For What?' from January 20 to the end of February 1906. The subject is borrowed from a book by S.V. Maksimov, *Siberia and Hard Labour* (See Diary, 1898, note 147), vol. 3, pp. 73–5. The story is published in *Circle of Reading*, vol. II.

16 Yuvachov's articles are contained in *IV*, no. 2, 1906.

17 Tolstoy's article 'Notes for Soldiers' was written in 1901 and published in England in 1902 in the Free Word edition (*PSS*, vol. 34). In Russia it was distributed in illegal editions, and in 1906 it was printed by several publishers.

18 V.V. Veresaev, 'Rasskazy o voine' (Tales of war), 1, Lomailo, in *Mir Bozhii* (God's World), no. 2, 1906 (*YaZ*, March 2).

19 Carbonel, former secretary to the French embassy in St Petersburg, declared himself in a conversation with Tolstoy to be in favour of the political struggle. After meeting him Tolstoy noted in his diary: 'Lost my temper with Carbonel' (*PSS*, vol. 55, p. 205).

20 E.F. Yunge's painting and Sofia Tolstaya's copy (in oils) are at the Yasnaya Polyana Estate Museum.

21 N.S. Askarkhanov, publisher and editor of the St Petersburg journal *Russkoe svobodnoe slovo* (Russian Free Word), published in nos 1–6 for 1906 some works of Tolstoy's that had been banned by the censors.

22 P.A. Sergeenko was preparing a second edition of his book *Kak zhivyot i rabotaet L.N. Tolstoy* (How L.N. Tolstoy lives and works), published in Moscow in 1908.

23 Sofia Tolstaya was preparing the 12th edition of the *Complete Collected Works* of Tolstoy, and wanted to include in it works previously banned by the censors. On the advice of N.V. Davydov and the lawyer Makarenko she decided not to pursue the idea (*YaZ*, March 19).

24 M.S. Sukhotin was elected as a delegate to the first State *Duma*.

25 At the end of March and the beginning of April 1906 Tolstoy read N.A. Sablukov's 'Zapiski o vremeni Pavla i ego konchine' (Notes on the reign of Paul and his death), and 'Zapiski Ekateriny Vtoroi' (Memoirs of Catherine II), *IV*, nos 1–3, 1906.

26 D.A. Khomyakov's brochure 'Samoderzhavie (Opyt skhematicheskogo postroeniya etogo ponyatia)' (Autocracy. An attempt at a schematic construction of this concept), 2nd edn, Moscow, 1905. Tolstoy read it from 4 to 7 February and found it 'very interesting and clever' (*PSS*, vol. 36, p. 509). After reading it he noted in his diary his thoughts on power and its origins (*PSS*, vol. 55, pp. 188–93). These notes formed the basis of his article 'Dve dorogi' (Two roads) (final title: 'O znachenii russkoi revolyutsii' (The meaning of the Russian Revolution), *PSS*, vol. 36), on which Tolstoy worked from April to September 1906. In November the article was published in an Intermediary edition.

27 M.M. Klechkovskii, one of the organisers of the educational cultural establishment 'House of the Free Child', which existed in Moscow between 1906 and 1909, visited Tolstoy to talk to him about children's education and methods of teaching them trades (*YaZ*, April 27).

28 A reference to a discussion between Tolstoy and his sons Ilya and Sergei about politics and land reform (*PSS*, vol. 55, pp. 224, 544–5).

29 See Daily Diary for September 19, 1905 and note 48.

30 Tolstoy was reading 'Revelation and Reason' (a translated excerpt from Rousseau's *Confessions*), which was included in the *Circle of Reading*, vol. II. Tolstoy was at that time correcting the proofs of this and of Kropotkin's *Rechi buntovshchika* (Speeches of an insurgent), St Petersburg, 1906 (*YaZ*, May 27).

31 In a conversation with Yu.D. Belyaev Tolstoy said that the State Duma made a 'comical, scandalous and repugnant impression' on him, and he gave Belyaev, to include in his article, a brief summary which he had translated from the *Standard*, of the Henry George scheme, as well as his conclusion to it (*PSS*, vol. 55, p. 230).

32 Returning the proofs to Belyaev on June 12, 1906, Tolstoy wrote that he had found his feuilleton 'extremely well written' (*PSS*, vol. 76, p. 160). Yu.D.Belyaev, 'U Lva Nikolaevicha Tolstogo' (With Lev Nikolaevich Tolstoy), *NV*, no. 10,808, June 16, 1906.

33 The Japanese writer Kenziro Tokutomi spent five days in Yasnaya Polyana. Tolstoy told V.V. Stasov, in a letter of June 21, 1906, that he had found him 'a good person, and very sensitive' (*PSS*, vol. 76, p. 162). Tokutomi's memoirs about his meeting with Tolstoy 'Pyat dnei v Yasnoi Polyane' (Five days in Yasnaya Polyana), are in *LN*, vol. 75, book 2, pp. 170–202. See also note 11.

34 The article 'Two Roads'. See note 26.

35 One of the visiting Japanese was a journalist called Shingoro Takaishi. He later recalled that he had not 'intended to engage in serious arguments with Tolstoy [. . .] and wanted only to present himself and his readers with a vivid picture of Tolstoy'. He was convinced, however, that 'this old man of almost eighty was still possessed of a strong will, was continuing to

learn, and had not abandoned the pen with which he had written so many great works' (*LN*, vol. 75, book 2, p. 460). For more details about this see A.I. Shifman's *Lev Tolstoi i Vostok* (Lev Tolstoy and the East), Moscow, 1971, pp. 283–4.

36 Tolstoy was visited by some peasants who had chopped down several oak trees in the Yasnaya Polyana forest, were arrested by the bailiff, and now wanted him to defend them. Sofia Tolstaya handed the matter over to the court, despite Tolstoy's plea that they be released, and the peasants were sent to prison. After the trial Sofia Tolstaya agreed to pardon them, but this proved to be legally impossible. See P. Sergeenko, 'V Yasnoi Polyane' (In Yasnaya Polyana), *Iskry* (Sparks), no. 36, 1906, p. 493; and Goldenweiser, p. 188.

37 The French writer A. Leroy-Beaulieu visited Yasnaya Polyana on May 9, 1905.

38 Tolstoy visited the district government offices to ask that public assistance be given to a poor widow from the village of Mostovaya, who was bringing up both her own children and those of her dead sister (*YaZ*, August 1 and 7).

39 We do not know what Tolstoy said about Chernyshevskii on this occasion. For their relationship see M.P. Nikolaev's book *L.N. Tolstoi i N.G. Chernyshevskii* (L.N. Tolstoy and N.G. Chernyshevskii), Tula, 1969.

40 For Tolstoy's attitude to the philosophical views of Herbert Spencer see his article 'What Then Must We Do?', chapter XXX (*PSS*, vol. 25), and a diary note of June 18, 1895 (*PSS*, vol. 53, p. 40–3). Various ideas of Spencer's were contained separately in the *Circle of Reading*, however.

41 M.O. Menshikov printed several articles critical of Tolstoy. Their conversation immediately turned into a bitter quarrel, with Menshikov challenging Tolstoy's views on religion and modern science (*PSS*, vol. 55, pp. 236, 555–6).

42 A. France, *Na belom kamne* (On the white stone), St Petersburg, 1906, chapter IV.

43 P.I. Biryukov was continuing his work on the second volume of his biography of Tolstoy.

44 M.V. Nesterov stayed in Yasnaya Polyana from 20 to 22 August and made several sketches of Tolstoy for a picture he had his in mind called *Na Rusi* (In Holy Russia). The sketches are in the GMT. Nesterov described his stay there in his book *Davnie dni* (Bygone days), Moscow, 1959, pp. 274–84.

45 See V.F. Snegiryov's memoirs 'Operatsiya. Iz zapisok vracha' (Operation. From a doctor's notes), in *Mezhdunarodnyi tolstovskii almanakh* (International Tolstoy Almanac), Moscow, 1909, pp. 332–40. Tolstoy wrote in his diary on that day: 'They have just operated. They say it was a success. But it's hard. This morning she was so spiritually beautiful' (*PSS*, vol. 55, pp. 241–2).

46 Aleksandra Tolstaya wrote to Chertkov on September 29, 1906: 'It's terrible to move old people from one place to an unfamiliar setting and climate. Papa said yesterday that if it is essential for Maman's sake, then he'll go. But Maman is afraid to move him and thinks she'll feel calmer without him' (GMT). Sofia Tolstaya's trip did not take place.

47 In the village of Sudakovo, situated near the Likhvinskaya railway line, seventeen peasant households were burnt to the ground as the result of a flying spark from a passing steam engine. Tolstoy urged that financial help be given to the victims of the fire, and that money be made available to remove the houses near the railway line to a safe spot. He took the case to a barrister, B.O. Goldenblatt, and to the Vice-Governor of Tula province, V.A. Lopukhin (*PSS*, vol. 76, pp. 211–12).

48 Chertkov's letter to Sofia Tolstaya of October 18 (new style), 1906, in which he expressed his sympathy and hopes for her speedy recovery (GMT).

49 E. Adler, *Znamenitye zhenshchiny Frantsuzskoi revolyutsii 1789–1795* (Famous women of the French Revolution 1789–1795), Moscow, 1907. The book evidently appeared at the end of 1906 (*YaZ*, October 23 and 24).

50 On October 27 Andrei Tolstoy, at his father's request, went to Tula to ask the Governor to find places in the orphanage for the six children of the village policeman, who had shot himself. As there were no places in the orphanage, it was decided to organise a charity

concert in aid of the orphans. It is not known which excerpt was given, or whether the concert took place. The children were eventually taken into the orphanage (*YaZ*, October 28 and November 8).

51 The American writer L. Scott and his wife (*YaZ*, November 4).

52 Sofia Tolstaya was copying Pokhitonov's painting *The Place Where the Green Stick is Buried.* The original, in oils, is at the Yasnaya Polyana Estate Museum. Sofia Tolstaya's copy was given to A.A. Goldenweiser. See Goldenweiser, p. 196.

53 P. Sabatier sent Tolstoy his book *Po povodu otdeleniya tserkvi ot gosudarstva* (On the separation of Church and State), 2nd edn (Fischbacher, Paris, 1906), and in a letter of October 2 (new style) 1906, he asked him to write an article on this subject for a magazine. Tolstoy's letter to Sabatier of November 7–20, 1906, on which he worked for about 2 weeks, was published in the paper *Siècle* at the end of November (*PSS*, vol. 76, pp. 223–31).

54 Durland visited Yasnaya Polyana with his wife (*YaZ*, November 10).

55 Tolstoy's article 'O Shekspire i o drame' (On Shakespeare and Drama) (*PSS*, vol. 35) was published in *RS*, nos 277–85, November 12, 18 and 23, 1906, not in translation from the English but from a manuscript which Chertkov gave to I.D. Sytin (*PSS*, vol. 35, p. 684; vol. 89, p. 49).

56 Tolstoy was re-reading the essays of Montaigne (*YaZ*, November 15). There are two editions of this book, with Tolstoy's notes, in the Yasnaya Polyana library: M. Montaigne, *Essais*, Paris, 1882, 3 vols, and Paris (n.d.), 4 vols.

57 Tolstoy wrote to Chertkov about this in a letter of November 16 (new style), 1906 (GMT).

58 A group of Dukhobors travelled to Russia from Canada to enquire about the possibility of later returning home.

59 Tolstoy had been working since March 1906 on a children's version of the *Circle of Reading*, and in these lessons with the peasant children he was testing whether the material he had prepared was accessible to them.

60 Tolstoy generally wrote a summarised version of his thoughts in his notebook, which he always carried around with him, then copied them into his diary, where he developed them. On December 29 Tolstoy transferred into his diary all his notes for the end of November and December (*PSS*, vol. 55, pp. 372–3 and 393–6).

1907

1 This sentence was written by Tolstoy himself. His letters to M.A. Stakhovich and Olga Tolstaya are dated January 1, 1907 (*PSS*, vol. 77, pp. 5–7).

2 Sofia Tolstaya was reading her memoirs covering the years 1876–8. Sukhotin was interested in the year 1876–7, when Tolstoy changed 'from being a non-believer to being an ardent orthodox believer'. In Sofia Tolstaya's memoirs there was no 'psychological explanation' for this 'extraordinary crisis', and Sukhotin mentioned this to Tolstoy. Tolstoy replied, 'Yes, I know, it would be hard to describe it in any more detail. For me too it's quite inexplicable, a sort of leap, something it would be impossible to amplify.' In 'Iz dnevnika M.S. Sukhotina' (From the diary of M.S. Sukhotin), *LN*, vol. 69, book 2, pp. 190–1.

3 Xenophon, *Vospominaniya o Sokrate* (Memories of Socrates) ('Memorabilia', *PSS*, vol. 56, pp. 3, 179). In the book *Ksenofont, Poln. Sobr. soch. v 5-ti chastyakh* (Xenophon, Complete Collected Works in 5 parts), vol. 2, St Petersburg, 1902 (YaPL, with Tolstoy's notes). Tolstoy was reading Xenophon simultaneously in Greek and in Russian translation (*YaZ*, January 13).

4 A reference to Shaw's *Man and Superman. A Comedy and Philosophy*, London, 1906 (YaPL, with Tolstoy's notes), sent to Tolstoy by the author. In the summer of 1908 Tolstoy re-read it, and on August 17 he sent Shaw a letter containing his views on it (*PSS*, vol. 78, pp. 201–4).

5 N.A. Morozov, 'V. nachale zhizni' (At the beginning of life), in *RB*, nos 5–6, 1906. Tolstoy

wrote Morozov a letter on April 6–11, 1907, saying that he had read this 'with the greatest interest and satisfaction' (*PSS*, vol. 77, p. 78). 'I found this Morozov most instructive,' said Tolstoy (*YaZ*, January 22).

6 Menshikov's article 'Pisma k blizhnim. Dve Rossii' (Letters to intimates. Two Russias), in *NV*, no. 11,085, January 21, 1907. Nesterov's painting *Svyataya Rus* (Holy Russia) was displayed at his personal show in January 1907 in St Petersburg. In his letter to Menshikov Tolstoy thanked him for his article and wrote that he had 'wept when he read it' (*PSS*, vol. 77, p. 17).

7 The 35th exhibition of the Fellowship of Wandering Artists opened in the Historical Museum.

8 Tolstoy had resumed work on 'Detskii zakon bozhii' (The law of God for children), which he had started in 1906.

9 After his talk N.F. Nazhivin wrote to Tolstoy, on February 10, 1907: 'My lecture was met with a sympathetic response from the audience.'

10 Camille Flammarion, *Nevedomoye v prirode (Yavleniya mediumizma)* (The unknown in nature. Phenomena of mediumism), excerpts published in an illustrated supplement to the newspaper *Rus* (Holy Russia), nos 4 and 6, 1907.

11 E. Renan, *Saint Paul* (1869), part of his *Histoire des origines du christianisme*, 7 vols, Paris, 1863–82.

12 A.A. Fet, *Moi vospominaniya, 1848–9* (My reminiscences), vols 1–2, Moscow, 1890 (YaPL).

13 Tolstoy was selecting philosophical sayings for a children's *Circle of Reading.*

14 Tolstoy was choosing stories for a children's *Circle of Reading.* In a letter of March 7 he asked I.I. Gorbunov-Posadov to send him 'any [. . .] good childrens' stories' (*PSS*, vol. 56, p. 185; vol. 77, p. 54). Tolstoy wrote six stories for the children's *Circle of Reading* (see *PSS*, vol. 40, pp. 401–22).

15 See 'From the Diary of M.S. Sukhotin', *LN*, vol. 69, p. 193. They may have talked about the *Narodnoe slovo* (People's Word), a religious newspaper published by Bodyanskii.

16 S.T. Semyonov, 'V rozhdestvenskuyu noch', (On Christmas Eve), Moscow, Intermediary, 1904.

17 The day before, Tolstoy had divided his pupils by age into two classes. On March 17 he wrote in his notebooks: 'Lesson with the 2nd class. Very good' (*PSS*, vol. 56, pp. 18, 187).

18 The play was performed in St Petersburg's Maly Theatre. A review, signed 'V. Sh.', was published in *NV*, no. 11,140, March 18, 1907.

19 The chapter 'Nikolai Nikolaevich Gué', *MZh* (1882, book 4, pp. 28–35).

20 Tatiana Sukhotina kept a diary from 1878 to 1929 (twenty-eight notebooks, manuscript, GMT). Excerpts from the diaries are published in T.L. Sukhotina.

21 M.O. Menshikov, 'Pisma k blizhnim. Velikopostnaya tema' (Letters to intimates. A Lenten theme), *NV*, no. 11,147, March 25, 1907.

22 On March 29 Tolstoy wrote in his notebook: 'I have been reading Chekhov for the past two days and am enchanted by him' (*PSS*, vol. 56, p. 189).

23 The diary of V.V. Nagornova, Tolstoy's niece, which she kept from 1864 to 1918 (nine notebooks, manuscript, GMT).

24 Tolstoy reworked N.S. Leskov's story 'Pod rozhdestvo obideli' (They sinned at Christmas) for the *Circle of Reading* and included it there, under the title 'Pod prazdnik obideli' (They offended before the holiday) (*Circle of Reading*, vol. 2, Moscow, Intermediary, 1906); see also the book *Tolstoi-redaktor* (Tolstoy as editor), Moscow, 1965, pp. 248–60. According to Makovitsky, Tolstoy read his arrangement to some children on that day (*YaZ*, April 16).

25 M.O. Menshikov, 'Beznogie lyudi' (Legless people), *NV*, no. 11,170, April 17, 1907.

26 It is not known whether the manuscript has been kept or whether the play was published.

27 On April 23, 1907 a telegram arrived in Yasnaya Polyana from St Petersburg, saying:

'Shaken by news of Lev Nikolaevich's death. Nemirovich-Danchenko' (*YaZ*, April 23).

28 D.P. Makovitsky noted that Tolstoy had explained to his wife the essence of the three-field system in peasant agriculture, but she did not understand and would not agree to give the peasants any additional land. To her observation that the peasants were all thieves and liars Tolstoy replied: 'We who are unfit for real life, curse the peasants without whom we would perish' (*YaZ*, April 25, published in *PSS*, vol. 56, p. 563).

29 Knut Hamsun's *Drama of Life*, which had just been on tour in St Petersburg, was performed at the Moscow Public Art Theatre.

30 See Daily Diary for February 9, and note 11. From 1 to 17 May Tolstoy worked on his article 'Pochemu khristianskie narody voobshche i v osobennosti russkii nakhodyatsya v bedstvennom polozhenii' (Why the Christian people in general, and the Russians in particular, are at present in a wretched condition) (*PSS*, vol. 37). It was not published in Tolstoy's lifetime.

31 'Pervye nedeli tsarstvovaniya imperatora Alexandra III. Pisma K.P. Pobedonostseva iz Peterburga v Moskvu k E.F. Tyutchevoi' (The first weeks of Tsar Alexander III's reign. K.P. Pobedonostsev's letters from St Petersburg to E.F. Tyutcheva in Moscow), *Russkii arkhiv* (Russian Archive), no. 5, 1907. Reprinted in an illustrated supplement to *NV*, nos. 11,197 and 11,200, May 16 and 19, 1907.

32 Vyacheslav Andreevich Behrs, Sofia Tolstaya's younger brother, a railway engineer, was killed on May 19 by maximalist Socialist Revolutionaries. Details of the murder were published in *RV*, nos 114, 115 and 120, May 20, 22 and 27, 1907.

33 News of the dissolution of the 2nd Duma was published in *NV*, 1907, no. 11,215, June 3, 1907. The Manifesto was also there – no. 11,216, June 4, 1907.

34 There are two editions of the works of Vauvenargues in the Yasnaya Polyana Library, both containing Tolstoy's notes. On June 13, according to Makovitsky, Tolstoy was looking through the proofs of the selected thoughts of Vauvenargues, included in the book *Izbrannye mysli Labruyera, s pribavleniem izbrannykh aforismov i maksim Laroshfuko, Vovenarg i Monteske* (The selected thoughts of La Bruyère, with additional aphorisms and maxims of La Rochefoucauld, Vauvenargues and Montesquieu), Moscow, Intermediary, 1908. He also used Vauvenargues, *Oeuvres*, Paris, 1820 (*YaZ*), June 13), as a source.

35 L.D. Semyonov.

36 M.V. Nesterov visited Yasnaya Polyana at the invitation of Sofia Tolstaya. He did a series of sketches and started work on a large portrait in oils of Tolstoy, which he finished in the autumn of 1907. M.V. Nesterov, *Davnie dni* (Bygone days), Moscow, 1959, p. 278. The portrait is now in the GMT.

37 For the weekly readings of his *Circle of Reading*, Tolstoy wrote a story on June 4, 1907 called 'Shut Palechek' (Palechek the clown), based on a Czech legend by Jan Gerben called 'Brother Ivan Palechek, Fool of the Czech King Jiri'. The censorship laws prevented the story from being published in Tolstoy's lifetime (*PSS*, vol. 40). The author of the legend is mistakenly named there as A. Shkarvan; see also *Tolstoy as Editor*, pp. 281–6.

38 A.D. Rotnitskii, one of the organisers of this visit to Tolstoy by pupils from the Tula schools, recalled: 'The organisers had no small cause for alarm after this excursion [. . .] Lyubomudrov, the Black Hundreds mayor, planned to dismiss the women teachers in the town who had taken part in the excursion, and other organisers were threatened with exile. However the inspector of popular schools [. . .] sent the governor a letter justifying the visit. Why was Tolstoy's *ABC* allowed in the schools, when children were not allowed to see him? Evidently this simple truth appeared quite convincing to the governor, and the excursion was hushed up' (manuscript, GMT).

39 'I am giving the peasants 200 acres of Yasnaya land for 90 rubles, and Papa is very pleased about this,' Sofia Tolstaya wrote to Tatiana Sukhotina on June 22, 1907 (GMT).

40 Mr and Mrs Barrow visited Yasnaya, with the writer Alice Fletcher, who wrote a letter on

August 17, 1907 thanking them for their hospitality and for the discussion on religious matters (GMT).

41 Tolstoy resumed his work with children on October 22, 1907 (*YaZ*, October 22).

42 'Ne ubii nikogo' (Thou shalt not kill anyone), was written by Tolstoy (from July 9 to August 5) after N.E. Felten, editor of the Obnovlenie (Renewal) publishing house, was arrested on 3 July for publishing Tolstoy's article ('Ne ubii') (Thou shalt not kill). The article was published in the paper *Slovo* (The Word) (no. 245, September 6, 1907) with various passages censored, and was reprinted by other papers (*PSS*, vol. 37).

43 E.R. Stamo.

44 Vsesvyatskii, a student at Kharkov University.

45 Tolstoy had made the acquaintance of V.K. Syutaev, a peasant in the Tver province, in 1881, and acknowledged his influence in the period of his religious search.

46 A correspondent for the *Golos Moskvy* (Voice of Moscow), G.O. *Klepatskii* (not Kenchitskii), visited Yasnaya Polyana, and Tolstoy had a discussion with him about political matters.

47 I.E. Repin, *Vospominaniya, stati i pisma iz-za granitsy* (Memoirs, articles and letters from abroad), St Petersburg, 1901 (YaPL).

48 Tatiana Sukhotina's letter to the newspaper editors of August 5, 1907 about the fire on her estate, and about the peasants' attitude to it. Edited by Tolstoy and with a preface by him, it was published in *Voice of Moscow*, no. 188, August 14, 1907 (*PSS*, vol. 90). 'Tanya's article touches me,' wrote Tolstoy after receiving a copy of the paper (*PSS*, vol. 56, p. 208).

49 The Czech pedagogue, Karl Veleminsky, translator of Tolstoy's works, visited Yasnaya Polyana and discussed philosophical and moral questions with Tolstoy. He described his meeting with Tolstoy in his book *U Tolstého* (At Tolstoy's), Prague, 1908.

50 V.F. Ilinskii came to talk to Tolstoy about the Russo-Japanese War and patriotism (*YaZ*, August 19).

51 N.T. Izyumenko, *V distsiplininarnom batalione* (In the disciplinary battalion), Free Word edition, Christchurch, 1905; E.I. Popov, *Zhizn i smert Drozhina* (Life and Death of Drozhin), 3rd edn, Free Word, 1903 (YaPL).

52 Sofia Tolstaya wrote to the governor about the raid on the orchard and asked for protection.

53 The Yasnaya peasants D.A. Zhidkov, M.A. Vlasov and A.V. Egorov were arrested. In a letter of September 11, 1907 to D.D. Kobeko, the governor, Tolstoy pleaded for their release, but they were sentenced to two months in prison (*PSS*, vol. 77, p. 194).

54 The doctor was from Krasnoyarsk (his surname is unknown). Tolstoy talked to him about religion, working on oneself and the reconstruction of the social order (*PSS*, vol. 56, p. 212; D. Troitskii, 'Pravoslavnoe-pastyrskoe uveshchanie grafa L.N. Tolstogo' (Count L.N. Tolstoy's orthodox-pastoral admonishment), *Khristianin* (Christian), 1913, p. 37.

55 D.E. Troitskii.

56 On that day Tolstoy wrote in his notebook: 'Guards and an unpleasant conversation' (*PSS*, vol. 56, p. 213). The cause of this conversation was evidently the guards, who had been sent to Yasnaya Polyana at Sofia Tolstaya's request, and who were checking the passports of all Tolstoy's visitors. At Tolstoy's request that they stop doing so the village policeman 'rudely replied that if the countess wanted to be protected from suspicious people they would have to look at everyone's passports' (*YaZ*, September 12; see *PSS*, vol. 56, p. 599).

57 L.B. Yavorskaya, a dramatic actress and proprietress of the New Theatre in St Petersburg, made a tour in 1907 of the towns of Russia. She sent Sofia Tolstaya a telegram on September 13, 1907 asking her to buy some peasant clothes in Tula for a production of Tolstoy's *The Power of Darkness* in Tbilisi (GMT).

58 At Sofia Tolstaya's request, four peasants from Yasnaya Polyana and four from Grumond were imprisoned for stealing oak trees.

59 Tolstoy was working on a new *Circle of Reading*, subsequently titled *Na kazhdyi den* (For every day) (*PSS*, vols 43–4).

60 Repin stayed in Yasnaya until September 29, 1907 and painted a portrait of Tolstoy and his wife. It is now at the IRLI.

61 Tolstoy was reading both stories for the *Circle of Reading* (vols 1 and 2, Moscow, Intermediary, 1906; *PSS*, vols 41–2). Tolstoy included France's story, abbreviated and reworked, in the *Circle of Reading* under the title 'Ulichnyi torgovets' (The street trader). Chekhov's story 'Beglets' (The fugitive) was put in without changes.

62 After reading Kuprin's stories 'Nochnaya smena' (Night shift) and 'Allez!' Tolstoy said: 'The main thing in art is a sense of moderation [. . .] Kuprin's great quality is that there's nothing superfluous' (Gusev, p. 52).

63 Paul Loyson, *Le Droit de vierge*, Paris, 1903 (YaPL).

64 Ugo Arlotta, correspondent for the Rome paper *Italia*. An account of his meeting and conversation with Tolstoy is published in *Birzhevye vedomosti* (Stock Exchange Gazette), no. 10,252, December 13, 1907.

65 Mikhail Sukhotin noted in his diary on October 16, 1907, after the arrival of two threatening telegrams: 'the family has been terribly alarmed. [. . .] But L.N. is not afraid and still calmly goes out to meet people who want to see him without taking any special precautions [. . .] Courage is one of L.N.'s fundamental qualities' (Iz dnevnika M.S. Sukhotina' (From the diary of M.S. Sukhotin), *LN*, vol. 69, book 2, p. 197). 'Goncharov' did not visit Yasnaya Polyana.

66 S.A. Zabolotnyuk.

67 L.L. Tolstoy's play *Moya Rodina* (My country) was performed at the Korsh Theatre in Moscow.

68 On October 22, 1907 Tolstoy's secretary, N.N. Gusev, was arrested in the flat of the district police officer and was later taken to Krapivna district jail. His arrest came after an informer had reported that at some meetings of young peasants he had 'cursed the Tsar'. During a search of Aleksandra Tolstaya's estate at Telyatinki, where Gusev lived, police found a censored version of Tolstoy's pamphlet 'The One Thing Necessary' (Not 'Where Is the Solution?'), published by Renewal, St Petersburg, 1906; in the margins Gusev had inserted the text of the censored passages, including several sharp denunciations of the Tsars (*PSS*, vol. 36, pp. 168–9).

69 Published in an anthology of stories by Nazhivin called *V doline skorbi* (In the vale of despond), Moscow, 1907.

70 Lev Nikolaevich and Sofia Tolstoy were badly shaken by their son Andrei's decision to leave his family and marry E.V. Artsimovich, wife of the governor of Tula and mother of *five* (not six) children (see Tolstoy's letters to his son at the beginning of May, and on June 10, 1907, and his letters to E.V. Artsimovich (June 2) and to her husband (July 2 and 21), *PSS*, vol. 77). Andrei Tolstoy married E.V. Artsimovich on November 14.

71 V.A. Lopukhin, Vice-Governor of Tula province, promised to help Gusev. For a detailed account of this meeting with Lopukhin see Tolstoy's letter to Chertkov of November 2, 1907 (*PSS*, vol. 89, p. 76).

72 Tolstoy had finished work on the fourth edition of his new *Circle of Reading* and observed in his diary: 'I've finished a rough version, but there's still a mass of work to do on it' (*PSS*, vol. 56, p. 78).

73 Letter to Andrei Tolstoy of November 22, 1907 (*PSS*, vol. 77, p. 247).

74 News of the attempt on the Moscow Provincial Governor-General S.K. Gershelman on November 21, 1907 was in *NV*, no. 11,386, November 22, 1907.

75 For Tolstoy's unrealised plan to compile a children's 'Geography' see E. Zaidenschnur, 'Detskaya Geografiya. Materialy Tolstogo dlya uchebnoi knigi' (A children's geography. Tolstoy's materials for a textbook), *Yasn. Sb.*, 1965, pp. 17–24.

76 See *PST*, p. 768.

77 Sverchkov's painting was exhibited at the autumn show, which opened in December 1907 in the Stroganovskii educational institute.

78 Evidently letters from F.A. Zmiev (November 30, 1907) and T.S. Trukhtanov (December 8), to which Tolstoy replied on December 18, 1907 (*PSS*, vol. 77, pp. 267–9).
79 A.P. Arapova, 'Natalya Nikolaevna Pushkina-Lanskaya', illustrated supplement to *NV*, nos 11,406, 11,409, 11,413, December 12, 16, 19, 1907.
80 Tolstoy particularly liked the 'old French folk-dances and the oriental folk-songs'. He said to Wanda Landowska, 'I thank you, not only for giving me so much pleasure with your music, but for confirming my views on art' (Gusev, p. 69).

1909

1 Tolstoy's letter to Tatiana Sukhotina of January 3, 1909 (*PSS*, vol. 79, p. 9), and Sofia Tolstaya's of January 3–4 (GMT).
2 Tolstoy had started work in December 1908 on the story which was subsequently called 'Kto ubiitsy? Pavel Kudryash' (Who are the murderers? Pavel Kudryash). On January 5, 1909, after writing two rough versions, he started writing on the same subject in dramatic form (*PSS*, vol. 37). See also Diary, January 14, 1909, and note 1.
3 See Diary, January 14, 1909, and note 2.
4 In October 1905 V.A. Scheierman gave his land away to the peasants, leaving himself a small allotment. His 'Otkrytoe pismo k gg. zemlevladeltsam' (Open letter to Messrs landowners), appealing to them to renounce their rights to the land, along with an accompanying letter from Tolstoy of January 16, 1906, was published in *Novosti dnya* (News of the Day), no. 8102, January 20, 1906 (*PSS*, vol. 76, pp. 83–5). After this meeting Tolstoy noted in his diary: 'Yesterday Scheierman was here, a strong, sympathetic man, and we had a good talk together' (*PSS*, vol. 57, p. 13).
5 Tolstoy noted in his diary on January 22: 'I spoke to him frankly but too cautiously, and didn't tell him what a sin his work was. And I should have done so, for it spoilt Sonya's account of his discussion with her. He would like apparently, if not to convert me, then to destroy or belittle my – in their opinion – harmful influence on the faith and the Church [. . .] They're sure to think of some way of assuring people that I "repented" before my death' (*PSS*, vol. 57, p. 16; see also Gusev, pp. 234–5).
6 Possibly a reference to a letter from S. Alekseev, to which Tolstoy replied on January 23, 1909 (*PSS*, vol. 79, pp. 44–5).
7 M.P. Novikov, *Na voinu* (To war), Moscow, 1906. Tolstoy first read it in September 1904 in a manuscript which the author sent him. He liked the story for its 'seriousness, its sincerity and its profundity [. . .] and the beauty, power and picturesqueness of the peasant language' (Gusev, p. 237; see also *PSS*, vol. 90, p. 330).
8 'Zapiski senatora Esipovicha' (Notes of Senator Esipovich), *Russkaya starina* (Russian Antiquity), nos 1 and 2, 1909.
9 This summary of Tolstoy's article 'Zakon nasiliya i zakon lyubvi' (The law of violence and the law of love) was published in *RV*, no. 37, February 15, 1909, under the title 'Novaya statya L.N. Tolstogo' (A new article by L.N. Tolstoy).
10 The poet, Baskin-Seredinskii, who visited Yasnaya Polyana on several occasions.
11 'Nomer gazety' (An issue of a newspaper), an analysis of no. 680 of the St Petersburg paper *Slovo* (The Word), for January 16, 1909. On February 20 Tolstoy noted in his diary: 'I've revised "An Issue of a Newspaper" – no good' (*PSS*, vol. 57, p. 29). The article was not published in his lifetime (*PSS*, vol. 38).
12 N.G. Molostvov and P.A. Sergeenko were working on an illustrated biography of Tolstoy, which appeared in several separate instalments under the title: *Lev Tolstoi. Kritiko-biograficheskoe issledovanie* (Lev Tolstoy. Critical biographical research). Only three instalments appeared.
13 On February 13 Tolstoy wrote twelve letters (*PSS*, vol. 79, pp. 80–9). On February 26 he

dictated to Gusev a small article called 'O gosudarstve' (On government). It was not published in his lifetime (*PSS*, vol. 38).

14 Tolstoy's letter to V.I. Timiryazev of February 27, 1909 (*PSS*, vol. 79, p. 94).

15 L.N. Tolstoy *Detstvo i otrochestvo* (Childhood and Boyhood, with 26 illustrations by G. Roux and Bennet), Moscow, printed by I.N. Kushneryov and Co., 1909.

16 A.A. Korsini, a traveller and geography teacher from Moscow, gave a lecture about India, together with a slide show. She was accompanied by N.P. Rudakova.

17 V.G. Chertkov was deported on the instructions of the police department.

18 In her letter of March 6, 1909 Sofia Tolstaya wrote: 'Chertkov's expulsion and the punishment inflicted on all who dare to read and encourage others to read Tolstoy's books are expressions of petty resentment towards an old man whose name has glorified the name of Russia in the eyes of the entire world' (GMT).

19 M.P. Novikov read his article 'Novaya vera' (The new faith). Tolstoy observed in his diary that there was 'a lot of good in it, but it's long and monotonous' (*PSS*, vol. 57, p. 37). Tolstoy tried to get it published, but was unsuccessful (see his letter to A.M. Khiryakov of May 1, 1909 – *PSS*, vol. 79, pp. 178–9).

20 The letter was printed in *RV*, no. 57, March 11, 1909, and reprinted by other papers.

21 The Society of the Tolstoy Museum, established in St Petersburg in January 1909, had organised an exhibition devoted to Tolstoy.

22 Baba Bharati's book *Shree Krishna: The Lord of Love*, New York, 1904 (*PSS*, vol. 57, pp. 40, 47). In it he marked a series of sayings to be translated and included in a book about Krishna on which S.D. Nikolaev was working at the time. Tolstoy edited the Krishna legend which formed the basis of Baba Bharati's book, and the translations of the sayings, and also wrote an introduction to the book (*PSS*, vol. 39). The manuscript was sent to the Intermediary publishing house, but the book was not published.

23 A.I. Kuprin, 'Kak ya byl aktyorom' (How I became an actor).

24 See letters of 1845, 1851 and 1858 (*PSS*, vols 59, 60), and also a letter of December 25, 1858 (*PSS*, vol. 60, pp. 276–7).

25 *Les Livres sacrés de l'Orient*, Paris, 1852 (YaPL, with Tolstoy's notes).

26 M.D. Groshev's letter of April 6, 1909, to which Tolstoy replied on April 10 (*PSS*, vol. 79, p. 152).

27 Tolstoy was continuing to work on his article 'Neizbezhnyi perevorot' (An inevitable upheaval), (*PSS*, vol. 38).

28 A. Mazon, then a French teacher in Kharkov, visited Tolstoy on April 19, 1909. They discussed contemporary French literature and Tolstoy's attitude to I.A. Goncharov (*YaZ*, April 20).

29 In a letter of April 1909 Bulgakov asked Tolstoy to explain his views on education and upbringing. Tolstoy's reply, on which he worked from April 9 to May 3, took the form of an article, and was published under the title 'O vospitanii' (On Education) in *Svobodnoe vospitanie* (Free Education), no. 2, 1909–10 (*PSS*, vol. 38).

30 Tolstoy observed in his diary: 'Mogilevskii played magnificently. I could not stop weeping' (*PSS*, vol. 57, p. 56).

31 Nazimov told Tolstoy that during the suppressing of the 1905 armed Moscow uprising by the Semyonovskii regiment, he had saved eleven people from being shot. 'Had a good talk' with Nazimov, wrote Tolstoy in his diary (*PSS*, vol. 57, p. 59). For details of this conversation see N.N. Gusev. 'Epizody iz zhizni L.N. Tolstogo' (Episodes from the life of L.N. Tolstoy), *Krasnaya niva* (Red Cornfield) no. 37, 1928.

32 P.L. Uspenskii, a lawyer.

33 Tolstoy was selecting material for some booklets on the teachings of Confucius and Lao-Tzu, which had been proposed for publication by the Intermediary (*PSS*, vol. 57, p. 57).

34 A.I. Kuprin, 'Yama' (The pit), in the almanac *Zemlya* (Land), 3rd edn, no. 3, 1903. On that evening the reading was interrupted by Tolstoy's remark, 'It seems Sofia Andreevna

was right [. . .] It is indeed loathsome.' From what he read he liked the discussion between the police-officer and the brothel proprietress (in vol. 1, ch. 2). See Gusev, pp. 252–3.

35 Chertkov received notification that the Minister of Internal Affairs, P.A. Stolypin, had refused him the right to enter the province of Tula. Chertkov and his family then moved to the village of Kryokshina, in the province of Moscow, and lived on the estate of some relatives.

36 There was news in the papers of the imminent trial of N.A. Felten for publishing in the Renewal publishing house Tolstoy's articles 'Thou Shalt Not Kill', 'Notes to Soldiers' and so on. The trial took place on May 12, 1909, and Felten was sentenced to 6 months' imprisonment. In an account of the Felten case in *RV*, no. 107, May 13, 1909, Tolstoy's letter of February 27 to the prosecutor of the St Petersburg 19th district was mentioned (*PSS*, vol. 79, pp. 93–4).

37 Two excerpts from Dostoyevsky's *Notes from the House of the Dead* were included in the *Circle of Reading* under the title 'Oryol' (Oryol) and 'Smert v gospitale' (Death in hospital) (*PSS*, vol. 41; Gusev, p. 254).

38 Sofia Tolstaya met a passer-by who said to her: 'Before it was Tsar Nikolai Palkin, now it's Nikolai Veryovkin' [i.e. untranslatable puns of popular peasant origins: roughly 'Before it was Tsar Nicholas the stick, now it's Tsar Nicholas the rope'] (Goldenweiser, p. 267).

39 Tolstoy told S.P. Spiro of the contents of his article 'O "Vekhakh" ' (On the "Landmarks" group), and dictated several excerpts from it. 'L.N. Tolstoi o "Vekhakh" ' (L.N. Tolstoy on the 'Landmarks' group), *RS*, no. 114, May 21, 1909 (*PSS*, vol. 57, p. 71; see also Gusev, p. 256).

40 S.V. Gavrilov. He corresponded with Tolstoy between 1908 and 1910. Tolstoy wrote about him in his diary: 'A very interesting man visited, who had walked all the way from Simbirsk. He said many good things' (*PSS*, vol. 57, p. 71; see also Gusev, p. 257).

41 I.I. Mechnikov (Elie Metchnikoff) and Tolstoy discussed religion, science, literature and art. As they were saying goodbye Tolstoy said to Mechnikov that 'he had expected the meeting to be pleasant, but had not expected it to be so pleasant'. For more details about this see Tolstoy's diary entries for May 30 and 31, 1909 (*PSS*, vol. 57, p. 77); Goldenweiser, pp. 267–72; Mechnikov's essay 'Den u Tolstogo v Yasnoi Polyane' (A day with Tolstoy at Yasnaya Polyana), in I.I. Mechnikov, *Sobr. soch.* (Collected works), vol. 13, Moscow, 1954; S.P. Spiro, 'Tolstoi o I.I. Mechnikove' (Tolstoy on Mechnikov), in *RS*, no. 125, June 3, 1909.

42 See Diary, February 14, 1902, and note 22.

43 Henry George the son came with a photographer. 'A pleasant man,' wrote Tolstoy in his diary (*PSS*, vol. 57, p. 79). Henry George wrote about his meeting with Tolstoy in his article 'My farewell to Count Tolstoy', *New York World*, November 14, 1909.

44 According to B.S. Troyanovskii, Tolstoy 'especially liked the balalaika transcription of the Russian folk-songs' and found his art most 'distinctive and original'. B.S. Troyanovskii, 'U Tolstogo v Yasnoi Polyane' (With Tolstoy in Yasnaya Polyana), in the Leningrad newspaper *Smena* (Change), no. 269, November 20, 1940.

45 Tolstoy was talking to Matveev, Marshal of the Nobility for the Mtsensk district, whom he met on the train. They discussed the land question and the teachings of Henry George (Gusev, p. 266).

46 On June 11 Tolstoy noted in his diary: 'Went for a ride, very tired. But mainly a tormenting sense of the poverty – not the poverty, the humiliation and oppression of the people [. . .] Then at dinner [. . .] Conversations in French and games of tennis, when all around are starving, half-naked slaves, crushed by work. I cannot bear it, I want to run away' (*PSS*, vol. 57, p. 82).

47 Letters of June 20, 1909 to Tolstoy (*PST*, p. 774) and to Tatiana Sukhotina (GMT).

48 Lyova Tolstoy destroyed his unfinished bust of his father. On June 25, 1909 Sofia Tolstaya

wrote to her husband: 'Lyova suddenly took your bust today and smashed it, after working terribly hard on it for a month' (*PST*, pp. 778–9).

49 *MZh*, book 6, pp. 60–73. For Sofia Tolstaya's meeting with Alexander III on April 13, 1891; see also Diary, April 22, 1891.

50 Tolstoy's letter of June 19, 1909 (*PSS*, vol. 84, p. 386).

51 'Wrote a little of "On Science",' wrote Tolstoy in his diary (*PSS*, vol. 57, p. 93; vol. 38).

52 According to Gusev, Tolstoy 'had a long talk with him and did not agree with his views' (Gusev, p. 271).

53 In a letter of 12 (25) July to the organising committee of the 18th International Peace Congress, due to open on August 14, 1909 in Stockholm, Tolstoy thanked them for choosing him as an honorary member and said that 'if his strength allowed' he would 'do all he possibly could to be in Stockholm', or would say 'what he wanted to say' in a letter (*PSS*, vol. 80, pp. 22–3).

54 At Tolstoy's request, Gusev read out his unfinished article – the letter 'O nauke' (On science), written in response to the peasant F.A. Abramov's letter of June 22, 1909 (*PSS*, vol. 38). For more details see Gusev, pp. 272–3). See also Daily Diary, November 11, and note 92.

55 This book – Elie Metchnikoff, *Essais optimistes*, Paris, 1907 (YaPL) – was sent to Tolstoy by the author.

56 I.K. Parkhomenko's portrait is reproduced in *PSS*, vol. 57. The whereabouts of the original are not known.

57 V.A. Molochnikov, in a letter to Tolstoy of June 12, 1909, reported some information received from a friend about the oppression of the peasants on the estate of B.A. Vasilchikov, a wealthy landowner and member of the Government Council, and asked Tolstoy to write to him about it. Tolstoy expressed his indignation about Vasilchikov in a letter to Molochnikov of June 16, 1909 (*PSS*, vol. 79, p. 234). V.A. Molochnikov then sent Vasilchikov a sharp letter quoting Tolstoy's words (see further *PSS*, vol. 80, pp. 28–9.)

58 Sofia Tolstaya's book *Kukolki-skeletsy i drugie rasskazy* (Skeleton dolls and other stories) was published in Moscow in 1910 (YaPL).

59 S.P. Spiro was interested in Tolstoy's proposed trip to Stockholm. See S.P. Spiro, 'U L.N. Tolstogo' (With L.N. Tolstoy), *RS*, no. 117, August 2, 1909.

60 Sofia Tolstaya was looking through the proofs of the 3rd edition of Molostvov's and Sergeenko's critical biographical study of Tolstoy, *Lev Tolstoi* (St Petersburg, 1909: YaPL). Molostvov wrote, in a letter of August 6, 1909, that her 'observations in the margins of the proofs and in her letter [. . .] had been used [. . .] Such as her observation that Lev Nikolaevich now tried to write without the words "which" or "who" ' (GMT).

61 On August 2, 1909 Tolstoy wrote to Chertkov: 'It seems we shall go to the congress. Sofia Andreevna is quite prepared to. I am preparing my speech, which I am still dissatisfied with' (*PSS*, vol. 89, p. 134). Tolstoy's journey did not take place. Because of a general strike in Sweden the Peace Congress was postponed. For more details see P.I. Biryukov's biography of Tolstoy, vol. IV, Moscow/St Petersburg, 1923, p. 191.

62 A visit from participants of the 11th All-Russian Forestry Congress, which took place in Tula. Professor N.S. Nesterov spoke for them, and expressed the hope that Tolstoy's 'living words for the good of humanity' would 'ring out for a long, long time'. Information about this was published in *RV*, no. 221, September 27, 1909.

63 On the instructions of the Minister of Internal Affairs, N.N. Gusev was sentenced on July 15, 1909 to two years' exile in the province of Perm under police surveillance, for 'revolutionary propaganda and the distribution of banned literary works'. For more details see Gusev, pp. 283–304.

64 V.I. Zasosov. Tolstoy noted in his diary on that day: 'A most happy impression' (*PSS*, vol. 57, p. 113).

65 Chertkov's article 'Stranitsa iz vospominanii. Dezhurstvo v voennykh gospitalyakh' (A page

from my memoirs. On duty in military hospitals), published in *VE*, no. 11, 1909. 'Lovely memoirs', was Tolstoy's response (*PSS*, vol. 57, p. 113; see also vol. 89, pp. 136–8).

66 Tolstoy's 'Zayavlenie ob areste Guseva' (Announcement of Gusev's arrest), and the article 'V Yasnoi Polyane' (In Yasnaya Polyana) (unsigned), *RV*, no. 183, August 11, 1909.

67 I. Shcheglov, *Podvizhnik slova. Novye materialy o N.V. Gogole* (Devotee of the word. New material about N.V. Gogol), St Petersburg, 1909.

68 On July 31, 1909 Maude sent Tolstoy the proofs of the second volume of his biography of him to look through and correct (GMT). See Daily Diary, September 24.

69 Tolstoy had received an enquiry from the newspaper *Morgen Post* as to whether he really intended to go to Berlin at the invitation of the concert director Jules Sachs, in order to read the speech he had prepared for the Stockholm Peace Congress. Sofia Tolstaya's entry may refer to the telegram Tolstoy sent in reply, in which he said that the speech would be read in Berlin by one of his friends (*PSS*, vol. 80, p. 59). The speech was not read. See Tolstoy's letter to E. Schmidt of September 22 (October 5), 1909 (*PSS*, vol. 80, pp. 105–6).

70 The illustrations to Sofia Tolstaya's book *Skeleton Dolls* were executed by A.V. Moravov, with her guidance.

71 Tolstoy's book had been published: *Na kazhdyi den. Uchenie o zhizni, izlozhennoe v izrecheniyakh, vzyatykh u myslitelei raznykh stran i raznykh vekov* (For every day. Teachings on life expounded through the sayings of philosophers of various countries and various periods), St Petersburg, June 1909 (YaPL).

72 A. Marukhin. Tolstoy's comment on him in his diary was: 'an exceedingly interesting man' (*PSS*, vol. 57, pp. 129–30).

73 B. Müller, accompanied by A. Zhashkevich.

74 Representatives of Pathé, the French cinematographic firm, received permission to visit Tolstoy and film him. But on September 2 a telegram was sent on Tolstoy's instructions asking them not to come (*PSS*, vol. 80, p. 286). They came none the less, and filmed Tolstoy's departure from Shchekino station. For more details see Goldenweiser, pp. 316–18.

75 See Goldenweiser, pp. 320–3.

76 On September 20, 1909 Tolstoy was filmed by a cameraman from the firm of A.O. Drankov.

77 The second volume of Aylmer Maude's *The Life of Tolstoy. Later Years*, came out in London in 1910.

78 Representatives of the Pathé firm showed the film taken of Tolstoy leaving Shchekino station on September 3.

79 E.Ek. *Rasskazy* (Stories), 2 vols, Moscow, 1907–8 (YaPL, with a dedication to Tolstoy from the author).

80 Tolstoy wanted to interest M.D.Chelishchev in Henry George's theory of a single land tax, since Chelishchev could raise this matter at the *Duma*. (See Tolstoy's letter to S.D. Nikolaev of October 7, 1909 – *PSS*, vol. 80, p. 129; see also vol. 57, pp. 149–50.) Chelishchev did not raise this in the *Duma*.

81 The editorial board of the *Neue Gesellschaftliche Correspondenz* sent Tolstoy a questionnaire asking his opinion on the death penalty. Tolstoy replied on October 12, 1909. On this day he wrote to Jan Styk, who had written asking his permission to translate the *Circle of Reading* into French (*PSS*, vol. 80, pp. 141–2).

82 L.N. Andreev's story 'Proklyatie zverya' (The curse of the beast), in *Zemlya* (Earth), book 1, 1908 (*YaZ*, October 13).

83 Possibly a reference to the memoirs of S.V. Belgardt (née Mengden), covering the years 1881–1897 and published under the title *Luchi proshlogo* (Rays of the past), literary supplement to *Niva* (Cornfield), no. 8, 1903.

84 In the Indian journal *The Vedic Magazine*, vol. 3 no. 4 1909, Tolstoy read an article called

'Plato and Shankara Acarya' by Pandit Prabhu Dutt Shastri M.A.B.T. (*PSS*, vol. 57, pp. 152, 373).

85 See Daily Diary, October 30, and note 89.

86 The Tolstoys received a visit from employees of the Gramophone firm, accompanied by the poet I.A. Belousov, representing the Society of Workers on Periodical Publications, and I.I. Mitropolskii, editor of the newspaper *Stolichnaya molva* (Capital Word). Tolstoy read several passages from his book *For Every Day*, into the phonograph, in Russian, French, German and English, and the recording was reproduced on gramophone records. For more details see I.I. Mitropolskii, 'Poezdka v Yasnuyu Polyanu' (A trip to Yasnaya Polyana), in the anthology *Zhivye slova nashikh pisatelei i obschestvennykh deyatelei* (Living words of our writers and social activists), no. 1, Moscow, 1910, pp. 145–57; I.A. Belousov, *Literaturnaya sreda. Vospominaniya* (The literary milieu. Memoirs), Moscow, 1928, pp. 211–29.

87 S.A. Tolstaya was interceding for the second volume of Biryukov's biography of Tolstoy (Intermediary, 1908). On November 2 the ban was revoked.

88 The story 'Khristiane' (Christians) in L.N. Andreev, *Melkye rasskazy* (Minor stories), vol. 3, St Petersburg, 1906. The copy in the Yasnaya Polyana Library contains Tolstoy's notes and at the end of the story a mark: '5+'. (See *Biblioteka L.N. Tolstogo v Yasnoi Polyane* (L.N. Tolstoy's library at Yasnaya Polyana), vol. 1, Moscow, 1972, p. 41.)

89 The court was investigating the case of S.S. Rezunov, a Yasnaya peasant who had divided his property with his stepmother. Tolstoy found his trip 'very interesting' (*PSS*, vol. 57, p. 163).

90 A.V. Moravov's oil portrait, *L.N. Tolstoy in his Study*, is at the GMT.

91 His diary entries covering these days contain an extensive description of Gorky's stories, and the observation: 'A great talent' (*PSS*, vol. 57, pp. 167–9).

92 *RV*, no. 258, November 10, 1909. See also Daily diary, July 12, and note 54.

93 The article was published simultaneously in the papers *Kievskie vesti* (Kiev News), nos 300–2, November 10–12, 1909) and *RV*.

94 S.M. Solomakhin and D. Graivoronskii were members of the 'khlyst' sect (i.e. they practised self-flagellation). Tolstoy had a 'good talk with them', and 'drew up some notes for their village community' in answer to a series of questions from Solomakhin (*PSS*, vol. 57, p. 171; vol. 80, pp. 195–7).

95 A reference to the Khokhlov children from the village of Novaya Kolpna (*PSS*, vol. 57, pp. 175, 177, 387–8). See Daily Diary for 1910, note 19.

96 *Knizhnaya letopis* (Literary Annals), no. 42, October 13, 1909, announced that Tolstoy's pamphlet *O razume i vere* (on reason and faith) (Moscow, 1909) had been removed from the shops.

97 The incident was described by Tolstoy in his sketch 'Zhivushchie i umirayushchie' (The living and the dying), which was included in the cycle *Tri dnya v derevne* (Three days in the country) (*PSS*, vol. 38, pp. 17–18).

98 Tolstoy's trip to enquire about an order to levy taxes was undertaken at the request of some Yasnaya Polyana peasants, whose property had been distrained for non-payment of taxes (*PSS*, vol. 57, p. 180). Tolstoy later discussed his conversation with the peasants and with the district clerk's assistant in the sketch 'Podati' (Taxes), included in the cycle *Three Days in the Country* (*PSS*, vol. 38, pp. 19–22).

99 Tolstoy had thought out the preface to the anthology *For Every Day* and started work on it in 1907. This work continued until 1910. There have been 105 editions of it, the last being published as the preface to the anthology *The Path of Life* (*PSS*, vol. 45, pp. 13–17).

100 In a letter to Sofia Tolstaya of December 2, 1909, O.A. Drankov requested permission to 'pay her a visit in order to demonstrate the picture made of Lev Nikolaevich during his journey through Moscow' in September 1909. From his next letter to her, of December 13, it is clear that Sofia Tolstaya asked him in her reply to delay his visit (GMT).

101 M.A. Bodrova, a peasant woman from the village of Demyonka, who had been left in a

wretchedly impoverished state after her husband's conscription into the army, appealed to Tolstoy for help. In a letter of November 29, 1909, Tolstoy asked her father, A.V. Bodrov, to take his daughter temporarily into his house, and said that he would try to ensure that her husband was allowed home. After visiting her, Tolstoy noted in his diary: 'Ghastly poverty' (*PSS*, vol. 57, pp. 180, 193; vol. 80, pp. 221–2).

102 'Son' (Dream), the fourth sketch in the cycle *Three Days in the Country*. Tolstoy started work on it on October 23, 1909. On December 28 he noted in his diary: 'I've had a good look through "Dream". I can leave it as it is – it's not too bad' (*PSS*, vol. 57, p. 195). He continued working on it until 1910 (*PSS*, vol. 38).

1910

1 Tolstoy was working on the cycle *Three Days in the Country* (*PSS*, vol. 38). On January 14 he wrote to Chertkov: 'My work is most unsuccessful; I've finished now and am glad to be done with it. All the pieces are at fault in being in a more or less fictional form. Taken all together they should make one totality, and however bad individually, they may be of some use together. Together they go like this: 1st day in the country: Vagrants. 2nd day in the country: The living and the dead. 3rd day in the country: Taxes. And 4th day: Dream. Two of these have been copied out, the other two will be copied over the next day or so and sent off to you' (*PSS*, vol. 89, p. 168).

Three parts of *Three Days in the Country* were published in a censored version in *VE*, no. 9, 1910; the editors published 'Dream' in an abridged form, and it was published first in full by Sofia Tolstaya in vol. XVI of the *Works of Count L.N. Tolstoy*, Moscow, 1911, pp. 487–96.

2 Stepan Andreevich Behrs died on January 1 (?), 1910. 'The children' are N.S. and T.S. Behrs.

3 Of this visit from René Marchand, correspondent of the French newspaper *Le Figaro*, Tolstoy noted in his diary: 'Marchand the Frenchman came. Heated discussion with him, replied to his questions' (*PSS*, vol. 58, p. 3). See also *LN*, vol. 75, book 2, pp. 62–4.

4 Sofia Tolstaya's letter to G.K. Gradovskii, which has not been kept, was in reply to a letter to Tolstoy from the journal *Ogonyok* (Flame). Gradovskii played a mediating role in this, and on December 15, 1909 he sent Sofia Tolstaya a letter and a questionnaire from *Ogonyok* (Flame) in which people were asked to give an autobiographical reply to the question: 'What do you wish for Russia in the coming year, 1910?' Tolstoy declined to answer.

5 A.O. Drankov filmed Tolstoy taking a walk. In September 1909 he had made a film of Tolstoy setting off to visit Chertkov, and in Kryokshina, and the farewell scene at the Kursk station on September 19. Fragments of the film are now at the GMT Gosfilmfond, and are included in the film *Zhivoi Tolstoi* (The living Tolstoy) (1960).

6 A.I. Sumbatov-Yuzhin, an actor at the Maly Theatre, first visited the Khamovniki Street house in 1898, at the invitation of Sofia Tolstaya. He wrote his memoirs of Tolstoy, 'Tri vstrechi' (Three meetings) (1908), for the *Mezhdunarodnyi Tolstovskii almanakh* (International Tolstoy Almanac), Moscow, 1909, pp. 325–9.

7 Letter from P. Polizoidi in Reshta of December 28, 1909. On January 14, 1910, Tolstoy replied: 'I thank you most warmly for your interesting and important information about the Bekhaists' (*PSS*, vol. 81, p. 48). The 'Bekhaists' were a religious sect which emerged in Persia in the 1840s. They were also called 'Babids', after the founder of the sect, Ali-Muhammed Baba.

8 Sofia Tolstaya was evidently protesting against the publication in the St Petersburg newspaper *Novaya Rus* (New Holy Russia), for November 1, 1909, of inaccurate and savagely censored excerpts from *For Every Day* ('March', 'April', 'May', 'December').

9 Lyova Tolstoy was in Paris. In a letter of January 26, he wrote: 'Dearest Maman, I received your telegram yesterday. I'm astonished that you are so worried. It [i.e. the flood] has been

terribly exaggerated by the newspapers. [. . .] They're talking much less about it now, and the curse of the day is Rostand's play *Chantecler'* [*sic*] (GMT).

10 N.N. Gusev's letter to Tolstoy of January 2 from Korepino, in the district of Cherdyn, province of Perm, where he was living in exile for distributing Tolstoy's banned works. The letter contained a detailed account of the story of S.N. Durylin, who visited Yasnaya Polyana on October 20, 1909, and it quoted extracts from his letter to Gusev: 'In a word, once one has talked to Tolstoy and seen him for a day, it is impossible not to leave him as a Tolstoyan, in the sense that one will always love him and carry around the image of him' (GMT).

11 Tolstoy and Makovitsky visited the district assizes of the Moscow Palace of Justice, which was trying the criminal case of some peasants accused of attempting to seize the mail, and the political case of a Socialist Revolutionary named I.I. Afanasiev, accused of harbouring illegal literature. As the newspaper *Tulskaya Molva* (Tula word) wrote: 'Tolstoy's mere presence served to defend the accused' (no. 679, January 17, 1910). The peasants accused of seizing the mail were acquitted; in the case of Afanasiev, a relatively light sentence was passed. For a more detailed account of Tolstoy's presence at the trial see *YaZ*, January 16.

12 L.N. Tolstoy, *Circle of Reading. Thoughts of Many Writers on Truth, Life and Conduct, Selected and Arranged for Every Day in the Year* (Odessa), *Odesskii listok* (Odessa Leaflet) edition. (In memory of the 36th anniversary of the publication of the *Odessa Leaflet.* Editor, V.V. Navorotskii.) YaPL.

13 V.F. Bulgakov, on the recommendation of Chertkov, started working as Tolstoy's secretary on January 17, 1910. On that day he made his first entry in his diary (first published under the title *U L.N. Tolstogo v poslednyi god ego zhizni. Dnevnik* (With L.N. Tolstoy in the last year of his life. Diary), Moscow, 1911). According to Bulgakov, Tolstoy was then preparing a new plan for a more popular edition of the *Circle of Reading* anthology (Bulgakov, pp. 50–1). His work on the children's *Circle of Reading*, started in 1906–7, was not finished. Part of the material, with a short introduction by Tolstoy, was published by I.I. Gorbunov-Posadov in *Svobodnoe vospitanie* (Free Education), no. 1, 1907, under the title 'Besedy s detmi po nravstvennym voprosam' (Talks with children on moral questions). Sofia Tolstaya included this article in vol. IV of *The Works of Count L.N. Tolstoy*, Moscow, 1911, pp. 403–13.

14 A.V. Golitsyn, in a letter of January 19, 1910, asked Tolstoy for his opinion about cooperation, and Tolstoy expounded his views on the subject in letters to Golitsyn (January 23: *PSS*, vol. 81, pp. 67–9) and V.F. Totomyanets (ibid., pp. 66–7). The latter, under the title 'Pismo L.N. Tolstogo o kooperativnom dvizhenii' (L.N. Tolstoy's letter on the cooperative movement), was published in *Zhizn dlya vsekh* (Life for All), no. 2, February, 1910, pp. 148–9, erroneously dated January 13.

15 See Daily Diary, 1909, note 86.

16 Beethoven's *Egmont* Overture in F Minor, Opus 84.

17 I.E. Repin, *L.N. Tolstoy Sitting in the Pink (or his Grandfather's) Chair*, oils, 1909; A.V. Moravov, *Tolstoy at Work in the Study at His Yasnaya Polyana Home*, oils, 1909 (GMT).

18 The opening of the peasant library of the Moscow Society of Literacy, in honour of L.N. Tolstoy's eightieth birthday, took place on January 31, 1910 in the village of Yasnaya Polyana, in the hut of a peasant named A. Eliseev. Tolstoy attended the opening, and a photographer from *R W*, named A.I. Savelev, took a photograph – 'Tolstoy Amongst the Peasants on the Porch of the Library'. See the article by A.S. Kuprianov, 'Torzhestvo v Yasnoi Polyane' (Celebration in Yasnaya Polyana), *RS*, no. 26, February 2. Tolstoy recorded the opening of the library in his diary (*PSS*, vol. 58, p. 14).

19 The orphans were Tatiana, Ivan and Pyotr Khokhlov, children from a peasant family in the village of Novaya Kolpna. Sofia Tolstaya placed the eldest, Tatiana, in the Sergievskii craft school, and Ivan in the Olginskii children's home; the youngest, Pyotr, was sent to the agricultural school in the town of Bobriki, after Tolstoy's death. See 'Vospominaniya Khokhlovykh' (Memoirs of the Khokhlovs), typewritten manuscript (GMT).

20 N.E. Felten, arrested for printing banned articles by Tolstoy, was sentenced by the St Petersburg Court of Justice to six months' imprisonment in the fortress. He enclosed a copy of the indictment in a letter to Tolstoy of January 3. Tolstoy sent this on to A.M. Kuzminskii, who was at the time a senator and president of the Petersburg circuit court, and asked him to help Felten (*PSS*, vol. 81, p. 23). In his reply of January 17 Kuzminskii refused to intercede for him. Tolstoy was enraged by the injustice of the trial and by this refusal from Kuzminskii. V.A. Molochnikov, a follower of Tolstoy's, forwarded to Yasnaya Polyana four letters to him from S.I. Smirnov, a soldier who had refused to do military service and had served a sentence in the Novgorod jail. Tolstoy replied to Molochnikov on January 29. On the envelope of Molochnikov's letter he had noted, 'Smirnov's marvellous letter' (*PSS*, vol. 81, pp. 80–1).

21 Without Tolstoy's knowledge the newspaper had published an excerpt from his diary for 1889, 'Poslednii etap moei zhizni' (The last phase of my life), which was distorted by a translation back from French into Russian. First published by Chertkov in *Listki 'Svobodnogo Slova'* (Leaflets of the *Free Word*), no. 2, 1899, pp. 48–52. Tolstoy sent Chertkov a telegram questioning him about the appearance of this article (*PSS*, vol. 89, p. 170).

22 A Czech quartet, consisting of Hans Wigan, Karl Hoffman, Josef Suk and Oskar Nedbal, played in the Khamovniki house on December 19, 1895. Tolstoy so liked the playing of this quartet that he attended their concert in the Small Hall of the Palace Assembly. See N. Gusev and A. Goldenweiser, *Lev Tolstoi i muzyka* (Lev Tolstoy and music), Moscow, 1953, pp. 38–9.

23 Rachmaninov frequently visited the Khamovniki Street house, and on January 9, 1900 he accompanied F.I. Chaliapin at a musical evening at the Tolstoys'. Rachmaninov's memoirs of Tolstoy are in the anthology *Vospominaniya o Rakhmaninove* (Reminiscences about Rachmaninov), vol. 2, Moscow, 1967, pp. 229–30.

24 The story 'Devil', written in 1889 (*PSS*, vol. 27), was not published in Tolstoy's lifetime. It first appeared in *Posmertnye khudozhestvennye proizvedeniya Lva Tolstogo* (Posthumous literary works of Lev Tolstoy), Moscow, 1911, vol. 1.

25 George Meyer, a cameraman from the Pathé company (Frères Pathé), made a film, of which a fragment is now kept at the Gosfilmfond. Parts of it are included in the film *The Living Tolstoy* (see note 5).

26 In a letter to Chertkov of February 17, Sofia Tolstaya thanked him for his invitation to move to Kryokshina (prompted by the typhus epidemic which hit the villages around Yasnaya Polyana); she wrote that such a move would be impossible owing to the serious illness of Aleksandra Tolstaya.

27 For a detailed account of Tolstoy's conversation with M. Levin, correspondent of the Norwegian newspaper *Morgenbladet*, see *YaZ*, February 20. See also Bulgakov, pp. 102–3.

28 *Barricade* was a much talked-about play by the French writer Paul Bourget. It was filled with the spirit of Catholicism, attacked the workers' movement and glorified violence, and it evoked a lively polemic in the French press.

I.D. Halpérine-Kaminskii, who lived in Paris and translated Tolstoy's works into French, sent him six newspaper cuttings with reviews of the play by representatives of various parties, then sent him the play itself. (Letters from I.D. Halpérine-Kaminskii of February 15 (28) and March 12 (new style), GMT.) Tolstoy's response to the play, and to the polemic surrounding it, are contained in his letter to Halpérine-Kaminskii of February 24–5 (*PSS*, vol. 81, pp. 111–12).

29 *Lev Tolstoi. Kritiko-biograficheskoe issledovanie N.G. Molostvova i P.I. Sergeenko. Pod red. A.L. Volynskogo* (Lev Tolstoy. Criticial biographical research by Molostvov and Sergeenko, edited by A.L. Volynskii), St Petersburg, 1910. Instalments 1–3, with illustrations by Samokish-Sudkovskii.

30 Of this visit from L.I. Shestov, author of the book *Dobro v uchenii gr. Tolstogo i F. Nitsshe*

(What is good in the teachings of Count Tolstoy and F. Nietzsche), Moscow/St Petersburg, 1907, Tolstoy noted in his diary: 'Shestov came. Of little interest – a "literary man", not a philosopher' (*PSS*, vol. 58, p. 21).

31 The Book *Die Greuel der christlichen Zivilisation. Briefe eines buddhischen Lama aus Tibet* (The horrors of Christian civilisation. Letters from a Buddhist Lama from Tibet), Leipzig, 1907, was sent to Tolstoy in 1909 by the author, a German writer called B. Freidank. It was written in the name of an invented character called Chong-Ka-Pa-Lama. At Tolstoy's suggestion it was sent on to A.A. Goldenweiser, and was published in the *Vegetarianskoe obozrenie* (Vegetarian review) (nos. 5–10, 1910), under the title 'Pisma buddista k khristianinu' (Letters from a Buddhist to a Christian).

32 In the 'Afterword' to *War and Peace* is printed Tolstoy's article 'Neskolko slov po povodu knigi *Voina i Mir* (A few words about the book *War and Peace*) (*The Works of Count L.N. Tolstoy*, vol. VIII, Moscow, 1911).

33 Tolstoy's letter to Z.M. Lyubochinskaya of March 25 was published in *RS*, no. 55, March 9, 1910, under the title 'O samoubiistve' (On suicide) (*PSS*, vol. 72, pp. 175–6).

34 Sofia Tolstaya undertook to read Tolstoy's banned works in connection with the preparation of the 12th edition of the *Works of L.N. Tolstoy*. On March 3 she wrote to Chertkov:

> Respected Vladimir Grigorevich!
>
> As I expect you know, I am publishing a new edition of the works of Lev Nikolaevich's works and have made up my mind to publish everything I possibly can, even at the risk of several volumes being seized.
>
> My request to you is this: I wonder if you could give me or tell me where to find those of Lev Nikolaevich's articles and works which I do not have and am unable to obtain, since over the past few years everything has been sent to you without my knowledge and I have not even had the chance to copy many of the things I would have liked to have, and which I now need for a more complete edition.
>
> I enclose a list of the works I do not have, and am relying on your friendly assistance. I am sure that you would wish for a wider distribution of Lev Nikolaevich's works and a more complete edition of them. [GMT. The list attached to the letter is missing.]

Chertkov replied on March 8 that he was 'happy to be of service', and to obtain and send the missing articles, although there would be some delay as some of the material had to be ordered from abroad. (The manuscripts of Tolstoy's banned works were kept in a special safe constructed by Chertkov in Christchurch, England.)

Without waiting for Chertkov's answer Sofia Tolstaya, possibly on Tolstoy's advice, turned to the *Polnoe sobranie sochinenii L.N. Tolstogo zapreschyonnykh russkoi tsenzuroi* (Complete collection of Tolstoy's works banned by the censor), edited by Chertkov, Russian Free Word edn, 1901–6.

35 V.Yu. Shimanovskii's letter to Tolstoy of March 7. Tolstoy's reply of March 10. See *PSS*, vol. 81, pp. 140–1.

36 S.A. Stakhovich brought to Yasnaya Polyana a typewritten manuscript of Tolstoy's letters to A.A. Tolstaya. In 1903 A.A. Tolstaya gave the originals of the letters to the Manuscript Department of the Academy of Sciences Library in St Petersburg. *Perepiska L.N. Tolstogo s gr. A.A.Tolstoi. 1877–1903* (L.N. Tolstoy's correspondence with Countess A.A. Tolstaya, 1877–1903) was published by the Society of the Tolstoy Museum in St Petersburg in 1911.

37 V.N. Meshkov did a charcoal sketch of Tolstoy and several drawings: *Tolstoy at Work, Playing Chess with M.S. Sukhotin*, as well as sketches of various rooms in the Yasnaya Polyana house (GMT). See V.N. Meshkov, '[. . .] Pamyatnoe. Listki iz memuarov' (Memorable events. Pages from my memoirs), in the newspaper *Sovetskoe iskusstvo* (Soviet art), no. 114, August 28, 1938.

38 A reply to Gusev's letter of March 9, in which he said he was threatened with arrest for distributing Tolstoy's banned works (*PSS*, vol. 81, p. 152).

39 The Finnish writer A. Ernefeldt urged Tolstoy, during his visit to Yasnaya Polyana, to visit

Stockholm in July for the Peace Congress. See Ernefeldt's letter to Chertkov, published in *PSS*, vol. 58, p. 345.

40 Sofia Tolstaya's copy of V.A. Serov's portrait of her (oils, 1892) hangs in the drawing-room of the house at Yasnaya Polyana (GMT).

41 A.P. Voitichenko, a student at the school of sculpture in the town of Nezhin. (See Bulgakov, p. 140.)

42 Tolstoy's tract *The Kingdom of God is Within Us* (*PSS*, vol. 28) was originally published abroad in 1893 in French and German translations, then in Russian in Paris and Berlin; it was banned from distribution in Russia by a secret circular from the Chief Office of Press Affairs (May 18, 1894, no. 2829). It was first published in Russia by Chertkov in 1906 in the Russian Free Word edition, and was published uncensored in vol. XIV of the *Works of Count L.N. Tolstoy*, Moscow, 1911.

43 The Czech writer and philosopher T. Mazaryk stayed two days in Yasnaya Polyana, March 29 and 30. Tolstoy wrote in his diary: 'Had two good talks with Mazaryk yesterday' (*PSS*, vol. 58, p. 31).

44 The Society of the Tolstoy House-Museum, one of whose founders was M.A. Stakhovich, was established in 1908 in St Petersburg. A Moscow branch of the Society was formed soon after the St Petersburg one. Its meetings were held in the building of Art and Literature Circle, on Bolshaya Dmitrovka. The official opening of the Moscow branch took place on March 19, 1911.

45 M.A. Stakhovich asked Sofia Tolstaya to take copies for the GMT of the letters in her possession between Aleksandra Tolstaya and L.N. Tolstoy. Their correspondence, comprising 119 letters from Tolstoy and 66 replies, was published in 1911.

46 Sofia Tolstaya was reading the proofs of vol. II of Aylmer Maude's book *The Life of Tolstoy*, London, 1910.

47 The story 'After the Ball' (*PSS*, vol. 34) was first published in the *Posthumous Works of Lev Nikolaevich Tolstoy*, vol. I, Moscow, 1911.

48 Shortly before the second All-Russian Congress of Writers, G.K. Gradovskii, one of its organisers, sent to Sofia Tolstaya a letter (dated April 1) appealing for her cooperation and asking if Tolstoy would send a message to the Congress. On April 6 Tolstoy wrote Gradovskii a letter containing a message of support (*PSS*, vol. 81, pp. 211–12). In a letter of April 12 Gradovskii asked for permission to read this message to the Congress, omitting the words 'rabble' and 'lost souls' in reference to the government. Tolstoy agreed (*PSS*, vol. 81, p. 242). However, in the event Stakhovich read out only the first part of the letter, which aggrieved Tolstoy and provoked Chertkov to send a letter of protest to the papers (*Re*, no. 121, May 5, 1910, and *Utro Rossii* (Morning of Russia), no. 138, May 5, 1910).

49 Tolstoy attended a session of the circuit hearings of the Moscow Court of Justice on January 19, and became interested in the case of a worker named Figner accused of murdering a peasant who had stolen some wood. Tolstoy asked for a meeting with the murderer, but the Tula prosecutor refused this. D.P. Makovitsky wrote, after talking to Tolstoy: 'L.N. wanted to understand his psychology. He was extremely moved by this tragic event: "why does brother attack brother? What was happening in this man's soul? What made him act this way?" ' (*YaZ*, January 16).

When Stakhovich heard that the Tula authorities had refused Tolstoy's request, he asked permission of S.S. Khrulev, Chief Administrator of Places of Imprisonment, for Tolstoy to visit prisoners in the Tula jail, but his request was turned down.

50 This manuscript is taken to be the third edition of *Childhood*.

51 Sergei Lvovich Tolstoy tells the story thus: 'Sergei Nikolaevich Tolstoy told us that when an old servant of his was invited to go for a swim, he replied, "No I won't go, my swimming days are over." ' Tolstoy applied the phrase to himself when referring to his literary labours (*DST*, IV, p. 290).

52 Two photographers from Mey's firm, Scherer and Nabholz, were invited to Yasnaya Polyana

by Sofia Tolstaya to take a new photograph of Tolstoy for the 12th edition of the *Works of Count L.N. Tolstoy*, which she was preparing. The photograph and a facsimile of Tolstoy's autograph, dated April 14, were reproduced in vol. I.

53 A notebook of thoughts and aphorisms, collected by N.S. Leskov, was sent to Tolstoy by P.A. Sergeenko. Bulgakov, asked by Tolstoy to select some of Leskov's sayings for the new edition of *For Every Day*, discovered that most of the thoughts belonged to Tolstoy himself. (See Bulgakov, pp. 156–7.)

54 *She Has All the Qualities* (*PSS*, vol. 38). First published in the *Posthumous Literary Works of L.N. Tolstoy*, vol. I, Moscow, 1911.

55 A retired colonel called Trotskii-Sanyutovich wrote some verses accusing Tolstoy of apostasy from the Orthodox Church and the government. After talking to Tolstoy he became ashamed of his verses and decided to burn them.

56 Harala Tatsuki, director of a high school in Tokyo, and Mitsutaki Hodze, an official at the Ministry of Communications. For a description of this visit see Bulgakov, pp. 178–80.

57 According to Bulgakov's memoirs,

> Lev Nikolaevich said, as he went out for tea, how much he had enjoyed her playing.
> She flushed: 'You're joking,' she said hesitantly.
> 'Not a bit of it. That adagio in "Quasi una fantasia" was so delicate . . .'
> How happy Sofia Andreevna was!
> 'I deeply regret how badly I play, never more so than when Lev Nikolaevich is listening to me,' she said later (Bulgakov, p. 185).

58 According to Makovitsky and Bulgakov, Sofia Tolstaya talked to Andreev about her work on *MZh* and the new edition of L.N. Tolstoy's *Collected Works* (*YaZ*, April 21; Bulgakov, p. 185). L.N. Andreev's reminiscences *Za polgoda do smerti* (Six months before his death) were published in the journal *Solntse Rossii* (Sun of Russia).

59 These letters do not appear in the *List of Letters Written on L.N. Tolstoy's Instructions*.

60 Makovitsky recounts Tolstoy's discussion with B.O. Sibor about the 'Kreutzer Sonata': Tolstoy agreed with Sibor that the finale of the sonata was a disappointment, and added that it contained the beginnings of decadence (*YaZ*, April 23).

61 Of this visit to Yasnaya Polyana by students of the Tula Technical College Bulgakov wrote: 'Lev Nikolaevich talked to them, showed them the Pythagorean theorem "in Brahmin" and gave them his books as keepsakes. The boys left in a state of great elation' (Bulgakov, p. 206).

62 The letter is dated May 4, 1910, when postal stamping was introduced (*PST*, p. 782).

63 Sofia Tolstaya was evidently going through Tolstoy's youthful works, which were published later in *PSS*, vol. 1, as 'Youthful Experiments'.

64 Tolstoy went to the village of Izvekovo to visit some peasant Old Believers, but did not find them.

65 Tolstoy worked for four years, on and off, on his preface to *For Every Day* (subtitled 'A New Circle of Reading'), and revised it more than a hundred times (*PSS*, vol. 45, pp. 521–6).

66 Makovitsky wrote: 'L.N. walked this afternoon to Zhelyabino (the village of Zhelyabukha); there he met some carpenters who were building a hut for a poor peasant, and he talked to them, mainly about vodka. They got out of it by making jokes, but he was well pleased with their conversation. Chertkov followed him unnoticed, and took photographs' (*YaZ*, May 14).

67 For Ivan Khokhlov's move to the orphanage, see note 19.

68 Vol. IV contains Tolstoy's pedagogical works and his works for children, vol. XI his peasant tales, and vol. XII his 'Reminiscences of Childhood', and plays and stories of the 1880s and 1890s.

69 Sergei Sergeevich's tutor was Maurice Kuez.

70 The 'dark one' was D.L. Maksimchuk, a Ukrainian, who had decided to refuse military service.

1 Tolstoy took with him the proofs of his anthology *The Path of Life*, consisting of thirty-one booklets. They were published by the Intermediary, with the exception of one, 'Sueverie gosudarstva' (The government's superstition), which was banned by the censors. See *The Path of Life*, Moscow, Intermediary, 1911.

2 Chertkov's letter of May 26, in which he recommended the actor P.N. Orlyonov to Tolstoy and asked that he be received at Yasnaya Polyana (*PSS*, vol. 58, pp. 397–8; Tolstoy's answer in *PSS*, vol. 89, p. 189).

3 Sergei Tolstoy explains this entry thus: 'L.N. didn't "drive" Sofia Andreevna anywhere, he merely said to her, when she complained about the difficulty of running Yasnaya Polyana, that she did not need to live there, and that she could live anywhere, even in Odoev (the chief town of Tula province)' (*DST*, IV, p. 296).

4 This note from Sofia Tolstaya's Tula acquaintance E.A. Shchelkan-Taneeva, née Maklakova, is no longer extant.

5 P. Trubetskoi, *Tolstoy at Work*, oils, 1910, and also four pencil drawings (GMT).

6 *She Has All the Qualities*.

7 P. Trubetskoi, *L.N. Tolstoy On His Horse*.

8 Ahmet the Circassian, who guarded the forest and meadows of Yasnaya Polyana, caught a peasant named Prokofii Vlasov stealing some felled wood, and brought him into the office to be charged; Vlasov was a former student of Tolstoy's, from his first peasant school in Yasnaya Polyana. Tolstoy referred to this episode in his diary: 'It has become insufferable here, I really have considered leaving' (*PSS*, vol. 58, p. 60).

9 'First Memoires', part of Tolstoy's unfinished autobiography *Moya zhizn* (My life) for the 1910–11 edition. (See *PSS*, vol. 23.)

0 S.T. Semyonov, a peasant writer, author of stories, tales and plays about Russian village life. Tolstoy was acquainted with him and corresponded with him. In 1894 he wrote a preface to Semyonov's *Krestyanskie rasskazy* (Peasant stories), in which he praised his work highly (*PSS*, vol. 29).

1 On this day Tolstoy wrote in his diary: 'More agitation and aggravation. Very hard' (*PSS*, vol. 58, p. 62).

2 The proofs of vol. II of Maude's *The Life of Tolstoy*, London, 1910.

3 This letter to the newspapers, dated June 7–10, was prompted by the increase in letters requesting financial help. (See *PSS*, vol. 82, pp. 51–2.)

4 Sofia Tolstaya's edition of the *Complete Collected Works* was planned to consist of twenty volumes. Eleven of these were ready by June 1910, and work was proceeding on the remaining volumes.

5 Karl Veleminsky. See Daily Diary, 1907, note 49.

6 P. Trubetskoi, *Peasant Ploughing* (Paris, Institute of Slavonic Languages).

7 The *ABC* and the story 'Sorok let' (Forty years) went into vol. XII of the 1910–11 edition.

8 Both these works went into vol. XII of the 1910–11 edition.

9 Letter from Otradnoe of June 14 (*PSS*, vol. 84, p. 393). It mistakenly indicates here that Sofia Tolstaya only received the letter on June 22.

0 The letter is not published. Sofia Tolstaya wrote: 'Belinkii has just brought your letter, darling Lyovochka, and I never imagined I could be so delighted. I thank you and kiss you. A storm cloud is looming, but Kolechka and I are going to the Nikolaevs – I need your preface to Henry George, and I simply haven't got it here in any of the cupboards. Well goodbye now my dearest husband, your "old wife" (as you write) who loves you still none the less, Sonya' (GMT).

1 Tatiana Sukhotina, in a letter of June 14, wrote: 'Since leaving you my ears have rung with your words – that your nerves are so agitated, your life is so hard, difficult and demanding, you have far too much work to do at your age. This is quite true, and people at your time of life very often live in peace [. . .] To be quite honest I think you have so little egoism that it is a real joy for you to make others happy [. . .] That said, I cannot help

asking why, for whom and for what reason you lead this life of drudgery, which makes you describe yourself as a "harnessed nag" [. . .] Papa constantly suffers from this' (*DST*, IV, p. 299).

92 No known letter of June 17. About a letter of June 18 Sofia Tolstaya makes the following observation: 'An urgent telegram arrived in Yasnaya Polyana from the editorial board of the *St Petersburg Gazette*, enquiring about Lev Nikolaevich's health. I was very alarmed and sent a telegram to the Chertkovs to enquire about it' (*PST*, p. 784).

93 Letter of June 18 in which Tolstoy wrote: 'Chertkov suddenly walked in this morning with your telegram, which arrived last night and which we found utterly incomprehensible. Absolutely nothing the least bit pleasant or unpleasant has happened here' (*PSS*, vol. 84, p. 394).

94 Letter of June 18 (*PST*, p. 784).

95 Sergei Tolstoy challenged K.V. Sumarokov to a duel after the two men had come into conflict over the latter's hunting of wolves in Nikolskoe-Vyazemskii. The duel did not take place, and in December 1910 they had a formal reconciliation.

96 'When Sofia Andreevna learnt that I had brought a letter from Chertkov, she begged Lev Nikolaevich to tell her what it contained,' wrote Bulgakov. 'Lev Nikolaevich replied that it was a business letter but that he could not, as a matter of principle, give it to her to read' (Bulgakov, p. 394). This refers to Chertkov's letter of October 26, in which he thanked Tolstoy for his letters to him, and for sharing with him what he 'experienced in the depths of [. . .] his soul' (GMT).

97 On this day Tolstoy wrote a rough copy of his farewell letter to Sofia Tolstaya (see note in his notebook for October 27, *PSS*, vol. 58, p. 233), worked on his letter to K.I. Chukovskii about capital punishment (see *PSS*, vol. 58, p. 123), and read the manuscript of P.N. Gastev's reminiscences of V.K. Syutaev.

98 See this Diary, 1910, note 155.

99 L.L. Tolstoy was abroad.

100 D.D. Obolenskii, an 'old friend' of the Tolstoy family, arrived in Yasnaya Polyana as a correspondent for *NV*. In his article 'Neskolko slov po povodu otezda L.N. Tolstogo' (A few words about L.N. Tolstoy's departure) (*NV*, no. 12,444, November 2, 1910) he wrote: 'Being an intimate of the Tolstoy family I hurriedly hired a troika and drove to Yasnaya Polyana to discover what had really happened.' His articles were published on October 29 and 30, and November 2.

101 Tolstoy set off from Yasnaya Polyana, accompanied by Doctor Makovitsky, to Shchekino station, and from there took a train to Shamordino to see his sister Maria.

102 These entries were made later, which meant that there was a chronological confusion of events. Tolstoy left Shamordino early on the morning of October 31. On arriving at the station of Kozelsk, he, Makovitsky and Aleksandra Tolstaya boarded a train, without tickets, and travelled south.

103 Doctor P.I. Rastegaev (Sofia Tolstaya has misspelled the name) was accompanied by a medical student called E.I. Skorobogatova.

104 See Diary, 1910, note 156.

105 At Tolstoy's request Aleksandra Tolstaya sent Chertkov a telegram on November 1: 'Got out yesterday at Astapovo. High fever. Lost consciousness. This morning temperature normal. Chills. Impossible to leave. Expressed desire to see you. Frolova' (*Smert Tolstogo* (The death of Tolstoy), Lenin Library, Moscow, 1928, p. 18). Wanting to keep his whereabouts a secret, Tolstoy and his daughter Aleksandra used pseudonyms in their correspondence. Tolstoy was 'Nikolaev' and Aleksandra 'Frolova'.

106 Tatiana Sukhotina recalled: 'Mother went up to him, sat at the head of the bed, leant over him and started whispering tender words to him, saying farewell and begging him to forgive her for all the wrong she had done him. His only reply was a number of deep sighs' (T.L. Sukhotina, p. 425).

7 'In order to attempt a true picture of Tolstoy's flight and the reasons which impelled him to this, I visited Yasnaya Polyana in my capacity as journalist,' wrote A. Ksyunin. 'I spent a whole day there talking to Sofia Andreevna and her daughters, visited the Yasnaya Polyana peasants and talked about L.N. with them, then went to the monastery where Tolstoy's last healthy days were spent.' He wrote a series of articles about these visits which were published in December 1910 in *NV*, and which formed a book, *Ukhod Tolstogo* (Tolstoy's departure), St Petersburg, 1911. 'A very good and truthful article by Ksyunin in *New Times* today, and very sympathetic to me,' Sofia Tolstaya wrote to Tatiana Sukhotina in Rome on December 11 (GMT).

8 Letters to Octave Mirbeau (May 26, 1903) and Paul Sabatier (December 7 (20), 1906) went into vol. XX of the 1910–11 edition.

9 The artist V.I. Rossinskii thought of doing an artistic documentary chronicle of the last days of Tolstoy's life. For this reason he came to Yasnaya Polyana after Tolstoy's 'flight' and also visited all the places where Tolstoy had been. The drawings he did were exhibited at the first Tolstoy exhibition, on October 11 in Moscow, and were made into the album *Poslednie dni L.N. Tolstogo* (The last days of L.N. Tolstoy), St Petersburg, 1911. The album was prefaced by the artist, who expounded the various accounts he had heard regarding Tolstoy's 'flight' and death.

10 The letter was published in *Letopisi* (vol. 2, pp. 252–3). Sofia Tolstaya wrote to Taneev: 'At the end I caused L.N. a lot of distress and grief with my nervous illness and my dislike of Chertkov, whom he did not see on my account, and this is now the chief cause of my unhappiness. I live alone here in this great house, with the same servants and the same furniture as before. Everyone has left, apart from Doctor Makovitsky, and he too will soon leave.'

11 M.A. Stakhovich visited at Sofia Tolstaya's invitation. She wrote to him on December 13: 'My greatest joy at present is to be with people like you, who valued L.N. highly and loved him utterly selflessly. There is also a lot for me to discuss with you, I want to unburden my heart and listen to your advice [. . .] Sasha wants me to be in Moscow by January 10 to give her the manuscripts which are in the museum' (GMT). Stakhovich's advice concerned Sofia Tolstaya's rights to Tolstoy's manuscripts, which she had put in the Historical Museum, and how her rights to her editions of his works were affected by the will. (See Diary, 1910, note 49.) On these questions Stakhovich consulted various eminent lawyers. See entries for 1911, and notes 4–6.

12 The unfinished autobiographical drama on which Tolstoy had worked since the 1880s, for two decades. First published in *Posmertnye khudozhestvennye proizvedeniya Lva Nik. Tolstogo* (Posthumous fictional works of Lev Nikolaevich Tolstoy), vol. 2, Moscow, 1911, an edition compiled by Aleksandra Tolstaya (*PSS*, vol. 31).

13 A reference to Tolstoy's letter to I.I. Gorbunov of August 4–6, 1889 (*PSS*, vol. 64, pp. 290–2). Sofia Tolstaya included it in vol. XX of her edition under the title 'O lyubvi k bogu i blizhnemu' (Love of God and one's neighbour).

14 The story was written in 1906 (*PSS*, vol. 36). First published in *Posthumous Works*, vol. 1, Moscow, 1911.

15 The tickets were bought on the journey, at the station of Volovo in Rostov on Don.

911

1 Maria Nikolaevna wrote to Sofia Tolstaya about this: 'When Lyovochka came to me he was very downcast at first; and when he told me how you had thrown yourself into the pond he sobbed violently and I couldn't look at him without weeping' (GMT – copy in Sofia Tolstaya's letter to Tatiana Sukhotina of April 25, 1911).

2 Sofia Tolstaya and her youngest son, Vanechka, had been allotted the Yasnaya Polyana property (see Diary, 1891, note 54). After Vanechka's death in 1895 the property was left to

Sofia Tolstaya and her sons. Immediately after Tolstoy's death the question arose as to the future of Yasnaya Polyana, since his heirs did not have the means to maintain it as a cultural and historical monument. There was a scheme to redeem the property with money collected in 'civilised countries', with a view to turning it into an international cultural monument, and selling the rest of the land to Americans for 1.5 million dollars. Mikhail Kuzminskii, who arrived in New York on January 1, conducted a series of negotiations with various foreign industrialists. From the interviews with Kuzminskii that were published in the papers (*Birzhevye vedomosti* (Stock Exchange Gazette), no. 12,108, January 5, 1911; *Odesskii listok* (Odessa Leaflet), no. 5, January 6), it became clear that this plan to sell Russia's national property to foreigners aroused deep indignation amongst the Russian people, and this was expressed in speeches, articles and letters. At the end of April there appeared an interview with Tolstoy's sons (Sergei Tolstoy was not party to this, and refused his share of the inheritance), in which they announced: 'We did indeed hold negotiations with American millionaires, but these concerned only the sale of the land, not the property. Our common desire was to sell everything to the nation' (see *Utro Kharkova* (Kharkov morning), no. 1328, April 24, 1911. Ilya Tolstoy did not go to America.

3 Vol. XX of the 1910–11 edition went under the general title *Mysli i pisma* (Thoughts and letters) and comprised the following sections: 'Dlya chego my zhivem?' (What do we live for?), 'Muzhchina i zhenshchina' (Man and woman), 'O soznanii dukhovnogo nachala' (The consciousness of spiritual origins) and so on.

4 On November 20, 1910, after Tolstoy's will had come into force, N.K. Muravyov sent a statement to the Historical Museum, where Sofia Tolstaya had deposited part of her archive and part of Tolstoy's. The statement proposed that 1) The stored property should be kept there temporarily; 2) No one should be admitted to the safe, and 3) The safe should be kept sealed up. The legal injunction which he drew up on January 10, 1911 and sent to the Kushneryov printing works stated that 'according to the terms of the will, the printing or publishing of the works of L.N. Tolstoy by any person besides Aleksandra Tolstaya is an infringement of her interests'. In consequence of this there must be the 'complete cessation on the part of the publishers of any further publication of L.N. Tolstoy's works [. . .] and an undertaking by Countess S.A. not to publish what the printers have already printed'. The printers did not agree to these demands, 'since it is Countess S.A. Tolstaya who has placed the order, she who buys the paper, she who puts her labour into reading the proofs and deciphering the manuscripts (and no one but her could possibly decipher them), and consequently it is she who owns the order' (*RS*, no. 12, January 16, 1911).

5 In her letter to N.S. Shcherbatov, president of the Council of the Historical Museum, Sofia Tolstaya asked to be allowed admittance to the manuscripts that were kept there as they were essential for her work on her memoirs. She also suggested that Aleksandra and Sergei Tolstoy and Tatiana Sukhotina should be given the opportunity to take copies from the manuscripts of all Tolstoy's unpublished works, which Aleksandra could use when taking advantage of her publishing rights; she suggested this so that the originals could be kept permanently at the museum and would not be spoilt by frequent handling. (See L.L. 'Spor o rukopisyakh L.N. Tolstogo' (The argument over L.N. Tolstoy's manuscripts), *Re*, no. 293, October 25, 1911). The Museum Council replied that it 'could not seal up the room [. . .] and the things that were in it could be given to no one but Countess Sofia Tolstaya [. . .] but in view of the argument that has developed the parties will not be allowed into the room separately' (*RS*, no. 12, January 16, 1911).

6 Sofia Tolstaya is referring to a series of articles sympathetic to her point of view which appeared in several papers. M.A. Stakhovich had consulted with the eminent lawyers G.F. Shershenevich and S.I. Filippov.

7 V.G. Chertkov, 'O poslednikh dnyakh Lva Nikolaevicha Tolstogo' (Lev Nikolaevich Tolstoy's last days), *RV*, nos 12 and 13, January 16 and 18, 1911. Republished by many papers, it appeared shortly afterwards as a separate edition (St Petersburg, 1911).

8 Two letters – from Aleksandra Tolstaya and V.G. Chertkov – to the editors of *RS* were published under the general heading 'Literaturnoe nasledie L.N. Tolstogo' (The literary heritage of L.N. Tolstoy). Aleksandra Tolstaya announced in hers that as a result of the violation of 'her father's posthumous wishes' she had had to resort to 'legal injunctions'; she also insisted that the 'original manuscripts, not the copies', be handed over to her, since this was the 'major condition of the will'. (See Diary, 1910, and note 49.)

Chertkov in his letter repudiated Sofia Tolstaya's assertion that the manuscripts had been given to her by Tolstoy, and also permitted himself some tactless and offensive remarks about her (*RS*, no. 22, January 23, 1911).

9 The anthology of sayings *For Every Day* was published in the newspaper *Novaya Rus* (New Holy Russia) throughout the whole of 1909 and up until May 1910 (when the paper closed down). See *PSS*, vols 43–4.

10 The plan for this novel was familiar to Sofia Tolstaya. (See Appendices, 'Various Notes for Future Reference', February 15, 1870 and January 16, 1873, and notes 11 and 24.) But this was evidently her first acquaintance with the texts of the rought versions which were kept. 'At our recent meeting', wrote A. Ksyunin after visiting Yasnaya Polyana, 'Sofia Andreevna told me that she had just found some pages written in pencil relating to Tolstoy's planned epic about Peter the Great. L.N. did not write this work [. . .], as he said, "I could not re-create the everyday life of the period"' (*NV*, no. 12,629, May 11, 1911).

11 Tatiana Sukhotina's letter of January 29 from Rome. She wrote: 'In your place, for love of the memory of my husband, who could not endure struggle and hatred, and also to save my daughter from a shameful and unworthy struggle with her own mother, I would open the doors of the museum to her and give her (and society at large) responsibility for the manuscripts' (GMT).

12 Some material about Tolstoy was published in the January and February editions of *VE*.

13 Letter of December 4, 1910 about the circumstances of Tolstoy's flight (IRLI); it was published, translated into French, under the title 'Tolstoy's Last Days', *Le Figaro*, February 11, 1923.

14 Diary, 1862–3. *PSS*, vol. 58.

15 'Diary for Myself Alone' (*PSS*, vol. 58).

16 Vols XVI, XIX and XX were seized after the censors had sent a report to the Moscow Committee on Press Affairs about the instigation of criminal proceedings against the publishers for including 'criminal works' in them.

17 Included in Volume XX were two appeals by Tolstoy to Nicholas II: 'To the Tsar and His Assistants' (1901) (see *PSS*, vol. 34) and 'To the Tsar on the Situation in Russia' (January 16, 1902) (see *PSS*, vol. 73, pp. 184–91). See note 28.

18 See note 5.

19 In a letter of March 1911 to Kasso, Minister of Education, Sofia Tolstaya repeated the contents of her letter to Shcherbatov (see note 5), and also asked that various things be returned to her – diaries, notes, letters to her (see *Re*, no. 293, October 25, 1911).

20 The newspapers printed Sofia Tolstaya's announcement: '*The Collected Works of L.N. Tolstoy* are now in print, price 25 rubles. Warehouse, 21 Khamovniki Street, Moscow.'

21 Sofia Tolstaya replaced the articles that were removed by the censors with letters from the two-volume *Pisma L.N. Tolstogo, sobrannye i redaktirovannye P.A. Sergeenko* (Letters of L.N. Tolstoy, selected and edited by P.A. Sergeenko), Moscow, Kniga (Book), vol. I, 1910; vol. II, 1911.

22 L.A. Kasso wrote in reply to Sofia Tolstaya (see note 19): 'In view of the argument that has arisen between you and [. . .] A.L. Tolstaya, it is hard for me to allow access to the various materials referred to.'

23 L.L. Tolstoy wrote about the problems or organising an exhibition of his sculptural works.

24 I.D. Halpérine-Kaminskii published two articles, 'Yasnaya Polyana bez Lva Tolstogo' (Yasnaya Polyana without Lev Tolstoy), *Sinii zhurnal* (Blue Journal), no. 19, 1911, and 'Spor

iz-za rukopisei Tolstogo' (The argument over Tolstoy's manuscripts), ibid., no. 20, in which he made use of various materials received from Sofia Tolstaya to defend her against 'all manner of accusations' from her opponents.

25 The text of this will is no longer extant.

26 'Yunost' (Youth), the first part of an autobiographical novel by E.I. Chirikov called *Zhizn Tarkhanova* (The life of Tarkhanov).

27 A line from a verse by A.A. Fet, 'To A.L. Brzeskaya' ('Spring again, again the leaves are trembling . . .') (1879).

28 It was announced in the press that the Moscow Palace of Justice had decreed that vols XVI, XIX and XX of the 12th edition should be destroyed because of the articles 'To the Working People', 'The Slavery of Our Time', 'A Great Sin', 'Thou Shalt Not Kill', 'Change Your Mind', 'I Cannot Keep Silent', 'The Law of Violence and the Law of Love', 'To the Tsar and His Assistants' and others, as they were found to contain 'blasphemy', 'inciting the people to adopt a hostile attitude to the government and an insolent disrespect for the higher authorities' (*RS*, no. 89, April 20, 1911). This was republished in many other newspapers.

29 On this day Sofia Tolstaya wrote to Tatiana Sukhotina: 'I visited the Censorship Committee at the Palace of Justice. I demanded, insisted and complained, and was eventually told that at 5 p.m. tomorrow I would be given a list of the banned articles with permission to reprint them; otherwise they would have destroyed 3 volumes' (GMT).

30 A major exhibition of the paintings of I.P. Pokhitonov opened in Moscow, at the Lemercier Gallery.

31 Sofia Tolstaya received permission to republish the last three volumes of the *Collected Works*. 'After consideration of S.A. Tolstaya's petition, the Committee For Press Affairs agreed that the articles banned by court of law from L.N. Tolstoy's famous three volumes be cut from the published volumes. In the execution of this decree there took place yesterday, April 28, in S.A. Tolstaya's warehouse, in the presence of representatives of the Censorship Committee, the police and one of the directors of the Kushneryov works [. . .] the removal of the seals from the confiscated books. These books will be taken to the printing works where the removal of the forbidden articles will proceed. The printing works are obliged to keep all the cut pages. After the cutting has been completed officials from the Censorship Committee will take the exact number of cut pages, and the entire mass will either be shredded in the office of the printing works' director, or burnt under the observation of Censorship Committee officials in the stoves of the Kushneryov company' (*RV*, no. 97, April 29, 1911).

32 Sofia Tolstaya wrote on May 3 to Tatiana Sukhotina: 'The Empress [. . .] has refused me an audience, and it is said she has not forgotten what was said about me long ago: that I deceived Alexander III by promising not to publish the *Kreutzer Sonata* separately, and then bringing it out in a separate edition. In fact it was brought out by some underground publishers' (GMT).

33 This meeting of the Society of the Tolstoy Museum heard reports on its activities, about preparations to open a Tolstoy Museum in Petersburg and the decision to publish the correspondence between Tolstoy and N.N. Strakhov.

34 A rough copy has been kept of Sofia Tolstaya's letter to the Minister of Justice, I.G. Shcheglovitov, in which she wrote: 'I beg you, esteemed Ivan Grigorevich, to hasten your decision about the Tolstoy manuscripts, a matter which is exhausting us and the whole of Russian society' (GMT).

35 She is probably referring to a lecture by K.I. Arabazhin, 'Drama zhizni i tvorchestva L.N. Tolstogo' (The drama of L.N. Tolstoy's life and work), *NS*, no. 3, 1912.

36 See notes 2, 49 and 90.

37 A.A. Shakhmatov visited Sofia Tolstaya in connection with her appeal to the Academy of Sciences for help in sorting and cataloguing Tolstoy's manuscripts, and about the possibility

of leaving them there for good. He told her that the Academy of Sciences had agreed.

38 E.A. Naryshkina, *Moi vospominaniya* (My reminiscences), 1st edn, St Petersburg, 1906; 2nd edn, St Petersburg, 1910.

39 In her letter to the Tsar, dated May 10, Sofia Tolstaya suggested that Yasnaya Polyana should be bought by the government. 'It is our most passionate wish to leave his cradle and grave in the protection of the state,' she wrote. 'I consider it my last duty to his memory to keep the material and spiritual wealth of the Russian state in its own hands and to preserve it untouched.' She referred also in her letter to the situation with the Tolstoy manuscripts, and explained that it was her desire to 'see that everything he wrote [. . .] stays in Russia and for Russia', to 'be kept permanently, free of charge, in some state or scientific safe in Russia' (GMT).

40 Vols XVI and XIX came out in an abridged edition, without the addition of new material; in vol. XX the removed passages were replaced by Tolstoy's letters (to Sabatier, Mirbeau and others), and the former contents table was retained.

41 The purpose of her meeting with N.I. Guchkov, mayor of Moscow, was to propose that the Khamovniki Street house be sold to the town.

42 Sofia Tolstaya wrote twice to Kasso, in February and in March (see note 19). Kasso replied on May 12 that he would not refuse her request. (See *Re*, no. 293, October 25, 1911).

43 The concluding chapter of the second volume of Maude's *The Life of Tolstoy*, London, 1910.

44 She is referring to the books V.F. Bulgakov, *U L.N. Tolstogo v poslednii god ego zhizni* (With L.N. Tolstoy in the last year of his life), Moscow, 1911 (with a dedication and notes written in the margins): Sofia Tolstaya's library; V. Lazurskii, *Vospominaniya o L.N. Tolstom* (Memories of L.N. Tolstoy), Moscow, 1911; Romain Rolland, *La Vie de Tolstoi* (The life of Tolstoy), Paris, 1911 (Sofia Tolstaya's library) and Maude's book, mentioned in note 43.

45 Sergei Tolstoy was working on a book called *Yasnaya Polyana. Kratkoe opisanie i svedenie dlya posetitelei. S kartoi, 4 planami i 5 fototipiyami* (Yasnaya Polyana. A brief catalogue and guide for visitors. With a map, 4 plans and 5 phototypes). It was published by the Moscow Tolstoy Society in 1914. The entire text, with the exception of two chapters, was written by Sergei Tolstoy.

46 Letter unknown.

47 The journal *Foi et vie* (May 16, 1911, Sofia Tolstaya's library) published the reminiscences of Maurice Denis Rochat about his visit to Tolstoy's estate in June 1899, 'Tolstoi v Yasnoi Polyane' (Tolstoy at Yasnaya Polyana). See *LN*, vol. 75, book 2, pp. 24–31.)

48 The album *Iz zhizni L.N. Tolstogo. Snimki isklyuchitelno gr. S.A. Tolstoi* (From the life of L.N. Tolstoy. Photographs exclusively by Countess S.A. Tolstaya). The phototypes were reproduced by Messrs Scherer, Nabholz & Co. in Moscow. It was published in aid of peasant victims of fire in the Yasnaya Polyana region.

49 *RS*, no. 121, May 28, 1911, announced that a session of the Council of Ministers had decided to acquire Yasnaya Polyana for 500,000 rubles, through the State Peasant Bank.

50 Many articles were written about V.G. Belinskii in newspapers and journals on this day, the hundredth anniversary of his birth.

51 M.M. Prishvin described his visit to Yasnaya Polyana in an essay called 'Otkliki zhizni. Smuta' (Echoes of life. Sedition), *RV*, no. 262, November 13, 1911. A new edition of the essay later formed the chapter 'Niagarskii vodopad' (The Niagara Falls), in the book *Glaza zemli* (Eyes of the world).

52 Probably Pascal's *Discours sur les passions de l'amour*. See Daily Diary, 1912, entry for July 19.

53 See Daily Diary, 1907, note 36.

54 The Tolstoys' offer to sell Yasnaya Polyana to the government contained a number of conditions, including the burial of Sofia Tolstaya and her sons beside Tolstoy's grave, and Sofia Tolstaya's right to live the rest of her life in the so-called 'Kuzminskiis' wing'.

55 This polemic was inspired by Chertkov's article 'Otvet na klevetu' (A reply to slander) (*RV*,

no. 148, June 29, 1911), in which he repudiated press reports that in a discussion with G.P. Georgievskii on January 31 he had demanded the manuscripts of Tolstoy's diaries from him, so as to 'tear out or destroy certain pages'. Chertkov insisted that his words had been misinterpreted. In reply, with Sofia Tolstaya's permission, *RS* published Georgievskii's letter to her of February 2, and his official open letter of April 24, reasserting her rights to the disputed manuscripts, and referring to something said by Tolstoy in his presence: 'I have given all my manuscripts to Sofia Andreevna, and they are her property' (*RS*, no. 153, July 5, 1911).

56 The painting *L.N. Tolstoy's Grave* (oils) is at the Estate Museum at Yasnaya Polyana.

57 A reference to Makovitsky's *Yasnopolyanskie zapiski* (Yasnaya Polyana memoirs) which he kept from 1904 to 1910. In 1911 he started tidying them up and copying them.

58 Chapter XXXIX of *Resurrection*, banned by the censors in Russia, was published in the anthology *Iz zhizni dukhovenstva* (From the life of the clergy), London, 1902.

59 S.D. Merkurov was preparing for the Tolstoy Exhibition (see note 85) a relief map of Yasnaya Polyana with the estate, the grave and all the places connected with Tolstoy.

60 See Daily Diary, 1909, and note 63. N.N. Gusev returned from exile on July 12, 1911.

61 At Tatiana Kuzminskaya's request Sofia Tolstaya sent a reprint of her memoirs to Charles Salomon in Paris. 'Moi poslednii priezd v Yasnuyu Polyanu' (My last visit to Yasnaya Polyana) was published in *NV*, no. 12,487, December 15, 1910 (see Tatiana Kuzminskaya's letters to S.A. Tolstaya of July 28 and August 18, GMT).

62 The application was addressed to N.I. Guchkov. Sofia Tolstaya wrote that she agreed to sell the Khamovniki Street house, as well as the furniture in Tolstoy's study and the other rooms. See V. Bulgakov, 'Istoriya doma Lva Tolstogo v Moskve' (The history of Tolstoy's house in Moscow), in *Letopisi*, book 12, p. 568.

63 This decision was prompted by Aleksandra Tolstaya, who, in accordance with the wishes expressed in Tolstoy's will (see Diary, 1910, note 49), announced in the press that the rights of the free editions of the *ABC*, the *Books for Reading* and various other works by Tolstoy would be made available to all publishing houses.

64 A letter asking him to read her application without delay.

65 E.F. Yunge, *Vospominaniya* (Memoirs), Moscow.

66 'On this unforgettable day for Russia,' wrote S. Spiro in his essay '28e v Yasnoi Polyane' (The 28th in Yasnaya Polyana), 'the anniversary of the birth of the great writer of the "Russian land", there gathered at his grave Tula police-officers, the Tula police-chief, the district police-officer, district sergeants, village policemen and approximately a hundred armed mounted police guards. The police from virtually the whole of Tula province were there' (*RS*, no. 199, August 30, 1911).

67 P.D. Dolgorukov's arrival was occasioned by the decision by the Moscow Society of Literacy to build a reading-room named after L.N. Tolstoy beside the Yasnaya Polyana peasant library.

68 On September 1 a terrorist attack was committed against P.A. Stolypin, President of the Council of Ministers.

69 V.A. Posse met Tolstoy in 1895, 1900 and 1909. His talk with Sofia Tolstaya gave him material for his lecture 'Love in the Works and Life of L.N. Tolstoy', which he read in the autumn of 1911 in Saratov and other towns. He also used this material for the chapter 'Tolstoy' in his book *Moi zhiznennyi put* (My life's path), Moscow/Leningrad, 1929.

70 Ch. Vetrinskii, *Lev Nikolaevich Tolstoi. Ocherk zhizni i deyatelnost* (An essay on his life and activity), 1st edn, Nizhnii Novgorod, 1910. The author described his book as a 'little book for people who are not fully acquainted with the activities of Lev Tolstoy'.

71 Letter unknown.

72 Sofia Tolstaya replied to Guchkov's query (of August 16) about the final price of the Khamovniki property and his request for an inventory of the furniture which was being sold along with the house. In her letter Sofia Tolstaya indicated the sum of 125,000 rubles,

which included Tolstoy's study; the other furniture she was 'obliged to keep in her possession [. . .] owing to changed circumstances' (V. Bulgakov, *Istoriya doma Lva Tolstogo v Moskve* (The story of Lev Tolstoy's house in Moscow), *Letopisi*, book 12, p. 568).

73 'Smert Sokrata. Iz razgovorov Platona' (The Death of Socrates. From Plato's Dialogues) in *Circle of Reading*, *PSS*, vol. 42, pp. 65–72.

74 On this day *The Living Corpse* was published for the first time in *RS*, no. 218, September 23, 1911. See note 79.

75 *Pisma Turgeneva k Viardo i ego frantsuzskim druzyam* (Turgenev's letters to Viardot and his French friends), Moscow, 1900.

76 To the Tolstoy Exhibition that was being organised in Moscow Sofia Tolstaya gave twelve photographs of Tolstoy and her children.

77 To Sergei Tolstoy she sent the deed of settlement drawn up between the Tolstoy brothers on February 20, 1851, the power of attorney over the property and some other material to be shown at the Tolstoy exhibition.

78 G.S. Burdzhalov, V.A. Simov and I.M. Polunin were making models of Tolstoy's study in Khamovniki Street and his room in Astapovo for the Tolstoy exhibition. The Yasnaya Polyana rooms were not exhibited.

79 The first separate edition, brought out by Aleksandra Tolstaya (Moscow, 1911).

80 Aleksandra Tolstaya was preparing a three-volume edition of the *Posthumous Works of L.N. Tolstoy* (two volumes came out in 1911). 'Tikhon and Malanya' and 'Idyll' were two versions of a story about peasant life Tolstoy had started in 1860, and which remained unfinished (*PSS*, vol. 7).

81 P.A. Sergeenko, *Tolstoi i ego sovremenniki* (Tolstoy and his contemporaries), Moscow, 1911.

82 The suitcase with which Tolstoy left Yasnaya Polyana on October 28.

83 A reference to her letter giving the Historical Museum permission to lend Tolstoy's writing-desk from the Khamovniki Street house to the exhibition.

84 Journalists on the *Solntse Rossii* (Sun of Russia) prepared a special issue for November 7 – the anniversary of Tolstoy's death – to include photographs by Chertkov, Sofia Tolstaya and their own photographer. The editors expressed their gratitude to Sofia Tolstaya and Chertkov 'for the friendly and practical help they had given to representatives of the journal when collecting material' (no. 53, November 7, 1911, p. 14).

85 On September 24 *The Living Corpse* opened at the Arts Theatre. Dress rehearsals (on September 20 and 21) were attended by Sergei, Ilya and Aleksandra Tolstoy, Tatiana Sukhotina, and many friends and followers of Tolstoy's. Andrei Tolstoy was not there. The solemn opening of the Tolstoy Exhibition took place on October 11 in Moscow, in the building of the Historical Museum.

86 Sofia Tolstaya's album *Iz zhizni Tolstogo* (From the life of Tolstoy) and her anthology of children's stories.

87 Sofia Tolstaya's visit to the exhibition was given wide coverage in the newspapers, which published her replies to journalists' questions about the exhibition.

88 K. Arabazhin, *L.N. Tolstoi (Kak lichnost, khudozhnik i myslitel). Publichnye lektsii o russkikh pisatelyakh* (L.N. Tolstoy (as personality, artist and thinker). Public lectures about Russian writers), St Petersburg, 1909.

89 Tolstoy's musical and poetic works were on display at the exhibition. Having familiarised herself with them, Sofia Tolstaya made a few revisions, on the basis of which an article was written by 'S.T.' (probably Sergei Tolstoy), which said: 'I: *Waltz ascribed to L.N. Tolstoy*. He himself played this waltz several times as his own composition. S.I. Taneev noted it down after hearing L.N. play it. But L.N. once expressed doubts as to whether he had in fact composed it. One may surmise, from S.A. Tolstaya's words, that the waltz was written by him in collaboration with his friend Zybin, a cellist and a rather good musician. II. *The refrain of a Sevastopol Song*. This is a somewhat variable refrain from an old gypsy song: "I'm

a young gypsy girl, But I'm not simple, For I can tell fortunes." L.N. frequently played the accompaniment to this song, or he and another person would play melody and accompaniment arranged for four hands. The song was generally played in D Major' (*TE*, 1912, p. 299).

90 On October 14 there was a meeting of the Council of Ministers at which the Minister of Finances read a report about all the financial and economic problems involved in buying Yasnaya Polyana at the price asked by the heirs – 500,000 rubles. Since the real price of the property was 200,000 rubles (which would be paid by the Peasant Bank), the remaining 300,000 would have to be paid for, he suggested, by the government. A firm opponent of any government involvement in the purchase of Yasnaya Polyana was K. Sabler, Chief Procurator of the Holy Synod, who said: 'The immortalisation of Tolstoy's memory at public expense will be seen as a desire to strengthen his teachings in the people's consciousness. The government must not glorify Tolstoy, in view of the Holy Synod's ruling on his defection from the Orthodox Church.' Quoted in the article by E. Zaidenschnur, 'Yasnaya Polyana v gody sovetskoi vlasti' (Yasnaya Polyana in the years of Soviet power), in the anthology *Yasnaya Polyana*, Moscow, 1942, p. 110. A paragraph entitled 'K vykupu Yasnoi Polyany' (On the purchase of Yasnaya Polyana) in *RV*, no. 260, November 11, 1911, said: 'the question remained open.'

91 I.D. Sytin offered to buy all the unsold copies of the last *Collected Works of L.N. Tolstoy* from Sofia Tolstaya for 169,000 rubles. See entry for November 14, and note 93.

92 A reference to A. Kogan's article 'Cherez god. Yasnopolyanskie zarisovki' (A year later. Yasnaya Polyana sketches), in *Solntse Rossi* (Sun of Russia), no. 53, November 7, 1911.

93 The agreement was concluded in 1912. See Daily Diary, 1912, entry for April 21.

94 See entry for November 17, and note 96.

95 In the offices of Speshnev Sofia Tolstaya completed a deed of purchase to enable the City *Duma* to buy the Khamovniki Street house. A commission was set up, headed by the architect A.A. Ostrogradskii, with responsibilities for taking over the house.

96 In her letter to the Tsar, sent on November 18 and delivered by Bogdanov, Sofia Tolstaya wrote: 'If the Russian government does not buy Yasnaya Polyana, my sons, some of whom will be left in a greatly impoverished state, will be forced, with much anguish in their hearts, to sell it privately, either in separate plots or as a whole. And the hearts of Lev Tolstoy's descendants and of the whole Russian people will tremble and grieve if this happens, and if the government does not defend the cradle and the grave of a man who has glorified the name of Russia to the entire world and who is so greatly loved by his people and his country. Do not let Yasnaya Polyana perish for ever by allowing it to be sold into private hands, rather than to the Russian government' (GMT). The Tsar's response to this letter was as follows: 'I consider the purchase of Count Tolstoy's estate by the government entirely impermissible. It is for the Council of Ministers merely to discuss the extent of the pension to be allocated to his widow' (December 20, 1911). Quoted in Zaidenschnur's article (see note 90), p. 110.

97 F.A. Strakhov, 'Dve poezdki iz Moskvy v Yasnuyu Polyanu' (Two trips from Moscow to Yasnaya Polyana), *Petersburgskaya gazeta* (Petersburg Newpaper), no. 305, November 6, 1911. The article recounts the history of the two wills drawn up by Tolstoy, in 1909, and 1910.

98 The role of Fedya Protasov was played by I.M. Moskvin. The cast included V.I. Kachalov (Karenin), K.S. Stanislavskii (Prince Abrezkov), M.P. Lilina (Anna), M.N. Germanova (Liza), A. Koonen (Masha), and others.

99 *Dni nashei skorbi. Sbornik statei i izvestii o poslednikh dnyakh Lva Nikolaevicha Tolstogo* (Days of our grief. An anthology of articles and items of news about the last days of Lev Nikolaevich Tolstoy), Moscow, 1911. Sofia Tolstaya's library, with margin notes.

100 *Posthumous Literary Works of L.N. Tolstoy*, brought out by Aleksandra Tolstaya. The royalties from this edition, according to Tolstoy's wishes, were to be used by his family to redeem the Yasnaya Polyana land, which was to be given to the peasants.

01 N.S. Shcherbatov refused, without written permission from Sofia Tolstaya, to give Tolstoy's writing desk to the exhibition being organised at the Moscow Tolstoy Museum. Her letter contained this permission.

02 The issue containing Strakhov's article 'Two trips from Moscow to Yasnaya Polyana'. See note 97.

03 The anthology *Perepiska L.N. Tolstogo s gr. A.A. Tolstoyi* (L.N. Tolstoy's correspondence with Countess A.A. Tolstaya), St Petersburg, 1911. Preparations for the publication of this book started in the spring of 1910, after Tolstoy had given his permission for the correspondence to be published. 'Your news that L.N. had agreed to the publication of Countess Aleksandra Andreevna's letters and those of N.N. Strakhov delighted all of us on the editorial commission as regards the fate of the forthcoming edition,' M.A. Stakhovich wrote to Sofia Tolstaya on May 7 (GMT).

04 Published in an illustrated supplement to *NV*, no. 12,848, December 17, 1911. Concerning these memoirs Sofia Tolstaya wrote to Tatiana Sukhotina on December 19: 'There are some slight inaccuracies. For instance he was told about the death of the Tsar by a little Italian with a monkey, not a bird; and Lev Nik. didn't go to Tula, *I* did, and surprised to hear the bells ringing I asked the reason, and they told me at the gates that our Tsar had been killed. Another mistake was where he says that L.N.'s mother was waiting for her husband and watching the road from the tower – *I* built the watch-tower and cleared the place for it, his mother waited on the bench by the lower pond' (GMT).

05 'Falshivyi kupon' (The forged coupon), the story on which Tolstoy worked, off and on, from the end of the 1880s to February 1904. First published in the *Posthumous Works of L.N. Tolstoy*, vol. 1, Moscow, 1911.

06 Tolstoy's library contains only one Gospel in French: *Evangile de notre Seigneur Jésus-Christ selon Saint Jean et d'autres* (Gospel of Our Lord Jesus Christ according to St John and others), Paris, 1893 (without Tolstoy's margin notes).

07 Shcherbatov's letter of November 30 and Sofia Tolstaya's reply. See *RS*, no. 250, December 7, 1911.

08 See Diary, 1895, note 22.

1912

1 A.I. Mey, proprietor of a photographic studio, for preparing the phototypes for the album *From the Life of L.N. Tolstoy* (see note 48 to the Daily Diary, 1911), and the Kushneryov company for printing the *Works of L.N. Tolstoy* (1910–11 edn).

2 The fortieth exhibition of the Fellowship of Wandering Artists.

3 The Tolstoy Museum was visited by members of a British group called the Interparliamentary Alliance.

4 Aleksandra Tolstaya suggested to I.D. Sytin that he buy from Sofia Tolstaya all the unsold copies of all her editions still in the warehouse. In accordance with her father's wishes, before availing herself of her rights to all his works written before 1881 (see Diary 1910, entry for July 22 and note 49), she offered Sofia Tolstaya the opportunity to sell all the unsold copies of Tolstoy's collected works, as well as of individual works.

5 The eighth exhibition of the Union of Russian Artists.

6 Sofia Tolstaya was 'graciously awarded [. . .] a pension from the State Treasury amounting to 10,000 rubles a year' (*TE*, 1912, p. 213).

7 Sofia Tolstaya's discussions with I.D. Sytin and the barrister Levitskii concerned the text of the agreement about the sale of books (see note 4). Her objections were to the parts inserted by Chertkov and Aleksandra Tolstaya, confirming their rights to the manuscripts in the Historical Museum. (See Sofia Tolstaya's letter to Tatiana Sukhotina of January 29 – GMT. See also Daily Diary, 1911, entry for January 24, and note 8.)

8 S.I. Fonvizin, *Dve zhizni. Molodost Mukhanova* (Two lives. The youth of Mukhanov), St Petersburg, 1912.
9 A reference to Tatiana Sukhotina's article 'Po povodu nasledstva L.N. Tolstogo' (About L.N. Tolstoy's legacy), originally intended for *RS*. The motivation to write this article came from a collective letter signed by L. Gurevich, D. Ovsyaniko-Kulikovskii, B. Modzalevskii, I. Ginzburg and others, published under the title 'Nasledstvo L.N. Tolstogo' (L.N. Tolstoy's legacy) in *RS*, no. 42, February 21, 1912. It condemned Sofia Tolstaya's position and demanded that the manuscripts in the Historical Museum be handed over to Aleksandra Tolstaya so that a new edition of L.N. Tolstoy's works could be published.

Tatiana Sukhotina refuted the opinions contained in this letter-article and showed that the main culprits for the conflict were Aleksandra Tolstaya and Chertkov. She particularly criticised Chertkov's behaviour and his role in the life of Tolstoy and his family (GMT).
10 'I have now decided not to publish this letter,' Tatiana Sukhotina told her mother in a letter of March 4. 'I have so far kept my hands clean of all newspaper polemics, and I want to continue to do so in future' (GMT). After refusing to publish the article she asked her mother to send her copy to Ginzburg, so that all signatories of the collective letter to *RS* could familiarise themselves with it. Tatiana Sukhotina's article and her letter to Ginzburg are contained in M. Stakhovich's article (in English): 'The Question of Tolstoy's Posthumous Work', published in *RO*, vol. II, no. 2, 1913.
11 *Lev Tolstoi i golod* (Lev Tolstoy and the famine), published under the editorship of Ch. Vetrinskii, Nizhnii Novgorod, 1912.
12 The GMT contains letters from Aleksandra Andreevna Tolstaya to Tolstoy which did not appear in the Tolstoy Society's anthology of their correspondence, but came from the Manuscript Department of the Academy of Sciences, where she herself had deposited them.
13 The texts were given to P.I. Biryukov, since Aleksandra Tolstaya and Chertkov had entrusted him with the editorship of their new edition of Tolstoy's works.
14 V. Semyonov, *Rasplata* (Retribution), St Petersburg, last edition 1912.
15 N.A. Sokolov later recalled: 'I visited Sofia Andreevna at Yasnaya Polyana in 1912 over Easter – it was a Tuesday (March 27). Three of us travelled from St Petersburg to see her [. . .] We were received immediately – to our great surprise, for we were quite unexpected. We were shown absolutely everything, to the very last corner of the house, given exhaustive explanations of almost every object, and above all we were told a lot about L.N. and S.A.'s life together' (N.A. Sokolov. 'S.A. Tolstaya', in *Vestnik literatury* (Herald of Literature), no. 1, 1921, pp. 6–7).
16 Almost all the newspapers contained obituaries of Maria Nikolaevna Tolstaya. Amongst the writers of articles dedicated to the memory of Tolstoy's sister were P.I. Biryukov, D.P. Makovitsky, I.L. Tolstoy, A.M. Khiryakov, V.A. Posse, Al. Ksyunin and others.
17 Maria Nikolaevna Tolstaya's funeral was attended by two members of the Tolstoy family, Ilya and Andrei.
18 Sofia Tolstaya, in response to a request from a 'young collector' called Ernst Yurgenson, who had already collected 400 autographs of Russian writers, sent him 'a piece of paper from the great writer's notebook' (see Yurgenson's letter to Sofia Tolstaya of April 18, GMT).
19 See note 48.
20 See note 4.
21 'I saw Kasso,' Sofia Tolstaya wrote to Tatiana Sukhotina on April 28. 'He refused to give me the manuscripts and instructed me to complain to the Senate about his refusal. His explanation was that he was afraid to take *sole* responsibility, and that it was the Senate, consisting of many judges, that should settle the argument' (GMT). See note 57.
22 On May 12 Sofia Tolstaya received an official reply from Kasso to this letter: 'I cannot agree to release the 12 boxes [. . .] of L.N. Tolstoy's manuscripts, at present in the

Historical Museum, in view of the argument that has arisen between you and Aleksandra Tolstaya about the rights to the ownership of these manuscripts. For the same reason, taking copies from the manuscripts and sorting them out may only be permitted with Aleksandra Lvovna's consent' (GMT).

23 'The Posthumous Notes of Old Fyodor Kuzmich', first in *RB*, no. 2, 1912, and almost simultaneously in several separate editions with 'Notes' by Chertkov.

24 Sofia Tolstaya gave Biryukov the manuscripts of the second and third versions of *Childhood*, the two original outlines of *Youth* and other material, from which he compiled the 'Appendices' to the new edition of Tolstoy's works (see note 13), *L.N. Tolstoy, Complete Collected Works*, vol. 1, 1913, pp. 373–410.

25 *Pensées de Pascal*, Paris, 1898 (Sofia Tolstaya's library, with margin notes).

26 Georges Bourdon, *En écoutant Tolstoi*, Paris, 1904 (YaPL). For the Russian version of this see *LN*, vol. 75, book 2, pp. 39–61. Bourdon was in correspondence with Tolstoy and Sofia Tolstaya (*PSS*, vol. 75, p. 172; *LN*, vol. 75, book 2, pp. 39, 40).

27 Aleksandra Tolstaya bought the Yasnaya Polyana land from her brothers in order to give it to the peasants, in accordance with her father's wishes. Sofia Tolstaya acquired for herself the house, the grounds, a little plot of land and the garden – about 170 acres in all.

28 A periodical publication which came out in 1911. Five numbers appeared, which formed the *Tolstovskii ezhegodnik* (Tolstoy Yearbook).

29 A letter of April 10, 1911, in which V.F. Snegiryov, a Professor of Medicine, expressed his opinion of Tolstoy's 'flight' and shared his impressions of their family life. 'There was not an hour, possibly not even a minute of your life in which you were distracted from him,' he wrote. 'Your entire being was filled with him and his life [. . .] he had much to be grateful to you for' (GMT).

30 See entry for July 30, and note 36.

31 A. Divilkovskii, 'Tolstoi i Russo' (Tolstoy and Rousseau), *VE*, nos 6 and 7, 1912.

32 See entries for March 10 and 11 and notes 9 and 10.

33 Georges Dwelshauvers, 'Rousseau et Tolstoi', a reprint from the journal *Revue de Métaphysique et de morale*, May 1912, sent to Sofia Tolstaya by the author with a dedication (Sofia Tolstaya's library).

34 *Discours sur les passions de l'amour*, by B. Pascal.

35 See entry for September 24, and note 48.

36 M.A. Stakhovich's letter of July 27, in which he referred to Tolstoy's own words and confirmed that the manuscripts deposited in the Historical Museum were 'the property of S.A. Tolstaya' (GMT).

37 'Diary for Myself Alone' (*PSS*, vol. 58).

38 'O Tolstogo' (On Tolstoy's religion), 2nd anthology, Moscow, 1912; this included articles by S.N. Bulgakov, N.A. Berdyaev and others.

39 I. Potapenko, 'Privratniki slavy' (The janitors of fame), *VE*, nos 7 and 8, 1912.

40 Grand Duke Nikolai Mikhailovich (Romanov), *Russkie portrety XVIII and XIX stoletii* (Russian portraits of the 18th and 19th centuries), vols 1–6, St Petersburg, 1906 (YaPL).

41 Tatiana Kuzminskaya was probably reading the opening chapters of her memoirs *Moya zhizn doma i v Yasnoi Polyane* (My life at home and at Yasnaya Polyana), a history of the Behrs and Islenev family lines.

42 Ch. Vetrinskii, *A.I. Herzen*, St Petersburg, 1908.

43 See note 48.

44 See entry for September 18 and note 46.

45 See 'Vlast tmy' (The power of darkness), an excerpt from Sofia Tolstaya's unpublished book *My Life* (*TE*, 1912, pp. 17–23).

46 No. 37 of the journal *Iskra* (Spark) published photographs of L.N. and S.A. Tolstaya's twenty-four grandchildren on the occasion of their fiftieth wedding anniversary.

47 A.E. Gruzinskii was commissioned by the Tolstoy Society to study the Yasnaya Polyana

library, the books it contained and Tolstoy's margin notes in them. He published the results of his work in an article entitled 'Yasnopolyanskaya biblioteka' (The Yasnaya Polyana Library). See *TE*, 1912, pp. 133–4.

48 'Zhenitba L.N. Tolstogo' (L.N. Tolstoy's marriage), excerpt from Sofia Tolstaya's memoirs *My Life* in *RS*, no. 219, September 23, 1912.

49 Sympathetic responses to Sofia Tolstaya's memoirs appeared too in the press. For instance an anonymous author wrote in the newspaper *Trudovaya kopeika* (Worker's Kopeck): 'These contain the real Tolstoy, his soul [. . .] This is a Tolstoyan piece, as lovely as *Childhood* and *Boyhood* (no. 71/228, September 26, 1912).

50 By Anatole France, first published in Paris, 1912.

51 Tatiana Kuzminskaya's letter of September 25, 1862 (GMT).

52 See entry for November 12, and note 62.

53 See Daily Diary, 1911, note 57.

54 Letter of October 4. Naryshkina considered that Sofia Tolstaya's Memoirs contained 'so much poetry, freshness, seriousness and youthful purity', and well conveyed the 'atmosphere' of the time (GMT).

55 A reference to the film *Ukhod velikogo startsa* (The flight of a great old man), scenario by I. Teneremo, produced by A.Ya. Protazov; the role of Tolstoy was played by V.I. Shaternikov. The preview in St Petersburg was attended by Lyova Tolstoy and Tatiana Kuzminskaya, who protested against its screening. Outraged responses to the film, which depicted the last days of Tolstoy's life in a distorted and disrespectful fashion, appeared also in the press. See entries for October 23 and 24 and notes 56 and 58.

56 After Sofia Tolstaya's complaint the police department ordered all cinematograph proprietors to destroy the film.

57 In this complaint against L.A. Kasso, Minister of Education, which Sofia Tolstaya sent to the Senate, she disputed the actions of the Museum in forbidding her access to the manuscripts, and on the basis of existing civil laws and supplementary documents, she proved her right to them. Sofia Tolstaya's application was discussed by the Senate on April 3.

58 The film was banned everywhere.

59 E.I. Chirikov, 'Izgnanie' (Banishment), the second part of his autobiographical novel *Zhizn Tarkhanova* (The life of Tarkhanov). See Daily Diary, 1911, note 26.

60 Chertkov published an article in *Re*, no. 306, November 7, 1912 called 'Blago lyubvi. Obrashchenie L.N. Tolstogo k lyudyam-bratyam' (The blessing of love. L.N. Tolstoy's attitude to his fellow-men), with his own 'Note', in which he again developed the idea that Tolstoy's 'flight' was prompted merely by family circumstances. Stating that Tolstoy's article was written when he was 'seriously ill', Chertkov explained that 'this illness [. . .] was the direct consequence of the shock he suffered from those spiritual crises which periodically attacked him in connection with the agonisingly painful conditions of his family life and the circumstances of his life in general.' Further on Chertkov sought to prove that Tolstoy was 'on the point of leaving his family on several occasions' but stayed to 'carry his cross'.

61 E. Rod, a French writer and author of novels and philosophical works in which Tolstoy was very interested. There are several of his novels, with dedications, in the Yasnaya Polyana library (*LN*, vol. 75, book 2, p. 72).

62 *Solntse Rossii* (Sun of Russia) (nos 145–6, November 7, 1912) published 'Pervoe predstavlenie komedii grafa L.N. Tolstogo "Plody Prosveshcheniya"' (The first performance of Count L.N. Tolstoy's comedy *The Fruits of Enlightenment*), from *Zapiski gr. Sofii Andreevny Tolstoi (Moya Zhizn)* (The memoirs of Countess Sofia Tolstaya (My life)); P. Boulanger's article 'On zhiv' (He is alive); A. Khiryakov's 'L.N. Tolstoi i narodnye izdaniya' (L.N. Tolstoy and peasant editions); Sergei Gatov's 'Den s Tolstym' (A day with Tolstoy), and so on.

63 M. Menshikov, 'Falsh tolstovschiny' (The hypocrisy of Tolstoyism), *NV*, no. 1317,

November 10, 1912, in which he attacked Tolstoy and his philosophy of life from a defensive position and in an unworthy form.

64 A reference to an interview with Chertkov in which he used the letters of Sofia Tolstaya and Tatiana Sukhotina to Aleksandra Tolstaya, and the evidence of Goldenweiser and Olga Tolstaya to support Aleksandra Tolstaya's claim to the disputed manuscripts (*RV*, no. 267, November 18, 1912).

65 V.F. Bulgakov, in accordance with the decision of the Tolstoy Society, worked from 1912 to 1916 on cataloguing the books in the Yasnaya Polyana library and all Tolstoy's margin notes and observations. On the basis of his catalogue a bibliographic guide was published in Moscow: *Biblioteka Lva Tolstogo v Yasnoi Polyane* (Lev Tolstoy's library in Yasnaya Polyana), published by Kniga (The Book). Part 1, 1972; part 2, 1975.

66 Sofia Tolstaya sent Sergei Tolstoy a typewritten copy of excerpts from Tolstoy's diary for 1897 (see Sofia Tolstaya's letter to Sergei Tolstoy of December 4, GMT).

67 'Chetyre poseshcheniya gr. L.N. Tolstogo monastyrya "Optyna pustyn" ' (Count L.N. Tolstoy's four journeys to the Optyna Pustyn Monastery), from Sofia Tolstaya's memoirs, *MZh*, published in *TE*, 1913, pp. 3–7.

68 In November and December N.N. Gusev visited Moscow, Petersburg, Saratov and other towns, where he read his lecture 'Odinochestvo velikoi dushi' (The solitude of a great soul), based on personal memories, Tolstoy's unpublished diaries and Aleksandra Tolstaya's diaries. In this lecture he gave a general description of the writer's spiritual life, talked about his last months, his illness and death, and the 'real reasons for his flight from Yasnaya Polyana', which included the 'shattering of his last illusion, the illusion of family life'.

69 This priest, Grigorii Lavrentevich Kalinovskii (he told his name to no one but Bulgakov), 'announced that he did not recognise the Synod's prohibition against praying for L.N., as he considered that L.N. had brought nothing but good to people'. See 'V osiroteloi Yasnoi Polyane 1912 goda' (Orphaned Yasnaya Polyana in 1912), *Golos minuvshego na chuzhoi storone* (Voice from the past in another land), no. 3/XVI, 1926, p. 119.

70 Sofia Tolstaya had started to prepare a volume of Tolstoy's letters to her.

71 *'Voina i Mir.' Pamyati L. Tolstogo. Sbornik* (*War and Peace.* Memories of L. Tolstoy. An anthology), edited by T.I. Polner and V.P. Obninskii, Zadruga (The Clan), Moscow, 1912.

72 A. Pankratov's article condemned the funeral service at Tolstoy's grave (see note 69), on the grounds that this act appeared to accept Tolstoy back into the bosom of the Church which he did not recognise and from which he had been excommunicated (*RS*, no. 294, December 21, 1912). Sofia Tolstaya responded with a letter justifying the priest's 'selfless' action, since, in her words, Tolstoy 'was distinguished by his supreme religious tolerance' (ibid., no. 298, December 28). The story of the service over Tolstoy's grave was given wide publicity by the press.

73 On December 20 the Moscow Committee on Press Affairs placed a ban on the book, and the publishers were tried in court. The ban was subsequently lifted and the court trial cut short.

74 See Daily Diary, 1913, note 3.

1913

1 A reference to the issue of the journal *Iskra* (Spark) which published portraits of Tolstoy's twenty-four grandchildren, and the issue of the journal *SR* which published Sofia Tolstaya's memoirs. See Daily Diary, 1912, notes 46 and 62.

2 Probably the last three volumes of the 1910–11 edition of the *Works of Tolstoy*.

3 In 1913 a supplement to *Sovremennyi mir* (Contemporary World) (nos 1–7, 9–12) published the correspondence between Tolstoy and N.N. Strakhov. Strakhov's letters were sent to the journal by Sofia Tolstaya. See *Sovremennyi mir*, no. 12, 1913, p. 458.

4 The Yasnaya Polyana library contains several novels by M. Prévost, sent to Tolstoy by the

author, who was a great admirer of his work (see *LN*, vol. 75, book 2, p. 72). Tolstoy had a very negative opinion of Prévost's works (see *PSS*, vol. 30, p. 88).

5 The anthology *Voina i mir* (War and peace), edited by T.I. Polner and V.P. Obninskii.

6 Leonid Andreev, 'On. Rasskaz neizvestnogo' (He. The story of an unknown man), *Sovremennyi mir*, nos 1 and 3, 1913.

7 D.P. Makovitsky was reading his *Yasnaya Polyana Memoirs*. See Daily Diary, 1911, note 57.

8 V.V. Baryatinskii, *Tsarstvennyi mistik (imperator Aleksandr I i Fyodor Kuzmich)*, (The royal mystic. Emperor Alexander I and Fyodor Kuzmich), Prometei publishing house. On reading this book on February 9, Sofia Tolstaya wrote to her sister: 'Very interesting, but unconvincing' (GMT).

9 Several newspapers published an announcement that in connection with the Senate's imminent discussion of Sofia Tolstaya's complaint against the Minister of Education, L.A. Kasso, the senators had already reviewed the question privately and had come to the conclusion that 'The Senate had not the right to enter into discussions as to the ownership of the material kept in the Historical Museum' and would only debate the issue of 'the legality of the Museum's action in putting a ban on this property, without being granted any special legal powers to do so'. (See 'Rukopisi Tolstogo' (Tolstoy's manuscripts), *RV*, no. 31, February 7, 1913.)

10 There are two stories known to be written by Sofia Tolstaya, 'Po povodu Kreitzerovoi Sonaty' (About the Kreutzer Sonata), 1891, and 'Pesnya bez slov' (Song without words), 1895–1900.

11 See Daily Diary, 1914, note 10.

12 Ilya Tolstoy, 'K vystavke khudozhnika Saltanova' (On the artist Saltanov's exhibition), *RS*, no. 2, February 20, 1913. The exhibition displayed several paintings by Saltanov of Yasnaya Polyana and its surroundings. In his article Ilya Tolstoy discussed the exhibition 'with open and enthusiastic partiality', and shared many of the memories it evoked of his father and his childhood.

13 In the preface to the first volume of his biography of Tolstoy, Biryukov wrote: 'I wish to express my deep gratitude to Sofia Andreevna Tolstaya, who gave me access to the valuable collection of biographical material which she had collected and given to the Moscow Historical Museum' (P.I. Biryukov, *Biografiya L.N. Tolstogo* (Biography of L.N. Tolstoy), vol. 1, Moscow/Petersburg, 1923, p. xv).

14 In the first edition of the book *Pisma gr. L.N. Tolstogo k zhene* (Count L.N. Tolstoy's letters to his wife) (Moscow, 1913), Sofia Tolstaya included 656 letters and 7 notes. In her introduction she wrote: 'I am publishing *all* the letters – apart from those relating to living people, and the six last ones, for which the time is not yet ripe' (p. iii). In fact there are 840 epistolatory documents from Tolstoy to his wife, including unsent letters, notes and telegrams (see *PSS*, vols 83, 84).

15 'The forest was sold on contract to the merchant Chesnokov,' Sofia Tolstaya wrote to Tatiana Sukhotina on February 28. 'I have bought 200 *desyatinas* of land from my sons – with the estate – for 150 thousand rubles, and have sold my own land to Sasha' (GMT).

16 Aleksandra Tolstaya and V.G. Chertkov had started preparing a separate edition of part of Tolstoy's diaries, a copy of which N.L. Obolenskii gave to the Tolstoy Museum (thirty-four notebooks, 1895–1910). The editing and the compilation of the notes were entrusted to various people, including N.N. Gusev. The first volume (1895–9) came out only in 1916.

17 Possibly Repin's painting *L.N. Tolstoy and S.A. Tolstaya* (1907).

18 Ilya Tolstoy had started work on his book *Moi vospominaniya* (My reminiscences).

19 A possible reference to N. Bernstein's article 'L.N. Tolstoi i muzyka' (L.N. Tolstoy and music), *Artist*, no. 3, 1913, Sofia Tolstaya's library.

20 Sofia Tolstaya was intending to publish the letters she received from the Academy of Sciences on November 8, and from F. Koni on November 10, 1910. See A.F. Koni, *Sobr. soch.* (Complete works), vol. 8, Moscow, Yuridicheskaya Literatura (Legal literature)

publishing house, 1969, pp. 434–5, 268–9. Both these letters expressed condolences at Tolstoy's death. For Snegiryov's letter see Daily Diary, 1912, note 29. The letters never appeared in print.

21 See Sofia Tolstaya's letter to Tolstoy of November 11, 1886 (*PST*, p. 375) and Daily Diary, 1907, entry for May 20 and note 32.

22 Sofia Tolstaya was probably reading the memoirs of Maria Vatatsi, née Mertvago, 'Byl minuvshaya' (Bygone days) in *IV*, nos 3 and 4, 1913. The author was a niece of E.D. Zagoskina, a friend of the Tolstoys. Vatatsi describes episodes of Tolstoy's life in the Caucasus and recalls Zagoskina, whom Tolstoy met then and later (*PSS*, vol. 83, p. 271).

23 Tolstoy's sons had sold 175 *desyatinas* of forest for felling. See note 15.

24 A reference to Aleksandra Tolstaya's 'Obyasnenie' (Explanation), in which she invoked Tolstoy's will to reaffirm her exclusive rights to the disputed manuscripts, and urged that the Senate should not investigate Sofia Tolstaya's complaint (*RS*, no. 77, April 3, 1913).

25 Sofia Tolstaya's complaint was investigated by the Senate on April 3. N.A. Dobrovolskii, Senate Chief Procurator, proposed that Kasso's instructions be revoked, but because his proposal was not accepted unanimously it was decided to move the discussion to a general meeting of the Senate. See 'Spor o rukopisyakh L.N. Tolstogo' (The argument over L.N. Tolstoy's manuscripts), *RS*, no. 78, April 4, 1913.

26 On April 14, *RS* started publication of Tolstoy's diaries from October 28, 1895, with an introduction by Chertkov (*RS*, no. 87, 1913).

27 Probably Tatiana Sukhotina's memoir 'Nikolai Nikolaevich Gué', which went into her book *Druzya i gosti Yasnoi Polyany* (Friends and guests at Yasnaya Polyana), 1st edn, Moscow, 1923.

28 V. Mikulich, 'Teni proshlogo' (Shadows of the past), nos 2, 3, 4, 1913.

29 The Stupin warehouse contained goods and furniture taken from the Khamovniki house after it was sold.

30 Sofia Tolstaya made several notes correcting factual errors in Makovitsky's memoirs for 1905 (GMT).

31 The published correspondence between Tolstoy and N.N. Strakhov consisted of 220 letters from Strakhov and 70 from Tolstoy. Sofia Tolstaya's allegations against Chertkov are unfounded, however. Chertkov only had copies of some of the letters, which he took at the behest of A.M. and E.D. Khiryakov in 1893. P.A. Sergeenko had published these letters from Chertkov's copies in his two-volume edition *Pisma L.N. Tolstogo* (The letters of L.N. Tolstoy), Moscow, 1910 and 1911, so these letters were not included in the journal edition. Originals of 100 of Tolstoy's letters were subsequently given to the Tolstoy Museum by the Bakhrushin Museum. They are all included in *PSS*.

32 The Preface to *Count L.N. Tolstoy's Letters to His Wife.*

33 In 1888 Sofia Tolstaya had started making copies of Tolstoy's letters to her. Since the originals of the letters were kept at the Historical Museum, she had to prepare another copy for her edition of *Count L.N. Tolstoy's Letters to His Wife*, and it was this copy which went to the printers.

34 Osman, the old Circassian who guarded the house at Yasnaya Polyana between 1912 and 1913. He and his brother had been exiled from the Caucasus to Central Russia in their youth for participating in a bloody vendetta. Sofia Tolstaya petitioned for them to return to their native land. See entry for November 8.

35 Sofia Tolstaya's letter (*RS*, no. 143, June 22, 1913), in which she referred to the 'unbecoming behaviour of the public visiting Yasnaya Polyana and the grave of Count Lev Nikolaevich', and announced that she was allowing access to his grave and rooms 'only once a week'.

36 Sofia Tolstaya's letters were not included in *Count L.N. Tolstoy's Letters to His Wife.*

37 Sofia Tolstaya was writing to S.V. Chefranov, director of the Kushneryov print-works, at the

request of Tatiana Sukhotina, who wanted them to publish someone's work (see Sofia Tolstaya's letter to Tatiana Sukhotina of June 9, GMT).

38 Sofia Tolstaya read the first chapters of Ilya Tolstoy's *My Reminiscences* some time before their publication in *RS* on September 29. She provided her son with material and shared her memories with him, and judging from the content of his memoirs, Ilya Tolstoy received invaluable information from her. See I.L. Tolstoy.

39 Sofia Tolstaya was reading Sergei Tolstoy's essay on Yasnaya Polyana, intended for his *Yasnaya Polyana. A Brief Catalogue and Guide for Visitors*. See Daily Diary, 1911, note 45.

40 A reference to A. Moshin's essay *Iz vospominanii L.N. Tolstogo* (Memories of L.N. Tolstoy) no. 6, 1913, in which the author narrated the account by the Kuzminskiis' tutor, F.F. von Gafferberg, of his visit to Yasnaya Polyana, and made a number of errors.

In connection with this Sofia Tolstaya wrote a letter to the editors of *ZV*, in which she said: 'The old woman he saw in the office was Agafya Mikhailovna, who had been Countess Pelageya Nikolaevna's maid, and who appeared in *Childhood* as "Gasha". She died shortly before her seventieth year. She was a tall, straight-backed, austere woman, strict with people but tender with animals. Natalya Savishna, who also appeared under another name, was in fact the nurse of L.N.'s mother, Princess M.N. Volkhonskaya' (*ZV*, no. 7, 1913, p. 1003).

41 'Professor Vengerov left only yesterday,' Sofia Tolstaya wrote to her daughter Tanya on July 12. 'He is one of these people who is preparing a very grand and costly edition of Tolstoy's works (Brockhaus and Efron), with a biography, commentaries and illustrations, and I have given him various pieces of information for it' (GMT). The planned academic twelve-volume edition of the collected works of Tolstoy, edited by S.A. Vengerov, came to nothing.

42 Aleksandra Tolstaya had sold Telyatinki and bought a small farm not far from Yasnaya Polyana, called Novaya Polyana.

43 See note 34, entry for August 18 and note 46.

44 An article for the monthly art and literature magazine *Argus*, which first appeared in Petersburg in 1913. Sofia Tolstaya refused to write anything for this magazine.

45 On the basis of this discussion he wrote his article 'Tolstoi i Turgenev. Iz vospominanii S.A. Tolstoi' (Tolstoy and Turgenev. From A.S. Tolstaya's memoirs), signed 'B.P.' (*RS*, no. 193, August 22, 1913). Sofia Tolstaya recalled her meetings with Turgenev 'when she was a little girl', and the circumstances of the writers' 'reconciliation'.

46 See note 34. The application was sent to the Vice-Regent of the Caucasus, I.I. Vorontsov-Dashkov. Her plea was successful. See entry for November 6 and V. Bulgakov, *O Tolstom* (About Tolstoy), Tula, 1964, pp. 241–3.

47 At the end of July S.A. Vengerov appealed to Sofia Tolstaya to write her autobiography (the letter is not known). Attached to this letter was a questionnaire concerning not only her personally, but also Tolstoy's life and work, and the reasons for their separation and their family drama. See *Nachala* (Beginnings), no. 1, 1921, p. 131.

48 Sofia Tolstaya's companion was A.T. Kudryavtseva.

49 Possibly a reference to the book *En regardant passer la Vie [. . .] par l'auteur d'"Amitié amoureuse"*, by Ermina Leconte de Nouis, who was on friendly terms with Maupassant.

50 L.L. Tolstoy's bust of Bulgakov is at the Tolstoy Museum.

51 *Count L.N. Tolstoy's Letters to His Wife* was published on A.A. Levenson's engine-press.

52 Dr L.A. Landau, *Moisei. Analiz ego psikhicheskoi zhizni* (Moses. An analysis of his psychological life), Yurev, 1913. (In the series Psychiatric Analyses, issues 1, 2 and 3. Sofia Tolstaya's library.)

53 *Count L.N. Tolstoy's Letters to His Wife* was first published abroad only in 1925, with the appearance of the anthology *Leo Tolstoy. Briefe an Seine Frau*, Paul Zlonnoy Verlag, Berlin/Vienna/Leipzig, ed. D. Umanskii, with a preface by Tatiana Sukhotina.

54 An article for the *TE*. See Daily Diary, 1912, note 67.

55 On September 28 Sofia Tolstaya wrote to Bulgakov: 'Today I corrected all the inaccuracies

and the passages unsuitable for publication, which were pointed out to me' (Bulgakov, *O Tolstom* (About Tolstoy), p. 288).

56 Not wanting to name Chertkov, Sofia Tolstaya ironically referred to him, both in her published statements and her autobiography, as a 'close person'.

57 A second edition of *Count L.N. Tolstoy's Letters to His Wife* was published in 1915.

58 An index of newspapers and magazines published in French throughout the world.

59 Dr L.A. Landau, *Graf L.N. Tolstoi. Analiz ego psikhicheskoi zhizni i literaturnykh tipov* (Count L.N. Tolstoy. An analysis of his psychological life and literary characters), Yurev, 1913. In the series *Psychiatric Analyses*, issue 6. (Sofia Tolstaya's library.)

60 See Daily Diary, 1912, note 67.

61 N.V. Davydov, *Iz proshlogo* (From the past), Moscow, 1913. Sofia Tolstaya's library.

62 Davydov's memoirs contained an extremely positive appraisal of Chertkov's personality and activities.

63 Sofia Tolstaya's letter is not known. In reply to her Davydov wrote on November 3: 'Allow me to thank you most warmly and sincerely for your extremely valuable letter, and for your corrections to my article about Lev Nikolaevich' (GMT). In her own copy of the book Sofia Tolstaya wrote her corrections of various factual errors in the chapter on Tolstoy.

64 The news of M. Beilis' acquittal in Kiev by jury appeared in the press; he had been charged with ritual murder.

65 *RS*, no. 240, October 18, 1913, published an article about a letter written by Duma member N.A. Shamin, who suggested that the Town Council should collect information about all the houses in Moscow in which Tolstoy had lived. In reply to this, Sofia Tolstaya published a 'Note', in which she described five houses in Moscow in which Tolstoy had at various times stayed (*RS*, 1913, no. 247, October 26, 1913).

66 On October 19, 1910, Kh. Dosev wrote A.K. Chertkova a letter criticising Tolstoy for 'submitting to S.A.', describing this as 'not a virtue but a weakness', and expressing his regret that 'in the eyes of the world his external life effaced all the sense and meaning of his words and ideas' (Goldenweiser, II, pp. 324–5). Chertkov replied to him on October 19, 1910 (ibid., pp. 325–33), for which Tolstoy, who knew the contents of both letters, thanked him (see *PSS*, vol. 89, p. 228).

67 A letter was sent to *RS* to correct a mistake that had appeared in the piece called 'V Yasnoi Polyane' (In Yasnaya Polyana) (no. 258, November 8, 1913). Referring to remarks made by Sofia Tolstaya, the author stated that an argument had arisen over the distribution of the forest amongst the peasants – whether to divide it 'amongst the children or the souls'. In her letter she explained that it was a question of whether to divide it 'amongst the *stoves* or the souls' (ibid., no. 267, November 17, 1913).

68 Tatiana Kuzminskaya, *Moi vospominaniya o grafine Marii Nikolaevne Tolstoy* (My reminiscences of Countess Maria Nikolaevna Tolstaya), St Petersburg, 1914. Sofia Tolstaya was probably reading it in manuscript. In a letter to Tatiana Kuzminskaya of December 2 she wrote: '[. . .] I read with great pleasure [. . .] your memoirs of Mashenka [. . .] The second part is especially good and interesting' (GMT).

69 Tolstoy's letters to S.A. Rachinskii were published in a supplement to *NV*, no. 13,529, November 9, 1913.

70 Sofia Tolstaya's letter is unknown, but judging from Golubev's reply, dated December 8 (GMT), she was referring to the last three volumes of Tolstoy's works which were sent to him (1910–11).

71 See note 31.

72 On December 4 a chapter from Ilya Tolstoy's memoirs was published, entitled 'Moya zhenitba. Pismo otsa. Smert Vanechki' (My marriage. Father's letter. The death of Vanechka) (*RS*, no. 278, 1913).

73 V.V. Rozanov, *Literaturniye izgnaniki* (Literary exiles), vol. 1, St Petersburg, 1913. The

anthology consisted of an essay 'N.N. Strakhov, ego lichnost i deyatelnost' (N.N. Strakhov, his personality and activity), and a section called 'Nekrologi i zametki' (Obituaries and notes), about Strakhov.

74 *Re*, no. 337, December 9, 1913, published a short memoir by Aleksei Sergeenko called 'Kak pisalos zaveshchanie L.N. Tolstogo' (How Tolstoy's will was written).

75 See Daily Diary, 1912, notes 69 and 72.

76 On December 13 the Senate investigated Sofia Tolstaya's complaint against Minister of Education Kasso. 'In view of the fact that a two-thirds majority vote was not obtained, the matter has been referred to the Ministry of Justice to be settled' (*RV*, no. 388, December 14, 1913).

77 The painting, *Portrait of Countess Sofia Andreevna Tolstaya* (1892, Yasnaya Polyana), was shown at a posthumous exhibition of the works of V. Serov, which opened on February 9, 1914 in the Arts Salon in Moscow. (It is now at the Yasnaya Polyana Estate Museum.)

78 A.E. Gruzinskii, 'L.N. Tolstoi v pismakh k zhene' (L.N. Tolstoy in his letters to his wife), *Vestnik vospitaniya* (Herald of Education), no. 8, 1913; separate edition Moscow, 1913.

1914

1 A.S. Pankratov, 'U velikikh mogil' (At the great graves), Moscow, 1914.

2 See Diary, September 26, 1878.

3 On January 16 Sofia Tolstaya wrote to Tatiana Sukhotina: 'I'm still working on the same thing – now I'm copying out my letters to my husband. I shan't publish them, but if some of them are needed for publication and for a biography of Papa, then there'll be a complete copied version of them. It won't ever be necessary to publish them as a whole: the details of our family life and children are of no interest to the public, but there are one or two interesting things' (GMT).

4 Vladislav Yakubovskii, *Polozhitelnye narodnye tipy v raznykh proizvedeniyakh L.N. Tolstogo i obraz Karataeva* (Positive peasant characters in various works of L.N. Tolstoy and the image of Karataev), published in *Yubileinyi sbornik k 50-letiu Rizhskogo Politekhnicheskogo instituta* (Jubilee anthology for the 50th anniversary of the Riga Polytechnic Institute), Riga, 1912. Sofia Tolstaya's library.

5 E. Chirikov, 'Vozvrashchenie' (The return), the final part of his trilogy *Zhizn Tarkhanova* (The Life of Tarkhanov).

6 Probably a reference to the publication of *Count L.N. Tolstoy's Letters to His Wife* in England. The correspondence has not been kept.

7 A reference to the events of early 1911, when there were student demonstrations at the university, and on the instructions of Minister of Education L.A. Kasso the university was put under police control. Enraged by Kasso's action, the rector handed in his resignation, as a consequence of which his staff were removed from their posts and dismissed. As a sign of protest 125 teachers resigned.

8 N. Timkovskii, *Dusha L.N. Tolstogo* (The soul of L.N. Tolstoy), Moscow, 1914.

9 Paul Déroulède, French writer and political activist, visited Yasnaya Polyana on July 15, 1886. Tolstoy referred to this visit, and his argument with him, in the tract 'Khristianstvo i patriotizm' (Christianity and patriotism) (*PSS*, vol. 39, pp. 49–52). The essay 'Paul Deruled v Yasnoi Polyane' (Paul Déroulède in Yasnaya Polyana) (*RS*, no. 33, February 9, 1914) was written by Ilya Tolstoy after hearing of Déroulède's death.

10 Sofia Tolstaya suggested to Gusev that they prepare a new edition of *Count L.N. Tolstoy's Letters to His Wife*. Gusev conveyed his consent via Makovitsky and pointed to the serious shortcomings of the first edition: the absence of dates in many letters, inaccurate references to the volumes of the *Complete Collected Works*, major gaps in the commentaries and the text (see Makovitsky's letter to Sofia Tolstaya of March 25, 1915, GMT). Gusev did not participate in the preparation of a second edition, however.

11 Chertkov was searched when S.M. Belinkii, who was living with him, was arrested and charged with distributing 5,000 copies of various works of Tolstoy's.
12 Golubkov sent B.I. Gladkov's pamphlet 'Graf L.N. Tolstoi kak bogoiskatel' (Count L.N. Tolstoy as Godseeker), St Petersburg, 1914.
13 L. Andreev, 'Polyot' (Flight), *Sovremennyi mir* (Contemporary World), no. 1, 1914.
14 *Mont-Oriol*, a novel by Guy de Maupassant, 1887.
15 N.N. Strakhov, 'Tolki ob L.N. Tolstom' (Rumours about Tolstoy), *VFP*, no. 5, 1891.
16 See Daily Diary, 1913, note 53.
17 Ilya Tolstoy visited Moscow, Nizhnii Novgorod and various other towns, lecturing on 'Personal Memories of My Father'.
18 This discussion with N.A. Dobrovolskii was occasioned by a letter Sofia Tolstaya received from the Minister of Justice, I.G. Shcheglovitov, on January 31, in which he wrote: 'I have been appointed, as Chief Procurator of the First Department of the Ruling Senate, to take all measures necessary for the speedy despatch of the case you have raised concerning the surrender of your late husband's manuscripts' (GMT).
19 Repin's painting *The Duel* (1913) and two sketches were shown at the forty-second Wanderers' Exhibition.
20 Leonid Semyonov, 'Lermontov i Lev Tolstoi' (Lermontov and Lev Tolstoy) (written on the hundredth anniversary of Lermontov's birth), Moscow, 1914. Sofia Tolstaya's library.
21 A rough draft has been kept of Sofia Tolstaya's letter to the Tsar (undated), asking him to help Andrei Tolstoy find a position.
22 The suggestion that Sofia Tolstaya should write a new chapter to her autobiography was made by S.A. Vengerov, in a private conversation with her in St Petersburg. 'I gave Vengerov my Autobiography today,' she wrote to Bulgakov on March 7. 'He commented that I did not write enough about Lev Nikol.'s growing fame with the publication of *War and Peace* and *Anna Karenina*, and that I should write more about my influence on and participation in my husband's creative work. He wants me to write another chapter in this spirit, but I do not feel capable of it' (V. Bulgakov, *O Tolstom* (About Tolstoy), Tula, 1964, p. 290).
23 According to Bulgakov, 'The cause of this disagreement was S. A–na's harsh and irritable words about L. N–ich' (ibid., p. 291). From the written explanation that followed it is clear that the 'disagreement' occurred over a discussion about the last months of Tolstoy's life and about his relations with Chertkov (ibid., pp. 291–2).
24 'Diary for Myself Alone' (*PSS*, vol. 58).
25 Letter of March 15, in which Kuzminskii wrote that at a meeting in the office of the Minister of Justice a majority had accepted the proposal that the manuscripts stored in the Historical Museum be handed over to Sofia Tolstaya, and that this proposal be discussed in the next few days at a general session of the Senate (GMT).
26 As well as the new chapter Sofia Tolstaya sent Vengerov a letter in which she wrote: 'However hard I try, however hard I search for material for this chapter, I have been able to find almost nothing and have merely used whatever I could' (*Nachala* (Beginnings), no. 1, 1921, p. 134).
27 Bulgakov read a lecture on 'The Work of Cataloguing the Yasnaya Polyana Library' on March 29, to the annual general meeting of the Tolstoy Society.
28 Tatiana Sukhotina, *Maria Montessori i novoe vospitanie* (Maria Montessori and the new education), Moscow, 1914; Sofia Tolstaya's library, with the dedication: 'To dearest Mother, not to read, but with the author's esteem. Kochety, April 1914.'
29 *Sobranie pisem svyatitelya Feofana* (Anthology of letters from the Prelate Feofan), in 7 vols: vol. 1, Moscow, 1899; vol. 7, Moscow, 1900. Feofan's letters are on Orthodox religious matters. In several of them he speaks out extremely sharply against Tolstoy, especially his work 'What I Believe', which he attacks for its denial of Christianity.

30 Feofan, 'Chto est dukhovnaya zhizn i kak na nee nastroitsya?' (What is the spiritual life, and how to embark on it?) *Letters*, Moscow, 1904 (YaPL).

31 Photographs of the houses in which Tolstoy lived.

32 Sofia Tolstaya's letter is not known. N.M. Zhdanov, the lawyer who conducted all her affairs, asked her in a letter of June 29 how to dispose of the money left in Tolstoy's current account. This money was divided up amongst the heirs. (See Zhdanov's letter to Sofia Tolstaya of October 18, GMT.)

33 On June 28 there was an attempt on the life of the 'village elder', G. Rasputin, but he was not killed.

34 See Diary for 1910, note 11.

35 She is probably referring to Lyova Tolstoy's article 'Za svoe velikoe' (For my own greatness), *NV*, no. 13,780, July 24, 1914.

36 M. Sivachev, 'Schastlivitsa' (Lucky woman), *VE*, no. 7, 1914.

37 Levushka was Lyova Tolstoy's 2-year-old son.

38 A.S. Sukolyonova, the younger Tolstoy children's nurse.

39 The proof pages of the 'booklets', separate editions of sections of the *Put zhizni* (Path of life) anthology.

40 'Detsvo Tani Tolstoi v Yasnoi Polyane' (Tanya Tolstaya's childhood in Yasnaya Polyana), first published in Russian in T.L. Sukhotina.

41 Ilya Tolstoy was a correspondent for the newspaper *RS*, in which in 1914 he published a series of war communiqués: 'Vpechatleniya' (Impressions), *RS*, no. 183, August 10; 'V Galitsii. V pokorennoi strane' (In Galicia. In a subjugated land), no. 207, September 10; and 'Kartiny voiny' (Pictures of war), no. 219, September 24.

42 Tatiana Kuzminskaya was reading her memoirs about Maria Nikolaevna Tolstaya. Sofia Tolstaya became acquainted with them in manuscript and supplied her sister with essential material. See Daily Diary, 1913, note 68.

43 Sofia Tolstaya was reading A.L. Leroy-Beaulieu's obituary article about Tolstoy, which included his reminiscences of his visit to Yasnaya Polyana on May 9, 1905. See *LN*, vol. 75, book 2, pp. 402–3.

44 Bulgakov's article 'O voine' (On war), appealing to people to refuse to take part in military activities. Published in *ZV*, no. 5, 1917. It was distributed in hectographed and manuscript versions.

45 P. Kropotkin, *Pisma o sovremennykh sobytyakh* (Letters about contemporary events), review articles which were published in *RV* from September 1914 to 1917. Sofia Tolstaya read the first two letters, *RV*, no. 216, September 7, 1914, and no. 229, October 5, 1914.

46 This information was in fact false.

47 See note 40.

48 'Shved Abraam von Bunde' (The Swede Abram von Bunde), *RM*, no. 11, 1914, one of the essays in Tatiana Sukhotina's cycle of memoirs, *Druzya i gosti Yasnoi Polyany* (Friends and guests at Yasnaya Polyana). Bunde visited Yasnaya on May 26, 1892.

49 M.G. Veselova-Ilstedt, *Kolychevskaya votchina* (The Kolychev patrimony), in two parts, St Petersburg, 1911.

50 M.I. Tolstoy, a cadet at the Tiflis military academy, enlisted in the Intermanland infantry regiment, went to the front and was taken prisoner. He tried twice to escape. See Ilya Tolstoy's article 'Vnuk L.N. Tolstogo' (L.N. Tolstoy's grandson), *RS*, no. 82, April 11, 1915. He returned in 1918. See Daily Diary, 1918, entry for November 24.

51 Letter of April 18 (GMT). In the newspapers there also appeared an announcement that 'The Senate has decided to propose to the Minister of Education that the ban on the manuscripts be removed forthwith, and they be handed over to Countess S.A. Tolstaya' (*Utro Rossii* (Morning of Russia), no. 280, November 13, 1914). This ended the 'dispute over the manuscripts'.

52 Bulgakov's appeal *Come to Your Senses, Brothers!* with a call to 'love your enemies', was

distributed in typewritten manuscript. The appeal was signed by twenty Tolstoyans, fellow-thinkers of Bulgakov. (Published in the anthology Val. Bulgakov, *Opomnites lyudi-bratya!* (Come to your senses, brothers!), Moscow, 1922. Bulgakov also took part in copying and circulating the appeal. S. Popov's appeal was of a similar nature.

53 Sofia Tolstaya wrote a letter describing in detail this nocturnal visit by the police, and expressed her indignation at what happened. Published under the title 'Iz Yasnoi Polyany' (From Yasnaya Polyana), *NV*, no. 13,879, October 31, 1914, and also in other papers.

54 There exists a rough draft of Sofia Tolstaya's letter of October 29 to the Minister of Internal Affairs, V.F. Dzhunkovskii: 'Yesterday,' she wrote, 'police again appeared in my house, 6 of them, as though out to catch a criminal, and they arrested and probably took off to prison Valentin Fyodorovich Bulgakov, who was living with me. The charge is the usual one of spreading harmful thoughts. I must confess that I feel personally outraged that a police lieutenant-colonel should have demanded that I unlock some bookcases belonging to me personally in the room where Bulgakov was staying, and then searched them [. . .]' In her letter she asked that Bulgakov be released on bail 'on the recognisance of Sergei Lvovich' and her, so that 'work on the library could be finished' (GMT).

55 Dzhunkovskii's telegram of November 3 read: 'Bulgakov properly arrested in your house for circulating criminal appeals to popultion not to participate in war, and writing them on your typewriter, but arrest and search could of course have been freely conducted by day, not night, and I offer deep sympathy that you were disturbed at such an hour' (GMT).

56 The second volume of V. Karenin's monograph *George Sand, sa vie et ses oeuvres* was published in Paris in 1912. In the preface to the Russian edition the author pointed out that after the publication of the French edition 'readers of the Russian journals read a re-translated version of certain chapters, including "New Material from the Life of George Sand and Chopin"'. (See V. Karenin, *Zhorzh Sand, ee zhizn i tvorchestvo* (George Sand, her life and work), Paris, 1916, pp. vii–ix.

57 In the second edition of *Count L.N. Tolstoy's Letters to His Wife* (1915) Sofia Tolstaya inserted seven new letters, from June to October 1910.

58 The exhibition of V.D. Polyonov's paintings opened in Moscow for the seventieth anniversary of his birth.

59 Sergei Tolstoy was present during the police search of October 28 and, enraged by police lieutenant-colonel Demidov's demand to search Tolstoy's bookcases, he said to him: 'I would advise you to change your occupation and find some other' (Bulgakov, *Come to Your Senses, Brothers!*, pp. 156–7).

60 Sofia Tolstaya was reading *M.S. Gromeka o L.N. Tolstom* (M.S. Gromeka on L.N. Tolstoy), Intermediary, with a preface by I.I. Gorbunov-Posadov (Sofia Tolstaya's library), which was contained in the article 'Poslednie proizvedeniya gr. L.N. Tolstogo' (The later works of Count L.N. Tolstoy), *RM*, nos 2, 3, 4, 1883; no. 11, 1884.

61 Grand Duke Konstantin Konstantinovich, President of the Academy of Sciences, wrote an official letter to Sofia Tolstaya on December 2, asking for her consent to take copies from the manuscripts in the Historical Museum, or to hand them over to the Academy of Sciences (GMT). There exists a rough draft of Sofia Tolstaya's reply of December 8, in which she wrote: 'My personal plans are to transfer the entire archive from the Historical Museum to the Rumyantsev Museum [. . .] I stipulate only that free access to copy the manuscripts is given to me, my heirs, or those people whom we appoint. I have decided on this museum because Lev Nikolaevich always worked there and made use of its material, especially for *War and Peace*. He loved this museum and Moscow – he always referred very negatively to Petersburg . . . ! Count L.N. Tolstoy's diaries, like my own, I have decided to give to the Rumyantsev Museum on condition that they are never let out of the museum and that only those passages are published to which I, and after my death my heirs, give our consent' (GMT).

62 D.P. Makovitsky was arrested for signing the appeal *Come to Your Senses, Brothers!* (see notes 52 and 59).

1915

1 See Daily Diary, entry for December 6, 1914, and note 61.
2 Apart from the telegram (text unknown), Sofia Tolstaya received official notification from the Ministry of National Education that 'in executing the decree of the Senate' N.S. Shcherbatov had been instructed to give her all materials kept at the Historical Museum (GMT).
3 From the correspondence of L.N. Tolstoy (letters to S.S. Urusov, 1869–89). With commentaries by A.E. Gruzinskii (*VE*, no. 1, 1915). The same issue contained 'Zametki o Tolstom' (Notes on Tolstoy) by D.N. Ovsyaniko-Kulikovskii.
4 Sofia Tolstaya received a copy of the Senate's decree of December 18, 1914 (GMT).
5 See Daily Diary, October 26 and 28, 1914, note 62.
6 Forty-third exhibition of the Fellowship of Wandering Artists.
7 F.V. Bergholz, *Dnevnik kamer-yunkera Bergkholtsa, vedennyi im v Rossii v tsarstvovanie Petra Velikogo* (The diary of gentleman of the bedchamber Bergholz, kept in Russia during the reign of Peter the Great), Moscow, 1862 (YaPL, with Tolstoy's margin notes).
8 Ilya Tolstoy wrote in a letter of February 4 that the first issue of the newspaper *Novaya Rossiya* (New Russia), organised as a 'joint-stock' company', would appear on February 10, and he asked Sofia Tolstaya 'to write a short article about the time in 1876–7 when Papa decided to go off to war' (GMT). The newspaper was never published. There exists a rough version of Sofia Tolstaya's article, in which she describes Tolstoy's state of mind during the Russo-Turkish War. 'Gloomy and preoccupied,' she recalled, 'he couldn't do anything, and kept saying: "I can't work or write while this war is going on. It's just as though there was a fire blazing somewhere, and it's impossible to do anything." [. . .] The idea of going to war took a greater and greater hold on him, and eventually assumed quite an acute form. Lev Nik. started seriously planning to go off to war. "I can't sit at home when I know there are battles to be fought," he said' (GMT).
9 The anthology *Russkii byt po vospominaniyam sovremennikov XVIII veka* (Everyday Russian life in the memories of contemporaries of the eighteenth century), Moscow, 1914.
10 *Den pechati* (Day of the Press), a one-issue newspaper published in aid of the victims of war. It appeared on February 9 and contained a section entitled 'From the War' consisting of three sketches: Ilya Tolstoy's 'Alye bashmaki' (Scarlet shoes), his impressions of a 'wild' Caucasian division; V. Bryusov's 'Neutolimoe' (Insatiable) and V. Obolenskii's 'V tserkvi' (In church).
11 'Iz dnevnika L.N. Tolstogo' (From L.N. Tolstoy's diary), *Ezhemesyachnyi zhurnal* (Monthly Journal), no. 1, 1915. Its publication was evidently organised by Chertkov.
12 'Iz perepiski L.N. Tolstogo' (From L.N. Tolstoy's correspondence) (Letters to L.D. Urusov, 1885), *VE*, no. 2, 1915. This also contains the article 'Zametki o Tolstom (Bez zaminki)' (Notes on Tolstoy. (Without a Hitch)), by D.N. Ovsyaniko-Kulikovskii.
13 'Lev Nikolaevich Tolstoi o sebe. Izvlechennye, sobrannye L.P. Nikiforovym.' (Lev Nikolaevich Tolstoy on himself. Selected and arranged by L.P. Nikiforov), *Monthly Journal*, nos 3, 7–9, 10, 11, 1914.
14 A reference to the Tolstoys' agitation for the release of Bulgakov and Makovitsky on bail. See entry for December 7 and note 39.
15 M. Aldanov, *Tolstoi i Rollan* (Tolstoy and Rolland), Moscow, 1915.
16 A reference to the organisation of a special place in the Rumyantsev Museum where the Tolstoy archive could be stored, and where people could pursue their studies of his legacy. The 'study' existed there until 1939, when all the materials were transferred to the GMT.
17 In a letter of May 17 Maude thanked Sofia Tolstaya for Strakhov's letter and article. See Daily Diary, 1911, note 97.
18 *Pisma I.S. Turgeneva k grafine E.E. Lambert* (I.S. Turgenev's letters to Countess E.E. Lambert), Moscow, 1915. Preface and notes by G.P. Georgievskii.

19 'Iz perepiski L.N. Tolstogo. Pisma k G.A. Rusanovu' (From L.N. Tolstoy's correspondence. Letters to G.A. Rusanov) (1885–1906), *VE*, no. 3, 1915; the same issue also contains D. Ovsyaniko-Kulikovskii's article 'Zametki o Tolstom. Pautina lyubvi' (Notes on Tolstoy. The web of love).

20 The letter has not been kept. The letter to I.F. Kostsov, a book-dealer, probably contained a request to send the separate edition of Tolstoy's short story 'Tri startsa' (The three elders).

21 D.P. Ovsyaniko-Kulikovskii, 'Tsennost zhizni. Etyud' (The value of life. A study), *VE*, no. 5, 1915.

22 N. Morozov's memoirs, 'Za svet i svobodu' (For light and freedom), in *GM*, no. 4 (continuation in no. 5), 1915.

23 'Ukazatel lits i proizvedenii' (Index of people and events) to the second edition of *Count L.N. Tolstoy's Letters to His Wife*, Moscow, 1915.

24 N.N. Apostolov visited Yasnaya Polyana to examine Tolstoy's library and to explore the literary sources of *War and Peace*. In the article 'Materialy po istorii literaturnoi deyatelnosti L.N. Tolstogo' (Material for a history of L.N. Tolstoy's literary activity), *Pechat i revolytsiya* (Revolution and the Press), no. 4, 1924, he recalled: 'In the Yasnaya Polyana library, scattered amongst five shelves, we found books belonging to the category of "sources" for *War and Peace*. These were the Russian and French memoirs which Tolstoy used' (p. 92).

25 There were disturbances in Moscow on April 28 and 29, after German and Austrian citizens were expelled from the city and the shops and businesses belonging to them were attacked. There is a rough draft of Sofia Tolstaya's letter to the Minister of Internal Affairs, N.A. Maklakov, in which she urges him to take measures to avert further disturbances.

26 Igor Arnoldi, 'Na zakate' (At sunset), *VE*, no. 6, 1915.

27 D. Darskii, the author of a book about Fet's poetry, *Radost zemli* (Joy of the earth), Moscow, 1915. Fet and Sofia Tolstaya had an active correspondence, particularly in the 1880s (GMT).

28 A reference to the Novogeorgievskii fortress.

29 Untrue. As early as 1913 *Re* (no. 264, September 27) had published a letter from Chertkov: 'Today my trusted assistant Aleksei Sergeenko and I took approximately 25 *poods* [900 pounds] of L.N. Tolstoy's papers from my fire-proof safe in England and gave them to the Academy of Sciences. These form the archive of the manuscripts he gave or sent to me in the course of almost 30 years to keep. The only papers remaining in the safe in England are L.N.'s personal correspondence with me, which I hope shortly to publish, some of his own hand-written letters given to me personally by their owners, copies of his general correspondence, exact copies of all his works of the final period, and also the originals of those works of his which it might be foolish to keep in Russia in the present circumstances.'

30 Tatiana Sukhotina suffered from antritis and underwent two operations.

31 See Appendices, 'L.N. Tolstoy's Marriage'.

32 Sofia Tolstaya's letter was prompted by the publication of chapters 1–5 of Sergeenko's article 'Iz skazki o schastie' (A story about happiness), about Tolstoy's marriage (*RV*, no. 15,097, September 19, 1915). The letter was not published.

33 I.V. Denisenko asked Sofia Tolstaya in a letter of October 3 'to give something from her memoirs or from Lev Nikolaevich's works' for 'an evening [. . .] at the Gogol Society on November 7'. In a letter of November 9 Denisenko thanked her 'for the excerpts sent', and informed her that one of them, 'Poezdka v Kryokshina' (The visit to Kryokshina), was read aloud at the evening on November 7 (GMT). The text of the 'second article' is not known.

34 Maybe the manuscript of Giuseppe Mazzini's biography, written in Tolstoy's lifetime by L.P. Nikiforov, the translator of his works. The manuscript was not published and its present whereabouts is not known.

35 G. Sienkiewicz, *Kamo gryadeshi* (Quo Vadis), 1896.

36 The Daily Diary for this year contains a note by Sofia Tolstaya: 'The little leather diary in

the museum finishes on November 8, 1861' (see *PSS*, vol. 48, pp. 3–39).

37 V.F. Bulgakov was released from prison on the security of Aleksandra Tolstaya.

38 *Turgenevskii sbornik* (A Turgenev anthology), Ogni publishing house, Sofia Tolstaya's library, dedication by the editor, N.K. Piksanov, with the date November 15, 1915. Sofia Tolstaya's criticism refers to N. Bogdanova's memoirs *Dva intimnykh pisma I.S. Turgeneva* (Two intimate letters from I.S. Turgenev).

39 D.P. Makovitsky was released on the security of Tatiana Sukhotina.

40 Sofia Tolstaya's criticism refers to 'Vospominaniya o Turgeneve' (Memories of Turgenev) by N.A. Ostrovskaya, who mistakenly indicates that Turgenev simultaneously received two letters from Tolstoy written after their argument in May 1861. In fact Tolstoy's second 'placatory' letter, declining to fight a duel, was written on October 8, 1861 (see *PSS*, vol. 60, p. 406).

41 A.E. Kaufmann, one of the editors of an anthology prepared by the mutual insurance fund for writers and scientists and dedicated to the memory of G.K. Gradovskii, asked Sofia Tolstaya to give material about him from Tolstoy's diary and her own to be published in it. She allowed him to publish sixteen letters from Gradovskii to her and four from her to him.

42 After the appearance in print of L.N. Tolstoy's diary, edited by Chertkov, many newspapers carried excerpts from the diary entries and from the editor's preface.

43 Probably the play *Raketa* (The rocket).

44 A.V. Amfiteatrov, 'Lev Tolstoi', *Sobr. soch.* (Collected works), vol. XX, St Petersburg, 1913. As a student at Moscow University Amfiteatrov had worked under Tolstoy's supervision on the 1882 census. His memoirs contain several vivid and interesting facts about Tolstoy, but they also tend mainly to attack the writer, defaming his character and accusing him of hypocrisy, dishonesty and so on. The essay (first published in 1907) was included in Amfiteatrov's *Collected Works* in a new edition, in which the anti-Tolstoy bias was even more pronounced.

1916

1 Letters unknown. The letter was not published in *NV*.

2 There exists an incomplete rough draft of Tatiana Sukhotina's sketch 'Kurzik', in which she described the life and death through drink of a poor peasant. She sent the story to Korolenko to publish in the journal *Russkie zapiski* (Russian notes), but it was not published.

3 *Dnevnik Lva Nikolaevicha Tolstogo* (The diary of Lev Nikolaevich Tolstoy), vol. 1, 1895–9, Moscow, 1916, edited by V.G. Chertkov. This edition contains 112 cuts, 55 for reasons of censorship and 57 for intimate reasons. The diary was published with the maximum completeness allowed at that time.

4 The film of Tolstoy's story 'What People Live For' was produced by A.A. Khonzhenkov's film company. Ilya Tolstoy wrote the script, and directed and played the part of the gentleman; the angel was played by A. Vertinskii. For an account of his visit to Yasnaya Polyana and the shooting of the episodes in which he took part see Aleksandr Vertinskii, 'Chertvert veka bez rodiny' (A quarter of a century without a homeland), in the journal *Moskva* (Moscow), no. 5, 1962, p. 213.

5 Tatiana Sukhotina kept a diary from 1879 to 1919. It was published in a French translation (Tatiana Tolstoi, *Journal*, Paris, 1953). Excerpts from it are included in T.L. Sukhotina.

6 The play *Udalos* (Successful). See Daily Diary, January 1, 1917, and note 1.

7 Gusev did a literary re-working of *Yasnopolyanskie zapiski* (Yasnaya Polyana notes), as Makovitsky, a Slovak by nationality, had an insufficiently fluent grasp of Russian. A copy of Gusev's reworked version of the notes is not at the GMT. It was partially published. First instalment, Moscow, 1922; second, Moscow, 1923; *GM*, no. 3, 1923; *Yasn. sb.*, 1955 and 1960.

8 Charles Salomon's letter to Tatiana Sukhotina of May 8 (new style), 1915, about the death of his nephew Lucien at war on August 22, 1914. Lucien Salomon visited Yasnaya Polyana in 1910.
9 V. Bulgakov went to Moscow to work as assistant curator of the GMT.
10 K. Mulford, *K zhizni* (To life), 1st edn, St Petersburg, 1912; 2nd edn, St Petersburg, 1913.
11 L.L. Tolstoy was working on his lecture 'Edinoe chelovechestvo' (One humanity). See note 22.
12 Tatiana Sukhotina left for Moscow to appear as a witness in the trial of Bulgakov, Makovitsky and the other Tolstoyans.
13 She wrote this protest after a German submarine in the Black Sea sank the hospital ship *Portugal*, which was carrying wounded soldiers and officers.
14 From March 21 to 28 the case of the Tolstoyans who had signed Bulgakov and Popov's *Appeal* was heard in the Moscow circuit court. See Daily Diary, October 26, 1914, and notes 52–4. Bulgakov, Makovitsky, Tregubov and the others were aquitted. S. Popov, who was also accused of 'inciting the military ranks to violate their obligations of service', was sentenced to a term in prison. (See *RS*, no. 73, March 20, 1916.)
15 M. Menshikov, 'Pisma k blizhnim. Sredi filosofov' (Letters to intimates. Amongst the philosophers), *NV*, no. 14,394, April 3, 1916).
16 See entry for May 16 and note 22.
17 A reference to the memoirs of V.V. Nagornova (signed V. Nagornaya) 'Original Natashi Rostovoi v romane *Voina i mir*. Molodost T.A. Kuzminskoi' (The original of Natasha Rostova in *War and Peace*. The youth of T.A. Kuzminskaya). See supplement to *NV*, no. 14,400, April 9, 1916; no. 14,413, April 23; no. 14,427, May 7 and no. 14,434, May 14. In her preface to these memoirs Varya Nagornova wrote that they were based on her own memories and diary, letters, her mother's tales and those of Tatiana Kuzminskaya. See no. 14,400. See also *Voprosy literatury* (Questions of Literature), no. 9, 1977.
18 Sofia Tolstaya and Tatiana Kuzminskaya's letters about V. Nagornova's education are unknown. Kuzminskaya replied on April 18 to one of them, in which Sofia Tolstaya probably expressed her suspicions that her sister had helped to write them: 'I am very glad you liked the article [. . .] but anyone who says it was written by me would be quite wrong [. . .] I simply gave it the literary polish it lacked. It is enormously successful, and many, many people are reading it' (GMT).
19 The manuscript of Ustinya Suvorova's memoirs has not been kept.
20 Probably one of the two Molokans who visited Tolstoy on May 8, 1897, V.I. Tokarev or V.T. Chipelev.
21 L.L. Tolstoy, 'My prosnemsya (povest iz sovremennoi zhizni)' (We are waking up. A tale of contemporary life), *VE*, nos 3, 4, 5, 1916.
22 A reference to his lecture 'Edinoe chelovechestvo. Kak unichtozhit bedstviya i stradaniya nastoyashchego i pribilizitsya k bogatsvu i vechnomu miru narodov' (One humanity. How to abolish poverty and suffering and hasten on the perpetual peace and wealth of nations.) The lecture was intended to be delivered at public meetings abroad. (Lyova Tolstoy was planning to leave for foreign parts.)
23 The anthology *Come to Your Senses, Brothers!* (see Diary, 1914, notes 52 and 59), which tells the story of the writing of the *Appeal*, the collection of the signatures and the interrogation and arrest of Bulgakov and his co-thinkers. When the first part came out in Moscow in 1922 Bulgakov was named as the only author, but the preface mentions that he made use of Tatiana Sukhotina's verbal accounts.
24 V.M. Popov supervised the Manuscripts Department at the GMT in Moscow.
25 I. Nazhivin, *Iz zhizni L.N. Tolstogo* (From the life of L.N. Tolstoy), Moscow, 1915. Sofia Tolstaya's Library, with a dedication dated May 30, 1916.
26 The GMT contains the manuscripts of two unfinished novels by Lyova Tolstoy, hand-copied by Sofia Tolstaya and with the author's corrections. One of them is entitled *Chto est*

istina? (What is the truth?) and the other, untitled, is dated May 27 and is set during the war, 1914–1916.

27 Sofia Tolstaya was reading her poem 'Starost' (Old age), which she sent to P.A. Sergeenko with a letter dated August 5 (GMT). There are two notebooks in the Tolstoy Museum containing verses written at various times by her.

28 On August 9 Sofia Tolstaya's new will was legally ratified by the notary, P.P. Kosyakov.

29 A reference to S.S. Abamelek-Lazarev's 'Vospominaniya o L.N. Tolstom' (Memoirs of L.N. Tolstoy), about his visits to Yasnaya Polyana during 1884 to 1887 and in 1904. These memoirs were not published and are now at the GMT.

30 Abamelek-Lazarev's memoirs tend mainly to attack Tolstoy for remaining an 'old Russian nobleman'.

31 There exists a rough draft of Lyova Tolstoy's memorandum to the Tsar entitled 'O tverdykh tsenakh, monopolizatsii khlebnoi torgovli i uchrezhdenii osobogo prodovolstvennogo vedomstva' (On fixed prices, the monopolisation of the bread industry and the establishment of a special provisions department) (GMT). It is not known whether this memorandum was given to the Tsar.

32 A reference to Tatiana Kuzminskaya's memoirs *My Life at Home and at Yasnaya Polyana.* She wrote to Sofia Tolstaya on September 25: 'I have received the manuscript. I thank you with all my heart for copying it out. It is beautiful, clear and literate' (GMT).

33 Probably Lyova Tolstoy's story 'Odol' (in *Ves mir* (All the World), no. 46, 1916), or 'Khot by v boyu' (Into the battle!) *Ogonyok* (Flame), no. 45, November 6, 1916.

34 The publication of a new *Tolstoy Yearbook* did not in fact take place.

35 Probably a reference to Lyova Tolstoy's 'L.N. Tolstoi i pisateli kotorykh on chital' (L.N. Tolstoy and the writers he read), *Birzhevye vedomosti* (Stock Exchange Gazette), nos 15,906 and 15,908, November 5 and 7, 1916. Lyova Tolstoy recalled his father's pronouncements about Pushkin, Lermontov, Turgenev, Goncharov, Gogol and other Russian writers, and his discussions with him about literature in general.

36 Tatiana Sukhotina, 'Agafya Mikhailovna', first published in *Druzya i gosti Yasnoi Polyany* (Friends and guests at Yasnaya Polyana), Moscow, 1923. The complete essay first appeared in 'Tanya Tolstaya's Childhood at Yasnaya Polyana' in T.L. Sukhotina, pp. 62–9.

37 A.S. Volzhskii, 'O pravde i krivde (k voprosu o semeinom razlade L.N. Tolstogo)' (On truth and falsehood. The question of L.N. Tolstoy's family disharmony), in *Bogoslovskii vestnik* (Theological Herald), no. 6, 1916. The author explains Tolstoy's 'family disharmony' in terms of the fact that Tolstoy was searching for 'God', whereas Sofia Tolstaya wanted 'worldly things' (p. 349).

38 Volzhskii referred in extremely hostile terms to Chertkov, describing him as a 'faceless, alien, deathly individual, who doesn't smell quite human' (ibid., p. 370).

39 Ilya Tolstoy left Petersburg for America on November 2. On this day he wrote to his mother: 'I deeply regret that I was unable to visit Yasnaya to say goodbye before leaving, but I had so much to do writing and translating my lectures' (GMT).

40 Tatiana Sukhotina helped to organise in the large auditorium of the Polytechnic Museum an evening in memory of Tolstoy at which she gave a lecture entitled 'On Popular Education and Tolstoy's Attitude to It'. Three Yasnaya Polyana peasants, coached by her, sang some of Tolstoy's favourite folk-songs, and O.A. Ozarovskaya read excerpts from Sukhotina's memoirs 'Tanya Tolstaya's Childhood at Yasnaya Polyana'. A third of the money collected was donated to the Society to Aid War Victims.

41 On 7 November there was a musical evening in memory of Tolstoy at the Polytechnic Museum, at which excerpts from Tatiana Sukhotina's memoirs 'Tanya Tolstaya's Childhood at Yasnaya Polyana' were read. She wrote to her mother on November 8: 'We had the second Tolstoy concert yesterday. Everything went smoothly, I wouldn't say it was a brilliant success but was all quite satisfactory. A full house both evenings. Stakhovich spoke well yesterday, and actors from the Maly Theatre read *The Fruits of Enlightenment.* My

memoirs, as I predicted, were quite appropriate for the children's evening but not for the larger gathering' (GMT).

42 Announcements for this evening were placed in all the Moscow newspapers.

43 'V Yasnoi Polyane' (In Yasnaya Polyana), in the book by A. Izmailov, *Literaturnyi Olimp* (Literary Olympus), St Petersburg, 1911. About his visit to Tolstoy on June 14.

44 Tatiana Sukhotina-Tolstaya, 'Starushka Schmidt' (Old Woman Schmidt), *GM*, nos 5–12, 1919, with the author's date April 3, 1918; subsequently in the book *Friends and Guests at Yasnaya Polyana.*

45 *Mémorial de Sainte-Hélène. Par M. le comte de Las Cases*, Paris, 1837 (YaPL, with Tolstoy's notes). N.N. Apostolov (Ardens), in his book on *War and Peace*, referred to this work as a major source for Tolstoy's image of Napoleon, and quoted texts from it in Sofia Tolstaya's translation. See N.N. Ardens, *Tvorcheskii put L.N. Tolstogo* (L.N. Tolstoy's creative path), Moscow publishing house of the Academy of Sciences of the USSR, 1962, pp. 172–3. See Daily Diary, May 31, 1915, and note 24.

1917

1 On January 1 there was a family performance of Tatiana Sukhotina's children's play *Udalos* (Successful).

2 V.I. Sreznevskii was compiling a biographical outline called *Nit zhizni Tolstogo* (The thread of Tolstoy's life). A short extract from this, entitled *Kanva zhizni Tolstogo* (An outline of Tolstoy's life), came out in 1928 in Leningrad.

3 The book *Publitsist-grazhdanin. Literaturnyi sbornik posvyashchennyi pamyati G.K. Gradovskogo* (Publicist and citizen. A literary anthology dedicated to the memory of G.K. Gradovskii), Petrograd, 1916. In his essay 'Dva dnya v Yasnoi Polyane' (Two days in Yasnaya Polyana) Gradovskii described his visit to Tolstoy in October 1909 and referred sympathetically to Sofia Tolstaya, who made an 'enchanting impression' on him (p. 147).

4 *Religiya* (Religion), an anthology of articles about Buddhism, Judaism, Christianity and Islam. Published by *Zhizn dlya vsekh* (Life for All), Petrograd, 1916. On July 7, 1887 Tolstoy wrote to P.I. Biryukov: 'Ah, how good it would be if someone could expound the teachings – the genuine, fundamental teachings of the faiths, 3 or 6 of them' (*PSS*, vol. 64, p. 56). In 1886 Tolstoy had the idea of writing such a work, but his plan was not realised. There exists a rough draft of it (*PSS*, vol. 26, pp. 572–7).

5 See Daily Diary, 1916, note 7.

6 L. Sulerzhitskii, *V Ameriku s dukhoborami. Iz zapisnoi knizhki* (To America with the Dukhobors. From my Notebook), Moscow, 1905 (YaPL, with a dedication). Sulerzhitskii helped Tolstoy in his work resettling the peasant Dukhobors exiled by the Tsarist government.

7 *Bednost ne porok* (Poverty is no sin), a play by A.N. Ostrovskii.

8 Eleven letters from L.N. Tolstoy to Sofia Tolstaya in 1911, were first published in *PSS*, vol. 84.

9 The article was not published. The text is unknown.

10 Tatiana Kuzminskaya's letter of March 1 about her husband's death (GMT).

11 He was probably reading the article 'The Meaning of the Russian Revolution' (1906), *PSS*, vol. 36.

12 *Pensées inédites de Tolstoi, trad. du manuscrit par W.L. Bienstock*, Paris, 1910. Bienstock translated Tolstoy's works into French.

13 A. Fet, *Moi vospominaniya* (My memoirs), vols. 1–2, Moscow, 1890–2.

14 Ernest Crosby, poet and journalist, was personally acquainted with Tolstoy and corresponded with him. He described his visit to Yasnaya Polyana in May 1894 in an essay entitled 'Two Days with Count Tolstoy' in the *Progressive Review*, no. 2, 1897. It is possible that Makovitsky read the book Ernest Crosby, *Tolstoi i ego zhizneponimanie* (Tolstoy and his

understanding of life), (1st edn, 1906; 2nd edn, 1911), which was prefaced by an article by Tolstoy entitled 'Pervoe znakomstvo s Ernestom Krosbi' (First acquaintance with Ernest Crosby) (see *PSS*, vol. 40, pp. 339–40), and a short biographical sketch of I.I.Gorbunov-Posadov called 'Ernst [*sic*] Crosby, poet novogo mira' (Poet of a new world).

15 Sofia Tolstaya received thanks from the Bibliographical Society of Moscow University.

16 Lyova Tolstoy was much published in the journals *Ogonyok* (Flame) and *Ves mir* (All the World) throughout 1916. See Daily Diary, 1916, note 33. *Ves mir* also published his stories 'Vanechka pomog' (Vanechka helped) (no. 11) and 'Esli by vy znali' (If only you knew) (no. 42).

17 V. Polents, *Krestyanin* (The Peasant), translated from the German by V. Velichkina, with a preface by L.N. Tolstoy. Moscow, 1904 (YaPL). Tolstoy described the novel in his preface as a 'magnificent work of art', and of 'great importance' (*PSS*, vol. 34, pp. 272, 271).

18 The newspaper carried information about the July events in Petrograd, where the Provisional Government fired on peaceful demonstrations of workers, soldiers and sailors.

19 Alphonse Karr, *Clothilde*, vols 1–2, St Petersburg, 1858 (YaPL).

20 Paul Hyacinthe Loyson, publicist and playwright, the author of an article called 'L'Investiture de Tolstoi'. Tolstoy was in correspondence with him (see *PSS*, vol. 74; Loyson's letters, *LN*, vol. 75, book 1, pp. 440–7). Loyson sent Tolstoy many of his plays and comedies (YaPL). See *LN*, vol. 75, book 1, p. 522. 'Some Frenchmen arrived,' wrote Tatiana Kuzminskaya in her diary on July 21, 'including the playwright Loyson. Tanya had been eagerly waiting for him – she says he is very clever and interesting. Yesterday she read us his French play *L'Apôtre*. Very theatrical' (GMT).

21 G.P. Danilevskii, 'Poezdka v Yasnuyu Polyanu' (A visit to Yasnaya Polyana), first published in *IV*, no. 3, 1895, about his visit to Yasnaya on September 28, 1885. His memoirs were included in vol. 14 of *Sochineniya G.P. Danilevskogo* (The works of G.P. Danilevskii), St Petersburg, 1901 (YaPL, with Tolstoy's margin notes).

22 *Chernyi god. (Pugachevshchina)* (The black year. (The Pugachov incident)), a novel by G.P. Danilevskii.

23 V.A. Posse, *Iz istorii kommunistecheskikh idei* (A history of communist ideas), St Petersburg, 1917.

24 V. Bulgakov arrived in Yasnaya Polyana alarmed by news in the papers that the peasants 'had chopped down the orchard, smashed the beehives and destroyed the crops'. On his return to Moscow he published an article entitled 'V Yasnoi Polyane' (In Yasnaya Polyana), in which he wrote that at a general meeting on September 20 the Yasnaya peasants had condemned the plunderers and resolved to 'help in every way possible to guard both the house and the property of the estate' (*RS*, September 24, 1917).

25 Sofia Tolstaya wrote to the Ministry of Internal Affairs asking that measures be taken to protect Yasnaya Polyana. At the same time A.P. Sergeenko and A.L. Volynskii (L. Andreev was to have been the third member of the delegation, but arrived too late to take part in the discussion) also appealed to the Ministry, suggesting that they discuss ways of securing 'the historic estate and the Tolstoy family from further attacks'. 'As a result of the discussions,' it was announced in the press, 'It has been decided that the most expedient measure would be to send to Yasnaya Polyana a person acquainted with the local peasants and close to the late L.N. Tolstoy, who would organise a defence force from the ranks of the peasants who revere the memory of the great teacher. P.A. Sergeenko has been chosen to fulfil this task.' At the same time the Tula Regional Commissar was urged to 'pay serious attention to Countess Tolstaya's requests and personally do everything possible to avert unwarranted actions by the local citizens against her estate'. See 'Yasnaya Polyana v opasnosti' (Yasnaya Polyana in danger), *RV*, no. 16,463, September 27, 1917.

26 Valentin Bulgakov, *Khristianskaya etika. Sistematicheskie ocherki mirovozzreniya Tolstogo* (The Christian ethic. A systematic outline of Tolstoy's world view), Moscow, 1917.

27 *The Light Shines Even in Darkness*. See Daily Diary, 1910, note 12.

28 See Daily Diary, 1916, note 45.
29 P.A. Kropotkin, *Pisma o tekushchikh sobytiyakh* (Letters about current events), Moscow, 1917.
30 Peasants in the province of Tula, dissatisfied with the Provisional Government's agrarian policies, unleashed a great wave of lootings against aristocratic estates. Several young Yasnaya Polyana peasants and some soldiers recently returned from the front incited the people to loot Yasnaya Polyana. Those who disagreed with them informed Sofia Tolstaya. Tatiana Sukhotina informed the secretary of the commission of enquiry, E.D. Vysokomirny, about the situation, after which the Presidium of the Soviet of Workers' and Soldiers' Deputies decided to despatch soldiers there immediately to safeguard the estate.
31 'After the October Revolution the protection of the house in Yasnaya Polyana where L.N. Tolstoy lived,' announced the Military-Revolutionary Committee of the Commissariat for Internal Affairs, 'was made the responsibility of a detachment of Red Guards and all the property was registered' (*Yasn. sb.*, 1910–60, pp. 133–4).
32 'Vanechka. Istinnoe proisshestvie iz ego zhizni' (Vanechka. A true episode from his life), a short story by Sofia Tolstaya, included in her anthology *Skeleton Dolls*.
33 Tolstoy's short story from book III of the *ABC*. See *PSS*, vol. 22, pp. 421–32.
34 'P.A. Sergeenko has taken a lot of trouble for us and helped us a great deal,' wrote Sofia Tolstaya to Sergei Tolstoy on November 12. 'Thanks to his intercession they are now selling us flour at Kosaya Gora. Sergeenko raised some interest there in the defence of Yasnaya Polyana, and they are sending us 15 militiamen every night for three nights' (GMT).
35 Letters written during Lyova Tolstoy's serious illness and cure abroad.
36 A short story by Tolstoy (*PSS*, vol. 25).

1918

1 The Constituent Assembly was dissolved on January 6 on the decision of the Executive Committee of the Party. The ministers A.I. Shingarev and F.F. Kokoshkin of the overthrown Provisional Government were assassinated by anarchist sailors.
2 Yasnaya Polyana was in an exceptional position compared to other aristocratic estates in Tula province. 'The safety of this historic estate is guarded even more carefully at present than ever before,' wrote Bulgakov. '[. . .] the Tula political organisations are directly involved in the protection of Yasnaya Polyana, and have assigned a special permanent guard to the estate [. . .] The inhabitants are being belped with their provisions [. . .] A few days ago a telephone was installed there, linking Yasnaya Polyana with Tula and Moscow [. . .] The shadow of Lev Nikolaevich guards the estate and keeps it safe' (V. Bulgakov, 'In Yasnaya Polyana', *RV*, December 29, 1917).
3 It is not known who gave this order, but it was never carried out and Yasnaya Polyana remained intact.
4 Tolstoy's play (1886) – *PSS*, vol. 26.
5 A reference to Tolstoy's tract *Soedinenie i perevod chetyryox Evangelii* (Collation and translation of the four Gospels) (1880–1), first Russian edition, Intermediary, 1907–8 (*PSS*, vol. 24). See also Appendices, 'Various Notes for Future Reference', note 45.
6 P.A. Sergeenko, 'Deizi' (Daisy), Moscow, 1890.
7 The question of the publication of Tolstoy's complete works was again discussed in April 1917 at a meeting of the directors of the Tolstoy Society. At this meeting an editorial commission was elected, which included Sergei and Aleksandra Tolstoy. V.F. Bulgakov, N.N. Gusev, N.V. Davydov and others. To finance the edition it was decided to make a collection. After the October Revolution, as A.V. Lunacharskii observed, the question, '*on Lenin's personal initiative*', was made 'a matter of administrative order' (*LN*, vol. 69, book 2, p. 432). 'The first volumes of the *Complete Works of L.N. Tolstoy* will shortly be appearing,' it

was announced in the press. 'These will probably amount to no fewer than 60 volumes. L.N.'s unpublished diaries will also be included along with his other writings in this edition, as well as his letters to various people, which alone will take up several volumes (most of his letters are appearing in print for the first time), and a significant amount of previously unpublished material. This edition will be more complete than any others so far published' (*Sovetskaya pravda* (Soviet Truth), no. 24, January 31, 1918). it was also announced here that a committee had been set up to supervise the publication of Tolstoy's collected works.

The Tolstoys played an active part in the preparation of this edition. On February 13, 1918 Sergei Tolstoy wrote to his mother: 'If we all work together on this, then in the first place the edition will be without rivals, and in the second place various questions connected to father's literary legacy will be laid to rest once and for all. I plan to sort out manuscripts in the Rumyantsev Museum in the most energetic fashion; I shall keep a strict watch to make sure that they don't take any of them away, and shall see that no one makes use of them besides the publishing committee (editorial committee)' (GMT). So in 1918 work began on the preparation of the *Complete Works of L.N. Tolstoy* in 90 volumes, which was known as the 'Jubilee Edition', vol. I of which appeared in 1928.

8 These rumours were caused by the start of an Austro-German offensive against the centre of Russia.

9 L.N. Tolstoy, 'Iz zapisok knyazya Nekhlyudova. Lyutsern' (From the notes of Prince Nekhlyudov. Lucerne) (1857) (*PSS*, vol. 5).

10 See Daily Diary, 1916, note 8.

11 E.D. Vysokomirnyi was secretary of the provincial committee of enquiry.

12 See Diary, March 1, 1898, and note 57.

13 Maria Mikhailovna Tolstaya, Sergei Nikolaevich's wife.

14 This decision was changed and on the orders of the Soviet of People's Commissars the pension was continued. The decision (March 30, 1918) was taken at a meeting chaired by Lenin.

15 'Pokhorony Lva Tolstogo do ego smerti' (Lev Tolstoy's funeral before his death), *Byloe* (The past), no. 2, 1917. The article contained secret documents discovered at the police department with instructions as to what should be done if he died; these were drawn up in 1901–2 when he was seriously ill in the Crimea.

16 On March 25 Sofia Tolstaya wrote to Sergei Tolstoy: 'I always realised that this was out of the question – all the more so with the present high costs. I am writing to Georgievskii to say that I shall let you and Sasha take copies from the manuscripts at your own discretion and in the best possible way' (GMT).

17 The story is not known.

18 On April 15 to 20 (new style), the provincial meeting of land committees decided on the basis of the Sovnarkom (= Soviet of People's Commissars – i.e. the government) decision of March 30 (*Yasn. sb.*, 1910–60, p. 135), 'to make L.N. Tolstoy's Yasnaya Polyana estate ineligible for reapportionment amongst the citizens of the adjacent hamlets, and to use it as a historical monument, purely for cultural and educational purposes.' The peasants at first agreed with this decision, but then decided that the land should be taken, and convened a meeting on April 27 (new style) at which it was decided to take the land (40 *desyatinas*) and use it for tillage. Several days later, however, the Yasnaya peasants went back on their decision, and delegates were sent to the estate with an apology. (See E.D. Vysokomirnyi, *Yasnaya Polyana v gody revolyutsii* (Yasnaya Polyana in the years of the Revolution), Moscow/Leningrad, 1928, pp. 12–14.)

19 'A solemn event took place at Yasnaya Polyana: all the peasants from the village appeared at the estate, met Sofia Andreevna with festive greetings and asked her to accompany them to Lev Nikolaevich's grave. When they got there they all took off their caps, silently knelt on the ground and chanted "Eternal Memory". Then, having walked Sofia Andreevna home, they told her that there would be no more misunderstandings and went back to the village.

As they left they said they had decided to put up a monument to Lev Nikolaevich in the village' (ibid., p. 14).

20 'A commission arrived in Yasnaya Polyana today headed by Kalinin, who leads our soldiers,' noted Tatiana Kuzminskaya in her diary on May 6 (GMT).

21 V. Bulgakov, *L.N. Tolstoi v poslednii god ego zhizni* (Lev Tolstoy in the last year of his life), Moscow, 1918, 2nd edn. 'Thank you for sending me your book,' Sofia Tolstaya wrote to Bulgakov on May 23. 'I shall try to read it, as I find it very interesting' (V. Bulgakov, *O Tolstom* (About Tolstoy), p. 311). Sofia Tolstaya read the first edition of the book in 1911.

22 Georgii Nelyubin, *Velikii Knyaz Konstantin Konstantinovich. Zhizn i tvorchestvo 1858–1915.* (Grand Duke Konstantin Konstantinovich. His life and work, 1858–1915), Petrograd, 1916. Sofia Tolstaya's library.

23 See note 7. The request was made verbally via M.V. Bulygin. On June 3 (new style) Sergei Tolstoy wrote to his mother: 'Mikh. Vas. will tell you how we have been working in the museum. We have been working with love and enthusiasm, and are being very careful with the manuscripts. There is so much interesting material there. Much of it is new to me. I have taken on the editing of the diaries, not all of them, of course – I have chosen only the bachelor diaries for now, Tanya can do the period up to 1900, and the period from 1900 until the illness in the Crimea Sasha could do with Gusev and Bulgakov, and I could help. Mikh. Vas. will tell you what information we need to revise the diaries. I need to know precise details from you, with dates, of everything you have copied, so as not to re-copy any of the diaries [. . .] I should like to bring copies of some of them with me, and maybe some photographs too, so that you, Tanya and I can underline the parts that are unsuitable for publication' (GMT).

24 Lyova Tolstoy, in his own words, had returned from a journey 'around the world'. 'After writing two lectures, one entitled "On L.N. Tolstoy's Life and Teaching", and the other "The Problems of Our World",' he wrote in his essay 'Vokrug sveta' (Around the world), 'I left for Japan, planning to go from there to China and India [. . .] I travelled around all the major towns of Japan with my lecture' (*Vestochka* (Piece of news), nos 2 and 3, August 26 and 27, 1918).

25 T.I. Polner was a member of the editorial committee preparing a new *Complete Collected Works* of Tolstoy. Later he wrote the book *Lev Tolstoi i ego zhena. Istoriya odnoi lyubvi* (Lev Tolstoy and his wife. The story of a love), Paris, 1928, which made use of information and material supplied by Sofia Tolstaya. In this book he also described his visit to the writer's home. 'Sofia Andreevna [. . .] met me calmly, wearily and with dignity. She was already 74 years old. Tall, slightly stooping and extremely thin – she glided softly through the rooms like a shadow, and looked as though a strong gust of wind would have blown her off her feet [. . .] When she talked she did not smile but she spoke very eagerly. She seemed half-dead, although she was happy to read us her memoirs about happy times in Yasnaya Polyana' (p. 235).

26 The Tula archive contained Tolstoy's official letters, and documents and material about his military and public activities.

27 In 1917 Tolstoy's friends in Tula initiated the establishment of the educational Yasnaya Polyana Society in Memory of L.N. Tolstoy, whose purpose was to protect the writer's estate, his grave and all his memorabilia, and to turn Yasnaya into a cultural centre. In April 1918 the Society was legally ratified and officially recognised. From the very beginning of its existence the Society worked on a series of measures designed to protect Yasnaya Polyana and perpetuate the writer's memory – the construction of an asphalt highway, a library, a school, etc. P.A. Sergeenko was elected president of the Society, and Vysokomirnyi secretary.

28 Tolstoy's short story 'Polikushka' (1861–3); *PSS*, vol. 7.

29 'Once we read Salias' novel *Novgorodtsy* (The Novgorodians),' recalled M.P. Sergeenko. ('V Yasnoi Polyane posle revolyutsii' (In Yasnaya Polyana after the Revolution), GMT).

30 K. Arsenev, 'Khronika' (Chronicle), *VE*, nos 1–4, 1918 (the journal closed after this issue). Arsenev's review contained an analysis of the events of February–March 1918, after the dissolution of the Constituent Assembly.
31 Sofia Tolstaya drew up a domestic spiritual will (GMT).
32 Goncharov's novel *Obyknovennaya istoriya* (An ordinary story), 1847.
33 Everything at Yasnaya Polyana was declared public property, inventoried and taken under the protection of the government. See the text of the 'Document of Protection' of May 27, 1919, and V.A. Zhdanov's article 'Yasnaya Polyana v pervye gody revolyutsii' (Yasnaya Polyana in the early years of the Revolution') (*Yasn. Sb.*, 1962, pp. 26–7).
34 Sergei Tolstoy was reading his reminiscences 'Turgenev v Yasnoi Polyane' (Turgenev in Yasnaya Polyana), published in *GM*, nos 1–4, 1919. These reminiscences were included in the text of S.L. Tolstoy.
35 P.I. Biryukov had been working from 1909 on the third volume of his *Biography of Lev Nikolaevich Tolstoy*. The volume was published in Berlin in 1921; 2nd edn, Gosizdat, 1923.
36 See Daily Diary, 1915, note 29.
37 Ovid's poem (translated by A.P. Barykova), in *PSS*, vol. 41, pp. 511–13. The *Circle of Reading* contains extensive quotes from the sayings of Socrates, as well as 'The Trial of Socrates and His Defence' (from Plato's *Apology*) (ibid., pp. 348–51).
38 There is no precise information about Sofia Stakhovich's work on the manuscripts of *War and Peace* – it is possible that she was working on an analysis of them. Thus Sofia Tolstaya wrote on October 29, 1917 to Sergei Tolstoy, who was planning to systematise his father's manuscripts: 'But you evidently have a very hazy notion of what a vast and complicated job this is. For instance the manuscripts of *War and Peace*, which were once left in a ditch, and were all stuffed anyhow into two drawers. They're all scraps and cuttings, and it's hard to think how to put them in order. It's inconceivable that one could do it on one's own' (GMT). For the volumes of *War and Peace* (*PSS*, vols 9–12) S.A. Stakhovich translated texts from other languages and assisted greatly in taking copies from the manuscripts (see *PSS*, vol. 13, p. 7).
39 N.V. Davydov wrote in a letter of January 4, 1919: 'On the instructions of Aleksandra Lvovna and the editorial commission of the Tolstoy publishing company I have prepared Lev Nikolaevich's comedy *The Infected Family* for publication, correcting the errors in the names and providing several versions of one of them. But an introductory article (a short one) still needs to be written, describing the times in which the comedy was written, and if possible some details of its publication and subsequent fate' (GMT). Sofia Tolstaya's reply is not known.

1919

1 N.V. Gogol, *Dead Souls*. (See *Sochineniya i pisma* (Works and letters), vol. 4, St Petersburg, 1857; Tolstoy's notes.)
2 *Vospominaniya o L.N. Tolstom uchenika yasnopolyanskoi shkoly Vasiliya Stepanovicha Morozova* (Reminiscences of Tolstoy by Vasilii Stepanovich Morozov, a pupil at the Yasnaya Polyana School), edited and annotated by P.A. Sergeenko, Moscow, Intermediary, with the date 'July 12, 1917' under I.I. Gorbunov's introduction. V. Morozov was Tolstoy's 'favourite pupil' and appeared as Fedka in his story 'Komu u kogo uchitsya pisat, krenstyanskim rebyatam u nas, ili nam u krestyanskikh rebyat?' (Who should teach whom to write, should we teach the peasant children, or should they teach us?) Tolstoy found a 'genuine creative talent' in him (*PSS*, vol. 8, p. 306). Tolstoy wrote an introduction to Morozov's story in 1908 (*PSS*, vol. 37).
3 *Count Lev Nikolaevich Tolstoy's Letters to His Wife* (1915 edition). P.A. Sergeenko presented it to Sofia Tolstaya with the inscription: 'To Countess Sofia Andreevna Tolstaya (for her comments),

Let these bygone missives
Transport you to the past,
Kindle memories in your soul
And melt them into legends
For the instruction of others.

P. Sergeenko, Yasnaya Polyana, XI. 4'

Between the pages were pasted some blank sheets of paper, for additions, corrections and observations. The title page bore a note saying, 'I have started making new notes from January 4, 1919, Countess Sofia Tolstaya' (Sofia Tolstaya's Library). Her notes were extensive and detailed, referring to facts about Tolstoy's life, recalling judgements of his, information about the way several of his works were written, and descriptions of his children, friends and guests at Yasnaya Polyana. Only a part of this valuable material was used; the notes to vols 83 and 84 of *PSS* (Tolstoy's letters to his wife).

4 I.L. Tolstoy, *Moi vospominaniya* (My memoirs), Moscow, 1914.

5 'K politicheskim deyatelyam' (To political activists), 1903, an article by Tolstoy (*PSS*, vol. 35), which appeared as a separate edition in London, Free Word publishing house.

6 Sergeenko's assumptions were without any foundation, and contradicted the government's decision about the inviolability of Yasnaya Polyana. See Daily Diary, 1918, notes 2 and 23. A children's home was to be built in Telyatinki.

7 Sofia Tolstaya's request was inspired by the Commissariat of Education's decision to take stock of all the books on the market, in view of the dearth of books in the country. All the publishing houses had to provide information about editions sold and in stock. Her request was granted. See Diary entries for February 3 and 8.

8 On February 2 Sofia Tolstaya and Tatiana Sukhotina sent the following appeal to the directors of the Yasnaya Polyana Society (see Daily Diary, 1918, note 27): 'Being unable to continue running the Yasnaya Polyana estate on our own, and to maintain in their proper state the grounds and house in which Tolstoy lived and worked, and fearing that these may lapse into decay and dilapidation, we consider that the best solution in the present circumstances would be to hand over the management of the estate and the entire property to the Yasnaya Polyana Society in Memory of L.N. Tolstoy. In view of this we are appealing to the Society to take on the management of the Yasnaya Polyana property.' The proposal was accepted at a general meeting of Society members, and the running of the estate was entrusted to N.L. Obolenskii. At the end of March the Society petitioned the Soviet government to allow them to take on the management of Yasnaya Polyana (E.D. Vysokomirnyi, *Yasnaya Polyana v gody revolyutsii* (Yasnaya Polyana in the years of the Revolution), Moscow/Leningrad, 1928, pp. 20–1). On May 27 the Commissariat of Agriculture issued a decree ordering that the estate be handed over 'to its control and in accordance with its instructions' (*Lev Tolstoi, Materialy i publikatsii* (Lev Tolstoy. Materials and publications), Tula, 1958, p. 10). Yasnaya Polyana remained under the control of the Society until June 1921, when the Executive Committee of the Party passed a resolution to nationalise it.

9 On February 24 the management committee of the Society appealed to the Soviet of People's Commissars for an extended loan in order to carry out various measures needed to turn Yasnaya Polyana into a state cultural and educational centre. The Soviet government assigned the money to carry out the projected changes.

10 G. Flaubert, *Madame Bovary*, translated from French, reprinted from the journal *Biblioteka dlya chteniya* (Library for reading), no. 8, 1858, YaPL.

11 A.I. Kuprin, *Sochineniya* (Works), vol. IV, Moscow, 1908 (YaPL).

12 A reference to her book *Friends and Guests at Yasnaya Polyana*. It was not yet in print. (It was published in 1923 by the Kolos (Wheat ear) publishing house.)

13 V. Doroshevich, 'Sofia Tolstaya', *RS*, no. 251, October 31, 1910.

14 Work unknown.
15 'Ioann Damaskin' (Johannes Damascenus), a poem by A.K. Tolstoy.
16 Sergei Tolstoy was sorting out and systematising his father's diaries, and preparing them for the planned collected works. See Daily Diary, 1918, note 23.
17 'The official service and merit list of ensign Count Tolstoy, assigned to the 12th St Petersburg rocket brigade', published in V. Fyodorov's article 'L.N. Tolstoi v voennoi sluzhbe' (L.N. Tolstoy in military service), in the journal *Bratskaya pomoshch* (Fraternal Aid), no. 12, 1910, pp. 41–4.
18 In this letter, enclosed in an envelope with the inscription 'To be opened after my death', Sofia Tolstaya wrote: 'The circle of my life is closing, I am slowly dying, and to all those with whom I have lived, recently and in the past, I want to say farewell and forgive me.

'Farewell my dear children whom I love so much, especially my daughter Tanya, whom I love more than anyone else on earth – I beg her to forgive me for all the pain I have caused her.

'Sasha too – forgive me for not giving you enough love, and thank you for your kindness to me in recent days.

'Forgive me, sister Tanya, for being unable, despite my unchanging love for you, to comfort you and make things a little easier for you when your life was so lonely and hard. I beg Kolya to forgive me for being unkind to him occasionally. Whatever may have happened, I should have realised how difficult his life was, and have been more charitable towards him. Forgive me, all you who have served me throughout my life, and thank you for your services. And for you, my dearest, precious, dearly beloved granddaughter Tanyushka, I have very special feelings. You have made my life so happy. Farewell, my darling! Be happy, I thank you for all your love and tenderness towards me. Do not forget your granny, who loves you so much, S. Tolstaya.' (Quoted in S.L. Tolstoy, p. 270.)
19 *Mezhdunarodnyi Tolstovskii almanakh, sostavlennyi P. Sergeenko. O Tolstom* (International Tolstoy Almanac, compiled by P. Sergeenko. About Tolstoy), Moscow, 1909.
20 The text of the will is unknown.
21 *Father Sergei* (1890–8), an unfinished work of Tolstoy's (*PSS*, vol. 31).
22 Denikin's offensive on the southern front, which started in July 1919, and the departure of the Red Army, put the central region of Russia in peril. The troops grouped in the village of Yasnaya Polyana had been quartered there for military manoeuvres against the volunteer army which was marching in the direction Kursk–Oryol–Tula–Moscow.
23 On October 8 there was an extraordinary meeting of the directors of the Yasnaya Polyana Society, which Tatiana Sukhotina attended. In an appeal addressed to the Soviet of People's Commissars they wrote: 'The battles approaching from the South raise alarming questions about the fate of L.N. Tolstoy's former estate at Yasnaya Polyana – his house, his grave, his library and all the things that are historically connected to the great writer's life [. . .] may fall into the range of battle and be irrevocably destroyed [. . .] ' The presidium of the Party Executive Committee then stated that they 'accepted this appeal and [. . .] would send it to the Revolutionary Military Committee Council [. . .] so that all possible measures could be taken' (Vysokomirnyi, *Yasnaya Polyana in the Years of the Revolution*, pp. 25–7). The day after this statement troops were despatched from Yasnaya Polyana, and news of this was sent to Denikin's headquarters. In this way the danger to Yasnaya Polyana was averted.
24 The seizure of Kursk by Denikin's army was accompanied by terror and excesses.
25 In reply to a letter from N.V. Davydov (which is unknown), Sofia Tolstaya wrote: 'I cannot be sure exactly when Lev Nikolaevich had the idea of writing "Polikushka", as this was before my marriage, but I remember that he gave me the story to copy shortly after I had arrived in Yasnaya Polyana. He based the character of Polikushka on a Yasnaya servant. The lady, my sister Tatiana Andreevna and I have decided, was based on Countess Elizaveta Aleksandrovna Tolstaya, whom I have never seen, however. She was the sister of

Tatiana Aleksandrovna Ergolskaya, and she lived at her estate in Pokrovskoe, in Chern district' (GMT).

26 Davydov's letter is unknown. Davydov was the author of the article 'Lev Nikolaevich Tolstoi i sud' (Lev Nikolaevich Tolstoy and the law), for the journal *Yuridicheskii vestnik* (Legal Herald) no. 3, 1913, in which Tolstoy's attitude to the law is discussed in terms of his journalistic writings and his novel *Resurrection*. Davydov was evidently intending to continue his research into this question in a biographical form.

27 'The organisers of the Yasnaya Polyana Society devoted several meetings to a discussion of questions that arose in connection with relations between P.A. Sergeenko and the members of L.N. Tolstoy's family [. . .] Sofia Andreevna never complained about anyone or anything, and never grumbled. The only thing that troubled her was Sergeenko's impertinence' (Vysokomirnyi, *Yasnaya Polyana in the Years of the Revolution*, pp. 29, 30).

28 In October 1919 the Red Army won a series of victories over Denikin's army: Oryol was taken, and Voronezh, and the danger threatening Tula and Yasnaya Polyana was averted.

29 On June 13, 1921 the Presidium of the All-Russian Central Executive Committee passed a resolution about the nationalisation of Yasnaya Polyana, and it was declared a 'national property of the RSFSR' (*Yasn. sb.*, 1972, p. 6). In the years of Soviet power Yasnaya Polyana has been converted into a cultural and historical monument of national and international significance.

APPENDICES

Our Trip to Troitsa

1 Lyubov Aleksandrovna Behrs, Sofia Tolstaya's cousin.

2 Lyubov Aleksandrovna Behrs, Sofia Tolstaya's mother.

3 Elizaveta Andreevna Behrs, Sofia Tolstaya's elder sister and Elizaveta Aleksandrovna Behrs, a cousin.

4 Aleksandr Andreevich Behrs, Sofia Tolstaya's elder brother.

L.N. Tolstoy's Marriage

1 Tatiana Kuzminskaya describes A.M. Islenev in chapter 3 of her memoirs (Kuzminskaya, pp. 33–7).

2 Islenev's daughters from his second marriage were called Aglaya (Adèle), Olga and Natalya.

3 Maria Nikolaevna Tolstaya separated from her husband, V.P. Tolstoy, in 1857, then went abroad and spent the next two winters in Algeria; she returned to Russia from Switzerland in the summer of 1862.

4 Zaseka was a huge strip of crown forest adjacent to Yasnaya Polyana, some one half to four miles wide, running through the whole of Tula province. (In the sixteenth and seventeenth centuries the trees in this forest were chopped down to make barricades against the onslaughts of the Tartars.)

5 Natalya Petrovna Okhotnitskaya.

6 The 'room under the vaults' had many different functions over the years. From the end of 1862 to 1864 it was Tolstoy's study, where he wrote the beginning of *War and Peace*; between 1864 and the 1880s it was the older children's nursery, then the Tolstoys' sons' room; between 1887 and 1902 it was Tolstoy's study again; and from 1902 onwards Tolstoy's daughters lived here. See N.P. Puzin, *Dom muzei L.N. Tolstogo v Yasnoi Polyane. Ocherk-putevoditel* (The Tolstoy House Museum at Yasnaya Polyana. An essay and guide), Moscow, 1971, pp. 74–8.

7 Evdokia Nikolaevna Bannikova, married name Orekhova.

8 Aleksei Stepanovich Orekhov.
9 Nikolai Dmitrievich Bannikov.
10 After the death of his first wife Sofia Petrovna Kozlovskaya (in 1830), Aleksandr Mikhailovich Islenev gambled away his Krasnoe estate at cards (see Kuzminskaya, p. 114).
11 Sofia Petrovna Kozlovskaya.
12 Sofia Petrovna Kozlovskaya had six children by Aleksandr Mikhailovich Islenev.
13 Elizaveta Aleksandrovna Ergolskaya.
14 Tolstoy was actively involved in pedagogical work throughout 1859 to 1862. Twenty-one schools were opened in his district from the autumn of 1861 on, with him serving as arbitrator. Students banned from the universities were invited by Tolstoy to teach there, and he himself held classes for peasant children at Yasnaya Polyana. For details see Gusev, *Materialy*, II, chapters 7, 9 and 10, and *PSS*, vol. 8.
15 *Yasnaya Polyana. Shkola. Zhurnal pedagogicheskii, izdavaemyi gr. L.N. Tolstym* (Yasnaya Polyana School. A pedagogical journal published by Count L.N. Tolstoy); first appeared in 1862, nos 1–12 (the last issue appeared in March 1863).
16 Between July 6 and 7, while Tolstoy was away in Samara province taking the *kumis* cure, Yasnaya Polyana was searched on the orders of police chief V.A. Dolgorukov. They were looking for a secret printing press, banned works and so on, but they did not find anything incriminating. When he learnt about the search Tolstoy was extremely angry. 'I keep telling myself,' he wrote to Aleksandra Tolstaya on August 7, 1862, 'what a blessing it was that I wasn't there. If I had I would certainly have been arrested – as a murderer' (*PSS*, vol. 60, p. 438).

In his letter to Alexander II (August 22), Tolstoy wrote that he would like to know 'who was to blame for what occurred' so that 'they could be if not punished, then at least publicly exposed as guilty' (ibid., p. 441). The letter was submitted by Tolstoy via S.A. Sheremetev, aide-de-camp to the Tsar. Dolgorukov's explanation for this business completely satisfied the Tsar.
17 In young Sofia Behrs' story 'Natasha' there were two heroes, Dublitskii and Smirnov, and a heroine called Elena, who had two sisters, the elder called Zinaida and the younger Natalya. The story tells of the pure love between Elena and Smirnov and her attraction for Dublitskii, a man considerably older than she. See 'Povest Soni' (Sonya's story) in Kuzminskaya, pp. 101–2. Tolstoy made this note about the story on August 26, 1862 (*PSS*, vol. 48, p. 41). Sofia Tolstaya later regretted that she had burnt it.
18 On August 23, 1863, Tolstoy too made his first note in his diary about his feelings for Sofia Behrs. 'I am afraid of myself – afraid it may be the desire for love, not love itself. I try to see only her weaknesses, but it won't go away' (*PSS*, vol. 48, p. 40) But in a letter to Aleksandra Tolstaya he humorously confessed: 'Toothless old fool that I am, I have fallen in love' (*PSS*, vol. 60, p. 444).
19 See *PSS*, vol. 48, pp. 44–5.
20 See *PSS*, vol. 83, pp. 16–17.
21 O.D. Zaikovskaya.
22 She is referring to negotiations with the Petersburg publisher F.T. Stellovskii over his publication of the *Sobranie sochinenii Tolstogo* (Collected works of Tolstoy). The negotiations on this occasion were unsuccessful, and only in 1864 did Stellovskii bring out his *Sochineniya grafa L.N. Tolstogo v dvukh tomakh* (Works of Count L.N. Tolstoy in two volumes).
23 Compare with this note in Tolstoy's diary: '[. . .]doubts about her love, and the thought that she has deceived herself [. . .] On the wedding day fear, distrust and the desire to run away' (*PSS*, vol. 48, p. 46).
24 The Behrs' apartment was situated in the Kremlin, in the building of the 'Ordonnanzhaus' (the administration of army quarters).
25 *Anna Karenina*, part 5, chapters 1 to 6.

26 Mitrofan Andreevich Polivanov (see Diary, 1862, note 1).
27 Stepanida Trifonovna Ivanova, the housekeeper.
28 Sofia Tolstaya's first letter from Yasnaya Polyana, of September 25, 1862, has been kept. 'I haven't managed to look around properly yet,' she wrote to her sister Tanya. 'It still feels strange that Yasnaya is now my home' (GMT). This was the first letter she 'solemnly signed Countess Sonya Tolstaya'.
29 See Tolstoy's diary notes: 'Unbelievable happiness. She is writing beside me again. It cannot be that this will last all our lives' (*PSS*, vol. 48, p. 46).

'arious Notes for Future Reference

1 A.S. Pushkin, *Sochineniya* (Works), with additional material for a biography – portraits, and photographs of his handwriting and his drawings. Vol. I, St Petersburg, published by P.V. Annenkov, 1855 (YaPL).
2 Tolstoy wrote to Fet on August 30, 1869, that he had 'ordered all the works' of Schopenhauer, 'had read them and was still reading them', and was 'endlessly delighted' by them. 'I am sure that Schopenhauer is the greatest genius of all' (*PSS*, vol. 61, p. 219).
3 Tolstoy considered Hegel a 'weak thinker' (see *PSS*, vol. 48, p. 345), but in a letter to N.N. Strakhov he admitted that in reading extracts from Hegel he 'hadn't understood a word of it' (*PSS*, vol. 61, p. 348).
4 This idea came to Tolstoy at the time he was still writing *War and Peace*, and after he had finished the novel he worked hard on his *ABC*, which came out in 1872.
5 There exists a rough draft of Tolstoy's notes for this proposed novel, whose heroes were to be people 'with the characters of Russian folk heroes' (see *PSS*, vol. 90, pp. 109–10). The idea of this novel continued to interest him throughout that year, as evidenced by his note on Ilya Muromets and his comrades in his notebook, December 30, 1870 (*PSS*, vol. 48, p. 90). For more details see E. Zaidenschnur, 'Rabota L.N. Tolstogo nad russkimi bylinami' (Tolstoy's work on Russian folk epics), in *Russkii folklor. Materialy i issledovaniya* (Russian folklore. Materials and research), Moscow–Leningrad, 1960, pp. 329–66.
6 In a letter of February 4 Tolstoy announced to Fet: 'I have been reading a great deal of Shakespeare, Goethe, Pushkin, Gogol and Molière, and very much want to talk to you about it all' (*PSS*, vol. 61, pp. 226–7). Also of this period is a note of Tolstoy's on a separate piece of paper – some reflections on drama and comedy, on tragedy, and on *Boris Godunov*, which he considered 'weak' (*PSS*, vol. 48, p. 344).
7 The plan was never realised.
8 Sofia Tolstaya later added a postscript to this note in her Diary: 'His praise for Shakespeare was short-lived. At heart he has never liked him, and always says: "This is just between us, mind".' See Tolstoy's article 'O Shekspire i o drame' (On Shakespeare and drama', 1903–4 (*PSS*, vol. 35).
9 *Istoriya tsarstvovaniya Petra Velikogo* (A history of Peter the Great), N.G. Ustryalov's unfinished work, which took him twenty-three years: vols I–III (1858); vol. VI (1859) and vol. IV (1863).
10 His note about Lieutenant V.M. Mirovich, which he wanted to turn into a play, has not been kept.
11 On this day Tolstoy wrote a first draft of his novel on the Peter I period. This work continued with one interruption until 1873. All this time Tolstoy was studying the period, and he wrote twenty-five versions of the first chapter. The work was interrupted for almost five years while he wrote *Anna Karenina*. In 1879 Tolstoy returned to it once again, and wrote another eight versions of the beginning. The novel remained unfinished (*PSS*, vol. 17).
12 This is the first reference to *Anna Karenina*, which Tolstoy started writing in 1873. See note 26.

13 The journal *Zarya* (Dawn), which the editors sent to Tolstoy free of charge, published four articles by Nikolai Strakhov on *War and Peace* (nos 1–3, 1969; no. 1, 1870). The articles were published separately under the title N.N. Strakhov, *Kriticheskii razbor* Voiny i Mira (Critical analysis of *War and Peace*), St Petersburg, 1871; they were reprinted in the anthology: N.N. Strakhov, *Kriticheskie stati ob I.S. Turgeneve i L.N. Tolstom* (Critical articles on I.S. Turgenev and L.N. Tolstoy), St Petersburg, 1885. Sofia Tolstaya wrote in *MZh* (book 2, p. 261): 'Lev Nikolaevich said that Strakhov in his article had attached to *War and Peace* the great significance that it would acquire later, and which it would retain for ever afterwards.' See also Sofia Tolstaya, 'Avtobiografiya' (Autobiography), in *Nachala* (Beginnings), no. 1, 1921, p. 147.

14 The German paper *Moskauer Deutsche Zeitung* was sent to Yasnaya Polyana by F.F. Ries, proprietor of a Moscow printshop, where the first two editions of *War and Peace* and *Anna Karenina* were printed.

15 The beginning of this novel has not been kept.

16 In a letter to Fet of November 17, 1870, Tolstoy wrote: 'You simply cannot imagine how hard I found this preliminary work, ploughing deep furrows in the field I must sow' (*PSS*, vol. 61, p. 240).

17 Tolstoy spent several days in Moscow; he stayed in the hotel Rossiya, on the Kuznetskii Most.

18 Sergei Tolstoy later recalled his lessons with his father: 'He would sometimes shout and lose his temper, especially during lesson times, but I do not remember him ever swearing; the only thing that ever happened was that he would dismiss me from the room' (S.L. Tolstoy, p. 88).

19 In the winter of 1870 Tolstoy was fascinated by Greek and in three or four months had mastered the language to the point where he could without difficulty 'read Xenophon without a lexicon', and after that 'Homer and Plato' (see his letter to S.S. Urusov, December 29–31, 1870 – *PSS*, vol. 61, p. 245). He continued to read classical Greek throughout 1871 too, and on February 13 he wrote jokingly to Fet: 'I am living in Athens at present. I speak Greek in my sleep at nights' (ibid., p. 249).

20 Books I–IV of the *ABC* (see *PSS*, vol. 22).

21 The *ABC* 'failure' was due to several reasons. The tsarist administration was suspicious of Tolstoy's pedagogical activities and the Ministry of Education would not allow the *ABC* to be used as a textbook in schools (see *PSS*, vol. 61, pp. 338–40). Some sharply negative reviews of it appeared in the press. As a result of this and the book's high price it did not sell. To make it easier to sell it was broken up into twelve booklets: four Russian readers, four Slavonic readers, two arithmetic books and a 'Teacher's Guide'. But this did not help, and in 1875 Tolstoy started to re-work the *ABC* (*PSS*, vol. 21, pp. 547–94).

Although the *ABC*'s failure 'annoyed and upset' Tolstoy, he remained convinced that '*exegi monumentum* ['I have erected a monument' – title of famous Pushkin poem] with this *ABC*', and that '10 years from now it will be appreciated by the children who are studying from it' (*PSS*, vol. 61, p. 349; vol. 62, p. 9).

22 In a letter to P.D. Golokhvastov of December 6, 1872, Tolstoy named thirteen books on the Peter I period which he wanted (see *PSS*, vol. 61, p. 341), and at the same time he bought seven books in Moscow on account (*PSS*, vol. 17, pp. 629–30). Tolstoy made a similar request to Golokhvastov in January 1873 (see his letter of January 24 – *PSS*, vol. 62, pp. 5–6).

23 While he was working on the Peter I period Tolstoy read the following books: I.E. Zabelin, *Domashnii byt russkogo naroda XVI i XVII st.* (The home life of the Russian people in the sixteenth and seventeeth centuries), vol. 1, part 1, Moscow, 1862; vol. 2, Moscow, 1869. And G.K. Kotoshikhin, *O Rossii v tsarstvovanie Alekseya Mikhailovicha* (Russia in the reign of Aleksei Mikhailovich), St Petersburg, 1840.

24 In a letter to Fet, of January 30, 1873, Tolstoy complained: 'Work has started – it's

frightfully difficult. There is no end to the preparatory research involved, the plan keeps getting bigger and I feel I have less and less strength for it' (*PSS*, vol. 62, p. 8). We find the last reference to Tolstoy's work on a novel of the Peter I period in a letter to Fet of March 17, 1873: 'My work is not progressing' (ibid., p. 15).

In explaining why the novel was not finished, Tolstoy referred to the 'distance in time', to the fact that 'Tsar Peter was very far removed from him', and so on. The main reason was evidently that Tolstoy grew disillusioned with both Peter's personality and his government activity (see Gusev, *Materialy*, III, pp. 127–32).

25 Evidently an excerpt from 'In 179– I returned to Livonia' (A.S. Pushkin, *Works*, vol. 5, St Petersburg, 1855, pp. 517–18).

26 On March 18, 1873 Tolstoy started to write his novel *Anna Karenina*. In a letter to Strakhov of March 25, 1873 he wrote that the impetus for it had come from his reading of an extract from Pushkin's 'The guests were arriving at the country house' (Pushkin, *Sochineniya* (Works), vol. 5, pp. 502–6). In this letter he also announced that he had 'just finished a rough draft of the novel' (*PSS*, vol. 62, p. 16).

27 K.A. Islavin.

28 Tolstoy's family arrived at a farm in Samara on June 8. The journey was made for the sake of Tolstoy's health.

29 The Tolstoys returned from Samara to Yasnaya Polyana on August 23. For more details about the various stages of his work on *Anna Karenina*, see N.K. Gudzi's article 'Istoriya pisaniya i pechataniya *Anna Kareninoi*' (The history of the writing and publishing of *Anna Karenina*), *PSS*, vol. 20, pp. 577–643.

30 I.N. Kramskoi painted Tolstoy's portraits at Yasnaya Polyana from September 5 to October 13, 1873. He did two other portraits, one of which is now in the Tretyakov Gallery, the other at Yasnaya Polyana. He wrote to Repin on February 23, 1874 that 'Count Tolstoy, whom I have been painting, is an interesting, even rather an extraordinary man. I spent several days with him, and I confess I was in a state of great agitation throughout. He smacks of genius.' See his letter to Tolstoy of January 29, 1885, published in *Ivan Nikolaevich Kramskoi. Ego zhizn, perepiska i khudozhestvennye-kriticheskie stati* (Ivan Nikolaevich Kramskoi. His life, correspondence and articles of art criticism), St Petersburg, 1888, pp. 102, 513. Kramskoi's portrait was the first that had been painted of Tolstoy.

31 *Anna Karenina*, part 5, chapter 22, or 23 and 24.

32 Tolstoy referred to his ideas for a new novel in letters to Strakhov and Fet (of January 12 and 26, 1877 – *PSS*, vol. 62, pp. 304, 308), but it is only in Sofia Tolstaya's diary that the complete plan is revealed. In 1878 he tried to bring it to life and wrote some new openings for his unfinished novel *The Decembrists* – an account of how one of the Decembrists falls in with some emigrating peasants. See note 41 to Sofia Tolstaya's diary for January 8, 1878.

33 A.P. Bobrinskii came to Yasnaya Polyana in 1873 and expounded his views on goodness and faith in Christ.

34 His reflections about the meaning and purpose of life led Tolstoy to religion, in which he hoped to find salvation from the questions that tormented him. In a letter to Aleksandra Tolstaya (February 5–9, 1877), he wrote that for him 'the question of religion was the same sort of question as what a drowning man should grasp hold of to save him from inevitable death'; religion presented him with this 'possibility of salvation' (*PSS*, vol. 62, p. 310). In his 'Confession', written two years later, he described his search for religion, which led him to break with the teachings of the Church (*PSS*, vol. 23). In a letter to Aleksandra Tolstaya of March 3, 1882, he wrote: 'There can be nothing in common between us, because the holy faith which you profess I have professed with my whole heart and have studied with ceaseless energy, and I am now convinced that this is not faith but a vile lie, invented to destroy people' (*PSS*, vol. 63, p. 90). See Tolstoy's religious and philosophical works of 1875–8 in *PSS*, vol. 17.

35 In a letter to Fet of September 1–2, 1877, Tolstoy wrote: 'I have spent all this time hunting

around and trying to organise our teaching staff for the winter' (*PSS*, vol. 62, p. 341). In the autumn of 1877 the Tolstoys hired V.I. Alekseev to teach their children. See his memoirs about his life in the Tolstoy family in *Letopisi*, book 12, Moscow, 1948, pp. 232–325. 'Vasilii Ivanovich was the first teacher we had who genuinely wanted not only to teach us the usual subjects but to give us some sort of moral training too' wrote Sergei Tolstoy (S.L. Tolstoy, p. 59).

36 The Russo-Turkish War of 1877–8. Tolstoy suffered very much for the casualties borne by the Russian army in the early months of the war. (See his letter to N.N. Strakhov of August 10, 1887 – *PSS*, vol. 62, pp. 334–6.) 'This war upsets and grieves me inexpressibly,' he wrote to N.M. Nagornov at the beginning of September 1877 (ibid., p. 341).

37 Tolstoy and Strakhov left for the Optyna Monastery on July 25. On July 26 Tolstoy talked to Father Ambrosius and some other monks and attended vespers in the monastery. (See his letter to Sofia Tolstaya of July 26, 1877 – *PSS*, vol. 83, pp. 238–9; see also Gusev, *Materialy*, III, pp. 439–43.)

38 Tolstoy's plan to write to Alexander II about the reasons for Russia's reverses in the war with Turkey, and about the general situation at home, was eventually dropped. Instead of this he began an article 'O tsarstvovanii imperatora Aleksandra II' (On Alexander II's reign), which was never finished (*PSS*, vol. 17).

39 Seven parts of *Anna Karenina* were published in *Russian Herald*, from 1875 to 1877. The eighth part appeared as a separate volume in 1877, printed by F.F. Ries. In the summer of 1877 Tolstoy revised the journal text of the novel for a separate edition: *Anna Karenina*. Roman grafa L.N. Tolstogo v vosmi chastyakh (*Anna Karenina*. Novel by Count L.N. Tolstoy in eight parts), Moscow 1878. 'Second Edition' is written on the cover – the first edition was considered to be that published in the journal.

40 Tolstoy wrote a dialogue called 'Sobesedniki' (People talking), then tried to expound his views on the relationship between faith and reason in the form of an article (under the same title), which remained uncompleted. See *PSS*, vol. 17.

41 This entry, like that of March 3, 1877, refers to Tolstoy's renewed interest in *The Decembrists*. In letters to Tanya Kuzminskaya (January 14 and 25), Sofia Tolstaya wrote that Tolstoy was 'planning to write some historical work about the reign of Nikolai Pavlovich', and that 'it would be very good indeed, a historical novel about the Decembrists, something rather like *War and Peace*' (GMT; quoted in *PSS*, vol. 17, p. 475).

42 In Moscow, where Tolstoy went on February 8, he bought books he needed on the reigns of Alexander I and Nicholas I, he also made the acquaintance there of the Decembrists P.N. Svistunov and A.P. Belyaev, and the daughter of N.M. Muravyov, S.N. Bibikova. (See his letter to Sofia Tolstaya of February 9, 1878 – *PSS*, vol. 83, p. 242.)

43 In the autumn of 1879 Tolstoy had the idea of writing some works expounding the religious views he had formed as a result of his critical study of the Church's teachings. (See the outline plan in his notebook – *PSS*, vol. 48, p. 195.) From November to December he wrote 'Tserkov i gosudarstvo' (Church and State) (*PSS*, vol. 23), and 'Chto mozhno i chego nelzya delat khristiyaninu' (What a Christian can and cannot do) (*PSS*, vol. 90); his article 'Chi my? bogovy ili dyavolovy?' (What are we? God's or the Devil's?) remained unfinished (*PSS*, vol. 90), as did an untitled work beginning with the words: 'I have grown up, grown old and looked back on my life . . .' (published in Gusev, *Materialy*, III, pp. 592–601).

44 In February 1879 Tolstoy stopped working on his novel *The Decembrists*. On April 17 he wrote to Fet: 'God knows where my Decembrists are at present. I don't think about them at all now, and if I did think about them and write about them I flatter myself that the mere spirit with which I infused it would be intolerable for those who shoot people for the benefit of mankind' (*PSS*, vol. 62, p. 483). Gusev, *Materialy*, III, pp. 530–7.

45 In March 1880 Tolstoy started on a work entitled 'Soedinenie i perevod chetyryokh Evangelii' (Collation and translation of the four Gospels) (*PSS*, vol. 24). He formulated its contents as follows: 'An investigation of the teachings of Christ based not on

interpretation but simply on what has come down to us from the teachings of Christ, words attributed to him and written in the Gospels; a translation of the four Gospels, brought together here as one' (ibid., p. 801). This work continued off and on until the summer of 1881. First edition, vols 1–3, Geneva, published by Elpidine, 1892–4.

46 A.S. Pirogova killed herself on January 4, 1872 (information in *Tulskie gubernskie vedomosti* (Tula Provincial Herald), January 8, 1872). In April of that year A.N. Bibikov married the 'beautiful German woman', O.A. Firekel. There is some doubt about Sofia Tolstaya's assertion that it was Anna Pirogova's story that led Tolstoy to give his heroine this name, as in the rough drafts of *Anna Karenina* she bears the name Tatiana, Anastasia (Nana), and only in the fourth draft is she called Anna. See V.A. Zhdanov, *Tvorcheskaya istoriya 'Anny Kareniny'* (The creative evolution of *Anna Karenina*), Sovetskii Pisatel (Soviet Writer), Moscow, 1957, pp. 9–20.

47 Tolstoy's personal acquaintance with Turgenev began in June 1855, when Tolstoy arrived in St Petersburg from Sevastopol. Turgenev had known Maria Nikolaevna Tolstaya since October 1854. Turgenev always had a very high opinion of Tolstoy's literary talents, but closer acquaintance revealed differences of character, opinions and artistic direction, and there appeared between them what Tolstoy described as a 'gulf'. This led to a mutual coolness and eventually to a break in their personal relations for seventeen years.

48 The quarrel between Tolstoy and Turgenev took place on May 27, 1861 (see Fet's book *Moi vospominaniya* (My memoirs), part 1, Moscow, 1890, pp. 37–45, and also Gusev, *Materialy*, II, pp. 437–54.

49 See Tolstoy's correspondence with Turgenev for May to October 1861 in *Tolstoi. Perepiska*, pp. 110–12.

50 This entry has been broken off. Sofia Tolstaya wrote about Tolstoy's reconciliation with Turgenev on August 12, 1878.

51 Tolstoy's letter of April 6, 1878 (*PSS*, vol. 62, pp. 406–7). Turgenev's reply of May 20, 1878 (I. Turgenev, *Pisma* (Letters), vol. XII, book 1, p. 323). Turgenev expressed the hope that he would be 'visiting Oryol that summer' and would see Tolstoy.

52 There is no information about Turgenev's telegram. Turgenev's letter of August 4 has been kept. In this he wrote that he would be in Tula on Monday, August 8, and asked Tolstoy where they could meet – there or in Yasnaya Polyana (Turgenev, *op. cit.*, vol. XII, book 1, p. 340). On August 8 Tolstoy met Turgenev in Tula, they returned together to Yasnaya Polyana, and Turgenev spent two days there.

53 M.N. Antokolskii's sculpture *Khristos pered sudom naroda* (Christ before the people's court). Bronze copy (1874), in the Russian State Museum, marble duplicate (1876) there and in the Tretyakov Gallery.

54 This episode was recorded in Tatiana Sukhotina-Tolstaya's memoirs *Zarnitsy pamyati* (A summer lightning of memories) and *Kto boitsya smerti?* (Who is afraid to die?). (See T.L. Sukhotina, pp. 432–3.)

55 Turgenev stayed in Yasnaya Polyana from September 2 to 4. 'Turgenev stayed with us on his way back,' Tolstoy wrote to Fet on September 1878. 'He is exactly the same, and we now know the degree of intimacy that is possible between us' (*PSS*, vol. 62, p. 441).

The Death of Vanechka

1 An abridged version of the chapter 'The Death of Vanechka', from Sofia Tolstaya's *My Life* (*MZh*).

2 *Doch katorzhnika* (The convict's daughter), after Charles Dickens' novel *Great Expectations*, in a version by Varvara Sergeevna Tolstaya, Intermediary, no. 185, Moscow, 1895.

3 The exact text of this note in Tolstoy's diary on February 26 was: 'We buried Vanechka. A terrible – no, not a terrible, a great spiritual experience. I thank thee Father. I thank thee' (*PSS*, vol. 53, p. 10).

4 Letter to Tatiana Kuzminskaya of March 7, 1895 (GMT).
5 In November 1932 the cemetery was demolished and the remains of the Tolstoy children were transferred to the Kochakov cemetery, two miles from Yasnaya Polyana.
6 Both of Kasatkin's studies (of the graves of Tolstoy's children Aleksei and Ivan, at Nikolskoe cemetery) have been kept; one, in oils on canvas, is in Sofia Tolstaya's room, the other, on board, is in the Tolstoy Estate Museum in Moscow, in Tatiana Sukhotina's room. It was probably with reference to this study that Kasatkin wrote to her, on March 5, 1895: 'I sympathise deeply with Sofia Andreevna and am very pleased that she likes my study. It must not be given away without altering certain details – it would be most undesirable to leave it as it is. I have decided to copy it, with a few alterations, on to board, then give them both to you together.' Quoted from the book, K.A. Sitnik, *Nikolai Alekseevich Kasatkin. Zhizn i tvorchestvo* (Nikolai Alekseevich Kasatkin. Life and work), Moscow, 1955, pp. 157–8. An autographed copy is at the GMT.
7 There is no copy of N.A. Kasatkin's letter at the GMT.
8 Letter to Tatiana Kuzminskaya, March 7, 1895 (GMT).
9 There is no copy of Menshikov's letter in Sofia Tolstaya's archive.
10 On March 2, 1895 N.N. Strakhov wrote: 'Why has this extraordinary little boy died? I have so often thought how much better it would be if I had died, rather than he! He promised much – maybe he would have inherited not only your name but your fame. What a lovely child he was – words cannot describe him! I can well imagine Sofia Andreevna's grief!' (GMT). On March 8 Tolstoy replied: 'For me this death was as significant an event as the death of my brother – maybe more so. Deaths like these (of people whom one loves especially, and who are exceptionally pure in spirit), seem to reveal the mystery of life, and this revelation is ample compensation for the loss. These were my feelings' (*PSS*, vol. 68, p. 43).
11 A.V. Zhirkevich's letter, March 13, 1895 (GMT).
12 M.A. Stakhovich's letter, March 8, 1895 (GMT).
13 O.A. Golokhvastova's letter, March 3, 1895 (GMT).
14 S.A. Filosofova's letter, February 28, 1895 (GMT).
15 A.G. Dostoyevskaya's letter, March 5, 1895 (GMT).
16 Vanechka's story 'Spasyonny Taks' (Taks who was saved), in the journal *Igrushechka* (The toy) in the section 'Dlya malyutok' (For little ones), no. 3, 1895. Sofia Tolstaya described how it came to be written: 'One day, lying on the ottoman in the drawing room, he said to me: "Maman, I'm bored, I want to write like Papa. I'll tell you a story and you write it down." And he proceeded to dictate to me such a clever little story about his own childish life, which he called "Taks Who Was Saved"!' (*MZh*).
17 A.N. Peshkova-Toliverova's letter of March 5, 1895 (GMT).
18 Her letter to Tatiana Kuzminskaya, March 27, 1895 (GMT).
19 Sofia Tolstaya has quoted from two separate diary entries of Tolstoy for March 17. The exact text is: 'Sonya is suffering as much as before, and is incapable of rising to a spiritual level. It must be that suffering is necessary to her and is doing its work within her. I feel sorry for her. But I believe it must be thus. It is necessary, so that she may feel the hand of God, and grow to know and love it' (*PSS*, vol. 53, p. 14).

'I have thought about it recently. Sonya is suffering terribly. The reason is that she invested all her spiritual energies in her animal love for her little one: she put her soul into the child, in the desire to keep him alive. And she wanted to keep herself alive with the child, not to destroy her life for the world or God, but for her child. It's very strange' (ibid., p. 16).

20 In a letter to Tatiana Kuzminskaya of March 27 Sofia Tolstaya wrote: 'Lyovochka is being very kind to me, he takes me out for walks and has taken me to visit a political prisoner in jail [. . .] I find his kindness and affection very comforting, but it grieves me to see him becoming more and more old, bent and thin; he cries all the time, he never smiles and is

never cheerful. He is terribly unhappy about Vanechka and cannot see me' (GMT).

Sofia Tolstaya is here referring to her visit to the Butyrki prison, on March 22, to see N.T. Izyumenko, who was deported to Siberia after refusing to do military service.

1 The exact text of Tolstoy's diary entry for April 6, 1895 is as follows: 'Mashenka also became so much kinder after going into a convent. What does this mean? How can paganism be reconciled with Christianity? I cannot satisfactorily explain this to myself. What sort of a cult is this?' (*PSS*, vol. 53, p. 20).

Bibliography

Works translated from, or based on, those referred to in the Diaries, and works of general interest for further reading.

Gerald E. H. Abraham, *Tolstoy*, Duckworth, London, 1953.

Lady Cynthia Asquith, *Married to Tolstoy* (with portraits), Hutchinson, London, 1960.

John O. Bayley, *Tolstoy and the Novel*, Chatto & Windus, London, 1966.

Isaiah Berlin, *The Hedgehog and the Fox. Essays on Tolstoy's View of History*, Weidenfeld & Nicolson, London, 1953.

Sergei Andreevich Bers (= Behrs), *Recollections of Count Leo Tolstoy* (trans. Charles Edward Turner), Heinemann, London, 1893.

Pavel Ivanovich Biryukov, *Leo Tolstoy, His Life and Work. Autobiographical Memoirs, Letters and Biographical Material Compiled by P. Birukoff &C*, Heinemann, London, 1906.

—— *The Life of Tolstoy*, Heinemann, London, 1911.

Valentin Bulgakov, *The Last Year of Lev Tolstoy* (trans. Ann Dunnigan), Dial Press, New York, 1971.

Vladimir Grigorevich Chertkov, *The Last Days of Tolstoy* (trans. Nathalie A. Duddington), Heinemann, London, 1922.

Reginald F. Christian, *Tolstoy. A Critical Introduction*, Cambridge University Press, Cambridge, 1969.

John S. Collins, *Marriage and Genius. Strindberg and Tolstoy* (with portraits), Cassell, London, 1963.

Ernest H. Crosby, *Tolstoy and His Message*, Simple Life, London, 1903.

Emil J. von Dillon, *Count Leo Tolstoy. A New Portrait*, Hutchinson, London, 1934.

Anne Edwards, *Sonya. The Life of Countess Tolstoy*, Hodder & Stoughton, London, 1981.

Lily Feiler, 'The Tolstoi marriage: conflict and illusions', *Canadian Slavonic Papers*, Canadian Association of Slavists, September 1981.

Aleksandr Borisovich Goldenweiser, *Talks with Tolstoy* (trans. S. Koteliansky and V. Woolf), Hogarth, London, 1923.

Maksim Gorky, *Reminiscences of L.N. Tolstoy* (trans. S. Koteliansky and L. Woolf), Hogarth, Richmond, 1920.

Tatiana Andreevna Kuzminskaya, *Tolstoy as I Knew Him: My Life at Home and at Yasnaya Polyana* (trans. Nora Sigerist et al.), Macmillan, New York, 1948.

Aylmer Maude, *Family Views of Tolstoy*, Allen & Unwin, London, 1926.

—— *The Life of Tolstoy*, 2 vols, Oxford University Press, Oxford, 1930.

Tikhon Polner, *Tolstoy and His Wife*, New York, 1945.

N. Puzin, *Yasnaya Polyana, the Lev Tolstoy Estate Museum* (with portraits), Progress Publishers, Moscow, 1965.

Tatiana Sukhotina, *The Tolstoy Home, Diaries* (trans. Alec Brown), Harvill, London, 1950.
—— *Tolstoy Remembered* (trans. from French by Derek Coltman), McGraw Hill, New York, 1977.
Aleksandra Tolstaya, *A Life of My Father* (trans. Elizabeth Reynolds), Gollancz, London, 1954.
Sofia Tolstaya, *The Autobiography of Countess Sophie Tolstoi* (trans. S. Koteliansky and V. Woolf), Hogarth, Richmond, 1922.
—— *The Diary of Tolstoy's Wife, 1860–1891* (trans. Alexander Werth), Gollancz, London, 1928.
—— *The Countess Tolstoy's Later Diary, 1891–1897* (trans. Alexander Werth), Gollancz, London, 1929.
—— *The Final Struggle. Being Countess Tolstoy's Diary for 1910* (trans. Aylmer Maude), Allen & Unwin, London, 1936.
Ilya Lvovich Tolstoy, *Reminiscences of Tolstoy* (trans. George Calderon), Chapman & Hall, London, 1914.
Lev Lvovich Tolstoy, *The Truth About My Father*, John Murray, London, 1924.
L.N. Tolstoy, *Tolstoy's Love Letters* (ed. P.I. Biryukov, trans. S. Koteliansky and V. Woolf), Hogarth, Richmond, 1923.
—— *Tolstoy's Letters* (ed. and trans. by R. F. Christian), 2 vols, Athlone Press, London, 1978.
—— *Tolstoy's Diaries* (ed. and trans. by R. F. Christian), 2 vols, Athlone Press, London, 1985.
Sergei Lvovich Tolstoy, *Tolstoy Remembered by His Son* (trans. Moura Budberg), Weidenfeld & Nicolson, London, 1961.
Henri Troyat, *Tolstoy* (trans. Nancy Amphoux), Penguin, Harmondsworth, 1970.

Index

Name Index

Figures in italics refer to the notes

Vatatsi, Maria (née Mertvago), 'Bygone Days' 735, *975 n.22*
Veleminsky, Karl ('the journalist') (1880–1934), Czech pedagogue *945 n.49, 959 n.85*
Velichkina, Vera Mikhailovna (married name Bonch-Bruevich) (1868–1918), doctor, writer, revolutionary 172, *895 n.3*
Vengerov, Semyon Afanasevich (1855–1920), historian of literature, bibliographer 740–1, 747, 753, *976 n.41, 47, 979 n.22, 26*
Verdi, Giuseppe (1813–1901), Italian composer 298
Veresaev, V.V., writer, *Tales of War* 604, *939 n.18*
Verhaeren, Emile (1855–1919), Belgian symbolist poet 248
Verigin, Pyotr Vasilevich (1862–1924), leader of the Dukhobors from 1886 613–14
Verne, Jules (1828–1905) French writer, *Twenty Thousand Leagues Under the Sea 896 n.1*
Vertinskii, Aleksandr Nikolaevich (1889–1957), actor 775, *984 n.4*
Veselitskaya-Bozhidarovich, Lidia Ivanovna (pseudonym, V. Mikulich) (1857–1936), writer 179–80, 373–4
Veselova-Ilstedt, M.G., *The Kolychev Patrimony* 761, *980 n.49*
Viardot, Michelle Pauline (1821–1910), French singer 706
Vinogradov, Dmitrii Antipovich (1886–1958), artist 696
Vinogradov, Ivan Mikhailovich *913 n.10*
Visnev, V.A., architect 766
Vladimirov, S.A. marshal of the Oryol Nobility 606
Vlasov, Mikhail, Yasnaya Polyana peasant *945 n.53, 959 n.78*
Volkhonskiis, the 741
Volkhovskaya (Volkhonskaya) (née Zvegintseva), daughter of A.E. Zvegintseva 596
Volkonskii, Nikolai Sergeevich (1715–84), Tolstoy's grandfather 71, 390, 827
Volkov, Dmitrii Nikitich, member of the educational Yasnaya Polyana Society in Memory of L. N. Tolstoy 692, 794, 797, 800, 802, 809, 817
Volkov, Efim Efimovich, artist 616, 622
Volkov, Konstantin Vasilevich (1871–1938), *zemstvo* doctor in the Yalta district 418, 428, 434, 436–7, 448
Volkov, Nikola Nikolaevich (1839–1909), landowner in the Chern district 37
Volkovs, family of K. V. Volkov 417, 448
Volzhskii, A.S., 'On Truth and Falsehood (on the question of L. N. Tolstoy's Family Discord)' 782, *986 n.37, 38*
Vorontsov-Dashkov, Illarion Ivanovich (1837–1916), Minister of the Imperial Court and its Principalities 728, *894 n.104*
Vsesvyatskii ('the student') *945 n.44*
Vsevolozhskii, Ivan Aleksandrovich (1835–1909), Director of the Imperial Theatres 130, 171, 416
Vsevolozhskii, Mikhail Vladimirovich (1860–1909), friend of Sergei Lvovich Tolstoy 122
Vysokomirnyi, E.D., secretary of the Yasnaya Polyana Society in Memory of L. N. Tolstoy (1917–19) 798–9, 809, 811–12, 815, 817, *989–90 n.30, 11, 993 n.8*

Wagner, Richard (1813–83), German composer 300, 305
Ward, Mrs Humphry (1851–1920) English novelist, *Marcella* 176, *896 n.3*
Weber, Carl Maria von (1786–1826), German composer 56, 62, 410, 416, 590, 612, 707, 713, 753–4, 760, 813
Wells, Herbert George (1866–1946), English writer 787
Welsh, Anna, English music teacher to A. L. and S. A. Tolstaya 207, 260, 261, 263, 287, 297, 308, 342, 376, 405, 407, 760, 800, 806
Westerlund, Ernest Teodor (1839–1924), father of Dora Tolstaya 316, 321–2, 324–5
Westerlund, Nina (née Oluderus) (1839–1922), mother of Dora Tolstaya 316, 322
Williams, Howard, *The Ethics of Diet 892 n.84*
Wipper, nun 395
Witte, Sergei Yulevich (1849–1916), in 1898 Minister of Finances 283
Wright, C. Hagberg (1862–1940s) *923 n.7*
Wulf, Ekaterina Nikolaevna, Moscow friend of the Tolstoys 240, 241

Yakubovskii, V., *Positive Peasant Types in the Early Works of L. N. Tolstoy, and the Image of Karataev* 750, *978 n.4*
Yanzhul, Ivan Ivanovich (1845–1914), economist 399, *916 n.16*
Yartsev, Aleksandr Viktorovich (1850–*c.* 1919) 220
Yasinskii, Ieronim Ieronimovich (1850–1931), writer 422, *918 n.3*
Yavorskaya, L.B. *945 n.57*
Yazykova, doctor's assistant 693
Yazykovs, the, friends of the Tolstoys from Tula province 595
Yunge, Aleksandr Eduardovich 373, 605
Yunge, Ekaterina Fyodorovna (née Tolstaya) (1843–1913), artist, Tolstoy's first cousin once removed 305, 373, 387, 523, 605, 631, 645, 660, 664, 666, 668, 687, 689–90, 694, 700, 733, 737, *940 n.20, 966 n.65; Reminiscences* 700, 704, 717
Yuon, Konstantin Fyodorovich (1875–1958), artist 815
Yurev, Sergei Andreevich (1921–88), writer, translator, editor of the journal *Russian Thought* (1880–5) 853

Subject Index

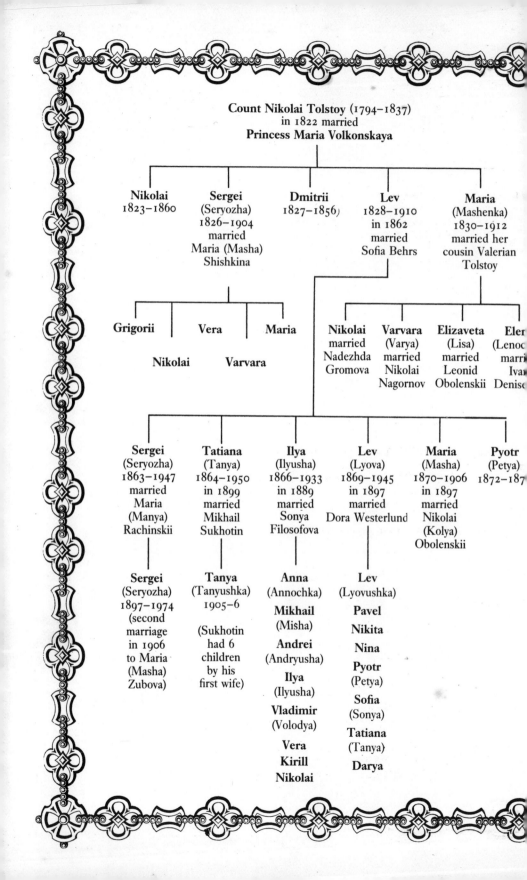

Count Nikolai Tolstoy (1794–1837)
in 1822 married
Princess Maria Volkonskaya

- **Nikolai** 1823–1860
- **Sergei** (Seryozha) 1826–1904 married Maria (Masha) Shishkina
  - **Grigorii**
  - **Nikolai**
  - **Vera**
  - **Varvara**
  - **Maria**
- **Dmitrii** 1827–1856)
- **Lev** 1828–1910 in 1862 married Sofia Behrs
  - **Sergei** (Seryozha) 1863–1947 married Maria (Manya) Rachinskii
    - **Sergei** (Seryozha) 1897–1974 (second marriage in 1906 to Maria (Masha) Zubova)
  - **Tatiana** (Tanya) 1864–1950 in 1899 married Mikhail Sukhotin
    - **Tanya** (Tanyushka) 1905–6
    - (Sukhotin had 6 children by his first wife)
  - **Ilya** (Ilyusha) 1866–1933 in 1889 married Sonya Filosofova
    - **Anna** (Annochka)
    - **Mikhail** (Misha)
    - **Andrei** (Andryusha)
    - **Ilya** (Ilyusha)
    - **Vladimir** (Volodya)
    - **Vera**
    - **Kirill**
    - **Nikolai**
  - **Lev** (Lyova) 1869–1945 in 1897 married Dora Westerlund
    - **Lev** (Lyovushka)
    - **Pavel**
    - **Nikita**
    - **Nina**
    - **Pyotr** (Petya)
    - **Sofia** (Sonya)
    - **Tatiana** (Tanya)
    - **Darya**
  - **Maria** (Masha) 1870–1906 in 1897 married Nikolai (Kolya) Obolenskii
  - **Pyotr** (Petya) 1872–187
- **Maria** (Mashenka) 1830–1912 married her cousin Valerian Tolstoy
  - **Nikolai** married Nadezhda Gromova
  - **Varvara** (Varya) married Nikolai Nagornov
  - **Elizaveta** (Lisa) married Leonid Obolenskii
  - **Eler** (Lenoc marri Iva Denise